CHINA'S WEST REGION DEVELOPMENT

Domestic Strategies and
Global Implications

CHINA'S WEST REGION DEVELOPMENT

Domestic Strategies and Global Implications

Edited by

Ding Lu
National University of Singapore

William A. W. Neilson
University of Victoria, Canada

World Scientific

NEW JERSEY · LONDON · SINGAPORE · BEIJING · SHANGHAI · HONG KONG · TAIPEI · CHENNAI

Published by

World Scientific Publishing Co. Pte. Ltd.

5 Toh Tuck Link, Singapore 596224

USA office: Suite 202, 1060 Main Street, River Edge, NJ 07661

UK office: 57 Shelton Street, Covent Garden, London WC2H 9HE

British Library Cataloguing-in-Publication Data
A catalogue record for this book is available from the British Library.

CHINA'S WEST REGION DEVELOPMENT
Domestic Strategies and Global Implications

ISBN 981-238-800-1

Printed in Singapore by World Scientific Printers (S) Pte Ltd

Table of Contents

Preface

The papers in this collection represent contributions to the Centre for Asia-Pacific Initiatives' interdisciplinary conference on West China Development: Domestic Strategies and Global Implications that was held on the University of Victoria campus from March 6 to 8, 2003. The conference attracted over 60 scholars, practitioners and government officials from across North America, China, Australia, Europe and Asia. The views expressed in this collection reflect those of individual authors and should not be seen as representative of the views of the editors or of any of the agencies involved in supporting this initiative.

Mounting an international conference of this scale and breadth requires substantial support. Much appreciation goes first to the Canadian International Development Agency's (CIDA) Conference Secretariat and China Program for their generous support of the conference. In particular, the guidance and intellectual contributions of then Senior Development Officer Gregory Chin were very warmly appreciated. CIDA's contribution allowed for the participation of several China-based scholars whose input into the conference was immeasurable. The International Development Research Centre (IDRC), under the guidance of Stephen Tyler, provided crucial support to several additional key presenters and facilitators and similarly enabled us to broaden the perspectives shared with the Conference audience. Finally, but not least of all, the Asia-Pacific Foundation of Canada through the good offices of Vice-President Yuen Pau Woo provided additional support to the conference, both financially and through their participation. Recognition should also go to long time CAPI and UVic benefactor, David Lam and his late wife Dorothy, who provided the support to allow us to invite eminent China scholar Dwight Perkins as our prestigious Lam Lecturer for 2003. Wing Thye Woo of the University of California Davis and Special Advisor to the United Nations Millennium Project provided valuable advice and support to the conference organizers. To all of these key contributors, we would like to extend a very warm "thank you".

The team at CAPI also worked tirelessly to ensure that the conference went off without a hitch. Heidi Tyedmers, CAPI's Program Officer and Stella Chan, CAPI's Secretary, both dedicated many hours to ensuring that all details were handled expeditiously. CAPI Research Assistant Jeanie Lanine worked many hours preparing briefs and reviewing proposals and also helped in note-taking throughout the conference. Several students and on-campus volunteers dedicated many hours over the three-day event by assisting with registration and logistics.

Finally, several individuals must be recognized for their contributions to this volume. First, we would like to thank the contributors for their work and interest in this important topic. Also Stella Chan, Fenwick Lansdowne, Helen Lansdowne and Kate Vallance all deserve special thanks for the hours they put into editing and formatting this publication and for helping to ensure that it was released in a timely manner. Staff of our publisher, World Scientific, also deserve our appreciation for their professional and attentive support in ensuring the successful publication of the papers.

Without the gracious and generous contributions of these organizations and individuals this conference would not have been the success it was, and this publication would not have come to fruition. We are indebted to all of you for helping us to mount this initiative, and for providing the support for what was in the words of one participant, "a wonderful atmosphere for relevant and strategic thinking on China's Western development."

Ding Lu
Department of Economics
National University of Singapore

William Neilson
Centre for Asia-Pacific Initiatives
University of Victoria, Canada

January 2004

List of Contributing Authors

Shuming Bao, Senior Research Associate Social Science, China Data Center, University of Michigan, Ann Arbor, 1080 S. University Ave., Ann Arbor, MI 48109-1106, U.S.A. E-mail: sbao@umich.edu

Robert Bedeski, Professor, Department of Political Science, University of Victoria, P.O. Box 1700 STN CSC, Victoria, BC Canada V8W 2Y2. E-mail: rbedeski@uvic.ca

Gene Chang, Director, Asian Studies Institute, Professor of Economics, Department of Economics, UH 4110-G, University of Toledo, Toledo, OH 43606, U.S.A. E-mail: gene.chang@utoledo.edu

Chen Zhilong, Centre for Economic Studies, Fudan University, 220 Han Dan Road, Shanghai 200433, People's Republic of China. E-mail: zhlchen@163.com

Greg Chin, Asian Branch, Canadian International Development Agency, 200 Promenade du Portage, Hull, Quebec Canada K1A 0G4. E-mail: greg_chin@acdi-cida.gc.ca

Dai Jian, Institute of Techno-Economic and Energy System Analysis, Energy Science Bldg., INET, Tsinghua University, Beijing 100084, People's Republic of China.

Sylvie Démurger, Honorary Associate Professor, HK Institute of Economics and Business Strategy, University of Hong Kong, Room 903, K.K. Leung Building, Pokfulam Road, Hong Kong. E-mail: demurger@hku.hk

Du Ping, Senior Research Professor and Director-General of Institute of Spatial Planning and Regional Economy (ISPRE),The State Development and Reform Commission (former SDPC), Room 903, Guo Hong Building, Muxidibeili, Jia 11 Xucheng District, Beijing 100038, People's Republic of China. E-mail: duping@mx.cei.gov.cn

Feng Jie, Department of Development Strategy and Regional Economy, Development Research Center of the State Council, No. 225 Chaoyangmen Nei Dajie, Beijing 100010, People's Republic of China.

Feng Zhiming, Professor and Director of Laboratory for Integrated Research on Regional Resource and Environment, Institute of Geographical Science and Natural Resources, Chinese Academy of Sciences, No. 15 Shuangqing Road, Beijing 100085, People's Republic of China. E-mail: fengzm@igsnrr.ac.cn

Glen Filson, Associate Professor, School of Environmental Design and Rural Development, University of Guelph, Guelph, Ontario, Canada N1G 2W1. E-mail: gfilson@oac.uoguelph.ca

Hou Yongzhi, Vice-Director, Department of Development Strategy and Regional Economy, Development Research Center of the State Council, No. 225 Chaoyangmen Nei Dajie, Beijing 100010, People's Republic of China. E-mail: yongzhi@drc.gov.cn

L. Kannenberg, Department of Agriculture, University of Guelph, 12 Evergreen Drive, Guelph, Ontario N1G 2M6 Canada.

Govind Kelkar, Coordinator, UN International Fund for Agricultural Development/Food and Agriculture Organization Gender Mainstreaming in Asia Project WFP, 2 Poorvi Marg, Vasant Vihar, New Delhi 110057, India. E-mail: govindkelkar@yahoo.com

Li Shantong, Senior Research Fellow, Development Research Center of the State Council, No. 225, Chaoyangmen Nei Dajie, Beijing 100010, People's Republic of China. E-mail: shantong@drc.gov.cn

Li Yu, Department of History, University of British Columbia, Suite 1297, 1873 East Mall, Vancouver, BC Canada V6T 1Z1. E-mail: liy@telus.net

Lin Ling, Professor of Economics, Vice President of Chinese Industrial Economics Institution and Sichuan Academy of Social Sciences, Qing Yang Palace, Chengdu 610072, People's Republic China. E-mail: linling6@yahoo.com, or linling6@163.com

Liu Shiqing, Professor of Economics, Secretary-General of West Development Research Center, Sichuan Academy of Social Sciences, Qing Yang Palace, Chengdu 610072, People's Republic China. E-mail: shiqingl@yahoo.com, or shiqingl@163.com

Ding Lu, Associate Professor, Department of Economics, National University of Singapore, AS-2 Level 6, 1 Arts Link, Singapore 117570. E-mail: ecslud@nus.edu.sg

Zhigang Lu, Department of Information Management, Tianjin University of Finance and Economics, No. 25 Zhujiang Road, Hexi District, Tianjin 300222, People's Republic of China. E-mail: lu732000@yahoo.com

Namgyal, Research Officer, Environment and Development Desk, Central Tibetan Administration, Dharamsala, Kangra District, HP, India 176215. E-mail: anamgyal@hotmail.com; ecodesk@diir.gov. tibet. net

William Neilson, Director, Centre for Asia-Pacific Initiatives, University of Victoria, P.O. Box 1700 STN CSC, Victoria, BC Canada V8W 2Y2. E-mail: wneilson@uvic.ca

Dwight Perkins, Harold Hitchings Burbank Professor of Political Economy, Department of Economics, Harvard University, Littaurer M-12, Cambridge, MA 02138 U.S.A. E-mail: dwight_perkins@harvard.edu

Qian Yihong, Center for Environment and Development, Chinese Academy of Social Sciences, 5 Jianguomennei Street, Beijing 100732, People's Republic of China.

Euston Quah, Associate Professor,Department of Economics, National University of Singapore, 10 Kent Ridge Crescent, Singapore 119260. E-mail: ecsquahe@nus.edu.sg

Jeffrey D. Sachs, Director, Earth Institute at Columbia University, 405 Low Library, MC 4335, 535 West 116th Street, New York, NY 10027, U.S.A. E-mail: sachs@columbia.edu

Shen Hong, Institute of Techno-Economic and Energy System Analysis, Energy Science Bldg., INET, Tsinghua University, Beijing 100084, People's Republic of China.

Shi Yulong, Section Chief, Urban Development, Institute of Spatial Planning and Regional Economy, State Development Planning Commission, B907, Guohong Building, Muxidi, Beijing 100038, People's Republic of China. E-mail: shiyl@mx.cei.gov.cn

J. Simpson, Department of Agriculture,University of Guelph, 12 Evergreen Drive, Guelph, Ontario N1G 2M6 Canada

Shunfeng Song, Professor of the Department of Economics, University of Nevada, Reno, NV 89557-0207, U.S.A. E-mail: song@unr.nevada.edu

Neal C. Stoskopf, Professor (retired) of Agriculture, University of Guelph, 12 Evergreen Drive, Guelph, Ontario N1G 2M6 Canada. E-mail: nstoskop@uoguelph.ca

Dodo Thampapillai, Department of Economics, National University of Singapore, 10 Kent Ridge Crescent, Singapore 119260. Permanent address: Personal Chair in Environmental Economics, Macquarie University, NSW 2109, Australia. E-mail: ecstj@nus.edu.sg; or dthampap@gse.mq.edu.au

Shandre M. Thangavelu, Department of Economics, National University of Singapore, 10 Kent Ridge Crescent, Singapore 119260.

Elspeth Thomson, Visiting Research Fellow, East Asian Institute, National University of Singapore, 10 Kent Ridge Crescent, Singapore 119260. E-mail: eaiebt@nus.edu.sg

Wang Shaoguang, Professor, Department of Government and Public Administration, Chinese University of Hong Kong, 3/F, T.C. Cheng Building, United College, Shatin, New Territories, Hong Kong. E-mail: wangshaoguang@cuhk.edu.hk

Wen Mei, Fellow, Research School of Pacific and Asian Studies, Economic Division, Australian National University, Canberra, ACT 0200, Australia. E-mail: rosemei.wen@anu.edu.au; meiwen@coombs.anu.edu.au

Wing Thye Woo, Professor of Economics, and Special Advisor, East Asian Economies, United Nations Millennium Project, Department of Economics, University of California, Davis, One Shields Avenue, Davis, CA 95616, U.S.A. E-mail: wtwoo@ucdavis.edu

Yaoqi Zhang, Assistant Professor, School of Forestry and Wildlife, Auburn University, 205 M. White Smith, AL 36849-5418, U.S.A. E-mail: yaoqi.zhang@auburn.edu

Zhao Xiusheng, Research Fellow, Institute of Techno-Economic and Energy System Analysis, Energy Science Bldg., INET, Tsinghua University, Beijing 100084, People's Republic of China. E-mail: zhaoxs@tsinghua.edu.cn; or zhaoxs@dns.inet.tsinghua.edu.cn

Zheng Yuxin, Director, Center for Environment and Development, Chinese Academy of Social Sciences, 5 Jianguomennei Street, Beijing 100732, People's Republic of China. E-mail: zhengyuxin@95777.com

1 Introduction: West China Development — Issues and Challenges

Ding Lu and William Neilson

China has been the world's fastest growing economy in the last two decades, in which its total GDP sextupled. This remarkable economic growth has been, however, mainly a coastal phenomenon. The country's western inland region, with a total area of 6.85 million km (71.4% of the whole nation), was largely left out of the boom. While its population (367 million by 2002) accounts for 28.8% of China's total, its share of the national GDP is under 17%. The per capita income of the western region is less than 40% of the level in the eastern region.

At the turn of the century, the Chinese government launched the West China Development Program, aiming to reorient the growth vigour towards the western region. A series of fiscal initiatives and institutional innovations have been proposed and implemented to boost the region's development prospects and close the income gaps between the western inland provinces and the rest of China. In the first three years of this program, 36 mega infrastructure projects with investment over 600 billion *yuan* (equivalent to US$ 72 billion) have taken off. China's banking sector has increased another 600 billion *yuan* of loans to the provinces in the western region.[1] To Chinese policy makers, the development of the west region is meant to reduce interregional disparities and to meet both environmental protection and national security goals. Outside of China's borders, the effects of this development will be far-reaching, both regionally and globally, with repercussions in several areas including the environment, regional governance and human security, poverty reduction, and trade and investment.

1

To study the major domestic issues and global implications of this development program, the University of Victoria's Centre for Asia Pacific Initiatives organized and hosted an international conference on March 6-8, 2003. About 65 scholars, policy-makers and development practitioners from Canada, China, U.S., and other countries attended the event, the first multi-disciplinary international symposium of this scale on the theme. All the papers were written and presented by specialists/professionals who have done significant research regarding China's regional development. Their areas of speciality include economics, political science, sociology, geography, history, environment, and regional planning. Several of the Chinese writers have been personally involved in regional policy making at central or local governmental levels. A number of non-Chinese authors have experience working on China-related projects or providing consulting and fieldwork services to the Chinese government and institutions.

This volume collects 24 of the papers presented at the conference. We group these papers around five major issues of the West China Development Program: (1) the goals and objectives; (2) the coordinating institutions and mechanism; (3) the effectiveness and efficiency of development strategies and policies; (4) the distribution of benefits and costs; and (5) sources of interregional disparity.

Part I, "Goals and Objectives", has four papers. They carry in-depth discussions on complements, tradeoffs and possible conflicts of priorities among the goals of the West China Development Program. These goals include achieving economic growth, improving inter-regional income equality, enhancing environmental protection, and consolidating national security and unity.

In **Chapter 2**, "Designing a Regional Development Strategy for China", Dwight Perkins (Harvard University, USA) leads the discussion by examining several goals of China's regional development strategy, i.e. the goal of binding the different parts of China to the homeland, the goal of extracting natural resources of mineral and energy industries for the interior region, and the goal of reducing inequality between the people of the coast and the people of the interior. After highlighting the differences in these goals, he recommends "a policy of allowing unfettered migration to the cities with families" from the interior to the coast and discusses its feasibility and benefits. In his opinion, "a true regional development strategy in a market economy focuses mainly on getting the market to work properly".

In **Chapter 3** "Eco-Environmental Protection and Poverty-Alleviation in West China Development", Zheng Yuxin and Qian Yihong (Centre for Environment and Development, China Academy of Social Sciences) point out that most areas of Western China are ecologically vulnerable with adverse geographic conditions. The problem of excessive exploitation of the environment is always precipitated by people's efforts to lift themselves out of poverty. Addressing the vicious cycle of "poverty – environment deterioration" should be a major goal of West China Development Program. To achieve this objective, public policy initiatives are necessary to internalize the external socio-economic impact of poverty alleviation and environmental protection. In contrast to Perkins' confidence on market, the duo argue that market mechanism is not sufficient to provide appropriate incentives for environmental protection. "The establishment of an ecological compensation mechanism must depend on non-market measures, particularly government interference at various levels", concluded Zheng and Qian.

Robert Bedeski (University of Victoria, Canada) places the contemporary West China development in a geopolitical perspective in **Chapter 4,** "Western China: Human Security and National Security". He reviews the western region of China as a frontier of national security concerns for the central governments of various eras. In particular, he discusses the changes in the geopolitical situation of this frontier since the incident of September-11 and signifies national security as a strategic goal of the West China Development Program. However, the author expresses concerns over the program's possible negative impact on human security in the western provinces and autonomous regions as it may transform them "into areas that more closely resemble the societies and economies of the eastern provinces".

Zhao Xiusheng, Dai Jian, and Shen Hon (Tsinghua University, China) discuss the goals of development at a micro level in **Chapter 5,** "Reconciliation between Ecosystem Preservation and Economic Development Initiative". The discussion is based on a project, Tarim Basin Water Management and Desertification, which is one of the many cooperative initiatives between Canada and China in regional development. Funded by Canada's International Development Research Centre (IDRC), Tsinghua University and Xinjiang Academy of Agricultural Sciences jointly undertook the project to address the chronic water stress and local development issues in Tarim Basin of Xinjiang Uighur Autonomous Region. In the paper the authors advocate a community-based water resource management approach to address the dual objectives of ecosystem preservation and economic development with local initiatives and participation.

Part II of this volume is about the "**Coordinating Institutions and Mechanism**" in the endeavour to develop West China. The five papers in this volume highlight the need for institutional reforms to coordinate interests and initiatives between the central and local governments, among different governmental branches and local authorities.

Chapter 6, "A New Pattern of Regional Cooperation in China", is the work of three researchers, Li Shantong, Hou Yongzhi and Feng Jie (Development and Research Centre of China's State Council). The authors propose to establish four supra-provincial "economic belts" that horizontally link provinces and regions across eastern and western parts of China. They believe that the launch of these "economic belts" will enhance inter-regional and inter-province coordination of local development plans, reduce inter-regional income disparity, help the nation to achieve sustainable growth, optimize industrial structure based on regional comparative advantages, and facilitate China's participation in international economic cooperation. They advise the Chinese government to guide and encourage regional specialization, industrial relocation and industrial restructure within these "economic belts" and, through overall planning of the economic belts in industrial development, infrastructure building and environmental protection, to eliminate inter-region blockade and trade barriers. With a supra-provincial administrative structure overlooking these "economic belts", it is possible to develop a welfare compensation mechanism for ecological projects between the upper reaches and the lower reaches within each belt.

In **Chapter 7** "The Political Logic of Fiscal Transfers in China", Wang Shaoguang (Chinese University of Hong Kong) empirically examines the central government's allocation of net fiscal transfers across provinces. He found that the patterns of transfers exhibit a discernible political logic. While equity considerations appear to play some role in central policies of regional redistribution, the concern of central policy makers about national unity is the most important determinant in the fiscal transfer system. On top of that, there exists an unequal per capita representation in the Central Committee of the Chinese Communist Party and this distribution of representation appears to have a positive and statistically significant effect on fiscal transfers. These findings support the hypothesis that "the distribution of fiscal transfers is largely determined by the interactions between central and regional politicians, both of whom are motivated to maximize their chances of staying in power within given institutional constraints". This political logic casts light on the coordination mechanism in China's regional development.

Policy coordination must work through the political structure, which is discussed in **Chapter 8** "The Politics of China's Western Development Strategy" by Gregory T. Chin (Canadian International Development Agency). He first outlines the "core structure" of decision-making and administration for the Western Development Initiatives inside the central government. He then discusses intra-bureaucratic tensions inside this structure and the central-local tensions in the implementation of central policies. He observes that in contrast to earlier regional development programs in earlier history of the People's Republic, the current Western Development Strategy has been introduced through a more institutionalized and consensual process of decision-making. Several recommendations are offered to the Chinese policy makers for strengthening the effectiveness and positive politico-developmental impact of the Western Development Initiatives.

Chapter 9 "An Introductory Environmental Macroeconomic Framework for China" illustrates the need for cognisance of the role of environmental capital in the formulation of plans for the development of West China. The three economists, Dodo Thampapillai, Euston Quah, and Shandre M. Thangavelu (National University of Singapore), internalize the environmental capital into a standard macroeconomic framework in the context of the Chinese economy. Although in this paper the authors confine China's environmental capital to its air shed and its stock of forest cover, their model can be extended to internalize more broadly defined environmental capital stock and also other external effects such as income distributional impact. This exercise is useful for coordinating regional development and answers directly to the call by the authors of Chapter 3 for "establishing the measuring criteria for 'environment value'" in economic growth.

Glen Filson, Neal C. Stoskopf, J. Simpson and L. Kannenberg (University of Guelph, Canada) describe another Canada-China joint project in West China in **Chapter 10** "The Western China Development Strategy: an Agroforestry Approach". This project involves a broad spectrum of people including administrators and scientists from China, and research personnel from the University of Guelph and a non-governmental organization, Resource Efficient Agricultural Production (REAP). The aim of the project is to reduce environmental degradation along the Yellow and Yangtze Rivers and alleviate poverty for local communities. Eleven sub-watershed areas along these rivers were chosen by China's Ministry of Water Resources as demonstration sites for a holistic approach consisting of biological, physical and social aspects to make major environmental, economic and social changes. The chapter provides a detailed account of involvement the two Canadian institutions in the project as well as their agroforestry approach for local development.

Part III concerns the questions of "**Effectiveness and Efficiency**". Several components of the West China Development Program, such as the projects of transportation, reforestation, and natural resource extraction, have come under scrutiny.

Chapter 11 "On the Urban-Rural Relationship in the Process of Western Region Development" is contributed by Shi Yulong and Du Ping, two leading experts at the Institute of Spatial Planning & Regional Economy under China's State Development and Reform Commission. With their experience of direct involvement in the government's regional policy making, the authors first review in this chapter the main consensuses and diversified views regarding the goals and policies of the western region development among Chinese policy makers and academia. They then give a brief account of the activities and achievements of the West China

Development Program in its first three years (2000-02) of practice and critically comment on the aspects that need to be improved. Based on these observations, the authors point out that the program should firstly be a development aid program to contain the growing regional disparity. They recommend that promotion of human development should be a major goal for this program and the small and medium-sized projects that can directly improve the life of local people should be given the top priority in the government's development plan. As for urbanization in the western region, the focus should shift from construction of hardware infrastructure to building up the rural people's capability of living and working in urban areas through improving their health and skills.

In **Chapter 12** "The Western Regions' Growth Potential", Ding Lu and Elspeth Thomson (National University of Singapore) examine the market access conditions across regions to estimate the extent to which China's ambitious plans for transport infrastructure development in the western region will increase its growth potential. They find that differences in the transportation-cost denominated market- and supply-access conditions are a major cause of inter-regional income disparity. Meanwhile, the extent of institutional reforms matters a great deal in growth-performance differences across provincial economies. The authors caution that, if overall market accessibility is not sufficiently improved, lower transportation costs could accelerate the decline of periphery centres and industries.

In **Chapter 13** "Measuring the Impact of the 'Five Mega Projects'", Lin Ling and Liu Shiqing (Academy of Social Sciences of Sichuan Province, China) critically examine the effects of five mega projects of West China Development, namely, the ecological environment construction project, the West-to-East natural gas transportation project, the West-to-East electricity transmission project, the Qinghai-Tibet railway project, and the South-to-North water diversion project. They observe that the West China Development Program benefits the whole country but continues to widen the East-West gap as the division of labour between the eastern and western regions remains the same. They also criticize that the environmental construction in the western areas lacks a powerful and sustainable development strategy and the prospect of investment returns and debt redemption for West China development is still gloomy. The authors thus call for a policy adjustment for western region industrial development.

The Grain-for-Green Policy is a major part of West China Development Program to restore ecological balance in the western region by turning low-yielding farmland back into forest and pasture. In **Chapter 14** "Grain-for-Green Policy and Its Impacts on Grain Supply in West China", Yaoqi Zhang (University of Alberta) and Zhimin Feng (China Academy of Sciences) assess the impact of this policy in the Upper Reaches of the Yangtze River and the Upper and Middle Reaches of the Yellow River. They show that the impact on grain supply at the country level is only about 2-3% so it should not be a threat to China future grain supply (2-3%) and the world market. They nevertheless caution that the impact on the local level can be significant and the associated socio-economic issues should be addressed properly. They also express concerns over the sustainability of the policy when state compensation for farmers expires in a few years. Therefore, the authors suggest that the Grain-for-Green policy should be gradually implemented, first target on those most ecologically sensitive farmlands. They also propose that Grain-for-Green policy be integrated with other socio-economic reforms and the best long-term strategy is to encourage emigration from environmentally vulnerable areas.

Education and human capital development are high on the agenda of West China development. Yu Li (University of British Columbia, Canada) addresses this issue in **Chapter 15** by reviewing the historical experience of Sichuan in the first two decades of the 20th century. Despite the fact that education reform in Sichuan achieved greater quantitative success than all of the coastal provinces in the early 20th century, it failed to result in social and economic development in the later years. The gap between the province and coastal China continued to enlarge through the decades. Yu observes that education is certainly a necessary, but not sufficient, requirement of economic growth. In China's western landlocked areas, "there might be some more important and urgent works than the expansion of education". The mismatch between what is taught in schools and what is needed in local development may cause failure of human capital accumulation and brain drains.

The issue of **Part IV, "Distribution of Benefits and Costs"**, drew serious attention from the audience at the conference. Multiple, reasoned criticisms were voiced over distributional implications for women, indigenous peoples, local communities and other social groups who will likely not share the economic advances predicted by the West China Development Strategy planners.

Chapter 16 "The New Challenges Facing the Development of West China" by Liu Shiqing and Lin Ling (Sichuan Academy of Social Sciences) scrutinizes the West China Development Program from the perspectives of local people. According to the authors, the first challenge is how to integrate the environmental protection with creating avenues for local peasants to better their economic prospects. The second issue is coordinating infrastructure construction with the technological transformation and development of manufacturing industry in the western provinces. They also argue that the exploitation of natural resources should be integrated with the development of processing industries in the region. Therefore they call for more state support in terms of preferential policies.

Since the 1980s, inter-regional income and opportunity disparity has led to increasing volume of voluntary inter-regional migration, a phenomenal factor in China's regional economic development. Shuming Bao (University of Michigan) and Wing Thye Woo (University of California at Davis) look into this issue in **Chapter 17** "Migration Scenarios and Western China Development". They first give an overview of historical distribution of population over last 50 years, especially after 1978. Then they describe the migration flows between urban cities, towns and rural areas, and between different regions in the past decade. In particular, they identify the net "gainers" and "losers" of migrants by region and analyze the types of migration by motivation, gender and employment sector. Applying Roberto Bachi's Migration Preference Index, the authors also identify the national "centres of attraction" to migration in recent years.

A major socio-economic impact of regional economic development falls on distribution of costs and benefits between men and women. Govind Kelkar, Editor of India's *Gender Technology and Development Journal*, provides her observation of changes in gender relations and ecological consequences of tourism development in Lijiang of Southwest China in **Chapter 18**. The case is of particular interest since the village under her study has both matrilineal systems and patrilineal systems being practised by different ethnic groups. Based on information collected from interviews with local residents, the author discusses ethnic, class and gender factors in determining who are able to take advantage of globalization in the context of the growth of tourist trade.

The Tibet Autonomous Region is of strategic importance to West China Development Program. In **Chapter 19**, Namgyal (Department of Information and International Relations, Central Tibetan Administration, India) raises doubts about the benefits of the program to the indigenous Tibetans. After lamenting some negative impacts of the development in the past decades on the environment and local communities, the author points out that a fundamental question for policy making is "how best to spread the benefits of rapid growth and modernization to the relatively poor Tibetan populations depending on subsistence agriculture and nomadic livestock production". He thus proposes that the rural population — herdsmen and farmers of the Tibetan plateau — should be made the centre of economic planning.

Developing West China has significant economic and geopolitical implications on China's neighbouring countries. Chen Zhilong (Fudan University, China) deals with this issue in **Chapter 20** "The Significance of West China Development to Asian Economic Integration". Citing trends of trade and investment in Asia, Chen predicts that West China development will facilitate economy integration from East Asia to Middle Asia and create many opportunities for businesses in these regions. He also observes that the central and regional governments in China have already taken initiatives in promoting economic co-operation at national, sub-national and enterprise levels across country borders.

There are four papers in **Part V "Sources of Interregional Disparity"**. The authors of these papers explore the causes and sources of interregional disparity. Their findings raise significant policy implications for the direction, pace and impact of the West China Development Strategy. **Chapter 21** "The Relative Contributions of Location and Preferential Policies in China's Regional Development" is the work of a team of economists: Sylvie Démurger (Centre National de la Recherche Scientifique, France),

Jeffrey D. Sachs (Columbia University), Wing Thye Woo (University of California at Davis), Shuming Bao (University of Michigan), and Gene Chang (University of Toledo). With a measure of the ability to participate in international trade (Geography), and a preferential policy index (Policy), the authors empirically investigate various factors that might have contributed to disparity of growth performance across provinces. The results suggest a failure of economic growth in the past two decades to cause convergence of per capita income across regions. The authors interpreted this failure by pointing out several Chinese institutions that have inhibited the income convergence process generated by factor movement and trade-induced factor price changes. They therefore propose reforms of these institutions, including the household registration system, the monopoly state bank system, and the decentralization-unleashed local protectionism.

In **Chapter 22**, Ding Lu (National University of Singapore) and Wing Thye Woo (University of California at Davis) examine the role of urbanization in regional growth disparity. They first review China's urbanization and regional development strategy before economic reform and show that the patterns of urbanization in the early 1980s did not reflect the location and size distribution pattern of a market economy. They then use econometric approach to gauge the impact of urban size distribution on economic growth. Based on their findings, they observe that under-urbanization and inefficient city-size distribution are partially responsible for China's growing interregional development disparity in recent years. They therefore recommend policies to remove institutional barriers to urbanization and factor mobility in regional economic development.

In **Chapter 23** "China's Regional Disparities in 1978-2000", Zhigang Lu (China's Tianjin University) and Shunfeng Song (University of Nevada at Reno) review China's regional development policies and strategies before and after China's opening-up. Applying a net-effect growth model to provincial data for the period of 1978-2000, the authors find that China's net growth in GDP is significantly affected by the increases in labour, fixed assets, human capital, domestic retail sales, exports and foreign direct investment. They also observe three main sources of uneven regional development in China: technology catch-up advantage, policy advantage, and the functioning of market mechanisms. They advise Chinese leaders to develop policies to strengthen development in cooperation among regions and provinces.

Chapter 24 "Development of West China: Marketization vs. FDI" is authored by Wen Mei (Australian National University). She does an econometric exercise to support her observation that various degrees of marketization and foreign direct investment flows are crucial factors associating with inter-regional growth disparity. This leads to the argument that the key to developing China's inland regions and to reducing inter-regional income disparity is to "accelerate development of a market mechanism" there.

From above preview of the chapters in this volume, one can identify many controversial viewpoints as well as consensuses. Some of the views are sharp and critical. For instance, the top-down and mega-project approach taken by China's central government in developing the west regions was questioned and challenged by several authors. Some papers have inquired into the sensitive issues of local ownership and participation by indigenous communities. On top of these, many policy proposals have been made to tackle these issues.

As this volume goes to print, it is worthwhile to update our readers with some recent adjustments in the Chinese government's regional policy since our conference was held in Spring 2003. These developments have taken place against the backdrop of the leadership succession in Beijing as a new generation of leaders, headed by Hu Jingtao (Party General Secretary and State President), and Wen Jiaobao (Premier) took the helm. One is that the new leadership has vowed to rejuvenate the "rustbelt" of heavy industrial base in provinces of Northeast China. This region used to be a stronghold of the centrally planned state-owned industrial base but has suffered from stagnation since the 1980s due to its tardiness in market-oriented reforms. Its superior geographic location, well-built infrastructure, and rich human capital, however, bode well for a market-driven resurrection once the institutional barriers are overcome. It seems that the new leadership has started a subtle shift of regional development focus to regions with better economic potentials and promise.

A second policy change with important implications for regional development is the decision taken at the Third Plenum of the 16th Central Committee of the ruling Communist Party in October 2003 to provide better protection for private property rights and to allow farmers to transfer their rights to land, thus letting some amass large holdings.[2] This policy change matches well the suggestion for using private property rights as leverage to sustain environment-friendly development put forward by some experts, including several authors of this volume.

The most recent sign for perhaps the most far-reaching policy adjustment is the announcement by Zhou Ganzhi, a leading adviser with China's Construction Ministry, that the government is mulling over a massive "West-to-East" campaign to migrate 100 million farmers in the undeveloped western region to the booming eastern coast – the Pearl River Delta, the Yangtze River Delta and the Beijing-Tianjin region.[3] Earlier, Wang Mengqui, Director of Economic Development Centre under the State Council, also revealed that the government has a plan to encourage 300-500 million farmers to migrate into urban areas before 2020.[4] This plan matches the trends of voluntary migration described in Chapter 17 and reflects a market-oriented emigration-urbanization approach recommended by several authors of this volume for West China development.

These adjustments are indications of growing "rethinking" among China's policy makers about the merits of a top-down and mega-project based approach of the West China Development Program in the past few years. Here again, we are glad to appreciate the fact that many critical views towards this program did not fall on deaf ears. That is the greatest reward to the authors as well as the editors of this volume.

Notes

1. *Lianhe Zaobao* (United Morning Post, Singapore), 9 December 2003, p. 1.
2. "CCP's Decision on Some Issues of Perfecting Socialist Market Economic System", Xinhua News Agency, 21 October 2003; "China endorses property rights", *The Washington Post*, 14 October 2003.

3. "Massive west-to-east migration proposed", *China Daily* (Beijing), 8 December 2003; "Eastward Ho!" *The Straits Times* (Singapore), 9 December 2003.

4. *Lianhe Zaobao* (United Morning Post, Singapore), 9 December 2003, p. 1.

Part I. Goals and Objectives

2 Designing A Regional Development Strategy for China

Dwight Perkins

China has long talked about the importance of developing regions other than those along its coast that saw the most development, not only since 1978, but also since the middle of the 19th century. When the Communists came to power there was a clear desire to develop China's interior to correct what was conceived as a capitalist-imperialist bias of just developing those areas that traded with the West.

In the late 1960s and early 1970s there was Mao's Third Front development effort to build a military industry and heavy industry capability somewhat out of reach of potential invaders both from the north and from the south. This was extremely expensive and produced few factories that could compete in the market economy of the 1990s. The issue of how to develop strategic regions such as Tibet or Xinjiang has also long been on the development agenda.

In the 1980s there was a conscious decision to put interior development on the back burner and concentrate on development in the coastal provinces where the rate of return on investment was presumed to be higher. It was only in the late 1990s that developing the west inland of China became a new focus of the national economic strategy.

What these various developments underscore is that before one can start talking about a regional development strategy for China, one must first define what one hopes to achieve through development of the less developed regions of China.

- Is the goal to improve the welfare of the people in the interior a good thing to achieve in its own right? Or is it a necessary policy to avert a revolt of the interior against the coast, which could abort the long-term growth in China? Historically coastal prosperity came to an unhappy end when the political forces of the interior backfired. The Communist Party in the 1930s and 1940s won the revolution with the support of the impoverished peasants of the interior.
- Is the goal instead to cement together the nation within its current borders as a true nation state and not as an empire? Clearly Tibet and the Northwest have long had elements that would have preferred to break away and form their independent states — those forces are much weaker nowadays than they were in the 1940s but they are still there.
- Is the real goal mainly to develop the natural resources of the interior so as to benefit economic growth and achieve a somewhat higher degree of energy and natural resource independence?

These are very different goals calling for very different strategies and China is not very clear about which takes priority in its present plans. Put differently, China at one time or another appears to be pursuing all goals at once but without a very clear sense of priorities.

I will take these different goals and their implications for an investment strategy in turn.

First, the strategic goal of binding the different parts of China to the homeland. Others may comment on whether this is a worthwhile goal or not, but most Han Chinese would take for granted that it is a worthy goal. There is no sentiment for allowing parts of present-day China to break away and form independent nations, either on the Mainland or on Taiwan island. A footnote to this regard is that Taiwan has only just recently recognized Mongolia as an independent country.

The solution to this problem has in recent times and historically involved two major kinds of development:

(a) The development of transport links between the populated coastal and central regions of China and the far western reaches of the nation. The railroad from Qinghai to Lhasa is the most recent example of this approach — earlier efforts included the railroad through Xinjiang and the now quite reasonable roads connecting the west inland to China's populous provinces.

(b) The movement of Han people into the regions formerly dominated by non-Han people. This happened in Mongolia and the Northeast some time ago and happened more because of unplanned migration into these regions by Han people than as a major government effort. Mongols and Manchus are now tiny minorities in these regions. A similar statement can be made about China's border areas with Southeast Asia.

The movement of retired military, the "sent-down" urban youth, and others to Xinjiang is a more recent phenomenon but the cities of the northwest are largely dominated by Han people even as the countryside is still largely but not entirely in Uighur hands. Parts of the northwest that were historically part of the Tibetan polity have also been integrated to a significant degree by both Han and non-Han, non-Tibetan people.

Tibet resisted this trend for some time largely because most Han people found it difficult to live at high altitudes and in what were in the pre-1980 period still quite primitive conditions. But this has changed as the Chinese government has invested large amounts of money to improve the quality of life particularly in the cities where most Han migrants choose to live. Much of the migration that has occurred has been spontaneous in the sense that Sichuan merchants and the like came without any specific encouragement from the state, and the government argued, and probably to some degree, believed that the investments were also improving the lives of the Tibetans even if a large number of Tibetans might not agree.

Second, the natural resource or energy development strategy for the interior has also been around for a long time. Back in the 1950s, China's only known source of petroleum was at Yumen in Gansu Province. Much of the natural resource development in the reform period, however, was focused off shore, but because the efforts to find oil and gas off shore proved to be somewhat disappointing, China's attention once again turned to China's interior.

This approach was often presented as helping the people of the interior to join in the growing prosperity being experienced on the coast, but much of what was happening had little to do with the people who actually lived in the interior.

I once attended in 1987 or 1988 a presentation of Sichuan government officials to a group of foreign investors (mostly small-scale American businesses). They talked at length about how much money they were spending on development projects in the province and how much new electric power was coming on line. But when one looked at what they were investing in concrete terms, much of the money was going to the development of a large mining and smelting operation in a remote western part of the province where relatively few Sichuanese lived.

The development of the Tarim Basin oil and gas similarly has little to do with the people of Xinjiang. The equipment and all of the skilled personnel have to be shipped in from outside. When the fields and pipelines are up and running they will employ relatively few people and even fewer of those people will be from the region. None of the people in the region actually live anywhere near this remote desert region so even the normal ancillary businesses that might develop to provide housing and meals to the shipped-in workers will also have to be shipped in. The GDP of Xinjiang will rise as a result of oil production in this area, but the incomes of the residents who were not shipped in will be little affected.

The impact of these investments on the people of the region will thus have no more impact than, say, building a pipeline to Kazakhstan or Siberia to ship gas and oil to China's coast. They may well be useful investments particularly if the cost of imported energy stays high or rises, but they have nothing to do with improving the regional distribution of income except in a very nominal sense.

What would a regional development strategy designed to reduce inequality between the people of the coast and the people of the interior look like? Put differently, what would an effort focused on raising the incomes of the people of the interior more than has been the case in the past look like?

I am not qualified to spell out all of the concrete details that would go into such a policy but I believe that any strategy with this purpose in mind would have all or at least some of the following characteristics:

(a) The investment would largely go to where most of the people are. Thus the big investments would go to Sichuan or Gansu or Guizhou, and not so much to Tibet or Xinjiang — at least the latter would not be getting much larger investments on a per capita basis than say the poorer regions of the poorest most populated provinces.

(b) The real investment issue, however, is not where government investment should be directed, but how China can change the private-market driven flow of investment away from the coast and toward the interior. Infrastructure investment can help in this regard but it is clearly not the whole story.

We have only one really good example of how development proceeds in a market economy of continental size — namely, the United States. (The U.S.S.R. regional development was not remotely market driven. The E.U. has been a continental sized market economy for too short a time and much of the labour flows from neighbouring regions, such as Turkey or the former Yugoslavia rather than from within the E.U., and there are many reasons why capital does not flow in large amounts in the opposite direction.)

The development pattern in the U.S. was that the labour moved from the poor agricultural south to the richer more industrialized north, particularly during and after World War II. During the post-WWII decades, capital moved from the north to the south, at least in industries that depended on low cost labour. First shoes and textiles left the Northeast and then machinery.

But in China, while there is movement of labour from the interior to the coast (and I will look at this migration at length in a moment), capital also appears to flow from the interior to the coast — at least capital that is responsive to market forces. Part of this is simply due to the nature of the Chinese banking system that has mainly lent to state-owned enterprises and there are more of these on the coast and the Northeast than in the interior, but that is not the whole story.

Foreign investors do not put much money in the interior and particularly not in non-resource based industries in the interior, but neither do Shanghai firms or Shandong firms, as far as I can tell. I do not fully understand the reasons why this is the case, but I suspect that the interior provincial governments have been slower to clear away the bureaucratic red tape involved in getting a piece of land on which to build, to get the necessary permits to do business, etc. Certainly this was the case the one time I tried to investigate this question in a very modest way in 1988 as part of a World Bank mission.

The challenge for China in this area is to find a way to remove these barriers much the way the American south did in the 1950s and 1960s (not all of the American methods such as union busting, were very attractive but they worked). If domestic firms started moving their more labour-intensive activities to the interior, the foreign investors might soon follow suit.

This said, it is important to realize that some areas in the interior are simply too disadvantaged to ever attract much profit-oriented investment. Few firms are going to build factories in the mountains of western Guizhou, however, much is invested in improving the infrastructure. The comparable situation in the United States would be parts of the Appalachian Mountains (West Virginia, etc.) where the government has poured in enormous sums to build infrastructure but the area remains poor. For these areas, the task is not to get more capital into the region but to get the people out.

That brings me to the final and, in my opinion, the most important component of a regional development strategy designed to help the people in the interior of the country and to help the poorer people in the country in general. The solution to much of the existing disparities in income across the regions is to move the people from the areas that are poor and lacking in opportunities to the areas that have a surplus of such opportunities.

Much of the emphasis by some writers and officials is to try to find ways to do more for the rural population of China in place — that is, helping them where they are now. This is a worthy goal but it is not going to be very effective in achieving major increases in the standards of living of these people. This is because:

- The basic problem is that China has five or more times as many people farming as it needs to produce current levels of agricultural output. Removing these people from the land would involve some additional capital investment but not very much, while the 10% of the population that remained on the land would be much better off.
- Having farmers shift to more lucrative non-grain crops will help and this is happening, but prices of farm products have come down dramatically in recent years, offsetting many of these gains and there does not seem to be much prospect of Chinese farm prices going back up in any major way. With the WTO rules, Chinese farm prices will follow world prices and there is little evidence that they will rise. Nor can China's government afford to follow the path of Japan or South Korea by subsidizing farmers with higher than world prices not only because the WTO agreements don't allow it but also because the Chinese government doesn't have the money.
- For a time it looked as though Township & Village Enterprises (TVEs) might be a partial solution to the problem of low rural incomes and for a time they were. But the development of TVEs appears to have run out of steam in recent years. Furthermore, these TVEs were disproportionately on the coast, near cities and not in the poorer regions of the interior provinces.

The biggest regional development challenge facing China, therefore, is how to remove perhaps as many as 600 million people from farming and the rural areas over the next two to three decades.

For 30 years China did its best to avoid dealing with this problem by following its own version of what can be called the "Hong Kong solution":

This approach focused until the last decade and a half on preventing rural people from migrating to the cities. The legal basis for this was the *hukou* (household registration) system that gave households permanent rural or urban status. If you had rural status, you could not stay long in the cities, could not get food ration coupons, could not send your children to urban schools, and could not have access to health care facilities, etc.

The "advantage" of this approach was that it reduced the need to invest in urban infrastructure but it also created two classes of citizens and there was rising inequality between these two classes during the Maoist period when China was supposedly an egalitarian nation.

This system continued into the reform period but the government over time relaxed its efforts to prevent migration and there was in fact a large flow of people into the cities — for construction work, for household service, and even for regular jobs since the factories needed more labour as they expanded rapidly and that abundant labour supply did not exist in the cities — especially with the one child policy which began affecting the growth of the labour force in the 1990s.

But while people could enter the cities, they still kept their *hukou* status and thus could not use local schools and health facilities and they couldn't afford the health facilities in any case since they lacked any kind of health insurance.

Schools did develop but without the help of urban governments in areas where there were large concentrations of migrants. These schools operate in abandoned buildings and the like and can be closed down by the authorities at a moments notice. Many urban authorities simply ignore these schools, but they can be hostile to migrants as well (example of the Shanghai official who said that rural migrants weren't interested in educating their children). These kinds of officials are trying to create modern cities on the pattern of New York and do not want to be distracted by the welfare needs of poor migrants.

Fortunately, there are others high in the government, probably including the new Party Secretary, Hu Jintao, who see the problem differently. Hu was Party Secretary and Governor in some of China's poorest provinces such as Guizhou and acquired an understanding of the migrant problems. The *hukou* system as a result is being partially abandoned in the sense that migrants with jobs will be allowed to change their residence status — but much depends on what one defines as a job and one suspects that most regions will define this as long term employment as a factory worker or something similar and will not include construction workers, retail service workers, household servants and the like.

The alternative approach of providing all of the migrants with all of the benefits that exist for current urban residents is not practical, however. The cost of housing is 160,000 *yuan* per family or USD 20,000. If 200 million families migrate over the next 3 decades, that will involve a total expenditure for housing alone of USD 4 trillion dollars or well over USD 100 billion per year, roughly 10% of China's total GDP at present. To that one would have to add all of the other infrastructure costs from roads to schools and health facilities.

There are still those in China who think that the way to deal with this problem is to let only those men and some women who have jobs to come without their families. But this approach both misses an opportunity and carries with it a major potential danger.

The opportunity lies in the ability to better educate the children of the migrants to make them more valuable for the economies of the urban areas in the decades ahead. Rural schools do not do this well and it is very hard to get good teachers, health workers, or almost any other skilled worker, to go to the poorer regions of the country. But one doesn't have to if the people of the poorer regions are allowed to bring their children to where the teachers and health workers prefer to live.

The danger is that keeping the families out will lead to tens of millions of males living in the cities without their families just as HIV/AIDS is beginning to break out into the heterosexual population. There is already a serious sexually transmitted disease (STD) problem because of the floating population that carries the problem back to their villages, but what if 5% of China's population became infected?

What will be the outcome of a policy of allowing unfettered migration to the cities with families?

- It could lead to a situation where large parts of the interior of China become depopulated, and, at least as far as the more mountainous regions are concerned, that is probably a good thing. But does one want the whole Chinese population crowding down into the coastal cities?
- This shift of the population eastward, however, does not have to occur if the there is a migration of capital westward. But that

migration of capital will not mainly be government investment in infrastructure. The large scale migration of capital, both domestic and foreign, just as in the American south, will have to come from companies pursuing higher profits by leaving the coastal cities with their high rents and expensive labour.

- For that shift to happen, China does not so much need a west-China infrastructure-investment policy although that will help. What it needs is to remove the barriers to capital flowing westward by changing the way the interior governments operate — specifically to remove the remaining barriers to creating a true relatively unfettered market system. This will involve getting rid of all kinds of government licences and permits. It will also involve recognition that the driving force for development is going to be the private sector, not state enterprises — this is much better understood on the coast that it is in the interior.

The bottom line of this discussion is that a true regional development strategy in a market economy focuses mainly on getting the market to work properly. The job of government in this process is not to guide the private sector that is responding to market forces. The job of government is to provide the infrastructure and services that the private sector cannot provide or at least is unable to provide at this time.

3   Eco-Environmental Protection and Poverty-Alleviation in West China Development

Zheng Yuxin and Qian Yihong

Introduction

Among all the great achievements attained by China in the two decades after it embarked on economic reform and opening up, the most remarkable are the tremendous changes brought about to China's rural areas by the rapid and sustained economic growth, which is most noticeably marked by the alleviation of poverty in the rural areas. In as little as six years, from 1978 to 1984, China's poverty-stricken population decreased from 250 million to 125 million and the incidence of poverty was reduced by half, from 30.7% to 14.8%. By 2000, the poverty-stricken population had dropped to 30 million, while the incidence of poverty declined to less than 3%.[1] Despite such a success, the distribution of the remaining poverty-stricken population has become more concentrated in China's central and western regions, especially the ecologically vulnerable areas.[2]

In such ecologically vulnerable areas with adverse geographic conditions, the impoverished people have to make a living within the constraints of scarce natural resources. The problem of excessive exploitation is always precipitated by their efforts to lift themselves from poverty, which is undoubtedly the most important factor contributing to the deterioration of eco-environment in these areas. The close interrelation between eco-environment deterioration and poverty is also evidenced by the fact that the former, in return, furthers the worsening of the living conditions of the poverty-stricken population. Although, in general, the vicious cycle of "poverty – environment deterioration" has been brought under initial control, China's environmental situation is still severe. Such a vicious cycle of poverty and environment deterioration still exists, especially widely in the impoverished western areas, resulting in a heavy toll of the country.

It is notable that the Chinese government's strategy of developing West China puts the ecological construction as the central task, which is the first time for a national economic program in China to do so. Some senior leaders of the Chinese government have also emphasized that environment protection should be given first priority in the West China Development Program. Nonetheless, if the problems of poverty in the western region, those caused by ecological vulnerability in particular, could not be effectively addressed, the claimed "great readjustment", "great restoration" and "great protection" of the eco-environment in the region can only be given lip service. It is perceivable that the work of poverty-eradication in the program is not only a must for realizing social justice, but also a prerequisite for improving the eco-environment.

Both poverty and environmental problems are typically results of market inefficiency. The solution thereof depends on reasonable policy-making and institutional arrangement, in which non-market factors are not only necessary but also determinant. This article will devote discussion to the interrelation between poverty-eradication and environment protection in the western region, with emphasis on the mechanism forming of a virtuous cycle between poverty eradication and environment protection, including the policy-making and institutional arrangement.

Regional Characteristics of Poverty in China

If Guangxi and Inner Mongolia, the two provincial regions previously belonging to the central region are taken into calculation, the western region covers an area of 6.83 million square kilometres, representing 71.2% of the total area of China. As a mountainous country, China has mountains and plateaux accounting for two thirds of its total area. Topographically, the west region is featured by most of the country's mountains, plateaux, deserts, apteriums, glaciers and areas permanently covered by snow. More than eighty percent of the impoverished counties of the western region find themselves located in one of these natural circumstances. Bad natural conditions render the poverty rate of the western region much higher than that of the central and eastern regions.

The distribution of absolutely impoverished population is concentrated in the western region

The "impoverished counties" are those counties to which the central government plans to give special support for poverty alleviation. According to the statistics of Poverty-Alleviation Office under the State Council, among the 592 counties defined in 1994 as "impoverished", 105 were in the eastern region, 180 in the central region, and 307 in the western region, respectively accounting for 18%, 30% and 52% of the total. Of the over 70 million impoverished population calculated by the State Statistics Bureau, 13.85 million are in the eastern region, 20.30 million in the central region, and 35.91 million in the western region, respectively representing 19.8%, 29% and 51.3% of the total impoverished population. In contrast, in 1995, the population of the western region was only 344 million, accounting for only 28.6% of China's total population.

The distribution of relatively impoverished population is also concentrated in the western region

The "relatively impoverished population" refers to the bottom 20% of rural population by income or the rural population whose income is 50% lower than the nationwide per capita rural income. By calculation in accordance with this definition, between 1994 to 1996, there were 150 to 180 million relatively impoverished persons in China's rural area. The western region is not only the area where the absolutely impoverished population concentrates, but also the area where the relatively impoverished population is distributed (see Table 3.1).

Table 3.1   The Distribution of the Relatively Impoverished
Population and Low-income counties among the Eastern,
Central and Western Regions

Type			Farmers with per capita net income			
			Below 500 yuan	Below 500-800 yuan	Below 800-1000 yuan	Below 1000 yuan
Relatively impoverished	Population (million)	East	0.00	0.24	0.93	1.17
		Central	0.23	8.71	15.79	24.73
		West	11.49	51.52	50.55	113.56
		Total	11.72	60.47	67.27	139.46
	Share of national total	East	0.00	0.39	1.38	0.84
		Central	1.92	14.41	23.48	17.73
		West	98.08	85.20	75.14	81.43
Low-income countries	Number	East	0	2	5	7
		Central	1	31	65	97
		West	44	206	148	398
		Total	45	239	218	502
	Share of national total	East	0.00	0.84	2.29	1.39
		Central	2.22	12.97	29.82	19.32
		West	97.98	86.19	67.89	29.29

Note: The levels of farmer's income on the basis of data of individual counties
are compiled from the *Yearbook on Rural Economy in China* (1997). In
1996, average net income of 1000 *yuan* was taken as a criterion for the
relative poverty populations in the rural areas.

Source: Chen (1998).

Interrelations between Poverty and Eco-Environment Deterioration in the Western Region

Like those in other countries, China's environment problems could be
divided into two categories: One is environment destruction related to

poverty which is generated by agricultural activities, e.g., reduction of forest, destruction of vegetation, erosion of water and soil and desertization, etc.; The other is the emission of pollutants in the process of industrialization or urbanization, e.g., waste gas, waste water, solid wastes and sound pollution, etc. In China, these two kinds of environment destruction not only exist simultaneously but also have mutual bearing on each other, thus yielding multiple pressures on China's environment.

In the case of the western region, it should be said that both problems are very serious, with the former being more acute. Given that the western region is located in the upper reaches of China's major rivers, water and soil erosion and land desertization are becoming increasingly worse, posing a severe threat to the development of the central and eastern regions, which are located in the middle and lower reaches of these rivers. This constitutes a major threat to the living conditions for the Chinese people as a whole.

Research indicates that, in the western region, eco-environment deterioration and poverty is highly interrelated with each other. This could be discerned from the typical regional characteristics of the distribution of China's poverty population. For the 592 impoverished counties defined by the State Council in the poverty-alleviation taskforce program, eco-environment deterioration and lack of resources are the leading causes of poverty. As for China's six major impoverished areas, albeit not completely disadvantaged in geographic location and climate, most of them are located in China's ecologically vulnerable areas. In these areas, the natural environment changes frequently and dramatically, the ecological system's responding capacity is relatively weak, and the environment deterioration is quite universal. In Gansu, Shaanxi and Guangxi, respectively 73%, 76% and 76% of their impoverished counties are located in the ecologically vulnerable areas, a reflection of the interrelationship between poverty and the ecological vulnerability (see Table 3.2). This finding has two implications. On the one hand, bad eco-environmental conditions and lack of resources constitute the leading cause for poverty; On the other hand, poverty exacerbates the deterioration of the eco-environment.

Table 3.2   The Interrelations between Poverty and Ecological Vulnerability

	Counties				Population			
Provincial territory	No. of EVCs	No. of ICs	Share of EVCs that are ICs	Share of ICs that are EVCs	Living in EVCs (1,000)	Living in ICs (1,000)	Share of EVC residents living in ICs	Share of IC residents living in EVCs
Hebei	35	49	0.83	0.59	10005	15801	0.87	0.55
Shanxi	41	36	0.68	0.78	5193	4666	0.71	0.79
Inner Mongolia	30	40	0.83	0.63	9478	8319	0.69	0.79
Liaoning	8	11	0.62	0.46	6014	4744	0.43	0.54
Jilin	5	6	0.60	0.50	1139	959	0.57	0.68
Zhejiang	11	3	0.27	1.00	2789	810	0.29	1.00
Anhui	24	17	0.54	0.77	11068	12650	0.74	0.64
Fujian	7	16	0.57	0.25	2208	4586	0.51	0.25
Jianxi	54	56	0.78	0.75	16474	20868	0.86	0.68
Shandong	13	14	0.77	0.71	10755	10488	0.72	0.74
Henan	28	26	0.64	0.69	16931	15672	0.68	0.73
Hubei	35	37	0.97	0.92	14072	14576	0.98	0.94
Hunan	37	28	0.65	0.86	12759	12401	0.64	0.66
Guangdong	12	25	1.00	0.48	6699	13133	1.00	0.51
Guangxi	44	49	0.91	0.82	12665	13703	0.86	0.79
Sichuan	57	51	0.68	0.77	35093	27980	0.74	0.93
Guizhou	30	31	0.37	0.36	12129	11997	0.59	0.60
Yunnan	30	42	0.70	0.50	5802	10700	0.78	0.42
Shannxi	35	34	0.74	0.76	6602	7904	0.86	0.72
Gansu	36	30	0.61	0.73	10845	8673	0.55	0.69
Qinghai	13	12	0.77	0.83	2276	2384	0.97	0.92
Ningxia	6	8	1.00	0.75	1650	1916	1.00	0.86

Notes: EVC=counties located in ecologically vulnerable areas;
IC=impoverished counties.

Source: Fu Min (1996).

Eco-environmental Goals and Poverty Alleviation

Historic experiences have told us that the downfall of the Chinese civilization in the past was closely related with the destruction of the environment. The rejuvenation of the Chinese civilization can not be achieved without effective improvements of the eco-environment.

In the mid-1990s, the Chinese government made "sustainable growth" the basic strategy of national development and began to pay comprehensive attention to environmental problems by publishing *China's 21st Century Agenda – a white book on China's Population, Resources and Environment*. The Agenda was the first government initiative to take an integrated perspective of the economy, society, resources and environment and contemplate these environmental and resource constraints and the potential crises facing China's development. The Agenda presents a comprehensive framework for evolutionary and sustainable development. Its publication was a significant event for China's environmental protection and development. In *China's 21st Century Agenda*, there are 450 actions of the government's "green departments"[3], including construction of laws and organizations, and policy measures, which are termed "green policies".

Recently, environmental problems have caught great attention in China. Three ecological events in the final years of 20th century sounded alarms. They were: (1) Yellow River discontinued for 227 days in 1997, (2) Yangzi River flooded seriously in 1998, (3) Sand and dust storms swept Beijing and other places in 2000. The three events marked the commencement of a new era, in which accumulated nationwide ecological destruction has begun to have a directly adverse effect on the people. Protection of the eco-system has become the first priority of national development.

In 1999, the State Council promulgated the "Construction Plan for China's Ecological Environment". The Plan worked out short-term (from present to 2010), mid-term (from 2011 to 2030) and long-term (from 2031 to 2050) goals for the eco-environment construction in China. According to the Plan, by the year 2010, man-made erosion of water and soil must be brought under control, the expansion of desert must be curbed, 600,000 square km of soil erosion and 22 million hectares of deserted land must be treated, and 5 million hectares of land must be returned to forest; By 2030, the nationwide eco-environmental situation must be improved significantly, so that 60% of water and soil erosion that are suitable for control will be controlled to different degrees, 40 million hectares of desertized land will be treated, and the area of forest be increased by 46 million hectares, thus expanding the nationwide forest coverage to 24%. By 2050, a sound ecological system that meets the requirement of sustainable development must be established.

Obviously, to translate such a great program into action, the key lies in the western region. Without the government-claimed "great readjustment", "great restoration" and "great protection" of the eco-environment in the region, the Plan will lead nowhere. Some major measures have been adopted in respect to eco-environment protection. For instance, the programs on Protection of Natural Forest, including Ban on Felling of Natural Forest, which went into effect in 1998, and the program on "Returning Cultivated Land to Forest and Grassland", which began in 1999, are both measures of great significance. From wanton felling of natural forests to resolutely banning the felling and giving state protection for forests, from indiscriminately destroying forest and grassland for the purpose of cultivation, to returning cultivated land to forest and grassland, it took China thousands of years to reach a turning point of great historical significance.

From 1999 to the end of 2002, China returned 115 million *mu* of land to forest, including 55.82 million *mu* of cultivated land and 59.66 million *mu* of wasteland. The government plans to arrange the return of 107 million *mu* of land to forest in 2003.[4] It is a great relief that the western region development program has been pioneered by these measures.

Yet, along with the overall protection of the natural forest and returning land to forest and grassland, new problems have come to the fore. The core problem is how to make overall arrangement for the living of the local residents and forestry-related workers. Given that the protection of natural forest and the returning of land to forest and grassland are mostly carried out in the impoverished areas, how to help the local people to get rid of poverty at the same time, namely practising green poverty-eradication, has become an imminent problem. Without addressing this problem, the eco-environment construction of the western region will be unsustainable.

Ecology Compensation: A Key Step in Green Poverty-Alleviation

Although in theory poverty-alleviation and ecological improvement should be consistent goals, in those areas suffering from both poverty and ecological vulnerability, there exist contradictions between the two goals. Poverty alleviation program may yield economic benefits but its negative externality (ecological destruction) is not necessarily internalized. On the other hand, the great positive externality of a ecological improvement program is also difficult to be internalized as it usually does not yield returns. Such a configuration results from the fact that the interests of the ecologically vulnerable areas and the ecologically benefited areas are separated from each other. In reality, it can be perceived that, in the eco-environment construction, the right of development and well-being of the local people are more or less prejudiced. The involved impoverished population is usually a disadvantaged group, and are constrained by the bad natural conditions and weak in market competitions. Eco-environment construction involves overall situation and benefit for more than a single village, a single county, or a single province. Therefore, those who suffer a loss from the eco-environment construction shall have compensation from the beneficiaries. If such compensation could be arranged through a system, the consistency between poverty-eradication and ecological improvement will be translated into reality, thus bringing about a win-win situation. We hold that the compensation has a broad sense which includes various kinds of assistance in favour of poverty-eradication. The core of the assistance shall be helping the poverty-struck population to raise its capacity to get rid of poverty and create a mechanism to increase income. Facing these challenges, China is gaining experience through organizational and institutional innovation, establishing a compensation mechanism at various levels.

Initiatives from the national level

Major input for the program of "Returning Land to Forest" comes from the national fiscal budget. The details of the policy for the program are: the central government provides farmers who return cultivated land to forest upstream of the Yangzi River and in up and middle stream of the Yellow River with 150 kg and 100 kg of grain per *mu* respectively (calculated according to 1.4 *yuan*/kg) for 5 years (in the case of economic forest) and 8 years (in the case of ecological forest) or more years, with 20 *yuan* of cash for daily expense, and with 50 *yuan* for seeds and saplings. The government also encourages farmers to return more wasteland to forest and grassland.

The programs on "Protection of Natural Forest" and "Returning Land to Forest" deal with 1.2 million of workers of forest industry and several million of farmers. By 2010, the central government will have spent at least 160 billion *yuan* on these programs. Obviously, most of the money is used as compensation for farmers.

However, the compensation mechanism still is not effective. China has to face the challenge of negative side effects of the two programs. From research on the following-up problems after the banning of felling of natural forest in the Dong and Miao National Autonomous Prefecture in the southeast part of Guizhou Province, a team of researchers from the Centre for Environment and Development of CASS concluded that the effectiveness of the program depends on how the economic compensations were given to the workers affected by the prohibition of forest felling.

In Leishan, Taijiang and Jianhe counties, our research team found that forestry and relevant industries took a fairly high share in the local financial revenue. For instance, Jianhe County's fiscal revenue from the forestry and relevant industry in 1998 was 14.35 million *yuan*, representing 49.1% of the total fiscal revenue of the locality. In 1999, the figure declined to 8.82 million *yuan*. Additionally, the revenue of the rural residents who mainly depend on forestry to make a living was also largely influenced. The average forestry-related revenue for a typical farmer was 311 *yuan* in 1998. The figure dropped to 216 *yuan* after the prohibition of felling. As a result, the incidence of poverty must have risen in some impoverished areas. Thanks to the reduction of felling quota, the local forest industry faced difficulties in repaying debts and generating capital. Economic returns declined by a wide margin for the forestry enterprises, state-owned wood-processing enterprises, and the town and township wood-processing enterprises. In short, the prohibition of felling has great influence on the entire county's economy and the bulk of the related employees, for whom the State should work out a policy to give proper compensation.

Similar problems also appeared in the process of returning land to forest and grassland. There have been many lessons in this regard. For example, assisted by the UN Grain and Agricultural Organization, the Xiji county in Ningxia returned land to forest and grassland in the early 1990s and consequently the vegetation was restored several years later. However, a few more years later, due to the unsolved poverty problem, farmers went back again to destroy forest and grassland to grow crops. The achievements of the eco-environment construction were thus ruined. So people worry about what will happen after the government stops providing grains for farmers who return their cultivated land to forest. To achieve the target of eco-system improvement is a very tough job and has no simple answer. No doubt, China faces severe challenges in this process.

Initiatives from the local level

In respect to establishing a compensation mechanism, some areas have tried some innovations. For instance, the County of Danfeng[5] under Shaanxi Province practices a policy requiring each person to construct one *mu* of "basic crop field" so as to ensure the realization of "returning land to forest." By choosing a proper area of land which is suitable for grain planting and turning it into field with adequate water, soil and fertilizer, the county raised the grain output of unit acreage of land and meets the rural people's demand for grain. Meanwhile, cultivated land on slope was transferred into forests to hold soil erosion and further environment destruction. The result proved the policy to be a good combination of eco-environment protection and economic growth in the mountain areas. The experience of the County of Danfeng in constructing "basic crop field" in promotion of returning land to forest suggests the merit of division of labour among local areas and ecological compensation mechanisms for poverty-eradication and ecological restoration.

Initiatives from interior regions

Ecology compensation mechanisms in large spheres, including the ones between the ecologically vulnerable areas in the upper reaches of the Yangtzi and Yellow Rivers and the ecologically benefited areas in the lower reaches, shall be built up as soon as possible. At present, in the process of implementing the preservation project for natural forests, the central government has suggested to use more grain from other areas to compensate for the returning of land to forest in the western region. Such a trans-regional environment-economy integration policy indicates that our poverty-alleviation strategy, or even the overall strategy of West China development, is being renovated by new thinking. Under such thinking, poverty-alleviation no longer equals the provision of subsistence goods, but becomes a part of the strategy of rendering protection to most of the ecologically vulnerable areas (especially those with great externalities). The western region is no longer seen as a region with mineral and forest resources, but a region adversely affecting China's overall eco-environment through water-soil erosion and desertization. This is a thinking of sustainable development, which is to integrate environmental goals and an ecology compensation principle into the poverty-alleviation program. Division of labour is the precondition for the raising of productivity and it will also become the precondition for sustainable development. Whether or not the eastern region should directly make eco-compensation to the western region is still a controversial issue in China.

The urgent need to establish the measuring criteria for "environment value"

Is the program of green poverty-alleviation and ecology compensation worthwhile? In absence of the awareness of the "environment value" and the "social cost", it is hard to make a reasonable judgement. The fact that the value of environment, especially the value of its ecological functions, cannot be put in the form of market value or calculated into gross national product (GNP) is a major reason that people can not comprehend the necessity of ecology compensation. In spite of all the difficulties, the work of evaluating eco-environment has become imperative in the process of promoting green poverty-alleviation and establishing division of labour and ecology compensation mechanism in various spheres and at various levels.

Conclusion

The externality of eco-environment makes the realization of ecological compensation through market mechanism infeasible. For this account, the establishment of an ecological compensation mechanism must depend on non-market measures, particularly on government interference at various levels. In ecological compensation, the principle of those who benefit shall pay indicates that ecological compensation is actually a redistribution of interests. Therefore, the difficulties in the process of implementation are beyond doubt.

Notes

1.   China's official poverty line on annual personal income is 100 *yuan* in 1978, 206 *yuan* in 1985, 268 *yuan* in 1990, 550 *yuan* in 1995, and 625 *yuan* in 2002.

2.   According to China's "Seventh Five-year Plan", the whole country is divided into east, west and central economic regions. The east region includes twelve provincial units, i.e., Beijing, Tianjin, Hebei, Liaoning, Shanghai, Jiangsu, Zhejiang, Fujian, Shangdong, Guangxi, Hainan, etc.; The central region includes nine provincial territories, i.e., Shanxi, Inner Mongolia, Jilin, Heilongjing, Anhui, Jiangxi, Henan, Hubei, Hunan, etc.; The western region includes nine provincial territories, i.e., Sichuan, Guizhou, Yunnan, Xizang, Shanxi, Gansu, Ningxia, Qinghai, and Xinjiang. The statistics are subject to such a division of region.

3.   The term "green department" refers to the government department that is in charge of protection of eco-system, resources and environment. Examples are State Environmental Protection

Administration, Ministry of Territory and Resources, State Forestry Bureau, Ministry of Agriculture, etc.
4.   One *Mu* = 99.17 square metres.
5.   The County of Danfeng is one of the CASS's poverty-relieving pilot areas that have received guidance from CASS expertise in their poverty relieving programs.

References

1.   Chen Fan (1998). "Some Problems Regarding Poverty in China", *Countryside Digest*, No. 9.
2.   Tang Jun (1999). "An Analysis of the Situation of Poverty and Counter-Poverty in China," *The Year of 1999: Analysis and Forecast of China's Social Situation*, Social Scientific Document Publisher House, January.
3.   Fu Min (ed) (1996). *Chinese Government's Action to Alleviate Poverty*, Hubei Scientific and Technological Publishing House.
4.   Li zhou and Sun Ruomei, et al (1997). *Research on the Relations between the Development Model and Ecological Changes in China's Rural Areas*, Shanxi Economic Publishing House.
5.   Shen Xiaohui (2000). "Development of Western Area: Do not let the successors regret again", *China's Green Time*, March 24 and April 7.
6.   Qian Yihong (1999). "Ecology Compensation Mechanism: A Key Step in Green Poverty-Relieving", *Research Report*, August.
7.   Qian Yihong (2000). "Pay Attention to the Follow-up Problems after the Prohibition of Felling of Natural Forest in China's Southern Areas", *Reference to Leaders*, No. 3.
8.   Qian Yihong (2000). "China Needs New Management Model for its Natural Preservation Zones: Viewing from the Problem of Regional Poverty-Relieving," *Research Report*, May.
9.   Taskforce of the Research Centre on Environment and Development, under CASS (1999). "Poverty and Environment in the Asia-Pacific Region (China Part)", *Research Report*, August.

4 Western China: Human Security and National Security

Robert Bedeski

The Geopolitics of Western China: the Frontier Region

Development of China's western regions has been overshadowed for the last two decades by phenomenal economic growth with central government emphasis on the coastal cities, with their more advanced infrastructure and easier access to global markets. From the standpoint of national defence, historic threats and conflicts have been more characteristic of the coastal regions during the nineteenth and twentieth centuries, from the intrusion of the Europeans, Americans, and later, the Japanese. During the quarter century when Mao Zedong dominated the Chinese state, the interior was developed in part as defence against possible invasion to provide base areas if the coastal regions were again occupied. From the early 1960s, a Soviet threat was added to the list of potential enemies, threatening the northern, western and northeastern sectors.[1]

Economic development in East Asia has been closely linked to national security. The program of rapid industrialization in Meiji Japan was tied to creating a modern military power in Japan that could prevent the dismantling of sovereignty occurring in nineteenth century China (Dower, 1975: 17). All strategic enterprises, including railways, telephones and telegraphs, and shipbuilding, were organized with state security the top priority. Even the highly nationalistic education system had the goal of transforming Japanese subjects into productive warriors not unlike the ancient Legalist program of Shang Yang, minus the industrial imperative. In modern times, Sun Yat-sen was impressed by the progress he saw in Japan, and envisioned regionally-even development and industrialization of China, once political order was restored. His death, the continued fragmentation under warlords, Japanese invasion, and the civil war between tl.e Nationalists and Communists postponed progress of economic development until the early 1950s. Major modern cities had been built in part with foreign capital and western technology, and were part of the emerging global markets before the onslaught of economic depression of the 1930s and Japanese invasions. Under the dictatorship of the Chinese Communist Party, China embarked on a program of industrialization inspired by Soviet central planning, and treated the nation as a great chessboard avoiding the concentration of industry in any particular city or region, to prevent having a hostage in event of war or all the industrial eggs in one basket. Deng's reforms merely reinforced the pre-eminence of the coastal industrial cities, with Hong Kong as the unclaimed crown jewel until 1997.

China's frontiers have historically been a zone of vulnerability, and security of the border, extending from Tibet to Shanhaiguan, preoccupied dynasties for millennia. The Great Wall was an attempt to fix the northern border between agrarian China and the nomadic Central Asian steppes. In the western flanks, formidable mountain ranges and deserts provided strategic buffers that spared China much of the migration and invasion which characterized European history after the fall of Rome. The eastern coast suffered pirates, but was not threatened by major military force until the mid-nineteenth century.

From the Opium Wars through World War II and the Korean War to the focus on retaking Taiwan, modern Chinese governments have held the western regions in secondary priority. During the Soviet-inspired industrialization of the 1950s and subsequent fear of Soviet military attacks in the sixties, dispersal of industries in the west was part of Beijing policy to correct the imbalances of uneven growth. In the post-Mao period, with Deng Xiaoping's economic reforms, the seaboard cities and ports were transformed into global entrepots, leaving the interior regions behind (Lai, 2002).

The rest of the People's Republic resembles nothing so much as a frontier. These vast and sparsely populated margins are home to the country's ethnic minorities, Tibetans, Uighurs, the myriad hill tribes of

Yunnan. Illiteracy and poverty rates are high, per capita income in 2000 was 35% below the national average and central control, often personified by Han settlers and military garrisons, is resented. In fact, the regions stunning natural beauty and famed hospitality belie a deeply troubled relationship with Beijing: during previous periods of imperial collapse, this Wild West was the first to bolt. Today, pro-independence sentiments simmer in the two largest provinces, Tibet and Xinjiang. Yet despite the area's outward backwardness, it is hard to imagine China without this region, which encompasses more than half the country's land mass (Pei, 2002).

Today, Western China is no longer the backwater of the past. The instability of the post-Soviet successor states poses new challenges for maintaining political order and military security on Central Asian borders (Rashid, 2002). China has supported formation of the Shanghai Cooperation Group (SCO)[2] to coordinate economic and security policies, although Mongolia has not joined, possibly fearful of losing its decade-old independence. After the September-11 incident and the overthrow of the Taliban regime in Afghanistan, the U.S. has become the dominant power in Central Asia, and there is little prospect of Russia and/or China dominating the SCO.[3] The rise of Islamic fundamentalism after the collapse of the Soviet Union has sharpened the need for cooperation in Central Asia. A new concern for China on its western flanks is the ability and apparent intention of the U.S. to project military force into a region once isolated from the mainstream of global power vectors.

National Security Issues for China

On the other hand, the September-11 incident has also reinforced China's ability to deal with dissidents when they perform terrorist acts. One of the expected consequences of globalization, and the decreasing isolation of Central Asia, is the rising importance of Western China's frontiers as buffers. Failure of China to respond to globalization will affect the ability to defend Western territories. If we look at how globalization affects China today, there are some clear influences:

1.   Economic globalization is the most apparent. Since the 1979 reforms, China has actively sought and expanded trade and investment. Accession to the WTO has been a major step forward in assimilating China into international trade and economic regimes.

2.   Through science and technology, and the information and communication technology (ICT) revolution, China is increasingly wired into the multitude of networks linking Chinese citizens to the world. Economic opportunities proliferate in nanotechnology, manufacturing, and genetic engineering, to name a few. Taking advantage of these opportunities requires greater openness, as well as substantial investment in education, infrastructure, and facilities.

3.   The U.S. war on terrorism, the subset conflicts with Iraq and possibly North Korea, and the Revolution in Military Affairs (RMA) all have a net effect on China's military and geo-strategic posture. To maintain a credible defence in the modern world, and even to preserve the option of force against Taiwan, China must adapt to the modern realities of warfare, requiring significant diversion of resources to its security budget.

4.   Chinese diplomacy must adjust to the complex realities of being a world power. The days when Beijing could play the part of wronged victim, and fall back on the bombastic ideology of anti-imperialism, are gone. China is a major nuclear power, with international entanglements stopping short of alliances, and growing international responsibilities. In practically every relationship, China must consider the role and interests of the U.S. before embarking on action.

5.   As China has moved toward greater "global citizenship", it has had to overcome the scars of the Tiananmen Event in 1989. Opening the country has made its abuses of human rights much more visible, and repressions in Tibet, against Christians and Falun Gong are continuing indictments of the Chinese regime. Few expect China to democratize in the next decade, but much of the world expects it to at least adhere to the requirements of civilized society.

6.   China has watched the increasing proclivity of the United Nations and the U.S. to intervene abroad for human security and

humanitarian purposes over the past decade with great concern. The doctrine of decreasing sovereignty[4] is a source of worry for China. For over a century, China has struggled to match the success of Japan in transforming itself into a viable modern sovereign nation-state (MSNS). Its incomplete territoriality is marked by Taiwan's secessionist tendencies, but in most other respects, China is a MSNS. Integration of Hong Kong and Macao has been an important milestone in the completion of Chinese territorial sovereignty.

Globalization is increasing the importance of China's western region, particularly Tibet and Xinjiang, which are most distant and remote from Beijing. From a strategic and military perspective, it is crucial for China to consolidate its hold on those areas. Economic integration and improved transportation and communication to those frontiers are underway, and will strengthen control.

Defending China is a vast problem; the country is the third largest country in the world, with fourteen bordering states and the longest land boundaries of any state. The ethnic geography imposes further strategic problems, with minority peoples largely occupying the territories outside China's core eastern areas. During the Sino-Soviet rift in the 1960s, both countries tried to encourage the other's minority grievances to threaten control of the frontier regions (Jenkins, 1990: 266-290, 268-9). Consolidation of these frontier regions has thus been a continuing concern of China.

Tibet

For much of the first half of the twentieth century, Xinjiang and Tibet were beyond control of Chinese governments. Great Britain exercised dominance over Tibet as part of its sphere of interest. Policy toward Lhasa was oriented toward resisting Russian southern penetration in Asia. With PRC incorporation of Tibet into China in 1950, direct western intervention came to an end, and China consolidated its natural borders in the southwest. Chinese legal and territorial claims subordinated Tibetan aspirations to independence (Heberer, 1989: 123). China has set up the Xizang Autonomous Region to provide special administration for Tibet, and grants special internal status to ethnic Tibetans. Minorities Institutes throughout the country as well as a multicultural face to official popular culture nourish an image of PRC multi-ethnicity, but the reality is tension between the PRC and its frontier peoples.

The drive to develop the region has been expensive, with more than 200,000 Han workers in Tibet since the 1950s. Taxes are virtually nonexistent, and Tibetan farmers receive tax-free leases on land, unlike the interior. The government encourages business with low interest loans, and imports from Nepal are duty-free. From 1952 to 1994, the central government invested USD 4.2 billion, and in 1994, Beijing initiated 62 infrastructure projects. In 1996, China provided USD 600 million to Tibet, a region with about 2.5 million people. Compare this to American aid of USD 800 million to all of Africa, with a population in the hundreds of millions. More than 90% of Tibets government revenue is estimated to come from outside (Hessler, 1999: 55-56).

The charge that China is exploiting Tibet as a colonial region is misleading. Beijing has spent an enormous amount of capital, human and financial, but self-sufficiency remains far off, although there is development of timber and mineral reserves. From Beijing's perspective, Tibet is important in part because of its military value, and will never again be allowed to come under foreign influence.

Plans to connect Tibet to central China by railways were discussed since the 1950s, but little was done due to the technical difficulties of high mountain peaks and permafrost swamps. In March 2001, the National People's Congress and State Council decided to construct the rail line, a move that will further consolidate Chinese control over the central Tibetan plateau. Completion of the Lhasa-Golmud line will increase Chinese ability to move troops and supplies around the region.

The line will be 1,118 kilometres long and will have 30 bridges and tunnels that have a total length of 20 kilometres, or 1.8% of the railways length. Projected cost in 1995 US dollars will be USD 2.34 billion. There are plans to construct three other lines connecting Lhasa to the western provinces:

- Chengdu-Kongpo-Lhasa
- Dali-Kongpo-Lhasa
- Lanzhou-Nagchu-Lhasa.

The projects are officially designed to enhance "national defence and domestic stability" and to further integrate the Tibetan economy with mainstream China. For construction of the first line, China will use about 67,000 outside workers and 16,000 local workers. The construction will place great pressure on local resources, and when completed, will undoubtedly damage the fragile Tibetan ecosystem with erosion, silting and pollution. Cheap and reliable transportation will also mean large-scale Han migration into central Tibet, further endangering the cultural identity of Tibet.

Xinjiang

While Tibet has historically been a barrier and buffer between South Asia and China, Xinjiang has been a geographical nexus, containing vital land routes through Russia and Central Asia to China. These are crucial communications that China has historically tried to control as far from its borders as possible in order not to face an open flank. This control not only offers military advantages, it also allows the Chinese to invest more to control the maritime access route to China. It also could allow China to gain access to the Indian Ocean and beyond.

Public attention has focused on Central Asia as an arena of terrorism and Islamic fundamentalism, and the response of the U.S. has emphasized this character. However, the possibilities for initiating large-scale economic projects throughout Central Asia and the Transcaucasus that connect these lands to Europe and East Asia deserve closer attention for at least three reasons (Blank, 2002: 282-314):

First, the Central Asian states are connections to the major players, and they are vulnerable to internal and external crises. So their economic and political stability directly concern their larger neighbours and the more distant major powers such as the United States and the E.U.

Second, the development and completion of major projects are essential to these states' security and prosperity, as well as to the major states that depend on this long-distance trade in energy. Major energy holdings are being developed, and the inherent difficulties of bringing them to market, the construction and completion of these pipeline and transpiration grids are important not just to the local states but also to the global economy.

Third, Central Asia has been insecure and unsettled since the collapse of the Soviet Union, and provides growing havens for terrorism, war, drugs and conduits for weapons of mass destruction (WMD).

Pakistan represents a demonstration of the cross-cutting forces in the region, with tribalism, widespread support for Islamic fundamentalism, drugs, and havens for terrorism. At the same time, the country is pulled in several directions. In 2002, Pakistani President Pervez Musharraf visited Russian President Vladimir Putin to discuss economic and security cooperation, the first visit by a Pakistani head of state in three decades.[5] Russia is also concerned that Chechen rebels have taken refuge in Pakistan.

Since the September-11 incident, Pakistan has also moved closer to the U.S. in allowing American armed forces access for the sake of search and destroy Taliban and its supporters, overcoming years of coolness over Pakistan's nuclear program. China has had a long-standing cooperative relationship with Pakistan, in large part because of mutual suspicion of India.

China's Xinjiang is not Pakistan, but both have been significantly influenced by Islam. During the Afghan resistance to Soviet invasion, Chinese aid to the mujahideen was funnelled through the Wakhan corridor from Xinjiang, and a few Chinese citizens reportedly joined the Taliban. China cannot ignore the dissident secessionist movement in the region, which it claims is sponsoring terrorism in the country.

Before the Communist takeover, it was estimated that about 94% of the Xinjiang population was Muslim and non-Han. China never completely ruled Xinjiang for over 2000 years, despite periodic occupation of the region. Only in 1884 was it integrated by force into the Manchu empire (Eberhard, 1982: 62). Beijing regards Xinjiang as integral territory of China, similar to Tibet. Landlocked, the common feature of Central Asia, means that practically all communication requires assent from adjoining powers, or the country that exerts sovereign power.

Xinjiang is further isolated by geography. It is a large depression surrounded on three sides by high mountain ranges. Drainage into the basin and evaporation produce salty lakes and marshes. Agriculture has been limited to oases separated from each other by long stretches of waterless desert. During the period of Communist repression of ethnic nationalism during the Great Leap Forward, many local people fled into adjacent Soviet Central Asia. During the post-1960 Soviet period, both China and the U.S.S.R. stationed large military forces to maintain defence against each other.

Ambitious oil exploration in the Taklamakan Desert produced a boom in the economy, growing a reported 10% annually in the first half of the 1990s. Korla (Kuerle), in the centre of the Autonomous Region, grew from 200,000 in the 1970s to over 300,000 by the mid 1990s, with Han Chinese at 61% of the town's population. This influx is part of the second Han wave of migration in the twentieth century. The first occurred in the late 1950s, when the government sent thousands of Hans to build roads, lay rail tracks and construct hospitals and schools. The two migrations have completely changed the demographics of Xinjiang. Before the 1950s, Uighurs made up 78% of Xinjiang's population. Now, they account for 48%, while the Han Chinese make up 38%.[6]

In the summer of 1958, the Chinese search for a site to test future nuclear weapons led them to the western deserts of Xinjiang. The Chinese rejected Soviet attempts to limit their nuclear program to weapons of 20 kilotons and chose a desert valley on the ancient silk road at Lop Nor.[7] The first underground test at Lop Nor took place on 22 September 1969. The last atmospheric test took place on 16 October 1980, and all tests since have been underground.

Conclusion

China's program of western development is undoubtedly driven in large part by economic considerations. Strategic and security interests also play an important part. In the past year and a half, U.S. intervention in Central Asia has awakened China and Russia to the fact that the region is no longer their exclusive sphere of influence. Since the collapse of the Soviet Union, Russia has been in retreat from Central Asia, and in any event, no longer able to safeguard its dominance as before. China recognizes the need to develop its western territory for economic reasons, and to exploit the natural resources where possible. Development of the region may also provide living space for tens of millions of surplus Han population. Full signification of the west will consolidate Chinese dominance of areas that have been only tenuously part of the past empire, although it will create tensions with the ethnic minorities in Tibet and Xinjiang.

From the standpoint of human security, there are likely to be major increases in threats to cultural security of minorities who are submerged by Han immigration to the western frontiers. Rapid development of urban centres, rail and road communications, agriculture, arboriculture, and industry will have negative effects on the often fragile environment of the west. Nevertheless, it appears that Beijing is determined to push ahead with its plans to transform its western provinces, and autonomous regions into areas that more closely resemble the societies and economies of the eastern provinces for better and worse.

Notes:

1. While in the *dongbei* (Northeast) several years ago, the author was told that the prestigious Harbin Institute of Technology had been deprived of full share of educational resources because the central leadership saw the region as vulnerable to Soviet intrusion during the sixties and seventies

2. The group consists of Russia, China, Kazakhstan, Kirghiztan, Tajikistan, and Uzbekistan.

3. At least one author considers the organization to have a future, see Tang (2002).

4. International Commission on Intervention and State Sovereignty, (2001). *The Responsibility to Protect*. Ottawa, IDRC.

5. "Pakistan urges Putin to be peace-maker with India" <http://www.alertnet.org>.

6. "Xinjiang Migration," <http://www.tibet.ca>.

7. The remoteness of the region was reaffirmed shortly before the first Chinese test. Part of the final test preparations included an aerial

inspection, and much to the surprise of the Chinese, the aerial photos revealed an encampment of over 200 inhabitants living close to ground zero! Search parties eventually rounded up the group, which turned out to be a group of Kuomintang (Chinese Nationalists), fugitives that had avoided surrender in 1949 [Wallace and Tinker (no date)].

References:

1. Blank, S. (2002). "Reconstructing Inner Asia". *The Journal of East Asian Affairs*, 16: 282-314.
2. Dower, J. W. (ed) (1975). *Origins of the Modern Japanese State.* Selected Writings of E.H. Norman. New York, Pantheon Books.
3. Eberhard, W. (1982). *China's Minorities*. Belmont, California, Wadsworth Publishing Company.
4. Heberer, T. (1989). *China and Its National Minorities*. Armonk, N.Y., M.E. Sharpe.
5. Hessler, P. (1999). "Tibet through Chinese Eyes", *The Atlantic Monthly*, 283: 56-66.
6. International Commission on Intervention and State Sovereignty, (2001). *The Responsibility to Protect*. Ottawa, IDRC.
7. Jenkins, A. (1990). "Defining and defending the Chinese state: geopolitical perspectives", *The Geography of Contemporary China. The Impact of Deng Xiaoping's Decade*. T. Cannon and A. Jenkins (eds). London, Routledge: 266-290.
8. Lai, H. H. (2002). "China's Western Development Program: Its Rationale, Implementation, and Prospects", *Modern China* 289:1(4): 432-463.
9. Minxin Pei, "The Chinese Split Personality", *Newsweek*, Oct. 28, 2002, in <http://www.taiwansecurity.org>
10. Rashid, A. (2002). *JIHAD The Rise of Militant Islam in Central Asia*. New Haven, Yale University Press.
11. Tang Shiping (2002). "The Future of the Shanghai Cooperation Organization", <http://www.ntu.edu.sg>

12.   Wallace, T. and Tinker, M. (no date). "The Last Nuclear Weapons Test? A Brief Review of the Chinese Nuclear Weapons Program", University of Arizona <http://www.iris.iris.edu>

5 Reconciliation Between Ecosystem Preservation and Economic Development Initiatives — The Case of Tarim Basin

Zhao Xiusheng, Dai Jian, and Shen Hong

Tarim Basin Background

Xinjiang Uighur Autonomous Region is the largest administrative province in the north-west part of China, accounting for one sixth of the country's total territory, where a number of ethnic minorities are living in a compact community, with the domination of Muslim Uighur people. The annual rainfall is 30-50 mm on average, while the evaporation can be as high as 2000-3000 mm, so water is the most important resource for irrigated agriculture. Some salient features of this remote province can be briefly described as follows:

- China's biggest administrative province
- A major agricultural area in Xinjiang, and also an important national petroleum base.
- Geographically located in the remote and outlying west region
- Multi-national ethnic groups living in a compact community
- Poverty-stricken region
- With relatively abundant natural resources
- With extremely fragile ecosystem
- Unique western features, ethnic folkways and Silk Road cultures
- Woman, gender, education and social stability are crucial issues

The Tarim Basin is geographically located in the south part of Xinjiang, occupying an area of 1.06 million m², with a population of around 8 million, over 80% being ethnic groups. The natural conditions are typically arid and the climate is extremely dry. The world's second-largest sand-dune, the Taklamagan Desert, sweeps across the central part of the basin covering an area of 330,000 km². Local people are ethnic groups of various Muslim minorities living in a relatively compact community and engaging in agricultural or live-stock production. In the south flows the Tarim River which is thought to be China's longest inland one, its mainstem running 1,321 km long if measured from the confluence of its three tributaries: Aksu River, Yarsant River and Hotan River. The upstream stretch is 495 kilometres from Xiaojiake to Yingbazha, the midstream stretch is 398 kilometres from Yingbazha to Kala and the downstream stretch is 428 kilometres from Kala to Tetema Lake, with a total drainage area of about 102 x104 km² as shown in Figure 5.1.

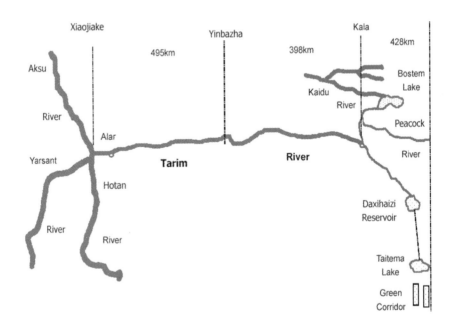

Figure 5.1.   Schematic Map of Tarim River Not Drawn to Scale

Major Problems and Physical Symptoms

Once fostering a resplendent civilization with a unique history of the Silk Road, the Tarim River has long been known to the world as Water of Survival for its critical role in maintaining the oasis culture and sustaining the local economy for all the ethnic groups in South Xinjiang.

However, with the expanded agricultural production and more increased human interventions, the fragile oasis-based ecosystem has been seriously damaged. The Great Reclamation Campaign launched in the 1960s by the ex-soldiers turned immigrants, along with the traditional behavioural patterns of local ethnic farmers in resource use have all combined to trigger even more conflicts and to intensify the long-existing practice of competing for use of the already scarce water resources. Still worse, due to the lack of an effective management system and inadequate engineering control over the entire river, the water inflow to Kala Point has kept declining ever since. Since 1979, the Tarim River had completely broken at the place of Daxihazi Reservoir, which is now the de facto ending point of this glorious lifeline. Currently, the 230 km segment further down from Yingsu has totally dried up and the water table between Tieganlike and Alagan has dropped to 10m, well below the critical level for the survival of the venerable diversiform-leafed poplar trees (Populus euphritica) and the natural vegetation which constitutes a green shelter belt to keep No. 218 National Highway open and stop the adjacent two great deserts, Taklamagan and Kuluke, from merging into one. As a result, the environmental degradation in the lower reaches has been deeply exacerbated, leaving the oasis economy at risk and the green corridor on the verge of extinction, thus threatening the subsistence and development of the people there. Some physical symptoms of the current environmental degradation can be summed up as follows:

- Shrunken and broken Tarim River, with the lakes dried up in lower reaches
- Deteriorated farmland and closed highway as a result of increasing desertification and sand-dune encroachment
- Frequent sandstorm disasters threatening the local people's survival and subsistence

- Degraded pasture-land and decreased live-stock carrying capacity
- Degenerated natural flora and green vegetation that help preserve the oasis-based culture

If reactions and responses are slow or too late, the environmental consequences and damage will be irreversible and likely to undermine the local economy and social stability. The current situation is largely attributable to the shrinking water inflow to the Kala Point. The surface water supply keeps tapering down every year, and such a phenomenon is even moving up to the lower part of the midstream sector.

The Leading Cause for Shrinking Downstream Inflow

The Tarim River is sourced by three tributaries — Aksu River, Yarsant River and Hotan River as shown in the sketch map above. According to the multi-year hydrological records, the natural run-offs of these sources show insignificant fluctuation and the incoming water flow generally remains invariable (Table 5.1).

Table 5.1.   Tributaries of Tarim River
(Unit: 10^8 m^3)

Tributaries	1957-1964	1965-1975	1976-1986	1987-1993	1957-1993
Aksu River	66.07	73.29	72.27	72.97	71.62
Yarsant River	63.42	64.10	66.90	62.40	63.93
Hotan River	45.31	43.50	45.23	39.80	44.00
Total	174.80	180.89	184.40	175.17	179.55

But, if measured at Alar Hydrological Station where these three source rivers converge to form what is called Tarim River, the average amount of flowing water is found to be reduced by about 10×10^8 m^3 from 1958 to 1993, and the total average water inflow for 37 years maintains a record of 46.8×10^8 m^3 (Table 5.2).

The declining water inflow from this point is attributable to the increasing water diversion and reservoir capacity at the source areas where the large irrigated oases are endowed with abundant sunlight and heat resources for economic expansion. Since 1979, Yarsant River had supplied little or no water down to Tarim River, and the inflows from the three source rivers had diminished to a certain degree.

Table 5.2. Inflow Records at Alar Hydrological Station –
Upper-most Point of Tarim River
(Unit: 10^8 m^3)

Tributaries	1957-1964	1965-1975	1976-1986	1987-1993	1957-1993
Aksu River	33.11	35.78	32.42	31.14	33.30
Yarsant River	5.95	1.80	1.80	0	2.35
Hotan River	11.51	10.75	12.53	9.3	11.16
Total	50.57	48.33	46.75	40.44	46.81

According to the experts with the Tarim River Administration, the variation of water distribution along the trunk river has produced a more significant impact on the inflow decrease at the downstream areas starting from Kala Point than the water supplies from three tributaries (Table 5.3).

Table 5.3.   Variation of Water Distribution along the Tarim River

Years for Comparison	Alar	Kala
1994 with 1966	-4.59%	-77.32%
1991 with 1965	+3.07%	-52.22%
1986 with 1968	-3.13%	-72.63%

Notes: + indicates increase, - denotes decrease.

Generally speaking, although the midstream water use amount fluctuates more or less, there is no such trend of steady increasing. However, the upstream withdrawal percentage keeps rising over the years, and it was more apparent in the wet year of 1994 when the water inflow to Alar Point was 49.02x108 m³ in the flooding season, but the downstream Kala station only measured an amount of 1.47x108 m³ incoming water. The waterflow recorded at Alar was 61.63x108 m³ for the whole year, while in Kala, the downstream section, only the amount of 2.65x108 m³ was available.

The long, unstable and zigzagging waterway of the Tarim River, compounded by the lack of recurrent maintenance necessary every year and constant canal-digging diversion for private use, has made it behave like an untamed horse, without forming a fixed running course. Every summer the flash floods even bring disastrous effects in the upstream and midstream regions, causing a significant loss of yearly run-off, while the annual water inflow to Kala Point downstream has diminished to the current level of 2×10^8 m³. Such imbalance in water demand and supply, including the common perverse practice of combatting flood in the upper reaches and struggling against drought in the lower parts of Tarim River, is attributable to the lack of institutional mechanism and infrastructure management.

In a word, the decreasing inflow from the source rivers, coupled with the considerable losses in the midstream areas, is contributing to the declining water-flows down to the lower reaches.

IDRC-funded Tarim Basin Projects and Subsequent Economic Priority for China's West

As early as the year 1992 when the World Conference on Development and Environment opened in Rio, the IDRC, with its insightful funding programs, supported the Chinese research team comprised of the Institute of Techno-Economic and Energy System Analysis (ITEESA), Tsinghua University, and the Institute of Agro-Economics and Information (IAEI), Xinjiang Academy of Agricultural Sciences (XAAS) to jointly undertake such a foresighted project of Tarim Basin Water Management and Desertification with the aim to address the chronic water stress and emerging issues in the Basin. There has been quite a successful implementation of two-phase studies by the present time and a series of useful outcomes that have been evolved into policy recommendations for the provincial and local governments.

Over the past decade, great changes have taken place across the basin with the initiative of building the national cotton-growing base, extraction of newly discovered petroleum and natural gas, the engineering miracle of the desert highway opening to traffic and the ban on the wasteland clearing as part of the national program to restore the eco-environment by converting the cultivated farmland back to forest and pasture. These changes have created significant impacts on the entire basin, particularly the water resources. So, how to establish the strong economic instruments and effective management institutions still remain an outstanding question. In January 1999, at the second session of the 9th National People's Congress of the PRC, the Xinjiang delegation motioned for listing the Tarim River issue high in the national program for large river management. They received a positive response from all participants and the motion was finally approved by the State Council. With the pressing need for remedial action prompted by both the severity and broad-based voices in relation to the Tarim issues, particularly in light of the current national initiatives for China's western economic development launched by the central

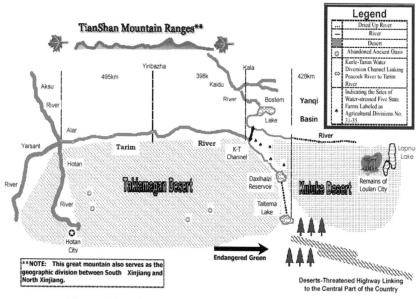

Figure 5.2. Schematic Map for Tarim River Watershed

government, a new program of Tarim Basin rehabilitation and ecosystem recovery has been formulated by the provincial government agencies with official approval and huge investments from the central authorities.

At present, the drive of pushing China's west socio-economic growth is gaining momentum and the ecosystem recovery program for the Tarim River basin initiated by the Xinjiang provincial government and supported by the central authorities is moving ahead in full swing, with positive results and tangible progress as scheduled and expected. According to the latest reports, which have aroused widespread concern and interest by the China Central Television (CCTV), on November 7, 2001, the Tarim River could be flowing down to the once dried-up Taitema Lake, to supply desperately needed water for ecological use in the lower reaches. These events will doubtless promote the sustainable development of the whole basin.

Outstanding Issues Addressed and Methodology Employed

This first-phase project was carried out from 1994 to 1997 with the research objectives focused primarily on the following four themes which were dealt with mainly from a macro-level point of view to address the major basin-wide issues.

- Water pricing and management system
- Techno-economic assessment of water-efficient technologies
- Scenario-based analysis of water allocation schemes for downstream green-belt preservation
- Evaluation of indigenous anti-desertification measures.

For the above points, water pricing and management schemes constitute the most important and crucial elements which are elaborated as follows:

Water pricing issues

The above-described physical manifestations of the environmental degradation over the entire Tarim River Basin can be more illustrative if analyzed in an economic point of view and examined for the institutional and managerial dimensions. In the Tarim Basin it used to be the following situations:

- Water underpricing, only 1/4 of its supply cost, causes little incentive to farmers for water conservation. The water resource that has long been regarded as God-given by local ethnic groups has never been priced either to reflect the delivery costs or react to the supply-demand imbalance in the Tarim Basin.
- No unique body with strong authorities to manage the water allocation over the whole river basin and also no set of rules and regulations for water rights allocation for different river stretches.

Recommended water pricing reforms

Three kinds of water supply costs were calculated for each prefecture on the basis of the data gathered during the field surveys as in Table 5.4. It can be seen from the table that the current water charge is far lower than the water delivery cost in each prefecture.

Table 5.4.   Water Supply Costs for Each Prefecture (unit: cent/m³)

Prefecture	Operational cost	Full cost with SLD	Full cost with DD	Present water rate
Akesu	1.34	3.33	4.68	0.60-0.66
Bayin	1.46	1.80	2.14	0.60-1.30
Hetian	1.48	2.51	3.54	0.30
Kashi	1.26	3.42	5.02	0.60

Notes: SLD- Straight-line depreciation, with re-estimated value of the fixed assets.
DD- Dynamic depreciation, r=7%, with re-estimated value of the fixed assets.

Table 5.5.   The ABIWs in Each Prefecture (unit: cent/m³)

	Akesu	Bayinguoleng	Kashi	Hetain
Grain crops	5.55	6.12	5.71	7.69
Cash crops	26.77	30.51	34.93	19.48
Average	13.55	16.40	14.78	10.50

On the other hand, we need to study how the water should be priced with more incentives to encourage farmers to use water in an efficient manner, while allowing for the affordability of local people. The average benefits of irrigation water(ABIWs) have been calculated by using the proportional method as shown in Table 5.5.

These values are very important for reference, but not enough for final decisions. Some other indicators are still needed to examine the economic tolerability of local farmers to water pricing levels. For example, the share of water charge in the gross and net agricultural production values and agricultural production cost. Moreover, the real disposable income and living standard of the farmers should also be taken into full account for making such an analysis. Now it has been set out in Xinjiang and the whole country that the water charge should not exceed 15% of the gross agricultural production value. The World Bank has such a regulation that the percentage of water bill in the agricultural value added should stay between 25% and 40%. In China, it is generally believed that the component of water fees in the total agricultural production cost should be within 5%-10%, and acceptable if no more than 15%.

Caveat: This part was completed before China's accession into the WTO, the domestic grain price is believed to have fallen following China's subsequent entry.

So, based on the above analysis, what's called a three-step water pricing reform has been suggested for implementation:

Step-1: Water should be priced to cover the operational costs. (In the current case: 1.5 cent/m³).

Step-2: Water should be priced to cover both the operational cost, maintenance and depreciation (in the current case: 2.5-3.0 cent/m³, still within the local farmer's affordable scope).

Step-3: Water should be priced to cover the full costs and include a reasonable margin of profits (in the current case: 4.0-5.0 cent/m³). Such price level seems a bit higher, but it could be in practice as the socio-economic reforms make progress and go deep.

Water management and institutional rebuilding

There are some key problems with the current water management institutions:

The water administration is incapable of exercising authorities of supervision over the basin-wide water use.

- The water administration by rule and by law remains to be well established, to make strict enforcement of water-related regulations and mitigate huge water loss and improve water use efficiency.
- The simple and separate way of water resource management and hydropower operation hampers the development of a water infrastructure industry.
- The simple and single investment channel cause insufficient funds and slow construction of water conservancy projects in the basin.
- The water management service system in the township and village level is not complete, farmers have little or no access to participation in the water management.

It is, therefore, suggested that a dual management system with the government's macro control on the one hand, and the promotion of water infrastructure commercialization on the other. Some main measures include as follows:

- The water allocation quota and water rights should be well-defined with the full consideration of the crop types, regions and ecological use.
- It is suggested that an unified and authoritative agency for water resource management in the Tarim River basin should be established in the principle of water administration by law.
- Separating government function from business management, to establish a virtuous circle of self-development of water conservancy enterprises gradually. It is suggested that water conservancy development companies be set up at all levels to

seek profitability by pursuing the economic development of water conservancy industry while developing a diversified business.

- The water infrastructure funds should be secured through multiple channels, and special construction funds can also be set up to engage the public support.

Outstanding Issues Addressed and Methodology Employed in 2nd Phase

National Actions for Tarim River Ecosystem Restorations

With the growing momentum of the on-going west economic development strategy, the Tarim River Basin has also been listed in one of the top-ten national rehabilitation programs for recovering the degraded ecosystems. In February, 2000, the Xinjiang provincial Development & Planning Commission initiated a set of remedial projects for rebuilding the water conservation facilities along the mainstem and recovering the Tarim River Basin ecosystem. The first-phase projects have been launched by the provincial government, with a good promise of reversing the overall decline of the ecosystem and promoting economic growth, especially the endangered downstream green-corridors which bear the brunt of the inexorable encroachment of sand-dunes and keep in check the possible union of the Taklamagan and Kuluke Deserts. Such programs are doubtless of great importance for maintaining the social-economic growth and political stability of regions, and for moving ahead with the on-going western economic strategy.

In March, 2000, this project proposal was approved at a regular working conference presided over by Premier Zhu Rongji, who heard reports by the Ministry of Water Resources and the Xinjiang provincial government on the details and planning of these projects. It was believed that these initiatives would facilitate the sustainable development and western economic take-off. Premier Zhu said that the Tarim River basin restoration programs are a practical step forward and should be well implemented with full financial support, and be completed by 2005 with the initial recovery of the downstream ecosystem.

The overall objectives of the Tarim River restoration project are to establish uniform management and allocation of water resources over the entire basin through strict water use quotas and to balance the ecosystem preservation with economic development. However, there still exist some concerns about the uncertainties in the balance between water supply and demand that may arise from the action plan to be initiated by the Xinjiang provincial government, as well as the relevant institutions and mechanisms needed to ensure the water allocation scheme as desired. Meanwhile, more efforts remain to be made to establish the community-based water management in the farmers' village, and it is still uncertain how to forge a strong macro-micro link. It is therefore of great importance to carry out this second-phase project activity so as to achieve a successful and effective implementation of the well-intentioned government blue-print.

Outlines and Structure of 2nd Phase Project Study

The IDRC has been a source of support and encouragement for orienting this well-begun research work toward an even more practical and useful project. So, the 2nd phase study was started from 1998 to 2001. At this stage, the project was carried out at both macro and micro layers with the objective covering five themes as described in the attached diagram:

- [Macro-1]. To develop a sound basin-wide water allocation scheme taking into account both the equity and efficiency, which could balance the water demand and supply for agricultural production.
- [Macro-2]. To put into place a set of rules and new institutions which would ensure an effective implementation of the basin-wide water allocation plan, based on the theory of game and economics of property rights.
- [Micro-1]. To understand the elastic responses from the local farmer to the water pricing levels and the associated willingness to adopt any water-efficient technologies.
- [Micro-2]. To understand the possible impacts of some non-technological factors like cultural practices such as the land

tenure, gender, education and local ethnic folkway, etc., on the behavioural patterns in relation to water use and conservation as well as anti-desertification measures.

- [Toicro-3]. To establish the institutional incentives at the village level to encourage the effective and efficient use of water resources in the community.

The framework and logic for the 2nd phase project study are well-organized to allow for the organic link between the macro and micro interconnections in the real case of Tarim Basin water use and management. After three more years of hard work on these interesting topics, the project study at this stage was finished in late May, 2001, with the following policy recommendations for the provincial government developed from the academic outputs:

- Water is a critical resource to maintain the watershed ecosystem, so the overall water use efficiency must be improved to make the best use of already scarce water resources by upgrading water conservation facilities and the basin-wide water management system.
- Market-driven mechanisms of water allocating and trading schemes would lead to the most efficient use of the Tarim Basin water resources and effective implementation of the planned restoration program for the Tarim watershed.
- The Tarim Basin water resources must be managed at the micro level by introducing the ideas of CBNRM relevant to the local socio-cultural conditions.
- The pace of pricing reform must be improved and more innovation is needed in management mechanisms in a bid to achieve efficient and effective use of Tarim Water resources.
- The water conservation potential and methodology needs further research to promote wider application of water-efficient technologies.
- Tarim water resources should be allocated in an equitable and enforceable way to ensure a reasonable balance between the economy and the ecosystem.

- New ideas and methodologies in this project study will greatly improve the scientific and practical results.
- A new and innovative system is essential for sustainable socio-economic development of the Tarim Basin[8].

Other policy recommendations for overhauling the current institutions and mechanisms to enforce the designed water property rights trading system have also been proposed for consideration and references, the main points including:

- Initial allocation and trade-off of water property rights.
- Institutional reform and agency rearrangement.
- Overhaul of water pricing system.
- Practical trade-offs of water property rights and investment mechanism for commercialization of water infrastructure.

The [Macro-1] theme addresses basin-wide water allocation, using the methods and ideas of system dynamics (SD) and integrated resource planning/demand side management (IRP/DSM) to make an assessment and simulation of the possible consequences which may arise from the remedial actions for both the Tarim River Basin and its surrounding ecosystem to be taken, and the water allocation quota system to be imposed, by the Xinjiang provincial government.

The overall objectives of the Tarim River restoration project are to establish uniform management and allocation of water resources over the entire basin through strict water use quotas and to balance the ecosystem preservation with economic development. The program will build a compound ecological system combining both natural and artificial environments, with the ecosystem rebuilding and water allocation as the key parts, through the broad and intensive construction of water conservation works. Some of the specific tasks are described as follows:

- Water use efficiency in the tributaries will focus more on agricultural production, with newly-lined canals and efficient field irrigation technologies.

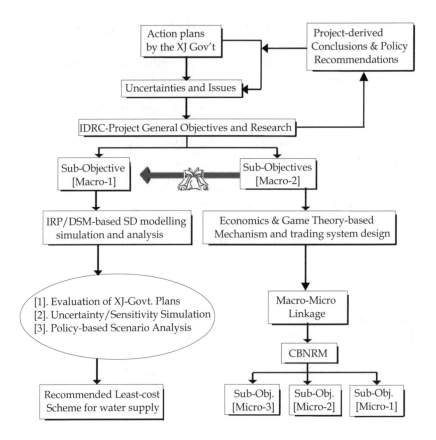

Figure 5.3.   Block Diagram for Research Objectives and Framework

- The focus along the mainstem regions will be on harnessing the uncontrolled river's course, with the construction or consolidation of necessary dikes to ensure efficient water delivery. The river bank will be protected, water control works will be constructed, and the river will be dredged to realize the target of delivering at least $3.0 \times 108 m^3$ water annually from Kala hydrological station to the lower reaches. The objective is to enable the water-head to pass through Alagan, along with other relevant management mechanisms and control measures, to revive the water-hungry "green shelter-belts" and to stop two deserts from joining hands.

- The plain reservoirs are to be scaled down to reduce the evaporation from large water surface areas, with more mountain reservoirs built to increase the control capability for reasonable water allocation.
- The crop structure is to be carefully changed to reclaim the unreasonable farmland for the development of forests and pastures, and to preserve the natural arid-region trees and restore the arid-region grassland.

After these measures begin to take effect, the total restored natural vegetation area will total as much as 1,950,000 *mu*, the downstream ecosystem can begin to recover, and about 3.0×10^8 m³ of water will flow annually down to Taitema Lake.

This government-designed program reflects the determination to reverse the inexorable degrading trends of the Tarim ecosystem and the long-term commitment to preserve the oasis-based environment through efficient use of scarce water resources. However, the water allocation scheme outlined therein is implicitly based on the following two assumptions:

- Multi-year average water flows from the three tributaries in recent years.
- Constant water demand for the current technical-economic conditions(efficiencies and irrigation standards).

So, this water allocation scheme set by the government could be an ideal and static balanced scenario in which the water supply(S_i) satisfies the water demand (D_i)

Water supply(S_i)-water demand(D_i)=0
{i= tributary, upstream. midstream, downstream}

However, the longer-term, overall economically strategic point of view is that Tarim Basin will undoubtedly experience more dynamic and vibrant socio-economic development in the foreseeable future. Additionally, greater variations of water flows from three tributaries would occur from year to year, due to a variety of natural factors. So, the equation only illustrates a pseudo steady state of the real system, without adequate reflection of the inherent interconnections or interdependences between the water use and future social-economic developments. A more thorough analysis of all possible scenarios is needed. For example, the water demand will change due to the inexorable local population increases, the agricultural productivity improvements, expansion of agricultural activities and restructuring of crop patterns, enhancement of water use efficiency, etc. Fluctuations of the natural water flows in different years will also cause uncertainties. All these elements will affect the balance between water supply and demand, leading to new conflicts over water use. Therefore, an in-depth study is needed to correct emerging imbalance by developing response measures including the deployment of a mix of feasible technologies with the least cost, to expand this government plan into a more realistic and enforceable scheme.

Therefore, it is apparently necessary to undertake an even more comprehensive and systematic analysis of any possible scenarios that would occur under some circumstances, to provide a better understanding of the future dynamic development of the Tarim Basin, and to prepare appropriate response measures to consequences that may take place.

The model includes three functional modules described below:

- Surface water allocation module reflecting the natural interconnections in the entire Tarim River system.
- Total water demand module related to the crop structures and agricultural scales.
- IRP/DSM-based water supply module driven by the gap between water supply and demand.

A quantitative and qualitative analysis of the simulated results derived from the SD+IRP/DSM model runs will be made under the combined scenarios as designed and shown in the above table, and the graphs, drawings and tables attached.

First of all, the possible results from the model simulations could be one of the following three cases, if looked at just from a qualitative point of view:

> *Case-A*: This would be the BAU situation in which the water supply equals the water demand with the mathematical equation Si-Di=0, as assumed in the government program for the ecosystem remedy over the entire basin, though only the static balance based on the two presumptions as described before, it can be believed to also cover all the special cases of dynamic balances between them. Actually, such phenomena could hardly take place in the real world.
>
> *Case-B*: This would be the most likely situation in which the water supply falls short of the water demand as previously described by the mathematical inequality Si-Di<0. It could be believed a more general case or probable occurrence, and the primary objective and focus of the model analysis and the project study. Under such circumstances, there would be a great gap between the surface water allocation and the demand for sustaining the socio-economic development due to various scenarios on the part of both the supply side and the demand side. Therefore, the originally planned water allocation scheme would be difficult to implement, and needs to be reconsidered for practical implementation. The solutions to resolving the water deficit problems have been attempted through the IRP/DSM methodologies, by identifying other water use potentials at both the supply side and the demand side with the competitive unit costs, to close the gaps between the surface water and the demand occurred in a dynamic process.
>
> *Case-C*: This would be the most ideal or desired situation in which the water supply exceeds the water demand as previously described by the mathematical inequality Si-Di>0. From a more

realistic point of view, it could be a special scenario which seldom or never happens. If this is the case, then the additional water can be used either for agricultural production or ecosystem preservation, or other social benefits, in light of the policy orientations.

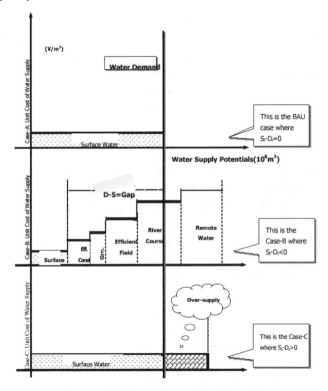

Figure 5.4. Illustration of the Three Cases

Some recommendations and conclusions based on the modeling exercises and the above analysis:

- The model simulations are based on the policy of top priority of water use to ecosystem. That is, surface water is firstly allocated for the use of ecosystem preservation, then for the farmland irrigation, with the objective of stopping the deterioration of the ever-worsening natural environment. Otherwise, the devastated oasis-based ecosystem would threaten the very survival of the local ethnic people, let alone the agricultural production. From a longer-term point of view, the surplus water could be guaranteed for the expanded wasteland once cleared without adequate allowance for the scant water supply in the event of dry years. If so, then either the agricultural production or the oasis environment could be left at risk.

- The government program for remedying the seriously degraded ecosystem should take into full account the impacts of other critical factors on the implementation of this blueprint, though some principles are clearly stressed therein, including planning the farmland subject to water constraints, and prioritizing the ecosystem protection in light of local conditions.
- Some undesired effects of the natural water flows during dry years should be anticipated before the event, by fully preparing for the worst situations that might occur in the foreseeable future. The IRP/DSM methodologies should be employed in light of local conditions to optimize the scarce water resources with improvement of water use being the top priority. Otherwise, the more water diversion, the more water loss. The development patterns of recklessly and extensively exploring new water sources should be replaced by the seeking of intensive improvement of water use efficiency.
- The water allocation scheme designed in the government program should be dynamically updated to allow for the changing needs of social-economic growth with the rapid development of the agricultural production and petroleum exploration, and the local population increase as well.
- The population increase would undoubtedly result in the growing need for the agricultural products which apparently could be satisfied by expansion of the farmland scale, or other means, like the restructuring of the crop patterns or improvement of productivity. The study shows that increase of the yields per unit area could largely offset the additional requirement of

agricultural products. It is very important both to readjust the crop mixes and develop some locally advantageous economic sectors, with the aim to improve the living standard of local ethnic groups.

- The simulation also shows that the improvement of water use efficiency could reflect the local capacity for future economic development. But the potentials from efficiency enhancement would depend on the water flows available. When the surface water is relatively plenty, this potential would be more obvious. So the upstream regions should deliver more water to the middle and lower reaches.

Some Caveats for the Model Runs

This model is formulated on the basis of the SD+IRP/DSM methodologies, by simulating the major structures and functions abstracted from the real agro-economic and ecological systems of the Tarim Basin. It is unavoidable that there would exist some errors derived from either the model calculation or the numerical rounding, or from the degree of accuracy of the raw data. Some data or parameter should also be amenable to the revivification of broad-based local and senior experts.

Additionally, the analysis is only for the agro-economic and ecological systems. But the spatial aspects should not be ignored as they would be more for the project outcomes, and require additional huge inputs of manpower and capital. If possible, such studies need to be followed up to be more useful for decision-makers.

The [Macro-2] topic deals with the necessary mechanisms and institutions needed to guarantee successful implementation of the water rights allocation scheme. Since water resource allocation in the Tarim River Basin is a benefit-conflict issue with several participating parties, the game theory and economic analysis have been employed to analyze the basin-wide water allocation conflicts and the competing use of the limited water resource. Some models of behavioural patterns in water use have also been developed to address the "gaming" issues in water allocation and use.

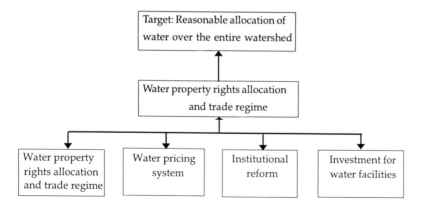

Figure 5.5.   Water Property Rights Allocation and Trade-off regime

- Model 1: Each prefecture goes his own way, or acts on his own will.
- Model 2: Command and Control model of water allocation.
- Model 3: Macro regulation and control model using water resource tax.
- Model 4: Macro regulation and control model using tax and transaction.

For the themes of [Micro-1], [Micro-2], and [Micro-3], a series of methodologies have been applied to the community level studies.

- The PRA method of understanding the possible response of local farmers in the pilot communities to water pricing, and the application of water conservation techniques and micro-schemes.
- DELPHI and AHP for the analysis of the impacts of the local traditions and cultural practices (non-technical factors) on the application of water-efficient conservation techniques. Some informal discussions with community groups, and visits to the county and the township governments have been arranged at various levels. At the same time, literature reviews have also been made. Please also see the following block diagram.

Experiences/Lessons Drawn and Caveats

As this IDRC-funded project was going on with the promise of useful and practical outputs, the blueprint of speedy economic development for China's western region was just being outlined by the central authorities. So, our research findings came at a most opportune moment with increasing attentions from the central and Xinjiang governments at various levels. Before launching of such economic movements and environmental rehabilitations, the policy impacts of our previous project study were less strong than what they are today. In other words, the objectives of our research project were well-aligned with the overall "governance framework" as well as the political determinations of the top leadership. At the same time, the research also generated some novel and original ideas suitable for the case of the Tarim Basin by employing the game theory and environmental/neoclassic economics, for example, well-defined, exclusive and transferable property rights, transaction costs, or the gaming process of staking out claims over water quotas, etc. More importantly, the team members have also established a better relationship with some relevant departments/organizations of the provincial governments, either through personal contacts, or even by taking advantage of the influential status of both Tsinghua University, a top seat of higher learning in China, and XAAS, a major academic institution in Xinjiang self-governing province.

The project team does not claim to be exhaustive even under the established research framework and objectives, due to both the physical limitations and the team capacity. For example, the project team is made up of the Beijing-based ITEESA, Tsinghua University, and the IAEI of Xinjiang Academy of Agricultural Sciences (XAAS) located in Urumqi, Xinjiang of China. The distance between these two cities is more than 3000 km, making it a bit inconvenient for face-to-face interaction or discussion with each other, even in case of necessity. It is always a tough job to make a field trip to the pilot communities by going all the way through the inhospitable deserts and sand-dunes to the remote and outlying oases. It often happens that the field task turns out to be insufficient for the subsequent office work or data need, but it is hard, if not impossible, to make up or update after the activity or event. Additionally, many of the team members are not well professionally trained in English writing, and most of us are unable to speak local ethnic language. Communications with the local Uighur people have to be conducted through interpreters. The knowledge base of the project team about all the aspects of the research work, including the local customs and folkway and basic theory of economics and gaming, needs to be substantially improved or increased to better deal with the real-life problems.

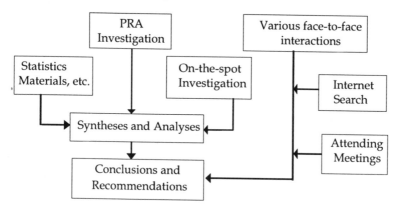

Figure 5.6. Workflow Chart for the Project

Follow-up Efforts to Fit Local Community Behaviours into the Basin-Wide Responses

The IDRC-aided project on the Tarim Basin Water Management and Desertification has been completed for both the 1st and 2nd phase studies as scheduled, with useful outputs that could be evolved into part of the provincial government policies, and positive impacts on China's west regional economic development initiatives and the on-going ecosystem recovery action plans for the Tarim River Basin. Some line agencies and officials of the Xinjiang provincial government and local authorities continue to show undiminished interests, particularly in water management at local levels and other related outstanding issues, in the hope that a project study of such significance may be followed by a closer link between the basin-wide water allocation and community-level management, and a more detailed study of all these issues cutting across the different levels.

Why Community-Based Water Management in Tarim Basin

It remains a big question as to what kind of appropriate community-based water resource management (CBWRM) should be established at this point to fit with the progress of basin-wide water allocation and ecosystem restoration.

- The chronic water shortage and increasingly damaged ecosystem necessitate stepped-up water management over the entire basin and at the community level particularly. So far, some important changes have already been instituted in the macro water planning and management, including water price hikes, reorganization of water control authorities, groundwater exploration and mainstream cannel construction in the middle reaches, etc. Some other response measures are expected to take shape, for example, a primary quota allocation scheme based on the equitable rights and the associated water trading system for efficient use, and gradual implementation of marginal water pricing proposals as discussed and suggested in our previous studies. These new changes either in place or yet to come need readjustments and improvements of water management and planning at various levels throughout the basin. However, the leadership is still uncertain how to begin such challenging tasks, and furthermore, the farmers' patterns of water use in the community would be greatly affected by these innovations. Even worse, the participatory capacity of local people still remains to be considerably enhanced. Unless rectified, these inadequacies would do more harm than good to the effective and efficient management of water over the basin, dilute incentives for the farmers to conserve water and increase incomes and apparently jeopardize the huge investments of 10.7 billion Yuan in the Tarim River ecosystem recovery initiative. It is necessary to carry out some studies on these topics, particularly on the community-based water management, as well as the inherent links to the macro policies and decisions.

- In the Tarim Basin, as in other parts of China, stakeholders and players at the grassroots are usually given short shrift when planning for "big-ticket" projects. In consequence, the government's ambitions, more often than not, turn out to be long shots. The link between the government's goals and local interests still remains to be reinforced or improved. Taking the Tarim Basin, for example, basin-wide ecosystem recovery projects have been launched by the provincial government to restore the damaged oasis-based living and farming environments, and some water management institutions or policies at the macro levels are being overhauled to fit with this on-going action plan. However, the community as a basic unit in the Tarim Basin, which used to be unreasonably ignored, is seen as essential to a successful implementation of the whole program.

- With China's entry into the WTO, and the growing momentum of speedy economic development in the west regions, as well as the inexorable transition to the market-driven economy, more deregulations and free choices are coming for local farmers and communities, who will become key actors in both the market and water management. However, due primarily to their incapacity and incompetence to keep up with the changing market situations and then cope with the associated risks, it is hard for those farmers to get an upper hand, or have a bigger say in the water decisions. So it is quite necessary for the project team to help build the farmers' capacity and offer more attractive choices by expanding the range of alternatives, so as to make them well-qualified indigenous "trouble-shooters" most suited to local cases.

- Within the context of China's switch-over from the centrally planned economy to the market one, the importance of the micro-level management has been increasingly recognized. However, in reality, the macro aspects are more emphasized, resulting in failure to make effective implementations of some well-meant policies. It is seen as avant-garde to carry out the demonstrable and innovative research work on community-based water management in the Tarim Basin, which would be ground-breaking to both Tarim Basin and the country as a whole.

Outstanding Issues on the Current Community Water Management in Tarim Basin

- At present, there is still a lack of mature and workable management measures to fit with changing situations of water shortage and environmental degradation in the entire basin, leading to inefficient water use. Some problems can be summarized as follows:
- The administrative orders dominate both the basin-wide and grassroots water management, with the farmer-participated community management only on a trial basis. Local farmers' participation in the community's water management is actually rare or little, with their voices left in the wilderness, resulting in little incentive for them to adopt and invest in water-efficient technologies. At present, governments at all levels are the main bodies to make investments and disseminations through command and control, with little success. So, it is therefore quite usual in the Tarim Basin that water resources are increasingly in short supply, and used in a wasteful manner.
- No apparent connection exists between effective water management in the community and the farmers' income or crop yield increase. Farmers care more for agricultural production than efficient use of natural resources and environmental preservation. This is one of the main causes for ever-increasing ecosystem deterioration over the basin.
- Since the water is managed through administrative means in the community, sometimes water distribution and fee charging

are not transparent or fair, thus causing de facto inequitable water use rights.

- Right now, there is no intermediary body both representing the farmers' own interests and acting as a liaison between the community and the governments. Some fragmented ideas of the farmers remain to be collected and reflected, the collective interests could hardly be ensured, for example, some farmers want to pick out the canal for irrigating their own farmland, while others would come out to oppose. If there is not any such an organization, the disagreement would not be solved. In addition, some public interest projects like water quality control and water infrastructure construction could not be initiated without collective decisions. The task division, responsibility, obligation and role of micro, mezzo and macro levels remain unclear.

Part II. Coordinating Institution and Mechanism

6 A New Pattern of Regional Co-operation in China: Four Economic Belts Across East to West

Li Shantong, Hou Yongzhi and Feng Jie

The West China Development Program has been launched at the turn of the century. It arose as a national initiative for coordinated development among China's eastern, central and western regions, as well as because of a need for the all-round propelling of the country's modernization course at the outset of the 21st century. With the backdrop of West China Development Program and better-coordinated regional development, China is forming four economic collaboration belts across the country, bringing a new pattern to regional economic co-operation.

Definition of the Economic Collaboration Belt and Its General Features

An economic collaboration belt is an economic area composed of cross-regional and geographically linked economic units with common interests and inner economic connections. It has four features:

(1)   It is a geographically linked belt-shaped area: This is a common feature of economic belts of various kinds as well as an important point that distinguishes the economic belts from other economic areas such as "economic spheres" and "economic zones".

(2)   It possesses convenient passages that adjoin various regions in the belt. Economic exchanges and links between different regions on an economic belt depend not only on the internal need for such exchanges and links, but also on the possibility and cost of facilitating these exchanges and links. The infrastructure (inclusive of transportation and communications and the institutions for cross-

regional exchanges) is vital to the formation and development of the economic collaboration belts.

(3)   There is a basis for the realization and possibility of the vertical division of labour among the regions within an economic belt. Different regions have different economic advantages within an economic belt and they are located at different points on an industrial value chain. Vertical industrial divisions of labour also mean that levels of development of different regions generally vary.

(4)   Complementary regional economic structures and co-operative economic links are the main feature of an economic belt. Competition exists as a main feature of economic relations among different regions of the same nature while collaboration exists prominently among regions of different natures. Different regions within an economic collaboration belt are basically regions of different natures, with complementary economic structures and co-operative economic links as a basis for forming an economic belt.

Forming Four Economic Collaboration Belts

As China becomes more open to the outside world and implements the West China Development Program, the country's eastern, central, and western regions are making good progress in exchanges and co-operations among themselves. The Pearl River Economic Belt, the Yangtze River Economic Belt, the Longhai-Lanxin Economic Belt (along the Lianyunguang-Xi'an-Lanzhou-Urumqi railway) and the Beijing and Tianjin-Huhehaote, Baotou and Yinchuan Economic Belt are taking shape. The four economic growth axes connecting the eastern, central and the western regions will constitute a new pattern for China's regional economic growth. The new trend of the economic belt development brings along the economic structural adjustment and the redistribution of the productive forces. It will change China's unbalanced regional development to a great extent and will stimulate China's regional economy to better-coordinated development.

The Pearl River Economic Belt

The Pearl River Economic Belt is an economic area emerging along the trunk streams of the Pearl River, which adjoins the six provincial territories and regions of Guangdong Province, Hong Kong, Macao, Yunnan Province, Guizhou Province and Guangxi Zhuang Autonomous Region. This belt is a natural connection for the south of China between the country's eastern and western regions. The Pearl River Economic Belt organically combines the Pearl River Delta Core Economic Zone within the river valley, the South-China Economic Zone and the Southwest Economic Zone. It plays an important role in enhancing development of the hinterlands and maintaining the growth of the export-oriented economy of Guangdong Province, Hong Kong and Macao. This belt facilitates the inland relocation of the Pearl River Delta industries and the inland expansion of the market by internationalizing the southwest regional economy and revealing the latter's resource advantages. The prospect for the formation of "China-ASEAN Free Trade Zone" has been recently highlighted by the conscientious initiatives taken by the Chinese government. This development has brought southwest border areas in provinces of Yunnan, Guangxi and Guizhou to the forefront of China's opening to the outside world, as well as economic cooperation with the ASEAN region. The planned construction of a Pan-Asian railway and the promotion of Lanchang River-Mekong River sub-regional economic co-operation are turning such prospects into reality. Such a great change in external environment has created good conditions for the development of China's southwest region. The new circumstances imply that the construction of the Pearl River Economic Belt will be a coordinated program to enhance regional co-operation and make full use of regional advantages by reorganizing the inter-region division of labour on the principle of comparative advantages. These tasks have become more pressing and of higher practical significance.

The Yangtze River Economic Belt

The Yangtze River Economic Belt is an economic area emerging along the trunk streams of the Yangtze River and traversing seven provinces and two Municipalities in the eastern, central and western regions of China. Trunk streams of the Yangtze River start from Sichuan Province in the west, flowing from Chongqing, Hubei Province, Hunan Province, Jiangxi Province, Anhui Province, Jiangshu Province, Zhejiang Province, to Shanghai and then into the ocean. The River meets on its way with 8 railway arteries from south to north. There are dense highway networks in the river valley, which connect east China, south China and the Sichuan Basin in the west. As the Gold Waterway offers developed inland water transport passages, co-operation between different regions on this economic belt began earlier and the co-operation is frequent and close. At the same time, this economic belt claims 40.8% of China's total population and 48.6% of China's Gross Domestic Product. In recent years, the provinces and regions in this economic belt experienced the fastest growth rates in the country, leading to an increasing weight of the belt in the national economy. Shanghai's successful bid of the right to hold the 2010 World Fair will further spur the development of the Yangtze River Delta, bringing new opportunities for co-operation between regions along the riverside.

Longhai-Lanxin Economic Belt

As part of the Europe-Asia Continental Bridge, the Longhai-Lanxin Economic Belt starts from Lianyungang of Jiangsu Province in the east and passes through Longhai-Lanzhou and Xinjiang railway to Xinjiang Autonomous Region in the uttermost west by way of Shandong Province, Henan Province, Shanxi Province, Gansu Province and Qinghai Province. This economic belt is the longest belt and traverses the whole of China from east to west. At the beginning of the 1990s, along with the construction and linking of the Europe-Asia Continental Bridge, the belt emerged as a point-axle network with close co-operation developed among the central cities along the route. The growing co-operation among China, Russia and the Central Asian countries has facilitated the opening of this belt to the world. However, this economic belt traverses a wide and long area where the difference of development levels among most sub-regions is relatively small. It links to the Central Asia where a number of transition economies are located, with underdeveloped institutions and relatively unstable security environment. As a result, the leading role of the east coast region in the belt's development has not yet been remarkable and the geographical advantages of west China as part of the continental bridge to the west have not become manifest. The internal motivation for the collaborations between different regions within the belt is thus not very strong and robust.

Beijing and Tianjin-Huhehaote, Baotou and Yinchuan Economic Belt

Beijing and Tianjin-Huhehaote, Baotou and Yinchuan Economic Belt is an economic area taking as its main axis. Beijing to Baotou and Baotou to Lanzhou railways and no. 110 state highway, which links the major cities including Beijing, Tianjin, Tangshan, Datong, Huhehaote, Baotou and Yinchuan. This economic belt covers six provinces and municipalities, including Beijing, Tianjin, Hebei Province, Shanxi Province, Inner Mongolia and Ningxia Autonomous Region. It traverses northeast, north, and west regions of China. The hinterland of the economic belt is a famous energy, chemical and heavy industrial base in China. North Shanxi, north Shaanxi and west Inner Mongolia are the most important production areas of coal, oil and natural gas. The Grand Beijing Area in east China, inclusive of Beijing, Tianjin and Tangshan, is known as one of the three growth centres of China, with the other two being the Pearl River Delta and the Yangtze River Delta. Beijing's success in its bid for hosting the 2008 Olympic Games is likely to bring in more business opportunities to the information-intensive, knowledge-intensive and capital-intensive Grand Beijing Area. It would also be a boost to the development of the Beijing and Tianjin-Huhehaote, Baotou and Yinchuan Economic Belt.

Table 6.1, Table 6.2 and Figure 6.1 show the basic conditions, relative indicators and the main covered areas of the four economic belts.

Table 6.1.　Comparison of Sphere, Population, Land Area and
GDP of the Four Economic Collaboration Belts

Economic Belt	Region	Population (10,000)	Share of China total (%)	Land area (10,000 km²)	Share of China total (%)	GDP (100 million)	Share of China total (%)
Pearl River	Guangdong	7783		18		10647.71	
	Yunnan	4287		38		2074.71	
	Guangxi	4788	16.2	23	10.0	2231.19	17.0
	Guizhou	3799		17		1084.90	
	Total	20657		96		16038.51	
Yantze River	Shanghai	1614		0.58		4950.84	
	Jiangsu	7355		10		9511.91	
	Zhejiang	4613		10		6748.15	
	Fujian	3440		12		4253.68	
	Anhui	6328		13		3290.13	
	Jiangxi	4186		16		2175.68	
	Hubei	5975	40.8	18	28.8	4662.28	48.6
	Hunan	6596		21		3983.00	
	Chongqing	3097		48		1749.77	
	Sichuan	8640		8.23		4421.76	
	Xizang	263		120		138.73	
	Total	52107		276.81		45885.93	
Longhai-Lanxin	Shandong	9041		15		9438.31	
	Henan	9555		16		5640.11	
	Shanxi	3659		19		1844.27	
	Gansu	2575	21.3	39	33.4	1072.51	21.0
	Qinghai	523		72		300.95	
	Xinjiang	1876		160		1485.48	
	Total	27229		321		19781.63	
Beijing, Tianjin, Huhehaot, Baotou, and Yinchuan	Beijing	1383		1.68		2845.65	
	Tianjin	1004		1.1		1840.10	
	Hebei	6699		19		5577.78	
	Shanxi	3272	12.0	15	16.8	1779.97	14.7
	Neimenggu	2377		118		1545.79	
	Ninxia	563		6.6		298.38	
	Total	15298		161.38		13887.67	
China		127627	100.0	960	100.0	94346.40	100.0

Table 6.2.   Main Cities and Connecting Passages Within the
Four Economic Collaboration Belts

| Economic belt | Main cities in | | | Main connecting passages | Growth centre in the east | Key districts for developing the west region |
	Eastern region	Central region	Western region			
Pearl River Economic Belt	Hong Kong, Macau, Guangzhou, Shenzhen, Zhuhai		Nanning, Guiyang, Kunming	The Pearl River water-ways (and other basic passages)	The Pearl River Delta	Nanning-Guiyang-Kunming Economic Zones
Yangtze River Economic Belt	Shanghai, Nanjing, Hangzhong, Ningbo, Suzhou, Wuxi, Changzhou	Wuhu, Hefei, Anqing, Jiujiang, Yueyang, Wuhan, Yichang, Jinzhou	Chongqing, Chengdu, Panzhihua, Mianyang	The Yangtze River waterways, Shanghai-Chengdu trunk lines of the state highways, railways along the Yangtze River	The Yangtze River Delta	The Yangtze River Upper Reaches Economic Belt
Longhai-Lanxin Economic Belt	Lianyun-gang, Rizhao, Yantai, Qingdao, Xuzhou, Jinan	Shijia-zhuang, Handan, Taiyuan, Zhengzhou, Kaifeng, Luoyang	Xian, Baoji, Tianshui, Lanzhou, Yinchuan, Xining, Hami, Wulumuqi	Longhai-Lanzhou-Xinjiang railways and state highway No. 312	The Yellow River Delta	Xizang-Longhai-Lanzhou Economic Belt
Beijing, Tianjin, Huhe-haote, Baotou, Yinchuan Economic Belt	Beijing, Tianjin, Tangshan	Zhangjia-kou, Datong	Huhehaote, Baotou, Eerduosi, Shizuishan, Yinchuan	Beijing-Baotou and Baotou-Lanzhou state highways No. 119, 110	Grand Beijing Area	Huhehaote-Baotou-Yinchuan-Jitong Economic Belt

Figure 6.1.   The Four Economic Collaboration Belts

Importance of the Construction of Four Economic Collaboration Belts

It was expressly put forward at the 16th National Congress of the Chinese Communist Party that "exchanges and co-operation between the eastern, central and western regions should be strengthened, mutual supplement of advantages and joint development should be realized, and a number of distinctive economic zones and economic belts should be formed". Construction of the above-mentioned four economic belts is an important measure in fulfilling this goal set by the "16th National Congress" and has both far-reaching historical significance and the important immediate effect of:

Reducing inter-regional disparity and promoting coordinated regional development

Within the four economic belts there is a world of difference between the levels of economic development in the eastern, central and western regions.

For example, Yunnan Province, Guizhou Province and Guangxi Zhuang Autonomous Region located at the upper and middle reaches of the Pearl River are lagging far behind the Guangdong Province, which is much more socially and economically developed. In 2001, GDP of Guangdong Province is 4.8 times that of Guangxi, and 9.8 times of Guizhou, and 5.1 times of Yunnan. In per-capita GDP, Guangdong is 2.9 times higher than Guangxi, 4.7 times higher than Guizhou and 2.8 times than Yunnan. As for the total import and export values (c.i.f.), Guangdong's is 98.2 times of Guangxi, 273 times of Guizhou and 88.8 times of Yunnan. Foreign direct investment inflow to Guangdong is 31.1 times of that to Guangxi, 421.8 times of Guizhou and 184.8 times of Yunnan. Guangdong's investment in fixed assets is 5.3 times of Guangxi, more than 5.3 times of Guangxi and 4.7 times of Yunnan.

Apart from the policy-related assistance by the government, economic exchanges and co-operation among different regions should be strengthened to reduce the disparity between eastern and western regions and to develop the economy of the backward regions in the west. Therefore, construction of the four economic collaboration belts will promote co-operation among the eastern, central and western regions of China and keep regional disparity from enlarging. It is an integrated part of the West China Development program, as well as an urgent need for the realization of joint development across regions.

Keeping the national economy on the track of long-term, fast-paced and sustainable growth

It was put forward at the 16th CPC National Congress that by 2020 the GDP should quadruple the level in year 2000 and the goal of constructing "a well-off society" should be fully achieved. In order to realize such an objective, it is necessary for the average annual growth rate for the national economy to reach no less than 7%. Long-term, fast-paced and sustainable growth requires huge input in the essential factors of production and consumption of large amount of energy. It will fuel great demands and market potential for the development of China's energy industry. To maintain long-term and fast-paced growth in the next phase of development, it is essential to enhance the harmessing of the ecological environment, building the state ecological safety system and realizing coordinated economic, social and environmental development. Sustainable and rapid economic growth of eastern region has to be backed by inland resources and markets in central and western regions. China's natural resources are mainly scattered in the vast central and western regions. Meanwhile, the lower development level and standard of living in the central and western regions imply a great potential there for growth and business. With the implementation of the West China Development Program and the construction of the infrastructure in the west regions, the basic conditions for cross-regional development within the four economic collaboration belts are being improved. Moreover, the west region is where China's ecological environment is most severely damaged. Ecological environments in many regions, including the source of the Yangtze River, the source of the Yellow River, the districts of the Loess Plateau where soil is washed away, and the desertized lands in Inner Mongolia, are increasingly deteriorating. This trend is increasingly affecting the east and central regions. Improvement of the ecological environment of the west region is a task that brooks no delay. Therefore, the construction of the economic collaboration belts across east to west regions is indispensable to achieving the sustainable and fast-paced growth of the national economy.

Facilitating the strategic adjustment of the industrial structure and the reasonable distribution of productive forces

The east, central and west regions within the economic belt have their respective advantages and disadvantages in natural resources endowment, geographical conditions, essential factors of production and social conditions. Natural resources of the east are relatively scarce, while social resources like talented people, technology, information and management, and the industrial basis and financing are relatively abundant and of superior quality; central provinces, especially western provinces, have relatively abundant natural resources, and the industrial basis of some key cities in central and western provinces and regions are very well built, but the intangible resources are of relatively inferior quality. Because of this, it becomes possible for the different regions within the economic belt to engage in economic integration by realizing mutual supplementation of comparative advantages. At present, the total economic volume of the east regions within these economic collaboration belts, having undergone economic expansion for years, has reached a certain scale and generated a greater market demand for energy, labour forces and various kinds of primary processed products. The labour-intensive processing industry initially supporting these regions are facing the pressure of a new round of adjustment of the economic structure and is developing a demand for transferring and spreading to the neighbouring areas. Accordingly, the adjacent central and west regions are well conditioned for supplying energy, labour forces and primary products of various kinds and are capable of and in need of taking in the shifting labour-intensive industries. At the same time, east, central and west regions within these economic belts have already formed the foundation for an extensive economic and technical co-operation. The East-West Co-operation Township Enterprise Demonstration Zones have been established in many districts in the upper reaches of the economic belts. The regions in these upper reaches have established a close relationship for economic and technical exchanges and co-operation with the regions on the lower reaches in terms of farm and sideline products such as flue-cured tobacco and vegetables, tourist products and energy products. Such co-operative plans as "Electricity of the West to be Delivered to the East", "Vegetables of the West to be Delivered to the East", "Tobacco of the West to be Delivered to the East" and "Labour Forces of the West to be Delivered to the East (labourers to move to the east)" are being implemented in an orderly way. Therefore, construction of the economic collaboration belts has helped different regions find their own roles in the regional economic division of labour and regional economic co-operation. It thus constitutes an industrial structure with regional comparative advantages and forms an interdependent co-ordinated relationship among the regions by facilitating the strategic adjustment of the industrial structure and the reasonable distribution of productive forces.

Enhancing China's openness to the outside world as well as its participation in regional economic co-operation

China has made systematic efforts to further open itself to the outside world. At the global level, China joined the WTO. At the level of Asia-Pacific regional economic co-operation, China has been an active promoter of APEC. At the level of Asian sub-regional economic co-operation, China is undergoing a negotiation with ASEAN for the establishment of China-ASEAN Free Trade Zone. At the same time, China has joined the regular dialogue between ASEAN and China, Japan and South Korea. Hence, China is entering into a new stage of openness of all-round and multi-level engagement. Geographically, an opening pattern composed of special economic zones, the coastal open cities, coastal open areas, capital cities of the provinces and the hinterland development zones, has emerged. The coastal open frontiers and the frontier clitellums have taken shape. The general trend of the all-round three-dimensional opening to the east, the north, the south and the west has also come into being. In such a pattern, development of each of the four economic belts has a different function. Development of the Pearl River Economic Belt is of primary importance in strengthening the opening to the south and in realizing the economic co-operation with Southeast Asia. Development of the Yangtze River Economic Belt is of primary importance in bringing the regions in the middle and lower reaches to further participation in the world economy and economic-trade co-operation with the economies in the Pacific region. Development of Longhai-Lanxin Economic Belt facilitates the realization of China's opening to the west and promotes China's exchange and co-operation with the Middle Asian countries. Developing Beijing and Tianjin-Huhehaote, Baotou and Yinchuan Economic Belt is of great importance in realizing the opening to the north and in further promoting China's participation in the economic co-operation in Northeast Asia.

Policy Proposals

Do a good job in spatial planning for national land development

China is vast in territory and the levels of development of its regions are diverse. The level of per-capita possession of natural resources is low and resource scarcity will constrain the country's economic modernization program. In order to build "a fully well-off society", China should achieve joint development of all regions and use the resources of various kinds rationally and comprehensively. To do a good job in spatial planning for national land development and ensure its smooth implementation by law and order will facilitate the joint prosperity of all regional economies and ensure an optimal process of modernization within the constraints of natural resources.

Make the formation and development of the four economic belts an important policy objective for China's regional development program in the 21st century

It has become a major challenge to China's regional policy makers to tackle the trend of growing inter-region disparity in development and to realize coordinated regional development. The launch of the four economic collaboration belts could be a practical and workable way for answering the challenge. The formation and development of the economic belts hinge on the economic basis and internal incentives of different regions within these belts. As a common background of administrative divisions, exchange and co-operation among these regions are hindered by regional politics, conflict in fiscal interests, cultural differences as well as communication barriers. Therefore, the formation and development of the economic belts must be coordinated and promoted by the Central Government. This job should be taken as an important objective for China's regional development program in the 21st century.

Strengthen the overall planning of the economic belts in industrial development, infrastructure building and environmental protection

Formation of the economic belts requires abandoning the existing model of functional division of labour across regions by administrative divisions. The issue of the development of all regions should be taken into consideration as a whole with a view to the development of city groups and economic belts. This calls for the breaking up of boundaries of administrative divisions to make overall planning for the functions of the economic zones and arrangement in a unified and planned way. At the same time, boundaries of administrative divisions should be broken up based on the evaluation and consideration of the regional economic performance. The concept of maximizing the beneficial results of all regions should be introduced. This calls for the implementation of a joint planning regime with joint programs for industrial development, layout of the economic belts, and overall framework for environmental protection. There should be rational division of labour across regions and redundant projects should be avoided. Construction of infrastructure and environmental protection should be coordinated in a unified way. Regional coordination and co-operation should be conducted with crucial resource development programs and in infrastructure construction in order to maximize overall advantages and to benefit from coordinated development of the economic belts.

Guide and encourage regional specialization, industrial relocation and industrial restructure within the economic belts and set up rational industrial structures

Coordination of all the sub-regions within each economic belt should be further strengthened. According to the geographic features of each region and its comparative edges, consistent policies should be formulated to encourage factor flows and guide them to promote industrial restructuring and rationalization of the layout of the productive forces within an economic belt. In order to give full play to geographical locations and regional economic advantages and to accelerate the optimization and industrial restructuring, domestic market demand should guide the integration of industrial advantages of different regions. Industrial groups with international competitiveness should be nurtured and an industrial structure with rational division of labour and ladder-shaped mutual supplementation should also be formed. To avoid redundant projects and homogenous industrial structures, each region should not pursue the nurturing and formation of leading industries and pillar industries within its own administrative boundary. Each region should bring its own advantages into full play and should look for its own place in the regional industrial structure so as to specialize in industries in which it has a comparative edge. At the same time, each region should devote effort to developing distinctive products and so raise the competitiveness of industries with true comparative advantages.

Eliminate inter-region blockade and trade barriers and establish a unified and open market

Local protectionism or blockade has a long tradition and institutional basis in China. It is a main factor that restrains the construction of the economic belts. In the long run, it is harmful to regional development and is all the more unfavourable to the maximization of the country's overall welfare. Local protectionism and regional blockade should be done away with and, through unified coordination within and across the regions, obstacles of various kinds should be broken up to facilitate the flows of fund, human resources and technology and to enhance assets restructuring and product circulation. This will ensure the formation of a unified market within the region, the realization of the opening of the markets, and the free flow of the essential factors within the region. Through promoting exchanges and co-operation within and across the regions, competitive, ordered, unified, open and outward-looking economic belts can be formed.

Set up a welfare compensation mechanism for ecological projects between the upper reaches and the lower reaches

Ensuring ecological safety is a challenge to both the upper reaches and lower reaches of the economic belts. At present, the deterioration of the ecology in the upper reaches of the four economic belts has not only affected the ecological safety of these areas themselves but also severely affected the ecological safety of the lower reaches. Improving the ecological conditions of the upper reaches will bring benefit to the entire group of economic belts. However, construction of ecological projects in the upper reaches not only needs the injection of huge funds but also is likely to affect the local economic development and the livings of local residents. That will thus have incentive consequence on the upper reaches' initiatives in improving ecological environment. In order to ensure the continuity of the ecological program, a welfare compensation mechanism for ecological projects must be set up between the upper and lower reaches to let the welfare-gaining lower reaches undertake a certain (even the principal) amount of ecological program cost.

Establish a higher coordinating mechanism to organizationally secure the development of economic belts

Attempts should be made to establish a higher coordinating mechanism composed of the all concerned state ministries and commissions and all the concerned provincial and regional governmental departments within the economic belts so as to provide a reliable organizational structure to secure the development of the economic belts. Meanwhile, the role of various kinds of non-governmental organizations should be brought into full play.

7 The Political Logic of Fiscal Transfers in China

Shaoguang Wang

Introduction

In virtually every large country, the state transfers large amounts of money across regions. Intergovernmental fiscal transfers are quantifiable expressions of the complex relationship between national and sub-national governments. Perhaps no data can provide a more objective and revealing picture of the inner operating logic of central-local relations in a country than the flows of fiscal resources between different tiers of government (Schumpeter, 1954; Treisman, 1996).

In the last decade or so, China scholars have paid considerable attention to central-provincial fiscal relations in the country (World Bank, 1990; Oksenberg and Tong, 1991; Wong, 1991; Ma, 1994; Wong, Heady and Woo, 1995; Montinola, Qian and Weingast, 1995; Chung, 1995; Huang, 1996; Wang and Hu, 2001). Due to the lack of reliable data, however, little research has been devoted to fiscal transfers, not to mention discerning and explaining the distributive patterns of fiscal transfers among China's 31 provincial units.[1] There is, of course, a vast literature on fiscal transfers in the West. Economists and political scientists have developed a range of theories concerning possible determinants of intergovernmental transfers in electoral democracies. Yet no one has ever attempted to test whether and to what extent those theories can be applied to analyzing a different political setting, such as China's.

This paper attempts to fill those gaps. Its focus is on ascertaining the factors that are the most influential in affecting intergovernmental transfers in China. This will be achieved with a set of newly released public finance data that covers all of China's 31 provincial units for 1998 (Ministry of Finance 1999). The patterns of allocation of fiscal transfers between the centre and provinces exhibit a perceptible political logic. In particular, the concerns of central politicians about national unity and unequal provincial representation in central decision-making have visible effects on provinces' shares of central transfers. These political factors are significant even after controlling for other possible determinants of fiscal transfers, including provinces' taxable potential and fiscal needs.

A broad concern is to investigate the extent to which theoretical frameworks that were developed in the context of electoral democracy are helpful in analyzing undemocratic systems. The findings of the case study suggest that Chinese politicians tend to allocate fiscal transfers according to their ranking order of preferences, as do their counterparts in electoral democracies, and that institutional structure matters in the process of transfer allocation in China every bit as it does under an electoral democracy.

Analytical Framework

Wherever intergovernmental transfers exist, they are normally justified as mechanisms of fiscal equalization. if the goal of transfers were indeed to offset regional inequalities in fiscal capacity and needs, then a high degree of progressivity would be expected in the distribution of such transfers. That is, regions with low per capita income and high per capita needs would receive more per capita central transfers than those with the opposite characteristics. Empirical studies, however, find that the real world rarely functions according to abstract ethical principles. The actual distribution of transfers fails to meet the equity objective not only in third world democracies like India (Rao and Singh, 2000) or newly democratizing countries like Mexico, Argentina, Brazil (Kraemer 1997), and Russia (Treisman, 1996; 1998a; 1998b), but also in mature industrial democracies such as the United States (Stein, 1981; Rich, 1989; Atlas et al., 1995) and Japan (Meyer and Naka, 1999).

Why does actual distribution deviate widely from the normative prescription? Case studies of electoral democracies all come to the same conclusion that politicians often use intergovernmental transfers to achieve goals other than equalizing fiscal resources and outcomes among regions. Numerous attempts have been made to explore possible determinants of intergovernmental transfers. Two groups of actors who may influence the distribution of transfers are central allocators and the regional recipients of transfers. The first group consists of central politicians and bureaucrats. Motivated to get re-elected, central politicians tend to use transfers as rewards for their constituencies, especially during periods that are immediately before national elections (Nordhaus, 1975; Tufte, 1978; Johnston, 1978). Bureaucrats are notorious for their desire to perpetuate and expand their programs. They tend to strategically use their fiscal transfer authority to gratify their patrons within the legislature (Arnold, 1981) or their loyal clientele groups in society (Anton, Cawley and Kramer, 1980). The second group includes regional governments and their representatives in central decision-making organs. Assuming that all regions try to lobby for as many central subsidies as possible, it is not surprising to find that regions with greater bargaining power typically receive a disproportionate share of central transfers than do others (Peliserro and England, 1980). Similarly, studies have found evidence that, as far as the distribution of central largesse is concerned, the name of the game for regional representatives in the national legislature is pork-barrel politics—each trying to acquire as much central spending or as many grants as possible for their own constituencies. Consequently, unequal regional representation in national decision-making organs is often related to the unequal distribution of central spending across regions (Kraemer, 1997; Atlas et al., 1995; Meyer and Naka, 1999).

The underlying assumption of all of the studies that are cited above is that electoral competition frames the incentive structures and defines the choice of both central and regional actors in the game of distributing central transfers. China is obviously not an electoral democracy, and neither central nor provincial leaders have to stand for competitive election. Does the absence of electoral competition mean that Chinese politicians are free to neglect public opinion and are totally exempt from accountability to others? To what extent are the theories that were developed in the context of electoral democracies instructive for investigating the patterns of intergovernmental transfers in China?

I believe that the political logic of intergovernmental transfers is, in essence, more or less the same everywhere, although its manifestations may vary across different institutional settings. In the case of China, even though central politicians are not popularly elected, they, just like their counterparts elsewhere, care a great deal about their political legitimacy and survival. So do provincial leaders. Preoccupied with this concern, Chinese central politicians tend to use fiscal transfers to reward prospective supporters or to neutralize potential threats. In the same vein, provincial politicians are inclined to extract as many central transfers as possible to please their constituents and make their own lives a little easier. The allocation of fiscal transfers is thus as likely to become a focus of contention in intergovernmental relations in China as in electoral democracies.

More specifically, the model that is tested in this study posits that the distribution of central transfers in China is the function of three factors: the nature of transfers, the objectives of central allocators, and the ability of the regions to influence central decision-making.

The Nature of Transfers

Intergovernmental transfers can be divided into two broad categories: formula-based transfers and discretionary transfers. Formula-based programs are calculated according to elaborate formulae, which normally, but not necessarily, include stringent needs-based eligibility criteria. The receipt of such transfers is subject to neither competition nor bargaining. Whichever region meets the basic requirements for programs receives money. Although formula-based programs are not completely immune from the penetration of political interest, the presence of binding rules nevertheless substantially reduces the probability of political intervention (Kraemer, 1997). In contrast, discretionary transfers are prone to be hijacked by political interests. They are often allocated strategically with the intention of building and maintaining political support (Stein, 1981).

The Objectives of Central Allocators

The objectives of central allocators have an ethical (egalitarian) dimension as well as a political dimension. The prevailing models of inter-governmental transfers assume that politicians are selfishly motivated: they care for nothing but power and personal material gains. Yet I do not think it right *a priori* to rule out the possibility that politicians genuinely care for distributive equity in the nation. Central politicians' equity concerns are perhaps not mere rhetorical masks for self-interest. They may allocate central transfers in such a way to somehow narrow gaps in public services and living conditions between provinces. Of course, I have no intention of suggesting that central politicians are benevolent in nature. Their egalitarian motive is almost always mixed with political motives. It is not very like them to sacrifice much of their political interest to achieve greater regional equality. Whenever their political goals are at odds with the equity principal, the former may very well compromise the latter in determining transfer policies.

In electoral democracies, national politicians have a propensity to use redistribution to gain or solidify the support of high "clout" groups of voters. Chinese politicians do not have to worry about their performance at the ballot box, but their desire to stay in power is as strong as, and probably stronger than, that of their counterparts in electoral democracies. To stay in power, central politicians tend to spare no effort to preserve national unity, without which it is simply impossible for them to maintain their political pre-eminence in the country. To preserve the nation, central decision makers may distribute more per capita transfers to provinces with secession possibilities than to others.[2] Provinces that pose no such threat benefit much less, because central decision makers may take for granted their support for national unity.[3] Thus, intergovernmental fiscal transfers may become an instrument for counter-acting centrifugal forces.

Provinces' Ability to Influence Central Decision-Making

A province's capacity to effectively lobby for central largesse depends on two factors: its possession of bargaining chips and the degree of its representation in key national decision-making organs. A province's bargaining power ultimately depends on the objectives of central policy makers. It may use its potential to promote and threaten those objectives as leverage to extract a larger share of centrally bestowed benefits (Treisman, 1996). As a result, provinces with greater potential to do so tend to gain from the political process. Other things being equal, I expect that provinces with large populations and economies would possess greater bargaining power vis-à-vis central politicians.

Scholars of communist systems often assume that all important decisions are made by one or a few top party leaders. Even if that were true, top leaders would not be completely free from political influence. Recent studies have established that those actors who are given the right to choose top leaders by the party constitution, or what Susan Shirk calls the "selectorate " (1993), could have some bearing on the central decision-making process. Who constitutes the selectorate in China? They are primarily the members of the Central Committee of the Chinese Communist Party (CCP), who hold the formal authority to select the Politburo, the Standing Committee of the Politburo, and the Party General Secretary. Although the Central Committee seldom initiates policy measures, major changes in policies, programs, and top leadership are subject to its approval and endorsement (Wang, 1999: 76).

Provincial party and government officials make up the largest bloc in the CCP Central Committee. However, provincial representation in the committee is by no means equally distributed. Because the Central Committee functions as "the final veto gate" in policy-making (Shirk, 1993: 81-82), I would expect the top central leadership to allocate transfers somewhat in accordance with the relative weight of each province's representation in the committee.

Data and Research Design

China's Ministry of Finance (1999) recently released information about allocation of central transfers to provincial governments.[4] This article utilizes only the data for the fiscal year 1998.[5] Such data make it possible for us to ascertain the factors that best explain why some provinces receive more per capita central transfers than others. In particular, I am interested in the extent to which variations in per capita central transfers can be explained by two political variables: the concerns of central politicians about national unity, and provincial representation in central decision-making.

Dependent Variables

There are many types of budgetary flows between the central and provincial governments in China. For the sake of parsimoniousness, I distinguish four types of net central transfers:[6]

1. Old transfer: this is a preset amount, fixed in 1994, that reflects the sum of transfers that a province received under the pre-1994 fiscal system.

2. Returned revenue: primarily designed to compensate provinces for what they would have to sacrifice for accepting the new 1994 fiscal system, returned revenue is allocated according a predetermined formula, and thereby no longer subject to negotiation.

3. New transfer: this consists of many kinds of discretionary central transfers that were introduced under the 1994 system.

4. Transitional transfer: first introduced in 1995, this is a kind of formula-based transfer, the aim of which is to address horizontal fiscal imbalance.

The dependent variables in this study are per capita old transfer (OLD), per capita returned revenue (RETURN), per capita new transfer (NEW), and per capita transitional transfer (TRANSITIONAL).

Independent Variables

To test the hypotheses that were outlined in the previous section, I use multivariate regression to estimate the effects of possible determinants on the allocation of the four types of central transfers.

1.   *Central Allocators' Equity Concern*

To ascertain the extent to which central policy-makers are motivated by a concern for equity, I include the following independent variables in the models.

Per capita GDP (PCGDP): this is a proxy for relative fiscal capacity, which refers to each province's potential ability to raise revenue, or the relative richness of each province's taxable resources. A major source of fiscal disparity in any country arises from asymmetries in the distribution of taxable resources, which in turn arises from unequal distribution of income. The lower the per capita GDP, the lower the taxable resources. If central transfers were allocated on equity-based criteria, then a negative regression coefficient would be expected.

The following four variables are measures of fiscal need, or the extent to which a province, through no fault of its own, faces conditions that augment the scope of services that its governments must provide, or increase per unit costs of providing public services.

Per capita cost of natural disasters (DISASTER): China is a country that is prone to natural disasters. In each year, however, some areas may incur greater losses than others. Central decision makers are supposed to take this factor into consideration when they allocate fiscal transfers. If they do, then I expect a positive coefficient.

The share of agriculture in the regional economy (AGRICULTURE): this is an indicator of underdevelopment. If central transfers were targeted to subsidize underdeveloped regions, then one would expect a positive regression coefficient.

Dependency ratio (DEPENDENCY): this ratio refers to the share of the population that is below and above the working age. It serves as an indicator of fiscal need. Regions with a larger dependent population are expected to receive larger per capita transfers.

Population density (DENSITY): This is a proxy for the unit costs of social services. Fiscal disparities can be the result of differences in revenue bases as well as in the unit cost of provision. There may be many environmental factors that affect costs of provision. Population density is just one of them. Presumably, the lower the population density in a region, the higher the unit cost of delivering any particular level of social services to the population. If central policy were to compensate cost differences, then one would expect a negative coefficient.

2.   Central Allocators' Political Concerns

The proportion of minorities in the population (MINORITY): Regions with a high concentration of non-Han inhabitants might be thought more likely to cultivate separatist aspirations. If the central government uses fiscal transfers as an instrument to pacify potentially troublesome provinces, then a positive coefficient would be expected.

The instances of labour disputes (INSTABILITY): This is an indicator of social stability. If social stability were a major concern for central leaders, then one would expect a positive regression coefficient.[7]

3.   Provinces' Bargaining Power

I consider two simple proxies of a province's importance in national politics: the overall economic size as measured by provincial gross domestic product (GDP) and its demographic size (POPULATION). Beijing is more likely to yield to pressure from provinces with noteworthy political and economic weight. Consequently, provinces with greater bargaining power are expected to extract more per capita transfers from the central government than are others.

4.   Provincial Representation in Central Decision-Making

POSITION measures the ratio of the total number of a province's leaders in the Central Committee to its population.[8] Table 7.1 indicates that substantial differences exist among provinces in the population per member of the Central Committee. Some provinces are over-represented in that their numbers of Central Committee members are larger than they would be if Central Committee members were allocated to provinces in proportion to population sizes. If per capita representation were to have a positive effect on per capita central transfers, then the expected sign of this coefficient would be positive.

Table 7.1.   Unequal Distribution of Per Capita Representation
in the Central Committee (millions of residents
represented per member)

Most Over- represented	Most Under- represented	Mean	Std. Deviation
2.48	65.7	21.3	16.3

In addition to provincial leaders, there are also Central Committee members who, in terms of their positions, are not tied to any particular province. To control the possibility that they favour the provinces of their origins in national policy-making, I include another indicator of provincial representation, BIRTHPLACE, which measures the ratio of the total number of the Central Committee members that originally came from a province to the population of that province.[9] A positive regression coefficient on this variable is also expected.

Determinants of Central Transfers

In this section, I conduct regression analyses on the four types of central-provincial transfers. My main purpose is to investigate the extent to which fiscal transfers in China are governed by equity considerations, and whether political considerations override ethic considerations.

Per Capita Old Transfer (OLD)

Column 1 of Table 7.2 displays the results that are obtained when OLD is regressed on the set of explanatory variables that were detailed in the preceding section. OLD is a remnant of the pre-1994 system, which may give us some idea about the patterns of fiscal flows between the central and provincial governments under the pre-1994 fiscal system. As can be seen from column 1, none of variables that signify central allocators' equity concern appear to have a statistically significant effect on OLD. Moreover, the two variables that measure provincial bargaining power (POPULATION and GDP) lack statistically significant effects.

As expected, the influence of political representation (POSITION) on OLD is positive and statistically significant. Provinces with greater per capita political representation in the Central Committee were able to receive larger per capita transfers than did provinces with smaller per capita representation under the old system.[10] Interestingly, the native places of Central Committee members do not appear to be determinants of central transfers under either old or new fiscal system. In this and the other three regressions that are reported in Table 7.2, the coefficient of BIRTHPLACE either bears a "wrong" sign or is not statistically significant, or both. The Chinese people are known for strong emotional ties to their "old homes" (*lao jia*) or "ancestral homes" (*yuan ji*), even when they have never lived and worked there. For this reason, some believe that a province should be able to influence national policy by enlisting the assistance of central officials of local origin (Shirk 1993: 100). However, Chinese politicians seem to be just as pragmatic, hard-nosed, and no-nonsense as their counterparts in the West. The Western adage that "where you stand is where you sit" can certainly be applied to them. That is probably why POSITION appears to have an effect on the decisions on OLD, NEW, and TRANSITIONAL, whereas BIRTHPLACE does not.

The most important determinants of OLD are the political concerns of the central leaders. The ethnic composition variable (MINORITY) has a positive coefficient that is statistically significant ($p = 0.000$), which implies that residents of provinces with big proportions of non-Han population were able to secure significantly larger OLD than did residents of other provinces under the pre-1994 system. To my surprise, however, the variable that measures social instability (INSTABILITY) is negatively correlated with OLD. This is also true in the cases of RETURN, NEW, and TRANSITIONAL. Rather than to calming down less stable provinces by allocating them more per capita transfers, central policy makers seem to have penalized such provinces.[11] Those provinces that are capable of maintaining social stability find favour in the eyes of the central allocators. Perhaps it is not politically wise for the central government to reward troublesome provinces with financial concessions.[12]

Table 7.2. Explaining Central-Provincial Transfers in China, 1998

Variables	1 OLD (Beta)	2 RETURN (Beta)	3 NEW (Beta)	4 TRANSITIONAL (Beta)
Central Leaders' Concern Over Equity				
PCGDP	-0.516 (-1.491)	0.947 (3.291)***	-1.039 (-2.218)**	-1.656 (-3.552)***
DISASTER	0.115 (1.487)	-0.067 (-1.039)	0.286 (2.732)**	0.206 (1.979)*
AGRICULTURE	-0.111 (-0.816)	-0.081 (-0.710)	-0.403 (-2.182)**	-0.488 (-2.658)**
DEPENDENCY	0.066 (0.614)	-0.048 (-0.531)	-0.289 (-1.984)*	-0.233 (-1.608)
DENSITY	0.059 (0.251)	0.204 (1.039)	1.139 (3.563)***	1.081 (3.398)***
Central Leaders' Political Concerns				
MINORITY	0.423 (3.966)***	0.180 (2.028)*	0.717 (4.974)***	0.719 (5.011)***
INSTABILITY	-0.433 (-2.809)**	-0.058 (-0.451)	-0.340 (-1.631)	-0.215 (-1.037)
Provincial Bargaining Power				
POPULATION	-0.194 (-0.872)	0.149 (0.804)	-0.698 (-2.320)**	-0.793 (-2.650)**
GDP	0.337 (1.552)	-0.410 (-2.369)**	0.509 (1.729)	0.775 (2.648)**
Provincial Representation				
POSITION	0.262 (1.978)*	-0.172 (-1.565)	0.506 (2.826)**	0.567 (3.183)***
BIRTHPLACE	0.118 (1.220)	-0.034 (-0.426)	-0.083 (-0.636)	-0.265 (-2.036)*
R^2	0.924	0.948	0.862	0.863
Adjusted R^2	0.881	0.917	0.782	0.784
Number of observations	31	31	31	31

Notes: t-ratios in parentheses: *$p<0.1$; **$p<0.05$; ***$p<0.01$ (all two-sided)

Per Capita Returned Revenue (RETURN)

In essence, returned revenue is a kind of side payment for the provinces not to resist the new 1994 fiscal system. Rich provinces did very well under the old system, which allowed them to retain much of taxes that they collected locally. To defuse the opposition of these provinces to the new system, central policy makers had to design the mechanism of returned revenue in ways that would be acceptable to them (Wang, 1997). Thus, the distribution of RETURN is not expected to conform to the equity principle. Indeed, the equity consideration appears to play no role whatsoever in allocating RETURN. All of the five indicators of provincial fiscal capacity and fiscal needs take the "wrong" signs from the perspective of fiscal equalization (Column 2 of Table 7.2). While four of them are not statistically significant, one, PCGDP, is significant at the level of 0.01. This is impressive evidence that the distribution of RETURN is biased in favour of provinces with higher per capita income, namely, those with vested interests in the old fiscal system.

Another variable that plays a clear role in affecting the distribution of RETURN is the ethnic composition of the province. The coefficient on MINORITY is positive and significant. Central policy makers appear to be more generous to provinces with large non-Han populations when they design the formula for allocating RETURN.

All other explanatory variables in the regression on RETURN are insignificant or related to the dependent variable in ways that contradict my expectations. For instance, one of the two variables that measure provincial bargaining power (POPULATION) carries the "right" sign, but it is completely insignificant (at $p = 0.43$). As for the other measure of provincial bargaining power, GDP is negatively related to the receipt of transfers and is statistically significant. It is quite puzzling why economically powerful provinces tend to fare worse in obtaining favourable formula with regard to the distribution of per capita returned revenue.

Per Capita New Transfers (NEW)

Old transfers and returned revenue are relics of the pre-1994 fiscal system. Anchored at fixed amounts or allowed to increase only by small margins, the relative weight of these two kinds of transfers will steadily diminish as the overall size of public finance grows. New transfers and transitional transfers will eventually become the main mechanisms of fiscal transfers in China.

New transfers are composed of various kinds of discretionary central grants. Political factors are therefore more likely to play a noticeable role in allocating NEW than in the cases of OLD and RETURN. Column 3 of Table 7.2 reports the regression results for NEW, which is helpful in our understanding of the underlying logic of fiscal transfers in contemporary China.

What are the key determinants of NEW allocation? Central leaders' concern over equity is one of them. This is manifested by NEW's negative relation with per capita GDP (PCGDP) and positive relation with per capita cost of natural disasters (DISASTER). The relationships are statistically significant. Other things being equal, poorer provinces seem to receive more per capita new transfers from Beijing, and so do provinces that suffer substantial losses from natural disasters.

The coefficients of the other three variables that measure provincial fiscal needs are statistically significant but carry the "wrong" signs. A province with a less developed economy and a larger dependent population receives less rather than more per capita new transfer, which obviously violates the equity principle. Because the cost of the provision of public services increases with a more dispersed population, provinces with low density are expected to obtain special help from the central government. Surprisingly, DENSITY has a positive coefficient and is statistically significant, which implies that central policy makers actually give preferentiality to high-density provinces along the country's coast over low-density provinces in the central and western regions.

Why do the coefficients of AGRICULTURE, DEPENDENCY, and DENSITY have the "wrong" signs? A possible reason for such unexpected results is that Chinese fiscal transfers may contain a strong urban bias: fiscal transfers benefit mostly urban residents, not rural residents. Consequently, in per capita terms, more urbanized provinces, namely those that are characterized by the small relative size of agriculture in the local economy, low birth rates, and high population densities, normally receive significantly more in new central transfers.[13]

If the role of central leaders' concern over equity is somewhat inconsistent and equivocal in determining the allocation of new transfers, then the role of their concern over national unity is unmistakable. MINORITY has a positive coefficient and a T-statistic of 4.97 (significant at $p = 0.000$), which confirms that central policy makers are inclined to use new transfers as instruments to appease provinces with high concentrations of non-Han inhabitants, and which thereby pose greater secession threats.

Pressure politics, however, does not play a major role in the allocation of new transfers. I assume that Beijing is more likely to yield to pressure from provinces with big populations. Contrary to my expectation, although the coefficients of POPULATION is statistically significant, it carries the "wrong" sign, which suggests that less populous provinces tend to do better in obtaining per capita new transfers.[14] A possible explanation is that, unlike in electoral democracies, a larger population in China does not mean greater political influence in terms of votes. With a population of 1.3 billion, China has reason to treat a large provincial population as detrimental to its economic and social development. Thus, a province's demographic size might not serve it as an effective bargaining chip in dealing with Beijing. Yet a province's economic size is still expected to have a positive effect on its receipt of per capita transfers. Indeed, the coefficient of GDP has the "right" positive sign, but is not statistically significantly different from zero at the conventional level.

In the column 3, the variable of provincial political representation again has a positive coefficient and relatively high T-statistic ($t = 2.826$). This suggests that per capita provincial representation in the key central decision-making body matters a great deal in determining the distribution of the central government transfers in China, just as it does in electoral democracies.

Transitional Transfers (TRANSITIONAL)

Comparing columns 3 and 4 of Table 2, it becomes immediately clear that the coefficients of all variables share exactly the same signs in both regression, while the levels of significance only change marginally in some of them. Evidently, similar factors more or less affect the allocation of these two types of transfers, including central leaders' concerns over equity and national unity, the urban bias of China's fiscal system, and provincial political representation.

The only noteworthy difference between the two regressions is the role of GDP, which is used to measure provincial bargaining power. While GDP is positively related to both transfers, its coefficient is statistically significant in the case of TRANSITIONAL, but not in the case of NEW. The two kinds of transfers differ in that new transfers consist of mostly discretionary grants, whereas transitional transfers are allocated according to some predetermined formula. Supposedly, formula-based transfers are less prone to the influence of political factors. How could provinces' negotiation advantages have more visible effects on the allocation of formula-based transfers than on the allocation of discretionary transfers? I do not have a plausible explanation for this surprising result, except to point out the possibility that a bias could have been built into the formula by economically powerful provinces in the process of negotiating such rules.

In sum, the regression results that are reported in Table 7.2 suggest that political factors are quite decisive in determining the distribution of various kinds of central transfers in China.

Conclusion

China scholars have paid considerable attention to intergovernmental fiscal relations in the country. Little research, however, has been devoted to the distribution of net fiscal transfers between Beijing and the provinces. This paper examines the allocation of per capita central net transfers across provinces in China in 1998. Foremost among the conclusions drawn is that the patterns of transfers exhibit a discernible political logic. The per capita central transfers that are obtained by a province are determined, to a large extent, by various political factors. The influence of these political factors remains significant even after controlling for other possible determinants. More specifically, the empirical findings suggest five conclusions.

First, equity considerations appear to play some role in central policies of regional redistribution. In three of the four regressions that are reported in Table 7.2, per capita central transfers are negatively related to per capita GDP and positively related to per capita cost of natural disasters, which means that the variance in the net per capita flow of fiscal resources can to some extent be explained by indicators of social needs. When provinces with less per capita income and high per capita disaster costs receive, *ceteris paribus*, more per capita transfers, it is reasonable to conclude that Chinese central leaders are indeed motivated by a concern for equity in their policies of regional redistribution.

However, this conclusion needs to be qualified, because the other three indicators of fiscal need (AGRICULTURE, DEPENDENCY, and DENSITY) are almost always correlated with per capita central transfers in ways that violate the equity principle. This is probably due to the inherent urban bias of China's public finance. For provinces at similar levels of per capita income, the more urbanized tend to receive more per capita central transfers. The Chinese central government must use per capita GDP as the summary index of social needs in making their decisions with regard to fiscal transfers. Other aspects of social needs are thus largely overlooked.

Second, the concern of central policy makers about national unity is the most important determinant in the Chinese transfer system. All four regressions in Table 7.2 reinforce each other and point to this conclusion.

Why does national unity figure so prominently in the allocation of fiscal transfers in China? Because China's 55 minority nationalities hold importance for the country's long-term development and national security which is disproportionate to their populations. Although minorities account for less than 9 percent of China's overall population, they are scattered over nearly two-thirds of the country's landmass, which is known as West China. These areas happen to be resource-rich, holding plenty of coal, oil, and gas, in addition to unlimited hydroelectric potential. To the extent that energy is a bottleneck for

China's future development, West China seems to hold the key. More important, China's ethnic groups live mostly along the country's borders. Put differently, China's border areas are mostly inhabited by minority peoples. From a security point of view, these areas have enormous strategic value as China's outposts for national defense.[15]

What worries Chinese political leaders is probably twofold. First, there have been persistent economic gaps between coastal regions where the Han Chinese dominate and western regions that are most heavily populated by minority nationalities. China's market-oriented reform only widens the existing gulf (Wang and Hu, 1999). With little sign that eastern prosperity has trickled down to the west, central decision-makers have reasons to worry that such disparities may fuel age-old resentments along ethnic, linguistic, and cultural lines. Second, separatist activities and ethnic unrest in some of China's border areas, especially Xinjiang and Tibet, constitute another evil omen for those who are holding the reins of power in Beijing. In particular, the creation of several new nations on China's Central Asian frontier has raised Chinese concern about the influence of separatist sentiment spilling over from the other side of the border into China's Muslim areas. Beijing's challenge is to convince China's minorities that they will benefit more from cooperating with their national government than from breaking away. To do so, central policy-makers have to take into account the interests of minority nationalities. Fiscal transfers are political instruments to appease ethnic or religious independence sentiments, real or potential. This is something that the Chinese government is willing and even happy to admit. In fact, whenever the issue of fiscal transfers comes up, the central government never tires of emphasizing that ethnic regions deserve preferential treatment (Information Office of the State Council 1999).

Table 7.3.   Fiscal Transfers to Minority-Concentration Provinces in 1998
(Unit: *Yuan*)

Provinces	Minority as % of the Population	Per Capita GDP	Per Capita Transfers	Per Capita Transfers	Per Capita Revenue	Per Capita Expenditure
Tibet	96.18	3716	1613.39	1676.27	145.60	1812.80
Xinjiang	62.42	6229	324.25	445.21	377.43	842.66
Qinghai	42.14	4367	466.20	598.85	255.66	882.68
Guangxi	39.24	4076	72.39	181.30	257.13	426.21
Yunnan	33.41	4355	79.89	388.92	408.42	796.31
Ningxia	33.27	4270	389.01	510.76	332.40	844.94
Guizhou	32.43	2342	95.30	193.40	179.90	366.44
Inner Mongolia	19.42	5068	264.32	397.67	332.56	729.22
Beijing	3.83	18482	-49.59	541.27	1845.94	2258.09
Tianjin	2.31	14808	-112.10	373.76	1061.78	1444.29
Hebei	3.94	6525	19.38	143.79	315.81	460.59
Shanxi	0.29	5040	40.22	175.71	330.08	520.86
Liaoning	15.62	9333	64.27	300.25	638.02	941.02
Jilin	10.24	5916	172.09	350.62	355.24	721.17
Heilongjiang	5.67	7544	152.83	306.94	418.05	689.58
Shanghai	0.47	28253	-478.49	642.69	2606.64	3218.42
Jiangsu	0.23	10021	-60.74	153.48	413.93	593.02
Zhejiang	0.51	11247	-6.33	204.98	445.62	645.17
Anhui	0.58	4576	55.41	143.00	258.61	393.26
Fujian	1.55	10369	73.23	208.71	571.10	774.56
Jiangxi	0.27	4484	136.53	216.65	232.97	420.24
Shandong	0.60	8120	46.28	148.93	399.92	553.62
Henan	1.18	4712	36.37	127.19	224.38	348.78
Hubei	3.97	6300	57.64	182.67	286.84	475.59
Hunan	7.95	4953	72.20	190.60	241.08	422.06
Guangdong	0.56	11143	14.81	233.68	902.85	1163.32
Hainan	17.00	6022	150.59	235.12	450.13	734.09
Chongqing	5.70	4684	66.37	173.13	233.14	412.19
Sichuan	4.56	4339	54.84	144.28	233.16	379.28
Shaanxi	0.48	3834	101.71	208.81	260.48	463.86
Gansu	8.30	3456	123.50	282.01	215.56	500.06

Source: Ministry of Finance (1999)

The concern about national unity that underlies fiscal transfers is evident in Table 7.3. Per capita locally collected revenue is generally lower in the eight minority-concentrated provinces than in the other provinces. Thanks to central transfers, however, per capita expenditure is generally much higher in those eight provinces than in the rest of the country, with the exceptions of Beijing, Tianjin, Shanghai, and Guangdong. As a matter of fact, a province with a large non-Han population is likely to receive more per capita transfers than one with a predominantly Han population, even when the former has higher per capita GDP than the latter. For instance, there were ten provinces whose per capita GDP were lower than Xinjiang's, but Xinjiang received a level of per capita transfers that was several times higher than those ten provinces (Table 7.3). The only explanation for such a large discrepancy is Xinjiang's predominantly non-Han population. More striking is a comparison between Shaanxi, Gansu, and Ningxia (in China, they are often lumped together and called the Shaan-Gan-Ning region)–three neighbouring provinces that resembles one another in almost every aspect except one: Ningxia is inhabited by a large number of Chinese Muslims, whereas Shaanxi and Gansu are the legendary birthplace of the Han Chinese. That difference seems to be crucial in explaining why Ningxia received far more per capita transfer than its two neighbours, despite the fact that its per capita GDP was higher (Table 7.3).[16]

More interestingly, when allocating fiscal transfers, the central government seems to have given first priority to those provinces that are most susceptible to ethnic separatism, namely the provinces that are mainly inhabited by Tibetans and Muslims (Tibet, Xinjiang, Qinghai, and Ningxia). On the other hand, provinces where minorities make little trouble (e.g., Guangxi and Guizhou) do not seem to have found much favour with Beijing as far as fiscal transfers are concerned.

Maintaining national unity certainly entails a high price, but, in the view of Chinese policy makers, the price is one worth bearing.[17]

Third, the most exciting finding of this study is that political representation does count in China. My investigation in this regard focuses on the role that is played by unequal per capita representation in the Central Committee of the Chinese Communist Party. As can be seen from

Table 7.2, the variable that reflects a province's per capita political representation (POSITION) appears to have a positive and statistically significant effect on all kinds of per capita central transfers, except for returned revenue.

Scholars who study policy making in communist systems usually assume that all decisions are made by one or a few persons at the very apex of the ruling party. If that were true, then formal representation would have no bearing. How could the unequal representation in the CCP's Central Committee affect the distribution of central transfers in China?

I believe that institutional arrangements matter as much in China as in electoral democracies, especially after the last strongman, Deng Xiaoping, died in 1997. Although Chinese politicians are not elected by popular vote, they nevertheless have to operate within an increasingly institutionalized political setting. For this reason, the CCP Central Committee deserves special attention. Composed of less than two hundred of China's most powerful political figures, the Central Committee as a collective body rarely initiates policy, but any changes in major policies and programs need its formal endorsement. That is why Susan Shirk calls it "the final veto gate in policy-making" (Shirk 1993: 80). More important, the CCP constitution grants the Central Committee the formal authority to select top party leaders (including the members of the Politburo and the Standing Committee of the Politburo, as well as the Party General Secretary), which sets "the context in which Chinese officials compete with one another to advance their careers and make economic policies" (Shirk, 1993: 9). To build a winning coalition among the groups that are well represented in the Central Committee, the incumbents of the Politburo have to take into account interests, preferences, and opinions of the Central Committee members when making key decisions. As provincial party and government officials constitute the largest bloc in the Central Committee, it is natural for top leaders to promote policies that appeal to key segments among them. They respond to the incentive structure of China's leadership selection system in very much the same way as Western politicians respond to the incentive structure of their electoral systems. To the extent that the "anticipated reaction" of Central Committee members may condition and shape decisions of the Politburo (Chang, 1990: 179), representation (albeit non-electoral) in this body certainly carries some weight. Thus, it is by no means surprising that over-represented Chinese provinces are likely to receive larger per capita transfers than do under-represented provinces.

Fourth, political factors may have an effect on the distribution of discretion-based as well as formula-based transfers, albeit at different stages of decision-making. It is generally believed that, as long as transfers are calculated according to certain elaborate formula, the possibility of political influence will be reduced to the minimum. This view is based upon the assumption that such formulae contain stringent needs-based eligibility criteria, and thereby embody the equity principle. However, a very important caveat must be kept in mind: it is possible for political factors to influence the design of formulae. In other words, biases could be built into such formulae by politically powerful forces (Kraemer, 1997). This probably explains why such political variables as MINORITY and POSITION appear to have impinged upon the distribution of formula-based OLD and TRANSITIONAL. Nevertheless, whether they conform to the equity principle or not, once formulae fall into place, the scope of subsequent bargaining is restricted.

Of course, when rules for allocating transfers are vague, there is much room for bargaining. Thus, I expect to see provincial bargaining power come into play in the game of allocating discretionary central transfers. In the regression analyses, however, the variables that measure bargaining power add little to the explanation, which is quite perplexing. One possibility is that the variables are not adequate for assessing provincial bargaining power.

Finally, even though China's political system is very different from electoral democracy, this study echoes the results of prior investigations that focused on electoral democracies in the West and elsewhere (Stein 1981; Rich 1989; Atlas et al. 1995; Kraemer 1997; Treisman, 1996, 1998a, 1998b; Meyer & Naka 1999; Rao & Singh 2000): the distribution of fiscal transfers is largely determined by the interactions between central and regional politicians, both of whom are motivated to maximize their chances of staying in power within given institutional constraints. I find that the objectives of central leaders and provincial representation are key determinants of the distribution of central budgetary transfers. This suggests that the underlying political logic of intergovernmental fiscal transfers in China is essentially the same as in other countries.

Appendix

Intergovernmental Transfers in China

During Mao's era, the central government enjoyed considerable control over the distribution of resources. The fiscal system was arranged in such a way that rich provinces had to remit large proportions of their revenue to the central government, and poor provinces were allowed to "retain all their revenues and receive additional direct subsidies from the central government" (Lardy, 1980: 172-73). Acting as a redistributor in between, the central government could use fiscal transfers to influence the behaviour of sub-national governments.

In the first 15 years of economic reform, however, the central government's ability to allocate transfers was critically enfeebled. Under the fiscal contract system that prevailed from 1980 to 1993, all of the provinces, both rich and poor, were compelled to become financially more independent. Most taxes were collected and most expenditure undertaken on a jurisdiction-by-jurisdiction basis (Wang, 1997). As fiscal surpluses from rich provinces drained off, what was available for the central government to redistribute became increasingly limited. The result was growing fiscal gaps between provinces. With larger tax bases, rich provinces could afford to either directly invest more with their budgetary capital or offer more generous tax concessions to potential investors. The same fiscal autonomy, however, worked to the detriment of poor provinces, because with less central subsidies they were hard up even for resources to support daily government operation and to provide such basic services as health and education, not to mention conducting productive investment (West and Wong, 1995; Selden, 1997).

By the early 1990s, there was a growing concern that a widening income gap between the prosperous coast and the laggard interior might eventually cause the break up of the Chinese nation state (Wang and Hu, 2001). To arrest this dangerous trend, China overhauled its fiscal system at the beginning of 1994. The new system was called the tax-assignment system (*fenshuizhi*). One of the manifest goals of the 1994 reform was to restore the central government's redistributive ability so that it could again transfer surpluses from more developed provinces to less-developed provinces.

The post-1994 Chinese fiscal flows between the central and provincial governments can be divided into four broad categories.

Returned revenue

Because strict adherence to the new rules would have lowered the revenue income of every province, when the 1994 system was introduced the central government made a pledge of compensating each and every province for what it would have to sacrifice to accept the new system. For this purpose, each province's net loss in accepting the new system was calculated.[18] Thereafter, in every year a province was supposed to receive central compensation (or "returned revenue") amounting to:

$$R_t = R_0 * (1 + 0.3 * G_t)^t$$

where R_t was the central compensation in year t; R_0 was the compensation baseline or the calculated net loss of the province for the first year; G_t was the average growth rate of VAT and consumption tax in the province in year t; and t represented the first, second, third...year after the introduction of the new system. As the mechanism of "returned revenue" was primarily designed as a kind of side payment for the provinces not to resist the new system, its distribution was not expected to conform to the equity principle.

Old system subsidies (or remittances)

Even after 1994, some of the revenue-sharing contracts that had been negotiated under the old system remained effective. The provinces continued to remit a certain amount of their locally collected revenue to, or receive a certain amount of subsidies from, the central government as they had under the pre-1994 regime. The only difference was that the amounts of remittance or subsidies were now fixed. Normally, a province that received subsidies did not have to remit to the central coffers. Shandong was the only exception. Among the other 30 provinces, sixteen were on the recipient side and fourteen on the remitting side. The former group included all eight of the provinces in which minority nationalities were concentrated (Tibet, Xinjiang, Inner Magalia, Ningxia, Guangxi, Qinghai, Yunnan, and Guizhou) and other poor provinces such as Sichuan and Jiangxi. Rich provinces such as Shanghai, Beijing, Guangdong, and Liaoning all belonged to the latter group. Thus, the mechanism contained elements of fiscal equalization. However, the significance of the mechanism will diminish, because as time goes by the relative size of such transfers will become smaller and smaller in the ever growing public finance.

New system subsidies (or remittances)

These were "new" because they were introduced after 1994. All of the transfers in this category were for specific purposes, such as disaster relief, subsidies to certain regions (e.g., Beijing, Chongqing, Xinjiang, and Yan'an), subsidies to certain projects (e.g., education, environmental protection, and industrial restructuring), and the like.

"Transfer of the transition period"

First introduced in 1995, this transfer was specifically designated to address horizontal fiscal imbalance. Unlike other "new system subsidies", this was the only formula-based type of transfer, the allocation of which was supposedly determined by objective measurements of fiscal capacities and the fiscal needs of the provinces.[19]

The net central transfers to the provinces can be calculated by subtracting the provincial remittances of taxes to the central coffers from the total of all central transfers to the provinces. In 1998, this figure amounted to 272.4 billion *yuan*, which accounted for about a half of the central revenue, or 3.4 percent of China's GDP. However, the bulk of the central transfers took the form of "returned revenue"–a kind of de facto provincial entitlement about which the central government could exercise little discretional power. If the "returned revenue" were to be excluded, then the net central transfers were barely 65 billion *yuan*. As for the most redistributive "transfer of the transition period," its size (6 billion *yuan*) was too small to be significant.

Given the heterogeneity of different forms of central subsidies, it may be useful to distinguish four concepts of net central transfers.

- Old Transfers = Old subsidies — Old remittances
- Returned Revenue = Returned revenue
- New Transfers = New Subsidies — New remittances
- Transitional Transfers = Transfers of the transition period.

Notes

1. Ma Jun (1994; 1997) dealt with the issue of intergovernmental fiscal transfers. However, his focus was on what constitutes a transfer system that is both desirable and feasible. Using Ma Jun's estimates, Martin Raiser (1998) studied the impact of fiscal transfers on capital flows and investment rates. Neither made efforts to investigate the determinants of transfers.

2. Wherever and whenever national unity is at stake, this seems to be the case. The most obvious example in this regard is Germany. East and West Germany were formally unified on October 3, 1990. However, unification posed a new challenge, the crux of which was a regional disparity. While the "old" Federal Republic had enjoyed a high degree of interregional balance, now it now became politically imperative to extend this interregional equality to the eastern part of the country and to establish equivalent living conditions throughout the "new" Federal Republic. For this reason, in each year after since 1990, the federal government has transferred at least DM 150 billion, or 5 percent of the West Germany GNP to East Germany. Without such an infusion of resources to narrow the overall income differential, the process of German unification would have been much bumpier and more problematic. As enormous as it seems, the fiscal sacrifice was a necessary political price to pay for consolidating the newly unified country (Heilemann and Reinicke, 1995; Renzsch, 1998). National unity may come at a high price, but central policy makers everywhere seem to view such a price as something worth bearing. In post-Soviet Russia, for instance, despite its inability to collect taxes and to make ends meet, Moscow still tried to placate separatist demands by central largesse. As a result, it was those regions that had posed serious threats to the country's political stability and territorial integrity that were rewarded with larger net per capita central transfers. As Treisman points out, "the practice of appeasing mobilized anti-centre regions was one reason why, despite separatist pressures, economic crisis, and weakened central institutions, Russia did not disintegrate in the early 1990s, as all three

other post-communist federations had done" (Treisman, 1998: 198). According to Melanie Beresford, who is a Vietnam specialist at Macquarie University in Australia, when the Vietnamese government allocates fiscal transfers, the most important consideration is to appease minority nationalities (Personal communication, July 23, 2001).

3. Several recent studies have taken into consideration the secession threat in their models of distributive politics (Persson and Tabellini, 1996; Bolton and Roland, 1997).

4. All the provincial governments also made transfer arrangements with county governments within their respective jurisdictions. In addition to money from Beijing, some provincial governments provided funds from their own budgets to finance downward transfers. Details of such arrangements varied greatly from province to province, but funds flowing to and from counties largely fell into the same four categories mentioned below. Regrettably, due to the unavailability of data on some key independent variables (e.g., county representation in provincial decision-making and incidence of labour disputes), it is not possible to conduct a sub-provincial level of analysis in the same way as reported in this paper. However, in a separate research on provincial-county transfers (including 2133 counties in 31 provincial units) that uses a model containing only five independent variables (per capita GDP, the agricultural share of county economy, whether a county is an autonomous area, GDP, and population), I found evidence that provincial governments followed the same political logic as the central government does in allocating fiscal transfers. Specifically, at any given income level, minority nationality autonomous counties tended to receive much more per capita provincial transfer than others. The results of the county level of analysis are available from the author on request.

5. Unless noted otherwise, all other data come from State Statistical Bureau (2000).

6. A detailed description about the four dependent variables is provided in Appendix.

7. I only have data on labour disputes in urban China (State Statistical Bureau, 2000). Regrettably, no data on the incidence of farmers' protests are available.

8. The data on the Central Committee of the Chinese Communist Party come from www.china-vip.com.

9. POSITION and BIRTHPLACE are not highly correlated (Pearson coefficient 0.379).

10. The current 15th CCP Central Committee did not come into being until 1997. Due to the lack of background information on the members of the 14th Central Committee that served between 1992 and 1997, I assume that the relative shares of each province's representation were more or less the same in the 14th as in the 15th Central Committees.

11. On the contrary, in Russia, regions with more strikes tend to receive more central transfers (Treisman, 1996: 319).

12. Alternatively, instances of labour disputes might be interpreted as a sign of overall stability rather than instability, because a high number of reported labour disputes might indicate that the process for addressing workers' grievances has been largely institutionalized.

13. For a detailed discussion of the urban bias in China's public finance, see Wang and Wang, 2001.

14. This is also true in Russia (Treisman, 1996: 325). However, in a case study of fiscal politics in India, population was found to have a positive effect on per capita transfers (Rao and Singh, 2001: 23).

15. Unfortunately, no information is available on exactly how much money goes toward developing natural resources, providing infrastructure, or suppressing separatist elements in those areas.

16. A comparison of those three provinces suggests that developing natural resources is not the main reason why the central government allocates more per capita transfer to minority areas, because Ningxia is not known for being more richly endowed with natural resources than its two neighbours.

17. In a study of fiscal transfers from 1978 to 1992, Martin Raiser (1998) noted that the poor provinces all received some subsidies, but the poorest provinces had not necessarily received the highest levels of subsidies. Rather it was provinces with predominantly non-Han

populations that were given the highest levels of subsidies, even though their income levels exceeded those of the poorest provinces. This finding led Raiser to suspect that fiscal transfers in China might have been motivated largely by political concern rather than by concern over equity. This study provides systematic evidence to support his conjecture.

18.   The net loss of a province was calculated according to the following formula:

$$R = S + 75\%V - T$$

Where R was the net loss of the province for the first year or the compensation baseline; S was revenue from consumption tax; V was revenue from VAT; and T was the province's actual revenue in 1993.

19.   Every year after 1995, the Ministry of Finance issued a detailed guideline on how the distribution formula was designed. For a collection of those yearly guidelines, see Zhang Hongli 1999.

References

1.   Anton, Thomas J., Jerry P. Cawley and Kevin L. Kramer (1980). *Moving Money: An Empirical Analysis of Federal Expenditure Patterns.* Cambridge, MA: Oelgschalger, Grinn and Hain.

2.   Arnold, R. Douglas (1981). "Legislators, Bureaucrats, and Locational Decisions". *Public Choice*, Vol. 37: 109-132.

3.   Atlas, Cary M., Thomas W. Gilligan, Robert J. Hendershott, and Mark A. Zupan (1995). "Slicing the Federal Government Net Spending Pie: Who Wins, Who Loses, and Why". *The American Economic Review*, Vol. 85, No. 3: 624-629.

4.   Bolton, Patrick and Gerard Roland (1997). "The Breakup of Nations: A Political Economy Analysis". Quarterly Journal of Economics, Vol. 112, No. 4: 1057-91.

5.   Buchanan, James M. (1950). "Federalism and Fiscal Equity". *American Economic Review*, Vol. 40, No. 4 (September), pp. 583-99.

6.   Chang, Parris H. (1990). *Power and Policy in China*, 3rd ed. Dubuque, Iowa: Kendall, Hunt.

7.   Chung, Jae Ho (1995). "Studies of Central-Provincial Relations in the People's Republic of China: A Mid-Term Appraisal". *China Quarterly*, No. 142: 491-510.

8.   Dixit, Avinash and John Londregan (1998a). "Fiscal Federalism and Redistributive Politics". *Journal of Public Economics*, Vol. 68, No. 2: 153-180.

9.   Dixit, Avinash and John Londregan (1998b). "Ideology, Tactics, and Efficiency in Redistributive Politics". *Quarterly Journal of Economics*, Vol. 113, No. 2: 497-530.

10.   Ferejohn, John (1974). *Pork Barrel Politics: Rivers and Harbors Legislation 1947-68.* Stanford: Stanford University Press.

11.   Gabris, Gilbert, and Harry Specht (1974). "Picking Winners: Federal Discretion and Local Experience as Bases for Planning Grant Allocation". *Public Administration Review*, Vol. 35: 565-574.

12.   Heilemann, Ullrich and Wolfgang H. Reinicke (1995). "Together Again: The Fiscal Cost of German Unity". *The Brookings Review*, Vol. 13, No. 2 (Spring): 42-47.

13.   Huang Yasheng (1996). "Central-Local Relations in China during the Reform Era". *World Development*, Vol. 24, No. 4: 655-672.

14.   Information Office of the State Council (1999). *National Minorities Policy and Its Practice in China*, Beijing.

15.   Johnston, Ronald (1978). "The Allocation of Federal Money in the United States: Aggregate Analysis by Correlation". *Policy and Politics*, Vol. 6: 279-297.

16.   Kraemer, Moritz (1997). "Intergovernmental Transfers and Political Representation: Empirical Evidence from Argentina, Brazil and Mexico". Inter-American Development Bank Office of the Chief Economist Working Paper 345.

17.   Lardy, Nicholas R. (1980). "Regional Growth and Income Distribution in China". In Robert F. Dernberger, ed., *China's Development Experience in Comparative Perspective.* Cambridge, MA: Harvard University Press, pp. 172-73.

18.   Lieberthal, Kenneth (1995). *Governing China: From Revolution Through Reform.* New York: W.W. Norton & Company, Inc.

19. Lieberthal, Kenneth and Michel Oksenberg (1988). *Policy Making in China: Leaders, Structures, and Processes*. Princeton: Princeton University Press.

20. Ma, Jun (1994). "Macro-economic Management and Inter-governmental Relations in China". Policy Research Working Papers 1408 (1994), World Bank, Washington, DC.

21. Ma, Jun (1997). "Intergovernmental Fiscal Transfers: A Comparison of Nine Countries". Macroeconomic Management and Policy Division, Economic Development Institute, World Bank, 1997.

22. Manion, Melanie (2000). "Politics in China". In Gabriel A. Almond, G. Bingham Powell, Jr., Kaare Strom and Russell J. Dalton, eds. *Comparative Politics Today: A World View*. New York: Longman.

23. McAuley, Alastair (1997). "The Determinants of Russia Federal-Regional Fiscal Relations: Equity or Political Influence?" *Europe-Asia Studies*, Vol. 49, No. 3: 431-444.

24. Meyer, Steven A. and Shigeto Naka (1999). "The Determinants of Japanese Local-Benefit Seeking". *Contemporary Economic Policy*, Vol. 17, No. 1: 87-96.

25. Ministry of Finance (1999). *1999 nian quanguo dishixian caizheng tongji ziliao* [Public Finance Data of Prefectures, Municipalities, Counties, 1999] Beijing: China Financial Economic Press.

26. Montinola, Gabriella, Yingyi Qian and Barry R. Weingast (1995). "Federalism, Chinese Style: The Political Basis for Economic Success in China". *World Politics*, No. 48: 50-81.

27. National Bureau of Statistics (1999). *China's Statistical Yearbook*, 1999. Beijing: China Statistics Press.

28. Nordhaus, William D. (1975). "Political Business Cycles". *Review of Economic Studies*, Vol. 42: 169-90.

29. Oakland, William H. (1994). "Fiscal Equity, An Empty Box". *National Tax Journal*, Vol. 47, No. 1 (March): 199-210.

30. Oksenberg, Michel and James Tong (1991). "Evolution of Central-Provincial Fiscal Relations in China, 1971-1984: The Formal System." *China Quarterly*, No. 125: 1-32.

31. Peliserro, John, and Robert E. England (1980). "Washington Grantsmen: A Study of Municipal Representatives in the Nation's

Capital". University of Oklahoma Bureau of Government Research, 1980.

32.   Persson, Torsten and Tabellini, Guido (1996). "Federal Fiscal Constitutions: Risk Sharing and Redistribution". *The Journal of Political Economy*, Vol. 104. No. 5: 979-1010.

33.   Rao, M. Govinda and Nirvikar Singh (2000). "The Political Economy of Central-State Fiscal Transfers in India", paper presented at the Columbia University-World Bank Conference on Institutional Elements of Tax Design and Reform, February 18-19, 2000, at Columbia University.

34.   Raiser, Martin (1998). "Subsidizing Inequality: Economic Reforms, Fiscal Transfers and Convergence across Chinese Provinces". *The Journal of Development Studies*, Vol. 34, No. 3 (February): 1-26.

35.   Renzsch, Wolfgang (1998). "Financing Germany Unity: Fiscal Conflict Resolution in a Complex Federation". *Publius*, Vol. 28, No. 4 (Fall): 127-146.

36.   Rich, Michael J. (1989). "Distributive Politics and the Allocation of Federal Grants". *American Political Science Review*, Vol. 83: 193-213.

37.   Schumpeter, Joseph A. 1954. "The Crisis of the Tax State." In Richard Swedberg, ed., Joseph A. Schumpeter, *The Economics and Sociology of Capitalism*. Princeton: Princeton University Press, 1991: 99-140.

38.   Selden, Mark (1997). "China's Rural Welfare System: Crisis and Transformation", paper presented at the PRC Political Economy: Prospects under the Ninth Five-Year Plan Conference, National Cheng Kung University, Tainan, Taiwan, June 7-10, 1997.

39.   Shirk, Susan (1993). *The Political Logic of Economic Reform in China.* Berkeley: University of California Press.

40.   State Statistical Bureau (2000). *China Statistical Yearbook* (CD-ROM). Beijing: China Statistical Publishing House.

41.   Stein, Robert M. (1981). "The Allocation of Federal Aid Monies: The Synthesis of Demand-Side and Supply-Side Explanations". *American Political Science Review*, Vol. 75, No. 2: 334-343.

42.   Tannenwald, Robert and Jonathan Cowan (1997). "Fiscal Capacity, Fiscal Need, and Fiscal Comfort Among U.S. States: New Evidence". *Publius*, Vol. 27, No. 3: 11-125.

43. Treisman, Daniel (1996). "The Politics of Intergovernmental Transfers in Post-Soviet Russia". *British Journal of Political Science*, Vol. 26: 299-335.

44. Treisman, Daniel (1998a). "Deciphering Russia's Federal Finance: Fiscal Appeasement in 1995 and 1996". *Europe-Asia Studies*, Vol. 50, No. 5: 893-906.

45. Treisman, Daniel (1998b). "Fiscal Redistribution in a Fragile Federation: Moscow and the Regions in 1994". *British Journal of Political Science*, Vol. 28: 185-222.

46. Tufte, Edward (1978). *Political Control of the Economy*. Princeton: Princeton University Press.

47. Wang, James C.F. (1999). *Contemporary Chinese Politics: An Introduction*. Upper Saddle River, NJ: Prentice Hall.

48. Wang, Shaoguang (1997). "China's 1994 Fiscal Reform: An Initial Assessment". *Asian Survey*, Vol. XXXVII, No. 9 (September): 801-817.

49. Wang Shaoguang and Hu Angang. 1999. *The Political Economy of Uneven Development: The Case of China*. Armonk, NY: M.E. Sharpe.

50. Wang Shaoguang and Hu Angang (2001). *The Chinese Economy in Crisis: State Capacity and Fiscal Reform*. Armonk, NY: M.E. Sharpe.

51. Wang Shaoguang and Wang Youqiang (2001). "Gongmingquan, suodeshui yu yusuanjiandu, jiantan nongcun feigaishui di silu" [Citizenship, Income Tax and Budgetary Supervision: On the Fee-to-Tax Reform]. *Zhanglue yu guanli* [Strategy and Management], No. 4: 1-14.

52. West, Loraine A. and Christine P.W. Wong (1995). "Fiscal Decentralization and Growing Regional Disparities in Rural China: Some Evidence in the Provision of Social Services". *Oxford Review of Economic Policy*, Vol. 11, No. 4: 70-84.

53. Wong, Christine P. W. (1991). "Central-Local Relations in an Era of Fiscal Decline—The Paradox of Fiscal Decentralization in Post-Mao China". *China Quarterly*, No. 128: 691-714.

54. Wong, Christine P. W., Christopher Heady and Wing T. Woo (1995). *Fiscal Management and Economic Reform in the People's Republic of China*. Hong Kong: Oxford University Press.

55. World Bank (1990). *China: Revenue Mobilization and Tax Policy*. Washington, DC: World Bank.

56.   Zhang Hongli (1999). *Zhongugo guoduqi caizheng zhuanyi zhifu* [Fiscal Transfers in the Transition Period]. Beijing: Zhongguo caizheng jingji chubanshe.

57.   Zhang Tianlu (1999). "Xiandai zhongguo shaoshu minzu renkou zhuangkuang" [Analysis of the Contemporary China minority nationality population situation], paper presented at the Contemporary Migration and Ethnicity in China Conference, 7-8 October 1999, Institute of Nationality Studies, Chinese Academy of Social Sciences, Beijing.

8 The Politics of China's Western Development Initiative

Gregory T. Chin

In 1999, a new phase of China's development was launched: "the Great Western Development" (*xibu da kaifa*). In this latest modernization and development effort, the government intends to reduce the disparities between coastal and interior regions in China, spur the overall development of China's western regions, and do so in an ecologically sustainable manner. Whereas much has been written on the economic and environmental aspects of the Western Development Initiative (WDI),[1] less attention has been given to the politics of China's WDI.

This paper examines the politics of policy decision-making and policy implementation in the WDI.[2] The purpose is to discuss the policy *content* and *context* challenges that set the 'limits of the possible' for the WDI, and explore potential government institutional, policy decision-making and implementation adjustments that could be undertaken in order to enhance the impact and chances for "success" of the WDI. This paper is both descriptive and prescriptive – the aim is to contribute practical, strategic knowledge.

The main argument is that China's WDI faces significant *dual* challenges of policy-making and policy implementation. This can be seen, first, in decision-making tensions inside the political "Centre" involving political elites and intra-bureaucratic negotiations over the WDI; and second, in central-local political tensions over WDI policy implementation. Cumulatively, the tensions hinder the effectiveness, consistency and coherence of this latest regional development initiative in China. In the first part, we outline the "core structure" of decision-making and administration for the WDI inside the national Centre. In the second section, we discuss intra-bureaucratic tensions inside the political Centre on the WDI. In the third section, we examine central-local tensions in the implementation of the WDI, focusing on one case study in particular, the "focal belts strategy" of the Office of the Leading Group for Western Region Development. This paper concludes by offering implementation recommendations which aim to strengthen the effectiveness and positive politico-developmental impact of the WDI.

The Core Structure

This section examines the main processes and institutions in the core structure of decision-making for the WDI. The organizational framework for decision-making on China's WDI is largely an extension of standard Party and bureaucratic processes for policy decision-making in China. We see a complex matrix of Party elites, and relevant bureaucracies and interests, which interact to produce decisions through extensive bargaining and coordination. The Party elite – the Party General Secretary and the member of the Politburo Standing Committee – set the main *priorities* and basic general line on the WDI. Once the basic strategic decisions are made by the political elite, the majority of formal policy formulation responsibility then rests with the bureaucratic State Council structure. At this stage, the bureaucracy works out the details, under the direction and supervision of the leading State Councils' organs inside which the Party-bureaucratic elite overlap. Much effort is then placed on gaining *consensus* on the decisions taken, and interdepartmental consultation mechanisms are set up to facilitate the drafting of policy, legislation and regulations. The final stage of policy decision-making – prior to policy implementation – is that of "legitimation", in which the National People's Congress (China's legislature) provides official sanctioning for the decisions taken. In the simplest terms, this structure has a *core* where most formal decision-making authority lies, and a set of organizations beside and beneath the core, that become involved depending on the issue. Policy implementation responsibility lies with the bureaucratic line-ministries, and extends to the Judiciary in cases where the interpretation of laws are challenged.

In the lead up to the official launch of the Western Development Initiative, all major pronouncements on the WDI were made by the Party elite. Since the formal initiation of the WDI in 1999, the government has attempted to institutionalize the decision-making, policy review, administration, and program/project evaluation processes for the WDI by establishing a core decision-making structure which consists of three main levels. The Office of the Western Region Development Leading Group (LG) is at the base of this core structure. At the next level is the Western Region Development Leading Group (*Xibu diqu kaifa lingdao xiaozu*).[3] This LG is the focal point of senior-level coordination for the Party's Central Committee and the State Council. At the highest level are the Party elite, Jiang Zemin, Zhu Rongji and Wen Jiabao (discussed in detail below).

The State Council formally established the Western Region Development LG on 16 January 2001 in order to carry out the decision made by the Party Central Committee, to speed-up the development of China's western region. Reflecting the priority the leadership attaches to Western development, Zhu Rongji and Wen Jiabao, the Premier and Vice Premier, were assigned as Chair and Vice-Chair of the LG. Other members of the Lead Group include top officials from the relevant national commissions, line ministries, and bureaus of the State Council. In total, the WRDLG includes the Chair and the Vice-Chair, seventeen Ministers and two ministerial level Party officials.[4]

Not all Leading Groups are of equal rank; some consist mainly of ministerial-ranking officials, while others consist of mainly vice-ministerial officials. The WRDLG, along with the Central Financial and Economic Affairs Leading Small Group, would be considered among the most important LGs. The WRDLG is the most comprehensive LG. Similar to other leading small groups, the Western Region Development LG falls under the category of the Chinese Communist Party Central Committee's "decision-making consulting bodies" (*juece zixun jigou*).[5] According to Lu Ning, all leading small groups are:

...composed of leading members of the relevant government, party, and military ministerial ranking agencies, and in most cases have no permanent office or staff. They convene regular meetings to discuss issues, exchange ideas, and put forward proposals as policy alternatives for the Politburo and its Standing Committee to use to make decisions.[6]

The Western Region Development LG provides a regular forum for the members of the central leadership – the politicians – to meet with leading officials of various government, party, and even certain defence institutions – the top bureaucrats. When appropriate, department-level bureaucrats, academics (and even influential journalists) are also invited to attend some of the LG meetings. The Western Region Development LG is not a decision-making body *per se*; but its policy preferences and recommendations are likely to have an impact on the final outcome of the decision-making process. The decisions of the central leadership will, at times, be made based on the recommendation of the LG. At other times, the central leadership has merely formalized the positions taken by the LG.[7] Decisions of the LG involve cross-ministerial jurisdiction and interests, and the Western Region Development LG therefore plays a *key consensus-building* and *macro-coordinating role* in the eventual decision-making process.

Unlike most LGs (e.g. Foreign Affairs LG), the Western Region Development LG is a standing *institution* and has permanent staff. The *Office of the Western Region Development LG* was set up in March 2001 to carry out the day-to-day work and plans of the WRDLG. It receives basic directives and guidance from higher levels, determines the specific implications of the directives/guidance, collects reports and analysis from research institutes, negotiates with other interested domestic bureaus and industries, attempts to reach a working consensus, and then reports back up the hierarchy on the results of the discussions. The provinces, autonomous regions and municipalities of the western regions were also instructed to establish WDI LGs and Offices. Some provinces and municipalities in the coastal regions have also created new institutions or reorganized existing institutions which are specifically responsible for supporting China's western regional development, through enhanced east-west cooperation.

Currently, the Office of the WRDLG has 3 main functions:

(1)   to study and put forward proposals on development strategy, development plans, important issues, relevant policies, laws and regulations with regard to western development so as to promote sustained, rapid and healthy economic development of the west;

(2)   to study and put forward proposals on rural economic development, important infrastructure construction, protection and construction of ecology and environment, structure readjustment, resource development and the arrangement of important projects and organizing and coordinating the implementation of the plan for changing arable land into forest and grass;

(3)   to study and put forward policy proposals on deepening of reform, opening wider to the outside world and introducing domestic and foreign capital technology and talent, coordinate the comprehensive development of economic work on the one hand and science, education and culture work on the other.[8]

On the instruction of the CCP Central Committee and the State Council, the Office of the Western Region Development LG has the task of focusing on four issue-areas and objectives: first, making an overall plan on west development; second, formulating policy and measures for speeding up west development; third, speeding up infrastructure construction in the west; and, fourth, strengthening protection and construction of ecology and environment in the west.

Since 2001, efforts have been undertaken to examine whether and how to *enhance* the role of the Office of the WRDLG in policy implementation, and to strengthen its administrative and project implementation coordination capacity. Certain foreign aid officials are supportive of such institutional capacity strengthening of the WRDLG Office, and are actively encouraging their donor institutions to allocate foreign aid dollars to such an initiative. However, heretofore, this organ has appeared most effective when it has focused on administering the policy "consultation" processes on behalf of the WRD Leading Group, and in generating policy options for the WDI. There are significant policy content and policy context factors that inhibit the WRDLG Office from effectively playing a more expansive policy implementation role, as will be discussed in detail below.

Western Region Development Lead Group

> **Western Region Development Lead Group**
> Chair: Premier Zhu Rongji
> Vice Chair: Vice Premier Wen Jiabao

Members:
Zeng Peiyan, Minister of SDPC
Chen Zhili, Minister of Education

Li Rongrong, Minister of SETC
Xu Guanhua, Minister of Science and Technology

Xiang Huaichen, Minister of Finance
Fu Zhihuan, Minister of Railways
Du Qinglin, Minister of Agriculture
Sun Jiazhen, Minister of Culture
Dai Xianglong, President of PboC
Wang Guantao, Minister of Construction
Shi Guansheng, Minister of MOFTEC

Tian Fengshan, Minister of Land and Resources
Huang Zhendong, Minister of Communications
Wang Shucheng, Minister of Water Resources
Wu Jichuan, Minister of Information Industry
Zhou Shenxiang, Director of Forestry Bureau
Zhang Xuezhong, Minister of Human Resources
Xie Zhenhua, Minister of SEPA

Liu Jibin, Minister of State Commission of Science, Technology and Industry for National Defence
Li Dezhu, Minister of State Ethnic Affairs Commission
Liu Yunshan, Minister of Propaganda of CCP
Xu Guanchun, Director of National Bureau of Broadcast and TV

State Developing Planning Commission

> *Office of Western Region Development Lead Group*
> Director: Zeng Peiyan
> Vice Director: Wang Chunzheng, Li Zibin, Duan Yingbi, Wang Zhibao

Department of Comprehensive Planning	Department of Agriculture, Forestry and Ecology	Department of Social Economy	Department of Human Resources and Regulatory

Offices in Western Provinces

Offices in Eastern and Mid Provinces

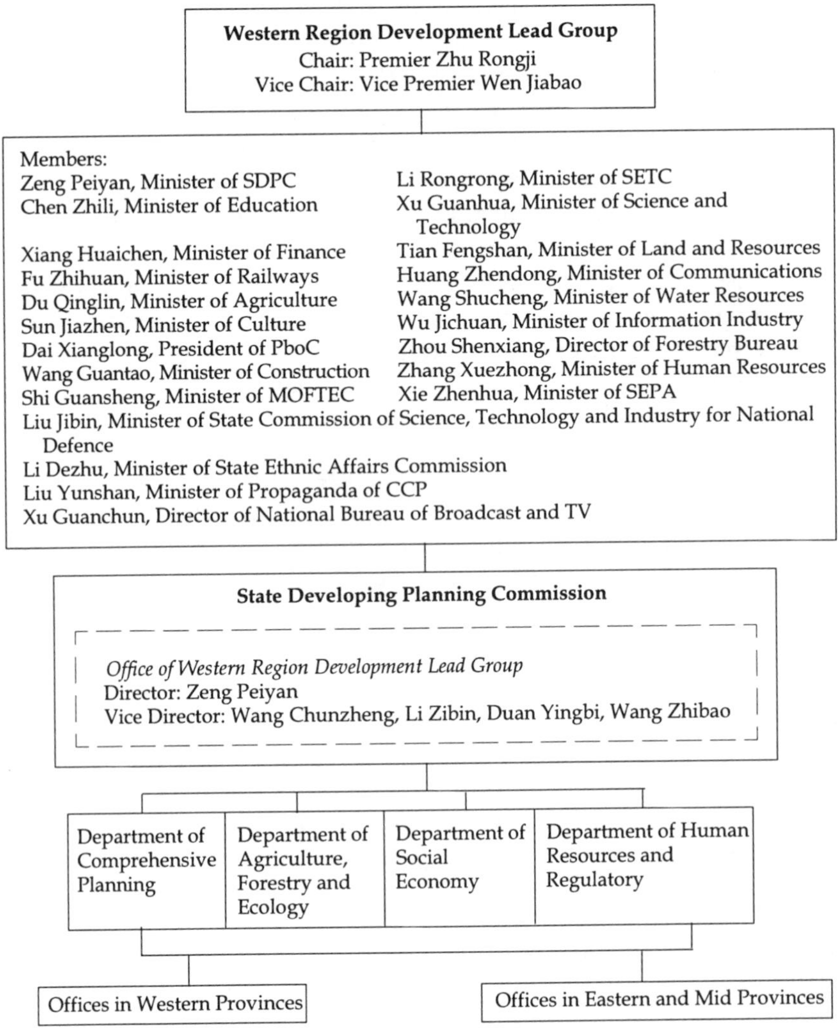

Figure 8.1. Organization Chart (accurate as of February 2003)[9]

The Office of the Western Region Development LG reports directly to one of the four SDPC Vice-Ministers because of the importance of its work (see Figure 8.1). The Office of the Western Region Development LG is actually located within the State Development Planning Commission. Below the Chair and Vice-Chair, SDPC Minister Zeng Peiyan is the Director of the Office of the Western Region Development LG, while SDPC Vice-Ministers Wang Chunzheng, Li Zibin, Duan Yingbi and Wang Zhibao are Vice-Directors. The Office is mainly staffed by officials of the SDPC, and it is generally regarded as a bastion of SDPC influence. The Office has four main Departments: Department of Comprehensive Planning; Department of Agriculture, Forestry and Ecology; Department of Social Economy; and Department of Human Resources and Regulation.

Despite its formal policy administrative authority, the Office of the WRDLG does not actually have final authority to make major decisions on the WDI. This authority rests with the Party Leading Group, chaired by Premier Zhu Rongji. Moreover, the Office's consensual decision-making coordination capacity has been heavily reliant on the personal prestige and influence Zhu Rongji, Wen Jiabao, and the Directors of the Office (Chairman of the powerful SDPC Zeng Peiyan, and his Vice-Directors Wang Chunzheng, Li Zibin, Duan Yingbi, and Wang Zhibao). Zeng Peiyan is one of the most respected senior bureaucrats in the Party elite, and known widely as one of Jiang Zemin's five closest advisors, and chief economic advisor and speechwriter.[10] At the November 2002 Party Congress, Zeng was promoted from being a member of the Central Committee to an alternate member of the Politburo Standing Committee (which means that he has a high probability to be promoted to the Standing Committee as part of the "Fifth Generation" leadership).[11] Wang Chunzheng is a long-serving (Executive) Vice Chair of the SDPC.[12] Li Zibin, is seen as one of the most promising younger senior bureaucrats in the Chinese government, and, as the former Mayor of Shenzhen (1995-2000) has strong ties with the international business community.[13] In addition to being SDPC Vice-Minister, Duan Yingbi is currently also Deputy Director of the influential Central Financial and Economic LG. Wang Zhibao is reputed to be Zhu Rongji's lead advisor on forestry and land management issues, and the former Minister of the State Forestry Administration. Wang Chunzheng,

Duan Yingbi, Wang Zhibao were all members of the Premier's core team that accompanied Zhu Rongji on an inspection tour to Sichuan province to examine ecological conditions and the situation of "national minorities" in June 2001.

At the apex of the core WDI decision-making structure is the Premier and the paramount leader. All the major pronouncements and decisions on the WDI have been made and sanctioned by the Party elite. Deng Xiaoping sanctioned the WDI until his death in 1997, and likely sanctioned the Party's decision in the mid-1990s to begin the strategizing that led to the official start-up of the WDI in 1999. During the 1980s, Deng Xiaoping proposed that China undergo development in two stages: first on the coast; and then in the interior.[14] He promised the interior regions that their patience would be generously rewarded. In 1992, Deng explicitly noted that the state might need to address regional inequality by assisting the less-developed regions around the end of the century, at the point when the nation's overall living standard had reached a "comparatively well-off level".[15] The post-Deng leadership, led by Jiang Zemin, paid greater attention to regional inequality in the 1990s. In March 1994 and March 1995, then Vice Premier Zhu Rongji highlighted the central government's concern for the interior region, by declaring at NPC sessions that the government would increase investment in the interior regions. In numerous speeches from 1996 to 1999, Jiang Zemin announced the need to reduce the gap in development between regions. The Party elite decided the timing for the start of the campaign. In 1999, Jiang announced that the "time is ripe" for "speeding up the development of the central and western regions", and that this "should become a major strategic task for the Party".[16] On 17 June, he gave a speech at a conference in Xian (on SOE reform in the five northwestern provinces), in which he first used the phrase "great western development" (*xibu da kaifa*), which is seen as symbolizing the birth of the western development policy. The Party leadership's continuing emphasis on the WDI is reflected in the stress on western regional development in the Tenth Five-Year Plan, as well as in statements of Party leadership at the Sixteenth Party Congress. Jiang Zemin, as Party General Secretary, has kept Deng's promise.

WDI officials note that the Premier (Zhu Rongji) has the authority to make major economic decisions, and Jiang Zemin has tended to defer to the opinion of Zhu on economic decisions. The Premier solicits and receives input from interested parties, including reports from the Office of the WRDLG, the SDPC, the Central Financial and Economics Affairs LSG, and select academics. Zhu also serves as the final arbiter of conflicting interests at the Vice Premier level. Zhu Rongji's relationship with Wen Jiaobao, in this regard, is key for elite decision-making on the WDI. Wen is Zhu Rongji's most trusted Vice Premier, and was put in charge of the most pressing economic and socially sensitive files: rural/agrarian development and financial reform. Wen Jiabao is also the Director of the influential Central Financial and Economic Affairs LSG, and can thus ensure macro-coordination on core issues of the WDI.

Players from the various levels outside the core structure have voiced their interests and attempted to affect outcomes through both *formal* and *informal* channels. The formal process consists of inter-bureaucratic consultation through the WRDLSG, and its Office's attempts to forge assent or consensus on issues affecting particular units or industries. The representatives from the various units take part directly in these discussions, and significant operational issues facing an impasse can be taken to the LSG meetings for resolution. The informal voicing of interests has occurred through the usual ways: personal networks, particularly informal ties between ministers and State Councilors and Vice Premiers. Local officials also rely on personal ties to central officials. The key difference between "lobbying with China's characteristics" and economic lobbying elsewhere is that most Chinese interests reside within the governmental or quasi-state structure, rather than in the private sector. In that each line-minister's raison d'etat is *de facto* to see that ministry flourish, and the inherent government-industry links in the government bargaining structure, has meant that industry (and regional) protectionism would be given voice inside the decision-making channels of the WDI.

Intra-Bureaucratic Tensions at "the Centre"

The WDI cuts across a multiplicity of thematic and sectoral areas. Inherent in such a cross-cutting regional development initiative are fundamental issues of intra-bureaucratic contestation inside the national "Centre" (*zhongyang*). To better understand the real terrain of decision-making on the WDI at the political centre requires moving the level of analysis both downward and horizontally inside the Centre, viewing central policies in their interactive relationship between the "core structure" of decision-making and the multitude of subordinate functional bureaucratic entities inside the Centre. Such an approach disaggregates "the Centre", examining the fissures in central authority in the national capital, and sheds light on the specifics of *fragmented authority* in the Centre.

The Office of the Western Region Development LG must be responsive to 'external' domestic interests as other bureaus or industries interested in a particular aspect of the WDI become more actively involved in the consultations. Fulfilling this "coordination" (*xietiao*) function has consumed a growing amount of its time. Interagency disputes that cannot be resolved at the Office level have often been referred to the Deputy Directors of the Office (the respective SDPC Vice-Ministers), and, at times, even to SDPC Chair and Director of the Office of the WRDLG, Zeng Peiyan, to lead the bureaucratic bargaining to reach consensus. The Chair, Premier Zhu Rongji, and Vice-Chair, Vice Premier Wen Jiabao, only tend to intervene on the most important decisions during the major meetings of the WRDLG, and do not get involved at the day-to-day level bureaucratic bargaining. The Office of the WRDLG is also responsible for conducting the public relations campaign on behalf of the government's western development initiative. Officials from the Office have given presentations in public, met with foreign officials and industry executives, discussed the WDI on radio and television, as well as published books and reports on the China's WDI.[17] Despite the *expansive* (cross-cutting and multi-sector) formal authority of the Office of the WRDLG, its actual capacity to carry out its "coordination" mandate on policy consultation is rather limited. The Office must solicit the interest of "peripheral" or lower ministerial-ranking units inside the political Centre in order to fulfill its responsibilities. Although the Office of the WRDLG has the formal authority to discuss, negotiate and coordinate most issues of the WDI, the Office itself does not actually possess policy implementation capacities. Such administrative capacity continues to be mainly housed in the respective line-ministries and even large-scale Chinese state enterprises in the sectors most relevant to the WDI, such as the energy, transportation, telecommunications, construction, and mining sectors. For example, in the area of *infrastructure*, the Ministry of Construction controls the government resources that are centrally allocated for the major infrastructure projects – including those in the western regions – and approved by the SDPC's national plans. This division of administrative control has persisted after the formation of the Office of the WRDLG. Sub-central levels of government also play a large role in raising funds and administering infrastructure projects in their respective locales – projects in which the WRDLG does not have a role in their day-to-day management. Many of these projects have been funded through either major international or state treasury bond issues or through capital markets (both international and domestic), and whereas the Ministry of Finance's Department of State Treasury Bonds and Finance and the SDPC's Department of the Foreign Capital Utilization have the authority to approve these projects, the Office of the WRDLG has limited influence over these powerful Departments.

On the *environment management* of China's western development, the Office of the WRDLG must deal with a host of interested ministries and bureaus, including powerful SDPC's own Department of Regional Economy, and the State Environmental Protection Agency (SEPA), which formally has the mandate for environmental "management", i.e. protection. Even though SEPA's own enforcement capacities are limited, it regularly coordinates with stronger bureaucratic units, such as the Ministry of Land and Water Resources (MLWR), China's powerful state energy and power companies, and other sector-specific units such as the Ministry of Agriculture (MOA), and the State Forestry Administration (SFA), on matters of mutual interest that affect the protection of China's fragile environment. SEPA, along with the MLWR, MOA, and the SFA all have large bureaucratic stakes and interests in the WDI's "environmental" initiatives such as the conversion of farmland to grasslands, re-forestation, the prevention of desertification, and creating eco-tourism zones.

With regards to energy initiatives that are included under the WDI, such as the trans-Continental pipeline project, on matters pertaining to the regulation of the energy sector in relation to ecological considerations, the Office of the WRDLG has had to deal not only with a multitude of powerful bureaucratic entities such as the State Economic and Trade Commission (Power Department), the SDPC's Department of Transport and Energy, and the MLWR, but also a cross section of some of China's most powerful state corporate entities, particularly, China National Petroleum Corporation (CNPC), whose large onshore oil and gas exploration and production assets lie in the north and west of China. Consultation has also extended to Sinopec, China National Offshore Oil Corporation (CNOOC), Sinochem, and even foreign joint ventures partners involved in the western pipeline project, such as Royal Dutch Shell Corporation. In the context of China's transitional economy, the Chinese state energy companies actually possess enormous influence over China's "environmental management" policy decision-making and regulatory process.[18]

On the human capital development initiatives of the WDI, the Office of the WRDLG has had to coordinate in a Central context controlled by the Ministry of Labour and Social Security (employment and labour policy and re-employment programming), the Ministry of Education, the Ministry of Agriculture (rural skills training); the SDPC's Department of Rural Economy which plays a policy role on China's rural under-employment problem, and a marginally effective Leading Group created under the SETC in 1996, that has been charged with handling issues relating to enterprise mergers, bankruptcies and re-employment.[19]

We have seen that the *excessive fragmented authority* on decision-making and administration presents a significant challenge to the Office of the WRDLG, especially if there is need for a timely decision, or quick-responsive action on a particular matter. This highly bureaucratic decision-making process – a product of the need to generate consensus among potentially antagonistic units – generates seemingly endless coordinating meetings, and could lead to stalemate at key moments on project implementation. At the same time, the broad representation and participation in decision-making on the WRDLG offers the potential for more broadly consensual (and representative) decisions when the various interests eventually line up. In addition to seeking official NPC sanction, striking a balance between various sector and social interests in decision-making –at least at the central level – is key to building the socio-political legitimacy for the decisions that are taken on the WDI.

As discussed above, to date, the Office of the WRDLG has been *most* effective when limiting its role to *studying* and *recommending strategies*, development plans, major issues and policies, laws and regulations, for developing China's western regions. It has experienced difficulty in trying to stretch its role to policy implementation. Part of the reason for this difficulty may lie in the fact that the Office of the WRDLG is located inside the SDPC. As a national Commission, the SDPC is mainly responsible for *developing* policy which macro-coordinates China's overall economic development. Its reach is strongest in monitoring and ensuring horizontal integration and adjustments. Its capacity to oversee policy implementation is generally limited to regulatory supervision. It is difficult for a Leading Group inside a national Commission to coordinate activities inside a particular issue-area (unlike a ministry). This, in turn, has made it difficult for the WRD Leading Group to generate policy momentum.

A bureaucratic interest model in which economic interests of ministries dictate their positions appears to aptly describe the way in which most line-ministries have participated in the various components of the WDI. It is true that the views of certain ministries toward the WDI have evolved over time as circumstances have changed. For example, the Ministry of Agriculture has softened its often negative views on the WDI as it has come to face more serious bureaucratic institutional challenges in the internal negotiations over China's entry into the WTO, and China's heightened integration into global agricultural markets.[20] Such shifts do not, however, negate the fact that narrow economic interests have had a strong influence on bureaucratic positions on the WDI.

On the defining issue of *poverty alleviation* in China's western regions, the Office of the WRDLG must deal with the Poverty Alleviation Lead Small Group (PALSG), which has the mandate for the Chinese government's poverty alleviation initiatives. The Office of the PALSG is housed inside the Ministry of Agriculture. The Office of the PALSG has been given significant financial resources, and has administrative authority over the use of these funds for the implementation of the government's various poverty alleviation campaigns (it can also use a portion of these funds to build up its own institutional capacities). To date, the Office of the WRDLG has had limited interaction with the Office of the PALSG.[21] Not having any direct control over poverty alleviation funds itself, the WRDLG Office needs to apply leverage to its institutional authority to influence the distribution of funds from the Poverty Alleviation Office. This is a challenge for the WRDLG Office because the mandate of the PALSG Office is to fight poverty in poverty-stricken counties across the country, not solely in the western regions. Due to the WDI, the PALSG Office does pay particular attention to the poverty situation in the western regions of the country, but it must help alleviate the situation of poor counties in relatively well-off coastal regions. Officials in the PALSG are proud of the fact that the scope of their institutional efforts is national. At the level of institutional culture and orientation, this contrasts with the Office of the WRDLG which focuses on poverty in the west.[22] Moreover, whereas officials of the Office of the WRDLG theorize poverty alleviation from a cross-cutting sectoral perspective, the campaigns of the Office of the PALSG reflect the sectoral proclivities of the Ministry of Agriculture, with emphases on basic food issues and rural poverty inside agricultural zones.

To briefly summarize that we see is that beneath the core structure of decision-making on the WDI, is a number of bureaucratic institutions that feed into policy decision-making on the WDI. The combination of the core structure and these 'peripheral' bureaucratic institutions provides comprehensive cross-representation for the four main sections of the Chinese state, following Zhu Rongji's 1998 administrative reorganization: (1) "macro-control departments" (SDPC, SETC, PBOC, MOF) concerned with economic coordination, finance, and banking; (2) "specialized economic administrative departments" (MOR, MOA, MOC, MOFTEC, MOLR, MOWR, MII, SFA, SEPA) covering issues from construction, transportation, water supply and foreign trade; (3) "social departments" (MOE, MOST) covering education, technology, national resources and social welfare; and (4) "State political affairs departments" (MOCulture, MOCommunications, SEAC, CCP Propaganda Department, National Bureau of Broadcast and Television, SCSTI for National Defence) covering foreign affairs, defence, health and ethnic minorities.[23] Beneath the central level, nearly all industrial sectors, and provincial and local governments – a huge number of entities – are in some manner affected by the WDI, and have been interested in decisions on the WDI. This also includes the officials of the coastal provinces who have been strongly encouraged through successive campaigns (such as twinning arrangements) to provide development support for their interior counterparts.

Central-Local Tensions

In all organizations and polities there tends to be a disjuncture between leadership intention, organizational behaviour, and the actual results of action; what Lampton calls the "policy implementation problem".[24] One basic task of the public-policy analyst is to describe and explain the state's "steering mechanism" and "the external forces" that buffet the entire ship of state in the course of policy implementation. This involves understanding the interrelationships among the content of policy, the institutional structures in which the policy is implemented, and the wider socio-political context in which these structures and processes operate.[25]

The study of the "implementation problem" in the WDI moves the level of analysis downward by viewing central policies in its interactive relationship with the multitude of territorial entities, and the often tenuous hold that Beijing has over the hinterlands. Lampton writes, "it is precisely these circumstances of diversity, conflict, fragmented authority, and central policy that diverges from local reality, which the implementation approach is most useful in analyzing".[26]

The issue of central-local coordination has been a perennial challenge in the long history of Chinese state administration. This special legacy has carried over into the modern period -- and into the WDI. The fact that the current WDI is situated within the specific dynamics of post-Mao decentralization of power and authority in the reform period adds further complexities. Early in the reform period, Deng Xiaoping chose to decentralize a certain degree of authority over economic activities (both domestic and international) in order to build political support for the reforms.[27] Jae Ho Chung argues that the post-Mao decentralization reforms, in combination with the centre's incentives that reward compliance, have spawned three trends in the behaviour of local governments: "bandwagoning"; "pioneering"; and "resistance".[28] *Bandwagoning*, the primary response of most local officials to central directives, is the response wherein local leaders neglect the needs of their own localities, opting to forcefully implement central directives, even at local expense. *Pioneering* has involved a smaller subset of officials, who have anticipated state policies, or gained knowledge on forthcoming policies through personal connections to the centre, and implemented them in advance and in more extreme fashion. Resistance involves non-compliance with central instruction.

We see all three forms of behaviour in western-local responses to the WDI. A tempered form of "bandwagoning" behaviour can be seen immediately after the launch of the WDI, when, in the interior, all local governments initially hailed the "golden opportunity" presented by the WDI, and they launched their own development initiatives. Pioneering behaviour on the part of local governments and social forces can help alleviate the onus on the centre of shouldering the main responsibility for, and activity of, trade and investment promotion. To date, the success of the centre in investment promotion, especially attracting foreign investors, has been limited, at best. In early-2001, SDPC Vice-Chair Li Zibin (former Mayor of Shenzhen) lead a high-profile tour of 50 overseas Chinese investors to China's western provinces to survey possible investment projects. By the end of the tour, only one Hong Kong millionaire agreed to invest in a cement factory in Sichuan.

In a sense, the "pioneering" behaviour of western officials predates the official launch of the WDI in 1999. We need to remember that sub-central level officials were key in pushing for preferential treatment to alleviate the growing east-west differences starting in the early 1990s. In 1995, during meetings over the Ninth Five-Year Plan, leaders from several interior provinces urged national leaders to provide aid and adopt policies to reduce regional inequality.[29] At sessions of the NPC and the Chinese People's Political Consultative Conference in 1996 and 1997, legislators and satellite Party representatives from the interior regions demanded that the central government address the alarming disparity and take action on its promise to help the interior regions through concrete policies, laws, projects, and investment.[30] Although the official launch of the WDI came from Beijing, the current WDI efforts respond, *politically*, to the pent up frustrations of officials from the interior regions, and implicitly, to the rising social unrest in the interior regions in the 1990s.

The first type of behaviour – bandwagoning – does not present a problem to the centre's efforts to provide guidance, and a coordinated and comprehensive framework for developing the west. The challenges come from the third form of behaviour, resistance, and less so from "pioneering", which only becomes an issue (to a nationally-coordinated approach) when the pioneering goes too far beyond the bounds of the basic guidelines laid down by the centre. The main issues in the central-local tensions are over which level of government and/or actors are the main driver of, and which are the ultimate arbiters on new initiative, i.e., design direction from the centre vs. local initiative.

The reality of China's regional differences has translated into cross-cutting tensions between central directives vs. local initiative, both in terms of levels of government and specific industries. This can be seen in the construction sector where the efforts of central officials to encourage the Shanghai commercial and real estate developers to 'go west' have encountered stiff resistance from China's powerful developers from the Shanghai area, from the Shanghai municipal units that are tied to these firms, and even from the Ministry of Construction, which relies heavily on the Shanghai area as a leading-edge 'model' site for experiments on housing and commercial real estate reforms. The Shanghai developers have argued that they have been ordered by the centre to operate in a commercial profit-oriented manner, responding to market demand.[31] Their position is that they have been instructed by the government at all levels that they must follow the money and seek profitable ventures only, and that there is no money to be made in the west. It is much safer to develop in the coastal regions, even though there has been commercial over-development in many of China's boom coastal cities, or even in the bigger metropolises in central China, such as Wuhan.

While resistance has been a common response to many central initiatives throughout China's political history, the more typical response to *certain* central initiatives of the WDI has been bureaucratic "foot-dragging". Outright resistance has diminished in recent years, most likely because of the central government's strongly improved capacity to monitor local performance through the development of a comprehensive auditing system, and by strengthening the statistical system, especially the capacity of the National Statistics Bureau.[32] In the case of the WDI, foot-dragging is rooted in central-local tensions, particularly *local frustrations* on the process and results of national comprehensive planning on the WDI. These tensions are not surprising considering the vastness of the country, the differences across regions, and the long traditional of stressing centralized control in both imperial China and the Soviet systems.[33]

One means whereby the Centre has attempted to counter local "foot-dragging" or excessive or non-centrally-integrated local initiatives has been to develop new channels and institutions of policy coordination influence. This is reflected in the creation of the Office of the Leading Group for Western Region Development, and even more to the point, the information and knowledge capacities of the Office's Department of Comprehensive Planning. The Office has aimed to develop a source of informal authority that is less studied than resources such as formal legal grants of authority, finances and status: control of strategic information and WDI policy-related knowledge. The influence and "informal authority" of the Office of the WRDLG is rooted in its ability to influence the flow of information that relates to policy coordination on the WDI, particularly strategic information that affects the State Council and Party leadership's ability to coordinate the implementation of the WDI, including the behaviour of lower-level units in implementing the policies of the WDI.[34] In so doing, the Office of the WRDLG, in essence, is drawn into competing with sub-central (and other Central line) bureaucratic units to persuade the Central leadership and other top officials of the wisdom of the institutes' policy proposals; what Halpern calls, "competitive persuasion".

Case Study: Focal Belts Strategy

One of the best examples of central-local tensions in the WDI is Office of the WRDLG's Focal Belts Project, formulated by its Department of Comprehensive Planning. The basic economic developmental rationale behind the strategy which underpins this project is sound. The Office has tried to strategize how best to maximize the impact of the WDI, keeping in mind that there are limits to the resources that can be dedicated to any one campaign – even one as worthy as the WDI. The centre, in weighing its limited resources against the vastness of the undeveloped interior, has proposed a strategy of targeting key geographical areas (*zhongdian quyu*), particularly "focal belts", that will become areas of concentrated development. Each of the focal belts have been selected on the criteria of having relatively firm economic bases, high population densities, being main communication lines, that are close to transportation routes and hubs (e.g. the Eurasian "Land Bridge" (*Ouya dalu quiao*), the Yangtze River, and the waterways in the southwest with outlets to the ocean). The three focal belts are:

(1) Xi-Long-(Qing)Hai-Lan(zhou)-Xin(jiang) Line;
(2) the upper reaches of the Yangtze River;
(3) and Nan(ning)-Gui(yang)-Kun(ming) Belt.[35]

The plan is to concentrate resources in these areas as loci of growth which will, in turn, generate further spin-off growth in the surrounding regions (what economic geographers have called "growth corridors"). Such "focal belts" or "growth corridors" already exist in other parts of China: in the southeast region (Pearl River Delta), in the lower Yangtze River basin (Shanghai, lower Jiangsu and upper Zhejiang), in the northeast (Beijing, Tianjin, Qingdao and Bohai Rim), and in the far northeast region (Dalian and the interior of Liaoning). The aim is to concentrate economic development/business concentration along main communication lines, which foremost means infrastructure construction, but also telecommunications, and information technology networks. In addition, major cities in western China (e.g. Chongqing, Xian, Chengdu) are seen as playing a "driving role" in (gradually) promoting the development of neighbouring areas. The plan also calls for creating new sectorally-specialized centres, such as an agricultural science base in Yangling (Shaanxi), a high-tech base in Minyang (Sichuan), and a salt and potash base in a new Lop Nor town.[36]

The leading bureaucratic unit in research and further developing the Focal Belts strategy for China's western development is the Department of Comprehensive Planning of the Office of the WRDLG. Its *formal* function is to work together with related departments of the SDPC, other agencies of the State Council and the provinces, autonomous regions and municipalities in the west, on western development.[37] It formulates development strategies and plans, provides suggestions on policy, law, regulations, and provides consultation. The Department also takes charge of the comprehensive work of the Office, drafts important documents and conducts "propaganda" on western development inside China and abroad. It works as a "contract agency" and collects information for member units of the Office of the WRDLG and local Development Offices of all provinces, autonomous regions and municipalities in the western region.

The Comprehensive Planning Department organizes scientific studies on the focal belts. Its approach is to *integrate* the development of the economic belts, infrastructure projects, and environmental management considerations. Outside of the belts, the Department's strategy is to promote "ecological construction" projects, focusing on the protection of natural forests, converting less-productive farmland into forests and grasslands, desertification and soil erosion prevention, and restoring natural grasslands. In formulating the various elements of such a "comprehensive" design, the Department is calling for the use of project funds to finance the development of information technology, satellite photo imagery, and more sophisticated data, for the investigations. Information technology is seen as vital for providing the necessary information on the resources and ecological environment of the three belts in a "macro, synchronous, accurate and regular manner".[38] It has also argued for learning from the experiences of developed countries in regional development. Foreign experts have been asked to introduce methods that developed-country governments use in applying information technology in regional planning, and methods commonly used internationally.

The Department's proposals are being forwarded to the State Council and the Leading Group for Western Region Development to help guide decision-making on the WDI. The results of the ongoing research programme on the "Major Economic Belts in China's Western Development" will be integrated into the draft of the Overall Plan of Western Development in the Tenth Five-Year Plan. This research is expected to generate new strategic information in four areas:

(1) contextual background, significance and importance of the major economic belt;

(2) current situation of the 3 economic belts in the west, and policy proposals for the infrastructure construction plan;

(3) proposals for methods, principles, and criteria for identifying economic belts; and

(4) proposals for the future development direction of the three belts.

The implementation of the focal belts strategy has encountered resistance at a number of levels. There is debate over whether the growth zones, which appear to already possess "natural" or existing comparative advantages, need to be the main focus of public attention; that a pro-poor growth strategy which focuses resources on the areas of chronic or high poverty would be more effective in alleviating poverty in the western regions. This is the approach preferred by most international donors. The focal zones approach is based on lessons drawn from the actual experience of China's one successful *regional* development campaign, the special economic zones and the coastal development strategy. Part of the reason for the success of the Chinese government's opening up strategy is that it went against the advice of the IFIs in not relying on small-scale private sector growth as the backbone of China's development. Rather, in theorizing from a view of the long-term tendency of capitalism to lead to centralization and concentration of capital, and comparative advantage built around oligopolistic firms, the government aimed to foster economies of scale, and industrial and capital concentration, in focused geographical locales, which would then provide spin-offs for surrounding regions: the coastal development strategy. The focal zones approach extends this strategy to the development of the western region. The question is whether the approach that was successful on the coast – with its various "natural" comparative advantages[39] – can be transferred to the western regions.

However, even if we assume that the focal zones approach has a degree of merit, the real problem for the focal zones strategy is not at the level of economic logic, but at the level of politics. There has been little buy-in from sub-central government levels to this approach, for what it leaves 'outside' its zones of concentration. Many provincial governments see significant parts of their jurisdictions being left out of Beijing's grand strategy of fostering spatially-concentrated belts of high dynamism. From the perspective of the local stakeholders, the regional spin-offs that are envisaged in the centre's calculations are too indirect to elicit their enthusiasm and political support. For provincial and local governments, the focal zones strategy leaves too much of their territory outside the scope of activities. In contrast to the central officials, who take a "nationally"–comprehensive approach to the western region, provincial, municipal, township and county governments have incentives to keep a spatially-broad tax base in their respective locales – to spread their fiscal risk. In addition, the human movement involved in making this plan operational would be massive, even if it was implemented over a long-period and at a gradual pace. This is politically de-stabilizing. Yet it is sub-central levels of government that are charged for maintaining public security, unless in times of crisis. Migration also means that citizens who contribute part of the local tax could flow into other locales, thus reducing the tax base of their current administrative locales.

The fiscal implications of the focal belts strategy coincide with a period in which China's local governments and municipalities are still responding to fiscal restraints and increased social welfare responsibilities. The 1994 fiscal re-centralization severely deteriorated the fiscal balances of most cities.[40] The 1995 Budget Law then imposed stringent restrictions on local governments' alternative fiscal tools for raising additional revenues. Local governments were further restricted in terms of bond issuance and borrowing from capital markets (domestic and international). These new rules were enforced by a new auditing system that monitored local adherence.

For the municipalities which would potentially receive large waves of migrants inside the focal belts, there is hesitancy to take on the challenge of absorbing new migrants into their jurisdictions. During the 1990s, China's municipalities faced enormous pressure as they became responsible not only for fostering economic growth but also managing the social dislocation that rapid and market forces unleashed. They have had to build new social infrastructure (including public health and sanitation), foster environmentally sound infrastructure planning and land use programs, and develop new regulatory structures. In addition, they have often faced these new social challenges without the necessary injections of centrally-allocated adjustment funding, as the centre has focused mainly on developing the appropriate new regulatory frameworks. The 1990s has also been a decade of increased social and spatial mobility. Rising urban crime, growing and increasingly organized worker unrest, and uneven social safety nets have all created a serious challenge to government. New models and forms of community governance are currently under experimentation. Reforms of the hukou (residence permit) system, re-employment programs, unemployment insurance programs, urban health care systems, pension systems, housing arrangements, are all under consideration. Falkenheim argues that, "social welfare issues are the single most pressing task facing local leaders, with perhaps the exception of maintaining economic growth and public order".[41] Municipalities caught between an eroding tax base and rising welfare demands are often unable to meet their statutory obligations, let alone take on more residents, unless, of course, the necessary funds are provided from the outside to cover the adjustment costs.

At the same time, there are issues over actually how and to what degree sub-central stakeholders are involved in the comprehensive planning process. Sub-central levels – particularly large municipalities and small-medium sized cities and towns – have been asked to be drivers of growth. Although the central government's primary emphasis in WDI is on infrastructure development, a secondary focus has been encouraging urban growth. Emphasis was placed on "making the most of central cities" as "engines of growth" in Zeng Peiyan's planning report to the March 2000 NPC session, and reiterated in the State Council's 2001 implementing measures.[42] In the view of Chinese analysts who argue that much of coastal China's growth has been due to the emergence of small and medium sized cities, located adjacent to metropolitan centres, fostering smaller cities is particularly critical to the west. Urbanization is seen as ensuring both rapid and efficient growth and the absorption of surplus labour. According to Zeng's report, "the west will be encouraged to accelerate the construction of small and medium sized towns and cities with comprehensive functions".[43]

In order to become "engines of growth", areas have been encouraged to formulate their own growth and development strategies, tailored to their particular comparative advantages. Chongqing has chosen to capitalize on its 'hub' functions, which Chongqing municipal boosters declare is in accordance to the "laws of regional development".[44] Pu Haiqing, Mayor of Chongqing noted that the city is "improving its various functions" so as to "step up its overall hub functions" by becoming a "transportation hub, a financial centre, a commerce and trade centre and a science and education centre". Economically advanced provincial capitals such as Xian stress technological development, while slower growing municipalities such as Guiyang or Yinchuan are searching for customized growth strategies. Having been encouraged by the centre to be innovative and self-directed, local governments would prefer their role to be more directive than responsive in the design and implementation of WDS programming in their respective locales. The stress on local initiative, "new thinking", reliance on the local private sector and market forces, has fuelled growing local competition in the western region. The extent of mutually under-cutting local competition became so fierce by late-2000 that, in early-2001, the centre had to formulate 'unified' policies to rein in ambitious local governments.[45] These central-local dynamics, created out of fiscal necessity, presents particularly serious challenges to efforts in nationally-comprehensive regional development planning.

In the end, these issues will be resolved in the process of defining the conditions for the control of resources, i.e., who has them, which level will control them. This brings us back to the public policy issue of fiscal authority and power, and control over fiscal redistribution. In situations of 'real scarcity' – as in many small and medium sized cities especially in areas of chronic poverty – and where market-led dynamics do not appear to be encouraging the private sector to go west, public funds need to be marshaled. This brings us back to 'the State', to state power, state capacity, and the developmental role of state institutions. To date, the (even limited) effectiveness of the Office for the WRDLG's Programme in developing "Major Economic Belts in China's Western Development" was highly dependent on the personal ties between the senior officials of the Office and senior Party leaders and top officials in the other line-bureaucratic units in the inaugural period of the WDI (1999-2002). In order for sub-central bureaucratic levels to begin adjusting their local policies to comply with the "Focal Belts" strategy, the Office of the WRDLG will need to demonstrate that it has the ear of "Fourth Generation" senior leaders, and the capacity to control the flow of information and strategic policy-related knowledge that will affect the future policy process of the WDI.

Concluding Remarks

This paper has examined the prospects for, and current 'roadblocks', 'obstacles', operational 'problems' in China's Western Development Initiative. The gains to date on the WDI have already been significant. Investment levels, infrastructure construction, re-forestation and farmland conversion to grasslands have all registered major gains since only 1999. At the same time, significant challenges lie ahead on all aspects of the WDI. While many analysts have cited issues such as "*structural* factors of underdevelopment" (poor infrastructure, human capital, slow information flow, large state sector), *cultural* roadblocks such as "predatory and wasteful habits", "inefficiency and unfamiliarity with the market and legal norms", and *political* obstacles such as "government inefficiency in the west", "ethnic tensions" and lack of "political support or indifference of local residents" to the centre's initiative, as main impediments to the WDI,[46] this paper has emphasized the political decision-making and bureaucratic challenges which currently inhibit the WDI. These challenges have emerged both inside the 'centre' and in central-local tensions. We have also examined the particular political character of the WDI, in comparison with China's earlier western development initiative, the Third Front strategy. The current WDI represents a democratic advance on the political process of the previous campaign. We see a much higher level of political institutionalization, and more bureaucratically inclusive decision-making, this time.

In considering future prospects, it is important to note that the WDI also faces other 'political' challenges in the form of the government's other 'big State-led' campaigns. The government currently has three other high-profile campaigns in the works or planned for the near future: (1) government institutional capacity building and reorganization as required under the conditions of China's WTO admission; (2) the forth-coming South-North Water Diversion Project; (3) the Beijing Olympics (2008) and Shanghai Expo (2010). The estimated cost of these projects is enormous. Although all the funds are not expected to come from public sources, the costs to the state will nonetheless be significant. Moreover, these major state-led projects may produce contradictory outcomes. For example, the successful bid for the Olympic Games will intensify the tensions between water supply and water demand in Beijing.[47] This could fuel an acceleration of the water diversion project to "guarantee" that Beijing has a supply of sufficient and clean water for a "successful" Olympic Games; thus leaving less funds for other WDI initiatives that are actually focused on the western regions of the country.

It is true that one of three routes under examination in the South-North Water Diversion project involves the west, moving water from the water-rich southwest to the water-scare north. The "western route" will divert water from the upper reaches of the Yangtze, Yellow, Yarlung Zangbo, Nu, and Lancang Rivers to Lanzhou, transferring it westward to Xinjiang and eastward through the Sanggan River channel to the north.[48] Therefore the South-North Water Diversion project can be seen as complementary, rather than a source of competition for state funds. Nonetheless, the overall cost of the South-North Water Diversion project is staggering. China's development efforts already face the reality of the limited fiscal capacity of the Chinese state.[49] Even if the state's fiscal capacity improves gradually over the next five years, these other big State-led campaigns will consume a significant share of the state's overall development budget.

Despite the decision-making and administrative "inefficiencies" of the WDI, it represents as a democratic advance in Chinese decision-making and governance processes in two senses. First, in comparison to the decision-making process behind the Chinese government's last major campaign to 'push west', the "Third Front strategy", the current WDI has been introduced through a more institutionalized and consensual process of decision-making. Despite the excessive pluralization of decision-making, the ensuing bureaucratic slowdowns, and potential "economic inefficiencies" of a multi-tiered state-led regional development initiative, the WDI has politico-developmental merit with respect to the ongoing process of governance reform in China – in what may be called the shift from "hard" to "soft" authoritarianism. In contrast to the WDI's heavy emphasis on macro-coordination and consensus-building, the start of the Third Front strategy was preceded by Mao's unilateral decision to go against the Third Five-Year Plan in 1965. In one speech, Mao negated the state economic plan.[50] The State Planning Commission (SPC), in 1963-64, had formulated the Third Five-Year Plan (1966-70), which was guided by the CCP Central Committee's policy of "readjustment, consolidation, filling out, and raising" in order to continue to ameliorate the worst excesses of the Great Leap Forward. The Plan placed primary emphasis on fostering agriculture, light industry, and the standard of living, while relegating national defence to a secondary priority. The Plan was passed by the National People's Congress and the Party's Central Work Conference in 1964.

In 1965, Mao had Li Fuchun (supported by Liu Shaoqi) replaced by Yu Qiuli as the Chair of the SPC. At the Hangzhou Conference later that same year, Mao Zedong suddenly declared that it was very possible that China could soon be threatened by new "imperialist war"; that it was necessary to prepare to fight a war; and that factories along the coast and in large cities should be moved to the "Third Front" areas of the southwest and northwest. Mao added that new factories should be primarily constructed in the Third Front areas, and that it was necessary to scatter the factories, place them in mountains and caves. In contrast to the Third Five-Year Plan drawn up by the SPC and already passed through the official channels, Mao argued that it would be necessary to strengthen national defence and subordinate agricultural investment to the construction of the Third Front (an interior industrial base). Mao further decided to have Yu Qiuli organize a "little planning commission" (*xiao jiwei*) to replace the SPC and to formulate a new Third Five-Year Plan geared to preparing for war, the national defence industries, and the construction of the Third Front. Although the post-Deng Party elite has clearly been in the lead of the WDI, their "measured and incremental" approach[51] and more consensual, institutionalized framework for decision-making contrasts sharply with the unilateralism of the Third Front strategy.

Remedial Considerations

(1)   *The effectiveness of the Office of the WRDLG could be enhanced by focusing its mandate to coordinating policy and proposals on comprehensive planning on the WDI; and limiting its administrative duties (on policy implementation).*

This would mean dividing up oversight responsibilities on WDI policy implementation and assigning it to other Departments inside a *further strengthened* SDPC, such as giving the Department of Regional Economy specific responsibility for "economic development issues" in the WDI. The Department of Regional Economy has extensive experience in dealing with the issue of regional economic development gaps, having been created in the mid-1980s to enable the SPC to deal with the growing gap between coastal and interior regions caused by the coastal development strategy. A key test of the policy influence and capacity of the Office of the WRDLG will be on the long-term development policy decision that needs to be made on the WDI: whether to have market-led or pragmatically state-led development in the west.[52] This refers to the point that if the Chinese government follows a market-led approach to WDI, it is very likely that China's central regions will benefit more the WDI than the 'western regions'. The basic logic is that the western regions have abundant natural resources. Thus it would make sense for China's dragonhead (*longtou*) and other large-scale enterprises to shift their processing facilities closer to the source of the raw inputs and cheap sources of energy. Yet China's central regions, especially the larger cities of central China, such as Wuhan, Yichang, Changsha and Jiujiang, have relatively more skilled workforces than the cities of western China, excluding Chongqing and Chengdu, and are located closer to end-markets (meaning lower distribution costs than western locales). Theorizing from simple cost-benefit analysis calculations, it is quite likely that large, coastal-based Chinese firms might actually set up in central China – a half-way point between the interior and the coastal markets, where the distance of shipping the energy is not as far as the coast, and where a more immediate supply of skilled labour resides.[53] The main challenge for the Office of the WRDLG, particularly for the Department of Comprehensive Planning, is to macro-coordinate across a huge number of bureaucratic entities – both inside the centre and at the various sub-central levels – when generating its strategy, policy and planning suggestions in response to this basic question.

(2)   *There is a need to balance policy implementation "efficiency" calculations with democratic development considerations.*

In order for the WDI to continue contributing to China's democratic development, there is need for a more participatory and systematically-inclusive central-local consultation mechanism for policy implementation on the WDI.

There is an inherent tension between the needs of public administrative and decision-making efficiency and democratic participation considerations. In the reform period, China's provinces, municipalities and counties have certainly gained greater influence. Not only has their direct access to the centre increased, they collectively constitute a major constituency to which competing national officials will seek to appeal. Susan Shirk has described the approximately 300 member Central Committee as being a "Selectorate", consisting of representatives from 3 major groupings: the national bureaucracy; the military apparatus; and the provinces and large cities. National leaders must build coalitions of support within and across these three groupings. However, within this structure, the representatives from the coastal regions have been a very powerful bloc of interest, and they have 'checked and balanced' the proposals of interior representatives. The WDI requires a more fundamental redistribution of influence and orientation inside the upper ranks of the Party.

Existing Party institutions and mechanisms could be reformed to accommodate the needs of the WDI. Hu Angang has proposed a "one-province, one-vote" system for membership in the CCP Politburo.[54] According to Hu, this would guarantee every province a voice in Party policy-making, would lead to a more "genuine" effort on the part of the central government to ease interior local dissatisfaction, especially with regard to the growing disparity between coastal and interior provinces.

Despite the potential economic drawbacks from "adding another layer of government into the mix",[55] from a governance reform and democratic development standpoint, it would be beneficial to systematically include the legislative organ at the apex of the political system, the National People's Congress, into the decision-making process on the WDI. Currently, the NPC and its "Special Committees" have played a limited role on the WDI. Research indicates that the NPC's Overseas Chinese Committee has been one of the more active NPC units on the WDI, focusing on the promotion of overseas Chinese investment and trade in the western region. Hu Angang has suggested that the Financial Committee of the National People's Congress should be expanded to thirty members (each province would have one representative on the Committee).[56]

The WDI is leading to a more "spatially" inclusive decision-making system in China. The most important *political* challenge in the WDI is whether China can develop the 'right' institutional mix and the new "consultation mechanisms" that would provide more geographically-inclusive and participatory methods of comprehensive planning on the WDI, and China's future development more broadly. This challenge is particularly acute with respect to the inclusion of China's "national minorities" within the participatory planning process. Such new arrangements would provide the political and bottom-up legitimacy necessary to sustain the WDI over the long-term – such that the west will reach a commensurate level of development by mid-century, as China's leaders hope. In developing such consultation mechanisms, the Chinese government could draw on its new inter-bureaucratic and public consultation mechanisms being developed to meet its WTO commitments.

(3)   *The political reality facing WDI implementation is that it must compete with the other massive state-led projects that the Chinese government will fund in the future.*

All signs indicate that the WDI has been spurred, foremost, by domestic "developmental" considerations. As such it differs from the Third Front strategy in that the latter was motivated foremost by Mao Zedong's geo-strategic military calculations, with the economic rationale following the military considerations. Naughton has written:

The massive diversion of resources to the Third Front was a response by the Chinese leadership to a world environment that they perceived to be extremely threatening. During the 1960s, China's strategic position was fundamentally altered by the collapse of its alliance with the Soviet Union and the gradual increase in hostility between the two countries…and when the spectre of super-power "condominium" against China seemed a very real possibility. The timing of the decision to begin the Third Front shows clearly that it was triggered by American escalation of the war in Vietnam. However, the Third Front was not a response to the threat to China's southern flank, but rather to a potential threat to the Chinese heartland.[57]

The WDI, in contrast, has not been *primarily* motivated by geo-strategic military considerations.[58] It is first and foremost a development strategy that responds to the problem of China's domestic uneven regional development. There is an undertone of national social security concerns, in anticipation of potentially worsening ethnic conflict that could rise if the current inequalities and inequities are not addressed. However, the prime rationale for the WDI is a combination of socio-economic, human, and ecological developmental concerns. While the LG does include Ministers from the political organs of the "State political affairs departments" (i.e., Minister of the CCP Propaganda Department, Minister of the State Ethnic Affairs Commission, Minister of Culture, Minister of Communications, Minister of Human Resources, Director of the National Bureau of Broadcast and Television), its membership does not include representatives from the armed forces – although the State Commission of Science, Technology and Industry for National Defence is part of the military industrial establishment.

While the development objectives in the WDI are sound, the reality is that the WDI will have to "compete" with other state-led "big" projects. At the same time, the political realities of China's societal context – pressures from the 'bottom-up' demanding greater equity or ecological accountability – may work in favour of the WDI. Social and community-based pressure from outside the official corridors of power may keep the issues of the WDI on the centre of the political agenda. In addition, top leaders in the new "Fourth Generation" of leadership have spent significant time in the west. Even many of the Party elites not usually identified with 'the west' have spent periods of time in the interior rural regions of China as part of the 'sent-down' youth of the Cultural Revolution period.[59] This life experience may lead the current elite to connect with the situation of those in the west, and in the rural regions, and they may be more active in bringing about the needed adjustments.

Notes

The author thanks Dwight Perkins for his suggestions on this paper, and Charles Pellegrin and Li Delai for their research assistance on the WDI. This paper is the responsibility of the author, and does not reflect the views of the Canadian International Development Agency or the Government of Canada.

1.   Hongyi Harry Lai, "China's Western Development Program: Its Rationale, Implementation, and Prospects", *Modern China*, 28(4), October 2002, pp.432-466; Asian Development Bank, *The 2020 Project: Policy Support in the People's Republic of China* (Asian Development Bank, 2003); OECD, Foreign Direct Investment in China: Challenges and Prospects for Regional Development (Paris: OECD, 2002).

2.   This paper applies the bureaucratic politics model of "fragmented authoritarianism" and the "policy implementation problem" approach in studying the politics of the WDI. On "fragmented authoritarianism", see: Kenneth Lieberthal and Michel Oksenberg, *Policy Making in China: Leaders, Structures, and Processes*(NJ: Princeton U.P, 1988); Kenneth Lieberthal and David M. Lampton (eds.), *Bureaucracy, Politics and Decision Making in Post-Mao China* (CA: University of California Press, 1992). The "implementation problem" in post-Mao China has been addressed at length in the ground-breaking book, David Lampton (ed.), *Policy Implementation in Post-Mao China* (CA: University of California Press, 1987). For useful studies of Chinese government decision-making which integrate the two aforementioned approaches, see: Carol Lee Hamrin and

Zhao Suisheng (eds.), *Decision-Making in Deng's China: Insider's Perspectives* (NY: M.E. Sharpe, 1995).

3. The literal English translation for Xibu diqu kaifa lingdao xiaozu is "Western Region Development Leading Small Group". However, due to the unprecedented large size of this Leading "Small" Group, it is less misleading to refer to this decision-making body in English as the "Leading Group" for Western Region Development.

4. Chen Yao, *Xibu kaifa da zhanlie yu xin silu* (Grand Strategy and New Thinking in Western Development), (Beijing: Zhongguo zhongyang dangxiao chubanshe, 2000), pp. 264-265.

5. Under the reform package of the Second Plenum of the Thirteenth Party Congress in December 1987, the roles of the CCP Central Committee were redefined into three categories: decision-making consulting bodies (*juece zixun jigou*); executive bodies (*banshi jigou*); and service institutions (*shiye jigou*). Lu Ning, "The Central Leadership, Supraministry Coordinating Bodies, State Council Ministries, and Party Departments", in David M. Lampton (ed.), *The Making of Chinese Foreign and Security Policy in the Reform Era* (CA: Stanford U.P., 2001), p. 46.

6. Ibid.

7. The author's interview: Beijing, December 2002.

8. This information is from the official website of the Office of the WRDLG (online: www.chinawest.gov.cn)

9. I would like to thank Lynn Maisonneuve for help on this chart.

10. The four others are Zeng Qinghong, You Xigui, Jia Tingan, Teng Wensheng. See: Bruce Gilley, *Tiger On the Brink: Jiang Zemin and China's New Elite* (CA: University of California Press, 1998), p. 218.

11. One of Zeng Qinhong's most important previous positions was Director of the Office of the Central Finance and Economic LSG, starting in 1992.

12. Wang Chunzheng was a participant at the World Economic Forum in 1999, and gave a keynote address at the East Asia Economic Summit.

13. Li Zibin was a participant at the World Economic Forum (Davos, Switzerland) in 2000, and gave the keynote address at the China Business Summit.

14.   Du Ping, Shi Peihua, Xiao Jincheng, and Yang Jie, *Xibu qiujin: Xibu da kaifa de zhengce Beijing yu shangye jiyu* (Getting gold in the west: the policy background and commercial opportunities in great western development), (Beijing: Zhongguo yanshi chubanshe, 2000), p. 25; Fang Li and Chen Zishun, *Zhongguo xibu xiandaihua fazhan yanjiu* (A study of the modernization and development of China's west), (Shijiazhuang: Hebei remin chubanshe, 2000), pp. 6-7; *Beijing Review*, February 7, 2000. (cited in Lai, "China's Western Development Program", 2002, p. 433).

15.   Deng Xiaoping, *Deng Xiaoping wenxuan* (Deng Xiaoping Selected Works), (Beijing: Renmin chubanshe, 1993), p. 374. (cited in Lai, "China's Western Development Program", 2002, p. 433).

16.   Du, Shi, Xiao and Yang, *Xibu qiujin*, (2000), p. 27.

17.   For a recent example of the written publications, see: Office of the Western Region Development Lead Group, *The Overall Plan of Western Development and Related Policy Measures* (Beijing: China Planning Press, 2002).

18.   Philip Andrews-Speed, Stephen Dow and Zhiguo Gao, "The Ongoing Reforms to China's Government and State Sector: The Case of the Energy Industry", *Journal of Contemporary China*, 9(23), 2000, pp.5-20.

19.   State Council of the People's Republic of China, "Supplementary Notice of the State Council Concerning Experiment of Merger and Bankruptcy of State-Owned Enterprises and Employed Reemployment in Selected Cities", (1996).

20.   See: Gregory T. Chin, "Back from the Margin: China's Ministry of Agriculture in the Globalization Era" (2003, unpublished mimeo).

21.   The author's discussion with officials of the Office of the Poverty Alleviation Leading Small Group: March 2003.

22.   The author's interviews with officials of the Office of the Poverty Alleviation Leading Small Group and the Office of the Western Region Development Leading Small Group: May 2002, March 2003.

23.   Laurence J. Brahm, *China's Century: The Awakening of the Next Economic Powerhouse* (Singapore: John Wily & Sons (Asia), 2001), pp. 409-410.

24.   Lampton (ed.), Policy Implementation in Post-Mao China, (1987).

25. Lampton, "The Implementation Problem", (1987), p. 3 (Introduction) Lampton cites the writings of Merilee S. Grindle, (ed.), *Politics and Policy Implementation in the Third World* (NJ: Princeton University Press, 1980); James G. March and Johan P. Olson, "Organizing Political Life: What Administrative Reorganization Tells Us about Government", *American Political Science Review*, 77(2), 1983, p. 292.

26. Lampton, "The Implementation Problem", (1987), p. 5.

27. Susan S. Shirk, *How China Opened Its Door: The Political Success of the PRC's Foreign Trade and Investment Reforms* (NY: Brookings Institution, 1993).

28. Jae Ho Chung, *Central Control and Local Discretion in China* (NY: Oxford U.P, 2000).

29. Lai, "China Western Development Program", (2002), p. 438.

30. *Zhongguo nianbao*, 1997, pp. 3, 82, 83; 1998, pp. 1, 130, 131, 4, 73. (cited in Lai, "China Western Development Program", (2002), p. 439).

31. The author's discussion with a senior official of the Canadian Mortgage and Housing Corporation involved in Canada-China trade: Vancouver, April 2002.

32. Victor C. Falkenheim, "Central-Local Policy Dynamics in China: Implications for Municipal Programming", (Research Paper for the China Integrated Municipal Development Project, Federation of Canadian Municipalities, 2003), p. 9.

33. The flip side of the political equation is that both systems also consciously fostered competition among various bureaucracies in order to maximize control by the top leaders. (Kenneth Lieberthal, *Governing China: From Revolution Through Reform* (NY: W.W. Norton & Company, 1995), pp. 157-158.

34. This dimension of informal authority, i.e. control over policy-related information flows, was first studied by Nina Halpern. See: Nina P. Halpern, "Information Flows and Policy Coordination in the Chinese Bureaucracy", in Lieberthal and Lampton (eds.), *Bureaucracy, Politics and Decision-Making in Post-Mao China*, (1992), pp. 125-148.

35. The author's discussions with officials from the Department of Comprehensive Planning, Office of the Western Region Development Lead Small Group: November 2001, May 2002.

36. Falkenheim, "Central-Local Dynamics", (2003), p. 32.
37. Information from the Department of Comprehensive Planning, Office of the Western Region Development Lead Small Group: July, 2002.
38. The author's discussion with officials from the Department of Comprehensive Planning, Office of the Western Region Development Lead Group: July 2002.
39. Wing Thye Woo, Stephen Parker, and Jeffrey Sachs (eds.), *Economies in Transition: Comparing Asia and Europe* (Cambridge: MIT Press, 1997), especially T.W. Woo and J. Sachs' chapter on China.
40. Falkenheim, "Central-Local Dynamics", (2003), p. 15.
41. Falkenheim, "Central-Local Dynamics", (2003), p. 23.
42. Cited in Falkenheim, "Central-Local Dynamics", (2003), p. 30.
43. *Beijing Review*, May 1, 2000.
44. This paragraph draws on information from Falkenheim, "Central-Local Dynamics", (2003), pp. 31-32.
45. Falkenheim, "Central-Local Dynamics", (2003), p. 30.
46. Lai, "China's Western Development Program", (2002), pp. 458-461.
47. Li Shantong, Lu Zhongyuan, Hou Yongzhi, Liu Yong and Feng Jie, "Major Issues in the Implementation of the South-to-North Water Diversion Project", *China Development Review*, 4(3), July 2002, p. 105.
48. Lai, 'China's Western Development Program", (2002), p.453. The "eastern route" will use the Grand Canal to move water from the lower reaches of the Yangtze to Shandong, Hebei, Tianjin and Beijing. The "middle route" will use an elevated canal through the Danjiangkou Reservoir to transport water from the Three Gorges Reservoir to the north.
49. Wang Shaoguang and Hu Angang, *The Political Economy of Uneven Development: The Case of China* (NY: M.E. Sharpe, 1999), pp. 183-190; Wang Shaoguang and Hu Angang, *Zhongguo guojia nengli baogao* [A Report on China's State Capacity] (Shenyang: Liaoning chuban she, 1993). Wang Shaoguang and Hu Angang convincingly argue that the limited fiscal capacity of the Chinese state in the reform era has, in fact, further intensified regional disparities in resource distribution, thus highlighting the political causes of uneven regional development in China, which is the root developmental

problematique to which the WDI responds. (Wang and Hu, *Political Economy of Uneven Development*, (1999), pp. 191-198)

50.   Wang Lixin and Joseph Fewsmith, "Bulwark of the Planned Economy: The Structure and Role of the State Planning Commission", in Hamrin and Zhao (eds.), *Decision-Making in Deng's China*, (1995), p. 58.

51.   With regard to the timetable for implementation of the WDI, Jiang Zemin warned against "rushing headlong into mass action". Jiang stated that it might take the country decades or even the entire twenty-first century to develop the west. He urged officials to conduct project analysis, adopt policy measures and prepare for long-term efforts. (*People's Daily*, September 4, 2000). These statements are likely informed by memories of the enormous economic losses caused by earlier mass campaigns, such as the Third Front strategy. In 1977-78, the SPC investigated the losses caused by the Third Front and determined that direct losses (ineffective investment) exceeded RMB 150 billion (more than US$50 billion). Indirect losses were two to three times as great. (Wang and Fewsmith, "Bulwark of the Planned Economy", (1995), p. 58.)

52.   The author's discussion with Chen Xiwen, Vice-Chair of the State Council's Development Research Centre: Ottawa, November 2002.

53.   The author's discussion with Hu Dayuan, senior analyst of the China Economic Research Centre, Peking University, Beijing, November 2001.

54.   Hu Angang, *Zhongguo fazhan qianjing* (Prospects of China's Development), (Hangzhou: Zhejiang remin chubanshe, 1999), p. 312.

55.   The author thanks Dwight Perkins for raising this point.

56.   Hu Angang was among the first scholars to appeal to the Chinese leadership to reallocate resources to China's interior regions. Hu has recently claimed that the difference in GDP per capita between Shanghai (China's richest region) and Guizhou (China's poorest province) has increased from 7/3 times in 1990 to 12 times in 2000. See: *Shijie ribao* (World Daily), January 12, 2000, p. A9.

57.   Barry Naughton, "The Third Front: Defence Industrialization in the Chinese Interior", *China Quarterly*, 115, September 1988, pp. 368-369.

58.   For the security considerations that lend strategic credence to the WDI, see: Robert Bedeski, "Western China: Human Security and National Security" (paper presented at Western China Development Conference, March 2003).

59.   Cheng Li, *China's Leaders: The New Generation* (Lanham: Rowman & Littlefield, 2001), pp. 175-242.

9 An Introductory Environmental Macroeconomic Framework for China: Implications for West China Development

Dodo J Thampapillai, Euston Quah, Shandre M Thangavelu

Introduction

The literature of Environmental Economics recognizes two distinct functions of environmental capital, namely, a source function and a sink function. The source function deals with the provision of resources and raw materials for the formation of output. The sink function pertains to nature's role as a receptacle for the residuals that stem from the formation and consumption of output. Recent assessments of China's performance (Yu-shi et al, 1997), make explicit the rapid degradation of environmental capital resulting in the significant loss of both source and sink capacities. In this paper, we illustrate the need for cognisance of the role of environmental capital in the formulation of plans for the development of West China. We choose forestation as a vehicle for expanding sink capacity and such choice follows the evidence that China's capacity for forest cover is approximately 300 million hectares, whilst current forest cover is nearly less than half of this (Hongchang, 1997).

We consider a simple environment-economy relationship and illustrate its internalization within an introductory Keynesian model of income determination. In this standard model, output is determined by aggregate demand and price level is held constant. The illustration permits the demonstration of a policy approach that differs from the standard practices in macroeconomics. We confine China's environmental capital to its air shed and its stock of forest cover. These endowments act together as a sink for various atmospheric emissions that originate from economic activities. The depreciation of the environmental capital stock is valued in terms of the cost of pollution abatement as illustrated below. We then examine the viability of expanding the capacity of the sink by facilitating investments in forestation and evaluate the role forestry in sustainable development. In the illustration below the investment is funded by way of a marginal increase of the income tax.

Central to the analysis is the distinction between a macroeconomic equilibrium that ignores the role of environmental capital, namely $Y \equiv$ GDP and that which includes this role, namely $Y \equiv$ GDP $- C_{EM}$, where C_{EM} represents the depreciation allowance of environmental capital. In the literature of environmental economics, $(Y \equiv$ GDP$)$ is referred to as an unsustainable equilibrium as opposed to $(Y \equiv$ GDP $- C_{EM})$, which is regarded as a sustainable equilibrium; (Thampapillai and Uhlin, 1996, 1997). Regardless the type of equilibrium, the imposition of an additional tax is likely to prompt a regressive effect on the economy. Hence the basis for the test of viability is that the returns from the environmental capital investment must surpass the setback caused by the tax increase. The lead up to this evaluation also includes the tests of two hypotheses that are relevant to the analyses here. These are:

- The time-paths of $(Y \equiv$ GDP$)$ and $(Y \equiv$ GDP $- C_{EM})$ do not show show the possibility for convergence.
- The regressive effects of a broad-based income tax may be over-stated when C_{EM} is ignored.

As illustrated below, analyses of these two hypotheses become useful in testing the hypothesis that is central to this paper, that is:

- The returning of tax earnings as environmental capital investments may more than offset the regressive effects prompted by the imposition of the tax.

Conceptual Premises

Consider first the macroeconomic equilibrium that is not adjusted for environmental capital

$$Y \equiv GDP = C + I + G + X - M \tag{1}$$

If we suppose that all components of GDP excluding C are constant and denote the constant term as Φ, then (1) could be rewritten as:

$$Y \equiv GDP = \Phi + C \tag{2}$$

In the context of a tax increase, C is defined as:

$$C = \beta(Y - \Delta T) = \beta(Y - \tau Y) \tag{3}$$

Where, ΔT represents the additional tax earnings; t is the rate of tax increase, which is defined by $(\Delta T/Y)$; and β is the marginal propensity to consume. A specific assumption in (3) is that the autonomous consumption component of C is also included in Φ. When (3) is substituted into (2) we get:

$$Y = GDP = \Phi + \beta(Y - \tau Y) = \Phi + \beta Y - \beta \tau Y \tag{4}$$

From here it follows that equilibrium income (Y_T^*) will be:

$$Y_T^* = \Phi/[1 - \beta(1 - \tau)]$$

Consider now the macroeconomic equilibrium, which is adjusted for the depreciation cost of environmental capital:

$$Y \equiv GDP - C_{EM} \tag{6}$$

If we retain the assumption about GDP; that is, C being the only variable as in equation (4), and further assume that C_{EM} is a constant proportion, γ, of GDP, then (6) could be rewritten as:

$$Y = \Phi + \beta(Y - \tau Y) - \gamma[\Phi + \beta(Y - \tau Y)] \tag{7}$$

From (7), it is possible to derive the following definition for equilibrium income:

$$Y_T^{**} = [\Phi(1 - \gamma)]/\{1 - [\beta(1 - \tau)(1 - \gamma)]\} \tag{8}$$

In some earlier analyses (Thampapillai, 2002), the equilibrium values of income, in the absence of tax increases, have been defined as follows:

$$Y^* = \Phi/(1 - \beta), \tag{9}$$
when C_{EM} is excluded; and

$$Y^{**} = \Phi(1 - \gamma)/[1 - (\beta(1 - \gamma))], \tag{10}$$
when C_{EM} is included.

The different equilibria stemming from the internalization of C_{EM} into the Keynesian framework, with respect to a given time period, are also illustrated in Figure 9.1.

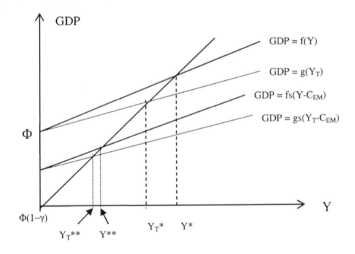

Figure 9.1.   Equilibria within a Simple Model of Income Determination

Consider the first hypothesis. For this we need to estimate the time trends of Y^* and Y^{**}. We would naturally expect $(Y^* > Y^{**})$. If this hypothesis is to be confirmed, then the difference $(Y^* - Y^{**})$ must increase over time. The test of the second hypothesis would involve comparing $(Y^{**} - Y_T^{**})$ against $(Y^* - Y_T^*)$. If this hypothesis true, then it follows that $(Y^{**} - Y_T^{**}) < (Y^* - Y_T^*)$.

The third hypothesis, that is the test of the responsiveness of the economy to an investment in environmental capital, depends on how the responsiveness would be manifested. An important type of response to an environmental capital investment could be a reduction in C_{EM}. This is considered in the next section.

The Relationship Between C_{EM} and Forestation

There is substantive scientific evidence to support the existence of an inverse relationship between air pollution and the extent of forest cover. That is, to some extent forests can assimilate atmospheric pollutants and hence extend the sink capacity of air sheds. We demonstrate this inverse relationship by way of a simple procedure that is illustrated in Figure 9.2. The surveys of land use in most countries, for example through the application of Geographic Information Systems (GIS), reveal that forest cover in several countries has been gradually decreasing rather than increasing. Although China is an exception to this trend, in the first instance we estimate a general relationship between C_{EM} and the cumulative extent of deforestation (X_L) from panel data gathered from countries that display deforestation.

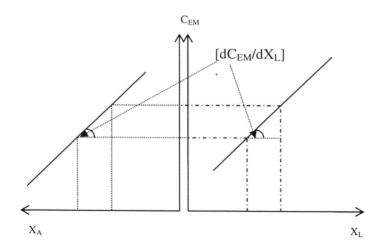

Figure 9.2. Relationships between C_{EM} and X_L and X_A

Table 9.1.   Estimation of C_{EM} for China
(All monetary estimates are in billion *yuan* at 1994 price)

Year	Energy (10^9 KWh)	NO_X ($Y10^9$)	SO_2 ($Y10^9$)	CO ($Y10^9$)	Particulates ($Y10^9$)	CO_2 ($Y10^9$)	C_{EM} ($Y10^9$)
1984	5994.88	3.263	0.683	0.363	0.042	309.366	313.717
1985	6505.02	3.541	0.741	0.394	0.045	335.692	340.413
1986	6816.21	3.711	0.776	0.413	0.048	351.751	356.698
1987	7256.86	3.950	0.827	0.439	0.051	374.491	379.758
1988	7758.86	4.224	0.884	0.470	0.054	400.397	406.028
1989	7899.94	4.301	0.900	0.478	0.055	407.677	413.411
1990	7916.85	4.310	0.902	0.479	0.055	408.550	414.296
1991	8281.23	4.508	0.943	0.501	0.058	427.354	433.364
1992	8588.86	4.676	0.978	0.520	0.060	443.229	449.462
1993	9190.35	5.003	1.047	0.556	0.064	474.269	480.939
1994	9975.75	5.431	1.136	0.604	0.070	514.799	522.040
1995	10319.53	5.618	1.175	0.625	0.072	532.540	540.030
1996	10562.12	5.750	1.203	0.639	0.074	545.059	552.725
1997	11021.77	6.000	1.255	0.667	0.077	568.780	576.779
1998	10864.00	5.914	1.237	0.658	0.076	560.638	568.523
1999	10849.79	5.906	1.236	0.657	0.076	559.905	567.779
2000	10747.39	5.851	1.224	0.651	0.075	554.620	562.420

Notes: NO_X: [(0.541/10^6) tons per KWh] @US\$116.75/t;
SO_2 : [(0.425/10^6) tons per KWh] @US\$116.52/t;
CO : [(0.333/10^6) tons per KWh] @US\$79.03/t;
Particulates: [(0.0.0745/10^6) tons per KWh] @US\$40.70/t;
CO_2: [(498.6/10^6) tons per KWh] @US\$45/t.
Source: http://www.eia.doe.gov/pub/international/ielf/tablee1

This relationship, $C_{EM} = g(X_L)$, is illustrated in the right hand panel of Figure 9.2. We then assume that C_{EM} will decline with reforestation at the same rate as it increases in the context of deforestation. It is then possible, as illustrated in the left hand panel of Figure 9.2, to define the inverse relationship between cumulative forestation (X_A) and C_{EM}. As indicated, this inverse relationship is defined in terms of the rate of change of $[C_{EM} = g(X_L)]$; that is $[dC_{EM}/dX_L]$ being the same for $[C_{EM} = f(X_A)]$ as well.

To empirically illustrate the relationships in Figure 9.2, we first need to develop a method for measuring C_{EM}. The literature in environmental accounting reveals a wide array of methods involving different proxies; [Lawn and Sanders, 1993; Lutz, 1993; Ahmed, 2000; and Quah and Tan, 2002]. If one assumes that energy consumption is the main source of air pollution, then a weak proxy is to equate C_{EM} to the cost of energy consumption. A somewhat better proxy for the valuation of air quality can be drawn from the findings of the Industrial Pollution Project of the World Bank (Hartman, Wheeler and Singh, 1997). Using scientific data and a range of approximations, it is possible to estimate the quantities of key pollutants that would emerge from energy consumption of economies that are typically dependent on fossil fuels. These pollutants, namely NO_X, SO_2, CO, CO_2, and Particulates, are regarded as important because of their impacts on the productivity of economic systems. The World Bank project also identified abatement costs for the emissions of these pollutants. We have used this information to estimate the value of C_{EM} as the sum of the pollution abatement expenditure for each year from 1984 to 2000 for the Chinese economy. In Table 9.1, we present this data on C_{EM}.

As indicated, the Chinese economy has displayed positive rates of forestation (approximately 1% per year) over the past decade. Hence, we use panel data on countries that have displayed significant rates of deforestation and estimated a generalized association between CEM and cumulative deforestation $[C_{EM} = g(X_L)]$ in Chinese *yuan*. The analysis yielded the following linear equation, which satisfied the standard criteria of r^2 and t (shown in parentheses)

$$C_{EM} = 47.7 + 64.86 \ (X_L) \qquad\qquad (11)$$
$$(20.177) \qquad (33.54) \qquad\quad r^2 = 0.98$$

Hence, it follows that for every unit of forest added, C_{EM} will diminish by:

$$dC_{EM}/dX_L = 64.86 \qquad\qquad (12)$$

In this formulation, a unit of forestation is a million hectares and that of C_{EM} is a billion *yuan*. We use this simple relationship to adjust the value of equilibrium income, in the next section. However, following the advice of experts in tropical forestry, we assume that forestation that commences in a given year has a lag time of six years before it could become functional in terms of assimilating pollutants.

The Tests of Hypotheses

To analyse the hypotheses, we estimate trends for the coefficients that determine Y^*, Y_T^*, Y^{**} and Y_T^{**} and project the time paths of these equilibrium income values. These coefficients are: Φ, β, γ and τ and were estimated from the macroeconomic aggregates presented in the Appendix for the time period 1984-2000. For illustrative purposes we equate τ to be equal 4% each year. The following time-trend equations {where ($T = 1, ...$) and (1984 =1)}were obtained for Φ, β and γ:

$$\Phi(T) = 574.92 + 155.62T \tag{13}$$
$$(R^2 = 0.91)$$

$$\Phi(T) = 0.0001T^3 - 0.0025T^2 + 0.0107T + 0.5053 \tag{14}$$
$$(R^2 = 0.861)$$

$$\Phi(T) = 0.00007T^3 - 0.0019T^2 + 0.008T + 0.1584 \tag{15}$$
$$(R^2 = 0.985)$$

We nominate 1998 as the initial year and project the values of the coefficients for a ten year period until 2007 using the trend equations (13), (14) and (15). We then simulate the values of Y^*, Y_T^*, Y^{**} and Y_T^{**} for each year in the period 1998-2007. Recall that Y^* represents the equilibrium which is based on standard macroeconomic data, that is $\{Y \equiv GDP\}$, whilst Y^{**} represents the sustainable equilibrium $\{Y \equiv GDP-C_{EM}\}$. Hence if the first hypothesis is true the projected paths of Y^* and Y^{**} should not show any showing sign of convergence. This is confirmed in Figure 9.3 and Table 9.2; that is the projected paths of Y^* and Y^{**} reveal a strong tendency to diverge rather than converge. This implies that sustainability considerations have been excluded from standard macroeconomic practices in China.

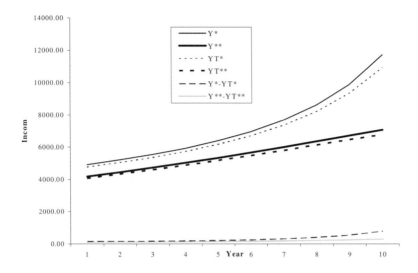

Figure 9.3.   Trends in Y*, Y$_T$*, Y** and Y$_T$**

Table 9.2.   Projected Values of Coefficients and Equilibrium Income
(All monetary values are in billion *yuan* at 1994 price)

	1998	1999	2000	2001	2002	2003	2004	2005	2006	2007
Φ	2753.6	2909.22	3064.84	3220.46	3376.08	3531.7	3687.32	3842.94	3998.56	4154.18
β	0.44	0.44	0.45	0.46	0.47	0.49	0.52	0.55	0.60	0.65
γ	0.090	0.087	0.087	0.089	0.095	0.105	0.118	0.137	0.160	0.189
τ	0.04	0.04	0.04	0.04	0.04	0.04	-	-	-	-
Y*	4912.76	5202.47	5533.20	5919.96	6383.21	6952.17	7670.73	8608.74	9885.19	11721.3
Y**	4175.30	4443.79	4723.46	5016.70	5325.71	5652.02	5995.63	6353.65	6717.98	7071.78
Y$_T$*	4763.35	5043.44	5360.51	5727.91	6163.61	6692.88	7352.99	8201.88	9335.45	10925.6
Y$_T$**	4066.89	4327.25	4597.04	4878.10	5171.97	5479.44	5799.74	6129.25	6459.47	6773.99
I$_{KN}$	9.8	10.4	11.1	11.8	12.5	13.2	0.0	0.0	0.0	0.0
XA	-	-	-	-	-	9.8	20.2	31.3	43.1	55.5
Φ_{CEM}	-	-	-	-	-	63.7	131.5	203.5	279.9	360.9
γ(I)	0.090	0.087	0.087	0.089	0.095	0.095	0.101	0.113	0.132	0.158
Y$_T$**(I)	4066.9	4327.3	4597.0	4878.1	5172.0	5577.3	6214.2	6695.4	7186.9	7659.8

Notes: I$_{KN}$: Million Hectares Forested Each Year
XA: Cumulative Forested Area with Sink Capacity
Taxation for the first six years.

An observation of the time paths of $(Y^*\text{-}Y_T^*)$ and $(Y^{**}\text{-}Y_T^{**})$ reveals that $(Y^*\text{-}Y_T^*)$ is always in excess of $(Y^{**}\text{-}Y_T^{**})$ and that this difference tends to increase over time as income increases. This observation confirms the second hypothesis; that is in the absence of sustainability considerations, the regressive effects of a tax increase appear to be overstated.

Given that the regressive effects of a tax increase are less when national income is better accounted for in terms of C_{EM}, it is pertinent to consider whether the investments of the additional tax earnings in environmental capital could viably offset the regressive effects. This is the gist of the third hypothesis. To illustrate this, we consider a hypothetical scenario where the Chinese economy supposedly finances a forestation programme from 1998 by means of an addition to government revenue, from a marginal tax of 4%. Note that some commentators claim that West China has substantive tracts of land that are suitable for forestation. Using data from forestry sources, the extent of forestation that would have become feasible each year was estimated at 16, 000 *yuan* per hectare. Further as indicated, the reduction in C_{EM} becomes effective after six years. We use equation (12) to estimate this reduction, which is denoted in Table 9.2 as (ΔC_{EM}). The reduction in C_{EM} in turn prompts the need to revise the value γ which is denoted as $[\gamma(I)]$. This is then used in revising the value of equilibrium income now denoted as $(Y_T^{**}I)$.

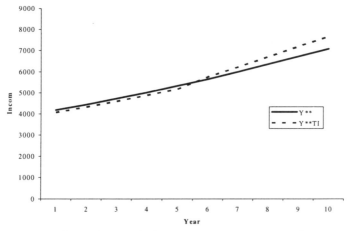

Figure 9.4.   The Response to Investments in Forestry

In order to evaluate the economic viability of forestation, we consider the following options with respect to the financing of forestation by recourse to taxation:

- A marginal tax increase of 4% for only the initial year (1998) enabling the forestation of 9.8 Million Hectares
- A marginal tax increase of 4% for the first two years (1998-99) enabling the forestation of 20.2 Million Hectares
- A marginal tax increase of 4% for the first three years (1998-2000) enabling the forestation of 31 Million Hectares
- A marginal tax increase of 4% for the first four years (1998-2001) enabling the forestation of 43 Million Hectares
- A marginal tax increase of 4% for the first five years (1998-2002) enabling the forestation of 55.5 Million Hectares
- A marginal tax increase of 4% for the first six years (1998-2003) enabling the forestation of 68 Million Hectares

In Table 9.2 and Figure 9.4 we illustrate the six-year taxation option. In all options, the path of $Y_T^{**}(I)$ exceeds that of Y^{**} from six years after the commencement of the supposed forestation program. A simple cost-benefit analysis of the six investment options using an 8% discount rate displays a positive NPV. For this simple exercise, we define the net change in welfare as $[(Y_T^{**}I) - (Y^{**})]$. As indicated in Table 9.3 below the highest welfare gains are attained for 4-year taxation option.

Table 9.3.   Net Present Value of Welfare Gains

Duration of Tax Increase (Years)	Extent of Feasible Forestation (10^6 Hectares)	NPV of Net Welfare Gain (10^9 *Yuan*)
1	9.8	181.75
2	20.27	315.89
3	31.3	396.83
4	43.05	419.08
5	55.5	377.63
6	68.7	264.89

However, one should note that such ranking of the investment options are invariably influenced by a range of factors such the length of time period, the discount rate and the tax rate.

Some Further Policy Analyses

The above analysis reveals that forestation by recourse to a marginal tax is a possible policy measure. However, it is by no means a confirmation of the utmost desirability either of forestation or the use of marginal taxes. The analysis merely illustrates another dimension, which is often ignored in standard macroeconomic policy analysis.

For illustrative purposes, we now consider a simple extension to the above analysis. Macroeconomic planners are often interested in achieving a certain level of target income, for example, for satisfying employment objectives. Suppose that the planned target income for 2004 is that defined as Y^* in Table 9.2, namely 7,671 billion *yuan*. The policy of forestation, as illustrated above within the context of sustainability leads to an income of 6214 billion *yuan*; that is a shortfall of 1456 billion *yuan*. This shortfall is marginally higher when the tax-funded reforestation policy is not adopted; that is, $[(Y^{**}) < Y_T^{**}(I)]$. This simple example illustrates the potential conflict between the goals of sustainability and employment. As illustrated, this conflict is marginally alleviated by the adoption of forestation, which essentially enhances the efficiency of environmental capital (ECE). In Figure 9.5, we illustrate the impact of forestation on the coefficient that describes the depreciation of environmental capital, namely, the ratio (C_{EM}/GDP). This ratio in the context forestation $[\gamma(I)]$ begins to decline well below $[\gamma(0)]$ – the ratio that prevails in the absence of forestation.

The exploration of the relationship between ECE and Y^{**} reveals that if sustainability and employment (as defined by Y^*) are to be reconciled, ECE has to be as high as 95%; that is, the value of γ must fall by 95%. Clearly, this type of efficiency gain cannot be achieved by the policy of reforestation alone. For the time period considered in Figure 9.5, the value of ECE due to forestation ranges between 14 and 16 percent.

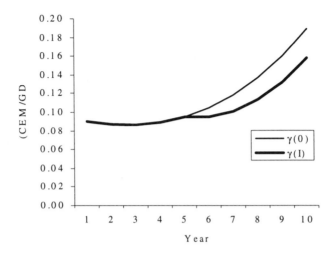

Figure 9.5.   Relationship between ECE and Y**

Concluding Remarks

By way of simple conceptual premise, we have illustrated the internalization of environmental capital into a standard macroeconomic framework. As indicated, such internalization demonstrates a potential deviation for the path pursued in public policy analysis. There are, of course, several alternatives to the policy option considered here; for example, the adoption of cleaner production technologies and changes in consumption behaviour. Inevitably the reconciliation between sustainability and higher output for employment will involve trade-offs between adoption rates of the different alternatives in terms of achieving the desired targets. Nevertheless forestation has an explicit role in West China development in terms of lowering (γ), the rate of environmental capital depreciation. In this context it is important to note that we have considered only one aspect of forestation in terms of ECE; that is the improvement of the quality of air-sheds. However, forestation plays a much wider role in terms of ECE. This includes bio-diversity benefits, moisture retention in soils and improvements in the quality of ground water tables; (Hongchang, 1997). Had these benefits too been included and quantified, then the net welfare gains identified above would no doubt be much larger.

Several extensions to the framework that was presented above are possible. First, it is useful to drop the assumption of output determination by aggregate demand and consider a general equilibrium framework where both aggregate supply and demand are made explicit. Such a general equilibrium framework would permit a more robust analysis in terms of simulations of the types of initiatives considered here. In considering tax initiatives such as those presented above, it is also important to internalise distributional issues, since economies such as China display acute inequalities of income. One possibility for this internalization is to formulate a weighted income determination model with the weights elicited from a standard Lorenz Curve. Finally, the type of analysis presented here is a useful teaching tool in the classroom. Hence, it is useful to consider the internalization of environmental capital within other standard frameworks used in teaching, such as the IS-LM model and those of aggregate supply.

References

1.   Ahmed M. (2000). "A Review of Natural Resource Valuation Through National Income Accounting", 19 *Economic Papers* 55.

2.   Hartman, R. S., Wheeler, D. and Singh, M. (1997). "The Cost Air Pollution Abatement", 29 *Applied Economics*, 759.

3.   Hongchang, W. (1997). "Deforestation and Dessication in China: A Preliminary Study", in Yu-shi, M., Datong, N., Guang, X., Hongchang, W. and Smil, V. *An Assessment of the Economic Losses from Various Forms of Environmental Degradation in China*, Occasional Paper of the Project on Environmental Scarcities, State Capacity and Civil Violence, Cambridge: American Academy of Arts and Sciences and the University of Toronto.

4.   Lawn, A. Phillip and Sanders, D. Richard. (1997). "A Sustainable Net Benefit Index for Australia 1966-67 to 1994-95" 16 *Working Paper in Economics*, Nathan, Brisbane: Griffith University.

5.   Lutz, E. (1993). "Toward Improved Accounting for the Environment" in Lutz. E (ed), *An UNSTAT - World Bank Symposium*, Washington, DC: The World Bank.
6.   Quah, E. and Tan, K. C. (2002). *Siting Environmentally Unwanted Facilities: Risks, Trade-Offs and Choices*, London: Edward Elgar.
7.   Thampapillai, D. J. and Uhlin, H-E (1996). "Sustainable Income: Extending Some Tisdell Considerations to Macroeconomic Analyses", 23 *International Journal of Social Economics*, 137.
8.   Thampapillai, D. J. and Uhlin, H-E (1997). "Environmental Capital and Sustainable Income: Basic Concepts and Empirical Tests", *Cambridge Journal of Economics*, 379.
9.   Thampapillai, D. J. (2002). *Environmental Economics: Concepts, Methods and Policies*, Melbourne: Oxford University Press.
10. Yu-shi, M., Datong, N., Guang, X., Hongchang, W. and Smil, V. (1997). *An Assessment of the Economic Losses from Various Forms of Environmental Degradation in China*, Occasional Paper of the Project on Environmental Scarcities, State Capacity and Civil Violence, Cambridge: American Academy of Arts and Sciences and the University of Toronto.

Appendix

Table A9.1.   Macroeconomic Aggregates and Energy Consumption

C= Consumption, I = Investment, G= Government, X = Exports ,
M = Imports, EC = Energy consumption
Estimates of C, I, G, X, M and GDP in billion *yuan* at 1994 price; EC
in 10^{15} BTUs

	C	G	I	X–M	GDP	EC
1984	971.281	269.580	652.542	0.264	1893.667	20.46
1985	1068.864	275.776	788.662	-85.481	2047.820	22.20
1986	1107.204	292.473	822.861	-54.558	2167.979	23.26
1987	1143.097	285.726	828.798	2.301	2259.923	24.76
1988	1315.499	297.638	947.029	-26.024	2534.142	26.47
1989	1411.660	336.685	1009.393	-30.803	2726.935	26.96
1990	1453.486	359.185	1027.792	81.343	2921.806	27.01
1991	1506.820	413.368	1097.981	90.269	3108.437	28.26
1992	1593.135	446.487	1232.059	35.289	3306.971	29.31
1993	1766.781	506.983	1689.720	-76.498	3886.986	31.36
1994	2081.000	598.600	1926.000	63.400	4669.000	34.04
1995	2438.256	605.492	2160.803	90.403	5294.953	35.21
1996	2655.007	648.393	2218.589	120.479	5642.468	36.04
1997	2644.436	661.963	2159.022	216.760	5682.181	37.61
1998	2598.059	667.441	2079.094	214.763	5559.357	37.07
1999	2587.629	675.559	2002.968	147.709	5413.865	37.02
2000	2609.686	711.838	1961.582	136.225	5419.332	36.67

Sources:

http://www.adb.org/Documents/Books/Key_Indicators/2002/default.asp
http://www.eia.doe.gov/pub/international/iealf/tablee1.xls

10 Enhancing the Western China Development Strategy (WCDS): Innovative Approaches

N.C. Stoskopf, G. Filson, J. Simpson, L. Kannenberg

An interdisciplinary team comprised of Canadian and Chinese biological scientists and extensionists has initiated work with western Chinese farmers to change practices which have contributed to the redevastation of land and water degradation. For example, soil erosion from deforestation, non-sustainable agricultural practices, and desertification has resulted in enormous annual depositions of sediment into the Yellow River. These depositions, aggravated by excessive local water use, are so significant that the Yellow River has ceased to flow for extended periods causing serious downstream problems. On the Yangtze River, land degradation along its tributaries is a direct threat to the Three Gorges Dam project and has global climate change implications as well.

In response to these environmental problems, the Chinese Ministry of Water Resources and local Soil and Water Conservation Bureaus have embarked on an ambitious three-phase program known as the West China Development Strategy (WCDS), possibly the most significant environmental remediation project in Chinese history. It not only has immense global implications offsetting greenhouse gas emissions through carbon sequestration throughout much of western China but also should reduce poverty, enhance food security and increase the sustainable management of natural resources.

Phase I of the WCDS is well underway and has involved identification of and investment in eleven subwatershed demonstration sites, typically about 10 km² in area, in six provinces of western China. Phase II is designed to increase the participation of the farmers and other rural people. Work has begun at two of the eleven sites. Phase III expands the WCDS to the total (landmass of about 2.7 million km2) of which the eleven watersheds are representative.

This paper summarizes efforts that are being made to develop a cooperative agroforestry systems approach to environmental remediation and protection in western China. It involves a broad spectrum of people including administrators and scientists from China, and research personnel from the University of Guelph and a non-profit, non-governmental organization, Resource Efficient Agricultural Production (REAP).

The West China Development Strategy

A long history of intensive agricultural practices has resulted in extensive soil and water degradation in western China. Now China is aggressively seeking to reduce environmental degradation along the Yellow and Yangtze Rivers. Land degradation in the loess plateau and desertification have resulted in sand and dust storms of increasing severity and frequency. Beijing, for instance, experienced more than 40 serious dust storms in 2000 and the dust storms have been starting earlier every year and with increased frequency and severity. Loss of vegetative cover and reduced carbon sequestration could affect climate change on a global basis. Reduced air and water quality affects health and living conditions over an extended area. Although environmental degradation remains very serious and ground water contamination continues to worsen in many areas, much more effort is now going into preventing further nationwide environmental pollution. Though water quality remains good in big rivers like the Yangtze and Pearl, the Yellow River has some of the worst water quality problems (Zi, 2000).

Eleven demonstration sites were identified by the Ministry of Water Resources and the Department of Water and Soil Conservation through remote sensing, and ground level geographical and geological assessment to be used for projects to demonstrate immediate land degradation amelioration through biological, engineering and socio-economic inducements and improvements (see Appendix). The eleven demonstration sites are located in Inner Mongolia Autonomous Region and the provinces of Shanxi, Shaanxi, Gansu, Sichuan and Yunnan. Each demonstration project, generally about 10 km² in area, was carefully selected to represent a unique set of environments typical of extensive ecological circumstances in the region. Overall, the eleven subwatersheds represent about 2.7 million km² of fragile soils.

With respect to the eleven subwatersheds, a three-phase project has been initiated. Phase I, the identification of the eleven subwatersheds, is in place. A holistic approach consisting of biological, physical and social aspects is intended to make major environmental, economic and social changes. The 'hardware' of the project includes reforestation with selected trees and shrubs, development of economic agroforestry systems, terracing, creation of feedlots with stored feed, introduction of conservation tillage systems, development of agri-tourism, and construction of small scale dams.

Phase II is designed to extend the demonstration concepts to local stakeholders within the eleven sites and is the 'software' of the project. The approach involves the development of a sustainability index based on ecological, economic and social indicators to determine the degree of sustainability and threshold levels for inputs. Wang (1996) suggested parameters suitable for the sustainability of subwatersheds. Included are parameters such as floods, landslides, land-use structures, combinations of plant and animal species, agroforestry design, and management systems (Stoskopf et al., 2001). Most parameters have been quantified in the eleven subwatersheds. Professor Wang, the most senior member of the Chinese team, assessed the extent to which his parameters were followed in the construction of each demonstration project as the Chinese and Canadian teams visited each subwatershed project in February, 2001 (see Appendix). Phase III involves expanding successful concepts developed in Phase II to farmers outside of the eleven demonstation sites, an area of 2.7 million km².

Canadian Involvement in WCDS — REAP

REAP has already initiated a separately funded exploratory project, aimed at poverty alleviation, at two of the eleven demonstration sites: Dingxi

County in Gansu Province and Zhungar County, Inner Mongolia. REAP is using a participatory community planning approach and farmer-to-farmer training to raise the capacity of the farmers and farm organizations within each of the two sites. The use of participatory methods and REAP's agro-ecological village model is unique within China but has increasingly been used in other parts of the world including such southeast Asian countries as the Philippines and Indonesia. This approach is based on the realization that community organizational work and ecological land management can provide the basis of sustainable community development in environmentally degraded areas (REAP, 2002).

REAP's project in Dingxi and Zhungar Counties has the following purpose:

> The project aims to improve the economic and social well being of marginalized farming communities with a focus on women, while at the same time protecting and enhancing the natural resource base through the use of participatory development methods and the agro-ecological village development model (REAP, 2002: 8).

By promoting the adoption of ecological, gender sensitive practices, REAP intends to remediate degraded land by reducing soil erosion and diversifying farm activities, improving food and water security in these extremely dry areas. The capacity of both men and women will be raised through fostering increased participation, entrepreneurialism, the communities' comparative advantages and a broader range of markets for the communities' production.

Participatory Rural Appraisals (PRA) have been conducted in both Zhungar and Dingxi Counties. These PRAs have been conducted to facilitate and strengthen the capacity of farmers. They involve group animation among stakeholders to share information, analyze and jointly act to plan appropriate ecologically oriented farm endeavours. PRAs can also lead to increased capacity of local organizations to conduct their own appraisals flexibly and dynamically. In Dingxi County, for example, the REAP/Chinese PRA group conducted an initial open meeting, a final meeting and a follow-up meeting. They used semi-structured interviewing and focus group discussions to encourage local farm villagers to identify their strengths, weaknesses, opportunities and threats. Farmers ranked their problems, opportunities, and adopted a Village Resource Plan (VRMP). They will now proceed to implement and evaluate the plan including extensive farmer-to-farmer training once the trainers themselves have been trained. Their goals include:

- Increased capacity of farmers via farmer-farmer training;
- Increased economic activity;
- Improved status of women;
- Landscape restoration through contour farming, revegetation of sloping land and controlled grazing.

Canadian Involvement in WCDS-University of Guelph

The University of Guelph team, after inspecting most of the eleven sites in 2001, has concluded that our major contribution to the success of the WCDS will be through two programs: the creation of a sustainability index for each subwatershed and a system of capacity building for agroecological consciousness-raising among farmers within the eleven subwatersheds.

Sustainability Indices

The Chinese have provided excellent suggestions for identifying ecological, economic and social factors (e.g., Wang, 1996) but have not assigned numerical values. An index or degree of sustainability can be produced by summarizing assigned numerical values of salient input/ output factors for a number of environmental, production and socio-economic factors. Threshold levels need to be established to identify acceptable and/or unacceptable levels of soil erosion, physical degradation and water quality (e.g., nitrate levels in water, farm runoff of waste). Numerical values could be assigned from existing data. For social acceptability it is possible to interview random samples of farm and non-farm rural people in each subwatershed to assess their perceived absolute and relative quality of life. Capacity building will also be done to strengthen the agro-ecological sensitivity of subject matter specialists, extension workers and farmers.

Attention to threshold levels of farm equity, viability, economic profitability, and the degree to which off-farm employment was resorted to in order for the operation to continue are essential. Other socio-economic indicators include health care facilities, educational opportunities, availability of potable water, recreational facilities, social amenities (including news facilities), police protection and social services. These aspects can also be applied cumulatively at the rural community level (Stoskopf *et al.*, 2001, Stoskopf *et al.*, 2003).

Economics of food production indicators might include crop yield, livestock productivity, energy output/input, crop rotation, ratio of perennial to annual crops, cost of production inputs (machinery, fertilizers, pesticides, tillage), labour, irrigation water use efficiency, soil compaction, soil water holding capacity, seed costs (Stoskopf *et al.*, 2003: 4).

Additionally, and no less important than the economic level, is the need to establish social threshold levels of acceptability. What are the minimum levels of perceived well-being or quality of life in both absolute and relative terms below which would be considered unacceptable for most members of the farm and rural village household individually and the rural community collectively? A measure of the quality and quantity (calories per person) of food and fibre produced on the farm must be included as an indicator of food security.

Finally, the interactive effects of the environmental, economic and social consequences of the proposed changes to the farming system must be assessed. Are they positive or negative in the cumulative sense? Trade-offs among the ecological, economic and social consequences of these systems can be identified from the sustainability index.

Capacity building through Participatory Technology Development (PTD)

Capacity building is not defined through the instruments used, but through its goal of enhancing the capability of people and institutions in a sustainable manner to improve their competence and problem-solving capacities. Capacity Development is:

> The process by which individuals, groups, organizations, institutions
> and societies increase their abilities to: (1) perform core functions,

solve problems, define and achieve objectives, and (2) understand and deal with their development needs in a broad context and sustainable manner (UNDP: 1997).

Capacity building programs have the potential to empower program participants to address the causes of their environmental problems and their economic marginalization through increasing their social capital. Social capital is defined by the World Bank as "the institutions, relationships and norms that shape the quality and quantity of a society's social interactions" (World Bank, 2002, URL#1).

Formidable challenges for farmer adoption of the dramatic changes required mean farmer participation is essential if the WCDS is to succeed. Each of the eleven subwatersheds has an instrumental and strategic rationality but an insufficient communicative rationality. The development of learning platforms with subject matter specialists (SMSs) complements village extension workers (VEWs) and farmers. This approach is more participatory than the traditional diffusion of innovative extension schemes such as the training and visit system. Agricultural extension using participatory training and development (PTD) methods have been shown in Indonesia and elsewhere to increase people's capacity to change and improve their quality of life by reclaiming their environment and improving their economic returns as they gain more confidence and strengthen their farm organizations (Röling and Van de Fliert, 1998). Whether this can be achieved within a Communist political structure such as in China remains to be seen.

It will be essential to train a core of Chinese village extension workers and/or local officials in capacity building/leadership training. Outreach/ distance education techniques developed by the University of Guelph's Prof. Janakiram[1] in Russia, India, Egypt and Cameroon can also help to disseminate some of these concepts to remote western Chinese regions. We could be involved in developing distance learning curricula in capacity building and agroecological/forestry principles as well as in community/ site monitoring and evaluation from the specified demonstration sites for dissemination to larger watersheds.

Capacity building innovations could then be evaluated by the communities within each subwatershed and eventually disseminated to each entire region. Many ideas will be unique to each subwatershed but some of the concepts will have a wider application. Capacity building/ leadership training will eventually be needed in each of the eleven subwatersheds.

Training must be coordinated among the eleven subwatersheds and eventually spread throughout the six provinces from provincial authorities trained in the capacity building methods. Our Chinese counterparts have admitted that they lack experience and know-how in this area and would like Canadian input.

Once master facilitators (including, for example, Seabuckthorn Institute personnel and provincial and county Soil and Water Conservation officials) have attended workshops in Canada and China, they could work with the Canadian team to train the VEWs in agroecological methods such as minimal grazing and tillage systems, animal husbandry and agroforestry. The master facilitators would then educate other VEWs who will, in turn, train other VEWs to run the Agroforestry Capacity Building (ACB) farmer groups. Farmer-to-farmer training could later be conducted by two farmers selected from each of the ACB farmer groups within each of their villages to develop the knowledge base throughout all eleven demonstration projects. We expect that Chinese farmers in each subwatershed would acquire knowledge of sustainable agricultural methods designed to introduce environmentally friendly best management practices that will raise their incomes significantly.

The proposed PTD is based on the identification of about 20 farmers selected for gender equality and leadership potential by county officials or extension workers, in each of 2 to 6 villages per subwatershed, to participate in ACB farmer groups. Each group would be facilitated by one male and one female extension worker.

The first stage involves an intensive month-long workshop with subject matter specialists and village extension workers in facilitation, agroecosystem analysis and watershed design. Once these master facilitators from both the county and provincial levels have taken the workshop provided by our Canadian Rural Extensionists both in Canada and in China.

These are platforms for raising the awareness of farmers and extension workers and creating opportunities for them to interact with guest subject matter specialists from the county and provincial levels. Each of the village based ACBs could be subdivided into four small groups of farmers who will participate in action research on animal husbandry, cropping, ecological protection, and forestry (five people in each with at least two women per group). Although women historically have been responsible for household and child care duties in China, they are currently involved in most aspects of farming. The weekly dialogue sessions would initially last for three months. Guest speakers from the county and provincial levels would be invited to speak about the special features of the subwatershed's ecological, economic and social design.

Farmer-to-farmer education would later be conducted by two farmers selected from each ACB farmer group to encourage farmer-to-farmer learning throughout each of their villages as a way of scaling up the participation. Each of the two farmers from each ACB group would need about one week intensive workshop education sessions to be conducted by the village extension workers who had facilitated the ACB group. This is the method by which the farmer-to-farmer education could be initiated. Each farmer facilitator would be encouraged to work through existing farmer organizations and or facilitate their creation in order to better understand the subwatershed's ecological, economic and social design while encouraging the other farmers to develop their own PAR projects. This procedure would allow the facilitation/education to be scaled up throughout the subwatersheds. It could also form the basis for the later expansion of these techniques throughout other parts of the subwatershed which hold similar prospects for adaptation. By these methods, a critical mass of close to half of the affected population in each subwatershed could be reached, effectively diffusing the environmental protection concepts throughout the subwatersheds in such a way that the farmers have increased participation, commitment and a raised level of confidence regarding their abilities to make relevant local adjustments as they implement the plans.

We intend to monitor the total numbers of SMSs, VEWs and farmers involved in education and capacity building throughout Phase II. We also intend to use random interview surveys in each of the eleven subwatersheds to ensure that these numbers are being achieved and that participants are providing extension services of the highest possible quality.

Desired Outcomes

The most immediate beneficiaries of these programs would be the farm and non-farm households in the eleven demonstration subwatersheds. Chinese farmers in the demonstration sites would acquire increased knowledge of agroforestry methods designed to prevent soil and water degradation through participating in agroforestry capacity building circles and undertaking appropriate measures to reduce land degradation while increasing their income. Over the life of the projects, they should see improvements in environmental quality, family income or their quality of life including gender equality issues. Secondary beneficiaries would be the people along and at the ends of the Yellow and Yangtze Rivers who would have a more regularized access to water resources, will experience fewer dust storms and will find less silt in their water.

The implications for reducing the greenhouse effect by carbon sequestration on the vast area of Central Asia and as a template to poverty alleviation, enhanced food security and sustainable management of natural resources are awesome. While that part of western China which was once the lush, green heartland for agricultural production may be irrevocably lost, there is still time to prevent the Yellow River from becoming a permanently continental river if siltation can be minimized. There is also considerable potential to arrest gully development and generate alternative agroforestry development which can be done in harmony with ecosystem health in contrast to the extractive nature of the intensive cropping and grazing patterns that have developed over the past several hundred years. Thus, not only will this reduce siltation into the Yellow and Yangtze Rivers, it will transform fragile grazing and cropping areas into economic shrubbery and forests. If this can be accomplished with these demonstration projects, what is learned from this experience over the next five years can be spread throughout the Yellow and Yangtze watersheds so that land degradation can be severely reduced and the impoverished people trying to live off their increasingly failing agriculture can be usefully employed in more economically productive agroforestry and agri-tourist alternative sustainable livelihoods.

As for the project risks, there have been discussions on the measures to mitigate and/or monitor the anticipated risks. One considerable risk is that the farmers will not want to participate in the fundamentally sound ecosystem health and agroecological solutions being provided because the approaches to getting them to understand and participate have been insufficiently participatory. We have criticized our Chinese colleagues for being too instrumentalist and strategic in their rationality and insufficiently communicative in their dealings with farmers and other local rural residents. They have admitted to having placed too little emphasis on interacting with farmers in a manner that ensures farmer participation. This is partly due to a shortage of extension workers and insufficient training in how to facilitate farmer involvement in their demonstration projects.

The Participatory Technology Development approach that we are advocating is now becoming widely accepted as a more successful approach to achieving farmer involvement than some of the alternative extension strategies (commodity focused approach, training and visit system, top-down diffusion of innovation, etc.). It places more emphasis on the protection of indigenous knowledge systems where they can be shown to have advantages over more expensive, high input, so-called 'modern', scientific approaches to farming. This is especially true in China where farmers are often restricted to one-tenth of a hectare or less of land.

If the independent and cooperative initiative, which the PTD approach is designed to encourage, fosters new farm organizations within civil society, critics may allege that this could be threatening to some authorities. We do not believe that this is likely to be the case, however, because of more relaxed government attitudes in accepting constructive input. We intend to carry out random and ongoing quality of life interviews of farmers and other rural people within the eleven subwatersheds to determine their extent of understanding of the function of the demonstration projects, the perceived impact of these projects on their absolute and relative well-being and the economic impact of the changes they are undergoing over the course of the first (2001-2003) and second (2002-2005) phases of this project.

Development Priorities to be Fulfilled by this Project

Basic Human Needs

China has huge cities and continues to experience significant rural to urban migration which is generating unemployment in many of its urban areas. It is essential to minimize this migration while protecting its fragile western land and water system; hence, China has developed the WCDS. As a major part of this strategy, these eleven subwatersheds have been selected as reflecting the problems of western China. Farm and non-farm rural families within these demonstration areas often have annual incomes in the order of $C120 per capita.

To illustrate these circumstances, consider the efforts to rehabilitate the desertification environment in Pingchuan Township of Linze County, Gansu Province (in the Hexi Corridor), one of the 11 subwatershed demonstration sites (site 7, Appendix). This is a partially desertified area which suffers from an increasing frequency of dust storms, degradation and blowouts of sections of the sand dune fixing species *Haloxylon ammodendron*, which does not regenerate naturally. This poses a continuing threat to the sustainable livelihoods of the already impoverished residents. Literally they are in a life and death struggle with encroaching desertification. The people within this demonstration site have had the good fortune, however, to work with the Cold and Arid Regions Environmental and Engineering Research Institute which has set up the "Hydrological and Ecological Research Station of Desert Oasis" in Pingchuan township. Within this 14 km², area there are 1824 people in 456 households of whom 1042 make up the labour force, the majority of whom are indigenous to the area but there are growing numbers of immigrants to the outskirts of Yigongcheng village. Per capita income in the village is 1500 *yuan*/year or about C$300 per capita/year while that of the immigrants is only about C$116 per capita/year. Soil erosion through overgrazing and severe wind erosion have combined to threaten the lives of the local people, especially the immigrants. The only reason the latter would immigrate to the area is that growing desertification had forced them out of even dryer areas nearby. "The original margin of the oasis has become an immigrant village with imperfect protective systems and impoverished soils" (Demonstration Plot for Comprehensive Rehabilitation of Wind Erosion and Desertification Environment in Pingchuan Township of Linze County, Gansu Province, 2001: 6).

Phase I involves the stabilization of shifting sand by means of mechanical and biological measures. It includes the conversion of some of its croplands to grassland and ephedra-planting areas. (The ephedra plant, which has medicinal uses, grows in western China) Grain production has been more than self-sufficient but per capita cropland has been reduced from 2.3 *mu* to 1.3 *mu* (15 *mu* = 1 hectare).

Besides ephedra, other leguminous forages like *Lycium chinensis* will be planted on sandy land along with other nitrogen-fixing forages and grain crops. Drought tolerant plants have been started on the sand dunes and in interdune depressions at the margin of the oasis and a 10-50 m wide sandbreak forest has been established along the main canal which is at the oasis margin. "Selected tree species mainly include poplar species, *Hippophae rhammoides*, elm and *Tamarisk ramosissima*, and among the poplar species the triploid *Populus tomentosa* will be first selected for its high resistance to yellow spot beetles" (Demonstration Plot...Pingchuan Township, 2001: 8). This is part of a comprehensive management conception of water-ecology-economy to use water saving measures and establish an insect resistant forest windbreak system to improve agricultural production conditions. This plan is designed to increase the average overall income from 940 *yuan* to 1500 *yuan* by improving 80% of the desertified, wind-eroded lands but, of course, this requires careful monitoring of the demonstration site's ecological, economic and social aspects of sustainability. A concerted effort is needed to undertake capacity building with the residents in order to get them to establish and maintain the appropriate biological and engineering control mechanism and agro-forestry activities that will allow for a sustained increase in income.

We are skipping a detailed accounting to support health care efforts, family planning and sanitation because the issues associated with protecting the land and water from further erosion are so crucial to meeting these people's basic human needs. Although smaller in area and having fewer people than many of the other subwatersheds (see Appendix I), the challenges facing the meeting of their basic human needs are not unlike those in the other demonstration plots.

Women in Development and Gender Equity

We are hoping to enhance gender equity and promote conditions more conducive for children to be able to stay in school for longer periods of time thereby improving their human rights. To illustrate how the project is designed to contribute to enhanced gender equity, consider the case of Fuxing Watershed's Eco-Environment Rehabilitation Project in Dingxi County, Gansu Province. It is important to realize that whereas many of the women participate equally with men in the farming and engineering work such as terrace construction and masonry projects, women tend to do more of the household labour, a phenomenon not unlike the Canadian situation. Nevertheless, the work that women do must be recognized so that they can look towards establishing a more equal overall workload with the men.

Dingxi County is one of the most impoverished counties within China. The demonstration site (#8 below) has four villages with 325 families and 768 people in its labour force of which 373 are women and 395 are men. The families have a per capita net income of approximately $C254 from crop production (31%), forestry (0.5%), livestock (10%), off-farm employment (14.5%), and service employment (44%). Examples of poor management in the past include excessive tree cutting, over-grazing of animals and cropping highly sloped land with annual tillage for annual crops. All of these exacerbate gully formation on the hilly landscape.

Some of the economic projects deserve mention. Twenty technical demonstration households have been selected of which five will plant Chinese herbs, five will develop sunlight greenhouse vegetables, nursery and edible fungus, five will focus on irrigation and another five will each raise livestock including cattle, sheep, pigs, chickens and rabbits. A household innovation will include the use of solar energy stoves for each household to partially replace the use of wood stoves, thereby saving wood.

The key to gender equity will be to ensure that the twenty households, including both women and men, participate fully in the training courses which will be run by SMSs and VEWs employed by the Gansu Provincial Soil Conservation Research Institute. By beginning with these 20 households, the eventual intention is to eventually train 800 farmers within Dingxi County, concentrating on young farmers and balancing the training so that relatively equal numbers of men and women technicians are trained in the areas of infrastructure (e.g., road, cistern and canal design and construction), agricultural techniques (e.g., household yard orchards, cash crop cultivation, greenhouses), forestry techniques (e.g., orchard construction, fruit tree grafting and pruning) and livestock techniques (e.g., construction of livestock and poultry sheds, grass cultivation). Women will be as involved as men in each of these aspects though they will specialize in their areas of greatest interest. Considering the extent to which training is already proceeding, Dingxi County demonstration site may be the most likely choice for gender sensitive Agroforestry Capacity Building circles to be developed and monitored in order for the most effective ACB approach to be developed in the other subwatersheds (Stoskopf et al., 2001). The biggest advantage that this project will bring is that, by reducing the amount of farmland, women labourers will be somewhat freed from heavy farm activities, leaving the heaviest tasks to men. The project planners also hope to increase their income by selling seeds to other counties. This will enable more children, especially among the poorest families, to be able to pay the tuition needed for them to go to school for a longer time.

Infrastructure Services

Phase I involves massive infrastructure construction. As in the discussion of two of the eleven demonstration subwatersheds, in Phase I, the Chinese are undertaking extensive investments in infrastructural services including roads, terraces, stone masonry terrace walls, water storage reservoirs, check dams to help manage water and silt movement, solar energy heating, discharge and water gully head protection earth works, canals and water storage retaining walls, etc. Our experience from speaking with farmers at the China-Canada Link Project for Soil and Water Conservation in Yufeng Demonstration Watershed near Chengdu City is that they want to be involved in suggesting infrastructural works. Farmers told us that they would like to see wells for drinking water sunk inside the demonstration project so that they would not have to continue to walk almost two kilometers to carry water for their own consumption. The Director of the Yufeng Demonstration Small Watershed demonstration project, Madame Fan (Assistant Director to the Director Madame Wang of the Gansu Soil and Water Conservation Bureau), specifically indicated to the Canadian team that she felt that one of the most important things that we might be able to help Chinese officials accomplish was to develop "a suitable method to achieve the participation of the local farmers in the ecological management of her group's project". We feel that the PTD will foster this kind of participation in the design of infrastructure projects during Phase II of the project, thereby improving the extent to which their basic human needs are met.

Human Rights, Democracy and Good Governance

Dingxi County is illustrative of how the workload of women and children may be eased by the demonstration project and increased income obtained to in turn enable more children to be able to go to school. Every demonstration project is aimed at increasing per capita income and if these relatively impoverished Chinese farmers and rural non-farm workers can succeed, the results will benefit everyone, including women and children. These are the social benefits which our interview surveys of people's quality of life will be designed to monitor, but the prospects do appear real.

   The second function of the ACB circles is to promote the development of farmer organizations distinct from the state, thereby providing one of the central building blocks of rural civil society. Farm organizations are certainly intended to foster co-operation with state initiatives but in the long run, it is hoped that farm organizations will continue informally on their own.

Private Sector Development

China has opted for a "socialist market economy". The state is withdrawing from its earlier omnipresent role in all walks of Chinese life. This does not necessarily mean that China's strong central state will weaken but it does mean that it is encouraging more of its citizens to develop their own methods of survival. These demonstration projects are designed to encourage rural initiative, initially in close cooperation with governments at the federal, provincial and municipal levels. After five years, farmers will cease receiving money and/or grain, as they are presently receiving as part of government strategy of reward and punishment. Of course, it remains to be seen whether the ACB circles and the encouragement to be independent of government may have unforeseen consequences which will be of concern to authorities but for now, the Ministry of Water Resources and the provincial Bureaus of Soil and Water Conservation are committed to this as part of their Development Strategy.

Environment

Most fundamentally, of course, these demonstration projects are designed to halt some of the most serious land degradation that exists anywhere in the world. If they are successful this will make a major contribution to the global environment as well as the sequestering of carbon throughout the Yellow and Yangtze River watersheds. If environmental changes are successful, they will prevent the Yellow from becoming a continental river and they will permit the Chinese to be able to feed themselves for the foreseeable future.

Concluding Remarks

The construction and development of the demonstration projects (Phase I) is well underway in every subwatershed but should be completed some time in 2003. Phase II has started in Inner Mongolia and Gansu in 2002 under the aegis of REAP and will run to 2005. Final assessments of the value of the Sustainability Indices and Participatory Technology Development will occur some time later as funding becomes available. Our

Chinese partners intend the best features of Phase I and II, determined through intensive monitoring, to be propagated in other parts of the Yellow and Yangtze watersheds before the end of Phase II.

Note

1.   Professor Jana Janakiram has developed a Canadian International Development Agency funded model of distance education techniques based on training and collaboration between recipient countries and the University of Guelph's School of Environmental Design and Rural Development. Suitable farmer and village extension worker materials, credentials and evaluation developed in host country institutions are implemented in remote centres and villages.

References

1.   Demonstration Plot for Comprehensive Rehabilitation of Wind Erosion and Desertification Environment in Pingchuan Township of Linze County, Gansu Province (2001). 'Basic Condition and General Planning Consideration,' Linze County: Cold and Arid Regions Environmental and Engineering Research Institute, Chinese Academy of Sciences.
2.   Dingxi Bureau of Soi Conservation (Feb. 2001). Preliminary Design Report Fuxing Watershed Eco-Environment Rehabilitation Project in Dingxi County, Gansu Province, Lanzhou: Gansu Provincial Soil Conservation Research Institute.
3.   Röling, N. and E. Van de Fliert (1998). "Introducing integrated pest management in rice in Indonesia: a pioneering attempt to facilitate large-scale change" in N. G. Röling and M. A. E. Wagemakers (eds), *Facilitating Sustainable Agriculture: Participatory Learning and Adaptive Management in Times of Environmental Uncertainty.* Cambridge: Cambridge University Press.
4.   Samson, R. (Sept. 2002). *The Western China Agro-ecological Village Development Project: 2002-2003 Annual Workplan.* Submitted to the Sustainable Communities Program Shell Foundation by Resource

Efficient Agricultural Production (REAP)-Canada in Partnership with the Ministry of Water Resources, PRC.

5.   Stoskopf, N. C., G. C. Filson, J. Simpson and L. Kannenberg (Mar. 6-8th, 2003). "Enhancing the Western China Development Strategy (WCDS): Innovative Approaches". Paper presented to the Conference on West China Development: Domestic Strategies and Global Implications, Victoria, B. C.

6.   Stoskopf, N. C., G. C. Filson, L. Kannenberg, K. C. Tan and J. Simpson (April 30, 2001). "Capacity Building for Sustainable Development in Eleven Subwatersheds of Western China" (A Component of the Western China Development Strategy). Proposal to CIDA's Bilateral Responsive Program. Guelph: Univ. of Guelph.

7.   UNDP (1997). "Capacity Development," in *Capacity Development Resource Book*. Management Development and Governance Division. New York: UNDP.

8.   Wang, L. (1996). "Theoretical basis and index system of sustainable watershed management" in L. Wang (ed), *Combating Desertification in China*. Beijing: China Forestry Publishing House.

9.   World Bank (2002) http://www.worldbank.Org/poverty/scapital/whatsc.htm (retrieved, Dec. 20, 2002).

10.   Zi, M. (July 10, 2000). "China's Environmental Situation Remains Severe". *Beijing Review* 12.

Appendix

Demonstration Sites for Ecological Environmental Rehabilitation Established in Western China by the Central Government of China (see Stoskopf, *et al.*, 2001)

Site 1: ZHAO HE GRASSLAND, XI LA MU REN TOWN, DA MAO BANNER, INNER MONGOLIA AUTONOMOUS REGION (110° long; 41° lat).
Demonstration area: 13.3 km²
Topography: Hilly grassland
Elevation: 1585 to 1960 m
Precipitation: 281 mm/y
Frost-free period: 110 days
Socio-economic: 15 families with approximately $575 (Can.) income per capita; 2200 livestock
Basic problems: over-grazing and soil degradation, desertification and consequent serious wind erosion of 2500 to 6000 t/km²
Chinese investment: Approximately $504,000 (Can.)
Project development period: 2001 to 2003

Site 2: DESHENGXI WATERSHED, ZHUNGEER COUNTY, INNER MONGOLIA AUTONOMOUS REGION (Also known as the Erdos Plateau) (110°31' long., 39°50' lat)
Demonstration area: 41.3 km² and representing 32,000 km²
Topography: Severely gullied sandstone with annual erosion rate of 11000 t/km² and with a gully density of 8.25 km/km²
Elevation: 1200 m
Precipitation: 350 mm/y
Frost-free period: 140 days
Socio-economic: 65 families with $200 (Can.) per capita per year
Basic problems: soil erosion by water, wind and gravity. "Most serious area of soil erosion in the world." The area is the major contributor to Yellow River sediment load (350 mt/yr)
Chinese investment: no information provided.
Project development period: 2001-2003

Site 3: **LANG-WO WATERSHED, JINGLE COUNTY, SHANXI PROVINCE** (112° long, 38°31' lat)
Demonstration area: 9.55 km²
Topography: hilly, loess 10-30 m thick
Elevation: 1280 to 1833 m
Precipitation: 450 to 550 mm/y, 70% from July to Sept. via heavy storms
Frost-free period: 90 to 120 days
Socio-economic: Population of 512 in 4 villages, $320 (Can.) annual per capita income, primarily from cropping (29%), livestock (41%) and 30% from specialty crops.
Basic problems: soil erosion via water and gravity; low productivity
Annual sedimentation: 6130 t/km²
Chinese investment: $820,000 (Can.) approx.
Project development period: Work initiated in 1993; current program 2001-2003.

Site 4: **YINGWANG WATERSHED, YICHUAN COUNTY, SHAANXI PROVINCE** (110° long, 36° lat)
Demonstration area: 10 km²; area of representation: 497 km²
Topography: part of Huanglong Mountains, basic rock and red soils covered with thick loessial deposits; gully density: 0.8 km/km².
Elevation: 1198 to 1351 m
Precipitation: 575 mm/y, 60% in storms from June to September
Frost-free period: 150 to 200 d
Socio-economic: 14 villages with 1487 families; per capita income: $120 (Can.) from crop production (47%), forestry (28%), livestock (23%), side-line industry (2%).
Basic problems: mainly water erosion, but gravity and wind erosion also serious; some areas exceed annual soil losses of 2500 t/km²
Chinese investment: $211,000 (Can.) approx.
Project development period: 2001 to 2003

Site 5: NIUWUCHUAN WATERSHED, FUXIAN COUNTY, SHAANXI
PROVINCE (109° long, 36° lat).
Demonstration area: 10 km²; area of representation: 497 km²
Topography: part of Huanglong Mountains, red soils with thick
loess cover; deeply gullied with density of 0.75 km/km².
Elevation: 1020 to 1526 m
Precipitation: 560 mm/y with 60% from July to September.
Frost-free period: 150 to 200 d
Socio-economic: 9 villages with 1520 families with per capita
income of $138 (Can. approx.) from crop production (70%),
forestry and orchards (9%), livestock (8%) and side-line
industry (13%).
Basic problems: Severe water erosion primarily, but also gravity
erosion, with losses of 1513 t/km² annually and a total eroded
amount of 530,000 tons annually
Chinese investment: $211,000 (Can.) approx.
Project development period: 2001 to 2003

Site 6: ZHAO YUANWAN PROJECT, JINJITAN TOWNSHIP, YULING
CITY, SHAANXI PROVINCE (109°50' long, 38°30' lat)
Demonstration area: 9.39 km²
Topography: Desert grassland of fixed or semi-fixed dunes 3-8 m
high, with some (0.7 km²) moving dunes; in middle reach of
Yudong Irrigation Area with ground water level at 1.5 m
Elevation: 1200 m
Precipitation: 414 mm/y
Frost-free period: 155 d
Socio-economic: unoccupied, but scheduled for resettlement of
farmers moving due to dam project; plans for 160 families after
sustainable practices in place
Basic problems: Wind erosion, with up to 230 soil-eroding
incidents per year
Chinese investment: $1.1 million (Can.) approx.
Project development period: 2001-2003

Site 7: **PINGCHUAN YIGONGCHENG OASIS, PINGCHUAN TOWNSHIP, LINZE COUNTY, GANSU PROVINCE** (99°25' long, 39°20' lat)

Demonstration area: 14 km²; area of representation; oases totalling 10947 km²

Topography: juncture of low mountain, desert, and oasis; demonstration area is typical of oases of Hexi Corridor region.

Precipitation: 117 mm/y

Frost-free period: 1532 d

Number of gale days: 15

Socio-economic: one village and an immigrant area; 456 families with per capita income of $300 (Can., approx.), but immigrant area $116, from irrigated crop production (42%), livestock (33%), other (25%).

Basic problem: wind erosion resulting in desertification at margin of oases (4656 km² overall of which 39% is severe), blown sand within oases, and frequent (sometimes catastrophic) sand and dust storms; overall 2400 km² of oases are newly desertified each year

Chinese investment: information not provided

Project development period: ongoing

Site 8: **FUXING WATERSHED, DINGXI COUNTY, GANSU PROVINCE** (104° 35' long, 35°45' lat)

Demonstration area: 19.3 km²

Topography: loess-covered (up to 100 m thick) rolling hills with gully density of 1.08 km/km² in area of 1.58 km²; 54% of area has slopes greater than 25°

Elevation: 1840-2285 m

Precipitation: 352 mm/y with 60% from July to September often as severe storms

Frost free period: 141 d

Socio-economic: 4 villages with 325 families with per capita net income of $254 (Can. approx.) from crop production (31%), forestry (0.5%), livestock (10%), off-farm employment (14.5%), and other employment (44%).

Basic problems: water and gravity erosion at annual rate of 5400 t/ km², totalling 104, 300 tons; 40% of area is strongly to severely eroded

Chinese investment: $729,500 (Can.) approx.

Project development period: some work initiated in 1993 with intensification of effort since 1999. Current program: 2001 to 2003.

Site 9: **YUFENG WATERSHED, SUINUNG CITY, SICHUAN PROVINCE** (105°30' long, 30°45' lat)

Demonstration area: includes 2 small watersheds, 2 other areas, and an experimental station; total demonstration area: 16 km²; area of representation 42.4 km²

Topography: low mountains, hills, hillocks, mainly covered by brown podzolic soils with thin top soil; soil erosion, averaging 4250 t/km², occurs in about 40% of the area, with half of that being highly or severely eroded.

Elevation: 282-427 m

Precipitation: 993 mm/y, 81% May-October; semi-tropical, wet monsoon climate

Socio-economic: available data confound urban and rural populations, but rural per capita income is $280 (Can., approx.), with income from crop production (56%), livestock (34%), forestry (1%), and other (9%)

Basic problems: extensive water and gravity erosion

Chinese investment: $1.56 million (Can.) approx.

Project development period: Preliminary projects were initiated in 1980s; current program: 2001-2003.

Site 10: **YUZIGOU WATERSHED, KAIXIAN COUNTY, CHONGKING CITY, SICHUAN PROVINCE** (108°20' long, 31°20' lat).

Demonstration area: 11.1 km²

Topography: steep hills with yellow soil developed from limestone as main type; annual erosion rate: 5323 t/km²; 70% of watershed affected

Precipitation: 1232-1376 mm/y

Socio-economic: 7 villages with populations of 3824 and per capita income of $90 (Can. approx.) from crop production (primarily), forestry, and livestock.

Basic problems: severe soil erosion and potential to impinge on performance of nearby Three Gorges Reservoir because of annual 22000 ton sediment load due to erosion

Chinese investment: $454,000 (Can.) approx.

Project development period: 2001-2003

Site 11: **LAOLONGQING RAVINE, DONGCHUAN DISTRICT, KUNMUNG CITY, YUNNAN PROVINCE** (103°05' long, 26°02' lat)

Demonstration area: 10.3 km²; demonstration area is typical of many areas of South China

Topography: high mountains, large gullies with steep slopes; 64% of area subject to erosion, much of it severe; frequent landslides and rockslides, with threatening debris flows

Elevation: 1387-2670 m

Precipitation: 846 mm/y, 88% from May to September, some severe

Frost-free period: 258 d

Socio-economic: 4 villages of 681 families with per capita income of $218 (Can., approx) from crop production (39%), forestry (2%), livestock (22%) and side-line industry (37%).

Basic problems: water and gravitational erosion in 64% of area, of which over 60% is severely eroded (annual erosion rates of 6500 to 18,000 t/km²); overall erosion rate is 5163 t/km²; debris flows occur frequently and threaten the 4 villages, their 1249 farmers, and farmers' livelihood

Chinese investment: Information not provided

Project development period: a history of 50 years of some control measures, especially since 1985; current program: 2001-2003.

Part III. Effectiveness and Efficiency

11 On the Urban-Rural Relationship in Western Region Development Program

Shi Yulong and Du Ping

The Background

The Chinese government launched the Western Region Development Strategy in 1999. In October, 2000,the State Council set out the policies pertaining to the development of the western region, including the policies for increasing financial inputs, improving the investment environment, expanding opening up to the outside world, attracting talents, and developing science and education. One year after that, the Office of the Leading Group for Western Region Development of the State Council (OLGWRDSC hereafter) further developed 70 concrete measures to implement the strategy. In February 2002, the overall plan of Western Region Development during the Tenth Five-year Plan (2001-05) period was formulated. These documents provide the information of the overall design, policies, and measures to be taken and the basic goals of the development plan implemented currently.

The Start Point of Western Region Development

The enlarging development gap among different regions in China since the mid-1980s is the most important start point of Western Region Development. Many researches conclude that the 1990s witnessed the most rapid development after 1949, and the development gaps enlarged not only among provinces, but also among the eastern, central and western regions in the same period (Wang and Li, 2000; Lu and Liu, 2001; Zhou and Qi,

2002). Some research further shows that this trend will continue in the near future if no new measures are undertaken (Yang *et al*, 2002) and it has been proved by the existing phenomenon of "club convergence" found by Cai and Du (2000).

The regional development gap in China can be viewed from two perspectives: first, there are very large gaps among the eastern, central, and western region; second, there is a large gap between urban and rural areas. Research by Tsui (1993) has shown that the development gap between the western region and other parts of the nation can in large part be attributed to interregional rural disparity. However, recent research regarding regional development gap in China is only based on disparity among provincial administrative areas, or among the eastern, the central and the western regions, while other research focused on urban-rural development gap without looking into regional disparity issues. It is obvious that the western rural region is the least developed in China if we divide the western region into urban and rural area. If it was linked with the trend of enlarging regional disparity, we believe that narrowing the urban-rural gap in West China should be a key step to reach the goal of western region development.

The Goals of Western Region Development

Regarding the goals of Western Region Development, both government leaders and academic community believe that they should include: (1) to eliminate regional disparity; (2) to facilitate harmonious regional development; (3) to maintain and improve ecological environment in the western region. It is expected that by the middle of the 21st century, the regional disparity in China will be narrowed considerably, the relative underdevelopment of the western region will be reversed, and the western region will be transformed into a prosperous and advanced new region with stable living conditions, united ethnic groups, and beautiful landscape as well (SDPC and OLGWRDSC, 2002).

It must be mentioned that there are also some scholars who emphasized that 'enriching local people first' should be a priority in western development with poverty eradication as the most important task (Hu and

Wen, 2000). Yet, this argument failed to be included in the official documents.

It is obvious that although the overall target of the two opinions is consistent, the different emphases will lead to different policy implications. The former pays more attention to transforming the physical landscape, whereas the latter focuses more on the improvement of people's lives. We think the absence of urban-rural relationship is a missing link in the development plan.

Understanding of the Urban-Rural Relationship in West Region Development

The western region has a fragile ecological environment, poor conditions for agricultural production, and surplus labour with limited land resources. The unfavourable environment leaves little room for agricultural restructuring efforts to increase farmer incomes. Providing labour services to urban sectors becomes a major means of employment for the rural surplus labourers. Therefore, urbanization is a rational choice that can facilitate the development process in West China.

Up to now, both the government and academic circles shared the consensus that urbanization is an effective way to promote the western region development. The functions of agglomeration and conglomeration of major cities in the developing process is then emphasized. The model is described as 'to connect key points (major cities) by lines (major transportation routes) and to promote adjacent areas by the development of key points' in the overall plan. Some scholars further suggest focusing on the large and medium-sized cities, especially the prime cities in western provinces. They think it will promote the development of adjacent areas greatly by urban expansion (Lu and Liu, 2001; Li and Liu, 2001; Gu, 2001; Chen, 2002; Liu and Liu, 2002; Gao and Jing, 2002). Other scholars propose to "give priority to cities, and focus on developing metropolis in West China" (Liu and Song , 2001).

These arguments have received positive responses in policy making. However, what we need to think about is the approach to promote urbanization in West China. What is the channel that links development and urbanization? How can rural people migrate to urban areas and settle there? What are the effective ways to accommodate the immigrants in urban areas? Will the process intensify urban construction only as it has currently done or will it also improve the capacity of rural people to adapt to urban life? These are the key questions we shall discuss in this paper.

Reviews of the Activities and Achievements of the Western Region Development in the Past Three Years

In the past three years, the central government has invested about 200 billion *yuan* for infrastructure construction in western region, over 50 billion *yuan* for ecological improvement and environment protection, and 10 billion *yuan* for education, public health, and culture development. The total reached 260 billion *yuan*. The fiscal transfers from the central government to western region reached 300 billion *yuan* at the same period.

Comparatively speaking, there have been remarkable achievements in the past three years. The growth of GDP and the investments have been extraordinary. In the year of 2000 and 2001, the GDP of the western region increased by 8.5% and 8.7% respectively and is higher than the national average of 7.2%. In the first three-quarters of 2002, the western GDP increased by 9.6%. Figure 11.1 shows the growth of fixed assets investments in western region, which is obviously higher than the national average in 2000-2001, and is also slightly higher than other regions, although in 2002 the performance is not as good as we expected.

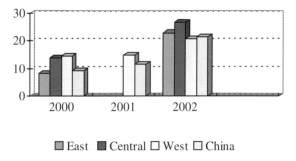

■ East ■ Central □ West □ China

Figure 11.1.   Regional Investment Increase (2000-2002)

Note: data of 2002 are first half of this year;

Source: National Bureau of Statistics of China, China Statistical Yearbook 1999-2002; and www.xinhuanet.com.cn 2002-11-2

The Basic Thinking of Western Region Development

In March 2000, Premier Zhu Rongji, on behalf of the central government, proposed that the major tasks of Western Region Development are: (1) Infrastructure construction, (2) Ecological improvement and environmental protection, (3) Industrial development that takes account of local characteristics, (4) Science, technology, education, culture and public health development, (5) Further opening to the outside world (Zhu, 2000).

As a matter of fact, the Chinese government started to undertake active fiscal policies to offset the negative impacts of the Asian Financial Crisis in 1998 by expanding domestic consumption, boosting the national economy, and increasing employment opportunities. More than 100 billion *yuan* of long-term construction bonds have been issued every year since then to increase domestic demands. The central government has chosen five major fields for investing, including: (1) infrastructure of water conservancy, communication, telecommunication, (2) technological innovation and improvement of enterprises, (3) ecological improvement and environment protection, (4) education and culture development, (5) grain storage facilities.

Comparing the two lists of investment areas above, we can find that infrastructure construction, ecological improvement and environment protection, and science, technology, culture and education development are listed in both. In the past few years, there are about 160 billion *yuan* of national debts, accounting for one third of the total volume issued by central government that have been input to West China. We can conclude that the national debts have played key roles for the rapid increases of investments in the western region in the past few years.

The basic thinking of the central government for western region development is to rely on the function of market mechanism by promoting physical infrastructure quickly, improving the environment of investment, and attracting financial inputs from the outside world. This is consistent with China's marketization process and thus received strong support from the academic community. Following this way of thinking, it is easy to understand that urban construction has played a key role in the process of promoting urbanization.

The Major Characteristics of the Practices in the Past Few Years

In the past few years, the Chinese government has input many financial sources to improve the environment of investment. All these projects shared some common characteristics as below:

(a)   Compared to small and medium-sized projects, mega-projects have attracted more investments

Consistent with the overall plan and the goals of development, a large amount of state capital went to large projects in the past few years. Ten high-profile projects were launched first in 2000, and the total investments were over 100 billion *yuan* (Table 11.1). After that, another 12 large projects were started in 2001 with the total investments reaching more than 200 billion *yuan* (Table 11.2). In 2002, the corresponding numbers increased to 14 and over 300 billion *yuan* (Zeng, 2002). In the past three years, a total of 36 mega-projects were started with the investments over 600 billion *yuan*. Both the number of projects and the average project-scale increased year by year.

These high-profile projects include not only the large infrastructure projects that will cost more than 10 billion *yuan* each, such as Qinghai-Tibet railway, but also a group of some medium-sized projects, such as the project for education, increasing the coverage of radio and television programs in the western region. The construction of these mega-projects has created a good atmosphere for western development, and made great contributions to the rapid increases of the investments and GDP in West China in recent years and it definitely will benefit long-term development in West China. However, the effect on local economic development is uncertain. What we have seen in the working fields of these projects is that more and more instruments have taken the place of human power, and that employment opportunities for local people have not increased significantly after these projects started.

Table 11.1.   The 10 High-Profile Projects started in 2000

Project	Budget for investment (billion *yuan*)
1. Railway from Xi'an to Nanjing (Xi'an—Hefei line)	23.23
2. Railway from Chongqing to Huaihua	18.23
3. Highway (includes national highway trunk lines and the roads connect poverty counties)	N/A
4. Airport construction in West China	5.0*
5. First underground line in Chongqing (Jiaochangkou–xinshancun line)	3.26
6. Natural gas pipeline from Sebei to Lanzhou through Xining	2.25
7. Water conservancy project	
7.1 Water conservancy project in Zipingpu, Min Jiang river, Sichuan	6.2
7.2 Water conservancy project in Shapotou, Ningxia	1.3
8. Converting cultivated land back into forestry and pasture, ecological improvement and project of seedling	N/A
9. Potassic manure project in Qinghai	0.72
10. Infrastructure of higher education in western region	0.61*

Note   : * for the year of 2000
Source: *China Economic Herald*, 14 April 2000.

Table 11.2.   The High-profile Projects Started in 2001

Project	Budget for investment (billion *yuan*)
1. Qinghai-Tibet Railway	26.0
2. Pipeline for natural gas from Xinjiang to Yangtze river delta	40.0
3. Longtan hydropower station in Guangxi	24.3
4. Baise water conservancy project in Guangxi	5.33
5. Nierji water conservancy project in Inner Mongolia	5.45
6. Aluminium with electrolysis and other base of production for nonferrous metals in western region	N/A
7. Industrialization of Y7-200A plane	N/A
8. Ecological improvement, includes converting cultivated land back into forestry and pasture, protecting natural forests etc.	N/A
9. Project for education, increase the coverage of radio and Television program	N/A
10. Xiaowan hydropower station in Yunnan	29.60
11. Renovation of the Talim River in Xinjiang	10.70
12. Comprehensive renovation of the Heihe River in Gansu	2.30

Source: www.cei.gov.cn, 11 May 2001.

(b)   *Compared to the physical infrastructure projects, inputs for human development are insufficient*

From Tables 11.1 and 11.2, we can find that the projects related to human development only constitute a small share in the total investments, and most of them are invested in higher education, broadcasting and television development. However, that which are most in short supply in West China are public services such as basic education, health care, clean water, and energy for living purposes. These shortages affect the daily lives of local people in the western region, especially the lives of the rural residents.

Compared to the large physical infrastructure projects, the human development projects can not only provide basic public services for local people and benefit human resource development, but also help to build up development capacity of the western region. The rural residents can receive professional training that helps them to improve the adaptive capacity to work and live in urban areas, which will finally facilitate urbanization in the west.

Compared to the large physical infrastructure projects, the same amount of investments in human development projects usually could benefit more people and improve their living standards directly. According to the information provided by OLGWRDSC, from 1999 to 2001, the input of 2.8 billion yuan has provided accessible clean water to 13 million rural people in West China. Since 2001, the central government has input about 3 billion *yuan*, which is less than the investments of the first phase of urban light rail system in Chongqing, for the 'Primary and Middle School Building Renovation Project'. With this money, 14,853 schools in 26 provinces in central and West China could have repaired or reconstructed the classrooms.[1] By the end of 2002, about 9 million square metre classrooms will be reconstructed, and 1.8 million children can receive education in a safe space.[2] Nevertheless, it is just such projects that received insufficient inputs from the central and local governments since most of the government resources have been put into physical infrastructure projects. Table 11.3 lists the sources of capital inputs in school renovation projects in Yunnan Province in 2002, showing that 23.4% of the total 740 million *yuan* was raised from non-government sources.

Table 11.3.   The Distribution of Sources for Classroom Reconstruction in Yunnan 2002

Item	Government Budge				Raised fund	Total
	central	provincial	municipal	county		
Amount (million *yuan*)	219.54	191.92	59.72	98.81	173.68	743.67
Share (%)	29.5	25.8	8.0	13.3	23.4	100

Source: www.xinhuanet.com, 20 August 2002.

(c)   *Compared to the investments in urban infrastructure, the investments in rural infrastructure are insufficient*

The strategy of facilitating west development through urbanization has become in practice the promotion of urban construction. Many western cities constructed waterworks, gas stations, and environmental facilities, and have completed some comprehensive renovation projects for urban rivers, and projects for air pollution control. These projects have definitely improved the urban environment greatly in West China. After that, many cities that have some disposable financial resources competed to invest in projects for 'urban beautification'. Magnificent squares, large grassland, beautiful street lamps, and pathway trees were planned by many cities.

The urban environment has been improved greatly in many western cities, but the employment opportunities failed to increase correspondingly. Rural people still have to face the situation of insufficient jobs and the lack of working skills. The result of migration from rural to urban areas was not as significant as it could have been. The thinking of promoting west development through urbanization met new difficulties: the surplus rural labour could only participate in the urban construction as temporary workers. It seems that there is still a very long journey before the agglomeration effect can work.

Some Cases about the Way of Promoting Urbanization by Local Governments

Guided by the thinking of using urbanization to promote west development, western cities started a large scale of urban construction in the past few years. Some large but irrational projects have been started or planned for construction. Here are some examples reported by the news media.

Case 1:   In a small town with a built area of about 3 square kilometres in Changan county, Shanxi province, 2 squares have been completed. The local government released a grand plan that will construct a third square over 10 thousand square metres, 4 street gardens, 2000 square metres grassland, 4 music fountains, and one large sculpture. The investment of the projects will cost over 10 million *yuan*.

Case 2:   Yumen is a small city in Gansu province. Although uncovered channels for drainage can still be found in its residential areas, in 2002 the city spent more than 10 million *yuan* to construct an office building for the municipal government, a main road 80 metres wide, and the largest square in the province.[3]

Case 3:   On December 24, 2002, the "Digital Guizhou Overall Plan for Construction" passed examination by leading experts in Beijing. According to the plan, Guizhou, the poorest province in China, will invest 26 billion *yuan* before 2010 to construct a comprehensive information system.[4]

Case 4:   At the beginning of 2003, the government of Gansu Province declared that it would invest 300 million *yuan* to construct the largest logistic centre of northwest China in Lanzhou, the capital city of the province. The centre will occupy over 13 hectares and the total construction area will be 50 thousands square metres.[5] But the latest research shows that 60% of the completed space of the logistic centre in China is not fully utilized yet. (Yan and Hu, 2002).

These four cases provide us with a typical scenario of urban infrastructure projects in the western region. It is difficult to understand what is going on. If these can be the ways to promote urbanization and the western region development process, we will definitely have to face a disappointing outcome in the near future.

The Effect of the Way to Promote Urbanization in West China

Many scholars agreed that promoting urbanization is one of the most important ways to implement the strategy of Western Region Development, and most local governments have done it by large-scale construction of urban infrastructure. Unfortunately, it seems that this work failed to achieve the desired results. Table 11.4 shows the share of people living in municipal districts of the total population in western provinces. In Sichuan, Guizhou, Shanxi, Ningxia, and Guangxi, the share decreased in 2001. Other provinces only had limited growth.

Table 11.4.   Percentage of People Living in Municipal Districts in the Western Provinces

Region	1999	2000	2001
Chongqing	42.47	44.06	44.19
Sichuan	33.46	35.61	33.56
Guizhou	27.31	25.68	24.15
Yunnan	20.69	20.57	20.84
Tibet	8.97	8.92	9.01
Shanxi	28.88	29.65	29.56
Gansu	27.01	27.35	27.53
Ningxia	31.74	34.30	32.04
Qinghai	16.98	15.78	17.32
Xinjiang	36.47	34.38	36.53
Guangxi	29.11	31.10	29.51
Inner Mongolia	33.60	33.54	34.00
Total	30.33	31.04	35.86

Source: Department of Urban and Rural Plan, Ministry of Construction, *Urban Population Statistics, 1999-2001*.

The limited growth will become even less if the increased population is excluded because of reclassification of the administrative divisions. In 2001, eight counties or cities of the county level, including Changshou in Chongqing, Xindu in Sichuan, Zhaotong in Yunnan, Shangzhou in Shanxi, Wuwei in Gansu, Guyuan in Ningxia, Dongsheng, and Hailaer in Inner Mongolia, upgraded their status to urban district. Millions of people in these eight counties were reclassified as "people living in municipal districts" in Table 11.4.

This unexpected decision to reclassify arose from the "urban-biased" belief that simply constructing urban infrastructure would be enough to absorb more people into the urban areas. The reality is that the increase of urban infrastructure alone did not lower the barrier for rural migrants.

Shifting the Emphasis of Western Region Development from Urban to the Rural Area

After three years of hard work and a great deal of investments, dozens of mega-projects have been launched. We believe it is time to shift the emphasis of West China development to rural areas based on the following observations.

Insufficient Growth of Investment in the Western Region

As mentioned above, the growth of the absolute volume of investment is the most remarkable achievement of west development in the past three years. The share of investments in the western region of nationwide investment, however, has decreased from 18.56% in 2000 to 15.13% in 2001 after a short period of rise (Table 11.5). In nine western provinces, even the absolute volume of investment in fixed capital assets decreased in 2001. Guizhou, Tibet and Qinghai were the only exceptions.

According to the latest statistics, with a total investment of 1,930 billion *yuan*, China had completed more than 4,600 projects by issuing domestic bonds by the end of 2001. In the meantime, a total of 370 billion *yuan* was invested in West China, less than 20% of the total. It is necessary to broaden the fields of investments in the western region if we consider that the increase of investments plays a key role in Western Region Development.

Table 11.5.   Investment in fixed assets of West China
(100 million RMB *yuan*)

Region	1998	1999	2000	2001
Chongqing	493	525.3	572.6	568.5
Sichuan	1145.3	1224.4	1418	1169.4
Guizhou	278.4	311.9	397	413.4
Yunnan	660.4	664	684	513.6
Tibet	41.3	53.6	64.1	85.0
Shanxi	517.6	587.8	653.7	632.3
Gansu	301.5	355.5	395.4	383.6
Qinghai	108.8	117.2	151.1	178
Ningxia	106.8	128.1	157.5	151.9
Xinjiang	514.8	526.7	610.4	608.6
Inner Mongolia	316.8	348.2	423.6	418.3
Guangxi	562.3	578.8	583.3	458.4
Sub-total	5047	5421.5	6110.7	5581
Total in China	28406.2	29854.7	32917.7	36898.4
Share of west (%)	17.77	18.16	18.56	15.13

Source: National Bureau of Statistics of China,
China Statistical Abstract 2002.

Failure to Narrow the Urban-Rural Income Gap in West China

Although great progress has been made in the western region in terms of GDP and investment growth, these achievements have so far failed to narrow the income gap of the residents between West China and other regions. In 2000-2001, the per capita disposable incomes of urban population in west region increased 5.3% annually, lower than the average level of 7.5% for the whole country. In the same period, the per capita net income of rural population in the western region increased by 2.6% annually, lower than the average 3.2% for the whole country. Figures 11.2 and 11.3 show the change of per capita income of the west region as a percentage of the national average in recent years. The trend does not favour the west region.

Figure 11.2. Growth of Urban Residents' Per Capita Disposable Income: Rate of West China as a Percentage of the National Average

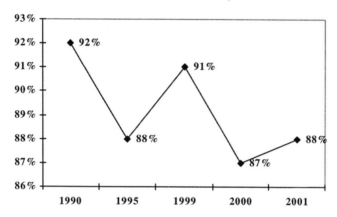

Source: National Bureau of Statistics of China, *China Statistical Yearbook 1999-2002.*

Figure 11.3. Growth of Rural Residents' Per Capita Net Income: Rate of West China as a Percentage of the National Average

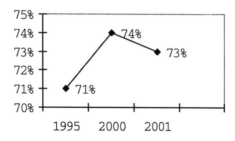

Source: National Bureau of Statistics of China, *China Statistical Yearbook 1999-2002.*

In Table 11.6, we can easily find that the income gap between West China and the national average is larger than that between urban and rural areas. The per capita net income of rural residents in West China was only 25.2% of the per capita disposable income of urban residents in this country. According to the latest research, the development gap among the cities and prefectures within the west provinces has grown larger and larger. By the end of the 1990s, the average gap in per capita GDP between the richest city and the poorest city/prefecture in west provinces (such as those in Sichuan, Guizhou and Shanxi) was about 4 times, similar to the per capita income gap (4.7 times) between Guangdong, the richest province and Guizhou, the poorest province in China. What shocked us is that the per capita income gap between the richest and poorest cities reached 10-30 times in Gansu and Xinjiang, much larger than the gap (12 times) between Shanghai and Guizhou (Fan *et al*, 2001).

Table 11.6.   Per Capita Income of Urban and Rural residents (2001)

Item	Per capita net income of rural residents	Per capita disposable income of urban residents	Per capita rural income as percentage of per capita urban income
West China	1721.19	6017.49	28.6
National	2366.40	6838.06	34.6
Per capita income in West China as percentage of National	72.7	88.0	

Source: National Bureau of Statistics of China,
China Statistical Yearbook 2002.

The growing income disparity is a consequence of the development strategy, which emphasized the construction of physical infrastructure projects, especially large projects in urban areas. Public services such as primary education, public health, water and energy for residential use are short of supply and less emphasized. Without holding to the principle of 'enriching local people first', the West China development would be a failure despite the great improvement of infrastructure in some places of the western region.

Policy Recommendations

(1) The function of market mechanism should not be over-emphasized for Western Region Development. The Western Region Development program should firstly be a development aid program to contain the growing regional disparity. After the first round of large-scale construction of physical infrastructure in western cities, the focus should be shifted to the rural areas. The central government must pay more attention to the improvement of the environment for human settlement in West China.

(2) Promotion of human development should be a goal for the Western Region Development program. From the analyses above, we can find that rural areas in West China are the most difficult place for development and thus are also the best place to test the effect of the planned strategy. If we only concentrated on narrowing the development gap with other regions and harmonizing regional development by constructing grand infrastructure in the western region, the life of local people, especially that of the rural residents, may be ignored to some extent.

(3) Providing equal access to public services for all residents is the responsibility of government. There are multiple causes of the underdevelopment of the rural areas in West China: insufficient infrastructure, weak capacity of R&D, and lack of human capital. If the basic living conditions such as education, public health, clean water and energy for residential use cannot be met, it is difficult to initiate industrial development. As for urbanization, it needs a precondition for rural people to move to urban areas smoothly. Our recommendation is that the small and medium-sized projects that can directly improve the life of local people should be given top priority in the development plan.

(4)   It is rational to promote the urbanization process in West China. Nevertheless, the starting point should not be construction of urban infrastructures, especially irrational projects. Most of the rural residents are unable to share the benefits of large projects in urban areas at this stage. Our suggestion is that the development path should return to the track of poverty alleviation. Urbanization should be promoted through improving the health and skills of the rural people to build up their capability of living and working in urban areas. It is necessary to start more projects that can benefit the daily life of rural residents in the near future.

Notes

1.   Xinhuanet, 10 May 2002.
2.   Xinhuanet, 7 November 2002.
3.   Xinhuanet, 25 December 2002.
4.   *Guizhou Daily*, 25 December 2002.
5.   Xinhuanet, 1 February 2003.

References

1.   Cai, F. and Du,Y. (2000). "Convergence and Divergence of Regional Economic Growth in China", *Economics Research*, 10: 30-37.
2.   Chen, D.S. (2002). "On the Strategical Allocation and Urbanization in the Development of West China",*Tech-economics and Management Research*, 2: 3-4.
3.   Fan, J., Cao, Z.X., Zhang,W.Z., and Xu Y.D. (2001). "The Consideration of Strategic Innovation of West Development Based on the Theories of Economic Geography", *Acta Geographica Sinica*, (56) 6: 711-721.
4.   Gao, X.C. and Jing, J. (2002). "Promoting the Development of Urban Economy by Institutional Innovation", *Guangming Daily*,10 September: 6.
5.   Gu, W.X. (2001). "Enhancing West Development Based on Central Cities", *Urban Studies* (Beijing), 2: 54-58.

6.   Hu, A.G., and Wen, J. (2000). "On the New Models and New Principles Implemented in the Process of West Development," *Management World*, 6: 34-48.

7.   Li, S.T., and Liu, Y. (2001). "Options of Urbanization in West Development", *Urban Studies* (Beijing), 3: 1-7.

8.   Liu, C., and Liu, J.Q. (2002). "The Road of Urbanization in West China", *The Economists* (Chengdu) 5: 83-88.

9.   Liu, F.Y., and Song, L. (2001). "Some Understandings on the West Development", in Chen, D.S. (ed) (2001). *West Development: Great Strategy, New Think Way*, Beijing: Economic Science Press.

10.   Lu, D.D., and Liu, Y. (2001). *Regional Development of China, 2000 – A Development Report of the West*, Beijing: The Commercial Press.

11.   SDPC and OLGWRDSC (2002). *Overall Plan of Western Region Development During the Tenth Five-Year Plan Period*, Beijing: China Planning Press.

12.   Tsui, K.Y. (1993). "Decomposition of China's Regional Inequalities", *Journal of Comparative Economics* 15:1-21.

13.   Wang, M.K., and Li S.T. (2000). *Studies on the Unbalanced Problem of Social and Economic Development among China's Regions*, Beijing: The Commercial Press.

14.   Xi, B.Z. (2002). "The Progress and Outline of West Region Development", *Macro-economy Management*, 2:21-23.

15.   Yan, J.R. and Hu S.W. (2002). "Chinese Economic Forecast Report: Integration of Regional Economy", *Shanghai Stock News*, 9 December: 1.

16.   Yang, X.G., Fan, J., and Zhao Y.X. (2002). "Analysis on the Factors of China's Regional Economic Increase in 1990's", *Acta Geographica Sinica* (57) 6: 701-708.

17.   Zeng, P.Y. (2002). "The Historical Change of National Economy and Social Development", *Macro-economy Management*, 10: 4-6.

18.   Zhou, Y.C. and Qi, Q.W. (2002). "Characteristics of Dynamic Variation of the Inter-Provincial Economic Difference in China in Recent 10 Years", *Geographical Research*, (21) 6: 781-790.

19.   Zhu, R.J. (2000). "Report of the Central Government of China", *People's Daily*, 17 March: 1.

12 The Western Region's Growth Potential

Ding Lu and Elspeth Thomson

Introduction

When China opened its doors to foreign trade and investment two decades ago, it was eastern China which benefited first and most. For a variety of economic, historical, political, geographical and social reasons, it made most sense for foreign companies to start doing business in the eastern provinces. Despite the systematic efforts of the government of the People's Republic to relocate industrial bases away from the coastal cities to the interior of the country in earlier decades, by 1980 the coastal provinces were still China's most industrialized areas, with better infrastructure and human capital stock. Immediate access to maritime shipping routes gave the coastal cities a head start in the race to wealth. On top of this, the central government in Beijing granted preferential policies to attract foreign investment through the 1980s to the early 1990s. Most of these policies, in particular the establishment of 'special economic zones', favoured the coastal regions much more than the rest of the nation. At the same time, some national security rules have not exactly encouraged business in the west: foreigners have long been forbidden to travel in many parts of the interior and west.

It is therefore not surprising that after the launch of the economic reforms in 1978, the development gap between the east and west started to widen at an alarming rate. The increasing inter-regional disparity became of great public concern in the 1990s when officials and citizens living in the west began to express frequently their anger and frustration over the fall in their incomes relative to those in the east (Yang, 1997: 92). It is estimated that some 60 to 100 million people have left the west in search of better opportunities.

The central government began in the early 1990s to look to the western region as the focus of the next phase of development.[1] Deng Xiaoping, China's reform leader, decreed that by the end of the 20th century, by which time the eastern region was expected to have achieved a modest level of prosperity, it would be time to begin allocating more resources to the development of the central and western regions, and that the eastern region must accept this as being in the interest of the country as a whole (Deng, 1993: 374). The 'strategic decision' to make serious plans for the development of the west was formally endorsed at the Central Economic Work Conference held in November 1999. The main objectives of the western development programme were broadly identified as: reducing the economic disparity between east and west, mitigating ethnic tensions, developing the region's natural resources, providing markets for industries in the east plagued with production over-capacity, and restoring damaged ecosystems which have led to serious desertification and flooding in recent years.[2]

As a first step in encouraging investment, developing untapped resources, and reducing the economic disparities, the Chinese leadership chose to make a series of major infrastructure projects – roads, railways, airports, electric power, pipelines, telecommunications, water systems, ecological recovery, industrial parks, urban development – the foundation of the development programme. Construction of this infrastructure is regarded as an indispensable precondition for resource evacuation, business development, and modernization (Guo, 2001; Wang and Wei, 2001; CASS/ NDSRG, 2001).

The particular focus of this article is the transport infrastructure component of the western development programme, specifically, the potential of the new or expanded links to encourage investment and sustain economic development in the region. In committing large sums of money for which there are many other pressing and less risky uses in a developing country as China, the government cannot assume that because new transport infrastructure contributed to growth in eastern China, it will likewise promote economic growth in the west. It is the aim of this article to examine what new transport infrastructure can and cannot do for the west.

We first construct an index to measure the economic gravity between each provincial/regional economy and China's three most developed regions: Beijing-Tianjin, Shanghai, and Hong Kong-Guangzhou. We then use this gravity index to project an income level for each province/region which corresponds with its market potential.

We also use freight traffic data to construct proxies for market- and supply-access conditions in each provincial/regional economy. Based on these results, we then estimate (a) whether the status-quo regional development levels have matched the pattern of market- and supply-access conditions across provinces/regions; and (b) the extent to which China's ambitious plans for infrastructure development in the western region will increase its growth potential.

After reviewing the relevant literature we outline our methodology which is designed to overcome data constraints. In Sections 3 and 4, we examine the gravity effect of China's three growth hubs on the economic potential of the western provinces/regions, and present our findings regarding the market- and supply-access conditions of each of the provincial/regional economies, and discuss their impact on the growth potential of the western region. We summarise our key findings and their policy implications in the final section.

Literature and Methodology

Relevant literature

Over the past half-century, econometric techniques, ranging from the very basic to the highly sophisticated, have been employed in an attempt to predict the relationship between the availability of transport infrastructure and economic growth, investment in industry and services, and increased employment (Sahoo and Saxena, 1999; Fox and Porca, 2001). There is much debate over the opportunity costs, direction of causality among the various requirements for economic growth, and best sequencing of transport projects in relation to other crucial infrastructure (Kessides, 1993; World Bank, 1994).

Literature on economic gravity has drawn much attention in recent years. Early studies on the issue include the model by Harris (1954), which relates the market potential (MP) for goods and services produced in a location i to the distance-weighted economic activities in all locations:

$$MP_i = \sum_j^R \frac{GDP_j}{d_{ij}} \tag{1}$$

Lermer (1997) uses (1) to evaluate potentials in per capita income growth in post-reform Eastern European economies based on their access to Western European markets. Based on a model developed by Krugman and Venables (1995), Redding and Venables (2000) derive a set of theory-consistent measures of both market and supply access. According to their measurement, per capita income or average wage rate in an economy is determined by its market- and supply-access conditions:

$$y_i = f(MA_i, SA_i) \tag{2}$$

where y_i is per capita income or average wage.

Market access in economy i is defined as the sum of all foreign trading partners' import demand for economy i's export, which is the sum of transport-cost-weighted (or distance-weighted) imports of all trading partners, plus economy i's demand for its own output. A simplified form of market access could be written as:

$$MA_i = \sum_i (Y_i)^\gamma (T_{ij})^\delta + Y_i^\gamma (T_{ii})^\sigma \tag{3}$$

where Y_j is the income at economy j; T_{ij} is the transportation cost factor between economies i and j. For economy i, Tii is the average transportation cost factor within its territory. γ is the elasticity of import (from economy i) to income level in economy j. δ and σ are parameters for the transport cost factor for inter-economy and local transport, respectively.[3]

Similarly supply access is the sum of economy i's trading partners' exports that come to economy i as its import, plus this economy's demand for its own output. For economy i, this could be written as:

$$SA_i = \sum_j (Y_j)^\varphi (T_{ij})^\delta + Y_i^\varphi (T_{ii})^\sigma \tag{4}$$

where φ is the elasticity of export (to economy i) to output (income) level in economy j. To estimate the parameters, one must know pair-wise trade volumes between each pair of trade partners, the transportation cost (usually being replaced by distance as a proxy), and their income (GDP) levels. This would allow running the following regression:

$$\ln (X_{ij}) = \alpha + \varphi \ln(Y_i) + \gamma \ln(Y_j) + \delta \ln(T_{ij}) + u_{ij} \qquad (5)$$

where X_{ij} is the pair-wise trade volume between economy i and j while   is constant and u_{ij} is the error term.

Data constraints and methodology

Data

Table 12.1 provides the means and standard deviations of the key variables, namely, per capita GDP, freight traffic, GDP growth per annum, waterway's share in non-port freight traffic, state-owned enterprise (SOE) share in industrial output, and proportion of population with education of/above secondary level.

This information puts the western region's poverty and remoteness into national perspective. Per capita GDP is only a third that of the wealthy eastern region, and per capita freight traffic is just about half. The mean railway distance to the three hubs is over 1,000 kilometres longer, there is much less water transport available, state industry dominates the economy, and only slightly more than a third of the population has secondary education or above.

Constraints and Methodology

The major data constraint in this study is the non-availability of pair-wise trading data among Chinese provinces/regions. This constraint makes it impossible to run regression (5) to estimate the parameters. To overcome this barrier, we decided to treat China's three economic hubs, namely, Shanghai, Beijing-Tianjin, and Hong Kong-Guangzhou, together accounting for 28% of China's total GDP in 2001, as the country's gravity centres. We then calculated each province.

Table 12.1.   Key Variables: Means and Standard Deviations

	Year	West Region		Central Region		East Region	
		Mean	Standard Deviation	Mean	Standard Deviation	Mean	Standard Deviation
Per capita GDP (yuan, current price)	1996	3572	844	4161	495	8991	4182
	2001	5273	1215	5949	978	14748	8523
Freight traffic (10,000 ton)	1996	23864	17193	45949	16639	52640	28731
Per capita freight (ton)		8.48	3.78	9.16	6.66	15.32	5.70
Freight traffic (10,000 ton)	2001	26129	17715	53111	23879	57341	29996
Per capita freight (ton)		9.08	4.68	10.48	8.94	17.13	9.31
Real GDP Growth Rate Per Annum	1996-2001	9.20	0.95	9.75	0.64	10.23	1.19
Mean Railway Distance to the Three Hubs (km)	2000	2598	870	1199	142	1560	479
Waterways' share in non-port freight traffic	1996-2001	1.53	2.39	6.06	4.99	12.09	11.57
SOE Share in Industrial Output	1998	79.97	7.62	66.05	8.66	52.22	20.67
Proportion of Population with Education of/ above Secondary	1998	36.58	11.37	47.27	4.98	54.13	9.80

Note: The East region is comprised of Beijing, Shanghai, Tianjin, Hebei, Shandong, Jiangsu, Zhejiang, Guangdong, Fujian, Liaoning, Jilin, Heilongjiang, and Hainan. The Central region is comprised of Hubei, Hunan, Henan, Shanxi, Anhui, and Jiangxi. The West region is comprised of Xinjiang, Neimengu, Chongqing, Qinghai, Ningxia, Guangxi, Yunnan, Sichuan, Shaanxi, Gansu, Tibet, and Guizhou.

Source: China State Statistical Bureau, *China Statistical Yearbook*, Beijing: China Statistical Press, 1996-2002; *Zhongguo xinbian jiaotong luyou dituce* (China Newly Compiled Transport Tour Mapbook), Xian Map Press, 2001; National Railway Transportation Information Service, http://www.he183.com/lieche. Ministry of Communications web site, http://www.moc.gov.cn.

region's market potential index, as defined by (1) the railway distance for dij, and GDP data of the hubs. As for each hub, the 'distance' to itself (or within its own territory) is approximated by $d_{ii} = 1/3 \cdot (\text{Area}/\pi)^{\frac{1}{2}}$, which gives the average distance between two points in a circular area (Redding and Venables, 2000). Finally we assume that a provincial economy's per capita GDP is a function of its market potential, so we estimate the following equation by regression:

$$\ln \quad y_i = \alpha + \beta_1 \ln MP_i + \Sigma \beta_k x_k + \varepsilon_i \qquad (6)$$

where yi is per capita GDP; α, β_1, β_k are parameters, x_k is one of the other variables that may affect the per capita GDP, and ε_i is the error term.

Second, we used freight traffic data by region as a proxy for each province/region's total export and import of goods, which is a sum of $(Y_j)^{\gamma}$ and $(Y_j)^{\varphi}$. We defined a proxy for market access condition as:

$$M_i = d_{ii}F_i + \Sigma_j d_{ij}F_j \qquad (7)$$

where F_j is province j's freight traffic, and a proxy for supply-access condition as:

$$S_i = d_{ii}F_i + \Sigma_j d_{ij}F_i \qquad (8)$$

We then estimated the following equation to evaluate provincial/regional per capita GDP potential:

$$\ln \quad y_i = \alpha + \beta_1 \ln M_i + \beta_2 \ln S_i + \Sigma \beta_k x_k + \varepsilon_i \qquad (9)$$

To evaluate the growth potentials, we also ran the following regression:

$$\ln \quad G_i = \alpha + \beta_1 \ln M_i + \beta_2 \ln S_i + \Sigma \beta_k x_k + \varepsilon_i \qquad (10)$$

where G_i is growth rate of GDP in province/region i during a period, M_i and S_i are initial levels of M_i and S_i, and x_k refers to other relevant factors. An alternative version of (10) is

$$\ln \quad G_i = \alpha + \beta_1 \ln Mg_i + \beta_2 \ln Sg_i + \Sigma \beta_k x_k + \varepsilon_i \qquad (11)$$

where Mg_i and Sg_i are the growth rate of M_i and S_i during the period.

Gravity of the Three Hubs

Figure 12.1 provides the estimated market potential of each province/ region in descending order and per capita GDP in 2001. Not surprisingly, Shanghai was found to have the highest market potential and highest per capita GDP. Guangdong has the next highest market potential, but per capita GDP is considerably less than that of Beijing which has the third highest market potential. After the largest four (Shanghai, Guangdong, Beijing and Tianjin), which are themselves assumed here to be the gravity hubs, the next six provinces among the top ten all border one of the hubs: Hainan (rank 5), Hunan (rank 7), and Jiangxi (rank 9) all border Guangdong; Zhejiang (rank 6) and Jiangsu (rank 8) both border Shanghai; and Hebei (rank 10) borders Beijing. Most of the provinces/regions which make up the western region have low market potential indices. The area with the least market potential is Tibet, but it is Guizhou, considerably higher up the list, which has the lowest per capita GDP.

Table 12.2 provides the estimates for the model (6): the determinants of per capita GDP. The R squared value in Regression I suggests that the 3-hub market potential index alone can explain over 53% of the per capita GDP differences across provinces/regions. With the education factor included, Regression II explains over 63% of the cross-province/region per capita GDP differences. The positive and significant coefficient estimated for ln MPi implies that a one-percentage point increase in the 3-hub market potential index is associated with a 0.3 percentage point increase in per capita GDP. Meanwhile, a one-percentage point increase in the proportion of population with secondary or higher education is associated with 1.78 percentage point increase in per capita income.

Figure 12.1.   Market Potential Index and Per Capita GDP (2001)

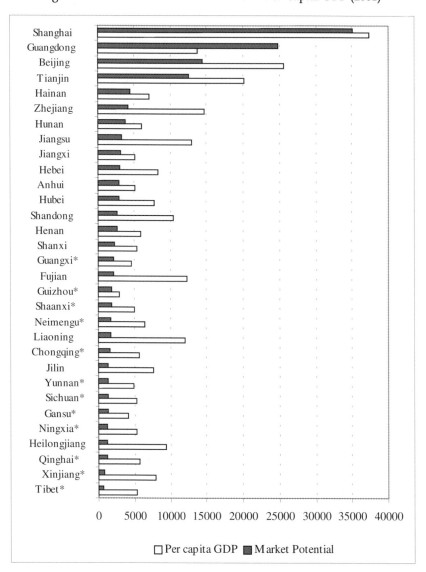

Notes: (a) * denotes the provinces/regions making up China's western region.
        (b)   market potentials are calculated according to (1).

Table 12.2.   Estimates for Model (4): Determinants of Per Capita GDP

	I	II
Constant	7.4967	7.1582
Ln MP$_i$	0.4480 ***** (5.7729)	0.3002 ***** (3.3676)
Education		1.7873 **** (2.6994)
R^2 F-statistics Prob>F N	0.5347 33.3263 0.0000 31	0.6308 23.9190 0.0000 31

Notes: (1) 'Education' refers to proportion of population with secondary and above education.
(2) Figures in brackets are t-statistics.
(3) Significance level: ***** 99; **** 95; *** 90; ** 80; * 70.

The per capita GDP that is projected by the growth potential index for each province/region is presented in column 3 of Table 12.3. Most of the provinces/regions making up the western region fall very low in terms of projected per capita income, but there is no clear trend in their real per capita incomes as percent of the estimated ones. Two regions and one province in the west, Xinjiang, Tibet, and Qinghai overshot their projected per capita income by 127–197%, while most of other western provinces/regions achieved per capita income levels well below the projected ones, with Guizhou and Shanxi being the lowest.

Table 12.3.   Per capita GDP Projected

2001 Per capital GDP	Actual	Projected by 3-hub Market Potential Model	Real Value as of Projected (%)	Projected by Market and Supply Conditions	Real Value as of Projected (%)
Shanghai	37382	25866	145	38553	97
Guangdong	13730	16097	85	10601	130
Beijing	25523	21640	118	17216	148
Tianjin	20154	15769	128	15793	128
Hainan	7135	9462	75	13097	54
Zhejiang	14655	8955	164	11137	132
Hunan	6054	8783	69	7298	83
Jiangsu	12922	8781	147	12342	105
Jiangxi	5221	7775	67	7189	73
Hebei	8362	9101	92	8045	104
Anhui	5221	7304	71	7120	73
Hubei	7813	8470	92	9688	81
Shandong	10465	7839	133	7104	147
Henan	5924	8500	70	7589	78
Shanxi	5460	8519	64	8037	68
Guangxi	4668	6644	70	5819	80
Fujian	12362	6524	189	7148	173
Guizhou	2895	5387	54	4341	67
Shaanxi	5024	6812	74	6267	80
Neimengu	6463	7603	85	7016	92
Liaoning	12041	8639	139	9757	123
Chongqing	5654	5916	96	5849	97
Jilin	7640	7657	100	8934	86
Yunnan	4866	4739	103	3338	146
Sichuan	5250	5817	90	5307	99
Gansu	4163	5415	77	4639	90
Ningxia	5340	6079	88	6845	78
Heilongjiang	9349	7426	126	8025	116
Qinghai	5735	4529	127	4674	123
Xinjiang	7913	5236	151	5253	151
Tibet	5307	2692	197	4148	128

Two observations can be made from the above results. First, these results confirm a fundamental thesis in transportation/geographic economics, i.e., the higher the transport costs between a centre and a periphery location, the lower the potential income level that periphery location may achieve. Transportation distance or cost is found to be a major cause of income disparity in China.

Second, those provinces/regions with per capita incomes well below their 3-hub-gravity projected levels may be constrained in reaching their potential by factors other than transportation costs, while provinces/regions with per capita incomes above their potential, may have as a result of various particularly favourable factors, been able to overcome their transportation constraints.

Indeed, there are many factors affecting per capita income, and concomitantly, economic growth and development. For instance, quantity and quality of local human and physical capital stock, entrepreneurial competence, and connections with foreign capital and expertise are important determinants of a provincial/regional economy's growth potential. The central government's fiscal policy in terms of taxes or subsidies is also pivotal, as are inter-regional differences in policies towards business and the degree of marketization in social-economic institutions. Growth potential also depends on factors such as the existence of a desire for growth and change on the part of the peoples in the target area, resource prices (including labour costs), political and social stability, reliability of legal and financial infrastructure, access to new technologies, and an awareness of the transport options. To identify and capture some of the most relevant factors, we proceed to use freight traffic data to construct a market- and supply-access model for further analysis.

Impact of Market- and Supply-Access Conditions

After working out the proxies for market- and supply-access conditions based on (7) and (8), we ran several regressions according to (9), (10), and (11). Table 12.4 provides a summary of the impact of market- and supply-access conditions on income and growth.

Compared to the three-hub model in the previous section, these results should be more robust because they take into account the gravity effects of all the provincial/regional economies. The projected per capita GDP levels are displayed in column 5 of Table 12.3. At least six observations can be made here.

Table 12.4.   Impact of Market- and Supply-Access Conditions on per capita GDP and GDP Growth

	Per Capita GDP 2001 (logarithm)		GDP Growth Rate per annum 1996-2001 (logarithm)		GDP Growth Rate per annum 1996-2001 (logarithm)	
Constant	5.9629		0.0361		0.0817	
ln Mi	0.3844 (1.8095)	***	0.0154 (2.9474)	*****	0.3664 (2.7406)	****
ln Si	-0.1963 (-2.5377)	****	-0.0078 (-3.6674)	*****	-0.0758 (-1.7996)	***
Initial per capita GDP			0.0034 (0.6005)		0.0034 (0.5719)	
Waterway share	2.1626 (3.4260)	*****	-0.0343 (-1.7595)	***	-0.0273 (-1.2462)	*
Education	2.9652 (4.1604)	*****	-0.0026 (-0.0995)		-0.0056 (-0.2773)	
SOE share			-0.0402 (-2.8966)	*****	-0.0327 (-2.9915)	*****
R^2 F-statistics Prob > F N	0.7376 18.2685 0.0000 31		0.6675 8.0283 0.0001 31		0.5845 5.6262 0.0009 31	

Notes: (1) Figures in italics refer to the per annum growth rate of the variable.
(2) Waterway share refers to the share of waterway freight traffic in total non-port freight traffic.
(3) SOE share refers to the share of state-owned enterprises in total industrial output.
(4) Significance level: ***** 99; **** 95; *** 90; ** 80; * 70.
(5) In growth rate analysis, per capita GDP, M and S are initial year (1996) values. Waterway share, education, and SOE share are 1998 values.

First, M_i, the proxy for market-access conditions, is significant and positively correlated with per capita GDP level. It also has a significant positive impact on growth. This is as would be expected. This confirms what is known to be the case almost universally, i.e., anything which increases market access and, in particular, reduces transportation distance/ costs, generally encourages investment and helps sustain growth by improving the movement of people and goods in terms of access, speed, frequency, capability (quantities, types and combinations), dependability, safety (lower incidence of harm to fragile goods and passengers), and efficiency (fewer transferrals en route). It also enables economies of scale in that more goods will be able to be produced and shipped, making for more efficient use of the region's resources.

The fundamental economic contribution that transport infrastructure can make in any location is to facilitate transactions between producers and consumers by reducing the time, effort and money required to bridge distances. It enlarges the area that consumers and industry can draw upon for resources and products/services, and expands the market to which a given enterprise can distribute its products economically. Consumers and producers alike benefit from a wider field from which to obtain what they need at lower costs.[4]

Second, S_i, the proxy for supply-access conditions, has a significantly negative, but much smaller, impact on per capita GDP level and growth. This corresponds well with the definition of supply-access conditions which determine an economy's tendency to import goods and services from other economies, a 'leakage' in national income accounting.

Third, according to the convergence hypothesis, we would expect the coefficient for initial per capita GDP to be negative and perhaps significant. The estimated coefficient is, however, insignificantly positive and very small. The absence of evidence for conditional convergence for this period (1996-2001) is possibly due to other factors associated with the initial level of per capita income, such as better legal and financial infrastructure and quality of local governance, which are favourable to economic growth but not taken into account in this analysis.

Fourth, education level continues to display strong and positive correlation with per capita income level, as in the three-hub-gravity analysis.

It, however, failed to display a significant impact on growth during the period under investigation. A possible reason is the fact that the length of the sample period (five years) is not long enough to allow the labour force quality effect to be significant. Another possible explanation is the existence of the large mobile ('floating') labour population across regions, which makes the actual quality of the labour input different from what is reflected by the statistics.

Fifth, waterway share is significantly and positively related to per capita income, indicating that provincial/regional economies with better access to waterway transport are generally richer. However, it is negatively (less significantly) related to growth. This may be explained by two factors: the provincial economies with better access to waterway transport tend to be more open to international trade and would have thus been more affected by the Asian Financial Crisis of 1997-98 and the world economic slowdown of 1999-2001. Another factor may have been the West China Development Plan launched in the autumn of 1999. With state capital investment amounting to hundreds of billions of *yuan*, the growth in the western provinces/regions, which all have little or no access to waterway transportation, was boosted. This factor may also explain the insignificant convergence effect presented earlier.

Sixth, the share of SOEs had a significantly negative impact on growth. This is consistent with the findings of Démurger et al (2002) on the provincial/regional growth factors in the 1990s, and reflects the efficiency problems of the SOEs and their restructuring in recent years. Hundreds of SOEs have either been closed or merged, and hundreds of thousands of workers have been laid off. The economies of the provinces/regions that were dominated by SOEs would most certainly have been affected.

Of the above findings, the first and second are most relevant to the evaluation of the transportation infrastructure development in Western China. Basically, our results suggest that if the transportation-cost reduction improves market- and supply-access conditions by the same proportions, the combined (net) effect on income and growth should be positive since the absolute value of coefficient M is larger than that of S. There is, however, one problem in this process: For any particular location, the transportation-cost reduction may not have an equal effect on the market- and supply-access conditions. Tibet is an important example. The 1,907-km long Tibet-Qinghai railway is a major transport project launched as part of the western development programme. In order to learn more about this project's net impact on Tibet's income potential, we estimated the following regressions using year 2001 data.

$$\ln \text{PCFreight}_i = 1.2736 + 4.3265 \text{ TelPen}_i + 0.1017 \text{ ln RailDen}, \quad (12)$$
$$(5.0234) \qquad (6.1593)$$
$$R^2 = 0.77, \quad \text{F-statistics} = 46.78, \text{Prob} > F = 0.0000, N = 31$$

where PCFreight is per capita freight traffic (in tons), TelPen is telephone penetration rate,[5] and RailDen is railway length (km) per 10,000 square km. Figures in brackets are t-statistics.

$$\ln S_i = -4.9755 + 1.1643 \ln \text{Freight}_i \qquad (13)$$
$$(17.2724)$$
$$R^2 = 0.91, \text{F-statistics} = 298.33, \text{Prob} > F = 0.0000, N = 31$$

$$\ln M_i = 3.9079 + 0.3390 \ln \text{Freight}_i \qquad (14)$$
$$(5.1507)$$
$$R^2 = 0.48, \text{F-statistics} = 26.53, \text{Prob} > F = 0.0000, N = 31$$

Construction of the Tibet-Qinghai railway will raise Tibet's rail density from nil to 15.63 kilometres per 10,000 square kilometre. At the same time, we assume that Tibet's telephone penetration rate could rise from its 2001 level of 5.7%, to that of Qinghai in 2001, 9.1%. From (12) we estimated that Tibet's per capita freight traffic would reach 1.95 tons, equivalent to a gross freight traffic of 5,093 thousand tons per year, almost three times its actual freight traffic in 2001. Next, we use this freight traffic figure to project indices for market- and supply-access conditions according to (13) and (14). The projected indices of M and S are 412.98 and 9.79, much higher than 374.35 and 2.21, their values calculated from the actual 2001 data.

However, when we applied these results to the model in column one of Table 12.4, we projected Tibet's potential per capita GDP to be only 3,212 *yuan*. This is not only much lower than 5,307 *yuan*, the actual per capita GDP of Tibet in 2001, but also lower than 4,148 *yuan*, the predicted per capita GDP using the actual M and S data in 2001. In other words, the net effect of the Tibet-Qinghai railway project would be to reduce the per capita GDP potential according to these estimates.

This counter-intuitive result is obtained because although both M and S would increase after the railway is built, they would increase disproportionately: while M would increase from 374.35 to 412.98 by 10%, S would increase more than four fold from 2.21 to 9.79. Such disproportional impacts are a result of the value gap between the estimated coefficients for freight in (13) and (14) respectively, which are regression outcomes from the data of all provinces/regions. The limit of such a prediction, which is based on average conditions rather than local conditions, is obvious. Is this result totally absurd and incomprehensible?

Ideally new transport links have a stimulating effect on investment, employment, incomes, and consumption. They are expected to trigger self-reinforcing agglomeration, multiplier-accelerator processes, and economies of scale. However, geographers and transport economists have observed that a central area in which a new link is built may grow at the expense of surrounding areas (Holtz-Eakin and Schwartz, 1995; Stephanades, 1990; Thompson, Weller and Terrie, 1992). In the vocabulary of regional planning, for every spread effect there is a countervailing backwash effect. Myrdal (1957), the economics Nobel Laureate who devised this concept, observed that reductions in transport costs resulting from a new transport link in one area could cause peripheral areas to become less economically attractive. Labour and resources begin to flow at an accelerating rate to the centre benefiting from the new transport link and forces of agglomeration and economies of scale take root. As it is usually the best resources the periphery has to offer that are made available, and the most able among the labour force who self-select, the surrounding areas rapidly deteriorate economically. In extreme cases, any fledgling economic activity would leak out, and the target region never recovers. Our numerical exercise above, though oversimplified, illustrates this phenomenon, and should possibly be regarded as a warning.

Concluding Remarks

In this paper we set out to determine whether or not the status-quo regional development levels match the pattern of market- and supply-access conditions across regions, and to estimate the extent to which China's ambitious plans for infrastructure development in the western region will increase its growth potential. The main findings are as follows:

(1) Transportation distance or cost between each provincial/regional economy and the nation's growth centres is a key determinant of the income and growth potentials of each. Differences in the transportation-cost denominated market- and supply-access conditions are a major cause of inter-regional income disparity.

(2) The education level of a province/region's residents, and its access to waterway transportation can explain a significant part of status quo per capita income differences. However, they did not appear to be a major constraint on growth over the five-year period under investigation.

(3) The extent of institutional reforms matters a great deal in growth-performance differences across provincial economies. This is indicated by the significantly negative impact of state-owned enterprise shares in industrial output on growth rate.

(4) Whether an infrastructure project which reduces transportation costs will raise per capita income potentials in a specific region, depends on the relative magnitudes of its impacts on market - and supply-access conditions.

No matter what techniques are employed by academics or business people attempting to determine the feasibility of various business locations, there can be no doubt that the cost structure of most economic activities will be dominated by transport costs. If any periphery-located industry is to succeed, the costs of all the inputs, equipment, storage, advertising, and packaging must be kept considerably below what they would be in centres closer to the market destinations in order to counteract the high cost of shipping.

The new rail and road transport links planned for western China are crucial in the government's goal to reduce regional disparities, but they are not all that matters. As pointed out by Hu Angang, a leading Chinese economic strategist, 'Infrastructure spending alone will not solve the problem'.[7] Market-access conditions can be improved by institutional changes and policy reforms. Without sufficient improvement in overall market accessibility, lower transportation costs could actually accelerate the decline of periphery centres and industries, as warned by Myrdal.

The cautious opinion that public infrastructure projects in the development of western China may not yield immediate economic benefits is also shared by Chinese leaders, who have stressed repeatedly that economic progress there will take much longer than it did in the east. They have pleaded for all involved to be patient. President Jiang Zemin himself noted in 1999 that the Chinese government is prepared to 'spend decades or even a whole century of effort to build a western region marked by economic prosperity, social progress, stable lifestyle, national unity, and beautiful mountains and rivers.' The government seems not to be expecting the outlays of its huge investment to be recouped, assuming that the societal gains over the long run will greatly outweigh financial returns. It recognizes that transport infrastructure per se, can be at the same time unprofitable, certainly in the short run, but economically beneficial in longer terms with many non-quantifiable benefits. Indeed, the government is very much hoping that the new transport infrastructure will also contribute to the social and political unification of this multiracial region.

There are certainly many issues beyond the ambit of our simple gravity analysis. There is no doubt that the transport infrastructure projects will not have a uniform effect across the western region. It is a vast area with enormous economic disparities within itself, and there are thousands of villages and townships for which a new, or more direct linkage is not planned. Moreover, in western China, some of the construction of the new transport infrastructure will be ahead of demand and some behind. Planning ahead of demand means planning for the provision of services – food, lodging, medical, educational, financial – in advance of the consumers' being ready, able or even present to make use of them. It involves risk in that under- or over-estimating service capacity can cause great financial loss. Planning behind demand means planning for services for which demand is immediate. While much of the existing land transport is either non-existent or very poor, the government faces the risk that some of the new links will be woefully under-utilized or, on the other hand, hopelessly under scale. Estimating future usage involves making assumptions about population growth and the relative attractiveness of the west to potential investors, entrepreneurs, and job-seekers.

Notes

1. The region targeted for development was initially comprised of six provinces: Sichuan, Guizhou, Yunnan, Shaanxi, Gansu and Qinghai; three autonomous regions: Xizang (Tibet), Ningxia and Xinjiang; and one centrally administered municipality: Chongqing. Two more autonomous regions – Inner Mongolia and Guangxi – were added later, and Xian (Shaanxi), Chengdu (Sichuan), Guiyang (Guizhou), Kunming (Yunnan) and Lhasa were designated 'economic development zones'. Other economic 'belts' are now being considered along main railway lines and the upper reaches of the Yangtze River.

2. 'Chronicle of Events in Developing Western China', a bulletin (special issue) published online by the Hong Kong Trade and Development Council, July 2000. http://www.tdctrade.com/alert/chwest07d.htm (5 Sept. 2001).

3. Once   is estimated, one may want to set   to be a fraction of   in order to capture the likelihood that internal transport costs are less than external transport costs (Redding and Venables, 2000).

4. Beyond that, we would also expect that the construction of transport projects may have a positive short-term effect on per capita GDP by creating temporary employment in planning, construction and supporting services. There will also be certain backward linkages, i.e., the expansion and creation of industries producing the materials needed for the construction, such as cement, and a wide variety of metal and synthetic building materials.

5. Telephone penetration rate is the number of local telephone subscribers divided by the population, calculated from data in *China Statistical Yearbook 2002*.

6.   Backwash effects (or polarization effects) are negative externalities resulting from an investment such as a transport infrastructure project, while spread effects (trickle down effects) are positive externalities from such an investment.
7.   'China's Noisy Campaign to Develop West Falling on Deaf Ears', *Agence France-Presse Online*, 23 Oct. 2000 (25 Aug. 2001).
8.   *Xinhua News Agency*, 18 June 1999.

References

1.   Chinese Academy of Social Sciences Northwest Development Strategy Research Group (CASS/NDSRG) (2001). "Xibei da kaifa de zhanlue xuanze" (Strategy Choices in the Western Development Programme), *Zhongguo gongye jingji* (China Industrial Economy), 1: 35-42 and 2: 38-47.
2.   Démurger, Sylvie, Jeffrey D. Sachs, Wing T. Woo, Shuming Bao, and Gene Chang (2002). "The Relative Contributions of Location and Preferential Policies in China's Regional Development". *China Economic Review* 13 (4): 444-465.
3.   Deng Xiaoping (1993). *Deng Xiaoping wenxuan* (Selected Works of Deng Xiaoping) III, Beijing: People's Press.
4.   Guo Mingan (2001). "Xibu kaifa zhong zhengfu zi de zhongdian" (Government Investment Focal Points in the Western Development Programme), *Touzi yanjiu* (Investment Research), 4: 47-9.
5.   Fox, William F. and Sanela Porca (2001). "Investing in Rural Infrastructure". *International Regional Science Review*, 24 (1): 108-11.
6.   Kessides, C. (1993)." The Contributions of Infrastructure to Economic Development: A Review of Experience and Policy Implications", *World Bank Discussion Paper* No. 213.
7.   Krugman, Paul and A. Venables (1995). "Globalization and the inequality of nations". *Quarterly Journal of Economics*, 110: 857-880.
8.   Harris, C. (1954). "The market as a factor in the localization of industry in the United States". *Annals of the Association of American Geographers*, 44: 315-48.

9.   Holtz-Eakin, D. and A.E. Schwartz (1995). "Spatial Productivity Spillovers from Public Infrastructure: Evidence from State Highways". *International Tax and Public Finance*, 2: 459-68.

10.   Lermer, E. (1988). "Measures of openness". In R. Baldwin (ed), *Trade Policy Issues and Empirical Analysis*, Chicago: University of Chicago Press: 137-200.

11.   Myrdal, Gunnar (1957). *Economic Theory and Underdeveloped Regions*, London: G. Duckworth.

12.   Redding, Stephen and Anthony J. Venables (2000). "Economic Geography and International Inequality". *CEPR Discussion Paper* no. 2568. London: Centre for Economic Policy Research.

13.   Sahoo, Satyananda and K.K. Saxena (1999). "Infrastructure and Economic Development: Some Empirical Evidence". *Indian Economic Journal*, 47 (2): 54.

14.   Stephanades, Y.J. (1990). "Distributional Effects of State Highway Investment on Local and Regional Development". *Transportation Research Record*, 1274: 156-64

15.   Thompson, G.L., B. Weller and E.W. Terrie (1992). "New Perspectives on Highway Investment and Economic Growth". *Transportation Research Record*, 1395: 81-7.

16.   World Bank (1994). *World Development Report. Infrastructure for Development*. Oxford: Oxford University Press.

17.   Wang Luolin and Wei Houkai (2001). "Wo guo xibu kaifa de zhanlue ji fazhan qianjing" (The Strategy and Prospects for China's Western Development Programme), *Zhongguo gongye jingji* (China Industrial Economy), 3: 5-19.

18.   Yang Dali L. (1997). *Beyond Beijing: Liberalization and the Regions in China*. London: Routledge, 1997.

13 Measuring the Impact of the "Five Mega- Projects"

Lin Ling and Liu Shiqing[1]

After experiencing great development along the eastern seaboard, the Chinese government initiated the West China Development Strategy in 1999. The strategy of opening up the eastern coast first started with setting up five "special economic zones" including Shenzhen, Zhuhai, Shantou, Haikou and Xiamen in the early 1980s and the practice was expanded to include the whole eastern coastal regions. The West China Development Strategy started with five grand projects – the project of environmental treatment and protection, the project of the West-to-East natural gas transportation, the project of the West-to-East electricity transmission, the project of South-to-North water diversion (west line), and the project of the Qinghai-Tibet railroad. The five projects are expected to lay a foundation for the future development of the West. This paper attempts to evaluate the effects of the "Five Grand Projects".

Policy Goals of West China Development

West China has ten features: (1) a long history: actually, the region has been regarded as the cradle of Chinese civilization; (2) a vast region: it makes up about 70% of the territory of China; (3) low density of population: only about 28% of the national average density; (4) 90% of minorities of China reside in the West; (5) the long continental borderline, which makes up 90% of the national borderline of China; (6) the region is rich in natural resources such as oil, gas, hydro-power, non-ferrous and rare minerals; (7) the region is located at the upper reaches of the major rivers of China and its fragile ecological environment implies large potential impacts on the lower reaches of these rivers and the rest of the country; (8) the regional infrastructure is backward: the status of railways, roads, aviation, and communications lags behind the national level; (9) educational, scientific and health standards seriously lag behind the national level; (10) low per-capita GDP: equivalent to 67% of the national level, and 39% of the eastern region's level. Despite the existence of some kind of advantageous industries in resource exploitation, arms manufacturing, and mechanical equipment manufacturing in the West, the industrialization level is generally still in the primary stage of development. Consequently, the level of economic development is low. There is a striking contrast between the region's magnificent history and its reality of backwardness and also a contrast between the prosperity of the eastern region and the poverty of the western region. If this situation persists, the political stability of China will be in jeopardy.

Against this backdrop, the Chinese government set the policy goals for the West China Development as: (1) Narrowing the gap between the eastern and western regions by promoting the mutually beneficial development among the regions and improving the infrastructure and ecological environment; (2) Raising the living standard of the local people; and finally (3) Realizing the objective of building "a well-off society in an all-round way" in the western region.

Since 2000, to achieve these policy goals, the government has taken serious measures in the western region, and congruently has successively executed a series of grand construction projects. The central government implemented 10 grand projects in 2000 and 12 key projects in 2001 (Li Zibing, 2001). On top of these, the government declared the plan to build 3 large-scale hydro-power stations in Xiluodu and Xiangjiaba along the Jinsha River, and in Pubugou along the Dadu River.

Vice-premier Li Lanqing announced that during the past three years the total amount of investment in key projects of the West China Development is more than 600 billion *yuan* (72,500 million dollars) and the long-term national bond issued for developing the west region is up to 160 billion *yuan* (USD 19.3 billion). It was estimated that the investment of the planned grand projects in the West China Development program would be more than 600 billion *yuan* within the next 3 years; and to be more than one trillion *yuan* within the next 5 years; and up to be 1.8 trillion *yuan* in the next 10 years (Zhao Ai, 2001). As for the scale of the investment of the Western Region Development from the outside of the mainland China, it was estimated to reach USD 100 billion by 2005. Zeng Yinquan, the chief of government's Office of Hong Kong Affairs, projected that it will go up to USD 220 billion (2 trillion *yuan*) in the next five years. Thanks to the fast rise of investment, the growth rate of GDP of the western region accelerated year after year. In 2000, the growth rate of GDP reached 8.5%, 8.7% in 2001, and 9.9% from January to September of 2002.

The Five Mega-Projects of West China Development

The investment projects in West China Development Program can be classified into three categories: (1) the projects that have a western region foothold and benefit the whole country, such as the ecological construction, West-to-East natural gas transportation, West-to-East electricity transmission project, Qinghai-Tibet railway, South-to-North water diversion. (2) The projects that improve infrastructure conditions of the western region, such as railway, highway, airport, hydro-power station, hydro-engineering, city infrastructure construction, scenic spots and traffic construction, etc. (3) The projects that improve the western people's living standards, such as "networks of paved roads to county level", "electricity supply to township level", "broadcasting and television networks to village level". Presently, 98% of western villages and towns have electricity and 97% of administrative villages have access to broadcasting and television. In the past three years, the nation invested 2.8 billion *yuan* to solve the problem of supplying drinkable water for 3 million inhabitants of rural villages. Within the above-mentioned three categories, the following five major projects are most remarkable.

The ecological environment construction project

The western region is located at the upper reaches of the Yangtze River, the Yellow River, and the Pearl River, which are the top 3 main rivers of China. As the western region's ecological destruction was very serious and the environment is now extremely fragile, the western region has become the origin of the nationwide natural calamities in three categories: the Yangtze River flooding, the siltation of Yellow River, and northern sandstorms. West China Development Program started with treating the ecological environment and advanced in three aspects of prohibiting logging of natural forest, "grain for green or grass" in hilly areas, and natural grassland restoration. It is rare anywhere in the world to implement projects on such a large scale, and the accomplishment of the projects is expected to build up vegetation coverage to stop soil and water erosion as well as control the sandstorms.

There are many aspects to the ecological environment construction policies. One main policy is "grain for green" that stands for the government's intention to encourage peasants to turn planting grain in hilly fields with slope of more than 25 degrees into planting trees or grass. Any peasant who complies with the government's policy gets compensation in the forms of cash, free plantlet providing, free grains in three or five or eight years. After the transaction of turning grain into green, the peasants are likely to profit from the grown trees and the grass planted. The policy is welcome by the peasants because it removes the worry of the profit loss due to stopping grain planting business. In fact, with assistance from the policy, the peasants were able to engage in more profitable business. At present, "grain for green project" has fully been implemented in the western region. After a success of the first two years of a pioneer project the ecological environment construction project will be implemented in 25 provinces and autonomous regions. The restoration of natural pasture will be started in Inner Mongolia, Xinjiang, Sichuan and other western territories in 2003. To guarantee the implementation, the State Council issued the "Regulations of Turning Farming into Foresting" to provide a legal foundation and operational standards for the project.

The planned scale of "grain for green" assigned by the country is 5,728,666 hectares in 2002 and the finished scale is 4,132,000 hectares. According to preliminary statistics, the "grain for green project" has already affected 13,330,000 peasant households with a population of more than 53 million, within the average area of cultivated land conceding into forestry per household as 0.29 hectare. About 4,100,000 peasant households with more than 16 million population have benefited from the implementation of the "grain for green project" during the 3 years of the pioneer project. On average each household was subsidized with 870 kg of grain and 146 *yuan*. For example, Bai Zhanfu, a peasant who lives in Jinfuping village, Luoyuan Township, Wuqi County, Shaanxi Province has a family of four. He contracted 1.73 hectare cultivated land in which he conceded 1.333 hectare land to forestry in 1999 and was then subsidized 2,000 kg of grains with a subsidy of 400 *yuan* every year. After conceding the land, his family cultivated the remaining 0.4 hectares of land – growing vegetables in greenhouses, and raising pigs and sheep. In 2001, the total gross income reached 20,000 *yuan* and income per capita, of 5,000 *yuan*, was ten times more than that of villagers like Bai Zhanfu in 1998.

After the implementation of "grain for green" policy, the problem of soil erosion and land desertification was alleviated. According to data from the National Forestry Department, in Hongya County of Sichuan Province, the amount of soil erosion decreased by 4.96 tons and the soil moisture increased to 18 cubic metres per mu since 1999 after implementing the "grain for green" policy. The soil erosion in Hongya County decreased year by year, and the tendency of reoccurring natural calamity has significantly declined. Particularly, the impact of drought is a serious concern. For example, Sichuan province suffered from a serious drought in 2001 and the counties neighbouring Hongya County suffered bitterly. However, Hongya County itself was barely affected, and eventually had a good harvest. The local people cheerfully said "the sky of Hongya gets bluer, the land gets greener, the peasants get richer, and the river gets clearer since the implementation of 'grain for green'policy three years ago".

Evidence in Wuqi county of Shanxi province also shows the vegetation coverage reached 49.6% in 2001, with a coverage net increase of 27.4% since 1997. The amount of soil erosion dropped to 8,800 tons per square kilometres in 2001, with a net decrease of 42.5% on the basis of 1997. The newly grown dense vegetation has covered the past bald mountains, consequently giving animals greater amounts of grazing land. In such areas, the run-off of precipitation was turned into soil moisture, and the mud remained in the reaches, thus improving a good local climate (Zhang Hongwen, 2002). Sichuan's supervision of the ecological environment project shows that 34,000 sq. km of soil erosion area has been controlled already, the total amount of silt held is up to 560 million tons in the past four years, and that the coverage rate of forest in Sichuan has risen from 24.23% to 26.62%, by 2 percentage points within four years.

The West-to-East natural gas transportation project

The western region is the region that contains the most abundant natural gas in China, with the major producing bases found in Xingjiang, Qinghai, Shanxi, Chongqing, and Sichuan. After the West China Development Program was launched, the country decided to implement the West-to-East natural gas transportation project in order to closely combine the development of the western region with the prosperity of the eastern region. The West-to-East natural gas transportation project includes three pipelines: from Tarim Basin of Xinjiang to Shanghai, from Shaanxi to Beijing and Tianjin (has been accomplished), from Chongqing and Sichuan to Hubei and Hunan. The engineering of the pipeline from Xinjiang to Shanghai commenced in July 2002, starting from Lunnan county of Xinjiang and passing ten provinces and cities, with a designed full length of 4000 km. The designed annual volume of transferring natural gas is estimated at 12 billion cubic metres. The investment of the pipeline engineering is more than 40 billion *yuan* and the total investment in the three lines including the upper, middle and lower sections is more than 140 billion *yuan*. The three pipelines go through the Gobi desert, the Loess plateau, the Taihang Mountains, and across the Yellow, Huai, and Yangtze Rivers. In the near future it will be the longest, the most expensive, and the most important gas-transferring pipeline in China.

The West-to-East natural gas transportation grand project also includes the storing station project, antiseptic project, tunnel project, communication project, automatic system project and other projects. These projects, however, require support from the hi-tech sector. They also involve in the sectors of steel, machinery, electronics and communications, building materials and building construction. The investment in pipeline project accounts for 26% of the total investment. If China's domestic industrial sector is able to execute the entire project properly, it will directly generate domestic expenses of tens of billion *yuan*. In addition, the project will create important opportunities for international investors and manufacturers in China's western regions.

The West-to-East natural gas transportation project is significant for several reasons. First, the project can exploit the resources and then consequently benefit the western region people. Second, the project can supply ten provinces and cities with high quality natural gas, especially the Yangtze River Delta where Shanghai is situated. The utilization of the gas, for electricity generating, resident life, and chemical industry and so on, will greatly promote the development of the region. Third, the project can improve atmospheric quality of particular regions along the pipeline, specifically the Yangtze River Delta. Experts believe that if the Yangtze River Delta is supplied with 10 billion cubic metres per year of gas, the region can reduce burning of 9 million standard coal every year. Thus, the region can reduce the emission amounts of sulfur dioxide about 200,000 tons and the emission amount of nitrogen oxygen about 120,000 tons, and the emission amount of carbon dioxide about 25 million tons. Fourth, the construction of the pipelines, through the desert regions, arid and half-arid regions, and the sandstorm-origin regions from Xinjiang to Yingyang of Henan will consequently bring special benefit to the land to these areas, especially in regard to soil erosion control and desertification. Fifth, the project can create conditions for possible international cooperation concerning natural gas with Central Asia and Russia in the future (Yan Sanzhong, 2001).

The West-to-East electricity transmission project

The western region origins of China's main rivers such as the Yangtze River, the Yellow River, the Pearl River, the Lancang River, and the Brahmaputra River. In theory, the total reserve of hydro-energy in the twelve provinces of the western region collectively is about 557 million kilowatts that accounts for 82% in the nation. The exploitable hydro-energy is about 291 million kilowatts that accounts for 76.85% in the country. However, the exploitation rate is only 11.4%, far below the exploitation rate of hydro-energy in developed countries (more than 50%). Along with the "Three Gorges" hydropower station, exploiting clean, cheap and renewable energy resources from the western region and transmitting them to the eastern region are important strategic measures for developing China.

In line with the strategic plan of West China Development Program, the West-to-East electricity transmission project is divided into three lines: the south line, middle line, and north line. The south line relies mainly on Yunnan, Guangxi, Guizhou to transmit electricity to the areas such as Guangdong; the middle line relies mainly on Sichuan to transmit electricity to eastern and central China; the north line relies mainly on the hydro-power of the Yellow River and the thermal power of Inner Mongolia and Shanxi, to transmit electricity to Beijing, Tianjin, Tangshan, and Shandong. The West-to-East electricity transmission project consists of hydropower station construction and transmitting and distributing grid construction. Currently, the south line, the middle line, and the north line are advancing side by side. Some projects, to be commenced in the near future, such as the Longtan hydropower station on the Hongshui River of Guangxi, the Xiaowan and Luozhadu hydro-power stations on the Lancang River of Yunnan, can be classified in the "world class" category. Collectively, the total electrical capacity exceeds 4 million kilowatts. The Xiluodu and Xiangjiaba hydropower stations on the Jinsha River of Sichuan are scheduled to commence construction, and their total capacity is expected to be over 20 million kilowatts, exceeding the "Three Gorges" hydropower station on the Yangtze River (16 million kilowatts installation)(CECC, 2000). The West-to-East electricity transmission project will benefit the whole nation. When the grand project is finished, the whole country will be able to use clean, cheap, and renewable energy resources. The problems of the eastern and central parts of China lacking electrical power will be solved thoroughly, and the regions will be guaranteed power for further development. To the western region, the total investment of the West-to-East electricity transmission project from 2001 to 2010 is above 526,500 million *yuan* (excluding investment in the "Three Gorges" hydro-power station). Such huge investments generate various market opportunities for the western region and the whole country. The experience in constructing the "Three Gorges" hydro-power station shows that these opportunities will generate business opportunities for the building materials market (steel, timber, and cement markets), the engineering machinery market, the vehicle transport market, the generating equipment market, transmission and transforming power equipment market, project construction market, installment and construction market, goods and materials transport market, consumer goods supplying market, and the labour market.

Taking construction of the Longtan hydropower station of Guangxi as an example, according to calculation by the experts, if the investment is 100 *yuan*, Guangxi's economy can obtain 132 *yuan* increments. The gross investment of the Longtan hydropower station is 24,300 million *yuan*, so GDP per each person of Guangxi will increase by about 700, while providing 58,000 direct employment opportunities and about 30,000 indirect employment opportunities. When the project is completed, there will be chances of utilizing the abundant low-priced electric power to develop high energy consuming industries and other manufacturing industries.

The Qinghai-Tibet railway project

The construction of the Qinghai-Tibet railway has special implications on West China Development. First, the project can open up new channels for developing Tibet, and eventually will connect Tibet with the inner lands of China. Second, the project can create more favourable conditions for strengthening national defence.

For a long time, Tibet has made contact with the inner lands mainly via the Sichuan-Tibet unpaved roads and Qinghai-Tibet roads. The success of the Chengdu-Lhasa aviation line, opened in the 1980s, created air transportation between Lhasa and the inner lands. Later, the southwest aviation corporation opened a route from Lhasa to Khatmandu, Nepal. Since then, Tibet has established connections with the world through aviation. However, poor roads remained an obstacle, leaving undiminished the need to meet the huge demands of socio-economic development in Tibet, and the needs of national defence. Thus, the necessity of building a railway system in the region became imperative.

The history of building the railway can be traced back to 1955 when the country made the first attempt at this project. In 1959, Qinghai-Tibet railroad's first section was completed from Lanzhou to Xi'ning. However, expansion beyond the first section was curtailed due to the project's forced suspension at the beginning of the Cultural Revolution in 1966.

In 1973, the country dispatched more than 1700 scientific and technical personnel to Qinghai and finished a series of preparatory jobs such as research, designing, and surveying. The construction materials had been transported to Naqu, 400 kilometres from Lhasa. However, because of two technical difficulties encountered due to the frozen soil and the high elevation, the Qinghai-Tibet railway construction was suspended for the second time. In that period, the railway was built successfully from Qinghai to Golmud, and became operational in 1984.

The Fourth Session of the Eighth National People's Congress listed Tibet railway construction in agenda for the third time in 1996 and proposed four phases of development: the Qinghai-Tibet phase, the Gangsu-Tibet phase, the Yunan-Tibet phase, and the Sichuan-Tibet phase. On February 8, 2001, the Xinhua News Agency reported that the State Council had made the decision to build the Qinghai-Tibet railway. As Premier Zhu Rongji pointed out, as the overall wealth of China had grown substantially, the country had sufficient economic power to build the Qinghai-Tibet railway after twenty-years of reform and "opening-up." In addition, feasible solutions to the technical problems of building the railway on frozen soil of the plateau had been put forward through intensive scientific research and experimentation. The conditions of building the Qinghai-Tibet railway had matured, and the material preparations for such a project were formalized. One year later, ceremonies were held at the same time in Lhasa and Golmud on June 29, 2002, declaring the formal launch of the Qinghai-Tibet railway construction (Zhong Tianlu, 2001). The total length of railway from Golmud of Qinghai to Lhasa of Tibet is 1142 kilometres and gross investment is more than 26 billion *yuan*. The time limit of construction for this railway is 7 years and it is estimated that it will start operation in 2007.

The Qinghai-Tibet railway construction is ending an age of stagnation of development for the Tibetan Plateau. The railway will not only facilitate Tibetan business progress but also make the economic and social contacts between Tibet and the inner lands more convenient as well as widen the scope for cultural exchanges. Moreover, it will bring unprecedented opportunities to socio-economic development of the regions along the railway line. Now, the regions along the railway line have already begun to draw development plans for local economies. Gongbaozhaxi, the secretary of the Party committee in Naqu county, said: "Naqu has the biggest pasture of Tibet. The construction of the Qinghai-Tibet railway will greatly promote the economic development of Naqu, where we have more than 8 million heads of livestock, because the railway will provide an enormous economic corridor. The abundant animal resources, the tourism resources, and the mineral resources of northern Tibet will be changed into economic advantages quickly "(Duan Bo and Liu Ximei, 2001). The Qinghai-Tibet railway construction will exert a great influence on national unity and stabilizing borderland control.

The South-to-North water diversion project

China is a country short of water resources and suffering from the uneven distribution of these water resources. At present, the total Chinese water resource are about 280 billion cubic metres, and on average each person has only 2,300 cubic metres, which is below the average level of the world community. With the major river systems located in the South, the North seriously lacks water. Water quality of the South is superior to that of the North, too. In October 1952, Mao Zedong said: "Water in the South is at a surplus while water in the North is scarce. If possible, borrowing some water from the South to the North is right." Aligning with this optimistic plan, many scientific workers have carried on a five-decade investigation, analyzing and comparing more than fifty different strategic schemes. Experts have now formed the South-to-North water diversion scheme consisting of east, middle, and west lines. The east line of South-to-North water diversion project formally began on December 27, 2002. The middle line is tentatively scheduled to start at the end of 2003 and the west line will be implemented in 2010. The gross investment of the South-to-North water diversion project is nearly 500 billion *yuan*. It will be the greatest hydro-engineering project in the world after the "Three Gorges Projects". According to the current plan of procedures, after South-to-North water diversion project is finished, four horizontal and three vertical patterns of river networks will link the Yangtze River, the Yellow River, Huai River, and the Hai River. Thus, the ultimate goal of distributing water resources to the North from the South, and to the East from the West will be achieved. By 2050, the total volume of transferred water will amount to 44.8 billion cubic metres, corresponding to an increase in the Yellow River's total water supply in the Huang-Huai-Hai plain and the Northwest.

Among the three lines of South-to-North water diversion project, the west line is the most influential for western development. The planned west line of South-to-North water diversion project is mainly to divert water from the Yangtze River source to the Yellow River. According to the investigation from the water conservancy committee of the Yellow River, in recent years, the all reaches of the Yellow River are becoming more arid, causing the influx water to decrease. Meanwhile, the demand for water by economic development is increasing, aggravating the depletion of the Yellow River source. It is estimated that by 2010, the water deficit amount in the upper and middle reaches of the Yellow River will reach 4 billion cubic metres in normal years, and up to 10 billion cubic metres in a year with water flux below the average.

To solve this problem, the west line scheme of South-to-North water diversion proposes a three-stage water project. The first stage plans to divert water from the five tributaries of the Yalong River and Dadu River to the Jiaqu tributary of the Yellow River by opening a long tunnel passing through the Bayankala Mountain and flowing to the Yellow River automatically. The total amount of diverting water per year will be 4 billion cubic metres and the total length of the diversion channel will be 260 kilometres. The second stage of the project plans to divert 5 billion cubic metres water from the Yalong River. The third stage plans to divert 8 billion cubic metres of water directly from the Jinsha River. The designers of the west line project of South-to-North water diversion expect that the Yellow River will stop riverbed silting and that the riverbed in the lower reaches will be cleaned. In addition, it is expected that the drying out problem of the Yellow River will be finally alleviated (Hang Zhenjun and Wan Libing, 2002).

However, it must be pointed out that the west line scheme would raise many issues regarding the Yangtze River, because the significant decrease of water in the upper reaches of the Yangtze River may trigger serious consequences such as the deterioration of the ecological environment and the loss of power generation capabilities along the Yalong River, Dadu River, and Jinsha River. Specialists acknowledge that quite a number of different views have been mentioned concerning the west line of the South-to-North water diversion project, creating a call for further debate on the subject.

Probing the Political Objectives and Effects of the Five Projects

From the discussion above it is easy to comprehend that the Chinese government's promotion of West China Development is based on the western region's regional economic cooperation and development, which will ultimately benefit the whole nation. The policy has proved advantageous so far and has achieved some significant successes. However, some problems do exist and need to be addressed in order to identify a solution.

The West China Development Program benefits the whole country, but continues to widen the East-West gap

The five mega-projects are implemented in the western regions and bring to the western region some definite benefits, indeed. However, these projects are intended to benefit the nation as a whole. Take the environmental construction project as an example. Measures such as the prohibition of logging the natural forest, returning woods and grassland from farms, and the recovery of natural grasslands are all being implemented in the western region, yet they significantly benefit the eastern territories by solving the problems of regional floods in the middle and lower reaches of the Yangtze River, conserving soil and water along the Yellow River's reaches, alleviating the Yellow River's drying out in the eastern region, and quenching the sandstorms occurring in Beijing. Similarly, take transporting gas and electricity from the western region to the East as another example. Natural gas and water-electricity are both dominant resources needed in the western region. They benefit the eastern economy more by providing it with clean, cheap energy and chemical raw materials. Only the Qinghai-Tibet railway construction is completely in the western region, having great significance to the development of the Tibetan Plateau.

A priority is the promotion of national unity, to consolidate the parametres of China's frontier as well as national defence. Transferring water from South to North is vital to Chinese overall development in the long run. The problem is, however, that the rivers in the western region line project undertake the task of providing electricity to the eastern region. Meanwhile, these rivers have also assumed the duty of transferring water to the Yellow River. The five mega projects are a double-edged sword as regards China's regional development. The western region is more of a benefactor than a beneficiary, while the eastern region is more a beneficiary than a benefactor. Using our preliminary analysis above, about 40% of the investments of the Five Projects is utilized to purchase equipment and materials from China's eastern and central provinces, because the western region is unable to produce them. In this sense, The West China Development actually drives the development of China's eastern and central provinces. What exists is a concern that West China Development is not directly benefiting western territories so much as China's eastern and central provinces. From the view of the benefited part, the western region is beneficiary and yet is mainly a contributor while the eastern and the middle regions are the contributors and yet are mainly beneficiary. According to our preliminary analysis, about 40% of the total investment in the five big projects is invested in buying the equipment and materials of the East and the Middle because the western region can't make these products. In this meaning, West China Development Program has driven the development of the eastern and middle provinces further. The original fear that the West China Development Program would have a negative impact on the development of the eastern and middle regions has been proved to be unfounded. From data of the past three years, per capita GDP of the western region rose from 4123 *yuan* (USD 498) in 1998 to 5007 *yuan* (USD 605) in 2001, to 5489 *yuan* (USD 663) in 2002. However, the gap of per capita GDP and growth rate between the western and the eastern regions did not dwindle but expanded further as showed in Table 13.1.

While absolute disparity between the eastern and the western regions continues to expand, the disparity in growth rate is also expanding. Since

West China Development Program started three years ago, the gap of incremental index between the eastern and western regions has expanded by 8.39 percentage points (Table 13.2). That indicates that the growth gap between the eastern and western regions is not checked.

Table 13.1.   The Gap of Per Capita GDP between the Western and Eastern Regions

	1998		1999		2000		2001		2002	
	Yuan	USD	Yuan	USD	Yuan	USD	Yuan	USD	Yuan	USD
East 11 (provinces)	10032	1212	10770	1301	11334	1369	12811	1548	14105	1704
West (12 (provinces)	4123	498	4321	522	4687	566	5007	605	5489	663
National	6307	762	6547	791	7084	856	7543	911	7972	963
West below National	2184	264	2226	269	2397	290	2536	306	2483	300
West to National Ratio	1:1.53		1:1.52		1:1.51		1:1.51		1:1.45	
West below East	5909	714	6449	779	6647	803	7804	943	8616	1041
West to East Ratio	1:2.43		1:2.49		1:2.42		1:2.56		1:2.57	

Table 13.2.   Gap of Incremental Index between the Eastern and Western Regions (1998 to 2002, 1998=100)

	1998	1999	2000	2001	2002
East	100	107.36	120.51	132.85	144.59
West	100	104.82	113.70	124.59	136.20

As shown by these figures, the western region development has accelerated during the past these years while the eastern region has developed even faster. The greater disparity lies in that the growth of the western region is mainly propelled by the investment in infrastructure construction while the growth of the eastern region is mainly propelled by the manufacturing industry and service-trade sectors with high added values. The eastern region catches the opportunity of a new round of international industry relocation to China and upgrades its industries rapidly, achieving fast growth rate and high profits. This tendency suggests a further enlargement of the disparity between the eastern and western regions.

Division of labour between the eastern and western regions remains the same

During the years of centrally planned economy, the division of labour between the eastern and western regions was that the western region exploited resources and the eastern region manufactured products. In the periods of the First Five-Year Plan, the Second Five-Year Plan, and the Third Front Construction (1964-1977), the western region built some heavy industries or national defence industries. For a period of time, it was perceived that economic cooperation in exploiting mineral and coal resources throughout the western region should be jointly conducted by the eastern and the western regions while the consumer products that the western region needed were basically purchased by the eastern region. Since the period of Reform and Opening up, this mutual dependence has changed greatly. As the east coastal areas implement the strategy of opening to the outside world, a great number of material industries have been established in the East, such as steel and iron, oil refining, and machinery manufacturing. The eastern region directly obtains resources and technological equipments from international markets. Eastern areas such as Guangdong and Shanghai cooperate with Hong Kong and Taiwan enterprises in the form of capital and technologies to develop new consumer goods, such as "white goods" (home electronic durables), fashion apparel, cosmetics, processed foods, office supplies, etc. Currently, products from

Guangdong and Shanghai dominate 70% of the western region's consumer goods market. It is true that transmitting gas and electricity from the West to the East and transferring water from the South to the North contributes to the rebuilding of mutual dependence between the eastern and western regions. The division of labour, however, remains the same while the high value added products are still dominated by the eastern region.

In terms of capital, in the period of the centrally planned economy, the amount of loans exceeded the amount of deposits for a long time in the western region banks. So the western region banks were known as the "banks of debit balance" where the funds were allocated by the state budget directly to make up for the shortfall of funds. Now fundamental restructures have taken place in the banking system and the bank operations are commercialized. Although the western region still badly needs funds, the situation of "credit balance" persists year after year because there are not enough investment projects with good market prospects and high rate of returns to justify banking loans to enterprises. For example, the amount of "credit balance" of Sichuan banks is up to more than 90 billion *yuan* in 2002 alone. A large amount of funds flows from the western region to the eastern and middle regions. The outflow of capital and rural migrant workers started in the 1980s and still continues. To reverse this situation, the traditional west-east pattern of industry-labour division must be changed. We should speed up the development of manufacturing industries suitable for the western region while implementing infrastructure construction and ecological environment construction.

The environmental construction in the western areas lacks a powerful and sustainable development strategy

In China, the success of "grain for green" strategy depends on the successful agricultural harvest that fills national granaries. The environmental policy cannot be executed unless the government has surplus food to trade with peasants and has sufficient financial strength to compensate farmers. Without these two preconditions it is impossible to let farmers return farmlands to forests and grasslands. Experts reckon that these two tasks can be executed within the time span of the policy. Yet, when the time span of the policy expires, farmers will return to the old personal modes of production and rely on the returns from the wood and grass business to purchase food. It is usually unknown to a peasant whether the returns from wood and grass business would be sufficient to make a living. If, when the policy period is expired and the woods in the formerly forestland have not yet grown into forests, could the period of "grain for green" policy be extended? Could peasants cut down the woods occasionally and engage in the timber business after the woods in retreated cultivated land grow into forests? How can the peasants of the western region rely on the woods for their living? How will the eastern and the middle regions compensate the western region for ecological environmental improvement in the upper reaches of rivers?

If farmers' welfare cannot be assured when the expiry date of the policy comes, the achievements of the environmental protection policy might all be lost. The loss refers to not only several years of painstaking efforts but also the imponderable environmental cost. At present, China still has no sustainable development strategy to prevent these problems from emerging.

The prospect of investment returns and debt redemption for West China development is gloomy

In the last three years, most West China development projects have been financed mainly by the central government-issued bonds and banks' policy loans. The local governments' investment is considerably less since much of the local budgets are tied in civil servant hiring, education, and health care. Foreign capital, Hong Kong-Taiwan capital, eastern region capital and capital from western region non-governmental organizations have risen to some extent, but these funds are still insufficient. In recent years, the western provinces' GDP has increased rapidly, propelled by the central government's debt finance and policy loans. An analysis of Sichuan provincial GDP data shows that, in 2002, fixed capital investments contributed about 50% of GDP growth. The figure is even higher for other western provinces. There is still a great gap between the western and eastern regions regarding the fixed capital investment.

Table 13.3.   Fixed Capital Investment in the Western and
Eastern Regions, 1999- 2002 (100 million *yuan*)

	Total GDP	%	Per Capita	Investment in state sector (*yuan*)	%	Per Capita (*yuan*)
1999						
Eastern	17330	59.8	3735	8120	53.9	1750
Western	5421	18.7	1512	3334	22.1	930
National	29855	100	2371	15948	100	1267
2000						
Eastern	18752	58.8	3817	8250	53.0	1679
Western	6111	19.1	1720	3490	22.4	982
National	32918	100	2541	16504	100	1274
2001						
Eastern	20874	57.9	4356	8384	50.6	1749
Western	7159	19.8	1964	3924	23.6	1077
National	37213	100	2916	17607	100	1380
2002						
Eastern	18456	42.7	3896	20874.	57.9	4356
Western	5672	13.1	1558	7159	19.8	1964
National	43202	100	3363	37213	100	2916

Table 13.3 indicates, though the percentage of the investment in the western state sector is increasing, the increase is very limited. The percentage of the western region is far below 29%, the ratio of western region population to the total population. Figure 13.1 shows the persistent regional gap in per capita fixed-capital investment.

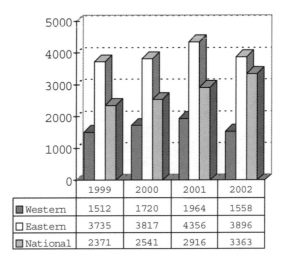

	1999	2000	2001	2002
■ Western	1512	1720	1964	1558
□ Eastern	3735	3817	4356	3896
▨ National	2371	2541	2916	3363

Figure 13.1.   Per Capita Fixed Capital Investment by Region (*yuan*)

The Chinese government has pursued an expansionary fiscal policy for 5 years, issuing bonds worth 0.8 trillion *yuan*. If policy loans from banks are included, the total expansionary budget is estimated to be above 2.5 trillion yuan. If there are no alternatives of financing, the investments to the western region from the government will decrease, leading to a significant drop in the GDP growth of the western region. If this situation emerges, it will suppress the impetus of West China development. In the meantime, some national investment items have entered their debt redemption time. The predecessors raised loans for the successors to pay. The issue becomes a concern. Many local governmental officers and the heads of enterprises, however, have not prepared for this, nor have they thought of repayment of debts. The West China Development actually needs 50 to 100 years to effectively take shape, whereas now many provinces are pushing for establishing "the all-around well-off society" by 2020. Frankly, the goals are set too high. However, it would be reasonable to understand that the objective of establishing an "all-around well-off society" is the final phase in the process, and such conditions require the investment of capital from both domestic and international sources. Without a long-range sustainable investment strategy, and without viable political guarantees, it would be dangerous to proceed since the plan has no reliable sources of investment. Therefore, one of the most important issues in West China development is to establish long-term and stable investment channels to answer the challenge of the growing financial pressures.

Call for a Sustainable Development Strategy

The West China Development Program has been implemented for over three years. To formulate a sustainable development strategy, we need to attend to the following issue.

Policy adjustment

The basic goal of West China Development Program is to narrow the disparity between the western and eastern regions progressively, to enrich the western region people, and to bring about coordinated development in regional economy. Everyone understands that it is a slow task to narrow the disparity and is impossible to achieve the goal in one move.

Through more than two decades of high-speed development, the eastern region has already obtained the strong capability of self-accumulation and self-development. It is important to let the eastern region seize the opportunity and accelerate its development for the national interests of China. However, it is also crucial to let western region people see the prospect of narrowing the gap between the western and eastern regions. At the present, the eastern region has already entered the period of self-sustained growth propelled by the manufacturing and service sectors while the western region still relies on infrastructure investment to generate growth. The western region's ability of self-accumulation and self-development is very weak. Once central government reduces the public-debt financed investment to the western region, the growth may slow and inter-regional disparity will be widened further.

The choice that we face now is whether to continue the West China Development Program according to the present policies or to adjust the policy in order to accelerate the pace of the West China development appropriately. We believe that policy adjustment is necessary. Our suggestions are as follows.

First, to strengthen the investment in the western region further because the economic growth of the western region is to be pulled by investment over a pretty long period. The first step is to make investment in the western region reach the national per capita investment level. The second step is to make investment in the western region exceed the national per capita investment level.

Second, to adjust investment structure and strengthen investment in western manufacturing industry and agriculture. It is right to make infrastructure investment a priority, but infrastructure construction must develop along with manufacturing industry in proportion. Western region infrastructure construction should be sequenced according to the needs of manufacturing and other industries suitable for western regions. It is necessary to develop the infrastructure and manufacturing industry at the same time and to strengthen investment in manufacturing industry and agriculture.

Third, focus must be placed on solving the problems of the poverty and compulsory education of the western region. There are 28,200,000 people below the poverty line in the whole country, most of whom live in the western region. Most of children of school age who cannot enter the schools also reside in the western region. Most of the areas not accessible by highway, electricity grid, and broadcasting network are also part of the western region. Most of the areas with abominable living conditions are also found in the western region. Therefore, the central government's use of poverty alleviation funds, fiscal transfer payments, tax rebates, and investment in education should favour the western region to solve these problems. Especially it is very necessary to make the school-aged children in the western region enjoy free compulsory education with the aid of government assistance.

Finally, the local government of the western region should make efforts to adjust the industrial structure and develop manufacturing industries and agriculture to accord with local characteristics. Efforts should be made to attract the outside funds and mobilize the inside funds for developing these sectors. Poverty alleviation and compulsory education should be high on the agenda.

Adjustment of industrial pattern

The industrial pattern with the western region exploiting natural resources and the eastern region processing and manufacturing goods has taken shape for a long time in China. It is one of the important reasons that cause the widening of the gap between the eastern and western regions. This problem must be solved by significant governmental policy adjustment, otherwise it will cause the lopsided development of provincial industries that will harm the local people's interests. The adjustment of the industry pattern is not a very complicated concept. What needs to take place is the central government's support and endorsement for the western territories to develop processing of raw materials, to better utilize hydro-electricity, gas, water, labour and mineral resources. The government also needs to promote the production of high technology of the western arms industries. For example, in the West-to-East natural gas transmission project, the central government can establish some natural gas chemical engineering projects in the western region. In the West-to-East electricity transmission project, the central government can arrange some energy-intensive projects in the western region. In the western cities with high-tech arms industries, the central government can build some new high-tech industries.

If the country really wants to develop the western region, the country should strategically adjust the industrial patterns of the nation in favour of the western region, and allow western region people to enjoy the added value of processing resources right in the land they inhabit. With the western electricity, gas, and water being transported to the East, South, and North respectively, the western region is unable to utilize its low-priced electricity, gas, and water to develop manufacturing industries. Is this fair? The gap between the western and eastern regions is not narrowing but is widening.

Environmental construction and economic compensation

It is right to put environmental construction at the top of West China Development Program's priorities, because the ecological destruction of the western regions often leads to nationwide disasters. If the treatment and improvement of the ecological environment in the western regions are not carried out, the whole country's well being is in jeopardy. However, specific conditions must be analyzed.

The western ecological environment was formed under the influence of multiple factors: either due to barren land, bad weather, or lack of rainfall. Because there has been a low population density in the region a kind of ecological balance has occurred. If the ecological environment construction in these regions is carried out without sufficient technical support, the effort will be short-lived and will destroy the ecological balance rather than protect the environment. In some inhabitable areas, the major destructive factor of the ecological balance is caused by human presence. If the local population could migrate out from these areas, the ecological balance would resume naturally. Other kinds of "bad land" were formed by unreasonable human behaviours such as the destructive logging of forests, overgrazing of pastures, and inadequate farming techniques. These regions are generally densely populated, and the people make a living at the risk of destroying the environment.

It is correct for the environmental construction in the western region to put emphasis on prohibiting the logging of natural forests, on providing grain for giving up farmland, on natural grassland recovery, and on the regulation of irrigation works. But environmental construction projects need long-term and unremitting efforts to implement national laws and policies as well as to gain support from local people. If the policies fail or the laws are not enforced, the achievements of ecological construction could be destroyed overnight.

Among all the policies of ecological construction, the most important policy concerns the supply of grain. According to the data available, it needs dozens of million tons of grain every year to ensure the implementation of "grain for green policy". A plan must be made for buying grain for the ecology of the future.

After peasants implement the policy of grain for green and grass, they should be able to not only make a living by the income of forests and crops but also get rich by doing so. Thus, peasants must be able to shift the forestry and crop industries into both the ecological carrier and the renewable goods sectors, so that timber forests and bamboo groves can be harvested accordingly, and perennial economic forests can be established. Agriculture needs to be conducted in the mode of industrialization within an adequate scale. Furthermore, the forestry industry and grass industry need to be developed ahead of industrialization in order not to create an imbalance in the long run. Provided that the forestry industry and grass industry develop well and peasants get rich, the ecological environment will benefit. A new policy combining ecological protection with poverty alleviation is a practical means of internalizing the externalities of West China development.

The construction of the ecological environment in the western region is a great cause that benefits the middle and lower river regions as well as the whole country. The input is very large and the rewards emerge very slowly. Despite its importance, there are many benefits unnoticed and uncountable. To make this cause successful, it paradoxically needs to depend solely on western region efforts. It is therefore necessary to build a compensation mechanism in advance for the sustainable development of environmental construction. In China, ecological environment construction is a newly established system, yet with no definitive compensation mechanism. The more serious problem, however, is that there is no sense of environmental compensation. The situation already begins to attract public attention, and it is expected to be solved to some extent by the western region environmental construction project.

Government and Market in West China Development

Is West China Development a step-by-step market economy process, or a planned-economy type of process? This is the problem put forward by a scholar and is worth serious consideration. (Liu Ji, 2002)

On the one hand, the primary things West China Development should be concerned with are the environment and infrastructure, both of which need long-term investments. On the other hand, although the influence of the market economy to allocate resources is increasing, it is still far from forming a nationwide resource allocation mechanism. Although the government no longer has as much control of the economy as it did in the previous centrally planned economic system, it still has the power and means to mobilize labour resources and allocate financial resources. When the East-West gap becomes wider and development in the western region is required for national growth, the combination of the government's influence along with the strength of the growing market will become the optimal option. Otherwise, if West China development is delayed until the market economy becomes mature, China will be harmed by economic factors of imbalance, as well as political, social, and ethnic discord.

Today, the primary problems of West China development are how to increase direct governmental investments and introduce new funding sources after national debt financing phases out, as well as how to increase the market's influence. There are many options in this respect. Some social common projects such as the logging ban, Grain for Green project, recovery of natural grasslands, maintenance of dams along great rivers, nine-year compulsory education, etc, must entail sufficient gratuitous investments. Some projects can absorb long-term investment from the government in advance, while others can implement governmental-investment-led joint stock system and/or building proprietary limited liability companies. Some can be established by governmental investments and later transferred. Some can practice the build-operate-transfer (BOT) mode, letting investors return the property to the proprietor after running it for some years. Some can list on the stock market. After national debt issuance phase out, the government can issue a regional West China Development bond, as well as establish a West China Development Bank to develop channels for stable West China Development funds. Alternatively, some areas which possess preponderant industries and high-tech industries can be chosen to set up western special economic zones, whereby special economic policies can be implemented, eventually forming a political enclave for capital and production elements to flow into, so that the economy in the special zones can rapidly improve. The western region has cheap electricity, gas, water, labour and resources. It therefore should use these assets to create an investment environment where production and transportation costs are lower than in the eastern region. Foreign and domestic capital will be likely to rush to the western region for rich profits and promising markets.

The focal points of West China Development Program

The western region is vast in territory and it differentiates from the rest of China in terms of natural environment, density of population, natural resource endowment, and development level. People in the western region really are very afraid of being poor, and everyone is afraid of missing the opportunities available through West China development. They all want to take advantage of this chance to experience the dream of becoming wealthy overnight. This sentiment raises a dilemma for the Chinese government at many levels: the poorer people are, the stronger the desire of enjoying wealth is; on the other hand, the more wealth that is obtained, the larger the gap between the rich and the poor. Deng Xiaoping broke egalitarianism using an unbalanced development strategy. At the same time he opened up people's vision to prosperity and consequently his strategy achieved the goals it set. Now at a time to turn to develop China's western region, Deng Xiaoping's unbalanced development strategy is still valuable and must be further pursued. It is important for the western region people to get rid of all mental obstacles, to understand the policy of "allowing some to get rich first" and the need to build cities first and develop rural sectors next. The limited resource should go to key areas, key industries, and assist key projects, as Guangdong did by developing the Pearl River Delta first, as Jiangsu did developing the Wuxi-Changzhou district first, and as Shandong did by developing the Jiaodong Peninsula first.

While moving forward with sequence, the western region must utilize domestic as well as international resources to develop progressively. The relationship between western and coastal provinces is improving. The western region is both the Chinese frontier and the borderland to Central and South Asia. Several big passages going out to sea and leaving the country have already connected the western region with neighbouring countries. The establishment of the China-ASEAN Free Trade Areas and the Shanghai Co-operation Organization lays the foundation for the western region's cooperation with these countries. Furthermore, cities like Kunming, Urumuqi, Chengdu, and Chongqing are becoming the major centres of West China Development. These growing economic centres will promote the growth of the western region and enhance the region's interaction with the global community.

Notes

1. The authors thank Fu Shi, Zhang Xingzhou, McNally Christopher, William Nitzke and Jiang Yu for translating the paper from Chinese into English.
2. The so-called "a well-off society in an all-round way" (*xiao kang* in Chinese) is an official term used in Chinese government documents to describe a middle-class level of living standard for majority of people.

References

1. Du Shouhu (2001). *Environmental Economics*. The First Edition. Beijing: Chinese Encyclopedia Press.
2. Duan Bo and Liu Ximei (2001). "Qinghai-Tibet Railway: The Most Splendid Breakthrough", 9 *Western Development Jounal*.
3. Hang Zhenjun and Wan Libin (2002). "The Construction of South-to-North Water Diversion Project Begins Today", November 25, <www.cctv.com.cn>.
4. Li Zibing(2001). speech in the "2001 Chinese Western Forum", September 6.
5. Liu Ji(2002). "The Key Times of Chinese Economic Development", 8 *Business Weekly*.
6. Liu Wangyong (2002). "To solve the problem of education development bottleneck, China is actively making high school education accessible to all school-age youth", October 12, <www.chinanews.com>.
7. The Planning Department of Chinese Economic and Commercial Council (2000). *The Tenth Five-Year Plan of Electric Industry*.
8. Yan Sanzhong (2001). speech in the "2001 Chinese Western Forum," September 6.

9.   Zeng Yingquan (2001). "220 billion dollars will be required in the following five years to develop West China", May 28, <www.homeway.com.cn>

10. Zhang Hongwen (2002). "Grain for Grass project achieving an initial success", *People's Daily*, December 30.

11. Zhao Ai (2001). "WTO – opening the markets – anti-monopoly", speech at the Third International Forum of China Basic Field Reforms, October 22.

12. Zhong Tianlu (2001). "Let the history tell the future", 3 *Qinghai Economic Research*.

14 "Grain for Green" Policy and Its Impacts on Grain Supply in West China

Zhiming Feng and Pengtao Zhang

Introduction

"West China" consists of China's South-West (Chongqing, Sichuan, Guizhou, Yunnan, Tibet) and North-West (Shaanxi, Gansu, Qinghai, Ningxia and Xinjiang) regions. Accounting for more than half of China's total area, West China is known for its backward economy and vulnerable ecology and environment. The gap between the eastern and western regions has been becoming larger since the economic reform. For decades, due to the shortage of grain supply and lack of economic opportunities in the region, farmers have to cut down huge tracts of forest, much of it on steep slopes, to turn it into farmland, and also plough up large areas of grassland. This has resulted in severe soil erosion and flooding, and caused land degradation (Zhao and Ma ,1999; Peng, 2001).

To develop the vast western region has become the national development strategy since 1999. The strategy was proposed to be part of the great outline to develop the whole country, and it is of great importance in terms of economy, polity, and environment because it will promote economic development and maintain long-term stability in the country (Feng, 2001). It was proposed in the strategy to accelerate agricultural restructuring and rural development and increase farmers' income, upgrade the industrial sector and revitalize enterprises and traditional industries with high technologies, step up infrastructure construction, enhance environmental protection.

Among the six biggest tasks for promoting development of West China, declared in the 16th National Congress of CCP on November 12,

2002, ecological environmental protection and construction was one of top priority. An important step to improve the environment is to shift some farmland to forest and grassland. The primary plan is to shift about 15 million hectares of farmland to forest and afforest 17 million hectares of barren mountains and land. The slope farmland with severe water shortage and soil erosion will be returned to forest as soon as possible. The principle plan is stressed on the treatment of 67 million hectares of degrading grassland.

The "Grain for Green" policy was a concrete step to restore ecological balance in the western region by turning low-yielding farmland back into forest and pasture. In recent years, China's grain output has grown steadily. After several consecutive bumper harvests, the country now has huge stockpiles of grain (Hu A, 2001). This makes it possible for implementing a massive farmland-to-forests campaign. To compensate the loss, farmers will receive subsidies in the form of grain and money for turning cultivated land back into forest and pasture. To minimize the loss from land use changes, the trees to be planted can be fruit and other commercially valuable trees if the natural conditions are suitable. While the government provides the seedlings, the farmers are allowed to retain all the profits from planting trees and grass on cultivated land. In return, they will be responsible for taking care of the restored forests and pastures. The policy is welcomed by most of the farmers and the implemented areas were larger than planned (Xu and Cao, 2002).

According to a notice issued by the State Forestry Administration Bureaus, the State Development Planning Commission and the Ministry of Finance on March 29, 2002, for every hectare of forest and pasture redeveloped, farmers in the upper reaches of the Yangtze River will receive 2 250 kg of grain every year, while farmers in the upper and middle reaches of Yellow River will receive 1 500 kg of grain every year. The government has put no time limit on grain aid to ensure that farmers will not cultivate re-developed forests and pasture areas in the future. The government will also give 300 *yuan* to farmers for re-developing every hectare of forest and pasture every year to help cover medical and educational expenses (see SFAB, 2000).

The theoretically economic justification of land use change from farmland to forests is straightforward, i.e., the relative scarcity changes of the product from the land and input factors (see, e.g., Park *et al.*, 1998; Zhang, 2000; Zhang *et al.*, 2000). Most developed countries have had similar a experience (see Mauldin *et al.* 1999; Mather, 1992; Pfaff, 2000). This study is not intended to make such justification. In practice, it is not easy to decide how much and what kind of land use should be changed. So far, this policy has been implemented for 4 years. During this time, about 6.4 million hectares of land has been taken out of cultivation, about half of the abandoned land was forested, and similar amount of barren land was planted with trees. The total investment was about 23 billion *yuan*. About 13 million households have been involved in this program (*China Green Time*, January 1, 2003). There is little doubt this policy will have a significant impact on West China, and the rest of the country, in terms of economy and environment. It will also have some impact on the world. One of the most direct impacts is in the change of grain supply. To know the impact of this "grain for green" policy is important for policy makers. This study attempts to estimate such an impact.

The Cultivated Slope Land and "Grain for Green" Policy

As noted above, the "grain for green" policy is intended to return cultivated slope land to forests and grassland. In order to estimate the effect, we must know the scope of the slope land and the amount of such land that is to be returned to forest and grassland under the "grain for green" policy.

The Cultivated Slope Land in West China

In total there are 38 million hectares of cultivated land in West China, accounting for 28% of all cultivated land in China, but the cultivated slope land in the West accounts for the majority in China (For more details of the slope land and its distribution, see Figures 14.1-14.3). In West China, the cultivated slope land accounts for more than half of the total agricultural land in all the rest of the provinces except for Xinjiang and Tibet. As we know, the upper reaches of two largest rivers in China, the Yangtze River and Yellow River, are located in West China, and this region is critical not only to itself (such as biodiversity, land degradation), but also to the middle and lower reaches of the two rivers that cover almost half of China. For instance, it is believed that desertification, resulting from deforestation, and grassland degradation, cause increasingly frequent damaging floods and sandstorms in Northern China (Song, 1994; Zhu, *et al.* 2000; Ma, 2001; Peng, 2001; Bao, *et al.* 2001).

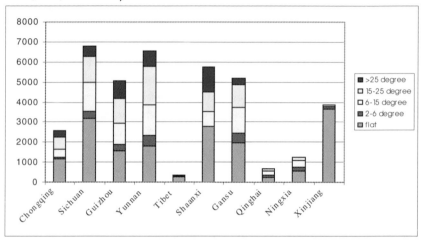

Figure 14.1.   Cultivated Slope land in West China

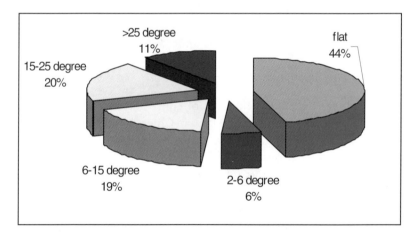

Figure 14.2.   Structure of Cultivated Land in West China

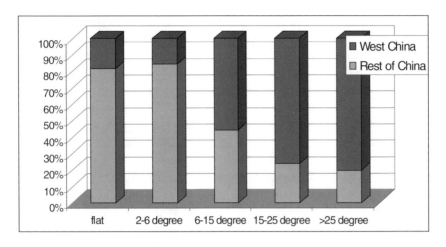

Figure 14.3.   West China's Share of Cultivated Slope Land in China

Regulations on Slope Land Farming and "Grain for Green" Policy

A number of laws and regulations clearly prohibit new land reclamation for agricultural purposes on the deep slope land. The most recent and specific one is the "regulation on converting farmland to forests", that was approved by the State Council on the 6th of December, 2002. This regulation has been in effective since 2003. Generally speaking, it requires already cultivated land over 25 degree slope to be gradually shifted to forest and grassland, and restored with vegetation, or changed into terraced land (e.g., see Water and Soil Conservation Law, article 14). Based on these regulations and laws, it is estimated the total land of 4 million hectares (about 10% of the total cultivated land) should no longer be ploughed. About 38% is located in the North-West, and 62% in the South-West.

It is more problematic and controversial to determine how much land with slope between 15 and 25 degree should be returned to forests and grassland. Since West China is very much local food self-sufficient and depends on agricultural land to survive, it is not feasible to use the same percentage rate of reconversion or a specific degree of slope as a threshold for action. This is not only an ecological problem, but also a socio-economic problem. For those less than 15 degree slope, it is generally believed that they should be kept in agricultural use in the near future, but accordingly implemented by ecological and environmentally friendly farming.

In order to simulate the potential impacts, three scenarios (assumptions) are made at the county level: (A) retaining 0.133 hectare (2 *mu*) per person; (B) retaining 0.1 hectare (1.5 *mu*) per person; (C) retaining 0.067 hectare (1 *mu*) per person. After keeping such an amount of a agricultural land, the rest of cultivated slope land is to be converted into forests and grassland. For each scenario, we must have some information about the population. It may be more realistic to use population some years ahead. Here we use the forecast in "China's population across millennia" (each province has its own volume) (CCCP, 1994).

To calculate the required cultivated land conversion, the procedure illustrated by Figure 14.4 is used. Based on these assumptions, the returning rate is listed in the Table 14.1 and Figure 14.5. It is important to note that our analysis is at county level rather than provincial level.

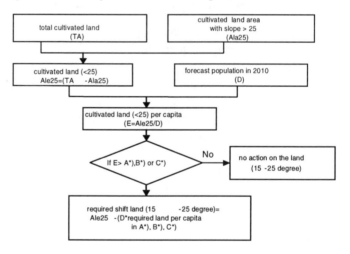

A*=0.133; B*=0.1; C*=0.067

Figure 14.4.   Computing Procedure to Calculate the Requested Land of Returning to Forests

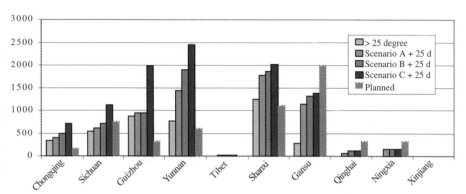

Figure 14.5.   Scenarios of Converting Land Use and the Planned Target

Table 14.1.   The Percentage of Slope Land that Should Be Shifted to Forests and Grassland

Provinces	Total cultivated (hectare)	Planned shift		Land slope >25 degree (%)	Scenario (%)		
		area	%		A	B	C
Chongqing	2575.43	183	7.11	13.21	15.51	19.15	27.59
Sichuan	6794.23	769	11.32	7.93	8.92	10.56	16.65
Guizhou	5063.72	333	6.58	17.28	18.78	18.78	39.28
Yunnan	6567.51	613	9.33	11.85	21.99	28.94	37.49
Tibet	360.55	0	0.00	1.68	3.46	4.45	5.56
Shaanxi	5759.11	1116	19.38	21.49	30.88	32.35	35.15
Gansu	5166.16	2000	38.71	5.50	22.07	25.60	26.87
Qinghai	681.43	333	48.87	0.83	9.44	17.60	19.06
Ningxia	1261.46	333	26.40	0.66	12.20	12.60	12.63
Xinjiang	3841.05	0	0.00	0.00	0.03	0.03	0.03
West China	38070.65	9462	24.85	10.70	17.21	19.81	26.31

Note: The proposed land to be converted is assembled by the authors from different sources, particularly the strategic planning by each provincial government.

When the scenarios are compared with the provincial strategic planning (see Figure 14.6 and Table 14.1), some general circumstances can be observed. First let us see the North-West region: in Shaanxi more than 20% of cultivated land has slope > 25 degree, which is approximately equal to the planned converting land area. For those that have < 25 degree slope, land use does not need to change, but more ecological and environmental friendly farming must be practised. In Gansu, the scenario C still cannot meet the requirement of the planned strategy. That means some slope land < 15 degree is required to be shifted to forests and grassland. In Qinghai, the proposed land use change accounts for half the cultivated land, more than the Scenario C. The reason lies in the fact that the planned land use change covers not only the slope land, but also some too dry land, high altitude land and newly reclaimed land. The situation of Ningxia is quite similar to Qinghai. Xinjiang has very little deep slope farmland, and low slope farmland. But the planning is mostly intended for the land that is prone and vulnerable to desertification. This land is usually planted in cotton. So there will be no big negative impact on grain production.

Now let us see the South-West region. In Chongqing, the desired land for change is much less than the amount of 25 degree slope land. But it should be noted that this amount is only in the first period. It is planned in the second period (2010-2030), that another 180 000 hectares should be returned to forest and grassland. In Sichuan, due to different data sources, there is some gaps between the slope land > 25 and the planned conversion land, otherwise they should be quite close. It is proposed to concentrate only on the slope land > 25. In Guizhou, the proposed land use change is also divided into two periods: the first period is 0.2 million hectares before 2010, the second period is 0.3 million hectares during 2011-2030. In Yunnan, the main target of land use change is the slope land > 25 degree. It is also proposed to implement 80% of the total before 2010.

Estimates and Analysis of Loss in Grain Production

If we know the average output of various categories of slope land, then the loss can be simply estimated by the product per unit and the amount of land change. Unfortunately, we do not have such data. An alternative way to estimate the loss is to develop a grain production function. A simple and straightforward method is to develop production as function of various slope lands and other associated variables. Since the socio-economic and natural conditions as well as data vary too much from one region to another, it is necessary to divide the whole region into 7 regions that do not corespond to the provincial boundary (Figure 14.6). In each region, there are some similarities. The observation points for conversion are based on the county level. There are two kinds of variables used:(1) the share of various slope land; (2) the social economic variable. Assuming the climate within each region is the same, the factors about it do not need to be included here (see Table 14.2). The data used are mainly assembled from "*China Statistical Yearbook 1997*" (see, CSB, 1997) and "China Rural Statistical Materials" (see, MoA, 1990-1999).

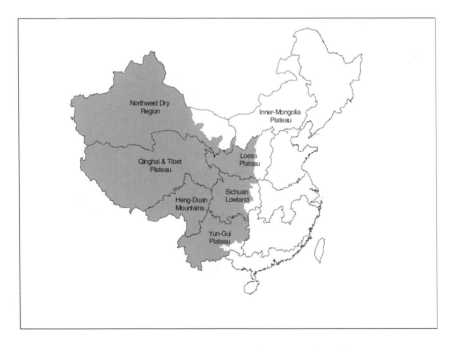

Figure 14.6.   Seven Agricultural Zones in West China

The approach used here is to first estimate the output per unit of land from statistical regression. Then the total production is the product of production per unit and the total remaining cultivated land. It is expected that the impact of returning cultivated land to forests will be negative as the total cultivated land declines when marginal land is first shifted to forests and grassland, but positive in grain output per unit of land due to land quality increase and probably more input available and also ecological improvement. The variables chosen as well as the simple regression results are listed in the Table 14.2.

Based on these parameters and the land use changes in the scenarios, we can calculate the grain production loss for each region. The formula can be simply expressed as:

$$\Delta P = P_t - P_0 = (\Sigma Y_{ti} * A_{ti}) - (\Sigma Y_{0i} * A_{0i}),$$

where, ΔP is the loss or gain resulted from the land use change; P_t is the total grain output at time t; P_0 is the initial total production; Y_{ti} is the production per unit at time t in county i. Y_{0i} is the production per unit at initial time in county i. A_{ti} is the total agricultural area at time t in county i. A_{0i} is the total agricultural area at initial time in county i. For comparison purposes, the 1996 production is used as the initial level. The impact on the total grain production is the sum of all regions (see Table 14.3). By re-organizing the outputs, we can also get the grain production loss by each province (see Table 14.4).

From Table 14.3 or Table 14.4, we can see that the total loss of grain production, under scenarios A, B and C, are 8, 9.6 and 15.4 million tons, accordingly accounting for 7.84%, 9.48% and 15.16% of the total grain production, respectively. At the current time, the grain production from West China is about 20% of the whole of China.

Table 14.2.   Regression Results of Average Grain Production
Per Unit by Different Zones (kg/ha)

Variable	Loess Plateau (1)	Sichuan Lowland (2)	Yun-Gui Plateau (3)	Qinghai & Tibet Plateau (4)	Heng-Duan Mountains (5)
Constant	1637 (0.00)	1872.62 (3.30)	422.73 (2.44)		
S0: < 2 degree land (%)				2219.21 (13.15)	4581.52 (5.27)
S2: 2-6 degree land (%)	-16.096 (1.99)			1286.98 (2.11)	1202.92 (2.02)
S6: 6-15 degree land (%)	-8.479 (2.20)			1014.64 (1.45)	1425.93 (2.26)
S15: 15-25 degree land (%)	-5.461 (1.10)	-18.136 (3.30)	-3.88 (1.32)	486.92 (0.87)	1689.43 (5.75)
S25: > 25 degree land (%)	-11.468 (1.33)	-19.503 (1.98)	-10.151 (2.75)		
I: water irrigated land (%)	40.385 (13.70)				
L: labor input (person/ha)		893.338 (10.18)	715.248 (16.59)		
M: mechanical input (kw/ha)					
F: fertilizer use (kg/ha)					
T: ladder land (%)		0.917 (0.16)		2355.6 (8.23)	2471.082 (5.92)
R^2	0.80	0.71	0.66	0.33	0.28

Notes: (1) The values in parentheses under the parameters are t value.

(2) Two other regions, Inner Mongolia and Northwest dry region, use
the same model as in the Loess Plateau since the natural
characteristics are the same and the sample size is too small.

Table 14.3.   Estimated Grain Production Loss by Changing Land Use
(by regions with Scenario A)

	Scenarios	Converted land (1000 ha)	of total (%)	1996 production (1000 tons)	Estimated loss (1000 tons)	% of Total
Loess Plateau	A	2095	22.3	15652	1494	9.55
	B	2370	25.2	15652	1874	1.97
	C	2514	26.7	15652	2159	3.79
Sichuan	A	1776	17	48684	3597	7.39
Lowland	B	1995	19.1	48684	4044	8.31
	C	2612	24.9	48684	6010	2.34
Yun-Gui	A	2411	20.5	23877	2597	0.88
Plateau	B	2870	24.4	23877	3341	3.99
	C	4504	38.3	23877	6749	8.27
Qinghai-Tibet	A	59	9.5	972	20	2.06
Plateau	B	74	11.9	972	25	2.57
	C	80	13	972	27	2.78
Heng-Duan	A	152	20.8	1443	206	4.28
Mountain	B	202	27.6	1443	287	19.89
	C	253	34.6	1443	381	26.40
Inner-	A	0	0.1	1666	0	0.00
Mongolia-	B	0	0.1	1666	0	0.00
Plateau	C	1	0.5	1666	2	0.12
Northwest	A	43	0.9	9142	38	0.42
Dry Region	B	47	1	9142	47	0.51
	C	47	1	9142	47	0.51
Total	A	6537		101435	7952	7.84
	B	7550		101435	9619	9.48
	C	10010		101435	15377	15.16

Table 14.4.   Estimated grain production loss from shifting land use (by province)

Provinces	Scenario A		Scenario B		Scenario C	
	Prod. Loss (1000 tons)	%	Prod. Loss (1000 tons)	%	Prod. Loss (1000 tons)	%
Southwest						
Chongqing	1315.00	10.32	1546.00	12.14	2279.00	17.89
Sichuan	1653.00	4.84	1892.00	5.54	3188.00	9.33
Guizhou	1038.00	9.85	1038.00	9.85	3129.00	29.67
Yunnan	1464.00	11.71	2186.00	17.49	3344.00	26.74
Tibet	11.00	1.42	15.00	1.94	20.00	2.56
Northwest						
Shaanxi	1539.00	12.58	1657.00	13.54	2025.00	16.56
Gansu	776.00	12.36	1022.00	16.28	1108.00	17.63
Qinghai	73.00	5.86	173.00	13.88	193.00	15.49
Ningxia	81.00	3.13	87.00	3.36	88.00	3.42
Xinjiang	2.00	0.03	2.00	0.03	2.00	0.03
West China	7952.00	7.98	9618.00	9.65	15376.00	15.43

Conclusions and Discussions

Based on the assessment above, the total loss in grain production for the country from the three scenarios will be around 2-3% (total output in China was 460 million tons in 2000). Since the process of converting land use will last a long period of time (10-30 years), the impact on the total grain market should be very small. Since the model does not include the mechanical input and fertilizers, the average use per unit of land is likely to increase when total land decreases, so the loss in production might be slightly overestimated. In addition, the ecological and environmental improvement may play some positive role in the remaining cultivated land. All these factors are not included in this study, so the estimates here are very preliminary. We must be cautious in using these estimated figures. In addition, for policy making, it is far from enough to investigate the impact of grain loss alone. Cost-benefit analysis of such policy is another important field.

Although the impact at the country level may be small, the impact at the local level may be significant, for instance, in Gansu, Yunnan, and Shaanxi and Chongqing. As we know, the population migration and labour flow from one place to another and even the grain transportation from the East to the West, especially at county and village level, still face big challenges, and local self-sufficiency becomes more important. This concern has already been pointed out in many other empirical studies (see, e.g., Hou and Xiao, 2000, Lu *et al.*, 2001). How to redistribute the demands and supply of the grain at the country level needs to be carefully studied.

As we can see, the marginal impact resulting from this policy varies, for instance, as seen in Table 14.3, the marginal impact in the Sichuan lowland is much larger than in the Loess Plateau. Potential improvement can be made by implementing different criteria in provincial and even county levels. From this assessment, several policies have been recommended: First, "Grain for Green" policy should be gradually implemented, first on the deep slope land and other ecologically sensitive cultivated land. Second, "grain for green" policies should be integrated with other policy and economic reforms. The best long term strategy is to encourage the population to emigrate from environmentally sensitive areas to higher population capacity areas. Third, converting cultivated land to forest should be coordinated with the improvement of remaining cultivated land and infrastructure development and other resource management. So far, the average grain supply in West China still cannot reach 400 kg, the required general standard in China. The constraints in transportation and other limited economic opportunities in West China makes the reliability of a local food supply become more important.

So far, this policy has been well implemented. The key reason for the success is cash and food compensation, which generally exceeds the farmers' net yield, and in some cases, gross yields, on the targeted land (CCICED, 2000). But the problem is "can we continue to keep such compensations when the converted land area increases?" What will happen when the compensation stops after five or eight years? So far, the policy implementation is strict and swift. The abrupt introduction of the policy, with necessary planning in advance, may lead to problems. Therefore, follow up monitoring and evaluation become important.

References

1.   Bao, Y., Zhang, R., Song, F. (2001). Primary study on forbidding cultivation for restoring forest or grass in sand region. *Journal of Inner-Mongolia Normal University* 30(1): 79-84 (in Chinese).
2.   CCICED (China Council for International Cooperation on Environment and Development). *2001 Forest/Grassland Taskforce Report* to the CCICED 2001 Annual Meeting. The 5th meeting of the 2nd phase of CCICED. Beijing (in Chinese).
3.   China's Ministry of Agriculture (MoA) (1990-1999). China Rural Statistical Materials. *China Agricultural Press*, Beijing (in Chinese).
4.   China's Statistical Bureau. *1997 China Statistical Yearbook*. China Statistical Press.
5.   Feng, Z. and Zhang, P. (2002). "Converting Cultivated Land to Forests and its Impact on Grain Production in West China", Institute of Geographical Science and Natural Resources Research, Chinese Academy of Sciences. Beijing (in Chinese).
6.   Feng,G. (2001). "Suggestions on Turning Cultivated Land to Forest or Grassland and Economic Development in West China". *Forestry Economy* (1): 50-52, 55 (in Chinese).
7.   Hou, Z. and Xiao, W. (2000). "Shifting Farm Land to Forests and Food Security in West China". *China Food and Nutrition* (3rd issue of 2000): 45-46 (in Chinese).
8.   Hu, A. (2001). "Region and Development: The New Development Stratagem of West China", *China Planning Press*, 206-238 (in Chinese).
9.   Lu, X., Lu, S., and Zhou, X. (2001). "Shifting Farm Land to Forests and the Dynamic Demand and Supply of Grain in West China", *Social Sciences of Gansu* (2nd issue of 2001): 10-14 (in Chinese).
10.   Ma, H. (2001). "Study on Agricultural Reversion of Farmland and Sustainable Development in West Region", *Journal of Adult Education Institute of Politics and Law* (1): 85-88, 92 (in Chinese).

11.   Mather, A.S. (1992). "The Forest Transition", *Area* 24, 367 -379.
12.   Mauldin, T.E., Plantinga, A.J., and Alig, R.J. (1999). "Land Use in the Lake States Region: An Analysis of Past Trends and Future Changes", U.S. Forest Service, Pacific Northwest Research Station, Research Paper PNW-RP-519. 24 pp.
13.   Park, P.J., Barbier, E.B., and Burgess, J.C. (1998). "The Economics of Forest Land Use in Temperate and Tropical area", *Environmental and Resource Economics* 11 (304): 473-487.
14.   Peng, K. (2001). "Study on Changing Cultivated Land to Forest (Grass) in West China", *Zhong-nan Forestry Investigating and Planning* (1): 56-61 (in Chinese).
15.   Pfaff, A. (2000). "From Deforestation to Reforestation in New England, United States". In Palo, M. Vanhanen, H. (eds), *World Forests from Deforestation to Transition?* pp. 67-82. Kluwer Academic, the Netherlands.
16.   Song, X. (1994). "Primary Study on Reclamation of Sloping Land and Returning Cultivated Land to Forest", *Shaanxi Forestry Science and Technology* (3): 63-65 (in Chinese).
17.   State Forestry Administration Bureau (SFAB) (2000). The 111th document issued Department of Planning, Forestry Administration Bureau: Appendix: Implementation Proposals for "Grain for Green" policy in the Upper Reaches of the Yangtze River and the Upper and Middle Reaches of the Yellow River (in Chinese).
18.   The compiling committee of China's population across millennia (CCCP) (1994). "China's Population Across Millennia", *China Statistical Press*, Beijing (in Chinese).
19.   Xu, J. and Cao, Y. (2002). "Sustainable Development Issues Involved in Converting Cultivated Land to Forests and Grassland", *International Economic Review* ¾ : 56-60 (in Chinese).
20.   Zhang, Y. (2001). "Deforestation and Forest Transition: Theory and Evidence from China". In Palo, M. Vanhanen,H.(eds),*World Forests from Deforestation to Transition?* Kluwer Academic, pp. 41–65.
21.   Zhang, Y., Uusivuori, J., Kuuluvainen, J. (2000). "Econometric Analysis of the Causes of Forest Land Use Change in Hainan, China", *Canadian Journal of Forest Research* 30: 1913-1921.

22. Zhao, X., Ma, Y. (1999). "The Ecological Function and Operating Measures of Turning Farmland to Forest", *Forest Resource Management* (3): 36-39 (in Chinese).
23. Zhu, B., Wang, D., Meng, Z. (2000). "Considering on Farmland Abandon and Afforestation on Slope Land in the Upper Reaches of Yangze River", *Study and Development of World Science and Technology* (22 S): 29-31 (in Chinese).

15 Education and Development: A Historical Experience of Sichuan

Yu Li

Since the Chinese government proposed the ambitious "Development Strategy of the West Region" in November, 1999, many articles have been published in Chinese newspapers and journals to contribute ideas for Chinese policy makers. One of the suggestions frequently offered in the articles is that to cause a rapid economic development, the government should invest more in education in West China because the shortage of men of talent, and the backwardness of the people's mentalities are the major obstacles to economic growth in the region.[1] *Xibu kaifa*, jiaoyu xianxing (Education pioneers the Western Exploration) has become one of the catchwords in discussing the strategy of the exploration.

Undoubtedly, education is important to economic development and heavier investment of education in West China is necessary. A World Bank paper published in 1989 reviewed more than one hundred studies on the connection between education and economic development, finding that most of the studies, which covered many nations throughout the world, including both rich nations and poor nations, reported a positive relationship between education and development.[2] It is also true that West China is underdeveloped not only in economic development but also in education. In the region there is indeed a shortage of men of talent, and people's mentalities need to change. Statistics show that investment in education in West China is lower than that of China's average.[3] Despite all of these facts, however, there are some potential problems in overemphasizing the instrumental function of education to development in underdeveloped regions like West China.

Though education is important, it is not necessarily always the most important factor to development. There might be some more urgent problems that need to be resolved first, taking into account the resource that is available to an underdeveloped region. In addition, though education is important, what is more important, as some scholars have already suggested, is the type of education sought and what the education is used to accomplish.[4] There is no reason to assume that education will be the same everywhere and that the type of education in industrial and advanced regions can always be applied to an underdeveloped region and be useful to its people. With regard to the relations between education and development, the contents of education – that is to say the types of knowledge, skills, and values taught – are often more important than the statistic growth of schools and enrolled students.

In this paper, I am going to examine the experience of Sichuan, a province of West China, in its effort to promote development through expanding education in the first two decades of the twentieth century. What is interesting with the case is that this populous, remote, closed, and backward province used to be the leader of China in the establishment of modern education. In quantitative expansion such as the number of schools and enrolled students, education reform in Sichuan achieved greater success than all of the coastal provinces in the early twentieth century. The expected social and economic development, however, did not follow in the later years. The gap between the province and coastal China continued to enlarge. At the end of the 20th century, almost one hundred years after the Qing educational reform, when the Chinese government proposed the "Development Strategy of the Western Region", Sichuan was still placed by the government in the category of backward, poor, and remote provinces of the western region, which need a "great exploration." Sichuan's experience mocks the proposition that education always works to promote development, and it is worth studying why it does.

Unfavourable Geographic Location

The basic fact with the case of Sichuan was that the backwardness of the province was much less due to its underdevelopment in education than to its unblessed geographical location. Indeed, Sichuan is a prisoner of geography. Two of the three major unfavourable geographic factors for a nation or a region's economic development (tropical climate, distance from the coastal areas, poor communications) identified by economic geographers, apply to Sichuan. Though not in the tropical zone, Sichuan is situated in the deep hinterland of China, more than one thousand kilometres away from the nearest coast. And the province is almost totally landlocked. The landform of Sichuan is like a basin. In the middle is a large plain called Chengdu Plain or Chuanxi Plain, which is surrounded by high mountains on all sides. The capital city of Sichuan, Chengdu, is located at the west of the plain. Before modern means of transportation were introduced to this province, its connection with the outside world relied on the Yangzi River and several narrow mountain paths leading to the neighbouring provinces, Shaanxi to the north, Hubei and Hunan to the east, and Guizhou and Yunnan to the south. The land paths that run over high mountains and along deep valleys are very dangerous roads and not very useful for large scale transportation. In his famous poem "Shu Dao Nan" the great Tang Sichuan poet, Li Bo (701-762BCE) sighs, "going to Sichuan by land path is more difficult than climbing up to the blue sky."[5]

Because of its special geographic environment, Sichuan in history had relatively loose connections with other parts of China and is viewed by modern scholars like William Skinner as one of the independent macro region, the so-called Upper Yangzi Region. In traditional agriculture economy, the landlocked geographic location didn't seem to be a big problem to the province. Sichuan basin possesses rich land and plenty of rainfall and it has an excellent irrigation project, the Dujianyan project, which was built two thousand years ago during the Qin dynasty (220-207BCE). Since its construction, agriculture in the greater portion of Sichuan plain has no longer been at the mercy of weather. The province therefore has become one of China's most important regions of grain production, known as "The Storehouse of Heaven". As late as the early twentieth century, outside visitors were still impressed by the wealth of the province, describing the province as "one of the fairest and richest corners of the Chinese Empire" and "a magnificent garden".[6]

The geographical location of Sichuan, however, has become a serious problem in modern times when access to global markets is regarded as the main engine of development for any country or region. Sichuan was obviously, compared to the coastal provinces, at a comparative disadvantage in participating in the international flow of capital, goods, technology and ideas since its distance from the seacoast would make transportation costs to and from the province very high. Ricardo Hausmann's discussion of the disadvantages of inland regions in economic development is highly relevant to the case of modern Sichuan though his focus is at the global level and his units of analysis are countries: "A recent study found that shipping goods over 1 additional kilometre of land costs as much as shipping them over 7 extra kilometres of sea. Maritime shipping is particularly suited to the bulky, low-value-added goods that developing nations tend to produce; therefore, countries lacking cheap access to the sea will be shut out of many potential markets."[7] This offers an explanation for the common phenomenon throughout the world that the coastal regions of a country are often the more developed regions. Though Sichuan has the Yangzi River to connect it to the coast, the narrow Three Gorges seriously reduced the value of the river as an important means of transportation in modern times. It was due to its unfavourable geographic location that Sichuan was excluded from the maritime commercial revolution which occurred on the coast of China.[8] If Sichuan's connection to the outside world is not substantially improved, the expansion of education alone will be of little help for the economic development of the province.

In the first decade of the twentieth century, the Sichuan government and people, following orders from the central government, took great pains to expand education. Local governments in prefectures and counties transformed all the traditional educational institutions under their jurisdictions, such as academies and charitable schools, into modern schools. Many Buddhist and Daoist temples were commandeered and used as schoolhouses and their lands and properties were transformed into education funds. Throughout the province special taxes for development of education were levied and teacher-training centres were established. Those local magistrates who did not make enough efforts to expand new education under their jurisdictions were punished and those who did outstanding work were rewarded.[9]

There were individuals in all social classes like officials, gentry, merchants, monks, and common people who were active in making donations to new schools. Even many widows were enthusiastic donors. From the connection of memorials of Xiliang, the Sichuan provincial governor of the time, we have learned that the governor submitted quite a number of memorials to the Qing emperor asking him to reward those Sichuan widows who donated their lands to new schools. Social organizations like *hanghui* (guilds), *tongxianhui* (associations of people from the same place), *zongqinghui* (associations of people who have the same family name) participated in the campaign of donation to the new schools.[10] Many of these individuals and organizations not only donated to the public schools but also founded private schools. With great enthusiasm in the new school system, resources levied for modernization and development from the province at the time were mainly used to expand education.

The establishment of new schools became a massive social movement in Sichuan at the turn of the twentieth century. The result of the movement was the emergence of the largest provincial new school system in China. The Qing government statistics of national education development in 1907 and 1909 showed that Sichuan ranked top of all the provinces of China in total number of schools and students. In 1909, for example, Sichuan had 10,661 schools, second only to Zhili (11,201), but far ahead of the southern coastal provinces, Jiangsu (1,357), Zhejiang (2,165) and Guangdong (1,294). In the number of students, Sichuan was the largest (345,383). The coastal province Jiangsu had only 44,708, while Zhejiang had 76,114; Guandong 86,437. Sichuan's record in the scale of school system remained at least until 1922. According to the statistics of the year, the total enrolled students in Sichuan numbered 556, 379, second only to Zhili (610, 916). Considering the rate of total population to the number of students, Sichuan was still far ahead of the coastal provinces.[11]

In contrast to its outstanding performance in schooling expansion, the first decade of twentieth century saw little improvement in Sichuan's transportation capacity. The transportation of goods into and out of Sichuan in early twentieth century was still mainly via the Yangzi River. The first modern steamboat did not come to Chongqing until 1909 and before that year the transportation along the Yangzi River between Hankou and Chongqing relied on about 2,500 old-fashioned junks whose total freight tonnage was around 80,000.[12] This transportation capacity was too little, for as early as 1907, steamboats in all the treaty ports in China already numbered 91,380 and their total freight tonnage was 74,130,376.[13] Due to the small capacity of transportation Sichuan had no significance in China's commercial economy. In the first decade of the twentieth century, Sichuan's proportion in the total of China's international trade was tiny, only about 4.22 percent.[14] Some researchers found that before 1911, the per capita possession of commercial goods in Sichuan was about only one fourth of that in Hubei province.[15]

Sichuan people and government did not totally ignore the problem of transportation and communication in their province. A railway connecting Chengdu and Hankou, the capital city of Hubei province, was planned and the Chuan-Han Railway Company declared to be established in 1904, the same year that the new school system was being organized in the province. Stocks of the company were sold to all Sichuan taxpayers. Unfortunately, a quarrel over who had the right to monopolize the construction of the railway occurred between the Qing court and Sichuan Provincial Assembly in 1910. People in Sichuan launched a railway protection movement, which later developed into a military confrontation with the Qing court and was one of the triggers of the 1911 revolution. Construction of the railway was thus suspended and it was not resumed until the 1950s, almost half a century later. The fact that it was the clash over a railway that caused the 1911 revolution symbolizes how critical transportation was to the development of the province. Without substantial improvement of its connection with the outside world, Sichuan's good performance in education failed to narrow the gap between it and the coastal provinces in development. It demonstrates that education is a necessary, but not by itself a sufficient, economic growth.

The Motives for Modern Education

Backward transportation and communication not only hindered the flow of capital and goods into Sichuan, it also impeded the spread of modern skills, knowledge, and values into the province. Education expanded in Sichuan in the first two decades of the twentieth century, but it was not accompanied by a radical change of the purpose and contents of education. And it was also not accompanied by a change of people's attitude toward education.

Making a sweeping statement about the positive relationship between education and development is useless unless the kind of education is clearly indicated. There was education expansion in pre-modern Europe but it was caused by the rivalry between the religious sects for control of people's minds and behaviour.[16]   There was also education expansion in late imperial China but it was mainly intended to spread Confucian moral principles. Economic development may not benefit from this kind of education, in fact, it may be impeded by it. Some scholars have already pointed out that education concentrating on Confucian classics might be one of the major reasons for China's failure to industrialize before the European countries.[17]

In the first decade of the twentieth century, the proclaimed goal of establishing a new school system was to modernize the country, as can be seen in Yuan Shikai's memorials about the end of the examination system[18] and in the 1906 Educational Rescript.[19] It was the assumption of such Qing reformers that Japan and Germany were ascendant because they had systematized school systems and educational doctrines and China had not, and that Prussia had defeated France (1871) and Japan had defeated Russia (1905) because they had centrally controlled schools and school textbooks. But the goal of the central government was not necessarily the goal of the local government and local people. Though the Sichuan provincial government spared no effort to expand schooling, it did it mainly in obedience to an administrative order from above. Its greatest concern was not the actual instrumental function of education to local development but how perfectly the provincial government carried out the order and therefore demonstrated the government's administrative effectiveness. In such a mindset, it stressed quantitative expansion rather than reform of education contents.

Local people who participated in the establishment of new schools had varied motives. Personal benefits from donations were the main motives of many people, not their interest in modern education or their understanding of the need for education for modernization and development. The Qing regime offered different rewards such as certificates of merit, honorific arches, or even official posts to donors according to the amount they donated. If the donor was already an official, and his donation was large enough, his official rank would be elevated. Certificates of merit and honorific arches might be employed by holders to promote their social prestige in the local society. Reward of official posts to donors was in fact the continuation of purchasing an official post in the second half of the nineteenth century.[20]

As I mentioned before, the most surprising donors for new schools in Sichuan were widows. Why were these widows so concerned with new schools, which seemed to have nothing to do with them? Widows were not, of course, more eager advocates of modern education. The real reason was that after the death of the husband of the family, if the widow had no children, the clan of the husband would covet the land of the family. In such a case, if the widow contributed some land or money to the official or public schools, she could get certain rewards from the government, such as a certificate of merit, or an honorific arch, which was a sort of protection for the property that was still in her hands. It is evident that the purposes and motives of many school founders and donators had little to do with development and modernization.

There were also problems with the contents of the new education. In the first two decades of the twentieth century Sichuan education authority was certainly concerned more with the numbers of the schools than with what was taught in schools. There was a serious lack of standard and qualified textbooks for many new schools. As late as 1913, about ten years after the education reform and two years after the revolution, many elementary schools, especially those in countryside, were still using traditional *mengxue* readers edited in late imperial China to teach students.[21]

A lack of qualified teachers in those modern schools was also a problem. It would be an undue expectation that after just a few months of training, those men of the old education system who grew up in *sishu* (traditional private schools) and knew nothing but Confucian classics could become qualified teachers in the new schools. Some contemporary records demonstrated how low the quality of the teachers could be in even some city schools. Guo Moruo, the famous writer of modern China, who had his primary and secondary school education respectively in Jiading city and Chengdu city, Sichuan, in the early twentieth century, said in his autobiography that his primary school mathematics teacher, a returned student from Japan, knew almost nothing about mathematics, but the teacher's knowledge about Confucian classical learning was one of the reasons for Guo's later interest in that subject. When Guo entered middle school, he found that his geography teacher, though familiar with *Shanhai jing, Huainanzi,* and *Dixinxun,*[22] was confused about the relative geographic positions of China, Japan, and Korea. The teacher was also interested in teaching students how to identify directions by employing The Five Elements (*wuxing*) and The Eight Trigrams (*bagua*).[23]

The norms and values the students learned to accept in such modern schools were also not the sort one would be expected to follow in a modern industrial society, rather, it was still the values and norms of the traditional Confucian society. This was clearly reflected in strict campus regulations of the new schools of the time.[24] Moral Character Cultivation and Confucian Classic Reading were still the two most important courses in the new schools, not only in Sichuan but also in the whole of China.

The school system was still practicing gender discrimination. The earliest girls' *sishu* in Sichuan was founded in 1903 by several returned students from Japan. The name of the *sishu* was Girls' *Sishu* for Fair Behaviour (*shuxin lushu*), which reflected the purpose of the school: training good wives and mothers. Confucian classics were the major courses of the students. It was not until 1907 that the name of this school was changed to Girls' School for Fair Behaviour (*shuxin luxue*). The name of the school changed but its purpose did not.

Although the new school system in Sichuan was established as early as 1904, modern girls' schools were not permitted in Sichuan until 1907 when the Qing regime issued Regulations for Primary Girls' Schools and Regulations for Girls' Normal Schools which called for the localities to open girls' schools. Before 1907, although there were some girls' schools in Sichuan, they were in fact *sishu* rather than new schools. In 1905, a lady Zhou, nee Zhang, applied to transform the girls' *sishu* she had opened into a new girls' school, but her application was rejected by the provincial Board of Education, which claimed:

> According to the combined regulations for *mengyang* (elementary school) and *jiajiao* (family teaching), Chinese girls should be taught in families. To establish girls' schools will cause many problems, and therefore it is not appropriate. China had different customs from those of the West, which should not be adopted incautiously. Therefore, this board will not ratify any applications for founding girls' schools.[25]

After 1907, though girl schools were established and girls were allowed to receive a school education, there were still many social restrictions that hindered them in going to school. The number of female students enrolled in schools before 1949 was much smaller than that of the male students.

Students enrolled into the schools at this period not because they were interested in new knowledge but because they viewed the new school system as a new path of social mobility that replaced the abolished civil service examination system. This explains the phenomenon of the sudden increase of enrollment in new schools in 1905, the year when the civil service examination system was abolished. In 1904, Sichuan had only 170 new schools and 6,308 enrolled students, while in 1905, the number of schools sharply increased to 2793, and that of enrolled students to 145,876.[26]

It was not the enthusiasm for modern education but the abolition of the civil service examination that was the major driving force for young men in Sichuan to go to new schools. This kind of attitudes toward new education was partly the result of the encouragement of the Qing policy. The Qing court decided to offer civil service examination titles and official posts to the graduates of the new schools. A student who graduated from an upper primary or middle school would get a *shengyuan* or *gongsheng* title, while those who graduated from higher schools would receive a *juren* title and be appointed to a post of county magistrate. Those graduated from universities would be eligible for *jinshi* title and might be assigned to positions in *Hanlin* academy. It is evident that to many students of the time the modern school was merely a new ladder of success replacing the abolished civil service examination. Such attitudes toward modern education can be found in other societies. For example, in his study of educational development in South Asia after World War Two, Gunnar Myrdal found that there was, throughout the region, a dislike for manual work that affected the way people approached education and the use they made of it. Myrdal was, of course, right to point out, "The notion that education is valuable because it affords an avenue of escape from manual work cannot be regarded as legitimate from a development point of view."[27]

Students going to modern schools didn't mean that their attitude toward education had changed. It is well known that the great mass fervour of Chinese students to go to study in Japan in the first decade of the twentieth century was stimulated by the defeat of China by Japan in the first Sino-Japanese War in 1894.[28] What is not so well known is that the effect of the abolition of the examination system was equally, if not more, important. The climax of the fervour, after all, did not really come until 1905, ten years after the war. The Qing government and educational reformers encouraged students to study in Japan for the purpose of strengthening China, but did the students departing for Japan cherish the same purpose when they responded to the government call? Some present-day historians like Paula Harrell think the students did, believing "they went to Japan looking for solutions to China's backwardness."[29] But the general validity of this point of view is very doubtful. A careful examination of Sichuan students' motivations for studying in Japan suggested that many of them were more concerned with the change of their educational identity and the symbolic significance of having been to Japan than the study there, *per se*. The year when there were the most Chinese students in Japan was also the year the quality of the students was poorest.

Most of the students who went to Japan during 1905-1906 studied in the common schools and short-cut schools which were opened particularly for Chinese students. The common schools, just like their Chinese copies, were middle schools and primary schools. The short-cut schools were either normal schools or law and administration schools (*fazheng xuetang*), some of which were so lax that students in them needed to study only for several months or even just several days.[30] The Qing Education Ministry reported to the emperor in 1907: "In recent years, we have investigated carefully the number of students studying in Japan, and found that though the total has been over ten thousand, 60 percent of them study in short-cut schools; 30 percent of them are students in common schools; 5-6 percent of them have dropped out of schools without finishing their courses; 3-4 percent have entered higher schools or advanced specialist schools; and those who have entered universities are just one percent."[31] It is hard to believe that the students in those poorly qualified short-cut schools could find any "solutions to China's backwardness."

It is more valid to argue that to many students who had a traditional educational background, studying abroad, as well as entering domestic new schools, was very much a new path of advancement that replaced the civil service examination. Though Sichuan was a closed, conservative, and backward province in inland China, it was one of the provinces which sent the most students to Japan. One of the reasons for this contradictory phenomenon was that Sichuan had a larger surplus student population from the old education system than most of the other provinces, and many of the students regarded study in Japan as a new social *chulu* (exit).

The Sichuan case suggests that statistical growth of education does not mean modernity. If there is not significant change of the contents and purpose of education, quantitative education expansion means very little. This partly explains why Sichuan had more schools and enrolled students than coastal China, but the new school system did not provide Sichuan with larger dynamics for development in the early twentieth century.

No Escape from Socio-economic Setting

The expansion of education without considering its social setting might even cause some pathologic outcomes. Expansion of education in Qing China had caused relative surplus of the student population in the nineteenth century. This was because on one hand, the expansion of schools in the Qing produced a larger number of students than ever before in Chinese history,[32] while on the other hand, the Qing regime purposely restricted the number of upper degree holders for political reasons,[33] and the pre-industrial society with its limited choices of occupations was unable to absorb all the career-seeking students. Since the aim for a student to obtain education in society was to become a political elite member, a surplus of the student population resulting from educational expansion caused serious troubles to the whole mechanism of elite recruiting. This was different from the case of an industrial society where students could be absorbed by the large number of modern political, cultural, social, and especially, economical, institutions.

The problem of the growth of schooling in Sichuan in the first two decades of the twentieth century was similar. With modest improvement of its communication to outside world and little development of modern industry, the modern educational reform and expansion of schooling took place in a socio-economic setting that differed little from that of the 19th century. It was interesting to see how the students tried to reach a compromise between modern education and unchanged social reality through specialty selection. Sichuan students' three preferred specialties at the time were law and administration, military subject, and pedagogy. For example, the local gazetteer of Shuangliu county, a county near Chengdu, recorded 82 students graduated from higher schools or specialist schools between the years 1905 and 1915, of whom the specialty distribution was as follows:[34]

Specialty	Number
Law and Administration	27
Military	26
Normal school	11
Science and technology	10
Higher School (no specialty indicated)	3
Agriculture and Sericulture	2
Police	2
Business	1
Total	82

Undoubtedly, the distribution of specialties indicates the influence of the examination system on the students' occupation choice. Obviously, the first two specialties, law and administration, and military, corresponded with the abolished civil service examination and the military examination, while schoolteacher was the most popular job of the failed examination participants in traditional China.

But more important, the specialty distribution reflected that there was little change of social reality. Sichuan society was still basically a traditional agricultural society and there was therefore no urgent social requirement for the skills and knowledge in science and technology that would be imperative to modern industrial society. The lack of interest in the study of science and technology can also be found in other parts of the world where the social setting was still largely that of an agrarian society. For example, in 1810, forty-five percent of the students in French public *lycees* and *colleges* were majoring in law, whereas only five percent studied science.[35] In 1963 at the new University of Abidjan of the Ivory Coast, an African country, 550 students were majoring in law, while only 44 were in science.[36]

The focus of reform in early twentieth century Sichuan was mainly on the construction of new governmental, military and educational institutions rather than on development of modern industrial economy. This, to a great extent, decided what was taught and what the students wanted to learn in schools. To satisfy the interest for law and administration, and military education, a large number of specialist schools on law and on the military were founded. In Chengdu alone, there were nearly fifty private law and administration schools opened in the first two years after the founding of the Republic, and many of them were poorly qualified. Guo Moruo writes in his autobiography:

> "The great number of privately founded law and administration schools exhibited most clearly the Chinese opportunist psychology, and eagerness for official posts. In Chengdu city whose girth was just 22 *li*, there were a good number of privately founded law and administration schools when we went there for the first time before the revolution, but within the first one or two years after the revolution,

all of a sudden, the numbers of this sort of school increased to about fifty. Three month short-cut, six month short-cut, and one year short-cut schools! The educational institutions of the time produced the talents of law and administration faster than paper-flower-making craftsworkers produced paper flowers. There were plenty of admirable rumours such as father and son, grandfather and grandson, studying in the same law and administration schools. China was thus 'reformed' and thus 'self-strengthened'".[37]

Not only in Sichuan but also in the whole of China at the time, education in law and administration was poor. In 1914, the Education Ministry of the Chinese government condemned the blind passion for law and administration education, warning that "a great number of law and administration schools recruited unqualified students and attached no importance to education, while the enrolled students were concerned only with diplomas and official posts."[38] The ministry then sent two inspectors to inspect the privately founded law and administration schools in several provinces. When the inspectors returned to Beijing, they submitted to the ministry a very negative report of the schools they had inspected, accusing them of "being bent solely on profit."[39] This kind of school could contribute very little to development.

Sichuan students' interests in the study of military subjects in this period also had little positive effect on the development of the province. During the reform period in the first decade of the twentieth century, the military service examination system was abolished as well. Just as the civil officials in the modern government were trained in law and administration schools, the officers in the new army would now be trained in modern military schools. This change offered the young men of education in Sichuan a new chance. To study in a military school became one of their popular choices. In about ten years between 1902 and 1912, there were at least eight military schools established in Sichuan, which trained 2,830 military officers. The most important military factions in Sichuan during the later Warlord period, such as the *Wubei* faction, the *Sucheng* faction, the *Baoding* faction,[40] and the *Junguan* faction, were formed around the students who graduated from these schools.[41] Viewed from this perspective, these military schools offered one of the preconditions for Sichuan warlordism in the following decades. Ironically, the expansion of education in the first decades of the twentieth century contributed more to the military disturbances instead of to the economic development, of Sichuan.

Another negative consequence of blind education expansion in the pre-industrial Sichuan social environment was brain drain. One of the characteristics of the new education system in early twentieth century China was that it tended to change the geographical distribution of high level students in favour of more developed areas such as cities and coastal China. The able and ambitious ones now felt that Sichuan, the closed and backward province, was not a place for them. Many left Sichuan to seek careers in other parts of China, especially in the cities of coastal provinces and in treaty ports. There was a great number of eminent Chinese in the twentieth century, such as Deng Xiaoping, Guo Moruo, Zhang Daqian, who were from Sichuan. But most of them left Sichuan very young. The brain drain problem makes the argument that education benefits development less valid. If there was not some basic change of the socioeconomic environment, and more opportunities for those who had modern knowledge and skills, the jobless school graduates would be forced to leave Sichuan. In this sense, Sichuan itself did not benefit from its education expansion, coastal China did.

Conclusion

This paper is not intended to belittle the importance of education to development or to deny the connections between the two. Based on the study of the historical experience of Sichuan in the early twentieth century, it argues that education is certainly a necessary, but not a sufficient, cause of economic growth. In landlocked areas like West China, there might be some more important and urgent work than the expansion of education, such as improvement of means of transportation and communication, which should have priority too. After all, the real goal of the exploration of the western region was nothing else but to incorporate this region into the world capitalist market, so as to cause a smoother flow of capital, goods, technology, and modern values to the region. Without substantial improvement of transportation and communication, it was almost impossible to achieve the goal. The paper also attempts to point out that though education is important, more important is the type of education sought and what the education is used to accomplish. The case of Sichuan shows that in underdeveloped regions, without adequate attention to the contents of education, that is, what is taught in schools, growth of schooling alone contributes very little to development.

Though the paper is about the story of a province in the western region nearly one hundred years ago, it could become a present-day story if the Chinese policy makers fail to realize all the potential problems with an overemphasis of education expansion in the region. It is obvious that some basic geographic and socio-economic obstacles of the region, which existed one hundred years ago, have not yet been totally removed. These obstacles could still divert the aim of education expansion and impede the healthy development of education. Actually, recent studies show that similar problems have already begun to appear in West China, along with the outcry for increasing education investment in the region.[42] On one hand, it is certain that investment in education is insufficient in West China; on the other hand, there has been a serious waste of educational resources. Curricula in many schools of West China take little consideration of the needs of local society, but are blind copies of that of developed areas. Since there are not enough economic and technical institutions which make use of their skills, many students who graduated from colleges and universities in West China found that their skills and knowledge are not needed by local society, and they have to be crowded into government or public organizations which have little to do with their training.

Some students who cannot find proper jobs in West China choose to migrate to east coast provinces where there are more opportunities. Now it is not only manual labourers but also college and university students who migrate from the west region to East China to find jobs. This phenomenon has been euphemistically described as "Peacocks flying to the east." (*kongque dongnanfei*). According to a recent study of 4 million domestic educated migrants in the late 1990s, 76.3% of them are migrants to East China while only 13.97% of them are those to West China. Undoubtedly, there has been another wave of "brain drain" from West

China since the beginning of the reform era. It is therefore understandable that some scholars argue that in West China it is more important to keep and use men of talent now available to the region than train more men of talent.[43]

In China, the view that education is most critical to development is not novel at all. Indeed, throughout modern Chinese history, the Chinese elite has steadfastly believed in the instrumental value of education to China's development and modernization. However different their political ideologies and concepts of modernization might be, Chinese modern reformers, intellectuals and political leaders, have all assumed that modernity should begin with people's minds and that education could reform the people. The idea was reflected in the educational guidelines designed by the late Qing educational reformers like Zhang Zhidong and Yuan Shikai, in the concept of "new people" proposed by Liang Qichao and Sun Yat-sen, in the articles written by the intellectuals of the May 4th Movement, in the liberal intellectuals' Rural Reconstruction, in Chiang Kai-shek's New Life Movement and even in Mao Zedong's Cultural Revolution. The present idea, "education should pioneer the Western Exploration", is just the most recent version of the view. After so many examples of failure, however, it is time to argue that strategy of development of West China should no longer rest on clichéd slogans but on a solid and detailed study of historical experience and careful investigation of the socio-economic setting of the region.

Notes

1.   See Zhou Jin, 2000; Zhong Li-xia and Zheng Chang-de, 2000.
2.   See Tilak, 1989.
3.   Wang Bida, 2002:50.
4.   Porter, 2000: 15. Also see Woodside, 1992: 23-46.
5.   Li Bai, 1997:81.
6.   Adshead 1984:3.
7.   Hausmann, 2001: 46.
8.   According to Hao Yen-ping, the revolution was essentially limited to the coastal areas. Hao Yen-ping, 1986: 337.

9.   About the records of reward and punishment of Sichuan local magistrates concerning their works in education reform, see *Sichuan Xuebao* 1904, vol. 16; 1905, vol 12: *gongdu*.

10.   Xiliang 1959:582.

11.   We don't have the population figures of the provinces of China in the early 20th century, but we have those in 1947. The populations of Sichuan and coastal provinces in the year were as follows: Sichuan 48,107,821; Jiangshu 37,089,667; Zhejiang 19,942,112; Guangdong 29,101,941. See Ho Ping-ti, 1959: 94-95.

12.   Yan Zhongping and others, 1955: 235.

13.   Yan Zhongping and others, 1955: 221.

14.   Zhang Xuejun and Zhang Lihong, 1990: 106.

15.   Wei Yingtao, 1990: 254

16.   See Strauss, 1976: 69.

17.   Eastman, 1988: 153.

18.   *Guangxu Chao Donghua Lu*, IX, 4979-4982.

19.   *Guangxu Chao Donghua Lu,X*, 5474-5479.

20.   Yu Li, 1999: 69.

21.   *Wendu Monthly* 1913, February , no. 7 *faling*: 7.

22.   All are ancient Chinese pre-scientific geographic books.

23.   Guo Moruo, 1978: 64; 95.

24.   For the regulations, consult Shu Xincheng. 1961: 3 Vol.

25.   *Sichuan xuebao*, 1905: No.15: 62.

26.   Yu Li, 1999: 83.

27.   Myrdal, 1968: 1538.

28.   Shu Xincheng, 1933: 4; Huang Fuqing, 1975: 2.

29.   Harrell, 1992: 5.

30.   Saneto Keishu, 1982: 37.

31.   Shu Xincheng, 1933: 55.

32.   For discussion of Qing education expansion, See Woodside and Elman, 1994: 525.

33.   For a detailed analysis of how the civil service examination system, as the major elite recruiting mechanism, was weakened in the Qing dynasty, see Woodside.1994: 472-474.

34.   *Shuangliu xianzhi*,1920.2: 104a-105b.

35.   Stearns, 1998: 36.
36.   Abernethy,1969: 11.
37.   Guo Moruo, 1978: vol.1, 296.
38.   Jiaoyu zazhi.1914: vol.5, no.10, *jishi*, 85.
39.   Jiaoyu zazhi.1914: vol.5, no.10, *jishi*, 93.
40.   This faction was formed around the students who had studied in the Sichuan Land Force Primary School. Because most of the students who graduated from that school were finally sent to Baoding Officer School in Hebei., the faction was thus named.
41.   See Zhang Zhonglei, 1962: 355-364.
42.   Wang Bida, 2002.
43.   Cai Raoyun, 2001: 53

References

1.   Abernethy, David B. (1969). *The Political Dilemma of Popular Education: An African Case*. Stanford: Stanford Univ. Press.
2.   Adshead, S.A.M. (1984). *Province and Politics in Late Imperial China: Viceregal Government in Szechwan*. London: Curzon Press.
3.   Cai Raoyun (2001). "Luelun xibu kaifa de renli zhiyuan zhanlue" (A brief Comment on the Strategy of Human Resources for the Exploration of the West Region), in *Shehui Kexue Yanjiu*, Chengdu: Social Science Academy of Sichuan, Vol. 5.
4.   Eastman, Lloyed E. (1988). *Family, Fields, and Ancestors Constancy and Change in China's Social and Economic History 1550-1949*. New York: Oxford University Press.
5.   *Guangxu Chao Donghua Lu*, IX, X
6.   Guo Moruo (1978). *Moruo zizhuan* (Moruo's Autobiography) Vol.1 *Shaonian Shidai* Vol.2 *Xuesheng shidai*. Hong Kong: Joint Publishing Co.
7.   Hao Yen-ping (1986). *The Commercial Revolution in Nineteenth Century China: the Rise of Sino-Western Mercantile Capitalism*. Berkeley : University of California Press.
8.   Harrell, Paula (1992). *Sowing the Seeds of Change: Chinese Students, Japanese Teachers 1895-1905*, Standford: Standford University Press.

9.   Hausmann, Ricardo (2001). "Prisoners of geography". In *Foreign Policy*, Washington; Issue 122, Jan/Feb.

10.   Huang Fuqing (1975). *Qingmo liuri xuesheng* (The Overseas Students in Japan at the End of the Qing Dynasty), Taipei: Institute of Modern History Academia Sinica.

11.   *Jiaoyu Zazhi* (1914). Vol. 5, No.10; No.11.

12.   Li Bo. "Shudaonan" (The Tough Roads to Sichuan), in *Tangshi sanbai shou*, Zhanghua: guangming guoxue chubanshe.

13.   Myrdal, Gunnar (1968). *Asian Drama: An Inquiry into the Poverty of Nations*, 3 vols. Harmondsworth: Penguin Books.

14.   Porter, Michael E. (2000). "Attitude, Values, Beliefs, and the Microeconomics of Prosperity." In Lawrence E. Harrison, ed. *Culture Matters: How Values Shape Human Progress*. New York: Basic Books.

15.   Saneto Keishu (1982). Translated by Tan Ruqian and Lin Qiyan. *Zhongguoren liuxue riben shi* (A History of Chinese Students in Japan) Hong Kong: Zhongwen daxue chubanshe.

16.   Shu Xincheng (1933). *Jindai zhongguo liuxue shi* (The History of Overseas Study in Modern China) Shanghai: Zhonghua shuju.

17.   Shu Xincheng (ed) (1961). *Zhongguo jindai jiaoyushi ziliao* (Documentary Materials in Modern Chinese Educational History) 3 Vol. Beijing: Renmin jiaoyu chubanshe.

18.   *Shuangliu xianzhi*, 1920.

19.   *Sichuan xuebao* , vol. 12, 1904; vol. 16, 1905.

20.   Stearns, Peter N. (1998). *Schools and Students in Industry Society: Japan and the West 1870-1940*. Boston Bedford Books.

21.   Strauss, Gerald (1976). "The State of Pedagogical Theory C. 1530: What Protestant Reformers knew About Education", in Stone, Lawrence, ed. *Schooling and Society: Studies in the History of Education*.

22.   Tilak, Jandhyala B.G. (1989). *Education and Its Relation to Economic Growth, Poverty , and Income Distribution: Past Evidence and Further Analysis*. World Bank Discussion Papers, Washington DC: The World Bank.

23.   Wang Bida (2002). "Pingqiong de jiaoyu yu jiaoyu langfei" (Education in Poverty and Waste in Education) in *Shehui Kexue Yanjiu*, Chengdu: Social Science Academy of Sichuan, vol. 2.

24. Wei Yingtao (ed) (1990). *Sichuan jindai shigao* (A Draft of Sichuan History) Chengdu: Sichuan Renmin chubanshe.

25. *Wendu Monthly* (1913) February, no. 7.

26. Woodside, Alexander and Elman, Benjamin (eds) (1994). *Education and Society in Late Imperial China 1600-1900.* Berkeley: University of California Press.

27. Woodside, Alexander and Elman, Benjamin (1992), "Real and Imagined Continuities in the Chinese Struggle for Literacy." In Ruth Hayhoe (ed) *Education and Modernization: The Chinese Experience.* Oxford: Pergamon Press.

28. *Xiliang yigao* (1959). 2 vols. Beijing: Zhonghua shuju.

29. Yan Zhongping *et al.*, (eds) (1955). *Zhongguo jindai jingjishi tongji ziliao xuanji* (Selected Statistics Data in Economic History of Modern China) Shanghai: Kexue chubanshe.

30. Yu Li (1998). "Social Change During the Ming-Qing Transition and The Decline of Sichuan Classical Learning in the Early Qing", in *Late Imperial China.* John Hopkins University, Volume 19, No.1, June.

31. Zhang Xuejun and Zhang Lihong (1990). *Sichuan jingdai gongye shi* (The History of Modern Sichuan Industry). Chengdu: Sichuan People's Publishing House.

32. Zhang Zhonglei (1962). "Qingmo Minchu Sichuan de Junshi xuetang ji chuanjun paixi." (Sichuan Military Schools and the Factions of Sichuan army during the Late Qing and Early Republic) in Zhongguo renmin zhengzhi xieshang huiyi quanguo weiyuanhui, ed., *Xinghai geming huiyilu,* Vol. 3.

33. Zhong Li-xia and Zheng Chang-de (2000). "Development of Human Resource and Accumulation of Human Capital in Western Region of China" in *Journal of Sichuan University* (Social Science Edition), No. 5.

34. Zhou Jin (2000). "Xibu dakafa yu renli zhiben youxian jinei zhanlue" (The Great Exploration of the Western Region and the Strategy of Accumulation of Human Capital), in *Shehui kexue*, No. 6.

Part IV. Distribution of Benefits and Costs

16 The New Challenges Facing the Development of West China[1]

Liu Shiqing and Lin Ling

Since the inception of the China's Western Region Development Program, there has been an upsurge of development never seen before in West China. As a consequence, the Program has already achieved considerable progress. However, it is also facing a series of new challenges:

Environmental Protection versus Improving the Living Standards of Local People

Owing to long-term natural changes, great destruction by Man, and a deficiency in its treatment and protection, the ecological environment of the western region is seriously threatening the economic and social development of the whole country. The Yangtze River often floods, the lower reach of Yellow River is short of water with increasing frequency and the sand storms of northern China become more devastating. These phenomena make treating and protecting the ecological environment the priority in the Western Region Development Program. As a result, the central government has taken such actions as implementing the "Natural Forest Protection Project" and the "Grain for Green Project" in sloping fields and has given financial support to these projects. Many provinces have also put forward the "Beautifying Hill and Water Project" and "Ecological Barrier Project of the Upper Waters of the Yangtze River ". These efforts have gained support nationwide and praise from the international community. However, cutting natural forests and growing grain in sloping fields are the sources of livelihood upon which poor local peasants depend. Logging is also the financial mainstay of local counties. At the early stages of implementing these actions, there was a "shut-down effect". The living standards of local peasants fell sharply and their livelihood was threatened. Some local counties dependent on forestry lost most of their fiscal revenues (Lin Ling and Liu Shiqing, 2000). Now, after the central government's compensation policies have taken effect, the situation is getting better. However, these policies only give local peasants short-term compensation and cannot make them rich. Peasants are not only the protectors of the environment, but also its destroyers. Once the livelihood of these peasants is threatened, some will cut woods, and destroy the forest and grass for their living. Such examples have often taken place in the past. The solution to this challenge is to integrate the treatment and protection of the environment with creating avenues for local peasants to better their economic prospects. Only by doing so will the western region attain economically, socially, and ecologically sustainable development.

To reach this aim is not easy. A series of policies need to be implemented by focusing on the fostering of industrialization and commercialization. It must include new regulations on property rights, such as on woods right, the distribution of proceeds from state-owned forest protection and breeding, the auction and long-term tenancy of desolated hills and slopes suitable for forests, and the paid transaction of contracted land. It should further include efforts to commercialize and industrialize the forest and grassland industries, the processing of forest products, the planting and processing of Chinese traditional medicinal herbs with modern technology, the development of crop farming, seedling growing, and processing industries. Peasants must be able to attain profits from the development of these enterprises. In order to make these enterprises successful, we must foster individually-run enterprises, encourage entrepreneurs of non-public enterprises to move into rural areas, with the necessary fiscal and policy support from the government.

Infrastructure Construction versus Western-Region Industrialization

In terms of infrastructure, West China is a laggard among the rest of China. It is therefore necessary to strengthen the western region's infrastructure during the implementation of the Western Region Development Program.

However, infrastructure construction must be accompanied by the exploitation of resources and the development of manufacturing industries. For example, the construction of the Chengdu-Kunming railroad fostered the setting up of the Panzhihua Steel Base and the construction of the double-track railroad of Longhai is to exploit the petroleum and natural gas reserves of Xinjiang. Similarly, the large-scale railroad construction in East China during the 1980s solved the transportation bottlenecks of the eastern coastal regions, and the construction of large-scale power plants in Guangdong allowed the province to develop its external economy.

The large-scale infrastructure construction in the western region must also have definite goals. If we do not consider demand when constructing expressways or airports, these projects might be left with insufficient uses upon completion. Infrastructure requires big investments and, generally, the return on these investments is low. If demand is insufficient, the investment return period will be very long. Indeed, expenditure might not be recouped at all. This will lead to the waste of scarce capital. For example, there are five airports in the small Pearl River Delta region and there is a TV relay tower every eight kilometres in the Suxichang region. Care must be taken to not create a similar situation in the western region.

The policy of fostering infrastructure construction in the western region in the past two years is right. Nonetheless, there is a drawback in neglecting the technological transformation and development of the manufacturing industry. The country has decided to implement many grand projects in the western region including the western region-East natural gas transmission project, the western region-East electricity transmission project, the Qinghai-Tibet railroad project, the HuaiHua railroad project, several expressways, airports, and the "Three Gorges Power Plant" under construction. We estimate that the whole investment amounts to over a thousand billion *yuan*. The construction of these projects is very important for the future development of the western region. However, because the western region does not have the ability to produce the engineering and construction equipment and materials that these projects need, equipment and materials have to be purchased from the eastern region and other countries. So, 50-60% of the whole investment will be used to acquire goods and services from the eastern region. In terms of the whole country, this is a good layout, in that the western and eastern regions are complementary. Yet in terms of Western Region Development Program, the procurement of equipment and materials from firms in China's eastern region will not be a boost to the development of the western-region manufacturing industry. This might widen the big gap between the western and eastern regions, 70% of the daily industrial consumer goods consumed in the western provinces are now made in and imported from the eastern regions. If this situation lasts, the East-West gap will grow larger.

Accordingly, we should adjust the proportion between the investment in infrastructure and the investment in technological transformation to develop the western region's manufacturing industry. We should let the western region get more resources for the development of manufacturing. In other words, infrastructure construction in the western region should develop gradually and orderly on the basis of actual demand. At the same time, the manufacturing industry of the western region should be actively strengthened, especially for the following important industries: heavy equipment manufacturing, electrical equipment manufacturing, transmission and distribution, equipment manufacturing, steel, automobiles, engineering machine manufacturing, motorcycle manufacturing, material industries, electronics information industries, daily consumer goods industries, farm products processing industries, etc.

There are two wrong ideas concerning the western region development. One emphasizes only infrastructure construction, while it neglects the development of manufacturing industries. The other is to restrain the development of the western region's manufacturing industry in order to avoid the construction of redundant industries.

Western Region Resource Exports versus Local Utilization

China has formed a regional layout under which the western region explores and supplies resources and the eastern region processes resources and manufactures goods. When China was a centrally planned economy, the government administrated the prices of resources and supplied them to the eastern region for processing at low cost. Until the early 1990s, the policy of supplying the eastern region with raw materials from the western region at low prices was still an important part of policies supporting the development of the eastern region. Prices for raw materials from the western region were artificially low, while prices for processed products of the eastern region were high. So the eastern and the western regions got different revenues from their different products. This is the fundamental reason why the eastern region developed faster than the western region. Now that China has become a surplus economy with excess supply since the mid-1990s, products such as general goods, energy resources, and raw materials are in surplus. This has a big impact on the energy industry, the raw materials industry, the consumer goods industry of the western region and many industries of the western region are running in the red. Since the reform and opening-up of China, because many resources can be purchased from the international market, the demand of the eastern region for the western region energy resources lessened. But there is no change in the layout of regional division of industry that the western region explores and supplies resources and the eastern region processes and manufactures goods.

Many experts suggest changes for this industrial division of labour between the eastern and western regions. Nonetheless, in view of the many grand projects under construction, it can be seen that the layout is basically retained. For example, the West-East natural gas transmission project is to transmit natural gas from Xinjiang to East China via a 4000-kilometre pipeline. While the project is necessary, it might be more wise to exploit the natural gas directly to develop the natural gas industry of the western region so that the use of natural gas can add greater value to the western region's industries. If the western region only extracts and transmits the natural gas to the eastern region, the provincial governments in the western region can benefit very little in fiscal revenues.

Another case is the West-East electricity transmission project, which is important for improving the environment of the eastern region. If the western region only generates and transmits the electricity to the eastern region and does not develop local industries, especially the high energy-consuming industries, the western region will gain little from the tax revenues and the development of new industries.

In conclusion, the Western Region Development Program should integrate the exploitation of natural resources with the development of processing industries. The western region is rich in non-ferrous metals, rare earth metals, and precious metals. These resources are important raw materials for high energy-consuming industries, the products of which are in high demand. If the western region makes use of its ample energy resources such as hydro-energy and natural gas to develop high energy-consuming industries, the western region can develop better. One interesting example is the large-scale relocation over the past several years of the ceramics industry of Foshan County in Guandong province to Jiajiang County in Sichuan province. As a result, Jiajiang County has become the capital of ceramics in West China. Electricity prices and labour costs are high in Foshan County, while these costs are much lower in Jiajiang County which has, in addition, ample natural gas. So Jiajiang County has been able to attract producers from Foshan County. This shows that the rich natural resources and cheap electricity of the western region have distinct advantages, enabling the western region to attract capital and industrial know-how from the eastern region. Strategically, the western region should not only export its characteristic resources directly to the eastern region, but should also use these resources to attract capital and industrial know-how from the East.

The Need for Policy Support

The scarcest resource in western region development is capital. The current situation is that funds from the central government and the issuance of national bonds have started to flow in increasing amounts to the western region. However, other sources of capital have remained less significant. In addition, capital from the western region continues to flow to the eastern region, because of a new phenomenon of deposit surplus in the banking sector in the western region. It is estimated that new loans only take up 70% of newly added deposits in Sichuan province, Yunnan province, Guizhou province and the Tibet Autonomous Region during 1999. In Sichuan province, the four major state-owned commercial banks, which formerly had a loan surplus, have now experienced a deposit surplus with total surplus deposits amounting to 60 billion *yuan*. This abnormal situation signifies that the financial situation of the western region has not improved but worsened.

In western region development, the central government topped up the loans for poverty alleviation and the Ministry of Finance has increased the appropriation used for subsidy the interests of loans. However, because the loans for poverty alleviation are offered by commercial banks, the commercial loans need collateral. Because the poor in the western region have no collateral, most people cannot get loans for poverty alleviation. According to a recent survey that we took in Guanyuan town of Sichuan province, only 30% of the total loans for poverty alleviation have been borrowed. Therefore, for poor peasants, which account for 80% of all the poor in the country, poverty alleviation loans are only a nice cake drawn on paper. The loans cannot help poor farmers to develop their productive forces.

As water flows down to low places, capital flows to where the returns are high. Therefore, to create conditions that attract domestic and overseas capital to the western region and let the western region retain its capital are pivotal problems that Western Region Development Program must address. Under the conditions of a market economy, the aim is to let all capital flow freely and thus allow capital to obtain the highest returns. However, the capital markets of the western region are not only unable to attract domestic and foreign capital flows but also are unattractive to local capital. Because the eastern region has the ability to accumulate, develop and expand by itself, it can continue to attract large amounts of capital. For instance, most investments in the high-technology industry will concentrate in the eastern region.

The speed of development of the eastern region will exceed that of the western region, at least in the next few years and the gap will widen further. Under these circumstances, the Western Region Development Program must build a good environment to attract the capital. While the western region must strengthen reforms, central policy support is also very important and necessary. It was central government's policy support that made the eastern region develop so fast in the 1980s. At that time, the eastern coastal region not only got the preferential policies of the planned economy, but also the gains from initiating the market economy. So there was a big policy difference between the eastern and western regions. It was the policy difference that made the eastern region attract all kinds of capital and other factors of production such as high quality talented people and cheap labour forces. So the eastern region developed at a high speed in the last twenty years. Now, the economic, political, and cultural environments have changed greatly. But the nature of capital is unchanged. In order to attract the capital to invest in the western region, the western region must have more preferential policies. If there is no policy difference between the western and eastern regions, why would capital be invested in the western region if it can get more profits in the eastern region? Some think China has entered the period of a market economy and there is no need to implement preferential policies for western region. The western region must depend on itself to attract capital because the market economy is free and fair. We disagree with this view because it is not practical. The development of the market economy in China is very unbalanced and the western region lags far behind the eastern region. We need to cultivate the market economy in the western region actively. But the cultivation of the market economy in the western region will be slow and need a long time. So the western region must develop the market forcefully by gaining active policy and financial support from the central government.

The market is not omnipotent for the economic development and is also not almighty for western region development. In the early 1980s, Deng Xiaoping put forward a "two-step sequential strategy". The first step was to let the eastern region develop first, the second was to let the western region develop and become rich. In the last twenty years, the western region observed the sequential strategy and the central government gave the eastern region many preferential policies and financial support. The eastern region indeed develops and becomes rich. Now it is time for second part of this "sequential strategy" to be practiced and to construct a "special policy region " in the western region as constructed in the eastern region in the early period of coastal opening-up. This will allow all kinds of capital and factors of production to flow into the western region.

How can we construct a "special policy region" in the western region? As well as encouraging the eastern region to collaborate with the western region and give the latter financial and technological aids, the central government should strengthen further the national financial support to the western region and improve the efficiency of using the financial funds. The central government should also cease to collect the agricultural tax from the western region and should give the western region more preferential policies to attract foreign capital and capital from Hong Kong, Macao, and Taiwan.

The Priority of Developing Education

We often say that the scarcest resource for the western region development is capital. However, in the long run, the scarcest resource for western region development is education or human capital. The western region generally lacks talented people that have knowledge and working skills, especially the high-quality talented people. Furthermore, many talented people of the western region have left or are leaving the western region for the eastern region because the latter gives them better living and working conditions. The Chinese government announced in 2000 that China has "basically"achieved the goal of a "well-off" standard of living and nine-year compulsory education. This is a great achievement. But what does the word "basically" mean? An expert that often helps draft out the governmental documents tells us that the word "basically" means only 75%. So it means that there is still 25% of the whole population do not have a "well-off" standard of living. With the whole population of China amounting to 1.2 billion, this 25% approximates 300 million people. Where do these people live? Most of them live in the western region. In addition, there is an estimated 30 million people in poverty. Where are they from? Most of them are in the western region. There are 25 percent of children who cannot enter the schools for education. Where are they? Most of them are in the western region.

There is a city called Kunshan near to Shanghai with a population of 200,000. In this city, all the young can enter the senior high school and 28% of them enter the colleges and university. In contrast, in many places in the western region, for an average class-size of 40 pupils in the first grade of elementary school, there are only 8 students who will make it to enter the third grade of elementary school. In the western region, a student must have a score above 500 in the National Entrance Examination for University to be admitted into a university. However, for a student living in Beijing or Shanghai, it only takes a score above 400 to qualify for university entrance. In other words, the competition for tertiary education is not a levelled playing ground for students from the western region (He Fang, 2001). How can the western region develop with a laggard education system on an unfair basis?

Basic education is the basic public service of modern society. In China, people of the western region, especially peasants, often do not have access to basic education. This big gap in educational levels between the eastern and western regions must be rectified for the western region development to be successful. According to the research of Li Shouxing of the National Planning Council, of an average student in the western region, his/her knowledge level is only 35%, the ability to acquire knowledge is only 14%, and the ability to convey the knowledge is only 31%, respectively, of that of his/her counterpart in the eastern region (Li Shouxing, 2001). Some parts of the western region are isolated from the world and up-to-date knowledge. It is these factors that block the development of the western region. The western region is an important part of our country. It is not only the duty of the western region but also the duty of the whole country to provide equal access to elementary education in the region. Therefore, we suggest that the central government offers funds to support nine-year compulsory education in poor western counties and further stipulate that most of the educational budget be used in the western region. It is also the duty of the eastern region to give financial aid and educational support to the western region.

We commend the aspirations and enthusiasm of the government and the people of the western region to develop. However, we must attend to the imperfection of current policies and the widening income gap between the eastern and western region. We must take seriously the importance to the new challenges and make efforts to deal with them.

Note

1. We thank Fu Shi and Christopher McNally for translating this article.

References

1. Li Shouxing(2002). "The Implications and Countermeasures of Exploitation of Western Human Resources", *Western Development*, April 25, 2002 < www.qhei.gov.cn>
2. He Fang (2001). "The Biggest Unfairness for Chinese Education: There Is Regional Discrimination in National Entrance Examination for Chinese Universities", July 18,2001 <www.eastday.com>
3. Lin Ling and Liu Shiqing (2000). "Paying Attention to the Phenomenon of Coming Back to Being Poor in the Protection of Natural Forests Project and Grain for Grass Project", *Chinese Industrial Economy* 44.

17 Migration Scenarios and Western China Development: The Evidence from 2000 Population Census Data

Shuming Bao and Wing Thye Woo

Introduction

In China's history, many efforts have been made regarding western region development by the central government, from Yuan dynasty to the current Chinese government. Migration has always been one of the core policies for western development, with many people moved by the government from East or Central China to Western China to open wild land in the west. After thousands of years development, there is now great population pressure on the limited arable land in the west. With the development of a market economy and the reform of the household registration system, more and more rural labourers have been moving from their traditional living places to nearby cities or other provinces for new opportunities. Although there has been increasing immigration from other regions to the west, especially in recent years, the net loss of migration in the western region has been expanding since 1982, from 0.44 million for 1982-1987 to 6.63 million for 1995-2000.

The primary goals of the Chinese government for western development are to improve the regional economy and the welfare and life quality of local people in the west region. Those goals are related but not necessarily consistent. What will be the future trend of the migration in the west? How may it may affect the local economy? If the loss by migration continues at an accelerated rate in the future, will the west be able to keep its labour force to meet its increasing demands for labour? Can the government play any active role in relocating the human resources under the market economy? To answer those questions, it is important to have a better understanding of the current status of migration in the west: the spatial patterns of migration, the motivation of migration, the components of migration, and its potential trend under different scenarios.

In this paper, we will try to conduct a comprehensive study on different migration scenarios in China primarily based on the 2000 population census data with a focus on the changes on the migration patterns from 1982 to 2000. We will first give an overview of historical distribution of population over last 50 years, especially after 1978. We will then describe the migration flows between cities, towns and rural areas, and between different regions. A comparison will be given to changes in spatial patterns of migration in different regions over last ten years, such as changes in migration distance, places of origin and destination. We will also apply Roberto Bachi's Migration Preference Index for inter-provincial migration and investigate the changes in the migration patterns in western regions and other regions by grouping all provinces in several regions. Finally, the paper will compare the current migration in China with some results from 2000 U.S. Census data and briefly discuss the policy implications for western China development under different migration scenarios.

A Historical Review of Regional Distribution of Population in China

In hundreds of years China's history, the massive Chinese population has been historically characterized by its high birth and low mortality rates, a paradigm that has shifted in recent years. From 1949 to 1978, the regional distribution of population was strictly controlled by the government's household registration policy. There has been small scale of migration from east regions to sparsely populated western region controlled by the government. Although there have been movements of people, mostly from east coast regions to central and western regions, the regional population growth was mainly dominated by natural population growth rates, which was much higher in western than eastern provinces.

After 1982, the inter-province migration grew rapidly as a result of the relaxed household registration system. Meanwhile, there has been consistent decline in the natural population growth across the country after the government passed birth control legislation and other restrictive measures that have effectively slowed the birth rates. The changes in regional distribution of population are primarily affected by the inter-province migration. From 1978 to 1983, as a result of the implementation of household responsibility system in the rural area and the improvement in agricultural productivity, some farmers were released from their homeland. Since there were still very limited job opportunities in cities, migration was on a very small scale, mostly in short periods within short distances.

Since 1984, the government has gradually relaxed restrictions to migration by encouraging small start-up enterprises and allowing farmers to apply for work permissions in urban cities as temporary residents. From 1984 to 1988, the volunteer migration grew rapidly with the urban economic system reform. In 1985, Beijing conducted the first survey on mobile population. Starting from 1986, a regular statistical system for mobile populations in all major cities in China was established. From 1989 to 1995, migration kept growth at an annual rate between 10% and 20%. A significant difference from the previous migration is a greater percentage of long distance migration. A crisis broke out in 1989 as the limited supply of job opportunities could not meet the huge demand by those farmers who were seeking jobs in urban centres.

From 1992 to 1993, the government sped up the market-oriented reform by encouraging foreign investment, which greatly stimulated the demand for labour and led to many problems for cities due to "blind migration", especially in those coast regions. Guangdong province announced its regulation on mobile populations by establishing collaborative relationships on labour management with eight other provinces. Starting at the end of 1994, a series of policies and regulations for restricting 'blind migration' were implemented by the government in the whole country. After 1996, the flow of migration into cities, especially in coastal regions has been slowing down but has still kept a stable growth. The adjustment of agriculture policies by the government effectively improved agricultural revenue and enhanced the attraction of rural labour by the agriculture. As a result of the government's policy for developing the western region and the adjustment to the industrial structure in the east region, many enterprises gradually expanded or moved to inland or West China, which offered job opportunities in those regions. Some early birds from other regions to coast regions returned to their original places for new business opportunities. In another side, the state enterprise reform led to the laying-off of many workers in cities and a rise in the unemployment rate, which made it more difficult for new migrants. Some western provinces such as Xingjiang, Qinghai, Tibet, Yunnan and Ningxia have had a positive net migration as a result of the west development.

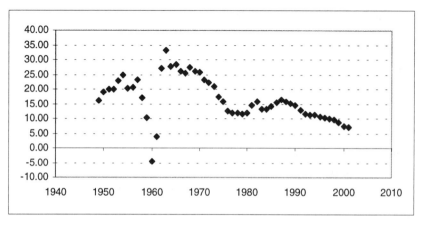

Figure 17.1.   The Natural Population Growth Rates from 1949 to 2001

According to 2000 population Census, China has a population of 1.26 billion (Communiqué on Major Figures of the 2000 Population Census No. 1) in 31 provinces and municipalities and autonomous regions on mainland. With some of the world's most congested urban centres as well as many nearly desolate tundra and desert regions, the regional distribution of China's population is featured by its significant spatial variation and diversity. About 38.9% of China's population is in the eastern region (including Beijing, Tianjin, Hebei, Liaoning, Shanghai, Jiangsu, Zhejiang, Fujian, Shandong, Guangdong, and Hainan), 32.9% in the central region (including Shanxi, Jilin, Heilongjiang, Anhui, Jiangxi, Henan, Hubei, and Hunan), and 28.1% in the west region (including Inner Mongolia, Guangxi,

Sichuan, Chongqing, Guizhou, Yunnan, Tibet, ShannXi, Gansu, Qinghai, Ningxia, and Xinjiang). The provincial population ranges from 92.56 million in Henan province, 90.79 million in Shandong province, and 86.42 million in Guangdong province to 5.18 million in Qianghai province and 2.62 million in Tibet.

For a nation with such a monolithic geographical span, China has an extremely concentrated population. Much of the nation's land is uninhabited, especially in the west region. The Sichuan Basin has a characteristically high suburban concentration in the Chengdu Plain and Chongqing areas, with more than 100 million inhabitants. Northwest Arid China is composed mainly of sparsely located but densely populated oases and gravel, the Gobi desert, and stony mountains. In stark geographic contrast to these arid deserts and mountains is the Tibetan Frigid Plateau, spanning roughly 25% of China's land area. Because of its near arctic climate and its "wild" environment, both of which are not conducive to human populations, only around 1% of the Chinese population resides there.

Although there has been a great improvement in education in China with a national illiteracy rate of only 9.01% for people 15 and older in 2000, the illiteracy rates are still very high in some western provinces, such as Tibet (47.25%), Qinghai (25.44%), Guizhou (19.85%), Gansu (19.68%) and Ningxia (15.72%). The female population in those regions have even higher illiteracy rates. The ethnically dense mountain regions in the west are characterized by illiteracy and poverty.

About 70% of China's population is of working age (between 15 and 64 years old). Employment is highest in Eastern China, especially in Yangtze Delta and Pearl River Delta. Although unemployment rates are relatively low in China, the under-employment rates are high in rural area and cities. About 50.0% of employment is in the primary industry, which is dominated by agriculture. Employment in the secondary industry, mainly manufacturing, accounts for 22.3% of total employment while the employment in the tertiary industry accounts for about 27.7% of all employment. Most provinces in the west region have a high percentage of employment in the primary industry, mostly from 56% to 73% and a low percentage of employment in the secondary industry, mostly under 15%.

Changes in Spatial Patterns of Migration: Evidence from 2000 China Population Census
The migration flows between cities, towns and rural regions

Table 17.1 summarizes the migration flows between cities, towns and rural regions during 1982-1987, 1985-1990, 1990-1995 and 1995-2000. The migration flows in Tables 17.1a-17.1c are based on the total migration, including both intra-province and inter-province migration. Table 17.1d is a little different from Tables 17.1a-17.1c since the detailed migration flows are not available in the provincial census data. Table 17.1 revealed a basic fact that the percentage of migration from rural areas has been decreasing consistently while the percentage of migration from cities has been increasing from 1982 to 2000. It indicates an important change in the nature and quality of the migration as a result of people's increasing mobility and market opportunities for job re-allocation. The local migration follows a two-stage trend: rural => towns => cities. About 35.11% of emigrants from towns moved to cities while about 39.30% of emigrants from rural areas moved to towns. The city has become the primary attraction for migration since 1990, which absorbed 59.40% (or 85.77 million) of all migration from 1995 to 2000 and 54.5% of inter-province migration. Other migration absorbed by towns and townships are 19.16% and 21.43% for 1995-2000 respectively. Most immigrants in cities are from the same province, accounting for about 73.05%. Only 26.95% of the immigrants in cities are from other provinces. About one third of inter-province migration flows into towns and rural areas in other provinces.

Table 17.2 summarized the migration flows by intra-province migration and inter-province migration to cities, towns and rural areas of seven regions. It reveals the regional difference in migration flows to cities, towns and rural areas between southwest and northwest as well as other regions. Although the city is also the primary attraction for immigration in northwest and southwest, the rural districts in northwest appear relatively more attractive than towns (attracted 31.18% of total immigration in northwest) while the towns appear more attractive than the countryside in southwest (about 23.97% of total immigration in southwest). There is a mixed attraction in the plateau, the rural area appeared more attractive to intra- province migration (about 28.79% of intra-province migration) while the town appeared more attractive to inter-province migration (about 26.39% of total inter-province migration). In all 12 western provinces, the city appears to be a relatively weak attraction while both towns and rural areas in the west attracted about 46% to 51% of migration in the region.

The migration flows between regions

Tables 17.3-17.5 summarize the inter-province migration flows between east, central and west regions. To keep the data consistent and comparable with previous tables in other papers, we adopted the definition of three regions defined by the State Commission of Planning and Development for the 7th Five-year plan. The east region includes Beijing, Tianjin, Hebei, Liaoning, Shanghai, Jiangsu, Zhejiang, Fujian, Shandong, Guangdong, Guangxi, and Hainan. The central region includes Shanxi, Inner Mongolia, Jilin, Heilongjiang, Anhui, Jiangxi, Henai, Hubei, and Hunan. The west region includes Chongqing, Sichuan, Guizhou, Yunnan, Tibet, Shaanxi, Gansu, Qinghai, Ningxia, and Xinjiang.

From Table 17,3, we found that the east region has experienced an increasing inflow of immigration, especially after 1990, and has become the primary attraction for immigration. The percentage of immigration absorbed by the east regions has increased from 52.97% in 1982-1987 to 79.18% in 1995-2000 (see Figure 17.2) while the central and west regions have experienced a shrinking share of immigration from 27.32% and 19.72% in 82-87 to 9.03% and 11.79% in 95-00 respectively.

The percentage of emigration from the east has declined from 35.16% in 82-87 to 23.58% in 95-00 while the percentage of emigration from the central region has increased from 38.09% in 82-87 to 48.99% in 95-00 (see Table 17.4), which indicated a significant shift of migration from central to east. We found not much change in the percentage of emigration from the west, which remains at around at 27% from 1982 to 2000. The percentage of migration from east and central regions has been declining from 1982 to 2000 while the percentage of inter-province migration within the west region has been increased from 51.98% in 1982-1987 to 57.58% in 1995-2000. Table 17.5 revealed that the east region has been the only region with a positive net migration since 1982, which has increased by 21 times from 1.11 million in 1982-1997 to 23.58 million in 1995-2000. The central region experienced a loss of migration at 0.67 million in 82-87 and 16.95 million in 95-00 while the west region had a loss of migration at 0.44 million in 1982-1987 and 6.63 million in 1995-2000.

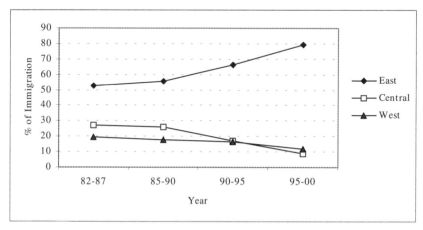

Figure 17.2.   Changes in Percentages of Immigration in East, Central and West Regions

Table 17.1.   Migration Population by Period: 1985-1990, 1990-1995, 1995-2000 (in 10,000 persons)

17.1a.   1987 1% population sample survey (1982-1987)

Total	Migration	From City	From Town	From Rural
Sum	3044.0	546.0	428.0	2070.0
%	100.0	17.9	14.1	68.0
To:				
City	36.6	59.8	23.6	33.2
Town	39.8	26.1	49.8	41.3
Rural	23.6	14.0	26.6	25.6
Total	100.0	100.0	100.0	100.0

17.1b.   1990 population census (1985-1990)

	Migration	From City	From Town	From Rural
Sum	3384.0	629.0	637.0	2118.0
%	100.0	18.6	18.8	62.6
To: City	61.7	67.8	65.3	58.8
Town	20.1	19.8	24.9	18.7
Rural	18.2	12.5	9.7	22.5
Total	100.0	100.0	100.0	100.0

17.1c.   1995 1% population sample survey (1990-1995)

	Migration	From City	From Town	From Rural
Sum	3323.0	1027.0	311.0	1986.0
%	100.0	30.9	9.4	59.8
To : City	61.4	80.6	65.6	50.8
Town	10.0	8.7	18.8	9.3
Rural	28.6	10.7	15.6	39.8
Total	100.0	100.0	100.0	100.0

17.1d.   2000 population census (1995-2000)

Province	Total	From City	From Town	From Rural	Inter-county	Inter-province
Sum	14439.1	4534.4	1429.4	8475.3		
%	100.0	31.4	9.9	58.7		
To: City	59.40	89.58	35.11	29.89	65.01	54.50
Town	19.16	3.83	32.80	39.30	15.48	20.02
Rural	21.43	6.58	32.09	30.81	19.52	25.48
Total	100.00	100.00	100.00	100.00	100.00	100.00
Of those to:						
City	100.00	32.06	8.52	4.92	27.54	26.95
Town	100.00	4.25	24.68	20.05	20.33	30.69
Rural	100.00	6.53	21.59	14.05	22.91	34.92
Total	100.00	21.26	14.42	9.77	25.17	29.38

Sources: 1a-1c are from Shanping Yan (1998).
        1d are derived from the 9.5% 2000 population Census sample data.

Table 17.2.   Percentage of Migration Flows to Cities, Towns and
Rural Areas by Seven Regions

Region	Overall			Intra-Province			Inter-Province			Total
	City	Town	Rural	City	Town	Rural	City	Town	Rural	
National	59.40	19.16	21.43	61.44	18.81	19.75	54.50	20.02	25.48	100
Metropolis	81.57	9.73	8.69	85.29	9.24	5.46	78.13	10.19	11.68	100
Coast	56.75	21.66	21.59	62.35	20.09	17.56	48.84	23.87	27.29	100
Northeast	67.23	11.60	21.17	67.91	11.58	20.51	62.79	11.73	25.48	100
Central	60.31	17.42	22.27	60.98	17.86	21.15	54.21	13.44	32.35	100
Northwest	48.52	20.30	31.18	49.42	21.99	28.59	45.82	15.21	38.97	100
Southwest	53.80	23.97	22.23	53.24	24.29	22.46	56.77	22.23	21.00	100
Plateau	53.04	21.56	25.39	51.89	19.32	28.79	55.54	26.39	18.07	100

Notes: The Metropoles include Beijing, Tianjing, and Shanghai.

Coast region includes Hebei, Jiangsu, Zhejiang, Fujian, Shandong,
Guangdong, and Hainan.

Northeast includes Jilin, Heilongjiang, and Liaoning.

Central includes Shanxi, Anhui, Jiangxi, Henai, Hubei, and Hunan.

Northwest includes Inner Mongolia, Shaanxi, Gansu, Ningxia, and
Xinjiang.

Southwest includes Chongqing, Sichuan, Guizhou, Yunnan, and Guangxi.

Plateau include Tibet and Qinghai.

Table 17.3.   Changes in the Inter-province Immigration Flows
by Region (1982-2000)

Region	In\Out	East (12)	Central (9)	West (10)	Total
1982-87	All	52.95	27.32	19.72	100
	East	53.35	33.72	12.93	100
	Central	61.94	25.13	12.93	100
	West	39.64	22.03	38.34	100
1985-90	All	55.87	26.29	17.84	100
	East	61.65	27.81	10.55	100
	Central	60.13	27.36	12.51	100
	West	42.5	22.86	34.65	100
1990-95	All	66.17	17.29	16.54	100
	East	69.74	19.74	10.52	100
	Central	72.26	16.72	11.03	100
	West	52.94	15.35	31.71	100
1995-2000	All	79.18	9.03	11.79	100
	East	77.93	13.23	8.83	100
	Central	86.21	7.83	5.96	100
	West	67.7	7.55	24.75	100

Table 17.4.   Changes in the Inter-Province Emigration Flows
by Region (1982-2000)

Region	In\Out	All	East (12)	Central (9)	West (10)
1982-87	Total	100	100	100	100
	East	35.16	35.42	43.4	23.05
	Central	38.09	44.56	35.04	24.97
	West	26.75	20.02	21.56	51.98
1985-90	Total	100	100	100	100.01
	East	38.4	42.37	40.61	22.71
	Central	34.13	36.73	35.51	23.93
	West	27.47	20.9	23.88	53.37
1990-95	Total	100	100	100	100
	East	31.5	33.2	35.95	20.03
	Central	41.06	44.84	39.7	27.37
	West	27.44	21.96	24.35	52.6
1995-2000	Total	100	100	100	100
	East	23.58	23.21	34.58	17.66
	Central	48.99	53.34	42.47	24.76
	West	27.43	23.45	22.95	57.58

Table 17.5.   Net Migration by Region 1982-2000 (in 10,000)

Region		East (12)	Central (9)	West (10)	Net migration
1982-87	East	0.00			111.42
	Central	73.50	0.00		-67.45
	West	37.92	6.05	0.00	-43.97
1985-90	East	0.00			193.31
	Central	108.94	0.00		-86.68
	West	84.37	22.26	0.00	-106.63
1990-95	East	0.00			369.41
	Central	249.93	0.00		-253.31
	West	119.48	-3.38	0.00	-116.10
1995-2000	East	0.00			2358.50
	Central	1659.21	0.00		-1695.21
	West	699.29	-36.00	0.00	-663.30

Note: The three regions were based on the definition by the State Commission of Planning and Development for the 7th Five-year plan. The east region includes Beijing, Tianjin, Hebei, Liaoning, Shanghai, Jiangsu, Zhejiang, Fujian, Shandong, Guangdong, Guangxi, and Hainan. The central region includes Shanxi, Inner Mongolia, Jilin, Heilongjiang, Anhui, Jiangxi, Henai, Hubei, and Hunan. The west region includes Chongqing, Sichuan, Guizhou, Yunnan, Tibet, Shaanxi, Gansu, Qinghai, Ningxia, and Xinjiang.

Sources: 1980 and 2000 China Population Census; 1987 and 1995 1% population sample survey.

Table 17.6 gives more details about the migration flows between the seven regions, including north-coast (Beijing, Tianjing, Hebei, and Shandong), east-coast (Shanghai, Jiangsu, and Zhejiang), south-coast

(Guangdong, Fujian and Hainan), northeast (Jilin, Heilongjiang and Liaoning), central (Shanxi, Anhui, Jiangxi, Henai, Hubei, and Hunan), northwest (Inner Mongolia, Shaanxi, Gansu, Qinghai, Ningxia, and Xinjiang), southwest (Chongqing, Sichuan, Guizhou, Yunnan and Guangxi), and plateau (Tibet and Qinghai). In terms of places of attraction (see Table 17.6a), both north-coast and south-coast seem to be primary attractions for the cross region migration. About 38.38% of emigration from northeast was attracted by north-coast. About 49.08% of emigration from central regions and 56.58% from southwest region were attracted by the south-coast. In terms of immigration origin (see Table 17.6b), the immigration from the central region has been the primary source for all coast regions (29.80% for North-coast, 56.34% for east-coast, and 51.59% for South-coast) and the northwest region (28.46%) while immigration from the southeast region is the primary source of immigration for northwest (22.20%) and plateau region (41.65%). Both central and southwest regions account for about 72.6% of all emigration in the country in 1995-2000 (see Table 17.6b). Table 17.6c further revealed that all coast regions, northwest and plateau regions have a gain of net migration in 1995-2000 while the central and southwest regions have a loss of net migration in 1995-2000.

Table 17.6.   The Migration Flows Between Regions, 1995-2000

Region	Total	North-coast	East-coast	South-coast	North-east	Central	North-west	South-west	Plateau
National	100	100	100	100	100	100	100	100	100
North-coast	12.17	50.55	14.63	9.53	38.38	8.32	18.84	4.06	13.76
East-coast	22.07	9.93	43.75	18.86	4.88	28.52	7.71	14.92	10.11
South-coast	41.47	7.30	12.44	33.02	6.56	49.08	16.22	56.58	5.87
Northeast	4.10	11.28	3.92	2.33	35.64	1.43	7.96	0.78	1.22
Central	6.09	9.29	10.98	14.57	2.77	4.78	12.23	4.61	13.45
Northwest	6.61	8.52	7.04	3.09	9.92	4.32	29.95	5.05	34.36
Southwest	6.93	2.73	6.71	18.37	1.74	3.35	4.38	13.22	16.33
Plateau	0.55	0.38	0.53	0.23	0.11	0.22	2.70	0.79	4.91

Table 17.6 *cont'd.*

Region	Total	North-coast	East-coast	South-coast	North-east	Central	North-west	South-west	Plateau
National	100	5.89	7.88	3.21	5.06	43.60	5.05	29.06	0.27
North-coast	100	24.46	9.47	2.51	15.95	29.80	7.82	9.68	0.31
East-coast	100	2.65	15.61	2.74	1.12	56.34	1.76	19.65	0.12
South-coast	100	1.04	2.36	2.55	0.80	51.59	1.97	39.64	0.04
Northeast	100	16.20	7.52	1.82	43.92	15.15	9.80	5.52	0.08
Central	100	8.98	14.19	7.67	2.30	34.17	10.13	21.98	0.60
Northwest	100	7.59	8.39	1.50	7.59	28.46	22.87	22.20	1.41
Southwest	100	2.32	7.62	8.50	1.27	21.06	3.19	55.40	0.64
Plateau	100	4.08	7.61	1.33	0.97	17.10	24.85	41.65	2.42

Net migration (in 10,000)

Region	Total	North-coast	East-coast	South-coast	North-east	Central	North-west	South-west	Plateau
North-coast	266.41	0.00	24.07	-5.27	54.13	130.62	19.06	43.16	0.63
East-coast	601.99	-24.07	0.00	-15.91	-2.62	490.73	-7.01	161.49	-0.61
South-coast	1623.15	0.00	0.00	0.00	10.90	887.82	30.53	672.34	0.36
Northeast	-40.43	0.00	0.00	0.00	0.00	20.43	-4.24	5.88	-0.09
Central	-1590.79	0.00	0.00	0.00	0.00	0.00	-53.65	-5.10	-2.44
Northwest	66.35	0.00	0.00	0.00	0.00	0.00	0.00	52.89	-1.84
Southwest	-938.49	0.00	0.00	0.00	0.00	0.00	0.00	0.00	-7.83
Plateau	11.81	0.00	0.00	0.00	0.00	0.00	0.00	0.00	0.00

Region	Total	North-coast	East-coast	South-coast	North-east	Central	North-west	South-west	Plateau
National		-	-	-	+	+	-	+	-
North-coast	266.41		+	-	+	+	+	+	+
East-coast	601.99	-		-	-	+	-	+	-
South-coast	1623.15	+	+	+	+	+	++		
Northeast	-40.43	-	+	-		+	-	+	-
Central	-1590.79	-	-	-	-		-	-	-
Northwest	66.35	-	+	-	+	+		+	-
Southwest	-938.49	-	-	-	-	+	+		-
Plateau	11.81	-	+	-	+	+	+	+	

Table 17.7 summarizes the changes in inter-province migration from 1985 to 2000. Although the total population of migration has increased in the last ten years, the relative percentage of intra-province migration has continued to ncrease from 68% in 1990 to 70% in 2000 while the percentage of the inter-province migration is declining with an exception of Beijing, Shanghai, Guangdong, Fujian, Zhejiang, and Yunnan.

In sum, the current scale of inter-region migration is still a small percentage: only 11.37% (or 144.39 million) for all intra- and inter-province migration. The majority of migrants were moving within local regions, mostly within the same city or county, which accounts for 5.28% of total population. The total intra-province migrants, including migrants moving within the same city/county or between cities/counties of the same province, account for 8.21% (or 101.97 million) while the inter-province migrants account for only 3.41% (or 42.42 million). It demonstrated a strong tendency of local concentration of population within the province.

The east-coast region has been the primary attraction for inter-province migration. Which account 73.27% (or 31.08 million) of inter-province immigration by Guangdong, Fujian, Hainan, Zhejiang, Shanghai, Jiangsu, Beijing, Hebei, and Tianjin. The western region absorbed 14.09% (or 5.97 million) inter-province migrations. Although the central regions (ten provinces including Liaoning, Jilin, Heilongjiang, Shanxi, Anhui, Jiangxi, Shandong, Henai, Hubei, and Hunan) have a percentage of 43.52% (or 540.72 million) of national population, they only absorbed 12.64% inter-province migration (or 5.36 million).

Clearly the east-coast regions are gainers of migration while the central and southwest regions are losers of migration. The south-coast region absorbed about 41.47% of total migration, while the east-coast and north-coast absorbed 22.07% and 12.17% respectively. The coast regions (south, east and nouth) have a net gain of 24.9 million from migration, about 5.63% of the total population of the region. The central region has a net loss of 15.9 million due to migration, about 4.6% of the total population of the region. The migration in the west is in contrast for southwest and northwest. While southwest has a net loss of migration, the northwest has a net gain of migration, especially Xinjiang province, which has a net gain of about 1.25 million.

Table 17.7.   Percentage of Inter-province Immigration in 1990, 1995 and 2000

Region	1985-1990	1990-1995	1995-2000	Change
Total	32.08	31.58	29.38	-
Beijing	51.82	47.50	53.11	+
Tianjin	45.56	38.03	33.69	-
Hebei	37.57	34.90	19.06	-
Shanxi	33.14	31.65	17.94	-
Inner Mongolia	29.53	35.34	14.31	-
Liaoning	27.19	26.70	16.12	-
Jilin	19.42	20.93	10.46	-
Heilongjiang	17.40	20.93	10.26	-
Shanghai	43.02	54.24	58.22	+
Jiangsu	31.89	30.09	27.88	-
Zhejiang	38.21	31.60	42.90	+
Anhui	21.72	15.97	6.47	-
Fujian	34.58	32.56	36.29	+
Jiangxi	20.67	17.45	7.52	-
Shandong	27.16	23.52	13.84	-
Henan	26.21	20.13	9.16	-
Hubei	25.29	23.28	10.69	-
Hunan	17.73	13.17	7.94	-
Guangdong	47.61	44.99	59.53	+
Guangxi	12.97	13.25	13.24	-
Hainan	44.82	40.61	39.03	-
Chongqing			15.36	NA
Sichuan	16.68	11.17	8.04	-
Guizhou	26.96	33.31	16.91	-
Yunnan	24.72	24.96	30.08	+
Tibet	51.22	62.15	50.83	-
Shaanxi	23.51	29.95	18.01	-
Gansu	25.51	26.11	14.64	-
Qinghai	27.35	29.82	23.81	-
Ningxia	41.53	41.94	28.53	-
Xinjiang	66.97	72.68	49.87	-

Source: 2000 China Population Census.

Migration by motivation and sex group

Tables 17.8a and 17.8b summarize the migration in several groups by their motivation and sex in 1985-90 and 1995-2000. Table 17.8a and 17.8b indicate a significant increase in the percentage of female migration from less than 50% (41.9% for intra-province migration and 46.3% for inter-migration) in 1990 to 52.29% in 2000, primarily for job and training. This change might be due to the increase in the educated level of female population (see the chart for illiterate female vs. the migrant female). Figure 17.3 suggests an inverse relationship between female migration and female illiteracy rates in 12 western provinces. While the illiteracy rates of females are declining from the age group of 34 to 15, the illiteracy rate of males is rising from the group of 34 to 15.

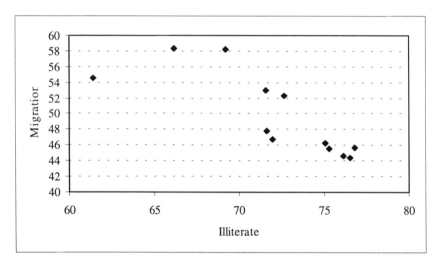

Figure 17.3.   Female Illiteracy Rate vs. Female Migration in Western Provinces

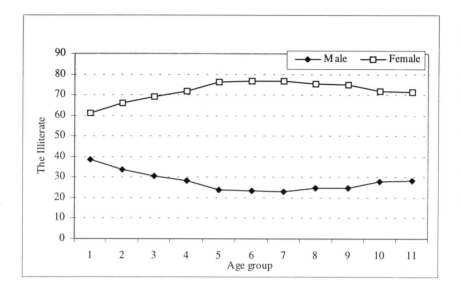

Figure 17.4.   Illiterate Population by Age and Sex in Western Provinces

Table 17.8c indicates that most migrants are in the profession of Sales and Service Workers, Agriculture and Related Workers, and Production and Related Workers, which account for 71.30% for intra-province migration and 90.76% for inter-province migration. Most professional migrants move within the same provinces or regions. Most inter-province migrants work in production sectors. In terms of regional difference, a larger percentage of migrants find jobs in production in east coast regions than the west while migrants to west are in service and agriculture. Figure 17.5 demonstrates a spatial tendency of migration in production from east (high) to west (low) and a reverse direction for migration in agriculture related fields.

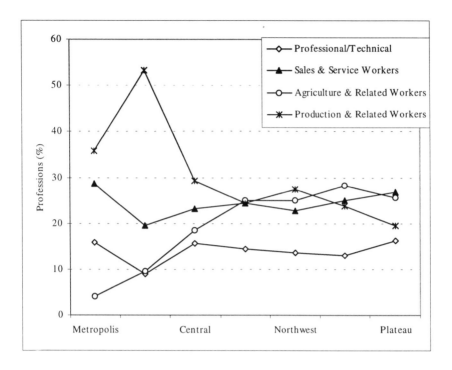

Figure 17.5.   Percentage of Professions of Migrants by Regions

Table 17.8d further reveals the motivation for different age groups. About 64.64% of total migrants are between 15-34. The job related migrants are mostly in an age range of 20-34. The training related migrants are mostly between 15 and 24. For working and business, the age group of 15-34, accounting for 78.84%. For "job transfer", the majority is age group 20-39, accounting for 73.73%. Group age of 20-29 accounts for 79.7% for "assign and employ". Group of 15-24 accounts for 94.91% for "learning and training". Group of 20-29 accounts for 78.39% for "marriage migration". Group of 0-14 accounts for 49.33% for "member of family in connection with movement". Both children (0-14) or aged people (65 and over) account about 40.08% who "go and live with relatives or friends".

Table 17.8.   Migration by Motivation

Table 17.8a. Migration by motivation and sex in 1985.7-1990.6.

	Intra-province migration			Inter-province migration		
	Total	Male	Female	Total	Male	Female
Total	100.00	58.10	41.90	100.00	53.70	46.30
Work and business	100.00	72.40	27.60	100.00	67.10	32.90
Job transfer	100.00	78.00	22.00	100.00	69.20	30.80
Job assignment	100.00	78.10	21.90	100.00	68.60	31.40
Study/training	100.00	71.30	28.70	100.00	60.70	39.30
Retirement	100.00	81.20	18.80	100.00	86.40	13.60
Marriage	100.00	8.40	91.60	100.00	9.30	90.70
Moving with family	100.00	39.20	60.80	100.00	40.00	60.00
Live with relatives or friends	100.00	46.90	53.10	100.00	40.90	59.10
Other	100.00	65.80	34.20	100.00	70.80	29.20

Source: Zhaoliang Hu, 1994.

Table 17.8b.   Migration by motivation and sex in 1995-2000

Motivation	Total	Male	Female
Total	100.00	47.71	52.29
Work and Business	100.00	56.96	43.04
Job transfer	100.00	67.74	32.26
Job assignment	100.00	58.60	41.40
Study/training	100.00	52.66	47.34
Moving housing	100.00	52.19	47.81
Marriage	100.00	11.11	88.89
Moving with family	100.00	39.63	60.37
Live with relatives or friends	100.00	45.11	54.89
Other	100.00	52.95	47.05

Source: 2000 China population Census (L7-5)

Table 17.8c.   Group of Migration by Motivation and Regions

National	Total	Metro-polis	Coast	Central	North-east	North-west	South-east	Plateau
Total	100	100	100	100	100	100	100	100
Male	50.89	58.66	50.11	53.38	48.22	54.24	48.9	52.22
Female	49.11	41.34	49.89	46.62	51.78	45.76	51.1	47.78
Administrator/ manager	3.16	4.68	2.47	5.06	3.66	3.59	2.89	3.8
Professional/ Technical	11.76	15.8	8.99	15.6	14.35	13.6	12.92	16.22
Clerical & Related Workers	7.16	11.04	6.17	8.32	7.81	7.46	6.77	7.55
Sales & Service Workers	22.29	28.64	19.45	23.11	24.5	22.77	25.1	26.89
Agriculture & Related Workers	15.93	4.04	9.59	18.54	24.93	24.98	28.24	25.61
Production & Related Workers	39.58	35.78	53.26	29.23	24.51	27.45	23.88	19.6
Not Stated	0.12	0.02	0.06	0.15	0.24	0.15	0.21	0.32

Table 17.8d.   Age Group of Migration Categorized by Moving Motivation

Age Groups	0-14	15-19	20-24	25-29	30-34	35-39	40-44	45-49	50-54	55-59	60-64	65+	Total
Total	11.0	15.7	19.5	18.0	11.4	7.7	4.6	3.9	2.6	1.7	1.4	2.4	100
Work $ business	0.0	15.2	24.8	22.1	16.8	9.9	4.6	3.3	1.7	0.9	0.5	0.3	100
Work transfer	0.0	2.4	15.1	22.7	19.5	16.5	9.2	6.9	4.0	2.1	1.1	0.8	100
Assign and employ	0.0	7.3	49.2	30.5	5.7	3.0	1.6	1.3	0.7	0.4	0.2	0.2	100
Learn & train	3.2	67.6	27.3	1.2	0.4	0.2	0.1	0.0	0.0	0.0	0.0	0.0	100
Pull down and move	13.7	5.4	4.9	9.9	12.6	13.2	10.9	9.6	6.1	3.9	3.4	6.5	100
Marriage	0.0	1.0	33.0	45.4	11.2	3.8	1.8	1.4	0.9	0.6	0.4	0.5	100
Move with family	49.3	8.3	5.8	8.4	7.5	5.4	3.3	3.1	2.4	1.8	1.6	3.0	100
Go with relatives or friends	27.8	7.5	9.1	9.1	7.1	4.8	3.3	3.9	4.7	5.0	5.5	12.3	100
Other	15.2	9.0	11.7	12.5	11.5	9.5	6.7	6.2	5.1	4.0	3.5	5.2	100

The Preference of Migration

To identify the regional migration patterns and the preference of local regions by migration, Robert Bachi (Shryock, 1976) proposed the Migration Preference Index (MPI) in 1956, which is defined as:

$$I_{ij} = \frac{M_{ij}}{(P_i / P_t)[P_i /(P_t - P_i)]\sum\limits_{i,j} M_{ij}} K$$

where I_{ij} is the migration preference index, M_{ij} is the total migrants from place i to j, P_i is the population at place i, P_j is the population at place j, P_t is the total population of all places, K is a constant, usually assigned to 100.

Respectively, the regional immigration preference index and the emigration preference index are defined as:

$$I\cdot_j = \frac{M\cdot_j}{(P_j / P_t)\sum\limits_{j} M\cdot_j} K$$

and

$$I_{i\cdot} = \frac{M_{i\cdot}}{(P_i / P_t)\sum\limits_{i} M_{i\cdot}} K$$

If a region's immigration preference index is greater than 100, it will indicate that the region has a stronger attraction to immigrants than average in the country. The higher the immigration preference index, the stronger the attraction of the region to immigration. In contrast, the higher the emigration preference index, the greater the pressure on emigration in the region or the higher the population mobility in the region.

Applying Roberto Bachi's Migration Preference Index, Table 17.9 gives the migration preference index from 1982 to 2000, derived from the migration data from the 1990 and 2000 population census data and 1987 and 1995 sample survey data. The index table allows us to compare changes in the attraction to migration by different provinces in last twenty years.

Grouping all provinces in several regions, we can compare the changes in the migration patterns of western regions and other regions. In Table 17.9, Hainan province was a part of Guangdong province in 1987. Tibet was excluded in the 1990 population census. The 1987 and 1995 population were used for calculating the indices 1982-1987 and 1990-1995. The average population from the 1982 and 1990 census were used for calculating the 1985-1990 index. The 2000 population was used for calculating the 2000 index.

Based on Table 17.9, those provinces with an immigration preference index higher than 200 include Beijing (532), Tianjing (219), Shanghai (560), Zhejiang (235), Guangdong (518) and Xinjiang (224), which shows a spatial pattern of regional attraction centered in Beijing, Shanghai, Guangdong and Xinjiang. Those provinces with an emigration preference index higher than 100 include Anhui (215), Jiangxi (267), Hubei (138), Hunan (199), Guangxi (163), Sichuan (237), and Guizhou (133), which shows two clusters of primary emigration origins in central and southeast regions.

Table 17.9 calculated the changes in the migration preference index from 1990-1995 to 1995-2000. Only four provinces with a greater immigration preference index from 1990-1995 to 1995-2000, which include Zhejiang, Fujian, Guangdong, and Yunann. It suggests that those regions appeared stronger attraction to immigration within the last 5 years. The provinces with higher emigration preference index include Anhui, Jiangxi, Hubei, Guangxi, and Sichuan, which suggests a great pressure of emigration from those regions from 1995 to 2000.

The analysis in the migration preference index can help us to identify the national centres of attraction to migration. Figure 17.6 shows the percentage of net migration to regional population by provinces with four national centres of attraction for immigration.

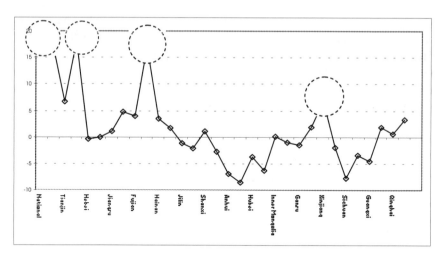

Figure 17.6. Percentage of Net Migration by Provinces, 1995-2000

Table 17.9. The Migration Preference Index by province from 1982 to 2000

	Popu-lation	Migrants Im-	Migrants Em-	1982-87 In	1982-87 Out	1985-90 In	1985-90 Out	1990-95 In	1990-95 Out	2000 In	2000 Out	Changes (90-00) In	Changes (90-00) Out
National	124261	4242	4242	In	Out	In	Out	In	Out	In	Out	In	Out
East													
Beijing	1357	246	9	306	227	647	127	681	115	532	20	-149	-95
Tianjin	985	74	8	73	37	285	84	270	75	219	25	-51	-50
Hebei	6668	93	122	95	82	88	109	87	72	41	54	-46	-18
Liaoning	4182	67	31	118	111	139	76	117	53	73	25	-44	-28
Shanghai	1641	55	50	179	99	509	101	573	97	560	25	-13	-72
Jiangsu	7304	105	36	99	91	120	94	153	71	102	69	-51	-2
Zhejiang	4593	31	61	77	87	81	152	119	132	235	95	116	-37
Fujian	3410	39	117	69	71	87	82	122	78	184	70	62	-8
Shandong	8997	313	14	91	82	74	65	66	48	34	36	-32	-12
Guangdong	8523	254	172	140	132	208	41	329	37	518	15	189	-22
Guangxi	4385	369	148	66	80	35	144	30	139	29	163	-1	24
Hainan	756	23	433			237	167	168	164	148	46	-20	-118
Shanxi	3247	215	81	123	125	110	78	58	52	60	28	2	-24

Table 17.9 *cont'd.*

	Popu-lation	Migrants		1982-87		1985-90		1990-95		2000		Changes (90-00)	
		Im-	Em-										
National	124261	4242	4242	In	Out	In	Out	In	Out	In	Out	In	Out
Central													
Inner Mongolia	2332	25	368	126	132	120	144	136	123	69	63	-67	-60
Jilin	2680	103	110	159	170	97	145	64	127	34	67	-30	-60
Heilongjiang	3624	48	307	107	133	104	173	68	185	31	95	-37	-90
Anhui	5900	61	281	68	73	62	97	29	141	11	215	-18	74
Jiangxi	4040	35	431	63	67	61	80	35	144	18	267	-17	123
Henai	9124	1506	43	51	54	58	71	34	92	15	99	-19	7
Hubei	5951	43	244	130	127	82	66	53	74	30	138	-23	64
Hunan	6327	38	12	88	97	46	89	37	123	16	199	-21	76
West													
Chongqing	3051	40	101							39	97		
Sichuan	8235	54	694	121	124	44	123	39	144	19	247	-20	103
Guizhou	3525	41	160	77	78	60	99	51	132	34	133	-17	1
Yunnan	4236	116	34	75	83	69	77	60	69	81	24	21	-45
Tibet	262	11	2	11	72		258	172	135	122	22	-50	-113
Shaanxi	3537	43	80	115	122	98	113	53	85	35	67	-18	-18
Gansu	2512	23	59	84	100	92	129	67	119	27	68	-40	-51
Qinghai	482	12	9	76	137	237	236	122	181	76	58	-46	-123
Ningxia	549	19	9	153	119	207	128	111	125	102	48	-9	-77
Xinjiang	1846	141	16	140	150	233	190	396	105	224	25	-172	-80

Comparison with the U.S. Experience

The current migration accounts for only 11.62% of total population in China while it accounts for about 45% of total population in the U.S. A significant difference between the U.S. and China is that the inter-province migration has a much higher percentage than the inter-state migration in the U.S. It is expected that the migration will keep increasing in the future. The speed of local concentration will be much faster than the inter-province migration. The inter-province migration will require better education and skills.

Table 17.10.   U.S. Migration Trends

Year	Popu-lation (for 1+)	Migra-tion	Migra-tion %	Intra-county	Intra-state/inter-county	Inter-state	Inter-country	Total
90-95	24180.5	10661.6	44.1	56.7	20.0	18.5	4.9	100.1
85-90	23044.6	10764.9	46.7	54.5	20.7	20.1	4.7	100.0
80-85	21610.8	9012.6	41.7	53.1	21.8	20.8	4.3	100.0
75-80	21032.3	9762.9	46.4	54.0	21.1	20.9	4.0	100.0

Source: Jason Schachter, *Current Population Reports: 1990 to March 1995.*
The U.S. Census Bureau, September 2000 (www.census.gov).

Almost 50% of migration cases in China are job related while the figure for U.S. is only 16%, which is much lower than that in China. A majority of migration cases in the U.S. are housing related. Job related migration accounts for about 16% of the total migration cases and 7% of the total population. The job related migration accounts for 50% of the total migration and 6% of the total population of the country, which is pretty close to that in the U.S.

Table 17.11.   U.S. Migration Motivation

	1999-2000		1998-1999		1997-1998	
	Number	%	Number	%	Number	%
Total	41642	100.0	41207	100.0	41304	100.0
Family	10969	26.3	10537	25.6	11136	27.0
Work	6725	16.1	6602	16.0	7080	17.1
Housing	21471	51.6	21027	51.0	19173	46.4
Others	2478	6.0	3041	7.4	3915	9.5

Source: Jason Schachter, *Current Population Reports: 1990 to March 1995.*
The U.S. Census Bureau, September 2000 (www.census.gov).

References

1.   Jason Schachter, Current Population Reports: 1990 to March 1995. The U.S. Census Bureau, September 2000 (www.census.gov).
2.   Narayana, M. R., 1990. "Policy and Non-policy Economic Determinants of Inter-regional Migration of Workers in a Developing Country: Some New Evidence Based on a Polytomous Logit Model for India". In *Population Research and Policy Review*, 1990, Vol. 9: 285-302.
3.   Population Census Office of the State Council and the National Bureau of Statistics, 2002. *Tabulation on the 2000 Population Census of the People' s Republic of China*, Vol. 1-3. China Statistical Press.
4.   Shryock, Henry S., Jacob S. Siegel and Associates, 1976. *The Methods and Materials of Demography*. New York. Academic Press: 394-395.
5.   陈奕平, 2002. 当代美国人口迁移特征及原因分析, 人口研究2002, Vol. 26(4): 59-65.
6.   胡兆量, 1994. 迁移八律与中国人口迁移, 云南地理环境研究, 1994, Vol. 6(1): 45-53.
7.   全国人口抽样调查办公室, 1997. 1995全国1%人口抽样调查资料,中国统计出版社.
8.   王桂新, 2000. 中国经济体制改革以来省际人口迁移区域模式及其变化, 人口与经济, 2000, Vol. 3: 8-22.
9.   严善平, 1998. 中国九十年代地区间人口迁移的实态及其机制, 社会学研究, 1998, Vol. 2: 67-74.

18 Gender Relations, Tourism and Ecological Effects in Lijiang, China

Govind Kelkar

Introduction

Research on the indigenous societies that are likely to be affected by tourism has tended to focus on economic development. Only a few mention the role of women or pay attention to gender relations. (Kelkar and Nathan, 1991; Kelkar, Nathan and Walter, 2003; Bosu Mullick, 2000; Sarin, 2000; Bolles, 1997; Vivan, Kothari and Hall, 1994). This invisibility compounds patriarchy as the invisible mediator in reproducing idealized images of the past and conceals the unequal benefits to be enjoyed from many tourism endeavours. This paper explores changes in gender relations as a result of economic development through tourism and forest management programs. We look at changes in gender relations in indigenous societies of matrilineal Mosuo and patrilineal Naxi in two situations: (1) the Chinese indigenous forest communities and the role of women and men in collective management of forests; and (2) current situation of development of tourism as a leading industry, where women play a significant role as workers and local managers, but where their social, economic and political position have come under increasing stress.

An initial intellectual curiosity drew us to study forest-based societies in which women were/are not exposed to extreme inequalities in social, political and economic spheres. We also looked into the manner in which gender relations were transformed in the shift from matrilineal to patrilineal societies within forest-based communities. If male domination was not always the rule, how did gender/social relations change from societies without male domination to ones where male domination was presented as the norm?

Since 1993, we have made regular visits to Lugu Lake and Lashi Lake in Yunnan, China. This study is based on our fieldwork in Luoshui village in Ninglang County, Lugu Lake and several visits to Naxi villages around Lashi Lake, 8km away from Lijiang Dayan town. These visits were related to our collaborative work with Chinese scholars (He Zhonghua, Yang Fuquan, Yu Xiaogang and Xi Yuhua) on forest management, watershed ecosystem and gender relations in matrilineal Mosuo and patrilineal Naxi. Focused group discussions and individual interviews were the main methods of data collection, supplemented by local government data. The one- to two-hour interviews were largely structured around questions designed to elicit information from women and men respondents on matters related to their work/contributions, Chinese and foreign visitors to the area, and changing relationship with the state, the family and the community.

These interviews were conducted to address the following major questions: How do gender relations within and outside the household affect management of forests and the tourism industry? What is the extent of women's centrality in provision of livelihood, through an analysis of their role and status in management of tourism and natural resources? What can we learn about gender relations from forest dwelling societies that are characterized by cultural valuation of women's economic, political and ritual roles and absence of institutionalized male control? Does the structure of gender relations within the household and in the community change as members respond to broad religion-cultural, social and economic restructuring of the indigenous societies, largely as a result of tourism.

About Luoshui

Lugu Lake with its scenic Yougning plateau in Yunnan is inhabited by matrilineal Mosuo people and, for purposes of development of tourism is called 'the Kingdom of Daughters'. Lashi Lake, with biological resources in the wetland, is adjacent to Yangtze valley and Lanchang (upper Mekong) valley. Lashi Lake inhabits Naxi and Yi and is 8 kilometres away from

Lijiang Dayon town, the World Cultural Heritage site. These two are now the most popular tourist destinations in Southwestern China.

People come not just to see scenery, but also to acquaint themselves, in however limited a fashion, with different cultures. This is what makes the mountain cultures, the matrilineal cultures of the Mosuo in Yunnan, for instance, something interesting to see and observe. The result is that the music, dance and other performances of these people have got new functions, as they are staged for tourists. Every minority nationality in Yunnan now stages these shows for tourists to see and even participate in. These, of course, are not their original functions. Often formerly sacred performances now become mere tourist attractions. But what must be seen is that the alternative is the slow or rapid but sure extinction of these cultural practices, which is what was occurring before the intrusion of tourism.

Luoshui Village is located by Lugu Lake to the southeast of the Yongning plateau, 20 kilometres away from the seat of district government. It is part of the larger Luoshui Administrative Village. The village is divided into two parts, the Upper Village and the Lower Village. The former sits next to the mountain slope, and its inhabitants are mostly Pumi. The latter is located near the lake, and its inhabitants are mostly Mosuo. According to late 1998 statistics, there were 76 households comprising of 485 people in both Upper and Lower Villages, of which the Mosuo made up 33 households and Pumi 21 households. The rest were Hans and Bais. During my investigation in the Lower Village in 1993 and 1996, I found that of the 33 Mosuo households, 31 (94%) were matrilineal families. Pumi in the Upper Village commonly followed the axia (the visiting marriage) practices of Lower Village Mosuo.

With the development of tourism, drastic changes have taken place in transportation, communications, housing and other local infrastructure. The way of life and the mode of thinking have also undergone important changes. Now the former dirt highway to the district seat is asphalt. Once impassable, the road around the lake can today reach Yanyuan County town in the dry season. Thirty-two out of 33 households have built new wooden houses and telephones, refrigerators, washing machines and television sets and small appliances are increasingly popular. Each family has a flush toilet, and some households even have water heated with solar energy equipment. However, they still retain their matrilineal system, axia, funeral customs, and sacrificial rites. "In fact, they have even further consolidated these practices, not for themselves, but as tourist attractions," (He Zhonghua, 2001)

After the economic reform in China, people began to seize political power. However, men were the main political leaders. In the former Village People's Committee of Luoshui Village, the ratio of women in the committee members was 6 to 0, and without a seat for a woman committee director. In April 1999, it began to offer a woman director's seat, but the ratio was still 8 men to 1 woman. Women are always considered to be of poor ability or less educated, incapable of participating in political affairs. In reality, some of the women are no less qualified, and some of the men are no more educated, yet the seats of village heads or officials are always for those said to be abler.

The gender division of labour tended to be equal in the past. This has reportedly changed now, the power of men is now being consolidated and strengthened. Although of equal labour value, women's activities and capacity in forestry are not valued or recognized. They have fewer opportunities to join in scientific and technological training in the development projects of village communities. In this regard, woman committee member Cao Xuezhen complained, for example, that while women usually plant, weed and fertilize apple trees, it is not the women but the men who receive technical training for this activity.

The development of tourism has also ushered in the trade in women's bodies. Beginning in 1977, some people from outside the community opened beauty parlours and set up sex trade businesses, which seriously disturbed the village. In 1998, these beauty parlours were ordered to close their doors in the community. As a result, they moved to the administrative district about one kilometre away and continued their trade.

Gender Relations and Forest Management

Gender relations are complex, dynamic and socially embedded having many interlocked dimensions. Cultural traditions of women's exclusion from community management confers authority and prestige on men. Men hold virtually all-formal positions of power and decision-making in villages under patrilineal systems, though women often exercise considerable influence in certain areas of village life. In matrilineal systems, women have an especially effective, indirect power in maintaining the lineage and therefore owning children. They have rights over ancestral property and control and knowledge of ritualistic activity, including being the spiritual heads of the community, for example, *Syiem Sad* among Khasi in India and *Bobolizan* among Rungus in Sabah, Malaysia.

In most patrilineal societies, women's major responsibility in reproduction and/or income-earning does not necessarily lead to social empowerment or gender equality within the household (Kelkar and Nathan, 1991; Munshi, 1986; Yang, 2000; Chhakchhuak, 2000). However, the presence of rights to forest and women's rights to access forest resources can mitigate, to some extent, this inequality in gender relations. K. S. Singh (1999) and Bosu Mullick (2000) found that in forest-based (patrilineal) communities, because of their involvement in gathering from forests and their marginal dependence on agricultural produce, women are economically more independent and have a higher status than in the rest of India. Among the patrilineal Naga of Northeast India, for example, women's role in swidden agriculture and in the processing of forest products for sale has kept gender relations relatively balanced.

In the more male-dominated society of Enzong village (a mixed Naxi and Han village, 8 kilometres from the town of Lijiang) women have no right to forests, land or trees, all of which are inherited from father to son, and forest distribution is carried out on the basis of the (male) head of household (Xi Yuhua, 2000). A woman, after marriage, acquires access to her husband's forest. Furthermore, women are allowed neither to climb trees nor to cut trunks even if these are needed for house construction. Spirits were supposed to reside in trees and a menstruating woman might pollute the tree and thus bring down the wrath of the forest spirit.

What we are dealing with is a whole complex of social behaviour, of practices that constitute incorporated social or gender relations. The complex of practices deals with knowledge, with religious rites and symbols, marriage and inheritance systems, economic rights, control over sexuality and reproductive powers, norms of behaviour, accepted forms of social excellence and ability, and differential access to social knowledge – all of which together constitute gender relations.

Still, in matrilineal systems, women's control over forest lands has generally enhanced gender equality by giving women a greater say in how forest lands are used. In the Chota Nagpur villages of Central India, Samar Bosu Mullick (2000) notices present day practices that socially acknowledge women's knowledge of forests and agriculture. When the Munda (the headmen) go from one village to another, his wives lead them. Women's knowledge of seeds, herbs, and plants is considered precious both in the family and community. Their knowledge of the roots of a particular plant is used to brew rice beer, the most sacred and popular drink of the people. Their role in the preparation of cultivable land is also very important; they are seen working with men in field preparation and reclamation of forest land. Women's contribution to the development of agriculture is further confirmed by the 'myth of the preparation of the first plough.' The Supreme Being's wife is described as the real inventor of the technology of plough-making. Thus women's right to the newly-reclaimed forest land and its produce received a permanent place in the customary law of the Munda people.

Matrilineal societies often associate women with forests through specialized roles in healing and religious ceremonies. Indra Munshi's interviews with the Warlis in India suggest that many women have a fair knowledge of medicinal properties of trees, roots, herbs and medicinal plants useful for reproductive health, childbirth, abortion and so on. And common ailments are treated at home. In the Tamang village Chisapani in Nepal, Suman Subba finds "The women shamans are accepted as equally knowledgeable and powerful as the male shamans" (2000: 9). There is no gender difference in carrying out rituals and healing people; except that the women shamans do not sacrifice animals and ask for help from a male member of the family. The women having a 'soft heart' was the stated reason for this difference in the sacrificial ceremonies. Both women and men, however, acquire the knowledge of shamanic treatment of diseases. This can be acquired either by learning from the senior shamans or through a spiritual knowledge relationship with a *Ban Jhankri* (the forest shaman) a female or male spirit who stays in the forest – in its trees, springs, caves, cliffs, hills and so on. Also, this knowledge can be acquired through spiritual transference into a new body, usually done at the deathbed of a senior shaman (grandmother or grandfather), to a member of the family. In either case, women's role in spiritual life, associated with knowledge of forests, places her in a position of relative power in the household and the community.

Thus, before the advent of state pressure on matrilineal societies, gender relations were relatively equal. Based on women's role in production, their special knowledge of forests, and their place in the cultural and religious life of matrilineal communities, women enjoyed considerable space within the household and the community to make decisions about resource use. Unfortunately, maintaining this position of power has been difficult, particularly in the face of pressures from the state in favour of centralizing androcentric systems and patriarchy as an invisible mediator through tourism; its distinct expression of modernity that privilege men through acts of travel, sightseeing, recreation and gender-specific employment in tourism industry.

To describe indigenous women as silent observers of the male appropriation of traditional power and resources oversimplifies both the women's voices of resistance and the range of ways in which they have expressed resistance. There are indigenous women who would speak publicly about the growing male dominance and control of resources, even as they challenged central control over the forests they depend on. In fact, women faced struggle on two fronts, against patriarchy within and outside their own communities, and against the seizure of forests that were once their source of power and authority, and on which they still often depend for livelihoods today.

Of course, many women are silent but would speak if power and resource inequalities did not create obstacles. Some choose not to speak publicly but instead exercise informal resistance in what James Scott describes as 'off stage defiance' (1985: 23) "infrapolitics of subordinate groups ... a wide variety of low profile forms of resistance that dare not speak in their own name" (1990: 19). There are also women who keep quiet and show nothing but compliance to male dominance; this is done as a result of fear of insult and physical assault. Moreover, gender-based domination is complex. In the case of women, relations of domination have typically been both personal and community-based; joint reproduction in the family and home without any control over resources has meant that 'imagining an entirely separate existence for the women as a subordinated group requires a more radical step than it has for poor peasants, working class or slaves' (ibid.). It is not surprising, then, that women do not publicly speak out against their oppression and subordination, since like any other subordinated group, they may be socialized into accepting a view of their position and interest as prescribed from above, in maintaining the male hierarchy in gender relations.

Certainly women have played a variety of roles in community-based forest management. Yang Fuquan's (2000) study of Naxi in Longquan village in Yunnan shows that some women were elected to important roles in protecting the forest resources of the community. Importantly for the post of forest or mountain guard, villagers will elect a person who is honest and frank, and can act justly, and it is the choice of the village women that counts in this appointment. A forest guard has a specific privilege: the dying trees of the collective forests are considered as her property, and she can take them back to her house. If she confiscates the axes, machetes and sickles of people who fell trees or otherwise violate village regulations about the use of forests, she can take the money or gifts that people pay her to redeem their axes, etc.

Box 18.1

An 80-year old woman, who had been a forest guard for 22 years, from mid-1950s onwards, summarized her experiences of looking after the forest resource: "I, as a woman, could be successful in managing the pubic mountain of two villages for a long time. It is because (the people of the two villages) backed me up so that I could boldly manage the collective forests of the two villages". The villagers trusted her very much and gave her nine work points per day, which was the highest payment at that time. During the interview, the other male forest guard and villagers added: "[She] is a courageous and robust Naxi woman. When she was the forest guard, many men were afraid of her and also respected her". They further acknowledged that women are the 'backbone of the family' and their working time is 10 to 20 percent more than that of men. The women, however, said that their work was actually 20 to 50 percent more than that of men, and men subsequently agreed. (Ibid.)

There are also examples of Community Forest Management in India where women have played an active role in initiating forest protection and several cases where women's committees (Mahila Samitis) are managing forests. In Baghamunda village in Orissa, the Mahila Samiti took over the forest protection and management responsibility in 1998 after the local youth club proved to be ineffective. The Mahila Samiti deploys five members on a rotational basis for guard duty every day. The women combine their guard duties with household responsibilities of collecting fuel, fodder and other forest products (Vasundhara, 2000). It is important to note that village committees tend to treat this women's protection responsibility as an extension of women's daily tasks of fuel and Non-Timber Forest Products (NTFP) collection from forests. However, when it comes to the inclusion of women in decision-making about the management of forests, male resistance is summed up in a statement made by a leading member of the Forest Protection Committee of Lapanga village in Orissa, "We are not so modern that we would involve women in Forest Protection Committee" (ibid).

In the Xiang forest station in Lugu Lake, China, He Zhonghua (2001) learned that in afforestation programs, 80 percent are women, in putting out mountain fires, and planting trees women constitute a majority of 80 percent. Furthermore, in cutting firewood, women choose to cut the twigs but men would cut the full grown, and even young trees, at random. But, men chair all forest rituals and religious ceremonies and also dominate village and forest management committees. Women's interests, labour and skills are not considered in many of the decisions they make. In each case, women are prevented from gaining access to resources such as fuelwood or broom grass, which is the basis of their livelihoods, and are also excluded from the decision-making bodies that determine access in the first place. The state forest policies did not make any substantial difference to the lives of poor indigenous women. In many of the sites we visited, forest policy targeting communities has yet to address the question of culturally-embedded gender relations and the gender-specific exclusion of indigenous women from local forest management institutions such as protection committees.

Gender and Tourism

Studies that have followed the growth of tourism industry, have focused upon the motivations of tourists. Relatively, little attention has been paid to human institutions and understanding of gender relations in the communities that receive tourists. For women of the receiving communities, economics of tourism is seen in sex tourism, that "female bodies are a tourist commodity" (Bolles, p. 78). While sex tourism is an emerging phenomenon in Yunnan and does need an examination to check the growing trade in women's bodies; it is, however, only one of many roles women play in the tourism industry. The tourism industry has also provided various decent livelihood opportunities for women. In addition to having the sole responsibility for rearing and financially supporting their children and other dependents, Mosuo and Naxi women have function of hosts, tourist workers, house keepers, boat rowers, craft and snack vendors, small entrepreneurs and managers of cottages, guest houses, night clubs, etc.

Tourism means a higher level of income, though not necessarily for all. The satisfaction of needs through consumption is possible because of the higher income. A new system of production like tourism, "means disruption, but it also means survival and much more" (Goody, 1998: 197). Survival, as we will see below, not only on a material level but also on a cultural level, as cultural practices become means of earning an income.

"The becoming cultural of the economic, and the becoming economic of the cultural, has often been identified as one of the features that characterize what is now widely known as post-modernity" (Frederick Jameson, 2001: 60). If the cultural practices and artefacts of mainstream cultures can become economic sectors, then what about the cultural practices and artefacts of the national minorities of China? Tourism has provided an avenue for the continuation of cultural practices (e.g., tea ceremonies of the Bai) or cultural products (hand printed, embroidered or woven cloth) that were in danger of extinction in the face of seeming irrelevance or economic competition from mill-made cloth.

Besides, some of the idioms of the mountain peoples also establish themselves as artistic practices, perhaps with esoteric value, if not on par with those of the plains' peoples. In China, as a result of tourism, Naxi traditional orchestras have been revived. Having almost died out (only a handful of men in their sixties and seventies kept its embers flickering), now after a gap of more than thirty years, they not only perform regularly, but have also produced cassettes and CDs of their music. There are many similar examples in handicrafts, etc.

The Naxi pictographic writing, which too was in danger of extinction (only a handful of old Dongba priests existed who could read it) has now made its presence felt as an idiom in painting and sculpture. These are new and different functions, to be sure. But the alternative to extinction is to be able to use one's heritage in changed circumstances. Tourism does give some scope for such expressions of local culture.

Culture and Commodity

Long looked down upon as inferior to the cultural performances of the plains, the songs, dances, handicrafts, etc. of the mountain peoples have gained an international acceptance, something that has grown with tourism. While in earlier times the music and cultural performances of the mountain people were facing extinction under the onslaught of the "superior" plains' products, or were preserved in hothouse fashion with heavy-handed state patronage, the growth of tourism has led to new roles for these cultural creations.

But, as Arjun Appadurai puts it, "locality is no longer what it used to be" (1996: 11). Tourism transforms and recreates locality in a new way, a new way even for the local people. There is a selective picking of what is of value in the global system. Further, to the local people too, the cultural products or practices cease to have the old participatory or religious values. The commoditization of these products and practices means that their value now lies only in the money they can bring in exchange. The products and practices are also influenced by changing tastes. Thus, Hani villagers in Yunnan have no qualms about dressing up and pretending to be Dai, since that is what the unknowing foreign or Han tourists expect of them. This interaction is itself the medium of expression of the circuits that create wealth and thus of domination of use value by exchange value. Cultural products that have use value may still continue to exist; but the global circuits are dominated by those that have exchange value. That is the price of cultural existence in the globalized market system, symbolized in this case by mass tourism.

Is commoditization of cultural products or of major global flows, like environmental services, good or bad? Those who idealize the pristine beauty of the original cultural products, fail to note that they are both continually changing and even in danger of dying out. Commoditization, on the other hand, does enable them to exist. Even more important it enables the artists who produce these works, to exist and continue to produce such works. What is needed is for the works of these artists to not just be part of the 'exotic' that tourists buy as souvenirs, not in the margins, but as parts of the global artistic idiom. That would require a change in the terms of the interaction of the local with the global.

It is necessary to understand the ways in which the local of the indigenous people interacts with the global in order to be able to change the terms of that interaction. This is so for cultural products and for environmental services. In both cases there has been a forcible and free extraction, without acknowledgement of original authorship or compensation. African sculptures became part of the global artistic scene, via Matisse and Picasso, but the original African sculptors remained completely unknown and even the African influences on these modern works were quite unappreciated by the general audience.

In a world dominated by the commodity form, the existence of an object as a commodity does give it some value. Its non-existence as a commodity does not save it from appropriation by others – whether in the case of African sculptures or forests' environmental services, both of which have been forcibly extracted. Gaining the status of commodities, these products would then have an acknowledgement of their authorship and would enable the terms of the earlier forcible and free exchange to be improved in favour of the local producers. This is the improvement in the current terms of exchange between the global and the local that we are advocating. It is not a trivial change. For those who have been kept outside the commodities, though their products have been appropriated by other, forcible means, entry into acknowledged commodity production is a step forward, even a liberation from a very unequal exchange.

Of course, this does not provide a full solution to the problem of the integrity of artistic endeavour or of the value of the environment. The commodity form is ultimately inadequate for both of these concerns. Commodifying ethnicity is not a way to integrally promote culture, as only those practices are maintained that have commodity value (Pierre Walter, 2002). The spread or generalization of commodity relations has its effect on all forms of human relations, including sexuality, with the spread of commercial sex. How and when an overcoming of these commodity forms can be carried out is something that humanity still has to come to grips with at the beginning of the twenty-first century, particularly after the disastrous record of, so far, failed attempts to overcome the commodity form of production. But without going through the contradictions of commodity production, along with its positive role in promoting production and accumulation, it is unlikely that any post-commodity system could be fashioned.

Besides the possibilities for local cultural expression, though transformed as commodities, brought about through the market, the new communications media made available through globalization, the electronic media, also make possible the articulation of the overall cultural and political concerns and identities of these local identities. The monopoly of the nation-state over these projects, which was a feature of print capitalism, has been broken by the development of the electronic media (Appadurai, 1996). Whether it is the Zapatistas in Chiapas or other indigenous people's movements, the electronic media has made it possible for these currently non-state movements to articulate and communicate their positions to larger, even global, audiences.

Women's groups in various parts of Asia are able to keep in touch with each other and with groups in other parts of the world through e-mail and other such communication systems. The resulting networks of such organizations are able to work in very close coordination with each other in conducting campaigns on various issues affecting women. Indigenous women's groups, indigenous peoples' organizations, organizations of those protesting against large dams - all such groups are now networking with each other in a manner made possible by the new communications technology. (Kelkar and Nathan, 2002).

The discourse on community is very much a non-western contribution to the discussion on rights and development. But it should not be assumed that these communities are homogenous, possessing no further groups within them. Women and men form two obvious groups within these communities. They have more or less well-defined and different social roles. Women, for instance, even in matrilineal communities, are not the political representatives of the community. Thus, community, while a valid unit of analysis itself, needs redefinition in terms of the roles of women and men. These redefinitions come about through conflict and struggle, which are themselves part of cultural practice.

We should note that cultures are not static, something given for all time. They change and the sources of change may be varied. Many changes originate in ideas gained from other cultures, from inter-cultural discussion and communication. But whether a particular idea originates from an intra-cultural critique or from inter-cultural discussion, the ideas change the existing cultural practice of the group or community concerned. It is this changing cultural practice, resulting from intra-cultural critique and inter-cultural exchange that forms the basis for the recognition of new human rights. "Human rights clearly have become part of a much wider, globalized, cultural network of perspectives. This does not mean, however, that they simply constitute an influx of alien meaning or cultural form which enters into a vacuum or inscribes itself on a 'cultural tabula rasa'. They enter into various kinds of interactions with already existing meanings and meaningful forms; in this case particular conceptions of … men and women, for instance" (Ann-Belinda S. Pries, 1996: 307).

The need for various forms of public or collective decisions extends to many aspects of social life besides that of environmental services. The preservation of cultural heritage is one of them, but this does not include the preservation of negative cultural practices. Cultural heritage has value not merely as a tourist attraction, but is important for its various non-commercial use values and even existence or non-extractive value. While tourism may provide a valuable source of income for the preservation of cultural sites, their overall development depends on a combination of private and public decisions, combining commercial and non-commercial use values and non-use values. Enshrining commercial values as the only values will not only lead to problems of equity, but also will seriously affect the supply of various public goods, including environmental services and cultural heritage. A combination of private with public decision-making at various levels, from the village to a watershed and above is needed for any kind of social cohesion. The neglect of these public goods in the transition to a market economy, perhaps is not so much the result of poverty as of the neglect of necessary public functions in the first flush of individualized commercialization and the resulting paradox of isolation. Does the development of tourism represent an "advanced mode of self-activity of the individuals" (Marx, Feuerbach, in selected works, vol. 1, 1970)? This was always how Marx understood the meaning of more developed productive forces -as more developed forms of labour. In the examples discussed above, the shift from collection of wild plant/tree materials as firewood to the cultivation of these plants/trees, certainly represents a higher form of labour. The knowledge of plants needed for domestication and cultivation is higher than in collection.

In another example, the shift of weaving from being a domestic activity of women to being the main source of income - in that, too, there is a considerable advance in the forms of labour. From producing relatively fixed designs, specific to a particular community, women now learn to weave or embroider any design that is given to them, viz. any design demanded on the market. In the process there is a generalization of the capacity to weave or embroider. There is even some local development of the capacity to innovate and make new designs, a capacity largely concentrated among the local weaver-traders who over time become specialized trader-designers and also among older, more experienced women, who are able to make new designs and set up looms, etc.

These are all definite advances in the modes of labour, the modes of self-activity of the producers. While the older, ancient form of production gave satisfaction from a limited standpoint; the modern seems to give no satisfaction, following as it does the dictates of the market. But there is a higher human content in the labour, only with the capitalist form it appears as alienation, as sacrifice of the human end to the external end of income or wealth, to paraphrase Marx (Grundrisse, 487-88). But as Marx repeatedly insisted (e.g. Grundrisse, 515) this is also a movement in the dissolution of the limited presupposition of existing production. Something clearly visible in the transformation of decorative embroidery and weaving from being a subsidiary domestic activity of women into a commercial at production and even the main income source of women and their families.

Of course, these are still regarded as tourist souvenirs, not as genuine artistic products. That requires a change not only in the attitude of the users/consumers of these products but also in development perception of work and in particular the recognition of women's 'reproductive work' as work. It is only after the rise of the feminist movement that women's decorative embroidery or quilt-making is being recognized as art. The feminist artist Miriam Schapiro has coined the term 'femmage' to show the close connection between women and the making of collages. That women's decorative motifs are a basis for abstraction in art was recognized, for instance, by Wassily Kandinsky. (Broude, 1982). There is, however, still a strong tendency to dismiss women's domestic artistic work as 'mere decoration' and 'not art'. The shift from such artistic work being a domestic function of women to becoming a commodity, even if it is the mass souvenir, could help in changing opinions about the artistic function of women art producers.

Investing in Tourism

Along with some revenues, the net income of companies owned by the local governments, for instance in the timber trade, was available for local accumulation. In contrast, where the companies operating the timber trade are either 'national' or 'multi-national', the surplus would not necessarily be available for local accumulation. The national or multi-national company would decide on its sphere and location of investment on the basis of its comparison of likely profit rates nationally or globally. Local investment of surpluses from the timber trade is important in the context of the usual drain from the regions of the forest economy. Further, there is likely to be a local shift from low productivity sectors like forestry (or, agriculture) to higher productivity sectors like tourism or processing of raw materials; thus, increasing the productivity of the entire local economy.

Of course, local accumulation can have many meanings, the implications of which would be different for livelihoods of those in villages and in towns. Local investment in Lijiang County could be mainly in Lijiang town. The hotel industry that has come up in Lijiang town has been built mainly from timber surpluses. This, though local to Lijiang County, is still extractive from the villages of the County. At the same time, the development of Lijiang town as a growth centre has a more beneficial impact on the economy of the County as a whole than, say, if the surpluses were to be reinvested in Beijing or even the Provincial capital of Kunming, for that matter.

There would be backward (supply of agricultural and forest products, e.g., mushrooms) and forward link (development of 'Eco-tourist' sites outside the town), besides the increased demand for labour in the town, to cater to the needs of tourists in Lijiang. But some of these links are also biased towards those who are better off or better connected. For instance, not all ethnic communities can equally benefit from the increased demand for labour in the town. Only those who already have relatives in the town can easily go and take up jobs in town. Since the Naxi are the main nationality in Lijiang town, it is mainly Naxis from the villages who are able to migrate into town to take up the new jobs that are coming up. The Yi or Lisu cannot as easily migrate to the town, and thus do not benefit as much from the growth of urban employment.

In Suining County of Hunnan Province, a more wood-based investment has not only enabled local accumulation but has also substantially helped the raw material producers. In the town, a bamboo board plant has been set up. The money for this investment came out of local revenues and earnings of the Forest Department. This directly provides employment to skilled workers in the town. But there is also an increase in the processing done in the villages, contributing to both higher skill and higher incomes. What this example shows is that if the investment out of local revenues is related to the processing of the forest products, then the backward links to the forest producers could be stronger and directly benefit them with higher incomes. The examples of the tourist industry, in contrast, do not exhibit such strong backward connections to the forest dwellers.

Because the accumulation is local, or in the hands of the local government, does it give more scope to the local people to intervene in directing the accumulation or development process? Is it more likely that the local government will be more responsive to the needs or desires of the local population than distant governments? At one level it can be pointed out that it would be more feasible for local people to make their desires or grievances heard by local authorities rather than by distant authorities. This is not to say that the paramount local interests will not dominate the local government. But, since the local government has to live with the local people, it can be more susceptible to pressures from below.

Further, studies of China (e.g., Siu, 1989; Oi, 1989 and Nathan and Kelkar, 1997) have pointed out that there often is a close relationship between local cadres who run the local administration, and the people. The party-state apparatus is not monolithic in its economic operations. Farmers and others often do express their grievances and resentments in various ways and the local party-state apparatus is forced to take these into account. For instance, in the Yi villages of Laoshe Township, the local administration deliberately allowed the Yi to cut and sell timber, even though the township did not have any logging quota. This was explained on the basis of the poverty of the Yi and the fact that timber was the major source of cash income with which they could pay school fees and meet other cash expenses. Similarly, even after a village was prohibited from cutting timber, when its forest was declared part of a nature reserve, the local administration continued logging, since that was almost its only source of revenue (Harkness, 1998). We are not here considering the ecological consequences of such decisions. But what we wish to point out that is that where decisions are taken at local levels, (village or township) rather than in distant capitals, there is more scope for local needs to impress themselves upon decision-makers and be taken into account in implementing, if not framing, policies. This is a positive gain from devolution of decision-making power to local government levels.

Income from Tourism

The structure of the tourist trade largely determines the distribution of returns to various links along the chain. It often happens that the mountain economy acquires relatively limited benefits from externally developed 'package tourism', with the majority of local participation being restricted merely to supplying cheap labour for menial jobs, and only a few with capital being able to move into more lucrative sections of the tourist trade.

When a substantial portion of the benefits accrue to the mountain economies, as seems to be the case in Switzerland, tourism does have the potential to create an important avenue for local absorption of labour, and thus reverse the outmigration that is otherwise a feature of mountain economies.[1] In turn, the ability of the Swiss cantons to acquire a substantial portion of the income from tourism could be related to the strong political position of the cantons, which, among other things, enabled the rural cantons to use water revenues to develop infrastructure.

In microcosm we saw a similar situation in the Mosuo village of Luoshui on Lugu Lake, in Yunnan, China, where the guest houses in which tourists stay are all owned, most wholly and a few partially, by local villagers. The poorer villagers whose houses were not located on the lake shore have not benefited as much, but they supply most of the other amenities, like horse and boat riding, that tourists require.

In Luoshui village by 1996, tourism had replaced farming as the leading industry of the village and was the main source of income for most households. In 1996, annual per capita income was 2,000 *yuan*, and the collective village income from boating, renting horses, and other tourist activities alone came to 100,000 *yuan*. Luoshui is now known far and wide as a relatively wealthy tourist village and is, in fact, one of the 10 richest villages in Lijiang prefecture (He Zhonghua, 2001).

Not only have incomes gone up, there are also new types of jobs. In a purely agricultural economy, out-migration of the educated is a strong feature. Traditional agriculture does not need their type of education. But with the development of tourism many new kinds of jobs come up requiring education. Travel agencies and guides are some of them. As restaurants develop, specialized cooks also become necessary. Musicians and other entertainers also get new scope.

All of this leads to more of the educated staying back in the village. This is visible both in Lugu Lake, Lijiang and in Jing Hong, Xishuangbanna. In some cases, e.g., in the village of Nanjie, Henan, there are even instances of computer operators and chefs returning to the village from having worked in Beijing or other cities. Tourism can help promote a reversal of the drain of the educated from the villages.

Promoting Entrepreneurs

Due to a historically self-consumption based production system, the mountain communities usually have a paucity of entrepreneurial experience. Consequently when an opportunity does arise it is often identified and taken advantage of by outsiders. These opportunities may range from relatively simple matters, like operating pedicabs to setting up plants for refining medicinal herbs. In Tibet, for instance, each of the above was first taken up by outsiders (Tashi, 2001). After a while, however, as the author points out, "the locals imitated them." Now Tibetans own many pedicabs and also greenhouses for vegetable production.

While there is a learning-by-imitating process by the local communities from the entrepreneurial initiatives of outsiders, there are also other examples where mountain communities have insisted that outside investors must join in partnership with local investors. The Mosuo village on Lugu Lake, which is now a major tourist attraction in Yunnan, has a regulation that any outside investor has to take a local partner, and that the outside investor can only remain for a period of ten years, after which the full ownership can be bought over by the local investor.

On the other hand, in the Swat region of Pakistan there are no such restrictions on outside investments and outside investors dominate the tourist and hotel industry that has come up. In such a process the local community is reduced to the position of merely being workers in these enterprises. They learn neither management nor entrepreneurship. If such processes of exclusion continue, they will lead to the local communities being confined to some of the newly emerging classes, basically to the lower levels of the working class, since even skilled workers could be brought in from outside. Such an exclusion of the mountain communities from the new classes of entrepreneurs or managers will only exacerbate ethnic divisions and lead to ethnic conflicts.

Given the paucity of entrepreneurial ability, the mountain communities could also adopt collectively owned enterprises as a way of advancing into new fields. The township and village enterprises (TVEs) of China are good examples of collectively owned enterprises. Some of the most prosperous villages in China also have collective ownership of all their enterprises. For instance, there is the village of Liuminying which is now famous, having been named an 'ecological village' by UNEP. Besides entrepreneurship, such collective enterprises also require strong internal management systems in order to stimulate productivity, and should not have the prop of a 'soft budget constraint'.

One factor of technological development, the new computer and telecommunications based Information and Communication Technology (ICT) can both reduce the costs of connectivity and increase its benefits. But the reduction of costs, for instance, by using wireless rather than wired, land-based systems, may not be enough to remove the need for subsidies in wiring the mountain communities.

The benefits of being wired to the Internet and other forms of international communication, can be substantial for the mountain communities. They will be able to check on prices in different markets and decide where to sell their products. They can set up Internet web sites to promote community-based tourism (as has been done by some communities in the hills around Mae Hong Son in Northern Thailand and is being carried out for Dayak villages in Kalimantan). They can check on possible markets for their handicrafts. Overall, the problems of accessibility due to transport difficulties could be overcome, in the area of market information, through being wired.

Who Is Better Able to Take Advantage?

The changes in the economic system have been accompanied by changes in thinking" "People are aware of doing business and have a rough idea of interpersonal competition," (He Zhonghua, 2001).

There are ethnic, class and gender factors in determining who is able to take advantage of globalization and the growth of trade, particularly long-distance trade. Taking the ethnic factor first, it is related to the differential exposure of different communities to trade and their acquisition of the capabilities that are needed to take advantage of the growing sectors. For instance, in the tourism county of Lijiang, the valley-dwelling, more urbanized and better educated Naxi have benefited much more from the growth of tourism than the Yi or Lisu, who both live on upper slopes and are less urbanized and educated. As in other rural-urban migrations, connections count in getting urban jobs. Besides, in the case of China, there is the difficulty of legal urban residence for those who do not have relatives in the cities, putting the less urbanized Yi and Lisu at a disadvantage.

Within trades, too, there are both less and more profitable ones and the ability to enter one or the other is not just a matter of the amount of capital needed. The Dai village of Man Gue (Xishuangbanna, Yunnan) has a large daily tourist trade. In the market place there are two distinct kinds of trades – the sale of local trinkets and food stuffs and the sale of jade. The jade trade is completely dominated by the Han traders, who have come from outside the area and set up shop to take advantage of the tourist influx. The lower return sale of trinkets and food stuffs is in the hands of the Dai. There are a few Dai women (women handle business among the Dai) who have accumulated enough capital to be able to go into the jade trade. But, as one of them explained, there is a specialized knowledge that is needed to be able to enter the jade trade, and the Han traders have this.

While women often carry out small-scale or micro-trade among the indigenous communities, when it comes to larger-scale or long-distance trade it tends to be taken over by men. In long–distance trade there are the factors of the difficulty for women who are responsible for childcare to be away from home for long periods of time, and their generally lesser knowledge of the mainstream, national languages. Of course, this is not a universal pattern and there are communities where the women being more involved in the market, even if it is local, have a better knowledge of the market language than men. This is so in some communities in Jharkhand,

India. But on the whole, the long distance trade does tend to disadvantage and displace women.

At the class level, there is the obvious factor that those households with education, labour, space and start-up capital, as Pierre Walter (2002) points out in the study of the Hani village, are able to better take advantage of the growing market opportunities. Even as mere sellers of gathered products, there is a difference in the price realized by those from surplus and those from food insecure households. Those from food insecure households are forced into sales in inter-linked markets (for instance, combining sale of the product along with purchase of daily necessities, rather than dealing with the sale and purchase as separate transactions) and lose a portion of the price of the product, a portion that may be higher than the interest on borrowed capital.

Those who depend more on non-natural resource-based sources of income, like tourism or wage employment, also tend to favour the conservation of natural resources and the promotion of their ecological service functions, as compared to those who depend on transforming these natural resources into income, like those who collect fuel wood for sale. Restrictions to conserve these natural resources, like not harvesting the forests on the hills around Lugu Lake, benefit those who get their income from tourism, but have a negative impact on those who depend on these natural resources. The poorer sections of the village get less, and those with the privileges of external contacts and/or location get more of the benefits from the new sources of tourist income. The initial position of these sections is itself worse than that of those with more land, etc. and tends to further deteriorate. There are a few from among the initially poorer sections, as we saw among the Khasi in Meghalaya, who from working as wage labourers with timber traders, etc. themselves learn the ways of business and become successful as timber traders.

In distributing the benefits from the new sources of income, the more equal distribution of land, and related resources, education, etc. are important. Inequalities will nevertheless develop, but the base level of income on which inequalities develop would be higher.

Growing Masculine Domination and Challenges

In one way or the other, with the growth of markets, external economic relations dominate domestic relations of production, although the domestic sphere, contributed to and controlled by women, remains an important coping structure in times of economic crisis (as happened during the Asian crisis, see Nathan and Kelkar, 1999). Funds for accumulation are increasingly obtained through banks or government sources. Men's role in managing the family's external affairs easily extends into such economic matters. In the matrilineal, even matrifocal Mosuo of Yunnan, China, the growth of tourism on Lugu Lake has increased the say of men, who secure the finance for constructing guest houses, etc.

"At the same time, with the expansion of ties between Mosuo households and the larger society, men who traditionally had a larger role in the social arena, are enabled to give full play to their superiority in this sphere, thus expanding their power, whereas the women, whose traditional work is confined to household labour, find it difficult to step up in the same arena. The presence of men from other ethnic nationalities, brought up in the atmosphere of patriarchal systems and possessing strong business ability and economic skills, are naturally and imperceptibly remoulding Mosuo traditional culture, which constitutes a crisis for Mosuo culture" (He Zhonghua, 2001).

The increase in men's say in family economic matters is coupled with their continuing control over village and other community affairs. While earlier men's monopoly in village and community affairs was counter-balanced by women's role over the economic and domestic sphere, with the growth of the market and the growing domination of external economic relations over the domestic economy, women lose their countervailing power. All hierarchies are step-by-step controlled by men.

The change to male domination is as much a patriarchal change as any of the others we have discussed here. The first phase of this change which establishes men's monopoly over the spiritual and material management of community affairs predates the spread of the market. But the second phase of this civilizational change, in which men use their domination of external relations to establish control over economic affairs, is very much the product of the spread of market-processes in which the external economy dominates the domestic sphere.

To illustrate this point we will again take the example of the Mosuo. Before the contemporary period, men's external role was limited to long-distance trade and the monkhood in pre-Liberation China. Long-distance trade along the 'Silk Road' was a chancy affair, and did not yield a regular income. The monkhood, of course, was a way of using surpluses, rather than of accumulating. With Liberation, men's roles changed to taking up education and political affairs. Until the growth of the market system, these roles too did not yield any substantial income. But with the growth of the market and the rise of the tourist trade, these external connections are now crucial in securing bank loans and other sources of finance. Women's management of domestic affairs has now turned more into drudgery. Though accumulation and inheritance are in the female line, it is men who are increasing their roles in families' strategic decision making.

The new norms of masculine domination are the product of two processes. On the one hand, there is the 'learning' from other communities and the state. On the other hand, there is also the internal struggle between the genders within these communities. The civilizational change we see is neither merely imposed from outside, nor is it entirely the result of internal conflicts. Both the internal and the external work together to bring about this change.

Simultaneously, and sometimes often in the same communities, there are also struggles to overcome these new patriarchal norms. Taking account of gender relations is not something that develops by itself. The large-scale entry of women into managing the tourist sector, for instance, among the Dai in Xishuangbanna, has reinforced their earlier domestic control. The main cash income is now also earned through women's activities and controlled by them. Even if the communities already had a practice of household cash being handled by women, the advance of women as the main cash earners does seem to make a difference to the say that women have over the use of household income.

The change in men-women relations with regard to control over household income among the Mosuo, however, has occurred largely in relations between brothers and sisters. Brothers, who are often the source of new investment funds, now have more influence than formerly on household spending. But since husbands and wives still continue to live and work with their mothers, there is no change in the economic relationship of wives and husbands. Even in matters of child care, it is uncles who spend more time with their sisters' children than do husbands with their own children.

There were attempts, for instance during the Cultural Revolution, to force husbands and wives to live together. But soon after, with the market opening, this 'nuclear family' approach was abandoned and women and men returned to their mothers' homes. As He Zhonghua points out, this form of family relationship has an added boost through its exotic value for tourists (Ibid.).

Tourism and Ecological Effects

In contrast to the transformations in Luoshui village where tourism has emerged as the main source of income, the Mosuo village of Zhengbo has been largely unable to participate in this development. The village retains its traditional agricultural structure with animal husbandry as a sideline activity. But one-crop farming and animal husbandry do not produce much income. In some households, people migrate to take up odd jobs to earn some money. They also sell some of their grain, livestock, mushrooms, and medicinal herbs in order to buy daily necessities, such as woven bamboo articles, brooms and butter. Villagers commonly keep a dozen pigs, and four or five horses for home consumption or use, but seldom sell them. At most they may sell a few chickens or piglets, and in case of urgent need a horse or cow may be sold. People still rely on the natural economy for self-sufficiency.

Farming as a single-product economy may solve the problem of obtaining food, but it is incapable of improving the living standard of villages to any great extent. Until now, only three households own a washing machine or telephone, and the whole village has only one truck to haul wood and it is not in use. Sixty percent of the households do not have television sets.

The provision of firewood is an urgent problem in the neighbouring village of Zhengbo. Firewood is in very short supply because there are no trees around the village. People go into the state forests to collect firewood.

Only one type of fuel is used here. Besides firewood, just a small quantity of sunflower stems and corn cores are used. But the consumption of firewood is very high, as not even improved stoves are in much use. In Zhengbo we witnessed a busy, early morning scene with people rushing about to collect and transport firewood. They came overburdened with firewood when the sun was setting. Many villages now cut branches or twigs, since there are no large trees left.

Fierce floods also pose a problem for Zhengbo, located as it is in the lower valley of two large rivers. Deforestation of the upper valley causes floods in the lower valley every year. The old people can recall a time when the rivers rose in summer, but at most it was clean water, and there were no floods at all. Now, floods with mud and sand cascade downwards, inundating the houses and fields, and there is no water fit to drink.

While in general it may be true that the stability of forest ownership and policy are closely related to the benefits available to the villagers, the Mosuo village of Luoshui is an exception. Although the ownership of the forest was taken back by the state, the villagers receive a rich return from the ecological effect of the forest because the village is situated in the natural protection zone. These ecological functions, including the scenery the forested hillside provides, are important to the village's main economic activity, i.e., tourism. Therefore, the division of ownership, the fact of non-ownership by the village community has little to do with their fundamental interest. As a result of this it is not difficult to manage the state forest and enforce the rules for its use.

On the other hand, in the nearby village of Zhengbo, there is a great dependence on forest products, like firewood, for the economy of the village. At the same time there is a large area of state forest. Deforestation has spread over both the collective and the state forests.

This relationship between forest use and the development of non-farm sources of income has two aspects to it. On the one hand, there is less reliance on the direct transformation of natural resources, as in agriculture or animal husbandry, for earning an income. Agricultural products are inputs into, for instance, cooking for tourists; but there is a substantial value addition in the process. The raw material is increasingly a smaller part of the total value of the meal supplied.

The second aspect is that since it is women who are largely involved in the tourist sector, as managers of small businesses, running restaurants, and so on, there is an increase in the opportunity cost of their labour. This promotes the adoption of labour-saving equipment like improved stoves, which also simultaneously consume less fuel, and therefore require less wood. In contrast, in villages where such non-farm income for women has not developed, there is very little adoption of labour-saving domestic equipment like improved stoves. (For a review of the relevant Asian experience in this regard see Nathan and Kelkar, 1997.)

Besides the comparison of the two Mosuo villages given above, there is a similar strong contrast between the adoption of improved stoves in tourism-dominated Dai villages and non-tourist related Dai villages in Xishuangbanna, with the former showing a universal adoption of labour-saving equipment, not only improved stoves but also piped water, and the latter continuing with the traditional three-stone or tripod fireplaces. As one must expect, the growth of women's cash earning activities leads to a saving of women's labour time in domestic labour, like fetching fuel wood and water.

There is also a shift from household-based collection of fuel wood from forests to either cultivation of firewood trees in the home garden or even the purchase of firewood. In general the development of tourism, means a shift from an all-round to a specialized economy. Such development of specialized economic activities need not lead to a loss of sustainability. In fact, specialized commercialization may actually promote sustainability. Take the case of fuel wood. Where fuel wood is collected from common land, often through women's labour given the very low opportunity cost of this labour, there is an overuse of labour in the collection of fuel wood and a lack of measures to increase the area-wise productivity of the product. But as commercial activities which involve the use of women's labour develop, then that community or village may cease to collect fuel wood and instead purchase it.

The development of tourism itself requires some direct attention to forest condition as part of the scenery that attracts tourists. The Hani village of Manmo has preserved its own forest in order to provide a 'walk in the rainforest'. Cutting of trees or even collecting branches is not allowed in this forest. While this has meant some moves to growing of fuel wood trees, perhaps by those directly involved in the tourist trade, there has also been a shift in the area of wood extraction. The 'other side of the hill', not visible to tourists has been denuded. Thus, there could also be a displacement of the problem.

There may be either a simple displacement of the problem, with extraction shifted elsewhere, or an intensification of production, with a saving in the use of land and labour. The crucial factor in this case is the shortage of labour. So long as labour is available and has a low opportunity cost, extensive methods of collecting fuel wood continue. But when the opportunity cost of labour, in particular the opportunity cost of women's labour, goes up then there is a movement to reduce the labour cost of collecting fuel wood. From gathering fuel wood the move is made to cultivating fuel wood, which is more sustainable than collection.

The environmental service function of forests, as scenery or recreational value, becomes more important than its direct income value. This holds true even in the case of what are state-owned forests. The tourist village of Luoshui is very mindful of the condition of the state forest on the hills above. It is important to protect the road leading into the village and as part of the attractive scenery around the lake. Thus, unlike in many other parts of China or Asia, the villagers do not make a distinction between this state-owned and other village-owned forest, protecting the latter and denuding the former. As a result it is not difficult to enforce the state forest rules for its protection.

Displacement of the costs of tourism can occur in other ways, too. The old town of Lijiang, Dayan, is in an old Chinese architectural style, with the added attraction of canals flowing by the side of streets through most of the old town. One can still see people washing clothes or vegetables in these canals. The water for these canals comes from Lashi Lake, about 50 kilometres away. The water-bearing capacity of the lake has been increased so that enough water is supplied to the town through the year. This has meant the flooding of former fields, depriving Naxi farm families on the banks of the lake of some of their income. They are paid some compensation per *mu* of land flooded. But, as is to be expected, the compensation is much lower than the income loss.

As in the larger case of loss of timber income following the ban on logging, the assignment of property rights over the lake water to the villages around the lake would enable them to sell the water that is crucial to Lijiang town. We would mention that Swiss mountain cantons have long had and continue to have the right to sell water to downstream power companies. This right has enabled the otherwise neglected uplands to share in the overall national development, and perhaps even provide the capital for investment in mountain tourist facilities. A similar right of local communities over, say, water would spread more widely the benefits of tourist development instead of making the upland communities bear only the costs, as they now do.

A factor that affects the environment is the density of tourist traffic. With the high incomes generated by tourism there is a tendency to keep pushing the tourist traffic to such an extent that it strains the 'carrying capacity' of the area. It may be difficult to clearly specify a concept like 'tourist carrying capacity', but that should not be reason to ignore this factor. People walking around grasslands obviously affect the state of the grass. To keep increasing the number of people who can go up to and walk around Alpine meadows would affect the very meadow itself.

The Naxi 'Suicide Meadow' overlooking 'Jade Dragon Mountain' is a place visited by tourists to Lijiang. The place has great significance in Naxi history. In 1993, when we first visited Lijiang, one could only go up on horseback, and the ride was managed by young women and men, organized in a cooperative. Now there is a cable car ride up the mountain. The numbers who visit have increased from maybe a hundred per day to a few thousand each day. Such large numbers tramping on the grasslands would completely destroy the meadow in a short time. The local authorities have responded very well to this problem – they have set up a slightly raised fenced boardwalk only on which one can go around the meadow. This allows large numbers to go up the mountain without destroying the meadow. What this means is that, as in other things, a new combination of private and public decisions and investment is needed in order for tourist development to be sustainable.

Recessions

The Chinese economy has not yet been subject to the recessions and financial collapses that are a part of the global capitalist system. Of course, there were local recessions in forest areas of Yunnan, when the logging ban was declared (See Dev Nathan and Yu Xiaogang 2002 for an analysis of the effects of the logging ban in Yunnan). But so far, the Chinese government's very Keynesian policy of stepping up government expenditures when private investment falters or there is a deflation, has meant that there has been no recession in China after the reform. But it is likely that such a policy will not always work in the future, as has been the case with Japan for more than a decade now.

Further, recessions in other parts of the global economy, as for instance, the downturn in tourism after the September 11 incident, can affect local tourism. Of course, tourists coming to Lijiang are still largely Chinese. But this could change. In any case, local economies need to prepare to meet the risks of recessions emanating from any number of global points.

With the dismantling of China's state-financed welfare systems the local communities are left exposed to sudden drops in income and well-being. Even if recessions originate in urban locations, they are felt in rural areas too, as a substantial portion of rural income is due to remittances from urban migrants, or, as in the following case, depends on urban spenders. In the Asian crisis two distinct rural effects were felt (Nathan and Kelkar, 1999). The drop in remittance income forced upland communities to turn to local resources to try to maintain income. The result was a larger clearing of forest land for agriculture. In fact, there is a clearly inverse relationship between urban remittances and clearing of forest land.

The gender effect also calls for comments. Since women in most cultures have the gendered responsibility of household food security, they had to put in more of the effort in trying to make up for lost urban incomes. In the absence of state schemes of income and employment support, it was largely left to the so-called coping strategies of women to deal with the rural effects of the Asian crisis.

With local recessions following the logging ban, there was the opposite relationship. Young women and men, deprived of logging income, were forced to migrate into nearby cities in search of jobs. Many ended up in barbers' shops or other low paid jobs in the tourist centres. But here, too, there was a gender difference. Boys did not tend to remit money home, while girls were much more prompt in this matter.

Learning from these lessons, it is necessary to devise insurance and state-cum-community (village) schemes to deal with the income and employment uncertainty that is a part of the capitalist economic system. A *laissez-faire* approach would only result in putting the main burden on rural women.

Conclusions

With the increase of income-earning opportunities as a consequence of tourism and technological change, women have been freed from the hard life of collecting and selling firewood. The example of the tourist village of Luoshui shows that when people have other channels of earning incomes, they demand less of local forests as a direct source of livelihood, which is obviously advantageous to the protection of forests and in turn promotes the development of the ecological service function of forests. However, it is also true that demands for firewood and timber are merely displaced to other non-local forests, just as tourism-related social ills, such as women in commercial sex, are displaced to areas outside the local community. At the same time, those households that have not benefited as much from the new sources of income have greater difficulty in meeting their fuel and other timber needs, as they are restrained from gathering wood from the nearby forests. The overall ban on logging, instituted in 1998, has also led to a fall in income of forest-dependent communities (more so Lisu and Yi than Mosuo and Naxi).

Liberalization of social relations as a consequence of economic reform policies and tourism, however, is much less seen in the case of gender relations. Men have taken over the social position of women in Naxi and Mosuo society, and women now have to put their ecological wisdom and energy into services related to entertainment of tourists and family affairs. In our interviews, men acknowledge that women-managed forest plots do better than those managed by men. However, women's representation in forest management committees or in political governance, whether at the village or higher levels, is usually non-existent. There is a growing tendency for men, even in matrilineal Mosuo society, to dominate important functions and positions of power.

The embedded violence of the trade of women's bodies does raise the question: What has been done to change women's gender identity of subordination, including that of sexual subordination? Have the progressive, gender sensitive policies attempted to use the threat point to dismantle patriarchal powers and structures that deny poor, rural and indigenous women control over their lives?

The women's movements in the south as well as the north are seen to be divided over the issue of sex work and the sex trade. We do not wish to discuss these positions of concern here. We, however, would like to say that the only way to understand this particular form of trade in women's bodies is to understand it as an aspect of masculine domination. Masculine domination legitimizes domination by embedding entitlement to women's sexual service in the biological nature of men. To erase such an institutionalized strategy of masculine power, we must "turn the stregnth of the strong against them" (Bourdieu, 32).

What this means is that we have to take account of just and equality-based gender relations in policies and practices of economic development. This calls attention to halting the emerging patriarchy in both Mosuo and Naxi societies, through measures like: (1) women's adequate representation in governance of their communities and resources; (2) development of capabilities (i.e. education, management and negotiating skills) of rural poor women to manage resources and the tourist industry at higher levels; and (3) redefining of gender roles with a positive analysis of cultural systems of Mosuo and Naxi societies to check the favour of boys in education and the concept of male-headship and to introduce the concept of dual-headed household system.

Note

1.   "The older members of the community [in some Swiss rural cantons] could remember the hard times associated with the lack of

employment in the valleys as agriculture increasingly failed to provide an adequate source of income. The arrival of the tourist industry has been the one thing that helped reverse out-migration and had been a major factor in encouraging improvements in infrastructure" (Funnell and Parish, 2001, 280).

References

1. Appadurai, Arjun (1996). *Modernity At Large*, University of Minnesota Press.
2. Bolles Lynn A. (1997). "Women as a Category of Analysis in Scholarship on Tourism: 1 Jamaican Women and Tourism Employment", in Erve Chambers ed. *Tourism and Culture, An Applied Perspective*. State University of New York Press.
3. Bosu Mullick, Samar (2000). "Gender Relations and Witches among the Indigenous Communities of Jharkhand, India", *Gender, Technology and Development*, Vol. 4. No. 3. Sage Publications, New Delhi: 333-358.
4. Bourdieu, Pierre (2001). *Masculine Domination*, Stanford, Stanford University Press.
5. Broude, Norma (1982). "Marian Schapiro and Femmage: Reflections on the Conflict between Decoration and Abstraction in Twentieth Century Art", in Norma Broude and Mary D. Gerrard, eds. *Feminism and Art History, Questioning Litany*. New York. N.Y. Harper Row.
6. Chhakchhuak, Linda (2000). *Gender Relations among the Mizos*, unpublished.
7. Goody, Jack, 1998. *Food and Love: A Cultural History of East and West*. London, Verso Press.
8. He Zhonghua (2000). "Forest Management in Mosuo Matrilineal Society, Yunnan, China", in *Gender, Technology and Development* Vol. 5, No. 1. Sage Publications, New Delhi.
9. Jamieson, Frederick (2001). "Philosophy of Globalization", in Frederick Jamieson and Masahi, eds., *Cultures of Globalization*. Duke University Press.

10. Kelkar, Govind and Nathan, Dev (1991). Gender and Tribe: Women, Land and Forests in Jharkhand, Kali for Women, New Delhi and Zed Press, London.

11. Kelkar, Govind and Nathan, Dev (2002). *Gender Relations and Technological Change in Asia, Current Sociology.* Sage, London, Vol 50 (3).

12. Kelkar, Govind and Nathan, Dev and Walter, Pierre (eds) (2003). *Patriarchy at Odds, Gender Relations in Forest Societies.* Sage Publications, New Delhi (in press).

13. Kinnaird Vivan, Uma Kothari and Derek Hall (1994). "Tourism: Gender perspectives", in V. Kinnaird and D. Hall, eds. *Tourism: A Gender Analysis.* Chichester, UK, Wiley Publishers, pp 1-34.

14. Marx, Karl (1970). *Selected Works,* Vol. 1, Moscow, Foreign Languages Press.

15. Marx, Karl (1975). *Grundrisse.* London, Penguin Books.

16. Munshi, Indra (1986). "Tribal Women in the Warli Revolt 1945-47: Class and Gender in the Left Perspective", *Economic and Political Weekly,* Vol. XXI, No. 17, April 26.

17. Nathan, Dev and Govind Kelkar (1997). "Woodfuel: The Role of Women's Unpaid Labour," in *Gender, Technology and Development,* Sage Publications.

18. Nathan, Dev and Govind Kelkar (1999). "Agrarian Involution, The Domestic Economy and Women: Rural Dimensions of the Asian Crisis", in *Economic and Political Weekly,* Bombay.

19. Nathan, Dev and Yu Xiaogang (2002). "Timber and Local Accumulation in China", mansucript.

20. Preis, Ann-Belinda (1996). "Human Rights as Cultural Practice: An Anthropological Critique", in *Human Rights Quarterly,* 18, The John Hopkins University Press.

21. Sarin Madhu (2000). "India Country Chapter", in Antonio Contreras, Liu Dachang, David Edmunds, Govind Kelkar, Dev Nathan, Madhu Sarin, Neera Singh and Eva Wollenberg, eds., *Creating Space for Local Forest Management,* CIFOR, Bogor, unpublished manuscript.

22. Scott, James (1985). *Weapons of the Weak: Everyday Forms of Peasant Resistance.* Yale University Press, New Haven, USA.

23. Scott, James (1990). *Domination and the Arts of Resistance: Hidden Transcripts*. Yale University Press, New Haven, USA.

24. Singh, K. S. (2000). *Shamanism, Witchcraft and the Position of Women in Tribal Society*, unpublished.

25. Singh, K.S. (1999). *Changing Attitude to Forest and Nature: A Historical Review with Focus on Jharkhand*, unpublished.

26. Subba, Suman (2000). "Transition of Gender Relations in Tamang of Nepal", Kathmandu, Nepal, unpublished.

27. Tashi, Townsend, Janet G. (1995). *Women's Voices from the Rainforest* (International Studies of Women and Place), Routledge.

28. Vasundhara (2000). "Women's concerns in community, forest rights debate in Orissa," in Contreras, Antonio, Liu Dachang, Edmunds, David, Kelkar, Govind, Nathan, Dev, Sarin, Madhu, Singh, Neera and Wollenburg, Eva, eds., *Creating Space for Local Forest Management*. CIFOR, Bogor, unpublished.

29. Walter, Pierre (2002). "Ecotourism and the Forest Management in Manmo Hani Village, Xishuangbanna," Manuscript.

30. Xi Yuhua (2000). *Tensions in Local Forest Management: A Case Study of Enzong Village*, unpublished.

31. Yang Fuquan (2000). *The Investigation of Use and Management of the Forest Resources in Longquan Administrative Village of Baisha Township of Lijiang County, Yunnan, China*, unpublished.

32. Yu Xiaogang (2002). "Gender Relations, Livelihoods and Supply of Eco-system Services: A Study of Lashi Watershed, Yunnan, China", manuscript.

19 China's West Development Strategy and Rural Empowerment: Is There A Link? A Case Study of the Tibetan Plateau Region

Namgyal

Geography of the Tibetan Plateau

Grasslands account for more than 60% percent of the Tibetan Plateau's area. Grassland ecosystems support a moderate diversity of animal species, including birds, rodents, ungulates, carnivores and domestic animals. Grasslands are becoming increasingly settled, either seasonally or permanently, with a population of more than 10 million people in the Tibetan Plateau region including 6 million Tibetans who are primarily pastoralists reliant on using natural rangelands for some form of livestock management.

The present environmental situation in China and Tibet offers unprecedented opportunities for international cooperation among Tibetan, Chinese and foreign researchers, academics, NGOs, government agencies and multilateral institutions. In the Tibetan Plateau region, the chance for truly sustainable development projects has not yet been lost, but the opportunity must be pursued promptly and intensively if it is to be realized. Overall, a principal obstacle to effective environmental management and sustainable economic development is a severe shortage of available or reliable biodiversity data to inform research and policy decisions. However, traditional Tibetan lifeways offer models for a variety of sustainable development strategies, and further research is needed on the lessons they offer. At the same time, it is necessary to recognize that both Tibetan and Chinese communities play a role in environmental destruction and that policies are needed to provide them with economic development alternatives. Cooperation between Tibetan and Chinese colleagues, and local communities, offers the best opportunity to successfully achieve environmental conservation and sustainable development goals.

A Brief Historical Background

Prior to 1950, Tibetans and Chinese had totally different historical experiences. Tibet was never colonized by any foreign colonial power except for a brief invasion by British from India in 1904; whereas China suffered a long period of colonial exploitation from the European powers and even Japan. The rise of Communism in China was largely the result of a surge of nationalistic fervour that arose from decades of humiliations at the hands of European powers and Japan. Historically, the Communist Party of China (CPC), after its claim of "peaceful liberation" of Tibet in 1951, was the first regime to assume total control over Tibet and rule Tibet directly from Beijing. Since then, Tibet has undergone a series of development and social experiments similar to those which happened in China. The Tibetans, however, saw the CPC under Chairman Mao as another ruler of China. Initially, Tibetans believed naively that Mao would uphold and honour the historical Cho-Yon (meaning "priest-patron" in Tibetan) relationship of the past (Smith, 1996: 88, 223, 614). It was a relationship that was based strongly on support and patronage of Tibetan Buddhism by successive Chinese emperors since the Yuan Dynasty. Prior to 1950, Tibet was very much a traditional subsistence society with the Dalai Lama as both secular and religious ruler, a system which has been in place for more than three centuries. This traditional system under the rule of Dalai Lama had strong religious influence over whole of ethnic Tibet, though its secular influence was concentrated in central and western Tibet. Today, northeast and east Tibet (traditionally called Kham and Amdo provinces) have been incorporated into the provinces of Sichuan, Gansu and Yunnan, with major portions of Amdo made into a new province of Qinghai.

Tibet differs from mainland China in both social and natural conditions. Tibet is largely grassland suited to extensive land use, which necessitates pastoral production as the one major livelihood in the region. Arable land fit for cultivation constitutes less than 2% of the total land area in the Tibetan Plateau region (Environment and Development Desk, 2000: 45). Thus livelihood on the Tibetan Plateau was a mix of farming along the river valleys and lowland and an extensive nomadic pastoralism over the vast rangelands complementing each other and forming the base of the economy. Tibet's nomadic pastoralism was different from the agricultural and farming practices of lowland China, where animals are fenced, reared and fattened for the market. Tibet's comparative advantage is that vast extent of grassland enabling the nomads to take animals to forage. Herd size has both survival and social value.

China's Development Policies from the Early 1950s

After assuming effective control over the Tibetan Plateau in the middle of the twentieth century, China implemented a dual policy of agricultural intensification and industrialization to transform the traditional economy that was primarily based on subsistence farming and livestock management. Later, after the introduction of Deng's economic reforms and opening up policies in the Tibetan Plateau in the 1980s, priority was given to improving transport and urban infrastructure and services, and to encouraging migration of Chinese migrant entrepreneurs and semiskilled workers. The policy assumed that the Tibetan Plateau has an extremely low quality of human resource, and that the migrants from more developed areas of China could provide the range of skills needed for Tibet's rapid economic expansion and modernization process (Qun, 1997). The result of this policy was rapid urban growth and modernization, which improved living standards for Chinese migrants and also the few Tibetans employed in urban areas (Holcombe, 2001).

The reliance on migrant entrepreneurs and semiskilled immigrant workers did help to spearhead rapid growth and modernization in the Tibetan Plateau, but unfortunately, this has not helped to perform its catalytic role of transforming and benefiting the Tibetans, except for a small proportion who live in the urban areas. All available statistics show poverty is widespread in rural areas (UNDP, 2002). These policies, however, contributed to a rapidly increasing income disparity between people living in urban and rural areas, and between Chinese and Tibetan ethnic populations, as most Tibetans live in rural areas, dependent on traditional agriculture and livestock management (Fischer, 2002).

Agriculture intensification and impacts

China's effective control over the Tibetan plateau in the middle of the twentieth century led quickly to a push for traditional production systems to intensify. Grain production was given the highest priority and marginal dryland pastures were converted to cropland, but not as extensively or as disastrously as in Inner Mongolia. The staple crop of the entire plateau is barley, which is unfamiliar and unappealing to Chinese tastes. Instead, wheat, the staple of northern China, was introduced, initially with catastrophic results (Becker, 1996: 171 and Tibet Information Network, 1997: 80).

What actually happened was that as nomads were collectivized and stripped of all decision-making powers, herd numbers were increased dramatically, to the long-term detriment of pasture quality. All through the 1960s and 1970s, with Tibetan herders powerless to do anything about it, herd numbers were held far above historic levels, in an effort to make the rangeland yield more than it sustainably could (Goldstein and Beall, 1990, and Miller, 1995). This set off uncontrollable degradation and erosion, which persists today in a frigid climate blasted by blizzards and gales, in which the hardy grasses and sedges withstand both the elements and grazing pressure. If grazing pressure is excessive, however, even the hardiest of sedges which keep most of their biomass below the surface, die off, exposing the soil to wind, hail and blizzard, with the result that it soon erodes, often to bare rock on upper slopes, with no prospect of recovery. Chinese scientists have documented the dramatic and unstoppable increase in such erosion in great detail, without acknowledging state failure as the cause.

In areas on the plateau closest to China there are other impacts of state policy that originate not in the revolutionary era but in the reform era that began in the late 1970s. In the provinces of Qinghai, Gansu, Sichuan and Yunnan herds were not only redistributed to individual families after the communes were disbanded, but each family was allocated land use rights to specified pastures, on which the family was expected to settle, build permanent housing and fencing, usually by going into debt. These policies of sedentarization have had further impact on pasture quality by reducing mobility and flexibility of rangeland management in a highly unpredictable climate in which flexibility is essential (Williams, 1996, and Humphrey and Sneath, 1999).

The result has been further degradation of the rangelands which, as the World Bank has noted, intensified in the 1990s (World Bank, 2001: 18). All indicators of economic progress, such as grown weight of herd animals, carcass weight of slaughtered animals, quantity and quality of forage, extent of pest species invasion, spread of desertification all show steady and serious decline of viability and livelihood. This is especially true in what China thinks of as "inner" Tibet, those portions of the plateau absorbed into the Chinese provinces of Qinghai, Gansu, Sichuan and Yunnan. It is in these provinces that Tibetans are small minorities, and substantial numbers of Chinese settlers have moved in, in response to state initiatives to establish new industries.

In central and western Tibet, known in China as Tibet Autonomous Region (TAR), the policies of fencing and sedentarization of nomads have not yet been implemented to the same extent, and rangeland degradation has not yet reached crisis point. Statistically, it is hard to disaggregate Tibetan nomads from available Chinese data on the provinces that incorporate northeastern and eastern Tibet. However, in TAR statistics the economy of Tibetans and the economy of Chinese settlers are readily distinguishable, because of the spatial inequality. In rural TAR there are almost no non-Tibetans, while in urban areas the populations are mixed. Statistics for rural TAR correlate strongly with the actual ethnic divide, and can be taken as a surrogate for the development status of the Tibetans. Today, the traditional community-based livestock management system has been totally abolished but no new mechanisms and systems of management are in place due to official neglect. The neglect of agriculture sector after the reforms of 1990 continues and presently the investment in the agricultural sector is dismal (Tashi, Partap and Lui, 2002: 154-155).

Transfer of outside migrants and their role in modernization process

Further, the Chinese state planners and economists very early on negatively evaluated the skills of Tibetans saying that Tibet has an acute shortage of quality of human resources and that the Tibetan economy was agrarian and subsistence based with no need to embrace materialism as the means of economic development. To counter this "extremely low quality of human resources" in Tibet, Beijing has taken up the task and responsibility of improving the quality of human capital through transfers of skilled cadres and personnel called "pioneers" to the Tibetan area to help in the development of the society. The alternative would have been to invest in education of the Tibetan population but the UNDP China Human Development Report 2002 shows this has not been done. Migration initially began as elsewhere in China during Mao's chairmanship when young educated Chinese youths were sent to the countryside to help the peasants. In the case of Tibet the state sent in large number of skilled and technical personnel to modernize and develop Tibet's society and economy. But this has had a huge underside, which is the influx of Chinese settlers into the Tibetan region, which in spite of its vast land area could not support the increase in population due to the fact Tibet's highland has less than 2% of arable land, and more than 60 % grassland. Tibet lost food security and famines and starvation occurred (Becker, 1996: 171-72, and Tibet Information Network, 1997: 29).

Moreover, due to political reasons and a mistrust and lack of faith in Tibetans' administrative capability, a new administrative and bureaucratic system was built and staffed in such a manner that decision-making powers were firmly in the hands of non-Tibetans. Tibetans were given high sounding titles and positions which were symbolic with no real decision making power. This institutional arrangement, the first in the history of Sino-Tibet relationship, necessitated the presence of a large influx of Chinese into the Tibetan region to carry out the necessary development work. The new arrangement means that for 40 years Beijing has had to pump in enormous funds and subsidies to sustain the burgeoning population of urban cadres and sojourners in Tibet (Tibet Statistical Bureau, 2001).

China has little historic experience of managing rangelands and areas best suited to extensive land use, and has made the bringing of feed to animals a defining characteristic of civilized rural production, whereas the bringing of animals to available forage is a sign of primitivity and enslavement to nature. The Chinese complaint is that Tibetan nomads fully utilize winter pastures but not the higher summer pasture growth. This scientific judgement is based on satellite reconnaissance of summer pastures high on mountain slopes, not all of which are consumed by domestic herds as much pasture is left by Tibetan herders for the use of herds of wild species (Wu, 1997: 115). Tibetans, if asked, would respond that the wider picture of risks and their management makes it dangerous to stock pastures at a rate that would consume all available summer feed, and that maintenance of biodiversity is part of the Tibetan definition of quality of life to be shared with all sentient beings. But Tibetans are not asked, and cannot be asked.

Urbanization and extraction enclaves

Beijing's focus and thrust of development has been on industrialization and development of pillar industries so that the economy in the region will eventually take off. Central subsidies and special treatment given to Tibet every year prop up the economy for the final take off. However, it appears that the economic take off is nowhere in sight, at least in the foreseeable future. In fact, this policy of central support and subsidies has propped an artificial economy in a few urban areas and resource extraction enclaves, excluding the majority of the population from any social services. Employment opportunities are restricted to these concentrations of resources and capital.

The inflow of central government funds was not restricted by requirements that projects generate adequate rates of return, even in the mid- to long-term. The state was willing to finance projects that fulfilled non-economic objectives such as border security, transmigrating excess population from unsustainably overcrowded area, stability in inter-ethnic relations, populating the plateau with loyal subjects, and assimilation of indigenous minorities into the national economy.

Since industrialization in the Tibetan region was not based on regional comparative advantages or rate of returns but was for political and stability reasons, the new industries performed dismally, requiring increasing central funds and support to keep them going. Successive Five-Year Plans announced the renewal of the pillar industries strategy for Tibet, with liberal subsidies and capital inflows, not only from state revenues and loan raisings, but in recent years also from requiring wealthy provinces to directly invest in Tibet. The steady and accelerating influx of capital has been successful in some ways, especially in creating employment. The beneficiaries are overwhelmingly non-Tibetan settlers and sojourners who save a high proportion of the high wages available, remitting much to Chinese provinces where their families remain (Holcombe, 2001). The very public capital inflow from state funds becomes an unpublicized capital outflow, with little capital reinvested in Tibet. This is one reason why, despite urban employment creation, industrialization has largely failed, loss-making enterprises are common, the traditional indigenous pastoral and farming economy remains undercapitalized and poverty remains common. Tibet's potential comparative advantages, in specialist production of animal products, are not utilized, despite rapidly growing urban demand in China's wealthiest markets for exactly what Tibet is best able to produce. It is clear that the above development strategy that is repeated in each Five-Year Plan with variations, has failed to create industries that create wealth or are self-sustaining without ongoing subsidies.

Industrialization and urban-biased economic development: Solution or the problem?

Some economists say that progress is inevitable, Tibet's turn will come even though it may be slow and faltering, but the direction is certain. However, it cannot be assumed that rural Tibet is progressing, as the degradation of the rangelands, the acceleration of desertification and the extent of erosion are now undermining actual progress in increasing yields and incomes in rural areas. The early period of agricultural intensification of 1950-1980 impacted negatively on the agricultural sustainability and growth due to misguided policies and historical inexperience in managing pastoral production systems. Today, the economy on the Tibetan Plateau remains largely a command economy, chronically dependent on massive external inputs aimed at generating pillar industries and eventual economic take-off. At a time when China is taking seriously the need to increase farmers' incomes, the gap between rural and urban areas is widening. This has happened in spite of China's rhetoric on opening up, liberalization and increasing utilization of the comparative advantage of the Tibetan Plateau. These contemporary trends have not affected the rural areas in Tibet in any positive way despite the obvious comparative advantage enjoyed by a region specializing in pastoral produce, just as urban China develops a demand for the very commodities and local advantages offered by its unique biodiversity and culture. Due to a stress on industrialization, the environment has been damaged and polluted to an unprecedented degree.

In spite of China's intentions and efforts to modernize the economy on the Tibetan Plateau, the failure is so extensive that leading Chinese economists such as Hu Angang (2001) openly question the validity of this 50-year-old experiment in economic take off. Writing in *China Tibetology* in 2001, he says industrialization has been seen as the only way to promote the development of a regional economy and to relieve poverty. Hu (2001) goes on to critique the high Stalinist development state model. Problems in China's economic development prior to reform and opening up originated during the early 50s when the strategy of giving precedence to heavy industry was adopted – a model of economic construction indiscriminately copied or inherited from the former Soviet Union. To adapt to this tactic of industrialization, Hu says China used the slogan 'industry as the guiding factor, agriculture as the base' as an economic developmental strategy for many years. It was also known as 'squeeze agriculture for industry', an economic strategy whereby policies in agriculture were adopted, which sacrificed agricultural development for the process of state industrialization. Hu goes on to point out that this exhausted policy of compulsory sacrifice is exactly what is proposed for Tibet, although it has actually been attempted in Tibet for years without success.

However, Tibet's 'Tenth Five-Year Plan' (*Tibet Information Network*, 2001: 25) lists processing industries, the mining industry and the forestry industry as mainstay industries in the exploitation of natural resources as a guide for the traditional strategy of industrialization. It was even proposed in the 'Tenth Five Year Plan' that the pursuit of an increase in GDP be the main target of so-called 'leap-style development'. The only industries which appear to be thriving are commercial brewing, quarrying and cement production, and maintenance of transport equipment on which the long supply lines to interior China depend. These are the only industries where output is climbing rapidly, and the inherited debt burden is not crippling, although in the case of the recently corporatized state transport enterprizes, that may be a result of leaving much inherited debt in the state parent organization to give this semi-privatized operation its best commercial chance.

Widening Inequality – a transitional phase or development failure?

Kanbur and Zhang have shown that in the past fifty years, inequality throughout China worsened at times when the central government policy was to extract as much as possible from the rural workforce, to be allocated by command economy mechanisms to heavy infrastructure and heavy industry (Kanbur and Zhang, 2001). In the 1960s, Kanbur and Zhang state, "To ensure low food cost for urban workers, agricultural product prices had to be suppressed as well... Under the planned system, the central government had large powers to allocate and utilize financial resources... In particular, we find that heavy-industry prioritizing development policy plays a key role in forming the enormous rural-urban gap in the pre-reform period."

One aspect of the region's economy that is reminiscent of the 1960s is the heavy burden of extraction of surpluses from the rural population, in the form of taxes, charges, fees and unpaid compulsory labour. Although these exactions are not counted in official statistics, there is consistent evidence from social science researchers and interviews of Tibetan farmers and nomads who escaped into exile that Tibetans experience the cadres as rent-seeking, and sometimes even predatory. As the central state downshifts responsibility for financing local services to users, and requires cadres operating local commodity marketing bureaus to finance their own salaries from local revenues, the pressure on nomads and farmers intensifies.

This leaves Tibet doubly disadvantaged, suffering both from its interior location, and, within Tibet, from the urban bias of the state investments on which the TAR economy depends in the absence of adequate internal revenues. For these reasons it is the Tibetans who are most disadvantaged, as they are the rural population whose livelihoods are compromised by cadre rent-seeking, yet who must pay up front for basic human services such as healthcare and education in the absence of any responsibility taken by the government beyond the most local level.

PRC Western Region Development Strategy in the Tibetan Plateau Region

President Jiang Zemin announced China's campaign to develop the western region in 1999. A year later, it was officially announced that exploitation of minerals and other natural resources was critical for the continued development of China's economy, but also helping to ensure the continued stability of local society while contributing to China's ethnic and national unity. Central to the Western Region Development Strategy is investment in "hard infrastructure" such as highways, railways, pipelines, mineral extraction, dams, power stations and irrigation facilities. Limited priority is given to "soft infrastructure" such as health, education and local human capacity building that would enable more local employment and participation in the modernization process. The Western Region Development Strategy to date has also given limited priority to investment in local agriculture and livestock, although the majority of the western region population, including particularly the non-Chinese ethnic populations experiencing most acute poverty, are in these two main traditional sectors.

An example is one of the largest ongoing projects in 2001, the upgrading of the *Yangpachen*-Lhasa segment of the Gormo to Lhasa highway. This 80 kilometre section of the road passes through a river gorge and is being completely rebuilt with extensive stone abutments and lining work carried out by very large numbers of migrant Chinese masons and other highway workers at an estimated cost of about 400 million RMB ($48 million). During June and July 2001, large numbers of Chinese road construction workers were also engaged in the upgrading of main roads in Lhasa itself. The construction work was consistent with a pattern seen in most Tibetan urban areas over the last decade with central or other provincial government financing. This pattern includes emphasis on the introduction of modern road and urban building construction designs, techniques and materials unfamiliar to local Tibetan workers, and the employment of migrant Chinese workers familiar with the techniques involved (Holcombe, 2001).

With the implementation of major infrastructure development and natural resources exploitation projects, Chinese migrants are encouraged to go West and carry out the essential planning, management and skilled manpower roles. The initial selection of priority infrastructure investment projects under the Western Region Development Strategy does not appear to correspond with the priority needs of the poorest populations in the traditional agricultural and livestock sectors. To the extent that the Western Region Development Strategy is oriented toward the infrastructure needs of the modern sector, and is a source of additional employment for Chinese migrants, it will further exacerbate income disparities between Chinese migrants and local Tibetans. It would also further social exclusion traps referred to in the preceding section.

The evidence so far suggests that China's official Great Western Region Development campaign, announced in 2000, may redirect development projects and even some Foreign Direct Investment (FDI) and Chinese investment capital into key cities of China's western half, but Tibet remains far beyond these major hubs. The central government may use its diminishing share of national Gross Domestic Product (GDP) to finance major integrative infrastructure projects such as the railway to Lhasa currently under construction. But even China's President says that the railway project is uneconomic, and is being implemented for national and political reasons, with little prospect of generating a positive rate of return.

A major reason for doubting whether the current state of development is just a transition stage comes from examining available data on the size, scale and financing of the urban tertiary sector.

Based on the latest *Tibet Autonomous Region's Statistical Yearbook* (Tibet Statistical Bureau, 2001) wages paid to urban workers show a remarkable concentration of wealth. The wages paid to employees of state enterprises in TAR alone in 2000 were 2.2 billion *yuan*. Taking 1978 as a base year, (table 4-13) by the mid 1980s, when Wang and Bai (1991) did their fieldwork the wage bill had more than tripled. There was a sharp spike in 1994, the year the Party held a Work Conference of all state stakeholder agencies operating in Tibet to redouble efforts, and wages jumped in a year from six times to ten times the 1978 base. By 2000 the wages index was well over 20 times the 1978 base. Even after correcting for inflation, this is a massive blowout in wages concentrated in a few hands, 54,604 persons who are mostly Chinese.

Of the wages paid to state sector employees, the largest share was consumed by government agencies and party agencies followed by propaganda workers, mass media broadcasters, education and cultural work unit employees. It might be expected that many school teachers would be in rural areas, but such is the prevalence of *minban* (community schools) untrained and locally hired teachers in rural schools, who are not on state payrolls, that very little of this expenditure is in rural areas. The other major category of employees taking a major proportion of the total wage expenditure are transport, storage, post and telecommunications staff. Their employment is highly concentrated in urban centres and in the narrow transport corridors connecting them. Together the above sectors consumed 65.2% of the total state sector wage spending. The urban bias is further confirmed by geographic disaggregation, with the biggest seven cities in TAR taking 61.7% of the total wage outlay. The only distinctly rural employment in the state sector, in farming, forestry, animal husbandry, mining, quarrying, geological prospecting and water conservancy accounted for only 7% of total wages.

These statistics can be compared with the overall disbursement of central finances for all aspects of government activity. Total spending in TAR in 1999 was 5.325 billion *yuan*, including the current construction boom, which uses public finance to build administrative office blocks, highways, hydropower stations and power grids. Official statistics fail to reveal the sectoral end use of a third of that amount. Capital construction used 21.8%, while labour-intensive service sectors (government administration, culture, education and health care) consumed a further 39.45%. By contrast, the only specifically rural expenditure, on support for agricultural production, received 2.67% of government spending in 1999 and 2.3% in 2000.

The wages paid to state employees are 36.8% of all official outlays for all purposes. High wages contribute to inflation, which saw CPI increase in urban areas by 1999 to 250.7 on a base of 100 in 1990. This has a flow-on effect in rural areas, where inflation was hardly any less, being 242 in 1999 using 1990 as the base 100 year (table 7-1). The sharpest inflation, urban and rural, was in 1993, 1994 and 1995, in years which were nowhere near as inflationary across China (Tibet Statistical Bureau, 2001).

The initial Western Region Development Strategy investment in the TAR is for railway construction facilitating mineral resources exploitation, and again is likely to be of main benefit to outside migrant workers with the needed skills. It is not clear to what extent the physical infrastructure and natural resource projects of the Western Region Development Strategy in Tibet will be accompanied by social investments developing local Tibetan skills and capacities in areas essential for transport and natural resources development. In the longer run, the Western Region Development Strategy should adopt a more balanced and equitable distribution of investment and income generation between urban and rural sectors and ethnic groups. This will require further measures to increase the commercial value to rural producers in the agricultural, livestock and rural industry sectors. Such efforts would also have the advantage of promoting more sustainable development in Tibet which invests in local human resource capacity and is less reliant on outside capital, expertise and markets for its prosperity.

However, to date, priorities for Western Development Strategy investment in the region appear to favour transport needed for natural resources development. There are also indications that major construction foreseen under the Western Region Development Strategy will again rely on the skills of migrants, particularly Chinese, and will not give priority to local training which would enable Tibetans to participate substantially from Western Region Development investment. It is crucial that development including that associated with the Western Region Development Strategy, should give greater priority to Tibetan capacity building as an integral part of investment.

An Alternative to Present Development Strategy

Since China is at a very early stage of this massive program to develop the western region, it is wise to pay attention to an ancient Chinese proverb: "To know the road ahead, ask those coming back." China could draw on its own experiences (Great Leap Forward in the 1950s) as well as parallel international experiences to learn and avoid debacles associated with large-scale economic development, especially in fragile environments. Western provinces, to most Chinese people living in the east, invoke an image of vast uninhabited wastelands, inhospitable mountains, arid lands and true deserts. Because of its spatial scale and the time proposed to fulfill it, the Western Region Development Strategy will play a significant role in the regional and global environmental changes. Few people realize that several of the world's major rivers have their origins in the Tibetan Plateau (including the Mekong, Irrawady, Indus, Ganges, Brahmaputra, Yangtze, and Yellow rivers). Land use, resource exploitation, climatic and desertification-related changes on the Tibetan Plateau would adversely affect the water flow that in turn goes to meet the needs of about 2 billion people downstream.

So it is imperative that as China carries out this ambitious Western Development Strategy, it draws upon experiences within China as well as those of other countries around the globe about the costs, benefits and consequences of massive and rapid development activities in arid and semi-arid areas. Further, the proposed "leap-forward" development style, mega-project schemes, unequal distribution of affluence, and radical population shifts generally pose great risks and have huge negative impacts on both the social and environmental stability in the western region. This would be in contradiction to what Beijing hopes to achieve through the ambitious West Development Strategy.

Much information about these issues already exists in and outside China. It is crucial that China understands the constraints of fragile western environments and respects the social capital of the region's inhabitants. This would help to maximize the economic, social and environmental benefits. A major factor for the failure of development efforts in the region has been a lack of clear rural development strategy. If China is really serious about the threats to social stability and national unity due to widening income inequality, it is high time that the rural areas got the top most priority for income generation that enhances rather than disrupts the traditional subsistence economy (CIDA, 1999).

Although the Tibetan Plateau is characterized by physical, economic and cultural uniqueness, which are viewed as constraints, there are natural and comparative advantages offered by the very nature of the Plateau's natural and social conditions. The Plateau is the water tower of Asia, the importance of which is now gradually appreciated by the people living downstream in China and rest of Asia.

China doesn't have to look far to find sustainable development alternatives. The Tibetan farmers and herders have maintained sustainable livelihoods on the fragile ecology for a thousand years, and the first right step is to involve and listen to the very people that the state is attempting to develop. Just across the Himalayas, Nepal, Bhutan and South Asia have much experience of different development alternatives such as community-based development, social forestry, participatory rural development, eco-tourism and gender sensitive development (National Environmental Secretariat, 1992 and Ladakh Project, 1986). Their experience gives a wealth of information and guidance on approaching development work in land-locked mountainous regions with fragile ecology. What is essential is a decentralized arrangement that allows and facilitates genuine popular participation and self-administration, which will satisfy the people's desire to participate and get involved in improving their living and economic conditions (CIDA, 1999).

For the Western Region Development Strategy to succeed, political and business leaders must acknowledge obstacles and deal with them objectively. Lower-level cadres who have closely administered their regions for decades will have to adopt a fresh approach. These individuals may either be too close to a situation to realize problems that an outsider can spot immediately, or, because of local conflicts, be unable to confront such problems. It may be up to Beijing to impose on local cadres a change of approach, that is less rent-seeking and extractive, and more respectful of traditional modes of production and their use of comparative advantage. The change in development thought and implementation is necessary if

China is to catch up with the world's best practice. It calls for a detailed analysis going well beyond the official reports, but to the people themselves to determine which solutions have and have not worked in China over the past 20 years.

The main stakeholders in the whole West Region Development Strategy scenarios, the local inhabitants—the farmers and herders in the Tibetan Plateau – don't figure anywhere in the whole process. In fact, the local cadres are already using the Western Region Development Strategy to justify their development plans. Consequently, the central government is taking steps to ensure that local leaders do not initiate programs that are inconsistent with the strategy's goals.

According to Hu and Wang *empowerment* is the pith and marrow of China's effort to reduce regional disparities. They say:

> "The central government has to first empower itself so that it can effectively enforce its policies, including regional policies. Then the government is advised to focus on empowerment of backward regions rather than on restraining advanced regions. How should China empower the backward regions? Purely income subsidies are not recommended, except for those living in absolute poverty. Instead, the emphasis should be placed on enhancing the long-term development capabilities of backward regions. This is to be done by investing in human capital, upgrading infrastructure, and offering investment incentives". (Wang and Hu, 1999: 216)

At present, the central government's role is largely that of an overseer whose job is to draw the master plan and ensure that development schemes fall within the parameters of the plan. Premier Zhu has mentioned that the Western Region Development Strategy is to be a "long-term" program – one with a timeline of 20 or 30 years. This statement is likely an effort to make sure participants understand that the program will take a long time to produce results. However, projects implemented so far are by and large extensions of existing programs that local governments have resubmitted under the plan. The key issue is whether the major players in the Western Region Development Strategy, the central government, provinces and local leaders are able to make an honest evaluation of both old and new business and development methods.

Finding an appropriate development model for the Tibetan Plateau

The fundamental question for the policy makers at the central government level is how best to spread the benefits of rapid growth and modernization to the relatively poor Tibetan populations depending on subsistence agriculture and nomadic livestock production. The experience of the past fifty years of development in the Tibetan Plateau region has shown that:

1. Urban-oriented growth strategies, relying on economic reform and opening up to outside expertise and resources, have resulted in growing income disparities between urban and rural populations. This also means disparities between Chinese and other non-Tibetan migrants and local ethnic Tibetan populations who live predominantly in rural areas;

2. Policies relying on market forces and outside trained and experienced migrants to promote rapid economic growth have had other unintended impacts on Tibetans, including a lower priority for Tibetan training, and the effective exclusion of Tibetans from most skilled and semi-skilled job opportunities that offer higher wages and the possibility to rise above the poverty line;

3. Overall poverty alleviation programs have not achieved their results and programs directed to poor Tibetan communities in rural areas have lacked adequate financing needed to overcome the negative economic and social impacts of urban-biased economic reform and opening up policies;

4. Education for most Tibetans is compromised by an effective barrier to higher general, vocational and technical education due to financial limitations and failure to implement a 1980 decision on the use of the Tibetan language above the primary school level;

5. Failure to employ and benefit the local Tibetans on major transport and building construction projects, which continue to employ largely Chinese and other non-Tibetan migrant labourers citing lack of requisite skill and experience on the part of local Tibetans. (Holcombe, 2001)

In the case of the Tibetan Plateau, two issues are particularly significant, i.e., an appreciation for and an understanding of traditional relations between nature and economy, and tied to this aspect, the importance of achieving sustainable uses of land and natural resources, to ensure an ecologically sustainable development. China has neglected and undervalued the importance of traditional modes of exchange and production. Development planners see traditional knowledge as irrelevant to the new situation and this knowledge is systematically devalued by the process of specialization and competitive production for the market. The common assumption that the modern scientific knowledge of the centre is sophisticated, advanced and valid, and that whatever rural people – the Tibetan farmers and herders – may know will be unsystematic, imprecise, superficial and often plain wrong needs to be discarded. At present the development methods based on disseminating this modern scientific, and sophisticated knowledge to inform and uplift the rural masses, has not yet lifted the Tibetan rural masses out of poverty and food insecurity. Knowledge flows in one direction only – downwards – from those who are strong, educated and "enlightened", towards those who are weak, ignorant and in darkness. But studies and experiences around the world show that indigenous systems have shown that there are workable models of how to achieve a greater measure of equality without doing irreparable damage to the environment. In her study of the Ladakhis in India, Helena Norberg-Hodge (1998: 65-74) calls for a reassessment of the very nature of development. For her, the momentum of development and progress, supported by massive investments from government and industry, are becoming a global monoculture...rooted in a narrow scientific world view, ...[is] an alien culture which destroys diversity and self-reliance in the name of development.

In the case of the Tibet Plateau, too, Chinese researchers and high-level officials are aware of the implications of economic development in fragile ecosystems. However, like the rest of China, economic concerns here supersede everything. This conventional model needs to be questioned and an alternative way of investing in human capital in the rural areas is the answer for China in the long run both from economic and social stability points of view.

Making the Tibetan Plateau an ecological safe haven could ensure stable and perennial flow of water downstream, prevent natural disasters like floods, sandstorms and droughts in China and beyond, and provide clean and beautiful natural surroundings for tourism. This itself is a sound utilization of comparative advantage that the Tibetan Plateau possesses. A development model that emphasizes an understanding and mutual respect for different cultures, which shows sincere understanding and appreciation of Tibetan culture and its traditional relations to the environment is necessary and critical. In their study of the nomads of Western Tibet, Goldstein and Beall (1990) note that traditional pastoral system, rather than being destructive, is sophisticated. They also emphasize that besides the need to protect the Changtang area, it is equally important to protect the nomadic pastoralists who reside there. Thus Goldstein and Beall (1990) write: "it would be indeed tragic if after surviving the destructive Cultural Revolution, these nomads' way of life is destroyed by modern notions of 'conservation' and 'development' that are based on faulty evidence, and flawed assumptions."

In the pursuit of modernization and regional economic development, China should realize that the Tibetan Plateau has different economic system based on extensive land use, with a different conception of resources, land and social organization. Unless China recognizes the relevance of traditional Tibetan economic and environmental relations, and bases development on indigenous Tibetan agricultural and pastoral practices, social and environmental problems will worsen rather than improve in the coming decades.

China may eventually attain such wealth that it may look within the human mind, as the Tibetans do, to find the sources of abiding happiness and to appreciate the traditional wisdom. But by then it might be too late.

The existing patterns of Chinese state orchestrated policies will result in learning the hard way at great cost if China persists with top-down approaches that denigrate or ignore traditional knowledge of land stewardship in the Tibetan Plateau.

An alternative – based on popular participation and genuine autonomy

Tibetans have based their entire civilization on the cultivation of wisdom through myriad explicit methods. If given a chance, Tibetans know how to restore health to their unsustainably managed land. If the nominal autonomy ascribed to Tibetan lands were actualized, the local people could restore sustainability. Genuine autonomy is the key. The traditional model of sustainability worked for a very long time. It was known not only to scholars and specialists but was widely understood and practiced. It is knowledge that is both an insight into the human condition, and an embodied everyday experience confirming and deepening such insight. Traditionally, lands were developed sustainably by maintaining a steady human population that did not command all living beings to serve human use. Valleys were farmed intensively, while the vast grasslands were used lightly, yet extensively, by a mobile people who lived harmoniously with huge herds of wild animals unafraid of human presence. Religions also taught people to be moderate in their needs and not to forever chase after greater and greater material wealth. Biodiversity flourished.

The theory and practice of sustainability remain the key to the future of the Tibetan Plateau. If sustainability is to be restored, then the rural farmers and herders must regain agency: a chance to speak for themselves and not to be spoken for by the world's most determined development state.

This broad, inclusive model of sustainability can serve not only the local inhabitants but the world. If given a chance, Tibetan herders and farmers can demonstrate in practice how China can live sustainably, rather than repeating all the mistakes of other countries and only then attempting to repair damage that is often irreparable. They could even teach the Chinese people to moderate their wants rather than to make insatiable demands. The spiritual traditions have many ways of teaching people to find happiness in strength of mind rather than material possessions.

A time-tested, demonstrable and replicable practice of sustainability is available to the world. It is not necessary to work strenuously to bridge the gulf between the human world and the natural world, between culture and nature, between man and the biosphere. Programs promoting sustainable development that are predicated on such separations make hard work of what can be achieved by a more spacious, inclusive, relaxed, non-anthropocentric worldview. The dichotomies and dualism underlying China's policies are illusory.

On the Tibetan Plateau and in Inner Mongolia, Buddhism taught people to think of the needs of future generations, not just the immediate needs. It also taught that humans are not separate from nature, that all sentient beings have a legitimate right to life, and that no species is privileged or lives apart in a realm exempt from interdependence. Sustainability and mindfulness of long term consequences have become an explicit part of life. Tibetan philosophers wrote long treatises on how the selfish human instinct is an ignorant misunderstanding of reality. Meditators taught all who would listen the practical methods to overcome false distinctions between self and other, human and animal, subject and object. By example and in the lives of popular saintly singers and poets, the Tibetans learned how to embody in daily life a worldview that fostered compassion for all that lived. This has helped the herders to conserve landscapes, moving herds so as to maintain the sustainability of pastures. Traditional stewardship of the land was careful, thoughtful and consistent.

Only Tibetans know how to live in the Tibetan Plateau and maintain long-term sustainability for all mind-possessors. Chinese people feel afraid in Tibet, fearful that they will die, fearful that they will be unable to breathe. This is not their homeland, and they know it with every breath they take. Slowly China is learning that it cannot simply impose its will on Tibet, but no Chinese scientist or policy maker has ever acknowledged or studied how we sustainably managed a high-risk environment for millennia. There is no Chinese scientific literature on Tibetan nomadic risk management strategies (Wu, 1997: 115). The subject does not exist, despite a massive Chinese scientific literature on all other aspects of grasslands and livestock production.

Only when the farmers and herders are able to be the stewards of our own lands will they be able to reassert their traditions, which value sustainability ahead of selfish exploitation for a human few.

Recommendations

It is obvious that the rural population – herdsmen and farmers of the Tibetan plateau – should be made the centre of economic planning. Angang (2001) says, "the choice of road to modernization should always be built upon the basic principle of 'the wealth of the people at root, investment in the people', to make the people who constitute the population's absolute majority – the peasant farmers and herdsmen – the principal, direct and general beneficiaries." Some Tibetan economists and social scientists have for some years advocated investment in strengthening the sustainable yields, varieties, and added value of the products of traditional economy. This will not only create wealth but also reduce the need for subsidies. Agriculture and animal husbandry consume materials much less than industry, and it has the peculiarity of being labour-intensive, and with large elasticity for substituting funds. It is obvious that agriculture, animal husbandry and characteristic industries must be the main development priorities since they have far greatest potential with comparatively less investment for benefiting the vast number of farmers and nomads and uplifting their living standards.

Putting farmers and herdsmen first is not exactly new thinking in development circles globally, but in China, with strong traditions of centrist control of the countryside, this is a new approach. Tibet was until the 1950s part of the global economy, exporting considerable surpluses of wool via Calcutta to Europe. Tibet's integration into the global economy was abruptly cut by policy directive from Beijing once Tibet was incorporated unto China, and thereafter Tibetan surpluses, often extracted coercively, were redirected eastward. Chinese planners and economists, whose historic experience is based on intensive use of irrigated lowlands, persist in making assumptions about productivity in the Tibetan plateau rangelands that are grounded in the biases of irrigated agriculture and plentiful supply of labour. Historically the trade links of "outer" Tibet were not with China but with India and

Nepal, which are much closer than Chinese markets, and, despite the intervening Himalayan chain, accessible (van Spengen, 2000:89-91). Unfortunately, only trade across the Nepali-Tibetan border is once more encouraged, after decades of restrictions. The nearest access to seaport from Tibet, the Indian seaport of Kolkatta around 410 kilometres from the Tibetan border, has been closed since the 1960s.

The most important and necessary precondition for successful West Development Strategy in the Tibetan Plateau is the active participation of Tibetans themselves. At present Tibetan people are not free to speak their minds, and usual methods of consultation, surveys and appraisal will not work reliably in Tibetan areas as long as Tibetans feel the omnipresence of state power which makes them afraid to speak their minds.

The rhetoric of participation is common. Asking for active Tibetan participation to be structurally inbuilt ensures the employment of competent Tibetans in all phases of the project cycle. If Tibetans are part of the project team they will be able to go with the team into Tibetan areas and not only discern the actual needs and true feelings of local populations, but also help resolve any difficulties with implementing agencies of the Chinese government. This contributes to promoting governance, rule of law, transparency and accountability. Tibetan staff or consultants will not add greater complexity but will help find solutions, and workable ways of satisfying the requirements of all parties. This has been the experience of the Tibetan non-governmental organizations (NGO). They have often worked skilfully and successfully inside Tibet, meeting basic human needs of deprived and excluded Tibetan populations, while maintaining good relations with the cadres as well. China has welcomed the investments of many such Tibetan NGOs.

Secondly special attention be paid to the experience of NGOs operating in Tibet. Special attention should be given to those NGOs that are largely Tibetan. By their very nature, NGOs are not required to identify potential projects from lists presented to them by the government of China, enabling them to make their starting point an assessment of actual needs in specific areas. They are best able to be culturally sensitive, as they are from the outset a partnership of a local Tibetan community with Tibetans and their supporters from the wider world.

Education and Health

The lesson to be learned from their NGO experience is that what Tibetan communities all over Tibet most keenly want, and feel deprived of, are education, health and food security, delivered in ways suited to a dispersed and often mobile population. The delivery of basic human services should be the top priority. By any measure Tibetans are poor, with low Human Development Index scores, and this should be the focus of all outside development aid. Targeted poverty alleviation has been lacking. The *UNDP China Human Development Report 2002* has a wealth of evidence of the systemic exclusion and deprivation of all areas of the Tibetan plateau. The task is to translate these findings into delivery of appropriate development projects.

Investment by the state in human capital formation in Tibetan areas has been much neglected. The quality of teachers, relevance of the curriculum, state of school buildings are all low. The model adopted is one of centralization, which is quite inappropriate for a largely mobile pastoral population who must send children away from the family to boarding schools where little is learned but bad habits. If outside development staff are able to ask Tibetan nomad parents to speak frankly, this is what they will tell you.

It is Chinese policy to emphasize minority languages in minority areas, and there is much scope for improvement in Tibetan areas to ensure real functional literacy is attained, both in Tibetan and Chinese languages. At present the burden of paying for education has been downshifted to the lowest and poorest levels of government, who in turn shift responsibility to villages and to parents. Central government support does not materialize because these lower levels are unable to come up with the counterpart funding required. Much the same applies to the provision of health care, except that the entire financial burden has been shifted onto individuals and families, which is often a cause of immiserization, a descent into absolute poverty.

Micro Credit

UNDP's emphasis on micro credit is especially appropriate for Tibetan areas. One of the simplest ways for Tibetans to empower themselves is to allow local Tibetan communities access to micro finance, for projects they want and need, to strengthen local life and economies. Tibetans are an entrepreneurial people, but Chinese banks, loaded with massive debts, very seldom make loans to Tibetans, who are not considered credit worthy.

If Tibetans can have access to micro finance, they can regain some control over the processing, marketing and transportation to market of what they produce. The profits of such enterprise can not only repay micro credit loans but also finance the construction of much needed schools and medical clinics in remote areas. In this way Tibetans need not depend on central government assistance, which seldom arrives, or on external donors.

Renewable Energy

UNDP China in its Five-Year Plan for 2001 to 2005 gives high priority to renewable energy. This is highly suited to Tibet, both because Tibet is sunny, and because portable solar power is compatible with the key goal of maintaining the mobility of the customary Tibetan nomadic way of life. This is definitely preferable to the present Chinese policy of using access to fixed grid electricity for nomads as an inducement to sedentarize.

Rule of Law

A further opportunity, in line with UNDP China's expressed goals for 2001 to 2005, is legal education. UNDP China is strongly committed to promoting the rule of law, which is best achieved through an educated population. Education of Tibetans, in both rights and responsibilities under Chinese law, is almost entirely lacking, and is much needed.

General Recommendations

We seek projects that are local, specifically targeted, emphasize flexible decentralized service delivery, give preference to human services rather than large scale infrastructure projects, small rather than big. Based on the actual experience of successful NGOs in Tibet, these basic principles mean the top priorities are:

- decentralized and culturally sensitive education;
- decentralized health care with financial support until affordable locally financed health insurance schemes can be implemented. Emphasis on prevention, hygiene and health education, primary health care, provision of clean water, with curbs on reliance on expensive drugs;
- support for pastoral mobility and rangeland quality. This includes flexibility of land tenure including guaranteed access to seasonal pastures, employment of local Tibetan communities in grassland regeneration, decentralized veterinary care, introduction of hybrid breeds suited to Tibetan conditions, encouragement of producer marketing and small scale value adding under local control. This also means provision of portable solar power rather than connecting pastoral families to a fixed grid, which forces them to settle, to the great detriment of rangeland quality, causing erosion, loss of production and poverty;
- support for Tibetan farming communities to minimize dependence on chemical fertilizer and pesticides, while maintaining productivity, with guaranteed access to suitable land. Local cooperatives under community control should be encouraged, to add value by processing rural products and improve incomes; and
- provision of off-farm employment opportunities that do not break up families or require depopulation of the countryside.

References

1.   Becker, Jasper (1996). *Hungry Ghosts: China's Secret Famine*. London: John Murray.
2.   CIDA (1999). *Providing for Basic Human Needs in the Tibet Autonomous Region*. Summary Report of the CIDA Appraisal Mission to the Tibet Autonomous Region (Xizang Province).

3. Fischer, Andrew (2002). *Poverty by Design: The Economics of Discrimination*. Montreal: Canada Tibetan Committee.

4. Environment and Development Desk (2000). *Tibet 2000: Environment and Development Issues*. India: Central Tibetan Administration.

5. Goldstein, Melvyn C. (1990). *Nomads of Western Tibet: The Survival of Way of Life*. Berkeley: University of California Press.

6. Goldstein, Melvyn C.; Beall, Cynthia, B.; and Cincotta, Richard P. (1990). "Traditional Nomadic Pastoralism and Ecological Conservation on Tibet's Northern Plateau", 6(2) *National Geographic Research* 139.

7. Holcombe, Arthur (2001). "On Local Ethnic Population Living Standards in China: The Case in Tibet". Available online 1 Feb <www.ksg.harvard.edu > (Draft paper to be presented at the Conference on Financial Sector in China September 11-13, 2001).

8. Hu Angang and Wang Shaoguang (1999). *The Political Economy of Uneven Development: The Case of China*. New York: M. E. Sharpe.

9. Hu, Angang (2001). "The Problem of Selecting the Correct Path for Tibetan Modernization (Part 1)", 1 *China Tibetology* 3 (In Chinese).

10. Humphrey, Caroline and Sneath, David (1999). *The End of Nomadism?* Durham: Duke University Press.

11. Kanbur, Ravi and Zhang, Xiaobo (2001). *Fifty Years of Regional Inequality in China: A Journey Through Revolution, Reform and Openness*. Available online 4 Feb <www.people.cornell.edu>.

12. Ladakh Project (1986). *Ecology and Principles for Sustainable Development*. Proceedings of a conference co-hosted by the Ladakh Project and the Ladakh Ecological Development Group in Leh, Ladakh from September 2-4.

13. Li, Lifeng (2001). "Exploring the Sustainable Development Strategy in Lhasa Distric, Tibet". *UNU/IAS (United Nations University/Institute of Advanced Studies) Working Paper* No. 96 <www.ias.unu.edu> February 1, 2003.

14. Miller, Daniel (1995). "Herd on the Move: Winds of Change among Pastoralists in the Himalayas and on the Tibetan Plateau". *Discussion Paper Series* No. MNR 95/2 Kathmandu: ICIMOD.

15. National Environmental Secretariat (1992). *Bhutan: Towards Sustainable Development in a Unique Environment.* Bhutan: National Environmental Secretariat.

16. National Bureau of Statistics (2002). *China Statistical Yearbook.* China: China Statistical Press.

17. Norberg-Hodge, Helena (1998). "Development and Globalization: Social, Psychological and Environmental Costs", in Akiner, Shirin; Tideman, Sander G. and Hay, Jon, eds., *Sustainable Development in Central Asia.* Britain: Curzon Press.

18. Qun Zheng (1997). "The Chief Constraining Factor on Tibet's Economic Development is the Low Quality of its Workforce", 30 (4) *Chinese Education and Society* 29.

19. Smith, Warren (1997). *The Tibetan Nation.* India: HaperCollins Publishers.

20. van Spengen, Wim (2000). *Tibetan Border Worlds: A Geohistorical Analysis of Trade and Traders.* London: Kegan Paul International.

21. Tashi, Nyima. Partap, Tej. Liu Yanhua, 2002. *Making Tibet Food Secure: Assessment of Scenarios.* Kathmandu: ICIMOD.

22. Tibet Information Network (1997). *A Poisoned Arrow: The Secret Report of the 10th Panchen Lama.* London: Tibet Information Network.

23. Tibet Information Network (2001). *News Review: Reports from Tibet.* London: Tibet Information Network.

24. Tibet Statistical Bureau (2001). *Tibet Statistical Yearbook.* China: China Statistical Press.

25. UNDP (2002). *China Human Development Report 2002,* 4 Feb <www.unchina.org/undp>

26. Wang Xiaogang and Bai Nanfeng, 1991. *The Poverty of Plenty.* New York: St. Martin's Press.

27. Outline of the Tibetan Autonomous Region's Five-Year Plan for Economic and Social Development and its Long-Term Target for 2010.

28. Williams, Dee Mack (1996). "The Barbed Walls of China: A Contemporary Grassland Drama", 55(3) *The Journal of Asian Studies* 665.

29. World Bank (2001). *China: Air, Land and Water.* Washington, DC: The World Bank.

30. Wu Ning (1997). *Ecological Situation of High-Frigid Rangeland and Its Sustainability: A Case Study on the Constraints and Approaches in Pastoral Western Sichuan/China.* Berlin: Dietrich Reimer Verlag

31. Wu Ning and Richard, Camille E. (2000). "The privatization process of rangeland and its impacts on the pastoral dynamics in the Hindu Kush Himalaya: The case of Western China, China", in Eldridge D. and Freudenberger D. (eds), *People and Rangelands.* Townsville, Australia: Proceedings of VI International Rangelands Congress.

20 The Significance of West China Development to Asian Economic Integration

Chen Zhilong

Introduction

As early as 1990, Li Guo Ding, a famous economist in Taiwan, noted that the rapid growth in the Asia-Pacific region, including Japan, "Four Little Dragons", countries in ASEAN, Australia, New Zealand and China, had surpassed that of the USA and the European Union. He also pointed out that trade within the Asia-Pacific region is developing rapidly. "Since 1986, because export from Japan and other countries in the Asia-Pacific Region to America has declined in general, the trade between Japan and newly industrialized Asian countries and the trade among those new industrialized countries has increased gradually, while trade between Japan and ASEAN, and that between new industrialized countries and ASEAN grew dramatically" (Li, 1996).

It is reported that trade within the Asian region, except Japan has started to boom since the later seventies, and accounts for 40% of the total volume at present. Last year, the contribution rate of the demand between countries and regions in Asia to Asian export increase exceeded one third. There is a new trend for export to move from developed countries to the Asian region. In 2002 Japan's export to other Asian regions increased by 14%, while its export to China increased by 32%, but export to America only increased by 1%, and to countries in the E.U. declined by 2% (Wen, 2003).

In my paper I regard the Western Region Development Program as a new driver to promote the Asian economy's integration. West China development pushes economy integration from East Asia to Middle Asia. It is a long-term course and not as fast as that in East Asia, but the trend is definite and inspiring. This paper wishes to draw people's attention from East Asia to other, vaster, Asian areas, and the discussion of the paper is the development of West China.

My contention concerning Asian economy conformity is that the trade volume between countries in Asia accounts for a larger and larger percent of the total foreign trade volume of Asian countries. Since at least the 1980s, the trade between Asian countries has been growing, and the proportion of its volume has been increasing compared with that of their trade volume with countries outside Asia. If we would believe the phenomenon observed by Li (1990) to have appeared primarily in East Asia over a decade ago, it may appear in extended Asian areas such as South Asia, Middle Asia and North Asia after the beginning of the 21st century.

The forces promoting Asian economy conformity come from many sources. The first is the Japanese economy. In the latter half of 20th century, as the economy in Japan grew up, it played an important role in Asian economy conformity. The second one is the new industrialized economies in East Asia, such as South Korea, Taiwan, Hong Kong and Singapore. Finally, due to the economic reform in countries such as China, Russia and India at the end of the 20th century, the economic growth rates of those countries have improved to different extents, and their opening has been promoted greatly, too. Therefore, these countries have begun to function in promoting the integration of the Asian economy.

In view of its geographic location, China has a special position in Asia. China may trade with countries in Northeast Asia, East Asia, Southeast Asia conveniently by the sea, and across its borders with countries in South Asia, Middle Asia and North Asia. Because the Chinese economy was closed before the 1980s, it not only was laggard in development, but also had a very limited effect on the economy of surrounding countries. But since the 1990s, the influence of China's economy on Asia has been more and more obvious. China began to attract a lot of foreign direct investment and from 1980 to 2000, China utilized at least 300 billion dollars of FDI, an 80% of that from related countries in Asia. In respect to trade, Japan, Korea, Hong Kong, Taiwan, and ASEAN are all important trade partners of China. Furthermore, there were some dramatic changes at the beginning of the 21st century, such as that China and ASEAN started to build a free trade zone.

At the turn of the century, China launched the strategy of West China Development. It is reasonable to expect that its implementation will promote the integration of the Asian economy further. My judgement is based on the following.

First, West China Development will inaugurate a new and strong domestic demand, which will certainly enable China to keep a high economic growth rate at the beginning of the 21st century, and reinforce China's economic strength.

Second, West China Development will create new room and new industrial fields to absorb and utilize FDI, providing new investment opportunities for some countries with investing capability in East Asia and Southeast Asia.

Third, the Chinese central government has substantially adjusted and developed the foreign relationship with all neighbouring countries of West China, and will continue to do so in future.

Forth, the Chinese central government has and will give more purviews in term of opening and developing the local economy to all the local governments in West China.

Finally, the Chinese central government and local governments will provide funds together to reinforce infrastructures that are indispensable to international trade in West China, such as the railway, road, river transport, oil and gas pipelines, and the information network across the border.

There are large populations and large economic scales in countries around West China. For the growing productivity in China, there is the market, and there are the chances. On the other hand, for all the neighbouring countries of China, the boom of the Chinese economy brings market and chances, too, and the implementation of West China Development will help to turn potential opportunity to reality.

I focus on the issue of West China Development and Asian regional economic integration in this paper, but this focus does not downgrade the significance of economic co-operation between Asian countries and countries outside Asia. For all the Asian countries, to strengthen the trade and economic co-operation with developed countries such as those in America and Europe is the most important thing. The economic growth in Asia must be part of the growth of the whole world. Hence, the West China Development Strategy contains many elements about attracting the investment from American and European multinationals, and many elements about expecting the governments of all developed countries to help.

Background: Asian Economic Development and China

An important trend of the world economy in the late 20th century was that the Asian economy developed more rapidly than that of other regions. East Asia drew the attention of the whole world (Table 20.1).

Table 20.1   The Achievement of Selected Asian countries

	Per capita GDP growth (%)	
Region or Country	1965-1995	1995-2025
East Asia	6.6	2.8
Hong Kong	5.6	2.1
Korea	7.2	3.5
Singapore	7.2	2.5
Taiwan	6.2	3.1
People's Republic of China	5.6	6.0
Southeast Asia	3.9	4.5
Indonesia	4.7	5.0
Malaysia	4.8	3.9
Philippines	1.2	5.3
Thailand	4.8	3.8
South Asia	1.9	4.4
Bengal	1.6	3.9
India	2.2	5.5
Pakistan	1.6	4.4
Sri Lanka	2.3	3.9
Papua New Guinea	0.4	1.5

Source: Fog, Harrigan and Connor, 1999: 80.

Table 20.2.   Asia in the World

Proportion of Asia in the world	1992	2022
Income:		
Including Japan	22.97	27.86
Not including Japan	7.32	14.78
Population:		
Including Japan	52.56	50.72
Not including Japan	50.28	49.19
Trade:		
Including Japan	27.02	36.50
Not including Japan	17.05	28.08
Investment		
Including Japan	32.91	28.45
Not including Japan	10.19	14.09

Source: Fog, Harrigan and Connor, 1999: 69.

According to estimates by Jacques de Lajugie, around 1970, the OECD contributed almost 70% of global GDP growth while the developing countries in Asia accounted for only 10%. But from 2020 to 2030, Asia will take up more than 50% of world economic growth, and the share of the OECD will reduce from 40% to less than 20% (Fog, Harrigan and Connor, 1999: 34).

The rapid development of the Asian economy allows China to benefit much, though West Europe and North America are also important external sources of growth for China. This can be seen from the fact that 76.2% of the the foreign investment in China comes from Asia (Table 20.3).

Table 20.3.   Distribution of Original Places of Foreign Investment
in China (1979-98)

Country or region	Contractual investment volume (US$ billion)	Proportion (%)	Actual investment volume (US$ billion)	Proportion (%)
Hong Kong	297.628	51.99	138.434	51.76
Japan	32.543	5.68	21.912	8.20
America	46.594	8.14	21.433	8.02
Taiwan	40.400	7.06	21.265	7.96
Singapore	31.091	5.43	12.177	4.56
Korea	14.837	2.59	7.562	2.83
Virgin Islands	16.917	2.96	6.736	2.52
United Kingdom	15.055	2.63	6.540	2.45
Germany	8.397	1.47	3.438	1.29
Macao	8.883	1.55	3.328	1.24
Others	60.149	10.50	24.487	9.14

Source: Wang, 2000: 413.

The import and export of China in 2001 was US$ 509.8 billion, more than half of which was traded with countries and regions in Asia. Allowing for the fact that China's trade of US$ 56 billion with Hong Kong includes some transfer trade of the countries in Europe and America, Asia accounts for about 40% of China's foreign trade volume in recent years. Neighbouring Asian economies also benefit China by trading parts for processing with China, which account for about half of China's trade. According to Chinese Customs, China's import and export of parts for processing amounted to US$ 302.17 billion in 2002, and 65% of it came from Japan, Taiwan, ASEAN, and Korea. At the same time, China exported US$ 46.8 billion, US$ 28.15 billion and US$ 26.14 billion of parts for processing respectively to America, Japan and European Union, altogether accounting for 56.2% of the total export amount of parts for processing.[1] It can be seen that rapid growth of

China's export to America and Europe has been driven by profound co-operation between China and other Asian economies.

However, we must point out that only the eastern coastal region in China has participated greatly in the Asian economic integration which began in East Asia in the late 20th century. This can be testified by the distribution of areas where foreign companies have directly invested. Between 1979 and 1998, 88% of FDI entered the eastern region of China, 9% entered the middle region, and only 3% entered Western Region (Wang, 2000). This reflects the bias in space and slowness in time of Asian economic integration, in a way. There are all kinds of reasons for this. For instance, it is because China and the former Soviet Union used to be rivals, China and India kept aloof from each other for too long, and that the economic co-operation between China and ASEAN was very limited. Of course, it is also related to China's inward-looking economic policy in the 1950s-1970s.

Launch of the Western Region China Development Strategy – A Turning Point

The launch of the Western Region China Development Strategy is a turning point in China's overall development strategy as it turns from a coastal-region-biased policy of more than twenty years standing to a new policy that encourages the eastern region to explore economic opportunities in West China. Meanwhile, the development of West China will benefit the Asian economy by extending the process of Asian economic integration from East Asia to Southeast Asia, South Asia, Middle Asia and North Asia.

According to the overall plan of West China Development by the Chinese Government (2000), the Western Region Development program covers Chongqing Municipality, Sichuan Province, Guizhou Province, Yunnan Province, Tibet Autonomous Region, Shanxi Province, Gansu Province,Qinghai Province, Ningxia Hui Autonomous Region,Xinjiang Uighur Autonomous Region, Inner Mongolia Autonomous Region and Guangxi Zhuang Autonomous Region. The strategic goal of the Western Region Development Program is as follows: Through the hard work of several generations, by the middle of 21st century when modernization is basically attained nationwide, the regional disparities between the western region and other regions should be diminished considerably, the relative underdevelopment of the western region should be reversed, transforming it into a prosperous and advanced new West where life is stable, ethnic groups are united and the landscape is beautiful.

The main tasks of the Western Region Development Program in the Tenth Five-Year Plan period include speeding up infrastructure construction, intensifying ecological improvement and environmental protection, consolidating and reinforcing the fundamental position of agriculture, actively conducting industrial restructuring, accelerating the development of science, technology and education and promoting social undertakings. There are some priority areas in the Western Region Development Program, the first being is the economic zone along the western part of Longhai Railway and Lanzhou-Xinjiang Railway. Relying on communication trunks such as the Longhai and Lanzhou-Xinjiang railways and the highway connecting Lianyungang and Huo'erguosi, major cities located along the Asia-Europe continental bridge including Xi'an, Lanzhou, Urumqi, Huhhot, Yinchuan and Xi'ning should play a pivotal role to support the development of Northwest China and promote the economic and technological communion and co-operation with Middle Asia region, by taking full advantage of their economic and technological strength. The second area is the economic zone of the upper reach of the Yangtze River. Major cities located along the Yangtze River such as Chongqing and Chengdu should play an important role in the development of Sichuan and Chongqing, by relying on communication arteries including the Yangtze River waterway, Shanghai-Chengdu highway and railroads along the Yangtze River. Another one is the Nanning-Guiyang-Kunming economic zone. Major cities located along the route to the sea in Southwest China including Nanning, Guiyang and Kunming should play a pivotal role in the development of Yunnan, Guizhou and Guangxi, by relying on communication arteries such as the Nanning-Kunming Railway, the highway connecting Chongqing and Zhanjiang. The last one is Tibet, Xinjiang and other ethnic minority regions.

As an important part of the national economy, the western region plays a key role in work division between areas all over the country.

The western region has extensive resources, good conditions and great potential for exploration. Hence, the western region is an important basis for the nation's long-term development.

Table 20.4.   Percentage Shares of Basic Resource in Different Areas

	Water	Energy	Mineral resources	Arable land resources	Infield resources
Western region	46.45	35.77	31.57	42.72	23.70
Include: Southwest	38.25	17.32	25.92	26.56	11.72
Northwest	8.20	18.45	5.67	16.16	11.98
Northeast region	5.74	3.33	17.66	11.83	16.97
Middle and lower reaches of Yellow River region	6.17	54.45	25.52	23.61	31.19
Middle and lower reaches of Yangtze River region	22.36	5.19	21.91	13.36	21.07
Southeast coastal region	19.28	1.26	3.32	8.08	7.08

Source: Liu, 1993: 120.

The territorial advantages of the western region include a long border, an assemblage of diverse peoples, convenient communication with interior and exterior areas, and this is an important gateway to China's western development. The border line of Xinjiang is about 5000 kilometres, that of Tibet about 2500 kilometres, that of Yunnan is 4060 kilometres, that of Guangxi is about 1020 kilometres, and that of Inner Mongolia is 4200 kilometres. There are 14 countries around those provinces. At present, there are the new Asia-Europe continental bridge and Great Southwest Entrée to the Sea as transport channels in the western region. The connection of those in north Xinjiang and railways in the former Soviet Union in September 1990 (from Urumqi to Alan Mountain) marks the completion of the new Asia-Europe continental bridge. It begins at Lianyun Port in China in the east and reaches Rotterdam in Holland in west. Its total length is

10900 kilometres, and its length within China is 4331 kilometres. Trading with countries in Europe, the Soviet Union, the Middle East and West Asia across the continental bridge will bring much benefit to the western region.

The western region possesses a complete industrial system, good technological equipment and abundant labour. In the past half century when the industrialization of New China took place, nearly 3000 big or middle-scale industrial firms were built in the western region, 800 of which are large companies, and make up more than 450 billion dollars of industrial fixed capital.

Table 20.5.   Preponderant Industries with National Importance
in Western Region

Sichuan	(a) hydroelectricity; (b) steel industry; (c) electronic industry; (d) mechanical industry; (4) chemical industry for agriculture
Guizhou	(a) hydroelectricity; (b) aluminium industry; (c) phosphate industry
Yunnan	(a) energy industry with hydroelectricity; (b) phosphate and salt industry; (c) industry of nonferrous metal such as lead, zinc and copper
Shanxi	(a) coal mining industry; (b) electronic industry; (c) mechanical industry
Gansu	(a) nonferrous metal industry; (b) energy industry; (c) oil extraction and refinery industry
Qinghai	(a) chemical industry of potash; (b) nonferrous metal industry; (c) energy industry; (d) oil industry
Ningxia	(a) energy industry with coal as main; (b) chemical industry of coal
Xinjiang	(a) oil industry; (b) textile industry

Source: Chen, 1996: 110.

Based on resources and industrial advantages, five zones will be founded in each direction through the implementation of the Western Region Development Strategy. The five zones in the southwest region include (1) the zone of energy for West-East electricity transmission, (2) the zone of nonferrous metal containing mainly aluminium, copper, lead and zinc, (3) the biggest zone of phosphor and chemical industry phosphor all over the country, (4) the zone of tropical and sub-tropical crops, and (5) the zone of tourism. The five zones in the northwest region are listed as follows: (1) the comprehensive energy zone of coal, hydroelectricity, oil and gas, (2) the chemical zone of oil and natural gas, (3) the zone of nonferrous metal containing mainly nickel, aluminium, lead and zinc, (4) the biggest zone of commercial cotton throughout the country, (5) the zone of livestock product.

Trade Relationship between China and Countries around the Western Region

China has been busy in improving her relations with countries in Asia in recent years and thus creating good external conditions for the implementation of the Western Region Development Strategy. Meanwhile, the strategy drives the Chinese government to actively develop trade and economic co-operation with adjoining countries. From the perspectives of the Western Region Development Program, the countries around China can be classified into four groups: (1) countries in Southeast Asia; (2) countries in South Asia; (3) countries in Middle Asia; (4) Russia and Mongolia.

Countries in Southeast Asia

China's neighbours in the Southwest include Vietnam, Laos and Burma. China works with ASEAN to co-operate with countries on West China Development. The general economic condition of all the Southeast Asian countries except Brunei in 2000 is listed in Table 20.6.

Table 20.6.   Economic Conditions of Countries in Southeast Asia (2000)

Country	Popu-lation (million)	Area (1,000 km²)	GDP Total (US$ billion)	GDP Per capita (US$)	Household consumption (US$ billion)	Investment (US$ billion)
Indonesia	210	1905	153.255	730	103.066	27.586
Singapore	4	1	92.252	23063	36.871	28.598
Malaysia	23	330	89.321	3884	38.200	23.223
Thailand	61	513	121.927	1999	71.625	26.824
Philippines	76	300	75.186	989	49.007	15.037
Vietnam	79	332	31.344	397	20.846	2.194
Laos	5	237	1.709	342	0.882	0.427
Cambodia	12	181	3.207	267	2.705	0.481
Burma	46	677	6.2	135		
Total	516	4476	574.401	1113	323.213	124.37

Sources: World Bank, *World Development Report*, 1999, 2000, 2002 and
World Bank, *World Development Indicator*, 2002.

Total GDP of the nine countries in Southeast Asia in 2000 was
US$ 574.4 billion, and their average per capita was US$ 1113, the total
household consumption and investment was US$ 450 billion. In the
1990s, political relations between China and ASEAN countries
developed rapidly. In 1994, ASEAN allowed China to take part in the
"ASEAN Regional Forum". In June 1996, China became a formal
dialogue partner of ASEAN. Bilateral trade volume between China and
ASEAN was US$ 9.1 billion in 1992, 20.3 billion in 1995 and 39.4 billion
in 2000, with an annual increase rate of 20.1% from 1992 to 2000. The
share of ASEAN in China's foreign trade rose to 8.3%, and ASEAN
became China's fifth biggest trade partner. The share of China in
ASEAN's foreign trade rose to 3.9%, and China became its sixth biggest
trade partner.

Table 20.7.   Trade between China and Countries in Southeast
Asia (US$ million)

Country	1992	1995	1999	2000
Indonesia	2025.58	3490.17	4829.98	7463.77
Singapore	3267.05	6898.62	8563.33	10820.67
Malaysia	1475.11	3346.08	5279.34	8044.87
Thailand	1318.80	3362.51	4215.61	6624.04
Philippines	364.67	1305.92	2286.81	3141.73
Vietnam	31.53	54.22	31.72	40.84
Cambodia	12.95	57.34	160.12	223.55
Burma	390.31	767.40	508.21	621.26
Total	9065.07	20334.45	27093.27	39447.14

Sources: National Statistics Bureau (1993) *China Statistics Annual 1993*,
National Statistics Bureau (2001) *China Statistics Annual 2001*,
Beijing: China Statistics Press.

In November 2000, at the ASEAN meeting of China, Japan, and Korea in Singapore, the Chinese Premier, Zhu Rongji, first put forward the proposal of building a China-ASEAN free trade zone. In November 2001, the meeting of leaders of China and ASEAN in Brunei approved of a report by economists from both sides, and agreed to found a China-ASEAN free trade zone in ten years, to cover an area with a population of 1.7 billion. The Chinese government actively responded to the suggestion by Asian Development Bank of building a highway between Kunming in China and Bangkok in Thailand. Chinese government maintains an active attitude towards a co-operative development project for an international area along the Large Mekong, as proposed by the United Nations.

Countries in South Asia

For a long time South Asia has been regarded as one of the poorest areas in the world. However, economic growth in some countries in South Asia has sped up since the 1990s. From 1990 to 2000, India achieved a GDP growth rate of 6% per annum, Pakistan made 3.7%, and both Bengal and Nepal reached an annual growth rate of 4.8%. These all exceeded the 2.8% annual growth rate of global GDP in the same period (Table 20.8). In 2000, total GDP of the four countries was US$ 594.4 billion, per capita GDP was US$ 457, and total consumption and investment reached nearly US$ 500 billion. The import volume of India from 1990 to 1999 grew by 7.7% per annum. This is another large market in China's neighbourhood.

Table 20.8.   Economic Conditions of Countries in South Asia (2000)

Country	Popu-lation (million)	Area (1,000 km²)	GDP Total (US$ billion)	Per capita (US$)	Household consumption (US$ billion)	Investment (US$ billion)
India	1016	3287	479.404	472	298.779	81.499
Pakistan	138	796	61.673	447	47.401	9.251
Bengal	127	144	47.864	377	36.579	11.009
Nepal	21	140	5.45	260	4.112	1.145
Total	1302	4367	594.391	457	386.871	102.9

Sources: World Bank, *World Development Report, 1999, 2000, 2002* and World Bank, *World Development Indicator, 2002.*

Table 20.9.   Trade between China and Countries in South Asia (US$ million)

Country	1992	1995	1999	2000
India	339.43	1162.81	1987.73	1914.21
Pakistan	643.02	1011.49	970.61	1162.50
Bengal	220.72	678.04	715.14	918.44
Nepal	35.68	56.60	215.36	204.21
Total	1239.01	2905.94	3888.84	4199.36

Sources: World Bank, *World Development Report, 1999, 2000, 2002* and World Bank, *World Development Indicator, 2002.*

The trade volume between China and the four countries in South Asia increased by 2.5 times in eight years. With improved relations, there is huge potential for trade growth between the world's two most populated continental economies. Since the 1990s, with domestic reforms and more openness to the world economy, countries in South Asia have picked up their developing speed and created an optimistic prospect for themselves.

Countries in Middle Asia

Middle Asia is located in the middle of Asia-Europe continent between the Caspian Sea in the west and West China in the east, and between Russia in the north and Iran and Iraq in the south. Five countries in the region are members of the Commonwealth of Independent States. The countries that border on China include Kazakhstan, Kirghiz, Tajikistan and Afghanistan.

Table 20.10. Economic Conditions of Countries in Middle Asia (2000)

Country	Popu-lation (million)	Area (1,000 km²)	GDP Total (US$ billion)	GDP Per capita (US$)	Household consumption (US$ billion)	Investment (US$ billion)
Kazakhstan	15	2725	18.264	1218	11.677	2.557
Kirghiz	5	199	1.304	261	2.103	0.235
Tajikistan	6	143	0.987	165	0.752	
Turkmenistan	5	488	4.404	881	1.513	2.026
Uzbekistan	25	447	13.517	541	4.884	2.433
Afghanistan	20	652				
Total	76	4654	38.476	506	20.929	7.251

Sources: World Bank, *World Development Report, 1999, 2000, 2002* and World Bank, *World Development Indicator, 2002.*

Total GDP of the five countries (excluding Afghanistan for missing data) in 2000 was US$ 38.476 billion. Their per capita GDP was US$ 506, and consumption and investment amounted to nearly US$ 30 billion. Because of economic transformation, the annual GDP growth rate of the five countries from 1990 to 2000 was negative. Fortunately, these economies began to resume positive growth by the end of the 1990s. The country that grew most rapidly in 1999-2000 was Kazakhstan with a rate of 17.6%. Slowest growth occurred in Uzbekistan with a rate of 4%.

Under the centrally planned economic system of the former Soviet Union, the five countries in Middle Asia functioned mainly as suppliers of raw material to Russian industries. With the industrial structure of a natural resource economy and underdeveloped manufacturing and processing industries, the region depends strongly on external trade partners to supply it with many kinds of industrial products. The total foreign trade volume of the five countries was US$ 26.66 billion in 2000, including US$ 16.1 billion of exports and US$ 10.56 billion of imports. The trade between China and the countries in Middle Asia increased rapidly in 1990s (Table 20.11).

Table 20.11.   Trade between China and Countries in
Middle Asia (US$ million)

Country	1992	1995	1999	2000
Kazakhstan	369.10	390.99	1138.78	1556.96
Kirghiz	35.48	231.04	134.87	177.61
Tajikistan	2.76	23.86	8.04	17.17
Turkmenistan	4.50	17.06	9.49	16.16
Uzbekistan	52.52	118.56	40.34	51.46
Afghanistan	25.67	48.24	19.58	25.29
Total	490.03	830.29	1351.10	1844.65

Sources: World Bank, *World Development Report, 1999, 2000, 2002* and World Bank, *World Development Indicator, 2002.*

Russia and Mongolia

Both Russia and Mongolia share with China a long borderline.

Table 20.12.   Economic Conditions of Russia and Mongolia (2000)

Country	Popu- lation (million)	Area (1,000 km²)	GDP Total (US$ billion)	Per capita (US$)	Household consumption (US$ billion)	Investment (US$ billion)
Russia	146	170750	251.092	1720	114.596	35.153
Mongolia	2	1567	0.975	488	0.643	0.254

Sources: World Bank, *World Development Report, 1999, 2000, 2002* and World Bank, *World Development Indicator, 2002.*

The annual GDP growth rate of Russia from 1990 to 2000 was -4.8%. Its economy fell into serious recession but has risen since the end of the 1990s with an annual growth rate of 8.3% in 1999-2000. In 2000 the total GDP of Russia still reached US$ 251.1 billion and its consumption and investment amounted to US$ 149.7 billion. Mongolia is an inland country specializing in farming and animal husbandry with a weak economy that grows slowly. The annual GDP growth rate of Mongolia from 1990 to 2000 was only 1%. The country's foreign trade was US$ 0.84 billion, nearing its total GDP, indicating the economy's high dependence on foreign trade.

Table 20.13.   Trade between China and Russia (US$ million)

Country	1992	1995	1999	2000
Russia	5862.40	5463.32	5719.93	8003.24
Mongolia	183.87	161.45	263.10	322.61

Sources: World Bank, *World Development Report, 1999, 2000, 2002* and World Bank, *World Development Indicator, 2002.*

Since the collapse of the Soviet Union in 1991, the relationship between China and Russia has improved from time to time. Russian President Yeltsin visited China twice in December, 1992 and in April, 1996. China and Russia decided to develop a strategic, forward-looking co-operation partnership with equality and trust. After President Putin started his term in 2000, China and Russia finished surveying their shared border and began the process of disarming in border areas. In contrast to the improved political relationship, the economic relationship developed more slowly. Trade volume between the countries was US$ 5.86 billion in 1992 and did not reach US$ 8 billion dollars until 2000, equivalent to only 5% of Russia's total foreign trade and 2% of China's total foreign trade. The economic and trade relation of China and Russia has large potential room for growth, given the size of the two economies and their complementary economic structures.

West China Development Strategy and Asia's Economic Integration

The Chinese economy has grown rapidly in the last two decades. With an annual growth rate of 9.3%, China's GDP grew two times between 1989 and 2001, reaching 9593.3 billion *yuan* at the end of the period. China has become the sixth largest economy in the world. After being the largest host economy for FDI among the developing countries for several years, China took over the US.. as the world's No. 1 host economy for FDI in 2002. By the end of 2002, China had altogether utilized US$ 447.966 billion of FDI. The total trade volume in 2002 reached US$ 620.79 billion, 21.8% higher than the previous year.[2]

By launching the Western Region Development Program, the Chinese government reinforced its support to the western region by means of an investment project, preferential tax policy and fiscal transfer payment. It pledges to improve the investment environment of the western region, and to guide foreign capital and domestic capital into the projects in West China. The central government also urges the local governments in the western region to adapt their local policies for self-sustained development.

From a geographic perspective, China has a special location in Asia, connecting East Asia, Southeast Asia, South Asia, Middle Asia, North Asia and Northeast Asia. In West China, Guangxi and Yunnan connect with Southeast Asia, Yunnan, Tibet and Xinjiang border on Bengal, India and Pakistan, Xinjiang meets the countries in Middle Asia and Russia, and Inner Mongolia joins Mongolia and Russia. West China development will have positive effects on the flows of commodity, capital, technology, and even labour, in a vast area of Asia. Intra-Asia economic co-operation and interaction will be boosted by West China development in the following levels.

The national level

At the beginning of this century, a series of important co-operative arrangements between China and the countries around took place. These co-operative arrangements will have long-term and positive effect on Asian economic integration.

In November 2001, China and ASEAN countries agreed on the completion of China-ASEAN free trade zone in ten years. A year later, China and ASEAN signed the "Agreement on China-ASEAN Economic Co-operation Framework". As is prescribed in the agreement, China and ASEAN will begin reducing the tariff of general products by 2005. China and the old members of ASEAN will complete the free trade zone by 2010. China and the new members in ASEAN will set up the free trade zone by 2015. This action has already influenced the China-ASEAN trade. According to Chinese Customs, the trade between ASEAN and China shot up by about 30% from 2001 to 2002. ASEAN 's export to China rose 28% in 2002, as compared to the rise of 4.7% in 2001.[3]

Since the mid-1990s, China has built a co-operation framework – the Shanghai Co-operation Organization – with countries in Middle Asia and Russia. On 26 April 1996, China, Russia, Kazakhstan, Kirghiz and Turkmenistan signed a convention in Shanghai to peacefully solve their border disputes based on mutual trust. On 24-25 April 1997, these countries approved a new convention in Moscow. In the following five years, China solved the border problems with the four countries respectively. On 7 July 2002, the leaders of the six countries in the Shanghai Co-operation Organization met in St. Petersburg and approved the "Charter of Shanghai

Co-operation Organization", formally giving birth to the organization. The organization has created a good and safe environment for West China Development, improving the stability and prospect of West China. At the same time, the Shanghai Co-operation Organization set the stage for West China and the countries in Middle Asia and Russia to extend bilateral and multilateral trade and economic co-operation. In 1992 the trade volume between China and the five countries in Middle Asia was half a billion dollars, but by 2000 it exceeded US$ 1.8 billion. In the first meeting of the presidents in the Shanghai Co-operation Organization in September 2001, leaders of the member countries decided to begin the multilateral economic and trade co-operation of the six countries, and to begin the process of making trade and investment convenient. Detailed discussions and planning started at the first meeting of ministers of the Economic and Trade Department in the Shanghai Co-operation Organization in June 2002 and at the Investment and Development Forum held by Shanghai Co-operation Organization in October 2002. In these meetings, attention was focused on the co-operation in energy and the China-Kirghiz-Uzbekistan railway project.

The sub-nation level

Since the 1980s, local governments in China have gained greater autonomy in regional economic development. After the launch of the Western Region Development Program, all provinces and localities in the western region responded zealously, especially in respect of international economic co-operation between local jurisdictions and development of border trade with neighbouring countries.

Take Yunnan province, for example. The provincial government of Yunnan proposed in 2000 the strategy of developing Yunnan into an economic gateway to Southeast Asia and South Asia. China, Burma, Laos and Thailand signed a convention on opening up the Lantsang-Mekong River to commercial navigation in April, 2000. With the active co-operation of Yunnan province, the opening commenced formally in April, 2001. Yunnan province has made great efforts to build a Kunming-Bangkok highway. Now Yunnan is promoting the projects of China-Burma transport infrastructure. Yunnan province has signed with Thailand the convention of co-operating on the construction of Jinhong Power Plant, in which Thailand pledged to invest 70% of the funds and Yunnan agreed to make all kinds of preparation for the start of the project in 2006. Yunnan province also made great progress in co-operation in tourism with the countries in Southeast Asia. The Chamber of Commerce of Yunnan signed the convention of co-operation in industry and commerce with its counterparts of Laos, Thailand and Burma. The border trade in Yunnan province is very active. In addition, Yunnan advocates actively the development of "sub-national economic co-operation among China, India, Burma and Bengal", and has held four special international forums for it, so far. The governments of Guangxi, Tibet, Xinjiang and Inner Mongolia have also made many initiatives for economic co-operation in trade, investment, and tourism with neighbouring countries.

The enterprise level

With the backdrop of the Western Region Development Strategy, the enterprises from the eastern region started to seek investment opportunities in the western region and more and more enterprises in the western region started to take part in international businesses. For example, according to my survey in Yunnan, by the end of 2001, the enterprises from Shanghai had invested in 956 projects in Yunnan province. The number of business people from Zhejiang province doing business in Yunnan amounted to 150,000. Their businesses involved 16 industries, with a turnover of 20 billion *yuan* in 2001. Business people from Zhanjiang have established more than 900 small-and-medium-sized enterprises in Guangdong province. According to my survey in Xinjiang, there were more than 370 enterprises that engaged in border trade, about one third of which were joint ventures between Xinjiang and the enterprises from the eastern region.

The famous shipping company COSCO has dominated the whole international shipping business in some Middle Asia countries. China's Oil and Natural Gas Company won the tender of a major oil and gas extraction project in Kazakhstan. Konka Electron Company from Shenzhen established a joint venture in India to produce and sell colour TVs. Huawei Company from Shenzhen carries on many communication projects in Middle Asia.

Based on my surveys in Guangxi, Yunnan, Xinjiang and Inner Mongolia, I believe that the Western Region Development Program will promote international economic co-operation and economy integration of the vast continental areas in Asia in nine ways. The first one is the key infrastructure projects such as the construction of multinational railways, roads, pipelines and river projects. The second is the co-operative exploration of multinational drainage areas. The third is international trade and mutual market opening. The other ways include contract and management of international engineering projects, international labour flows, multinational direct investment and joint ventures, international exploration of natural resources and the establishment and management of organization for sub-national economic integration. The last concern is on policies towards multinationals from the more developed countries in Asian countries.

It can be predicted that economic integration in Asia will develop to an unprecedented scale in the 21st century. This trend will greatly benefit the countries in Asia. The Western Region Development Strategy in China is one of the important driving forces.

Notes

1.   *Jiefang Daily*, 26 January 2003: 1.
2.   *International Business Daily*, 15 January 2003: 1.
3.   *International Business Daily*, 16 January 2003: 8.

References

1.   Chen Dongsheng, Wei Houkai, etc. (1996). *The Boost of China's West*, Shanghai: Shanghai Far-east Press
2.   Chinese Government (2000). *The Overall Plan of West China Development and Related Policy Measures*, Beijing: China Planning Press.
3.   Colm Fog, Francis Harrigan, David O'Connor (1999). *The Future of Asia in the World Economy*, (ADB/OECD 1998) Beijing: Xinhua Press.

4. Li Guo Ding (1996). "The status and prospect of economic development in Asia-Pacific region", *The Review and Study of World Economy*, first edition, Nanjing: Southeast University Press.

5. Liu Zaixing (1993). *Territorial Economy in China: Data Analysis and Contrast Research*, Beijing: China Price Press.

6. Wang Luolin (2000). *Report of Foreign Investment in China in 2000*, Beijing: China Financial Economy Press.

7. Wen Donghui (2003). "Asian Economy: Future Development Depends on Itself", *Eonomy Daily*, 16 April.

Part V. Sources of Interregional Disparity

21 The Relative Contributions of Location and Preferential Policies in China's Regional Development[1]

Sylvie Démurger, Jeffrey D. Sachs, Wing Thye Woo,
Shuming Bao, and Gene Chang

Introduction

Regional disparity has increased quite markedly in the 1990s. Figure 21.1 shows the coefficients of variation of per capita provincial incomes constructed from two samples.[2] The first sample consisted of 28 provinces that had complete income data for the 1952–98 period, and the second sample differs from the first by omitting Beijing, Shanghai, and Tianjin, the three metropolises that have province-level status. The coefficients of variation of GDP per capita (measured in 1995 prices) from these two samples are denoted Cov28 and Cov25 respectively. Cov25 differs from Cov28 by having a smaller dispersion in regional incomes, and not showing an upward trend during the 1966-78 period. These two differences mean that the three metropolises have always been substantially richer than the other provinces, and that the gap between these two groups widened substantially during the period of orthodox socialist economic management. This paper will focus on the common finding in Cov25 and Cov28 that there is a clear upward trend in provincial income inequality from 1992 onward, and that the 1998 level of provincial income disparity is highest since 1952.

This recent rise in regional inequality has elicited significant policy responses from the government. The budgets for infrastructure investments in the poor provinces have increased substantially every year, and a Western Region Development Office has been established under the State Council (the Chinese cabinet) to formulate a comprehensive development strategy and to coordinate its implementation.

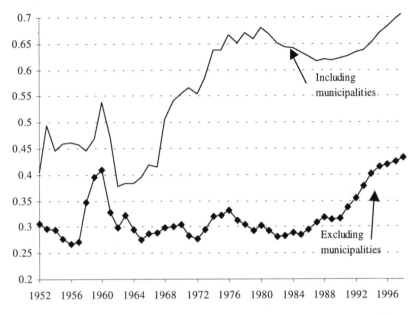

Figure 21.1: σ-convergence across Chinese provinces, 1952-98

Notes: Hainan and Tibet excluded due to missing data. Sichuan province includes Chongqing. GDP per capita is calculated at constant 1995 prices. Convergence is measured by the coefficient of variation.

Sources: NBS (1999), except for Sichuan, for which sources are SSB (1997), and 1977 to 2000 issues of *China Statistical Yearbook*.

The origin and consequences of China's regional disparity growing has been extensively studied in recent years.[3] One prominent view is that preferential policy treatment of the coastal provinces, especially the establishment of Special Economic Zones (SEZs), was largely to blame for this sustained rise in regional disparity. According to Hu Angang, an advocate for the abolition of SEZs: "If Deng Xiaoping knew the disparities were as big as they are, he would be more militant than I am in trying to eliminate them ... In America, the deep differences between the North and the South more than 100 years ago led to the Civil War," and "We must cease subsidizing rich coastal cities. Preferential treatment should be reserved for the poor".[4]   Hu Angang's diagnosis is consistent with the common finding in provincial growth regressions that the coastal variable has a positive coefficient that is statistically significant, e.g., Jian, Sachs, and Warner (1996), Chen and Fleisher (1996), Zhang (2001), and Bao, Chang, Sachs, and Woo (forthcoming).

Our thesis here is that the high coastal growth has been due to more than the preferential policies, it came also from advantageous location that enabled export-oriented industrialization; and we propose to quantify the relative contributions of geography and preferential-policy.[5]   The other major innovations in this paper are to construct a preferential policy index, explore the links between topographical features and income level, show that the geography and policy variables affect income growth with different time lags, and to quantify the impact of geography and policy variables on provincial growth rates in the 1996-99 period.

The Regional Implications of China's Economic Policies

Industrialization was shallow in 1949 and largely a coastal phenomenon. Naturally, just like the Soviet Union in 1917, China in 1949 saw its most important economic task to be industrialization, and its industrialization program in the 1952-78 period was directed by three principles: state ownership, central planning, and regional self-sufficiency. The self-reliance principle was motivated, first by the perception that it was an effective way of reducing poverty in the inland provinces, and then increasingly by the perception that China faced potential security threats from U.S.-backed forces in East Asia and the growing military presence of the United States in Vietnam. The result was that China, in 1964, accelerated its massive construction of military-industrial complexes in western China, popularly referred to as the "Third Front industries". However, from 1972 onward, China began reducing its discrimination against investments in the coastal provinces because the Soviet Union was fast becoming a bigger threat than the United States, and an invasion through the traditional land route by the Soviet Union had become much more likely than a coastal landing by armed forces supported by the United States. Coastal enterprises, especially those in Guangdong, were expanded, and export earnings jumped from US$2.6 billion in 1972 to US$3.4 billion in 1973, and then to US$9.8 billion in 1978.

The process of increased economic interaction with the outside world accelerated in 1979 when China embarked upon market-oriented reforms, of which the Open Door Policy was a key component.[6]   The Open Door Policy consisted of attracting foreign direct investment and promoting foreign trade in targeted economic zones. Table 21.1 summarizes the establishment of these various types of economic zones up to 1994, and reveals that the coastal provinces benefited disproportionately.   The leading role of this selective open-door policy in regional growth has been emphasized by a great number of studies (e.g., Mody and Wang, 1997; Berthélemy and Démurger, 2000; Chen and Feng, 2000; Lemoine, 2000; and Démurger, 2000). Most of them have found that foreign direct investment (FDI) had an impact on economic growth that went beyond an addition to the capital stock: it also provided competition to domestic firms and hence forced them to raise their productivity, generated demonstration effects that enabled domestic firms to improve their operations, and provided a training ground for future managers of domestic firms in the same industries.

Two other post-1978 policy changes – fiscal decentralization and price deregulation – also had significant regional impact. Fiscal decentralization was meant to encourage local initiatives in economic development,[7] and it took the form of individually negotiated tax contracts between the central government and the provinces.[8] Fiscal decentralization lowered state revenue from 35% of GDP in 1978 to 14% in 1992, and hence forced the centre to reduce fiscal provinces to the poorer provinces. Price deregulation in the industrial sector initially took the form of a dual track price system for industrial inputs. Since the central and western provinces were the main suppliers of raw industrial materials, the continuation of artificially low prices for these industrial inputs meant that the dual track pricing system was in effect transferring income from the interior producers to the coastal factories. The elimination of the dual track price system in the 1990–91 period was an equitable move from the viewpoint of regional disparity.

Table 21.1.   Timeline of China's Regional Preferential Policies, 1979-94

Year of	Number and type of	Location
1979	3 Special Economic Zones	Guangdong
1980	1 Special Economic Zone	Fujian
1984	14 Coastal Open Cities	Liaoning, Hebei, Tianjin, Shandong, Jiangsu, Shanghai, Zhejiang, Fujian, Guangdong, and Guangxi
	10 Economic and Technological Development Zones	Liaoning, Hebei, Tianjin, Shandong, Jiangsu, Zhejiang, and Guangdong
1985	1 Economic and Technological Development Zone	Fujian
	3 Coastal Open Economic Zones	Pearl River delta, Yangtze River delta, and Fujian
1986	2 Economic and Technological Development Zones	Shanghai
1988	Open Coastal Belt	Liaoning, Shandong, Guangxi, and Hebei
	1 Special Economic Zone	Hainan
	1 Economic and Technological Development Zones	Shanghai
1990	Pudong New Area	Shanghai
1992	13 bonded areas in major coastal port cities	Tianjin, Guangdong, Liaoning, Shandong Jiangsu, Zhejiang, Fujian, and Hainan
	10 major cities along the Yangtze River	Jiangsu, Anhui, Jiangxi, Hunan, Hubei, and Sichuan
	13 Border Economic Co-operation Zones	Jilin, Heilongjiang, Inner Mongolia, Xinjiang, Yunnan, and Guangxi
	All capital cities of inland provinces and autonomous regions	
	5 Economic and Technological Co-operation Zones	Fujian, Liaoning, Jiangsu, Shandong, and Zhejiang
1993	12 Economic and Technological Development Zones	Anhui, Guangdong, Heilongjiang, Hubei, Liaoning, Sichuan, Fujian, Jilin, and Zhejiang
1994	2 Economic and Technological Development Zones	Beijing and Xinjiang

Topography and Income

Our knowledge of changes in China's economic structure and policy regime in the 1952–98 period suggests two major channels through which geography has influenced provincial income levels (a) agriculture, and (b) international trade and FDI. China was a predominantly agricultural economy until the middle of the 1980s. For example, taking a province from each of the regions, the agricultural share of employment in 1978 and in 1998 were, respectively, 53% and 49% for Heilongjiang, 74% and 41% for Guangdong, 82% and 59% for Anhui, 77% and 60% for Gansu, and 83% and 70% for Guizhou. Given the large size of the agricultural sector in many provinces during 1978–98, agricultural productivity was an important determinant of provincial income per capita. Since differences in provincial topographical features, such as elevation and flatness of arable land, help shape differences in agricultural productivity across provinces, they should also help to explain differences in provincial income.

Geography also affects provincial income through physical location. The low cost of water transportation makes the coastal provinces and areas along navigable rivers that flow to the sea better suited to be platforms for producing manufactured exports. When allowed by the government, domestic firms located in these regions would naturally expand production to service foreign markets, and foreign firms would relocate their production there, given the low cost of Chinese labour. Hence, provinces with easy access to sea transportation received boosts to their incomes from international trade whenever China did not cut itself off from the international economy.

Table 21.2 summarizes some key geographical and economic characteristics of China in the following six regional groupings:

1. *The province-level metropolises* of Beijing, Tianjin, and Shanghai are highly industrialized, and over 71 % of their population lives within 100 kilometres of the coast or navigable waters.[9]
2. *The northeastern provinces* of Heilongjiang, Jilin, and Liaoning constituted the industrial heartland of China in 1978, and were the rich provinces of the central plan period.

Table 21.2.   Geographical Characteristics by Regions

Region	Metro-polises	North-east	Coast	Central	North-west	South-west	Total
GDP per capita growth rate, 1979-98 (%)	8.5	7.9	10.7	8.4	7.7	7.8	9.0
GDP per capita level in 1978 (*yuan*/person)	3,645	1,700	1,154	941	1,045	814	1,355
Population density (person/km²)	1,104	138	333	264	46	126	290
Distance from the coast (km)	77	380	86	492	1,383	656	547
Pop100 km (% of population)	65	17	60	0	0	4	24
Pop100 cr (% of population)	71	18	82	57	0	4	41
Slope >10 (% of area)	1.4	2.2	2.6	2.7	5	14.1	4.3
Average slope (%)	1.2	1.6	2.4	2.4	2.8	5.2	2.7
Average elevation (metres)	135	314	267	428	1,971	1,428	804
Temperature (Degrees)	10.9	4.5	16.4	14.9	6.8	16	12.2
Rainfall (mm)	63	50	103	90	26	98	74
Arable land (%)	36	21	29	24	8	10	21

Notes: GDP per capita compound annual growth rate throughout 1979-98 and GDP per capita levels in 1978 are calculated at 1995 constant prices.

Pop100cr = proportion of the population distribution of a province in 1994 within 100 km of the coastline or ocean-navigable river, excluding coastline above the winter extent of sea ice and the rivers that flow to this coastline. Pop100km = proportion of the population distribution of a province in 1994 within 100 km of the coastline, excluding coastline above the winter extent of sea ice. Slope >10 measures the percentage of area within a province with a slope greater than 10 %.

Temperature and rainfall are averages throughout the 1951-88 period. Arable land is available for 1994.

Metropolises = Beijing, Tianjin, and Shanghai. Northeast = Liaoning, Jilin, and Heilongjiang. Coast = Hebei, Jiangsu, Zhejiang, Fujian, Shandong, Guangdong, and Hainan. Central = Shanxi, Anhui, Jiangxi, Henan, Hubei, and Hunan. Northwest = Inner Mongolia, Shaanxi, Gansu, Qinghai, Ningxia, and Xinjiang (Tibet is excluded due to missing data). Southwest = Sichuan, Guizhou, Yunnan, and Guangxi.

Sources: NBS (1999) for economic and population variables; GIS calculations made by Bao Shuming for geographical data, except arable land; Wang and Hu (1999, table 4.1, p. 83) for arable land.

3. *The coastal provinces* of Hebei, Shandong, Jiangsu, Zhejiang, Fujian, Guangdong, and Hainan have 82 % of their population living within 100 kilometres of the sea or navigable rivers, and had the highest GDP per capita growth rate in the 1979-98 period.

4. *The central provinces* are Shanxi, Henan, Anhui, Hubei, Hunan, and Jiangxi comprise the agricultural heartland of China, and had about the same income level as the coastal provinces in 1978. The two large rivers and their many tributaries endow 57 % of the population with easy water transportation.

5. *The northwestern provinces* of Inner Mongolia, Shaanxi, Ningxia, Gansu, Qinghai, Xinjiang, and Tibet are arid, and only 8% of the land is arable, which explains why they have the lowest population density in China.

6. *The southwestern provinces* of Sichuan, Yunnan, Guizhou, and Guangxi have rainfall and temperature conditions that are ideal for crop cultivation, but suffer from being too mountainous, 14 % of the land has a slope greater than 10 degrees.

We use three benchmark years – 1952, 1978, and 1998 – for our econometric exploration of the role of geography in provincial income determination. The 1952 distribution of provincial GDP per capita was a market outcome, the 1978 distribution reflected the biases of central planning, and the 1998 distribution was the joint result of the post-1978 marketization and internationalization of the economy. There are two types of explanatory variables:

1. The ability to participate in sea-based international trade
    *   Distance from the coast [*Distf* = $1/(1+$distance in km$)$]
    *   The proportion of the population distribution of a province in 1994 within 100 km of the coastline or ocean-navigable river, excluding the coastline above the winter extent of sea ice and the rivers that flow to this coastline [*Pop100cr*].[10]

2. Topography
    *   Percentage of area within a province with a slope greater than 10 % [*Slope10*]
    *   Average slope of a province [*Slavge*]
    *   Average elevation [*Elavge*]

The regressions in Table 21.3 show three robust results that suggest a common hypothesis: economic internationalization has become much more important in determining provincial income in the post-1978 period. The first is that the two proxies for easy coastal access increased greatly in statistical significance and in magnitude in 1998. For example, *Pop100cr* was significant in 1998 but not in 1952 and 1978, and its estimated coefficient rose from 0.23 in 1978 to 0.70 in one case and from 0.16 to 0.55 in the other case. These developments mean that the post-1978 reform have made the ability of a province to engage in international trade and to host FDI an important determinant of provincial income.

The second robust result is that the "steepness" of land within a province was a greater challenge to raising provincial income in 1952 and 1978 than in 1998. To see how economic internationalization caused both the magnitude and statistical significance of the coefficients of *Slope10* and *Slavge* to decrease, one must know that the inland parts of the southern coastal provinces have fairly rugged mountains, which render agricultural activities arduous. After 1978, the income base of the southern coastal provinces moved rapidly from agriculture to industry, hence reducing "steepness" of the terrain as an obstacle to raising income.

The third robust result is that the R^2 is highest in 1998 and lowest in 1978. For example, the specification with *Pop100km* and *Slope10* reports an R^2 value of 0.35 for 1998, 0.14 for 1978, and 0.23 for 1952. This specification fits the data better in 1998 than in 1978 because China had pursued autarkic policies in the two decades prior to 1978, hence weakening the trade channel through which geography asserts itself. The finding that the statistical fit in 1998 is much higher than in 1952 suggests at least two explanations. One, the world today is more integrated economically than in 1952, so the gains from economic internationalization in 1998 are now greater than in 1952. Two, favourable geographical location could have a positive, but slow and cumulative, impact on income, hence yielding a substantial lag between geographical advantage and higher income level. Both of these explanations would predict that the coefficients and statistical significance of the geography variables in a growth regression would be larger in the later subperiods of the estimation period. This prediction is borne out in the growth regressions reported in the next section.

Table 21.3.   Relation of GDP Per Capita with Physical Geography in 1952, 1978 and 1998

Log of GDP per capita in year	Distf	Slope 10	Pop 100cr	Slavge	Elavge	R²
1952	10.4820	-0.0152				
	1.87	2.05				0.36
1978	15.6354	-0.0139				
	1.64	2.20				0.33
1998	23.9460	-0.0124				
	3.29	2.30				0.49
1952		-0.0164	0.2316			
		1.93	1.33			0.23
1978		-0.0182	0.2279			
		2.47	0.99			0.14
1998		-0.0111	0.7011			
		1.77	3.10			0.35
1952	9.4092			-0.0699	0.0000	
	1.87			2.21	0.18	0.40
1978	15.1829			-0.1001	0.0001	
	1.72			2.30	0.86	0.39
1998	20.7180			-0.0425	-0.0001	
	3.09			0.88	1.39	0.55
1952			0.1621	-0.0786	0.0000	
			0.72	2.16	0.17	0.28
1978			0.1936	-0.1159	0.0000	
			0.68	2.24	0.37	0.21
1998			0.5461	-0.0582	-0.0001	
			1.99	1.15	0.71	0.39

Note: Distf=1/(1+distance in km), i.e. the inverse of distance from the sea; Pop100cr=Percent of provincial population living within 100 km of coast or navigable part of rivers that flow to sea; Slope10= Percentage of area within a province with a slope greater than 10 %; Slavge= Average slope of a province; Elavge= Average elevation; Constant term not reported, and italicised figures are the absolute t-statistics. GDP in 1995 prices. N=28 in 1952, Hainan data unavailable, Chongqing data included in Sichuan, and Tibet data unavailable. N=29 in 1978 and 1998, Chongqing data included in Sichuan, and Tibet data unavailable.

Provincial Differences in Growth Rates (1978–98): Geography and Policy

As mentioned earlier, our analysis of post-1978 regional growth will replace the black box of regional dummies that is common in the literature with two variables:

1. transportation cost and pure geography effect [*Pop100cr*]
2. a preferential policy index for each province [*Policy*]

> We must stress that Policy is restricted to open-door preferential policies and does not take into account other factors, such as the business environment.[11] Table 21.4 reports the preferential policy index that is constructed by giving to each province a weight that reflects the type of economic zone that it hosts:

> Weight = 3: SEZ and Shanghai Pudong New Area
> Weight = 2: ETDZ and BECZ
> Weight = 1: COC, COEZ, OCB, MC, BA, and CC
> Weight = 0: No open zone

Equations 1 through 3 in Table 21.5 regress the provincial output growth rate in the different subperiods of the reform era on the initial income level and the coast dummy.[12]   The estimated coefficients have the theoretically expected signs but the low t-statistics of the output coefficient mean that conditional convergence does not characterize provincial output growth. The interesting result is that the coefficient of the coast dummy increases markedly in size over the subperiods, from 0.015 in 1979–84 to 0.023 in 1985-91, and then to 0.032 in 1992-98. The growing influence of the coast on output growth is confirmed by the monotonic increase in its t-statistics over time, from 2.98 in 1979–84 to 5.11 in 1992–98.

Equations 4 to 6 replace the coast dummy with *Policy* and *Pop100cr*. As will be seen, the magnitude of the Policy coefficient is stable over time (0.01), while the magnitude of the geography coefficient increases over time (from zero to 0.04). It therefore appears that the secular rise in the *Pop100cr* coefficient is responsible for the secular rise in the coast coefficient.

Table 21.4. Preferential Policy Index

	1978	1979	1980	1981	1982	1983	1984	1985	1986	1987	1988	1990	1991	1992	1993	1994	1995	1996	1997	1998	Average
Beijing	0	0	0	0	0	0	0	0	0	0	0	0	0	2	2	2	2	2	2	2	0.67
Tianjin	0	0	0	0	0	0	2	2	2	2	2	2	2	2	2	2	2	2	2	2	1.43
Hebei	0	0	0	0	0	0	1	1	1	1	2	2	2	2	2	2	2	2	2	2	1.24
Shanxi	0	0	0	0	0	0	0	0	0	0	0	0	0	1	1	1	1	1	1	1	0.33
Inner Mongolia	0	0	0	0	0	0	0	0	0	0	0	0	0	2	2	2	2	2	2	2	0.67
Liaoning	0	0	0	0	0	0	1	1	1	1	2	2	2	2	2	2	2	2	2	2	1.24
Jilin	0	0	0	0	0	0	0	0	0	0	0	0	0	2	2	2	2	2	2	2	0.67
Heilongjiang	0	0	0	0	0	0	0	0	0	0	0	0	0	2	2	2	2	2	2	2	0.67
Shanghai	0	0	0	0	0	0	2	2	2	2	2	2	2	3	3	3	3	3	3	3	1.76
Jiangsu	0	0	0	0	0	0	2	2	2	2	2	2	2	2	2	2	2	2	2	2	1.43
Zhejiang	0	0	0	0	0	0	2	2	2	2	2	2	2	2	2	2	2	2	2	2	1.43
Anhui	0	0	0	0	0	0	0	0	1	1	1	1	1	1	1	1	1	1	1	1	0.62
Fujian	0	0	3	3	3	3	3	3	3	3	3	3	3	3	3	3	3	3	3	3	2.71
Jiangxi	0	0	0	0	0	0	0	0	0	0	0	0	0	1	1	1	1	1	1	1	0.33
Shandong	0	0	0	0	0	0	2	2	2	2	2	2	2	2	2	2	2	2	2	2	1.43
Henan	0	0	0	0	0	0	0	0	0	0	0	0	0	1	1	1	1	1	1	1	0.33
Hubei	0	0	0	0	0	0	0	0	1	1	1	1	1	1	1	1	1	1	1	1	0.62
Hunan	0	0	0	0	0	0	0	0	0	0	0	0	0	1	1	1	1	1	1	1	0.33
Guangdong	0	3	3	3	3	3	3	3	3	3	3	3	3	3	3	3	3	3	3	3	2.86
Guangxi	0	0	0	0	0	0	1	1	1	1	2	2	2	2	2	2	2	2	2	2	1.24
Hainan	0	0	0	0	0	0	0	0	0	0	3	3	3	3	3	3	3	3	3	3	1.57
Sichuan	0	0	0	0	0	0	0	0	1	1	1	1	1	1	1	1	1	1	1	1	0.62
Guizhou	0	0	0	0	0	0	0	0	0	0	0	0	0	1	1	1	1	1	1	1	0.33
Yunnan	0	0	0	0	0	0	0	0	0	0	0	0	0	2	2	2	2	2	2	2	0.67
Tibet	0	0	0	0	0	0	0	0	0	0	0	0	0	1	1	1	1	1	1	1	0.33
Shaanxi	0	0	0	0	0	0	0	0	0	0	0	0	0	1	1	1	1	1	1	1	0.33
Gansu	0	0	0	0	0	0	0	0	0	0	0	0	0	1	1	1	1	1	1	1	0.33
Qinghai	0	0	0	0	0	0	0	0	0	0	0	0	0	1	1	1	1	1	1	1	0.33
Ningxia	0	0	0	0	0	0	0	0	0	0	0	0	0	1	1	1	1	1	1	1	0.33
Xinjiang	0	0	0	0	0	0	0	0	0	0	0	0	0	2	2	2	2	2	2	2	0.67

This large difference in the temporal profiles of the policy coefficient and the geography coefficient continues to hold in Equations 7 to 9, which are more sophisticated specifications. The initial size of the agricultural sector is added because of its large share, and because China's economic reform started with the large-scale deregulation of this sector. The square of this term is also included because Tian (1999) had found a diminishing role for agriculture. The agriculture variables received no statistical support however. The insertion of the initial size of the state sector variable is based on Sachs and Woo's (1994) argument that the maintenance of the existing state-owned sector would require the state to give state-owned enterprises (SOEs) priority access to capital, raw materials, and skilled manpower, hence making it difficult for new non-state enterprises, like rural industrial enterprises, to emerge. This SOE variable has the theoretically expected sign and strong statistical support in two of the three cases.

The results in Table 21.5 are confirmed in Table 21.6, which adds a metropolis dummy to prevent possible distortions caused by the presence of the atypical provinces of Beijing, Shanghai, and Tianjin. The contrasting time profiles of the *Pop100cr* and *Policy* coefficients emphasize the intuitively sensible point that the time lag between impact and effect could differ substantially among variables. In such situations, estimations based on averaging the variables over the entire time period or on pooling the data set would understate the coefficients of the slower-acting variables. This point is clearly seen in equations 10 to 12 of Tables 21.5 and 21.6.

The Economic Mechanisms of Preferential Policies and Geography

Table 21.7 constructs the two standard deviations confidence interval (2SDCI) for the coefficients of coast, *Pop100cr*, and *Policy* in 1979-84 and 1992-98. For the 1979-84 coast coefficient and 1979-84 *Policy* coefficient, their 2SDCIs overlap with the 2SDCIs of their counterparts in 1992-98. In contrast, the 2SDCI of the 1979-84 *Pop100cr* coefficient does not overlap with the 2SDCI of the 1992-98 *Pop100cr* coefficient. The important finding here is that the geography coefficient unambiguously increased over time, supporting the view that geography is a slow-acting variable.

Table 21.5.   Disentangling Influence of Geography and Policy

	period	Initial GDP	Coast	Pop 100cr	Policy	Initial agricul. share	Sq. agricul. share	Initial SOE size	R²
Sub-Period Averaged									
Eq 1	1979-84	-0.004 / 0.93	0.0153 / 2.67						0.22
Eq 2	1985-91	-0.0005 / 0.14	0.0226 / 3.41						0.35
Eq 3	1992-98	0.0105 / 1.55	0.0318 / 5.17						0.48
Eq 4	1979-84	-0.0083 / 1.55		0.0123 / 1.97	0.0056 / 3.10				0.23
Eq 5	1985-91	-0.0073 / 1.14		-0.0093 / 1.06	0.0115 / 2.66				0.32
Eq 6	1992-98	-0.0072 / 1.12		0.0408 / 7.57	0.0104 / 1.57				0.72
Eq 7	1979-84	-0.0073 / 0.43		-0.0018 / 0.20	0.0042 / 2.05	-0.0919 / 0.61	0.1949 / 0.96	-0.1034 / 2.69	0.39
Eq 8	1985-91	0.0160 / 0.92		-0.0067 / 0.60	0.0106 / 2.37	0.2927 / 1.46	-0.4045 / 1.22	0.0528 / 0.97	0.42
Eq 9	1992-98	-0.0153 / 1.51		0.0328 / 5.85	0.0117 / 2.43	-0.0729 / 0.49	0.1213 / 0.38	-0.1143 / 3.13	0.82
Entire Period Averaged									
Eq 10	1979-98	0.00136 / 0.46	0.02480 / 5.95						0.60
Eq 11	1979-98	-0.0091 / 2.40		0.0124 / 3.18	0.0130 / 8.31				0.71
Eq 12	1979-98	-0.0089 / 1.06		0.0082 / 1.54	0.0116 / 6.43	-0.0096 / 0.09	0.0195 / 0.13	-0.0492 / 1.68	0.76

Table 21.6.   Effects of Including the Metropolis Dummy

	Period	Initial GDP	Coast	Pop 100cr	Policy	Initial agricul.	Sq. (initial agricul.)	Initial SOE size	Metropolis dummy	R^2
Sub-Period Averaged										
Eq 1	1979-84	-0.0141 1.77	0.0174 2.95						0.0187 1.87	0.27
Eq 2	1985-91	0.0007 0.09	0.0222 3.06						-0.0023 0.18	0.35
Eq 3	1992-98	0.0001 0.01	0.0375 5.01						0.0196 1.29	0.51
Eq 4	1979-84	-0.0135 1.70		0.0120 1.87	0.0061 3.14				0.0099 0.78	0.24
Eq 5	1985-91	-0.0012 0.11		-0.0089 1.01	0.0109 2.44				-0.0104 0.68	0.33
Eq 6	1992-98	-0.0048 0.45		0.0408 7.44	0.0098 1.36				-0.0039 0.37	0.72
Eq 7	1979-84	-0.0089 0.58		-0.0007 0.08	0.0036 1.73	0.0871 0.38	-0.0643 0.21	-0.0949 2.47	0.0251 1.37	0.42
Eq 8	1985-91	0.0148 0.82		-0.0073 0.62	0.0107 2.31	0.3569 1.66	-0.4952 1.43	0.0490 0.84	0.0100 0.46	0.42
Eq 9	1992-98	-0.0180 1.63		0.0318 6.03	0.0121 2.60	0.1544 0.49	-0.3064 0.51	-0.1273 4.00	0.0230 0.94	0.83
Entire Period Averaged										
Eq 10	1979-98	-0.0067 1.00	0.0265 5.83						0.0152 1.67	0.63
Eq 11	1979-98	-0.0122 2.14		0.0121 2.88	0.0133 8.37				0.0056 0.55	0.72
Eq 12	1979-98	-0.0104 1.27		0.0089 1.74	0.0116 6.08	0.1427 1.40	-0.2001 1.36	-0.0411 1.46	0.0217 2.03	0.79

Table 21.7.   The Two-Standard Deviation Confidence Interval (2SDCI)
for the Coefficients

Variable	Table No.	Eqn. No.	Range of the 2SDCI for 1978-84		Range of the 2SDCI for 1992-98		Overlap of 2SDCIs?
Coast				0.0268	0.0195	0.0441	yes
Coast	6	1 and 3	0.0056	0.0292	0.0225	0.0525	yes
Pop100cr	5	4 and 6	-0.0002	0.0248	0.0301	0.0516	no
Pop100cr	5	7 and 9	-0.0198	0.0162	0.0216	0.0440	no
Pop100cr	6	4 and 6	-0.0008	0.0248	0.0298	0.0518	no
Pop100cr	6	7 and 9	-0.0179	0.0165	0.0213	0.0423	no
Policy	5	4 and 6	0.0020	0.0092	-0.0028	0.0236	yes
Policy	5	7 and 9	0.0001	0.0083	0.0021	0.0213	yes
Policy	6	4 and 6	0.0022	0.0100	-0.0046	0.0242	yes
Policy	6	7 and 9	-0.0006	0.0078	0.0028	0.0214	yes

To summarize, Tables 21.5 to 21.7 show that conditional convergence is only hinted at, rather than statistically supported; the *Policy* coefficient generally is temporally stable in magnitude statistical support across time; the *Pop100cr* coefficient increases in magnitude and statistical significance over time; and all the specifications fit the data best in the 1992–98 subperiod (as shown by R^2 being highest in 1992–98). We attribute the third and fourth findings to the slow-acting nature of geographical forces.

By government intent and design, the main growth mechanism of the provincial preferential policies is FDI. Geography, in comparison, manifests itself through two growth mechanisms: FDI and rural industrial enterprises. As most FDI in China, up to now, has been export-motivated, FDI would (ceteris paribus) prefer provinces that provide easier access to sea transportation (which is what the *Pop100cr* variable is designed to proxy for). Since a large and growing proportion of China's exports are produced by rural enterprises (in many cases, initially as subcontractors to SOEs and foreign funded enterprises), it has been natural for these export-oriented rural enterprises to be established in the coastal provinces. In turn, these rural enterprises generated agglomeration effects and backward economic links that induced new rural enterprises (not necessarily export-oriented) to locate themselves in the same localities, thus making the coastal region a major growth area. The disproportionate concentration of rural enterprises in the seven coastal provinces explains why, in 1988, the coastal region accounted for 53% of the investment by China's rural enterprises when it accounted for 40% of national investment, and 31% of investment by China's SOEs. The 1998 numbers are 56%, 43%, and 35% respectively. The opening of trade, in brief, allowed geography to establish FDI and rural industrial enterprises as its main growth mechanisms.[13]

Table 21.8 presents evidence to support the proposed effects of Policy and *Pop100cr* on FDI. The correlations among FDI, *Policy* and *Pop100cr* reported in Part A display two noteworthy results. First, the FDI-*Policy* link is stronger than the FDI-*Pop100cr* link. The correlation coefficient of FDI-*Policy* is larger than the correlation coefficient of FDI-*Pop100cr* for all time periods, suggesting that Policy had a greater influence than *Pop100cr* in determining the location of FDI. This suggestion is bolstered by the fact that the FDI-*Policy* correlation coefficient is always strongly statistically significant (with the weakest link at the 0.1% significance level in 1985–91), which is not true of the FDI-*Pop100cr* correlation coefficient.

Second, geography became a bigger determinant in the location decision of FDI over time. The FDI-*Pop100cr* correlation coefficient rose from 0.211 in 1979–84 to 0.389 in 1985–91, and then to 0.597 in 1992–98. (These figures are still smaller than the smallest FDI-*Policy* correlation coefficient, 0.604 in 1985–91.) The tightening of the FDI-*Pop100cr* link over time is due to the gradual extension of preferential policies to other provinces, and to geography having a longer lag on FDI compared to *Policy*.

Table 21.8.   The Role of Preferential Policy and Geography Nexus
in the Location of Foreign Direct Investment

Part A: Degree of correlation among Pop100cr, Policy and FDI for different
periods (italicized numbers refer to the level of statistical significance
that the correlation is zero)

		FDI	Policy	FDI	Policy
		1979-84			**1985-91**
Policy		0.8229		0.6039	
		0.000		0.001	
Pop100cr		0.211	0.2925	0.3886	0.6593
		0.272	0.124	0.038	0.000
		1992-98			**1979-98**
Policy		0.7539		0.8000	
		0.000		0.000	
Pop100cr		0.5968	0.4909	0.5642	0.581
		0.001	0.007	0.001	0.001

Part B: Addition of FDI tends to reduce significance of policy and
geography variables

	Period	Initial GDP level	Pop 100cr	Policy	Initial size of agri.	Sq. (initial size of agri.)	Initial SOE size	Metro-polis dummy	FDI	R²
Eq 1	1979-84	-0.0089	-0.0007	0.0039	0.0862	-0.0629	-0.0946	0.0250	-0.0864	
		0.56	0.08	1.25	0.37	0.20	2.39	1.34	0.12	0.42
Eq 2	1985-91	-0.0103	-0.0049	0.0035	0.4773	-0.7293	0.0099	0.0171	1.0713	
		0.52	0.55	0.98	2.13	2.25	0.16	0.86	4.32	0.61
Eq 3	1992-98	-0.0183	0.0331	0.0133	0.1602	-0.3245	-0.1230	0.0240	0.0276	
		1.62	4.72	2.26	0.49	0.52	3.43	0.96	0.37	0.83
Eq 4	1979-98	-0.0095	0.0084	0.0090	0.1741	-0.2501	-0.0471	0.0223	0.1068	
		1.11	1.66	1.77	1.72	1.70	1.46	2.05	0.72	0.79

Dependent Variable: Average Growth Rate of Per Capita GDP of Province in
indicated period constant term not reported, absolute t-statisitic in italic. N=29,
Tibet (missing data), and Chongqing data included into Sichuan

To make our point that FDI is one of the economic growth mechanisms enabled by the *Policy* and *Pop100cr* variables, Part B of Table 21.8 reports the regression results of adding FDI into the preferred specification in Table 21.6. FDI received strong statistical support in only one of the four cases, and its presence reduced the t-statistics of *Policy* and *Pop100cr* in every case. The results support our hypotheses that FDI into China and its distribution within China has largely been induced by *Policy* and *Pop100cr*.

Growth Quantification and Simulation

Table 21.9 uses the minimum and maximum values of the estimated coefficients of *Pop100cr* and *Policy* in 1992-98 from Tables 21.5 and 21.6 to quantify the range of the growth contributions from geographical location and preferential policies to the growth rates of provinces in the different regions in the 1996–99 period. It is surprising that there is only one case, the coastal region, where the range of the growth contributions from *Pop100cr* overlaps with the range from *Policy*; (2.6 to 3.3 percentage points) and (2.4 to 2.9 percentage points) respectively. Furthermore, there is only one case, the central region, where geography was unambiguously more influential than preferential policies – and this occurred largely because of the Yangtze being navigable for a long way upstream. Understandably, *Policy* has had more impact than *Pop100cr* in the growth of the western provinces.

The metropolises resemble the coastal provinces in enjoying large boosts from *Pop100cr* and *Policy*. There is, however, no overlap in the two ranges for the metropolises because they are so pampered that their lowest growth contribution from *Policy* equals the highest growth contribution to coastal growth from *Policy*.

The growth decomposition yields two important observations for economic policy. First, the faster growth of the coastal provinces could not be largely attributed to the more preferential policies that they had received. The coastal location was probably marginally more important than preferential policies in promoting growth. Second, despite the significant easing of regulations on FDI and international trade in the interior provinces since 1992, the regional differences in *Policy* in 1996–98 were still quite large, causing at least a one and a half percentage point growth gap between the metropolises and the central, northwestern, and southwestern provinces.

The last four columns in Table 21.9 simulate the growth consequences of Policy. The central provinces would have shown the highest growth rates (8.7 to 9.0%) in 1996–99, but the coastal provinces would still have grown faster than the northeastern, northwestern, and southwestern provinces. Furthermore, because the preferential policies had a positive impact on the growth of the inland provinces, the elimination of preferential policies to equalize policy treatment across provinces would have been a negative shock to the inland provinces. Since the troubling aspect about the preferential policies was not their effectiveness, but the unequal access to them, the solution lies in increasing the access of the inland provinces to the preferential policies rather than in denying these policies to everyone. For the counterfactual growth scenario of *Policy* = 2 for all provinces, the outcome would have been a higher national GDP growth rate and a reduction in the coefficient of variation for provincial income (because the poorer provinces would have grown faster, and the growth rates of the metropolises would have been at least one percentage point lower).

Table 21.9.   Contributions of Geography and Preferential Policy to Growth in 1996-99, and Policy Simulations

Location of Province		Metro-polis	North-east	Coast	Central	North-west	North-west
Average actual value in 1996-99 period	*GDP growth*	9.88	9.19	10.72	10.28	9.32	8.80
	Pop100cr	0.71	0.18	0.82	0.57	0.00	0.04
	Policy	3.00	2.00	2.43	1.33	1.33	1.50
Range of Geography Effects on GDP growth, (% points)	*Minimum*	2.25	0.56	2.60	1.82	0.00	0.12
	Maximum	2.88	0.72	3.34	2.34	0.00	0.16
Range of Policy Effects on GDP growth, (% points)	*Minimum*	2.94	1.96	2.38	1.31	1.31	1.47
	Maximum	3.63	2.42	2.94	1.61	1.61	1.82
Counterfactual GDP GDP growth when policy=0, (%)	*Minimum*	6.25	6.77	7.78	8.67	7.70	6.99
	Maximum	6.94	7.23	8.34	8.98	8.01	7.33
Counterfactual GDP GDP growth when Policy =2, (%)	*Minimum*	8.67	9.19	10.20	10.94	9.97	9.29
	Maximum	8.90	9.19	10.30	11.09	10.12	9.41

What is to be Done?

The presence of only conditional convergence and not unconditional convergence in China stands in marked contrast with Barro and Sala-Martin's finding of unconditional convergence in the United States. We see several Chinese institutions that have been inhibiting the income convergence process generated by factor movement and the Stolper-Samuelson mechanism. The household registration (*hukou*) system makes it illegal for rural labour to move to urban areas. The monopoly state bank system favours the SOEs, and most SOEs are located on the coast and in the northeast. The decentralization reforms of 1984-88 unleashed local protectionism, and it appears from the recent research of Young (2000) and Poncet (2001) that the decentralization reforms that restarted in 1992 might have brought local protectionism to new heights. The crucial point here is that there are other important factors that contributed to the widening of regional disparity besides geographical location and selective economic internationalization.

The government clearly recognizes the great importance of providing infrastructure to overcome production bottlenecks and facilitate international economic integration. Infrastructure construction stands first in the following list of priority tasks in the strategy to develop the western provinces (State Council 2000):

- developing infrastructure
- improving and protecting the environment
- strengthening agriculture
- restructuring industry
- promoting tourism
- enhancing science, technology, education, culture, and public health

In our opinion, science, technology, education, and public health have been given too low a ranking in the above priority list. This concern stems from our belief that, once a market economy is in place, technological advancement is the fundamental engine of sustainable development. The ultimate prize of western development efforts is the successful incubation of two or three centres of endogenous growth in western China. If the incubation effort is too ambitious, the next objective is to create sufficient local scientific capacity to hasten the diffusion of new technologies from the coastal provinces and foreign countries to western China. Finally, human capital formation has a much lower wastage rate than physical capital formation because humans can move and contribute to the technological progress there and bridges and tunnels cannot .

It must be recognized that the so-called "preferential policies" are in essence "deregulation policies" to marketize and internationalize these coastal economies so that they could operate in an economic environment closer to those of their East Asian neighbours (and competitors). The adjective "preferential" gives the misleading sense that the prosperity of these coastal economies had been mostly sustained by a steady flow of state subsidies, and this has not been the case. There was certainly pump priming in the beginning (i.e., state funds to build the infrastructure that would make these economic zones attractive as export platforms), but there have not been significant steady transfers to prop up failing enterprises in order to maintain the living standard in the region, as in the case of the northeastern provinces. The state should accelerate the extension of these deregulation policies to the other provinces rather than to reverse them for the coastal provinces as has been proposed. Furthermore, deregulation must be expanded to cover the household registration system, the monopoly state bank system, and local protectionism. An effective strategy to develop the western provinces must therefore encompass physical capital formation, human capital formation, and institutional capital formation.

Notes

1.   Reprinted from *China Economic Review* 13, Sylvie Démurger, Jeffrey D. Sachs, Wing Thye Woo, Shuming Bao, and Gene Chan, "The relative contributions of location and preferential policies in China's regional development: being in the right place and having the right incentives", 444-465, Copyright (2002), with permission from Elsevier.

2.   Unless otherwise indicated, the income data are from the National Bureau of Statistics (NBS 1999). The three main components (primary,

secondary, and tertiary sectors) of provincial GDP are recalculated at 1995 prices, and then summed up to obtain the real GDP series of the province, measured in 1995 prices. GDP data for Tibet and Hainan were available only after 1978. Chongqing data were consolidated with those of Sichuan by updating Sichuan data from the State Statistical Bureau (SSB 1997) from 1996 onward with data on Chongqing and Sichuan in subsequent years of the China Statistical Yearbook.

3. To cite but a few recent papers: Tsui (1996), Chan, Hseuh, and Luk, (1996), Raiser (1998), Tian (1999), Wu (2000), Démurger (2001), Kanbur and Zhang (2001), and Zhang, Liu, and Yao (2001). Besides the English-written literature, there is also an important Chinese-written literature that is not cited here.

4. The first quote is from "Deng's Economic Drive Leaves Vast Regions of China Behind," *New York Times*, 27 December 1995, and the second is from the *South China Morning Post* ("Clash over shrinking coffers," 23 September 1995) which also reported that "Mr. Hu slapped the SEZs in the face by accusing them of ripping off the rest of China – and widening the regional gap – by abusing the special policies granted them by the Centre ... [and he] concluded that the zones 'should no longer be allowed to remain special.' "

5. This paper is hence a follow-up to the Bao, Chang, Sachs and Woo (forthcoming) paper. The latter used real GDP data from the individual provincial yearbook, and this paper recalculated provincial GDP as described in footnote 1. The estimations here differ from those in Demurger, Sachs, Woo, Bao, Chang, and Mellinger (2001) by using a sample that included Beijing, Shanghai, and Tianjin. Wang and Hu (1999) discussed how China's heterogeneous geographical conditions can help explain regional economic disparities, but did not include geographical variables in their regressions.

6. There is a keen controversy about what are the fundamental economic mechanisms in the rapid growth of China after 1978. Some economists (the experimentalist school) believe that the growth was enabled by the discovery of new nonstandard economic mechanisms,

e.g., collectively owned rural enterprises and fiscal contracting, while others (the convergence school) see the growth as the result of moving toward a private market economy, whereby best international practices are adopted and modified according to local conditions. See Sachs and Woo (2000) and Woo (2001a) for a review of this debate.

7. The evidence on this front is mixed; e.g., Chen (forthcoming) and Zhang and Zou (1998) found negative relationships between fiscal decentralization and economic growth. See the review in Woo (2001a).

8. For details, see Wong, Heady, and Woo (1995).

9. Chongqing was granted province-level status in 1997, but we have included its data under Sichuan province.

10. The assumption is that the distribution of population across China did change much in 1952-98 because of the household registration system that kept people in the places where they were born.

11. Disentangling geography and policy is clearly not an easy task because preferential treatments are obviously related to geography; for example, Shenzhen was made an SEZ because it is located next to Hong Kong. Fortunately, the correlation between them appears far enough because of different types of zones, and different timing in establishments of the zones. The coefficient of correlation between the average value of the policy index over 1978–98 and the proportion of provincial population in 1994 with easy access to sea transportation [Pop100cr] is 0.54, more details given in Table 21.8.

12. The subperiods correspond to different policy episodes: 1979-84 was agricultural decollectivization, 1985-1991 was Oskar Lange-type of market socialism, and 1992-1998 was socialist market economy with Chinese characteristics (which include privatizing most SOEs, and giving state and private capital equal constitutional protection).

13. Woo (1998) found that rural industrial enterprises accounted for almost 30 % of the increase in output during 1985–93. Woo (2001b) showed that the contribution from rural enterprises to industrial output growth nearly always equaled to that of the SOEs in 1984-87 and exceeded it from 1988 onward.

References

1.   Bao, Shuming, Gene Chang, Jeffrey D. Sachs, and Wing Thye Woo (2002). Geographic Factors and China's Regional Development Under Market Reforms, 1978–98. *China Economic Review China* 13: 89–111.

2.   Barro, Robert J., and Xavier Sala-i-Martin (1995). *Economic Growth*, McGraw-Hill, New York.

3.   Berthélemy, Jean-Claude, and Sylvie Démurger (2000). Foreign Direct Investment and Economic Growth: Theoretical Issues and Empirical Application to China. *Review of Development Economics* 4 (2):140–55.

4.   Chan, Roger C.K., Tien-Tung Hseuh, and C. Luk (eds) (1996). *China's Regional Economic Development*. Hong Kong: Hong Kong Institute of Asia-Pacific Studies, Chinese University of Hong Kong.

5.   Chen, Baizhu, and Yi Feng (2000). Determinants of Economic Growth in China: Private Enterprise, Education and Openness. *China Economic Review* 11 (1):1–15.

6.   Chen, Jian, and Belton M. Fleisher (1996). Regional Income Inequality and Economic Growth in China. *Journal of Comparative Economics* 22 (2):141–64.

7.   Chen, Yu (forthcoming). Decentralization, Local Provision of Public Goods and Economic Growth: The Case of China. In Sustainability of China's Economic Growth in the 21st Century, edited by Ross Garnaut and Ligang Song. Canberra, Australia: Asia Pacific Press.

8.   Démurger, Sylvie (2000). *Economic Opening and Growth in China*. Paris: OECD Development Centre Studies.

9.   Démurger, Sylvie (2001). Infrastructure Development and Economic Growth: An Explanation for Regional Disparities in China? *Journal of Comparative Economics* 29 (1):95–117.

10.   Démurger, Sylvie, Jeffrey D. Sachs, Wing Thye Woo, Shuming Bao, Gene Chang, and Andrew Mellinger (2001). Geography, Economic Policy, and Regional Development in China. University of California. manuscript.

11.   Jian, Tianlun, Jeffrey D. Sachs, and Andrew M. Warner (1996). Trends in Regional Inequality in China. *China Economic Review* 7 (1):1–21.

12.   Kanbur, Ravi and Xiaobo Zhang (2001). Fifty Years of Regional Inequality in China: A Journey Through Revolution, Reform and Openness. Cornell University. Unpublished manuscript.

13.   Lemoine, Françoise (2000). *FDI and the Opening Up of China's Economy.* Centre d'Etudes Prospectives et d'Informations Internationales (CEPII). Paris.

14.   Mody, Ashoka, and Fang-Yi Wang (1997). Explaining Industrial Growth in Coastal China: Economic Reforms ... and What Else? *The World Bank Economic Review* 11 (2): 293–325.

15.   National Bureau of Statistics (NBS) (1999). *Comprehensive Statistical Data and Materials on 50 Years of New China.* Beijing: China Statistics Press.

16.   National Bureau of Statistics (NBS), formerly State Statistical Bureau (SSB), 1997-2000 issues of *China Statistical Yearbooks.* Beijing.

17.   Poncet, Sandra (2001) "Is China Disintegrating? The Magnitude of Chinese Provinces' Domestic and International Border Effects," CERDI manuscript, April.

18.   Raiser, Martin (1998). Subsidising Inequality: Economic Reforms, Fiscal Transfers and Convergence across Chinese Provinces. *Journal of Development Studies* 34 (3): 1–26.

19.   Sachs, Jeffrey D., and Wing Thye Woo (1994). Structural Factors in the Economic Reforms of China, Eastern Europe, and the Former Soviet Union. *Economic Policy* 18 (April): 101–45.

20.   Sachs, Jeffrey D., and Wing Thye Woo (2000). Understanding China's Economic Performance. *Journal of Policy Reform* 4 (1):1-50.

21.   State Council (2000). *Circular of the State Council on Policies and Measure Pertaining to the Development of the Western Region.* Beijing: China Planning Press.

22.   State Statistical Bureau (SSB) (1997). *The Gross Domestic Product of China, 1952–1995.* Dalian, China: Dongbei University of Finance and Economics Press.

23.   Tian, Xiaowen (1999). China's Regional Economic Disparities Since 1978: Main Trends and Determinants. East Asian Institute Occasional Paper 21. Singapore: National University of Singapore.

24.   Tsui, Kai-yuen (1996). Economic Reform and Interprovincial Inequalities in China. *Journal of Development Economics* 50 (2): 353–68.

25. Wang, Shaoguang, and Angang Hu (1999). *The Political Economy of Uneven Development, The Case of China.* Armonk, New York: M. E. Sharpe.

26. Wong, Christine P.W., Christopher Heady, and Wing Thye Woo (1995). *Fiscal Management and Economic Reform in the People's Republic of China.* Oxford: Oxford University Press.

27. Woo, Wing Thye (1998). "Zhongguo Quan Yaosu Shengchan Lu: Laizi Nongye Bumen Laodongli Zai Pei Zhi de Shouyao Zuoyong" in *Jingji Yanjiu*, vol. 3, 1998.

28. Woo, Wing Thye (2001a). Recent Claims of China's Economic Exceptionalism: Reflections Inspired by WTO Accession. *China Economic Review* 12 (2/3): 107–36.

29. Woo, Wing Thye (2001b). China's Rural Enterprises in Crisis: The Role of Inadequate Financial Intermediation. University of California. manuscript.

30. Wu, Yanrui (2000). The Determinants of Economic Growth: Evidence from a Panel of Chinese Provinces. University of Western Australian, manuscript.

31. Young, Alwyn (2000). The Razor's Edge: Distortions and Incremental Reform in the People's Republic of China. *Quarterly Journal of Economics*, vol. 115 (4): 1091-1136.

32. Zhang, Tao, and Heng-fu Zou (1998). Fiscal Decentralization, Public Spending, and Economic Growth in China. *Journal of Public Economics* 67: 221–40.

33. Zhang, Wei (2001). Rethinking Regional Disparity in China. *Economics of Planning*, vol. 34 (1-2): 113-138.

34. Zhang, Zongyi, Aying Liu, and Shujie Yao (2001). Convergence of China's Regional Incomes, 1952–1997. *China Economic Review* 12 (2/3): 243–58.

22 Urbanization and West China Development[1]

Ding Lu and Wing Thye Woo

Introduction

Two features are notable in China's economic growth over the past two decades. One is the hyper-growth rate of GDP, which averaged over nine per cent per annum. The other is the widening per capita income gap between the coastal and the inland areas, due to the uneven pace of market opening and regional growth (Table 22.1). A visitor who travels from the east coast city of Shanghai to the inland provinces and regions of the west will find him/herself going from the "First World" to the "Third World". Many factors have contributed to the regional disparities in growth performance. Although the vast territories of western China boast rich mineral resources, they are severely constrained by their land-locked geographic locations. The quality of local human capital, underdeveloped market institutions, and state policies all favour the coastal open cities and are partially responsible for the relatively slow growth and development of the west. (Bao et al, 2002; Démurger et al, 2002).

In this paper, we assess the role of urbanization in China's regional development. Urbanization is the process of transferring labour and other inputs from predominantly rural agricultural activities to urban manufacturing and service industries. As it is integral to the process of economic development, it is essential to identify the distinct features of urban systems which may affect the environment for economic growth. Specifically, we attempt to evaluate the impact of the varying pattern of city-size distribution on local economic growth performance.

Role of Urbanization in Regional Development

Literature review

The literature of urban economics is rich in explaining paces and patterns of urbanization occurring as a result or consequence of economic change. In other words, the central issue to cope with is "what makes cities grow". Many empirical studies have been conducted to estimate the quantitative impact of various factors on the level of urbanization (e.g., World Bank, 1983; Perkins, 1990; Fay and Opal, 2000). There is also a substantial body of literature on the determinants of individual cities' size and location. A number of empirical studies aim to identify determinants and sources of change in the system of cities over time (e.g., Pred, 1977; Heilbrun, 1987; Glaeser and Shapiro, 2001).

A number of rigorous and testable theoretical models such as those by Henderson (1988) were developed in the last two decades for applying neoclassical economic analyses to reveal the determinants of city size and size distribution of cities. In this vein, empirical works by Rosen and Resnick (1980), Alperovich (1993), Jones and Visaria (1997), and Rappaport and Sachs (2001) investigated the relevance of a wide set of economic, demographic, geographic and policy variables in explaining variations in city-size distribution and the clustering of economic activity across countries and regions.

With an incremental understanding of "what makes cities grow" or "why cities are distributed the way they are", researchers have increasingly turned their attention to the policy issue of "what kinds of cities are desirable" or "what patterns of city growth should be pursued". Starting in the 1980s, there were studies on the phenomenon observed in some developing countries, of *over-concentration* of city population (Renaud, 1981; Henderson, 1988; Ades and Glaeser, 1995; Moomaw and Shatter, 1996, etc.). Hansen (1990) adapted Williamson's (1965) hypothesis of an inverse U-shape relationship between regional disparity and economic development to an urban context, and hypothesized that a high degree of spatial or urban concentration in the early stages of economic development is helpful to growth. This hypothesis is related to the "centre-periphery" model developed by

Friedmann (1972), and assumes that the concentration of resources in urban centres is an integral process of industrialization, which gives rise to a dualistic spatial structure with the largest urban centre forming the core and small towns forming the periphery. The emergence of the dualistic spatial structure increases core-periphery disparity in resource allocation through the early stages of development until at some point industrialization matures and the development process starts to trickle down to the periphery.

Duranton and Puga (2001) proposed a theoretical model to demonstrate that diversified large cities tend to act as a "nursery" for new firms while the successful firms aim to relocate to specialized smaller cities if the relocation is not too costly. Their model implies that such a city system consisting of nursery centres and satellite cities is conducive to innovation and growth.

As noted by Henderson (2001), however, "no research to date has attempted to directly quantitatively examine whether urbanization promotes growth or whether there are optimal degrees of urbanization or urban concentration". Henderson himself used cross-country data to show empirically that economic development is not strongly affected by urbanization per se, but by the degree of urban concentration.

Features of China's urbanization

In the context of China's post-reform economy, this study attempts to assess the impact of different levels and patterns of urbanization on economic growth. This issue is of particular interest since China is not only the most populous country in the world, but also has the largest urban population (in absolute numbers). Moreover, China has had one of the most centrally planned urbanization policy regimes in the world. The changes in public policy have influenced the country's urbanization process in a magnitude and depth rarely observed in other parts of the world. With its vast territory of over 30 provinces and regions with very different city systems, China provides an ideal case study for testing the impact of the levels and patterns of urbanization on economic growth performance.

Table 22.1.   Development Level, Urbanization, and Geographic
Characteristics by Region

Region	Metro-polises	North-east	Coast	Centre	North-west	South-west	National
Per capita GDP growth rate, 1978-98 (%)	8.5	7.9	10.7	8.4	7.7	7.8	9
Urbanization, 2000	79.3	51.8	41.6	30.6	33.3	27	36.22
Per capita GDP, 2000	25000	8878	10548	5521	5276	4312	7078
Relative Per capita GDP, 2000 (National =100)	353	125	149	78	75	61	100
Population density, 1994 (persons/km²)	1104	138	333	264	46	126	290
Distance from coast (km)	77	380	86	492	1383	656	547
Pop100cr (% of population)	71	18	82	57	0	4	41

Notes:
  GDP per capita compound annual growth rate over 1979-98 was calculated at
    1995 constant prices.
  Per capita GDP in 2000 is nominal value.
  Urbanization is defined as urban residents divided by total population.
  Pop100cr = proportion of the population distribution of a province/region within
    100 km of the coastline or an ocean-navigable river, excluding the northern
    coastline which ices up in the winter, and rivers which flow to this coastline.
  Metropolises = Beijing, Tianjin, and Shanghai.
  Northeast = Liaoning, Jilin, and Heilongjiang.
  Coast = Hebei, Jiangsu, Zhejiang, Fujian, Shandong, Guangdong, and Hainan.
  Centre = Shanxi, Anhui, Jiangxi, Henan, Hubei, and Hunan.
  Northwest = Inner Mongolia, Shaanxi, Gansu, Qinghai, Ningxia, and Xinjiang
    (Tibet excluded due to missing data).
  Southwest = Sichuan (including Chongqing), Guizhou, Yunnan, and Guangxi.

Sources: NBS for economic and population variables; GIS calculations made by Bao
    Shuming for geographical data, except arable land; Wang and Hu (1999,
    table 4.1, p. 83) for arable land.

China's current urbanization and urban size distribution retain distinct legacies of the pre-reform regime (1949-1978). Zhou (1997: 244) observed that most Chinese cities in the 1980s tended to have similar industrial structures. He noted that a convergence of structures among mega cities would conform to their functions of agglomeration and conglomeration. Such a convergence among smaller cities, however, might reflect the influence of Mao's self-sufficiency policy. Using China's population census data, Goldstein (1985) observed several trends in the changes of city size distribution from 1953 to 1982. First, due to policies designed to relocate industry and develop urban places in inland areas, the urban population growth in the central south and western regions was two to three times that in the north and eastern regions.[2] Second, there was a substantial upward shift to larger size categories in overall city size distribution (see Figure 22.1). The distribution in the number of cities city among different size categories evolved from a hierarchical pattern in 1953 to a "peaked-at-median" pattern in 1982. Meanwhile, the share of smaller cities' in total urban population dropped sharply. Third, both eastern and western regions were characterized by big city growth, with the western region showing gains in its share of million-plus big cities. There was a limited shift westward in the location of big cities. Finally, the newly industrializing inland provinces generally displayed the highest four-city primacy indices over the period.

Heavy-handed state planning and manipulation were behind these inter-regional shifts of urbanization (Kirkby, 1985; Kwok, 1988). Through a series of powerful policy instruments, government development strategy profoundly affected the pace and pattern of urbanization. For instance, there were several waves of state sponsored migrations from the coastal regions to the west, and from urban to rural areas from the 1950s through the 1970s. The household registration system, or *hukou* system, introduced in the 1950s, segregated the urban and rural residents and became an effective leverage for rationing basic consumer goods and controlling the urban population. On top of these, state ownership and central planning allowed direct state command over the direction of capital investment.

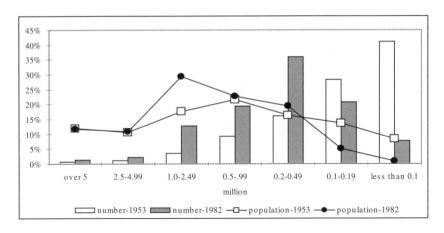

Figure 22.1. Percentage Distribution of Cities and City population
              (by size class)
          Source: Goldstein (1985).

Urbanization policy in the pre-reform period was dominated mainly by ideological or national security considerations rather than economic rationale. Mao's government made preparing the nation for the Third World War a high priority. Huge amounts of state capital were pumped into the central and western regions to build "socialist new cities" and industrial bases. Rural market towns were suppressed by the development of self-sufficient People's Communes. Provinces/regions and localities were encouraged to build their own autarkic-like industrial sectors to ensure local self-sufficiency in wartime. Traditional commercial connections between urban and rural areas as well as large and small cities were severed.

The result was that the patterns of urbanization in China in the early years of economic reform did not reflect the location and size distribution pattern of a market economy (ref. Figure 22.1, which compares the hierarchical pattern of city distribution in 1953 with the "peaked-at-median" pattern in 1982). The regional difference in city size distribution is revealing. The legacy is more profound in the inland regions than in the coastal. It has been erased in different degrees due to the varying advancement of market-oriented reforms and openness between the inland and coastal regions. It is immediately apparent that interregional differences are large not only in terms of levels of urbanization (Figure 22.2) but also in city size distribution (Figure 22.3). The eastern region appears to have a more even distribution of cities of different sizes compared to the west and central regions.

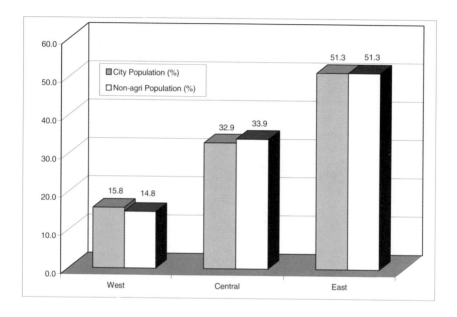

Figure 22.2.   Shares of Total Urban Population by Region (1998)

Note: The "east" region includes Beijing, Tianjin, Hebei, Liaoning, Shanghai, Jiangsu, Zhejiang, Fujian, Shandong, Guangdong, and Hainan. The "west" region includes Inner Mongolia, Guangxi, Sichuan, Guizhou, Yunnan, Tibet, Shaanxi, Gansu, Qinghai, Ningxia, and Xinjiang. The "central" region includes: Jilin, Heilongjiang, Anhui, Jiangxi, Henan, Hubei, and Hunan.

Source: *China Statistical Yearbook,* various issues.

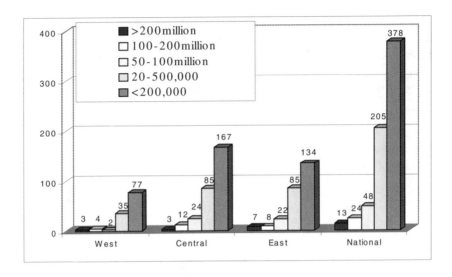

Figure 22.3.   Regional Distribution of Cities at Different Scales (1999)

Note: Regions are defined as the same as in Figure 22.6.
Source: *China Urban Yearbook,* various issues.

It has long been noted in the large and wealthy European and North American economies that they share a common pattern in urbanization. It is summed up as the Pareto distribution, which is described by:

$$\log R = a + b * \log x \tag{1}$$

where   b = the Pareto Coefficient (PC) to be estimated empirically
        R = rank of city
        x = size of city

Empirically, b around -1 is observed in these large wealthy economies (a finding popularized as "Zipf's Law" or "rank-size rule"). Note that the larger the absolute value of the Pareto Coefficient, PC, the lower the disparity in city size, e.g. "b = -infinity" means that all the cities are of the same size.

To gauge the degree of a province's deviation from Zipf's Law in urban size distribution, we define "root mean squared error of Zipf-Law deviation (RMSEZ)" as

$$\text{RMSEZ} = \sqrt{\frac{\sum_i (x_i - \hat{x}_i)^2}{n-1}} \tag{2}$$

where x_i is the size of the ith city and $\hat{x}_i$ is the Zipf's Law-predicted size of the city.

Accordingly, we defined the following versions of coefficient variance from Zipf's Law based on RMSEZ:

-- "Coefficient variance of Zipf-Law deviation normalized by mean city size (CVMN)" = RMSEZ divided by mean city size;

-- "Coefficient variance of Zipf-Law deviation normalized by median city size (CVMED)" = RMSEZ divided by median city size.

Table 22.2 shows the urbanization patterns in different regions in the 1985, 1993, and 2000. A clear division is seen in the regional PCs reported in Part A. The northwest and southwest regions have absolute PCs less than 1, whereas the northeast, coastal and central regions have absolute PCs greater than 1. Furthermore, since 1985, the northwest and southwest regions saw their degree of deviation from Zipf's Law (measured by CVMN and CVMED in Part B and C respectively) increase. Contrarily, in the rest of the country these indices generally experienced a sharp reduction. The opposing trends resulted in much higher index values for the northwest and southwest regions in 1993 and 2000. The inescapable fact is that the northwest and southwest regions have a comparatively lower number of small and medium towns and cities compared to the other three regions. The rapid growth of towns and cities with a population of less than a half million between 1982 and 2000 (Table 22.3) simply did not occur in the northwest and southwest regions.

Table 22.2.   Regional Features of City-Size Distribution

	1985	1993	2000
Part 1: Estimated size of Pareto Coefficient, b			
Northeast	-1.12	-1.13	-1.12
Coast	-1.00	-1.08	-1.14
Central	-1.09	-1.21	-1.28
Northwest	-0.87	-0.91	-0.93
Southwest	-0.78	-0.84	-0.84
Part 2: Coefficient variance of Zipf's-Law deviation normalized by mean city size (CVMN)			
Northeast	0.20	0.06	0.06
Coast	0.20	0.12	0.12
Central	0.20	0.14	0.14
Northwest	0.16	0.19	0.18
Southwest	0.17	0.16	0.17
Part 3: Coefficient variance of Zipf's-Law deviation normalized by median city size (CVMED)			
Northeast	0.30	0.09	0.10
Coast	0.31	0.19	0.18
Central	0.28	0.21	0.20
Northwest	0.29	0.35	0.35
Southwest	0.33	0.31	0.35

Notes: Northeast = Liaoning, Jilin, and Heilongjiang.
Coast = Hebei, Jiangsu, Zhejiang, Fujian, Shandong, Guangdong, and Hainan.
Centre = Shanxi, Anhui, Jiangxi, Henan, Hubei, and Hunan.
Northwest = Inner Mongolia, Shaanxi, Gansu, Qinghai, Ningxia, and Xinjiang (Tibet excluded due to missing data).
Southwest = Sichuan (including Chongqing), Guizhou, Yunnan, and Guangxi.

Table 22.3.   Percentage Shares of Urban Population Living in
Different Size Classes of Cities (1952-2000)

City size	1952	1965	1982	1985	1992	1996	2000
Over 1 million	40.1	43.0	43.3	39.4	39.6	35.2	37.7
0.5-1.0 million	19.0	20.5	20.5	19.3	13.1	14.8	13.9
Others	40.9	36.5	36.2	41.3	47.3	50.0	48.4

Source: 1952-1985, Zong (1988: 15); 1992-2000, compiled from
China Statistical Yearbook and *China Urban Yearbook*, various issues.

Methodology and Data

Given the importance of urbanization and its size distribution feature, we seek to investigate the impact of different types of city-size distributions on growth and factors that influence the speed of urbanization and city-size distribution. The statistical analyses are based on data from various issues of the China *Statistical Yearbook* and *China Urban Yearbook*.

We estimate a model by regressing the logarithmic per annum growth rate of per capita GDP during the period under investigation on a number of exogenous variables:

$$y_{\tau i} = a_\tau + b_{\tau 1}x_{\tau 1} + ... + b_{\tau n}x_{\tau n} + u_{\tau i} \tag{3}$$

where $y_{\tau i}$ is the logarithmic per annum growth rate of per capita GDP in the ith province during period τ and $x_{\tau 1} ... x_{\tau n}$ are exogenous variables in period τ. Note again that the residual, $u_{\tau i}$, represents growth not accounted for by these exogenous variables.

The estimation of (3) is based on the foundation work of Démurger et al (2002) and Bao et al (2002). The empirical results of Démurger et al (2002) show that geographical and policy factors, among others, played a major role in causing China's provincial/regional differences in income growth during the period 1979 to 1998. The regression models with the following variables were found to explain over 80% of the interregional growth differences over the whole period:

- *Initial GDP level*: a variable included according to the (conditional) convergence hypothesis that assumes the faster growth potentials for the less developed provinces in catching up with the more developed ones.
- *Initial share of the agricultural sector*: a variable included because China's economic reform started with the large-scale deregulation of this sector. The larger initial size of the agricultural sector also implies the potential of an abundant local supply of rural labour.
- *A squared term of the agricultural sector share*: a variable added because Tian (1999) found a non-linear correlation between agriculture and growth.
- *Initial size of the state sector*: a variable included by Sachs and Woo (1994) who argued that the maintenance of the existing state-owned sector would require the state to give state-owned enterprises (SOEs) priority access to capital, raw materials and skilled manpower, hence making it difficult for new non-state enterprises, like rural industrial enterprises, to emerge.
- *Pop100cr*: a proxy for provincial access to water transportation. It is the proportion of a province/region's population distribution in 1994 within 100 kilometres of the coastline or an ocean-navigable river, excluding the northern coastline which ices up in the winter, and rivers which flow to this coastline.
- *Policy:* a proxy constructed to measure the difference in provincial/regional access to the preferential treatment of foreign investment.[3]
- *Education*: the proportion of provincial/regional workforce with post-primary education (ED2).

To reflect the development of land transportation, we added TRANS, an index for the density of the road-railway network (length of roads and railways per square kilometre).

Note that we also follow Démurger et al (2002), and divide the 20-year period of 1978 to 1998 into three sub-periods:

- Period 1 (1979-84): the first reform phase when the emphasis was on agriculture.
- Period 2 (1985-91): the second reform phase of market socialism reform, when the government attempted to operate the economy along the parallel (dual) tracks of a centrally planned socialist system and a market-based system.
- Period 3 (1992-98): the third reform phase after the top Communist leadership reached consensus that the ultimate goal of reform should be a (socialist) fully-fledged market economy with a substantially diversified ownership structure.

We expanded the models of Démurger et al (2002) to include several indices of city-size distribution in estimate (3):

(1) Pareto coefficient, which measures the disparity of city size distribution.
(2) CVMN and CVMED, which measure the degree of deviation of city system from Zipf's Law or rank-size rule.[4]

Estimated coefficients for the variables 1) should indicate whether a more evenly/unevenly distributed city system had been more favourable for growth during the periods under investigation. Based on the definitions of the two variables in (2), we expect that *a city-size distribution with a smaller deviation from the rank-size-rule pattern would be more conducive to market-oriented economic growth*. This implies that their estimated coefficients in the regression model would have negative signs.

This hypothesis about the relationship between city-size distribution and growth is based on the urban economics literature of industrial agglomeration (Marshall, 1890; Glaeser, 1997; Duranton and Puga, 2001, etc.). These economists interpret the statistical regularity found in the hierarchy of city systems as reflecting the degree of agglomeration that works best for firms and industries, and the kinds of benefits which agglomeration provides. Large metropolitan areas provide a large, diverse economic base for modern services and innovative industries that derive important benefits from such an environment. They therefore provide enough benefits to justify the high labour and land costs in these areas. In contrast, smaller urban areas are more lucrative bases for those industries with standardized products or services. With lower labour and land costs, smaller cities and towns tend to specialize in production of goods that are exported outside the city (World Bank, 1999: 126-128). Therefore the rank-size-rule pattern of city-size distribution arises from the natural complementarity that exists among cities of different sizes where resource allocation is determined by the division of labour according to the comparative advantages of large and small cities/towns.

To find the determinants of the changes in the Pareto coefficient and variables that measure the degree of deviation from the rank-size rule, these variables are regressed on exogenous variables used in (3). In addition to these variables, we designed EDEQ, an index for equality in educational opportunities between the urban and rural residents. The rationale for constructing this index arises from the observation that ED2, the proportion of provincial workforce that had a post-primary education, has a much higher correlation with URBAN than ED1, the proportion of the provincial/regional workforce that had only a primary education. In period 1985-91, the ED2-URBAN correlation was 0.75 while the ED1-URBAN correlation was only 0.44. The respective figures for the 1992-98 period were 0.82 and 0.44. The difference in their correlation with urbanization reflects the fact that urban residents have greater opportunities to complete post-primary education.

The following steps are required to construct the EDEQ index: First, we regress ED2 and ED1 on URBAN respectively. We then use the estimated models to project $\hat{ED}2$ and $\hat{ED}1$. The index is then constructed by finding the percentage difference between the projected ED2-to-ED1 ratio and the real ratio between the two:

$$EDEQ_i = \frac{\frac{ED2}{ED1}_i}{\frac{\hat{ED2}}{\hat{ED1}}_i} - 1 \tag{6}$$

This index therefore presents the relative abundance of post-primary educated labour supply that is not explained by national differences in urban-rural educational opportunities. In other words, a province/region with a positive EDEQ would have higher opportunities for post-primary education for its rural residents than the national average.

Results and Interpretation

Due to the unavailability of city size data for most provinces/regions before 1984, we had to skip the period 1978 to 1984. Regression results in Table 22.5 show that for both periods 1985-91 and 1992-98, the estimated coefficients of Pareto indices were negative, indicating that more evenly distributed city systems were more favourable to growth. This result, however, is only significant for the 1992 to 1998 years.

Table 22.4.   Effects of City-size Distribution on Economic Growth

1985-91	I			II			III		
Per Capita GDP	0.0242	1.11	*	0.0153	0.95		0.0221	1.05	
Policy	0.008	1.17	*	0.0107	2.14	***	0.0097	1.75	**
Pop100Cr	-0.0011	-0.1		-0.0004	-0.02		-0.0059	-0.46	
Agriculture share	0.6274	1.84	***	0.4574	1.73	**	0.6148	2.09	***
Squared Agri. share	-0.991	-1.82	***	-0.6292	-1.48	**	-0.9522	-2.03	***
SOE Share	0.0766	1.31	*	0.0447	0.84		0.0874	1.15	*
Land transport	-0.0101	-0.17		-0.0396	-0.71		-0.0144	-0.25	
Post-primary-education rate	-0.0089	-0.12		0.0748	1.05		0.004	0.05	
Pareto coefficient	-0.0143	-0.09							
Squared Pareto coefficient	-0.0129	-0.18							
Dummy for vicinity to metropolis				0.006	0.83		0.0049	0.32	
CVMN				-0.2159	-1.96	***			
CVMED							-0.0561	-0.93	
N	23			23			23		
F-Stat.	3.29			5.54			2.23		
R²	0.62			0.75			0.63		

Table 22.4. *cont'd.*

1992-98	I			II			III		
Per Capita GDP	-0.0199	*-1.36*	**	-0.0363	*-2.09*	***	-0.0225	*-1.42*	**
Policy	0.0111	*1.39*	**	0.0203	*2.17*	****	0.0147	*1.78*	***
Pop100Cr	0.0287	*2.87*	****	0.0451	*3.76*	*****	0.035	*3.4*	*****
Agriculture share	0.5305	*1.21*	*	0.9222	*2.35*	****	0.7631	*2.05*	***
Squared Agri. share	- 1.134	*-1.38*	**	-2.0356	*-2.53*	*****	-1.646	*-2.22*	****
SOE Share	-0.0564	*-1.06*		0.0995	*1.06*		0.0311	*0.43*	
Land transport	0.0518	*1.38*	**	0.0587	*1.64*	**	0.056	*1.66*	**
Post-primary-education rate	-0.0232	*-0.47*		0.0112	*0.27*		-0.0169	*-0.41*	
Pareto coefficient	-0.1111	*-1.92*	***						
Squared Pareto coefficient	-0.0448	*-1.83*	***						
Dummy for vicinity to Metropolis				0.007	*1.03*		0.0045	*0.68*	
CVMN				-0.1348	*-3.11*	*****			
CVMED							-0.0427	*-2.85*	****
N	23			23			23		
F-Stat.	20.57			72.72			35.9		
R²	0.86			0.9			0.89		

Notes: Estimates for intercepts are not displayed. Numbers in italic are t-statistics.
The three metropolises, Tibet, Ningxia, Qinghai and Hainan are not included.
Chongqing is included in Sichuan. "Pop100Cr", "land transport", and "policy"
are average values in the period while the rest are initial-year values.
***** 99% significant; **** 95% significant; *** 90% significant; ** 80% significant;
* 70% significant.

As for the two measurements of deviation from the rank-size rule,
CVMN and CVMED, their estimated coefficients for both periods were
negative, suggesting that the provinces/regions with city-size distribution

patterns closer to the rank-size rule tended to grow faster. This effect became more significant (at over 95% level) for both variables in the 1992-98 period. These findings confirm our earlier expectations regarding the signs of the coefficients for these two variables. Overall, the R-square values and estimates' significance are much higher for the period after 1992. This corresponds well with the fact that market mechanisms improved after China abandoned the two-track economic reform model.

The regression results in Table 22.5 shed some light on what might have helped reduce the provincial/regional deviations from Zipf's Law-defined city distribution. The education equality index EDEQ appeared to have a significant role in reducing the deviation over period 1992-98, but its role between 1985 and 1991 was ambiguous. The rate of post-primary education and the access to land transportation displayed some marginal effects on reducing the deviation. Preferential policies aimed at facilitating openness to foreign investment also made a significant impact between 1992 and 1998. Between 1985 and 1991, it appeared more difficult for the cities in provinces/regions with higher shares of state-owned enterprises to evolve closer to the Zipf's Law-distribution, but this was not the case from 1992 to 1998.

Table 22.5.   Determinants of Changes in City Distribution

Regress Changes of CVMN on	1985-91			1992-98		
Per Capita GDP	0.0535	0.52		0.0388	0.65	
Policy	-0.0029	-0.19		-0.0579	-2.25	****
Pop100Cr	0.0593	0.96		0.0031	0.07	
Agriculture share	0.2483	1.12	*	0.0965	0.39	
SOE Share	0.4226	1.46	**	-0.2054	-0.74	
Land transport	-0.0524	-0.23		-0.1692	-1.59	**
Post-primary-education rate	0.0508	0.12		-0.1631	-1.58	**
EDEQ	0.2399	1.83	***	-0.185	-2.38	****
CVMN(initial)	-1.6077	-4.13	*****	0.0126	0.1	
N	23			23		
F-Stat.	8.47			1.82		
R²	0.76			0.62		

Table 22.5. *cont'd.*

Regress Changes of CVMED on	1985-91			1992-98		
Per Capita GDP	0.0187	*0.12*		0.0201	*0.38*	
Policy	-0.0125	*-0.4*		-0.0415	*-1.56*	**
Pop100Cr	0.0594	*0.54*		-0.0179	*-0.46*	
Agriculture share	-0.2121	*-0.76*		0.2355	*0.94*	
SOE Share	0.7524	*2.13*	****	-0.2541	*-1.09*	*
Land transport	0.1261	*0.38*		-0.0781	*-0.75*	
Post-primary-education rate	-0.272	*-0.41*		-0.0429	*-0.44*	
EDEQ	0.0562	*0.31*		-0.1487	*-1.75*	***
CVMED(initial)	-0.0414	*-0.14*		-0.0026	*-0.05*	
N	23			23		
F-Stat.	3.16			2.78		
R²	0.4			0.61		

Note: Same as Table 22.4.

Policy Implications

With rapid industrialization, urbanization is an urgent challenge to China. According to literature cited by Zhu (1999), more than 200 'one million plus' cities (over six times the current number of such cities) would be needed to absorb the (conservative) estimate of 120-175 million rural surplus labour and their dependents. This illustrates the necessity for China to rely on the development of cities and towns of all sizes.

The speed and scale of China's urbanization is, however, still not sufficient to absorb this rural surplus labour. Qiu Xiaohua, head of China's State Statistics Bureau, also pointed out that China's current urbanization rate, based on international experience, should reach about 45% but it is in fact only 37.7%. The gap is equivalent to over 100 million residents.[5] According to China's National Economic Research Institute, one third of the rural labour force is surplus (or underemployed), and each employed farmer works only two-thirds of his available time. Meanwhile the employment rate in the rural areas is only 44%. If urbanization grows at the rate it did between 1989 and 1997, the country's urban population would increase by only 160 million in the first decade of the century, absorbing only 70 million rural labourers (Zhao, 2002).

In China's urbanization experience, government development strategies and policies have significantly affected the pace and pattern of urbanization. In the past, the state has played a pivotal role in China's urbanization process using the instruments listed below:

- state sponsored migration
- centrally planned allocation of investment funds
- household registration system
- rationing of basic consumer goods according to household registration
- criteria of city-town designation and state approval of city-town blue-plans
- control over degree of fiscal and governance autonomy at local levels.

Since the early 1980s, the economic reforms and development of market institutions have greatly changed the relative importance and availability of these instruments. State sponsored migration in recent years has been used only in some poverty alleviation projects and the construction of the Three-Gorge Dams. The centrally planned allocation of investment funds continues to be highly important. However, with non-state financial market institutions playing a greater role in allocating funds, they will increasingly act as "seed money" rather than full-package funding in urban-related projects. The household registration system largely remains intact despite discussion of its abandonment and modification at the local level. As the market-oriented reforms ushered China into an era of supply abundance for foods and other basic consumer goods, the rationing of these goods completely ended in the early 1990s. Changes in the criteria for city-town designation as well as further delegation of local authority were interrelated and together triggered the urbanization boom after 1980.

The changing role of the state over the last twenty years fundamentally changed the nature of China's urbanization. Since the early 1990s, a series of market-oriented reforms, especially the development of the urban property market, made urban growth more demand-driven, or "spontaneous", and less supply-driven or state planned. Despite this though, state and local governments are still key players in urban development.

What roles should the central and local governments play in a market-based economy and mainly demand-driven urbanization process? Based on the "unhappy record of past government efforts to prevent rural-urban migration, or to steer urban growth to particular locations", the World Bank (1999) warns against active national government roles in deciding locations for households and firms. Rather, it recommends that national governments play "a more useful function by working to provide an environment conducive to economic growth regardless of location" and "to provide a level playing field so that large and small cities and rural areas can compete fairly with each other" (World Bank, 1999: 131). The findings of this study are useful in China's regional policy with respect to urbanization. The main findings are summarized below:

First, the pre-reform regional strategy has left behind unusual patterns of urbanization across regions.

Second, provinces/regions with more evenly distributed cities tended to grow faster after 1985. Those with city-size distribution closer to the rank-size rule also tended to achieve higher growth.

Third, under-urbanization and inefficient city-size distribution are partially responsible for China's growing interregional development disparity in recent years.

Finally, better local land transportation infrastructure, greater openness to foreign trade and investment (through preferential policies), and greater education opportunities for all residents are found to make for speedier growth. Openness and education opportunities are also found to be helpful in creating a city-size distribution closer to the rank-size rule.

Based on these findings and the relevant literature reviewed in this paper, our policy recommendations consist of the following:

- National and local governments should make urbanization a priority in the development agenda. The central government, however, should take a **size-neutral** stand towards urbanization and allow greater development of "urbanization from below" by relaxing centrally imposed land use constraints.
- A mainly market- (demand-) driven pattern of urban growth can lead to more balanced growth of cities of all sizes and thus help less developed regions catch up. It is therefore important to allow households and firms greater locational choice. Reforms are needed to revamp the household registration system (*hukou*) to allow freer flow of labour force across regions and city-town boundaries.
- Reforms are also needed to ensure that international trade and investment policies (in terms of openness) would provide a level playing field for urban development across regions.
- Central and local governments can expedite demand-driven urbanization by public investment in urbanization-related infrastructure, such as transport facilities. Private funding can possibly be mobilized through municipal bonds and build-operate-transfer (BOT) contracts.
- The awarding of city-town designation to local authorities should be continued as it has proven effective in promoting *in situ* urbanization in coastal provinces. Local authorities should also be encouraged to experiment with various reforms that facilitate rural-urban capital-labour flows according to local conditions.
- One of the major obstacles preventing rural residents from engaging in the urbanization process is their lack of knowledge and training for non-agricultural jobs. More opportunities for post-primary education and vocational training are crucial for the smooth and successful urbanization of the rural population. This is one of the few areas in which government intervention is still able, and ought to play, a pivotal and helpful role.

- Lack of capital is another major obstacle for rural residents trying to develop businesses in non-agricultural sectors and migrate to urban areas. To break this institutional barrier in western China, perhaps legislation similar to the U.S. 1862 Homestead Act could grant the necessary initial property rights to qualified residents and serve to launch the process of capital accumulation in the rural private sector.

Notes

1. We would like to thank Bao Shuming for his assistance in data collection and Du Ping, Wang Xiaolu, Zhao Yaohui, Zhao Guoliang, and Chen Zhilong for their valuable comments. We are also thankful to Elspeth Thomson for editing the manuscript.
2. Goldstein classified China into 6 regions: East (Jiangsu, Zhejiang, Shanghai, Anhui, Jiangxi, Fujian, and Shandong), Central-South (Shanxi, Henan, Hubei, Hunan, Guangxi, and Guangdong), North (Inner Mongolia, Shanxi, Hebei, Beijing, and Tianjin), Northeast (Heilongjiang, Jilin, and Liaoning), Southwest (Tibet, Sichuan, Yunnan, and Guizhou), and Northwest (Xinjiang, Qinghai, Gansu, Ningxia, and Shaanxi).
3. See Lu and Tang (1997) for a detailed discussion on regional differences among these preferential policies. Ref. Démurger et al (2002) for the technique to construct the "policy" proxy.
4. Due to the smaller number of cities in less developed provinces/ regions, we had to estimate these variables based on the largest eight cities in each.
5. *Lianhe Zaobao* (United Morning Post, Singapore), 15 July 2002.

References

1. Ades, A. F. and E. L. Glaeser (1995). Trade and circuses: explaining urban giants. *Quarterly Journal of Economics*, 110: 195-227.

2. Alperovich, Gershon (1993). An explanatory model of city-size distribution: evidence from cross-country data. *Urban Studies,* 30 (9): 1591-1601.

3. Bao, Shuming, Gene Hsin Chang, Jeffrey D. Sachs, Wing Thye Woo (2002). Geographic factors and China's regional development under market reforms, 1978–1998. *China Economic Review* (13)1: 89-111.

4. Démurger, Sylvie, Jeffrey D. Sachs, Wing T. Woo, Shuming Bao, and Gene Chang (2002). The Relative Contributions of Location and Preferential Policies in China's Regional Development. *China Economic Review* 13 (4): 444-465.

5. Duranton, Gilles and Deigo Puga (2001). Nursery cities: urban diversity, process innovation, and the life cycle of products. *American Economic Review,* 91 (5): 1454-1471.

6. Fay, Marianne and Charlotte Opal (2000). Urbanization without growth: a not so uncommon phenomenon. *World Bank Policy Research Working Paper,* no. 2412.

7. Friedmann, J. (1972). A general theory of polarized development. In N. M. Hansen ed. *Growth Centres in Regional Economic Development.* New York: The Free Press, pp. 82-107.

8. Glaeser, Edward L. and Jesse Shapiro (2001). Is there a new urbanism: the growth of US cities in the 1990s. National Bureau of Economic Research, Working Paper 8357.

9. Goldstein, Sidney (1985). Urbanization in China: New Insights from the 1982 Census. Honolulu: Papers of the East-West Population Institute no. 93.

10. Hansen, N. (1990). Impacts of small and intermediate-sized cities on population distribution: issues and responses. *Regional Development Dialogue.* Spring 11: 60-76.

11. Heilbrun, James (1987). *Urban Economics and Public Policy.* New York: St. Martin's Press.

12. Henderson, J. Vernon (1988). *Urban Development: Theory, Fact, and Illustration.* New York and Oxford: Oxford University Press.

13. Henderson, J. Vernon (2001). The urbanization process and economic growth: the so-what question. Brown University working paper.

14. Jones, Gavin and Pravin Visaria (eds) (1997). *Urbanization in Large Developing Countries*. Oxford: Clarendon Press.
15. Kirkby, R. J. R. (1985). Urbanization in China: Town and Country in a Developing Economy 1949-2000 AD. New York: Columbia University Press.
16. Kwok, R. Yin-wang (1988). Metropolitan development in China: a struggle between contradictions. *Habitat International*, 12(4): 195-207.
17. Lu, Ding and Zhimin Tang (1997). State Intervention and Business in China: the Role of Preferential Policies. London: Edward Elgar.
18. Marshall, Alfred (1890). *Principles of Economics*. London: Macmillan.
19. Moomaw, R. and A. Shatter (1996). Urbanization and economic development: a bias toward large cities? *Journal of Urban Economics*, 40: 13-37.
20. Perkins, Dwight H. (1990). The influence of economic reforms on China's urbanization. In Kwok, R.Y., A. G. Yeh, and X. Xu eds. *Chinese Urban Reform: What Model Now?* New York and London: M.E. Sharpe, 78-106.
21. Pred, Allan Richard (1977). *City-systems in Advanced Economies*. New York: Halsted Press.
22. Rappaport, Jordan and Jeffrey D. Sachs (2001). The U.S. as a Coastal Nation. Research Division of Federal Reserve Bank of Kansas City, working paper RWP 01-11.
23. Renaud, B. (1981). *National Urbanization Policy in Developing Countries*. New York and Oxford: Oxford University Press.
24. Rosen, Kenneth T. and Mitchel Resnick (1980). The size distribution of cities: an examination of the Pareto law and primacy. *Journal of Urban Economics*, 8: 165-186.
25. Sachs, Jeffrey D. and Wing Thye Woo (1994). Structural factors in the economic reforms of China, Eastern Europe, and the Former Soviet Union. *Economic Policy* 18: 101-145.
26. Tian, Xiaowen (2001). Privatization and economic performance: evidence from Chinese provinces. *Economic Systems* 25 (1):1-13, 2001.
27. Williamson. J. (1965). Regional inequality and the process of national development. *Economic Development and Cultural Change*. June: 3-45.

28. World Bank (1983). *World Development Report 1983.* Washington DC: World Bank.
29. World Bank (1999). *World Development Report 1999 D 2000.* Washington DC: World Bank.
30. Zhao Yanqing (2002). *Jiasu chengshihua shi jingji fazhan de xuyao* (Speeding urbanization is necessary for economic development), *Renmin Wenzhai (People's Digest)*, no. 5, http://www.people.com.cn/GB/paper2086.
31. Zhou, Yixing (1997). *Chengshi Dilixue (Urban Geography*, in Chinese). Beijing: Commerce Press.
32. Zhu, Yu (1999). New Paths to Urbanization in China: Seeking More Balanced Patterns. New York: Nova Science Publications, Inc.

23 China's Regional Disparities in 1978–2000

Zhigang Lu and Shunfeng Song

Introduction

For the past two decades, China's economic reforms have successfully improved its economic performance. During the period of 1978-2000, the Chinese economy achieved high growth rates in almost every aspect of economic indicators, including an average annual increase of 9.6 % in GNP and 8.3 % in per capita GNP (*China Statistical Year Book* 2001). As one of the major reform measures, the open door policy has promoted China's economic relationship with foreign countries and increased foreign trade and investment activities. Again, from 1978 to 2000, China's export increased from about 4.6 % of its GNP to about 23.38 % of the GNP, and the amount of foreign direct investment jumped from less than one billion to more than 40 billion U.S. dollars. People's livelihood improved remarkably. Real per capita income increased at an average annual rate of 8.4 % from 1980 to 2000. The shortages of consumer goods that existed in urban and rural markets before 1980 were remedied, and personal savings rose more than 5 times over the decade in real terms.

These improvements, however, are accompanied by an uneven development in China's different regions. In a large country with a diversity of local endowments, regional disparities in the course of growth and development are inevitable. Those regions influenced by the new market activities have experienced more rapid development than those still controlled by the state activities. An earlier study (Hu, 1996) showed that during 1979-1992 Guangdong recorded the highest average GDP growth, with 13.3%, followed by Zhejiang, with 12.5%, Fujian, with 11.6%, Shandong, Jiansu and Xinjiang, all with 11.1%, and Hainan with 12.0% (1987-1992). The lowest GDP growth was registered in Heilongjiang, which was 6.0%, followed by Qianghai, with 6.2%. A divergent pattern of regional development emerged.

There is a widespread concern in China that market-oriented economic reforms, though improving economic efficiency, may increase inter-provincial inequalities. The increasing economic disparities among China's regions may result in rising regionalism and the possibility of social and political instability. Rising regionalism in China has to do with the increase of local political autonomy during the post-Mao reform years. It has already been evidenced by the fact that many Chinese provinces have developed their own economic trading partners with various external regions and countries, such as Guangdong and Hong Kong, Fujian and Taiwan, Northeast China and the Russian Far East, Xinjiang and the Turkic republics, and Yunan and Burma and Thailand. In the long run, rising regionalism could be a hidden bomb to China's political integration. Increasing inequality may cause China's political and social instability.

This paper investigates regional disparities in China for the period of 1978-2000. It has three main contributions. First, the paper updates empirical evidence in previous studies on China's regional disparities by using various disparity measures (Jian *et al*, 1996; Tsui, 1996). Second, the paper aims to better understand the relationship between post-1978 reform policies and regional economic growth. Third, the paper uses a statistical analysis to determine factors that affect regional growth in the reform years.

An Examination of Regional Disparity in China

To evaluate China's regional disparities during the reform years, this study first examines regional economic development by focusing on the comparison of two economic indicators between China's three regions (the coastal, the central, and the western) in three different years (1980, 1990 and 2000). The indicators and years selected are based on the consideration of the importance and the availability of data. Measuring different aspects of economic performance, the two economic indicators are gross domestic product (GDP) and consumption expenditure. GDP is used to evaluate the regional economy as a whole. Consumption expenditure is used to evaluate both regional economy and people's livelihood.

Table 23.1 provides information on GDP in different regions and provinces. It shows that the share of national GDP for the coastal region increased from 52.23 % in 1980 to 54.01 % in 1990 and 59.40 % in 2000, while it decreased from 31.14 % to 28.89 % and 27.02 % for the central region, and from 16.63 % to 16.10 and 13.58 % for the western region. Among provinces, Table 23.1 shows that most provinces in the coastal region had increased shares of the national GDP but most provinces in both the central and the western regions had decreased their shares.

The consumption expenditure in Table 23.2 reveals a similar pattern. The coastal region increased its share from 48.85 % in 1980 to 51.54 % in 1990 and 54.37 % in 2000, while both the central and western regions decreased their shares. From 1980 to 2000, the central region decreased its shares by 4.51 percentage points, and the western region decreased its shares by 1.02 percentage points. Among provinces, Table 23.2 shows that most provinces in the coastal region increased their shares of the national consumption expenditure between 1980 and 2000, while most provinces in the central and western regions decreased their shares.

Table 23.1.   GDP by Regions and Provinces, 1980, 1990, and 2000

Region/Province	1980		1990		2000	
National	4395.87	100%	18329.4	100%	97209.37	100%
Coastal	2295.76	52.23	9898.83	54.01	57739.72	59.40
Beijing	139.07	3.16	500.82	2.73	2478.76	2.55
Fujian	87.06	1.98	523.3	2.85	3920.07	4.03
Guangdong	245.71	5.59	1471.84	8.03	9662.23	9.94
Guangxi	97.33	2.21	449.06	2.45	2050.14	2.11
Hainan	19.33	0.44	102.49	0.56	518.48	0.53
Hebei	219.24	4.99	896.33	4.89	5088.96	5.24
Jiangsu	319.8	7.28	1416.5	7.73	8582.73	8.83
Liaoning	281	6.39	1061.91	5.79	4669.06	4.80
Shandong	292.13	6.65	1511.19	8.24	8542.44	8.79
Shanghai	311.89	7.10	756.45	4.13	4551.15	4.68
Tianjin	103.52	2.35	310.95	1.70	1639.36	1.69
Zhejiang	179.68	4.09	897.99	4.90	6036.34	6.21

Table 23.1. *cont'd.*

Region/Province	1980		1990		2000	
Central	1369.08	31.14	5479.2	29.89	26266.18	27.02
Anhui	140.88	3.20	658.02	3.59	3038.24	3.13
Heilongjiang	221.04	5.03	715.23	3.90	3253	3.35
Henan	229.16	5.21	934.65	5.10	5137.66	5.29
Hubei	199.38	4.54	824.38	4.50	4276.32	4.40
Hunan	191.72	4.36	744.44	4.06	3691.88	3.80
Inner Mongolia	68.4	1.56	319.31	1.74	1401.01	1.44
Jiangxi	111.15	2.53	428.62	2.34	2003.07	2.06
Jilin	98.59	2.24	425.28	2.32	1821.19	1.87
Shanxi	108.76	2.47	429.27	2.34	1643.81	1.69
Western	731.03	16.63	2951.37	16.10	13203.47	13.58
Gansu	73.9	1.68	242.8	1.32	983.36	1.01
Guizhou	60.26	1.37	260.14	1.42	993.53	1.02
Ningxia	15.96	0.36	64.84	0.35	265.57	0.27
Qinghai	17.79	0.40	69.94	0.38	263.59	0.27
Shaanxi	94.91	2.16	374.05	2.04	1660.92	1.71
Sichuan	322.03	7.33	1186.22	6.47	5599.59	5.76
Tibet	8.67	0.20	27.7	0.15	117.46	0.12
Xinjiang	53.24	1.21	274.01	1.49	1364.36	1.40
Yunan	84.27	1.92	451.67	2.46	1955.09	2.01

Notes: (1) figures are based on current prices, 100 million *yuan*.
(2) Chongqing was separated from Sichuan in 1996; in this paper figures about Chongqing are added to Sichuan Province.
Source: State Statistics Bureau (1996, 2001).

The economic indicators evaluated in Tables 23.1-2 provide empirical evidence that the coastal region developed faster than the interior regions after the open-door policy announced in 1978, the industrial reform started in 1984, and Deng's south tour in 1992. To further evaluate regional disparities in China, we use both per capita output and livelihood indicators in the following analyses. The output indicator is per capita GDP. Livelihood indicators include per capita income and per capita consumption.

Table 23.2.   Consumption by Regions and Provinces

Region/Province	1980		1990		2000	
National	2576.39	100%	11578.58	100%	52421.2	100%
Coastal	1258.45	48.85	5967.49	51.54	28502.76	54.37
Beijing	57.44	2.23	230.96	1.99	1221.33	2.33
Fujian	67.91	2.64	376.65	3.25	2052.41	3.92
Guangdong	177.47	6.89	831.3	7.18	5336.22	10.18
Guangxi	77.79	3.02	346.68	2.99	1443.17	2.75
Hainan	19.1	0.74	66.29	0.57	284.51	0.54
Hebei	114.68	4.45	518.86	4.48	2240.68	4.27
Jiangsu	175.47	6.81	717.36	6.20	3710.72	7.08
Liaoning	157.43	6.11	1062.74	9.18	2587.52	4.94
Shandong	188.26	7.31	807.32	6.97	4099.74	7.82
Shanghai	81.24	3.15	316.8	2.74	1947.10	3.71
Tianjin	39.62	1.54	143.68	1.24	804.71	1.54
Zhejiang	102.04	3.96	548.85	4.74	2774.65	5.29
Central	867.59	33.67	3499.96	30.23	15285.46	29.16
Anhui	119.12	4.62	433.77	3.75	1947.78	3.72
Heilongjiang	132.25	5.13	435.91	3.76	1871.54	3.57
Henan	151.48	5.88	522.43	4.51	2758.60	5.26
Hubei	107.79	4.18	535.49	4.62	2146.54	4.09
Hunan	136.94	5.32	564.7	4.88	2383.27	4.55
Inner Mongolia	62.07	2.41	216.7	1.87	787.21	1.50
Jiangxi	81.02	3.14	310.12	2.68	1269.58	2.42
Jilin	76.92	2.99	279.73	2.42	1174.91	2.24
Shanxi			201.11	1.74	946.04	1.80
Western	450.35	17.48	2111.13	18.23	8632.98	16.47
Gansu	53.77	2.09	170.2	1.47	579.21	1.10
Guizhou	48.71	1.89	189.91	1.64	775.25	1.48
Ningxia	12.81	0.50	47.87	0.41	186.63	0.36
Qinghai	13.63	0.53	53.79	0.46	167.31	0.32
Shaanxi			300.64	2.60	956.45	1.82
Sichuan	213.52	8.29	841.53	7.27	3520.26	6.72
Tibet			20.05	0.17	66.16	0.13
Xinjiang	44.56	1.73	188.17	1.63	899.90	1.72
Yunan	63.35	2.46	298.97	2.58	1481.81	2.83

Notes: (1) Figures are based on current prices, 100 million *yuan*.
 (2) Chongqing was separated from Sichuan in 1996; in this paper figures about Chongqing are added to Sichuan Province.

Source: State Statistics Bureau (1996, 2001).

Table 23.3 shows the distribution of per capita GDP among three regions. In 1980, the per capita GDP for the three regions was 818.17, 409.41, and 369.78 *yuan*, respectively for the coastal, central, and western regions. The per capita GDP for the coastal region was twice of that for the central region and 2.21 times of that for the western region. In 2000, the per capita GDP for the three regions became 13698.08, 6045.22, and 4733.67 *yuan*, respectively. The per capita GDP for the coastal region became 2.27 times of that for the central region and 2.89 times of that for the western region. These results suggest an increasing economic gap between the coastal and interior regions between 1980 and 2000.

Table 23.3.   Relative Disparity among Coastal, Central, and Western Regions

Indicator	Year	Coastal	Central	Western	Coastal/ Central	Coastal/ Western
Per capita GDP	1980	818.17	409.41	369.78	2.00	2.21
	1990	2483.00	1440.51	1278.67	1.72	1.94
	2000	13698.08	6045.22	4733.67	2.27	2.8
Per capita income of urban area	1980	512.13	410.09	428.58	1.25	1.19
	1990	1801.96	1312.19	1512.03	1.37	1.19
	2000	7732.86	5191.07	5673.86	1.49	1.3
Per capita income of rural area	1980	248.25	189.95	171.56	1.31	1.45
	1990	936.22	640.71	553.46	1.46	1.69
	2000	3341.45	2070.66	1531.28	1.61	2.1
Per capita consumption of urban area	1980	557.18	422.60	604.90	1.32	0.92
	1990	1700.87	1235.51	1520.19	1.38	1.12
	2000	6011.93	4140.61	4610.90	1.45	1.30
Per capita consumption of rural area	1980	236.59	217.10	146.10	1.09	1.62
	1990	809.06	624.56	485.50	1.30	1.67
	2000	2337.03	1515.13	1237.39	1.54	1.89

Source: State Statistics Bureau (various years)

To have more precise pictures, we use both urban and rural data on per capita income and consumption. Due to the unavailability of data, some provinces are missing in our calculation. By using urban income data, Table 23.3 shows that in 1980 the per capita income for the coastal region was 1.25 times of that for the central region and 1.19 times of that for the western region. In 1990, these ratios changed to 1.37 and 1.19, respectively. In 2000, the two ratios increased to 1.49 and 1.36. Using rural income data, Table 23.3 shows that in 1980 the per capita income for coastal region was 1.31 times of that for the central region and 1.45 times of that for the western region. Both ratios increased to 1.46 and 1.69 in 1990, and 1.61 and 2.08 in 2000. These findings suggest a bigger income gap between the coastal and interior regions, especially for rural areas.

Table 23.4.   Per Capita Income and Consumption between Rural and Urban Residents

Year	Income			Consumption		
	Urban	Rural	U/R	Urban	Rural	U/R
1985	397.6	739.1	1.86	776.38	346.26	2.24
1986	423.8	899.6	2.12	925.93	371.16	2.49
1987	462.6	1002.2	2.17	1079.81	413.87	2.61
1988	544.9	1181.4	2.17	1398.99	505.79	2.77
1989	601.5	1375.7	2.29	1541.95	550.73	2.80
1990	686.3	1510.2	2.20	1667.89	547.09	3.05
1991	708.6	1700.6	2.40	1893.69	618.87	3.06
1992	784.0	2026.6	2.58	2327.54	715.29	3.25
1993	921.6	2577.4	2.80	2966.6	853.53	3.48
1994	1221.0	3496.2	2.86	3885.48	1137.74	3.4
1995	1577.7	4283.0	2.71	3537.57	1310.36	2.70
1996	1926.1	4838.9	2.51	3919.47	1572.08	2.49
1997	2090.1	5160.3	2.47	4185.64	1617.15	2.59
1998	2162.0	5425.1	2.51	4331.61	1590.33	2.72
1999	2210.3	5854.0	2.65	4615.91	1577.42	2.93
2000	2253.4	6280.0	2.79	4998	1670.13	2.99

Source: State Statistics Bureau (1996, 2001).

Table 23.3 also shows a regional disparity in per capita consumption among the three regions. Specifically, in 1980, the per capita consumption of urban residents in the coastal region was 1.32 and 0.92 times of that for central and western regions, respectively. Both ratios increased to 1.38 and 1.18 in 1990, and 1.45 and 1.30 in 2000. Table 23.3 shows that in 1980 the per capita consumption of rural residents in the coastal region was 1.09 and 1.62 times of that for central and western regions. In 1990 and 2000, both ratios increased to 1.30 and 1.67, and 1.54 and 1.89 respectively. No doubt, the gap of per capita consumption between the coastal and interior regions grew larger. Also, the gap of per capita consumption for rural residents is larger than the gap for urban residents among regions.

The issue of unequal regional development was further complicated when relating it to inequalities between China's rural and urban areas. The focus of this paper is to examine regional disparities. We are not attempting to have detailed literature on the urban-rural divide. However, it is helpful to provide a simple comparison of per capita income and consumption between farmers and urban residents. Table 23.4 shows income and consumption distributions between rural and urban residents from year 1985 to 2000. With regard to per capita income, it is clear that the ratios between urban residents and rural peasants started as 1.86 times in 1985 but increased to 2.79 times in 2000. The ratios of per capita consumption between urban and rural residents started as 2.24 times in 1985 but increased to 2.99 times in 2000. These findings indicate that urban-rural divide has been also enlarged.

To examine the trends of regional disparities in China, this paper applies two commonly used statistical measures: coefficient of variation (CV) and the Gini coefficient. In both cases, a larger coefficient indicates a greater regional disparity. Data used in our calculation come from various statistical yearbooks and China Regional Economy: A Profile of 17 Years of Reform and Opening Up, published by China Statistics Press. We use annual provincial level data for the period of 1978-2000.

Figure 23.1 presents the CV values of per capita GDP. It displays a downward trend from 1978 to 1990 and an upward trend after 1990. Chen and Fleisher (1996) argued that the tendency for measures of regional inequality to increase after 1990 is due to a widening of the gap between coastal and non-coastal provinces during this period. Figure 23.2 plots the CV values of per capita income for urban and rural areas. The overall trend after 1978 is evidently positive. We observe that over the period the income inequality in rural areas is larger than that in urban areas. Figure 23.3 plots CV values of per capita consumption for urban and rural areas. The two curves both display upward trends over the period of 1978-2000. Similar to the income pattern, we observe that the consumption disparity in rural areas is larger than that in urban areas. Figures 23.4-6 plot Gini coefficients for per capita GDP, urban and rural per capita income and consumption. Our calculated Gini coefficients show similar patterns as those in Figures 23.1-3, confirming the findings reached by coefficients of variation.

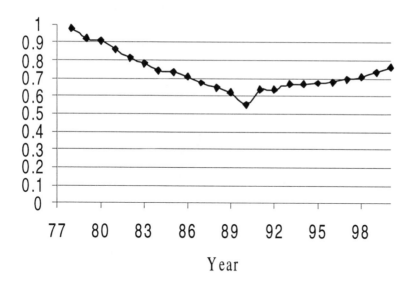

Figure 23.1.   CV of Per Capita GDP

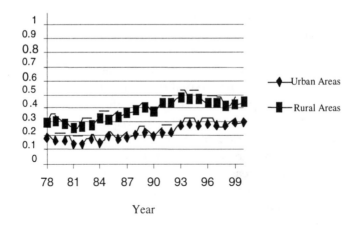

Figure 23.2. CV Values of Per Capita Income (Urban and Rural Areas)

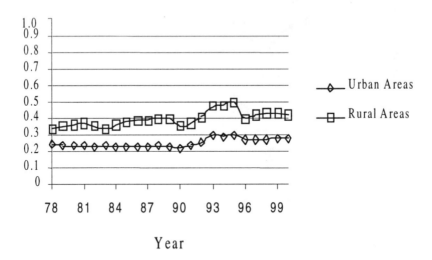

Figure 23.3. CV Values of Per Capita Consumption (Urban and Rural Areas)

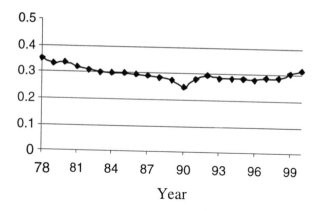

Figure 23.4.   Gini Coefficients of Per Capita GDP

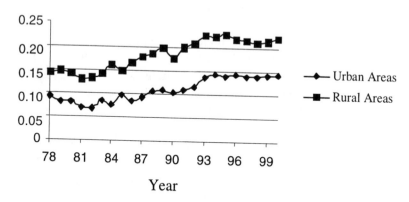

Figure 23.5. Gini Coefficients of Per Capita Income (Urban and Rural Areas)

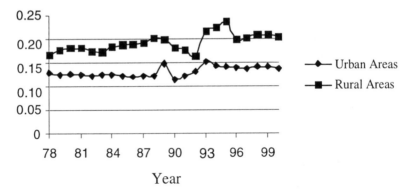

Figure 23.6. Gini Coefficients of Per Capita Consumption (Urban and Rural Areas)

The above different measures reveal that both inter-provincial and coastal-interior disparities in both output and livelihood indicators were widening. Three significant phenomena can be identified in the change in regional disparities: (1) a narrowing of inter-provincial output disparity from 1978 to 1990 and a widening of inter-provincial output disparity after 1990 (Figures 23.1 and 23.4), (2) a widening of inter-provincial livelihood disparity (Figures 23.2-23.3 and Figures 23.5-23.6), (3) a widening of coastal interior disparity in both output and livelihood indicators of development (Table 23.3). Overall, regional divergence appeared in China after 1990.

The issue of regional and income inequalities is especially important to the future fate of the reforms. One of the major policies emphasized in the success of economic development is the social equity policy. The social equity policy attempts to reduce the social adversity imposed by various inequalities (e.g., regional, class, or ethnic) and to affect the distribution of income resulting from economic growth. With regard to the Chinese experience, the emphasis on the impact of regional development has to do with the issue of whether China will stay united or break up because of increasing inequalities and regionalism.

A Policy Analysis of Uneven Regional Development

Both the tendency toward convergence and that toward divergence are due to the fact that some regions developed faster than others. The former implies that the faster developing are relatively backward regions; the latter implies that the faster developing are relatively advanced ones. No matter what kind of regions develop faster, a fundamental question remains: what lead some regions to develop faster than others? In other words, what are the sources of uneven regional development? Before we answer the question, it is crucial that we have a review on China's regional development policy before and after the reform years.

Traditional Development Policy

Traditional regional development in China was imbalanced between the country's interior and coastal regions. The coastal region covers a small area of land; it accounts for only 11.1% of the total land area of China. However, the population of the region accounts for over 37 % of the national total. With respect to the utilization of land resources, the index of reclamation and cultivation of land in the coastal areas is a very high 27.89% (Sun, 1988). In terms of major mineral and energy resources, the coastal region is poor, but it has rich resources of petroleum and iron ore. The imbalanced development stemmed from such economic and geographical factors as the long distance between the industrial production areas (mainly in the coastal region) and the raw material supply areas (mainly in the interior region). From the market consideration, the imbalance also was related to the fact that there is more concentration of human and financial resources in the eastern, coastal region than in the western, interior region. China's modern industry first developed and became concentrated along the coast. As a result, transport and communications in the region were well developed, and many cities possess considerable technical know-how. The degree of intensive farming and mechanization is also comparatively high.

To achieve a balanced development and to mitigate the difference between the coastal and the interior regions, the Chinese government emphasized and adopted a centrally directed investment in the interior region before open door reforms. The cornerstone of the strategies prior to the open door period had been a fundamental concern with regional self-sufficient and the creation of a self-reliant socialist economy, in which small and medium size cities were favoured over large ones, and "productive" cities over "consumptive" cities. The result was that the focus of state investment shifted further and further westwards from the early 1950s to the late 1970s. In his study of China's regional development, Yang (1998) estimated that, between 1953 and 1980, the Chinese government distributed about 60% of the country's investment in fixed assets in the interior region. The investment in the interior region ranged from 56 % in the First FiveYear Plan (1953-1957), to 60% in the Second Five Year Plan (1958-1962), to 71% in the Third Five Year Plan (1966-1970), and finally to 61% and 55% in the Fourth (1971-1975) and Fifth (1976-1980) Five Year Plans, respectively.

While emphasizing political and military considerations, the interior-oriented balanced development policy was inefficient from the economic point of view. From the ownership perspective, for example, the state's administrative organizations had taken the place of economic organization and the enterprises had become subsidiaries of the administrative organs of the state at all levels. This form of ownership was susceptible to the creation of bureaucratism, commandism, blind leadership, and "doing things in accordance with the wishes of higher-rank government officials". It also discouraged labours enthusiasm of production, the incentive to make suggestions, and the responsibility to take good care of properties in their enterprises. It is thus not surprising that the interior regions continued to develop more slowly than the coastal region, despite the tremendous resources invested by the central government. The traditional development policy intended to improve the equity distribution of China's industrial facilities and to promote even development among regions. But it was not economically efficient. The Chinese economy would have grown more rapidly if development policies were based on economic efficiency.

The New Regional Development Policy

One of the earliest reforms of the post-Mao period was the open door policy, which greatly expanded China's economic connections with the rest of the world. The period of 1978-2000 can be depicted as a more or less transitional one while progress was made from a centrally planned economic system towards a socialist market economy. Economic efficiency became a priority in China's regional development strategy, albeit with due regard also to equality of growth. To promote economic efficiency, the post-Mao reform leaders have gradually replaced the traditional balanced development policy and the interior-oriented strategy with a new, uneven, and coastal-oriented development policy. The uneven development policy allows differential development among different regions and especially gives preferential policies to the coastal region. The reformers believe that the faster development of the coastal region will become the engine of China's growth and eventually lead to the development in other regions.

Since its emphasis in 1978, the development of China's coastal areas has lasted more than a decade and extended from several isolated cities to most areas of the eastern, coastal region. The coastal development strategy is basically a two-tier combination of imported growth and exported expansion. The imported growth attempts to strengthen China's capability for obtaining advanced technology and capital, while the exported expansion is targeted to make China a global economic power. The major policy elements addressed in the coastal development strategy are (1) development of an export-oriented and labour intensive economy in the coastal region, (2) emphasis on the two principles embodied in the slogans "putting both ends (sourcing and marketing) toward the global marketplace" and "importing more (raw materials) and exporting more (products)", (3) assistance to foreign enterprises in exercising their managerial authority with regard to their operation and profits and losses, and (4) development of township enterprises to promote the regions' urban and rural development (Tzeng, 1991). Local and regional governments in the coastal areas have more authority and flexibility in setting their tax rates in order to attract investment (Song et al, 2000). The result of the coast oriented development strategy and policy is that both domestic and international investments in the coastal region have increased dramatically in the 1980s. The new, increased investments and the traditional superiority in technology, management, research and development in the coastal region have increased the region's share of the national growth since the mid 1980s.

Answer to the Question

What are the sources of uneven regional development? We identify in this research three main sources: technology catch-up advantage, policy advantage, and the functioning of market mechanisms. From our earlier analysis, the inter-provincial output disparity indicates a tendency toward convergence in 1978-1990, implying that backward provinces grew faster than more advanced ones in early reform years. We argue here that this is the most important reason for this is so-called "technology catch-up". That is, backward regions have an advantage in imitating and absorbing technology invented in advanced regions. The rationale lying behind the "technology catch-up" argument is that it is less costly to imitate and absorb a technology than to invent it. Since 1978, there has been inter-sectoral technology transfer from the military to the civilian sector, interregional transfers from the urban to rural areas, and above all, international transfers from abroad. The smaller the snowball is, the easier to double it. The divergence after 1990, however, may suggest a "saturated catch-up". The more advanced provinces may regain their faster developing steps because of other advantages they are holding, such as their access to foreign markets and attractiveness to foreign investors.

After 1990, our earlier analysis showed a tendency toward divergence: initially advanced coastal regions develop faster than initially backward interior ones. We argue that policy advantages enjoyed by coastal regions are largely responsible for this. After China opened up in 1978, its increasing economic contacts with foreign countries had to be carried out through coastal regions. Especially since the centre of gravity of the world economy shifted from the Atlantic to the Asia Pacific, coastal regions have become increasingly important in China's outward-looking socialist development strategy. This is reinforced by the close ties of coastal regions with overseas Chinese communities, especially with Hong Kong, Macau, and Taiwan. Between November 1987 and February 1988, Deng Xiaoping inspected developments along the coast in Jiangsu, Zhejiang, and Fujian Provinces. His message was direct:

Economic development in China's coastal areas is making the best use of good opportunities. Due to rises in labour costs, the developed world has been readjusting its industrial setup, and moving labour-intensive industries to places where labour costs are low. In this process, China's coastal areas are attractive since they have low-paid but fairly skilled labour, good transport facilities and infrastructure, and very importantly, a good scientific and technological development potential. So long as they do well, China's coastal areas should be able to secure sizable foreign investment (*Beijing Review*, 1988).

Soon after 1978, the Chinese government began to give a high priority to coastal regions in economic policymaking. In 1980, the government decided to establish four special economic zones (SEZs) in Guangdong and Fujian provinces, and gave them special policy treatments in relation to terms of foreign investment, arrangements of foreign trade, tax exemptions, and so on. In 1984, similar policy treatments were extended to 14 coastal cities, and a number of "economic and technological development districts" (ETDD) were established. Between 1985 and 1988, these policies were extended to other coastal cities and counties, and the "Hainan special economic zone" took shape. Not until 1992 were the policies extended to some of the interior regions. The policy advantages allowed coastal regions greater access to world markets than their interior counterparts, and have no doubt contributed to China's uneven regional development, and thereby to the widening coastal-interior disparity in the reform years.

The functioning of market mechanisms also affects regional development because it indicates not only the changing macro environment of China's transition to a market system or China's opening up to market forces but also the ability of individual regions to adapt to the transition or opening process. In labour-surplus developing countries undergoing a transition or opening process like China, the functioning of market mechanisms contributes to uneven regional development in many ways, but three of them are the most important. The first is the increase in market demand. Increasing market demand can lead to improved efficiency in resource utilization in labour-surplus developing countries and, therefore, can have a considerable impact upon regional economic growth. In other words, regional growth heavily depends upon whether a region can increase market demand for the commodities it produces. The second is uneven sector growth and the ensuing structural change introduced by market mechanisms through uneven resource allocation. The introduction of market mechanisms in post-1978 China brought about increasingly free flows of resources between sections. Uneven changes in market demand and competition have led to resource flows away from less efficient primary industry and state-owned enterprises. The improved efficiency in resource allocation and utilization has contributed significantly to China's growth, and must have a great impact on regional economic growth. To an extent, the speed with which a regional economy grows depends heavily on the extent to which market mechanisms lead to uneven sectoral growth and the ensuing structural change through resource reallocation in the regional economy concerned. The third is increasing regional autonomy and the corresponding relaxation of government intervention in regional income redistribution. Market oriented reforms triggered increasing competition between regions, and thereby led to increased regional autonomy and the corresponding relaxation of government intervention in regional income redistribution. Although the increasing regional autonomy and the relaxation of government intervention in regional income redistribution facilitated the economic growth of some regions, they inevitably hurt the regions which enjoyed subsidies from the central government in the previous period, and therefore led to widening regional disparities, especially in livelihood indicators of development.

A Growth Model: An Empirical Investigation

This section employs a growth framework for transition or opening economies to capture key mechanisms of China's growth. The growth framework is specified first, and then tested against China's growth performance in the period of 1978-2000.

Model Specification

In the growth literature, the Solow model is mostly used. It can be written as

$$\Delta Y/Y = \Delta L/L + \Delta K/K + \Delta A/A$$

where Y changes with variations in an economy's capital (K) and labour (L) inputs. The equation indicates that output growth depends on labour growth, plus capital growth and technical progress. The relationship between inputs and output, for a given state of technology, is summarized in the production function $Y = AF(K, L)$, where A denotes technology.

The Solow model, however, may not be appropriate to evaluate the economic growth in China. In this paper, we specify a net-effect growth model developed by Tian (1997). The theoretical framework of the model can be expressed mathematically as

$$\Delta Y = F(\Delta I, \Delta E)$$

where Y stands for GDP, I for various inputs such as labour, physical capital and human capital, E for efficiency in input allocation and utilization introduced by domestic as well as international market mechanisms. Δ stands for net increase, so and $\Delta Y = Y_t - Y_{t-1}$, $\Delta I = I_t - I_{t-1}$, and $\Delta E = E_t - E_{t-1}$. Economic growth thus is assumed to take place because either various inputs are increased or efficiency in input allocation and utilization is improved, or both. Better allocation of existing resources or improved utilization of existing resources would be thought of as productivity increases.

The distinction between the Solow model and net-effect model can be understood in the following points. First, the concept of growth in Solow model is different from the changes in GDP that an economy experiences due to fluctuations in aggregate demand during the business cycle. China is a developing country, and is experiencing a transition period. What determines economic growth is not only the supply side (especially various inputs such as labour, physical and human capital) but also the demand side (including both domestic and international markets).

Secondly, the Solow model focuses on long-run economic growth. This relates to the expansion of an economy's productive capacity, which is considered relatively constant from year to year, independent of fluctuations in aggregate demand and GDP. This can be shown graphically by an expansion in the *production possibilities frontier* and by a rightward shift in the aggregate supply curve. China is a labour-surplus developing country with enormous unemployment and underemployment, the long run supply curve is not vertical. If market demand increases due to non-price determinants (such as increase in disposable income, expansion of foreign trade), the market demand curve shall shift outward, and the economy shall be led to make fuller use of its resources than before to meet the rising demand. In that case, no matter whether the supply curve remains constant or is pulled outward, the aggregate supply (GDP) increases, and the output growth of the economy is thus accelerated.

Thirdly, Solow model is overshadowed by an "accumulative effect" since a net increase has to be divided by a previously accumulated level $(\Delta x/x)$. The net-increase model is accumulative effect free. We only consider the net increase (Δx). Underlying the "net-increase effect" argument is an assumption that what has an effect on net increase in GDP is ultimately the net increase in, rather than the previous accumulated level of, all the contributing factors. Experiments show that growth rate effect estimation is very sensitive to the previously accumulated level of the right hand variables. Since China experienced major policy shifts after 1978, we would not want to be affected by the previous accumulation of different variables. We are interested in what are really behind the net increase of output. Net increase effect estimation is highly recommended in our growth modeling.

Fourthly, the assumptions of degrees of government intervention in Solow model and net-increase model can be different. In Solow model, with economic foundations based on the role of markets, a theory generally free of outside intervention, and emphasizing the role of production in determining income and economic output. The government should play a minimal role in determining the condition of the economy. The government does have an important place in areas such as providing a legal framework, preventing abuses of the market, and to sustain national defence. However, extensive government intervention will hinder the efficient operation of the market in the determination of prices of goods and services and the allocation of resources towards their production. China is a developing country in transition period. In developing countries undergoing a strategic change like China, the development of domestic and foreign markets is not only a measure of the increase in efficiency but also a measure of the success of government policy reforms. In other words, China is a government policy – oriented economy. Good government policies and intervention measures should be directed to the correction of market failures and the provision of necessary legal, social, and physical infrastructure to ensure making full use of market mechanisms. In this case, net-increase is a good choice to evaluate dramatic changes of economy because of any policy change.

It should be noted that the assumption of government intervention should not be held against the assumption of major role of market mechanism in our net-effect model. Market mechanisms increase efficiency also by reallocating resources from sectors with lower productivity to sectors with higher productivity, and thereby output produced by the same amount of resources increases. This is especially true of developing countries where there exists a significant productivity gap between primary and non-primary industry due to enormous rural surplus labour, as is the case of China. This is also especially true of transition or opening economies where there exists a significant productivity gap between state-owned and non-state-owned enterprises due to previous adverse government intervention, as is the case of China. Resource flows between these sectors mean that they are efficiently utilized, and that output produced by available resources increases substantially.

Finally, technology changes in both Solow model and net-increase are assumed to be exogenous, or outside the influences of change in capital and labour inputs. Technology is also assumed to have a positive correlation with output; technological improvements lead to higher levels of output, Y, given capital and labour inputs. As a result, better technology, such as improvements in the quality of the existing capital stock, makes the labour inputs more productive and increases the output per worker (with a fixed supply of labour and capital).

To apply the net-increase effect model to China, a set of panel data was collected which covers all the thirty provinces and metropolitan cities in China for a period of seventeen years from 1978 to 2000. The increase in inputs is divided into three divisions: the increase in labour input (ΔL), the increase in physical capital input (ΔPc), and the increase in human capital input (ΔHc), which are measured respectively by the increase in the number of labourers employed, the new investment in fixed assets, and the new government expenditures on culture, education, science and health care. The increase in efficiency introduced by market mechanisms is divided into two divisions: the increase in efficiency through increased domestic market orientation (ΔDm) and the increase in efficiency through increased international market orientation (ΔIm), which are measured by the increase in the total value of retail sales and the increase in the total value of exports respectively (Tisdell and Chai, 1997). By substituting these for and in our net-increase model, we obtain

$$\Delta Y = F(\Delta L, \Delta Pc, \Delta Hc, \Delta Dm, \Delta Im)$$

where ΔY stands for the increase in GDP. We then specify the relationship in above equation with the familiar statistical model known as the exponential regression model:

$$\Delta Y_{it} = A\Delta L_{it}^{\beta_1}\Delta Pc_{it}^{\beta_2}\Delta Hc_{it}^{\beta_3}\Delta Dm_{it}^{\beta_4}\Delta Im_{it}^{\beta_5} e^{\mu_{it}}$$

where u stands for the stochastic disturbance term, e for the base of natural logarithms, i for the ith province and t for the tth time period. After log transformation, the equation becomes:

$$Ln\Delta Y_{it} = \alpha + \beta_1 Ln\Delta L_{it} + \beta_2 Ln\Delta Pc_{it} + \beta_3 Ln\Delta Hc_{it} + \beta_4 Ln\Delta Dm_{it} + \beta_5 Ln\Delta Im_{it} + \mu_{it}$$

where a stands for LnA. The equation can be used for the analysis of pooled cross-sectional and time series data in two ways: classical pooling to obtain invariant parameters for China in the period as a whole, and controlled pooling to obtain variant parameters for different regions and periods. Here, the analysis is confined to the former for illustrative purpose.

Before running the regression, a technical problem has to be addressed: there are negative and zero values in both dependent and explanatory variables which cannot be log-transformed, and which are therefore treated as missing data. In our empirical tests, about 1/3 observations are lost for each model due to this effect. Adding some value to the variables could be used to transform negative values into positive ones. However, the treatment of data would, especially in a multiple regression, distort the real relationship between variables in the model. It is preferable, therefore, to leave the data as they are. Such "objectivism" in data treatment has actually a very significant advantage for the net-increase effect model: it allows capture of the "net increase effect" in the true sense since all the decrease effects are excluded in the regression procedure. The effect on growth of an increase of 1 million labourers could be drastically different from that of a decrease of 1 million labourers. By excluding all the decrease effects, we can now safely say that what is being captured in the model is the "net increase effect" per se. The cost of the "objectivism" in the data treatment is, first of all, a loss of a considerable number of observations and, therefore, a considerable number of degrees of freedom. This would not do much harm to the estimation due to the large size of the sample. Ordinary least square (OLS) estimation is used with the normal statistical assumption that the errors it are independent and normally distributed, $N(0, \delta_\mu^2)$, for all individuals and in all time periods.

Results

The regression results are reported in Table 23.5, which shows that the adjusted R^2-value of 0.749 is reasonably high for this model, suggesting that the model fits the data quite well. The high t-values for most variables and the high F-values indicate that the multicollinearity problem is not serious. All variables are significant at 0.01 level. The logarithm of the model implies that the estimated coefficients are elasticities of the change in the net increase in GDP with respect to the change in the net increase in the explanatory variables. For example, the coefficient of the increase in physical capital input shows that a 1% change in the net increase in physical capital input could lead to a 0.32% change in the net increase in GDP, other factors held constant. All five variables have positive and significant estimated coefficients, supporting our assumptions.

Table 23.5.   Determinants of Real GDP Net Increase (1978-2000)
(Dependent variable: Ln(increase in real GDP)

Variable	Model 1		Model 2	
	Coefficient	t-Stat	Coefficient	t-Stat
Constant	1.66	10.72	1.82	13.04
Ln (increase in labour)	0.11	2.92	0.16	4.54
Ln (increase in fixed assets)	0.32	7.77	0.25	6.45
Ln (increase in human capital)	0.16	3.60	0.16	4.09
Ln (increase in retail sales)	0.28	5.69	0.21	4.64
Ln (increase in export)	0.11	2.99	-----	-----
Ln (FDI)	-----	-----	0.14	5.71
R^2-value	0.749		0.754	
F-value	104.48		121.67	

Note: All estimated coefficients are statistically significant at 0.01 level.

As shown in Table 23.5, increases in labour have the least impact. This is consistent with the fact that China is a labour-surplus developing country with enormous unemployment or underemployment. Reallocation of labour resources between sectors with different productivity levels may become more important in improving efficiency and, therefore, in accelerating economic growth. It is interesting to observe that the estimated coefficient of fixed asset investment is the greatest. Although this result is not surprising, it indicates that investment is still the most important instrument to stimulate China's economic growth.

The significant contribution to economic growth by human capital inputs (16%) deserves attention from policymakers. China began to reform its education system in the late 1970s, and Deng Xiaoping proposed that "science and technology are the prime productive force" soon afterwards. As a result, government expenditure on the improvement of human resources increased, elementary education strengthened, science and technology developed faster, cultural and education levels were enhanced. All have contributed significantly to China's rapid economic growth.

Therefore, China should continue to increase human capital input to maintain its growth momentum.

Our results show that the increase in domestic and international trade can lead to improved efficiency and accelerated economic growth. Therefore, China should devote major efforts to developing domestic and international trade in order to make full use of changing demand in domestic and international markets to promote economic growth and structural changes. The estimated coefficients show that domestic markets made a much greater contribution to China's GDP growth than that through international markets. This finding is consistent with the large size of China's population and territory. China is different from the "four small dragons" in East Asia which have to rely heavily on international markets owing to the small size of their population and territory. China should pay major attention to its huge domestic markets so as to ensure the sustainability of economic growth. It is worth mentioning that the market variables in the model should not be considered as a force contradicting government intervention. On the contrary, they should be considered as resulting from government intervention in China's special case, that is, from the reform and open-door policies adopted by the Chinese government. Since the opening-up, China has attracted a huge amount of foreign direct investment. In 1980, China received about $130 million of FDI. This amount increased to $2.97 billion in 1990 and $41.21 billion in 2000. In fact, China became the largest FDI recipient of the world in 2002, followed by the USA (People's Daily, August 10, 2002). One important feature of FDI in China is that most FDI went to the coastal region. For example, in 1990 and 2000, 93 and 86% of the total FDI went to the east coastal region (NBS, 1996, 2001). To investigate the impact of foreign investment on China's economic growth, we included a variable of Ln(FDI) into our model. For this model, we use data from 1985 to 2000 due to the fact that many provinces did not have FDI before 1985. Due to a high correlation between FDI and exports, we have to exclude the variable of exports from the new model. Our result shows a significant estimated coefficient on the FDI variable, confirming an important role of FDI in promoting China's economic growth.

Our empirical results suggest that China could narrow regional disparities by making greater efforts to improve education in the interior regions. Comparing with the coastal areas, education in the central and western regions is far behind. Today's education is tomorrow's productivity. In the past decades, the Chinese government helped the interior regions to build many factories and even sent many workers from the coastal areas. However, such efforts have been proven inefficient. We would argue that now China should pay more attention to education in its less developed areas and provide a greater support to improve education in these areas. Attracting FDI to the interior regions will also stimulate economic growth in China's less developed regions. The fast growth in the coastal region over the past two decades, as our empirical indicates, has evidenced the important role of FDI in promoting economic growth. With China's accession to the WTO, it is inevitable that more FDI will go to China. Here we would suggest that China should open more markets for foreign investment, especially in the interior regions. Although the coastal region contributes more than half of the national GDP, most Chinese people live in the central and western regions. With such a huge population and rich in natural and tourist resources, the interior regions will become more attractive to foreign investors. There is no reason that China should exclude FDI from many industries, such as mining, tourism, and services.

Conclusions

This study has used various measures to examine regional disparities in China. Our results provide empirical evidence to support two major findings about China's regional development. First, the post-1978 economic reforms have had positive effects on China's regional development because of the improved economic growth and development in all Chinese regions and provinces. Second, the regional growth and development records have shown some levels of difference between various regions and provinces. The eastern coastal region and provinces have grown faster than those in the central and western regions. The findings here support the effectiveness of China's post-Mao unbalanced regional development policy, which offered preferential measures and strategies in the coastal region. We have identified four significant phenomena of regional disparities: (1) a narrowing of interprovincial output disparity from 1978-1990, (2) a widening of inter-provincial output disparity after 1990, (3) an enlarging of inter provincial livelihood disparity, and (4) a widening of coastal-interior disparity in both output and livelihood indicators of development. The paper has reviewed development policies and strategies before and after China's opening-up. While the pre-reform policy aimed to achieve a balanced development and to mitigate the disparity between coastal and interior regions, the regional development strategies in early reform years gave a high priority to coastal region development. The new regional development policy has resulted in increasing economic differences among Chinese regions. The coastal region and provinces have grown faster than the central and western regions. This paper has argued three main sources of uneven regional development in China: technology catch-up advantage, policy advantage, and the functioning of market mechanisms. To promote economic integration within China and to avoid political disintegration, it is very important for Chinese leaders to develop policies to strengthen development in co-operation not confrontation among regions and provinces, and to maintain political and social stability.

Applying a net-effect growth model to provincial data for the period of 1978-2000, this paper has examined factors that affect economic development in China. We have found that China's net growth in GDP is significantly affected by the increases in labour, fixed assets, human capital, domestic retail sales, and exports. Foreign direct investment also plays an important role in stimulating China's growth. Specifically, the significant contribution of human capital to economic growth deserves attention from policymakers. The significant contribution to GDP growth by the domestic market, exports, and FDI suggests that improving the efficiency of market and further opening will be the main forces for China's future growth in the new century.

References

1.   Chen, Jian (1996). Regional Income Inequality and Economic Growth in China, *Journal of Comparative Economics* 22: 141-164.
2.   China State Statistics Bureau (1996). China Regional Economy, *A Profile of 17 Years of Reform and Opening-Up*, China Statistics Publication Press.

3.   China State Statistics Bureau (1996, 2001). *China Statistical Yearbook*, Beijing: China Statistics Publication Press.

4.   Fleisher, Belton M. and Jian Chen (1997). The Coast Noncoast Income Gap, Productivity, and Regional Economic Policy in China, *Journal of Comparative Economics* 25: 220-236.

5.   Hu, Angang, Wang Shaoguang, and Kang Xiaoguang (1995). *Disparities in China*, Liaoning People's Publication Press, Beijing.

6.   Jian, Tianlun, Jeffrey D. Sachs, and Andrew M. Warner (1996). Trends in Regional Inequality in China, *China Economic Review*, Vol. 7. No 1: 121.

7.   Solow, Robert M. (1956). A Contribution to the Theory of Economic Growth, *Quarterly Journal of Economics*, 65-94.

8.   Song, Shunfeng, George S-F Chu, and Rongqing Cao (2000). Intercity Regional Disparity in China, *China Economic Review*, 246-261.

9.   Sun, Jingzhi (1998). *The Economic Geography of China*, Oxford University Press.

10.   Tian, XiaoWen (1997). An Endogenous Model For China's Growth Since 1978, in *China's Economic Growth and Transition*, edited by Glement A. and Joseph C.H. Chai, Nova Science Publishers, Inc. Commack, NY.

11.   Tsui, Kai yuen (1996). Economic reform and Interprovincial inequalities in China, *Journal of Development Economics*, 50: 353-368.

12.   Tzeng, FW (1991). The Political-Economy of China Coastal Development Strategy – A Preliminary Analysis, *Asian Survey*, 31(3): 270-294.

13.   Yang, Dennis Tao and Hao Zhou (1999). Rural Urban Disparity and Sectoral Labour Allocation in China, *Journal of Development Studies*, 55(3): 105-133.

24 Development of West China: Marketization versus Foreign Direct Investment

Wen Mei

Introduction

The extended property rights theory on transitional economies points out that degrees of economic freedom, decentralization, market perfection, institution perfection of legislation, and policy consistency and persistency are key factors affecting firms' efficiency over different ownership types and the efficiency of resource allocation.[1] Since China's economic reform, the eastern coastal regions have been favoured by policies for prior development. With a geographical advantage in international trade and policies aimed at attracting foreign direct investment, eastern coastal regions are now more economically advanced than western regions. Confronting gradually enlarging regional income disparity, the Chinese central government advocated development of western China in 1999. In addition to reducing income inequality, developing western China is also a strategy for finding new forces for sustaining fast economic growth. As industrial growth has been pulling China's economic growth since economic reform (Wen, 2002a) and studies show that foreign direct investment has contributed to the growth (see Zhang, 2001, for example), utilization of FDI for developing western China, especially in resource tied or resource extensive industries, has been highlighted. Resembling eastern regions in the earlier period of economic reform, preferential policies for attracting FDI into western China have also been issued. Although extending and deepening economic reform to western regions is on the western development agenda, it seems that the contribution of a market mechanism and competition between diversified ownership firms based on this market mechanism to fast industrial growth have not been paid due attention regarding development of western China. This paper tries to draw deserved attention to the development of the market mechanism by providing empirical evidence of the significance of marketization and FDI in China's GDP growth.

After about a quarter of a century of market-oriented economic reform, China's eastern, middle, and western regions differ not only in their natural conditions, including geographical location, geological conditions, resource endowment, and climate, but also in per capita income, market conditions, infrastructure, human resources, international trade, as well as in both the condition for attracting foreign direct investment and the level of FDI inflow. Wen (2002b) argues that both ownership regime and industrial structure have important efficiency implications. However, the quality of institutions in transitional economies such as the level of marketization can affect efficiency gain from both industrial competition and ownership change of enterprises. In fact, Tian (2000) shows that optimal ownership composition in an economy depends on quality of institutions and consequential economic freedom, decentralization, and market perfection. Similarly, the efficiency of a foreign owned enterprise (or efficiency of FDI) depends on market conditions. Therefore, given the different initial conditions, the current optimal development strategy for western China can be different from those for eastern China in the earlier years of economic reform.

As is known, eastern China was given development priority in the earlier reform period due to its geographical advantage in international trade and in attracting foreign investments, especially investment from Hong Kong, Taiwan and Macau. Studies (Wei, 1995 and Zhang, 2001 for example) show that FDI and international trade contributed significantly to China's economic growth. However, efficiency of FDI depends both on the orientation of FDI and the economic system (as mentioned in the last paragraph). Zhang and Song (2000) show that before China's WTO accession, FDI inflow to China significantly promoted exports while more FDI may target at the domestic market after China's WTO accession (Sun et al., 2002). Based on an extensive and detailed analysis of import-substitute FDI induced inefficiency, Bhagwati raised the hypothesis that export-promoting FDI recipient countries attract a greater volume of FDI and enjoy greater efficiency therefrom.[2]   Although trade with Central, West, South and East Asia as well as Mongolia and Russia can be developed in western China, due to the relatively small market size of these economies (in terms of purchasing power) compared with high income OECD countries, western China dose not have geographical advantage in attracting export-oriented FDI. Although Bhagwati pointed out that import-substitute FDI may cause many inefficiency problems and may merely serve to redistribute income in favour of the new production agents, the efficiency of this FDI would improve with market perfection, other institution improvement and trade barrier reduction or removal. Therefore, the optimal policy priority for developing western China would be related to the relative significance of marketization and FDI. In other words, only when the relative significance for the development of western China is clear, can the promotive policies be more efficient.

Henceforth, China's transition and development towards a market economic system will be reviewed in the following section. Section 3 discusses the significance of the market system for economic growth. Regional differences in many economic aspects including marketization level, industrial development, per capita income, market size and international trade are examined in section 4. Empirical studies on relative significance of marketization and FDI will then be conducted in Section 5. Concluding remarks follow.

Transition and Development towards a Market Economic System

The market, a basic institution of a market economy for free trading and free contracting, has to gradually establish in transitional economies. Its size – determined by industrial structure, national purchasing power, transportation and transaction conditions – enlarges endogenously with economic growth. Industrial policies and legal regulations regarding enterprises' behaviour can improve the functioning of the market in the provision of information, fairness of competition, efficiency of resources and product allocation. Imperfection of the market in transitional economies is a major institutional shortcoming for achieving efficiency, which is easily neglected by economists who are devoted to market economies.

Since economic reform, a market system has been gradually established and developed in three stages in China. During the first stage, from 1979 to 1984, the Chinese had a 'taste' of the market. During this period, free markets were allowed for trading agricultural products. With the great success of radical agricultural reform – the gradual adoption of the household responsibility system nationwide – markets for agricultural products were activated. Free wholesale and retail markets for small industrial consumption goods were then allowed. Gradually, the government reduced the number of industrial products under central planning, raised the procurement prices of agricultural products according to the degree of shortage, adjusted the prices of some light industrial products according to market demand, and let the price of small consumption commodities be determined by the market.

Although establishment of the markets for intermediate goods and primary industrial inputs was not on the reform agenda during this period, due to the necessity for agricultural products and small consumption industrial goods, all Chinese were more or less involved in market transactions. People started to learn how the market works and gain the benefits of the market in product allocation. From purchasing most necessities through quotas and queuing at fixed prices, people began to compare different qualities and prices of consumption goods, and learnt to bargain for better quality at a lower price. Although the prices of some necessities increased due to shortages in the early years of economic reform, consumers realised that the market brought them the convenience of purchasing daily necessities, more variety of consumption goods and better-quality products as well as a higher income level.

The second stage was from 1985 to 1991. This was an important period for ideological change towards a market system. Due to the ideology of socialism that dictated state ownership of capital goods and land, most intermediate goods, labour, capital and land were still under central planning up to 1985. In 1984, the introduction of the dual-track system – which regulated that output under the plan should be sold at the planned price while output beyond the plan could be sold at floating prices within a 20% difference of the planned price – allowed state firms in more and more final product industries to transact with non-state marketized firms. In addition, the Central Governmental Decision on the Reform of the Economic System, passed in October 1984 at the third plenary session of the twelfth congress of the Chinese Communist Party, initiated the establishment and development of a market for intermediate goods from 1985 to 1991.

Although high inflation rates during 1988 and 1989 caused suspicion and dispute about the market system,[3] markets for capital, labour, technology, information and housing were gradually established during this same period. Most banks were restructured under state ownership. Workers in state-owned enterprises (SOEs hereafter), especially new employees, were shifted to the contract system. Free contracting for the application of most research and development results was allowed. Some departments, such as transportation, power, meteorology and banking, started to establish businesses and networks to share information.[4] With the reform of SOEs towards independent economic entities and the growth of collectives and individuals during this period, the market played a more important role in the economy for the efficient allocation of products and resources.

Comprehensive development for a sound market system occurred in the third stage – from 1992 to the present. Not only were the dual tracks merged to the market prices in 1992 and most intermediate goods opened to market competition, reform of the housing system towards a semi-commercial system was also executed nationwide. Two stock exchanges were also established in 1992 in Shanghai and Shenzhen, respectively. After Deng Xiaoping's southern tour, the fourteenth congress of the Chinese Communist Party, held in October 1992, officially declared that the aim of China's economic reform was to establish a socialist market system.

With the networking of product markets, the introduction of future markets and adoption of the Internet, a hierarchical network market system was gradually being established. Adoption of the Internet accelerated networking of the product market, while reducing transaction costs and extending the size of the market through e-commerce. It also promoted the development of service markets. The introduction of future markets facilitated inter-temporal optimization of economic agents.

In 1996, less than 10% of commodity categories were under government control. Over 90% of retail prices and 80% of agricultural and producer good prices (as a proportion of output value) were determined by the market. The number of production factors under central planning reduced from 256 in 1979 to less than 20 in 1996. The number of consumption goods under central control declined from 188 in 1978 to 14 in 1996. Although the market is playing an increasingly important role in transmitting information of different economic agents through the price signal at the national level, in each development stage, the marketization level in eastern, middle and western regions may vary to some extent due to prior development of eastern coastal regions and its inward transmission effect.

Significance of the Market System and FDI for Economic Growth

Along with the establishment and gradual improvement of a market system, China's economic reform was also characterized with ownership diversification. The state sector developed with gradually enlarged market transactions under government protections. Collectives, individuals, domestic private enterprises and foreign invested enterprises have also been growing largely based on market transactions. Due to their legitimacy, collectives, especially TVEs, have developed rapidly since 1978, compared with domestic private firms. As a feasible channel for absorbing a large amount of the labour force released from the agricultural sector under the urban system constraints and a way of cashing local resources (mainly land), collectives have developed even much faster than the state sector under local government support. In fact, up to 1997, 13.27 million people were employed in the collective industrial sector and it contributed 38% to gross industrial output value. Meanwhile, joint ventures and foreign owned enterprises have been encouraged since four special economic zones were first created in Guangdong and Fujian provinces. Favourable taxation policies, including tax-exemption in the first three years and allowing the duty-free import of inputs for export processing contracts, have encouraged overseas Chinese and foreign entrepreneurs to establish enterprises in eastern coastal regions. Adoption of the Coastal Development Strategy in 1987-88 promoted the export-oriented sector and foreign investment. After further openness policies were firmly released in late 1992 and several economic laws were discussed in 1993, FDI was stimulated to a new level in 1994. By 1999, the industrial share of different ownership sectors was substantially different from 1978, as shown in Figure 24.1.

In 1978, there were only state ownership, collective ownership and individuals, with collectives and individuals as a whole having a share of only about 0.224 in the gross industrial output value. But after more than two decades of market-oriented reform, collectives became the major industrial sector with an industrial output share of 0.354 while the share of all industrial SOEs and state-controlled share companies in the gross output value dropped to 0.282 in 1999. More importantly, enterprises with other ownership types, including foreign ownership and domestic private ownership, had a share of 0.261, which may be higher than the share of genuine state ownership if the private or foreign ownership in state-controlled share companies were separated out.

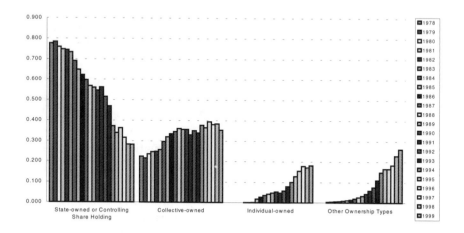

Figure 24.1.   Proportion of gross industrial output value by ownership, 1978–1999

Different ownership arrangement[5] of firms is believed to have efficiency implications.[6] The gradually improved market system provides a level playing field for the firms with different ownership types to exert their internal efficiency. Market competition works as an incentive and an information mechanism drives inefficient firms to make losses or even to go out of business, and promotes firms, who hope to survive, to improve internal efficiency by reducing costs. While development of different ownership agents increases market players, fast economic growth based on more and more market transactions significantly enlarged domestic market size. From a per capita GDP of 376 *yuan* in 1978 to per capita GDP of a 7517 *yuan* in 2001 (current price, or 2250 in 1978 prices), China's domestic market has enlarged dramatically with about a 32.6% population increase during the same period.   In turn, the enlarged market has been providing more chances for different firms to grow and different entrepreneurs to set up new businesses. Shortage had been a common feature of the centrally planned economies (Kornai 1980). After two decades of market-oriented reforms, China had eliminated shortages and the market had converted into a buyers' market. By June 1998, there was no shortage of any of the 610 commodities within state domestic trade statistics.[7]

Since China opened its door for FDI, export promotion and the technology spill-over effect of FDI have been noted. As state owned banks are inclined to lend to the state sector, domestic collectives and private firms didn't have advantage in technology, R&D compared with SOEs and foreign funded enterprises. Many TVEs in middle and western regions are geographically disadvantaged with their rural locations as well. Therefore, a lot of endeavour has been made to attract FDI and promote international trade including the efforts for WTO accession. FDI inflow to China promoted export.   More foreign entry and international trade exposed Chinese enterprises to rigorous international competition. In 1978, China had net imports of US$1.14 billion. Since 1995, however, China's net exports have surged to new levels, reaching US$24.11 billion in 2000.

It is the gradually strengthened industrial competition and the ownership diversification that contributed significantly to efficiency gains in China's economy. Although China's market is still far from perfection and relationship (*guanxi*) still plays an important role in conducting business, firms with different ownership types are observed to operate at significantly different technical efficiency levels. Several studies (Wen, et al., 2002, Zhang, et al., 2001) on the 1995 third industrial census data reveal that SOEs on average had the lowest technical efficiency among firms with different ownership types. Domestic stock-listing companies had a relatively high technical efficiency among domestic ownership types although their internal efficiency was not as high as joint ventures and pure foreign owned enterprises. Interestingly, joint ventures on average were observed to be more technically efficient than pure foreign enterprises due to imperfect market environment in 1995. But it is found that the labour productivity of pure foreign enterprises were higher than that of joint ventures due to improvement of the market system and operating environment in the following year. Since 1996, when most SOEs made losses and when the TVE law was issued, market competition has forced more and more SOEs to either sack more redundant workers, go bankrupt, or adopt ownership transformation in one form or another to increase internal efficiency for survival. Many collective TVEs have also gotten rid of their red hats and have had more-clearly-defined property rights for efficiency improvements. With more FDI inflow into China following WTO accession, the enlarging domestic market and increasing international trade, firms in China will engage in more and more intensified industrial competition.

A time series study in Wen (2002a) finds that both industrial competition and ownership diversification have contributed significantly to China's industrial growth. A rough estimate is that approximately 10% of average annual industrial growth is due to disembodied total factor productivity improvement from ownership diversification. These efficiency gains are all based on the establishment and gradual improvement of China's market system. However, China's market system is yet to be improved. Current institutional constraints are still restricting the market from functioning more efficiently. As an evidence, the contribution of competition to industrial growth seems still to be mainly through increase in inputs. The cost-reduction effect of competition can partly be offset by inefficient allocation of resources among different ownership groups at an aggregate level.

Regional Differences in Marketization Level, Industrial Development, Market Size and International Trade

China's economic reform during the past 25 years was first characterized with the nationwide success of agricultural reform, then with lasting and higher than two digits industrial growth with stablized annual agricultural growth at about 5% and enlarging eastern, middle and western regional differences. In the 21st century, when a westerner travels across China, he/she may feel as it travelling across economies at different development levels. Current Shenzhen, Shanghai and Beijing may make the tourist feel as it in Hong Kong or some other modern western metropolis in both municipal appearance and the lifestyle of locals, while western China would still project an exotic and far-eastern feeling and exhibit a lifestyle of low income standards.

After more than two decades of economic transition, eastern coastal China has become China's industrial core with the agglomeration of many manufacturing industries in Guangdong, Jiangshu province and Shanghai city (Wen, 2001). The industrial agglomeration follows market-oriented reform, induced by lower transaction and transportation costs in eastern regions and driven by the "home market effect" generated from the higher per capita income of the region as well as industrial linkages. Concentration of manufacturing industries in eastern coastal regions enlarges regional income and trade differentials with a positive acceleration rate so that the regional income disparity can no longer be ignored by the central government. By 2001, eastern China has a per capita GDP of 13,789 *yuan* while middle and western China have a per capita GDP of 6039 and 5192 *yuan* respectively. Yet, eastern regions have a higher GDP growth rate than middle and western regions.

Although billions of FDI has flowed into China since 1994, eastern regions are the major FDI recipient areas, especially for export-oriented FDI. In 2001, the actual utilization of FDI in eastern, middle and western regions was 3.394 billion, 467.6 million and 159 million U.S. dollars, respectively. While the actual utilization of FDI in middle and western regions was more than 18% of that in eastern region, exports and imports of the middle and western regions are just around one-tenth of eastern regions'.[8]   Table 24.1 gives out the figures of regional export and import value as well as growth rate of export, import and FDI in 2001.

Table 24.1.   Regional Export and Import and the Growth Rates in 2001

	East	Middle	West
Export (US$10,000)	2043521	152719	71874
Import (US$10,000)	1889167	123219	58238
Growth Rate of Export*	0.13	0.23	0.16
Growth Rate of Import*	0.17	0.14	0.11
Growth Rate of Average Utilization of FDI*	0.04	0.04	-0.08

Note: * The growth rate of export and import are calculated from data in U.S. dollars at current prices from SSY 2002, American consumer price index from the World Tables is used to deflate 2001 data to 2000 term. The growth rate of average utilization is calculated from data of current U.S. dollars. If the data are adjusted with American consumer price index, the growth rate of FDI in eastern, middle and western regions should be -0.08, -0.08 and -0.16, respectively.

It can be seen from Table 24.1 that it will be very difficult for middle and western regions to catch up with the eastern region in international trade and utilization of FDI, even though exports and imports of middle and western regions grows a little faster. The growth rate of FDI in western regions in 2001 is negative. Except for the impact of U.S. economic recession since 2000, the decline of FDI in western regions after the first trials of foreign investors under government advocacy in 2000 may be due to their realization about market conditions in the western regions. It was said that many domestic enterprises in eastern regions retreated from investing in western regions after their trial in the region in 2000, due to institutional and market shortcomings. In addition, business people in eastern regions feel that ideological changes towards conducting business are still required in western regions. With capital mobility across regions, improvement of institutions and market mechanism is a pre-requisite for western regions to attract more investment, no matter from domestic or foreign sources.

According to the marketization index of China's provinces compiled by NERI (2001), there are substantial regional differences in the marketization level in China. In eastern China, the government intervenes in economic decisions to a lower degree and more product prices are determined by the market. To an even larger extent, middle and western regions are less developed in factor markets, the non-state owned sector, intermediaries and the legal system as shown in the following Table 24.2.

The regional differences in marketization level reflect different regional investment environments. Although the huge amount of money invested in the middle and western regions for upgrading their infrastructure such as roads, highways and railway systems during the past several years will further connect regional markets and reduce transport costs, the reduced transportation costs may actually promote industrial agglomeration in eastern coastal regions, owning to the fact that China seems still on the upside of an upside-down U curve of industrial spatial concentration (Wen, 2001).[9] Therefore, a pertinent long run strategy for developing western China can be based on both infrastructure improvement and further regional marketization. When agglomeration of firms in eastern China pushes up wages and prices, and investments in the region generate a crowding out effect, improved infrastructure and market mechanisms in middle and western regions will naturally attract more and more investment. Firms would then be more likely to choose to locate in middle and western regions even without favourable policies.

Table 24.2.   Regional Changes in Institution and Marketization Levels

Index representing	1999	2000	Change
1. Reduction of Government Intervention			
Nationwide	**6.11**	6.05	**-0.06**
Eastern Region	7.08	7.11	0.03
Middle Region	5.59	5.47	-0.11
Western Region	5.52	5.40	-0.12
2. Development of Non-state Owned Enterprises			
Nationwide	**4.80**	**5.34**	**0.54**
Eastern Region	6.91	7.58	0.67
Middle Region	4.41	4.65	0.25
Western Region	2.99	3.60	0.61
3. Development of Product Market			
Nationwide	**7.23**	**7.44**	**0.21**
Eastern Region	7.94	8.16	0.22
Middle Region	7.70	7.88	0.17
Western Region	6.16	6.39	0.22
4. Development of Factor Market			
Nationwide	**3.43**	**3.60**	**0.17**
Eastern Region	5.41	5.66	0.25
Middle Region	2.41	2.59	0.17
Western Region	2.18	2.29	0.11
5. Development of Intermediaries and Efficiency Improvement of Legal System			
Nationwide	**5.01**	**5.26**	**0.25**
Eastern Region	6.13	6.43	0.30
Middle Region	4.72	4.92	0.20
Western Region	4.10	4.34	0.24

Note: This table is translated from table 3 of NERI (2001). Construction approach of these indices is provided in the NERI report.

Developing Western China: Marketization versus FDI

To see how marketization and FDI contributed to China's GDP growth, a regression is conducted according to new growth theory. Similar to Balasubramanyam et al. (1996), how FDI contributes to income growth is examined with cross sectional (regional) 2001 data. To test Bhagwati's hypothesis that EP regions (countries) attract a greater volume of FDI and enjoy greater efficiency therefrom, the cross-effect between FDI and export is included. As firms' internal efficiency varies with market environment, an increase in marketization level may increase total factor productivity. Therefore, one relatively objective marketization index – index of the development of product market are included in the regression. Regression results are shown in the following Table 24.3.

Table 24.3.   Contribution of Marketization and FDI Through
            Promoting Export to GDP Growth
            (Dependent Variable: GDP growth rate)

Explanatory Variables	Coefficient Estimate	T value (p-value)
Constant	4.895707	5.498274 (0.0000)
Growth rate of employment	-0.340950	-2.748420 (0.0120)
Ratio of total investment in fixed assets to GDP	5.959678	4.668459 (0.0001)
Cross effect b/w FDI_GDP		
Ratio and export_GDP ratio	31.88960	2.020516 (0.0563)
Growth rate of export	1.028288	2.876443 (0.0090)
Marketization level	0.247536	2.696299 (0.0135)
Regional export dummy	1.347328	2.436642 (0.0238)
FDI_GDP ratio	-16.00871	-1.293035 (0.2100)
Adjusted R-squared	0.751976	

From Table 24.3, it can be seen that marketization significantly (at 0.00135 level) contributes to GDP growth. FDI also significantly contributes to GDP growth through promoting exports (the coefficient of cross effect of FDI and export is significantly positive at 0.0563 level). As an approximate of percentage change of capital input, the ratio of total investment to GDP is also significantly positive in the regression, although the coefficient of labour input is significantly negative due to redundant workers in many enterprises. In addition, higher export regions have higher total factor productivity and fast growth of exports can also increase regional income. FDI level (the ratio of FDI to GDP) is negative in the regression but not statistically significant even at 0.1 level.

The above regression reveals that both market mechanism and FDI are very important to China's economic development, especially when FDI can promote exports. This confirms Bhagwati's hypothesis and the extended property rights theory. In the first two decades of economic reform, FDI inflow into eastern coastal regions is mainly export-oriented. However, according to Sun et al. (2002), more foreign directly invested projects in China are targeting at domestic markets, especially after China's WTO accession. The unit contribution of this FDI to China's income growth may not be as high as can be seen in the former period of economic reform.

As to western China, its geographical disadvantage to western countries and the current instability of Central East regions and Russia can make western China unattractive to export promoted FDI. This does not mean that foreigners will not have interests in investing in western China. Due to business opportunities emerging in the current development stage and the large population size of each Chinese province, import substitute FDI should come to western China.[10] Given favourable taxation policies for foreign invested enterprises in western regions, foreign businessmen will be more interested in investing into western China than domestic entrepreneurs in eastern coastal regions. However, to what extent import-substitute FDI can promote regional income growth is still a question which deserves further quantitative study. According to Bhagwati, import-substitute FDI may cause many inefficiency problems and may merely serve to redistribute income in favour of the new production agents. This can be true especially in transitional economies where the market is imperfect and distortion exists in resource allocation.

Nevertheless, an optimistic view of developing western China can still be held and the good will of reducing regional income disparity can be conducted more efficiently through searching for more approaches. So far, major projects commenced in western regions are infrastructure projects, which can pull the regional economic growth through the growth of the construction sector in the short run. In the long run, reduced transportation costs will increase production efficiency through triggering higher levels of specialization and division of labour, facilitating restructuring of economic organization, and increasing productivity. Although middle and western regions were once bases for industrial development during the 1960s due to security concerns, it's difficult and inefficient to use policy tilts to affect firms' spatial locations. Instead, to emphasize developing business sense and market mechanisms in the western region can be a more powerful approach for both attracting more domestic and foreign investment into the region and increasing the efficiency of capital investment. Although western regions have no comparative advantage in foot-loose industries in the short run, they have wonderful resources for developing tourist industries and developing resource extraction industries. If market mechanisms can be developed at a faster speed in middle and western regions, the regional market size can increase rapidly with the development of construction, tourist, and resource extraction industries. The enlarged market size and improved investment environment can itself attract more capital, human resources and advanced technology into the region for further development.

Although former sections provide the empirical evidence that competition and ownership diversification based on market mechanisms significantly contributed to China's industrial growth, many Chinese economists felt domestic private sector was relatively weak, especially compared with foreign sector after China's WTO accession. The weakness of the domestic private sector is partly due to the fact that pure domestic private ownership was not legitimized in the earlier years of economic reform so that this sector developed relatively late. This might be a lesson for developing western China. To give enterprises of different ownership types an equal policy ground and have them compete fairly in the market can generate more efficiency gains. This is where the government can play a very important role: to provide a fair market and to encourage and maintain fair market competition.

Concluding Remarks

China's transition towards a market-oriented economy has created fast income growth with different growth rates in eastern, middle and western regions. When the government puts effort into reducing regional income disparity, the significant contribution of competition and ownership diversification to income growth shouldn't be ignored. It is the establishment and improvement of market mechanisms and the encouragement of new entries of different ownership types that enables strong market competition. Current regional income disparity is partly due to different regional paces in the transition towards a market mechanism. In turn, to accelerate development of a market mechanism in middle and western regions will be the key to developing these regions and to reducing regional income disparity. Meanwhile, encouragement of new entries of more efficient ownership types and fairness of market competition will bring more efficiency gains and higher regional income growth.

Notes

1. Tian, Li Chang and Wang , Wing, Wen et al, literature here.
2. See Balasubramanyam et al., 1996.
3. The general consumer price index was 18.8% and 18.0% in the years 1988 and 1989, respectively.
4. A typical example of the establishing information market in the 1980s was the increase in small businesses that collect and provide information on the route of empty trucks and the demand for trucks for road commodity transportation.
5. Different arrangement of residual income rights and control rights.
6. See Hart and Moore, 1990 and Wen, 2002a, 2002b, for example.
7. Data provided in this paragraph are from the Editorial Office of China Economic System Reform Yearbook, Yearbook of China's Economic System Reform 1999.
8. Calculation of regional data uses the geographical regional definition as follows. Eastern region includes Liaoning, Beijing, Tianjing, Shanghai, Hebei, Shandong, Jiangshu, Zhejiang, Fujian, Guangdong, Hainan, and Guangxi; Middle region includes Heilongjiang, Jilin,

Shanxi, Inner Mongolia, Anhui, Jiangxi, Henan, Hunan and Hubei. Western region includes Sichun, Chongqing, Yunnan, Guizhou, Tibet, Shaanxi, Gansu, Qinghai, Ningxia and Xingjiang. This definition of western region is different from the one which government regulates for favourable policy effectiveness in developing western China. The latter includes inner Mongolia and Guangxi as well as some Chinese minority regions such as Xiangxi of Hunan, Ensi of Hubei, and Yanbian of Jilin.

9.   In economic geographical literature, the upside-down U curve of industrial spatial concentration describes how the degree of industrial concentration first increases with the reduction of unit transaction and transportation cost, then decreases with the improvement of transaction and transportation conditions after the unit transaction and transportation cost reaches a threshold value.

10.   Compared with many developed economies with a small population size, any Chinese province is a large market given the population size.

References

1.   Balasubramanyam, V. N., Salisu, M. and D. Sapsford (1996). "Foreign Direct Investment and Growth in EP and IS Countries," *The Economic Journal*, 106(434): 92-105.

2.   Hart, O. and J. Moore (1990). "Property Rights and the Nature of the Firm," *Journal of Political Economy*, 98(6): 1119-58.

3.   Li, X. and Liu, X. and D. Parker (2001). "Foreign Direct Investment and Productivity Spillovers in the Chinese Manufacturing Sector," *Economic Systems*, 25: 305-321.

4.   National Economic Research Institute (NERI, 2002). *NERI index of Marketization of China's Provinces 2001*, Beijing: Economic Science Press.

5.   State Statistics Bureau of the PRC (various years). *Statistical Yearbook of China*, China Statistical Publishing House, Beijing.

6.   Sun, Q., Tong, Wilson and Q. Yu (2002). "Determinants of Foreign Direct Investment across China," *Journal of International Money and Finance*, 21: 79-113.

7. Tian, G. (2000). "Property rights and the Nature of Collective Enterprises," *Journal of Comparative Economics*, 28: 247--68.

8. Wei, S. (1995). "The Open Door policy and China's Rapid Growth: Evidence from City Level Data," in Ito, T. and A. O. Krueger (eds.), *Growth Theories in Light of the East Asian Experience*, Chicago: The University of Chicago Press.

9. Wen, M. (2001). "Relocation and Agglomeration of Chinese Industry", Working Paper # 2001/07, Division of Economics, RSPAS, The Australian National University, Canberra, Australia.

10. Wen, M. (2002a). "Competition, Ownership Diversification and Industrial Growth", in *China 2002*, ed. by R. Garnaut and L. Song, Canberra: Asia Pacific Press, 63-80.

11. Wen, M. (2002b). "Privatization: Theory and Evidence", in Guoqiang Tian (ed). *The Frontiers of Modern Economics and Finance*, Beijing: Shangwu Press, 564-609.

12. Wen, M., Li, D. and Lloyd, P. (2002). "Ownership and technical efficiency – a cross-section study on the Third National Industrial Census of China," *Economic Development and Cultural Changes*, 50(3): 709-34.

13. Zhang, A., Zhang, Y. and Zhao, R. (2001). "Impact of ownership and competition on the productivity of Chinese Enterprises," *Journal of Comparative Economics*, 29: 327–46.

14. Zhang, K. H. (2001). "How Does Foreign Direct Investment Affect Economic Growth in China," *Economics of Transition*, 9(3): 679-93.

15. Zhang, K.H. and S. Song (2000). "Promoting Export: The Role of Inward FDI in China," China Economic Review, 11(4): 385-496.

Index

> I think of the New Testament church in its beginnings as an ideal organization. There was a structure, but it permitted everyone to share everything so no one was in need. As the organization grew and prospered, so did the people. People's needs come before the organization.

6. Should organizations attempt to select people for positions on the basis of their problem-solving styles? What would be the benefits of doing this? Would there be any dangers?

MANAGEMENT INCIDENTS AND CASES

Toughest Bosses in America

John Welch Jr., General Electric Company

Extraordinarily bright, penetrating in his questions, and determined to get results, John Welch, Jr., Chairman, General Electric, has carved out quite a reputation for himself since going to work for General Electric in 1960. According to former employees, Welch conducts meetings so aggressively that subordinates tremble. He criticizes, demeans, ridicules and humiliates people in meetings. "Jack comes on like a herd of elephants," says one former GE employee. Managers at GE used to hide out-of-favor employees from Welch's gunsights so they could keep their jobs. At one division that Welch was in charge of on his way to the top, these people were tagged "mummies."

Since taking over, Welch has announced the closing of 25 plants. This has earned him the nickname of "Neutron Jack." Employees joke that, like the aftermath of a neutron bomb, after Welch visits a plant the building is left standing but a lot of people are dead. A lot of people get shot up; the survivors go on to the next battle.

Most employees at GE agree that Welch is a doer, who doesn't want "I think" answers. Since taking over at GE, the stockholders' return on their money is around 18%, compared to 13.8% for other Fortune 500 companies. He is a person with many creative business ideas who has the ability to tap people's brains. Former employees at GE have said that at GE there had been more reviewers than doers until Welch's arrival. "I'd present plans to 35 people," says a veteran GE employee. "It was insane. And at times, incredibly provoking." For example, while head of GE's consumer products division, Welch instructed his general managers to cut inventories immediately. One month later he called a meeting to see what progress they had made. None had implemented his order. Welch then recessed the meeting and told the managers that he wanted action before the afternoon meeting. He got it.

Welch says that as chairman he is trying to promote risk-taking by making heroes out of risk-takers in the company, even if they have failed. He says, "the role for the mediocre is clearly short-lived." However, subordinates accuse him of missing the opportunity to get input from people who don't have the skill or courage to live up to his high standards. If you have a controversial idea, you must have the guts to put it forward.

John Smilow, Beatrice Companies, Inc.

John Smilow, a senior executive at Beatrice Companies, Inc., describes himself as tough but fair, and one who welcomes dissent and discussion. The long-time chairman of International Playtex division of Esmark has been described by subordinates as one who has all the answers and thinks that everyone else is wrong.

In the late 1970s and early 1980s, Playtex asked the Hay Associates, a consulting firm, to conduct two surveys to determine the level of satisfaction at Playtex. Both times, the firm got the same result: Morale was the lowest at Playtex that the firm had ever seen. Why? According to his subordinates, Smilow might have had something to do with the conditions. Former employees say that he has the uncanny ability to demoralize subordinates. As a former employee said, "He gives the impression that he thinks of employees as throwaways." Many of his subordinates have heard him use his favorite phrase, "Stupid is forever," behind an employee's back. According to a former Playtex manager, Smilow has little trust in people. He has risen to a senior executive because of his business knowledge and skills, not his interpersonal skills. When a former officer of Playtex was asked to characterize his boss's people skills, he replied, "The guy is a train wreck."

Smilow has been known to fire many people. Management turnover probably averaged somewhere in the high 30% range when Smilow ran Playtex. Under the former head of Playtex's International Division, Ralston Coffin, foreign sales and profits increased dramatically over four years. Smilow dumped him nonetheless. Once Smilow fired an employee with over 15 years of service and then refused to extend the man's medical insurance while he sought a job, even though he had a heart condition. After some discussion, personnel executives got Smilow to relent on the insurance and even allow the man to use a company office in his job search. Soon, however, Smilow forced the personnel department

to move the man's parking space. Smilow didn't want to see him in the parking lot.[13]

Questions

1. What are the problem-solving styles of these two men?
2. How would you like to work for either of them?
3. How can you account for their remarkable business success?

Roger Smith at General Motors

In 1980, the year before Roger Smith became the 10th Chief Executive Officer of General Motors, GM was in the red for the first time in more than 50 years. During 1981, Smith's in-house cost-cutting measures, including closing inefficient plants and the sale of the company's New York City office building, resulted in a profit of $33.4 million. In 1982, he consolidated and modernized GM plants, got wage concessions from the union, and saw GM's profits reach $926 million. In 1983, GM sold a record number of cars (4.1 million) and recorded record profits of $3.8 billion. In 1984, profits were slightly over $4.7 billion.

Smith began his GM career in the finance department at GM. "Being part of the finance staff," he says, "you're a little bit back from all the gung-ho spirit you normally get from other divisions, and you develop a more pragmatic attitude. Believe me, I've had my share of pet projects that just didn't fly. I've always felt that GM had not, in the past, quit early enough on some projects. One of my major roles is to manage change. Strategic planning is worthless without strategic management."

Traditionally, the word *change* has not been a commonly used term at GM. However, the radical reorganization of GM in late 1984 has changed this. Smith simplified GM's five separate car divisions (Cadillac, Buick,

Oldsmobile, Pontiac, and Chevrolet) into just two groups—one responsible for development and production of small cars, the other focused on the larger models. Smith also turned foreign rivals into partners when GM moved into joint ventures with Suzuki, Isuzu, and Toyota.

In 1985, Smith announced that a new car, the Saturn, will be made and sold by a new subsidiary. The goal of this new corporation is to produce the Saturn, a car that could get 45 miles per gallon, by the late 1980's. Creating the Saturn Corporation was an innovative step for GM. Not only will the car be built by a completely new organization, the first such addition since GM purchased Chevrolet in 1918, but they will be built under a new labor contract and sold by a new network of dealers. "We hope this car will be less labor intensive, less material intensive, less everything intensive than everything we have done before," Smith says.

Under Smith's leadership, GM has made some other business acquisitions. In 1984, GM bought EDS (Electronic Data Systems), an information processing company that devised governmental and industrial computer programs. EDS's annual growth rate has been about 20%. Some computer industry analysts say that after the eventual shakedown in computers, only a half dozen big international players will survive, including IBM, AT&T, and either ITT or GM–EDS. GM also has joined with a Japanese firm to produce robots.

Smith's management style has broken with GM's tradition. He has streamlined GM's penchant for paper pushing and has opted for a hands-on, more participative management style. This means that managers have more authority to make decisions. Smith describes the job assignment that had the greatest impact on his career:

> It was a worldwide operation and entailed everything from the production of a million valve lifters a day to marketing locomotives selling at half a million dollars a crack," he says.
>
> Since our automotive side was making good money, we never got into too much trouble or got much attention from others in the company. It was running my own thing—a pretty nice deal, being left alone.[14]

Questions

1. What is Smith's problem-solving style?
2. How have Smith's managerial experiences helped shape his problem-solving style?

REFERENCES

1. Adapted from Iacocca, L. *Iacocca: An Autobiography.* New York: Bantam Books, 1984; Leigh, J. Executives and the Personality Factor. *Sky,* May 1985, 34–38.

2. Jung, C. *Psychological Types.* London: Routledge and Kegan Paul, 1923.

3. For a text to determine your own style, see Hai, D. *Organizational Behavior: Experiences and Cases.* St. Paul, Minn.: West, 1986. For some of the more popular tests, see Myers, I. *The Myers–Briggs Type Indicator.* Palo Alto, Calif.: Consulting Psychologists Press, 1962; Keirsay,

D., and Bates, M. *Please Understand Me.* Del Mar, Calif.: Prometheus Nemesis Books, 1978. For some problems with these instruments, see Schweiger, D., Measuring Managers' Minds: A Critical Reply to Robey and Taggart, *Academy of Management Review,* 1983, *8,* 143–151.

4. Myers, I. *Gifts Differing.* Palo Alto, Calif.: Consulting Psychologists Press, 1980.

5. For articles written on managers' problem-solving styles, see Slocum, J., and Hellriegel, D. A Look at How Managers' Minds Work. *Business Horizons,* July–August 1983, 58–67; Isenberg, D. How Senior

Managers Think. *Harvard Business Review,* November–December 1984, 81–90; Mitroff, I., and Kilmann, R. Stories Managers Tell: A New Tool for Organizational Problem Solving. *Management Review,* July 1975, 18–28; McKenney, J., and Keen, P. How Managers' Minds Work. *Harvard Business Review,* July–August 1974, 79–90; Kiechel, W. How Executives Think. *Fortune,* February 4, 1985, 127–128.

6. For further information, see Hoy, F., and Hellriegel, D. The Kilmann and Herden Model of Organizational Effectiveness Criteria for Small Business Managers. *Academy of Management Journal,* 1982, *25,* 308–322; Hoy, F., and Boulton, W. Problem-Solving Styles of Students: Are Educators Producing What Business Needs? *Collegiate News and Views,* 1983, *36*(3), 15–21; Hai, D. Comparisons of Personality Dimensions in Managers: Is There a Management Aptitude? *Akron Business & Economic Review,* Spring 1983, 31–36; Henderson, J., and Nutt, P. The Influence of Decision Style on Decision Making. *Management Science,* 1980, *26,* 371–386; Fleming, J. A Suggested Approach to Linking Decision Styles with Business Ethics. *Journal of Business Ethics,* 1985, *4,* 137–144.

7. Menzies, D. Don Nyrop Keeps Tight Rein on Northwest. *Fortune,* August 14, 1978, 148–150; The Airline Report. *Dallas Morning News,* May 1, 1985.

8. Mok, P. Behind the Great Stone Face. *Texas Parade Magazine,* November 1976, 49–52.

9. Where Management Style Sets the Strategy. *Business Week,* October 23, 1978, 88–90; *Moody's Industrial Manual,* 1985, 5703–5704.

10. Stieglitz, H. Maneuvering in a Dogfight. *Across the Board,* March 1985, 19–23.

11. Kilmann, R. *Beyond the Quick Fix.* San Francisco, Calif.: Jossey-Bass, 1985; Agor, W. *Intuitive Management.* Englewood Cliffs, N.J.: Prentice-Hall, 1984.

12. Mitroff, I. Archetypal Social Systems Analysis: On the Deeper Structure of Human Systems. *Academy of Management Review,* 1983, *8,* 387–397.

13. Abstracted from Flax, S. The Toughest Bosses in America. *Fortune,* August 6, 1984, 18–23.

14. Abstracted from Fisher, A. GM's Unlikely Revolutionist. *Fortune,* March 19, 1984, 106–112; Kubit, D. Roger Smith—GM's Big Surprise. *Nation's Business,* February 1985, 32–36.

6 Learning and Reinforcement

LEARNING OBJECTIVES

When you have finished studying this chapter, you should be able to:

- Discuss the differences among classical, vicarious, and operant theories of learning.
- State the contingencies of reinforcement.
- List the methods used to increase desired behaviors and reduce undesired behaviors.
- List four reinforcement schedules.
- Describe the key steps used in behavioral modification.
- State two limitations of behavioral modification.

OUTLINE

Preview Case

Fran Tarkenton

Francis Asbury Tarkenton, former professional quarterback for the New York Giants and Minnesota Vikings, is now chairman of a management consulting company called Tarkenton Productivity Group. His company has been used by Boeing, GTE, Continental Group, and Southwestern Bell to design incentive programs that are aimed at raising productivity in their plants and offices. For the programs, Tarkenton charges these companies fees that range from $50,000 to $250,000. In his role as consultant, the problems Tarkenton encounters are performance problems. "If the marketing vice-president is interested in improving performance, he has to get involved, accept and acknowledge his responsibility for the performance he wants," Tarkenton emphasizes. "He has to learn to do things differently to fulfill that responsibility. He is going to have to learn about behavior—to control consequences, to use positive reinforcement, to give feedback, to manage people for long-range payoff, rather than to let them skate from sales campaign gimmick to sales campaign gimmick. And that means making a systematic change in how that marketing vice-president manages. It means arranging the management system so people know how they are doing and get rewarded when they are doing things correctly."

In discussing whether behavior management has a place on the gridiron, Tarkenton says, "Yes, we do have a performance feedback system." Managing behavior through consequences is an important part of managing the Vikings' offense. Extensive data is collected on twenty variables that, history and a good computer have proved, bear directly on the offensive team effort. During the Wednesday showing of Sunday's game films, the offensive unit is evaluated according to these twenty variables. Perfect performance on eleven or twelve of these critical variables usually leads to winning. "We get feedback on the variables, we get reinforced on the variables, and it gets our people to concentrate on the things that are important to our winning. We find the most effective reinforcement is social reinforcement, peer reinforcement of each other."

Tarkenton also comments on former Green Bay Packer Coach, Vince Lombardi. "Everyone thinks of him as very punitive, very negative, but he was no ranting, raving lunatic," Tarkenton emphasizes. "He was a very organized, systematic person. He pinpointed exactly what he wanted, and he gave feedback—sometimes loudly, but feedback. As a reinforcing agent, he was unbelievable. A nod from Lombardi could be a more powerful reinforcer than twenty minutes of gushing from anyone else."

He also talked about Ohio State Coach Woody Hayes' slapping Buckeye decals on his player's helmets when they perform well. "Some people think that's all Mickey Mouse, stars on the helmet," says Tarkenton. "It isn't. Recognition for doing a good job, especially from those who know good performance from bad performance, means a lot. Recognition means a lot to the fifty-year-old guy working on the plant floor, and to the guy sitting in the chairman-of-the-board chair, and to the college football player. It means a lot to know you did something well, and somebody saw it, and somebody acknowledged it. People don't just work from paycheck to paycheck, at least not any more. Those stars on the helmets—be they real stars or metaphorical stars—mean a lot."

Tarkenton comments further: "We're *all* reinforcing agents and feedback agents for each other, each *and* every one of us. I'm a great believer in feedback, positive and negative. When something isn't right, tell the performer what and why and how to correct it. And when it's right, deliver the positive reinforcement and positive feedback."[1]

Fran Tarkenton's behavior management system is based on specific principles drawn from an area of psychology called **learning theory**. The learning theory approach stresses the assessment of behavior in objective, measurable (countable) terms. Behavior must be publicly observable; this approach deemphasizes unobservable, inner, cognitive behavior. This chapter will explore the development, maintenance, and change of employee work behaviors.

Desirable work behaviors contribute to the attainment of organizational goals; conversely, undesirable work behaviors are detrimental to these goals. Labeling behavior as "desirable" or "undesirable" is entirely subjective and depends on the value system of the person making the assessment. For example, a secretary who returns late from a coffee break exhibits undesirable behavior from the supervisor's viewpoint, desirable behavior from the viewpoint of friends with whom the worker chats during the break, and desirable behavior from the worker's own viewpoint because of relief from physical fatigue.

Behavior that is viewed as undesirable by management, such as returning late from a break, becomes a potential target for management action to bring about change. By changing something in the environment, management can change the frequency of the undesirable behavior. However, a behavior should not be regarded as desirable or undesirable only in terms of whether the managerial objective is to increase or decrease its frequency. Rather, the work setting is the basis for determining whether a behavior is desirable or undesirable. The more a behavior deviates from organizational norms, the more it would be regarded as undesirable. However, norms may vary considerably from one organization to another. For example, a research and development laboratory may encourage scientists to question directives from top management because professional judgment is critical to the organization's final output. A military organization, however, would consider such questioning as insubordination and subject the questioner to severe sanctions.

A good manager does not try to change an employee's basic personality or fundamental beliefs. Rather, the manager should identify observable employee behaviors and the environmental conditions that affect these behaviors. The manager should then attempt to control external events in order to manage employee behavior. However, as we discussed in Chapters, 3, 4, and 5, this does not mean that events *within* the individual employee do not influence behavior. An individual's personality, values, and psychological functions influence the manner in which he or she behaves. Because managers often have a difficult time uncovering these characteristics in a subordinate, they focus on those behaviors that they observe.

TYPES OF LEARNING

Learning is a relatively permanent change in the frequency of occurrence of a specific employee work behavior.[2] In an organization, a manager wants employees to learn productive work behaviors. To a great extent, learning new work behaviors depends on environmental factors. The manager's goal, then, is to provide learning experiences in an environment that will promote the employee behaviors desired by the organization. Learning generally is considered to take place in one of three ways: classical conditioning; vicarious or observational learning; and operant conditioning.

Classical Conditioning

Classical conditioning involves reflexive responses or behaviors. A **reflex** is an involuntary or automatic response that is not under an individual's conscious control. Examples of reflexive behavior are shown in Table 6-1. In classical conditioning, an *unconditioned stimulus* (environmental event) is said to elicit a reflexive response. Sometimes a neutral environmental event, called a *conditioned stimulus,* can be paired with the unconditioned stimulus that elicits the reflex. Eventually, the conditioned stimulus alone elicits the reflexive behavior. In classical conditioning, environmental events that precede a reflexive response control it.

The name most frequently associated with classical conditioning is Ivan Pavlov, the Russian physiologist whose experiments with dogs led to the early formulations of classical conditioning theory. In Pavlov's famous experiment, the sound of a bell (the conditioned stimulus) was paired with the desire for food (the unconditioned stimulus), so that a dog eventually exhibited a salivation response (the reflex response) to the sound of the bell alone. This process is shown in Figure 6-1.

The distinction between reflexive and nonreflexive behavior has become somewhat blurred. Behaviors formerly thought to be exclusively reflex responses in some cases, have been shown to be under the individual's control. For example, biofeedback techniques can be effective in changing heart rate, blood pressure, muscle tension, and galvanic skin response—responses previously considered to be exclusively reflexive. Exciting new breakthroughs can be anticipated in this area of learning.

From a managerial viewpoint, classical conditioning is usually not considered applicable to the work setting. The type of employee behavior that managers have to deal with usually does not include reflexive responses that are amenable to change through the use of classical conditioning techniques. Instead, managers are interested in the voluntary behavior of employees and how it can be changed through the use of other techniques.

TABLE 6-1   Examples of Reflexive Behavior

	Stimulus (S) ———————————➤	Response (R)
The individual	is stuck by a pin and	flinches.
	is shocked by an electric current and	jumps or screams.
	has something in his or her eye and	blinks.
	hits an elbow on the corner of a desk and	flexes arm.

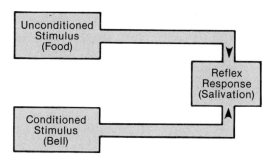

FIGURE 6-1.
Classical Conditioning

Vicarious Learning

In **vicarious learning**—also called observational learning, modeling, and imitation—a person does not learn through direct experience.[3] Vicarious learning occurs through observation of others who are performing the behavior and/or experiencing the consequences of the behavior. By observing others, a person learns a behavior without actually having performed it.

In Practice: Dick Hammil

When Dick Hammil first came to work for ADT Computer Systems, he had never worked with a computer. He was somewhat apprehensive when Joan Davis, his supervisor, took him into the computer room with all of its complex consoles and machines. Dick had been fairly confident when he applied for the computer operator job, but the first day he doubted that he would be able to learn to operate the complicated equipment.

Joan did two things to help Dick get started. First, she assigned him to work with Karen Stone, who had been operating the equipment for more than three years. Second, she took Dick to the personnel training cubicle and showed him how to check out and operate the slide-tape equipment that provided instructions on how to operate the computer.

During the first few days, Dick did not operate the computer at all. He observed Karen very closely, noting that she had fairly well-patterned ways of doing task assignments. In addition, the slide-tape modules presented him with an opportunity to observe most of the operating tasks in action. As Dick came in for his fifth day of work, he looked forward to actually operating the console, as Karen had promised. Although he had not yet actually performed the task, Dick felt that he had learned a lot from observing Karen and the slide tapes. He felt confident of being able to undertake most of the operating tasks.

While vicarious learning can be helpful in the development of a new behavior, it does not in itself result in performance. Performance is the actual accomplishment of the behavior, and it is necessary for sustained maintenance of learned behaviors. The consequences that follow the performance of a newly learned task, or behavior, are important in maintaining its frequency. That is, operant conditioning, which will be described in the next section, is an important subsequent support of vicarious learning.

The degree to which vicarious learning affects subsequent performance also depends on other factors. People are more likely to imitate models that they perceive as having high prestige, status, or expertise. They also tend to imitate other people that are similar to them rather than different from them.

Operant Conditioning

Operant conditioning attempts to provoke a change in the voluntary, or operant, work behavior of an employee.[4] Voluntary behaviors are called *operants* because they operate, or have some influence, on the environment; they generate some consequence in that environment.

The consequences that follow the behavior partly control it. Virtually all employee work behaviors in an organization are operant behaviors. Table 6-2 shows some examples of operant stimuli and responses. In fact, most behaviors in everyday life (such as talking, walking, reading, frowning, or working) are voluntary and thus are operant behaviors.

Operant work behaviors are of interest to managers because these behaviors can be controlled, or managed, by their environmental consequences. The frequency of an employee behavior can be increased or decreased by changing the environmental consequences of that behavior. The critical aspect of operant conditioning is what happens as a consequence of the response. Since the strength and frequency of operantly conditioned behaviors are determined mainly by consequences, managers must understand the effects of different kinds of consequences on the work behaviors of employees.

CONTINGENCIES OF REINFORCEMENT

A **contingency of reinforcement** is the relationship between a behavior and the preceding and following environmental events that influence that behavior. A contingency of reinforcement consists of an antecedent, a behavior, and a consequence.[5] Figure 6-2 depicts these elements of a contingency of reinforcement.

An **antecedent** is a stimulus that precedes a behavior and sets the stage for the behavior to occur. The probability of occurrence of a particular behavior can be increased by presenting or removing a particular antecedent. The manager who prepares a "to do" list is organizing the work for the employee and attempts to focus the employee's attention on specific behaviors the manager deems important. The "to do" list is an antecedent that the manager is using to influence the subordinate's behavior.

A **consequence** is what results from a behavior. A consequence is *contingent on* the behavior—the manager administers the consequence only if the

---

TABLE 6-2   Examples of Operant Behaviors and Their Consequences

	Response (R)	Stimulus (S)
The individual	works and	is paid.
	is late to work and	is docked pay.
	enters a restaurant and	eats.
	enters a football stadium and	watches a football game.
	enters a grocery store and	buys food.

Antecedent event: what comes before the behavior.
Consequence event: what comes after the behavior.

FIGURE 6–2.
A Contingency of
Reinforcement

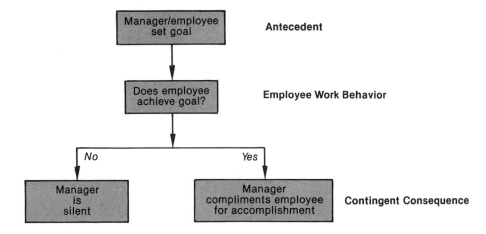

FIGURE 6–3.
The Logic of a
Contingent
Consequence

employee behavior occurs. That is, the occurrence of a consequence depends on successful performance of the employee behavior. Figure 6-3 shows the logic of a contingent consequence.

First, the employee sets a goal (say, selling $100,000 worth of equipment next month) that is agreed to by the manager. Next, the employee performs activities to achieve this goal (calling on four new customers a week, having lunch with a current buyer, attending a two-day executive training program on new methods of selling). If the employee reaches the sales goal, the manager provides the employee with a verbal consequence (praise) that is contingent on achievement of the goal. If the employee does not reach the goal, the manager may not say anything or may reprimand the employee.

To further understand the contingency of reinforcement concept, it is necessary to identify the types of contingency. First, the environmental event can be *presented* (applied) or *withdrawn* (removed); that is, it is possible to present or withdraw an environmental event contingent on an employee behavior. Also, it is useful to classify the environmental event as positive or aversive. **Positive events** are desired, or pleasing, to the employee, whereas **aversive events** are undesired, or displeasing. Figure 6-4 shows how these factors can be combined to produce various types of contingencies of reinforcement. It also indicates whether a particular type of contingency increases or decreases the future frequency of the employee behavior. Figure 6-4 forms the basis for the following discussion of the various types of contingencies of reinforcement. Note that reinforcement, whether positive or negative, always *increases* the frequency of the employee behavior. Extinction and punishment always *decrease* the frequency of the employee behavior.

Positive Reinforcement

Reinforcement is a behavioral contingency that increases the frequency of a particular behavior that it follows. **Positive reinforcement** (Box 1, Figure 6-4)

FIGURE 6–4.
Types of
Contingencies of
Reinforcement

	Event Is Added	Event Is Removed
Pleasant Event	**1** Positive reinforcement (increases likelihood that behavior preceding it will be repeated)	**2** Extinction (punishment by removal) (decreases likelihood that behavior preceding it will be repeated)
Unpleasant Event	**3** Punishment (decreases likelihood that behavior preceding it will be repeated)	**4** Negative reinforcement (increases likelihood that behavior preceding it will be repeated)

involves the presentation of a pleasant event contingent on the occurrence of a behavior. That is, a manager provides some positive reward contingent on an employee's behavior that the manager views as desirable or leading toward achievement of the organization's goals.[6]

REINFORCEMENT VERSUS REWARD   The terms *reinforcement* and *reward* are frequently confused in everyday usage. A reward is an event (consequence) that a person would define as desirable or pleasing. Thus whether a reward acts as a reinforcer is a subjective choice on the part of the receiver. The manager who singles out and praises an employee before his co-workers for finding an error in the group's report believed that he was reinforcing that behavior. Later, however, the manager finds out that the employee is being given the silent treatment by his co-workers, and that the employee's error finding behavior has decreased. To qualify as a reinforcer, a reward must increase the frequency of the behavior it follows. In this case, the reward did not act as a reinforcer because the frequency of the behavior decreased.

Whether or not a reward acts as a reinforcer can be determined empirically. If the frequency of a desired behavior increases as a result of the contingent administration of the reward, the reward can be said to be a reinforcer. If any contingent environmental consequence increases the frequency of a desired employee behavior, then that contingent environmental consequence is said to be a reinforcer.

PRIMARY AND SECONDARY REINFORCERS   An individual does not have to learn the reinforcing value of a consequence called a **primary reinforcer.** Food and water are primary reinforcers for hungry and thirsty people. This is not to say that primary reinforcers always reinforce. If an individual is satiated with a consequence, it may not be reinforcing. For example, food may not be a reinforcer to someone who has just completed a 12-course meal. An environmental event more likely reinforces if an individual is deprived of the event.

Most behavior in organizations is influenced not by primary reinforcers but by secondary reinforcers. A **secondary reinforcer** is an event that once had neutral value but that has taken on some value (positive or negative) for an individual because of past experience. Money is an obvious example of a secondary reinforcer. It cannot satisfy a basic human need, but it has a value that can be used to purchase both basic necessities and nonessentials by an employee.

Principles of Positive Reinforcement

Several factors potentially can influence the intensity of a positive reinforcement contingency.[7] These factors can be thought of loosely as "principles" because they help to explain optimum reinforcement conditions.

PRINCIPLE OF CONTINGENT REINFORCEMENT   The **principle of contingent reinforcement** states that the reinforcer must be administered *only* if the desired, or target, behavior is performed. According to this principle, a reinforcer loses effectiveness if it is administered when the desired behavior has *not* been performed. To determine whether the principle was followed, ask the question, "Was the reinforcer given only when the target behavior occurred?"

PRINCIPLE OF IMMEDIATE REINFORCEMENT   The **principle of immediate reinforcement** states that the reinforcer will have more effect if it is administered immediately after the target behavior has occurred. The more time that elapses, the less effective the reinforcer will be. Thus delivery of the reinforcer should follow completion of the target behavior as closely as is practical.

PRINCIPLE OF REINFORCEMENT SIZE   The **principle of reinforcement size** states that the larger the amount of reinforcer delivered after the target behavior, the more effect the reinforcer will have on the rate of the target behavior. The amount, or size, of the reinforcer is relative. A reinforcer that might seem large to one person may be small to another person, so the reinforcer's appropriate size must be determined in relation both to the behavior and the individual.

PRINCIPLE OF REINFORCEMENT DEPRIVATION   The **principle of reinforcement deprivation** states that the more a person is deprived of the reinforcer, the more effect it will have on the future occurrence of the target behavior. However, if an employee recently has had enough of a reinforcer and is satiated, the reinforcer will have less effect.

Organizational Rewards

What types of rewards are commonly used in organizations? Material rewards—salary, bonuses, fringe benefits, and so forth—are obvious. However, organizations offer a wide range of rewards, many of which are not immediately apparent. They include such things as verbal approval, assignment to desired tasks, improved working conditions, and extra time off. In addition, self-administered rewards are important. Self-congratulations for accomplishing a particularly difficult assignment can be an important reinforcer for the person. Table 6-3 contains an extensive list of organizational rewards.

A successful management program at Cosmopolitan Lady illustrates the use of organizational rewards and the importance of adhering to the principles of positive reinforcement.

TABLE 6-3   Rewards Used by Organizations

Material Rewards	Fringe Benefits	Status Symbols	Social/ Interpersonal Rewards	Rewards from the Task	Self- Administered Rewards
Pay	Medical plans	Corner offices	Informal	Sense of	Self-recognition
Pay raises	Company	Offices with	recognition	achievement	Self-praise
Stock options	automobiles	windows	Praise	Jobs with more	Self-congratu-
Profit sharing	Insurance plans	Carpeting	Smiles	responsibility	lations
Bonus plans	Pension	Drapes	Evaluative	Job rotation	
Incentive plans	contributions	Paintings	feedback	Output feedback	
Christmas	Product discount	Watches	Compliments		
bonuses	plans	Rings	Nonverbal signals		
	Vacation trips		Pats on the back		
	Recreation		Requests for		
	facilities		suggestions		
	Work breaks		Invitations to		
	Club privileges		coffee or lunch		
	Expense		Newspaper		
	accounts		articles		
			Formal awards or		
			recognition		
			Wall plaques		

In Practice: Cosmopolitan Lady

A major problem for most women's spas is employee turnover. A typical spa has about 400 percent turnover a year of its employees. There are several reasons for this. First, most spa employees are required to work 60–70 hours per week. Second, there is tremendous pressure on sales people to sell memberships.

Cosmopolitan Lady has designed a system that has drastically reduced employee turnover at its five locations in the Dallas/Fort Worth area. Each spa has two managers who handle separate sales teams. The two teams are called A and Z. Each team works alternate days, so no saleswoman works more than 36 hours per week. The primary financial incentive for the saleswoman is to meet her quota of selling six new, $2,500 memberships a month. If a saleswoman fails to meet her quota, she receives only one-half the full commission on her total sales. Once a saleswoman meets her monthly quota, she receives a bonus of $50, and becomes eligible to receive an additional $50 for every membership she sells above the $15,000 level. A saleswoman at Cosmopolitan Lady can be expected to earn between $20,000 and $35,000 per year.

Like the saleswoman, the managers of their respective teams also have sales quotas. Each manager has a monthly quota of $67,500. If the manager meets her quota, she receives one piece of fine crystal stemware. If a manager repeatedly does not meet her quota, she is demoted to saleswoman. In addition, the manager whose team finishes last in sales for the month receives the Horse's Butt Award, a small trophy in the shape of a horse's rear end. If a manager meets her quota throughout the year, she can earn up to $75,000.

At the end of every month, all saleswomen and managers are required to attend a company meeting. At these meetings, the outstanding saleswomen from the previous month are recognized. The number 1 saleswoman (in terms of total dollars) receives a plaque with her name engraved on it, $100 in cash, and the privilege of driving a brand new red Corvette. The number 2 saleswoman receives a plaque as well as $50 cash. The next five top saleswomen are recognized by name only, but are invited to the monthly Top Five Luncheon.

In addition to these programs, the owner has instituted a company-wide program. This program is known as the blue-chip program. If the owner sees an employee performing commendably, he will flip a blue plastic poker chip in the air to that employee. The blue chip is worth $5.00, redeemable at the end of the month. When the owner flips the chip, the employees nearby are expected to shout, "Ain't it great to be alive."[8]

Where Cosmopolitan Lady has used positive reinforcement, behavior change has been dramatic, sustained, and uniformly in the desired direction. Positive reinforcement was used selectively in areas where work could be measured and quantifiable standards set (if they did not already exist) and in areas where observation showed that the existing level of performance was far below standard. Other corporations, such as United Airlines, IBM, IT&T, Procter & Gamble, Ford Motor Company, and Emory Air Freight, have used positive reinforcement approaches with similar results.[9]

Negative Reinforcement

In **negative reinforcement** (Box 4, Figure 6-4), an unpleasant event is presented *before* the employee behavior and is then removed when the behavior occurs. This procedure increases the frequency of that specific behavior.[10] Negative reinforcement is sometimes confused with punishment because both use aversive events to control behavior. However, negative reinforcement is used to *increase* the frequency of a desired behavior, whereas extinction and punishment are used to *decrease* the frequency of an undesired behavior. Negative reinforcement is a form of social blackmail because the person will behave in a certain way or be punished.

Supervisors frequently use negative reinforcement when an employee has *not* done something that is desired. For example, when a supervisor yells at a messy worker until the employee cleans a machine, the procedure is negative reinforcement: the oral reprimand terminates when the worker begins to clean the machine, and the probability that he will continue to clean the machine *increases*. This type of procedure is also called *escape* because the employee begins cleaning the machine to escape the supervisor's reprimand. In escape, an aversive event is present until an employee performs a behavior, or *escape response,* to terminate it.

Avoidance is closely related to escape. A person prevents an aversive event from occurring by completing the target behavior before the aversive event is presented. After several encounters with an angry supervisor over a dirty machine, for example, the employee may clean the machine to *avoid* an oral reprimand from the supervisor. Escape and avoidance are both types of negative reinforcement that result in an increase in the target behavior and involve displeasing events.

Extinction

Whereas reinforcement increases the frequency of a desirable behavior, extinction decreases the frequency and eventually extinguishes an undesirable behavior (Box 2, Figure 6-4). In **extinction,** events that are reinforcers are stopped. Managers use extinction to diminish undesirable employee behaviors. That is, extinction reduces the occurrence of employee behaviors that do not lead toward achievement of organizational goals. The extinction procedure consists of three steps:

- Identifying the target behavior the manager wants to reduce or eliminate.
- Identifying the reinforcer that maintains the target behavior.
- Stopping the reinforcer.

Extinction is a useful technique for reducing behaviors that are undesirable or disruptive to normal work flow. For example, a group reinforces the disruptive behavior of a member by laughing at this behavior. When the group stops laughing (the reinforcer), the disruptive behavior will diminish and eventually stop.

Extinction can also be regarded as a failure to reinforce a behavior positively. In this regard, the extinction of behaviors can be quite unintentional. If managers fail to reinforce desirable behaviors, they may be using a process of extinction without recognizing it. As a result, the frequency of desirable behaviors may inadvertently decrease.

Although extinction may effectively decrease undesirable employee behavior, it does not automatically replace the undesirable behavior with a desirable behavior. Often when extinction is stopped, the undesirable behavior is likely to return if alternative behaviors have not been developed to replace the extinguished behavior. Therefore, when extinction is used, it should be combined with other methods of reinforcement to develop desirable behavior to replace the extinguished behavior.

Punishment

A **punishment** is an unpleasant event that follows a behavior and decreases its frequency (Box 3, Figure 6-4). As in positive reinforcement, a punishment contingency may include a specific antecedent that cues the employee that a consequence (punisher) will follow a specific behavior. Whereas a positive reinforcement contingency encourages the frequency of a target behavior, a punishment contingency suppresses its frequency.

To qualify as a punisher, an event must decrease the target behavior. In other words, just because an event is thought of as unpleasant, it is not necessarily a punisher. The event must actually suppress behavior before it can be defined as a punisher.

Organizations typically use several types of unpleasant events as punishers. Material consequences, for example, include such events as a cut in pay, a disciplinary layoff without pay, a demotion in salary grade or job classification, or a job transfer because of failure to adequately perform. The ultimate punishment is the firing of an employee for failure to perform. In general, unpleasant material events are not used widely in organizations except in cases of very serious behavior problems.

Interpersonal punishers tend to be used much more widely on a day-to-day basis. Examples include the oral reprimand from a manager to an employee because of unacceptable behavior or nonverbal punishers such as frowns, grunts, and aggressive body language. Sometimes a task itself can be unpleasant. The fatigue that follows hard physical labor can be considered a punisher, as can harsh or dirty working conditions. However, care must be exercised in labeling a punisher: in some fields or to some employees, harsh or dirty working conditions could be considered just "something that goes with the job."

The previously discussed principles of positive reinforcement have equivalents in punishment. For maximum effectiveness, a punisher should be directly linked to the target behavior (principle of contingent punishment); the punisher should be administered immediately (principle of immediate punishment); and in general, the greater the size of the punisher, the stronger the effect will be on the target behavior (principle of punishment size).

Potential Side Effects of Punishment

An argument against the use of punishment is the possibility of undesirable side effects, especially over long periods of time or through sustained periods of punishment. Even though the punishment may eliminate an undesirable employee behavior, the potential secondary consequences may be more of a problem than the original undesirable behavior. Figure 6-5 illustrates some potential side effects of punishment.

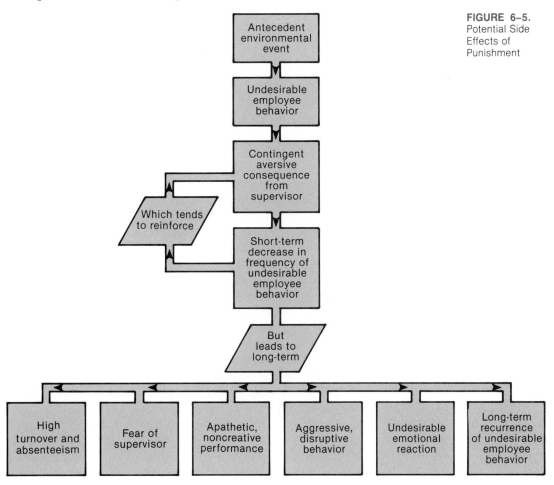

FIGURE 6–5. Potential Side Effects of Punishment

Punishment may cause undesirable emotional reactions. For example, a worker who has been reprimanded for staying at a break too long may react with anger toward the manager and the organization. This anger may lead to behavior that is detrimental to the organization. Sabotage, for example, typically is a result of a punishment-oriented behavioral management system.

Punishment frequently leads to only short-term suppression of the undesirable employee behavior rather than to its elimination. Continuous suppression of an undesirable behavior over a long period of time usually requires continued punishment. Another problem is that the control of the undesirable behavior becomes contingent on the presence of the punishing agent. When the punishing agent is not present, the undesirable employee behavior is likely to recur.

In addition, the punished individual may try to avoid or escape the punishment situation. From an organizational viewpoint, this reaction can sometimes be undesirable because an employee may avoid a particular job situation that is necessary for normal operations. Absenteeism is a form of avoidance that is likely to occur in situations where punishment is used frequently. Voluntary termination is the employee's ultimate form of escape. Organizations that depend on punishment are likely to have higher rates of employee turnover. While some turnover is desirable, excessive rates are undesirable because of increased recruitment and training costs and because useful, adequately performing employees are more likely to leave.

Another problem with punishment is its potential to suppress employee initiative and flexibility. Many an employee has said, "I'm going to do just what I'm told, and nothing more." This reaction to punishment is undesirable, because organizations depend on the personal initiative and creativity that individual employees bring to their jobs. An overuse of punishment tends to produce apathetic employees, who generally are not an asset to an organization. Sustained punishment can also lead to a generalized negative self-esteem on the part of the employee. Low self-esteem, in turn, undermines the confidence necessary for performing most jobs.

Punishment also tends to produce a conditioned fear of the punishing agent. That is, the employee tends to develop a general fear of whoever administers the punishment. This person becomes an environmental cue that indicates to the employee the probability of an aversive event. This is an obvious problem, especially if many day-to-day situations require a normal and positive interaction between the employee and this person. Responses to fear such as "hiding" or reluctance to communicate with a manager may well hinder an employee's normal performance.

Many managers rely on punishment because it often produces fast results in the short run.[11] In essence, the manager is reinforced for using punishment because the approach does produce an immediate change in an employee's behavior. However, this manager overlooks the long-term detrimental side effects of punishment, which can have a cumulative effect. A few incidents of punishment may not produce undesirable side effects, but the long-term, sustained use of punishment as a dominant mode of managing employee behavior will invariably result in unproductive organizational outcomes. Consider what happened at Joe Foster Realty. If Jim Turner, the president of the company, understands the potential side effects of punishment, how should he deal with the situation in Mary Spencer's department?

In Practice: Joe Foster Realty

Joe Foster Realty decided to form a new department to manage shopping malls. It was obvious to Jim Turner, president of the realty company, that leasing space in newly built shopping malls had the potential to bring in large profits. Jim decided that Mary Spencer was the logical person to head up this department, although Mary had little experience in leasing shopping mall space. Jim assigned four subordinates to Mary to help her find locations for new malls and lease space to tenants. Mary had been with the company for several years and knew everyone on a first-name basis. She had resolved that if she ever got to be a department head, she would run a tight ship and not tolerate the monkey business that was going on in some departments. Within the first month, Mary's subordinates knew she meant business. When the first shopping mall project was presented during her weekly staff meeting, Mary jumped all over Barry because he arrived five minutes late. Mary also became quite upset when Sally made a small mathematical error in her report. When Mary asked Roy Hall to work over the weekend on a special report for Jim, she said nothing to him Monday morning. Within a few weeks, Roy was transferred to another department at a lower salary because "he just couldn't perform."

After the first year, Esther Craig, personnel manager, was called into Jim's office. Jim said: "Esther, I'd like you to look into what's going on in Mary's department. When I appointed Mary to this job, I thought that she would make an excellent manager. Lately, however, I'm not so sure that I made the right choice. Look at some of these statistics. Her department has the highest turnover and absenteeism in the company. Three of her four assistants have written to me asking to be transferred out of her department as soon as an opening comes up in another department. In addition, when something unusual comes up, like when the newly constructed Gator Mall in Gainesville, Florida, had severe storm damage last month, her employees seem not up to the task. Her people don't seem to have any 'get up and go.' "

"Besides those problems, Mary has started smoking again and drinking a lot of coffee. I knew that running this new department wasn't going to be a piece of cake, but I'm worried about Mary's ability to take care of herself under these conditions. I know that she and her husband recently separated and that's probably adding strain to the office situation. I guess the bottom line of what I'm asking you to do is help me decide whether I should replace Mary as manager of this department."

Effective Use of Punishment

Positive reinforcement generally is more effective than punishment in the long-term management of employees. However, punishment also has an appropriate place in management, and this section examines some of the factors that influence its effective use.

The most common form of punishment in organizations is the oral reprimand. This is intended to diminish or stop an undesirable employee behavior. An old rule of thumb is "Praise in public; punish in private." Private punishment does indeed establish a different type of contingency than public punishment. In general, a private reprimand can be constructive and instructive in nature, whereas a public punishment is likely to cause undesirable emotional side effects and behavior.

Punishment should be connected as immediately, directly, and obviously as possible to the target behavior. An unnecessarily long time interval between the occurrence of the behavior and the punishment tends to lessen the effectiveness of the punishment. Verbal reprimands should never be delivered about behavior in general and, especially, never about a so-called bad attitude. An effective reprimand pinpoints and specifically describes the undesirable behavior to be avoided in the future. It focuses on the target behavior and avoids threatening the employee's intrinsic worth. The effective reprimand punishes *specific* undesirable behavior, not the person.

Unfortunately, punishment (by definition) trains a person in *what not to do,* but not in *what to do.* Therefore a manager must specify an alternative behavior to the employee. Then, when the employee performs the desired alternative behavior, it is essential for the manager to reinforce that behavior positively.

Finally, managers should strike an appropriate balance between the use of positive and aversive management. It is not the absolute number of aversive management incidents that is really important, but the ratio of positive to aversive incidents. When a manager uses positive reinforcement frequently, an occasional deserved punishment can be quite effective. However, if a manager never uses positive reinforcement, but relies entirely on aversive management procedures, the long-run side effects are likely to counteract any short-term benefits. Positive management procedures should dominate in any complete management program.[12]

Summary of Types of Contingencies of Reinforcement

Figure 6-6 demonstrates the use of the two types of reinforcement (positive and negative), extinction, and punishment. Remember, for a positive reinforcer to cause a behavior desired by the manager to be repeated, it must be of value to the employee. If the employee is consistently on time, the manager positively reinforces this behavior by complimenting the employee and/ or recommending a pay raise. The second method of obtaining the desired behavior from the employee is negative reinforcement. In this case, if the employee has been reprimanded in the past for coming to work late and then

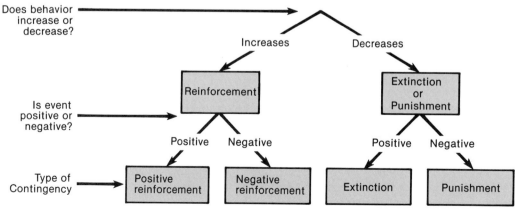

FIGURE 6–6.
Responses to Behavior: Reinforcement, Extinction, and Punishment

reports to work on time, the manager refrains from saying anything that would embarrass the employee. The manager hopes that the employee will learn to avoid unpleasant remarks by coming to work on time.

If the employee comes to work late, the manager can use either extinction or punishment in an attempt to stop this undesirable behavior. The manager who chooses extinction does not give the tardy employee praise or a pay raise but just simply ignores the employee. The manager who chooses punishment may reprimand, fine, and/or suspend the employee—and, ultimately fire the employee if the employee is consistently late.

Clay and Ellen Hamner recommend six guidelines for implementing these strategies:

- Do not give the same level of reward to all employees.
- Remember that failure to respond to behavior has reinforcing consequences; superiors are bound to shape the behavior of subordinates by the way in which they utilize the rewards at their disposal. Therefore carefully examine the consequences of nonactions as well as actions.
- Tell employees what behavior gets reinforced.
- Tell workers what they are doing wrong.
- Do not punish employees in front of others.
- Make the consequences equal to the behavior. In other words, do not cheat workers out of their just rewards.[13]

SCHEDULES OF REINFORCEMENT

The rules that describe when reinforcers that are contingent on employee behavior are applied are known as *schedules of reinforcement*. Deliberately or not, reinforcement is always delivered according to some schedule.[14]

Continuous and Intermittent Reinforcement

In the simplest schedule, known as **continuous reinforcement**, the behavior is reinforced each time it occurs. Unfortunately, the manager seldom has the opportunity to reinforce the employee every time the employee demonstrates the correct behavior. Therefore behavior is generally reinforced intermittently.

An **intermittent reinforcement** is delivery of a reinforcer after some, but not every, occurrence of the behavior. Intermittent reinforcement can be subdivided into interval and ratio and fixed and variable schedules. Reinforcers are delivered after the passage of a certain amount of time in an interval schedule. In a ratio schedule, reinforcers are delivered after a certain number of behaviors have been performed. Another distinction in intermittent schedules is that of fixed (not changing) and variable (constantly changing) schedules. Thus there are four types of intermittent schedules: fixed interval, variable interval, fixed ratio, and variable ratio.

Fixed Interval Schedule

A **fixed interval schedule** means that a constant amount of time must pass before a reinforcer can be provided. The first desired behavior to occur after the interval has elapsed is reinforced. For example, in an FI:1hr (fixed interval, one hour) schedule, the first target behavior that occurs after an hour has elapsed is reinforced.

Administering rewards under this schedule tends to produce an uneven pattern of responses. Prior to the reinforcement, the behavior is infrequent and unenergetic. Immediately following the reinforcement, the behavior becomes more frequent and energetic. Why? Because the individual rather quickly figures out that another reward will not immediately follow the last one. Therefore the person may as well relax until it is time to be rewarded again. A common example of administering rewards on a fixed interval schedule is the payment of employees on a weekly, biweekly, or monthly basis. Monetary reinforcement comes regularly at the end of a specific period of time. Such time intervals, unfortunately, are generally too long to be an effective form of reinforcement for newly acquired work-related behavior.

Variable Interval Schedule

In a **variable interval schedule,** the reinforcer is also dependent on the passage of a certain amount of time, but that time interval tends to vary around some average length of time. For example, a steel industry vice-president makes it a point to walk through the melting shop on the average of once a day at varied times, perhaps twice on Monday, once on Tuesday, not on Wednesday, not on Thursday, and twice on Friday. During this walk, this manager reinforces any desirable behavior observed.

Fixed Ratio Schedule

In a **fixed ratio schedule,** the target behavior must occur a certain number of times before it is reinforced. The exact number of behaviors is specified. A fixed ratio that reinforces after every response is designated FR 1:1.

Administering rewards under a fixed ratio schedule tends to produce a high response rate that is characterized by steady behavior. The person soon determines that reinforcement is based on the number of responses and performs the responses as quickly as possible in order to receive the reward.[15] The piece-rate system used in many manufacturing plants is an example of such a schedule. Production workers are paid on the basis of how many acceptable pieces they produce (number of responses). Other things being equal, the worker's performance should be steady. In reality, other things are never equal, and a piece-rate system may not lead to this type of behavior.

Variable Ratio Schedule

The **variable ratio schedule** means that a certain number of target behaviors must occur before the reinforcer is delivered, but the number of behaviors varies around some average. Managers frequently use variable ratio schedules with nonmaterial reinforcers. Praise and recognition, for example, can be given on a variable ratio schedule. Managers do not reinforce every behavior, and the number of behaviors that occur before they give verbal approval varies from one time to the next.

Table 6-4 summarizes the four types of reinforcement schedules. Which is superior? While the data are inconclusive, it appears that the ratio reward schedules—fixed or variable—lead to better performance than the interval

TABLE 6-4   Schedules of Intermittent Reinforcement

Schedule of Reinforcement	Nature of Reinforcement	Effects on Behavior when Applied	Effects on Behavior when Perceived	Example
Fixed interval	Reward on fixed time basis	Leads to average and irregular performance	Quick extinction of behavior	Weekly paycheck
Fixed ratio	Reward consistently tied to output	Leads quickly to very high and stable performance	Quick extinction of behavior	Piece-rate pay system
Variable interval	Reward given at variable intervals around some average time	Leads to moderately high and stable performance	Slow extinction of behavior	Monthly performance appraisal and reward at random times each month
Variable ratio	Reward given at variable output levels around some average output	Leads to very high performance	Slow extinction of behavior	Sales bonus tied to selling X accounts, but X constantly changing around some mean

Source: Steers, R. *Introduction to Organizational Behavior*. 2d ed. Glenview, Ill.: Scott, Foresman, 1984, 199. Used with permission.

schedules. This is probably because they are more closely related to the target behaviors, whereas interval schedules focus on the passage of time.

PROCEDURES FOR BEHAVIORAL MODIFICATION

Based on the viewpoint that it is the manager's responsibility to manage the behavior of subordinate employees, certain steps have been recommended for applying the principles of operant conditioning in organizations.[16] Figure 6-7 shows an appropriate, logical sequence for these steps, and the following paragraphs describe the steps in the diagram.

Pinpointing Target Behaviors (Box 1)

In the first and most critical step in applying operant conditioning principles, the manager identifies those performance-related behaviors that have a major impact on an employee's overall performance. The manager concentrates on these target behaviors, trying to increase desirable behaviors and decrease undesirable behaviors. Not all employee behaviors are necessarily "desirable" or "undesirable" from a managerial viewpoint. Many behaviors are neutral; they neither contribute to nor detract from the achievement of organizational goals.

The pinpointing procedure for identifying a target behavior consists of three activities:

- *Seeing* the behavior.
- *Counting* or measuring the behavior.
- *Describing* the situation in which the behavior occurs.

Training or orientation is necessary to enable managers to pinpoint behaviors. Frequently, the untrained manager confuses attitudes, feelings, and temperament with behaviors.

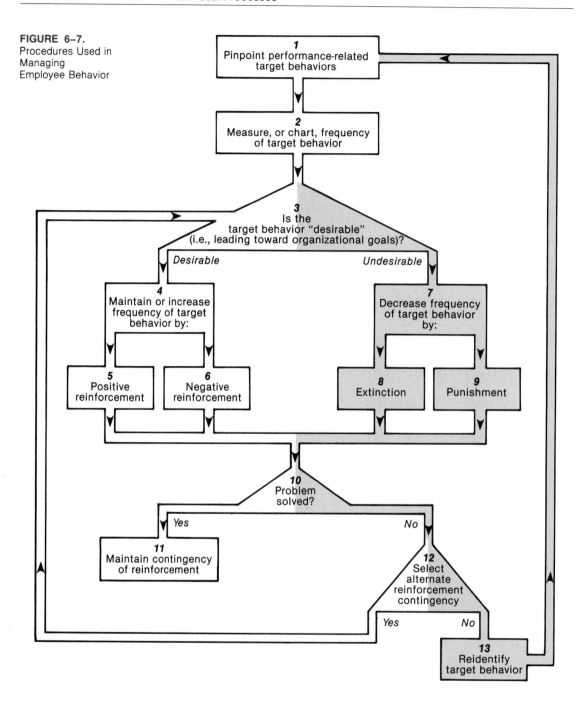

FIGURE 6–7.
Procedures Used in
Managing
Employee Behavior

Charting a Target Behavior (Box 2)

One of the best ways to keep track of an employee target behavior is through
charting, or measuring, it over a period of time. Figure 6-8 shows an example
of an employee behavior chart. The horizontal axis shows the time dimension, and the vertical axis shows the measurement of the employee behavior.
Each bar on the chart represents the measurement of the employee's behavior during one unit of time.

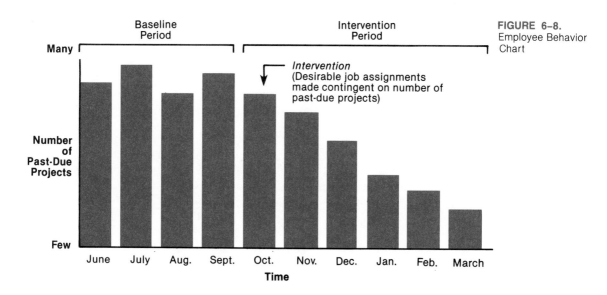

FIGURE 6-8.
Employee Behavior Chart

Typically, a chart is divided into at least two parts. The first is the *baseline* period; it measures behavior before any attempt is made to change it. In Figure 6-8, the baseline period covers the months of June–September. Usually, observations during the baseline period are made without the employee's knowledge.

The second part of the chart is known as the *intervention* period; it measures the employee's behavior after some type of positive reinforcement or punishment. During the intervention period (October–March in Figure 6-8), the employee might be made aware of the chart, which constitutes a type of feedback. Sometimes this feedback in itself has sufficient power to cause a change in behavior. However, the contingent administration of a reward or penalty frequently accompanies feedback.

Charting has two overall objectives. First, the baseline period provides an accurate picture of the actual frequency of a target behavior. Sometimes, charting a behavior reveals that the behavior is not as much of a problem as was originally thought. Observation alone may result in a distorted picture of the extent of a behavior. Second, by charting through an intervention period, the manager is able to determine whether the intervention strategy is actually working. Charting then becomes a means of evaluation. Sometimes a chart reveals no change in behavior, which means that the attempted intervention to manage behavior was not successful.

ACROSS CULTURES

Stopping Lateness in Mexico

Organizations have many behavioral problems to solve. In Mexico, workers' tardiness is one of the most important problems. In one plant, 131 workers accumulated 750 tardies during a year. Some companies have handled this problem by implementing monthly bonuses, annual bonuses, and/or punishment procedures. A common practice among companies in Mexico City is the suspension for one day without pay for each three tardies in a period of 30 days.

To correct this problem, the company made money contingent on punching in on time. In this study, money was used as a positive reinforcer. Twelve men with chronic tardiness records were experimentally exposed to a positive consequence. The target response was punctuality, which was defined as punching a time clock on or before 7:00 A.M. Each time the person punched in on or before 7:00 A.M., he received a slip of paper that read: "Mr. X, for arriving before 7:00 A.M. on September 6, 1971, has earned 2.00 pesos." Each Friday, the worker would be able to cash in his slips to the Supervisor of Industrial Relations. Along with the slips of paper, the worker also turned in his time cards. If the worker was late or absent for any reason, he would lose the money only for that day. This procedure had the effect of making the slips of paper conditioned reinforcers; they had value because of their association with cash.

Baseline punctuality figures covering the previous year were obtained from company records. All together, there were three experimental treatment periods and three baseline periods lasting 77 weeks. The baseline/treatment/baseline procedure allowed the workers to serve as their own control across time. To ensure that changes in tardiness were due to the presence or absence of the punctuality bonus plan, a control group of equivalent workers was selected. People in the control group received no treatment.

Tardiness increased during the baseline periods when the bonus plan was not in effect but decreased significantly when the workers were able to earn a bonus for punctual arrival at work. For those workers who received a bonus for punctuality, tardiness decreased from 15% during the first baseline period to an average of 1.2% during the last treatment condition. For those workers in the control group, tardiness continued to be 9.8%. More tardy arrivals at work were recorded for members of the control group than for workers in the treatment condition. The treatment procedures also reduced the frequency of tardiness, but did not change how late a worker would be if he were tardy.

Source: Herman, J., *et al.* Effects of Bonuses for Punctuality on the Tardiness of Industrial Workers. *Journal of Applied Behavioral Analysis,* 1973, *6,* 563–570.

Choosing a Strategy (Boxes 3–9)

After an employee's behavior has been identified and a baseline period charted, the manager must decide the strategy that should be implemented to change the behavior. In the case of a desirable behavior, the manager will use techniques to increase or maintain them. Positive reinforcement is the first alternative to consider, and the manager must make an educated guess as to which reward will have the desired effect of increasing the target behavior. Of course, negative reinforcement is another possible alternative.

If the target behavior were undesirable, however, the goal would be to decrease or eliminate it, and either punishment or extinction would be appropriate. The manager might also choose to use a combination strategy to punish or extinguish the undesirable behavior while reinforcing (increasing) other, desirable behaviors.

Did the First Attempt Work? (Boxes 10–13)

Experience gives the effective manager a valuable tool in choosing a strategy for controlling employee behavior: the ability to generalize from similar past situations or from similar incidents with the same employee. If the manager has indeed been successful in affecting the target behavior, the contingency of reinforcement must be maintained.

However, there is no guarantee that a chosen technique will be effective. Every manager encounters situations where the first intervention strategy fails. What does the manager do then?

The most important thing for a manager to do is to reidentify the target behavior (Box 13). What is the desired behavior? After this has been done, the manager must consider each step of the procedure again. However, the procedure can be simplified by an evaluation of the previous effort. The manager may conclude that a new reinforcement contingency is needed. The manager can then attempt several alternatives. For example, the reward can be changed in an attempt to increase the target behavior. The manager also can try a different type of reinforcement contingency; for instance, a change from a negative to a positive reinforcement contingency. Or the manager can choose a combination intervention strategy.

LIMITATIONS OF BEHAVIORAL MODIFICATION

There are two general limitations to the use of the behavioral modification techniques presented: individual differences and group norms.[17] We will state each limitation and briefly describe ways in which the effective manager can overcome them.

Individual Differences

Behavioral modification often ignores individual differences. People have different needs, values, abilities, and desires. When Cosmopolitan Lady set up its positive reinforcement system, the owners assumed that all employees valued money and praise and that all salespeople and managers had the ability to carry out sales-related behaviors. However, what is reinforcing to one person may not be to another.

An effective manager can account for these individual differences in two ways. First, managers can attempt to select and hire employees who value the rewards offered by the organization. Proper selection of employees can lead to hiring those employees whose needs most closely match the reinforcers provided by the organization. While this is not an easy task, it can be an effective method for managers to account for individual differences.

The second technique that managers can use is to allow employees to participate in determining their rewards. Thus, if the present contingencies of reinforcement are ineffective, the manager can ask employees what they would do to correct the situation. This method allows employees to have a greater voice in the design of their work environment and should lead to greater ego involvement of employees. However, if this method is used simply to exploit employees, they will find ways to lessen the impact of this method on their performance.

Group Norms

When workers feel that management has tried to exploit them, group norms emerge that aim to control the degree of cooperation with management. This control typically takes the form of restricting output. When this situation exists, the implementation of a program (particularly one that relies on praise and other nonmaterial rewards) is likely to meet with stiff resistance from the work group. Group members feel that there is little reason to cooperate with management since this behavior may likely lead to pressure to increase productivity, without a corresponding increase in pay.

The power of group norms can reduce the effectiveness of most reward systems. When employees and managers have a history of distrust, the principles covered in this chapter probably will not help. It is first necessary to build an atmosphere of trust between employees and managers. Once that has been done, the principles covered in this chapter have a better chance of working.

SUMMARY

The operant conditioning approach to learning focuses on the effects of reinforcement on desirable behaviors. Changes in behavior result from the consequences of previous behavior. People tend to repeat a behavior that leads to a pleasurable outcome, whereas they tend to avoid a behavior that leads to an unpleasurable result. In other words, when a behavior is reinforced, it is repeated; when it is punished or not reinforced, it is not repeated.

There are two types of reinforcement: (1) positive reinforcement, which increases a desirable behavior because the person is provided with a pleasurable outcome after the behavior has occurred; and (2) negative reinforcement, which also maintains the desirable behavior, but by presenting an aversive event before the target behavior occurs and stopping the event when the behavior occurs. Both positive and negative reinforcement increase the frequency of a desirable behavior. Extinction and punishment reduce the frequency of an undesirable behavior. Extinction involves stopping all things that reinforce the behavior. A punisher is an unpleasant event that follows the behavior.

There are four schedules of reinforcement. The fixed interval schedule gives rewards on a fixed time basis (for example, a weekly paycheck). The fixed ratio method ties rewards to certain outputs (for example, a piece-rate system). In the variable interval system, the reward is given around some average time during a specific period of time (for example, the plant manager walking through the plant on the average of five times every week). In the variable ratio schedule, the reward is given around some mean, but the number of behaviors varies (for example, a slot machine).

The steps that managers can use in applying the principles of behavior modification include pinpointing target behaviors, charting these behaviors, and choosing a strategy to obtain desirable behaviors and stop undesirable behaviors.

KEY WORDS AND CONCEPTS

Antecedent	Charting
Aversive events	Classical conditioning

Consequence
Contingency of reinforcement
Continuous reinforcement
Extinction
Fixed interval schedule
Fixed ratio schedule
Intermittent reinforcement
Learning
Learning theory
Negative reinforcement
Operant conditioning
Positive events
Positive reinforcement

Primary reinforcer
Principle of contingent reinforcement
Principle of immediate reinforcement
Principle of reinforcement deprivation
Principle of reinforcement size
Punishment
Reflex
Reinforcement
Secondary reinforcer
Variable interval schedule
Variable ratio schedule
Vicarious learning

DISCUSSION QUESTIONS

1. Explain what is meant by *learning.*
2. Compare and contrast the classical conditioning, vicarious learning, and operant conditioning theories.
3. Which type of learning is most important for managers? Why?
4. Identify the two types of reinforcement and give an example of each.
5. How can a manager use punishment effectively?
6. According to Hamner and Hamner, what are some guidelines for using operant conditioning? Can you identify those used at Cosmopolitan Lady?
7. What are the four schedules of reinforcement? Which are most effective in maintaining desirable behaviors over the long run?
8. How does a manager go about pinpointing target behaviors of subordinates?
9. What should a manager do when the first attempt at changing an employee's behavior fails?

MANAGEMENT INCIDENTS AND CASES

Paying Employees Not to Go to the Doctor

Companies are constantly searching for new ways to compensate their employees. Fringe benefits, which are rewards other than salary and cost a company an average 37 percent of an employee's salary, have been widely used to compensate employees for innovative behavior. Blue Shield of California and the Hartford Foundation have designed a unique system that basically pays employees for not going to the doctor. Each employee has a specific amount of money in an annual medical account. If there are still medical claims after this, the insurance plan takes over. At the end of the year, any money that has not been used for legitimate medical bills is paid to the employee in cash. These companies have two primary goals that they hope to achieve through this plan. The first is to teach employees to be more careful and knowledgeable about purchasing health care. The second is to reduce current costs. According to 1983 statistics, health care cost organizations well over $100 billion a year.

A more complex version of this plan has been established by Chemical New York Corporation. For each of its more than 20,000 employees, the company deposits $300 in an employee spending account. In addition, employees can allocate up to 50 percent of their profit-sharing monies to this account. During the year, employees can simply reimburse themselves for medical expenses from this account, or they can buy additional health insurance at a reduced rate. At the end of the year, if there is any money left over, employees can withdraw it and pay taxes on that amount. If they choose not to withdraw it, they can return it to the profit-sharing account that remains untaxed until the employee retires.

William Byrd Press, Inc., has started another system. Every individual has $1,200 in a Blue Cross account at the beginning of the year. For every $5.00 of unused money at the end of the year, the employee receives a lottery ticket. The lottery drawing awards one $5,000 and two $2,500 prizes.[18]

Questions

1. What kind of reinforcement schedules are these companies using?
2. What ethical concerns do these practices pose for you?

Cooper Aerobics Activities Center

Kenneth Cooper, a practicing physician and researcher in the U.S. Air Force during the 1960s, has gained notoriety for his exercise and fitness programs. He focuses on cardiopulmonary fitness in his best-selling book, *Aerobics,* and has opened centers to help people make needed changes in their behavior.

Cooper's famed Aerobics Center in Dallas, which opened in the early 1970s, includes a research and continuing education division, a medical clinic, and an activities center. Headed by William Grantham, the activities center appears to function like a commercial health club. The center's involvement with its clients, however, extends beyond the average fitness center. Four activities leaders work with Grantham to program and consult with the center's 2,200 clients. Their stated goal is to implement the Aerobics Exercise Program prescribed and supervised by Cooper. To accomplish this goal, the center provides guidance and facilities to reward and encourage fitness.

People who join the center are scheduled with one of the activities leaders for a general assessment of the clients' fitness in terms of where they have been, where they are now, and where they want to go. After these evaluations, the leaders determine the fitness-related activities that the clients can do, those that the clients can develop, and the activities that are impeding the client's fitness. All clients over the age of 30 are required to have a stress test prior to the interview to confirm the activities they are capable of undertaking.

The leaders also discuss the overall goal of the program, explaining that Cooper has designed a point system—called "aerobic points"—that directly relates to cardiovascular fitness. For example, jogging 2 miles in 20 minutes is worth 6 points. For general fitness, a client should achieve 30 points a week.

With the overall goal of 30 points, the activities leaders set specific week-by-week program goals for the clients during the first three months. These short-range goals are always measurable and objective. For example, a client's objective might be to get 10 points the first week, walk 8 laps a day for 2 weeks, and attend two classes. When clients reach a goal, a reward is given. There are many rewards, such as getting on the 100-mile-a-month list or the lost pounds list, and winning a sweatshirt or equipment bag.

To ensure that clients know how many points they have earned, the Aerobics Center has developed an elaborate computer system that acts as a source of immediate feedback. After the clients have completed their exercises, they enter their time and/or distance for each exercise into a CRT terminal. The screen then displays their points earned through the day's activities, as well as their total for the month. Each month the clients are mailed a computer print-out with their total points. This system also provides a means by which the staff can check on all clients' physical fitness. The four activities leaders can quickly scan all clients' aerobic points. If clients have not been logging in points, they receive a "we've missed you" card or telephone call. This alerts these clients that the staff knows they have missed aerobic points during that month.[19]

Questions

1. What types of reinforcers are used at the Aerobics Center?
2. What schedule of reinforcement is used with the clients?
3. Evaluate the limitations of the Aerobics Center reinforcement program.

REFERENCES

1. Abstracted from Rowan, D. Fran Tarkenton, Corporate Quarterback. *Fortune*, January 21, 1985, 118–122; December 1976 issue of *Training*.

2. Kazin, A. *Behavior Modification in Applied Settings*. Homewood, Ill.: Richard D. Irwin, 1975, 21–24.

3. Gioia, D., and Manz, C. Linking Cognition and Behavior: A Script Processing Interpretation of Vicarious Learning. *Academy of Management Review*, 1985, *3*, 527–539; Manz, C. and Sims, H. Vicarious Learning: The Influence of Modeling on Organizational Behavior. *Academy of Management Review*, 1981, *6*, 105–113.

4. Luthans, F. and Kreitner, R. *Organizational Behavior Modification*, 2d ed. Glenview, Ill.: Scott, Foresman, 1985.

5. Skinner, B. *Contingencies of Reinforcement*. New York: Appleton-Century-Crofts, 1969.

6. O'Hara, K., Johnson, C., and Beehr, T. Organizational Behavior in Management in the Private Sector: A Review of Empirical Research and Recommendations for Further Investigation. *Academy of Management Review*, 1985, 10, 848–864.

7. These principles are based on Thorndike's Law of Effect and can be found in Thorndike, E. *Educational Psychology: The Psychology of Learning*, vol. 2. New York: Columbia University Teachers College, 1913.

8. Wayne, S. *An Analysis of Performance Reward Contingencies at Cosmopolitan Lady*. Unpublished Paper, Cox School of Business, Southern Methodist University, Dallas, 1985.

9. O'Hara, *et al. Academy of Management Review*.

10. Miller, L. *Principles of Everyday Behavior Analysis*. Monterey, Calif.: Brooks/Cole, 1975, 276–277.

11. Beyer, J., and Trice, H. A Field Study of the Use and Perceived Effects of Discipline in Controlling Work Performance. *Academy of Management Journal*, 1984, *27*, 743–764; Arvey, R., Davis, G., and Nelson, S. Use of Discipline in an Organization: A Field Study. *Journal of Applied Psychology*, 1984, *69*, 448–460.

12. Luthans, F. and Kreitner, R. *Organizational Behavior*, 2d ed. Glenview, Ill.: Scott, Foresman, 1984.

13. Hamner, W., and Hamner, E. Behavior Modification on the Bottom Line. *Organizational Dynamics*, Winter 1976, 2–21.

14. Bandura, A. *Principles of Behavior Modification*, New York: Holt, Rinehart and Winston, 1969, 85.

15. Luthans, F., Paul, R., and Baker, D. An Experimental Analysis of the Impact of Contingent Reinforcement on Salespersons' Performance Behavior. *Journal of Applied Psychology*, 1981, *66*, 314–323.

16. Luthans, F. *Organizational Behavior*, 4h ed. New York: McGraw-Hill, 1985, 304–340.

17. For a general review of the arguments and limitations of these techniques, see Luthans, F., and Smith, P. Organizational Behavior Modification. In B. Karmel, *Point and Counterpoint*. Hinsdale, Ill.: Dryden Press, 1980, 47–94; Babb, H., and Kopp, D. Applications of Behavior Modification in Business Organizations: A Review and Critique. *Academy of Management Review*, 1978, *3*, 221–292; Luthans, F., and Kreitner, R. A Social Learning Approach to Management: Radical Behaviorists "Mellowing Out." *Organizational Dynamics*, Autumn 1984, 47–65.

18. Adapted from Paying Employees Not to Go to the Doctor. *Business Week*, March 21, 1983, 146–150.

19. Bessier, S. *Cooper Aerobics Center*. Unpublished paper, Cox School of Business, Southern Methodist University, Dallas, 1982.

7 Work Motivation

LEARNING OBJECTIVES

When you have finished studying this chapter, you should be able to:

- Describe a basic model of motivation.
- Identify four content and two process theories of motivation.
- Explain the basic dimensions of four content theories of motivation: needs hierarchy theory, ERG theory, achievement motivation theory, and motivator-hygiene theory.
- Describe the basic dimensions of two process theories of motivation: expectancy and equity.
- State the managerial implications for each of the six theories of motivation.

OUTLINE

Preview Case

Thank God It's Friday

It's 4:10 on a Friday afternoon. The weatherman has predicted that the weekend temperatures will be in the low 80s and that there will be lots of sunshine. The traffic patrol person on the local radio station indicates that traffic on I-30 is heavier than usual for this time of day because many people are leaving work early to get a headstart on the weekend. Your boss has just walked into your office and says that she needs the new figures on the computer project before you leave for the weekend. You look at her and want to scream. You and your secretary have been working nights all week to finish up bids on another project. Both of you have pushed the people in the word-processing center all week to get that project out. Now you realize that you will have to ask someone to stay a little longer. Your secretary's eyes are burning from lack of sleep. However, she says that she could work a little longer, but that you will have to personally go to the word-processing center and ask someone there to stay late.

When you enter the word-processing center, it's full of activity. Jane Bell is typing faster than ever. She's just about to finish a project for Andy Chen. For Jane, the entire week has been spent typing, proofreading, and then retyping. She looks tired, and her eyes are red because she's been watching the green CRT screen all week.

Next to Jane is Susan. Susan has been trying on new shades of lipstick since 2:30 when her work was finished. It has not been easy for her to decide which shade she'll wear tonight for her date with Dick Hansen. She's asked just about everyone in the center what they think about each shade of lipstick. Her behavior has gotten a good deal of angry stares from her co-workers. While Jane is tired and overworked, Susan has spent the last two hours checking her looks and staring at the clock. Five o'clock is fast approaching.

Does this story sound familiar to you? Perhaps you have had similar experiences with others who have worked very hard, or those who hardly seem to work at all. Studies have found that the best workers often produce two to three times as much work as the poorest workers. This chapter is concerned with one of the reasons why such differences exist: motivation.

THE ROLE OF MOTIVATION

Motivation is the term we use to describe the forces acting on or within a person that cause the person to behave in a specific, goal-directed manner. The specific motives employees have for working affect their productivity. In many respects, the job of management is to effectively channel employee motivation toward achieving organizational goals. Jack Pascal, the head of IBM's New York City financial branch, has a sign over his desk that reads, "New York Financial—The Difference Is People." This sign actually means that the performance of IBM employees determines the overall effectiveness of this $44.3 billion industrial giant. John Akers, chairman of the four-person corporate management committee that runs IBM, estimates that the company spends about $5 billion a year—about 15 percent of its 1984 gross revenues—to motivate people. Why?

One reason is productivity. The performance of U.S. firms is often compared with that of Japanese firms: between 1960 and 1980, Japan's manufacturing productivity growth was nearly three times the U.S. rate. Between 1977 and 1984, Japan's productivity increase was more than 40 percent. The techniques used by Japanese managers to motivate their workers seem to play an important role in their efforts to increase productivity.

Another reason is that organizations are striving to satisfy three behavioral requirements:

- People must be attracted not only to join the organization, but also to remain in it.
- People must perform the task for which they were hired.
- People must go beyond routine performance and engage in creative and innovative behavior at work.

In other words, for an organization to be effective, it must tackle the motivational problems involved in stimulating people's decisions to join the organization and their decisions to produce at work.[1]

In order to get people to join a company and remain in it, large corporations (such as Xerox, Kodak, Goodyear Tire and Rubber Company, IBM, GM, and Apple Computer) provide a broad range of benefits to employees. At Goodyear, for example, the company provides its employees with comprehensive medical insurance, disability income benefits, life and accident insurance, a company-paid pension plan, discounts up to 30 percent on all Goodyear products, paid vacations, tuition assistance, and the opportunity for employees to purchase Goodyear common stock. Goodyear also has a six-story activities hall across from its corporate headquarters in Akron, Ohio, which includes a gym, bowling lanes, racquetball and handball courts, and fully equipped conditioning rooms.[2]

To guarantee that employees will perform the tasks for which they were hired, IBM carefully screens applicants to determine whether they have the skills that the job requires. Once hired, people find their performance routinely evaluated. IBM employees who do not produce at work never get promoted and find themselves transferred from the corporate power centers; the company dismisses the least satisfactory workers.

Yet another reason for making large expenditures to motivate people relates to the ever-tightening constraints placed on organizations by unions, government agencies, increased foreign and domestic competition, citizen action groups, and the like. Management must look for new ways to maintain and increase its effectiveness and efficiency. Most of the profits that organizations could depend on in the past are disappearing because of these new constraints. Roger Smith, chairman and chief executive officer at General Motors, believes that the union and GM may have signed a historic agreement in 1984.[3] The contract calls for a $1 billion, six-year job security program that many people feel will address the hourly employee's traditional fear that automation means unemployment. With the new agreement, if a worker has been employed at GM for a year, the person will always have a job or get paid. While it may not be the same job, GM will retrain the worker.

The company also announced that 6,000 managers would receive performance bonuses. Managers now will be rewarded or penalized for how well they do. Smith hopes that these new incentives will help ease the strain between GM and the UAW (United Automobile Workers) and instill a spirit of entrepreneurship in managers.

Companies faced with today's problems require creative and innovative behavior of their employees in addition to top performance. For example, to maintain its growth of more than 10 percent a year, Control Data Corporation has devised a business strategy that involves applying the problem-solving capabilities of its computer technology and financial resources to four markets: general purpose computer systems; computer and data services; peripheral equipment (devices to store and retrieve data); and financial services (Commercial Credit Company). According to Thomas Kamp, president of Peripheral Products, when that division was founded in 1962, the software business was still in its infancy, and Control Data had little sales volume in the area. This business has grown from generating 29 percent of Control Data's revenues in 1976 to more than 50 percent in 1985. Most of the products that Control Data offered to its customers in 1985 were not even on the market in 1980. Salespeople at Control Data constantly must learn about new products and reach new customers.[4]

And finally, as technology increases the complexity of production processes, machines alone cannot increase production. People, too, must increase their knowledge about new production processes, and many employers are buying interactive computerized systems to train employees.[5] Typically, such interactive training systems include portable, off-the-shelf hardware—a Sony or Pioneer videodisc player, a personal computer such as an Apple II or IBM PC, and a video screen or two. The software is usually specially created for each course, with the course material contained on one or more videodiscs. At Ford dealerships, for example, a mechanic who needs to know more about carburetors can get a closeup view of an engine on a screen and then use a light pen to simulate what he would do with a vacuum gauge and a screwdriver to tune the engine. As the mechanic adjusts the carburetor, he or she hears the engine noise changing. When the mechanic thinks it is right, he or she touches a certain spot on the screen and the computer either congratulates or sends the mechanic back to the point of the mistake. Last year, the average Ford mechanic got 22 hours of training, compared with 8½ hours just a few years ago. Similarly, at 450 Sizzler restaurants around the country, a new employee can roll a videodisc system from the storeroom to a desk and take a lesson when business is slow. The screen will show a customer giving an order, which the employee tries to write down. Then the screen shows what the order slip should look like when correctly filled out.

To employers the cost savings and practicality of high-tech training are at least as appealing as its power to teach. The American Society for Training and Development estimates that companies spent $30 billion in 1984 to train employees. For many companies, the biggest cost is travel and living allowances for workers sent to schools and training centers in other locations. Interactive systems can be expensive to set up, but Ford believes that, when these systems are set up in all 4,000 dealerships, they will save millions of dollars in salaries and travel expenses alone.

THE MOTIVATIONAL PROCESS: BASIC CONSIDERATIONS

A basic management principle states that people's performance is based on their level of ability and motivation. This principle is often expressed by the following formula:

$$Performance = f(ability \times motivation).$$

According to this principle, no task can be performed successfully unless the person who is to carry it out possesses adequate ability to do so. **Ability** refers to a person's talent for doing goal-related tasks. This talent might include intellectual components, such as verbal and spatial skills, and manual components, such as physical strength and dexterity.

Regardless of how intelligent, skilled, or dexterous people are, their abilities alone are not sufficient to attain a high level of performance. People must also be motivated to achieve high performance. When managers discuss motivation in their organization, they are concerned with (1) what drives behavior, (2) what direction behavior takes, and (3) how to maintain this behavior.

The motivational process begins with identifying people's needs, as shown in Figure 7–1. **Needs** are deficiencies that an individual experiences at a particular time. These deficiencies may be psychological (such as the need for self-esteem), physiological (such as the need for water, air, or food), or sociological (such as the need for friendship). Needs are viewed as energizers. The implication is that when need deficiencies are present, the individual is more susceptible to motivational efforts because need deficiencies create tensions within the individual that the individual finds uncomfortable and wants to reduce.

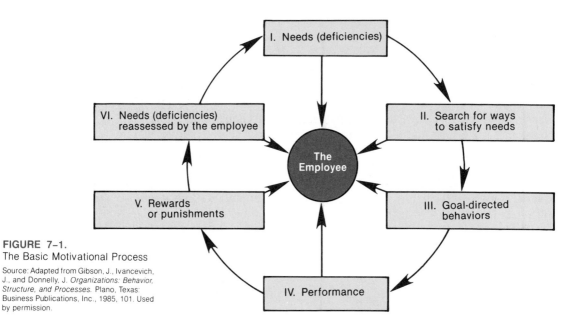

FIGURE 7–1.
The Basic Motivational Process

Source: Adapted from Gibson, J., Ivancevich, J., and Donnelly, J. *Organizations: Behavior, Structure, and Processes.* Plano, Texas: Business Publications, Inc., 1985, 101. Used by permission.

Motivation is goal directed. A **goal** is a specific result the individual wants to achieve. The goals that an employee seeks to reach are viewed as forces that attract the individual. The accomplishment of desirable goals can result in a significant reduction in need deficiencies.

Let us follow the motivational process shown in Figure 7–1. Some managers have a high need for power, a strong desire for advancement, and an expectation that working long hours will lead to a promotion. These needs, desires, and expectations create tensions within these managers that make them uncomfortable. Believing that some specific behavior can reduce this feeling, managers act. They direct their behavior toward the goal of reducing this state of tension. The initiation of this behavior sets up cues that feed information back to the managers on the impact of their behavior. For example, managers who have a strong desire to manipulate others (a high need for power) may attempt to increase their status in the organization by acquiring big offices (behavior) in hopes of gaining more influence (goal) in the organization. If they receive promotions and raises, the company is sending signals (feedback) to them that these behaviors are appropriate.

This general model of the motivational process is simple and straightforward. In the real world, of course, the process is not as clear-cut. First, motives can only be inferred; they cannot be seen. Suppose a supervisor notices two carpenters building packing crates for several large generators that the organization manufactures and ships to customers. The carpenters work the same shift, have similar abilities, and build the crates to the same specifications. When they have completed a crate, the carpenters place it on a conveyor belt and proceed to gather materials to begin the construction of another crate. After watching these two carpenters working for a week or so, the supervisor notices that one carpenter has completed about twice as many crates as the other. What can the supervisor conclude about the two carpenters? Since performance equals ability times motivation, and the supervisor knows that both carpenters have similar abilities, the difference in the carpenters' work output strongly suggests that they have different motivations. It would take more investigation, however, to determine what specifically motivates each carpenter.

A second complication centers on the dynamic nature of motives. At any one time, everyone has many needs, desires, and expectations. Not only do these factors change, but they may conflict with each other. Managers who put in many extra hours at the office to fulfill their needs for accomplishment may find that these extra work hours conflict directly with their needs for affiliation and their desire to be with their families.

A third complication is the considerable difference in the way people select certain motives over others and the difference in the drive with which people pursue these motives. Just as organizations differ in the products they manufacture or the services they render, people differ in terms of what motivates them to work. Some people work primarily for money, others for companionship, others for the challenge their work offers them, and still others for a combination of reasons. Organizations have tried numerous methods to motivate employees on the job by giving them interesting jobs, initiating participatory management, using pay-incentive systems, exercising close supervision, and so on. However, none of these methods alone can possibly work for all employees.

There is no shortage of motivation theories and managerial tactics that attempt to improve employee motivation.[6] There are two general categories of these theories: content and process theories.

CONTENT THEORIES OF MOTIVATION

Content theories attempt to explain the factors within a person that energize, direct, and stop behavior. These theories focus on specific things that motivate people. For example, an attractive salary, good working conditions, and friendly co-workers seem to be important to most people. Hunger (the need for food) or a steady job (the need for job security) are motivators that arouse people and may cause them to set specific goals (earning money to buy food or working in a financially stable industry). Four important content theories of motivation are Maslow's needs hierarchy, Alderfer's ERG theory, Herzberg's two-factor theory, and McClelland's achievement motivation theory.

Needs Hierarchy Theory

The most widely used theory of motivation in organizations is the **needs hierarchy theory**. Abraham H. Maslow suggested that people have a complex set of exceptionally strong needs, which can be arranged in a hierarchy.[7] Underlying this hierarchy are four basic assumptions:

- A satisfied need does not motivate. When a need is satisfied, another need emerges to take its place, so people are always striving to satisfy some need.
- The needs network for most people is very complex, with a number of needs affecting the behavior of each person at any one time.
- Lower-level needs must be satisfied, in general, before higher-level needs are activated sufficiently to drive behavior.
- There are more ways to satisfy higher-level needs than lower-level needs.

This theory postulates five needs categories: physiological, security, affiliation, esteem, and self-actualization. Figure 7–2 shows these five need categories arranged in Maslow's hierarchy.

PHYSIOLOGICAL NEEDS The needs for food, water, air, and shelter are all **physiological needs** and constitute the lowest level in Maslow's hierarchy. People concentrate on satisfying these needs before turning to higher-order needs. Managers should understand that, to the extent that employees are motivated by physiological needs, their concerns do not center on the work they are doing. They will accept any job that will serve to meet these needs. Managers who focus on physiological needs in attempting to motivate subordinates assume that people work primarily for monetary rewards and are primarily concerned with comfort, avoidance of fatigue, and the like. These managers try to motivate employees by offering wage increases, better working conditions, more leisure time, longer breaks, and better fringe benefits.

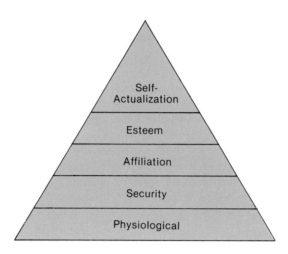

FIGURE 7–2.
Maslow's Hierarchy of Needs

SECURITY NEEDS   The needs for safety, stability, and the absence of pain, threat, or illness are all **security needs.** Like physiological needs, security needs that are not satisfied cause people to become preoccupied with satisfying them. People who are motivated primarily by security needs value their jobs mainly as a defense against the loss of basic need satisfactions. Managers who feel that security needs are most important to their employees focus on them by emphasizing rules and regulations, job security, fringe benefits, and employee protection against automation. Managers whose subordinates have strong security needs will not encourage innovation in solving problems and will not reward risk taking. The employees, in turn, will strictly follow the rules and regulations.

AFFILIATION NEEDS   The needs for friendship, love, and a feeling of belonging are all **affiliation needs.** When physiological and security needs have been satisfied, affiliation needs emerge and motivate people. Managers must realize that, when affiliation needs are the primary source of motivation, people value their work as an opportunity for finding and establishing warm, friendly, interpersonal relationships. Managers who believe that their subordinates are striving primarily to satisfy these needs are likely to act in a particularly supportive and permissive way, emphasizing employees acceptance by co-workers, extracurricular activities (such as organized sports programs and company picnics), and following group norms.

ESTEEM NEEDS   Both personal feelings of achievement or self-worth and recognition or respect from others meet **esteem needs.** People with esteem needs want others to accept them for what they are and to perceive them as competent and able. Managers who focus on esteem needs in their attempts to motivate employees tend to emphasize public rewards and recognition for services. Acknowledgment of difficulty of the work and the skills required for successfully doing it characterizes the managers' contacts with employees. These managers may use lapel pins, articles in the company paper, achievement lists on the bulletin board, and the like to promote their employees' pride in their work.

SELF-ACTUALIZATION NEEDS Self-fulfillment is the meeting of **self-actualization needs.** People who strive for self-actualization experience acceptance of themselves and others and increased problem-solving ability. To make work more meaningful, managers who emphasize self-actualization may involve employees in designing jobs, make special assignments that capitalize on employees' unique skills, or provide leeway to employee groups in designing work procedures and plans for implementation.

MANAGERIAL IMPLICATIONS Maslow's needs hierarchy theory specifically states the goals that people value and also suggests the types of behavior that will influence the fulfillment of various needs. It provides less complete information about the origin of the needs. The theory, however, implies that higher-level needs are potentially present in most people. Moreover, these higher-level needs will motivate most people if the situation does not block their emergence.

Maslow's work has received much attention from managers and psychologists.[8] Research has found that top managers generally are more able to satisfy their higher-level needs than are lower-level managers; top managers tend to have more challenging jobs and an opportunity for self-actualization. Lower-level managers, on the other hand, tend to have more routine jobs, which makes satisfying these higher-level needs more difficult. Employees who have little or no control over their work (such as assembly-line workers) may not even experience higher-level needs in relation to their jobs.

Studies have also shown that the fulfillment of needs differs according to the job a person performs, a person's age or race, the size of the company, and the cultural background of the employee.[9] More specifically, these studies have found the following:

- Line managers perceive greater fulfillment of security, affiliation, esteem, and self-actualization needs than do staff managers. The largest differences between line and staff managers occur in meeting esteem and self-actualization needs.

- Young workers (25 years old or younger) have greater deficiencies in meeting esteem and self-actualization needs than do older workers (36 years old or older).

- Black managers report a greater lack of fulfillment of every need than do nonblack managers.

- At lower levels of management, managers of small companies are less deficient in meeting their needs than are managers who work for larger companies.

- Workers in other countries have needs hierarchies that are different from those of U.S. workers.

ERG Theory

Clay Alderfer agrees with Maslow that individuals have needs that are arranged in a hierarchy.[10] Instead of the five categories of needs suggested by Maslow, Alderfer's **ERG Theory** holds that the individual has three sets of basic needs: Existence, Relatedness, Growth. Alderfer describes them as follows:

- **Existence needs.** These are material needs, which are satisfied by food, air, water, pay, fringe benefits, and working conditions.

- **Relatedness needs.** These are needs for establishing and maintaining interpersonal relationships with co-workers, superiors, subordinates, friends, and family.

- **Growth needs.** These are needs that are expressed by an individual's attempt to find opportunities for unique personal development by making creative or productive contributions at work.

The arrangement of these categories of needs is similar to Maslow's. The existence needs are similar to Maslow's physiological and safety needs; the relatedness needs are similar to Maslow's affiliation needs; and the growth needs are similar to Maslow's esteem and self-actualization needs.

However, ERG theory and Maslow's needs hierarchy differ with respect to the way people satisfy these different sets of needs. Maslow states that unfilled needs are motivators and that the next higher-level need is not activated until the lower-level need is satisfied. Thus a person progresses up the needs hierarchy as each set of lower-level needs has been satisfied. In contrast, ERG theory suggests that in addition to this **fulfillment–progression process,** a **frustration–regression process** is at work at the same time. That is, if a person is continually frustrated in attempts to satisfy growth needs, relatedness needs will reemerge as a major motivating force. The individual will return to satisfying this lower-level need instead of attempting to satisfy growth needs, and frustration will lead to regression. Figure 7–3 shows graphically these relationships. The *solid line* indicates a direct relationship between the set of needs, desire, and needs satisfaction. The *dotted line* represents what happens when a set of needs is frustrated. For example, if a person's growth needs are frustrated, then the importance of relatedness needs increases. The same behavior that has led to the frustration of growth needs now becomes the means for the person to satisfy his or her relatedness needs. The frustration–regression process assumes that existence, relatedness, and growth needs vary along a continuum of concreteness, with relatedness being the most concrete and growth being the least concrete. Al-

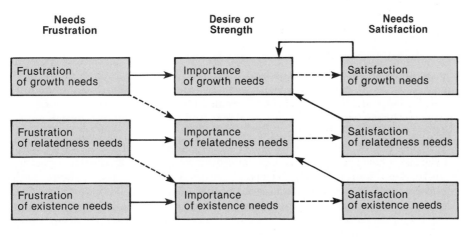

FIGURE 7–3.
Graphic Representation of Alderfer's ERG Theory

Source: Adapted from Landy, F., and Trumbo, D. *Psychology of Work Behavior,* rev. ed. Homewood, Ill.: Dorsey, 1980, 341.

derfer further assumes that when the lesser concrete needs are not met, more concrete need fulfillment is sought. (Note that the direction of the dotted lines in Figure 7-3 is downward from needs frustration to needs importance.)

MANAGERIAL IMPLICATIONS   Alderfer's ERG theory provides an important insight for managers. If a manager observes that a subordinate's growth needs are blocked, perhaps because the job doesn't permit the person to satisfy these needs or the company lacks the resources to satisfy these needs, the manager should attempt to redirect the subordinate's behavior toward satisfying relatedness or existence needs. The ERG theory states that individuals will be motivated to engage in behavior to satisfy one of the three sets of needs.

Because it is rather a new theory of motivation, very few research studies have tested ERG theory.[11] However, several studies have supported the existence of the three sets of needs in the ERG theory, rather than the five categories of needs in Maslow's hierarchy. Some of the most interesting findings are:

- Individuals with parents who had higher educational levels had greater growth needs than did individuals with parents who had lesser educational levels.

- Men had higher strength of existence needs and lower strength of relatedness needs than women.

- Blacks showed significantly greater strength of existence needs than did whites.[12]

Also, because it is a relatively new theory, ERG has not received a great number of criticisms. Some people have questioned the theory's universality, finding that it doesn't work in all organizations, while others say that the theory simply reflects common sense. We believe that it offers managers a useful way of thinking about motivating employees, but that a good deal of further research is required.

Managers should be sensitive to differences in desires among individuals, as suggested by the experiences of computer companies. You should be able to apply both the needs hierarchy and ERG theory to the situations described.

In Practice: **Are Computer People Different?**

The computer is becoming the central nervous system of more and more companies. But too often, the technical types who run the computer centers do not speak the language of business school trained managers. According to one executive recruiting firm, the greatest need is to find good managers who can motivate this new breed of computer people.

Who are these new employees? Just as composers, writers, and artists do not want to punch time clocks, many computer people don't like the 9 to 5 button down business environment. These people are often not motivated by money and job titles as are most general managers, but instead seek fulfillment and growth. Training and educational opportunities are often more important than money. "Money just keeps you in a style of living," says one computer consultant, "but learning is the key to excitement."

Not surprisingly, computer companies were among the first and most successful in developing new ways to manage and motivate technical employees. They reward their most creative employees with educational opportunities and recognition for individual input into major projects, as well as with financial incentives, such as stock options and bonuses.

Many computer employees are looking for ways to achieve, to learn more, and to grow. They want to do the next thing in their jobs, not because it means a promotion, but because they can get a "high" from moving ahead to bigger projects. The issue for management is not money, but for it to bring together interesting people to work on exciting projects. Andrew Heller says that he gets "offers that look like football contracts" to leave his job at IBM. He says that he turned down all these offers because "I do my job because I love it. No one could pay for the number of hours I put in." A 16-year veteran of IBM, he serves as an in-house consultant on 60 to 100 different projects at a time. "On any given day," he says, "I could have a discussion about fiber optics and protocols between micros and maxis in the morning and talk about the 1990 superprocessor in the afternoon." He often puts in 20 hours a day, taking time off to jog and eat dinner with his wife.[13]

Achievement Motivation Theory

David McClelland has proposed a theory of motivation that he believes is rooted in culture.[14] He states that we all have three particularly important needs: for achievement, affiliation, and power. McClelland suggests that when a need is strong in a person, its effect will be to motivate the person to use behavior that will satisfy the need. While he states that we all have these three needs, his research has focused mainly on ways that managers can develop their subordinates' desire for achievement. McClelland has studied achievement motivation extensively, especially with regard to entrepreneurship. **Achievement motivation theory** states that people are motivated according to the strength of their desire to perform in terms of a standard of excellence or their desire to succeed in competitive situations. McClelland indicates that almost all people feel they have an "achievement motive"; however, probably only 10 percent of the U.S. population is strongly motivated for achievement. The amount of achievement motivation that people have depends on their childhood, personal and occupational experiences, and the type of organization for which they work.

Motives are "stored" in the preconscious mind just below the level of full awareness; they lie between the conscious and the unconscious, in the area of daydreams, where people talk to themselves without quite being aware of it. The pattern of these reveries can be tested, however, and people can be taught to change their motivation by changing these reveries.

ASSESSMENT OF ACHIEVEMENT MOTIVATION McClelland measures the strength of people's achievement motivation by using the **Thematic Apperception Test** (TAT). In this method a person is presented with unstructured pictures that are capable of arousing many different kinds of reactions. Examples include an ink blot that a person can perceive as many different objects or a picture that can elicit a variety of stories. There are no right or wrong answers, and the subjects do not face a limited set of alternatives. A major objective of the test is to obtain the subject's own perception of the world. It is called a *projective* method because it emphasizes individual perceptions of stimuli, the meaning each subject gives to them, and how each subject organizes them.

One projective test involves looking at the picture in Figure 7–4 for 10–15 seconds and then writing a short story about it that answers these questions:

- What is going on in this picture?
- What is the man thinking?
- What has led up to this situation?

Write your own story about the picture. Then compare it with the following story written by a manager showing a strong achievement motive, whom McClelland would describe as a *high achiever:*

> The individual is a chief executive officer of a large corporation who wants to get a contract for his company. He knows that the competition will be tough, because all the "big boys" are bidding on this contract. He is taking a moment to think how happy he will be if his company is awarded the large contract. It will mean stability for the entire company and probably a large raise for him. He is satisfied because he has just thought of a way to manufacture a critical part that will enable his company to bring in a low bid and complete the job with time to spare.

FIGURE 7–4.
Sample Picture Used in a Projective Test

Source: (Photo © Hellriegel, Slocum, Woodman.)

CHARACTERISTICS OF HIGH ACHIEVERS   Self-motivated high achievers have three major characteristics. First, high achievers like to set their own goals. Seldom content to drift aimlessly and let life happen to them, they nearly always are trying to accomplish something. They are quite selective about the goals to which they commit themselves. For this reason, they are unlikely to accept automatically the goals that other people—including their supervisors—select for them. They do not tend to seek advice or help except from experts who can provide needed knowledge or skills. High achievers prefer to be as fully responsible for the attainment of their goals as possible. If they win they want the credit; if they lose they accept the blame. For example, assume that you are given a choice between rolling dice with one chance in three of winning and working on a problem with one chance in three of solving the problem in the time allotted. Which would you choose? A high achiever would choose to work on the problem, even though rolling the dice is obviously less work and the odds of winning are the same. High achievers prefer to work at a problem rather than leave the outcome to chance or other people.

Second, high achievers tend to avoid the extremes of difficulty levels in selecting goals. They prefer moderate goals that are neither so easy that attaining them provides no satisfaction nor so difficult that attaining them is more a matter of luck than ability. They gauge what is possible and then select as difficult a goal as they think they can attain—the hardest practical challenge. The game of ringtoss illustrates this point. Most carnivals have ringtoss games that require the participants to throw rings over a peg from some minimum distance but specify no maximum distance. Imagine the same game, but with people allowed to stand at any distance they wish from the peg. Some will throw more or less randomly, standing close and then far away. But those with a high achievement motive will seem to calculate carefully where they should stand to have the greatest chance of winning a prize and still feel challenged. These individuals seem to stand at a distance that is not so close as to make the task ridiculously easy and not so far away as to make it impossible. They set a distance that is moderately far away, but where they can potentially ring a peg. In other words, they set challenges for themselves and enjoy tasks that will make them stretch themselves a little.

Third, high achievers have a preference for tasks that provide more or less immediate feedback. Because of the importance to them of the goal, they like to know how well they are doing. This is one reason why the high achiever often decides on a professional career, a career in sales, or entrepreneurial activities. Golf would appeal to most high achievers: golfers can compare their scores to par for the course or to their own previous performance on the course; performance is related to both feedback (the golf score) and goal specificity (the handicap).

ROLE OF MONEY   McClelland points out the complex effect of monetary incentives on high achievers. High achievers usually value their services highly and prefer to place a high price tag on themselves. High achievers are self-confident, because they are aware of their abilities and inabilities and thus have confidence when they choose to do a particular job. They are unlikely to remain very long in an organization that does not pay them well if they are performing well. However, it is questionable whether an incentive plan actually increases their performance, since they are normally working at peak efficiency anyway. Thus they value money as a strong symbol of their achievement and adequacy, but money may create dissatisfaction if they feel that it alone adequately reflects their contribution.

When achievement motivation is operating, good job performance may become very attractive to people. However, achievement motivation does not operate when high achievers are performing tasks that are routine or boring, or when there is no competition. Let us look at how Kenneth Iverson's achievement motivation affects the way he runs Nurcor Steel company.

In Practice: Kenneth Iverson, Chief Executive of Nurcor

When Kenneth Iverson goes on vacation, he packs survival gear, rents a single-engine plane, and heads for the Alaskan woods. Being a loner and doing things his own way are his major strengths. When he couldn't find a cheap domestic supplier of steel 17 years ago, he started his company from scratch. Today, Iverson has built a $542 million steel company, while many steel companies have closed their doors.

He put his company together the same way he takes vacations—based on individual achievement. He has decentralized decision making and has only three management layers. Iverson believes that most people want to be recognized as capable, and on that assumption, should be given all the authority they can handle. His entire corporate staff consists of 15 people. Iverson hates middle management because they protect top managers from getting to know the workers.

At Nurcor, Iverson offers employees salaries at 50% below the market rate, but fantastic incentives based on performance. To motivate employees, Nurcor offers big chunks of stock, profit-sharing, and other incentives that promote their best work and productivity. Salaries are just the starting point. For example, in 1984, a typical worker earned only $15,000 in salary, but more than $15,000 in bonuses based on the company's performance. All employees also share the pain when profits fall. In 1983, Iverson earned no incentive pay, and his total compensation fell from $279,360 in 1982 to $106,716.[15]

MANAGERIAL IMPLICATIONS Most of the research to support this theory has been conducted by McClelland and his associates at McBer and Company.[16] Based on this research, they suggest that managers do the following things:

- Arrange tasks for workers so that they receive periodic feedback on their performance. Feedback will enable workers to modify their performance.
- Be good role models of achievement. Workers should be encouraged to use heroes to copy.
- Modify their self-images. The high-achievement person accepts himself or herself and seeks job challenges and responsibilities.
- Control their imaginations. Workers should think about setting realistic goals and the ways that they can attain these goals.

One of the major problems with the achievement motivation theory is also its greatest strength. The TAT method is valuable because it allows the researcher to tap the unconscious motivators of people. This method has some advantages over questionnaires, but the interpretation of a story is more of an art than a science. As a result, the reliability of this method is open to question.[17] The theory has also been questioned in terms of whether the three needs are permanent. Further research is needed to determine whether they are.

Motivator–Hygiene Theory

The motivator–hygiene theory is one of the most controversial theories of motivation, probably because of two unique features.[18] First, the theory stresses that some job factors lead to satisfaction, whereas others can only prevent dissatisfaction. Second, it states that job satisfaction and dissatisfaction do not exist on a single continuum. These features will be discussed later in this section.

Frederick Herzberg and his associates examined the relationship between job satisfaction and productivity in a group of accountants and engineers. Through the use of semistructured interviews, they accumulated data on various factors that these workers identified as having an effect on their feelings toward their jobs. Two different sets of factors emerged: motivators and hygienes.

MOTIVATOR AND HYGIENE FACTORS   The first set of factors, **motivators**, includes the work itself, recognition, advancement, and responsibility. They are associated with an individual's positive feelings about the job and are related to the content of the job itself. These positive feelings, in turn, are associated with the individuals' having experienced achievement, recognition, and responsibility in the past. They are predicated on lasting rather than temporary achievement in the work setting.

The second set of factors, **hygiene factors**, includes company policy and administration, technical supervision, salary, working conditions, and interpersonal relations. They are associated with an individual's negative feelings about the work and are related to the *context* or environment in which the job is performed. That is, these are **extrinsic factors**, or factors external to the job or the work itself. In contrast, the motivators are **intrinsic factors**, or internal factors associated with the job.

Viewed somewhat differently, extrinsic outcomes are largely determined by the company (for example, salary, policies and rules, and so on). They serve as a reward for high performance only if the organization recognizes high performance. On the other hand, intrinsic outcomes, such as feeling of accomplishment after successful task performance, are largely administered internally by the individual. The organization's policies have only an indirect impact on them. For example, by stating what defines exceptional performance, an organization may be able to influence individuals to feel that they have performed their tasks exceptionally well.

Figure 7-5 illustrates the motivator–hygiene theory. It shows the frequency with which accountants and engineers mentioned each factor in connection with high (satisfying) and low (dissatisfying) work experiences. Note that achievement was present in more than 40 percent of the satisfying experiences and in less than 10 percent of the dissatisfying experiences.

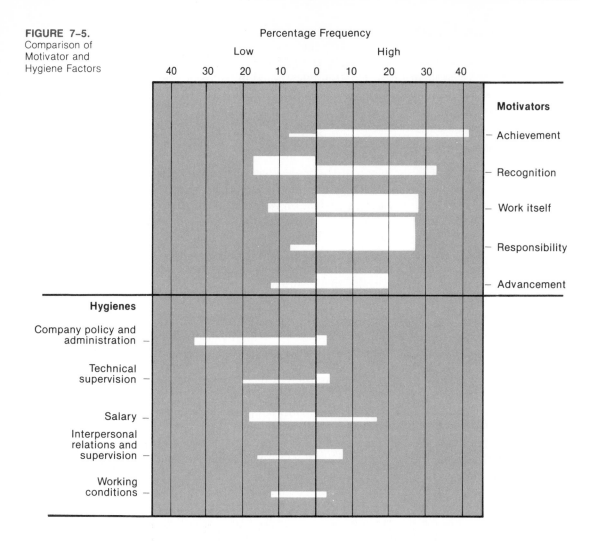

FIGURE 7–5.
Comparison of
Motivator and
Hygiene Factors

This theory also states that satisfaction and dissatisfaction are not on a single continuum but are separate and distinct continua, as indicated in Figure 7–6. Thus the concept is that a person can be satisfied and dissatisfied at the same time. This also implies that hygiene factors, such as working conditions and salary, cannot increase or decrease job satisfaction; they can only affect the amount of job dissatisfaction.

MANAGERIAL IMPLICATIONS   The research designed to test this theory has not provided clear-cut evidence that either supports or rejects it.[19] One aspect that appeals to managers is the use of common terms to explain how to motivate people. There is no need to translate psychological terms into everyday language. Therefore, among business people, it has become a very popular theory. In Chapter 13 we focus on how the principles of this theory can be applied to designing jobs that give the individual an opportunity to satisfy higher-order needs.

Despite its attractive features, several criticisms have been leveled at this theory. One major criticism is that Herzberg used a method-bound pro-

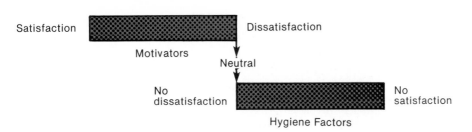

FIGURE 7–6.
Job Satisfaction
Continua

cedure; that is, the method he used to measure the factors determined the results. He asked two key questions: "Can you describe, in detail, when you felt exceptionally good about your job?" and "Can you describe, in detail, when you felt exceptionally bad about your job?" In response to such questions, people tend to give socially desirable answers, that is, answers the respondents think the researcher wants to hear or that sound "reasonable." Also, people tend to attribute good results from their job to their own efforts and to attribute reasons for poor performance to others.

A second major criticism of Herzberg's theory questions whether satisfaction and dissatisfaction really are two separate dimensions, as Figure 7–6 indicates. Research results are mixed. Some researchers have found factors that can contribute to both satisfaction and dissatisfaction, whereas others have found that motivators can contribute to dissatisfaction and hygiene factors can contribute to satisfaction. Although these findings raise serious questions about Herzberg's theory, they have not disproved the concept that satisfaction and dissatisfaction are two different continua.

Some evidence—although not strong—links experiences such as increasing job responsibility, challenge, and advancement opportunities to high performance. Unfortunately, Herzberg and other researchers have paid little attention to constructing a theory that explains why certain job factors affect performance positively or negatively. Similarly, few attempts have been made to explain why certain outcomes are attractive to employees or why people choose one type of behavior over another to obtain a desired outcome.

ACROSS CULTURES

Motivation in Zambia

Most of what we know about motivation has been tested in advanced nations. Today, as more and more underdeveloped nations attempt to industrialize and build their economies, their managers face a growing problem of how to motivate their workers. Problems of motivation continue to be major ones as is evident from the low productivity in these countries, despite the influx of capital and technology from industrially developed countries.

To study motivation in Zambia, the researchers asked 341 workers to state things that were bad or good about their job. The data in Table 7–1 indicate that the inadequacy of working conditions, poor pay, bad interpersonal relations, and poor supervision were most frequently named as

TABLE 7–1   Demotivating and Motivating Factors of Zambian Workers

Demotivating Factors, or Bad Aspects, of Working

1. Tribalism, favoritism, racial discrimination.
2. Bad interpersonal relations with supervisors, co-workers, subordinates.
3. Low pay, lack of bonuses or merit raises.
4. Supervisors who do not care to listen to problems of employees.
5. Death/sickness in family.
6. Fringe benefits (lack of transportation, housing).
7. Poorly defined work duties.
8. Domestic quarrels.
9. Too much work.
10. Lack of a chance to learn more about job and/or further training.

Motivating Factors, or Good Aspects, of Working

1. A lot of work.
2. Interesting work.
3. Work that has an urgent deadline.
4. Recognition.
5. Chance to learn more about job and/or further training.
6. Chance for promotion.
7. Achievement (work that allows achievement and proving oneself).
8. Responsibility.
9. Good interpersonal relations with co-workers.
10. Trust and confidence shown by superiors and co-workers.

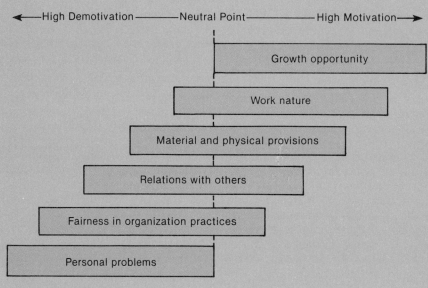

FIGURE 7–7.
Relative Frequency with Which Item Was Mentioned

bad, or demotivators. Those items dealing with the work itself, recognition by one's boss, and chance for promotion were listed as good aspects of their job, or motivators. These results are consistent with the motivator–hygiene theory.

The researchers then tabulated the frequency of mention for all items, either bad or good, that would lead workers to work harder. The results are shown in Figure 7–7. As can be seen from this figure, different groups of items had positive and negative impacts. Work nature and growth opportunity were the most important elements when workers reported what makes them work harder. Relations with others, fairness in organizational practices, and personal problems seemed to be most frequently mentioned as things that make them not want to work hard, or do little. Material and physical conditions were equally mentioned as motivators and demotivators. These data also support Herzberg's theory.[20]

Summary of Content Theories

The four content theories emphasize the basic motivational concepts of needs, hygiene-motivators, and achievement motivation. Figure 7–8 highlights the relationships among these four theories. The five-needs hierarchy theory served as the basis for the ERG theory. Therefore there are some important similarities between these two theories: self-actualization and esteem needs comprise growth needs; affiliation needs are similar to relatedness needs; and security and physiological needs are the building blocks of existence needs in ERG theory. A major difference between these two theories is that the needs theory offers a static needs system based on fulfillment–progression, whereas the ERG theory presents a flexible three-needs classification system based on frustration–regression.

The motivator–hygiene theory draws on both of the needs theories. That is, if hygiene factors are present, security and physiological needs (needs hierarchy) are likely to be met. Similarly, if hygiene factors are present, relatedness and existence needs (ERG theory) are not likely to be frustrated. Motivators focus on the job itself and the opportunity for the person to satisfy his or her own higher-order needs, or growth needs (ERG theory).

Achievement motivation theory does not have lower-order needs. The need for affiliation can be satisfied if a person encounters hygiene factors on

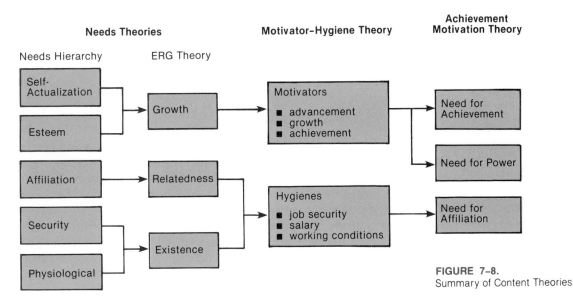

FIGURE 7–8.
Summary of Content Theories

the job. If the job itself is challenging and provides an opportunity for a person to make meaningful decisions, it is motivating. These conditions go a long way toward satisfying the need for achievement.

The content theories provide managers with an understanding of the particular work-related factors that start the motivational process. However, these theories promote little understanding of why people choose a particular behavior to accomplish work-related goals. This aspect of *choice* is the major focus of process theories.

PROCESS THEORIES OF MOTIVATION

Process theories attempt to describe and analyze how the personal factors (content theories) interact and influence each other to produce certain kinds of behavior. The fact that individuals exert more effort to obtain rewards that satisfy important needs than to obtain rewards that do not would be an example. The four best-known process theories of motivation are expectancy, reinforcement, equity, and goal-setting. In this chapter we cover the expectancy and equity theories. In Chapter 6, we discussed reinforcement theories, and in Chapter 15, we will present goal-setting.

Expectancy Theory

During the past two decades the **expectancy theory** approach to motivation has been developed.[21] Four assumptions about the causes of behavior in organizations provide the basis for this theory.

First, it is assumed that a combination of forces in the individual and the environment alone determines behavior. Neither the individual nor the environment alone determine behavior. As the In Practice about people who work with computers illustrated, people join organizations with expectations about their careers that are based on their needs, motivations, and past histories. These factors all influence how people respond to an organization.

Second, it is assumed that people make decisions about their own behaviors in organizations. Many constraints are placed on people's behavior (for example, rules, regulations, technology, and work-group norms). However, most people make two kinds of conscious decisions: (1) decisions about coming to work, staying with the same company, and joining other companies (membership decisions); and (2) decisions about how much to produce, how hard to work, the quality of workmanship, and so on (job-performance decisions).

Third, it is assumed that different people have different types of needs and goals. People want different kinds of outcomes from their work (for example, job security, promotion, good pay, and challenge). Not all employees want the same things from their jobs.

Fourth, it is assumed that people decide among alternatives based on their perceptions of the degree to which a given behavior will lead to a desired outcome. People tend to do the things that they perceive as leading to rewards they desire and avoid doing the things that they perceive as leading to outcomes they do not desire.

In general, the expectancy theory views people as having their own needs and ideas of what they desire from their work (rewards). They act on these needs and ideas when making decisions about what company to join and how hard to work on the job. It holds that people are not inherently motivated or unmotivated: motivation depends on the situation facing people and how it fits their needs.

In order to understand expectancy theory, it is necessary to define the important variables of the theory and explain how they operate. The four most important variables of the theory are: first- and second-level outcomes, expectancy, valence, and instrumentality.

FIRST- AND SECOND-LEVEL OUTCOMES   The results of behaviors that are associated with doing the job itself are called **first-level outcomes**. They include productivity, absenteeism, turnover, and quality of work. **Second-level outcomes** are those events (either positive or negative) that first-level outcomes are likely to produce, such as a pay increase, promotion, acceptance by co-workers, job security, and the like.

EXPECTANCY   The belief that a particular level of effort will be followed by a particular level of performance is called **expectancy**. It can vary from the belief that there is absolutely no relationship between effort and performance to the certainty that a given level of effort will result in a corresponding level of performance. Expectancy has a value ranging from 0, indicating no chance that a first-level outcome will occur after the behavior, to $+1$, indicating certainty that a particular first-level outcome will follow a behavior. For example, if you believe that there is no chance that you will get a high grade on the next exam by studying this chapter, your expectancy value would be 0. Therefore you would not study this chapter.

VALENCE   An individual's preference for a second-level outcome is called **valence**. For example, members of the United Auto Workers employed by GM preferred a small wage increase and guaranteed jobs over a large wage increase with no job security. An outcome is *positive* when it is preferred and *negative* when it is not preferred or is avoided. An outcome has a valence of *zero* when the individual is indifferent about receiving it.

INSTRUMENTALITY   The relationship between first-level outcomes and second-level outcomes is called **instrumentality**. It can have values ranging from -1 to $+1$. A -1 indicates that attainment of a second-level outcome is inversely related to the achievement of a first-level outcome. For example, if one of your desired second-level outcomes is to pass this course, but you receive a failing grade, it would be impossible for you to achieve your second-level outcome. A $+1$ indicates that the first-level outcome is positively related to the second-level outcome. For example, if you received an A on all of your exams, the probability that you would achieve your desired second-level outcome (passing this course) is approaching $+1$. If there is no relationship between your performance on a test and either passing or failing this course, your instrumentality would approach 0.

In summary, expectancy theory holds that work motivation is determined by individual beliefs regarding effort–performance relationships and the desirability of various work outcomes associated with different performance levels. Simply put, the theory is based on the notion that people will do what they can do when they want to do it. You can remember the important features of the model by the saying:

People exert **to** → task **and** → work-related
work effort **achieve** performance **receive** outcomes.

GENERAL MODEL OF EXPECTANCY THEORY On the basis of these four key variables, we can build a general expectancy model of motivation, as shown in Figure 7–9. Motivation is the force that causes individuals to expend effort. Effort alone is not enough, however. Unless an individual believes that his or her effort will lead to some desired performance level (first-level outcome), the person will not make much of an effort. The effort–performance expectancy is based on a perception of how difficult it will be to achieve a particular behavior (say, getting an A in this course) and the probability of achieving that behavior. For example, you may have a high expectancy that, if you attend class, study the book, take good notes, and prepare for exams, you could achieve an A in this class. On the other hand, if you believe that, even if you attend class, study the book, take good notes, and prepare for exams, your chances of getting an A are only 20 percent, the probability of your expending effort in these activities to achieve an A is much less.

The level of performance is important in obtaining desired second-level outcomes. In Figure 7–9, there are four desirable outcomes: passing the course, making the Dean's list, gaining admission to graduate school, and gaining further respect from other students and parents. In general, the more likely you feel that a particular level of performance (A, B, C, D, or F) will lead to these desired outcomes, the more likely you will try to perform at that level. If you really desire these four second-level outcomes and you can

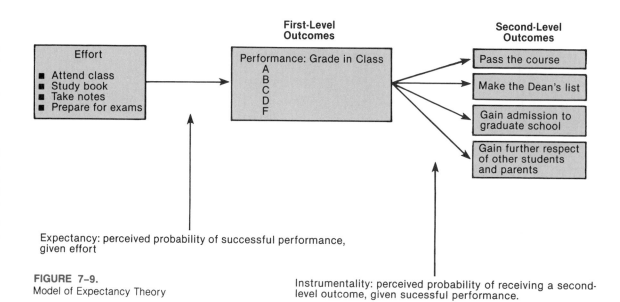

FIGURE 7–9.
Model of Expectancy Theory

achieve them only if you get an A in this course, the instrumentality between receiving an A and these four outcomes will be $+1.0$. On the other hand, if you believe that getting an A in this course means that you will lose some friends and that these friends are most important to you, the instrumentality between an A and this outcome will be negative. That is, the higher the grade, the more your friends will ignore you. Given this condition, you would *choose* not to get an A in this course.

EXPECTANCY THEORY FINDINGS   Researchers are still working on ways to test this model, which has presented some problems.[22] First, the theory attempts to predict choice or the amount of effort an individual will expend in one or more activities. However, there is little agreement about what constitutes choice or effort among different individuals. Consequently, this important variable is difficult to measure accurately. Second, since it is a within-person theory, expectancy theory does not specify which second-level outcomes are relevant to a particular individual in a given situation. Although researchers are expected to address this issue, comparison of study results at present is often difficult because each study is unique. Look at the second-level outcomes we chose (Figure 7–9). Would you choose these? What others might you choose? Finally, there is an implicit assumption that motivation is a conscious choice process. The individual is assumed to consciously calculate the pain or pleasure that he or she expects to attain or avoid when making a choice. Expectancy theory says nothing about unconscious motivation or personality characteristics. We know that people often do not make conscious choices about which outcomes to seek. Can you recall going through this process while trying to get an A in this course?

MANAGERIAL IMPLICATIONS   While there are still problems with the theory, it has some direct implications for motivating employees.[23] These implications can be grouped into six suggestions for managerial action.

First, managers should try to determine the outcomes that each employee values. This can be done by (1) using a questionnaire; (2) observing employee reactions to different rewards; and (3) asking employees about the kinds of rewards they want and the career goals they have. However, managers must understand that people can and do change their minds about desired outcomes. The effective manager correctly diagnoses these changes and also does not assume that all employees are alike.

Second, to motivate others managers should determine the kinds of performance they desire. They must define *good* performance and *adequate* performance in terms that are observable and measurable, so that subordinates can understand what managers desire of them. For example, a manager at a trucking company developed criteria for good driving. These criteria were used to measure a driver's performance over a 12-month period and included: (1) having no chargeable accidents (damages of more than $750); (2) having no moving violations; (3) being less than one hour late for all pickups and deliveries; (4) driving more than 100,000 miles per year; (5) averaging at least 5.6 miles per gallon of fuel; and (6) maintaining tire cost at or below 2.8 cents per mile.

Third, managers should make sure that desired levels of performance are reachable. Motivation is determined not only by expectancy, but also by instrumentality. This implies that the levels of performance set by managers as the points at which individuals receive desired outcomes must be attainable. If employees feel that the level of performance necessary to get a reward is higher than they can reasonably achieve, their motivation to perform will be low. For example, if the trucking company cannot get enough freight to guarantee its drivers 100,000 miles per year, that level of performance is too high.

Fourth, managers should directly link the outcomes desired by employees to specific performances desired by the managers. In Chapter 6, we discussed the application of operant conditioning principles to organizational settings. If an employee has achieved the desired level of performance and wants a promotion, the manager should try to get that person promoted. It is extremely important for employees to be able to see a clear demonstration of the reward process at work in a fairly short period of time if a high level of motivation is to be created and maintained. Concrete acts must accompany statements of intent in linking performance to rewards.

Many managers seem to forget that it is people's perceptions—and not reality—that determines motivation. It does not matter, for example, whether a manager feels that subordinates' pay is related to their motivation. The employees will be motivated only if *they* see the relationship. Too often, managers misunderstand the behavior of their subordinates because they tend to rely on their own perceptions of the situation and forget that their subordinates' perceptions are likely to be different.

Fifth, managers should analyze the situation for conflicts. Having set up positive expectancies for employees, managers must look at the entire situation to see whether other factors conflict with the desired behaviors (for example, the informal work group or the organization's formal reward system). Motivation will be high only when people see a number of rewards and few negative outcomes associated with good performance.

And sixth, managers should make sure that changes in outcomes or rewards are sufficiently large to motivate significant behavior. Trivial rewards result in minimal amounts of effort and thus only slight performance changes, if any. Rewards must be large enough to motivate individuals to make the effort required to bring about significant changes in performance.

Equity Theory

Feelings of unfairness were among the most frequently reported sources of job dissatisfaction found by Herzberg and his associates. Some researchers have made this desire for fairness, justice, or equity a central focus of their theories.[24] Assume that you just received a 5-percent raise. Will this rate lead to higher performance, lower performance, or no change in your performance? Are you satisfied with this increase? Would your satisfaction with this increase vary with the consumer price index, with what you expected to get, or with what others in the company performing the same job and at the same performance level received?

Equity theory focuses on an individual's feelings of how fairly he or she is treated in comparison with others. The theory has two key elements. First, it assumes that individuals evaluate their social relationships just as they would evaluate the buying or selling of a home, shares of stock, or a car.

The theory views social relationships as exchange processes in which individuals make contributions and expect certain results. For example, you expect to receive a grade in this course as a result of studying the book, attending class, taking notes, and preparing for exams for a certain period of time.

Second, people do not operate in a vacuum. Instead, each person compares his or her situation with that of others to determine the equity of their own situation. The extent to which people view an exchange favorably is influenced by what happens to them compared with what happens to others. These others may include co-workers, relatives, neighbors, and so on.

GENERAL MODEL   Equity theory is based on the relationship between two variables: inputs and outcomes. **Inputs** represent what an individual contributes to an exchange; **outcomes** are what an individual receives from the exchange. Some typical inputs and outcomes are shown in Table 7–2: the items in the two lists are not paired and do not represent specific exchanges.

According to the equity theory, individuals assign weights to various inputs and outcomes according to their perceived performance. Since most exchanges involve multiple inputs and outcomes, the weighting process is not precise. However, people generally can distinguish between important and less important inputs and outcomes. After they arrive at a ratio of inputs and outcomes for themselves, they compare it with their perceived ratios of inputs and outcomes of others in the same or a similar situation. Thus others become the objects of comparison for people in determining whether they feel equitably treated.

Equity exists whenever the ratio of a person's outcomes to inputs equals the ratio of outcomes to inputs for others. For example, an individual may feel properly paid in terms of what he or she puts into a job compared with what other workers are getting for their inputs. **Inequity** exists when the ratios of outcomes to inputs are not equal. For example, a person who works harder than others, completes all work on time while others don't, and puts in longer hours than others receives the same pay raise as the others. Someone in this situation believes that his or her inputs are greater than those of the others and therefore should receive a greater pay raise. Inequity can also occur when people are overpaid. In this case they might be motivated by

TABLE 7–2   Typical Inputs and Outcomes in an Organizational Setting

Inputs	Outcomes
Ability	Challenging job assignments
Age	Fringe benefits
Attendance	Job perquisites (parking space or office location)
Job effort (long hours)	Job security
Level of education	Monotony
Past experience	Pay
Performance	Promotion
Personal appearance	Recognition
Personality traits	Responsibility
Seniority	Seniority benefits
Social status	Status symbols
Training	Working conditions

Source: Adapted with permission from Belcher, D. and Atchinson, T. Equity Theory and Compensation Policy. *Personnel Administration,* 1970, *33*(3):28.

guilt or social pressure to work harder to reduce the imbalance between their inputs and outcomes and those of others.

CONSEQUENCES OF INEQUITY   Inequity causes tension within an individual—and among individuals. Since tension is not pleasurable, a person is motivated to reduce it to a tolerable level. In order to reduce a perceived inequity and the corresponding level of tension a person can choose among the six types of behavior described in the following paragraphs. This tension-reduction process is shown in Figure 7–10.

■ People can change their inputs either upward or downward to what might be an equitable level. For example, underpaid people can reduce the quantity of their production, work shorter hours, be absent more frequently, and so on. Figure 7–11 shows these relationships graphically.

■ People can change their outcomes to restore equity. Many union organizers attempt to attract nonunion members by pledging to improve

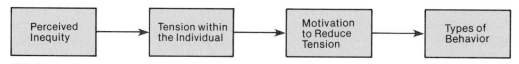

FIGURE 7–10.
Motivational Process of Inequity

Source: Adapted from *Introduction to Organizational Behavior* by Richard M. Steers, 2d ed. 167. Copyright © 1984 by Scott, Foresman and Company. Reprinted by permission.

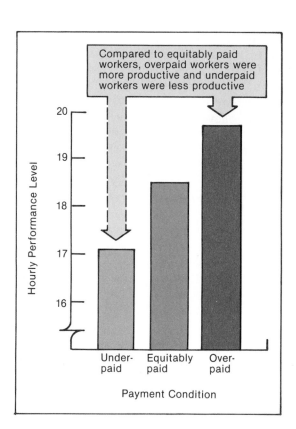

FIGURE 7–11.
Performance Levels for Underpaid and Overpaid Workers

Source: Based on data in Pritchard, R., Dunnette, M., and Jorgenson, D. Effects of Perceptions of Equity and Inequity on Worker Performance and Satisfaction. *Journal of Applied Psychology*, 1972, 56:75–94.

working conditions, hours, and pay without an increase in employee effort, or input.

■ People can distort their own inputs and outcomes. As opposed to actually changing inputs or outcomes, people can mentally distort them to achieve the same results. For example, people who feel inequitably treated can distort how hard they work ("This job is a piece of cake.") or attempt to increase the importance of the job to the company ("This is really an important job!"). By mentally distorting the input-outcome ratio, people achieve a more favorable balance.

■ People can leave the organization or request a transfer to another department. In doing so, they hope to find a more favorable balance in the new situation.

■ People can shift to a new reference group to reduce the source of the inequity. The star high school athlete who does not get a scholarship to a Big Ten university might decide that a smaller school has more advantages, thereby justifying his or her need to look at smaller schools when making a selection.

■ People can distort the inputs or outcomes of others. People may come to believe that the comparison group actually works harder than they do and therefore deserves greater rewards.

Keeping these six behaviors in mind, try to predict the effect on your behavior in the situation where a classmate gets a higher grade on an exam than you do, apparently with much less effort.

In Practice: Study Behaviors

You are a junior majoring in electrical engineering but are taking a course in organizational behavior to learn why people behave as they do in organizations. The mid-term exam is scheduled in two weeks and counts for 30 percent of your final grade. You spend 22 hours studying your notes, rereading all the assignments, and outlining major points from your notes and the instructor's lectures. You feel confident going into the exam when it comes.

After taking the examination, your roommate asks how you did and you say, "Really crashed it. Probably somewhere in the high 80s." The instructor returns your exam and you received a 73. You ask a fraternity brother who's majoring in personnel management what he got, and he says, "an easy 88." You know he hasn't been coming to class, and rumors around the house were that he even had to borrow the book to study for the exam.

According to equity theory, you can choose any or all of six of the behaviors in an attempt to reduce this perceived inequity. First, you can start cutting class and stop reading the textbook. Second, you can speak to the instructor and ask for suggestions about your study habits. Third, you can say to yourself that you really didn't try hard enough and, since you are not a business student anyway, the grade in this course will not affect your career in electrical engineering. Fourth, you can drop the course. Fifth, you can stop comparing your grade to those of business students and start comparing your grade to those of other nonbusiness students. Sixth, you can believe that your fraternity brother really studied hard but that you just didn't see him doing it.

EQUITY THEORY FINDINGS   Most of the research on equity theory focuses on pay and/or other compensation issues. A review of the studies, however, reveals some shortcomings.[25] First, the comparison person is always specified. The typical research procedure is to ask a person to compare himself or herself to some specific person. If the situation changes, would the subject choose a different comparison person? Do people also change comparison persons at various times during their careers?

Second, the research focuses mainly on short-term comparisons. Are the items that a person considers to be inputs or outcomes likely to remain the same over time? Longitudinal research, which examines what happens if inequity exists over an extended period of time, is needed. Do perceptions of inequity increase, decrease, or stabilize? Answers to these types of questions would help us to understand better the dynamic character of equity.

Third, the theory does not specify the action (from among the six possible actions) that a person would choose in order to reduce inequity in a given situation. That is, is one strategy used primarily when pay is involved, another when absenteeism or turnover is involved, and yet another when productivity is involved?

MANAGERIAL IMPLICATIONS   Despite these limitations, the equity theory is widely used by compensation specialists in large organizations and in setting pay scales for different jobs in most organizations. It makes two primary recommendations to managers. First, managers should treat employees equitably. When individuals believe that they have not been treated fairly, they will try to correct the situation and reduce tension by means of one or more of the six behaviors already discussed. A sizable inequity increases the probability that individuals will choose more than one of these behaviors to reduce it. For example, individuals may partially withdraw from the organization by being absent more often, arriving at work late, and not handing in assignments on time. The company, on the other hand, may try to reduce their inputs by assigning these people to monotonous jobs, taking away some perquisites, and giving them only small pay increases.

Second, people make decisions concerning equity only after they compare their inputs and outcomes with those of other people. These others may be employees of the company or employees of other companies. The latter presents a major problem for managers, who cannot control what other companies pay their employees. For example, the vice-president for personnel at a large corporation hired a recent graduate for $21,400. The new employee thought that this salary was very good until she compared it to the $25,000 that fellow business school graduates were getting at other firms. The company could not pay her any more for the job; she felt that she was being underpaid in comparison with her former classmates, which resulted in an inequity problem for her (and the company).

Summary of Process Theories

The expectancy and equity theories emphasize different aspects of motivation. Equity theory suggests that people are motivated by comparing their own situation with that of others who are in the same or a similar situation. Expectancy theory, on the other hand, is more internally oriented. That is, individuals assign probabilities to efforts leading to desired first-level out-comes (expectancy) and to the relationship of various performance levels to second-level outcomes (instrumentality).

Both theories emphasize the future role of rewards and an individual's decision-making processes. These theories suggest that managers who are concerned about improving the performance of their subordinates should take an active role in creating proper work environments and matching peo-ple to jobs. They should establish clear performance–reward systems. Moti-vation for high performance will not exist unless managers recognize such performance when it occurs and reward it quickly.

SUMMARY

Six widely accepted theories of motivation can be classified as either content or process theories. The four content theories—needs hierarchy, ERG, moti-vator–hygiene, and achievement—attempt to identify specific factors that motivate people. The needs hierarchy theory identifies five sets of hierarchi-cal needs and the ERG theory three sets of needs; the achievement theory stresses the building of achievement motivation; and the motivator–hy-giene theory focuses on the nature of the work environment and the work it-self. These theories are logical and easy to understand, but more research is needed to support their underlying assumptions. Although the use of each of the content theories can provide outcomes that people find desirable—and managers using them can generate actions that create desirable outcomes—no one knows why these outcomes occur. The trade-off for simplicity sacri-fices understanding of the complexity of the work motivation process. On the positive side, the content theories emphasize important factors in moti-vation, and the motivator–hygiene theory is a useful explanation for job en-richment.

The two process theories presented—expectancy and equity—are based on the assumption that people make conscious choices about their behavior and think out behavior in advance. Both models attempt to answer the ques-tion, "Why do outcomes become desirable?" The expectancy theory answers this question by stating that individuals choose among outcomes and assign probabilities, based on past experience or hunches, to the likelihood of reach-ing these outcomes through various performance levels. Equity theory an-swers the question by stating that outcomes become important only after individuals compare them to those that others in the same or similar situa-tions are getting. In general, the more the workers perceive that a given per-formance level directly relates to a desired goal or favorably compares with the rewards that others obtain, the more highly motivated the workers will be.

KEY WORDS AND CONCEPTS

Ability	Equity theory
Achievement motivation theory	ERG theory
Affiliation needs	Esteem needs
Content theories	Existence needs
Equity	Expectancy theory

Extrinsic factors
First-level outcomes
Frustration–regression process
Fulfillment–progression process
Goal
Growth needs
Hygiene factors
Inequity
Inputs
Instrumentality
Intrinsic factors
Motivation
Motivator–Hygiene theory

Motivators
Needs
Needs hierarchy theory
Outcomes
Physiological Needs
Process theories
Relatedness needs
Second-level outcomes
Security needs
Self-actualization needs
Thematic Apperception Test (TAT)
Valence

DISCUSSION QUESTIONS

1. What are the stages described in the needs hierarchy theory? How would you apply this theory in searching for a job?

2. Discuss the similarities and differences in the hierarchy of needs and the ERG theories of motivation. In your opinion, which is easier for managers to use? Why?

3. Discuss the achievement theory of motivation. Is achievement a need that can change? If so, how?

4. What is the value of the motivator–hygiene theory to managers?

5. Compare and contrast the basic motivational assumptions of the expectancy and equity theories.

6. How could a manager who understands equity theory apply this knowledge in establishing a pay system for a corporation?

7. Under what conditions are monetary rewards for employees a valid motivational approach?

8. Describe equity theory. State what you did when you found yourself in an inequitable situation.

9. The expectancy theory includes four key concepts: outcomes, expectancy, valence, and instrumentality. What do these concepts mean? How can a manager apply them to motivate subordinates?

10. Discuss the managerial implications of underpayment and overpayment using equity theory.

11. If high achievers tend to be superior performers, why don't managers simply hire only high achievers?

12. Explain the sequence by which needs are translated into behaviors.

MANAGEMENT INCIDENTS AND CASES

Motivating Willy Loman

Since Kenneth Olsen founded Digital Equipment Corp. in 1957, its salesmen have sold more than $20 billion worth of computers without earning a single cent in commissions. Not that DEC's marketers are underpaid. Their compensation—average annual earnings over $50,000—is up to industry standards. It's just that Olsen believes he can get more out of his salespeople by paying them a fixed salary.

"That means they are interested in the customer and not their paychecks," he explains. "The result is that our ratio of orders per person is among the best in the industry."

This strategy has served Olsen well, helping to make DEC the world's second-largest computer manufacturer. But in 1984, what with a disastrous first-quarter earnings decline, orders seem to have stalled. Could it be that DEC's more than 7,000 salesmen need a new brand of aggressiveness that doesn't come from a regular weekly paycheck?

During the 70's many firms in a variety of industries followed DEC's example, moving away from commission schedules toward fixed salaries. The result, according to the Chicago-based Dartnell Corp.: About 22% of all salesmen now receive only a salary, up from less than 9% a decade year. Some 21% still get paid solely through commissions, but that number has dropped sharply, from a peak of nearly 29% in 1973. The most popular form of compensation continues to be a blend of both approaches, typically 80% salary and 20% commissions. But as the popularity of full salaries grew, these combination plans declined, too.

Why? "Today's salesperson was raised in an affluent society," says John Steinbrink, a senior vice president at Dartnell who tracks sales force compensation. "They are used to a particular standard of living, and want the security of a fixed salary. They don't want to assume much risk."

Offering such security, of course, was also viewed as an element of "enlightened" management. Salaries, so the argument ran, made for more professional marketing and eliminated unseemly foot-in-the-door selling. Expenses rose accordingly: These days, for example, the average cost of a domestic sales call is $152, up 42% in just two years. And it typically takes a salesman five separate calls to land an order.

Experts think that many companies will reevaluate their sales compensation schemes. Studies show that building too much protection into pay plans tends to favor the least productive salesmen and provides little stimulus for putting forth extra effort. "You really should get the carrot as big as possible without making the guy die to reach it," explains Steinbrink. "Give him salary for the essentials, to help him pay the rent and put food on the table, but not much else. Hell, he's supposed to be a salesman."[26]

Questions

1. What is Dartnell's theory of motivation?
2. Using equity theory, what predictions can you make concerning salespersons' behavior on straight salary versus commissions?

Treetop Lumber Company

Mr. Don Wood is a production supervisor at the Treetop Lumber Company. His group of fifty people is responsible for processing walnut logs into high-quality lumber and gunstock. The process includes loading and unloading the lumber, stacking, sawing, and kilning. The band sawyers hold the only skilled position in the production process; all other positions are filled with semiskilled labor. Work in the sawmill subjects the employees to considerable amounts of dust and noise. Workers in the lumberyard do not have any weather protection throughout the year, and temperatures range from 25° F in the winter to 105° in the summer. Starting pay is the minimum wage.

Earlier in the week, Wood went through the personnel records of the company and obtained the following data:

- *Sex*—96 percent male and 4 percent female.
- *Age*—25 percent under 20 years, 18 percent 21 to 24 years, 40 per-

cent 25 to 29 years, and 17 percent 30 years or older.

- *Education*   10 percent completed elementary school, 15 percent completed junior high school, 52 percent completed senior high school, and 23 percent completed some college.
- *Tenure with the company*—50 percent three months or less, 20 percent one year or less, 20 percent five years or less, and 10 percent five years or more.

Wood was concerned that the needs of the employees, particularly those in his group, were not being met. He brought up this possibility at the next supervisors' meeting and was surprised at some of the comments from his colleagues: "We're meeting their needs. They are money motivated, not achievement motivated like we are." "All they care about is how big their paycheck is. They don't care about doing challenging work." "They are lazy. They avoid responsibilities. They are not dedicated. The point is, they simply don't care about their work."

Wood felt the supervisors were wrong in their assessments of the employees. He had gotten to know his workers and believed otherwise. After two weeks of debate, Wood finally convinced the other supervisors and his boss of the merits of bringing in a human resource expert from the nearby university, Dr. Amy Birch.

Wood explained to Birch that he felt employees' needs were not being met and told her how shocked he was to hear the views some of his fellow supervisors had about the employees. Birch said she would like to interview some of the employees and then administer a questionnaire to all of them. The questionnaire would involve the employees' ranking a list of sixteen job factors according to how important they were to them and the extent to which each factor was present in their particular job.

"On the basis of the interviews and the questionnaire, I should be able to determine many of the needs of your employees. From there we can try to figure out if these needs are being met," said Birch. "I'll have the results for you in time for your next supervisors' meeting, two weeks from now."

At the next meeting, all the supervisors were curious as to what Birch had to say.

"I think you will find the results of my study here quite surprising," she began. "The data I have collected seems to indicate that your workers' needs are not being met. According to the questionnaire, the workers do not feel they are lazy. If the job is right, they don't mind putting in some extra effort. A job is pleasant to them if it requires the use of their minds, provides feedback, and helps them to meet good people.

"The employees seem to demand work that is challenging enough to require creativity and the use of their talents—work that is of sufficient variety and complexity to develop new skills that will bring about opportunities for advancement and greater cooperation.

"The employees express a desire for friendship at work. They enjoy working with pleasant associates who provide assistance at work, share joy and sorrow, and provide recognition for a job well done.

"An analysis of their satisfaction with each of the sixteen items in the questionnaire suggests a similar conclusion regarding their desires. The three most significant sources of their dissatisfaction appear to be inadequate compensation, monotonous work, and poor recognition.

"As you can see, your understanding of what motivates your employees has been wrong. What is worse, your motivation and control programs were established on the basis of this misunderstanding. These have resulted in employee resentment and poor production. This, in turn, has reinforced the belief that employees 'simply don't care about their jobs.' It is a vicious circle—a self-fulfilling prophecy."

As Birch surveyed the astonished faces on some of the supervisors, she added, "Let's see if we can generate some ideas as to what the company can do to begin meeting some of these needs."[27]

Questions

1. How would the needs hierarchy theory and ERG theory interpret the results from this questionnaire? Are there differences in interpretation?
2. What would you suggest that the company do in order to meet its employees' needs?

REFERENCES

1. Katz, D., and Kahn, R. *The Social Psychology of Organizations*, 2d ed. New York: John Wiley & Sons, 1978, 402; Pinder, C. *Work Motivation*. Glenview, Ill.: Scott, Foresman, 1984.

2. *Goodyear Tire and Rubber Company, Annual Report, 1984*. Akron, Ohio: Goodyear Tire and Rubber Company, 1984.

3. Fisher, A. GM's Unlikely Revolutionist. *Fortune*, March 19, 1984, 106–112.

4. Kamp, T. Speech delivered at sales meeting. Minneapolis, April, 1985.

5. Main, J. New Ways to Teach Workers What's New. *Fortune*, October 1, 1984, 85–94; Lepper, M. Microcomputers in Education: Motivational and Social Issues, *American Psychologist*, 1985, *40*(1), 1–19.

6. Miner, J. *Theories of Organizational Behavior*. Hinsdale, Ill.: Dryden, 1980; Naylor, J., and Ilgen, D. Goal-Setting: A Theoretical Analysis of Motivational Technology. In B. Staw and L. Cummings (Eds.) *Research in Organizational Behavior, Vol. 6*. Greenwich, Conn.: JAI Press, 1984, 95–140.

7. Maslow, A. A Theory of Human Motivation. *Psychological Review*, 1943, *80*, 370–396; Maslow, A. *Motivation and Personality*. New York: Harper & Row, 1970.

8. Naylor, J., Pritchard, R., and Ilgen, D. *A Theory of Behavior in Organizations*. New York: Academic Press, 1980; Mitchell, T. Motivation and Performance. In J. Rosenzweig and F. Kast, *Modules in Management*. Chicago, Ill.: Science Research Associates, Inc., 1984, entire section.

9. For accounts of these studies, see Porter, L. Job Attitudes in Management. *Journal of Applied Psychology*, 1963, *47*, 141–148; Altimus, C., and Tersine, R. Chronological Age and Job Satisfaction. *Academy of Management Journal*, 1973, *16*, 53–66; Slocum, J., and Strawser, R. Racial Differences in Job Attitudes. *Journal of Applied Psychology*, 1973, *56*, 28–33; Slocum, J., Topicak, P., and Kuhn, D. A Cross-Cultural Study of Need Satisfaction and Need Importance for Operative Employees. *Personnel Psychology*, 1971, *24*, 435–445.

10. Alderfer, C. *Existence, Relatedness and Growth: Human Needs in Organizational Settings*. New York: Free Press, 1972.

11. Tracy, L. A Dynamic Living-Systems Model of Work Motivation. *Systems Research*, 1984, *1*, 191–203; Salancik, G., and Pfeffer, J. An Examination of Need-Satisfaction Models of Job Attitudes. *Administrative Science Quarterly*, 1977, *22*, 427–456.

12. Alderfer, C., and Guzzo, R. Life Expectancies and Adults' Enduring Strength of Desires in Organizations. *Administrative Science Quarterly*, *24*, 347–361.

13. "Computer People": Yes, They Really are Different. *Business Week*, February 20, 1984, 65–68.

14. McClelland, D. *The Achieving Society*. Princeton, N. J.: Van Nostrand-Reinhold, 1961; McClelland, D. *Assessing Human Motivation*. Morristown, N.J.: General Learning Press, 1971; Cornelius, E., and Lane, F. The Power Motive and Managerial Success in a Professionally Oriented Service Company. *Journal of Applied Psychology*, 1984, *69*, 32–40.

15. Scredon, S., and Nussbaum, B. Iverson: Smashing the Corporate Pyramid. *Business Week*, January 21, 1985, 71.

16. McClelland, D., and Burnham, D. Power is the Great Motivator. *Harvard Business Review*, 1976, *54*(2), 100–111; Stahl, M. Achievement Power and Managerial Motivation: Selecting Managerial Talent with the Job Choice Exercise. *Personnel Psychology*, 1983, *36*, 775–790; Cox, A. *The Making of the Achiever*. New York: Dodd & Mead, 1985.

17. For an excellent review, see Miner. J. *Theories of Organizational Behavior*. Hinsdale, Ill.: Dryden, 1980, 60–70.

18. Herzberg, F., Mausner, B., and Snyderman, B. *The Motivation to Work.* New York: John Wiley & Sons, 1959.

19. House, R., and Widgor, L. Herzberg's Dual-Factor Theory of Job Satisfaction and Motivation: A Review of the Evidence and Criticism. *Personnel Psychology,* 1968, *20,* 369–389.

20. Machungwa, P., and Schmitt, N. Work Motivation in a Developing Country. *Journal of Applied Psychology,* 1983, *68,* 31–42.

21. Vroom, V. *Work and Motivation.* New York: John Wiley & Sons, 1964.

22. Fusilier, M., Ganster, D., and Middlemist, D. A Within-Person Test Form of the Expectancy Theory Model in a Choice Context. *Organizational Behavior and Human Performance,* 1984, *34,* 323–342; Wanous, J., Keon, T., and Latack, J. Expectancy Theory and Occupational/Organizational Choices: A Review and Test. *Organizational Behavior and Human Performance,* 1983, *32,* 66–86; Kennedy, C., Fossum, J., and White, B. An Empirical Comparison of Within-Subjects and Between-Subjects Expectancy Theory Models. *Organizational Behavior and Human Performance,* 1983, *32,* 124–142.

23. Nadler, D., and Lawler, E. Motivation: A Diagnostic Approach. In J. Hackman, E. Lawler, and L. Porter (Eds.) *Perspectives on Behavior in Organizations.* New York: McGraw-Hill, 1977, 26–38.

24. Adams, J. Toward an Understanding of Inequity. *Journal of Abnormal and Social Psychology,* 1963, *67,* 422–436. Madigan, R. Comparable Worth Judgments: A Measurement Properties Analysis. *Journal of Applied Psychology,* 1985, *70,* 137–147.

25. Cosier, R., and Dalton, D. Equity Theory and Time: A Reformulation. *Academy of Management Review,* 1983, *8,* 311–319; Vecchio, R. Models of Psychological Inequity. *Organizational Behavior and Human Performance,* 1984, *34,* 266–282.

26. Abstracted from Byrne, J. Motivating Willy Loman. *Forbes,* January 30, 1984, 91.

27. Abstracted from Hoh, A. Interpreting Employee Needs: Assuming Versus Understanding. *Supervisory Management,* April, 1980, 29–34.

PART III

INTERPERSONAL AND GROUP PROCESSES

8 Interpersonal Communication

LEARNING OBJECTIVES

When you have finished studying this chapter, you should be able to:

- Explain why face-to-face interpersonal communication is an information-rich communication medium and is so important to managers.
- Describe the basic communication process in face-to-face interaction between two or more individuals.
- Evaluate the importance of communication networks for managers and the likely effects of five different communication networks for managerial effectiveness.
- Diagnose your own and other individuals' styles of interpersonal communication.
- Improve your effectiveness in giving feedback, engaging in self-disclosure, and listening to others.
- Explain and give examples of five types of nonverbal communication.

OUTLINE

Preview Case

Sperry Corporation and Listening

The following are brief excerpts of an interview conducted by John Di-Gaetani (hereafter J. D.), a faculty member in the Department of English, Hofstra University. The interview focused on the Sperry Corporation's campaign about listening with the two people most responsible for it: Kenneth E. Thompson (hereafter K. T.), Sperry's Group Executive Vice President, and Delmont J. Kennedy (hereafter D. K.), Director of Advertising.

J. D.: Tell me, what made you decide to start a campaign about listening?

K. T.: Well, we had been using as an advertising theme "making machines do more so man can do more" and it had been working at a couple of the divisions at Sperry. But it didn't really have the kind of impact for Sperry Univac that it had for the rest of Sperry. So we commissioned two research studies to find out what people thought about Sperry Corporation. The most positive thing that came back is that we were different because we would listen. And we would try to solve a customer's problems rather than just saying, "Here's our equipment. You want it or don't you?" The decision to buy a computer, as an example, is such a heavy, involved, expensive, long-term decision that a tremendous amount of thought goes into it before the decision is finally made. And the customers that were Sperry Univac customers and even some of those that were not would come back and say, the difference is that you listened.

And then we thought before we launch something like that over television, radio and the newspapers, we'd better make sure *our* people know what it's all about and make sure that more of them are listening. So we retained as a consultant and trainer Professor Lyman K. Steil from the University of Minnesota, who teaches listening. The first class that he held was for a group we call the Office of the Chairman—the chairman of the board, the president, and two group vice-presidents. And we went through a session with him and found we could improve our listening skills. Then we expanded from there and went through a fairly large part of the organization—you don't do 90,000 people in one summer of personal training. And then Del Kennedy and his people put together a number of pieces that went to all the employees saying, this is what we're going to do and why we're going to do it, and then we launched the campaign.

J. D.: You feel it has been successful.

K. T.: Oh, yes. Exceedingly so in our mind.

J. D.: What do you mean by successful?

K. T.: Well, let me try some stories from inside Sperry. One day I heard a personnel committee was in session, and I went in and asked them if there were any problems with the listening campaign and one of those present said, well yes. Some of our foremen are coming in and complaining that their people are coming to them and saying, "Now, look, you have to listen to me." And the individual then complained about some problem he has on the job or some improvement he would like to see put in to make the job more productive. With the listening campaign the foreman had to listen and had to respond, and to respond he had to think. Sometimes before he could respond he had to contact his superiors and discuss the issue, and sometimes the final answer to the employee was "No, we're not going to do that." But with reasons. And sometimes the answer would come back, "Yes, and thank you for the suggestion." So it's helped in that way. It's been used many times in conversations that I'm aware of where one of the people involved in the conversation just was not really tuned in and listening and then raises a question, and afterwards someone tells him he should have listened.

Everywhere I go in the corporation, and I do a lot of traveling, the listening thing is there. People are conscious of it.

J. D.: You said the initial response to the idea for the campaign was: "Isn't listening really a passive word? Is it an action word?"

K. T.: I guess if we had come into the market and said, "We listen," it wouldn't have had much impact. "Who doesn't?" people would say. But the way it appeared created the impact: "We understand how important it is to listen"—and then an example, like the Titanic, where someone didn't listen, with disastrous results.

D. K.: I think a couple of other things happened also. There was this concern about the passivity of the word. But as the internal training began to gain exposure inside the company, people, including myself, who had originally associated the word "listening" with the mechanical act of hearing, began to learn something. By our definition listening is more than that; it's understanding, evaluating, interpreting—and ultimately, responding to what you've heard. That total is our definition of listening. As our people began to understand that, they began to see that it's more than simply passively sitting there and having your ear drums beat on.

J. D.: Many times during our discussion on listening we've mentioned how difficult it is. Why do you think it is so difficult to listen well?

K. T.: Maybe our mouth was given more powerful muscles than our ears. We seem to want to use it more. Psychologically exactly why, I can't answer that. You would have better answers than I would.

J. D.: My own feeling is that it is more difficult for males to listen because our society has trained males to believe that power is in speaking. Now we all know enough about listening to know that is not true, but I think there is probably a little voice in most of us telling us the position of power is in speaking.

D. K.: Also, we're not trained to listen. We are trained to be good speakers. We are trained to be good writers and readers, but I've never had a course in listening in my life. I've had lots of courses on how to speak. We're just not trained, not sensitized to listening.

J. D.: Well, as you said, when this campaign first started, people confused listening with hearing. That's the problem. I think education has not done enough to sensitize people to a skill they assume they have.

Another question I wanted to ask concerns career development. My students, typical of this generation of college students, are very career oriented. I tell them that being a good listener can help them get a job, develop a career. Is this true? Some of them are skeptical.

K. T.: I think it's absolutely true. Being a poor listener will stop you from advancing, from promotions, from growth. You can't really learn anything from yourself; you can only know it from other people, and in order to learn you've got to listen.[1]

As demonstrated in the Preview Case, listening is a fundamental and active part of the process of effective interpersonal communication. Most often, the active part of interpersonal communication is thought of as only the words, emotions, gestures, and other cues provided by the sender. The most eloquent speaker is doomed to failure if the receiver does not actively listen. This is apparent in our definition of interpersonal communication. **Interpersonal communication** is the transmission and reception of ideas, facts, opinions, attitudes, and feelings—verbally, nonverbally, or both—which produce a response.[2] Through active listening, the messages intended by the sender are more likely to be accurately understood and interpreted by the receiver.[3]

Why is effective interpersonal communication—including active listening—so important to managerial effectiveness? First, many managerial tasks are partially or totally carried out through interpersonal communications of one type or another: one-to-one contact between superior and subordinate or between two peers, formal meetings of decision-making groups, and informal person-to-person communications. One study at Du Pont showed the distribution of first-level managers' time spent in communicating as follows: one-to-one and group meetings (administrative and technical), 53 percent; writing, 15.5 percent; reading, 14.9 percent; telephoning, 8 percent; and other, 7.7 percent.[4] Second, face-to-face interpersonal communication is probably the richest medium for processing issues, especially those that involve uncertainty and ambiguity. **Information richness** is the potential information-carrying capacity of data.[5] **Data** is simply the output of a communication channel. Words spoken face to face, telephone calls, letters and memos, and computer printouts represent forms of data. They become information when they reinforce or change the understanding of receivers with respect to their ideas, facts, opinions, attitudes, or feelings.

As shown in Figure 8-1, face-to-face interpersonal communication is considered to be the richest communication medium. Why? In brief, face-to-face interaction provides immediate feedback so that the receiver can check the accuracy of his or her understanding and make corrections if needed. The face-to-face medium also allows the sender and receiver to simultaneously

FIGURE 8–1.
Communication
Media and
Information
Richness

Source: Adapted from
Lengel, R. H. Managerial
Information Processing
and Communication-Media
Source Selection Behavior.
Unpublished Ph.D.
dissertation, Texas A&M
University, 1982; Holland,
W. E., Stead, B. A., and
Leibrock, R. C. Information
Channel/Source Selection
as a Correlate of Technical
Uncertainty in a Research
and Development
Organization. *IEEE
Transactions on
Engineering Management*,
1976, *23*, 163–167.

Information Medium		Richness of Information Transfer
Face-to-face discussion		Highest
Telephone conversations		High
Informal letters/memos (personally addressed)		Moderate
Formal written documents (impersonally addressed)		Low
Formal numeric documents (such as a computer printout of an income statement)		Lowest

observe multiple cues—body language, tone of voice, facial expressions—from each other that communicate beyond spoken words. Finally, face-to-face interaction enables the sender and receiver to more quickly identify and use language that is natural and more personal. Because of these characteristics, we almost always find that solving the important and tough management problems—and especially those involving uncertainty and ambiguity—requires extensive face-to-face interpersonal communication.[6]

In this chapter we develop the process, types, and patterns of verbal and nonverbal communication used by people in their work roles. The discussion focuses on interpersonal communication involving two to about ten people.

BASIC COMMUNICATION PROCESS

Accurate interpersonal communication between two or more people takes place only if the ideas, facts, opinions, attitudes, or feelings that the sender intended to transmit are the same as those understood and interpreted by the receiver. As discussed in Chapters 3 and 4, internal and external factors often lead individuals to inaccurate perceptions and poor interpersonal communication. Management and labor representatives may well disagree with each other while negotiating a new contract. But, so long as opposing viewpoints are being transmitted, received, and understood with the intended meaning, accurate interpersonal communication is taking place.

Sender and Receiver

Interpersonal communication obviously requires two or more people. Figure 8-2 presents a model of the communication process, which involves only two people. Since interpersonal communication often includes a number of exchanges between people, the labeling of one person as the *sender* and the other as the *receiver* is arbitrary. These roles shift back and forth, depending on where the people are in the process at any given time. This shifting of roles is particularly important for managers. Irving Shapiro, a former chief executive officer of Du Pont and a respected executive, illustrates these shifting roles and the importance of interpersonal communication to the achievement of organization objectives.

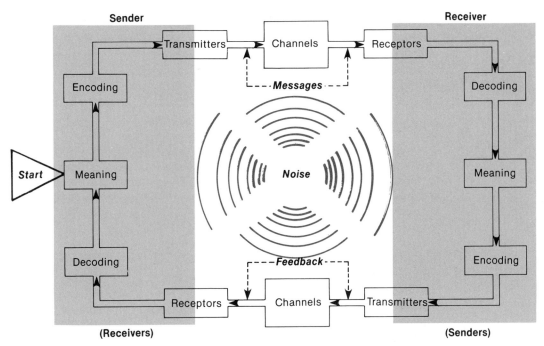

FIGURE 8-2.
Model of Interpersonal Communication Process

One important day-to-day task for the CEO is communication—digesting information and shaping ideas, yes, but even more centrally, the business of listening and explaining. Decisions and policies have no effect nor any real existence unless they are recognized and understood by those who must put them into effect. As with a board of directors, an operating business organization acquires a sense of purpose not just because one or two leaders have something in the back of their minds, but because that vision is shared and sold. It sounds banal to say that a CEO is first and foremost in the human-relations and communication business—what else could the job be?—but the point is too important to leave to inference. No other item on the chief executive's duty list has more leverage on the organization's prospects.[7]

The characteristics of the sender and receiver substantially influence the communication process. For example, the sender may have certain goals for communicating, such as adding to or changing the ideas, opinions, attitudes, or behavior of the receiver, or changing his or her relationship with the receiver.[8] If the receiver is antagonistic toward these goals, the probability of distortion and misunderstanding will be quite high. The less the goals of interpersonal communication are concerned with differences in attitudes and values, the greater is the probability of accurate communication.

Transmitters and Receptors

Transmitters and **receptors** refer to the means (media) available for sending and receiving messages, respectively. In interpersonal communication, they usually involve one or more of the senses—the ability to see, hear, touch, smell, and taste. Transmission can take place through verbal and nonverbal means. Once the transmitters are in operation, the communication process moves beyond the complete control of the sender; a message that has been transmitted cannot be brought back. How many times have you thought to yourself, "I wish I hadn't said that?"

Messages, Channels, and Noise

Messages include the data transmitted and the coded symbols that are intended to give particular meanings to the data. The sender hopes the interpreted meanings of these messages are as close as possible to the original and intended meanings. To understand the difference between the original meaning and the received message, think about an occasion when you tried to convey your inner thoughts and feelings of love, rage, or fear to another person. Did you find it difficult or impossible to transmit your true "inner meaning?" The greater the difference is between the interpreted meanings and the intended messages transmitted, the poorer is the interpersonal communication. For communication to occur at all, the sender and receiver must share something on some level. Words or nonverbal symbols have no meanings in and of themselves; their meanings are created by the sender *and* the receiver.[9]

Channels are the means by which messages travel from a sender to a receiver. For example, a conversation may be carried by the air in a face-to-face conversation or by a telephone line.

Noise is any interference with the intended message in the channel. A radio playing loud music while someone is trying to talk to someone else is an example of noise. Noise can be overcome by repeating the message or increasing the intensity (for example, the volume) of the message.

Meaning, Encoding, and Decoding

As Figure 8-2 indicates, the sender's message is transmitted through channels to the receiver's receptors. The senses—sight, hearing, touch, smell, and taste—are a person's only receptors for incoming messages. The received messages are changed from their symbolic form (such as spoken words) to a form that has meaning. **Meanings** represent a person's ideas, facts, opinions, attitudes, and feelings.

Encoding is the sender's translation of meanings into messages that can be transmitted. Vocabulary and knowledge play an important role in the sender's ability to encode. Professionals often have difficulty communicating with the general public because they tend to encode meanings in a form that can be understood only by other professionals in the same field. Consumer pressures to have contracts written in a form that can be understood by everyone is a reaction to self-serving encoding. Contracts that directly affect consumers often have been written on the assumption that the encoding and decoding will take place only by lawyers. Many consumers want this to change—and it is beginning to change.

The translation of received messages into interpreted meanings is called **decoding**. Through a shared language, people can decode many messages so that the meanings transmitted are reasonably close to the meanings received. Anyone who has tried to communicate with a person who speaks only another language probably already appreciates the importance of shared language in decoding messages.

The accuracy of interpersonal communication is evaluated in relation to the *ideal state*, where the sender's intended meanings are the same as the interpreted meanings of the receiver. The transmission of factual information of a nonthreatening nature most easily approximates this ideal state. For example, sharing the recipe for a cake will generally result in easier and more accurate interpersonal communication than the communication between a manager and a subordinate in a performance evaluation session.

Feedback

In the model of interpersonal communication, **feedback** is the receiver's response to the message that was sent by the sender. Feedback lets the sender know whether the message was received as intended and makes communication a process rather than just an event. Through feedback, interpersonal communication becomes a dynamic, two-way process. However, failures in interpersonal communication can occur at any point in the basic communication process.

COMMUNICATION NETWORKS

An **interpersonal communication network** is defined as "those interconnected individuals who are linked by patterned flows to any given individual."[10] The concept focuses on communication *relationships* among individuals rather than on the individuals themselves.

Role of Networks

Networks focus on the flow of verbal, written, or other forms of nonverbal signals (data) between two or more individuals. Networks emphasize the pattern of signal flow (for example, flow between member A and member B, or between member A and all other network members simultaneously) rather than whether the signal sent was received as intended by the sender. Of course, communication networks can influence the likelihood of a match between the intended messages sent and the messages actually received and interpreted.

The model of the interpersonal communication process in Figure 8-2 is based on the involvement of only two people, but, obviously, interpersonal communication often takes place among many individuals and larger groups. A manager must network with a variety of people both within and outside the organization. As illustrated by Figure 8-3, a manager's communication networks stretch laterally and vertically. Vertically, they include not only the manager's immediate superior and subordinates but also the superior's superiors and the subordinates' subordinates. Lateral networks include people at the same level (peers) and those at lower and higher levels (lateral superiors and lateral subordinates).[11] Managerial communication networks—as suggested in Figure 8-3—can be quite involved.

Group size places limits on the possible communication networks within a group. In principle, as the size of a group increases arithmetically, the num-

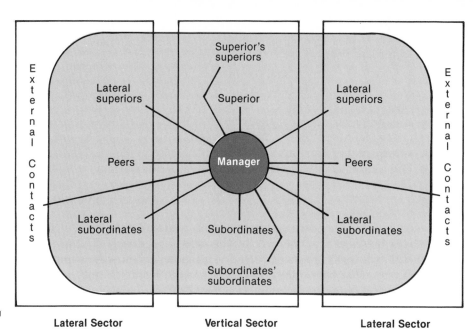

FIGURE 8–3.
A Manager's Interpersonal Communication Network

ber of possible communication interrelationships increases geometrically. Accordingly, a much greater variety and complexity in communication networks is possible in a 12-person group than in a 3-person group.

While every member theoretically may be able to communicate with all other members in a group, the direction and number of communication channels in an organization is often somewhat limited.[12] In committee meetings, for example, varying levels of formality in the rules and procedures influence who may speak, what may be discussed, and in what order. The relative status or ranking of group members also may differ, and the members having higher status will probably dominate the communication network. Even when an open network is encouraged, the members may actually use a more limited network arrangement.

Types of communication networks and their uses have been found to be especially important in understanding power and control relationships among employees and the rate of innovation in organizations.[13]

Managerial Guidelines and Implications

No simple guidelines exist to help the manager apply the research findings regarding communication networks under all conditions.[14] In problem solving, the level of complexity is one factor. Communication problems basically can be differentiated as simple or complex. Simple problems make few demands on network members in terms of (1) collecting, categorizing, and evaluating information; (2) generating goals or objectives to be achieved; (3) developing and evaluating alternatives; and (4) coping with human problems associated with the tasks at hand. Complex problems, in contrast, are characterized by a high degree of one or more of these types of demands.

Simple networks (such as superior-to-subordinate) are often effective for solving simple problems. All-channel or open networks (as in a group meeting) are often more effective for solving complex problems. Another qualifying factor in problem solving is the degree of member interdependence required to accomplish the group's task. Complex problems in which there is little member interdependence may be effectively handled through one of the more centralized communication networks (such as superior-to-subordinate). However, complex problems usually require member interdependence. Thus the higher the degree of member interdependence, the more likely it is that open networks will be the most effective.

Communication networks have several managerial implications. First, no single network is likely to prove effective in all situations for a work group with a variety of tasks and objectives. The apparently efficient and low-cost simple network of a superior communicating in a one-way fashion is likely to be ineffective if used exclusively. Dissatisfaction may become so great that individuals leave the group or lose their motivation to contribute. Second, groups that face complex problems requiring high member interdependence may deal with them ineffectively because of inadequate sharing of information, inadequate consideration of alternatives, and so on. Third, a group must consider trade-offs or opportunity costs. A work group committed to the exclusive use of the all-channel network may deal inefficiently with simple problems and tasks that require little member interdependence. In such cases, members may also become bored and dissatisfied with group processes. They simply come to feel that their time is being wasted. Another trade-off with the all-channel network is its implied labor costs; that is, more hours of time must be spent on processing a problem in group meetings with the all-channel network. A group should use the type of network that is most appropriate to its tasks and problems.

COMMUNICATION STYLES

The communication styles used by people can vary substantially. We will examine five basic styles of interpersonal communication and the possible effects of each.[15] The communication styles shown in Figure 8-4 provide a framework for evaluating and developing skills in feedback, self-disclosure, and listening in order to improve interpersonal communication. It serves as a diagnostic tool and should not be interpreted narrowly and mechanistically.[16]

Framework of Communication Styles

Figure 8-4 is based on two dimensions of interpersonal communication. One dimension, which is shown on the vertical axis and ranges from low to high, is *openness to others*. This dimension includes opening or revealing ourselves to others (self-disclosure) and being receptive to feedback from others, particularly about how others perceive us and our actions. The second dimension is *giving feedback*, which is shown on the horizontal axis and also ranges from low to high. Giving feedback is the degree to which we communicate our thoughts and feelings to one or more individuals. This can focus on the very personal or on the more abstract, such as reactions to others'

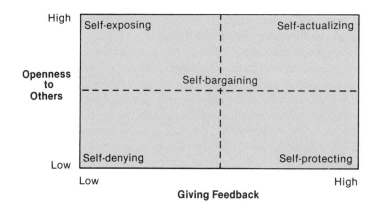

FIGURE 8–4.
Framework of
Communication
Styles

Source: Adapted from
Polsky, H. W. Notes on
Personal Feedback in
Sensitivity Training.
Sociological Inquiry, 1971,
41, 179. Used with
permission.

ideas or proposals. The emotional impact of feedback varies according to how personally it is focused.

Five Styles

The five interpersonal communication styles identified in Figure 8-4 are self-denying, self-protecting, self-exposing, self-bargaining, and self-actualizing. The **self-denying style** is used when individuals isolate themselves from others and withdraw. Introverted individuals are more likely to use this communication style than extroverted individuals. Self-denying individuals rank low in showing openness to others and low in giving feedback. In the extreme, their ideas, opinions, attitudes, and feelings are hidden from others.

When individuals only probe others or make evaluative comments to others, a **self-protecting style** is being practiced. However, the giving of feedback may be a defensive tactic to prevent self-exposure and comments from others. The self-protecting style ranks high in giving feedback to others but low in displaying openness to others. In the extreme, self-protecting individuals share only their ideas, opinions, attitudes, and feelings about others with others. Usually, they are quite willing to receive from others and share with others egotistical comments about themselves. But they almost never share or are receptive to comments about their limitations or personal characteristics that need improvement.

With the **self-exposing style**, individuals encourage others to focus on them by constantly asking for reactions to their behaviors. However, they may give little real thought to the feedback they receive. The self-exposing style ranks low in giving feedback but high in displaying openness to others. When feedback from others is taken seriously, these individuals may go through life on a roller-coaster ride of emotional highs and lows, depending on whether the most recent feedback from others was positive or negative.

With the **self-bargaining style**, individuals are willing to give feedback and open up if others in the interaction do the same. Individuals use themselves as a point of bargaining or negotiation. The self-bargaining style ranks as moderate in giving feedback and in displaying openness to others.

In the **self-actualizing style**, individuals spontaneously provide the appropriate amount of information about themselves, ask for feedback, and provide feedback in a constructive and nondefensive manner. The self-actualizing style ranks high in giving feedback and in showing openness to others. The self-actualizing style is desirable under ideal conditions, but situational factors can easily motivate people to use another style instead. One key situational factor is the approach that others take in communicating. If a superior is not receptive to receiving feedback, an employee, naturally, may be reluctant to give feedback.

To suggest that only one communication style is desirable in all situations would be simplistic and unrealistic. However, the self-actualizing style may be a desirable one to develop and use whenever possible. Thus the following sections on effective feedback, effective self-disclosure, and effective listening provide guidance for improving communication skills using the self-actualizing style.

Effective Feedback

Giving feedback is a crucial dimension in the framework of communication styles shown in Figure 8-4. Proctor & Gamble and many other organizations include the principles of effective feedback in their programs to build more effective working relationships.[17]

To the extent possible, people should offer feedback as follows:

- Feedback ideally should be based on a foundation of trust between the sender and receiver. If the organizational environment is characterized by extreme personal competitiveness, emphasis on the use of power to punish and control, and rigid superior–subordinate relationships, it will lack the level of trust necessary for effective feedback.

- Feedback should be specific rather than general, with clear and, preferably, recent examples. Saying "You are a dominating person" is not as useful as saying "Just now when we were deciding the issue, you did not listen to what others said, and I felt I had to accept your argument or face attack from you."

- Feedback should be given at a time when the receiver appears to be ready to accept it. Thus, when a person is angry, upset, or defensive is probably not the time to bring up other, new issues.

- Feedback should be checked with the receiver to determine if it seems valid. The sender can ask the receiver to rephrase and restate the feedback to see if it matches what the sender intended.

- Feedback should include only those things the receiver may be capable of doing something about.

- Feedback should not include more than the receiver can handle at any particular time. For example, the receiver may become threatened and defensive if the feedback includes everything the receiver does that annoys the sender.

Personal feedback helps people to look at their behavior by revealing to them the feelings aroused in others or by enabling them to see themselves as others do. However, someone who is given accurate feedback and who accepts it does not necessarily change in the direction implied by the feedback.

DIAGNOSING FEEDBACK PRACTICES Various types of interpersonal feedback take place within organizations.[18] This is true for all employees, but especially so for managers who maintain a wide-ranging interpersonal communication network. Table 8-1 provides a questionnaire that can be used to diagnose feedback practices by superiors and co-workers, as experienced by an employee in an organization.

The first seven items in Table 8-1 concern negative feedback from superiors and co-workers. Remember that negative feedback is not necessarily bad for the person who is receiving it, but that its effectiveness is largely determined by how the feedback is given.

The second section in Table 8-1 concerns the degree to which positive feedback is received from individuals at higher organizational levels (items 8–11). Positive feedback attempts to reinforce and reward certain behaviors so they will be repeated in the future. The third section (items 12–15) also concerns the degree to which positive feedback is received, but from individuals who are *not* in a hierarchical authority relationship. Thus the first three sections all concern the degree to which positive or negative feedback is received from sources external to the individual.

TABLE 8-1   Diagnosis of Feedback Practices

Read each of the following statements, and record your perceptions about the feedback practices you experienced in a previous job. Respond on the continuum that ranges from never to extremely often. Note that the midpoint is *occasionally.*

Negative Feedback

	Never	Occasionally	Extremely Often
1. Your supervisor tells you that you are doing a poor job.	_____	_____	_____
2. You receive a formal report of poor performance.	_____	_____	_____
3. The supervisor sharply criticizes your performance.	_____	_____	_____
4. The supervisor makes backhanded comments like "Have a hard night?"	_____	_____	_____
5. Co-workers kid you about doing too little.	_____	_____	_____
6. Co-workers tell you that you have done something wrong.	_____	_____	_____
7. You are told you should be doing something else.	_____	_____	_____

Positive Feedback from Hierarchical Authority

	Never	Occasionally	Extremely Often
8. You receive comments about completed jobs.	_____	_____	_____
9. Your supervisor tells you that you are doing a good job.	_____	_____	_____
10. You have a regular performance review with your supervisor.	_____	_____	_____
11. The supervisor treats you as an equal.	_____	_____	_____

Positive Feedback from Nonhierarchical Others

	Never	Occasionally	Extremely Often
12. Co-workers kid you about doing too much.	_____	_____	_____
13. Co-workers kid you about doing too well.	_____	_____	_____
14. You know more people are using the company's product or service because of your efforts.	_____	_____	_____
15. Co-workers like you very much.	_____	_____	_____

Internal Feedback

	Never	Occasionally	Extremely Often
16. You meet your own goals.	_____	_____	_____
17. You find better ways of doing the job.	_____	_____	_____
18. You know how much you can do without making a mistake.	_____	_____	_____

Source: Adapted with permission from Herold, D. M., and Greller, M. Feedback: The Definition of a Construct, *Academy of Management Journal*, 1977, *20,* 144–145.

By contrast, the fourth section (items 16–18) focuses on internal feedback, or the degree to which individuals observe and assess themselves. These items compare self-observation with self-perception.

The diagnostic questionnaire in Table 8-1 clearly shows that several forms of feedback are available to individuals in organizations. A lack of compatibility among these forms of feedback for a number of employees may indicate serious problems in interpersonal communication in an organization.

Effective Self-Disclosure

Self-disclosure is part of the dimension of openness to others in Figure 8-4. It plays a crucial role in communication style. **Self-disclosure** is any information that individuals consciously communicate verbally or nonverbally about themselves to others. However, people often unconsciously disclose much about themselves by what they say and how they present themselves to others.[19]

The ability to express one's real self to one or a few significant other individuals is often a prerequisite for the development and maintenance of a healthy personality. The relationship between self-disclosure and mental health appears to be curvilinear. Nondisclosing individuals may repress their real selves because revealing themselves is threatening. The self-protecting or self-denying communication styles may represent this personality type. Total-disclosure individuals who expose a great deal about themselves to anyone they meet may actually be unable to relate and communicate with others because of a preoccupation with themselves. This may be characteristic of the self-exposing style. A medium level of self-disclosure may be found in those who are quite open with a select few and moderately open with others, consistent with the specific requirements of their social relationships. These individuals would tend to make greater use of the self-bargaining and self-actualizing styles. A healthy openness in a work setting can facilitate discussions and sharing with superiors work-related problems that individuals are having. This assumes that the superiors are approachable and receptive.

S. M. Jourard expressed the ties among personality, self-disclosure, and communication style as follows:

> Healthy personality is manifested by a mode of what we call authenticity, or more simply, honesty. Less healthy personalities, people who function less than fully, who suffer recurrent breakdowns or chronic impasses, may usually be found to be liars. They say things they do not mean. Their disclosures have been chosen more for cosmetic value than for truth. The consequence of a lifetime of lying about oneself to others, of saying and doing things for their sound and appearance, is that ultimately the person loses contact with his real self. The authentic being manifested by healthier personalities takes the form of unself-conscious disclosure of self in words, decisions, and actions.[20]

Self-disclosure in interpersonal communication is often complicated by organizational levels. Individuals with formal power are likely to dampen self-disclosure to them. This is likely to be a consequence of their ability to allocate rewards—pay raises and promotions—or punishments—demotions and dismissal. (See Chapter 16.) Furthermore, even when we are able and willing to engage in "appropriate" forms of self-disclosure at work, the degree to which we perceive superiors as trustworthy in not using the revealed information to punish, intimidate, or suppress is likely to influence the amount and form of our self-disclosure.

Effective Listening

Effective listening is necessary to encourage maximum levels of feedback and openness to others. **Listening** is "an intellectual and emotional process that integrates physical, emotional, and intellectual inputs in a search for meaning and understanding".[21] Listening is effective when the receiver understands the sender's intended message. As demonstrated in the Preview Case, effective listening is an active process that requires considerable effort to master.

It has been estimated that as much as 40 percent of the workday of many white-collar workers is devoted to listening. However, tests of listening comprehension suggest that people often listen at only 25 percent efficiency.[22] Although exact percentages may vary, listening does require a substantial portion of most of the workday, particularly for those in white-collar and managerial jobs. Listening skills affect the quality and effectiveness of peer and superior–subordinate relationships. Employees who dislike their superior may find it extremely difficult to listen attentively to the superior's comments during performance-review sessions.

The following guidelines have been used by the Sperry Corporation and other organizations for increasing listening skills:

- We should have a reason or purpose for listening. Good listeners tend to search for value and meaning in what is being said, even if they are not predisposed to be interested in the particular issue or topic. Poor listeners tend to rationalize any or all inattention on the basis of initial interest.
- We should suspend judgment, at least initially. Good listening requires concentrating on the sender's whole message rather than forming evaluations on the basis of the first few ideas presented.
- We should resist distractions, such as noises, sights, and other people, and focus on the sender.
- We should pause before responding to the sender.
- When the message is emotional or unclear, we should rephrase in our own words the content and feeling of what the sender appears to be saying.
- We should seek the sender's important themes by listening for the overall content and feeling of the message.
- We should use the time differential between our rate of thought (400–500 words per minute) and the rate of speech (100–150 words per minute) to reflect on content and to search for meaning.[23]

Most of these guidelines for improving listening ability are interrelated—we cannot practice one without improving the others. Unfortunately, like the guidelines for improving feedback, the listening-skills guidelines are much easier to understand than to develop and use in day-to-day interpersonal communications.

Our discussion of communication styles thus far has been based on research and organizational experiences in the United States and Canada. Fundamental cultural differences can certainly modify the findings and guidelines presented. The styles of communication used in Japanese business organizations illustrate such differences.

ACROSS CULTURES

Communication within the Japanese Firm

One of the most frequently identified differences between Japanese and American business organizations concerns the nature of their interpersonal communications. Within the "typical" Japanese business organization, it is not uncommon to find employees willingly exchanging accurate and reliable task-related information with other members of the organization. Moreover, employees will readily admit to their supervisor when they have made mistakes. Likewise, employees will generally not hesitate to very *politely* and indirectly inform their superior, colleagues, or subordinates when they feel that mistakes or errors in judgment have been made by them. In fact, when it comes to the daily operations of the organization, there is very little that Japanese employees will *not* communicate with other members of the organization. However, an interesting characteristic of the process of communication within most Japanese business organizations concerns the "ambiguous" manner in which Japanese employees appear to communicate with one another. One aspect of the deliberate use of ambiguity when communicating with others involves the use of understatement. For the most part, the Japanese have mastered the art of saying something with considerably less emphasis or certainty than appears warranted. Consider the classic example of the president of a large corporation who stands before the company's Board of Directors and, knowing that the company has made a financial "killing" on the international market, calmly says to them, "It seems we have made a little bit of a profit on our recent international venture."

Another interesting aspect of the ambiguous manner in which Japanese employees communicate with one another concerns their deliberate use of evasive communication tactics. In general, Japanese employees will rarely (if ever) come right out with an explicit "no" to another's request. On the contrary, most employees will try to be very tactful and diplomatic in conveying a negative response. One of the typical ways to avoid saying "no" is to say "yes" and then follow the affirmative response with a detailed explanation which, in effect, means "no." An experience that happened to a friend of mine illustrates this first evasive tactic. On a recent business trip to Japan, my friend (Mr. Tomita) went into a bank in Tokyo and asked the teller to convert $2,000 of American Express traveler's checks into Japanese currency. Since the policy of that bank prohibited the teller from cashing more than $1,000 worth of foreign traveler's checks, the teller politely informed my friend that the bank's manager would have to authorize the transaction. The bank manager welcomed my friend into his office and had his secretary bring them both some tea. After a brief exchange of greetings, the manager asked what he could do for my friend. My friend explained that he wanted to convert $2,000 of traveler's checks into Japanese currency, but the teller had informed him that such a large transaction would have to be authorized by him (the manager). The manager smiled, nodded his head in agreement, and replied, "I don't see a problem here, Mr. Tomita, . . . let's see what we can work out." The manager then proceeded to carefully explain the rationale for the bank's policy, and provided my friend with about five reasons why the bank could not cash such a large amount of traveler's checks even if they wanted to. After about twenty minutes of explanation, it became quite obvious to my friend that the bank manager was *not* going to authorize the transaction, despite the fact that he appeared to my friend as initially responding in a positive manner.

The deliberate use of ambiguity in communication between Japanese employees is often attributed to their desire to display humbleness and tolerance when dealing with other members of the organization. However, the use of ambiguity can also be attributed to their desire to avoid embarrassing themselves and others. The Japanese appear to be particularly sensitive to the concept of "face" (i.e., one's dignity and self-respect) and thus make every effort to avoid or prevent the "loss of one's face" (i.e., the loss of self-respect and dignity resulting from public humiliation and embarrassment). So powerful is this desire to "save one's face" that it is not uncommon for an individual to voluntarily resign from a company (or in extreme instances, take his/her own life) rather than live with the shame of "losing one's face."

In using ambiguous messages to avoid the loss of "face," Japanese employees are normally careful to say things in such a manner that all parties are allowed to leave the interaction with their pride intact. That is to say, employees will attempt to phrase messages in such a way so as to preserve the opportunity to "save face" by saying, "Oh, I'm sorry if I offended you . . . it was not meant to sound that way." For example, in criticizing the work of subordinates, Japanese managers may say, "perhaps you could reflect a bit further on your proposal." What the managers *really* mean, of course, is, "You're way off base here . . . this proposal will never work . . . you'd better come up with a more acceptable idea." In phrasing the message in an ambiguous manner, however, managers are able to register their concern with proposals, while also allowing subordinates to leave meetings with their pride intact. Similarly, when questioning a decision made by superiors, subordinates will carefully select their words so that they can come close enough to the point to insure that the superiors understand the concerns, but *not* so close as to embarrass the managers or cause them to become defensive. For example, instead of saying, "I think the new schedule of yours will really cause dissention among the workers," the subordinate may say, "I'm wondering if all the workers would feel comfortable with this new schedule?" The latter question still raises some doubt about whether the new schedule is desirable, but does not "crowd" the superiors and force them to become defensive as does the first statement.[24]

NONVERBAL COMMUNICATION

So far, we have focused primarily on verbal interpersonal communication. The second major form of interpersonal communication—nonverbal communication—is more subtle in nature. Yet nonverbal communication, through its hidden messages, has a wide-ranging impact in organizations. In particular, nonverbal communication can influence the process and outcome of verbal communication.

Nonverbal communication includes nonword human responses (such as gestures, facial expressions) *and* the perceived characteristics of the environment through which the human verbal and nonverbal messages are transmitted. Even a person who is silent or inactive in the presence of others may be sending a message, which may or may not be the intended message (for example, boredom, fear, anger, or depression).[25] The actions of one departmental manager illustrate how the intended verbal messages of a sender may be less influential than the unintended nonverbal messages.

In Practice: Susan Rollich

Susan Rollich, a departmental manager, just wrapped up the usual monthly review and planning meeting with her five subordinates. These meetings typically last three hours and include reviewing the previous month's accomplishments and problems, as well as developing working plans for the coming month.

Unknown to her subordinates, Susan had attended a two-day communication skills seminar three days before the meeting. She learned about such things as the tendency of superiors to dominate communication flow when interacting with subordinates; the need for greater active listening by superiors; and the impact of nonverbal communication, such as frowns or smiles, as indicators of disapproval or approval. Based on exercises in the seminar and personal introspection, Susan had concluded that there was a need for major changes in how she communicated. For this staff meeting, therefore, Susan had decided to vary past practice by being almost exclusively a listener and by controlling her nonverbal responses by retaining a poker face.

What happened at this month's meeting? It was a complete disaster. One subordinate perceived Susan's new behavior as an obvious sign that she was terribly upset about something, and thus he became quite anxious. Another interpreted Susan's behavior as a sure indicator of complete boredom and became quite frustrated because of the inability to draw her out. A third subordinate suspected that Susan was afraid of something, such as getting fired or demoted, because the department had been having more than its share of problems over the past three months.[26]

The overriding implication is that Susan failed to communicate how her approach to communication would differ in this meeting from past approaches. Any radical change from a sender's behavior that receivers have learned to anticipate and interpret with reasonable accuracy may result in their misinterpreting messages, and different receivers may misinterpret differently. Or the sender's intended message may never be received by anyone. Over the long run, however, relearning can occur so the intended verbal and nonverbal messages more closely match the received or interpreted messages.

Types of Nonverbal Communication

Table 8-2 outlines the basic types of nonverbal communication and illustrates the numerous ways people can and do communicate without saying a word. Nonverbal communication is closely related to verbal communication.

TABLE 8–2   Types of Nonverbal Communication

Basic Types	Explanation and Examples
Body motion, or kinesic behavior	Gestures, facial expressions, eye behavior, touching, and any other movement of the limbs and body
Physical characteristics	Body shape, physique, posture, body or breath odors, height, weight, hair color, and skin color
Paralanguage	Voice qualities, volume, speech rate, pitch, nonfluencies (saying "ah," "um," or "uh"), laughing, yawning, and so on
Proxemics	Ways people use and perceive space, including seating arrangements, conversational distance, and the "territorial" tendency of humans to stake out a personal space
Environment (territory)	Building and room design, furniture and other objects, interior decorating, cleanliness, lighting, and noise
Time	Being late or early, keeping others waiting, cultural differences in time perception, and the relationship between time and status

Neither is adequate by itself for effective interpersonal communication. Verbal and nonverbal signals can be interrelated in the following ways:

- By repeating, as when verbal directions to some location are accompanied by pointing.

- By contradicting, as in the case of the person who says, "What, me nervous?" while fidgeting and perspiring anxiously before taking a test. This is a good example of how the nonverbal message can be more believable when verbal and nonverbal signals disagree.

- By substituting nonverbal for verbal messages, as when a manager returns to the office with a harried expression that says, "I've had a horrible meeting with my boss," without a word being spoken.

- By complementing the verbal message with nonverbal signals, as when a worker blushes with embarrassment while discussing poor work performance with a manager.

- By accenting a verbal message through nonverbal "underlining," as when a manager pounds the table, places a hand on the shoulder of a co-worker, or uses a tone of voice indicating the importance attached to the message.[27]

Nonverbal cues have been linked to a wide variety of concepts and issues. We briefly consider two of these: (1) status and nonverbal cues; and (2) gender differences and nonverbal cues.

Status and Nonverbal Cues

There are three main principles for relating the concept of environment (territory) in Table 8-2 to organizational status:

- Persons of higher status will have more and better territory. In corporations, executive offices tend to be spacious, located on the top floors of the building, and have carpets and furniture of fine quality. The most senior offices will be at the corners so they can have windows on two sides.

- The territory of higher-status people is better protected than that of lower-status people. Consider how much more difficult it would be for you to arrange to visit the governor of your state than for the governor to arrange to visit you. Top executive areas are typically least accessible and are often sealed off from intruders by several doors and a handful of assistants. Even junior-level managers and many staff personnel are "protected" by having an office with a door and a secretary who answers their telephone.

- The higher people's status, the easier they find it to invade the territory of lower-status people. A superior typically feels free to walk right in on subordinates, whereas subordinates are more careful to ask permission or make an appointment before visiting a superior.[28]

Managers often use their office spaces to influence the character of verbal interactions. Many managers set up their offices with two different areas. In one area, they talk across a desk to the people on the other side. This arrangement emphasizes the manager's formal power and status. Subordinates may well feel that here the managers have a "home court" advantage. In the other area, managers may group chairs around a coffee table or place them at right angles to one another. This arrangement often signals the manager's willingness and desire to play down differences in formal position power.[29] Thus it may encourage freer communication in terms of both self-disclosure and feedback.

Gender Differences and Nonverbal Cues

Physical differences between men and women contribute to differences in their nonverbal behavior. But, the contribution of physical differences is miniscule compared to that of learned differences. In addition to communicating gender, body language communicates status and power: many signs of dominance and submission are exchanged through nonverbal communication. Some nonverbal behaviors are associated with the subordinate position for either gender. But many of these same behaviors have been associated with women, regardless of status. In this section we describe a few of these nonverbal patterns, especially as they have been found to differ by virtue of gender.[30] These patterns reflect generalities and certainly do not apply to all men and women. Moreover, they are based on findings from the past, and we know that for some segments in society they are in the process of changing.[31]

USE OF SPACE   Women's general bodily demeanor is often restrained and restricted. Their femininity is gauged, in fact, by how little space they take up. Masculinity is judged by men's expansiveness and the strength of their gestures. Males control greater territory and personal space, a property associated with dominance and high status in both human beings and animals. Both observational field studies and laboratory studies have found that people tend to approach women more closely than men, to seat themselves closer to women and otherwise intrude on their territory, and to cut across women's paths.

EYE CONTACT   Eye contact may be greatly influenced by gender. It has been found that in interactions women look more at the other person than men do, and maintain more mutual looking. Some researchers have interpreted this finding in terms of women's traditional orientation toward social and interpersonal relations. However, it has been demonstrated that people maintain more eye contact with those from whom they want approval. Even if we do not have research evidence that women are more stared at and reciprocate by averting their gaze, we have the overwhelming personal reports of women who are stared at in public. Our language even has specific words—such as *ogling* and *leering*—for this phenomenon.

TOUCHING   Touching is another gesture of dominance, and cuddling to the touch is its corresponding gesture of submission. Just as the manager can put a hand on the worker, the master on the servant, the teacher on the student, the businessman on the secretary, so men more frequently put their hands on women, despite folk mythology to the contrary.

There is another side to touching, which is much better understood: touching symbolizes friendship and intimacy. The power dimension of touching does not rule out the intimacy dimension. A particular touch may have both components and more, but it is the pattern of touching between two individuals that tells us the most about their relationship. When touching is symmetrical—that is, when both parties have equal touch privileges—we have information about the intimacy dimension of the relationship: much touching indicates closeness and little touching indicates distance. When one party is free to touch the other but not vice versa, we have information about the status or power dimension: the person with greater touch privileges is of higher status or has more power.

BREAKING THE MOLD   Many women have been reversing these nonverbal interaction patterns. Women can stop smiling when they are unhappy, stop lowering their eyes, stop getting out of men's way on the street, and stop letting themselves be interrupted. They can stare people in the eye, address someone by first name if addressed by their first name, and touch when they feel it is appropriate. Men can likewise begin to become aware of what they are signifying nonverbally. They can restrain their invasions of personal space, touching (if it is not by mutual consent), and interrupting.

SUMMARY

Communication is the lifeblood of organizations. This chapter described one part of the total communication system in organizations: interpersonal communication. Its importance to organizations is reflected in such commonly heard statements as "He doesn't listen very well," "I just can't seem to communicate with her," "You never know what she is really thinking," and "Our basic problem is one of poor communication." Individuals' ability to engage in effective interpersonal communication plays an important part in determining their own sense of well-being, as well as the probability of their being viewed by others as good employees.

This chapter built upon earlier discussions, particularly from Chapter 4 on the perceptual process and from Chapter 5 on problem solving. Obviously, people's perceptions and tendencies to deal with problems in particular ways can influence interpersonal communication. By analyzing these dimensions within yourself, you should be able to improve your own communication effectiveness as well as have greater empathy for and understanding of the strengths and limitations of others.

Interpersonal communication involving face-to-face discussion was identified as the medium with the highest degree of information richness. An information-rich medium is especially important for processing task and social–emotional issues that involve considerable uncertainty and ambiguity. Important management issues usually contain significant doses of uncertainty, ambiguity, and people-related (especially social–emotional) problems.

The essential variables and relationships among the variables in the communication process were outlined. These essential variables include: senders, receivers, transmitters, receptors, messages, channels, noise, meaning, encoding, decoding, and feedback.

The interpersonal communication process may be repeated hundreds of times each day by managers through their many communication networks. Managers' communication networks, as illustrated in Figure 8-3, operate vertically and laterally. These networks can range from closed and centralized to open and decentralized (that is, an all-channel network).

A framework of communication styles was presented. Using this framework, five interpersonal communication styles were discussed: self-denying, self-protecting, self-exposing, self-bargaining, and self-actualizing. Although the latter two styles should dominate, it was recognized that special circumstances could warrant the use of any of the five styles. Guidelines for increasing your skills in the use of the self-actualizing style were presented in the discussions of effective feedback, effective self-disclosure, and effective listening. These guidelines were considered within their cultural context, namely North America, and contrasted to those of another culture, Japan.

Finally, the powerful role of nonverbal communication in the overall interpersonal communication process was discussed. Five types of nonverbal communication and some of the ways they are interrelated with verbal cues were examined. Some of the ties between organizational status and nonverbal cues and between gender differences and nonverbal cues were highlighted.

KEY WORDS AND CONCEPTS

Channels
Data
Decoding
Encoding
Feedback
Information richness
Interpersonal communication
Interpersonal communication network
Listening
Meanings
Messages

Noise
Nonverbal communication
Receptors
Self-actualizing style
Self-bargaining style
Self-denying style
Self-disclosure
Self-exposing style
Self-protecting style
Transmitters

DISCUSSION QUESTIONS

1. What is the difference between encoding and decoding?

2. Describe the various nonverbal forms of communication used by someone you have worked for or studied under. Was the nonverbal communication consistent or inconsistent with this person's verbal communication? Explain.

3. Is there one best communication network for a five-person group? Explain.

4. How would you compare the self-actualizing communication style with the self-exposing communication style?

5. Describe a situation in which you have used one or more of the communication styles presented in this chapter. Do you think the style was effective or ineffective? Why?

6. What types of problems and limitations prevent meaningful self-disclosure between superiors and subordinates?

7. What similarities and differences are there in this chapter's recommendations for improving feedback and listening skills?

MANAGEMENT INCIDENTS AND CASES

The Road to Hell

John Baker, chief engineer of the Caribbean Bauxite Company Limited of Barracania in the West Indies, was making his final preparations to leave the island. His promotion to production manager of Keso Mining Corporation near Winnipeg—one of Continental Ore's fast-expanding Canadian enterprises—had been announced a month before, and now everything had been attended to except the last vital interview with his successor, the able young Barracanian Matthew Rennalls. It was vital that this interview be a success and that Rennalls leave Baker's office uplifted and encouraged to face the challenge of his new job. A touch on the bell would have brought Rennalls walking into the room, but Baker delayed the moment and gazed thoughtfully through the window, considering just exactly what he was going to say and, more particularly, how he was going to say it.

Baker, an English expatriate, was 45 years old and had served his 23 years with Continental Ore in many different places: the Far East, several countries of Africa; Europe; and for the last two years, the West Indies. He had not cared much for his previous assignment in Hamburg and was delighted when the West Indian appointment came through. Climate was not the only attraction. Baker had always preferred working overseas in what were called the "developing countries" because he felt he had an innate knack—more than most other expatriates working for Continental Ore—of knowing just how to get on with regional staff. After only twenty-four hours in Barracania, however, he realized that he would need all of his innate knack if he were to deal effectively with the problems in this field that now awaited him.

At his first interview with Glenda Hutchins, the production manager, the whole problem of Rennalls and his future was discussed. Then and there it was made quite clear to Baker that one of his important tasks would be the grooming of Rennalls as his successor. Hutchins had pointed out that not only was Rennalls one of the brightest Barracanian prospects on the staff of Caribbean Bauxite—at London University he had taken first-class honors in the B.Sc. engineering degree—but, being the son of the minister of finance and economic planning, he also had no small political pull.

Carribean Bauxite had been particularly pleased when Rennalls decided to work for it rather than for the government in which his father had such a prominent post. The company ascribed his action to the effect of its vigorous and liberal regionalization program that, since World War II, had produced 18 Barracanians at the middle management level and had given Caribbean Bauxite a good lead in this respect over all other international concerns operating in Barracania. The success of this timely regionalization policy had led to excellent relations with the government—a relationship that gained added importance when Barracania, three years later, became independent, an occasion that encouraged a critical and challenging attitude toward the role foreign interests would play in the new Barracania. Hutchins, therefore, had little difficulty convincing Baker that the successful career development of Rennalls was of the first importance.

The interview with Hutchins was now two years in the past, and Baker, leaning back in his office chair, reviewed just how successful he had been in the grooming of Rennalls. What aspects of the latter's character had helped, and what had hindered? What about his own personality? How had that helped or hindered? The first item to go on the credit side, without question, would be the ability of Rennalls to master the technical aspects of his job. From the start he had shown keenness and enthusiasm, and he had often impressed Baker with his ability in tackling new assignments and the constructive comments he invariably made in departmental discussions. He was popular with all ranks of Barracanian staff and had an ease of manner that stood him in good stead when dealing with his expatriate seniors.

Those were all assets, but what about the debit side? First and foremost was his racial consciousness. His four years at London University had accentuated this feeling and made him sensitive to any sign of condescension on the part of expatriates. Perhaps to give expression to this sentiment, as soon as he returned home from London, he threw himself into politics on behalf of the United Action Party, which was later to win the preindependence elec-

tions and provide the country with its first prime minister.

The ambitions of Rennalls—and he certainly was ambitious—did not, however, lie in politics. Staunch nationalist that he was, he saw that he could serve himself and his country best—For was not bauxite responsible for nearly half the value of Barracania's export trade?—by putting his engineering talent to the best use possible. On this account, Hutchins found that she had an unexpectedly easy task in persuading Rennalls to give up his political work before entering the production department as an assistant engineer.

It was, Baker knew, Rennall's well-repressed sense of racial consciousness that had prevented their relationship from being as close as it should have been. On the surface, nothing could have seemed more agreeable. Formality between the two was minimal. Baker was delighted to find that his assistant shared his own peculiar "shaggy dog" sense of humor, so jokes were continually being exchanged. They entertained one another at their houses and often played tennis together—and yet the barrier remained invisible, indefinable, but ever present. The existence of this screen between them was a constant source of frustration to Baker, since it indicated a weakness that he was loath to accept. If successful with people of all other nationalities, why not with Rennalls?

At least he had managed to break through to Rennalls more successfully than had any other expatriate. In fact, it was the young Barracanian's attitude—sometimes overbearing, sometimes cynical—toward other company expatriates that had been one of the subjects Baker raised last year when he discussed Rennall's staff report with him. Baker knew, too, that he would have to raise the same subject again in the forthcoming interview, because Martha Jackson, the senior person in charge of drafting, had complained only yesterday about the rudeness of Rennalls. With this thought in mind, Baker leaned forward and spoke into the intercom: 'Would you come in, Matt, please? I'd like a word with you." Rennalls came in, and Baker held out a box and said, "Do sit down. Have a cigarette."

He paused while he held out his lighter and then went on. "As you know, Matt, I'll be off to Canada in a few days' time, and before I go, I thought it would be useful if we could have a final chat together. It is indeed with some deference that I suggest I can be of help. You will shortly be sitting in this chair doing the job I am now doing, but I, on the other hand, am ten years older, so perhaps you can accept the idea that I may be able to give you the benefit of my longer experience."

Baker saw Rennalls stiffen slightly in his chair as he made this point, so he added in explanation, "You and I have attended enough company courses to remember those repeated requests by the personnel manager to tell people how they are getting on as often as the convenient moment arises, and not just the automatic once a year when, by regulation, staff reports have to be discussed."

Rennalls nodded his agreement, so Baker went on, "I shall always remember the last job performance discussion I had with my previous boss back in Germany. She used what she called the 'plus and minus technique.' She firmly believed that when seniors seek to improve the work performance of their staff by discussion, their prime objective should be to make sure the latter leave the interview encouraged and inspired to improve. Any criticism, therefore, must be constructive and helpful. She said that one very good way to encourage a person—and I fully agree with her—is to discuss good points, the plus factors, as well as weak ones, the minus factors. So I thought, Matt, it would be a good idea to run our discussion along these lines."

Rennalls offered no comment, so Baker continued. "Let me say, therefore, right away, that as far as your own work performance is concerned, the pluses far outweigh the minuses. I have, for instance, been most impressed with the way you have adapted your considerable theoretical knowledge to master the practical techniques of your job—that ingenious method you used to get air down to the fifth shaft level is a sufficient case in point. At departmental meetings I have invariably found your comments well taken and helpful. In fact, you will be interested to know that only last week I reported to Ms. Hutchins that, from the technical point of view, she could not wish for a more able person to succeed to the position of chief engineer."

"That's very good indeed of you, John," cut in Rennalls with a smile of thanks. "My only worry now is how to live up to such a high recommendation."

"Of that I am quite sure," returned Baker, "especially if you can overcome the minus factor which I would like now to discuss with you. It is one that I have talked about before, so I'll come straight to the point. I have noticed that you are more friendly and get on better with your fellow Barracanians than you do with Europeans. In point of fact, I had a complaint only yesterday from Ms. Jackson, who said you had been rude to her—and not for the first time, either.

"There is, Matt, I am sure, no need for me to tell you how necessary it will be for you to get on well with expatriates, because until the company has trained sufficient men of your caliber, Europeans are bound to occupy senior positions here in Barracania. All this is vital to your future interests, so can I help you in any way?"

While Baker was speaking on this theme, Rennalls sat tensed in his chair, and it was some seconds before he replied. "It is quite extraordinary, isn't it, how one can convey an impression to others so at variance with what one intends? I can only assure you once again that my disputes with Jackson—and you may remember also Godson—have had nothing at all to do with the color of their skins. I promise you that if a Barracanian had behaved in an equally peremptory manner, I would have reacted in precisely the same way. And again, if I may say it within these four walls, I am sure I am not the only one who has found Jackson and Godson difficult. I could mention the names of several expatriates who have felt the same. However, I am really sorry to have created this impression of not being able to get on with Europeans—it is an entirely false one—and I quite realize that I must do all I can to correct it as quickly as possible. On your last point, regarding Europeans holding senior positions in the company for some time to come, I quite accept the situation. I know that Caribbean Bauxite—as it has been doing for many years now—will promote Barracanians as soon as their experience warrants it. And, finally, I would like to assure you, John—and my father thinks the same, too—that I am very happy in my work here and hope to stay with the company for many years to come."

Rennalls had spoken earnestly, and Baker, although not convinced by what he had heard, did not think he could pursue the matter further except to say, "All right, Matt, my impression may be wrong, but I would like to remind you about the truth of that old saying 'What is important is not what is true, but what is believed.' Let it rest at that."

But suddenly Baker knew that he did not want to "let it rest at that." He was disappointed once again at not being able to break through to Rennalls and at having again had to listen to his bland denial that there was any racial prejudice in his makeup.

Baker, who had intended to end the interview at this point, decided to try another tack. "To return for a moment to the plus and minus technique I was telling you about just now, there is another plus factor I forgot to mention. I would like to congratulate you not only on the caliber of your work, but also on the ability you have shown in overcoming a challenge that I, as a European, have never had to meet.

"Continental Ore is, as you know, a typical commercial enterprise—admittedly a big one—that is a product of the economic and social environment of the United States and Western Europe. My ancestors have all been brought up in this environment for the past two or three hundred years, and I have, therefore, been able to live in a world in which commerce (as we know it today) has been part and parcel of my being. It has not been something revolutionary and new that has suddenly entered my life. In your case," went on Baker, "the situation is different, because you and your forebears have only had some fifty and not two or three hundred years. Again, Matt, let me congratulate you—and people like you—on having so successfully overcome this particular hurdle. It is for this very reason that I think the outlook for Barracania—and particularly Caribbean Bauxite—is so bright."

Rennalls had listened intently, and when Baker finished, he replied, "Well, once again, John, I have to thank you for what you have said, and, for my part, I can only say that it is gratifying to know that my own personal effort has been so much appreciated. I hope that more people will soon come to think as you do."

There was a pause, and, for a moment, Baker thought hopefully that he was about to achieve his long-awaited breakthrough. But Rennalls merely smiled back. The barrier remained unbreached. There were some five minutes' cheerful conversation about the contrast between the Caribbean and Canadian climates and whether the West Indies had any hope of beating England in the Fifth Test before Baker drew the interview to a close. Although he was as far as ever from knowing the real Rennalls, he was nevertheless glad that the interview had run along in this friendly manner and, particularly, that it had ended on such a cheerful note.

This feeling, however, lasted only until the following morning. Baker had some farewells to make, so he arrived at the office considerably later than usual. He had no sooner sat down at his desk than his secretary walked into the room with a worried frown on her face. Her words came fast. "When I arrived this morning, I found Mr. Rennalls already waiting at my door. He seemed very angry and told me that he had a vital letter to dictate that must be sent off without any delay. He was so worked up that he couldn't keep still and kept pacing about the room, which is most unlike him. He wouldn't even wait to read what he had dictated. Just signed the page where he thought the letter would end. It has been distributed, and your copy is in your tray."

Puzzled and feeling vaguely uneasy, Baker opened the envelope marked "confidential" and read the following letter:

	14th August, 1985
FROM:	Assistant Engineer
TO:	The Chief Engineer Caribbean Bauxite Limited
SUBJECT:	Assessment of Interview Between Messrs. Baker and Rennalls

It has always been my practice to respect the advice given to me by seniors, so after our interview, I decided to give careful thought once again to its main points and to make sure that I had understood all that had been said. As I promised you at the time, I had every intention of putting your advice to the best effect.

It was not, therefore, until I had sat down quietly in my home yesterday evening to consider the interview objectively that its main purpose became clear. Only then did the full enormity of what you said dawn on me. The more I thought about it, the more convinced I was that I had hit upon the real truth—and the more furious I became. With a facility in the English language which I— a poor Barracanian—cannot hope to match, you had the audacity to insult me (and through me every Barracanian worth his salt) by claiming that our knowledge of modern living is only a paltry fifty years old, while yours goes back two hundred to three hundred years. As if your materialistic commercial environment could possibly be compared with the spiritual values of our culture! I'll have you know that if much of what I saw in London is representative of your most boasted culture, I hope fervently that it will never come to Barracania. By what right do you have the effrontery to condescend to us? After all, you Europeans think us barbarians, or, as you say amongst yourselves, we are "just down from the trees."

Far into the night I discussed this matter with my father, and he is as disgusted as I. He agrees with me that any company whose senior staff think as you do is no place for any Barracanian proud of his culture and race. So much for all the company claptrap and specious propaganda about regionalization and Barracania for the Barracanians.

I feel ashamed and betrayed. Please accept this letter as my resignation, which I wish to become effective immediately."[32]

cc: Production Manager
    Managing Director

Questions[33]

1. What were Baker's intentions in the conversation with Rennalls? Were they fulfilled or not, and why?
2. Was Baker alert to nonverbal signals? What did both Baker and Rennalls communicate to one another by nonverbal means?
3. How did Baker's view of himself interact with the impression he formed of Rennalls?
4. What kind of interpersonal relationship had existed between Baker and Rennalls prior to the conversation described in the case? Was the conversation consistent or inconsistent with that relationship?
5. What, if anything, could Baker or Rennalls have done before, during, or after the conversation to improve the situation?

REFERENCES

1. Excerpted from Di Gaetani, D. L. The Sperry Corporation and Listening: An Interview. *Business Horizons*, March–April 1982, 34–39. Copyright, 1982 by the foundation for the School of Business at Indiana University. Reprinted by permission.

2. Sigband, H. *Communication for Management.* Glenview, Ill.: Scott, Foresman, 1969, 10.

3. Axley, S. R. Managerial and Organizational Communication in Terms of the Conduit Metaphor. *Academy of Management Review*, 1984, *9*, 428–437.

4. Baird, J. E. *The Dynamics of Organizational Communication.* New York: Harper & Row, 1977, 6. Also see Macdonald, C. R. *Performance Based Supervisory Development: Adapted from a Major AT&T Study.* Amherst, Mass.: Human Resource Development Press, 1982, 114–133.

5. Daft, R. L., and Lengel, R. H. Information Richness: A New Approach to Managerial Behavior and Organization. In B. M. Staw and L. L. Cummings (Eds.) *Research in Organizational Behavior*, vol. 6. Greenwich, Conn.: JAI Press, 1984, 191–233.

6. Daft, R. L. *Organization Theory and Design.* St. Paul, Minn.: West 1983, 299–302. Also see Whitely, W. An Exploratory Study of Managers' Reactions to Properties of Verbal Communication. *Personnel Psychology*, 1984, *37*, 41–59.

7. Shapiro, I. S. Executive Forum—Managerial Communication: The View from Inside. *California Management Review.* Fall 1984, 157. Also see Shapiro, I. S. *America's Third Revolution.* New York: Harper & Row Publishers, 1984.

8. Herbert, T. T. Toward an Administrative Model of the Communication Process. *Journal of Business Communications*, 1977, *14*, 25–35; Sussman, L., and Deep, S. D. *COMEX: The Communication Experience in Human Relations.* Cincinnati, Ohio: South-Western, 1984; Kelly, C. M. Effective Communications—Beyond the Glitter and Flash. *Sloan Management Review*, Spring 1985, 69–79.

9. Broms, H., and Gahmberg, H. Communication to Self in Organizations and Cultures. *Administrative Science Quarterly*, 1983, *28*, 482–495; Rath, G. J., and Stoyanoff, K. S. Understanding and Improving Communication Effectiveness. In J. W. Pfeiffer and L. D. Goodstein (Eds.) *The 1982 Annual for Facilitators, Trainers, and Consultants.* San Diego: University Associates, 1982, 166–173.

10. Laumann, E. O. *Bonds of Pluralism: The Form and Substance of Urban Social Networks.* New York: Wiley Interscience, 1973, 7.

11. Kaplan, R. E., and Mazique, M. *Trade Routes: The Manager's Network of Relationships.* Technical Report Number 22. Greensboro, N.C.: Center for Creative Leadership, 1983.

12. Glazer, M., and Glazer, R. *Techniques for the Study of Team Structure and Behavior, Part 2: Empirical Studies of the Effects of Structure.* Pittsburgh: American Institute for Research, 1957.

13. Fidler, L. A., and Johnson, J. D. Communication and Innovation Implementation. *Academy of Management Review*, 1984, *9*, 704–711; Keller, R. T., and Holland, W. E. Communicators and Innovators in Research and Development Organizations. *Academy of Management Journal*, 1983, *26*, 742–749; Gronn, P. C. Talk as the Work: The Accomplishment of School Administration. *Administrative Science Quarterly*, 1983, *28*, 1–21; Brass, D. J. Men's and Women's Networks: A Study

of Interaction, Patterns and Influence in Organizations. *Academy of Management Journal*, 1985, 28, 327–343.

14. Guetzkow, H., and Simon, H. The Impact of Certain Communication Nets upon Organization and Performance in Task-oriented Groups. *Management Science*, 1955, *1*, 233–250. Also see Monge, P. R., Edwards, J. A., and Kirste, K. K. Determinants of Communication Network Involvement: Connectedness and Integration. *Group and Organization Studies*, 1983, *8*, 83–111; Penley, L. E., and Hawkins, B. Studying Interpersonal Communication in Organizations: A Leadership Application. *Academy of Management Journal*, 1985, 28, 309–326.

15. This section is adapted from Polsky, H. W. Notes on Personal Feedback in Sensitivity Training. *Sociological Inquiry*, 1971, *41*, 175–182. Also see Roloff, M. E. *Interpersonal Communication: The Social Exchange Approach.* Beverly Hills, Calif.: Sage, 1981.

16. Huseman, R. C., *et al.* Development of a Conceptual Framework for Analyzing the Communication–Performance Relationship. In R. C. Huseman (Ed.) *Proceedings of the Academy of Management*, 1980, 178–182.

17. Anderson, J. Giving and Receiving Feedback. In J. W. Lorsch and L. B. Barnes (Eds.) *Managers and Their Careers: Cases and Readings.* Homewood, Ill.: Irwin, 1972, 260–267. Also see Rasmussen, R. V. Interpersonal Feedback: Problems and Reconceptualization. In J. W. Pfeiffer and L. D. Goodstein (Eds.) *The 1984 Annual: Developing Human Resources.* San Diego, Calif.: University Associates, 1984, 262–266; Stone, D. L., Gueutal, H. G., and Mcintosh, B. The Effects of Feedback Sequence and Expertise of the Rater on Perceived Feedback Accuracy. *Personnel Psychology*, 1984, *37*, 487–506.

18. Baskin, O. W., and Aronoff, C. E. *Interpersonal Communication in Organizations.* Santa Monica, Calif.: Goodyear, 1980; Snyder, R. A., and Morris, J. H. Organizational Communication and Performance. *Journal of Applied Psychology*, 1984, *69*, 461–465; Liden, R. C., and Mitchell, T. R. Reactions to Feedback: The Role of Attributions. *Academy of Management Journal*, 1985, 28, 291–308.

19. Cozby, P. C. Self-disclosure: A Literature Review. *Psychological Bulletin*, 1973, *79*, 73–91.

20. Jourard, S. M. *Disclosing Man to Himself.* New York: Van Nostrand Reinhold, 1968, 46–47.

21. Chartier, M. R. Five Components Contributing to Effective Interpersonal Communications. In J. W. Pfeiffer and J. E.

Jones (Eds.) *1974 Annual Handbook for Group Facilitators.* La Jolla, Calif.: University Associates, 1974, 125–128.

22. Listening Is a 10-Part Skill. In Nicholas, R. G., *Successful Management.* New York: Doubleday, 1957, Chap. 5. Also see Rowe, M. P., and Baker, M. Are You Hearing Enough Employee Concerns? *Harvard Business Review*, May–June 1984, 127–135.

23. Reik, T. *Listening with the Third Ear.* New York: Pyramid, 1972; Brownell, J. *Building Active Listening Skills.* Englewood Cliffs, N.J.: Prentice-Hall, 1986.

24. Excerpts from: Hirokawa, Randy Y. Understanding the Nature and Functions of Communication Within Japanese Business Organizations. Unpublished manuscript. Iowa Ciy, Iowa: Department of Communication Studies, University of Iowa, 1985. Used with permission. Also see de Forest, M. E. Spanish-Speaking Employees in American Industry. *Business Horizons*, January–February 1984, 14–17; McKenzie, C. L., and Qazi, C. J. Communication Barriers in the Workplace. *Business Horizons*, March–April 1983, 70–72.

25. Watzlawick, D., Beavin, J. J., and Jackson, D. D. *Pragmatics of Human Communication: A Study of Interactional Patterns, Pathologies, and Paradoxes.* New York: Norton, 1967, 9. Also see Rasmussen Jr., K. G. Nonverbal Behavior, Verbal Behavior, Resume Credentials, and Selection Interview Outcomes. *Journal of Applied Psychology*, 1984, *69*, 551–556.

26. Adapted with permission from Fisher, D. *Communication in Organizations.* St. Paul, Minn.: West, 1981, 121.

27. Harper, R. G., Wiens, A. N., and Matarzzo, J. D. *Nonverbal Communication: The State of the Art.* New York: Wiley, 1978; Ekman, P., Friesen, W. V., and Bear, J. The International Language of Gestures. *Psychology Today*, May 1984, 64–69; Wieman, J. M., and Harrison, R. P. (Eds.) *Nonverbal Interaction.* Beverly Hills, Calif.: Sage, 1984.

28. Goldhaber, G. M. *Organizational Communication.* Dubuque, Iowa: W. C. Brown, 1979, 152–187.

29. McCaskey, M. B. The Hidden Messages Managers Send. *Harvard Business Review*, November–December 1979, 135–148; Stablein, R., and Nord, W. Practical and Emancipatory Interests in Organizational Symbolism: A Review and Evaluation. *Journal of Management*, 1985, 11, 13–28.

30. Excerpted with permission from Henley, N., and Thorne, B. Womanspeak and Manspeak: Sex Differences and Sexism in Communication, Verbal and Nonverbal.

In A. G. Sargent (Ed.) *Beyond Sex Roles*. St. Paul, Minn.: West, 1977, 201–218. Also see D. M. Hai (Ed.) *Women and Men in Organizations: Teaching Strategies*. Washington, D.C.: Organizational Behavior Teaching Society, 1984; Cohen, L. R. Nonverbal (Mis)Communication between Managerial Men and Women. *Business Horizons*, January–February 1983, 13–17; Dubono, P. Attitudes toward Women Executives: A Longitudinal Approach. *Academy of Management Journal*, 1985, *28*, 235–239.

31. Larwood, L., Gutek, B., and Gattiker, U. E. Perspectives on Institutional Discrimination and Resistance to Change. *Group and Organization Studies*, 1984, *9*, 332–352; Steckler, N. A., and Rosenthal, R. Sex Differences in Nonverbal and Verbal Communication with Bosses, Peers, and Subordinates. *Journal of Applied Psychology*, 1985, *70*, 157–163.

32. Prepared and adapted with permission from Evans, G. late of Shell International Petroleum Co. Ltd., London, for Shell-BP Petroleum Development Company of Nigeria, Limited.

33. Adapted with permission from Fisher, O. *Communication in Organizations*. St. Paul, Minn.: West, 1981, 171.

9 **Dynamics within Groups**

LEARNING OBJECTIVES

When you have finished studying this chapter, you should be able to:

- Describe why people do what they do in task groups.
- State the five stages of group development and the characteristics of each stage.
- Identify trouble spots and possible reasons why task groups may be operating at a less than optimal level.
- Discuss seven major factors that can influence group behaviors and outputs.
- Identify and discuss the six phases of effective group decision making.
- Describe how the nominal group technique can be used to increase the creativity of groups.

OUTLINE

Preview Case

The Engineering Group

Russ, the manager of engineering, met monthly with his section heads to review the status of all major projects and to determine how to staff new projects that were expected to be authorized. The group of five had developed standard ways for describing any project and had a solid base from which they could decide how much effort—in terms of engineering disciplines—would be needed on a project. When a rather large project was unexpectedly approved, Russ called a special meeting and, in two hours, the group decided how to shift work and people among the sections so that the new project could be handled. The section heads' feelings of accomplishment and pride in what they had accomplished more than compensated for the projects and people that some of them had agreed to give up. Furthermore, the section heads knew that the experience gained in the monthly meetings was excellent training. Participation in the group sessions helped demystify the role of the next higher level in the organization and increased understanding of what was expected and why.[1]

This Preview Case is a snapshot of an effective decision-making group. Russ and his subordinates participated in the decision-making process through open communication and with a recognition of the need to consider larger organizational goals and needs (the new project) as well as the goals and needs of each section. The engineering group is one of many examples of the increasing involvement of groups in the numerous organizational decisions made daily. What ingredients determine whether groups are efficient and effective—as illustrated by the Preview Case—or inefficient and ineffective? There is no simple checklist of ABCs for creating and maintaining effective groups or for changing groups that are ineffective.[2] However, in this chapter we do suggest ways for *diagnosing* groups and—based on the diagnosis—ways to manage groups in order to increase the probability that they will be efficient and effective. The chapter emphasizes (1) the relations between individuals and groups; (2) major factors that affect group behaviors and outputs; and (3) effective and efficient decision processes within groups. Group effectiveness and efficiency are stressed throughout the chapter. As might be expected, many of the other topics in this book, such as leadership and interpersonal communication, contribute to the skills needed for effective management of and participation in groups.

A **group** is "a number of persons who communicate with one another often over a span of time, and who are few enough so that each person is able to communicate with all the others, not secondhand through other people, but face to face."[3] Three conditions must be met for a group to exist. First, the members must be able to see and hear each other. Second, each group member must engage in two-way personal communication with every other member. Third, hierarchical distinctions between members must be minimal, unlike the formal organization's chain of command. However, distinctions between members in status or relative influence in the group may exist.

INDIVIDUAL–GROUP RELATIONS

People in the United States, Canada, and certain other countries strongly believe in the importance and centrality of the individual. Educational, governmental, and business institutions frequently proclaim that their reason for existence intimately relates to enhancing goals of the individual.

Individualism versus Collectivism

The cultural belief in *individualism* creates an uneasiness and ambivalence as to the influence that groups—in contrast to single individuals—should have in decision making and actions of organizations. The cultural belief in *collectivism* in such countries as China and Japan seems to have the opposite effect within organizations. The use of groups as part of the decision-making process is a natural consequence of their cultural values. Their ambivalence and uneasiness revolves around the relative influence and assertiveness of the individual in groups. The individualism versus collectivism difference between certain cultures might be characterized as the tension and ambivalence between "fitting into the group" versus "standing out within the group." Of course, even in societies that proclaim to value individualism, the potential impact of groups on individuals is substantial.

Individual versus Group Interests

The potential for individual members and the group to have incompatible interests certainly exists. However, these interests and relations need not always conflict and are often compatible.[4] The following observations reflect these potential conflicting and common interests:

- Groups do exist; they must be dealt with by any practical person—indeed, by any child—and they must enter into any adequate account of human behavior.
- Groups are inevitable and always present.
- Groups mobilize powerful forces that produce effects of the utmost importance to individuals.
- Groups may produce both good and bad consequences.
- Groups can be managed to increase the desirable consequences from them.[5]

The individual can best solve some problems; the group can best solve others; and the individual and group together can most appropriately tackle still other problems.

GROUP DIVERSITY

There are many different types of groups as well as different stages within a given group over time. This section describes several types of groups that are commonly found in organizations and the stages of development that have been observed for many groups.

Types of Groups

Individuals usually belong to many types of groups, and there are many ways of classifying groups, depending on a person's perspective. For example, a person concerned with the degree of difficulty in gaining membership or becoming accepted as a group member might develop a classification scheme that differentiates groups according to whether they are *open* or *closed* to new members.

FRIENDSHIP AND TASK GROUPS A person evaluating groups in an organization according to the primary purpose they serve might find useful the classifications of friendship group and task group. A **friendship group** serves the primary purpose of meeting its members' personal needs of security, esteem, and belonging. A **task group** primarily accomplishes organizationally defined goals. This chapter focuses on task groups, which sometimes are referred to as work groups. The engineering group discussed in the Preview Case is an example of a task group. Of course, a single group in an organization can serve both friendship and task purposes.

INTERDEPENDENCE IN TASK GROUPS Task groups can be further classified on the basis of the interdependencies between group members in accomplishing some task or objective. Three types of task groups have been identified: interacting, coacting, and counteracting.[6]

An **interacting group** exists when a group cannot perform a task until all members have completed their shares of the task. For example, the assembly team of a large luggage manufacturer consists of about ten people who perform the separate tasks required to assemble a complete piece of luggage. If one task is not undertaken, the task—the finished suitcase—cannot be completed.

When the group members perform their jobs in relative independence of each other, in the short run, a **coacting group** exists. *Relative* and *in the short run* indicate that if there were no interdependence over time, there would be no task group. For example, university faculty members may be independent in the day-to-day teaching of their courses, but they are highly interdependent in considering changes in courses or new course offerings.

A **counteracting group** exists when members interact to resolve some type of conflict, usually through negotiation and compromise. A labor–management negotiating group illustrates a counteracting group. The representatives from management and the union usually believe that at least some of their goals are in conflict.

Stages of Group Development

Based on a review of many studies on small groups, it has been suggested that most groups go though a five-stage developmental sequence: forming, storming, norming, performing, and adjourning.[7] The types of task-oriented behaviors and relations-oriented (social) behaviors often observed in groups differ from stage to stage. Figure 9–1 shows the five stages on the horizontal axis, starting with the forming stage and ending with the adjourning stage.

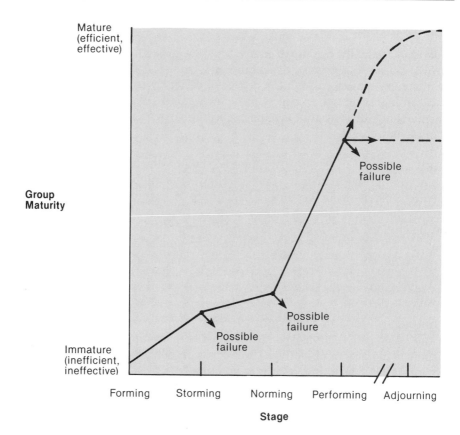

FIGURE 9–1.
Stages of Group
Development

Adapted from Tuckman, B.
W., and Jensen, M. A. C.
Stages of Small-Group
Development Revisited.
*Groups & Organization
Studies*, 1977, 2, 419–427.

The vertical axis indicates the level of group maturity, starting with an immature state (inefficient and ineffective) and ending with a mature state (efficient and effective). The figure also indicates that a group can fail (disband) during each stage or from one stage to another. It is difficult to pinpoint the developmental stage of a group at any specific time. Nevertheless, a manager must understand the developmental stages of groups because each stage can influence group effectiveness.[8] Let us consider the task and social-emotional behaviors we might find in each of these stages.

FORMING In the forming stage, task-oriented behaviors focus on the members' efforts to define goals and develop procedures for performing their tasks. Relations-oriented behaviors deal with feeling out and resolving dependency issues among group members. Group development in this stage involves getting acquainted and understanding leadership and other member roles. In this stage, individual members might: (1) keep feelings to themselves until they know the situation; (2) act more secure than they actually feel; (3) feel confused and uncertain about what is expected of them; (4) be nice and polite, certainly not hostile; (5) try to size up the personal benefits relative to the personal costs of being involved in the group, and the like.[9]

STORMING Things get serious in the storming stage. Conflicts over task behaviors emerge with respect to the relative priorities over goals, who is to be responsible for what, and the task-related guidance and direction of the leader. Relations-oriented behaviors are a mixture of expressions of hostility and strong feelings. Competition and conflict is a dominant theme at this stage. Some members may withdraw or try to isolate themselves from the emotional tension. The key is to manage conflict in this stage, not to suppress it or withdraw from it. The group cannot effectively evolve into the third stage if the leader and members go to either extreme. Suppressing conflict will likely create bitterness and resentment, which will last long after the members' attempts to express their differences and emotions; withdrawal can cause the group to fail more quickly.

NORMING   Task-oriented behaviors in the norming stage evolve into a sharing of information, acceptance of differences in opinions, and positive attempts to reach mutually agreeable or compromise decisions on the group goals and the rules by which the group will operate. Relations-oriented behaviors focus on empathy, concern, and positive expressions of feelings leading to group cohesion. Cooperation within the group is a dominant theme at this stage. A sense of shared responsibility for the group develops. The specific impacts of norms—positive and negative—on group behaviors and outputs is developed later in the chapter.

PERFORMING   This stage relates to how effectively and efficiently the group is able to perform its tasks. The roles of individual members are accepted and understood. The members usually understand when it is best for them to work independently of each other and when it is best to help each other in physically demanding tasks or decision-making tasks. The two dashed lines in Figure 9-1 suggest that groups differ after the norming stage. Some groups continue to learn and develop from their experiences and new inputs, thus continuing to improve their efficiency and effectiveness. Other groups—especially those that developed norms not fully supportive of efficiency and effectiveness—may perform only at the level needed for their survival. A minimally adequate level of performance may be caused by excessive self-oriented role behaviors by group members, the development of norms that impact negatively on task effectiveness and efficiency, poor group leadership, or other factors.

ADJOURNING   The adjourning stage involves the termination of task behaviors and disengagement from relations-oriented behaviors. Some groups—say, a task force created to investigate and report on a specific problem within six months—have a well-defined point of adjournment. Other groups—such as the engineering group in the Preview Case—may go on indefinitely. Adjourning for this type of group is more subtle and takes place when one or more key members—like Russ, the manager of engineering—move on to other positions or leave the organization.

The stages of group development are not easy to navigate, as suggested in Figure 9–1 by the points where failure is possible. However, this and other chapters in the book indicate ways in which both group members and leaders can progress through all the stages of group development. The next section reviews the primary factors that affect group behaviors and outputs. These factors also further explain why there can be so much diversity between groups and within a specific group over time.

FACTORS AFFECTING GROUP BEHAVIORS AND OUTPUTS

Figure 9–2 identifies seven factors that often influence the behaviors and outputs of a group. The two-way arrows between factors suggest their interrelationships. For example, the size of a group is likely to affect member composition and roles, which, in turn, is likely to influence the norms of the group. To avoid excessive complexity, we will discuss only some of the more important interrelationships among these factors.

Size

The size of a workable group can range from two members to a normal upper limit of 12–16 members. Twelve members in size is probably the upper limit to enable each member to react and interact with every other member.[10] Table 9–1 lists some of the possible effects of size on groups. It shows nine dimensions of groups in three categories (leadership, members, and group process). The likely effects of group size for each of these dimensions varies from low to moderate to high. The tendencies identified—"low to high," "moderate to high," and so on—indicate changes that may occur with increases in the number of group members. As shown in Table 9–1, members of groups of eight or more interact differently than they do in groups of two to seven members. A sixteen-member board of directors will operate differently than a board of seven members. Boards of directors often form subgroups of five to seven members to consider specific decisons in greater depth than is possible in a meeting of the entire board.

As with all factors that can affect groups, the tendencies identified in Table 9–1 need to be qualified.[11] For example, if considerable time were available to the group and members were sufficiently committed to the group's activities and goals, the tendencies identified might not be nearly as pronounced in a group of more than seven members as they would be in a hurried and less-committed group of the same size. And, if the group's primary

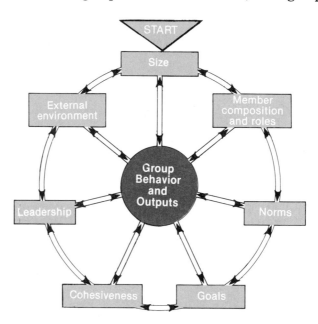

FIGURE 9–2.
Seven Factors That Affect
Group Behaviors and Outputs

TABLE 9-1   **Some Possible Effects of Size on Groups**

Category/Dimension	Group Size		
	2–7 Members	8–12 Members	13–16 Members
Leadership			
1. Demands on leader	Low	Moderate	High
2. Differences between leaders and members	Low	Low to moderate	Moderate to high
3. Direction by leader	Low	Low to moderate	Moderate to high
Members			
4. Tolerance of direction from leader	Low to high	Moderate to high	High
5. Domination of group interaction by a few members	Low	Moderate to high	High
6. Inhibition in participation by ordinary members	Low	Moderate	High
Group Process			
7. Formalization of rules and procedures	Low	Low to moderate	Moderate to high
8. Time required for reaching judgment decisions	Low to moderate	Moderate	Moderate to high
9. Tendency for subgroups to form within group	Low	Moderate to high	High

activity and goal were to tap the expertise of the members and to arrive at decisions based primarily on expertise rather than judgment, a larger group would not necessarily experience the tendencies identified.

Member Composition and Roles

Similarities or differences among individual members and the roles they prefer to assume in the group influence the process and outputs of a group.

PROBLEM-SOLVING STYLES   In Chapter 5, we discussed the differences in individual problem-solving styles. Recall that individuals are differentiated by their preference in obtaining information from the outside world (either by sensation or intuition) and by the two basic ways of reaching a decision (either by thinking or feeling). Combining the two information-input approaches and the two decision-making approaches resulted in a model comprised of four basic types of problem-solving styles: sensation-thinker, sensation-feeler, intuitive-thinker, and intuitive-feeler.

The particular combination of member personalities in a problem-solving group can affect its process and decisions.[12] For example, a task group with three strong sensation-thinkers and three intuitive-feelers who are all extroverts is likely to generate more conflict and divergence of opinion than a group consisting of members all of one type. While this divergence of viewpoint may be highly desirable, differences in group members can lead to conflict that escalates to the point where the task group cannot perform efficiently or effectively.

Managers can rarely alter the personalities of members of a task group. Thus they may find it more useful to focus on influencing the behavioral roles in the group. They can be classified according to whether they are task-oriented, relations-oriented, or self-oriented roles.[13]

TASK-ORIENTED ROLE   The **task-oriented role** of members facilitates and coordinates decision-making activities. It can be broken down into the following subroles:

- *Initiators* offer new ideas or modified ways of considering group problems or goals as well as suggest solutions to group difficulties, including new group procedures or a new group organization.
- *Information seekers* try to clarify suggestions and obtain authoritative information and pertinent facts.
- *Information givers* offer facts or generalizations that are authoritative or relate experiences that are pertinent to the group problem.
- *Coordinators* clarify relationships among ideas and suggestions, pull ideas and suggestions together, and try to coordinate activities of members of subgroups.
- *Evaluators* assess the group's functioning; they may evaluate or question the practicality, logic, or facts of suggestions by other members.

RELATIONS-ORIENTED ROLE   The **relations-oriented role** of members builds group-centered activities, sentiments, and viewpoints. It may be broken down into the following subroles:

- *Encouragers* praise, agree with, and accept the ideas of others; they indicate warmth and solidarity toward other members.
- *Harmonizers* mediate intragroup conflicts and relieve tension.
- *Gatekeepers* encourage participation of others by using such expressions as, "Let's hear from Sue," "Why not limit the length of contributions so all can react to the problem?" and "Bill, do you agree?"
- *Standard setters* express standards for the group to achieve or apply in evaluating the quality of group processes, raise questions of group goals and purpose, and assess group movement in light of these objectives.
- *Followers* go along passively and serve as friendly members.
- *Group observers* tend to stay out of the group process and give feedback on the group as if they were detached evaluators.

SELF-ORIENTED ROLE   The **self-oriented role** focuses only on members' individual needs, often at the expense of the group. This role may be broken into the following subroles:

- *Blockers* are negative, stubborn, and unreasoningly resistant; for example, they may try to bring back an issue the group intentionally rejected or bypassed.
- *Recognition seekers* try to call attention to themselves; they may boast, report on personal achievements, and, in unusual ways, struggle to avoid being placed in an inferior position.
- *Dominators* try to assert authority by manipulating the group or certain individuals in the group; they may use flattery or assertion of their superior status or right to attention; and they may interrupt contributions of others.
- *Avoiders* maintain distance from others; these passive resisters try to remain insulated from interaction.

Effective problem-solving groups are often composed of group members who play both task-oriented and relations-oriented subroles. Obviously, each individual member often performs two or more of these subroles. An individ-

TABLE 9-2 Questionnaire for Evaluating the Behaviors of Group Members

	Never	Seldom	Often	Frequently
Task-Oriented Behaviors				
1. Initiates ideas or actions	1	2	3	4
2. Facilitates introduction of facts and information	1	2	3	4
3. Clarifies issues	1	2	3	4
4. Evaluates	1	2	3	4
5. Summarizes and pulls together various ideas	1	2	3	4
6. Keeps the group working on the task	1	2	3	4
7. Asks to see if group is near decision (takes consensus)	1	2	3	4
8. Requests further information	1	2	3	4
Relations-Oriented Behaviors				
1. Supports and encourages others	1	2	3	4
2. Reduces tension	1	2	3	4
3. Harmonizes (keeps peace)	1	2	3	4
4. Compromises (finds common ground)	1	2	3	4
5. Encourages participation	1	2	3	4
Self-Oriented Behaviors				
1. Expresses hostility	1	2	3	4
2. Seeks recognition	1	2	3	4
3. Avoids involvement	1	2	3	4
4. Dominates group	1	2	3	4
5. Nitpicks	1	2	3	4

ual who is particularly adept at performing certain subroles valued by the group probably has relatively high *status*—the relative ranking of an individual in comparison with others in the group. A group dominated by individuals who are primarily acting out the self-oriented subroles is likely to be ineffective.

Table 9-2 provides a questionnaire for evaluating task-oriented, relations-oriented, and self-oriented role behaviors of group members. The point scale enables a ranking of how often each of these role behaviors is perceived in group members. In sum, group composition and member roles represent key factors influencing group behavior and outputs. Either too much or too little of certain attributes of members or roles can adversely influence group effectiveness.[14]

Norms

Norms are "rules of behavior, proper ways of acting, which have been accepted as appropriate by members of a group. Given a set of goals, norms define the kind of behavior which is [believed to be] necessary for or consistant with the realization of those goals."[15] Individuals may join groups in which many of the norms actually exist prior to group interaction. Take the case of Ginny, who is socializing the new packer by telling him that packing 80 pieces is the norm of production for ensuring a "fair day's work for a fair day's pay."

In Practice: **Eighty Pieces Is Fair**

For 18 years Ginny had been doing about the same thing: packing expandrium fittings for shipment. She was so well practiced that she could do the job perfectly without paying the slightest attention. This, of course, left her free to socialize and observe the life of the Company around her. Today, Ginny was breaking in a new packer.

"No, not that way. Look, Jim, if you hold it that way, well, then you have to twist your arm when you pack this corner, see. This way it's easier."

"But that's the way Mr. Wolf [the methods engineer] said we had to do it."

"Sure he did, Jim. But he's never had to do it eight hours a day like me. You just pay attention to what I say."

"But what if he comes around and says I should pack the other way?"

"Oh, that's easy. When he's here you do it his way. Anyway, after a couple weeks you won't see him again. Slow down. You'll wear yourself out. No one's going to expect you to do eighty pieces for a week anyway."

"But Mr. Wolf said ninety."

"Sure he did. Let him do it. Look, here's how to pace yourself. It's the way I was taught, and it works. You know the 'Battle Hymn of the Republic?' Ginny hummed a few bars. "Well, you just work to that, hum it to yourself, use the way I showed you, and you'll be doing eighty next week."

"But what if they make me do ninety?"

"They can't. Y'know, you start making mistakes when you go that fast. No, eighty is right. I always say, A fair day's work for a fair day's pay."[16]

This illustrates several themes about groups in organizations. First, group norms may be different than the standards management sets for lower-level employees. Second, peers may have as much, if not more, influence than higher management in pressuring workers as to the proper norms to follow. Third, workers are concerned with both task-oriented and relations-oriented behaviors. In their efforts to change task-oriented behaviors, managers must consider their possible impact on relations-oriented behaviors. The failure to do so is likely to lead to group resistance.

NORMS VERSUS ORGANIZATIONAL RULES   Norms differ from organizational rules. Norms are unwritten, and group members must accept and implement them to a substantial degree before they can be said to exist. Managers may write and distribute rules to employees in the form of manuals and memorandums, but these rules may be unacceptable and widely ignored. Some type of power or influence system must back up a norm. If a member consistently and excessively violates a group's norms, the other members use some type of negative sanction, positive sanction, or both, on the individual. Sanctions can range from physical abuse or threats to the application of rewards such as praise, recognition, and acceptance.

Group members may be only vaguely aware of some of the norms by which they operate. These subconscious group norms should be brought to the level of conscious awareness for at least two reasons. First, awareness increases the potential for individual and group freedom and maturity; self-awareness and awareness of the environment are necessary, though insufficient, conditions for freedom and maturity. Second, norms can have positive influences, negative influences, or both, on the effectiveness of individuals, groups, and organizations.[17]

CONDITIONS FOR NORMS ENFORCEMENT   Norms are not established for every conceivable situation in a group. Norms are generally formed and enforced with respect to those task-oriented behaviors and relations-oriented behaviors that are particularly important to the group. The four major conditions under which group norms are most likely to be enforced have been identified as follows:

- Norms are likely to be enforced if they aid in group survival and provision of benefits. For instance, a group might develop a norm not to discuss individual salaries with members of other groups in the organization, so that attention will not be brought to pay inequities in its favor.

- Norms are likely to be enforced if they simplify or make predictable the behavior expected of group members. When colleagues go out for lunch together, there can be some awkwardness about how to split the bill at the end of the meal. A group may develop a norm that results in some highly predictable way of behaving—split the bill evenly, take turns picking up the tab, or individually pay for what each ordered.

- Norms are likely to be enforced if they help the group to avoid embarrassing interpersonal problems. Task groups might develop norms about not discussing romantic involvements (so that differences in moral values do not become too obvious) or about not getting together socially in members' homes (so that differences in taste or income do not become too obvious).

- Norms are likely to be enforced if they express the central values or goals of the group and clarify what is distinctive about the group's identity. When employees of an advertising agency label the wearing of unstylish clothes as deviant behavior, they say: "We think of ourselves, personally and professionally, as trend-setters, and being fashionably dressed conveys that to our clients and our public."[18]

CONFORMITY TO NORMS Many popular writers criticize large-scale organizations for maintaining and encouraging conformity to norms in phrases like "It is best to keep opinions to yourself and play it safe" and "The most important thing is to appear to work hard, regardless of the results." Unfortunately, there is little data that demonstrates the extent to which conformity to such norms actually exists in organizations.

In task groups, the pressures to adhere to norms may result in conformity. Two types of conformity exist: compliance and personal acceptance.[19] **Compliance** occurs when a person's behavior becomes or remains similar to the group's desired behavior because of real or imagined group pressure. Considerable conformity in organizations and task groups results from compliance, even though the individuals do not necessarily believe personally in the desirability or appropriateness of the actions.

People may comply without personal acceptance for a variety of reasons. They may feel that the appearance of a united front is necessary for success in accomplishing the group's goals. For example, the president of a U.S. automobile manufacturing company would not announce, "After considerable argument and debate, the majority of my executive committee finally agreed to increase car prices by an average of 6 percent this year." Rather, the president might say, "After considerable study, the executive committee unanimously agrees that it is essential to raise the price of our cars by an average of 6 percent, even though the increased costs of producing a car exceed this percentage." On a more personal level, a person may comply because it is important in meeting a need to be liked and accepted by others. This may apply especially to members of lower status in relation to those of higher status, such as a subordinate and a superior. Finally, someone may comply because the costs of conformity are much less than the costs of nonconformity, which could threaten the maintenance of existing relationships in the group.

The second type of conformity is based on personal acceptance of the group's wishes. In **personal acceptance conformity**, the individual's behavior and attitudes or beliefs are consistent with the group's norms and wishes. This type of conformity is, by definition, much stronger than the compliance type of conformity. In brief, the person is a true believer in the group's goals and norms.

All of this helps to explain why some members of highly conforming groups may easily change their behavior (compliance type of conformity) whereas others may oppose changes and find them highly stressful (personal acceptance type of conformity). Without norms and some conformity to them, task groups would be chaotic and random environments in which few tasks could be accomplished. At the other extreme, excessive and mechanistic conformity threatens the important place claimed for the individual in certain societies, as well as the ability of groups to deal with change, uncertainty, and complex problems.

Goals

Group goals do not exist outside the minds of the members. In addition, they cannot be directly determined from the goals of individual members or determined by simply adding together the individual members' goals. **Group goals** are the objectives or states desired for the group as a whole, not just the objectives desired by each individual member. This definition rests on the idea that the whole is greater than and different from the simple sum of individual parts. Group goals refer to the group as a system and to desired states of the system, not just of individual members.[20]

RELATION TO GROUP NORMS A natural correspondence generally exists between group goals and group norms. It is logical, but not always true, that groups adopt norms to help them attain goals.[21] Some organizational development efforts help group members to assess whether the norms they follow are consistent, neutral, or conflicting in relation to group and organizational goals. For example, a task group may claim and believe that one of its goals is to improve its efficiency according to the productivity goals assigned to it by higher management. Close inspection of the members' behavior might actually reveal norms counterproductive to this expressed goal; norms that specify not to produce too much and not to make too many changes.

Even if the group's members are consciously aware of norms like these, they may rationalize them as being necessary in order to achieve their effectiveness goal. Members may claim that producing more than the norm will "burn them out" or reduce product or service quality and result in lower long-term effectiveness. If task group goals include such things as minimizing managerial influence and increasing the opportunity for social interaction among members, norms placing some restrictions on worker output could be perceived by the members as desirable.

PERVASIVENESS OF GOALS   We return again and again to the concept that goals are important to understanding or changing individuals, groups, and organizations. Each is partially defined as being a goal-oriented system. Determining the variables affecting group behaviors and outputs entails the constant assessment of group goals. Obviously, individual goals and the organizational goals within which the group functions are likely to influence both the types of group goals and the actual behavior and outputs of the group. Both compatible and conflicting goals may exist within and between individuals, groups, and organizations. For example, task groups typically have both relations-oriented goals and task-oriented goals. Effective task groups appear to be concerned with both types of goals, spending two-thirds or more of their time on task-oriented issues and roughly one-third or less on relations-oriented issues.[22] The pursuit of only one or the other over the long run can reduce effectiveness and efficiency, increase conflicts, and result in the dissolution of the group. The influence of goals on group behaviors and outputs becomes even more complex when the possible compatibilities and conflicts between individual member goals, group goals, and organizational goals are considered.

The management of Auburn Steel Company—a Japanese-owned firm located near Syracuse, New York—has attempted to bring individual, group, and organizational goals closer together through the creation of work teams. Management actively attempts to influence the formation of positive work norms. Let us take a look at these practices as described in an account provided by Martin E. Fanning, who was Vice President of Industrial Relations at Auburn Steel at the time the account was published.

In Practice: Work Teams at Auburn Steel

The teams are small work groups, with the supervisor clearly identified as the leader responsible for the workers' welfare and for the resolution of their problems. Daily personal contact at work is supplemented by informal meetings off the plant site, which supervisors often sponsor voluntarily. Workers are continually made to feel appreciated and an integral part of the company. At weekly meetings with foremen, the first question asked by a superintendent typically concerns employee morale.

Team development   Individuals become part of a team right from the beginning, since the company normally hires in groups of 10 to 15. A sense of camaraderie develops during that first week of tours, safety lectures, job demonstrations, movies, reviews of emergency procedures, and instruction in operating practices. The group receives a complete explanation of company policy and organizational principles, as well as of company benefits. Their responsibilities as Auburn Steel employees are defined, as is the team concept.

During the first week, new employees meet with every single company official, each one explaining his or her role at Auburn Steel. The President comes in, tells what he does, or what he tries to do. So do our vice presidents—marketing, finance, and so on. We give the employees a complete run down on the company: where it came from, how it got there, what we have done to date, and what our plans are. Employees are paid for this orientation.

Team performance and rewards   It is very easy to measure the productivity of a team. For example, in the melt shop we operate 24 hours a day. On any given day, three teams would be working, one from 7 A.M. to 3 P.M., one from 3 P.M. to 11 P.M., the other from 11 P.M. to 7 A.M., and a fourth team would be on its day off. At the end of an eight hour period, we have the data on how many tons were produced and what was good and what was bad.

When a team achieves a record, there's a reward; and there is a fair amount of competition. A lot of the rewards are going out to dinner. When a team achieves a production record, we take the whole team out and have an open bar and a dinner. Some may say: "Well, that's a pretty steep price to pay." But when you look at the production records and what they have achieved, it is really insignificant.

The first element of reward is personal pride. Then, there's the esteem of the other teams. And the team that set the record knows full well that the others are coming up right behind it. We feel it is genuine; we have tried not to make it manipulative. The thrust is the better a team does, the better the department does, the better the company does.

Social and Task Relations   There are team meetings, sponsored by the supervisor, at the local restaurant or a pizza place where they'll go and have a pizza and a couple of beers, sit in the back room, and talk over problems. These are voluntary, but attendance is high. About 60 percent of supervisors do this; 40 percent do not because they accomplish their communication in other ways. Some have meetings at their homes. Some teams have quarterly parties at somebody's home. They are involved, and they just can't help talking about work.[23]

Cohesiveness

Cohesiveness is the strength of the members' desires to remain in the group and their commitment to the group. It is influenced by the degree of compatibility between group goals and individual members' goals. A group whose members have a strong desire to remain in the group and personally accept its goals would be considered highly cohesive in relation to a group whose members do not. The Auburn Steel account clearly suggests that management is trying to create high group cohesiveness through the use of work teams that help integrate individual, group, and organizational goals.

RELATION TO CONFORMITY   No one-to-one relationship exists between cohesiveness and conformity. Low cohesiveness is usually associated with low conformity. However, high cohesiveness does *not* exist only in the presence of high conformity. For example, mature groups may have high member commitment and desire to stick together while simultaneously respecting individual differences in behavior and thought. This is more likely when cohesion is based on a common commitment to task-group goals. Moreover, in a group confronting complex problems, members may not only tolerate, but actually encourage and support, low or moderate conformity.[24]

RELATION TO GROUPTHINK When decision-making groups are both conforming and cohesive, a phenomenon called **groupthink** might take place. Irving L. Janis, who coined the term *groupthink,* focused his research on high-level governmental policy groups faced with difficult problems in a complex and dynamic environment. In business, decision making by groups rather than by individuals is quite common. Thus the possibility of groupthink exists in organizations in the private sector as well as the public sector.[25]

Figure 9–3 summarizes the initial conditions that are likely to lead to groupthink, its characteristics, and the types of defective decision making that will result from it. The initial conditions and the types of defective decision-making processes presented in Figure 9–3 are self-explanatory. Therefore we will concentrate on the eight characteristics of groupthink:

- An illusion of invulnerability is shared by most or all the members, which creates excessive optimism and encourages taking extreme risks.

- Collective rationalization discounts warnings that might lead the members to reconsider their assumptions before they commit themselves to their policy decisions.

- An unquestioned belief in the group's inherent morality leads the members to ignore the ethical or moral consequences of their decisions.

- Stereotyped views of rivals and enemies (outgroups) picture them as too evil to warrant genuine attempts to negotiate or too weak or stupid to counter whatever attempts are made to defeat their purposes.

- Direct pressure is exerted on any member who expresses strong arguments against any of the group's illusions, stereotypes, or commit-

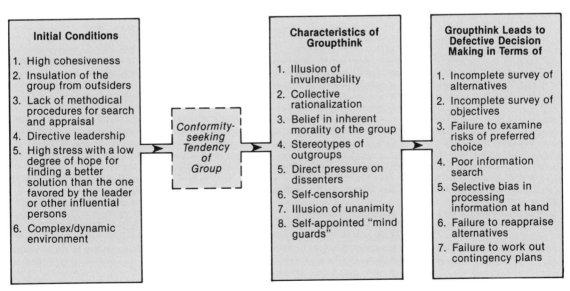

FIGURE 9–3.
Model of Groupthink

Source: Modified with permission of the Free Press, a division of the Macmillan Publishing Co., Inc., from *Decision Making: A Psychological Analysis of Conflict, Choice, and Commitment,* by Irving L. Janis and Leon Mann. Copyright © 1977.

ments, making clear that such dissent is contrary to what is expected of all loyal members.

- Self-censorship of deviations from the apparent group consensus reflects the inclination of the members to minimize to themselves the importance of their doubts and counterarguments.

- A shared illusion of unanimity results, in part, from self-censorship and is reinforced by the false assumption that silence implies consent.

- The emergence of self-appointed "mind-guard" members serves to protect the group from adverse information that might shatter the shared complacency about the effectiveness and morality of their decisions.[26]

The description of a committee that was formed to evaluate the desirability of creating a flexible work hours system in a firm illustrates a number of the characteristics and processes of groupthink.

In Practice: Flexible Work Hours Committee

Directive leadership   A company president who wanted to implement a flexible work-hours program asked a committee of lower-level managers and professionals to investigate the feasibility of flexible work schedules in the firm. The committee was composed of nine salaried employees, most of whom were young and all of whom held staff positions.

Cohesiveness   Five of the individuals saw membership on the committee as special because they had rarely been asked to consider corporate-wide policies. These group members felt honored to be a part of the group. Two other members had initiated the idea of appointing the committee and, therefore, were committed to making it a success. Thus, the members were considerably attracted to the group and highly valued membership in it. Such circumstances are conducive to a high frequency of groupthink symptoms. The committee was aware that the president favored flexible hours. However, several members expressed skepticism about implementing a flexible hours schedule.

Insulation   The committee discussed time accountability at several meetings, but the members insulated themselves between meetings and did not discuss the issue with other managers. (Insulation of group members from outside input is typically encountered in groupthink situations.) Moreover, most members were aware that the company president was quite receptive to automatic time accumulation (a factor that, in the end, facilitated concurrence).

Illusion of unanimity   Another symptom of groupthink is an illusion of unanimity which, in the case of the flexible hours committee, was apparent from the beginning of its discussions of time accountability. It was almost as if a decision had already been made and all that was needed was formal approval of the device. One of the more influential members of the group was unwilling to decide about the time accumulation device, and consistently refused to take a stand on the issue. Another member expressed some doubts about the accumulator's compatibility with the objective of flexible hours, but he was almost apologetic in presenting his concerns. In private conversations, however, he was much more aggressive and opinionated.

Self-censorship   Such behavior typifies the self-censorship symptom of group-think—that is, self-censorship on the part of individuals in raising objections to the apparent group consensus. Another incident suggesting self-censorship involved a committee member who held strong reservations about the accumulator. He expressed his feelings in the restroom rather than in the meeting room, where he sat quietly and did not raise questions or voice objections.

Morality of group   This group also expressed self-righteousness, which led its members to regard their actions as ethical and just. They viewed flexible hours as a benefit designed to give employees more self-determination and freedom. Under the old system, only management and professional employees were permitted some degree of flexibility, although by no means as extensive as that envisioned in the proposed program. Thus, the members saw the company-wide proposal as a noble cause; it had the president's support and was "right" for the employees involved. Even though many employees and managers might see the time accumulation device as a time clock, and thus, a regressive step, it would still be part of a positive program.

Illusion of invulnerability   The committee felt unlimited confidence and excessive optimism about flexible hours, and no time accumulation device was about to ruin the program. Indeed, the committee felt invulnerable in their ability to implement the program successfully. Three members of the group were aware of one outside manager's misgivings about the time accumulator but were reluctant to voice his concerns. Thus, the group tended to discount warnings that might have led it to reconsider its decisions.

At the committee's last meeting, the final details were discussed. At this late stage, bringing up the issue of a time accumulator seemed taboo. Nevertheless, an individual who had been sitting in on the meetings as an expert advisor suggested that there still appeared to be some unanswered questions.

Self-appointed mind guard   The committee moderator seemed surprised at this intervention, saying that she thought the issue had been settled and that the accumulator would be recommended. Nonetheless, she proposed taking a quick poll. At this point, she also noted the meeting had already gone past its scheduled period and it was time for lunch. The moderator started the poll by indicating why she favored the accumulator. Thus, the group leader—by suggesting a certain approach and preference—was acting as a mind guard. Several days later the president received the recommendation and expressed general agreement with it.

Constructive dissent   It appeared, then, that the company would implement the flexible hours program using the time accumulator. However, a manager who had earlier not felt free to voice his reservations quickly wrote a two-page letter to the moderator, asking that the committee reconsider the matter.

This formalized reservation, together with some coffee break banter by several other managers, prompted the group moderator to get more detailed views from other corporate managers who would be obliged to introduce accumulators in their departments. When she completed the survey of these managers, it was painfully clear that the use of accumulators in conjunction with the flexible hours program would meet with considerable resistance. Department managers would regard it as a threat to their automony in their departments.

On the basis of these developments, the group moderator proposed modifying the flexible hours recommendation so that each department would determine how to account for its employees' time. The president approved the change and the committee avoided a potentially disastrous problem.[27]

This example of groupthink points out how, under certain conditions, high group cohesiveness and conformity can hinder the effectiveness of decision-making groups. However, groupthink is not inevitable, and several steps can be taken to decrease it. For example, a leader should try to remain neutral and encourage criticism and new ideas. Small subgroups or outside consultants could be used to come up with different viewpoints. People holding or sympathetic to alternative views could be encouraged to present them. More will be said about increasing the effectiveness of decision-making groups later in the chapter.

IMPACT ON PRODUCTIVITY The degree of group cohesion is important because it can affect group productivity. In brief, **productivity** is the relationship between the inputs consumed (labor hours and costs, raw materials, money, machines, and the like) and the outputs created (products and services). It might be more appropriate to think of cohesion and productivity as potentially interdependent, particularly in groups with highly task-related goals. If the group is successful in reaching its goals, the positive feedback of its attainments may increase member commitment. For example, a winning football team is more likely to be cohesive than one with a mediocre record, everything else being equal. Of course, the cause-and-effect relationship applies both ways. Thus a cohesive football team also may be more likely to win games.

On the other hand, low cohesiveness may interfere with a group's ability to obtain task goals because members are not as likely to share or interact as frequently as necessary. High cohesiveness in task groups may actually be associated with low productivity if the group goals are contrary to organizational or managerial goals. Therefore the relationship between cohesion and productivity cannot be anticipated or understood unless the group's goals and norms are also known.[28]

Leadership

Studies of small groups within organizations have emphasized the importance of emergent, or informal, leadership, especially in accomplishing task goals. An **informal leader** is an individual who emerges over time with relatively high influence in the group.

MULTIPLE LEADERS Leadership in a group has been widely regarded as the province of a single individual. As mentioned earlier, task groups often have at least two major classes of goals: relations-oriented and task-oriented. It is quite possible therefore to have two leaders in a group: one who provides leadership with respect to relations-oriented goals and the other who provides leadership with respect to task-oriented goals. These two types of goals may require different personal skills for attainment, and they may conflict at times; thus they may create a combination of demands that any one person would find difficult to meet.[29]

Research suggests that informal task leaders of groups are unlikely to emerge unless the formal task leader abdicates task-related responsibilities or lacks the necessary skills to carry them out.[30] In contrast, relations-oriented leaders of task groups are much more likely to emerge informally.

EFFECTIVE GROUP LEADERS An effective group leader usually has important direct and indirect effects on the group. Virtually all the other factors affecting group outputs and behaviors (such as size, member composition and roles, norms, goals, and the external environment) are disproportionately influenced by the person or persons in group leadership positions. For example, the effective group leader often assumes a key role in the relations between the group and its external environment. This person probably influences greatly the selection of new group members, a universal process in task groups. Even when the task-group members themselves participate in the selection of new members, the group leader commonly screens potential members, thereby limiting the alternative choices. These behaviors provide only a sample of the effects and qualities needed for effective task-group leaders. We discuss leadership at length in Chapter 11.

External Environment

The final factor affecting groups that we consider is the group's **external environment**, that is, the conditions and factors not substantially controlled by the task group, representing givens for the members. The external environment for a task group might include technology, physical conditions, management practices, rules, leadership of the formal supervisors and managers, and organizational rewards and punishments.[31]

Up to this point the discussion of factors influencing group behavior and outputs has focused on the internal characteristics and dynamics of the group. The external environment can influence each of the factors already presented, as well as directly affect the behavior and outputs of a task group. For example, management may want to introduce a technological change, such as automatically controlled machines, and turn the problem over to a task group. The task group may consider this an external force, but, through united action, it may be able to influence the conditions under which the machines are introduced. Hence, two-way influences can exist between the external environment and the task group, rather than the external environment always influencing the group.

Groups are not easy to understand or manage. However, an understanding of the factors influencing group behavior and outputs can increase the effectiveness of both members and leaders in groups. This understanding also provides a good foundation for the consideration of decision processes within groups—the focus of the last two sections of this chapter.

EFFECTIVE GROUP DECISION MAKING

As suggested earlier, groups face different types of tasks and experience varying degrees of member interdependency for different problems over a period of time. Both individual and group decision making can be expected in effective groups. In Chapter 11, we discuss the criteria for deciding when to use (1) individual decision making; (2) group decision making; or (3) various combinations of individual and group decision making. In brief, costs are associated with the inappropriate use of either individual or group decision-making methods. In the inappropriate use of group decision making, organizational resources are wasted because the participants' time could have been used on other tasks; motivation is reduced because of boredom and a feeling that time is being wasted. On the other hand, the inappropriate use of individual decision making can result in poor coordination, lower quality and creativity in decision making, greater errors, and so on.[32]

Continuum of Group Decisions

As a group deals with making decisions of increasing importance to the group, it gains increasing autonomy. Table 9–3 shows examples of the types of decisions a group might make and the corresponding levels of group autonomy. Moreover, these types of decisions are generally thought to be cumulative. A group that can decide questions of recruitment for its membership will usually have an influence on the group's internal leadership and methods used to carry out its task.

Once the decision has been made that a high degree of group participation is appropriate and that the group should consider matters of important content, how should a manager proceed in order to obtain group decision making? Morris and Sashkin have developed a six-phase model for group de-

TABLE 9–3   Continuum of Group Decisions

Examples of Types of Decision	Autonomy of Group Decision (arbitrary point values)
Group has influence on its qualitative goals.	100 (High)
	—
Group has influence on its quantitative goals.	90
	—
	—
Group decides on additional tasks to undertake.	75
	—
Group decides when it will work.	65
Group decides methods to use.	60
Group decides internal distribution of tasks.	55
Group decides recruitment of new members.	50
Group decides internal leadership.	45
Group members individually decide how each will go about performing his or her own tasks.	40
	—
Group members influence some decisions about group functions.	30
	—
	—
	—
	—
	—
Group members have virtually no influence on decisions about group functions.	0 (Low)

Source: Adapted from Gulowsen, J. A Measure of Work-Group Autonomy. In L. Davis and J. Taylor (Eds.) *Design of Jobs.* Middlesex, England: Penguin Books, 1972, 374–390.

TABLE 9-4   Summary of the Morris and Sashkin Group Decision-Making Model

Phases	Activities
I. Problem definition	Explaining the problem situation; generating information; clarifying and defining the problem
II. Problem solution generation	Brainstorming solution alternatives; reviewing, revising, elaborating, and recombining solution ideas
III. Ideas to actions	Evaluating alternatives; examining probable effects and comparing them with desired outcomes; revising ideas; developing a list of final action alternatives and selecting one for trial
IV. Solution action planning	Preparing a list of action steps, with the names of people who will be responsible for each step; developing a coordination plan
V. Solution evaluation planning	Reviewing desired outcomes and developing measures of effectiveness; creating a monitoring plan for gathering evaluation data as the solution is put into action; developing contingency plans; assigning responsibilities
VI. Evaluation of the product and the process	Assembling evaluation data to determine the effects of actions and the effectiveness of the group's problem-solving process

Source: Reprinted by permission from *Organizational Behavior in Action* by Morris, W. C., and Sashkin, M. Copyright © 1976 by West Publishing Company, p. 3. All Rights Reserved.

cision making that managers and group members might well use.[33] Table 9–4 summarizes the model, and the following paragraphs expand on it.

Phase I: Problem Definition

Group members often assume that they know what the problem is in a situation, but they may be wrong and look at only a symptom or a part of the problem. Phase I encourages the group to fully explore, clarify, and define the problem. Even when the problem is identified, the group often needs to collect more detailed information for a sharper definition of the problem. Thus a key part of the problem definition phase is the generation and collection of information. Finally, the problem definition phase requires that the group identify or recognize the goals that it is trying to achieve by solving the problem that has been defined. When group members are clear about goals—which, in itself can be a major problem area—they can better determine whether the problem really exists and, if it does, the relative priority that should be assigned to solving the problem.

Phase II: Problem Solution Generation

Many people tend to be solution-minded rather than problem-oriented. They often tend to choose the first or one of the first solutions suggested. Phase II prolongs the idea-generating process and prevents premature decisions. Research has clearly shown that an eventual solution can be much better if as many ideas and alternative solutions as possible are considered. The more ideas generated, the more likely is the group to come up with a greater number of *good* ideas.

Phase III: Ideas to Actions

In Phase III, the group evaluates the ideas and comes up with a solution. Even though an idea may not work alone, it may provide a useful part of the solution. The group can take time to combine the good parts of various ideas. It then can carefully evaluate each alternative. Individuals will be more inclined to help and participate if they do not feel attacked or threatened. Rather than weeding out poor alternatives (and making those who suggested them feel defensive), the group should select the best ones and concentrate on those until everyone can agree on a solution.

Phase IV: Solution Action Planning

Now that there is a solution to try out, it probably will work more smoothly if the actions needed to put it into operation are planned carefully. In Phase IV, the group looks for implementation problems in advance, makes plans to involve those whose support will be needed, and assigns and accepts action responsibilities. Only if the group determines who is to do what and when can the agreed-on solution get a fair test.

Phase V: Solution Evaluation Planning

Unfortunately, most groups stop at Phase IV, losing the chance to learn from experience. Even if a solution is a tremendous success, a group benefits from knowing exactly what it was about the actions taken that made the solution work well, so that it can be repeated when appropriate. If a solution is a total disaster, group members may feel like hiding the fact that they had anything to do with it. However, a group that knows exactly what went wrong will avoid making the same mistakes in the future. In real life, solutions generally work moderately well; they are neither great successes nor great failures. By keeping track of exactly what is happening, we can make minor improvements or adjustments that will help significantly in other group problem-solving efforts. We should not base our monitoring on guesswork or trial and error, but on hard, accurate information about the effects of actions. Phase V offers the greatest potential for group learning in problem solving. In order to take advantage of this opportunity, a group must determine the kinds of evaluation information needed, who will obtain it, and when it must be specified and gathered.

Phase VI: Evaluation of the Product and the Process

When enough information has been collected to evaluate how well the solution worked, it is time for another group evaluation meeting. In Phase VI, the group can see the outcomes and whether the problem was solved. If the problem or some part of it remains, the group can recycle it by looking at the information, perhaps even redefining the problem, and coming up with new ideas or trying a previously rejected alternative. Phase VI also involves a review and evaluation of how well the group members worked together. As Figure 9–1 showed, open and constructive evaluation of the product and process usually occurs in mature groups.

Summary

Group decision making *rarely* proceeds so neatly or systematically as suggested in descriptions of these six phases.[34] Problem-solving groups often jump around or skip phases. However, the Morris and Sashkin model, if followed as closely as possible, should greatly improve the effectiveness of decision making in any group. The norms and values of the larger society often influence the group process and the roles of individuals in it. However, the Morris and Sashkin model implicitly assumes that *member expertise* and norms of *equality* among members underpin the group process. In contrast, group decision making in China illustrates the powerful influence of different societal norms and values on the functioning of decision-making groups.

ACROSS CULTURES

Group Decision Making in China

In working at the Institute of International Economic Management in Beijing (Peking) China, we had the opportunity to teach Chinese business people American management techniques. This experience has given us some insights into Chinese responses to Western management theory and application, as well as some knowledge of Chinese organizational behavior.

During the year, 200 students attended the Institute. The majority of the students worked as interpreters and employees in various import/export corporations in diverse regions of China. The remaining students were employed as engineers, scientists, commune workers, or in various other occupations. A number of decision-making groups of four to six members each were used in the training program.

We used group-observation sheets to organize our perceptions and comments on the discussions, and in a large class discussion we shared the observations we had made of the groups. We and the students then brainstormed to produce a list of behaviors and a set of assumptions that characterized the Chinese group meeting style, as shown in Table 9–5.

TABLE 9–5   Chinese Group Meeting Style

Behaviors	Assumptions
A leader is chosen to head the meeting.	Groups must have leaders or they will tend toward chaos. This reflects a *traditional* reliance on authority figures.
Participants speak in serial order.	Strict ordering of speaking is proper. This reflects *traditional* child-rearing practices.
Participants share, but do not debate, suggestions.	All people should be heard on an issue. This reflects *modern socialist ideals*.
	Conflict is to be avoided because it creates a loss of face for all involved. This reflects *traditional* Chinese culture.
The leader announces a decision without discussion.	Leaders make correct decisions after listening to the masses. This reflects a mixture of *traditional* deference to authority figures and *modern socialist ideals*.

Source: Lindsay, C. P., and Dempsey, B. L. Experiences in Training Chinese Business People to use U.S. Management Techniques. *Journal of Applied Behavioral Science*, 1985, *21*, 72. Used with permission of JAI Press, Greenwich, Connecticut and the authors.

The behaviors we observed in these groups were so pervasive that even as we discussed them with the students the behaviors were being practiced. The following list provides a summary of the surprising aspects of this Chinese group-process style as opposed to U.S. style: high dependence on authority and authority figures; participation by followers in "discussion," but not in decision making; strictly patterned "discussion" flows; and avoidance of public conflict. We traced each of these aspects to its root in either traditional Chinese culture or modern socialist development.

Students identified their high dependence on the leader as resulting from a traditional Chinese norm of deference to authority; one student said, "It is not right to disagree with the leader." They had a more difficult time explaining "discussion" without participation in decision making, for the general consensus of the students was that they had participated in arriving at the decision. Some students reported that they felt required to participate, but were afraid of being too outspoken. Although modern Communist ideals support participative decision making, ancient Chinese norms prohibit such boldness in the face of authority figures. Apparently, these two contradictory prescriptions for appropriate behavior had merged to produce the students' style.

Students insisted that strict patterning of discussion was "correct" polite behavior, an example of "right participation." In discussions of this point, students sometimes referred to the Confucian tradition of "five relationships," which defines social rules of interaction among the following five different pairs of related individuals: ruler and minister; father and son; husband and wife; brothers; and friends. This belief in the propriety of such behavior may stem from early experiences with traditional Chinese culture. This structured verbal interaction is reinforced by the childhood experience of being rebuked by elders for offering opinions.

Avoidance of conflict stems from the face-saving rituals of traditional Chinese culture, which perceive conflict as "confusion" and detrimental to social well-being. All of these aspects of the Chinese group style presented themselves repeatedly in subsequent interactions.[35]

The Morris and Sashkin Model (Table 9–4) has been proposed for improving the effectiveness of *interacting task groups,* especially in countries like the United States and Canada. However, interacting task groups—even if operating properly—are generally most effective in phase III (ideas to actions) through phase VI (evaluation of the product and the process). Phases I (problem definition) and II (problem solution generation) benefit from processes different from the usual face-to-face interactions. A variety of processes and procedures have been developed for improving the effectiveness of decision-making groups in addition to those noted in the Morris and Sashkin model.[36] The last section of this chapter considers one of the processes especially designed to improve the effectiveness of groups in Phases I and II.

STIMULATING GROUP CREATIVITY: NOMINAL GROUP TECHNIQUE

The **nominal group technique** (NGT) is a structured process designed to stimulate creative group decision making where the members lack agreement or there is incomplete knowledge concerning the nature of the problem.

This technique has a special purpose: to arrive at a group decision where individual judgments are essential inputs. That is, situations where group members must pool their judgments in order to solve the problem, determine a satisfactory course of action, and so on.

In Practice: Michelle's Task Force

Michelle was chairperson of a task force charged with producing fresh ideas about how to deal with a continuing absenteeism problem in one of the company's plants. She gazed dismally at the clutter left from the task force meeting just completed. It had been, she decided, an absolute disaster. As often happened, Roy had dominated much of the discussion. The meeting had ended with only a few ideas or solutions to the problem even being considered by the group. Those solutions seemed to reflect the personal opinion of Roy rather than the thinking of the entire task force. Michelle didn't want to be unfair to Roy. She had to admit that Roy was a talented person, who often had exciting plans and ideas. If she could just get him to shut up long enough to get input from others in the group! Don, for instance, had tried at least twice to get the group to consider some of his ideas, but had been "shouted down" on both occasions because some members seemed to think that his proposals were not feasible. Come to think of it, Michelle mused, we were particularly critical today concerning the "feasibility" of suggested solutions. Almost invariably, every new suggestion was greeted with a litany of reasons why it would not work, couldn't be done, violated this or that accepted "way of doing things," and so on. "What now?" Michelle wondered, "How will I get this task force off and running?"[37]

Some of the fault for the lack of progress by this task force lies with Michelle. She (and her group) have committed a classical mistake in group decision making: failing to separate the idea-generating phase from the task of evaluating ideas and making a decision to implement some particular proposal. Additionally, Michelle has perhaps been guilty of attempting to conduct a meeting in which judgment–idea generation is critically needed as though it were a "routine" meeting in which goals and techniques for achieving those goals were clear to all participants. The nominal group technique is a form of group decision making particularly well suited for situations such as this one.[38]

As a group decision-making process, the nominal group technique is most useful for (1) identifying the critical variables in a specific problem situation; (2) identifying key elements of a program designed to implement a particular solution to some problem; or (3) establishing priorities with regard to problems to be addressed, goals to be attained, desirable end states and so on. In all of these circumstances, it often seems beneficial to aggregate individual judgments into group decisions. However, NGT is not particularly well suited for routine group meetings that focus primarily on coordination of activities or an exchange of information. Nor is it appropriate for negotiating or bargaining situations.

The process of decision making using the nominal group technique consists of four distinct steps.[39] However, a number of useful ideas for modifying or tailoring these steps to special group conditions have been suggested.[40]

Step 1: Generation of Ideas

The first step in the process is to have group members generate key ideas. These ideas are written down independently by each participant in response to some statement of the problem, *stimulus question,* or other central focus of the task group. A stimulus question could be something as simple as: "What problems do you think we should consider over the next year?" The generation of ideas or solutions privately by individuals while in a group setting is advantageous in that it avoids direct pressures resulting from status differentials or competition among members, yet retains some of the social facilitation and creative tension generated by the presence of others. This step and the subsequent steps provide time for thinking and reflection and avoid premature choosing among ideas.

Step 2: Recording of Ideas

The second step is to record, in round-robin fashion, the ideas generated in step 1 on a flip chart or other device visible to all members of the group. This is done by asking for, and writing down, one idea from each group member in turn. The process continues until members are satisfied that the group list reflects all of the ideas which they generated individually. This round-robin process emphasizes the equal opportunity for participation from all members and serves to avoid losing ideas considered significant by individual members. The public listing depersonalizes ideas and makes potential conflict less threatening. Group members are often impressed and pleased with the array of ideas presented. This provides momentum and enthusiasm for continuing the process.

Step 3: Clarification of Ideas

During step 3, each idea on the list from step 2 is discussed in turn. The purpose of this discussion is to clarify the meaning of each idea and to allow group members to express agreement or disagreement with any item. The intent of this phase is to disclose the logic and thinking behind the ideas and to reduce misunderstanding, *not* to win arguments concerning the relative merit of the ideas. It is critical to note that differences of opinion will not be resolved at this step but rather by the voting procedure described next.

Step 4: Voting on Ideas

A nominal group will often list at least 12 and perhaps as many as 20 or 30 ideas. There are several ways to proceed at this point. Perhaps the most common voting procedure is to have the group members individually select a specific number (say, five) of the items they believe are most important. These five ideas are written on individual 3×5 index cards and group members are then asked to rank-order their five items from most to least important. The index cards are collected and the votes tabulated to produce the priority list for the meeting. An alternative to this single vote is to feed back the results of a first vote, allow time for group discussion of these results, and then to vote again. It has been shown that the feedback and discussion

seem to result in a final decision that more closely reflects the true preferences of the group.[41]

Regardless of format, the voting procedure determines the outcome of
the nominal group meeting: a group decision that incorporates the individual judgments of the participants. The procedure is designed to document
the group decision and to provide a sense of accomplishment and closure.

Conditions for Effectiveness

The potential advantages of the nominal group technique over the usual interacting group methods include greater emphasis and attention to idea generation, increased attention to each idea, and greater likelihood of balanced
participation and representation of each member in the group. However,
some research suggests that nominal groups may not be superior to interacting groups "when the task of problem identification is performed by persons
who are both (1) aware of the existing problems, and (2) willing to communicate them."[42] The nominal group technique may be most effective when there
are certain blocks or problems in a group, such as a few dominating members.

SUMMARY

Considerable information has been gathered during the past 30 years about
the functioning of groups and how they can be improved. Studying this information and techniques of group problem solving enables us to understand, diagnose, and improve the groups we join or lead. Unfortunately, no
simple and straightforward prescriptions can guarantee our success as
members or leaders of groups. However, a fairly broad foundation—in terms
of the key factors that can influence group behavior and outputs such as
those given in this chapter—can prove very useful.

A complex interrelationship exists between individuals and groups.
Groups have numerous classifications, depending on the classifier's perspective. In an organizational setting, useful classifications according to the
group's primary purpose include friendship and task (work) groups. Task
groups, in turn, may be interacting, coacting, or counteracting.

Major factors affecting groups are size, member composition and roles,
norms, goals, cohesiveness, leadership, and the external environment. As
group members, our behavioral roles may be task-oriented, relations-oriented
or self-oriented. Norms differ from rules in important ways and can be positive or negative in relation to organizational goals and productivity. In
groups, the pressures to adhere to norms may result in conformity—either
compliance conformity or personal acceptance conformity. Another factor
affecting groups, cohesiveness, is related to conformity, groupthink, and
productivity. Finally, a group can operate with both formal and informal
leaders.

The study of the concepts and techniques in group decision making—in
particular, the Morris and Sashkin group decision-making model and the
nominal group technique—can make both group members and leaders more
effective. Several themes running through discussion of group decision processes can be summed up in the form of the questions addressed in this chap-

ter. When should we use group decision making versus individual decision making? What is the relationship between group decision processes and the relative autonomy of groups? What are the factors that should be considered in group decision processes? Which phases of group problem solving should we follow to increase the effectiveness of interacting task groups? What is the nominal group technique, and when should we consider using it?

Although Chapter 10 focuses on relations between groups, much of the discussion has implications for behaviors within groups. Thus this chapter certainly has not presented all of the issues associated with the dynamics within groups, particularly task groups.

KEY WORDS AND CONCEPTS

Coacting group
Cohesiveness
Compliance
Counteracting group
External environment
Friendship group
Group
Group goals
Groupthink
Informal leader

Interacting group
Nominal group technique
Norms
Personal acceptance conformity
Productivity
Relations-oriented role
Self-oriented role
Task group
Task-oriented role

DISCUSSION QUESTIONS

1. Think of a group that you belong to and that is very important to you. Based on Figure 9–1 and the related discussion, at what stage of development is this group? What is the basis for your answer?

2. How would you assess the effects of size on a group of which you have been a member? Did group size affect your group in the ways shown in Table 9–1?

3. Identify three prevalent norms of a task group of which you have been a member. Do you think you or other group members conformed to these norms on the basis of compliance or personal acceptance? Explain.

4. Describe the leadership process of a task group of which you have been a member. Did there seem to be a task-oriented leader and a relations-oriented leader, or did one person perform both of these functions? Evaluate the group leader or leaders in terms of the types of behavior identified for effective group leaders in the chapter.

5. Using Table 9–3, describe and evaluate the content of group decisions that were made by a task group of which you have been a member. Should the group decisions have been changed for improved effectiveness? Explain.

6. What is meant by group cohesiveness? How is it related to group conformity?

7. What is meant by groupthink? Why is it likely to be a problem?

8. Is group decision making superior to individual decision making? Explain.

MANAGEMENT INCIDENTS AND CASES

Great Majestic Company

Robert Hoffman, the manager of the Great Majestic Lodge, was sitting at his desk and debating what he would say and what action he would take at a meeting with his bellmen, which was scheduled to begin in two hours.

He had just weathered a stormy encounter with Mr. Tomblin, the general manager of the Great Majestic Lodge and several other recreational and lodging facilities in the area.

Mr. Tomblin was visibly upset by an action taken by the bellmen at Great Majestic Lodge three weeks ago. At the end of the explosive meeting, Mr. Tomblin roared, "Bob, I don't care if you fire the whole damn bunch! I want you to do something about this right now!"

Background

Great Majestic Lodge was located in a popular park in the western United States. It was rather remote, yet offered all the modern conveniences featured at any fine metropolitan hotel. Because of its size and accommodations, the lodge was a favorite spot for large, organized tours. Most of the tours stayed one night and none stayed over two days. They were good moneymakers for the lodge because they always kept their schedules, paid their bills promptly, and were usually gone very early on checkout day.

Most of the employees hired by the Great Majestic Company were college students. This was an ideal situation, because the opening and closing dates of the lodge corresponded to most universities' summer vacations. The employees lived and ate at the company facilities and were paid $105 a month.

The Lodge Bellmen

The bellmen at the Great Majestic Lodge were directly responsible to the lodge manager, Mr. Hoffman. They were college students who, before being chosen for the bellman position, had worked for the company at least three summers. A total of seven were chosen on the basis of their past work performance, loyalty, efficiency, and ability to work with the public. Mr. Tomblin, the general manager, chose the bellmen himself.

The position of bellman was considered by the employees to be prestigious and important. In the eyes of the public, the bellmen represented the Great Majestic Lodge in every aspect. They were the first ones to greet the guests upon arrival, the people the guests called when anything was needed or went wrong, and the last ones to see the guests off upon their departure. Clad in their special cowboy apparel complete with personalized name tags and company insignia, the bellmen functioned as an effective public relations force for the Great Majestic Lodge, as well as providing prompt and professional service for each guest.

The bellmen all lived together in the back area of the most secluded employees' dorm at the Great Majestic Lodge. This facility was shared with most of the other lodge employees who had been with the company for two years or more. The older student-employees were especially close-knit, and all were looking forward to the time they would have the opportunity to be chosen as bellmen. The first-year employees usually occupied a dorm to themselves, adjacent to the seniority dorm. For the most part, a warm comradeship was experienced among all the staff at the lodge.

Traditionally, the bellmen had a comfortable relationship with Mr. Tomblin. This latest incident was of great concern to Mr. Hoffman. He realized that Mr. Tomblin was dead serious about firing them. It was midsummer, and it would be difficult to find qualified replacements. The bellmen this year had been especially productive.

The bellmen were paid a dollar per hour plus tips, which they pooled and divided equally at the end of each week. Daily tips averaged $20 per man. Hoffman was particularly concerned about the situation because it involved employees for whom he was directly responsible.

Organized Tours

The bellmen had the responsibility of placing the tour luggage in the guests' rooms as soon as the bus arrived. The front desk provided them with a list of guests' names and the assigned cottage numbers. Speed was particularly important, because the guests wanted to freshen up and demanded that their bags be delivered promptly.

On the morning of departure, the guests left their packed bags in their rooms while they went to breakfast. The bellmen picked up the bags, counted them, and then loaded them on the bus.

As payment for the service rendered by the bellmen, the tour directors paid fifty cents per bag. This was the standard gratuity paid by all tours. It was considered a tip, but it was included in the tour expenses by each company. On large tours, the tip could range as high as $75, although the average was $40.

The Jones Transportation Agency

The Jones Transportation Agency had a reputation throughout the area of being fair and equitable with their gratuities. However, one of their tour directors, Mr. Sirkin, did not live up to the company's reputation. On a visit to the Great Majestic Lodge, Mr. Sirkin had not given a tip. The bellmen knew their service to Mr. Sirkin had been very good. They were upset about the situation but assumed Sirkin had forgotten the tip in the rush before his tour departed. The tour was large and the tip would have amounted to $65.

Mr. Sirkin's tour also stayed at several other nearby resorts. Several of the Majestic Lodge bellmen knew the bellmen at the other lodges and, in discussing the situation, discovered that Mr. Sirkin had neglected the tip at each of the other lodges. It was apparent that Mr. Sirkin had

made a profit of more than $180 on his four-day tour through the region.

The Letter

Upon hearing of Sirkin's actions, the Majestic Lodge bellmen decided that some action had to be taken. They immediately ruled out telling Mr. Hoffman. On previous occasions when there had been a problem, Mr. Hoffman had done very little to alleviate the situation.

Roger Sikes, a first-year bellman and a business undergraduate, suggested that a letter be written directly to the president of Jones Transportation Agency. He felt that the agency would appreciate knowing one of their tour directors had misused company funds. After some discussion, the other bellmen present agreed. Sikes prepared a detailed letter, which told the Jones president the details of the Sirkin incident. The bellmen didn't expect to recover the money from the tour, but they felt that this was the appropriate action to take.

Five of the bellmen signed the letter as soon as it was completed. Two more opposed but, after more discussion and considerable peer-group pressure, agreed to sign the letter. It was mailed with the expectation of a speedy reply and justice for the offending Mr. Sirkin.

Reaction to the Letter

Three weeks after the bellmen's letter had been mailed to the Jones Transportation Agency, Mr. Tomblin was thumbing through his morning mail. He noticed a letter from his good friend Grant Cole, the president of the Jones Transportation Agency. Mr. Tomblin opened this letter first. Mr. Cole had written that there was a problem at the Great Majestic Lodge and he thought Mr. Tomblin should be made aware of it.

He enclosed the letter from the bell-men and suggested that, if the bell-men had any problems with any Jones directors in the future, it might be wise for them to speak to Mr. Tomblin before any action was taken. Mr. Cole informed Mr. Tomblin that Jones was investigating the Sirkin incident.

Mr. Tomblin was enraged. The bellmen had totally ignored their supervisor and had written a letter without first consulting any of the managers of the entire Great Majestic Company. This was not only a breach of company policy, but a personal humiliation for Mr. Tomblin.

Mr. Tomblin, yelling with outrage, leaped to his feet and charged through the lobby to Hoffman's office. He spotted bellman George Fletcher and ordered him to get out of his sight. The bewildered Fletcher quickly obeyed.

Robert Hoffman's meeting with Mr. Tomblin was an unpleasant experience. He had never seen Mr. Tomblin so upset at actions of employees. Mr. Tomblin was a proud man, and, because his pride had been hurt, he wanted revenge. He showed Hoffman the bellmen's letter and the reply from Grant Cole. Mr. Tomblin made it clear that he expected some quick action. Hoffman knew that the action had to meet Mr. Tomblin's approval. Hoffman's position as manager was suddenly placed in a precarious position.

There had been several employees in the lobby when Mr. Tomblin roared through. Hoffman knew the gossip would spread quickly throughout the lodge. The bellmen were well liked by the other employees and he knew they would be concerned about the bellmen's fate.

Hoffman called the still shaken George Fletcher into his office and told him to summon the off-duty bellmen for a meeting. After Fletcher left, Robert Hoffman attempted to think of alternatives that would

satisfy Mr. Tomblin and also provide the expected quality service to the guests.[43]

Questions

1. What norms and social factors appear to have played a part in the behaviors of the bellmen?
2. What organizational and environmental factors are relevant in this situation to the bellmen and Hoffman?
3. What should Hoffman do? Why?

Artisan Industries

Part I

In mid-October, 29-year-old Bill Meister, president of Artisan Industries, had to meet with his management group to consider increasing prices. A year before, he had taken over the failing $9-million-a-year, wooden-gift manufacturing company from his father. It had been a hectic year, but he had arrested the slide to bankruptcy. However, much work was still needed in almost every area of the company. People in his office for an 11:00 A.M. meeting are described in the following paragraphs.

Bob was the 30-year-old VP of finance. He had three years with the company, coming from the staff of a Big Eight accounting firm. He headed accounting and the office staff in general.

Cal was 35 years old and had been with the company eight years. Although he had a bachelor's degree in accounting, he had held many jobs in the company. Now he was installing a small computer system and reported to Bob.

Edith was Bill's 40-year-old sister and manager of the routine sales activity as it interfaced with the home office. The sales force was made up of independent sales reps. Only clerical people reported to Edith. She had no college training.

Bill called the meeting to order in the presence of a management consultant who happened to be visiting to discuss other plans for improvement.

Bill: OK. We've been discussing the need for a price increase for some time now. Bob recommends increasing prices 16 percent right away. I'd like to get all of your thoughts on this. Bob?

Bob: My analysis of profit statements to date indicates that a 16-percent increase is necessary right now if we are to have any profit this year. My best estimate is that we're losing money on every order we take. We haven't raised prices in over a year and have no choice but to do so now.

Cal: I agree. What's the sense in taking orders on which we lose money?

Bob: Exactly. If we raise prices across the board immediately, we can have a profit of about $300,000 at year's end.

Cal: It would've been better to have increased prices with our price list last May or June rather than doing it on each order here in the middle of our sales season, but we really have no choice now.

Bob: There's just no way we can put it off.

Bill [pausing, looking around the room]: So, you all recommend a price increase at this time?

Cal and Bob: Yes.

Bob: We can't wait to increase prices as new orders are written in the field or through a new price list. Right now we already have enough of a backlog of orders accepted at the old prices and orders awaiting our acknowledgement to fill the plant until the season ends in six to eight weeks. We must only accept orders at the new prices.

Cal: If we acknowledge all the orders we have now, like that 30-page one Edith has for $221,000, then the price change won't even be felt this year.

Bob: No, we should not acknowledge any orders at the old prices. I would hold the orders and send each customer a printed letter telling them of the price increase and asking them to reconfirm their orders with an enclosed mailer if they still want them.

Cal: Orders already acknowledged would keep the plant busy until they responded.

Bill: So, is this the best thing to do?

Bob: We're in business to make money; we'd be crazy not to raise prices!

Bill: Edith, you look unhappy. What do you think?

Edith [shrugging]: I don't know.

Bob [visibly impatient]: We're losing money on every order.

Edith: I'm just worried about trying to raise prices right in the middle of the season.

Cal: Well, if we wait, we might as well forget it.

Bob: Just what would you suggest we do, Edith?

Edith: I don't know. [Pause.] This order [picking up the 30-page order] took the salesman a month to work up with the customer. There are over 175 items on it, and the items must be redistributed to the customer's nine retail outlets in time for Christmas. I'm worried about it.

Bob: It's worthless to us as it is.

Cal: Look, in our letter we can mention inflation and that this is our first increase in a long while. Most customers will understand this. We've got to try. It's worth the risk, isn't it Edith?

[Edith shrugs.]

Bill: What do you suggest, Edith?

Edith: I don't know. We need the increase, but it bothers me.

Bob: Business is made of tough decisions; managers are paid to make 'em.

[All become quiet, look around the room, and finally look at Bill.]

Questions for Part I

1. Explain what happened at this meeting: What was each person's role? What was each person doing and trying to do? Diagram the interactions. Was it a good meeting? Why?

2. What is the decision going to be? Give all the specifics of the decision.

3. What do you think of the decision? Can you think of ways to improve upon it?

4. What would you do if you were there?

Part II

Consultant [calmly]: I think Edith has raised a good point. We *are* considering making a big move in the middle of our busy season. It will cause problems. If we can't avoid the increase, then what can we do to avoid or minimize the problems?

Bob [hostile and obviously disgusted]: It would be ridiculous to put off the price increase.

Consultant [calmly]: That may be true, but is it being done in the best way? There are always alternatives to consider. I don't think we are doing a good job of problem solving here. [Pause.] Even with the basic idea of an increase, it can be done poorly or done well. There is room for more thought. How can it be done

with the least penalty? [All quiet, as consultant looks around the group, waiting for anyone to add comments. Hearing none.] For example, by the time we mail them a letter and they think about it and mail it back, two or three weeks may pass. The price increase wouldn't take effect until the season is almost over. How can we get the increase to make money for us right away? And though we are bound to lose some orders, what can we do to minimize these? [Pausing to allow comments.]

Edith: Yes, that's what I meant.

Consultant: On this order, for example [picking up the $221,000 order], we could call them right now and explain the situation and possibly be shipping at the higher prices *this afternoon.*

Bob [with no hostility, and with apparent positive attitude]: OK. I will call them as soon as we leave here.

Cal: We have a pile of orders awaiting acknowledgement . . . .

Bob: Right, we can get some help and pick out the bigger orders and start calling them this afternoon.

Consultant: How about involving the sales force?

Edith: Yes, the salespeople know the customers best. We should call them to contact the customer. They got the order and know the customer's needs. But we will have to convince the salespeople of the necessity of the increase. I can start getting in touch with them by phone right away.

Bob: OK, we can handle the bigger orders personally by phone and use the letter on the small ones.

Consultant: What do you think about making them act *to keep* the order? Why not make it so *no action* keeps the order? Tell them that we are saving their place in our shipping schedule and will go ahead and ship if they don't contact us in five to seven days. Is it best to put the control in their hands?

Edith: That bothered me. Increasing the price is serious, and we need to handle it carefully if it's to work. I think most people will go ahead and accept the merchandise.

Bob: Edith and I can get together this afternoon on the letter. [All become silent again.]

Bill: OK, can you all get started after lunch? Let's meet in the morning to see how it's going.[44]

Questions for Part II

1. What do you think of the decision now? Is it improved? Why might you call the first decision "suboptimal"?

2. Would the group have made the new decision without help? Why?

3. It can be said that, initially, the group was not involved in problem solving. Why?

4. What did the consultant see that had to be done with the group? How could she do it? Did the consultant want to make the decisions herself? Could Bill have taken this role?

5. What does this incident say about the management team and the work environment at Artisan? What should and could be done about it?

6. What does the case illustrate about group problem solving? About communication?

REFERENCES

1. Reprinted, by permission of the publisher, from "A Closer Look at Participation," by S. R. Hinckley, Jr., *Organizational Dynamics*, Winter 1985, pp. 61–62. © 1985. Periodicals Division, American Management Association, New York. All rights reserved.

2. Gladstein, D. L. Groups in Context: A Model of Task Group Effectiveness. *Administrative Science Quarterly*, 1984, *29*, 419–517; Hinckley Jr., S. R. A Closer Look at Participation. *Organizational Dynamics*, Winter 1985, 57–67; Jewell, L. N., and Reitz, H. J. *Group Effectiveness in Organizations*. Glenview, Ill.: Scott, Foresman, 1981; Whitsett, D. A., and Yorks, L. Looking Back at Topeka: General Foods and the Quality-of-Work-Life Experiment. *California Management Review*, Summer 1983, 93–109; Yorks, L., and Whitsett, D. A. Hawthorne, Topeka, and the Issue of Science versus Advocacy in Organizational Behavior. *Academy of Management Review*, 1985, *10*,, 21–30.

3. Homans, G. C. *The Human Group*. New York: Harcourt, Brace and World, 1959, 2. Also see Miller, J. Living Systems: The Group. *Behavioral Science*, 1971, *16*, 302–398.

4. Gustafsan, J. B., *et al.* Cooperative and Clashing Interests in Small Groups, Part I: Theory. *Human Relations*, 1981, *34*, 315–339; Keller, R. T. The Harvard "Pareto Circle" and the Historical Development of Organization Theory. *Journal of Management*, 1984, *10*, 193–203; Swap, W. C. Destructive Effects of Groups on Individuals. In W. C. Swap and Associates (Eds.) *Group Decision Making*. Beverly Hills, Calif.: Sage, 1984, 69–96; Eddy, W. B. *The Manager and the Working Group*. New York: Praeger, 1985.

5. Cartwright, D., and Lippitt, R. Group Dynamics and the Individual. *International Journal of Group Psychotherapy*, 1957, *7*, 86–102. Also see Mossholder, K. W., Bedeian, A. G., and Armenakis, A. A. Group Process–Work Outcome Relationships: A Note on the Moderating Impact of Self-Esteem. *Academy of Management Journal*, 1982, *25*, 579–585; Wanous, J. P., Reichers, A. E., and Malik, S. D. Organizational Socialization and Group Development: Toward an Integrative Perspective. *Academy of Management Review*, 1984, *9*, 670–683.

6. Fiedler, F. *A Theory of Leadership Effectiveness*. New York: McGraw-Hill, 1967.

7. Tuckman, B. W. Development Sequence in Small Groups. *Psychological Bulletin*, 1965, *63*, 384–399; Tuckman, B. W., and Jensen, M. A. C. Stages of Small Group

Development Revisited. *Group and Organization Studies*, 1977, *2*, 419–427. Also see Srivastva, S., Obert, S. L., and Neilsen, E. H. Organizational Analysis through Group Processes: A Theoretical Perspective for Organization Development. In C. Cooper (Ed.) *Organizational Development in the UK and USA*. London: Macmillian, 1977; Obert, S. L. Developmental Patterns of Organizational Task Groups: A Preliminary Study. *Human Relations*, 1983, *36*, 37–52.

8. Kormanski, C. A Situational Leadership Approach to Groups Using the Tuckman Model of Group Development. In L. D. Goodstein and J. W. Pfeiffer (Eds.) *The 1985 Annual: Developing Human Resources*. San Diego: University Associates, 1985, 217–226.

9. Napier, R. W., and Gershenfeld, M. K. *Groups: Theory and Experience*, 3d ed. Boston: Houghton Mifflin, 1985, 459–460.

10. Berelson, B., and Steiner, G. *Human Behavior: An Inventory of Scientific Findings*. New York: Harcourt, Brace and World, 1964, 356–360.

11. Hare, A. P. Group Size. *American Behavioral Scientist*, 1981, *24*, 695–708; Markham, S. E., Dansereau Jr., F., and Alutto, J. A. Group Size and Absenteeism Rates: A Longitudinal Analysis. *Academy of Management Journal*, 1982, *25*, 921–927.

12. Bertcher, H. J., and Maple, H. J. *Creating Groups*. Beverly Hills, Calif.: Sage, 1977; Argyris, C. *Strategy Change and Defensive Routines*. Marshfield, Mass.: Pitman, 1985.

13. Hoffman, L. R. Applying Experimental Research on Group Problem Solving to Organizations. *Journal of Applied Behavioral Science*, 1979, *15*, 375–391.

14. Bales, R. F. *Interaction Process Analysis: A Method for the Study of Groups*. Reading, Mass.: Addison-Wesley, 1950; Bales, R. F. *Personality and Interpersonal Behavior*. New York: Holt, Rinehart, and Winston, 1970; Nicholson, N. A Theory of Work Role Transitions. *Administrative Science Quarterly*, 1984, *29*, 172–191; Pearce II, J. A., and David, F. R. A Social Network Approach to Organizational Design Performance. *Academy of Management Review*, 1983, *8*, 436–444.

15. Hare, A. P. *The Handbook of Small Group Research*, 2d ed. New York: Macmillan, 1976, 19.

16. Reprinted and adapted with permission from: *The Ropes to Skip and the Ropes to Know* by R. Richard Ritti and G. Ray Funkhouser. Grid Publishing, Inc., Columbus, Ohio, 1977, 188–189.

17. Allen, P. F., and Pilnick, S. Confronting the Shadow Organizations: How to Detect and Defeat Negative Norms. *Organizational Dynamics*, Spring 1973, 3–18; Pearce, J. L., and Peters, R. H. A Contradictory Norms View of Employer–Employee Exchange. *Journal of Management*, 1985, *11*, 19–30.

18. Feldman, D. C. The Development and Enforcement of Group Norms. *Academy of Management Review*, 1984, *9*, 47–53. Also see Spich, R. S., and Keleman, R. S. Explicit Norm Structuring Process: A Strategy for Increasing Task-Group Effectiveness. *Group & Organizational Studies*, 1985, *10*, 37–59.

19. Kiesler, C., and Kiesler, S. *Conformity*. Reading, Mass.: Addison-Wesley, 1969.

20. Bertcher, H. J. *Group Participation: Techniques for Leaders and Members*. Beverly Hills, Calif.: Sage, 1979.

21. Roethlisberger, F. J., and Dickson, W. J. *Management and the Worker: Technical versus Social Organization in an Industrial Plant*. Cambridge, Mass.: Harvard University Press, 1939. Also see Porac, J. F., Ferris, G. R., and Fedor, D. B. Causal Attributions, Affect, and Expectations for a Day's Work Performance. *Academy of Management Journal*, 1983, *26*, 285–296.

22. Mills, T. M. *The Sociology of Small Groups*. Englewood Cliffs, N.J.: Prentice-Hall, 1967.

23. Excerpts from Freedman, Audrey. *Japanese Management of U.S. Work Forces*, Report #865, New York: The Conference Board, 1982, 11–12. Used with permission.

24. Philip, H., and Dunphy, D. Development Trends in Small Groups. *Sociometry*, 1954, *22*, 162–174; Stokes, J. P. Components of Group Cohesion: Intermember Attraction, Instrumental Value, and Risk Taking. *Small Group Behavior*, 1983, *14*, 163–173; Watson, K. M. A Methodology for the Study of Organizational Behavior at the Interpersonal Level of Analysis. *Academy of Management Review*, 1982, *7*, 392–402.

25. Janis, I. L. *Victims of Groupthink: A Psychological Study of Foreign Policy Decisions and Fiascos*. Boston: Houghton Mifflin, 1972; Janis, I. L. *Groupthink*, 2d ed. Boston: Houghton Mifflin, 1982. For a study that questions the relation between groupthink and high cohesiveness, see Leana, C. R. A Partial Test of Janis' Groupthink Model: Effects of Group Cohesiveness and Leader Behavior on Defective Decision Making. *Journal of Management*, 1985, *11*, 5–17.

26. Huseman, R. C., and Driver, R. W. Groupthink: Implications for Small Group Decision Making in Business. In R. C. Huseman and A. B. Carroll (Eds.) *Readings in Organizational Behavior: Di-*

mensions of Management Actions. Boston: Allyn and Bacon, 1979, 100–110.

27. Adapted by permission of the publisher, from "Groupthink: When Too Many Heads Spoil the Decision", by C. W. Van Bergen, Jr. and R. J. Kirk, *Management Review*, March 1978, 46–48. © 1978 by AMACOM, a division of American Management Associations, New York. All rights reserved.

28. Seashore, S. *Group Cohesiveness in the Industrial Work Group*. Ann Arbor, Mich.: University of Michigan Survey Research Center, 1954. Also see Seers, A., *et al.* The Interaction of Job Stress and Social Support: A Strong Inference Investigation. *Academy of Management Journal*, 1983, *26*, 273–284; Brown, K. A. Explaining Group Poor Performance: An Attributional Analysis. *Academy of Management Review*, 1984, *9*, 54–63; Dorfman, P. W. and Stephan, W. G. The Effects of Group Performance on Cognitions, Satisfaction, and Behavior: A Process Model. *Journal of Management*, 1984, *10*, 173–192.

29. Bales, R. F. *Interaction Process Analysis*. Reading, Mass.: Addison-Wesley, 1950; Napier, R. W., and Gershenfeld, M. K. *Making Groups Work: A Guide for Group Leaders*. Boston: Houghton Mifflin, 1983.

30. Crockett, W. Emergent Leadership in Small, Decision-Making Groups. *Journal of Abnormal and Social Psychology*, 1955, *51*, 378–383. Also see Podsakoff, P. M., and Todor, W. D. Relationships between Leader Reward and Punishment Behavior and Group Processes and Productivity. *Journal of Mangement*, 1985, *11*, 55–73: Bennis, W., and Nanus, B. *Leaders: The Strategies for Taking Charge*. New York: Harper & Row, 1985.

31. Davis, T. R. The Influence of the Physical Environment in Offices. *Academy of Management Review*, 1984, *9*, 171–283; Fry, L. W., and Slocum Jr., J. W. Technology, Structure, and Workgroup Effectiveness: A Test of a Contingency Model. *Academy of Management Journal*, 1984, *27*, 221–246; Leatt, P., and Schneck, R. Criteria for Grouping Nursing Subunits in Hospitals. *Academy of Management Journal*, 1984, *27*, 150–165; Nelsen, N. E., and Reimann, B. C. Work Environment and Grievance Rates in a Manufacturing Plant. *Journal of Management*, 1983, *9*, 145–158; Oldham, G. R., and Rotchford, N. L. Relationships between Office Characteristics and Employee Reactions: A Study of the Physical Environment. *Administrative Science Quarterly*, 1983, *28*, 542–556.

32. Sashkin, M. Changing toward Participative Management Approaches: A Model and Methods. *Academy of Management Review*, 1976, *1*, 75–86; Sashkin, M. Participative Management is an Ethical Imperative. *Organizational Dynamics*, Spring 1984, 4–22; Zander, A. *Groups at Work*. San Francisco: Jossey-Bass, 1977.

33. Morris, W. C., and Sashkin, M. *Organization Behavior in Action: Skill Building Experiences*. St. Paul, Minn.: West, 1976.

34. Hare, A. P. *Creativity in Small Groups*. Beverly Hills, Calif.: Sage, 1982; Krantz, J. Group Process under Conditions of Decline. *Journal of Applied Behavioral Science*, 1985, *21*, 1–18; Seeger, J. A. No Innate Phases in Group Problem Solving. *Academy of Management Review*, 1983, *8*, 683–689.

35. Excerpts from Lindsay, C. P., and Dempsey, B. L. Experiences in Training Chinese Business People to use U.S. Management Techniques. *Journal of Applied Behavioral Science*, 1985, *21*, 65–78. JAI Press, Greenwich, Connecticut. Used with permission of publisher and authors.

36. Erffmeyer, R. C., and Lane, I. M. Quality and Acceptance of an Evaluative Task: The Effects of Four Group Decision-Making Formats. *Group and Organization Studies*, 1984, *9*, 509–529; Hart, S., *et al.* Managing Complexity through Consensus Mapping: Technology for the Structuring of Group Decisions. *Academy of Management Review* [to be published in July, 1985 issue]; Hackman, J. R. *A Normative Model of Work Team Effectiveness*. Technical Report #2. New Haven, Conn.: Research Programs on Group Effectiveness and Management, Yale School of Organization and Management, November 1983; Stumpf, S. A., Zand, D. E., and Freedman, R. D. Designing Groups for Judgmental Decisions. *Academy of Management Review*, 1979, *4*, 589–600.

37. Adapted from Woodman, R. W. Use of the Nominal Group Technique for Idea Generation and Decision Making. *Texas Business Executive*, Spring 1981, 50.

38. Major portions of this discussion of the nominal group technique are excerpted from Woodman, R. W. Use of the Nominal Group Technique for Idea Generation and Decision Making. *Texas Business Executive*, Spring 1981, 50–53.

39. Delbecq, A. L., Van de Ven, A. H., and Gustafson, D. H. *Group Techniques for Program Planning: A Guide to Nominal and Delphi Processes*. Glenview, Ill.: Scott, Foresman, 1975.

40. Bartunek, J. M., and Murninghan, J. K. The Nominal Group Technique: Expanding the Basic Procedure and Underlying Assumptions. *Group and Organization Studies*, 1984, *9*, 417–432.

41. Huber, G., and Delbecq, A. L. Guidelines for Combining the Judgments of Individ-

ual Group Members in Decision Conferences. *Academy of Management Journal,* 1972, *15,* 161–174.

42. Green, T. B. An Empirical Analysis of Nominal and Interacting Groups. *Academy of Management Journal,* 1975, *18,* 63–73.

43. The Great Majestic Company. Reprinted by permission from *Organizations and People*, Third Edition, by J. B. Ritchie and Paul Thompson. Copyright © 1976, 1980, 1984 by West Publishing Co., All rights reserved.

44. Prepared by and adapted with permission from Barnes, F. C. associate professor, University of North Carolina at Charlotte (presented at Southern Case Research Association).

10 Dynamics between Groups

LEARNING OBJECTIVES

When you have finished studying this chapter, you should be able to:

■ Describe the basic factors that often affect the dynamics between two or more groups within organizations.

■ Diagnose the causes of cooperative versus competitive and conflictual relations between groups within organizations.

■ Explain how intragroup dynamics can be affected as a result of winning or losing in intergroup competition.

■ Identify the conditions under which group power is likely to increase or decrease.

■ Describe the mechanisms for managing intergroup dynamics within organizations.

OUTLINE

Preview Case

The Drawing Division

The Drawing Division consisted of 250 employees and was part of a large corporation. The major task of the Drawing Division was to produce the engineering drawings needed to install electronic equipment. A large proportion of the customer requests that came to the division were routine and could be filled from the division files, which contained standard prints. The division was also responsible for the orders that required custom designs.

The division had three major departments—sales, production, and research. Each department was further divided into work groups. The sales department had 74 employees in five work groups; production had 123 employees in four work groups; and research had 53 employees in five work groups. Routine orders were received by the sales department, which verified or clarified all necessary information and then passed the orders to the production department. Production then obtained the appropriate drawings and sent them to the Manufacturing Division, a group outside the Drawing Division which was responsible for making the equipment. Nonroutine orders involved the research department. If the production department did not have an appropriate drawing on file, it would contact the research department which would create the drawing. The production department would add the copy of the new drawing to its files and pass the drawing on to the Manufacturing Division. To accomplish the tasks of the Drawing Division, its members had to interact with several other divisions in addition to the Manufacturing Division.

In each department within the Drawing Division, the day-to-day contact was highest among members of each work group and next highest among members of the departments immediately adjacent in the workflow. Members of departments at the beginning and end of the workflow reported the least amount of contact with each other. For example, the sales department had little contact with the research department, but extensive contact with the production department.

The Drawing Division brought together two different professional disciplines. The sales department personnel identified with customer service. Their objective was to meet customer needs at the lowest possible cost. The production department and the research department personnel identified with engineering. Their objective was to develop the best possible technical solution for customer problems. The existence of the Drawing Division testified to the need for bringing the two professional disciplines together. However, the major political struggle in the Drawing Division was due to members' perceptions of discrimination between the disciplines with regard to allocation of scarce resources (i.e., people, pay, promotions) at both the division and corporate levels. For example, higher management was perceived by the employees in production and research as favoring sales.[1]

The Preview Case touches on the importance of the dynamics between groups—both vertically and laterally—in accomplishing organizational goals. Work groups within each department had to interact and cooperate to accomplish their own goals. Each department within the drawing division—sales, production, and research—also had to interact and cooperate to accomplish their departmental goals. Finally, the drawing division as a whole had to interact and cooperate with the top management group, the manufacturing division, and other divisions to accomplish its goals. The Preview Case is one example of the general finding that organizations have an ongoing need to manage the dynamics between groups.

An understanding of intergroup relations is important to all managers because (1) groups often must work with and through other groups to accomplish their goals; and (2) other groups within the organization often create problems and demands on managers' own groups—whether they be called work groups, departments, or divisions. At the same time, managers should recognize that many of the behavior processes and issues discussed in other chapters, such as individual styles and motivation, intragroup processes, and leadership, also greatly affect intergroup processes, or dynamics. The factors affecting behaviors and outputs in intergroup relations are influenced by (and influence, in turn) interpersonal and intragroup dynamics. This constitutes a matrix of interactions that is implicit in our discussion of intergroup relations.

Chapter 9 focused on the dynamics within an interacting group of 12 or fewer individuals. This chapter focuses primarily on the dynamics between groups of various sizes. The meaning of group in this chapter goes beyond the definition involving face-to-face relations used in Chapter 9. In this chapter, *group* could indicate a work group (like the five work groups in the sales department in the Preview Case), a department (like the sales, production, and research departments in the Preview Case), or a division (like the drawing division and the manufacturing division in the Preview Case).

As noted in Chapter 9, groups are not always part of the formal organizational structure, as is a sales department or a drawing division. Therefore, in considering intergroup dynamics, the concept of coalition is useful. For our purposes, a **coalition** is an alliance of individuals formed to exert united action to achieve one or more common goals.[2] Coalitions can form on the basis of a variety of criteria such as religion, educational background, race, or occupation. In this chapter we discuss intergroup relations as they apply to groups such as departments, divisions, and various types of coalitions.

In the first section of the chapter we present six basic factors that independently—or in combination with other factors—often influence intergroup behaviors and outputs. In the second section, we discuss six mechanisms that independently—or in combination with other mechanisms—can be used to create effective intergroup behaviors and outputs between lateral groups. Although we consider some aspects of intergroup conflict in this chapter, we will deal with intergroup conflict much more extensively in Chapter 17. For example, we present the mechanisms for resolving or reducing intergroup conflicts in Chapter 17.

SOME FACTORS INFLUENCING INTERGROUP BEHAVIORS AND OUTPUTS

A variety of factors influence behaviors and outputs in intergroup relations, and two or more of these factors usually interact in group processes. Figure

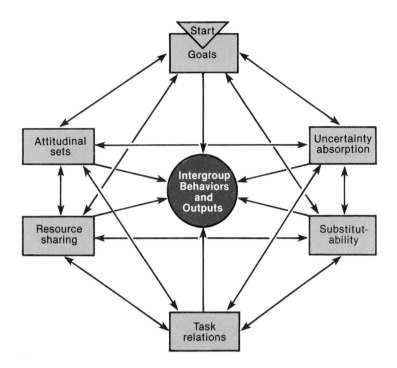

FIGURE 10–1.
Some Factors
Affecting Intergroup
Behaviors and
Outputs

10-1 identifies six basic factors that often affect the dynamics between two or more groups: goals, uncertainty absorption, substitutability, task relations, resource sharing, and attitudinal sets. The two-way lines connecting factors in Figure 10-1 reflect the idea that all of them—and possibly others not reviewed here—may interact and should be diagnosed to obtain a complete understanding of the dynamics between two or more groups.

Goals

The goals of groups can have a powerful impact on their behaviors and outputs, and, like individuals, groups use goals to reveal their preferences.[3] The ideal state exists in an organization when each group perceives its goals, the goals of the organization as a whole, and the goals of other groups as compatible with each other and mutually reinforcing. This is a win–win situation. Each group can attain its goal if the other groups attain theirs. In this situation, we usually find free-flowing communication, cooperation, mutual concern, respect for each other's problems, and rapid problem solving between groups. However, goals are not always perceived or designed to be compatible and mutually reinforcing.

GOAL CONFLICT When goal achievement by one group is perceived as preventing or reducing the level of goal attainment by one or more other groups, **goal conflict** occurs. Widespread goal incompatibility, a win–lose situation, is unlikely within an organization. A win–lose situation does exist, however, when one group attains its goal at the direct expense of another group. On occasion, confrontation between a union and management takes on the characteristics of extreme win–lose situations, particularly in bitter strike situations. These may include expressions of extreme hostility, some physical violence and property damage, unwillingness of the parties to listen to one another or compromise, and the like. Examples of strikes in recent years with win–lose characteristics include (1) the strike of Continental Airlines by the pilots' union; (2) the nearly year-long strike of the coal miners in Great Britain; and (3) the strike of the U.S. Federal Aviation Authority (FAA) by the flight controllers' union. In the case of the flight controllers' strike, the striking employees were fired and the union failed. The win–lose outcome between the groups in this strike was clear-cut: the FAA achieved its goals; the failed union and fired flight controllers did not attain their goals.

MIXED GOAL CONFLICT   Goal conflict between groups is more often mixed goal conflict than a total win–lose situation. For example, up to a certain level of goal attainment, no perceived or real conflict may exist between the groups. In the Preview Case, the production department in the drawing division may believe its efficiency goal is attainable so long as the sales department does not bring in an excessive number of nonroutine orders. The sales department, in its effort to increase its sales goal, increasingly promises clients customized features. This places extra demands on the production department. But, production comes to believe that sales is taking the easy way out by not trying hard enough to sell the drawings that are on file. This also makes it impossible for production to reach its efficiency goal for the year. Given this situation, the seeds for mixed goal conflict have been planted.

Goal conflict or mixed goal conflict often serves as a basis for the creation of coalitions in organizations.[4] Let us consider a brief example of the potential power of a coalition. Several years ago an executive of one of the divisions of a supplier of tools and equipment for oil and gas drilling issued a memorandum to the 8,000 employees under his jurisdiction forbidding women to wear slacks at work. At that time, the division had centralized computer operations. Twenty-eight of the women who kept the centralized computer system operating on a day-to-day basis walked off the job. These women were not members of a union. The whole division needed the information and reports from this computer center to perform their jobs. However, there was no other group of individuals who knew how to operate the computer system. This small coalition of women discovered that they had significant power. The executive reversed his order within 48 hours. These women immediately returned to work and resumed performing their jobs effectively.

INTERGROUP COMPETITION   Structured competition between groups represents an application of goal conflict. Intergroup competition relates most dramatically to goal conflict when the groups are interdependent. When Penn State and Pittsburgh, Texas A&M and the University of Texas, or UCLA and USC meet on the football field each year, each wants to win over its opponent. They are supposed to compete, not collaborate.

Outcomes are predictable when competing groups are interdependent and interact. The following questions and answers highlight these outcomes:

- *What happens within each competing group?* Each group becomes more cohesive and obtains greater loyalty from its members; members close ranks and bury some of their differences. Each group increases its task orientation relative to social and affective concerns. Leadership becomes more structured and authoritarian, and the group members more willingly accept this type of leadership. Finally, each group demands more loyalty and conformity so it can present a united front to the other group(s).

- *What happens between the competing groups?* Each group may begin to see the other as the enemy. Distortion of perceptions sets in, such as members perceiving their own group in positive terms and the other group in negative terms. Each group soon forms stereotypes and makes negative attributions of the other(s); for example, "They are dirty players." Each group feels and expresses increasing hostility toward the other. Interaction and communication decline. When the groups do interact, they tend to emphasize and listen only to their own concerns and to discount the statements of the other group(s).

- *What happens to the winner?* The winning group often becomes more cohesive and tends to release its tension in a victory celebration. Over time, the winner may become complacent ("fat and happy") and feel there is little need to reexamine its own internal functioning.

- *What happens to the loser?* The loser(s) may deny or distort the reality of losing. In sports, statements like the following are common: "The referees were biased" or "It was an unlucky day" or "The coach is terrible." When the losing group(s) accepts the loss, conflicts within the group(s) may surface, fights may break out, or some members may place the blame on other group members. As a result, there is more tension and less intragroup cooperation. Over time, the group may reevaluate its self-perceptions and stereotypes, which could lead to reorganization and other changes.[5]

SIGNIFICANCE TO MANAGEMENT   Thus the degree to which two or more interacting and interdependent groups perceive their goals to be compatible or conflicting can affect their behaviors and outputs. Complete compatibility in goals between groups is often not possible and may not always be desirable. The unique goals and specialization of group tasks inevitably creates some tunnel vision in the members of a group and naturally leads to a certain amount of goal conflict. The important questions, then, are to what degree goal conflict occurs between groups, what its effects are, and what mechanisms are available to manage it effectively.

Uncertainty Absorption

In its most basic sense, "**uncertainty** is the lack of information about future events".[6] One way of managing uncertainty involves creating particular groups or assigning particular people to deal with it. Some groups absorb particular types of uncertainty for other groups in the organization.[7] **Uncertainty absorption** occurs when one group makes particular decisions for another group or sets the decision-making premises for another group. For example, the accounting department may develop uniform procedures and guidelines for handling expense accounts. Thus accounting provides a sales manager with many ready-made answers about how to process expense accounts and how to determine what is an allowable expense. Accounting has absorbed the uncertainty that the sales manager otherwise might have experienced in handling expense account matters with sales representatives.

EFFECTS ON GROUP POWER   Uncertainty absorption often has an important impact on the relative power of groups. Power has three major dimensions: weight, domain, and scope.[8] The *weight* of a group's power is the degree to which the group can affect the behavior of another group. The *domain* of power for a group is the number of other groups it affects. The *scope* of a group's power is the range of behaviors or decisions that the group can determine for another group. In the previous example, the accounting department carries a heavy weight with respect to expense account procedures. Its domain in expense account matters is relatively encompassing, affecting virtually all members in marketing, as well as in other groups. Finally, the scope of behaviors affected in marketing by these procedures is probably small, relative to marketing's important behaviors and goals. The sources of power in organizations—as well as the relationships of individual and group power to decision making, information, and resources—will be discussed in chapter 16.

RELATION TO TECHNICAL EXPERTISE   The technical expertise of a group relative to others strongly influences the process of uncertainty absorption.[9] Recall the actions of the 28 women workers who kept the computer system operating on a day-to-day basis and walked off the job when told they could no longer wear slacks at work. These women shut down the centralized computer system for the whole division because only they had the needed technical expertise. These women had considerable power because of the uncertainty they absorbed for others with respect to a vital function: the centralized computer system.

The impact of technical expertise on uncertainty absorption and the amount of power it gives a group relative to others is normally limited to a specific area of knowledge and skills. Of course, the *importance* that others assign to this technical expertise influences the group's power. Let us look at the use of uncertainty absorption by a certain industrial relations department and the degree of importance given it by higher management. The uncertainty absorption and resulting power of the industrial relations department in relation to the production department occurred in one company of a conglomerate corporation.

In Practice: Industrial Relations Department

The most important tasks of the industrial relations department concerned the unions, including negotiating union–management agreements, processing grievances, and interpreting issues covered in the agreements. The mechanisms and practices by which the industrial relations department absorbed uncertainty for the production department stemmed heavily from the union's existence. A significant source of industrial relations' power relative to other departments within the scope of plant-level issues was industrial relations' use of the union as an "outside" threat that could adversely affect the whole organization.

One industrial relations manager recognized that the supposed antagonists, the unions, were a major source of industrial relations' internal power: "As I told one of the other industrial relations guys who was damning the unions, 'Don't bite the hand that feeds you.' " The union increased the need to maintain uniformity and coordination in industrial relations policies, practices, procedures, and rules. Without coordination, one plant might yield on union demands unimportant to them but of relevance to other companies or plants within the corporation.

To maintain and increase autonomy and power, the industrial relations department always claimed to possess the "bigger picture" that must be considered for decision making related to the organization's human resources. The inconsistent pressures of maintaining uniform labor relations policies, rules, procedures, and the like—while trying to give a reasonable amount of autonomy to managers within the companies and plants—created considerable uncertainty and some conflict. Because of these conflicting pressures (both within management and between management and the union), the industrial relations department played a key role in absorbing many of the uncertainties created.

The industrial relations department had superior knowledge of the bargaining agreements. They also had more skill and ability than others to apply that knowledge. Industrial relations people often asserted, "You never go by the wording in contracts. You go by the interpretation." Thus uncertainties in the meaning and interpretation of agreements were primarily absorbed by the industrial relations department. The industrial relations department was not part of the production department's chain of authority. Thus it could obtain information unavailable to others and bypass the plant's hierarchy. For example, industrial relations personnel regularly obtained extra information in their tours of the different manufacturing facilities. A key industrial relations representative was located in each manufacturing facility. Also, employees came to industrial relations personnel when they were afraid to go to their supervisors. Through such means, industrial relations could legitimately pick up bits and pieces of information and feelings about the true state of the organization that did not get into the plant managers' communication channels. This enabled the industrial relations department to absorb considerable uncertainty about emerging human resource problems in each of the plants.[10]

SIGNIFICANCE TO MANAGEMENT   Uncertainty absorption by groups is important for three reasons. First, uncertainty absorption forces higher management and others to decide which groups will have the discretion to make decisions that affect others. Second, uncertainty absorption influences the relative power of various groups—and individuals within those groups—in organizations. These power differences can be an important factor in understanding conflicts and other problems between groups. Third, uncertainty absorption requires the organization and others to make sure that the uncertainties being absorbed by groups are consistent with their knowledge and expertise.

Substitutability

Substitutability is the degree to which a group can obtain the services or goods provided by another group from alternative sources. If alternative services or goods are readily available, the power of the "service" group is probably weaker than if no alternatives existed.[11] In the case of the industrial relations department, there was no ready substitute for its services. However, if top management were willing to spend additional money, it could absorb some uncertainty by hiring external industrial relations consultants to evaluate the same issues as the industrial relations department, and provide independent diagnoses and recommendations. Top management could then more easily question and evaluate the activities of the industrial relations department.

LIMITS ON SUBSTITUTABILITY In order to utilize resources fully, organizations frequently have rules requiring that departments use the services provided by other departments within the organization.[12] For example, a marketing department that wants a new sales brochure printed has to go through the company's printing department rather than having the option to contract with an outside printing firm. The company might enforce this rule even if the marketing department could get the job done faster and at a lower price from an outside firm. From an organizational standpoint, the increased costs to marketing might be a less significant problem than low utilization of labor and equipment in the printing department.

SIGNIFICANCE TO MANAGEMENT Everything else being equal, the lower the substitutability of the services or activities of a group, the greater is its power within the organization.[13] Groups that provide vital and nonsubstitutable services often find the groups to which they provide these services trying one or two extreme strategies: (1) to win them over through the provision of extra rewards; or (2) trying to eliminate the service group or its management by complaints to higher management. Many managers of computer processing departments, for example, have been dismissed because they threatened higher management and other line groups. Computer processing departments provide vital and nonsubstitutable services. Thus the attempt to exercise too much power and control by a computer processing manager can create a backlash from others.

Task Relations

There are three basic types of possible task relations between two or more groups: independent, interdependent, and dependent. Relations between groups vary along a continuum from relative independence through varying degrees of interdependence to relative dependence. Figure 10-2 illustrates these three types of task relations between two groups.

INDEPENDENT TASK RELATIONS **Independent task relations** refer to the interactions between and mutual decision making by groups that occur only at the discretion of the group.[14] For example, some large organizations maintain internal consulting groups that contract, on mutually agreeable terms, to work with other departments. Corning Glass Company's Organizational Development Group operates principally in this way. For example, if a department at Corning wants to improve its problem-solving effectiveness in committee meetings, it can call in a representative from the Organizational Development Group to diagnose the problems and assist in changing the processes. Once groups start working together, their relations are interdependent for the duration of the project. However, if both groups have the freedom to withdraw from the relationship at will, they probably perceive a relatively independent task relationship, with neither group having much power relative to the other.

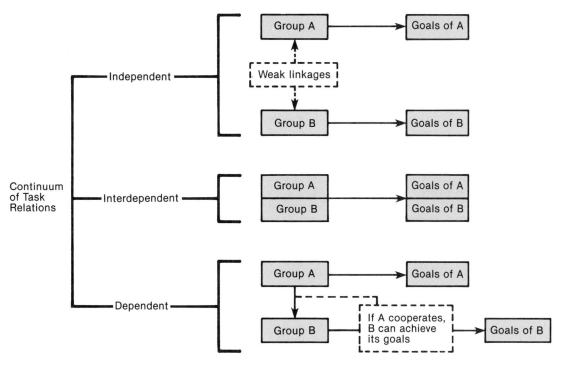

FIGURE 10–2.
Basic Types of Task Relations between Groups

INTERDEPENDENT TASK RELATIONS Interdependent task relations occur when collaboration, integration, and mutual decision making between two or more groups are necessary and desirable for each group to achieve its own goals.[15] For effective interdependent task relations to exist, no single group or individual within a group should dictate or unilaterally determine the outcome of all interactions.[16]

The top executives of "Organization M" were concerned about poor productivity for the firm as a whole. Let us examine what they decided to do about the situation.

In Practice: Organization M's Productivity Program

Concerned about poor productivity, Organization M's top executive established a top-level management task force. After eight months of study the task force determined that the problem was the performance of their 90 department managers. The task force believed that each department manager could independently deal with productivity improvement within his or her department.

A three-day training program was set up to "educate" (that is, fix) the department managers. Instead of the usual training approach (rumors were already circulating that the department managers were in for a "spanking"), the consultant helped device a mechanism for asking the department managers what they thought it would take to improve productivity.

The department managers leaped to the task. Nine key issues—budget processes, organization red tape, headquarters/field frictions, managerial skills, and so forth—emerged from their discussions. All department managers met in a series of workshops and devised ways to resolve the key issues. Most of these issues involved interdependent task relations between groups. For example, proposals for changes in rules, regulations, and procedures had to take into account the affect of the changes on many departments. The top level task force soon came to accept the view of department managers that the productivity problem could only be adequately dealt with by also recognizing the many interdependent task relations between lateral groups and vertical groups. The department managers also determined which aspects of their own departmental performance needed improving. A three-year action plan was mapped out.

Productivity improved markedly the first year. The organization's performance was termed the best ever. During the second year a new thrust was added—rank-and-file employees were brought into the picture. Productivity was improved even more.

Eighteen months later all original productivity goals were achieved and the department managers happily ended the program six months early. Many of the program activities (problem-solving groups, and so forth) continued and became a regular way of life for the organization.[17]

This experience represents a good example of collaboration, coordination, and mutual problem solving between vertical and lateral groups.

DEPENDENT TASK RELATIONS   When one group has the ability and power to dictate or unilaterally determine the behaviors and outputs from the interactions with one or more other groups, **dependent task relations** result. Dependent task relations often occur when (1) one group absorbs uncertainty for one or more other groups; (2) the services that one group provides for one or more other groups are not readily substitutable; or (3) one or more groups depend on another group for needed resources. A dramatic example of dependent task relations involves relations between the top-management planning and budget committee and lower-level organizational departments. Budget allocations and possibly the survival of the lower-level departments may depend on the stroke of a pen by the top-management planning and budget committee.

When individuals are dependent on the actions of another individual or group, they may unite by forming a coalition or joining an organization that represents their interests. One goal of such a coalition or organization is to reduce the dependency of the individual members on the unilateral actions of those who are perceived as having more power.[18] Some employees form or join unions to reduce their perceived dependency on the actions of higher management. They believe that "in unity there is strength," that is, less dependency.

SIGNIFICANCE TO MANAGEMENT   The diagnosis of task relations—independent, interdependent, and dependent—between two or more groups is essential. First, the achievement of important organizational goals—such as productivity, innovation, and profitability—is often influenced by the nature and degree of task relations between groups and individuals. The productivity improvement program at Organization M illustrates this idea nicely. Second, some degree of interdependent task relations between lateral groups—

such as the personnel department and production department—is inevitable and must be managed.[19] Third, there is no single set of "right" task relations that should exist between lateral or vertical groups within organizations.[20]

Resource Sharing

Resource sharing refers to the degree to which two or more groups must obtain needed goods or services from a common group and the degree to which these goods or services are adequate to meet the needs of all groups.[21] Consider the effects of resource sharing by groups that involved a word-processing department.

In Practice: The Word-Processing Department

Three departments used the same word-processing department to prepare most letters, memorandums, reports, and the like. These departments lacked the skills and resources to perform this type of work themselves. When the word-processing department had adequate resources (operators, word processors, paper, reproduction equipment, and so on) to meet the demands of the three departments, few, if any problems occurred among the departments over the sharing of the word-processing department.

Then each department expanded its work load and number of employees. But the word-processing department resources remained constant. This was a deliberate strategy by higher management. The word-processing department was currently staffed to meet peak demands from the other three departments and, consequently, was underutilized much of the time. Higher management felt that better planning, more realistic deadlines for the word-processing department, or both would result in much higher output with no additional personnel. This belief was reinforced by previous complaints from several word-processor operators who said they had to work frantically one day and were bored by inactivity the next day.

Initially, the three user departments responded by pressuring the word-processing department to the point where every job was urgent. Next, each department established priorities for its own materials. However, this did not solve the problem. Finally, representatives of the three departments and the word-processing department worked out a set of priorities and established mutual understanding through group problem solving.

SIGNIFICANCE TO MANAGEMENT   The need for two or more groups to share a common pool of resources can result in competition or cooperation between them.[22] In the situation involving the word-processing department, the groups initially cooperated, then competed, and eventually cooperated again when they confronted their problems. Management must encourage collaborative problem solving among groups who share a scarce pool of resources and help set priorities to minimize unnecessary competition and destructive conflicts. Management also holds a unique position to influence the attitudinal sets of groups toward each other when they experience difficulties in sharing resources and/or working together.

Attitudinal Sets

Attitudinal sets are the thoughts and feelings that two or more groups have toward each other.[23]

CAUSE AND CONSEQUENCE   The sets of attitudes that the members of a group hold toward another group and its members can be both a cause and a consequence of the behaviors and outputs between the groups. The intergroup dynamics might begin with the groups being trusting, cooperative, and open with each other. These attitudes often influence the other factors just discussed (goals, uncertainty absorption, substitutability, task relations, and resource sharing). If two groups trust each other, they tend to consider the other group's point of view more, avoid blaming the other when problems occur, and check with each other before making decisions that may have a mutual impact. If intergroup dynamics begin with attitudes of distrust, competitiveness, secrecy, and closed communication, the opposite tendencies can be expected.

The attitudinal sets of groups can also be a consequence of the other factors in intergroup dynamics. For example, if an organization evaluates its internal auditing group solely on the basis of its finding errors and reporting them to higher management, the other groups may have attitudes of distrust, competitiveness, and closed communication toward the auditing group. Of course, these attitudes are more likely to prevail if higher management uses the reports from auditing primarily to punish the other groups rather than to improve them. In such cases these other groups may appear to be cooperative and open in their communication with the auditing group, although in fact they are not.[24]

COOPERATION VERSUS COMPETITION   The attitudinal sets that groups hold about each other often become stereotypes; that is, standardized short-cut evaluations that reflect present or past perceptions of relations between groups or specific individuals within the groups. (Chapter 4).[25] A number of attitudinal and behavioral consequences have been identified for groups who stereotype their relationships as basically cooperative or competitive.[26] Recall that we discussed some of these outcomes for competing groups that "win" and "lose" earlier in this chapter.

Figure 10-3 summarizes some of the attitudinal and behavioral consequences for groups that stereotype their relationships with others as extremely cooperative versus extremely competitive. This figure could be used by group members to assess the ways in which they perceive other groups. In extremely competitive relationships, groups tend to be distrusting and unresponsive, to emphasize self-interests, to interact only when required, to resist influence or control from each other, and so on. On the other hand, a highly cooperative relationship tends to be characterized by trust, responsiveness, emphasis on mutual interests, easy and frequent interaction, acceptance of mutual influence or control, and so on.

Intergroup dynamics are probably rarely at one end or the other of all the continua in Figure 10-3. Intergroup problem solving and effectiveness tend to be greater when relations reflect the cooperative characteristics in Figure 10-3 than when they exhibit the competitive characteristics. This ap-

Under Extreme Conditions of Cooperation	Ambivalence	Under Extreme Conditions of Competition and Conflict
Trust		Distrust
Flexibility		Rigidity
Openness and authenticity		Closedness and deceptiveness
Mutual interests and goals		Self-interest and goals
Friendliness or neutrality		Aggressiveness or enemy status
Listening to each other		Listening to selves
Accepting mutual control		Resisting control of each other
Collaboration and compromise		Force and avoidance

FIGURE 10–3.
Some Attitudinal and Behavioral Consequences of Dynamics Between Groups and Individuals

plies especially to intergroup relations within organizations when effectiveness criteria are based on what is desirable for the organization as a whole.

SIGNIFICANCE TO MANAGEMENT   Attitudinal sets—whether cooperative or competitive—can significantly affect the ability and willingness of groups to work together to achieve organizational goals. If groups are *interdependent,* competitive attitudinal sets probably will reduce goal accomplishment. This is because the competitive and interdependent groups must expend considerable time and energy trying to "get one up" on the other. The next section of this chapter focuses on ways to maintain or create effective relations between interdependent groups, especially those groups that are in a lateral relationship to one another.

CREATING EFFECTIVE DYNAMICS BETWEEN LATERAL GROUPS

Lateral relations occur when two or more groups are *interdependent,* are able to influence each other, and are not in a hierarchical relationship. This section presents six major mechanisms for managing lateral relationships: superordinate group goals and rewards, hierarchy, plans, formal and informal linking roles, task forces, and integrating roles and groups. These six mechanisms are shown in Figure 10-4. The vertical axis shows the *additional resources required to use each mechanism,* ranging from low to high. Additional resources could include the extra time people spend in meetings, the

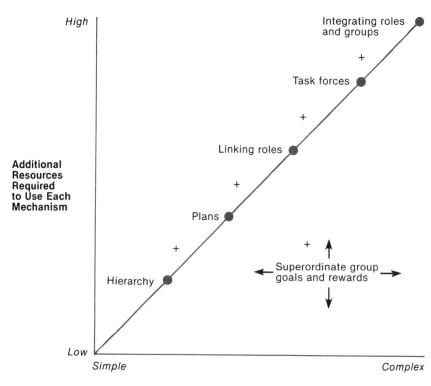

FIGURE 10–4.
Some Mechanisms for Creating Effective Intergroup Dynamics

increase in paper flow and memos sent between groups, the extra personnel that must be hired, and the like. The horizontal axis shows the *complexity of each mechanism,* ranging from simple to complex. The plus (+) signs between mechanisms suggest the probable use of the prior identified mechanism or mechanisms along with the new mechanism. With the exception of "superordinate group goals and rewards," these mechanisms tend to be related to each other in a hierarchy of complexity. For example, if linking roles are appropriate to integrate two or more groups, some uses of hierarchy and plans are probably appropriate as well.

Superordinate Group Goals and Rewards

Superordinate group goals are those common ends that might be pursued by two or more groups, and which cannot be achieved through the independent efforts or resources of each group separately.[27] These goals do not replace or eliminate the other goals of each group. Superordinate group goals can be qualitative or quantitative. An example of a qualitative goal would be "Marketing and production need to pull together for the good of the company." An example of a quantitative goal would be "Marketing and production need to work together if we are to reach company goals of launching the new X line within 9 months and achieving sales of 5,000 units per month of the X line within 15 months. The company's survival is at stake."

Superordinate group goals are likely to have a more powerful effect on the willingness of groups to cooperate if accompanied by superordinate group rewards. **Superordinate group rewards** are those tangible or intangible benefits received by the members of two or more groups, determined at least partially by the results of their joint efforts.

WIDE RANGE OF USE   As suggested by the multidirectional arrows in Figure 10-4, superordinate group goals and rewards can range widely in their degree of complexity and the resources required to use them. A company president might state:

> During this past year, we needed extensive cooperation among all our departments and divisions in order to achieve our company goal of a 20 percent increase in profits. I would like to express my appreciation to all of you for pulling together—even when we had to deal with several sticky issues involving some departments and divisions. Through everyone's efforts, we did it. I am pleased to report that profits are up 25 percent.

Based on Figure 10-4, the president's statement would fall at the *simple* end of the complexity continuum and the *low* end of the additional resources required continuum. But suppose that he added the following:

> Under our profit-sharing program, I am pleased to report that 90 percent of our employees will receive bonuses ranging from 10—35% of their salaries. As all of you should know, these bonuses are based on a weighted system of (1) individual merit rating; (2) achievement of departmental goals; and (3) overall company profitability.

These additional comments by the president suggest that the superordinate group goals and rewards are probably at the *complex* end of the complexity continuum and at the *high* end of the additional resources required continuum in Figure 10-4.

SCANLON PLAN   The Scanlon Plan is an example of a program based on superordinate group goals and reward mechanisms, as well as some of the other mechanisms for creating effective intergroup relationships. The **Scanlon plan** basically consists of a philosophy of management accompanied by a system of rewards and procedures. The philosophy includes building a genuine worker–management partnership (which could include a union). This philosophy includes creating greater employee commitment and identification with the firm, believing in significant employee participation, and sharing benefits of plantwide improvements with workers. The system of rewards and procedures includes a suggestion system, elected committees of workers, and a plantwide bonus formula based on productivity gains.[28]
Developed more than 40 years ago by Joseph Scanlon—the late official of the United Steel Workers of America—Scanlon plans give employees at the plant level incentives to improve production methods and suggest cost savings. The Scanlon plan is one type of gain-sharing system, which is different from profit sharing. Profit sharing awards the employee a proportion of *total* company profits. Gain sharing, on the other hand, usually rewards the

employee on the basis of the plant, division, or department productivity and efficiency targets toward which the employee works. Some observers believe that profit sharing is likely to have limited effectiveness because the individual worker in a large company will probably feel powerless to influence the overall profits of the firm to any noticeable degree. Moreover, company profits are perceived to be affected by many external factors (such as competitors' actions) that are well beyond the control or influence of workers.[29]

This type of plan has been quite effective in providing a process and incentive system to the employees and groups in a production plant to cooperate and work toward its superordinate goals. For a Scanlon plan to be successful, it is necessary to establish a network of committees that will involve almost everyone in productivity improvement. In addition, the organization must also be able to measure the difference between plant output and total payroll costs so that plantwide bonuses can be objectively determined. Let us consider the experience of the Dana Corporation with its Scanlon plan.

In Practice: Dana's Scanlon Plan

Dana's Scanlon plan has been used in 22 of the corporation's plants (approximately one-third of the major facilities), and it involves approximately 5,000 people. Each department within a plant has a production committee consisting of three or four employees, with their supervisor serving as chair. The committee solicits and evaluates suggestions. On average, 75 percent of the suggestions submitted to a plantwide committee are accepted and carried out.

Some suggestions have resulted in substantial savings. At one plant, a new process resulted in projected savings of $875,000 a year in a particular production operation. Cash rewards are computed from historical data and measurement of the ratio between plant output and total payroll. The ratio is used to estimate the allowable payroll each month. If the actual payroll is less than the allowed payroll, three-fourths of the difference is distributed to the employees as bonuses and one-fourth is retained for future investment in capital equipment. At the end of the month, all employees receive the same percentage bonus. Typical bonuses for a plan average 15 percent, with the range being from 0–30 percent.[30]

Hierarchy

Hierarchy is a mechanism for obtaining integration, or coordination, between two or more groups through the use of a common superior. The use of hierarchy to help integrate groups, or specific individuals within the groups, rests on the assumption that people at upper levels have more power than those at lower levels. As shown previously in Figure 10-4, hierarchy is probably the simplest mechanism and involves the least *additional* cost for achieving integration between two or more groups. Obviously, a hierarchy exists for many purposes other than creating effective intergroup relations.

The use of hierarchy to resolve intergroup integration problems may be especially appropriate when there are few integration requirements and only minor differences between the groups. Of course, the use of hierarchy does not necessarily prevent representatives of the involved groups from sitting down with the common superior and working through the issues together, or at least having an opportunity to discuss the problem and influence decisions.

Plans

Plans and planning processes can be used to help achieve effective intergroup relations. In the broadest sense, **planning** has been defined as:

> Figuring out as best as possible everything that is important to the business, such as: the organization's destination (vision and goals); the strategies for getting there; where the organization would like to be at specific times; the obstacles the organization may encounter; and the approaches the organization intends to use in dealing with these obstacles.[31]

Through accepted or agreed-on plans, two or more groups can act and make decisions on a day-to-day basis without constantly interacting with each other; yet they can be quite integrated and interdependent in terms of their goals. For example, a construction firm may start working on two sections of the same highway but many miles apart. So long as both construction crews make their decisions in relation to the requirements of the plan, the road surfaces being laid by each group should meet when and where they are supposed to meet (assuming virtual certainty regarding the accurate measurement and plotting of the path of the roadway by engineers).

Linking Roles

Linking roles are specialized positions in which people facilitate communication and problem solving between two or more interdependent groups. Creation of such a role is important when the exclusive use of hierarchy, plans, or both becomes too slow or time-consuming. For example, if minor issues were continually referred up the hierarchy, the common superior might become overloaded, and the response time might increase. Therefore a linking role to solve minor problems would reduce the common superior's load.

In the description of the industrial relations department presented earlier, a key industrial relations representative was located physically in each manufacturing facility but was a member of the industrial relations department located at company headquarters. While the industrial relations representatives served the manufacturing plant, they also served as the primary *link* between the industrial relations department and the managers of the production plant.

A linking role may be as simple as handling and tracking the flow of paper work between groups and following up on issues as required. In a more complex linking role—such as that of the industrial relations representatives just mentioned—the linking individuals may have expertise in helping the groups solve mutual problems, understand one another, and so on.[32]

BOUNDARY-SPANNING ROLES   Specialized linking roles can also link an organization to external groups or other organizations. These roles, often called **boundary-spanning roles,** provide an essential mechanism for facilitating the flow of information and decision making.[33] For example, a safety manager might fill a boundary-spanning role between an organization and the federal Occupational Safety and Health Administration (OSHA) with respect to safety and health issues. Boundary-spanning roles may also involve the representation of the interests and goals of a group or organization in relations with external groups. For example, boundary spanners in the collective bargaining process include negotiators representing management as well as those representing a union.[34]

Task Forces

Task forces are special groups that consist of one or more representatives from each of the interdependent groups who work on specific problems of mutual concern. Task forces are usually formed to work on temporary issues or problems and disband when the issues or problems are resolved. Some members of a task force may be engaged on a full-time basis and others on a part-time basis. The members often provide a linking role between their group and the task force. Members usually can provide information and ideas regarding common problems, serve as transmitters of ideas and information between the task force and their groups, and help to assess the impact of decisions by the task force on their groups.

Task forces can develop on a formal or informal basis. An informal task force can simply involve several people who get together to consider a mutual problem. Higher management usually creates and recognizes formal task forces, usually in writing, by stating the problem area and goals to be dealt with by the task force.

Integrating Roles and Groups

An **integrating role** is a position filled by one person who is permanently assigned to assist two or more groups in their relationships with each other. Whereas an integrating role is a position filled by one person, an integrating group has several people formally assigned to the task of ensuring integration between two or more groups. Examples of roles and groups that often serve the integrating function (in addition to those previously discussed) are product managers, program coordinators, project managers, group vice presidents, plant productivity committees, annual meetings between corporate and division general managers, boards of directors, union leaders, and union–management problem solving committees.

A Swedish firm—L. M. Ericsson Telephone—makes extensive use of roles and groups that serve to integrate human resources both vertically and laterally throughout the firm. The description of the company's approach is based on a presentation by B. Svedberg, president and chief executive officer.

ACROSS CULTURES

L. M. Ericsson Telephone of Sweden

L. M. Ericsson—one of the world's leading manufacturers of telecommunications equipment, including office automation systems—is a typical export-oriented Swedish manufacturer. While domestic production is substantial, the home market accounts for only about 20 percent of sales. To survive, the firm has had to compete throughout the world with the other major international companies in the field and with many regional and local competitors. Approximately 32,000 out of a total of around 66,000 Ericsson employees were located outside Sweden as of 1983.

Employees in Sweden are unionized to a higher degree than in any other free-market country. Ninety percent of the factory workers are affiliated with the Swedish Trade Union Confederation, and approximately 70 percent of the office personnel belong to the Central Organization of Salaried Employees, the largest union for white-collar employees. The Swedish Employers Confederation represents around 80 percent of the country's employers in the private sector.

The "federation" principle is applied. This means that—in one of Ericsson's units for example—all the factory workers are represented by the Metal Workers Union, all the Ericsson production foremen are represented by the Swedish Supervisors Union, and office employees are represented by the Swedish Industrial Salaried Employees Union or by the Union of Graduate Engineers. Thus, each Ericsson unit has to work out its own agreement with employees, based on local application of the contracts agreed upon by management and labor at the national level. Each unit also has to observe all the laws pertaining to joint consultation, negotiation, etc., that apply to each union organization.

The unions are represented on Ericsson's board of directors by two members and two deputy members, who are also entitled to attend board meetings and express their views. As a result, it is possible for all of the major unions to be represented on the board of directors, to obtain insight into company policies and operations, and to influence the decisions taken. Prior to each Ericsson board meeting, all current matters to be discussed are reviewed with the union representatives on the board.

Union representatives on boards of directors have not played the major role that was anticipated for them, partly because virtually all matters affecting employees are governed by the Codetermination Act, and, accordingly, are negotiated at other levels within the organization.

Each major Ericsson unit operating in the Swedish sector has another body—the Works Council. It consists of representatives of management and the unions. The Works Council serves as a vehicle for information and consultation, but has no decision-making power. These councils meet quarterly but normally have working committees—concerned with such matters as production, safety, and employee proposals—that meet monthly. The value of the councils and the working committees to the average employee depends to a large degree on the competence and diligence of the union representatives.

In actual practice, the compulsory consultation and negotiation requirements of the Codetermination Act of Sweden creates problems in maintaining contact with employees. This applies particularly to middle management. The union has to have advance information on all changes before such proposals can be discussed openly. Unfortunately, it occasionally happens that information reaches subordinates, via the union, even before managers have been informed and have been able to discuss the matter with their associates. Regular meetings between top management and middle management offer one way of partially preventing such unfortunate occurrences.

> The closest contact between representatives of management and the individual employees takes place in the so-called "shop floor groups". In these groups, foremen and workers—who participate on a rotating basis—meet at regular intervals for consultation and discussion related directly to the workplace. The issues covered deal with production, job transfers, changes in products, methods, and equipment, etc. Through shop floor groups, employees can have a direct influence on their work situation.[35]

The role of the integrating position or group usually consists of helping resolve nonroutine problems and conflicting goals that develop between groups. For example, conflicting goals and nonroutine problems often surface between production and marketing departments as well as between union and management groups. Intergroup issues could include interdepartmental conflicts, major capital investment decisions, schedules, cost estimates, standards of quality, human resource problems, authority and control problems, and the like.[36] The decision to use a role or a specialized group to achieve integration usually depends on the situation. An integrating group is usually a more costly integrating mechanism than a single integrating role. There is a tendency for managers to move toward integrating groups of increasing complexity when (1) the differences between the groups needing integration increases; (2) the need for integration increases because of interdependent task relations; and (3) the need to deal with nonroutine problems between the groups increases.

SUMMARY

This chapter focused on the dynamics between groups within organizations, with primary emphasis on groups that are in a lateral relationship with each other. For purposes of simplicity, we did not attempt to describe the vast array of impacts that individual and intragroup relations have on intergroup dynamics; however, they are significant and are implied throughout the discussion. We presented six basic factors that individually or in some combination often affect intergroup behaviors and outputs: goals, uncertainty absorption, substitutability, task relations, resource sharing, and attitudinal sets. When the goals of two or more interdependent groups are perceived as being incompatible, considerable conflict and poor coordination often occur. When one group absorbs uncertainty for other groups, its power usually increases. When substitutability of the services or activities of a group is not permitted, the group's power is often greater than it otherwise would be within the organization (everything else being equal). When task relations between two or more groups are highly interdependent, extensive collaboration, coordination, and mutual decision making is usually imperative. When resource sharing is required of two or more groups, there is a greater likelihood that they will come into conflict, and there will be a greater need for them to establish priorities and ground rules for sharing the common resource. When the attitudinal sets that two or more groups hold toward each other are characterized by trust, flexibility, openness, mutuality of interests, friendliness, and the like, high levels of intergroup cooperation often result.

Intergroup competition and conflict go hand in hand with opposing attitudinal sets.

In the second section we discussed six mechanisms for creating intergroup dynamics, especially the behavior and outputs between groups that are in lateral relationships with each other: superordinate groups and rewards, hierarchy, plans, linking roles, task forces, and integrating roles and groups.

This approach to the dynamics of group interaction is a highly contingent one. That is, only after careful diagnosis can we draw conclusions on the best mechanism or combination of mechanisms for creating effective intergroup dynamics. Managers can pay too little or too much attention to the dynamics between groups. Too little attention to the interfaces between groups can result in poor integration, duplication of effort, and destructive conflicts. Too much attention to intergroup dynamics can result in unnecessary paper work and meetings, an excessive expenditure of resources on achieving integration between groups, and a lack of sense of accomplishment for any of the groups.

KEY WORDS AND CONCEPTS

Attitudinal sets
Boundary-spanning roles
Coalition
Dependent task relations
Goal conflict
Hierarchy
Independent task relations
Integrating role
Interdependent task relations
Lateral relations

Linking roles
Planning
Resource sharing
Scanlon plan
Substitutability
Superordinate group goals
Superordinate group rewards
Task forces
Uncertainty
Uncertainty absorption

DISCUSSION QUESTIONS

1. Are there any conditions under which a department should be able to substitute services provided by a firm outside the organization for services provided by another group within the organization? Explain.

2. Can two or more groups with interdependent task relations also be characterized as being independent groups?

3. How serious a problem do you consider goal incompatibility to be between groups within organizations? Explain. Can you think of any examples where goal incompatibility occurred between a group of which you were a member and some other group? If so, describe the situation.

4. In what ways can a marketing research department absorb uncertainty for a sales department?

5. Utilizing the continua in Figure 10-3, how would you describe the intergroup dynamics between any two groups with which you are personally familiar? Does your diagnosis have any implications for the relative effectiveness or ineffectiveness of these groups? Explain.

6. Why might some managers object to the creation of a new integrating department in their organization?

7. Based on your work and school experiences, can you give any examples of superordinate group goals and rewards?

8. Based on your experiences in organizations, have the mechanisms used for integrating groups worked well or poorly? Illustrate and explain your position.

MANAGEMENT INCIDENTS AND CASES

Rushton Mining Company

The president of Rushton Mining Company and the president of the United Mine Workers of America signed a letter of agreement to collaborate on a quality-of-work-life *experiment* at Rushton Coal Mine in Pennsylvania. The experiment was designed by a team of researchers to improve employee skills, safety, and job satisfaction while simultaneously raising the level of performance and earnings.

After five months of deliberations by representatives of management and the union, the firm posted job bids requesting volunteers for an autonomous ("independent") work group. These miners would have direct responsibility for the production of an entire geographic "section" of the mine. The foremen of the section would abandon their traditional roles as "pushers" and develop new roles as advisors, consultants, trainers, and planners.

The autonomous work group employed an entire 27-man section, comprised of three shifts and three foremen. The group met with the research team two days a week for six weeks in an above-ground classroom where they received training in safety laws, good mining practices, job safety analysis, and group problem solving. On the remaining three days, the men mined coal in their new underground section and learned to work toward a common goal—safely maximizing production of the section rather than the shift. To encourage job switching and shared responsibility for the work, all 27 miners received the same rate of pay as the highest-skilled job classification on that section. This resulted in an increase to the top rate of $50 a day for 15 of the men.

Following the orientation period, the group met in the classroom with the research team at six-week intervals to discuss productivity, absenteeism, costs, health, and safety matters. During this time the research team developed several means for resolving intragroup conflict and enhancing intershift coordination. These included a "joint committee," comprised of one man from each shift, two local union leaders, one foreman, the mine's safety director, a training director, and two members of management. Biweekly foremen meetings, higher level management meetings, and underground visits by the research team occurred several times a week.

Seeds of conflict While intragroup coordination improved, inter-section hostility grew. At first, the other miners found the activities of the autonomous group and their association with the university research teams amusing, and humorously used such terms as "automatic miner" and "super miner" when the men of the autonomous section entered the waiting room before boarding the man-trip cars. In time, however, the good-natured banter changed to silent hostility—and eventually to open opposition—as other miners grew jealous of the privileged status of the autonomous section of the mine. Subsequent interviews with the men in the control sections suggested that they felt deprived because the research team gave them no information and little attention. Not only did the autonomous group work under generally favorable physical conditions, but it also received special training and, when requested, special tools and equipment. It had its own university researcher who spent an entire shift several times a week interviewing and observing the group's miners, sharing their danger and fatigue, and helping with training, development, and conflict resolution. It had the privilege of spending one day every six weeks out of the mine in a section conference with top management and top union officials. In addition, several of the miners attended quality-of-work-life conferences at the company's expense, enjoying rides to and from the airport in the mine president's helicopter and receiving honoraria for their presentations. Moreover, the president "treated" the autonomous section to a steak-and-lobster dinner at the conclusion of their training period.

A few of the men on the autonomous section aggravated this already-difficult situation by behaving in a haughty, arrogant manner toward other men in the mine who questioned their preferential treatment. For example, when one of the men on a control section complained of a "hard-nosed" boss who "works your tail off," the autonomous worker replied that he could tell his boss "where to get off." Another worker bragged that he had "retired" when he went into the autonomous section and planned to start bringing a sleeping bag with him into the mine so he could be more comfortable during his shift. Some evidence exists, however, that many of the autonomous workers felt stung by the criticism of their peers. In the early days of the experiment, the autonomous miners developed the habit of rubbing their hands—which were stained with coal dust—across their faces while pondering a problem. Although this seemed to be an unconscious action, it probably provided some protection against remarks from other miners that the autonomous workers did not look "dirty enough" to have worked very hard.

Growth and Spread of Conflict
About 10 months after the experiment began, the mine opened a new section. The men from the original autonomous section, many of whom had never attended a union meeting before, had by this time become enthusiastic proponents of "our way of working" and strongly influenced the favorable vote in the union hall that permitted the new section to be organized along autonomous lines.

When the company opened the new section, management and the researchers anticipated that experienced men would bid from other positions all over the mine to fill the vacancies. This, however, did not occur. Because of a reluctance to leave established patterns of working, a resentment toward being kept uninformed, and rising hostility toward the project, the older miners refused to place bids for jobs in the new section. New men who had been hired to fill the anticipated vacancies in other parts of the mine and who still wore the yellow hat of the inexperienced and uncertified miner obtained positions in the new autonomous section. The section thus consisted mostly of men with less than one year's experience who nevertheless drew the same or higher pay as miners with at least 40 years of experience.

Although it rapidly became one of the highest producers, the new section initially had the lowest production rate in the mine. This appeared to stem from the inexperience of the men and from the fact that they had to work with used equipment that continually broke down. Frequently, mechanics from other parts of the mine had to help the young, inexperienced mechanics from the new section repair their equipment. The combination of high pay, inexperience, and perceived low production of the new section increased the hostility and resentment the control group members felt towards the experiment.

As the weeks progressed, the members of the control sections became increasingly vociferous in their comments. They accused autonomous miners of "riding the gravy train" and being "spoon-fed," and called them "parasites" who were "carried" by the rest of the men in the mine. Rumors began to spread through the mine with increasing frequency and intensity. Some of the most widely circulated ones held that autonomy constituted a communist plot since everybody received the same top rate and that the company was being subsidized by the government and was "making out" at the expense of men.

An extremely damaging rumor defined the quality-of-work-life project as a management subterfuge in conjunction with "pinko" college people to "bust the union." This concept seemed especially credible since the company president had strongly resisted the unionization attempts led by "Jock" Yablonski 10 years earlier. Many of the older miners who had been involved in organizing felt greatly concerned that the project's committees, joint decision making, and universally high pay rate could cause a weaning away of the younger men from the traditional values of the United Mine Workers of America and possibly result in an independent or company union.

Although all of the men in the mine had access to general information regarding the purpose of the experiment, they could not learn about details. Effective refutation of the growing suspicions and rumors would have required the research team to spend considerable time with the control groups revealing the specifics of the experiment—and this would have disrupted the evaluation effort at an early stage.

The rumors and innuendoes continued until the talk inevitably became translated into action. Five months after the formation of the new section, the union membership voted to terminate the experiment unless the other men in the mine were given a chance to work at the top rate of pay.

Consequences of Conflict During the next two months, the research team feverishly interviewed and observed the men in the control groups at their jobs so that the team could perform the analysis required for a proposal for mine-wide autonomous working. In addition, the researchers made great efforts to explain the principles of autonomous working to all the miners and to refute the rumors that sprang up in the darkness and gloom of the underground environment. What appeared to be ridiculous speculation outside in the bright sunlight somehow seemed believable hundreds of feet underground.

This process culminated in a request by the local union for written proposals that would specify how the rest of the mine would become autonomous. The research team submitted proposals to the membership, who voted on them at a special election. The miners rejected the proposals by a vote of 79 to 75, and the experiment was terminated.[37]

Questions

1. What are the identifiable groups that played a part in this experiment and the eventual outcomes?

2. What appeared to be the goals and interests of each of these groups with respect to the quality-of-work-life experiment?

3. How did this quality-of-work-life experiment seem to impact the factors of uncertainty absorption, substitutability, and task relations within the autonomous ("independent") work group(s) and between the other groups at Rushton?

4. Why did the attitudinal sets between the groups deteriorate?

5. What actions might have been taken from the very beginning of the experiment to increase the probability of approval rather than rejection of the mine-wide autonomous group proposal? Your answer should indicate possible actions by each of the key groups.

REFERENCES

1. Reprinted from Studying Intergroup Relations Embedded in Organizations by C. P. Alderfer and K. K. Smith published in *Administrative Science Quarterly* (27, 1982,1) by permission of *The Administrative Science Quarterly*. Copyright © 1982 Cornell University.

2. Stephenson, W. B., Pearce, J. L., and Porter, L. W. The Concept of "Coalition" in Organization Theory and Research. *Academy of Management Review*, 1985, *10*, 256–268; Mintzberg, H. Power and Organization Life Cycles. *Academy of Management Review*, 1984, *9*, 207–224; Pearce II, J. A., and DeNisi, A. Attribution Theory and Strategic Decision Making: An Application to Coalition Formation. *Academy of Management Journal*, 1983, *26*, 119–128.

3. Richards, M. D. *Organizational Goal Structures*. St. Paul, Minn.: West, 1978; Zammuto, R. F. A Comparison of Multiple Constituency Models of Organizational Effectiveness. *Academy of Management Review*, 1984, *9*, 606–616.

4. Tichy, N. M. *Managing Strategic Change: Technical, Political, and Cultural Dynamics*. New York: John Wiley and Sons, 1983; Carper, W. B., and Litschert, R. J. Strategic Power Relationships in Contemporary Profit and Nonprofit Hospitals. *Academy of Management Journal*, 1983, *26*, 311–320; Murnighan, J. K., and Vollrath, D. A. Hierarchies, Coalitions and Organizations. In S. B. Bacharach and E. J. Lawler (Eds.) *Research in the Sociology of Organizations*. Greenwich, Conn.: JAI Press, 1984, 157–187.

5. Schein, E. *Organizational Psychology*. Englewood Cliffs, N.J.: Prentice-Hall, 1980, 172–176; Brown, L. D. *Managing Conflict at Organizational Interfaces*. Reading, Mass.: Addison-Wesley, 1983.

6. Saunders, C. S. Management Information Systems, Communications, and Departmental Power: An Integrative Model. *Academy of Management Review*, 1981, *6*, 431–442.

7. Thompson, J. *Organizations in Action*. New York: McGraw-Hill, 1967.

8. Kaplan, D. Power in Perspective. In R. L. Kahn and K. E. Boulding (Eds.) *Power and Conflict in Organizations*. London: Tavistock, 1964, 11–32. Also see: Astley, W. G., and Sachdeva, P. S. Structural Sources of Intraorganizational Power: A Theoretical Synthesis. *Academy of Management Review*, 1984, *9*, 104–113.

9. Fry, L. W., and Slocum Jr., J. W. Technology, Structure, and Workgroup Effectiveness: A Test of a Contingency Model. *Academy of Management Journal*, 1984, *27*, 221–246; Withey, M., Daft, R. L., and Cooper, W. H. Measures of Perrow's Work Unit Technology: An Empirical Assessment and a New Scale. *Academy of Management Journal*, 1983, *26*, 45–63.

10. Adapted with permission from Goldner, G. The Division of Labor: Process and Power. In M. N. Zald (Ed.) *Power in Organizations*. Nashville: Vanderbilt University Press, 1970, 97–143.

11. Kipnis, D. Technology, Power, and Control. In S. B. Bacharach and E. J. Lawler (Eds.) *Research in the Sociology of Organizations*. Greenwich, Conn.: JAI Press, 1984, 125–156.

12. Clegg, S. Organization and Control. *Administrative Science Quarterly*, 1981, *26*, 545–562.

13. Hickson, D., Hinnings, C., Lee, C., Schneck, R., and Pennings, J. A Strategic Contingencies Theory of Intraorganizational Power. *Administrative Science Quarterly*, 1971, *16*, 216–229; Beyer, J. M. Power Dependencies and the Distribution of Influence in Universities. In S. B. Bacharach and E. J. Lawler (Eds.) *Research in the Sociology of Organizations*. Greenwich, Conn.: JAI Press, 1982, 167–208.

14. Duncan, W. *Organizational Behavior*. Boston: Houghton Mifflin, 1978, 224–226.

15. Cheng, J. C. Interdependence and Coordination in Organizations: A Role–System Analysis. *Academy of Management Journal*, 1983, *26*, 156–162.

16. McCann, J. E., and Ferry, D. L. An Approach for Assessing and Managing Interunit Interdependence. *Academy of Management Review*, 1979, *4*, 113–119; Katz, R., and Allen, T. J. Project Performance and the Locus of Influence in the R&D Matrix. *Academy of Management Journal*, 1985, *28*, 67–87.

17. Adapted, by permission of the publisher, from Transforming Organizations Through Vertical Linking, by J. A. Hawley, *Organizational Dynamics,* Winter 1984, p. 70. © 1984. Periodicals Division, American Management Association, New York. All rights reserved.

18. Cook, K. S., and Gillmore, M. R. Power, Dependence, and Coalition. In E. J. Lawler (Ed.) *Advances in Group Processes.* Greenwich, Conn.: JAI Press, 1984, 27–58.

19. Nossister, V. A. New Approach toward Resolving the Line and Staff Dilemma. *Academy of Management Review,* 1979, *4,* 103–106.

20. Kmetz, J. L. An Information-Processing Study of a Complex Workflow in Aircraft Electronics Repair. *Administrative Science Quarterly,* 1984, *29,* 255–280.

21. Tushman, M. A Political Approach to Organizations: A Review and Rationale. *Academy of Management Review,* 1977, *2,* 206–216.

22. Komorita, S. S., and Hamilton, T. P. Power and Equity in Coalition Bargaining. In S. B. Bacharach and E. J. Lawler (Eds.) *Research in the Sociology of Organizations.* Greenwich, Conn.: JAI Press, 1984, 189–192.

23. Hackman, J. Group Influences on Individuals. In M. D. Dunnette (Ed.) *Handbook of Industrial and Organizational Psychology.* Chicago: Rand McNally, 1976, 1455–1525.

24. Sayles, L. *Managerial Behavior.* New York: Octagon, 1966, 231.

25. Sherif, M., and Sherif, C. *Groups in Harmony and Tension: An Integration of Studies on Intergroup Relations.* New York: Octagon, 1966, 231; Smith, K. K. Social Comparison Processes and Dynamic Conservatism in Intergroup Relations. In L. L. Cummings and B. M. Staw (Eds.) *Research in Organizational Behavior.* Greenwich, Conn.: JAI Press, 1983, 199–233.

26. Likert, R., and Likert, J. G. *New Ways of Managing Conflict.* New York: McGraw-Hill, 1976; Blake, R. R., Shepard, H. A., and Mouton, J. S. *Managing Intergroup Conflict in Industry.* Houston: Gulf, 1964; Blake, R. R., and Mouton, J. S. Overcoming Group Warfare. *Harvard Business Review,* November–December 1984, 98–108; Dalton, D. R., and Todor, W. D. Unanticipated Consequences of Union-Management Cooperation: An Interrupted Time Series Analysis. *Journal of Applied Behavioral Analysis,* 1984, *20,* 253–264; Schall, M. S. A Communication-Rules Approach to Organizational Culture. *Administrative Science Quarterly,* 1983, *28,* 557–581.

27. Sherif, M. Superordinate Goals in the Reduction of Intergroup Conflict. *American Journal of Sociology,* 1958, *68,* 349–358; Logan, G. M. Loyalty and a Sense of Purpose. *California Management Review,* Fall 1984, 149–156.

28. Schuster, M. The Scanlon Plan: A Longitudinal Analysis. *Journal of Applied Behavioral Science,* 1984, *20,* 23–38.

29. Research and Policy Committee. *Productivity Policy: Key to the Nation's Economic Future.* New York: Committee For Economic Development, 1983, 82–84.

30. Cowie, R. A. Testimony before the Subcommittee on Employment and Productivity, Senate Labor and Human Resources Committee (97th Congress, 2d session, April 2, 1982). Also see: U.S. Senate, Committee on Labor and Human Resources, *Productivity in the American Economy: Report and Findings.* Washington, D.C.: U.S. Government Printing Office, 1982.

31. Penchot III, G. *Intrapreneuring: Why You Don't Need to Leave the Corporation to Become an Entrepreneur.* New York: Harper & Row, 1985, 126.

32. Miles, R. *Macro Organizational Behavior.* Santa Monica, Calif.: Goodyear, 1980, 316–350.

33. Tushman, M., and Scanlan, T. Boundary-spanning Individuals: Their Role in Information Transfer and Their Antecedents. *Academy of Management Journal,* 1981, *4,* 289–305; Schwab, R. C., Ungson, G. R., and Brown, W. B. Redefining the Boundary Spanning-Environment Relationship. *Journal of Management,* 1985, *11,* 75–86.

34. Perry, J., and Angle, H. The Politics of Organizational Boundary Roles in Collective Bargaining. *Academy of Management Review,* 1979, *4,* 487–496.

35. Material from "Employee–Management Relations in a Highly Unionized Environment." by B. Svedberg from *Strategies for Productivity: International Perspectives* sponsored by the Japan Productivity Center. Reprinted/adapted with permission from UNIPUB, 205 East 42nd Street, New York, NY 10017.

36. Alderfer, C. P., Tucker, R. C., Alderfer, C. J., and Tucker, L. M. *The Race Relations Advisory Group: An Intergroup Intervention.* Working Paper #67. New Haven, Conn.: Yale School of Management and Organization, March 1985; Boyle, R. J. Wrestling with Jellyfish. *Harvard Business Review,* January–February 1984, 74–83; Davidson, W. H. Small Group Activity at Musashi Semiconductor Works. *Sloan Management Review,* Spring 1982, 3–14; Walton, R. E. From Control to Commitment in the Work-

place. *Harvard Business Review,* March–April 1985, 76–84.

37. Excerpted from Blumberg, M., and Pringle, C. D. How Control Groups can Cause Loss of Control in Action Research: The Case of Rushton Coal Mine. *Journal of Applied Behavioral Science,* 1983, *19,* 410–412. JAI Press, Greenwich, Connecticut. Used with permission. Also see: Blumberg, M. Job Switching in Autonomous Work Groups: An Exploratory Study in a Pennsylvania Coal Mine. *Academy of Management Journal,* 1980, *23,* 287–306; Blumberg, M., and Alber, A. The Human Element: Its Impact on the Productivity of Advanced Batch Manufacturing Systems. *Journal of Manufacturing Systems,* 1982, *1,* 43–52; Goodman, P. S. *Assessing Organizational Change: The Rushton Quality of Work Life Experiment.* New York: John Wiley, 1979; Susman, G. I., and Evered, R. D. An Assessment of the Scientific Merits of Action Research. *Administrative Science Quarterly,* 1978, *23,* 582–603.

11 Leadership

LEARNING OBJECTIVES

When you have finished studying this chapter, you should be able to:

- Explain the leadership process.
- List the sources of power a manager can use to influence subordinates.
- Describe the traits approach to leadership.
- State the two behavioral leadership dimensions found by the Ohio State Leadership Studies.
- Describe Fiedler's contingency model.
- Explain the leadership and contingency variables in House's path–goal model.
- State the situational variables in the Vroom and Yetton model.

OUTLINE

Preview Case

Thornton Bradshaw of RCA

When Thornton Bradshaw took over as chairman and chief executive officer of RCA in 1981, the company was a stumbling giant. It had acquired a number of companies over the years that led it down unfamiliar paths. RCA electronic products suffered from stiff competition with the Japanese, and NBC was lagging behind the other networks in television ratings. Earnings per share of common stock dropped from $3.35 in the 1970s to a minus $0.19 in 1981. However, since 1981, Bradshaw has sold off most of RCA's unprofitable businesses, earnings have risen to $3.19 per share (in 1984), and he has chosen a successor for when he retires from RCA.

This remarkable turn-about at RCA can be attributed to Bradshaw's leadership. When he took over in 1981, RCA did not have a consistent approach to running its many businesses. It did not know what it was, or what it wanted to become. RCA had become an extraordinarily diverse grouping of businesses: it was in carpets, frozen foods, steel furniture, financial services, car rentals (Hertz), consumer and commercial electronics, and broadcasting. There was no thought about what kind of company it was, or what its future should be.

The first thing that Bradshaw did was to hire a management consulting firm to study the basic industries in which RCA operated and future prospects of those industries. The consulting firm also assessed the strengths and weaknesses of RCA and how its businesses fit into each of the different industries. Within a short period of time, it became apparent to Bradshaw and his team that RCA had great strengths in electronics, communications, and entertainment. These strengths were derived from its people, who were mostly engineers and scientists; from its tradition, which centered on its laboratories, marketing, and manufacturing; and from its service company, which could fix electronic products ranging from computers to television sets. Unfortunately, these engineers and scientists knew little about freezing chickens, renting cars, or providing financial services.

Thus RCA's future lay in the electronics/communications market. With the deregulation of AT&T and the enormous need for information and control of that information, the market was tremendous.

RCA's biggest problem was that the businesses about which it had little knowledge were draining resources from its major growth businesses. Bradshaw soon realized that RCA could not supply the financial resources to compete successfully in the office furniture or finance business—or any of its other nonelectronic businesses—and, at the same time, finance putting satellites into orbit, construct new electronics plants, design new products, build more studios for the production of in-house TV shows, and produce more movies. To solve the financial problems at RCA, Bradshaw sold off most of the businesses that were not related to the communications/electronics market.

According to Bradshaw, a successful leader should do three things. First, a leader may not know as much about a business as the manager of that division, but the leader's role is to understand the problems of running the entire organization. For example, Bradshaw admits that he doesn't know the details of the Hertz operation but does understand and trust the managers who run that business. Second, a leader should have a clear "vision" of where the organization is going and hire people who agree with this vision. Third, a leader is a person whom others can follow with enthusiasm. This person sets the moral tone of the organization. Subordinates should say, "That's the way I want to live."[1]

A basic function of managers is to make decisions, and the extent to which subordinates are involved in the decision-making process is a basic issue in leadership. Even the most experienced managers have difficulty in deciding what style of leadership is most appropriate. In day-to-day work, managers are continually faced with issues such as those described in the Preview Case: responsibility and authority, delegation of decision making, control, performance evaluation, team building, and negotiating new business deals. Their experiences raise a number of questions about the leadership process: How can I get the job done most effectively? What is the *best* leadership style? When should I listen to my subordinates, and when should I give orders? If I become too friendly with my subordinates, will I lose their respect? How should I use my power to reward and punish people?

Although managers confidently discuss leadership characteristics—and many managers think that they can select good leaders on the basis of personal experience—the ability to develop more effective leaders remains a problem. Peter Drucker points out that leaders are the basic and the scarcest resource of any business enterprise.[2] As a result, many business failures can be attributed at least in part to ineffective leadership. Most organizations continually search for people who have the necessary ability to lead effectively. A quick look at the "Help Wanted" sections of the *New York Times*, *Washington Post*, or *Wall Street Journal* reveals hundreds of openings for people who are dynamic and effective leaders.

Each of us has a perception of leadership. We can give examples of what we consider to be good and poor leadership. Similarly, managers attempt to define effective leadership in trying to understand the leadership process. One way to begin understanding leadership is to study the behavior of individual leaders in business, government, military, civil rights, and religious organizations. Much can be learned about leadership through studying the biographies of outstanding and charismatic people such as Andrew Carnegie, Winston Churchill, Mahatma Gandhi, Joan of Arc, Golda Meir, George Patton, Martin Luther King, and Billy Graham. Most of the information we have about the leadership process, however, comes from numerous studies conducted in factories, offices, college laboratories, military units, and volunteer organizations. In this chapter, we will use the results of some of the more definitive leadership studies as we attempt to provide an understanding of the dynamics involved in the leadership process.

NATURE OF THE LEADERSHIP PROCESS

What is the difference between *leaders* and *leadership*? The popular definition of leaders is that they are people who draw other people to themselves. Leaders in this sense are people who command the trust and loyalty of others and whom others want to follow. However, most of the work in an organization is accomplished by individuals—managers of insurance offices, teachers, line supervisors at local mills, bank vice-presidents, newspaper editors, and so on—who may not be particularly charismatic. A **leader** in an organization, therefore, is someone who plans, organizes, controls, communicates, delegates, and accepts the responsibility for reaching the organization's goals. A leader is an individual who is given the authority and responsibility to accomplish the goals of an organization and is held accountable for the results. The manager of a local office of a large insurance company, for example, has the responsibility and authority to write insurance policies, train secretaries and other agents, handle client insurance claims, process changes in insurance policies, and investigate claims. A manager usually accomplishes these tasks by exercising leadership.

Leadership is the process of influencing group activities toward the achievement of goals.[3] This definition contains two important concepts. First, leadership involves a relationship between two or more people in which influence and power are unevenly distributed. This definition differentiates between being the *designated leader* of a group—the person who is in charge of a group and has been given the authority to exert influence on it—and engaging in leadership behavior as a member of the group. For example, the director of industrial relations may be the person that management designates to settle grievances brought against the company by employees. However, the first-line supervisor and/or the union shop steward may in fact be the leaders when they listen to employee complaints and take action to resolve problems before they reach the grievance stage.

The second concept in the definition of leadership is that leaders do not exist in isolation. If people want to know whether they are exercising leadership, they should look behind them. Is anyone following them? In most instances, people cannot coerce others into behaving in certain ways. Therefore leadership implies that followers must consent to being influenced. In accepting an individual as a leader, the followers voluntarily give up some of their freedom to make decisions in order to achieve a goal. An individual who finds it difficult to give up some decision-making freedom will not be a satisfied group member, just as an individual who finds it hard to make decisions for others will not find leadership very comfortable or rewarding.

Leader–Subordinate Relationships

Leadership is considered valuable by subordinates, and leaders become an integral part of a group or team only after proving their value to subordinates. For example, John Thompson, basketball coach at Georgetown University, demonstrated his leadership during the 1981–1982 through the 1984–1985 college basketball seasons. He led his team into the Final Four in three of the four years, winning the NCAA Championship in 1984. The players followed his advice both on and off the court because they knew it was sound, it resulted in deep psychological rewards and for some (Patrick Ewing, in particular) it yielded great economic rewards. The psychological rewards included a sense of achievement when the team won the championship, visited the White House to meet and be praised by President Reagan, appeared on the Today Show, and the like.

People in leadership positions also gain economic and psychological rewards. People at the top of many organizations are paid 10–20 times as much as the lowest-paid employees. (Notwithstanding the possibility that some people may not be worth that much more than others, it is clear that someone thinks so.) However, people seek leadership even when there are no economic rewards. The captain of a collegiate football team, a union steward, and the chairperson of a civic or church committee do not hold paid positions, but they usually exercise leadership. Leadership rewards people with influence or power over others; with this power, people believe that they can influence to some extent the well-being of others and can affect their own destinies.[4]

Leaders receive their authority from a group because the group has accepted them as leaders. To maintain a leadership position, a person must enable the group members to gain satisfactions that are otherwise beyond their reach. In return, the group satisfies the leader's need for power and prominence and gives the leader the support necessary to reach organizational goals.

Sources of a Leader's Power

In order to influence others, a person must appeal to one or more of their needs. (See Chapter 7.) If a robber is pointing a gun at a bank teller and seems ready to fire it, chances are that the teller will do what the robber asks. History demonstrates, however, that in many situations people refuse to obey an order even when faced with death. Thus effective leadership depends as much on acceptance of direction by the follower as on the leader giving it.

Because power and influence are central to a manager's job, Chapter 16 presents an in-depth discussion of the sources of a manager's power. Therefore, in this chapter, we will consider only briefly the sources of a leader's power.[5]

LEGITIMATE POWER Subordinates may do something because the manager has the right to request them to do it, and the subordinates have an obligation to comply. This **legitimate power** comes from the manager's position in the company.

REWARD POWER Subordinates may do something to obtain rewards that are controlled by the manager (promotions, pay raises, better assignments). Thus **reward power** comes from the manager's ability to provide something desired by subordinates in return for the subordinates' performance.

COERCIVE POWER Subordinates may do something to avoid punishments that are controlled by the manager (demotions, reprimands, no pay raises, termination). Unfortunately, **coercive power** does not encourage desired behavior. Chapter 6 described how workers whom managers reprimand for poor workmanship may suddenly slow production, stop working altogether, be absent more often, and so on.

REFERENT POWER Subordinates may do something because they admire the manager, want to be like the manager, and want to receive the manager's approval. **Referent power** is usually associated with individuals who possess admired personality characteristics, charisma, or a good reputation.

EXPERT POWER Subordinates may do something because they believe that the manager has special knowledge and expertise and knows what is needed to accomplish the task. Street gangs usually ascribe **expert power** to those who can fight the best; salespeople to those who sell the most. Expert power has a narrow scope: people tend to be influenced by another person only within that person's area of expertise.

EFFECTIVE USE OF POWER Figure 11-1 divides these sources of power into the personal and the organizational. Legitimate, reward, and coercive powers are organizational and are a part of the manager's job. Company rules and regulations prescribe them. A group probably will not achieve exceptional levels of performance if its manager relies solely on organizational power to influence subordinates. Reliance on referent and expert power—personal power—usually leads to higher job satisfaction and less absenteeism or turnover among subordinates. However, a manager must use all five sources of power at times, depending on the situation, to obtain both subordinate satisfaction and productivity.

LEADERSHIP MODELS

Many managers believe that they possess the intuitive ability to identify outstanding leaders. Often, they believe that people with pleasing personalities will be highly successful managers and recommend as managers those who have a great deal of personal charm.

A second reason for selection of a manager can be explained by attribution theory. (See Chapter 4.) Attribution is one way that people explain the behaviors of others. The manager thinks, "If these qualities enabled me to

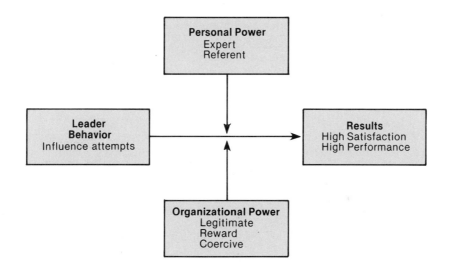

FIGURE 11-1. Sources of a Leader's Power and Effectiveness

Source: Yukl, G. *Leadership in Organizations*, 43. Copyright © 1981 by and adapted with permission of Prentice-Hall, Inc., Englewood Cliffs, N.J.

get this position and carry out my responsibilities successfully, I will pick others who have qualities similar to my own, and they will be successful also." Thus an individual's leadership success may depend on his or her manager's attribution process. If subordinates have a manager with similar personal qualities, the chances of their getting a favorable recommendation are greater than if they have a manager with dissimilar personal qualities. In other words, the leader attributes the potential for success to the subordinates because the subordinates possess characteristics similar to those of the leader.

Although some managers have the intuitive ability to select individuals who become good leaders, most managers do not possess this ability. Certainly, the attribution method of selection leaves much to be desired. However, there are several more objective ways to assess leadership effectiveness and leadership potential. In the remainder of this chapter, we present three general models for assessing leadership—traits, behavioral, and contingency—and then examine in more detail three contingency models: Fiedler's contingency, House's path–goal, and Vroom and Yetton's normative models. Managers should understand multidimensional character of leadership to avoid making premature conclusions about it.

Traits Models

The **traits model** is based on observed characteristics of a large number of successful and unsuccessful leaders. The resulting lists of traits are then compared to those of potential leaders to predict their success or failure.[6] There is considerable support for the notion that effective leaders have different interests and abilities and, perhaps, even different personality traits than do less effective leaders; however, most researchers have come to regard the traits approach as inadequate for successfully predicting leadership performance for at least three reasons.

First, although more than 100 personality traits of successful leaders have been identified, no consistent pattern or patterns have been found. The stereotypes of successful sales managers as optimistic, enthusiastic, and dominant and successful production managers as progressive, introverted, cooperative, and genuinely respectful of others, are just that: stereotypes. Many successful sales managers and production managers do not have all, or even some, of these characteristics. In fact, the list of personality traits never ends, and researchers often disagree over which traits are the most important for an effective leader. Furthermore, two leaders with different patterns of traits have been found to be successful in the same situation.

Despite these difficulties, the evidence does suggest that four traits generally are shared by most (but not all) successful leaders.[7] These traits, which are more likely to be found in middle-level and top managers than in first-line managers, are:

- *Intelligence*. Leaders tend to have somewhat higher intelligence than their followers.
- *Maturity and breadth*. Leaders tend to be emotionally mature and have a broad range of interests.

■ *Inner motivation and achievement drive.* Leaders want to accomplish things; when they achieve one goal, they seek another. They do not depend primarily on others for their motivation to achieve goals.

■ *People centered.* Leaders are able to work effectively with other people in a variety of situations. They respect others and realize that to accomplish tasks they must be considerate of others.

Individual differences in personality affect people's social perceptions and, consequently, play an important part in determining their behavior. Thus an assessment of leadership ability must in some way allow for such differences.

The second criticism of the traits model concerns the fact that it relates physical characteristics such as height, weight, appearance, physique, energy, and health to effective leadership. However, most of these factors also correlate with many situational factors that can significantly affect a leader's effectiveness. For example, military or law enforcement people must be a certain minimum height and weight in order to perform their tasks effectively. While these characteristics may help an individual to rise to a manager's position in such organizations, the number of inches of height or pounds of weight do not correlate highly with performance. In educational or business organizations, on the other hand, height and weight are not prerequisites for rising to an administrative position.

The final criticism of the model is that leadership itself is known to be complex. A relationship between personality and a person's interest in particular types of jobs could well exist, and a study relating personality to a measure of effectiveness would not reflect this. For example, one study found that high earners (a measure of success) in small firms were more aspiring, tended to have interests similar to those of personnel managers, were more open-minded, and described themselves as more considerate than low earners. In small firms, it should be noted, each individual is required to perform numerous jobs, and individuals who are predisposed to performing multiple jobs may seek out small firms that permit them to do so.[8]

Behavioral Models

Because of the failure of the traits model to predict successful leadership behavior, researchers turned to an examination of the structure and functions of groups. Their emphasis shifted from trying to identify traits that are important in leaders to studying leaders' behavior; that is, what they actually do and how they do it. Behavioral models suggest that effective leaders assist individuals and groups in achieving task goals in two ways: (1) by having task-centered relations with subordinates, in which they focus attention on the quality and quantity of work accomplished; and (2) by being considerate and supportive of group members' attempts to achieve personal goals (such as work satisfaction, promotions, and recognition), settling disputes, keeping people happy, providing encouragement, and giving positive reinforcement.

OHIO STATE UNIVERSITY LEADERSHIP STUDIES The greatest number of studies of leader behavior has come from the **Ohio State University leader-**

ship studies program, which began in the late 1940s under the direction of Ralph Stogdill.[9] The research aimed at identifying the leader behaviors that are important for the attainment of group and organizational goals. These efforts resulted in the identification of two dimensions of leader behavior: consideration and initiating structure.[10]

Consideration is the extent to which leaders are likely to have job relationships characterized by mutual trust, two-way communication, respect for subordinates' ideas, and consideration for their feelings. Leaders with this style emphasize the needs of the individual. They typically find time to listen to subordinates, are willing to make changes, look out for the personal welfare of subordinates and are friendly and approachable. A high degree of consideration indicates psychological closeness between the leader and subordinates; a low degree indicates greater psychological distance and a more impersonal leader.

Initiating structure is the extent to which leaders are likely to define and structure their roles and those of subordinates toward accomplishing the group's goals. Leaders with this style emphasize direction of group activities through planning, communicating information, scheduling, assigning tasks to subordinates, emphasizing deadlines, and giving directions. They maintain definite standards of performance and ask subordinates to follow standard rules and regulations. In short, leaders with a high degree of initiating structure concern themselves with accomplishing tasks by giving directions and expecting them to be followed.

Figure 11–2 illustrates these two dimensions of leader behavior. A leader may be ranked high, low, or moderate on consideration and initiating structure. For example, former President Jimmy Carter might be thought of as high on consideration and moderate on initiating structure. Tom Landry, coach of the Dallas Cowboys football team, might be rated high on initiating structure and moderate on consideration. The model indicates that a leader who emphasizes the consideration dimension generally fosters subordinate satisfaction, group harmony, and cohesion; and that a leader who empha-

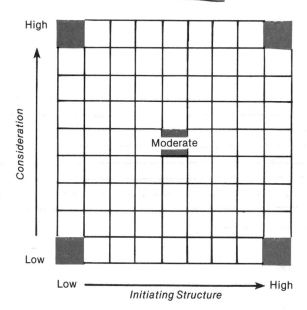

FIGURE 11–2.
Ohio State University
Leadership Grid

sizes the initiating structure dimension generally improves productivity, at least in the short-run. However, it has been shown that leaders high on initiating structure and low on consideration generally have a large number of grievances and a high turnover rate in their group.

The Ohio State University researchers made the underlying assumption that leader behavior is related not only to indirect measures of performance, such as absenteeism, grievances, and turnover, but also to direct measures of performance, such as the number of units produced. However, subsequent studies by others have failed to establish a significant relationship between the two dimensions of leadership behavior and group performance. This failure stems from the fact that individual productivity is influenced by other factors, including (1) individual social status within the group; (2) the technology used; (3) individual expectations of a certain style of supervision; and (4) individual psychological rewards from working with a particular type of leader.

WHEN CONSIDERATION IS EFFECTIVE   The most positive effects of consideration leader behaviors on subordinates' productivity and job satisfaction occur when:

- The task is routine and denies individuals any job satisfaction.
- Subordinates are predisposed toward participative leadership.
- Subordinates must learn something new.
- Subordinates feel that their involvement in the decision-making process is legitimate and affects their job performance.
- Few status differences exist between the leader and followers.

WHEN INITIATING STRUCTURE IS EFFECTIVE   The most positive effects of initiating structure leader behaviors on subordinates' productivity and job satisfaction occur when:

- A high degree of pressure for output is imposed by sources other than the leader.
- The task satisfies subordinates.
- Subordinates depend on the leader for information and direction on how to complete the task.
- Subordinates are psychologically predisposed toward being told what to do and how to do it.
- More than 12 people report to the leader.
- The task is nonroutine.

Let us consider how one manager effectively used initiating structure to revive a large telecommunications company in Italy.

ACROSS CULTURES

Italy's Most Talked-About Executive

The Italian press gives her star treatment, calling her "Lady Computer" and "the Manager in Jeans." Marisa Bellisario doesn't mind, though the labels are not quite accurate. She wears jeans to the office occasionally, but is recognized as the first woman to make it to the top of a major Italian industrial company.

Bellisario is president of Italtel, a $800 million company that is Italy's leading manufacturer of tele-communication equipment. When she arrived at Italtel in 1981, she characterized the company as "sedate and bureaucratic." Its payroll was too high and it was losing about $200 million a year. Because of the close relationship between the company and the government, numerous unprofitable practices had begun. She believed, however, that the company must carve out a place in the fiercely contested export markets for telephone gear. To be competitive, the company first had to become profitable.

Her strategy was to break up the company into product divisions and cut deadwood in staff positions [high initiating structure]. Because Italtel was a state-owned company, many thought that it was next to impossible to get rid of employees. During her first three years, more than 7,000 people were let go. Sales per employee have nearly trebled, absenteeism has dropped by a third, and there has been no labor trouble. Of the 29 senior executives now at Italtel, only ten were in the company before, and of these, only the general counsel and the chief accountant are in the same jobs. She said, "I was surrounded by people who had been there forever. This company was like a building without windows. I had to open it up to the world." Her subordinates say that her organizational abilities are truly remarkable, as well as her capacity to make decisions in a highly public arena [initiating structure].

Prior to working at Italtel, she worked at Olivetti in the corporate planning department. Working 12-hour days at least, she chaired meetings briskly in her impatient style. The president of Olivetti was impressed with her ability as a "housecleaner" and set her to turn around Olivetti's U.S. operation. The president gave her three years to fix the U.S. operation. However, within a year she returned to Italy and shortly thereafter resigned. She says, "I learned from this experience to manage a turnaround you need complete authority for a reasonable period of time."[11]

MAJOR WEAKNESSES OF THE MODEL   The major weakness of the Ohio State University research was the limited attention it gave to the effects of the situation on leadership style; it paid attention mostly to relationships between leader and subordinate and little attention to the situation surrounding the relationships. For example, if Italtel's financial and competitive conditions had been better, would Bellisario's style have worked? The importance of the situation is considered by the contingency, or situational, models of leadership.

Contingency Models in General

Research into the leadership process prior to the mid-1960s indicated no consistent relationship between leadership style and measures of performance, group processes, and job satisfaction. Although much of the research concluded that the situation within which a leader functions plays a significant role in the determination of the leader's effectiveness, researchers did little to identify key situational variables.[12]

Contingency leadership theorists, in contrast, direct their research toward discovering the variables that permit certain characteristics and behaviors of leaders to be effective in a given situation. For example, contingency theorists would hypothesize that effective college administrators and drill sergeants need substantially different characteristics and behaviors because each type of leader faces different situations.

Four contingency variables are frequently suggested for diagnosis and consideration as factors that influence a leader's behavior: (1) a leader's personal characteristics; (2) their subordinates' personal characteristics; (3) the group's characteristics; and (4) the structure of their group, department, or organization.[13] As suggested in Figure 11–3, these four contingency variables interact to influence the style of behavior that a leader will choose. The discussion of these variables is presented in the form of questions that leaders should ask when diagnosing the contingencies of a situation, with references to the chapters in which the topic or topics were covered.

LEADER'S CHARACTERISTICS   Chapters 3, 6, and 7 presented information about personality and attitudes, learning and reinforcement, and work motivation. The aspects of those topics that are important variables of leader characteristics include the following:

- *Personality*. How aggressive is the leader? Does the leader possess the intellectual ability to be a capable leader? Does the leader respond well to pressure?

- *Needs and motives*. What particular needs does the leader bring to the situation? What are the motivators in the situation? What are the hygiene factors?

- *Past experiences and reinforcement*. Has the leader received positive reinforcement using a particular leadership style in the past? Has the leader had previous experience in a similar situation?

SUBORDINATES' CHARACTERISTICS   The personalities of subordinates affect how they react to the leader's behavior. The same kinds of needs, motives,

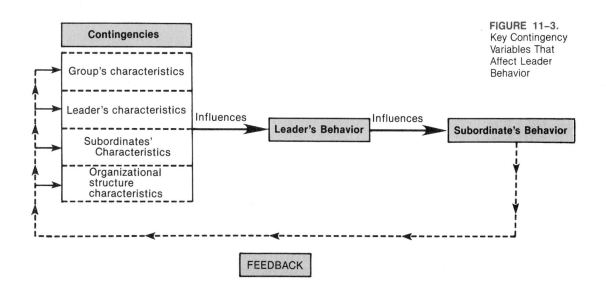

FIGURE 11–3.
Key Contingency
Variables That
Affect Leader
Behavior

and expectations affect subordinates' behavior as affect the leader's behavior in a situation:

- *Personality*. Will subordinates want to participate in decision making? Will they accept the leadership style of a highly initiating structure leader? How will aggressive subordinates react to a passive leader?

- *Needs and motives*. What kinds of needs do the subordinates bring to the situation? What are the motivators in the situation? What are the hygiene factors? What are the chances that the subordinates will experience intrinsic satisfaction from performing the task well?

- *Past experiences and reinforcement*. What kinds of behaviors in the past have led to successful task completion? If subordinates perform well, what is the probability that they will receive a significant reward (monetary or psychological)? What other types of reinforcement are the subordinates likely to expect?

GROUP'S CHARACTERISTICS   Chapters 9 and 10 discussed how groups operate in organizations, with Chapter 9 emphasizing group characteristics. Group characteristics that affect leadership include:

- *Group structure*. If the group is highly cohesive, what style of leadership will maintain this cohesion and, at the same time, result in high job performance? Do the members of the group all get along, or are there cliques within the group? What kind of communication network exists within the group?

- *Group task*. Does the task require the cooperation of all members? What kinds of decisions can the group make? Is the task better suited to a nominal or interacting group?

- *Group norms*. Do the group's norms agree with the organization's norms?

ORGANIZATIONAL STRUCTURE CHARACTERISTICS   Chapter 14 discusses organization design and how it relates to effectiveness. Organizational structure is the formal system of communication, authority, and responsibility that operates within a company. The characteristics of organizational structure that affect leadership include:

- *Hierarchy of authority*. What are the bases of leaders' power? What kinds of rewards and punishments do leaders control because of their position within the hierarchy? In a centralized system what types of decisions can managers at various levels make? In a decentralized system how much authority should be delegated to various levels of managers and employees?

- *Rules and regulations*. To what extent do formal, written statements specify acceptable and unacceptable decisions and behaviors? If rules and regulations are numerous how can leaders deviate from them when necessary?

No list of important situational factors or questions about them can be inclusive. The leadership process is very complex, and simple prescriptions (such as "democratic leaders have more satisfied workers than autocratic leaders") just do not work.

THREE CONTINGENCY MODELS

In this section we present and discuss three specific contingency models of leadership: Fiedler's contingency model, House's path–goal model, and the Vroom and Yetton normative model. Each provides at least a partial explanation of how contingency variables affect the leadership process.

Fiedler's Contingency Model

Fred Fiedler and his associates developed the first contingency model of the leadership process.[14] **Fiedler's contingency model** departs from the traits and behavioral models of leadership by specifying that a group's performance is contingent upon both the leader's motivational system and the degree to which the leader controls and influences the situation. The model's three contingency variables—group atmosphere, task structure, and the leader's position power—are shown in Figure 11-4. The three contingency variables—in combination—create eight situations.

GROUP ATMOSPHERE   A leader's authority depends partly on acceptance by the group. The **group atmosphere** measures a leader's perception of group acceptance. The leader who is accepted by and inspires loyalty in followers needs few signs of rank to get the followers to commit themselves to a task. When leader and followers get along well together, there is less friction in the group. In groups that reject the leader, the leader's basic problem is to keep from being undercut or having the task sabotaged. Only by maintaining tight control over group processes can the leader hope to maintain reasonable productivity.

TASK STRUCTURE   The extent to which a task performed by subordinates is routine or nonroutine is the degree of **task structure**. A routine task is likely to have clearly defined goals and only a few steps or work procedures, to be verifiable, and to have a correct solution. For example, an axle assembler in an auto plant who secures front and rear assemblies to chassis springs is performing a highly structured task; the goals are clearly defined, the method to accomplish the task is detailed and specific, and correct performance is verifiable.

   At the other extreme is the task that is completely nonroutine, and the leader may possess no more knowledge about how to perform the task than the subordinates do. Such a task has unclear goals and multiple paths to accomplishment; the task cannot be done by the "numbers." Unstructured

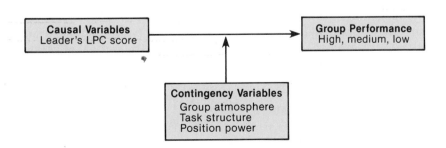

FIGURE 11–4.
Major Variables in Fiedler's Contingency Model

Source: Yukl, G. A. *Leadership in Organizations,* 137. Copyright © 1981 by Prentice-Hall, Inc., Englewood Cliffs, N.J. Adapted with permission.

tasks are difficult to manage and include those performed by detectives, policy makers, and marketing researchers.

LEADER POSITION POWER Leader **position power** is the extent to which a leader possesses reward, coercive, and legitimate power. In most business organizations, leaders such as supervisors and managers have high position power, including the authority to hire, discipline, and fire employees and to direct the actions of employees. In most voluntary organizations, committees, and social organizations, leaders tend to have low position power.

LEADERSHIP STYLE Fiedler was concerned with measuring the leadership style of an individual. He developed the **least-preferred co-worker (LPC) scale** to measure two different leadership styles: (1) task-oriented, or initiating structure; and (2) relationship-oriented, or consideration. Take a few minutes before reading on and complete the LPC scale that appears in Table 11–1.

To determine your LPC score, sum the ratings you checked to obtain a score between 18 and 144. Fiedler states that someone with a score of 64 or higher is a high-LPC person. The high-LPC person is the type who can work with difficult people. The high-LPC person has a sensitivity toward others and is classified as a "relationship-motivated" leader.

If your score is 57 or lower, you are considered a low-LPC leader. You tend to classify the least-preferred co-worker in negative terms. The low-LPC person is a task-motivated leader. A score of 58 to 63 indicates a mix of motivations in your leadership style.

MOST-LEAST FAVORABLE SITUATIONS In Figure 11–5, the three basic situational variables of leadership are plotted on a continuum of most favorable to least favorable situations for leaders. This results in a matrix of the eight combinations of situations and variables referred to previously. In the terminology of the model, each matrix block is called an *octant*. The Fiedler model assumes that the situation is most favorable for a leader in octant 1: group atmosphere is positive, leader position power is strong, and subordinates perform structured tasks. A leader will have somewhat less control and influence in octant 2, where group atmosphere is positive and tasks are structured, but leader position power is weak. In Octant 8, the leader has the least amount of control of and influence on the group. In this situation, group atmosphere is poor, leader position power is weak, and subordinates perform unstructured tasks.

Some typical groups of employees that might be placed in octants 1 and 5 are those in telephone offices, craft shops, meat departments, and grocery departments. Octants 2 and 6 might include basketball and football teams and survey parties; octants 3 and 7, general supervisors, ROTC groups, research chemists, and military planning groups; and octants 4 and 8, disaster groups, church groups, and mental health groups. The critical question is: What kind of leadership style is most effective in a particular group situation?

ASSESSMENT Figure 11–6 shows the average results of the studies conducted by Fiedler and his associates and represents the basic contingency model.[15] The horizontal axis is the continuum from Figure 11–5; the vertical axis represents the leader's LPC score. Points above the dashed midline indicate situations where high-LPC leaders performed better than low-LPC leaders.

TABLE 11-1   Least-Preferred Co-Worker (LPC) Scale

Throughout your life, you will have worked in many groups with a wide variety of different people—on your job, in social groups, in church organizations, in volunteer groups, on athletic teams, and in many other situations. Some of your co-workers may have been very easy to work with in attaining the group's goals, while others were less so.

Think of all the people with whom you have ever worked, and then think of the person with whom you could work *least well*. He or she may be someone with whom you work now or with whom you have worked in the past. This does not have to be the person you liked least well, but should be the person with whom you had the most difficulty getting a job done, the *one* individual with whom you could work *least well*.

Describe this person on the scale that follows by placing an *X* in the appropriate space.

Look at the words at both ends of the line before you mark your *X*. *There are no right or wrong answers.* Work rapidly; your first answer is likely to be the best. Do not omit any items, and mark each item only once.

Now describe the person with whom you can work least well.

										Scoring
Pleasant	8	7	6	5	4	3	2	1	Unpleasant	___
Friendly	8	7	6	5	4	3	2	1	Unfriendly	___
Rejecting	1	2	3	4	5	6	7	8	Accepting	___
Tense	1	2	3	4	5	6	7	8	Relaxed	___
Distant	1	2	3	4	5	6	7	8	Close	___
Cold	1	2	3	4	5	6	7	8	Warm	___
Supportive	8	7	6	5	4	3	2	1	Hostile	___
Boring	1	2	3	4	5	6	7	8	Interesting	___
Quarrelsome	1	2	3	4	5	6	7	8	Harmonius	___
Gloomy	1	2	3	4	5	6	7	8	Cheerful	___
Open	8	7	6	5	4	3	2	1	Guarded	___
Backbiting	1	2	3	4	5	6	7	8	Loyal	___
Untrustworthy	1	2	3	4	5	6	7	8	Trustworthy	___
Considerate	8	7	6	5	4	3	2	1	Inconsiderate	___
Nasty	1	2	3	4	5	6	7	8	Nice	___
Agreeable	8	7	6	5	4	3	2	1	Disagreeable	___
Insincere	1	2	3	4	5	6	7	8	Sincere	___
Kind	8	7	6	5	4	3	2	1	Unkind	___
									Total	___

Source: Adapted from Fielder, F., Chemers, M., and Mahr, L. *Improving Leadership Effectiveness.* New York: John Wiley and Sons, 1976, 7. Used with permission.

Types of Situations for Leaders

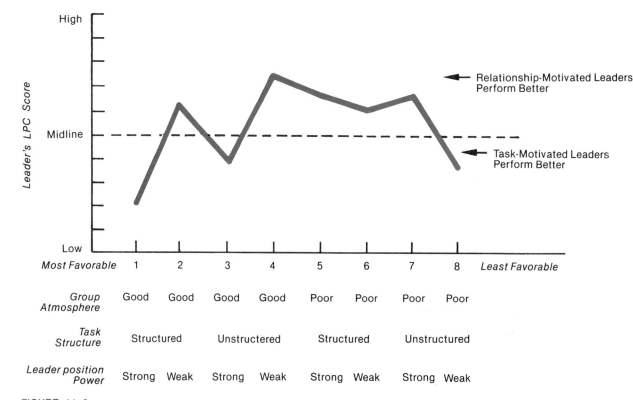

		Most Favorable ⟷ Least Favorable							
Contingency Variables	Group Atmosphere	Good	Good	Good	Good	Poor	Poor	Poor	Poor
	Task Structure	Structured		Unstructured		Structured		Unstructured	
	Leader Position Power	Strong	Weak	Strong	Weak	Strong	Weak	Strong	Weak
		1	2	3	4	5	6	7	8

FIGURE 11–5.
Continuum of the Three Basic Leadership Contingency Variables

Source: Adapted by permission of the *Harvard Business Review*. Exhibit from Fiedler, F. Engineer the Job to Fit the Manager. *Harvard Business Review*, September–October 1965, 118. Copyright © 1965 by the President and Fellows of Harvard College. All rights reserved.

FIGURE 11–6.
Relationships Among Leader LPC, Group Performance, and Leadership Style

Source: Adapted from Fiedler, F. What Triggers the Person–Situation Interaction in Leadership? In D. Magnusson and N. Endler (Eds.) *Personality at the Crossroads: Current Issues in Interactional Psychology*. Hillsdale, N.J.: Lawrence Erlbaum Associates, 1977.

Points below the dashed midline indicate situations where low-LPC leaders performed better than high-LPC leaders. The solid line represents the prediction of the relationship between a leader's LPC score and work-group effectiveness.

As Figure 11–6 shows, task-motivated (low-LPC) leaders performed more effectively than high-LPC leaders in the most favorable situations (octants 1, 2, and 3) and in the least favorable situation (octant 8). Low-LPC leaders are motivated basically by task accomplishments. In the most favorable situation, in which their group supports them, their power position is high, and the task is structured (octant 1), these leaders will strive to develop pleasant work relations by directing subordinates. They will be friendly and considerate toward co-workers. In the least favorable situation (octant 8), in which the task is unstructured, they lack group support, their position power is low, and they will devote their energies to achieving the primary goal of the company by telling people what to do.

Figure 11–6 also shows situations in which high-LPC leaders will probably perform more effectively than low-LPC leaders. High-LPC leaders obtain the best group performance under conditions that are moderately favorable (octants 4–7). Octants 4 and 5 describe situations in which (1) the group has a structured task, but it dislikes the leader, who must demonstrate concern for the emotions of subordinates; or (2) the group likes the leader but has an unstructured task, and the leader must depend on the willingness and creativity of group members to accomplish the goals.

There are several problems with Fiedler's contingency model.[16] In particular, critics have questioned the use of LPC, arguing that better and more stable measures of leader behaviors are needed. LPC is a unidimensional concept; that is, it implies that if individuals are highly motivated toward task accomplishment, they are unconcerned with relations among group members, and vice versa. In addition, critics say that Fiedler's model does not take into account the fact that leaders can influence both the task structure and group atmosphere because of their knowledge of the situation. That is, the task can be modified by the leader and therefore is not a separate variable in the model. The nature of the task as perceived by subordinates can be determined, at least in part, by the leader's style. Thus the leader of a group that engages in a highly unstructured task can use his or her style to give the task some structure.

MANAGERIAL IMPLICATIONS In spite of these criticisms, Fiedler's contingency model has four important managerial implications. First, both relationship-motivated and task-motivated leaders perform well under certain situations but not under others. Outstanding managers at one level who get promoted to another level may fail at the higher level because their leadership style does not match the demands of the situation. For example, a company may be surprised when its most successful floor supervisor, recently promoted to production manager, fails in the new position. The contingency model suggests that the supervisor's failure may not indicate a lack of intellectual ability, but rather a change in situation to one in which the individual's leadership style is no longer appropriate. The task has probably changed from a relatively structured to a less structured one. Assuming that this person's position power and acceptance by the group did not change, the contingency model would predict that two different leadership styles would be required of the same person in these different situations; that is, the supervisor has moved from a situation requiring a task-motivated style to a situation requiring a more relationship-motivated style.

Second, leaders cannot accurately be described as generally good or poor; instead leaders perform well in some situations but not in others. The floor supervisor promoted to production manager illustrates this point.

Third, leaders' performance depends both on their motivational bases and the situation. Therefore an organization can change leadership effectiveness by changing the motivational states of a manager or by modifying the favorableness of a manager's situation.

Fourth, leaders can do something about their situations. Table 11–2 presents some of Fiedler's suggestions for changing particular contingency factors. He is suggesting that leaders themselves can make changes that result in more favorable situations.

House's Path–Goal Model

Puzzled by the contradictory findings about leadership, Robert J. House developed a model based on the expectancy theory of motivation. (See Chapter 7.) **House's path–goal model** of leadership effectiveness does not indicate the one best way to lead but instead suggests that a leader must select a style most appropriate to the particular situation.[17]

The model states essentially that a leader should try to enhance subordinates' satisfaction with their jobs and increase their job performance. A leader can make job satisfaction easier to obtain and increase subordinates satisfaction by clarifying the nature of the task, reducing impediments to successful task completion, and increasing the opportunities for subordinates to obtain satisfaction. The model states further that the motivation of subordinates will increase to the extent that the leader performs these functions. Subordinates are satisfied with their jobs to the extent that perfor-

---

TABLE 11–2   **Leadership Actions to Change Contingency Variables**

Modifying Group Atmosphere

1. Spend more—or less—informal time with your subordinates (lunch, leisure activities, etc.).
2. Request particular people for work in your group.
3. Volunteer to direct difficult or troublesome subordinates.
4. Suggest or effect transfers of particular subordinates into or out of your unit.
5. Raise morale by obtaining positive outcomes for subordinates (e.g., special bonuses, time-off, attractive jobs).

Modifying Task Structure

If you wish to work with less structured tasks, you can:

1. Ask your boss, whenever possible, to give you the new or unusual problems and let you figure out how to get them done.
2. Bring the problems and tasks to your group members, and invite them to work with you on the planning and decision-making phases of the tasks.

If you wish to work with more highly structured tasks, you can:

1. Ask your superior to give you, whenever possible, the tasks that are more structured or to give you more detailed instructions.
2. Break the job down into smaller subtasks that can be more highly structured.

Modifying Position Power

To raise your position power, you can:

1. Show your subordinates "who's boss" by exercising fully the powers that the organization provides.
2. Make sure that information to your group gets channeled through you.

To lower your position power, you can:

1. Call on members of your group to participate in planning and decision-making functions.
2. Let your assistants exercise relatively more power.

Source: Fiedler, F. How Do You Make Leaders More Effective? New Answers to an Old Puzzle. *Organizational Dynamics*, Autumn 1972, *1*:3–8. Used by permission.

mance leads to things that they value highly. House's general model is shown graphically in Figure 11-7, and the following sections examine each of its parts.

LEADER BEHAVIORS   The model identifies four distinct types of leader behavior:

- **Supportive leadership** includes considering the needs of subordinates, displaying concern for their welfare, and creating a friendly climate in the work group. This is similar to what the Ohio State University researchers labeled *consideration*.

- **Directive leadership** involves letting subordinates know what they are expected to do, giving them specific guidance, asking them to follow rules and regulations, scheduling and coordinating their work, and setting standards of performance for them. This is similar to the Ohio State University researchers' *initiating structure*.

- **Participative leadership** includes consulting with subordinates and evaluating their opinions and suggestions when making decisions.

- **Achievement-oriented leadership** entails setting challenging goals, seeking performance improvements, emphasizing excellence in performance, and showing confidence that subordinates will attain high standards of performance.

In contrast to Fiedler, House believes that the same leader can practice these four styles at varying times and in different situations. Remember that Fiedler's model has been criticized for saying that leaders cannot be motivated toward accomplishing tasks and improving relationships among group members at the same time; in fact, Fiedler believes that it is easier for leaders to change the situation than to change leadership style.

CONTINGENCY VARIABLES: SUBORDINATES AND TASKS   House's model has two contingency variables: subordinate and task characteristics. The personal characteristics of the subordinates determine how they will react to a leader's behavior. For example, subordinates with high needs for belongingness and affiliation may find immediate need satisfaction in supportive leaders. On the other hand, subordinates with high needs for autonomy, responsibility, and self-actualization will probably be motivated more by directive leaders than by supportive leaders.

A routine task has the following characteristics:

- It does not provide employees with an opportunity to use a variety of skills.

- Employees do bits and pieces of a job rather than the whole job.

FIGURE 11-7
The Path–Goal Leadership Model

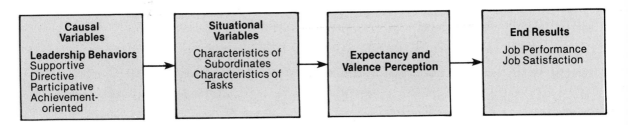

- It is not very important to the overall success of the organization.
- Employees make few decisions regarding scheduling and means for accomplishing the task.
- Employees receive little information about how well they perform the task.

A nonroutine task has the opposite characteristics. Figure 11–8 illustrates the application of supportive and directive leadership styles to routine and nonroutine tasks.

EFFECTS OF DIFFERENT LEADERSHIP STYLES When subordinates have a task that is tedious, boring, routine, or otherwise unpleasant, a manager can make performance of the task more pleasant by considering and supporting the employees' needs. For example, employees making Big Macs at McDonald's all day long cannot derive much self-esteem or self-actualization from

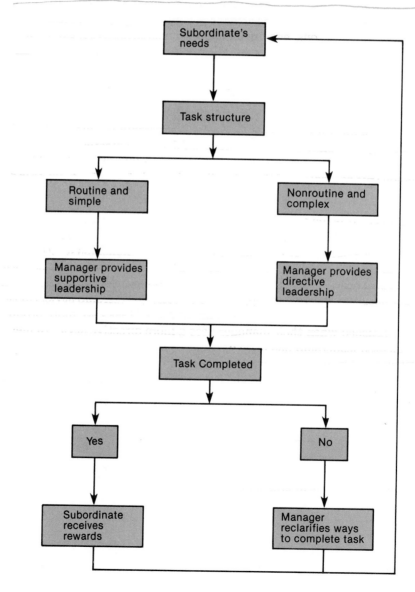

FIGURE 11–8.
Partial Version of House's Path–Goal Model

the performance of this highly structured and routine task. They would probably perceive a directive leadership style as excessive and unnecessary. A supportive manager, however, could increase employees' satisfaction with the work, which itself provides few satisfactions.

On the other hand, a more directive leadership style is appropriate for highly unstructured, complex, and nonroutine tasks. Directive leaders can help subordinates to cope with task uncertainty and clarify the paths to high job satisfaction and performance. For example, the manager of an industrial-relations team who gives subordinates guidance and direction on how to process a grievance for arbitration is attempting to clarify how to win the case for the company. The team members do not perceive this style of leadership as excessive, since it provides job satisfaction by helping them win the case.

Participative leadership involves sharing information, power, and influence between managers and subordinates. When the task is clear and subordinates are not ego-involved in the work, participative leadership will likely contribute to satisfaction and performance only for highly independent subordinates. For ambiguous, ego-involving tasks, participative leadership will have positive effects regardless of a subordinate's needs for self-esteem or achievement.

Achievement-oriented leadership is characterized by leaders who set challenging goals, expect subordinates to perform at their highest level, and show a high degree of confidence that the subordinates will assume responsibility for accomplishing challenging tasks. Leadership of this kind can induce striving for high standards and confidence in meeting challenging goals, especially among individuals who are working on unstructured tasks. This holds true regardless of the subordinate's needs for self-esteem or independence.

ASSESSMENT   It is too early to make anything but preliminary comments on House's path–goal model.[18] The research conducted so far has methodological limitations because of the complexity of the relationships addressed in the model. However, early research findings show that workers who perform highly routine or tedious tasks report higher job satisfactions when their manager uses a supportive (as opposed to directive) leadership style. On the other hand, subordinates who perform unstructured tasks are more productive and satisfied when their manager uses a more directive style. Achievement-oriented leadership has little effect on subordinates' performance and job satisfaction when they are performing routine and repetitive tasks. According to House, unless subordinates have some discretion over the what, when, and how of performing a task, the achievement-oriented leader can have little impact on subordinates' performance and satisfaction. Research has shown that participative leadership increases subordinates' efforts if they are performing an unstructured task; while participating in decision making about tasks, goals, plans, and procedures, subordinates learn more about the tasks and feel that they have a better chance of successfully completing them. If subordinates have a highly structured task and a clear understanding of the job, however, participative leadership has little effect on their performance.

We can gain some insight into how this model works by looking at how Joseph Lanier runs WestPoint Pepperell. We have identified the different styles of leadership he uses, depending on the circumstances.

In Practice: Joseph Lanier, WestPoint Pepperell, Inc.

In 1984, Joseph Lanier was named the best chief executive officer in the textile industry by the *Wall Street Transcript*. WestPoint Pepperell is the third largest textile manufacturer in the United States with sales over $1.4 billion and more than 22,000 employees in its 40 manufacturing plants. In an industry which is extremely competitive and suffers from heavy foreign competition, Lanier's leadership style has enabled WestPoint to retain its tradition as a low-cost producer of quality goods, such as Martex® towels, Cabin Craft® carpets, and Lady Pepperell® sheets.

To reduce the complexity of operating in this industry, Lanier operates the company as five autonomous divisions [directive leadership]. Each has a president, manufacturing and marketing vice-presidents, and a controller. Legal and financial operations are based in corporate headquarters. Corporate and division staff are very lean.

He has a good picture of where the company should go and a good grasp of when it should be there [achievement-oriented leadership]. By superior foresight and management skill, the company has created a manufacturing system where productivity per man hour has risen 50 percent over the past ten years, and quality is very high. He recently created a new international division with companies in Holland, United Kingdom, Belgium, Germany and France to manufacture cloth that can be tailored into Arrow shirts.

His employees describe him as enthusiastic. He gives freedom to managers, expects innovation, and tries not to second-guess his managers. Called a free-thinker, Lanier doesn't want to keep doing things the old way because they've always been done that way. He seeks advice and counsel from his managers [participative leadership] and is always searching for the facts. If he needs additional information, he goes right to the person. This approach not only gets him the answer quickly, but gives him an insight into the capability of the person.

His leadership style is also highlighted by his personal participation in training, promotions, and assignments of middle and upper management [supportive leadership]. The company prefers to promote from within and rewards are based on performance.[19]

MANAGERIAL IMPLICATIONS   The leadership style of a manager needs to vary according to the situation, as illustrated by Joseph Lanier's approach to management. Research findings support the notion that, while shop-floor personnel prefer a supportive manager in order to gain some satisfaction from performing routine and often boring tasks, middle-level and professional employees work better under a more directive leadership style. Job descriptions of positions at these higher levels are usually vague, and a directive leader can clarify the tasks and goals for the subordinates. It seems reasonable that different leadership styles are required for different occupational groupings and levels of an organization's hierarchy.

Vroom and Yetton Normative Model

Victor H. Vroom and Philip Yetton developed a normative theory of leadership that attempts to tell the manager which style of leader behavior is correct by varying the degree of subordinates' participation in the decision-making process.[20] Their model assumes that no single leadership style is appropriate for all situations. Instead, leaders should develop a range of leader behaviors, from autocratic to participative, and choose the style most appropriate to the situation. The Vroom and Yetton model has two contingency variables: (1) decision acceptance and quality, and (2) leadership style.

DECISION ACCEPTANCE   The degree of subordinate commitment needed to implement a decision effectively constitutes **decision acceptance**. In some cases, subordinates will be highly motivated to implement a decision even though they may not have any influence in making the decision. For example, few subordinates would refuse to accept a pay raise or take an afternoon off occasionally. Subordinates are more likely to implement a decision consistent with their values and preferences than one that they view as harmful to them (such as a reduction in the work force, demotion, and so on).

DECISION QUALITY   The extent to which decisions affect group processes such as communication, norms, and so on is called **decision quality**. For example, a decision on what time people go to lunch requires low decision quality, since it probably has little impact on the group's performance. Such decisions as the determination of the group's expected production rate, the assignment of people to tasks, and the determination of work rules and regulations require high decision quality. When decision quality is important and subordinates have relevant information that the leader does not have, a decision procedure that permits subordinate input will lead to a better decision than one that does not.

LEADERSHIP STYLES   Vroom and Yetton identify five leadership styles that can be placed on a continuum from highly autocratic to highly participative, as shown in Table 11–3. One leader can use all five styles, depending on the situation. The leader may be autocratic one time and participative the next. The key to effective management is the ability to correctly diagnose the situation before choosing a leadership style.

GUIDELINES FOR CHOOSING THE CORRECT LEADERSHIP STYLE   Vroom and Yetton suggested seven rules aimed at simplifying the selection of the appropriate leadership style. The manager who follows these rules should be able to discover quickly the most acceptable leadership style. The rules given in Table 11–4 indicate leadership styles that the manager should *avoid* in a given situation because decision acceptance and quality would be poor. The first three rules relate to the quality of the decision, and the remaining four relate to decision acceptance.

Vroom and Yetton also developed decision-process flow charts to simplify the application of their rules for managers. In Figure 11–9, the circled numbers indicate the preferred leadership style for each situation. A manager begins by answering question A: "If the decision were accepted, would it make a difference which course of action was adopted?" If the answer is no, the manager proceeds to question E, since questions B, C, and D are not relevant to this situation. Question E asks, "Is acceptance of decision by subordinates critical to effective implementation?" If the answer is no, the manager makes the decision autocratically and tells the subordinates what to do. Thus, by working down through the questions, the manager arrives at a

---

TABLE 11-3   Five Styles of Leadership

Leadership Styles	Degree of Subordinate Participation Encouraged by Leaders
	Low (Autocratic)
Leaders solve the problem or make the decision themselves using information available to them at the time.	1
Leaders obtain the necessary information from subordinates, then decide on the solution to the problem themselves. They may or may not tell their subordinates what the problem is in getting the information from them. The role played by subordinates in making the decision is clearly one of providing the necessary information to the leaders rather than generating or evaluating alternative solutions.	2
Leaders share the problem with relevant subordinates individually, getting their ideas and suggestions without bringing them together as a group. Then the leaders make the decision that may or may not reflect their subordinates' influence.	3
Leaders share the problem with their subordinates as a group, collectively obtaining their ideas and suggestions. Then the leaders make a decision that may or may not reflect their subordinates' influence.	4
Leaders share a problem with their subordinates as a group. Together they generate and evaluate alternatives and attempt to reach agreement (consensus) on a solution. The leaders' role is much like that of a committee chair: They do not try to influence the group to adopt "their" solution, and they are willing to accept and implement any solution that has the support of the entire group.	5
	High (Participative)

Source: Adapted, by the permission of the publisher, from Vroom, V. A. A New Look at Managerial Decision Making. *Organizational Dynamics,* Spring 1973, 67. Copyright © 1973 by AMACOM, a division of American Management Associations. All rights reserved.

---

leadership style most appropriate for a particular situation. If a manager has a choice of acceptable leadership styles, Vroom and Yetton recommend choosing the most autocratic one; it will save time without reducing the decision's quality or acceptance. Now use the In Practice: You're the President to practice choosing a leadership style.

In Practice: **You're the President**

You are president of a small but growing Midwestern bank, with its head office in the state's capital and branches in several nearby market towns. The location and type of business are factors which contribute to the emphasis on traditional and conservative banking practices at all levels.

When you bought the bank five years ago, it was in poor financial shape. Under your leadership, much progress has been made. This progress has been achieved while the economy has moved into a mild recession, and, as a result, your prestige among your bank managers is very high. Your success, which you are inclined to attribute principally to good luck and to a few timely decisions on your part, has, in your judgment, one unfortunate by-product. It has caused your subordinates to look to you for leadership and guidance in decision making beyond what you consider necessary. You have no doubts about the fundamental capabilities of these people but wish that they were not quite so willing to accede to your judgment.

You have recently acquired funds to permit opening a new branch. Your problem is to decide on a suitable location. You believe that there is no "magic formula" by which it is possible to select an optimal site. The choice will be made by a combination of some simple common-sense criteria and "what feels right." You have asked your managers to keep their eyes open for commercial real estate sites that might be suitable. Their knowledge about the communities in which they operate should be extremely useful in making a wise choice.

Their support is important because the success of the new branch will be highly dependent on your managers' willingness to supply staff and technical assistance during its early days. Your bank is small enough for everyone to feel like part of a team, and you feel that this has and will be critical to the bank's prosperity.

The success of this project will benefit everybody. Directly, they will benefit from the increased base of operations, and, indirectly, they will reap the personal and business advantages of being part of a successful and expanding business.

Leadership style you would use: _____. [Most managers would choose either leadership style 4 or 5, high participation.][21]

TABLE 11-4   **Rules Underlying the Vroom and Yetton Model**

Rules to Protect Decision Quality

Leader information rule. If the quality of the decision is important and you do not have enough information or expertise to solve the problem alone, rule out an autocratic style (1), since you might otherwise make a low-quality decision.

Goal congruence rule. If the quality of the decision is important and subordinates are not likely to make the proper decision for the organization, then rule out the highly participative style (5).

Unstructured problem rule. If the quality of the decision is important but you lack sufficient information and expertise and the problem is unstructured, eliminate the autocratic leadership styles (1, 2, and 3). Since the answer to the problem probably will arise while subordinates are openly talking about it, choose the more participative styles.

Rules to Protect Decision Acceptance

Acceptance rule. If acceptance by subordinates is critical to effective implementation, rule out the autocratic styles (1 and 2).

Conflict rule. If acceptance of the decision is important, subordinates will not accept autocratic leadership styles (1 and 2), and subordinates are likely to disagree over the correct solution, conflict is best resolved through the use of participatory leadership styles (3, 4, and 5).

Fairness rule. If the quality of the decision is unimportant but acceptance is important, use the most participatory style (5). An example of this rule is scheduling vacations for subordinates.

Acceptance priority rule. If acceptance is critical and not certain to result from an autocratic decision, and if subordinates are motivated to achieve the organization's goals, use a highly participative leadership style for best results.

Source: Adapted from Vroom, V. A New Look at Managerial Decision Making. *Organizational Dynamics*, Spring 1973, 2:67. Used with permission.

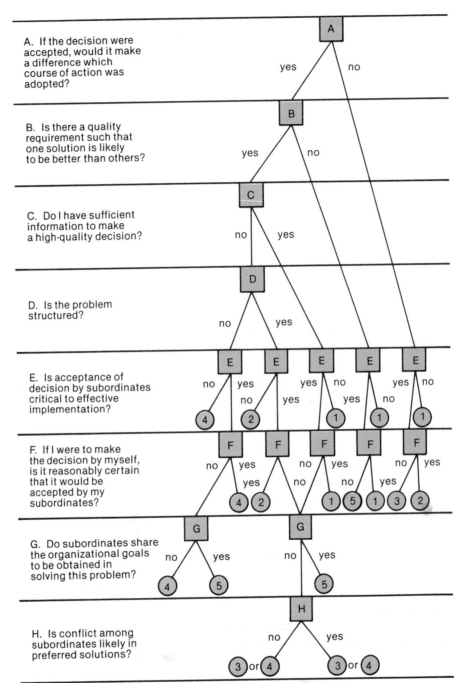

FIGURE 11–9.
Leadership-Style
Choices

A. If the decision were accepted, would it make a difference which course of action was adopted?

B. Is there a quality requirement such that one solution is likely to be better than others?

C. Do I have sufficient information to make a high-quality decision?

D. Is the problem structured?

E. Is acceptance of decision by subordinates critical to effective implementation?

F. If I were to make the decision by myself, is it reasonably certain that it would be accepted by my subordinates?

G. Do subordinates share the organizational goals to be obtained in solving this problem?

H. Is conflict among subordinates likely in preferred solutions?

ASSESSMENT   The Vroom and Yetton model is still relatively new and many studies will be needed to fully explore it.[22] To date, however, research results support the model. Managers who chose leadership styles indicated by the model had more productive subordinates than managers who did not. The research also indicates that most managers choose a more participative style than seems to be required in various situations. This is especially true for higher level managers. Although the model indicates that an autocratic leadership style can be effective, most managers tend to avoid its use.

Some limitations have been noted in the model. They focus mainly on the use of self-reported data. That is, managers are asked to list one situation in which they were effective and another one in which they were ineffective. The question is whether subordinates would rate the managers' behaviors in the same situation the same way. Secondly, there appears to be a cultural norm in the United States toward participation. That is, it is socially acceptable and desirable for managers to solicit participation from subordinates in making a decision. Thus there is a tendency for managers to want to appear more participative than they actually are in decision-making situations.

MANAGERIAL IMPLICATIONS   This model represents a significant conceptual breakthrough. It will encourage the training of future managers to choose leadership styles that will enable them to make high-quality, timely decisions. If a manager can diagnose a situation correctly, the choice of the best leadership style for that situation becomes easier. If the situation requires delegation, the manager must learn how to establish certain objectives and limitations—then let the subordinates determine how best to achieve the objectives within those limitations. If the situation calls for the manager alone to make the decision, the manager should be aware of potential positive and negative consequences.

Recall that a minor unresolved issue raised by the traits theorists was the extent to which a leader's personality or the situation itself influenced the choice of leadership style. Results from the use of this model indicate that about 30 percent of the time the situation is most influential in determining which leadership style is the best; about 10 percent of the time it is the manager's tendency to be autocratic or participative; and that about 60 percent of the time it is some combination of the leader's style and the situation.

Comparison of the Three Contingency Models

Choosing the most appropriate leadership style can be difficult.[23] A strongly stated preference for democratic, participative decision making in organizations prevails in the business community today. Evidence from Japanese management experience shows that this leadership style can result in productive, healthy organizations. Participative management, however, is not appropriate for all situations. Table 11–5 shows the differences in leader behaviors, situational variables, and outcomes among the three contingency models.

LEADERSHIP DIFFERENCES   Fiedler's model is based on the leadership style of a manager (high or low LPC) and the degree to which the situation is favorable for the manager. The leadership style of a manager is considered to be relatively rigid, and Fiedler recommends that the manager choose a situation that matches his or her leadership style. Vroom and Yetton, on the other hand, believe that managers can choose from among a variety of leadership styles, ranging from highly autocratic to highly participative. The manager's role in choosing a style is to improve the quality of the decision and the

TABLE 11-5   Comparison of the Three Contingency Leadership Models

Model	Leader Behaviors	Contingency Variables	Leader Effectiveness Criteria
Fiedler	LPC Task oriented: Low LPC Relationship Oriented: High LPC	Group atmosphere Task structure Leader position power	Performance
House's Path-Goal	Supportive Directive Participative Achievement oriented	Subordinate characteristics Task characteristics	Subordinate job satisfaction Job performance

Vroom and Yetton	Continuum of autocratic
	   to participative
		Decision quality
		Decision acceptance
			Quality of decision
			Acceptance of decision
			   by subordinates

Source: Reprinted with permission of Macmillan Publishing Company, Inc., from Hollander, E. P. *Leadership Dynamics.* Copyright © 1978 by The Free Press, a division of Macmillan Publishing Company, Inc.

probability that subordinates will accept and implement the decision on a timely basis. House's path–goal model states that managers should try to improve the job satisfaction and performance of subordinates by removing roadblocks that stand in the subordinates' way. The manager can choose a supportive, participative, directive, or achievement-oriented leadership style. Thus each of the three contingency models identifies different styles of leadership and views the manager's ability to choose among styles differently.

CONTINGENCY VARIABLES   All three models use different contingency variables. Fiedler's model holds that the way the variables (group atmosphere, task structure, and leader position power) are arranged in a situation determines whether and to what extent the situation is favorable or unfavorable to the manager. It assumes that a task-oriented manager will have the most control and influence when the group atmosphere is good, the task is structured, and the manager has high position power. As the combination of the three contingency variables changes, so do the leadership requirements.

House's model uses one of the same contingency variables as Fiedler's—task structure—and adds the characteristics of subordinates. Individuals who believe that rewards are based on their own efforts generally feel more satisfied with a participative style of leadership. If the task is unstructured, a directive style of leadership will lead to higher job satisfaction and performance than a participative style.

Vroom and Yetton's model deals with a different pair of contingency variables: decision quality and acceptance. These two variables make it useful for the manager to consider the situations in which either an autocratic style or a participative style would be more effective. If subordinates must implement a decision, they will be more highly motivated to do so if they have a voice in making the decision; participation increases understanding and generates commitment and involvement. Similarly, if it is highly unlikely that one individual will have all the information necessary to make high-quality decisions, a participative style again works best.

LEADERSHIP EFFECTIVENESS   All three models use somewhat different criteria for evaluating leadership effectiveness. Fiedler emphasizes performance; House emphasizes subordinate job satisfactions and performance; and Vroom and Yetton emphasize decision quality and acceptance. If a decision must be made with a group, the Vroom and Yetton model may best assist managers in choosing the most appropriate style of leadership. On the other hand, if improving individual performance is most important, perhaps either Fiedler's or House's model may be more useful.

SUMMARY

History relates the exploits of military, political, religious, business, and social leaders, and many legends and myths have grown up around them. The widespread fascination with leadership may be explained by its mystery, as well as by leadership's impact on everyone's life.

Leadership is a process by which individuals influence others toward achieving a goal. The ways in which managers attempt to influence others depends in part on the power available to them. The chapter discussed five sources of power—legitimate, reward, coercive, referent, and expert—that managers can draw upon to influence subordinates.

The chapter addressed three approaches to leadership: traits, behavioral, and contingency. The traits approach emphasizes the personal qualities of leaders and attributes the success of outstanding leaders to their possession of certain abilities, skills, and personality characteristics. However, research into this approach has not been able to determine why certain people succeed and others fail.

The behavioral approach emphasizes leaders' actions instead of their personal traits. The chapter focused on two leader behaviors—initiating structure and consideration—and how they affect the performance of subordinates. However, most research indicates a need to analyze also the situation in which the leader operates.

The contingency approach emphasizes the importance of the situation. The contingency models of Fiedler, House, and Vroom and Yetton were presented and evaluated. Fiedler focuses on the effective diagnosis of the situation in which the leader will operate. Thus he emphasizes understanding the nature of the situation and then matching the correct leadership style to that situation. According to this model, three contingency variables need to be diagnosed: group atmosphere, task structure, and the leader's position power. All leaders have a motivational system (LPC) that indicates the combinations of situations in which their styles probably will be effective.

House believes that leadership behavior is contingent on the characteristics of subordinates and the nature of the task. The leader's goal is to reduce the impediments that hinder employees in reaching their goals. For a routine task, a leader who is more considerate of employees will more likely have satisfied and productive employees than a leader who is not as considerate.

Vroom and Yetton base their model on an analysis of how a leader's style affects decision quality and subordinates' acceptance of the decision. These situational variables jointly affect group performance. Vroom and Yetton propose five leadership styles that managers can use. Their set of rules can help a manager to determine the leadership style to avoid in a given situation because decision quality and acceptance might be low.

KEY WORDS AND CONCEPTS

Achievement-oriented leadership
Coercive power
Consideration
Decision acceptance
Decision quality
Directive leadership
Expert power
Fiedler's contingency model
Group atmosphere
House's path–goal model
Initiating structure
Leader

Leadership
Least-preferred co-worker (LPC) scale
Legitimate power
Ohio State University leadership studies
Participative leadership
Position power
Referent power
Reward power
Supportive leadership
Task structure
Traits models
Vroom and Yetton normative model

DISCUSSION QUESTIONS

1. What is the major difference among the traits, behavioral, and contingency models of leadership?
2. It is possible to train leaders, or are leaders born? Explain.
3. Why are leadership models complex?
4. In Fiedler's contingency model, how can the organization design the job to fit the person?
5. How can subordinates influence a manager's choice of leadership style?
6. What are the similarities between the path–goal model and Fiedler's contingency model?
7. According to Peter Drucker, "Whenever anything is being accomplished, it is being done by a monomaniac with a mission." What are the implications of this saying for developing leaders?
8. Why were the Ohio State University leadership studies so important?
9. Is the manager's personality an important factor in the contingency theory of leadership? Why or why not?
10. Why is it difficult for managers to modify their leadership styles?

MANAGEMENT INCIDENTS AND CASES

Ned Norman

Ned Norman tried to reconstruct, in his own mind, the series of events that had culminated in that most unusual committee meeting this morning.

For example, each of the committee members had suddenly seemed to be stubbornly resisting any suggestions that did not exactly coincide with their own ideas for implementing the program under consideration. This unwillingness to budge from some preconceived position was not like the normal behavior patterns of most of the committee participants. Of course, some of the comments made in one of last week's sessions about "old-fashioned, seat-of-the-pants decision making" had ruffled a few feathers but Ned did not really think this was the reason things had suddenly bogged down today. Still, Ned thought it might be worthwhile to review in his mind what had taken place in this morning's meeting to see if some clues existed to explain the problem.

First, Ned recalled starting the session by saying that the committee had discussed in past meetings several of the factors connected with the proposed expanded-services program and it now seemed about time to make a decision as to which way to go. Ned remembered that Robert Roman had protested that they had barely scratched the surface of the possibilities for implementing the program. Then, both Sherman Stith and Tod Tolley, who worked in the statistics branch of Division Baker, had sided with Roman and were most insistent that additional time was needed to research in depth some of the other avenues of approach to solving the problems associated with starting the new program.

Walt West had entered the fray by stating that this seemed a little uncalled for, since previous experience had clearly indicated that expansion programs, such as this one, should be implemented through selected area district offices. This had brought forth the statement by Sherman Stith that experience was more often than not a lousy teacher, which was followed by Tod Tooley repeating his unfortunate statement about old-fashioned decision making! And, of course, Robert Roman had not helped matters at all by saying that it was obviously far better to go a little bit slower in such matters by trying any new program in one area first, rather than to have the committee members look "unprogressive" by just "trudging along on the same old cow paths!"

In fact, as Ned suddenly realized, if he hadn't almost intuitively exercised his prerogatives as chairman to stop the trend that was developing, he might have had a real melee on his hands right then. It was obvi-

ous that things were increasingly touchy among the members, so much so that despite his best efforts, everyone had simply refused either to participate or to support any of the ideas he (Ned) had offered to break the deadlock.

Feeling a little frustrated, early that same afternoon Ned had sought the counsel of his boss, who advised him to go talk to the division directors for whom the various committee members worked. In each area visited, Ned found that the division director was already aware of the committee problems and each one had his own ideas as to what should be done about them.

The director of Division Able stated that he was not much in sympathy with people who wanted to make a big deal out of every program that came along. He recalled the problem six years ago when the first computer had arrived in the agency and was hailed as the manager's replacement in decision making. He noted that, although the computer was still here, so was he, and that he had probably made better decisions, as a result of his broad background and knowledge than the computer ever would. The Division Able director told Ned that he had been on several deadlocked committees but that, when he was chairman, he had simply made the decision for the committee and solved the problem. He suggested Ned do likewise.

The Division Baker director stated that he knew Ned was one of those guys who wanted to use the best information available in estimating a program's performance. He told Ned that Sherman and Tod, who worked in Division Baker, had briefed him on the problems the committee had encountered and that, in his opinion, their investigative approach was the proper one to take. After all, stated the director, it logically followed that a decision could be no better than the research effort put into it. He also told Ned that, although he realized research might cost a little money, he had told Sherman and Tod to go ahead and collect the data they needed to determine the best way to implement the expansion program. The director flatly stated, "These are my men and my division will be footing the bill for this research, so no one else has any gripe about the cost aspects." He expressed the opinion that almost any price would be cheap if it would awaken some of the company employees to the tremendous values of a scientific approach to decision making.

The Division Charlie director stated, quite bluntly, that he was not particularly interested in how the expansion program was decided. He said it looked to him like the easiest way to get the thing moving was to do it a piece at a time. That way, he noted, you can evaluate how it looks without committing the company to a full-scale expansion. He concluded by saying, "It doesn't take a lot of figuring to figure that one out!"

The Division Delta director stated that the aspect of "time" was against the committee's looking at all angles and that a decision should be made after looking at two or three possible solutions. He stated that he needed Quentin Quinn, his representative on Ned's committee, for another job and hoped the committee would be finished very quickly.

Ned now realized that he had more of a problem than he had suspected. In view of the approaches and opinions expressed by the division directors, it seemed highly unlikely that any of the committee members would move from their present position. Therefore, Ned is now chairman of a deadlocked committee!

In pondering his dilemma, Ned considered various ways to break the impasse. First, as chairman, he could simply exert his authority and try to force a solution. This was guaranteed to alienate most of the committee members and the division directors, who had representatives on the committee.

Second, Ned considered returning to his boss, who had formed the committee, with the recommendation that the committee be disbanded. While the reasons for this recommendation would be easy to explain, Ned's failure to prevent this problem might be much more difficult.

As a third possibility, the idea occurred to Ned that he might ask each committee member to bring to the next meeting, in writing, his recommended plan for implementing the program. Since these would surely represent the thinking of the four division directors, this information could then be presented by Ned to his boss with a request for guidance. If his boss could be persuaded to make a choice, Ned's problem would be solved. Of the three ideas he had considered, Ned liked the last one the best. Accordingly, he reached for the telephone to call the first of his impossible committee members.[24]

Questions

1. Diagnose the situation facing Ned.
2. Which alternative should Ned choose?
3. How can Fiedler's and Vroom and Yetton's models help Ned make a decision?

West Virginia Cap Company

The West Virginia Cap Company, located in Parkersburg, West Virginia, manufactures a complete line of metal caps for glass containers, primarily for the food, drug, and cosmetic industries. The company employs approximately 500 people in five departments and normally operates on three shifts, five days a week. The process of manufacturing metal caps begins with decorating thin metal sheets with the customer's design in the lithography department. The decorated sheets are then transported in pallet loads by forklift trucks to the slitting department, where they are slit into strips. The strips are hand stacked onto pallets, bound with wire, and transported again by lift truck to the punch press department. Here, in a line consisting of several machines connected by conveyors, the decorated strips are converted into finished caps, with inserted paper discs, such as those commonly found on jars of peanut butter, deodorant, and salad oil packages. The caps in corrugated boxes on pallets are then transported again by lift truck to the packing department, where they are visually inspected for defects and packed into their final shipping cartons. From the packing department, they are transported on pallets by lift truck to the warehousing and shipping department for temporary storage or direct shipment to the customer.

West Virginia Cap Company has been in business for over 40 years and has been marginally profitable. The metal scrap business is very competitive and West Virginia Cap is far from the least cost producer, for several reasons. Its machinery, while well maintained, is of an older, less automated design and the packing department with over 75 employees, consists totally of manual operations in the processes of visually inspecting and packing caps. As a result, its labor costs are very high relative to its competitors.

The production and maintenance workers are represented by three labor unions: The Graphic Arts International Union for the lithography department; the International Association of Machinists for the machinists, electricians, and mechanics; and the Glass Bottle Blowers Association for the lesser skilled operators, inspectors, and packers. All three locals are headed by strong leaders, and local management, for the sake of labor peace, has made little change in manufacturing practices over the years.

Eighteen months ago, West Virginia Cap Company was purchased by the very large American Packaging Company (APC) to round out its line of packaging businesses. Recognizing the need for improvement, APC has made several changes. In addition to a new Plant Manager and Plant Manufacturing Engineer, APC brought in Jim DiNardo, age 34, an experienced manager, to manage the Packaging Department, with the goal of improving productivity. APC also installed an industrial engineering department to develop and install standards to measure performance as well as serve as a basis for a standard cost system.

About six months ago, Jim DiNardo hired Dave Anderson, age 28, to be the second shift supervisor in the Packing Department. Dave is a graduate industrial engineer whose career goal is to become Plant Manager, and while Dave had little production supervision experience, Jim felt Dave's industrial engineering education would be of great advantage in effecting productivity improvement. Because the packing department operations are almost totally manual, the department's output is controlled by the pace of the inspectors and packers. Jim felt that Dave could contribute to developing methods which would increase output. Dave has already made several changes in the operations which reduced the number of steps required in the inspection and packing process. Jim felt that Dave had excellent technical competence. With his industrial engineering background and above average intelligence, he had great potential. However, Jim was increasingly concerned about his interpersonal skills. Jim had a good relationship with John Lecinski, the local GBBA President, and through John and others, Jim learned about many gripes concerning Dave's handling of employees. Most of the gripes centered around Dave's constant criticism of the workers and his insensitivity to their problems.

In several counseling sessions with Dave, Jim tried to make Dave see that employee attitude, motivation, and morale were not improved by constantly criticizing individual workers. But in the following weeks, Dave continued to generate complaints with his, "I'll show you how" approach.

Three months ago, after the industrial engineering department had completed developing their standards, the accounting department began publishing daily Operating Performance reports. These reports compared the actual labor hours required to produce each department's output to the number of hours it should have taken, according to the new standards. For the packing department, these reports showed an actual performance of 80 percent of what the standard performance should have been. Moreover, they showed the first shift to be 90 percent, but Dave's second shift was just below 70 percent. The industrial engineering department was requested to study second shift operations individually to determine the causes of the substandard performance. Their reports indicated that almost all the employees were using the proper methods, but while some inspectors and packers were able to meet (and occasionally exceed) the standards, most were simply operating at a substandard pace.

Pressures were beginning to build on Jim for improved performance. Because the operating reports were read by all the managers, it was ap-

parent to them that the packing department was the poorest performer in the plant. Jim called Dave into his office on Friday afternoon, just before the second shift started at 3:00 P.M. He said, "Dave, we've got to find a way to improve our performance. Our packing department is on the bottom of the plant totem pole and we're not making much upward progress. I want you to put together a program for improvement for your shift and bring it in next Tuesday at 2:00 P.M. for review."

At the appointed hour, Dave appeared with a detailed program, the highlight of which was his recommendation to post on the departmental bulletin board each individual performance against the standard along with a statement that, "those employees who are not above 90 percent in 30 days will be subject to the plant's progressive discipline procedure."

Jim obviously realizes that adapting Dave's recommendation will generate a very negative reaction on the part of the employees, perhaps even a flurry of grievances by the local unions. However, he ponders the thought that allowing Dave to embroil himself in such a controversy will open his eyes and make him realize that his approach and his management style need drastic revamping if he is to succeed in manufacturing.[25]

Questions

1. What is Dave's leadership style?
2. If Dave's recommendation is adopted, what are some likely consequences?
3. What style of leadership might he choose in the present circumstances?

REFERENCES

1. Adapted from Stieglitz, H. His Master's Steadier Voice. *Across the Board*, February 1985, 38–43.

2. Drucker, P. *Management: Tasks, Responsibilities, and Practices.* New York: Harper & Row, 1974.

3. Bass, B. *Stogdill's Handbook of Leadership*. New York: Free Press, 1981, 9.

4. Bennis, W., and Nanus, B. *Leaders: The Strategies for Taking Charge*. New York: Harper & Row, 1985; Smith, J., Carson, K., and Alexander, R. Leadership: It Can Make a Difference. *Academy of Management Journal*, 1984, *27*, 765–776.

5. French, J., and Raven, B. The Bases of Social Power. In D. Cartwright (Ed.) *Studies in Social Power*. Ann Arbor, Mich.: Institute for Social Research, 1959, 150–167. For an excellent review of this literature, see Podsakoff, P., and Schriesheim, C. Field Studies of French and Raven's Bases of Power: Critique, Reanalysis, and Suggestions for Future Research. *Psychological Bulletin*, 1985, *97*, 387–411.

6. For an excellent review of the traits leadership studies, see Bass, B. *Stogdill's Handbook of Leadership*. New York: Free Press, 1981, 43–96.

7. Ghiselli, E. *Explorations in Managerial Talent*. Santa Monica, Calif.: Goodyear, 1971; Kenny, D., and Zaccaro, S. An Estimate of Variance Due to Traits in Leadership. *Journal of Applied Psychology*, 1983, *68*, 678–685.

8. Harrell, T. *Managers' Performance and Personality*. Cincinnati: Southwestern, 1961.

9. Stogdill, R. *Handbook of Leadership*. New York: Free Press, 1974.

10. Kerr, S., Schriesheim, C., Murphy, C., and Stogdill, R. Toward a Contingency Theory of Leadership Based Upon the Consideration and Initiating Structure Literature. *Organizational Behavior and Human Performance*, 1974, *12*, 62–82.

11. Ball, R. Italy's Most Talked-About Executive. *Fortune*. April 2, 1984, 99–102.

12. For an excellent overview of the research, see Schriesheim, C., and Kerr, S. Theories and Measures of Leadership: A Critical Appraisal of Current and Future Directions. In J. Hunt and L. Larson (Eds.) *Leadership: The Cutting Edge*. Carbondale, Ill.: Southern Illinois University Press, 1977, 9–45.

13. Szilagyi, A., and Wallace, M. *Organizational Behavior and Performance*, 3d ed. Glenview, Ill.: Scott, Foresman, 1983, 274–276.

14. Fiedler, F. *A Theory of Leadership Effectiveness*. New York: McGraw-Hill, 1967; Fiedler F., and Chemers, M. *Leadership and Effective Management*. Glenview, Ill.: Scott, Foresman, 1974.

15. Fiedler, F., and Mahar, L. The Effectiveness of the Contingency Model of Leadership Training: A Review of the Validation of Leader Match. *Personnel Psychology*, 1979, *32*, 45–62.

16. Rice, R. Leader LPC and Follower Satisfaction: A Review. *Organizational Behavior and Human Performance*, 1981, *28*, 1–16; Kabanoff, B. A Critique of Leader Match and Its Implications for Leadership. *Personnel Psychology*, 1981, *34*, 749–764; Singh, R. Leadership Style and Reward Allocation: Does Least Preferred Co-Worker Scale Measure Task and Relation Orientation? *Organizational Behavior and Human Performance*, 1983, *32*, 178–197.

17. House, R. A Path–Goal Theory of Leadership. *Administrative Science Quarterly*, 1971, *16*, 321–338.

18. Schriesheim, J., and Schriesheim, C. A Test of the Path–Goal Theory of Leadership and Some Suggested Directions for Future Research. *Personnel Psychology*, 1980, *33*, 349–370.

19. Dorsey, J., Joseph L. Lanier Jr. *Sky*, October, 1984, 73–79.

20. Vroom, V., and Yetton, P. *Leadership and Decision Making*. Pittsburgh: University of Pittsburgh Press, 1973.

21. Vroom, V., and Jago, A. Decision Making as a Social Process. *Decision Sciences*, 1974, *5*, 750.

22. Field, G. A Test of the Vroom-Yetton Normative Model of Leadership. *Journal of Applied Psychology*, 1982, *67*, 523–532; Field, G. A Critique of the Vroom-Yetton Contingency Model of Leadership Behavior. *Academy of Management Review*, 1979, *4*, 249–257.

23. For additional insights, see Lord, R., Foti, R., and DeVader, C. A Test of Leadership Categorization Theory: Internal Structure, Information Processing and Leadership Perceptions. *Organizational Behavior and Human Performance*, 1984, *34*, 343–378; Bass, B. *Leadership and Performance Beyond Expectations*. New York: Free Press, 1984; House, R. Cognitive and Affective Responses to Leader Behaviors: Toward a Clarification of Charisma. Paper presented at Texas A&M University, College Station, Texas, March 1985; Davis, T., and Luthans, F. Defining and Researching Leadership as a Behavioral Construct: An Idiographic Approach. *Journal of Applied Behavioral Science*, 1984, *20*, 237–251.

24. This case was prepared by Professor William Heier, Arizona State University, Tempe, Arizona. Used with permission.

25. This case was prepared by Donald Petersen, Loyola University of Chicago, Chicago, Il. Used with permission.

PART IV

ORGANIZATIONAL PROCESSES

12 Organizational Culture

LEARNING OBJECTIVES

When you have finished studying this chapter, you should be able to:

- Define the concept of organizational culture.
- Understand the nature and characteristics of organizational culture.
- Explain how organizational cultures are formed, maintained, and changed.
- State the possible effects of organizational culture on behavior and performance.
- Describe the process of organizational socialization.

OUTLINE

Preview Case

Two Contrasting Cultures: J. C. Penney Company and PepsiCo, Inc.

J. C. Penney Company cares about its employees and customers. J. C. Penney is a great place to work, and its customers will always receive satisfaction. These are the dominant values in Penney's corporate culture. Management actions have reinforced these values since founder James Cash Penney laid down the seven guiding principles, called "the Penney idea." These principles have brought forth tremendous loyalty from staff and customers. One store manager was reprimanded by the president for making too much profit, which was unfair to customers. Customers can return merchandise with no questions asked. Everyone is treated as an individual. Employees are encouraged to participate in the decision making process. Layoffs are avoided at all costs. Unsuccessful employees are transferred to new jobs instead of being fired. Long-term employee loyalty is especially valued.

PepsiCo has a completely different value system. Pepsi is in hot competition with Coke for a larger share of the soft drink market. Pepsi's values reflect the desire to overtake Coke. Managers engage in fierce competition against each other to acquire market share, to squeeze more profits out of their business, and to work harder. Employees who do not succeed are terminated. They must win to get ahead. A career can be made or broken on one-tenth of a point of market share. Everyone knows the corporate culture and thrives on the creative tension thus generated. The internal structure is lean and adaptable. The company picnic is characterized by intensely competitive team sports. Managers change jobs frequently and are motivated to excel. The culture is characterized by a go-go atmosphere and success at all costs.

One tangible indicator of the difference in culture between J. C. Penney and PepsiCo is the length of employee tenure. Penney's executives have been with the company thirty-three years on average, while Pepsi's executives have averaged only ten years.[1]

The effectiveness and success of an organization is not determined solely by the abilities and motivations of employees and managers; nor by how well groups of people can work together, although both individual and group processes are of critical importance to organizational success.

The organization itself has an invisible quality—a certain style, a character, a way of doing things—that may be more powerful than the dictates of any one person or any formal system. To understand the soul of the organization requires that we travel below the charts, rule books, machines, and buildings into the underground world of corporate cultures.[2]

The Preview Case described two firms—J. C. Penney and PepsiCo—that have very different organizational cultures. What is it about these companies that makes them so different? How did they get that way? The concept of organizational culture provides a useful way to address these questions.

This chapter introduces Part IV, "Organizational Processes." To this point in the book we have focused first on individual behavior and then on interpersonal and group behavior. We now shift our attention to the organizational level. In this chapter, we will examine the nature and characteristics of organizational culture, how cultures are formed, and how they are maintained or changed by managers and others; some possible effects of culture on behavior and performance; and, finally, how organizations socialize individuals into their particular culture.

NATURE AND CHARACTERISTICS OF ORGANIZATIONAL CULTURE

Organizational culture may be defined as a pattern of beliefs and expectations shared by organizational members.[3] These shared beliefs and expectations generate products and services, conversation and other verbal expressions, behaviors, and emotions. In turn, these things, sayings, doings, and feelings are perceived by employees and help them to understand and interpret the culture of the organization—to infer meaning from events and policies and to make sense of their work environment. Generally, the behaviors of individuals and groups within an organization are strongly shaped by norms stemming from shared beliefs, expectations, and actions.

Figure 12-1 shows the relationships among the content of an organization's culture, the manifestations of that culture, and employee perceptions and interpretations of that culture. Organizational culture also includes and is further defined by the following:

- *Observed behavioral regularities* when people interact, such as the language used and the rituals around deference and demeanor.
- The *norms* that evolve in working groups, such as "a fair day's work for a fair day's pay."
- The *dominant values* espoused by an organization such as "product quality" or "price leadership."
- The *philosophy* that guides an organization's policy toward employees and customers.
- The *rules* of the game for getting along in the organization, or the "ropes" that a newcomer must learn in order to become an accepted member.
- The *feeling* or *climate* that is conveyed in an organization by the physical layout and the way in which members of the organization interact with customers or other outsiders.[4]

None of these by itself represents the culture of the organization. Taken together, however, they reflect the culture of an organization and give meaning to the concept of organizational culture.

The common theme of a number of recent popular books is that strong, well-developed cultures are an important characteristic of companies with a record of high performance.[5] Strong, highly effective cultures are characterized by three major factors: (1) performance of managerial roles—particularly decisional, informational, and interpersonal roles—in ways desired by the company; (2) an internal environment that sets the tone and provides clear cues for desired employee behavior and performance; and (3) human re-

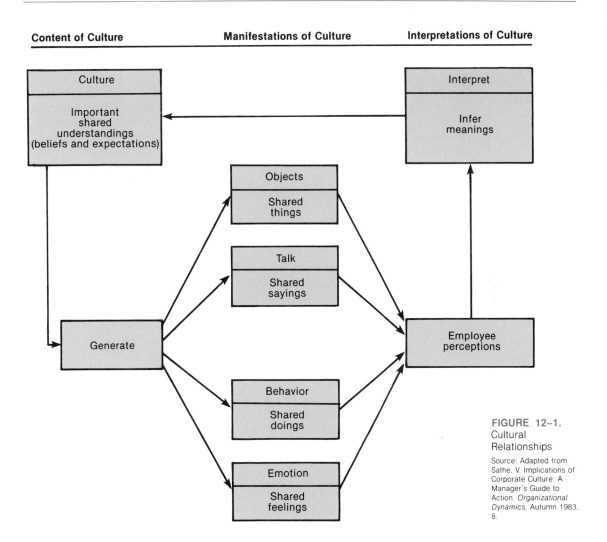

Content of Culture   Manifestations of Culture   Interpretations of Culture

FIGURE 12-1.
Cultural
Relationships

Source: Adapted from
Sathe, V. Implications of
Corporate Culture: A
Manager's Guide to
Action. *Organizational
Dynamics,* Autumn 1983,
8.

sources programs to implement and maintain the desired culture.[6] These
three factors can be seen clearly in two companies often identified as having
strong corporate cultures: IBM and Dana Corporation.

**In Practice: Examples of Strong Organizational Cultures—IBM
and Dana Corporation**

IBM's success is attributed primarily to its commitment to staying close to customers and giving clients quality service. IBM apparently understood long ago
that initiating and maintaining contacts with customers, clients, and outsiders
who could affect a department's or division's work was a critical role for all managers as well as other personnel to play. Currently, corporate officers at IBM still
make sales calls with much frequency. This interpersonal and informational role
is part of IBM's pervasive culture that influences managerial behavior down the
hierarchy. The relevant information gleaned from present or prospective client
contacts is then shared with relevant networks of managers and staff through-

out the organization. A customer orientation strongly influences product design, manufacturing, distribution, and personnel decisions.

IBM's culture also communicates customer service guidelines that serve as a frame of reference for a vast array of decisions. During their first year at IBM, fast trackers work for a senior manager in the sole capacity of responding to customer service letters. Customer satisfaction measures—collected on a monthly basis—account for a large part of incentive compensation, especially for senior executives. Information is also collected from IBM personnel on their perception of the quality of customer service. In essence, IBM has created a pervasive role model of what roles, activities, and behaviors managers should perform in order for them as well as IBM to be highly effective. In addition to ensuring that managers perform the various prescribed interpersonal, informational, and decisional roles, IBM has created an internal environment that sets the tone for employee behavior and performance. A careful design and integration of their human resources systems further increases the probability that actual behavior and performance will correspond to the culture desired by IBM.

Dana Corporation has similarly developed a culture to guide its managers' and employees' behavior and performance. At Dana, the most important roles, activities, and behaviors focus on productivity and improvement through people. All employees work in an environment that has been carefully shaped so that they look for opportunities to increase the effectiveness and productivity of the production process, their department, division, and so forth. Many of the interactions among managers, and between managers and workers, focus on information sharing about productivity improvement. Corporate results are communicated to all employees. Each month meetings are held between senior division managers and every manager within a division to discuss specific results. The various roles regarding interpersonal contacts and information sharing provide the context through which managers and subordinates are able to discuss and plan for implementing new programs and objectives.[7]

ORIGINS AND MECHANISMS OF ORGANIZATIONAL CULTURE

What establishes and sustains organizational culture? Can the culture of an organization be changed by managerial action? In trying to answer these questions, we will examine the formation of organizational culture and specific mechanisms that are used to maintain and change it. It is important to take a contingency approach to the examination of organizational culture because there is no evidence that any single organizational culture is the "best way." For example, both J. C. Penney and PepsiCo are highly successful firms, although they have very different cultures as the Preview Case indicated.

Forming Organizational Culture

Given the current state of knowledge, it is not possible to state with absolute precision the origins of any specific organization's culture. While external environment has an important influence on organizational culture, it has been noted that two organizations operating in essentially the same external environment may, nevertheless, evolve very different cultures. Edgar Schein suggests that organizational culture forms, in part, in response to two major sets of problems that confront every organization: (1) problems of external

---

TABLE 12-1   **Problems that Influence the Formation of Organizational Culture**

Problems of External Adaptation and Survival

■ *Mission and strategy.* Determining the organization's primary mission and main tasks; selecting strategies to use in pursuing this mission.

■ *Goals.* Setting specific goals; achieving agreement on goals.

■ *Means.* Methods to use in achieving the goals; getting agreement on methods to be used; deciding what the organizational structure, division of labor, reward system, authority system, and so on will be.

■ *Measurement.* Establishing criteria to use to measure how well individuals and groups are fulfilling their goals; determining the appropriate information and control systems.

■ *Correction.* Types of actions needed if individuals and groups do not achieve goals.

Problems of Internal Integration

■ *Common language and conceptual categories.* Identifying methods of communication; defining the meaning of the jargon and concepts to be used.

■ *Group boundaries and criteria for inclusion and exclusion.* Establishing criteria for membership in the organization and its groups.

■ *Power and status.* Addressing the issue of rules for acquiring, maintaining, or losing power; determining and distributing status.

■ *Intimacy, friendship, and love.* Setting rules for social relationships; for handling relationships between the sexes; determining the level of openness and intimacy appropriate in the work setting.

■ *Rewards and punishments.* Identifying desirable and undesirable behaviors.

Source: Adapted from Schein, E. H. *Organizational Culture and Leadership.* San Francisco: Jossey-Bass, 1985, 52, 66.

adaptation and survival, and (2) problems of internal integration.[8] Examples of these problems are listed in Table 12-1.

Problems of **external adaptation and survival** have to do with how the organization will find a niche in and cope with its constantly changing external environment. Problems of **internal integration** are concerned with establishing and maintaining effective working relationships among the members of the organization. An organizational culture emerges when members share knowledge and assumptions as they discover or develop ways of coping with the problems of external adaptation and internal integration. The approaches that have been developed have "worked well enough to be considered valid and, therefore, to be taught to new members as the correct way to perceive, think, and feel in relation to those problems."[9]

At least two additional types of influences on the origins of organizational culture are worth noting. First, early in the development of a new company, the entrepreneur/founder of the firm may be a strong determinant of the organization's culture. Later in the life of the organization, the then-current culture will reflect a complex interaction of the assumptions and ideas of the founder and the subsequent learning and experiences of other organizational members.[10] Second, the culture, mores, and societal norms of the country within which the firm is operating are determinants of organizational culture. In other words, the culture of the larger society influences the organizational culture of companies operating within it.[11] For example, some differences between U.S. and Japanese firms can be explained by differences between U.S. and Japanese societies.

The culture of Japanese organizations and the philosophy and practices of Japanese managers have received a great deal of attention. There are some intriguing differences between many Japanese and U.S. companies. Let us examine some of these differences.

ACROSS CULTURES

Japanese Management

Japanese firms have been very successful in international markets partly because of the quality of their products. For example, a new U.S. automobile is almost twice as likely to have a defect as a Japanese model.

A team of engineers and managers from the Buick Division of General Motors Corporation recently visited their dealer in Tokyo, who imports Buick automobiles and sells them to the Japanese. The operation appeared to be a massive repair facility, so they asked the dealer how he had built up such a large service business. He explained with some embarrassment that this was not a repair facility at all but rather a re-assembly operation where newly delivered cars were disassembled and rebuilt to Japanese standards. While many Japanese admire the American automobile, the dealer noted, they would never accept the low quality with which they are put together.[12]

Moreover, a typical U.S. color television set needs 50 percent more repairs than a Japanese set. And, in one quality test, computer memory chips made in the United States were three times more likely to fail than Japanese chips.

In addition to product quality, Japan also presents a productivity challenge to U.S. firms. Since World War II productivity in Japan has increased four times as fast as that in the United States. Despite some myths to the contrary, there is no evidence that the Japanese work harder or have personalities that cause them to be more committed to their organizations than U.S. employees. Instead, their greater productivity appears to stem from the superior organizational culture and management systems in many Japanese firms. Table 12–2 lists some typical differences between Japanese and U.S. organizations. The basic cultural orientation of **Japanese management** is to consider human assets as the most important assets of the organization. Many organizations throughout the world may claim a similar philosophy, but Japanese companies back up this cultural orientation with an integrated set of strategies and techniques, as Figure 12–2 indicates. These strategies and techniques have been described as follows:

TABLE 12–2 Some Contrasts between Japanese and U.S. Organizations

Japanese Organizations	U.S. Organizations
Lifetime Employment	Short-term Employment
Slow Evaluation and Promotion	Rapid Evaluation and Promotion
Nonspecialized Career Paths	Specialized Career Paths
Implicit Control Mechanisms	Explicit Control Mechanisms
Collective Decision Making	Individual Decision Making
Collective Responsibility	Individual Responsibility
Wholistic Concern for Employees	Segmented Concern for Employees

Source: Ouchi, G. *Theory Z: How American Business Can Meet the Japanese Challenge.* Reading, Mass.: Addison-Wesley, 1981, 58. Reprinted by permission of the publisher. © 1981

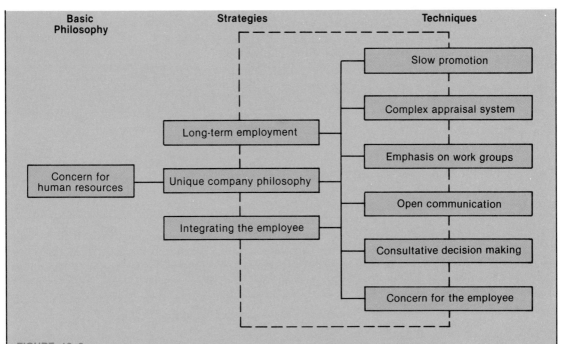

| Basic Philosophy | Strategies | Techniques |

FIGURE 12–2.
Japanese Management Philosophy

First, long-term and secure employment is provided, which attracts employees of the desired quality and induces them to remain with the firm. Second, a company philosophy is articulated that shows concern for employee needs and stresses cooperation and teamwork in a unique environment. Third, close attention is given both to hiring people who will fit well with the particular company's values and to integrating employees into the company at all stages of their working life. These general strategies are expressed in specific management techniques. Emphasis is placed on continuous development of employee skills; formal promotion is of secondary importance, at least during the early career stages. Employees are evaluated on a multitude of criteria—often including group performance results—rather than on individual bottomline contribution. The work is structured in such a way that it may be carried out by groups operating with a great deal of autonomy. Open communication is encouraged, supported, and rewarded. Information about pending decisions is circulated to all concerned before the decisions are actually made. Active observable concern for each and every employee is expressed by supervisory personnel. Each of these management practices, either alone or in combination with the others, is known to have a positive influence on commitment to the organization and its effectiveness.[13]

Japanese management practices and the organizational culture of Japanese firms have often been touted as potential cures for productivity problems in U.S. industries. However, it is important to note that Japanese management has been the target of recent criticism. Some evidence suggests that Japan also has serious problems with unemployment, productivity, and profits.[14] Among other things, a recent slowdown in Japan's economic growth has put pressure on the ability of Japanese organizations to offer long-term employment. To a certain extent, this concept is only meaningful for a minority of Japanese workers anyway—specifically, those employed by large corporations. In addition, the heavy reliance on consensual decision making in Japanese firms has not always been effective in terms of meeting competition in rapidly changing world markets. As a result, some Japanese corporations are seeking to limit the number of employees directly involved in the decision-making process in order to increase innovation and to shorten lead times in bringing new products to market.

William Ouchi has suggested that U.S. companies need to adopt a new approach to management—Theory Z—to improve their productivity.[15] The Theory Z (or Type Z) organization would draw characteristics from both successful Japanese and U.S. firms and blend them to fit the economic climate and culture of the United States. **Type Z organizations** would be characterized by:

- Long-term employment.
- Consensual decision making.
- Individual responsibility.
- Slow evaluation and promotion.
- Implicit, informal control with explicit, formalized measures of performance.
- Moderately specialized career paths.

This list of characteristics combines the features of both Japanese and U.S. organizations (Table 12-2). The Type Z organization would combine a cultural commitment to individualistic values (a feature of U.S. organizations) with a more group-oriented pattern of cooperation and decision making (a feature of Japanese organizations). Ouchi's Theory Z has been criticized particularly with regard to the lack of real data showing support for the notion that Type Z organizations are more productive than other organizational forms.[16] However, evidence suggesting that the Type Z organization can be effective is beginning to accumulate. For example, Charles Joiner of Mead Corporation successfully implemented the principles of Theory Z at both Chrysler Corporation and Mead Corporation. At Mead, a part of the business—a wholesale distribution company—with declining sales was reorganized as a Type Z organization. As a result, earnings were doubled and sales growth increased to 15 percent a year.[17]

Maintaining Organizational Culture

The ways in which an organization functions and is managed may have both intended and unintended effects on maintaining or changing organizational culture. In Figure 12–3, the basic mechanism for maintaining an organization's culture is shown: the organization attempts to locate and hire individ-

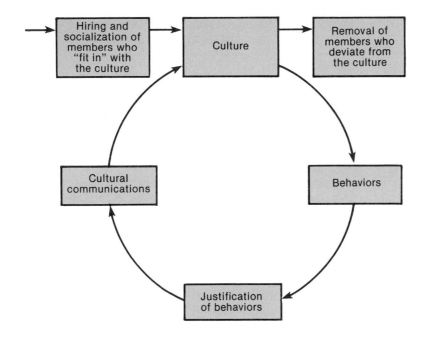

uals who, in some sense, *fit* the organizational culture. (The socialization of new employees into the culture of the organization will be addressed later in the chapter.) In addition, cultures are maintained by the removal of employees who consistently or markedly deviate from accepted behaviors and activities.

Specific mechanisms for maintaining organizational culture, however, are a great deal more complicated than Figure 12–3 suggests. The most powerful direct mechanisms for reinforcing the organization's culture are (1) what managers pay attention to, measure and control; (2) the ways managers (particularly top management) react to critical incidents and organizational crises; (3) managerial role modeling, teaching, and coaching; (4) criteria for allocating rewards and status; and (5) criteria for recruitment, selection, promotion, and removal from the organization.[18]

WHAT MANAGERS PAY ATTENTION TO, MEASURE, AND CONTROL   One of the more powerful methods of establishing and maintaining organizational culture consists simply of the processes and behaviors that the organization's managers pay attention to; that is, the things that get noticed and commented on. When things are systematically dealt with, this sends strong signals to employees about what is important and expected of them. For example, if a top manager emphasizes development opportunities for employees, monitors progress in developing subordinates, and rewards accordingly, this conveys to both the supervisor and the employee that such activities are an important aspect of the organization's culture. In contrast, if subordinate development is the subject of a pious platitude in some written corporate policy, but never receives any managerial attention—no monitoring of progress, no focus on the issue in meetings and conversations, and the like—supervisors and employees alike will not perceive subordinate development as an important aspect of the organization's culture.

REACTIONS TO CRITICAL INCIDENTS AND ORGANIZATIONAL CRISES When an organization, group, or department faces a crisis situation, the handling of that crisis by managers and employees reveals a great deal about the organization's culture. The manner in which the crisis is dealt with can either reinforce the existing culture or bring out new values and norms that change the culture in some manner. For example, an organization faced with a dramatic reduction in demand for its product might react by laying off or firing employees, or by reducing employee hours or rates of pay with no reduction in the work force. The alternative chosen indicates the value placed on human resources and can serve to reinforce and maintain the current culture or indicate a major cultural change.

ROLE MODELING, TEACHING, AND COACHING Aspects of the organization's culture can be conveyed to employees by the way managers fulfill their roles. In addition, managers may specifically incorporate important cultural messages into training programs and day-to-day coaching on the job.

CRITERIA FOR ALLOCATION OF REWARDS AND STATUS Employees also learn about the philosophy and values of their company through their experience with its reward system. The rewards and punishments attached to various behaviors convey to employees the priorities and values of both individual managers and the organizational culture. Similarly, the status system of an organization establishes and maintains certain aspects of its culture. The distribution of *perks* such as a corner office on an upper floor, carpeting, a private secretary, or a private parking space help to demonstrate which roles and behaviors are most valued by the organization. It is important *not* to assume that organizations will use rewards and status symbols effectively to maintain a desired culture. Organizations may do a good job of utilizing rewards and status symbols to reinforce the organization's culture; however, they may be quite inept at using rewards and status symbols in any consistent way. In any event, there is evidence that the reward practices of an organization and its culture may be strongly linked.[19] Thus one of the most effective mechanisms for influencing organizational culture may be through the reward system.

CRITERIA FOR RECRUITMENT, SELECTION, PROMOTION, AND REMOVAL As Figure 12–3 suggests, one of the fundamental ways that organizations maintain a culture is through the recruitment process. In addition, basic aspects of a culture are demonstrated and reinforced by the criteria used for assignment of personnel to specific tasks and jobs, who gets raises and promotions and why, who is removed from the company by firing or early retirement, and so on. Criteria used in these personnel decisions tend to become known throughout the organization and can serve to maintain an existing culture.

Changing Organizational Culture

The same basic mechanisms that are used to maintain the culture of an organization can serve as mechanisms to change that culture. That is, culture can be changed by (1) changing what managers pay attention to; (2) changing how crisis situations are handled; (3) changing criteria for recruiting new members; (4) changing criteria for promotion within the organization; (5) changing criteria for allocating rewards; and so on. For example, an organizational culture that tends to punish risk taking and innovation, and reward risk-avoidance behaviors, might be deliberately altered through changes in the reward system. Employees could be encouraged to set riskier and more innovative goals for themselves in counseling and goal-setting sessions. In performance-appraisal sessions and through merit raises individuals could be rewarded more for attempting challenging tasks, even if some failure were involved, than for attaining safe goals that required no innovative behavior, and so on.

Planned organizational change will be covered extensively in Chapters 20 and 21. Many of the specific techniques and methods for changing organizational behaviors that are presented in those chapters can also be used to change organizational culture. Indeed, any comprehensive program of organizational change is, in some sense, trying to change the culture of the organization. Consider an attempt to change the organizational culture of Procter & Gamble Company.

In Practice: **Cultural Change at Procter & Gamble**

Procter & Gamble, 148 years old in 1985, has been one of the most successful consumer products companies in the world. With 23,000 domestic employees and 64,000 worldwide, P&G is currently the 23rd largest corporation in the United States. For years P&G was a heavily bureaucratic organization with most important decisions highly centralized at the top. And there was a strict set of status symbols.

> A Procter & Gamble Co. manager remembers moving into his new office and discovering his ceiling had half a row of tiles too many. According to P&G tradition, brand managers' office ceilings measured 12 tiles by 12—only higher ranks got bigger offices and more tiles. His measured 12 by 12½. "People would come in and look at the ceiling and mutter things like, 'young whippersnapper!' ".
> When P&G designed its new headquarters in Cincinnati, it did away with ceiling tiles—and hoped to do away with exaggerated attention to rank as well, a prominant feature of the old culture. Pressed by competitors, and aided by new technology, P&G is, in fact, remodeling its corporate culture—a process bringing pain to some, relief to others, and wonderment to most.[20]

There also was a strict segregation of product brands with little coordination of functional activities across brands. In 1923, P&G introduced a program for production workers that guaranteed them 48 weeks of employment per year. The guaranteed-employment system and profit-sharing plans built employee loyalty that was the envy of their competitors.

Recently, however, Procter & Gamble has lost market share and suffered declines in profits. In 1985, P&G announced its first drop in annual operating earnings in 33 years. Competition has grown tougher and the mature stage of some important product areas has led to less growth potential. Procter & Gamble is fighting back both externally and internally. To meet the competition, P&G has introduced an unprecedented number of new products and is aggressively pursuing the development of still others. Internally, P&G seems determined to change aspects of its culture that it sees as obstacles to success. Among the changes underway are:

- *Implementation of a work team concept both for production workers and managers.* On the shop floor specific job titles and narrow skills are giving way to salaried technicians who are expected to have multiple skills and make most operating decisions. At higher management levels business teams are breaking down the barriers between brands and functions and allowing a decentralization of decision making.

- *Changes in the philosophy behind the lifetime-job tradition.* The company has trimmed its workforce by 4 percent companywide and 5 percent among production workers. Reduced hiring, early retirements, and some limited layoffs have occurred.

- *A reduction in corporate paternalism.* Top management is threatening to close facilities that don't improve productivity and product quality and is vigorously resisting union attempts to control or influence operations.

Some things at Procter & Gamble are not changing, such as maintaining close contact with consumers and distributors, an emphasis on high quality, and heavy expenditures on research. On balance however, P&G is moving toward a tougher yet more participative organizational culture.[21]

EFFECTS OF ORGANIZATIONAL CULTURE

Many of the effects of organizational culture can be summarized by four key ideas.[22] First, knowing the culture of an organization allows employees to understand the firm's history and current approach, which, in turn, provide guidance about expected behaviors in the future. Second, organizational culture can serve to establish commitment to corporate philosophy and values. This provides organizational members with shared feelings of working toward goals they believe in. Third, organizational culture with its related norms serves as a control mechanism to channel employee behaviors toward desired and away from undesired patterns. Finally, certain kinds of organizational cultures may be related to greater effectiveness and productivity.

Despite the repeated appearance of this latter theme in articles and books, there is little hard evidence that a strong culture–performance relationship exists. However, early results of research that has examined the culture–performance relationship are promising. For example, a study that examined this issue in 34 companies reported finding a strong relationship between organizational culture and performance. Specifically, firms with participative cultures and well-organized workplaces had better performance records than those firms without these characteristics.[23]

High degrees of participative management are often cited as a characteristic of successful cultures. **Participative management** refers to the sharing by managers of decision-making, goal-setting, and problem-solving activities with the employees of an organization.[24] However, despite its appeal, high levels of participation do not fit all settings and tasks; and to change an organization from a more traditional management approach to greater collaboration with employees may be extremely difficult to do.[25] Let us look at some of the possible effects of a corporate culture—that of Tandem Computer Corporation—where participation is a key aspect of its philosophy.

In Practice: **Tandem Computer Corporation**

It is 8:30 A.M. at the Tandem Computer Corp. assembly plant in Santa Clara, California. A young woman, dressed in blue jeans and sandals, calls to order a dozen workers—mostly middle-aged housewives and young Mexican women—seated around a table in a corner of the plant.

They gather like this every morning to discuss the previous day's performance and to air any gripes they might have. A supervisor reviews a quality report and announces dismally that the computer power supplies assembled at the plant the previous day showed a 30% failure rate. Everyone groans.

It is soon discovered that the fault lay primarily in poor components delivered by outside suppliers. "Let's invite the component people over to talk," suggests one matron with a hint of anger in her voice, and the task becomes hers.

This is just one small example of the "participative management" style that has made Tandem famous in the U.S. computer industry. Headquartered in Cupertino, California, Tandem is a leading producer of the kind of fail-safe on-line computer systems used by such businesses as airlines and banks to maintain uninterrupted access to the ever-changing records essential to their doing business. As the pioneer of such systems, known as fault-tolerant in the industry, and for several years virtually the only supplier to a booming market, Tandem has been one of the more spectacular—and colorful—success stories of Silicon Valley.

Not by accident, Tandem has shown that nurturing employees pays off. "To the degree that you get your assembly people involved in making decisions on how a product should be built, that adds up to the difference between high productivity and low productivity," says Robert C. Marshall, Tandem's chief operating officer.

Productivity at the Santa Clara power plant factory, for example, has increased eight-fold since participative management was instituted there 18 months ago: products now work their way through the factory in five days instead of 40. Companywide, Tandem's revenues per employee exceed $100,000 a year, higher than at either of its top two on-line systems rivals, IBM and Burroughs Corp.

Tandem has always operated with an "open door" policy but it is only within the past three years or so that the policy has been formalized into a clear-cut participative management scheme. Employees now have access to production information and are included in the decision-making process. Factory workers can use plant-floor computer terminals to call up information normally reserved for managers, such as overhead costs and projected hours for completion of a project.

Tandem employees are also encouraged to make their opinions known through a variety of forums. The "Popcorn Friday" beer parties are the most famous. Held at every Tandem location throughout the world, they begin at 4 P.M., an hour before normal quitting time, and go until about 6:30. Fifty to sixty percent of the workforce, from top to bottom, usually shows up.

Daily work group meetings are monitored by floor managers and led by a rotating worker "facilitator." These groups submit reports in writing to middle management for comment and decision. There are also hour-long factory meetings each week in which all employees, from plant manager on down, gather to discuss such matters as working conditions or how to improve the production process. Staff turnover at Tandem runs as low as 12 percent a year, far lower than the industry average of 21 percent.[26]

ORGANIZATIONAL SOCIALIZATION

Organizational socialization is the systematic process by which firms bring new employees into their culture.[27] Socialization provides the means by which individuals "learn the ropes" upon joining an organization. As such, organizational socialization includes learning work-group, department, and organizational values, rules and procedures, and norms; developing social and working relationships; and developing skills and knowledge needed to perform the new job.[28]

Process of Socialization

The process of organizational socialization is shown in Figure 12-4. Although this diagram is not intended to depict the socialization process of all organizations, Richard Pascale argues that many firms with strong cultures—such as IBM, P&G, AT&T, and Delta Airlines—frequently follow these seven steps for socializing new employees:

- *Step One.* Careful selection of entry-level candidates. Trained recruiters use standardized procedures and seek specific traits that tie to success in the business.
- *Step Two.* Humility-inducing experiences in the first months on the job cause employees to question their prior behaviors, beliefs, and values. For example, this might be accomplished by giving a new employee more work to do than can reasonably be done. The self-questioning promotes openness toward accepting the organization's norms and values.
- *Step Three.* In-the-trenches training leads to mastery of one of the core disciplines of the business. Promotion is tied to a proven track record.
- *Step Four.* Careful attention is given to measuring operational results and rewarding individual performance. Reward systems are comprehensive, consistent, and focus on those aspects of the business that are tied to success and corporate culture.
- *Step Five.* Adherence to the firm's values. The identification with common values allows employees to justify personal sacrifices caused by their membership in the organization.
- *Step Six.* Reinforcing folklore provides legends and interpretations of important events in the organization's history that validate the firm's culture and its goals. Folklore reinforces a code of conduct for "how we do things around here."
- *Step Seven.* Consistent role models and consistent traits are associated with those recognized as on the fast track to promotion and success.[29]

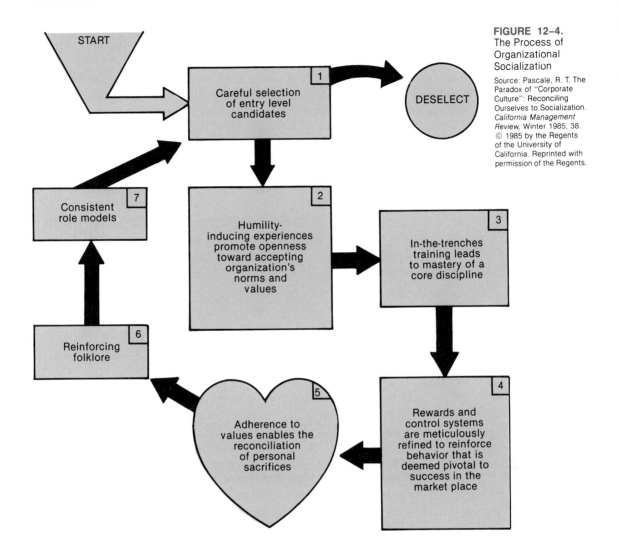

FIGURE 12–4.
The Process of
Organizational
Socialization

Source: Pascale, R. T. The
Paradox of "Corporate
Culture": Reconciling
Ourselves to Socialization.
*California Management
Review,* Winter 1985, 38.
© 1985 by the Regents
of the University of
California. Reprinted with
permission of the Regents.

Outcomes of Socialization

All organizations and groups socialize new members in some fashion, but the process can vary greatly in terms of how explicit and conscious it is. Organizations with strong cultures may be particularly skillful at socializing individuals into that culture.[30] If the culture is effective, this socialization process will contribute to organizational success. However, if the culture needs changing, a strong socialization process reduces the probability that the organization will be willing or capable of making needed changes.

The socialization process may affect employee and organizational success in a variety of ways.[31] Some possible outcomes of socialization are listed in Table 12–3. However, we do not intend to suggest that these outcomes are solely determined by the effectiveness of an organization's socialization process. For example, job satisfaction is a function of many things, including the nature of the task, the individual's personality and needs, the nature of

---

TABLE 12-3   Possible Outcomes of Socialization Process

Successful socialization is reflected in	Unsuccessful socialization is reflected in
■ Job satisfaction	■ Job dissatisfaction
■ Role clarity	■ Role ambiguity and conflict
■ High work motivation	■ Low work motivation
■ Understanding of culture, perceived control	■ Misunderstanding, tension, perceived lack of control
■ High job involvement	■ Low job involvement
■ Commitment to organization	■ Lack of commitment to organization
■ Tenure	■ Absenteeism, turnover
■ High performance	■ Low performance
■ Internalized values	■ Rejection of values

---

supervision, opportunities to succeed and be rewarded, and so on. Rather, the point here is that successful socialization may contribute to job satisfaction, whereas unsuccessful socialization may increase the probability of dissatisfaction.

SUMMARY

Organizational culture is the pattern of beliefs and expectations shared by organizational members. Culture includes behavioral norms, shared values, company philosophy, the "rules of the game" for getting along and getting things done, and ways of interacting with outsiders such as customers.

One explanation for the formation of any particular organizational culture is that it is a response to (1) problems of external adaptation and survival, and (2) problems of internal integration. The formation of an organization's culture is also influenced by the culture of the larger society within which the firm must function.

The primary mechanisms for both maintaining and changing organizational culture include (1) what managers pay attention to, measure, and control; (2) the ways managers and employees react to crises; (3) role modeling, teaching, and coaching; (4) criteria for allocating rewards; and (5) criteria for recruitment to, selection and promotion within, and removal from the organization.

A strong organizational culture can affect employee behaviors and commitment to the organization. A great deal of research remains to be done, but there is some evidence that highly participative cultures may be related to effective organizational performance.

Organizational socialization is the process by which new members are brought into the organization's culture. At firms having a strong culture, the socialization process is well developed and the focus of careful attention. All organizations socialize new members but, depending on how this is done, the effects could be either positive or negative in terms of job performance, satisfaction, and commitment to the organization.

KEY WORDS AND CONCEPTS

External adaptation and survival
Internal integration
Japanese management
Organizational culture

Organizational socialization
Participative management
Type Z organization

DISCUSSION QUESTIONS

1. Describe the concept of organizational culture.

2. List and explain the major influences on culture formation.

3. Describe Japanese management practices and cultural orientation and explain some of the important differences that typically exist between Japanese and U.S. firms.

4. Describe a Type Z organization. Do you think this organizational form is likely to be effective? Defend your answer.

5. List and describe the primary mechanisms for maintaining and changing organizational cultures. Which seems likely to be the most powerful for influencing organizational culture? Why?

6. While Japanese management practices and Theory Z ideas seem to suggest that organizations should move toward guaranteeing long-term employment, Procter & Gamble, AT&T, and some Japanese firms seem to be moving in the opposite direction. Explain this apparent contradiction.

7. Summarize the possible effects of a strong organizational culture.

8. Describe the process of organizational socialization. What are the implications of this socialization process for maintaining and changing organizational cultures?

9. Identify some potential outcomes of effective and ineffective organizational socialization.

MANAGEMENT INCIDENTS AND CASES

Waking Up AT&T: Life After Culture Shock

It has been, says one AT&T insider, "a cultural train wreck." As a regulated monopoly for 103 years, the American Telephone & Telegraph Co. created a pervasive corporate culture built around delivering good, cheap, universal phone service. The divestiture on "one-one-eighty-four" as AT&T people refer to the fateful date, split up the world's largest corporation and suddenly rendered that culture obsolete, an impediment to what the company had to do to survive. Amid reluctance, regret, and almost palpable pain afflicting employees and customers alike, the old Ma Bell leadership is gritting its teeth and working to generate new and potent habits before the company's competitive position is irreparably damaged.

Ironically, the old culture AT&T is trying to shed had much in it that enlightened American companies are striving to achieve today. AT&T was famous for guaranteeing lifetime employment, for the loyalty it inspired among employees, for promoting from within, for its consensual decision-making style, and for the high quality of its services and products—many of the characteristics that books on managerial excellence tell us are behind the Japanese success. The problem was that these values had grown up in a sort of cocoon of guaranteed profits, not in response to market needs or competitive pressures.

At the heart of the new culture to be forged is one overriding imperative: AT&T has to learn how to sell to survive. The old AT&T had no effective sales force and no sales ethic—Bell people simply waited for orders to come in. But the need to start selling became clear long before divestiture. The Federal Communications Commission's Carterfone ruling back in 1968 for the first time allowed customers to attach non-Bell equipment. Other companies began to sell equipment in competition with Bell.

To back up the new emphasis on sales, AT&T is changing its structure to point the corporation toward the market. Historically AT&T has been organized along functional lines—Bell Labs researched, Western Electric manufactured, and so forth. Insulated from the market, these units responded largely to their own inner needs. To banish this kind of thinking, AT&T is splitting up functional units to conform to the company's lines of business, and allowing product managers to stretch their authority across various functions to pull together the effort needed to get a product to market. A piece of Bell Labs, for example, is being assigned to work with Network Systems, the part of AT&T that makes equipment for other phone companies.

Along with the reorganization, AT&T is trying to develop a whole new way of treating its people, to make them independent and responsive, not waiting for headquarters to tell them what to do. The huge staff divisions at corporate headquarters—Ma Bell's "general departments"—used to issue tomes of detailed instructions on how every task should be performed. "You weren't measured by your successes but by how little trouble you caused," says one former executive. The general departments don't exist anymore, and nowadays employees are held accountable for what they accomplish. Instead of earning straight salaries as before, salesmen at Information Systems work on commission. For example, a salesman in Dallas, instead of earning a flat $25,000 a year, could earn $100,000 a year or more, or as little as his base salary of $12,500, in which case he would probably be fired. Annual personnel ratings, which used to lump about 90 percent of employees into a meaningless category of "satisfactory," are being sharpened to draw clearer distinctions between the performers and the nonperformers.

From corporate headquarters on down, AT&T is trying to reduce the intensity of supervision and flatten the chain of command. For example, in Information Systems one regional headquarters has cut the staffs of the groups reporting to it from 30 or so people to six and eliminated most of a level of management. Foremen in the region now supervise 15 technicians instead of eight.[32]

Questions

1. Although one out of every three of the one-million jobs in AT&T are being changed in the reorganization, corporate executives have been quoted as stating that the greatest challenge that AT&T faces is to change its culture. Explain why AT&T management might make such a statement.
2. Summarize both the new and old organizational cultures of AT&T.
3. Suggest some ways or mechanisms that AT&T might use to change its culture. Explain why each mechanism might be used.

The Hewlett-Packard (H-P) Way

Any group of people who have worked together for some time, any organization of long standing, indeed, any state or national body over a period of time develops a philosophy, a series of traditions, a set of mores. These, in total, are unique and they fully define the organization, setting it aside for better or worse from similar organizations. At H-P all of this goes under the general heading of the "H-P Way." It cannot be demonstrated to be unique and, although based on sound principles, it is not necessarily transplantable to other organizations. But what can be said about it is that it has worked successfully in the past at H-P and there is every reason to believe that being a dynamic "way" it will work in the future. If this is true, and if it differs from more conventional practices, then it is important that whatever this "way" is that it be conveyed to, and understood by, this very large body of new H-P people.

What is the H-P way? In general terms it is the policies and actions that flow from the belief that men and women want to do a good job, a creative job, and that if they are provided the proper environment they will do so. But that's only part of it. Closely coupled with this is the H-P tradition of treating each individual with consideration and respect and recognizing personal achievements. This sounds almost trite, but Dave Packard and Bill Hewlett honestly believe in this philosophy and have tried to operate the company along these lines since it first started.

What are some examples of this application of a confidence in and concern for people? One was a very early decision that has had a profound effect on the company. That decision was that we did not want to be a "hire and fire" operation—a company that would seek large contracts, employ a great many people for the duration of the contract, and at its completion let these people go. Now, there is nothing that is fundamentally wrong with this method of operation—much work can only be performed using this technique—it's just that Dave and Bill did not want to operate in this mode. This one early decision greatly limited the company's freedom of choice and was one of the factors that led H-P into the business in which it is now engaged.

There are a number of corollaries to this policy. One is that employees should be in a position to benefit directly from the success of the organization. This led to the early introduction of a profit-sharing plan, and eventually to the employee stock-purchase plan. A second corollary was that if an employee was worried about pressing problems at home, he could not be expected to concentrate fully on his job. This and the fact that in the early days Dave and Bill were very closely associated with people throughout the company and thus had a chance to see first-hand the devastating effect of domestic tragedy, led, among other things, to the very early introduction of medical insurance for catastrophic illness.

As the company grew and it became evident that new levels of management had to be developed, H-P applied its own concept of management-by-objectives. When stripped down to its barest fundamentals, management-by-objectives says that a manager, a supervisor, a foreman, given the proper support and guidance (that is, the objectives), is probably better able to make decisions about the problems he is directly concerned with than some executive way up the line—no matter how smart or able that executive may be. This system places great responsibility on the individual concerned, but it also makes his work more interesting and more challenging. It makes him feel that he is really part of the company, and that he can have a direct effect on its performance.

Another illustration of the H-P way occurred in 1970. During that time, orders were coming in at a rate less than our production capability. Hewlett-Packard was faced with the prospect of a 10-percent layoff—something it had never done. Rather than a layoff, a different tack was tried. The company went to a schedule of working nine days out of every two weeks—a 10-percent cut in work schedule with a corresponding 10-percent cut in pay for all employees involved in this schedule. At the end of a six-month period, orders and employment were once again in balance and the company returned to a full work week. The net result of this program was that, effectively, all shared the burden of the recession, good people were not turned out on a very tough job market, and the company benefitted by having in place a highly qualified work force when business improved.

The dignity and worth of the individual is a very important part of the H-P way. With this in mind, many years ago the company did away with time clocks, and more recently H-P introduced the flexible workhours program. Flexible, or gliding, time was originated within the company at the plant in Germany. Later it was tried for six months or so at the Medical Electronics Division in Waltham, and then made available throughout much of the company. Again, this is meant to be an expression of trust and confidence in H-P people as well as providing them with an opportunity to adjust their work schedules to their personal lives.

Many new H-P people as well as visitors often note and comment about another H-P way—that is the informality and everyone being on a first name basis. Both Dave and Bill

believe individuals operate more effectively and comfortably in a truly informal and personal name atmosphere. Hopefully, with increasing growth the company can retain this "family" way of operating with the minimum of controls and the maximum of a friendly "help each other" attitude.

Other examples could be cited, but the problem is that none by themselves really catch the essence of what the H-P way is all about. You can't describe it in numbers and statistics. In the last analysis it is a spirit, a point of view. It is a feeling that everyone is a part of a team, and that team is H-P. It exists because people have seen that it works, and they believe in it and support it. The belief is that this feeling makes H-P what it is, and that it is worth perpetuating.[33]

Questions

1. Summarize the organizational culture of Hewlett-Packard.
2. Is Hewlett-Packard a Type Z organization? Justify your answer.
3. List the major issues and ideas from Chapter 12 that appear, in one form or another, in this company statement.

REFERENCES

1. Shrivastava, P. Integrating Strategy Formulation with Organizational Culture. *Journal of Business Strategy,* Winter 1984, 103–104. Reprinted with permission. Copyright 1984, Warren Gorham & LaMont Inc., 210 South St., Boston, MA 02111. All rights reserved.

2. Kilmann, R. H. Corporate Culture. *Psychology Today,* April 1985, 63.

3. Schwartz, H., and Davis, S. M. Matching Corporate Culture and Business Strategy. *Organizational Dynamics,* Summer 1981, 30–48.

4. Schein, E. H. *Organizational Culture and Leadership.* San Francisco: Jossey-Bass, 1985, 6.

5. See, for example, Deal, T. E., and Kennedy, A. A. *Corporate Cultures: The Rites and Rituals of Corporate Life.* Reading, Mass.: Addison-Wesley, 1982; Ouchi,

W. G. *Theory Z: How American Business Can Meet the Japanese Challenge.* Reading, Mass.: Addison-Wesley, 1981; Pascale, R. T., and Athos, A. G. *The Art of Japanese Management: Applications for American Executives.* New York: Simon and Schuster, 1981; Peters, T. J., and Austin, N. *A Passion for Excellence.* New York: Random House, 1985; Peters, T. J., and Waterman, R. H. *In Search of Excellence.* New York: Harper & Row, 1982.

6. Albert, M., and Silverman, M. Making Management Philosophy a Cultural Reality, Part I: Get Started. *Personnel,* January–February 1984, 15.

7. Albert and Silverman, 15. Reprinted with permission of the publisher. © 1984 Michael Albert. Published by Periodicals Division, American Management Associations, New York. All rights reserved.

8. Schein, E. H. The Role of the Founder in Creating Organizational Culture. *Organizational Dynamics,* Summer 1983, 13–28; Schein, E. H. Coming to a New Awareness of Organizational Culture. *Sloan Management Review,* Winter 1984, 3–16; Schein, *Organizational Culture and Leadership.*

9. Schein, The Role of the Founder . . ., 14.

10. Schein, 13–28.

11. DeFrank, R. S., Matteson, M. T., Schweiger, D. M., and Ivancevich, J. M. The Impact of Culture on the Management Practices of American and Japanese CEOs. *Organizational Dynamics,* Spring 1985, 62–76; Gordon, W. I. Organizational Imperatives and Cultural Modifiers. *Business Horizons,,* May–June 1984, 76–83.

12. Ouchi, *Theory Z,* 3–4.

13. Hatvany, N., and Pucik, V. Japanese Management: Practices and Productivity. *Organizational Dynamics,* Spring 1981, 522.

14. Odiorne, G. S. The Trouble with Japanese Management Systems. *Business Horizons,* July–August 1984, 17–23; Sethi, S. P., Namiki, N., and Swanson, C. L. The Decline of the Japanese System of Management. *California Management Review,* Summer 1984. 35–45.

15. Ouchi, *Theory Z;* Ouchi, W. G., and Jaeger, A. M. Type Z Organization: Stability in the Midst of Mobility. *Academy of Management Review,* 1978, *3,* 305–314.

16. Sullivan. J. J. A Critique of Theory Z. *Academy of Management Review,* 1983, *8,* 132–142.

17. Joiner, C. W. Making the "Z" Concept Work. *Sloan Management Review,* Spring 1985, 57–63.

18. This section is based on Schein, *Organizational Culture and Leadership,* 223–243.

19. Kerr, J., and Slocum Jr., J. W. Linking Reward Systems and Organizational Culture. Paper presented at the American Institute for Decision Sciences annual meeting, Toronto, November 1984; Sethia, N. K., and Von Glinow, M. A. Managing Organizational Culture by Managing the Reward System. In Kilmann, R. H., Saxton, M. J., and Serpa, R. (Eds.) *Gaining Control of the Corporate Culture.* San Francisco: Jossey-Bass, 1985, 400–420.

20. Solomon, J. B., and Bussey, J. Cultural Change: Pressed by Its Rivals, Procter & Gamble Co. Is Altering Its Ways. *The Wall Street Journal,* May 20, 1985, 1.

21. The description of cultural change at Procter & Gamble is drawn from Rohon, T. M. Market Pressures Spur Internal Changes. *Industry Week,* October 15,

1984, 65–69; Solomon and Bussey, Cultural Change . . ., 1, 16.

22. The "key ideas" were drawn from Martin, J., and Siehl, C. Organizational Culture and Counterculture: An Uneasy Symbiosis. *Organizational Dynamics,* Autumn 1983, 52–64.

23. Denison, D. R. Bringing Corporate Culture to the Bottom Line. *Organizational Dynamics,* Autumn 1984, 5–22.

24. Sashkin, M. Participative Management is an Ethical Imperative. *Organizational Dynamics,* Spring 1984, 5.

25. Boyle, R. J. Wrestling with Jellyfish. *Harvard Business Review,* January–February 1984, 74–83.

26. Joseph, J. Is Tandem's Management Style as Fail-Safe as its Computers? *International Management,* October 1984, 58–62. Reprinted with permission from International Managment. Copyright, McGraw-Hill Publication Company. All rights reserved.

27. Pascale, R. The Paradox of "Corporate Culture": Reconciling Ourselves to Socialization. *California Management Review,* Winter 1985, 27.

28. Fisher, C. D., and Weekley, J. A. Socialization in Work Organizations. Technical Report for the Office of Naval Research. TR-ONR-4. Texas A&M University, February 1982.

29. Pascale, The Paradox of Corporate Culture . . ., 29–33.

30. Albert, M. and Silverman, M. Making Management Philosophy a Cultural Reality, Part 2: Design Human Resources Programs Accordingly. *Personnel,* March–April 1984, 28–35; Pascale, R. Fitting New Employees into the Company Culture. *Fortune,* May 28, 1984, 28–43.

31. See, for example, Feldman, D. C. The Multiple Socialization of Organization Members. *Academy of Management Review,* 1981, *6,* 309–318; Fisher and Weekley, Socialization in Work Organizations; Louis, M. R. Surprise and Sense Making: What Newcomers Experience in Entering Unfamiliar Organizational Settings. *Administrative Science Quarterly,* 1980, *25,* 226–251; Van Maanen, J., and Schein, E. H. Toward a Theory of Organizational Socialization. *Research in Organizational Behavior,* 1979, *1,* 209–264; Wanous, J. P. *Organizational Entry.* Reading, Mass.: Addison-Wesley, 1980.

32. Excerpted from Main, J. Waking Up AT&T: There's Life After Culture Shock. *Fortune,* December 24, 1984, 66–74. © 1984 Time Inc. All rights reserved.

33. Reprinted courtesy of Hewlett-Packard Company.

13 Job Design

LEARNING OBJECTIVES

When you have finished studying this chapter, you should be able to:

- Describe five approaches to job design.
- State how technology and job redesign are linked.
- Explain how the job characteristics enrichment model may increase work motivation and job satisfaction.
- Diagnose job design problems.
- Explain how the sociotechnical system model attempts to integrate the needs and goals of employees with those of the organization.

OUTLINE

Preview Case

Factory Jobs of the Future

Since the mid-1970s, scare accounts of the human impact of the factory of the future have hit the American public about once a month. These nightmare versions play on human feelings of powerlessness—victims confronting the relentlessness of the unfeeling, never-tiring machine. At best, the image is Charlie Chaplin, all by himself, fighting his way off an assembly line of machinery painted white in a factory also painted white. At worst, the image is that of the sorcerer's apprentice, unable to let go of the magical brooms and buckets, engulfed in uncontrollable, destructive "productivity."

These fears, however, have little to do with the actualities of the factory of the future. True, there is some bad news to report. Nearly everyone in the factory labor force and all their management are certainly in for change, and change may be painful. But there is good news, too. Overall, factory automation seems likely to result in relatively favorable trends in employment, job enrichment, and human productivity.

Qualitative changes in job content, organization, and work culture inside the factory will be as real and noticeable as the reduction in number of factory employees. Robotics, word processors, CAD/CAM (Computer Aided Design/Computer Aided Manufacturing) systems, modern materials handling, and manufacturing resource planning have been applied long enough in sufficient settings to provide many clues about the prospective impact of these technical and managerial innovations on organizations. Fortunately, the trends are consistent with the requirements of the information revolution and the preferences of the less submissive work force that is taking over factory jobs.

Average skill levels will be higher. General Motors believes that skilled tradesmen, who now number 16 percent of GM's plant force, will be up to 50 percent by the year 2000. These men and women will not be college graduates necessarily, but they will have received at least a couple of years of post-secondary education. Much of this education will be to make them competent to use, operate, monitor and control computer software.

The scope of typical production jobs—once just above the level of sweeping and cleaning—will be broader. Nearly everyone in the plant will be comfortable in accessing computerized information and inputting commands as well as data. Nearly everyone will have an integrated understanding of a broad range of operating and support functions. Being a skilled machinist in itself will not be enough. Skilled machinists will be succeeded by workers who understand a good deal about supply, parts inventory control, demand forecasting, scheduling, and finished goods inventory control, as well as tool operations and the maintaining of work quality and quantity. These workers will be monitors more than doers, troubleshooters more than fixers, and information manipulators rather than object manipulators.[1]

Whether or not you agree with this scenario of the design of factory jobs in the future, one thing does seem certain: the design of jobs—in the factory, office, and elsewhere—will increasingly be an important area of managerial concern. As noted in the Preview Case, the revolution in information technology already directly affects the tasks that many employees perform and how they go about performing them. For example, the recent introduction of word processors and microcomputers in offices as substitutes for electric typewriters has served to (1) expand the skills needed by secretaries to effectively use this new technology; (2) eliminate or substantially reduce the amount of time spent on routine tasks in preparing letters, memos, and documents; and (3) increase the productivity of secretaries in terms of both the quantity and quality of letters, memos, and documents produced. Along with the increasing impact of new technologies on the design of jobs, social forces and attitudes must increasingly be taken into account in how jobs are designed.

In effect, every time managers assign work, give instructions, or verify that a task is being done, job design occurs. Consciously or unconsciously, managers constantly change the tasks of their subordinates. Because tasks and the best means for performing them change over time, managers need to know how to formally design and redesign jobs—frequently in collaboration with their subordinates—to make jobs as motivating and productive as possible. The "ideal" state is approximated when jobs effectively use employees' competencies and skills and meet the needs of the organization to create products and services efficiently.[2] This ideal state is not always feasible, but, research clearly indicates that substantial improvements in employee-job-organization relationships are possible and beneficial to both employees and organizations. These benefits often extend to stakeholders external to the organization—customers, stockholders, suppliers, government, and others. For example, through improved design of production workers' jobs in automobile plants, the quality of cars has improved, which directly benefits car owners.

In this chapter, we review five major approaches to job design. We give two of them—the job-enrichment approach and sociotechnical system approach—in-depth coverage because they are usually the most effective methods of integrating employee and organizational needs. Before discussing these two approaches in detail, however, we present a framework for diagnosing the close relationship between technology and job design.

APPROACHES TO JOB DESIGN

Job design is the formal and informal specification of tasks that are performed by employees, including expected interpersonal relationships and task interdependencies with others. Ideally, the needs and goals of both employees and the organization are taken into account in the design or redesign of jobs.[3] Figure 13–1 provides an overview of five approaches to job design and highlights their overlapping, interconnected nature. It also indicates that many *contextual* factors, such as managerial style, unions, working conditions, and technology, affect job design. This chapter focuses on individual and group job design. But the design of the entire organization (the focus of Chapter 14) must be considered in order to appreciate the structural issues related to job design.

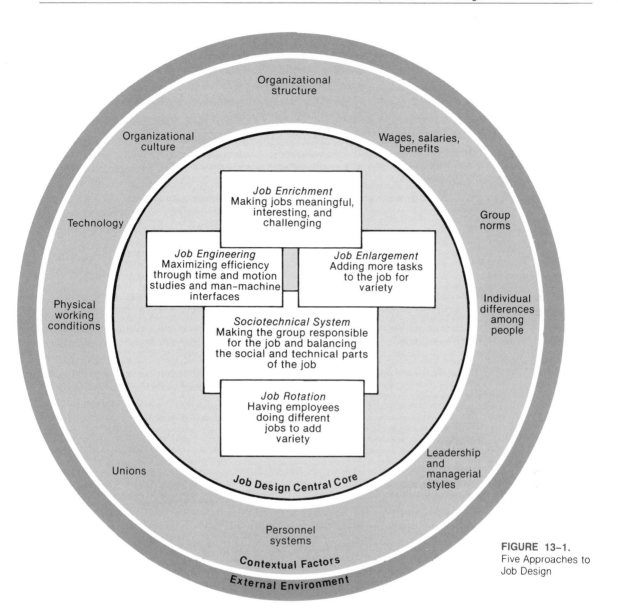

FIGURE 13-1.
Five Approaches to
Job Design

Job Engineering

Late in the nineteenth century, Frederick W. Taylor established the foundation for modern industrial engineering. Taylor's description of the application of his principles at a Bethlehem steel plant provides an interesting insight into job engineering. As you read that account, keep in mind that Taylor may have taken some "poetic license" and that his description may not be totally consistent with historical fact.

In Practice: Bethlehem Steel Plant

The Bethlehem Steel Company had five blast furnaces, the product of which had been handled by a pig-iron gang for many years. This gang, at this time, consisted of about 75 men. They were good, average pig-iron handlers, were under an excellent foreman who himself had been a pig-iron handler, and the work was done, on the whole, about as fast and as cheaply as it was anywhere else at that time.

We found that this gang was loading on the average about 12.5 long tons per man per day. We were surprised to find, after studying the matter, that a first- class pig-iron handler ought to handle between 47.5 and 48 long tons per day, instead of 12.5 tons.

Once we were sure that 47 tons was a proper day's work for a first-class pig-iron handler, the task which faced us as managers under the modern scientific plan was clearly before us. It was our duty to see that the 80,000 tons of pigiron was loaded on the cars at the rate of 47 tons per man per day, in place of 12.5 tons, at which rate the work was then being done. And it was further our duty to see that this work was done without bringing a strike among the men, without any quarrel with the men, and to see that the men were happier and better contented when loading at the new rate of 47 tons than they were when loading at the old rate of 12.5 tons.

We selected Schmidt as the most likely man to start with. He was a little Pennsylvania Dutchman who had been observed to trot back home for a mile or so after his work in the evening about as fresh as he was when he came trotting down to work in the morning.

Schmidt started to work, and all day long, and at regular intervals, was told by the man who stood over him with a watch, "Now pick up a pig and walk. Now sit down and rest. Now walk—now rest," etc. He worked when he was told to work, and rested when he was told to rest, and at half-past five in the afternoon had his 47.5 tons loaded on the car. And he practically never failed to work at this pace and do the task that was set him during the three years that the writer was at Bethlehem. One man after another was picked out and trained to handle pig-iron at the rate of 47.5 tons per day until all of the pig-iron was handled at this rate, and the men were receiving 60 percent more wages than other workmen around them.[4]

Modern industrial engineering concerns product design, process design, tool design, plant layout, work measurement, and operator methods. **Job engineering** is one aspect of industrial engineering and focuses mainly on the tasks to be performed, the methods to be used, the work flow between workers, the layout of the workplace, performance standards, and the interface between people and machines. These job design factors are often combined in the term *time-and-motion studies*. The central concern is with the time required to do each task and the efficiency of motion needed to perform it. Figure 13–2 shows an example of the results of a time-and-motion study.

Specialization of labor and efficiency are cornerstones of job engineering. High levels of specialization are assumed to (1) allow workers to learn a task rapidly; (2) permit short work cycles so performance can be almost automatic, with little or no mental direction; (3) make hiring easier, since lower-skilled people can be easily trained and paid relatively low wages; and (4) reduce the need for supervision owing to simplified jobs and standardization. Managers and industrial engineers now recognize that traditional job engineering creates fractionalized, boring jobs. Yet it remains an important job design approach because the immediate cost savings generated by time-and-motion studies can be visualized and measured.

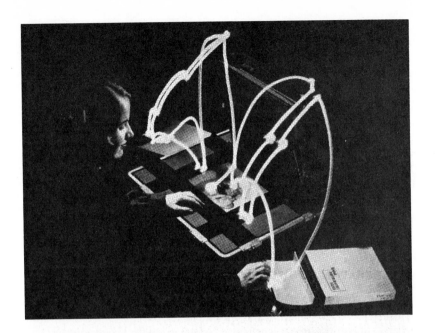

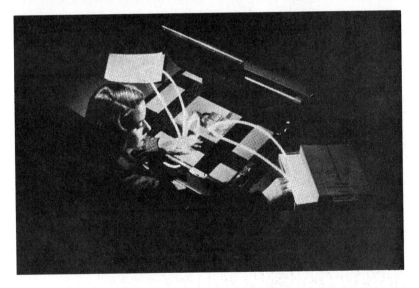

FIGURE 13–2.
Results of a Time
and Motion Study

Source: Reprinted with
permission from Barnes,
R. M. *Motion and Time
Study: Design and
Measurement of Work*, 5h
ed. New York: John Wiley
and Sons, 1964, 132.

Job Enlargement

Job enlargement expands the number of different tasks performed by employees. For example, one automobile assembly-line worker's job was enlarged from installing just one taillight to installing both taillights and the trunk. An auto mechanic switched from only changing oil to changing oil, greasing, and changing transmission fluid. Job enlargement attempts to add more tasks to the job so that it will have more variety and be more interesting.

Although this approach often has positive effects, employees may resist it. Some employees view job enlargement as just adding more routine, boring tasks to their job. Other employees may view it as eliminating the advantage of being able to perform their job almost automatically. These employees may value their opportunity to daydream about a big date that night or a vacation next month—or they may simply prefer to spend their time socializing with nearby workers. If an enlarged job requires more careful attention and concentration, some employees may find the enlarged job interesting, whereas others may view it negatively. The importance of individual differences should not be underestimated in attempting to anticipate or understand the reactions of employees to redesigned jobs.

Consider the job of a telephone operator at Bell Telephone. Do you think you could adapt to its demands?

In Practice: Bell Telephone Operators

In the early 1950s, AT&T used about a quarter of a million operators. The majority of those jobs have disappeared with automation, but Bell claims that the remaining 88,000 operators will continue to be needed for the predictable future.

Typical operators sit or stand (standing is a recent innovation) in front of button-laden consoles for six and a half hours a day. Their ears are plugged into machines that feed them a constant stream of unknown voices and numbers—up to two calls a minute, or 800 per shift. Their hands punch in the numbers on their computer consoles far faster than the eye can see.

"If there is as much as a 10-second lull between calls, they don't like it," says Edward Youngs, a Bell Labs psychologist who has studied 500 veteran operators. "They are extremely occupied by their work, but remember almost nothing of what has occurred afterwards. Operators have overlearned their jobs and can function at the level of peripheral awareness. The callers' information seems to pass from their ears to their hands without ever becoming part of a cognitive process. With time, their awareness of what they're doing just goes away."

"I never hear a word the callers say" says Chuck Bradley, a 28-year-old operator at Mountain Bell in Denver. Bradley has handled 650,000 long-distance calls in his two years on the job. "As the voices come into my mind, I just freeze the information in one part of my brain and hold it there. Then I pull it out whenever I need it. This allows me to distance myself from my work and ignore the fact that callers treat me like a rock. Who I am and what I do don't meet. My identity is separate from my job."

Operators must suppress their own feelings and personalities, always be "up" and pleasant to customers, and make callers believe they care. "Many operators like the sense of structure in their jobs," says Charles Thornton, director of operator services for AT&T. "There seems to be a sense of comfort in this, or perhaps a lack of discomfort. The job is unambiguous. Ambiguous situations make some people uncomfortable."[5]

Job Rotation

Job rotation involves moving employees from job to job to give them an opportunity to perform a greater variety of tasks. It is closely related to job enlargement. Both approaches focus on adding variety to the job to reduce employee boredom. If all tasks are similar and routine, however, job rotation may not have much impact. For example, rotating automobile assembly-line workers between the jobs of bolting bumpers on cars and bolting tire rims (wheels) on cars is not likely to have much effect on reducing boredom with job tasks. Job rotation may be of benefit if (1) it is part of a larger redesign effort, such as job enrichment or sociotechnical system approaches; and/or (2) it is used as a training technique to improve the skills and flexible use of employees.

Job Enrichment

Job enrichment adds tasks to employees' jobs that allow them to assume more responsibility and accountability for planning, organizing, controlling, and evaluating their own work.[6] The job-enrichment approach originated in the 1940s at International Business Machines (IBM). In the 1950s, the number of companies interested in job enrichment grew slowly.[7] However, successful and widely publicized experiments at AT&T, Texas Instruments (TI), and Imperial Chemicals led to an increasing awareness of and interest in job enrichment late in the 1960s.[8] Herzberg's two-factor theory of motivation—introduced late in the 1950s—was one of the first models to place special emphasis on job enrichment as a central strategy for increasing employee work motivation and job satisfaction. (See Chapter 7.)

The techniques used for enriching jobs are often specific to the job being redesigned. However, four concepts for implementing the job-enrichment approach apply to a wide variety of jobs: (1) client relationships; (2) employee scheduling of own work; (3) employee ownership of the product or service; and (4) direct feedback.[9]

CLIENT RELATIONSHIPS One of the most important approaches to job enrichment is putting employees in touch with the users of their output. Employees too often wind up working directly for their superiors rather than the customer or client. For example, in word-processing centers, certain operators can be assigned to specific clients or groups of clients, such as salespeople or engineers. Thus, when problems arise or peculiarities are encountered, the operator can work directly with the client.

SCHEDULING OF OWN WORK Most employees can very capably schedule their own work. The supervisor may set deadlines or goals, but within these guidelines, the employees could be allowed some freedom to set their own pace. **Flextime** is a form of scheduling that is becoming more common and allows each employee, within certain limits, to vary arrival and departure times to suit individual needs and desires. Flextime facilitates self-scheduling of work. With the new capabilities of information technology—such as computer hookups between home and office—there is speculation that an increasing number of jobs will be performed primarily in the employee's residence.[10]

OWNERSHIP OF PRODUCT OR SERVICE Employees who assemble entire television sets, assemble entire washing machines, or type whole reports identify more with their finished products. Allowing employees to build an entire product or complete an entire task cycle helps to create a sense of pride and achievement. Assigning people as much responsibility as possible for a certain geographical area may also create the feeling of ownership. The Indiana Bell Company found substantial improvements in performance and satisfaction when it assigned telephone directory compilers to their own city or part of the city.[11]

DIRECT FEEDBACK   The job-enrichment approach focuses on getting feedback to the employee directly from performance of the task.[12] Reports or computer outputs may be routed directly to the employees instead of just to their manager. A common technique is to let people check their own work so that they can catch most of their own errors. Obviously, this technique also increases autonomy. Direct communication with others may also improve the timeliness and accuracy of feedback. An organization could allow people in different divisions or companies to communicate directly in person or by telephone and letter. This can eliminate distortions and delays in feedback.

Sociotechnical System

The **sociotechnical system** approach to job design focuses simultaneously on the technical system and the social (human) system, recognizing that ideally they should be integrated. The fundamental goal of this approach is to find the best match *possible* (all things considered) among the technology available, the people involved, and the needs of the organization.[13] The sociotechnical system approach zeroes in on clusters of tasks that are highly interdependent. These clusters of tasks become the basis for forming natural work groups. After these work groups have been formed, the specific tasks to be performed by each member of the work group are considered. The last section of this chapter examines the specifics of this approach. The description of two contrasting chemical plants provides an insight into the sociotechnical system approach. One chemical plant operates according to the sociotechnical system approach, whereas the other operates according to more traditional job-engineering principles.

In Practice: Two Contrasting Chemical Plants

Consider the marked differences between two plants in the chemical products division of a major U.S. corporation. Both make similar products and employ similar technologies, but that is virtually all they have in common.

The first, organized by businesses with an identifiable product or product line, divides its employees into self-supervising 10- to 15-person work teams that are collectively responsible for a set of related tasks. Each team member has the training to perform many or all of the tasks for which the team is accountable, and pay reflects the level of mastery or required skills. These teams have received assurances that management will go to extra lengths to provide continued employment in any economic downturn. The teams have also been thoroughly briefed on such issues as market share, product costs, and their implications for the business.

Not surprisingly, this plant is a top performer economically and rates well on all measures of employee satisfaction, absenteeism, turnover, and safety.

With its employees actively engaged in identifying and solving problems, it operates with fewer levels of management and fewer specialized departments than do its counterpart plants. It is also one of the principal suppliers of management talent for these other plants and for the division manufacturing staff.

In the second plant, each employee is responsible for a fixed job and is required to perform up to the minimum standard defined for that job. Peer pressure keeps new employees from exceeding the minimum standards and from taking other initiatives that go beyond basic job requirements. Supervisors, who manage daily assignments and monitor performance, have long since given up hope for anything more than compliance with standards, finding sufficient difficulty in getting their people to perform adequately most of the time. In fact, they and their workers try to prevent the industrial engineering department, which is under pressure from top plant management to improve operations, from using changes in methods to "jack up" standards.

A recent management campaign to document an "airtight case" against employees who have excessive absenteeism or sub-par performance mirrors employees' low morale and high distrust of management. A constant stream of formal grievances, violations of plant rules, harassment of supervisors, wildcat walkouts, and even sabotage has prevented the plant from reaching its productivity and quality goals and has absorbed a disproportionate amount of division staff time.[14]

TECHNOLOGY AND JOB DESIGN

In the broadest sense **technology** refers to the actions, knowledge, techniques, and physical implements (computers, tools, equipment) used to transform inputs into outputs (goods and services).[15] A variety of useful models relate technology to job design.[16] We develop one of these models here.

Slocum and Sims have proposed that technology—especially as it relates job design and organization design—can be analyzed in terms of the three technology dimensions: work-flow uncertainty, task uncertainty, and task interdependence.[17]

Work-Flow and Task Uncertainty

Work-flow uncertainty is the knowledge that an employee has of when inputs will be received for processing. When work flow uncertainty is low, an employee may have little discretion (freedom) to decide which, when, or where tasks will be performed. **Task uncertainty** is the knowledge that an employee possesses about how to perform the tasks in the job. When task uncertainty is low, there is relatively complete *prespecified* knowledge about how the employee will go about producing the desired outputs. In contrast, with high task uncertainty, there are *few* (if any) *prespecified ways* for dealing with some or many of the tasks in the job. This means that experience, judgment, intuition, and problem-solving ability (that is, problem definition, solution generation, alternative evaluation, and so on are usually required.

We first consider the roles of work-flow uncertainty and task uncertainty in job design. Then, in the next section, we add a discussion of the effects of task interdependence in job design. Figure 13–3 shows the possible inter-

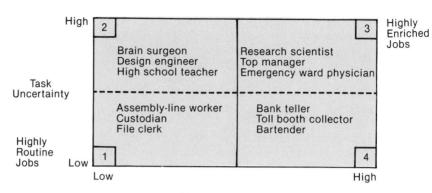

FIGURE 13–3.
Technology and Job
Design Framework

Source: Adapted from
Slocum Jr., J. W., and Sims
Jr., H. P. Typology for
Integrating Technology,
Organization, and Job
Design. *Human Relations*,
1980, *33*:196; Susman, G.
I. *Autonomy at Work: A
Sociotechnical Analysis of
Participative
Management.* New York:
Praeger, 1980, 132.

Work-flow Uncertainty

actions between the *work-flow uncertainty* dimension, ranging from low to high, and the *task uncertainty* dimension, also ranging from low to high. Remember, *low* task uncertainty means that the job can be performed in a highly predictable and standardized manner, such as the assembly-line job of bolting bumpers on automobiles.

Examples of jobs that can be categorized by each of the four cells are also shown in Figure 13–3; that is, low task uncertainty and low work-flow uncertainty, high task uncertainty and low work-flow uncertainty, and so on. We must be careful *not* to stereotype all employees that have a particular job label (high school teacher, bartender, assembly-line worker, manager) as occupying only a single position on the grid. Through job and organization redesign, it is often possible to modify most jobs so that they are characterized by more or less task uncertainty and more or less work-flow uncertainty. The job of top manager is generally characterized by high task uncertainty and high work-flow uncertainty. However, managerial jobs—including some top-manager jobs—could range from the extreme upper right corner in cell 3 to closer to the center of the matrix. Another important point is that some jobs do not clearly fit into a single cell. For example, an auditor's job in a public accounting firm might generally be plotted somewhere in the middle of the matrix.

From a technology perspective, job enrichment generally involves increasing the degree of task uncertainty and/or the degree of workflow uncertainty. Thus the assembly-line job shown in cell 1 of Figure 13–3 could be enriched, but still be generally classified as a cell-1 type of job. This framework also suggests how jobs could become too enriched. Some people who occupy cell-3 types of jobs could experience problems of stress, which can result from too much uncertainty (Chapter 18).

Task Interdependence

Task interdependence is the degree to which decision making and cooperation between two or more employees (or groups) is necessary for them to perform their own jobs. For example, when structural steel is being used for the frame of a high-rise building, there is a high degree of task interdependence between the crane operator, ground crew, and assembly crew in moving and joining the steel girders. (Recall the discussion of independent, interdependent, and dependent task relations in Chapter 10.)

Three types of interdependent task relations need to be kept in mind: pooled, sequential, and reciprocal. **Pooled interdependence** occurs when each employee is not required to interact with other individuals to complete the task or tasks. The requirement that each student write his or her own term paper for a course is an example of pooled interdependence. The bulk of the tasks—searching through the card catalog and business periodicals index, checking out and studying resource materials, creating an outline, writing the paper, and typing the paper—could be achieved independently by each student. When the instructor collects all of the papers, each student's paper is "pooled" and represents the term paper output for the whole class.

Sequential interdependence occurs when one employee must complete certain tasks before other employees can perform their tasks. In other words, the outputs from one employee become the inputs for other employees. The sequence of interdependencies can be a long chain in some mass production technologies. The traditional automobile assembly line is the best example of sequential interdependence.

Reciprocal interdependence occurs when outputs from one individual (or group) become the inputs for others, and vice versa. Reciprocal interdependencies are common in everyday life. A few examples include: (1) the three stooges; (2) Johnny Carson and Ed McMahon (3) a family; (4) a basketball team; (5) a surgical team; (6) a decision-making group; and (7) a class project assigned to a small group of students. Reciprocal interdependence usually requires a high degree of collaboration, communication, group decision making, and integration among interdependent individuals.

In the design of new jobs or the redesign of existing jobs, it is often necessary to consider and make changes in one or more of the three technological dimensions: task uncertainty, work-flow uncertainty, and task interdependence (pooled, sequential, or reciprocal). For example, *increases* in pooled interdependence *decreases* the amount of required job integration. The decrease in required job integration is achieved through a reduction in sequential and/or reciprocal interdependence. *Decreases* in the amount of job integration require *increases* in the amount of task uncertainty and/or work-flow uncertainty for the individuals involved. Following the explanation of the job characteristics enrichment model, we will expand on the linkages between changes in technology and job characteristics.

JOB CHARACTERISTICS ENRICHMENT MODEL

J. R. Hackman and G. R. Oldham developed the job characteristics enrichment model.[18] It has become one of the more popular approaches to job enrichment and is shown in graphic form in Figure 13–4.

General Framework

The **job characteristics enrichment model** defines job enrichment as increasing the amounts of five core job characteristics. The model suggests that the levels of these job characteristics can affect three critical psychological states. These psychological states, in turn, may create a number of positive personal and work-related outcomes.

As you will recall from chapter 7, employees may experience positive feelings toward their jobs to the extent that they (1) receive feedback (knowl-

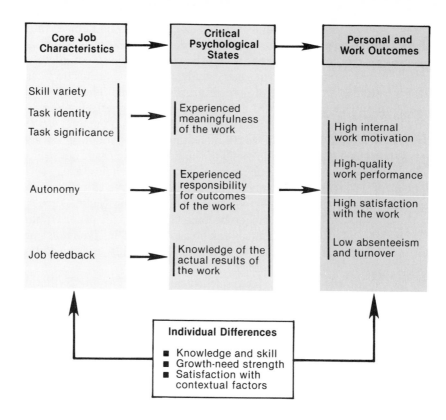

FIGURE 13-4.
Job Characteristics
Enrichment Model

Source: Hackman, J. R.
and Oldham, G. R. *Work
Redesign,* © 1980,
Addison-Wesley, Reading,
Massachusetts. (Adapted
from Fig. 4.6 on pg. 90).
Reprinted with permission.

edge of results) about task performance; (2) experience personal responsibility for tasks; and (3) feel a sense of meaningfulness about the tasks performed. If all three psychological states are present, a self-perpetuating cycle of positive work motivation based on self-generated rewards is activated. However, all three states must be present for maximum task-based motivation to occur. A job without meaningfulness, responsibility, or feedback is incomplete and thus would not provide strong motivation for an employee to perform the job tasks. Because of the in-depth coverage of motivation and outcomes in chapter 7, we will discuss further only the job characteristics and individual differences components of the model here.

Job Characteristics

The five job characteristics that are the key to job enrichment efforts are:

- **Skill variety** is the degree to which a job requires a range of personal competencies and abilities in carrying out the work.
- **Task identity** is the degree to which a job requires completion of a "whole" and identifiable piece of work, that is, doing a job from beginning to end with a visible outcome.
- **Task significance** is the degree to which the job is perceived by the employee as having a substantial impact on the lives of other people, whether those people are within or outside of the organization.
- **Autonomy** is the degree to which the job provides freedom, independence, and discretion to the employee in scheduling the tasks and in determining the procedures to be used in carrying out the tasks.

- **Job feedback** is the degree to which carrying out the job-related tasks provides the individual with direct and clear information about the effectiveness of his or her performance.[19]

Skill variety, task identity, and task significance may be especially powerful in influencing the experienced meaningfulness of work. Autonomy usually fosters increased feelings and attitudes of personal responsibility for work outcomes. Job feedback provides the knowledge of results the employee receives directly from performing the job; this is feedback from the work itself, *not* the performance-appraisal feedback often given to subordinates by superiors.

The job of surgeon can be used to illustrate these points. That job seems to rate high on all of the core job characteristics. It provides a constant opportunity for using highly varied skills, abilities, and talents in diagnosing and treating illnesses. Task identity is high because the surgeon normally diagnoses a problem, performs the operation, and monitors the convalescence. Task significance is also very high—much of the surgeon's work can mean life or death to the patient. Autonomy is quite high because the surgeon is often the final authority on the procedures and techniques of the job. However, the growing prevalence and threat of malpractice suits may have lowered the sense of autonomy among surgeons recently. Finally, the surgeon receives excellent feedback from the job, knowing almost immediately whether an operation is successful.

Individual Differences

According to Hackman and Oldham, three possible differences among individual employees should be considered in designing jobs or planning the redesign of jobs. As shown in Figure 13–4, the three major individual differences that are likely to influence the way in which employees respond to enriched jobs are (1) knowledge and skill; (2) strength of growth needs; and (3) satisfaction with contextual factors.[20] These differences can affect the relationship between job characteristics and personal/work outcomes in several important ways.

KNOWLEDGE AND SKILL   Employees with sufficient knowledge and skill to perform well an enriched job are likely to experience positive feelings about the tasks they perform. However, employees who are *not* competent to perform well an enriched job may experience frustration, stress, and dissatisfaction. These feelings and attitudes may be especially intense for employees who *desire* to do a good job but realize they are performing poorly. Thus it is important to diagnose the knowledge and skills of employees whose jobs are to be enriched. A training and development program may be needed to accompany the enrichment program.

STRENGTH OF GROWTH NEEDS   The **strength of growth needs** is the degree to which an individual desires the opportunity for self-direction, learning, and personal accomplishment at work. This concept is essentially the same as Alderfer's growth-needs concept and Maslow's esteem-need and self-actualization need concepts. (See Chapter 7.) Individuals who score high on growth-needs strength tend to have positive responses—that is, higher satisfaction with work, higher internal work motivation, and so on—when their jobs are enriched.[21] Some evidence suggests that individuals who score low on growth-needs strength are not impressed when their jobs are enriched. Their sense of satisfaction with work and internal work motivation does not appear to change after job enrichment. However, research has not shown job enrichment to be negatively related to satisfaction or performance for individuals with low strength of growth needs. Except in unusual cases, people's responses range from neutral to highly positive in an enriched job.[22]

SATISFACTION WITH CONTEXTUAL FACTORS   The degree to which employees are satisfied with contextual factors at work may affect their willingness or ability to respond positively to enriched jobs. In Figure 13–1, the ring surrounding the central core of job design shows a number of these contextual factors. Recall also the presentation of Herzberg's two-factor theory in Chapter 7. A number of contextual factors are included in the hygiene factors in the two-factor model, namely, company policy and administration, technical supervision, salary, interpersonal relations, and work conditions (lighting, heat, safety hazards, and the like). Thus employees who are extremely dissatisfied with their superiors, salary levels, and safety measures on the job are less likely to respond favorably to enriched jobs. In contrast, employees who are relatively satisfied with pay, job security, co-workers, and superiors are more likely to respond favorably to enriched jobs. Other contextual factors—such as employee satisfaction with the broader organizational culture, power and political processes, and work-group norms,—can all play a part in affecting employee responses to a job enrichment program.[23]

Job Diagnosis

There are a variety of useful methods for diagnosing jobs to determine whether job-design problems exist and the potential for job-enrichment success.[24] We will limit our consideration to two of these methods: the structural clues method and the survey method.

STRUCTURAL CLUES METHOD   The structural clues method involves checking for situational factors that are often associated with deficiencies in job design.[25] Analysis of five specific structural elements often gives important clues regarding job-design problems and possible employee acceptance of job enrichment:

- *Inspectors or checkers.* When inspectors or checkers examine work, rather than the workers themselves, autonomy is usually much lower. Feedback is also less direct and does not come from the job itself.
- *Troubleshooters.* The existence of troubleshooters usually means that all of the exciting and challenging parts of a job have been taken from the workers. Thus they do not have as much opportunity to experience a sense of responsibility for work outcomes. Task identity, autonomy, and feedback are usually poor.
- *Communications and customer-relations sections.* These sections usually cut the link between workers who do the job and customers or clients. Thus these sections may dilute feedback and task identity.

- *Labor pools.* Pools of word processors, computer programmers, and so forth are appealing because they seem to increase efficiency and the ability to meet erratic workloads. However, pools may destroy workers' feelings of ownership and task identity.
- *Narrow span of control.* A supervisor who has only a few subordinates (say 3–5) is more likely to become involved in details of their day-to-day tasks. Centralization of decision making and over-control may result from too narrow a span of control. Thus, autonomy may be seriously affected.

SURVEY METHOD   Several types of questionnaires are available for use in diagnosing jobs relatively easily and systematically.[26] One of these is the **Job Diagnostic Survey** (JDS). It was constructed by Hackman and Oldham to measure the job dimensions in their model (Figure 13–4) and the likely outcomes of job redesign.[27]

The five questions in Table 13–1 are taken from the JDS. They measure perceived skill variety, task identity, task significance, autonomy, and feedback from the job. The complete JDS uses several questions to measure each job characteristic.

You can develop your own job profile by answering the questions in Table 13–1. By using your scores (1–7) for each job dimension, you can calculate an overall measure of job enrichment called the **motivating potential score** (MPS). The MPS is calculated as follows:

$$\text{MPS} = \frac{\overset{\text{Skill}}{\text{variety}} + \overset{\text{Task}}{\text{identity}} + \overset{\text{Task}}{\text{significance}}}{3} \times \text{Autonomy} \times \text{Feedback}.$$

The MPS formula sums the scores for skill variety, task identity, and task significance and divides the total by 3. The combination of these three job characteristics is given the same weight as the job characteristics of autonomy and feedback. Why is this done? The job characteristics enrichment model (Figure 13–4) requires that both *experienced responsibility* and *knowledge of results* be present for high internal job motivation. This outcome can be achieved only if reasonable degrees of autonomy and job feedback are present.

ROLE OF SOCIAL INFORMATION   Use of the Job Diagnostic Survey and other self-report job-design questionnaires assume that employees can respond in a reasonably accurate and objective manner about the characteristics of their jobs. However, recent research suggests that employees perceptions of job characteristics may be partially the result of various social sources of information and influence.[28] For example, two employees performing the same tasks with the same job characteristics under different superiors might respond differently to the *descriptive* characteristics of their jobs on the JDS. The differences in perceived social information cues—praise or criticism by the two superiors—might account for some of the variation in the employees' responses on the JDS. The intricate and varied ways that social information in the work place can affect the perceptions of job characteristics is beyond the scope of our discussion here. To reduce possible distortions caused by social information influences, the employees' superior and possibly a trained job analyst should also rate the characteristics of jobs that are being considered for redesign.

TABLE 13–1   Selected Questions from the Job Diagnostic Survey

---

Please describe your job as objectively as you can.

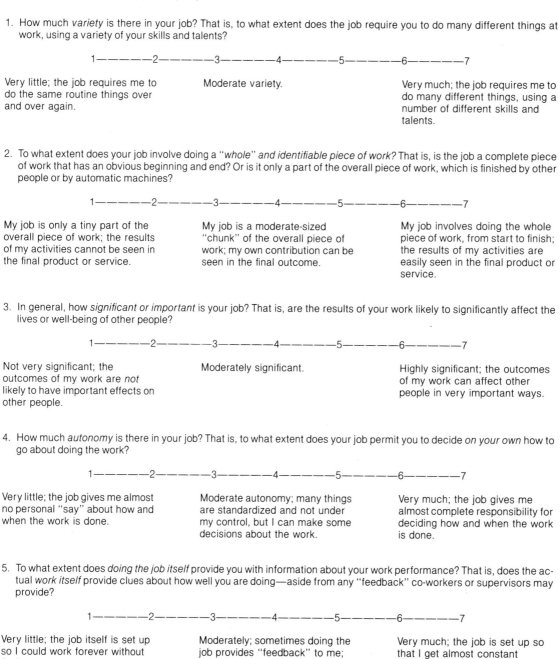

1. How much *variety* is there in your job? That is, to what extent does the job require you to do many different things at work, using a variety of your skills and talents?

1—————2—————3—————4—————5—————6—————7

Very little; the job requires me to do the same routine things over and over again.

Moderate variety.

Very much; the job requires me to do many different things, using a number of different skills and talents.

2. To what extent does your job involve doing a *"whole" and identifiable piece of work*? That is, is the job a complete piece of work that has an obvious beginning and end? Or is it only a part of the overall piece of work, which is finished by other people or by automatic machines?

1—————2—————3—————4—————5—————6—————7

My job is only a tiny part of the overall piece of work; the results of my activities cannot be seen in the final product or service.

My job is a moderate-sized "chunk" of the overall piece of work; my own contribution can be seen in the final outcome.

My job involves doing the whole piece of work, from start to finish; the results of my activities are easily seen in the final product or service.

3. In general, how *significant or important* is your job? That is, are the results of your work likely to significantly affect the lives or well-being of other people?

1—————2—————3—————4—————5—————6—————7

Not very significant; the outcomes of my work are *not* likely to have important effects on other people.

Moderately significant.

Highly significant; the outcomes of my work can affect other people in very important ways.

4. How much *autonomy* is there in your job? That is, to what extent does your job permit you to decide *on your own* how to go about doing the work?

1—————2—————3—————4—————5—————6—————7

Very little; the job gives me almost no personal "say" about how and when the work is done.

Moderate autonomy; many things are standardized and not under my control, but I can make some decisions about the work.

Very much; the job gives me almost complete responsibility for deciding how and when the work is done.

5. To what extent does *doing the job itself* provide you with information about your work performance? That is, does the actual *work itself* provide clues about how well you are doing—aside from any "feedback" co-workers or supervisors may provide?

1—————2—————3—————4—————5—————6—————7

Very little; the job itself is set up so I could work forever without finding out how well I am doing.

Moderately; sometimes doing the job provides "feedback" to me; sometimes it does not.

Very much; the job is set up so that I get almost constant "feedback" as I work about how well I am doing.

Technology and Job Characteristics

We will now bring together the earlier discussion of the technology and job design framework (Figure 13–3) with that of the job characteristics enrichment model (Figure 13–4).

As mentioned previously, in order to change one or more of the five job characteristics, it is usually necessary to make objective changes in one or more of the three technological dimensions: task uncertainty, work-flow uncertainty, and task interdependence (pooled, sequential, or reciprocal). Let us now consider a job redesign scenario where management decides to use a combination of vertical loading and the formulation of natural work groups. **Vertical loading** refers to delegating to employees responsibilities that were formally reserved for management or staff specialists. Hackman and Oldham explain the elements of vertical loading as follows:

> Jobholders can be given discretion in setting schedules, determining work methods, and deciding when and how to check on the quality of the work produced. Employees can make their own decisions about when to start and stop work, when to take breaks, and how to assign priorities. They can be encouraged to seek solutions to problems on their own, consulting with other organization members as necessary, rather than calling immediately for the supervisor when problems arise.[29]

Vertical loading serves to increase the amount of task uncertainty and possibly the amount of work-flow uncertainty that must be handled by employees in redesigned jobs. Moreover, some of the changes brought about by vertical loading tend to increase pooled interdependence and decrease sequential and reciprocal interdependence. For example, the reduction in the need to constantly check with a quality-control specialist for approvals before proceeding with other tasks serves to reduce sequential interdependence.

The formation of *natural work groups* combines individual jobs into a formally recognized unit (such as a section, group, or department), the criteria for which are logical and meaningful to the employee. The following are among the possible criteria for forming natural work groups:

- *Geographical.* Salespersons might be given a particular section of the city, state, or country as their territory.
- *Type of business.* Insurance claims adjusters might be assigned to business groups, such as utilities, manufacturers, or retailers.
- *Organizational.* Word-processing operators might be given work that originates in a particular department.
- *Alphabetical or numerical.* File clerks could be made responsible for materials in specified alphabetical groups (A–D, E–H,) and so on; library-shelf readers might check books in a certain range of the library's cataloging system.
- *Customer groups.* Employees of a public utility might be assigned to serve particular institutional or business accounts.[30]

Forming natural work groups on the basis of these criteria has the most direct impact on task interdependence. All of the criteria for forming natural

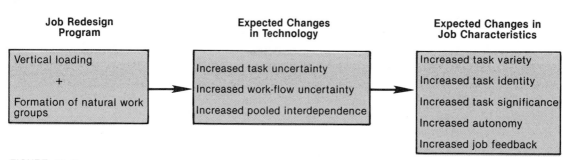

FIGURE 13–5.
Expected Technological and Job-Characteristic Links in a Job Redesign Program
Source: Adapted from Slocum, Jr., J. W. and Sims Jr., H. P. A Typology for Integrating Technology, Organization, and Job Design. *Human Relations*, 1980, 33:205.

work groups tend to increase the use of pooled interdependence and decrease the use of sequential and reciprocal interdependence.

Figure 13–5 shows the technological changes that will probably accompany a job-redesign program that employs vertical loading and the formation of natural work groups. These changes, in turn, can then be expected to lead to changes in job characteristics. Research that clearly points to the close and intricate links between technological dimensions and job-design characteristics is beginning to be published.[31]

SOCIOTECHNICAL SYSTEM MODEL

The important role of technology in job design and redesign has always been recognized in the sociotechnical system approach. Moreover, the sociotechnical system approach—unlike the job characteristics enrichment model—tends to focus on clustering jobs into work groups where there is a high degree of reciprocal or sequential interdependence between jobs, which cannot be reduced. Thus the increased use of pooled interdependence tends to occur between work groups rather than between individual jobs (as was the case with the job characteristics enrichment model).

As with job enrichment, there are several useful sociotechnical system models that can be applied.[32] We will draw on the model developed by Cummings.[33] The **sociotechnical system model** of job design deliberately designs work roles to integrate people with technology and to optimize relationships between the technological and social systems. This model centers on the creation of natural and self-managing (autonomous) work groups and reciprocal and/or sequential interdependence among jobs *within* each of the work groups. In addition, the model focuses on vertical job loading to the cluster of jobs within the group as a whole rather than to each individual job. Changes in technology are often difficult and costly in an existing plant. Thus the sociotechnical system model usually works best in the design of jobs for an entirely new plant.

Volvo's Kalmar plant in Sweden implemented the best-known and, to date, the most extensive sociotechnical project in the world. Numerous other organizations in Europe and the United States also have implemented sociotechnical system projects, including General Foods, GM, Weyerhauser, TRW, Rushton Mining, and the Tennessee Valley Authority (TVA).[34]

ACROSS CULTURES

Volvo's Kalmar Plant In Sweden

One of the most famous examples of the sociotechnical model of job design is the Kalmar automobile plant opened in 1974 by Volvo in Sweden. The plant is designed to produce up to 30,000 cars per year with one shift of assembly workers. When Pehr G. Gyllenhammar became Volvo's president, he saw that a new era was emerging: employees were demanding more meaningful work, job security, pay, and participation. When these demands were not fulfilled, people were leaving their jobs and going to work elsewhere. Turnover at Volvo was 52 percent per year, and absenteeism was a serious problem. To overcome these costly problems, Gyllenhammar decided on a risky course—to completely redesign the new, planned Kalmar plant. His goal was to make it possible for an employee to see a Volvo driving down the street and say, "I made that car."

Implementing this goal involved changing the conventional auto assembly line that moved through a plant to a system where the work remained stationary and the materials were brought to the work station. A special carrier to transport an entire car and position it for assembly was developed, as shown in Figure 13–6. The carrier moves around on an electric tape track and can be removed or held in place during assembly. Moreover, if problems arise, an automobile can be pulled out of the production flow for more work. The trolly can also be tilted in order to facilitate work underneath the automobile.

The Kalmar plant has approximately twenty-five work groups of twenty people each. They are organized to perform all the work on certain

(a)

FIGURE 13–6.
Application of the Sociotechnical Approach: (a) Traditional Assembly Line at Volvo; (b) Volvo's New Patented Car Carrier; and (c) Volvo's Car Carriers in Action.

Source: Pehr Gyllenhammar, *People at Work,* © 1977, Addison-Wesley, Reading, Massachusetts. Reprinted with permission.

FIGURE 13–6 continued.

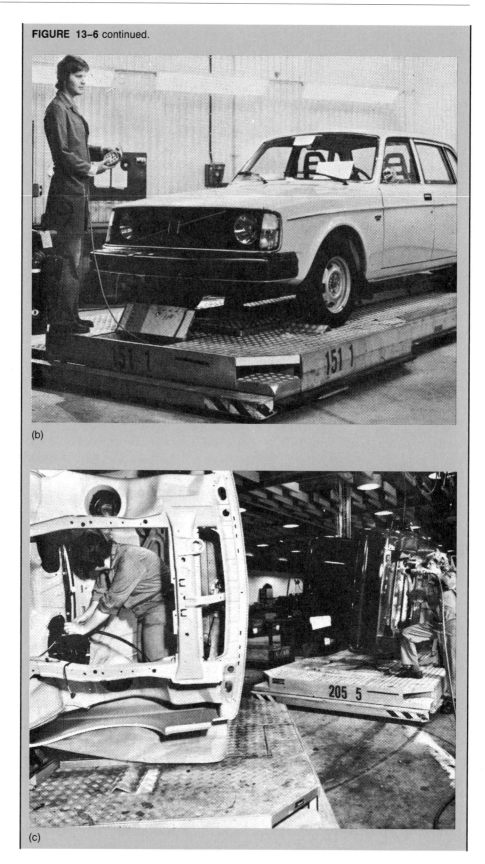

(b)

(c)

subsystems, such as electrical systems, instrumentation, steering and controls, and interiors. Each team has its own area of the shop floor and its own rest area. Management does not dictate responsibilities and work procedures: each group organizes itself. Teams can elect to organize themselves so members specialize in individual jobs, divide themselves into subteams to do parts of the job, or devise rotation schemes. The teams have substantial opportunities for self-control. They contract with management to deliver a certain number of such things as finished doors, brake systems, and interiors per day. The groups determine the pace of their work and break times. They conduct their own inspections, and a computer-based quality control system flashes the results directly back to the work stations on a television screen.[35]

Berth Jönsson, the vice-president of organization development at Volvo, responded to a series of comments by the editors of *New Management* (hereafter NM) some 10 years after the start up of the Kalmar plant. A few of these comments and his responses are presented as follows.

NM: We've heard from many observers that "Kalmar was a noble experiment which failed."

Jönsson: We, too, have heard this criticism. The statement is false. In reality, Kalmar was the start of a new philosophy at Volvo, a new strategy of production technology. It had the full commitment of top management from the start, and was never planned as an "experiment." It was stated from the beginning that a productivity standard lower than that of a traditional factory *would not be accepted.* No company can afford to experiment with extensive investments like the Kalmar Plant. The diffusion after Kalmar is also a proof that the new concepts are preferable to Volvo. Nine additonal Volvo plants have been built after Kalmar and they are all designed in an unconventional way.

NM: We have read that Kalmar did not meet productivity standards.

Jönsson: Again, this is wrong. Kalmar has achieved 20% higher productivity than the goal set for the project. Remember, we are in business, and we demand a return on our investments. We must continuously seek new ways of improving productivity. The contrary is not acceptable, and it is unheard of at Volvo. Our experience is that people are happier with the Kalmar design and work organization than with the traditional system. This is not to say that the organization of work is ideal, or that we have reached the only and final solution.

Absenteeism due to sickness is about half of what it is in our traditionally organized Torslanda Plant. To sort out another misunderstanding, there is still some demanding manual work which has to be done in Kalmar. A "laissez-faire" attitude about tasks just would not work in an auto factory. But, if our people had a choice, it would be an easy choice in favor of the new approach.

NM: Most business professors in America believe that the Kalmar plant is an isolated experiment and hasn't been disseminated throughout Volvo.

Jöhsson: I think this is the most widespread and most seriously inaccurate myth about Volvo. What has been going on in the company during the last ten to twelve years is broad-scale, organization-wide change. It is important to understand that we are *not* talking about one model for change but a variety of approaches. Redesign strategies vary from plant to plant on such factors as management style, social relations, demographic structure, and technology. Consequently, there is no standardized model of change which can be used as a normative tool within a company or between companies.[36]

FIGURE 13–7.
Sociotechnical System Model of
Job Design

Source: Adapted and further developed from
Cummings, T. Self-Regulating Work Groups:
A Socio-Technical Synthesis. *Academy of
Management Review*, 1978, 3:625–634.

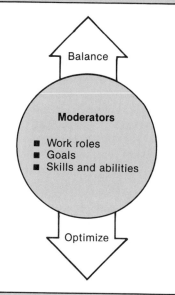

The Volvo Kalmar plant experience suggests that the sociotechnical system model is important not only for the purpose of job design, but also as part of the whole management process. Figure 13–7 presents a sociotechnical model of job design, which is based on the model developed by Cummings and consists of three major elements: the social system, the technological system, and moderators. You should keep the description of the Volvo approach in mind as you study this model.

Social System

The social system in the sociotechnical model includes those parts of the "human side" of the organization that can influence how individuals and groups go about performing tasks, as well as their attitudes toward work and the organization. The contextual factors shown in Figure 13–1 are illustrative of important social system influences, many of which have been addressed in previous chapters. Chapter 9 and chapter 12, in particular, presented the main elements and processes of the work-related social system. For example, if the organization is characterized by distrust, back-stabbing, and hostility, creation of self-managing work groups is likely to be very difficult until some degree of trust and cooperation is established.

Technological System

The three technological dimensions (task uncertainty, work-flow uncertainty, and task interdependence) need to be diagnosed. These technological dimensions are likely to vary with the type of production process being used or planned. Thus the type of production process (assembly line, process, batch, or unit) is an important technological characteristic and different production processes require different approaches to job design. In a process technology operation, such as an oil refinery, most of the work is automated; the relatively small number of workers spend much of their time monitoring dials and performing maintenance tasks. In contrast, small-unit technologies, such as plumbing, television repair, sales, and investment brokering, require relatively larger amounts of labor applied directly to the job.

Another technological characteristic is the physical work setting (amount of light, temperature, noise, pollution, geographical isolation, and orderliness). For example, if it is too hot or noisy, employees may have a more difficult time performing tasks that require intense thought and concentration.

Complexity of the production process is also an important technological characteristic. It may be quite easy for a person to learn to build an entire toaster, but one person probably could not build even a major subsystem of a complex jet aircraft. In general, the more complex the production process, the greater are the degrees of task uncertainty and work flow uncertainty and the requirement for reciprocal task interdependence.

Other important technological characteristics are the nature of the raw materials used in production and the time pressure inherent in the production process. For example, newspapers are published on a tight and rigid time schedule. Bottlenecks must be dealt with quickly and workers must speed up their pace if the production flow falls behind schedule by even 60 minutes.

Moderators

Work roles act as moderators in the sociotechnical system model. They establish a set of expected behaviors for each employee; they help to define the relationships between people who perform tasks and the technological requirements of those tasks; and they help to stabilize work relationships and provide the glue that binds the sociotechnical system together.

Goals also moderate the relationship between the social system and technological system. For example, autonomous work teams may have a goal of producing a certain number of subassemblies or cars per day. This goal, so long as it is compatible with the goal for the technical system, actually allows them to be somewhat autonomous of higher management. Thus, they can structure the work any way they want as long as they meet the common output goal.

A final moderator includes the skills and abilities of the employees. A higher level of sociotechnical mix would be possible in a country with a highly skilled and educated work force than in an underdeveloped country where skill and educational levels are quite low. If the skills needed are not available, it may be necessary to change the production process and simplify the jobs.

SELECTING JOB-DESIGN MODELS

It should now be apparent that the factors to be diagnosed in job design decisions can be quite complex.[37] Perhaps the most basic issue is the management philosophy and values that define the organizational culture of a company. Managers interested in improving both the quality of work life and organizational effectiveness would find the job-enrichment or sociotechnical models appropriate. Managers interested only in production and efficiency would concentrate on the job-engineering, job-enlargement, or job-rotation approaches.

Technology is a major variable in job design. Some jobs cannot be enriched without a redesign of the whole plant. When it is impossible to change a job, other techniques (such as flextime) may soften the effects of a nonenriched job.[38] Moreover, new information technologies, especially those involving robots and computers, are being used increasingly to eliminate boring and routine jobs, eliminating the need to redesign them.[39] Perhaps the best strategy for managers is to understand fully the various approaches to job design and to use the combination of approaches that best fits their organization or department.[40]

SUMMARY

Job design is a continuous managerial task. Ideally, jobs will be designed that are both efficient and satisfying to employees. There are five major approaches to job design: job engineering, job enlargement, job rotation, job enrichment, and the sociotechnical system. Job engineering includes traditional industrial engineering techniques that simplify a job in order to make it more efficient. Job enlargement and job rotation seek to make boring jobs more interesting by adding variety.

Job enrichment seeks to make jobs more meaningful and challenging, especially through vertical loading. Managers can enrich jobs in many ways; having employees establish client relationships, allowing employees to schedule their own work, providing employees with a sense of ownership of the whole product, and providing for direct feedback from the job itself. The job characteristics enrichment model focuses on modifying five job characteristics: task variety, task identity, task significance, autonomy, and job feedback. Technological dimensions that affect these job characteristics must usually be changed. The three technological dimensions involved are: task uncertainty, work-flow uncertainty, and task interdependence (pooled, sequential, and reciprocal).

Employees in properly designed jobs are more likely to be satisfied and perform better. Individual differences are important in redesigning jobs because some people may not want enriched jobs or may not want to work in groups. Also, some organizational or technological situations may not permit job enrichment.

The sociotechnical system model of job design attempts to integrate the technological system with the social system within an organization. Three moderators—work roles, goals, and skills and abilities—serve to balance the components of the social system and optimize the components of the technological system. This model seems to be most useful in the design of new plants, such as Volvo's Kalmar plant in Sweden.

Job design decisions, like other managerial decisions, contain many contingencies that must be diagnosed. Perhaps the best way to understand and balance these contingencies is by having a thorough knowledge of the various job design approaches that can be applied.

KEY WORDS AND CONCEPTS

Autonomy
Flextime
Growth-needs strength
Job characteristics enrichment model
Job design
Job Diagnostic Survey
Job engineering
Job enlargement
Job enrichment
Job feedback
Job rotation
Motivating potential score
Pooled interdependence

Reciprocal interdependence
Sequential interdependence
Skill variety
Sociotechnical system
Sociotechnical system model
Task identity
Task interdependence
Task significance
Task uncertainty
Technology
Vertical loading
Work-flow uncertainty

DISCUSSION QUESTIONS

1. Why do technological dimensions often need to be changed as a first step in changing job characteristics?
2. What are the characteristics of an enriched job?
3. Why do employees sometimes react adversely to the job-engineering approach to job design?
4. What are the similarities and differences between job enlargement and job rotation?
5. How would you rate each of the job characteristics present in a professional baseball player's job and a cook's job in a fast food restaurant. Which job has the highest motivating potential?
6. What clues might you look for in determining whether a job needs to be redesigned?
7. Why does the job characteristics enrichment model sometimes fail to bring about the intended personal and work outcomes?
8. How does the sociotechnical system approach to job design differ from the job-enrichment approach?

MANAGEMENT INCIDENTS AND CASES

Nissan's Plant in Smyrna, Tennessee

Nissan's first U.S. vehicle plant was opened in June 1983. Located on a 782-acre site in Smyrna, Tennessee, the plant has 3.4 million square feet and cost $745 million. It currently has a designed annual production capacity of 240,000 vehicles. When opened in 1983, the plant produced only small pickup trucks. In 1984, the decision was made to add assembly of the two-door Nissan Sentra car. The first Sentra car rolled out of the plant in 1985. By 1988, the Smyrna plant is also expected to produce the four-door Sentra model and have an annual production of 100,000 cars and 140,000 trucks. The work force in the plant is expected to total 3,000 employees by 1988, working two shifts per day. Only 78 acres of the 782-acre site is currently used. Thus a substantial amount of land is available for plant expansion.

Marvin Runyon is the president and chief executive officer of Nissan Motor Manufacturing Corporation USA. Runyon is 62 years old and a 37-year Ford veteran who took the Nissan job after retiring from Ford as vice-president of body and assembly operations. He oversaw 29 plants and 120,000 employees at Ford.

According to Runyon, the selection of plant workers, called "hourly technicians" by Nissan, begins with initial screening by the Tennessee Department of Employment Security. This yields applicants "who have the necessary skills to become maintenance, quality-control, material-handling, tool and die, or manufacturing technicians." Those who pass this first screening have their first interview with Nissan, at which the firm's working style is discussed. If the applicant "passes," he or she is familiarized with Nissan in more detail. Applicants are then enrolled in the state's preemployment training,

with no compensation. They are not yet Nissan employees, but the training is carried out in Nissan facilities.

Runyon comments: "We opened a 30,000-square-foot training center at our site, which houses both a shop area and classrooms. We have demonstration models of all the robots, a paint booth, a maintenance area, and a variety of other demonstration equipment that provides our employees with hands-on practice."

A major emphasis throughout the training program is cross-training. In explaining the program, Runyon notes that cross-training is "not traditional" in U.S. manufacturing.

> Because the new machine systems include complex interrelated subsystems that cannot be treated as independent skills, the workers must have a variety of skills to be able to work with equipment. A robot, for instance, may have a servo system that incorporates electronics and hydraulics and, at the same time, is directed by a programmable controller.
>
> Our manufacturing system depends on workers who want to expand their jobs. They are expected to participate in refining the manufacturing system and to make suggestions to increase productivity and quality. This requires an employee who is well-trained, shows initiative, and maintains a good working relationship with other employees.

Nissan has also invested in supervisory development. First-level supervisors have been taught leadership and team-building skills and ways of enhancing the self-esteem of their employees. Faculty members from local universities have been involved in this program to teach supervisors new ways of relating to subordinates. Runyon observes that trying to run an entire business with this orientation (that is, greater self-direction) requires a thoroughgoing conversion from conventional management practice.

First you have to teach the chief executive officer how to do it, then you have to teach every person down to the supervisor how to do it. They all have to be dedicated to the idea or it won't work. You can teach the supervisor, who can go out and do it and everything looks great. Then some problem develops all of a sudden. The general foreman or the superintendent or the manager to whom the supervisor reports just cannot accept that, because he has not been properly trained. A real training process, a real dedication to making the thing work, is necessary. It has to happen at all levels of management. You have to be careful and have "people facilitators" from outside the organization who come in and say: "You did it wrong; now go back and correct it."

The plant has "employee involvement groups" working on technical production problems. However, these groups are not exact copies of Japanese quality circles. Runyon points out that quality circles took many years to develop in Japan, and that they were generated and operated by employees.

Supervisors are not members of those circles in Nissan's Japanese plants. Seven or eight hourly employees are in a circle. They get together and come up with what they want. One of the reasons that they work very well in Japan is that they are given all of the information they need to solve the problems they raise. They ask management questions like: "How much does this piece cost?" "And how much time does it take

to do the job?" "How much does a minute of labor cost?" They are immediately given that information.

That is a very strange thing to me. In my U.S. management experience, you would not give the information to a production worker who asked: "What is my time on this job?" American management would respond: "You have enough time to do the job." "And how much does the material cost?" Response: "It's none of your business, you know, just put the part on."

For quality circles to be effective, people have to know material costs; they have to know labor costs; they have to know tooling costs. Because, if they are working on something, they need to know what it is they need to work on. If the material cost is the big thing, then they work on material.

Runyon provides an example. While he was at Nissan, he saw a computerized, automatic warehouse storage "machine" and inquired about its cost and savings from its use. The plant manager did not know, but the machine operator knew cost, payout time, and the number of people replaced. The operator knew more about the business aspects of the warehouse operation because it was a part of the operator's job.

Runyon describes a traditional U.S. auto plant job and notes how it contrasts with the typical job at the Smyrna plant.

One of the reasons we have low turnover is because the people who work in our operation have more responsibility for their jobs. In the normal automotive assembly plant in the United States today, a production operator does a production job. That consists of putting on five bolts to hold a wheel in place. Then, about 20 operators down the line, there is an inspector. That inspector checks to see that those bolts are on, and that they are tight. If something happens to the socket on one of those bolts and it becomes damaged, the production operator notifies the supervisor that he has a broken socket. And the supervisor notifies the maintenance employee, who then comes down and fixes the broken socket. In the meantime, the line is stopped and the production operator is standing there waiting for the socket to be fixed. He may not have noticed it immediately when it broke. The inspector may not have been watching for those nuts because he has several other things to look at. Some defective product may have gone by.

Our manufacturing technicians have the responsibility to put the nuts on, and a responsibility to check them because they will not be checked again in the plant. And, if that socket breaks, they also have a responsibility to replace it.

If people have responsibility to do their jobs, have something that is interesting to do, and have total control over it, I think they are much happier. In too much of industry today, we try to take all of the skills out of the job and just have a person do one simple thing. As a result, we have lost productivity in this country.

An example of cross-training (and the absence of work-rule restrictions) is graphically described by Runyon:

Consider the maintenance technician in the conventional U.S. plants. If you had a malfunctioning welding transformer, you would have to get a millwright to go up there on the rail where it is mounted and get it down to the floor. First, a pipefitter may have to go up and disconnect some pipes, so the millwright can bring it down. You might need a welder if the bracket broke. Four people: a welder, a millwright, an electrician, a pipefitter. Nissan trains its people in all of those skills so that one person can do that job.

There are only five levels of management at all of Nissan USA:

- president (Marvin Runyon);
- vice-presidents (six, plus General Counsel and an Organization and Development Department, reporting to the President);
- plant managers (three, and a director of supply, reporting to vice-president of manufacturing);
- operations managers (three to four report to each plant manager); and
- supervisors (three to eight report to each operations manager).

Supervisory ratios are affected by the level of technology in each area of the plant. In the highly automated and robotized body-construction area, each supervisor directs about 11 technicians. In the paint operation, which is somewhat less automated, 16 technicians report to each supervisor. In the trim and chassis area, the ratio is about 20:1 because "there is less automation and more handwork."[41]

Questions

1. What concepts and processes from the job characteristics enrichment model seem to be practiced at the Nissan plant? Identify specific descriptive statements in the case and link them to the concepts and processes in the job characteristics enrichment model.

2. What concepts and processes from the sociotechnical system model of job design seem to be practiced at the Nissan plant?

Identify specific descriptive statements in the case and link them to the concepts and processes in the sociotechnical system model.

3. How would you characterize Nissan's plant with respect to the three technological dimensions presented in this chapter, namely, task uncertainty, work flow uncertainty, and task interdependence (pooled, sequential, and reciprocal)?

REFERENCES

1. Excerpts from Hagedon, H. J. The Factory of the Future: What About the People? Reprinted by permission from the *Journal of Business Strategy,* Summer 1984. Published by Warren, Gorham & Lamont, Inc. 210 South St., Boston, Mass. Copyright © 1984. All rights reserved.

2. Brousseau, K. R. Toward a Dynamic Model of Job–Person Relationships: Findings, Research Questions, and Implications for Work System Design. *Academy of Management Review,* 1983, *8,* 33–45; Sims, R. R. Kolb's Experiential Learning Theory: A Framework for Assessing Person–Job Interaction. *Academy of Management Review,* 1983, *8,* 501–508.

3. Adapted from Griffin, R. W. *Task Design: An Integrative Approach.* Glenview, Ill.: Scott, Foresman, 1982, 4.

4. Taylor, F W. *The Principles of Scientific Management.* New York: Norton, 1911, 42–47.

5. Excerpted from Singular, S. A Robot and Liking it. *Psychology Today,* March 1983, 22. Reprinted with permission from *Psychology Today Magazine.* Copyright © 1983 (APA).

6. Aldag, R. J., and Brief, A. P. *Task Design and Employee Motivation.* Glenview, Ill.: Scott, Foresman, 1974.

7. Herzberg, F., Mausner, B., and Snyderman, B. *The Motivation to Work.* New York: Wiley, 1959.

8. Myers, M. S. *Every Employee a Manager.* New York: McGraw-Hill, 1970.

9. Hackman, J. R., and Oldham, G. R. *Work Redesign.* Reading, Mass.: Addison-Wesley, 1980.

10. Magee, J. F. What Information Technology Has in Store for Managers. *Sloan Management Review,* Winter 1985, 45–49.

11. Ford, R. N. Job Enrichment Lessons from AT&T. *Harvard Business Review,* January–February 1973, 96–106.

12. Herold, D. M., and Parsons, C. K. Assessing the Feedback Environment in Work Organizations: Development of the Job Feedback Survey. *Journal of Applied Psychology,* 1985, *2,* 290–305; Ashford, S. J., and Cummings, L. L. Feedback as an Individual Resource: Personal Strategies for Creating Information. *Organizational Behavior and Human Performance,* 1983, *32,* 370–398.

13. Huse, E. F., and Cummings, T. G. *Organization Development and Change,* 3d ed. St. Paul, Minn.: West, 1985, 204–205; Susman, G. I. *Autonomy at Work: A Sociotechnical Analysis of Participative Management.* New York: Praeger, 1976.

14. Reprinted by permission of the Harvard Business Review. Excerpt from "From Control to Commitment in the Workplace" by Richard E. Walton (March/April, 1985). Copyright © 1985 by the President and Fellows of Harvard College; all rights reserved.

15. Perrow, C. P. A Framework for the Comparative Analysis of Organizations. *American Sociological Review,* 1967, *32,* 194–208; Rousseau, D. M. Assessment of Technology in Organizations: Closed versus Open Systems Approaches. *Academy of Management Review,* 1979, *4,* 531–542.

16. Blacker, F., and Brown, C. Evaluation and the Impact of Information Technologies on People in Organizations. *Human Relations,* 1985, *38,* 213–231; Cummings, T. G. Designing Work for Productivity and Quality of Work Life. *Outlook,* 1982, *6,* 35–39; Thompson, J. D. *Organizations in Action.* New York: McGraw-Hill, 1967; Withey, M., Daft, R. L., and Cooper, W.H. Measures of Perrow's Work Unit Technology: An Empirical Assessment and a New Scale. *Academy of Management Journal,* 1983, *26,* 45–63; Woodward, J. *Industrial Organization: Theory and Research,* 2d ed. New York: Oxford University Press, 1980.

17. Slocum Jr., J. W., and Sims Jr., H. P. A Typology for Integrating Technology, Organization, and Job Design. *Human Relations,* 1980, *33,* 193–212. Also see Mills, P. K., and Moberg, D. J. Perspectives on the Technology of Service Operations. *Academy of Management Review,* 1982,

7, 467–478; Northcraft, G. P., and Chase, R. B. Managing Service Demand at the Point of Delivery. *Academy of Management Review,* 1985, *10,* 66–75.

18. Hackman, J. R., and Oldham, G. R. *Work Redesign,* 71–96.

19. Hackman and Oldham, 77–80.

20. Hackman and Oldham 82–88.

21. Loher, B. T., Noe, R. A., Moeller, N., and Fitzgerald, M. P. A Meta-Analysis of the Relation of Job Characteristics to Job Satisfaction. *Journal of Applied Psychology,* 1985, *70,* 280–289; Pokorney, J., Gilmore, D. C., and Beehr, T. Job Diagnostic Survey Dimensions: Moderating Effect of Growth Needs and Correspondence with Dimensions of Job Rating Form. *Organizational Behavior and Human Performance,* 1980, *26,* 222–237.

22. O'Connor, E. J., Rudolf, L. G., and Peters, L. H. Individual Differences and Job Design Reconsidered: Where Do We Go From Here? *Academy of Management Review,* 1980, *5,* 249–254; Ganster, D. C. Individual Differences and Task Design: A Laboratory Experiment. *Organizational Behavior and Human Performance,* 1980, *26,* 131–148.

23. Caldwell, D. F., and O'Reilly, C. A. Task Perceptions and Job Satisfaction: A Question of Causality. *Journal of Applied Psychology,* 1982, *67,* 361–369; Dunham, R. B., Pierce, J. L., Newstrom, J. W. Job Context and Job Content: A Conceptual Perspective. *Journal of Management,* 1983, *9,* 187–202; Ferris, G. R., and Gilmore, D. C. The Moderating Role of Work Context in Job Design Research: A Test of Competing Models. *Academy of Management Journal,* 1984, *27,* 885–892; Griffeth, R. W. Moderation of the Effects of Job Enrichment by Participation: A Longitudinal Field Experiment. *Organizational Behavior and Human Decision Processes,* 1985, *35,* 73–93.

24. Levine, E. L., Ash, R. A., Hall, H., and Sistrunk, F. Evaluation of Job Analysis Methods by Experienced Job Analysts. *Academy of Management Journal,* 1983, *26,* 339–348.

25. Whitsett, D. A. Where Are Your Enriched Jobs? *Harvard Business Review,* January–February 1975, 74–80.

26. Campion, M. A., and Thayer, P. W. Development and Field Evaluation of an Interdisciplinary Measure of Job Design. *Journal of Applied Psychology,* 1985, *70,* 29–43; Sims Jr., H. P., Szilagyi, A. D., and Keller, R. T. The Measurement of Job Characteristics. *Academy of Management Journal,* 1976, *19,* 195–212; Sashkin, M., and Lengermann, J. L. Quality of Work Life-Conditions Feelings Instrument. In J. W. Pfeiffer and L. D. Goodstein (Eds.) *The 1984 Annual: Developing Human Resources.* San Diego, Calif.: University Associates, 1984, 131–144.

27. Hackman, J. R., and Oldham, G. R. Development of the Job Diagnostic Survey. *Journal of Applied Psychology,* 1975, *60,* 159–170.

28. Adler, S., Skov, R. B., and Salvemini, N. J. Job Characteristics and Job Satisfaction: When Cause Becomes Consequence. *Organizational Behavior and Human Decision Processes,* 1985, *35,* 266–278; Arvey, R. D., Davis, G. A., McGowen, S. L., and Dipboye, R. L. Potential Sources of Bias in Job Analytic Processes. *Academy of Management Journal,* 1982, *25,* 618–621; Blau, G. J., and Katerberg, R. Toward Enhancing Research with the Social Information Processing Approach to Job Design. *Academy of Management Review,* 1982, *7,* 543–550; Griffin, R. W. Objective and Social Sources of Information in Task Redesign: A Field Experiment. *Administrative Science Quarterly,* 1983, *28,* 184–200; Thomas, J., and Griffin, R. W. The Social Information Processing Model of Task Design: A Review of the Literature. *Academy of Management Review,* 1983, *8,* 672–682.

29. Hackman and Oldham. *Work Redesign,* 138–139.

30. Walters, R. W., and Associates. *Job Enrichment for Results.* Reading, Mass.: Addison-Wesley, 1975.

31. Brass, D. J. Technology and the Structuring of Jobs: Employee Satisfaction, Performance, and Influence. *Organizational Behavior and Human Decision Processes,* 1985, *35,* 216–240.

32. Davis, L. E., and Taylor, J. C. (Eds.) *Design of Jobs.* Baltimore: Penguin Books, 1972; Lawler III, E. E. Increasing Worker Involvement to Enhance Organizational Effectiveness. In P. S. Goodman and Associates (Eds.) *Change in Organizations.* San Francisco: Jossey-Bass, 1982, 280–315; Susman, G. I. *Autonomy at Work: A Sociotechnical Analysis of Participative Management.* New York: Praeger, 1976; Thorsrud, E., Sorenson, B., and Gustavsen, B. Sociotechnical Approach to Industrial Democracy. In R. Dubin (Ed.) *Handbook of Work Organization and Society.* Chicago: Rand McNally, 1976, 648–687; Walton, R. E. From Control to Commitment in the Workplace. *Harvard Business Review,* March–April 1985, 76–84.

33. Cummings, T. G. Self-Regulating Work Groups: A Socio-Technical Synthesis. *Academy of Management Review,* 1978, *3,* 625–634. Cummings, T., and Molloy, E. *Improving Productivity and the Quality of Work Life.* New York: Praeger, 1977;

Cummings, T. Designing Work for Productivity and Quality of Work Life. *Outlook,* 1982, *6,* 35–39.

34. Goodman, P. S. *Assessing Organizational Change: The Rushton Quality of Work Life Experiment.* New York: John Wiley and Sons, 1979; Taylor, J. Experiments in Work System Design: Economic and Human Results. *Personnel Review,* 1977, 6:28–37; Walton, R. E. Work Innovations at Topeka: After Six Years. *Journal of Applied Behavioral Science,* 1977, *13,* 422–433; Whitsett, D. A., and Yorks, L. Looking Back at Topeka: General Foods and the Quality-of-Work-Life Experiment. *California Management Review,* Summer 1983, 93–109.

35. Adapted from Gyllenhammar, P. G. *People at Work.* Reading, Mass.: Addison-Wesley, 1977; Jönsson, B. The Quality of Work Life—The Volvo Experience. *Journal of Business,* 1982, *1,* 119–126.

36. Reprinted from New Management, Vol. 1, No. 2, 1983, pp. 30–33. Copyright © the Dean and Faculty of the Graduate School of Business Administration, University of Southern California.

37. Kiggundu, M. N. Task Interdependence and the Theory of Job Design. *Academy of Management Review,* 1981, *6,* 499–508.

38. Cohen, A. R., and Gadon, H. *Alternative Work Schedules: Integrating Individual and Organizational Needs.* Reading, Mass.: Addison, Wesley, 1978; Ronen, S. *Flexible Working Hours: An Innovation in the Quality of Working Life.* New York: McGraw-Hill, 1981.

39. Machine of the Year: A New World Dawns. *Time,* January 3, 1983, 12–32; Brody, H. Overcoming Barriers to Automation. *High Technology,* May 1985, 41–46; Collier, D. A. The Service Sector Revolution: The Automation of Services. *Long Range Planning,* December 1983, 10–20; Hollon, C. G., and Rogol, G. N. How Robotization Affects People. *Business Horizons,* May/June 1985, 74–80; Foulkes, E. K., and Hirsch, J. L. People Make Robots Work. *Harvard Business Review,* January–February 1984, 94–102; Wall, J. L., Daniels, J. P., Shane, H. M., and Wernimont, T. A. Robotics: Challenges for the Human Resources Manager. *Business Horizons,* March/April 1984, 38–46; Strassman, P. A. *Information Payoff: The Transformation of Work in the Electronic Age.* New York: Free Press, 1985.

40. Griffin, R. W. *Task Design: An Integrative Approach.* Glenview, Ill.: Scott, Foresman, 1982.

41. Most of this case was excerpted and adapted from Freedman, Audrey *Japanese Management of U.S. Work Forces.* New York: Conference Board, 1982, 3–6. Used with permission. Other sources used include Bylinsky, G. America's Best-Managed Factories. *Fortune,* May 28, 1984, 16–24; Bohn, J. Runyon Maps Success of Nissan's U.S. Plant. *Automotive News,* September 3, 1984, 3, 53; Mayer, M. B. First Nissan Car Built in U.S. *Automotive News,* April 1, 1985, 1, 54; Sentra in the Spring. *Automotive News,* October 22, 1984, E26, and E28.

14 Organization Design

LEARNING OBJECTIVES

When you have finished studying this chapter, you should be able to:

- Describe how environmental forces, strategic choice, and technological factors influence the design of organizations.

- Diagnose organizations with respect to their degree of mechanistic versus organic characteristics.

- Identify the key variables that affect interdepartmental relations and state their impacts on organization design.

- Describe the characteristics of three basic organizational structures and some of the managerial implications of each.

- State how organization design and different structures can influence the effectiveness of employees and the organization.

OUTLINE

Preview Case

Hewlett-Packard

On July 16, 1984, Hewlett-Packard (H-P) announced a sweeping structural reorganization designed to accelerate its transition from a company run by engineers for engineers to one with the marketing clout needed to reach a wider audience and compete with an increasingly aggressive IBM. H-P's overhaul unifies the previously fragmented marketing efforts of its two biggest businesses: computers and instruments. Its new structure, engineered by president and chief executive John A. Young, regroups H-P's dozens of product divisions under sectors that are focused on markets rather than product lines. Two major sectors will now sell computers. One will concentrate on business customers, while the second will market computers and instruments to scientific and manufacturing customers. H-P is merging its two biggest businesses because industrial customers increasingly are buying computers linked with instruments for testing and process control.

Hewlett-Packard's difficulties in the computer business are well known. It backed into the industry in 1968 by launching a minicomputer to be used for controlling instruments—and caught a wave. It is now the third-largest minicomputer maker, after IBM and Digital Equipment Corporation. Yet the company is still feeling its way. Its share of the minicomputer market has slipped slightly from 7 percent in 1979 to about 6 percent in 1985.

Many of the problems can be laid to fragmented product development. Traditionally, the company had been split into scores of small autonomous divisions. That structure enabled H-P to compete better with the relatively small, fast-moving companies of the instruments industries. Each division developed, manufactured, and sold its own products, sometimes in competition with other divisions. It was a hallowed organization structure. Moreover, H-P's depth of management came from attracting and training many young executives to run complete businesses. But it was exactly the wrong way to develop complex computer systems that are made from many different components, which must work smoothly together. Hewlett-Packard has floundered in computer aided engineering (CAE), for example, because ten highly competitive divisions were responsible for developing different components of CAE systems.

Young has some firsthand experience with the ways in which his organization had worked against effective product development. The first big computer project he chaperoned as chief executive fell flat. This project was a much publicized effort in 1981 to produce a 32-bit desktop work station for engineers. The basic computer was set to go on time, but parts of the system, such as software, that were being developed in other divisions held up its introduction for nearly a year. "I learned the importance of having everybody on the project working together," Young says. Now he's set up a single 800-person group to develop every basic component of the Spectrum line, a new family of computers. The group represents the first time the company has taken such a formally integrated approach.

Young had been thinking about the reorganization for some time. Since at least 1978, he and the board had wrestled with the problem of customers demands for complete systems of computers and instruments for solving broad problems, such as factory automation, rather than individual instruments. As the dividing line between computer systems and test and measurement equipment blurred, H-P's instrument and computer salesmen sometimes tried to sell the same customer different equipment for solving the same problems, with different discounts and other conditions of sale. At one time, a customer might be offered any of 16 types of purchase agreements, depending on the salesman involved.

The thrust of the reorganization is to combine most of the field force into one marketing group with a clear chain of command. One difficulty is the time required for implementation. In classic H-P fashion, Young issued no directives detailing how local field offices were to be set up. That task was given to each local office. "It does take longer," admits Ernest Arbuckle (a former Dean of Stanford Business School and a retired Hewlett-Packard director who lives next door to Young), "but the outcome will be better than the results of an authoritarian pronouncement." Young personifies H-P's renowned corporate culture. The company believes in participatory management, in giving everyone a sense of autonomy and achievement. It has 83,000 employees but has never laid off an hourly worker, seldom fires a manager, and still marks an employee's marriage with the gift of a silver bowl and the birth of a first child with a blanket. Practices like these have contributed to the company's success and strong corporate culture. Young is dedicated to preserving them. When asked what he most hopes to achieve, he replies, "To show that it's worth institutionalizing our founders' principles, hopefully by growing some and detracting nothing from the human elements that are so important."[1]

Organization design is the management process of diagnosing and selecting the structure and formal system of communication, authority, and responsibility that is intended to help achieve the organization's goals. In the Preview Case, we saw how major changes in the external environment (customer needs and demands), technology (new computer technology and its uses with H-P's line of instruments), and strategic choices (top management and the board of directors' decision to become an even larger producer of computer systems) came together to suggest the need for reorganization. This reorganization focused on changing the structure and authority relationships, improving internal communication among interdependent tasks and products, and clarifying authority and responsibility relationships internally and externally in dealing with customers—all for the purpose of becoming more competitive in the marketplace.

This chapter provides an overview of several key concepts and issues that are involved in designing organizations, as well as discussions of the three basic structural forms.[2] We begin by describing how environmental forces, strategic choices, and technological factors impact on the design of organizations.[3] Then we present a framework for diagnosing the extent to which organizations and their component parts can be characterized as mechanistic or organic. Next, we discuss three key variables in interdepartmental relations and their implications for organization design.[4] Finally, in the remaining sections of the chapter, we describe three structural forms of organization—functional, product, and matrix—each of which reflects a somewhat different approach to handling differentiation and integration.

In general, organization design should help link technology, tasks, and people so that inputs, such as raw materials, can be effectively and profitably transformed into outputs. Thus organization design requires a decision-making process that encompasses environmental forces, technological factors, and strategic choices (including desired organizational goals) in the selection of formal structural mechanisms.[5] Specifically, organization design should help achieve three goals:

- Facilitate the flow of information and decision making in order to better manage uncertainty and achieve organizational goals.
- Define clearly the authority and responsibility in jobs and units so the potential benefits from the division of labor and effective job design can be realized.
- Create the desired levels of integration (coordination) between departments (for example, between the production and marketing departments).

KEY CONTINGENCIES

Three key contingencies—environmental forces, strategic choices, and technological factors—can independently and in combination impact organization design decisions. Figure 14–1 conveys this idea and highlights the important variables for each contingency.[6]

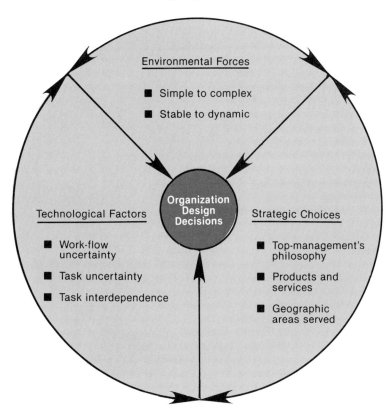

FIGURE 14–1.
Key Contingencies in Organization Design Decisions

Environmental Forces

In order to diagnose the impact of environmental forces on organization design decisions, managers need to understand: (1) the *characteristics* of the present and possible future environments; and (2) the *demands* of these environments on the need to process information, cope with uncertainties, and achieve desired levels of differentiation (division of labor) and integration (coordination).

TASK ENVIRONMENT AND STRUCTURE The **task environment** includes the external groups and forces with which the organization has direct contact and transactions.[7] Figure 14–2 shows the primary types of groups within the task environment of most for-profit organizations. It illustrates a simple

FIGURE 14–2.
Relationship of a Simple Functional Form of Organization to Environmental Forces

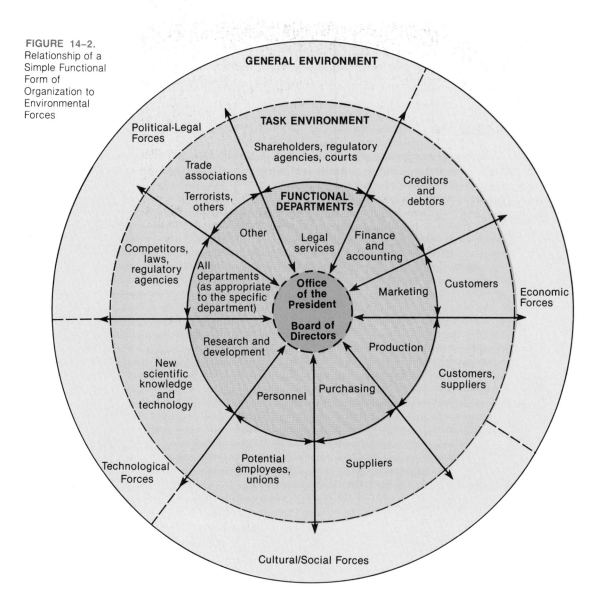

functional structure, in which separate departments specialize in dealing with each major group in the task environment; the departments are shown as interfacing with these respective groups. For example, the marketing department normally has more direct contact with customers than any of the other departments.

The placement of the office of the president and the board of directors in the center of Figure 14-2 conveys the fact that they are usually responsible for the following:

■ Setting the strategies and policies to be followed by the departments when they have contact with external groups.

■ Approving the strategic plan that is to be followed by each functional department.

■ Monitoring and evaluating functional department effectiveness in their internal and external activities.

■ Monitoring and diagnosing the forces in the task and general environments and making the key decisions suggested by this diagnosis (approve major new plant construction, set dividend policy, approve acquisition of a supplier, and the like).

So long as the firm only has one product, this illustrative functional structure is adaptable to and can operate in a variety of types of environments, which require different degrees of integration among departments and with top management.

ENVIRONMENTAL CHARACTERISTICS   After managers have defined the relevant groups and forces in the task environment, the next step is to assess their characteristics and relative importance to the organization.[8] The complexity dimension and dynamism dimension are used here to assess environmental characteristics.

The **complexity dimension** relates to whether the factors considered are few in number and similar to each other or many in number and different from each other. People in a planning department are typically confronted with a complex environment because they must take into account virtually all the groups shown in the task environment in Figure 14-2. At the other extreme, people in a custodial department face a simple environment. Rating an environment as simple or complex depends on both the number of factors and the number of subenvironments involved. Five factors in one subenvironment, such as the customer subenvironment, would not be as complex as five factors in three subenvironments, such as customers, suppliers, and competitors.

The **dynamism dimension** relates to whether the factors in the environment remain basically the same over time or change. In the Preview Case it was apparent that Hewlett-Packard had to consider both new and changing factors that created the need for increased integration in some parts of the organization.

BASIC TYPES OF TASK ENVIRONMENTS   Figure 14-3 classifies organization task environments in terms of complexity and dynamism. Four "pure" types of task environments can face an organization or its various parts: simple/stable, complex/stable, simple/dynamic, and complex/dynamic. The actual environment of an organization or one of its parts can be located anywhere on this grid.

The *simple/stable environment* (box 1, Figure 14–3) represents the easiest management situation. There are few surprises in the task environment and the manager's role focuses on making sure that workers consistently follow well-established routines and procedures. Managers need relatively less managerial skill, formal training, and job experience to operate successfully in this environment than are needed for success in the others.

The *complex/stable environment* (box 2, Figure 14–3) often results in some uncertainty for managers. However, risk, more than uncertainty, characterizes many of the decision-making problems in this task environment. Under conditions of risk, managers usually understand the task environment and the available alternatives fairly well. They cannot predict the future, but they can assign probabilities to the effects of various alternatives. This task environment is relatively stable, but managers may need considerable training and on-the-job experience to understand and manage it. For example, the registrar's office of a college or university must interact with academic departments, current and prospective students, the central administration, and governmental education agencies. But the nature of these interactions do not change frequently and are usually guided by the application of extensive rules and procedures.

The *simple/dynamic environment* (box 3, Figure 14–3) requires highly adaptable managers and structures. In this task environment, a number of changes take place, but managers can handle them with a reasonable level of intelligence and motivation. Computer-based information systems often help managers keep track of the changes. McDonald's, for example, frequently offers new menu items, but all must be relatively easy to make.

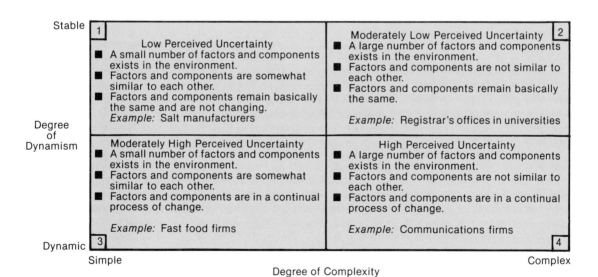

FIGURE 14–3.
Basic Types of Task Environments

Source: Adapted and reprinted by permission of the publisher from What is the Right Organization Structure? Decision Tree Analysis Provides the Answer by Robert Duncan, *Organizational Dynamics*, Winter 1979, p. 63. © 1979 AMACOM, a division of American Management Associations, New York. All rights reserved.

The *complex/dynamic environment* (box 4, Figure 14–3) represents the most difficult management situation because the task environment contains numerous uncertainties. Of all task environments, this one requires the most managerial sophistication, insight, and intuition. Proven decision-making techniques can aid managers in this situation, but they cannot substitute for human judgment. Managers cannot solve the problems and issues confronting them by merely using standardized rules and procedures.

The problems and opportunities confronting most complex organizations have become more numerous and diverse. One authority recently commented:

> The new managerial calculus suggests that only 20 percent of business factors are, in any sense, controllable, and that 80 percent are noncontrollable. What is beyond business' control is its environment—that "buzzing, blooming confusion" (to many managers) of global, national, and business events. This environment is the source of the shocks, surprises, and discontinuities that batter traditional business performance and make mincemeat of strategies that are inadequately attuned to the new externalities.[9]

Each type of task environment requires unique ways of structuring and managing an organization or its parts. Later in the chapter, we identify different structures and describe the type of task environment in which each is most likely to be effective. For now, we will simply note that a simple functional structure—such as the one illustrated in Figure 14–2—is usually adequate when an organization faces a simple and stable task environment.

Strategic Choices

Organization design decisions, including choice of structure, result in a particular distribution of control, power, rights, and responsibilities to different jobs, departments, and levels within an organization. Thus top-management's philosophy plays a role in the strategic choice between centralized and decentralized structure and management system.[10] A philosophy of centralization (everything else being equal) requires more levels in the hierarchy and more resources to be devoted to departments that help top management monitor and control lower-level departments. For example, the quality-control, personnel, and auditing departments may be given relatively large budgets and considerable authority (again, everything else being equal), if top management has a philosophy of centralization.

A second strategic choice that affects organization design is top-management's strategy of marketing and producing products and services within one region of or throughout a country or in a particular region of or throughout the world. Global organizations that have defined the world as their market usually need to create much more complex structures than those firms that produce and market domestically. However, domestic-oriented firms often contract with independent agents to handle international sales for them.

A third strategic choice involves top-management's decisions about the types of customers they want to serve. A firm that tries to sell to industrial, commercial, and residential customers often needs a different structure than a firm that only tries to sell to industrial customers.

These few examples of how strategic choices can impact organization design illustrate a key point: management often creates and modifies organizational structures in making strategic choices.[11] Again, the Preview Case clearly suggests that the strategic choices of John Young and the H-P board of directors to become a major "player" in computer systems led to some restructuring.

Technological Factors

In Chapter 13, we discussed ways in which three technological variables—work-flow uncertainty, task uncertainty, and task interdependence—relate to job design. These three variables are also important to organization design, particularly in terms of the creation of departments, the delegation of authority and responsibility to them, and the need for formal integrating mechanisms among them. The practices of homebuilding firms provides one example of the combined impacts of technology, environment, and strategic options on an industry and the organization design of its businesses.

In Practice: Homebuilding Firms

The size and organization of homebuilding firms are well-suited to the industry's exacting environmental conditions. An abundance of small, locally based general contractors and special tradesmen are able to produce most housing efficiently. These widely dispersed firms are sensitive to local demand and financial conditions as well as to local building codes and zoning laws. Such factors, which vary across geographical and governmental units as small as neighborhoods in some municipalities, make it difficult for housing firms to operate on a national scale.

Subcontracting is one way that these small contractors cope with the industry's demanding environment. It allows them to survive periods of low demand and to employ labor efficiently when the economy improves. General contractors with small permanent payrolls can ride out seasonal slumps or recessions. On the other hand, they can respond quickly to new opportunities simply by hiring subcontractors. Subcontracting also helps contractors estimate and fix construction costs, thereby reducing an additional uncertainty.

Subcontracting is also an efficient adaptation to the uniqueness of housing construction. It frees general contractors from the burden of finding productive employment for all their tradesmen all the time. For instance, contractors need not maintain masons on salary while building houses made entirely of wood. They are also relieved of training and sustaining new specialists when new techniques are discovered. Thus, in a peculiar way, the system facilitates the adoption of new technology. When a project requires a new technique, the general contractor merely seeks out a subcontractor who is properly equipped to provide it.

The nature of homebuilding technology and the peculiarities of the housing market work against large scale, hierarchical organizations. Most attempts at vertical integration in homebuilding (such as combining building crafts and subcontractors into large-scale national organizations) have failed. The historical conditions that fostered vertical integration in manufacturing and the beginnings of "big business" in the nineteenth century—the revolutions in transportation, communications, mass marketing, and mass production—could not stimulate the growth of large-scale housing firms.

In sum, three major factors have shaped the structure of many residential construction firms: the characteristics of the product, the site-bound technology it requires, and the cyclical fluctuations of the housing market (environmental turbulence). To date, the same factors have worked against the predominance of large-scale housing firms.[12]

WORK-FLOW AND TASK UNCERTAINTY   From an organization-design perspective, *work-flow uncertainty* is the degree of knowledge in a department (not just a single employee) about when inputs will be received for processing. When work-flow uncertainty is low, a department has little discretion to decide which, when, or where tasks will be performed. From an organization-design perspective, *task uncertainty* is the degree of well-defined knowledge in a department (not just a single employee) with respect to performing the tasks assigned to it.[13] When task uncertainty is low, there is relatively complete knowledge about how the department will go about producing desired outcomes. In contrast, with high task uncertainty, there are few (if any) pre-specified ways for dealing with some or many of the tasks assigned to the department. This means that key members of the department usually apply experience, judgment, intuition, and joint problem-solving activities (such as problem definition, problem solution generation, evaluating alternatives, and the like) in order to produce desired outcomes.

Parallel to the discussion of technology and job design in Chapter 13 (see, especially, Figure 13–3), we will first consider the roles of work-flow uncertainty and task uncertainty in organizational design and then discuss the effects of task interdependence on organization design.[14] Figure 14–4 shows possible interactions between work-flow uncertainty and task uncertainty, both of which range from low to high, yielding four combinations of these factors.

Examples of departments that may be characteristic of each of the four combinations are listed in each cell in Figure 14–4. We need to be careful not to stereotype a department as fitting into only one of these cells. Through organization redesign, it is often possible to modify most departments so that they can be characterized by more or less task uncertainty and more or less work-flow uncertainty. The office of the president and the planning depart-

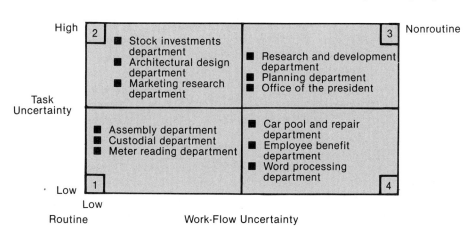

FIGURE 14–4.
Technology and Organization-Design Framework

Source: Adapted from Slocum Jr., J. W., and Sims Jr., H. P. A Typology for Integrating Technology, Organization, and Job Design. *Human Relations,* 1980, *33;*196; Susman, G. I. *Autonomy at Work: A Sociotechnical Analysis of Participative Management.* New York: Praeger, 1980, 132.

ment are generally characterized by high task uncertainty and high work-flow uncertainty. However, some of the specific tasks that they perform could be classified anywhere on the matrix. Another important point is that some departments do not fit clearly into any single cell. For example, the auditing department in a public accounting firm might generally be placed somewhere in the middle of Figure 14–4.

One of the implications of the framework in Figure 14–4 is that departments may be formed on the basis of similarities in technological characteristics. This is most often done by creating functional departments such as those shown.

TASK INTERDEPENDENCE   From an organization-design perspective, *task interdependence* is the degree to which decision making and cooperation between two or more departments is necessary for them to perform their own tasks and achieve departmental goals. As discussed in Chapter 13 for job design, there are three major types of task interdependence: pooled, sequential, and reciprocal. From an organization-design perspective, these types of interdependence can be characterized as follows:

- *Pooled interdependence* occurs when each department is relatively autonomous and makes a discrete contribution to the organization as a whole. For example, the many sales and services offices of State Farm Insurance do not engage in day-to-day decision making, coordination, and communication with each other. (However, the local offices are interdependent with regional offices that do coordinate and set policies for the local sales and service offices.)

- *Sequential interdependence* occurs when one department must complete certain tasks before one or more other departments can perform their tasks. For example, in a refrigerator factory, the fabrication department provides its outputs to the assembly department which, in turn, provides its outputs to the painting and finishing department, and so on.

- *Reciprocal interdependence* occurs when the outputs from one department become the inputs for another department and vice versa. For example, the planning, marketing, and research and development departments are likely to have many reciprocal interdependencies in the development of new products.

As shown in Figure 14–5, reciprocal interdependence is the most complex type, and pooled interdependence is the simplest type. Greater interdependence generally requires greater integration among departments.[15] Placing reciprocally interdependent departments under a common superior often improves integration and minimizes information-processing costs. Thus the marketing research, advertising, and sales departments are likely to be under the jurisdiction of the vice-president of marketing. These departments are more interdependent with each other than they are with the maintenance department, for example.

You will recall from the Preview Case that Hewlett-Packard had emphasized pooled interdependence *among* its business groups. Of course, *within* each business group, the types of interdependence found within and among departments varied widely. As of 1985, H-P had 53 separate business groups

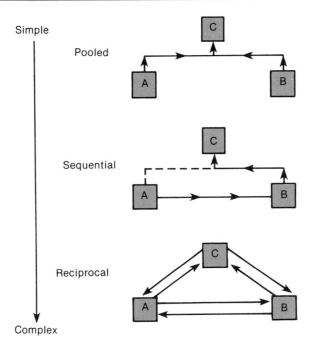

Simple

Pooled

Sequential

Reciprocal

Complex

FIGURE 14–5.
Types of Task
Interdependence in
Organization
Design

and divisions.[16] Recall that one of the strategic reasons for the reorganization at H-P in 1984 was to improve the integration among computer systems, instruments, and meeting customer needs. Thus Hewlett-Packard judged that there should be less pooled interdependence between some business groups and more reciprocal interdependence among them.

MECHANISTIC VERSUS ORGANIC SYSTEMS

A **mechanistic system** is characterized by extensive use of formal rules and regulations, centralization of decision making, narrowly defined job responsibilities, and a rigid hierarchy of authority. In contrast, an **organic system** is characterized by low-to-moderate use of formal rules and regulations, decentralized and shared decision making, broadly defined job responsibilities, and a flexible authority structure with fewer levels in the hierarchy.[17] Routine technology (that is, low task and work-flow uncertainty) and a simple/stable environment often lead to use of a mechanistic system. In contrast, nonroutine technology (that is, high task and work-flow uncertainty) and a complex/changing environment often lead to use of an organic system.

For our purposes, the mechanistic system is essentially synonymous with bureaucracy. Max Weber, a German sociologist and economist in the early 1900s, defined a **bureaucracy** as an organization having the following characteristics:

- The organization operates according to a body of laws or rules, which are consistent and have normally been intentionally established.

- Officials are subject to an impersonal order which guides their actions. In turn, instructions have authority only insofar as they conform with this generally understood body of rules; obedience is to the position, not to the individual occupying the position.

- Each occupant of a position has a specified sphere of competence, with obligations, authority, and powers to compel obedience strictly defined.

- The organization of positions follows the principle of hierarchy; that is, each lower position is under the control and supervision of a higher one.

- The supreme head of the organization occupies the top position by appropriation, by election, or by being designated as successor. Other positions are filled, in principle, by free selection, and candidates are selected on the basis of "technical" qualifications. They are appointed, not elected.

- The organization has a career ladder. There is promotion according to seniority or achievement. Promotion depends on the judgment of superiors.

- Officials in principle are excluded from any ownership rights in the organization and are subject to discipline and control in the conduct of their positions.[18]

The word *bureaucracy* often conjures up thoughts of rigidity, incompetence, red tape, inefficiency, and ridiculous rules. However, many of the characteristics of bureaucracy may make it a reasonable and attractive way to organize in certain situations.[19] Thus any discussion of a bureaucratic organization (mechanistic system) must distinguish between the way it should ideally function and the way some large-scale organizations actually operate.[20]

As Figure 14-6 shows, the relative and absolute degrees to which an organization emphasizes characteristics of a mechanistic or an organic system can vary substantially; this is true, also, of departments or divisions *within* a single organization. Organization B in Figure 14-6 represents a relatively mechanistic system across all the selected dimensions; Organization A, which is more varied in its emphasis in each dimension, represents an organic system. Organization B could be an automobile assembly plant and Organization A a research and development department. This pattern could also exist if the automobile assembly plant and the research and development department were part of the same organization, such as GM, Ford, or Chrysler.

Selected Dimensions	Organic System	Degree of Emphasis	Mechanistic System
	Low	Moderate	High
Hierarchy of authority			
Centralization			
Division of labor			
Rules			
Procedural specifications			
Impersonality			
	Key: ▽ Organization A		▼ Organization B

FIGURE 14-6. Possible Characteristics of Mechanistic and Organic Systems

The organic system emphasizes the technical competence of people, rather than their formal position in the hierarchy, as a basis for influence in decision making. It has a less rigid hierarchy and permits greater flexibility for coping with uncertainties in technology and the task environment in general. The organic system tends to be effective when the environment is complex/dynamic and when there is high task and work-flow uncertainty. In contrast, the mechanistic system may be more effective where the environment is simple/stable and where there is low task and work-flow uncertainty. The following paragraphs describe briefly each of the dimensions identified in Figure 14-6.

Hierarchy of Authority

Hierarchy of authority refers to the extent to which an organization structures decision making and defines the formal power allocated to each position. Higher-level departments or positions assign or approve goals and budgets for lower-level departments or positions.

The hierarchy-of-authority dimension is sometimes confused with centralization. **Centralization** is a relative concept: it prevails when all major, and possibly many minor, decisions are made only at the top levels of the organization.[21] Centralization is common in a mechanistic system, whereas decentralization and shared decision making among levels are common in an organic system. However, both systems have a hierarchy of authority. The hierarchy of authority dimension—in contrast to the centralization concept—implies a specification of the decisions that can be made by employees who occupy positions at each level in the organization.[22]

Division of Labor

Division of labor refers to the various ways of dividing up tasks and labor to achieve desired goals.[23] Adam Smith, the father of the capitalistic economic system, recognized the importance of this concept in organization design in *An Inquiry into the Nature and Cause of the Wealth of Nations*, published in 1776. Smith noted that the wealth of a nation could be increased if organizations used the proper division of labor. In general, he believed that the greater the division of labor used in the design of an organization, the greater would be the efficiency of the organization.[24]

The mechanistic system typically follows Smith's views. As noted in Chapter 13, the continued increase in the division of labor may eventually become counterproductive. Employees—especially those at lower levels—who perform only very routine and simple jobs that require few skills may become bored, alienated, indifferent and even hostile to their work. The results may be low productivity, high conflict, low product quality, and the like. From an organization-design perspective, the creation of departments having narrowly defined sets of tasks and few responsibilities may create excessive tunnel-vision. In addition, the managerial costs of integrating highly specialized departments is usually high. In contrast, the organic system tends to reduce these costs by delegating decision making to lower levels of the organization. Delegation also encourages a deeper sense of responsibility for achieving assigned tasks and linking them to the needs, tasks, and goals of the entire organization. The organic system takes advantage of the benefits from the division of labor, but it is much more sensitive to recognizing when increases in the division of labor may become counterproductive.

Rules

Rules are formal, written statements specifying acceptable and unacceptable behaviors and decisions by organization members. One of the ironies in the proliferation of rules that attempt to reduce individual discretion is that someone must still exercise discretion as to which rules apply to specific situations.[25]

Rules are an integral part of mechanistic and organic systems, alike. However, in a mechanistic system, the tendency is to create uniform rules to handle tasks and decisions *whenever possible.* In contrast, in an organic system the tendency is to create rules *only when necessary* (such as safety rules to protect life and property). There is also more of a tendency to question the need for new rules and the existing rules in an organic system. In a mechanistic system there is a tendency to accept the need for extensive rules and to formulate new rules in response to new situations, even if they are exceptional cases that are not likely to occur again in the same form.

Procedural Specifications

Procedural specifications are the predetermined sequences of steps that employees and departments must follow in performing tasks and dealing with problems. Procedural specifications often consist of a number of rules that must be implemented in a particular sequence. In order to obtain reimbursement for travel expenses in most companies, for example, employees must adhere to a well-defined set of procedures. Because procedural specifications are essentially made up of rules, they have many of the same positive and negative features that characterize rules and are most often embraced in a mechanistic system. Managers in organic systems are usually alert to the possibility that extensive rules and procedural specifications can make the organization too rigid and thus lower employees' motivation and their ability to innovate and create.

Impersonality

Impersonality is a measure of the extent to which organizations treat their members, as well as outsiders, without regard to individual characteristics. Of course, all organizations consider individual characteristics if they are related to predetermined and specified standards. And organizations often consider a person's ability to pass a physical examination when applying for a position as an appropriate individual characteristic to consider.

Managers in a mechanistic system are likely to place great emphasis on impersonal factors, such as degrees, certificates earned, scores on tests, courses or training programs completed, number of years of service, and the like, when making hiring, pay raise, and promotion decisions. Although such factors may be considered in an organic system, there is likely to be more emphasis (relative to the mechanistic system) on actual achievements and the pooling of qualitative judgments from several individuals about how well the person is likely to perform and fit into the organization. For example, at Hewlett-Packard (which operates as an organic system), a college graduate applying for a job typically goes through an extensive interview process, which involves several managers and many (if not all) of the employees with whom he or she would work. It is not unusual for the applicant to be "interviewed" casually and informally by a group of employees. The person responsible for filling the open position solicits the opinions and reactions from these employees before making a decision. In some instances, the manager may even call the employees and other managers who participate in the interview process together to discuss the candidate(s).

INTERDEPARTMENTAL RELATIONS

An essential part of organization design is to determine what the nature of relations among departments should be. Interdepartmental relations are affected by three key variables: (1) the desirable degree of differentiation between departments; (2) the desirable degree of integration between departments; and (3) the degree of uncertainty (including task, work-flow, and environmental) confronting each department. As Figure 14–7 shows, each of these variables can range from low to high. Thus diagnosis of these variables and their impact on effective operations is a necessary step leading to organization design decisions and the structural mechanisms to be used.

Differentiation

Differentiation is the degree to which departments differ in the extent of departmental structure (low to high), members' orientation to a time horizon (short to long) and to other people (permissive to authoritarian), and members' interface with the task environment (certain to uncertain).[26]

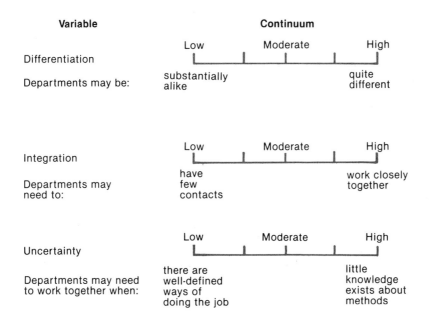

FIGURE 14–7.
Variables that Affect Relations between Departments

Production departments often have a high degree of formal departmental structure with many rules and procedures, tight supervisory control, and frequent and specific reviews of individual and departmental performance (mechanistic system). Research departments and sales departments often are just the opposite (organic system). Research and sales personnel tend to prefer open, interpersonal relationships with one another, whereas those in production tend to prefer more directive and structured relationships with co-workers. Sales and production personnel have short time horizons and think more about immediate problems and profits; research people tend to think several years into the future. In general, the greater the differences between departments, the more problems managers have in getting them to work together (such as marketing with production).

Integration

Integration is the degree of collaboration (cooperation) and mutual understanding required and achieved among departments.[27] The division of labor and task interdependencies create the need for integration. This need is greatest between departments that are reciprocally interdependent and least when they are in a pooled interdependent relationship.

Managers must be careful not to establish too much or too little integration among departments.[28] Too little integration will probably lead to a lower quality of decisions and the misuse of resources. The costs associated with too much integration are likely to far exceed any possible benefits. Moreover, with excessive integration, departments often obstruct rather than help each other in performing their tasks and achieving goals.

In Chapter 10, we presented four structural mechanisms for achieving integration among groups (departments): hierarchy, linking roles, task forces, and integrating roles and groups (departments). The use and monitoring of the effectiveness of one or more of these mechanisms can minimize the likelihood of too little or too much integration.

Uncertainty

Uncertainty is the gap between what is known and what needs to be known to make sound decisions and to perform tasks effectively. The following factors should be evaluated in determining the degree of uncertainty that will confront departments:

- The extent to which there is a clearly defined body of knowledge or guidelines that can be applied independently or jointly by departments to perform tasks.
- The frequency with which departments can be expected to face independent or mutual problems that they do not know how to solve and that they must take time to think through before taking any action.
- In general, the amount of actual thinking time that departments must spend before trying to implement solutions to independent or mutual problems.
- The probability that departments can be reasonably sure of the results of their independent and mutual efforts.[29]

Implications for Organization Design

The combinations of the three variables that affect relations among departments have several significant implications for organization design and management. First, the easiest situation to manage occurs under conditions of low uncertainty, low differentiation, and low integration requirements. In this situation, departments are practically independent of each other.

Second, increases in the degrees of uncertainty, differentiation, and desired integration must be accompanied by increases in the expenditure of resources, the number of formal mechanisms applied, and the use of certain behavioral processes to obtain integration.

Third, the most difficult interdepartmental situation to manage is likely to occur under conditions of high uncertainty, high differentiation, and high required integration. Managers must expend the greatest amount of resources and use the greatest variety of formal integration mechanisms and behavioral processes to manage interdepartmental relations under this set of conditions.

FUNCTIONAL STRUCTURE

The **functional structure** creates positions and departments on the basis of specialized activities, such as engineering, marketing, and manufacturing. This structure represents a common means of dealing with sequential interdependencies. Early writers on organization design spent considerable time and effort attempting to develop concepts and principles for creating effective functional structures. We consider four of these concepts: departmentalization, line and staff functions, chain of command, and span of control.

Departmentalization

Departmentalization of a typical manufacturing firm is according to function, such as engineering, manufacturing, shipping, sales, and finance, as shown in Figure 14–8. Tasks also can be divided functionally by the *processes* used, such as stamping, plating, assembly, painting, and inspection. Figure 14–9 shows an organization that incorporates both managerial function and process in its departmentalization. Thus an organization can use one, two, or even several types of functional classification.

Regardless of the functional division of labor, a common theme of the writers on functional structure was the desirability of standardizing and routinizing repetitive tasks whenever possible. Management can then concentrate on exceptions to eliminate any gaps or overlaps.

Line and Staff Functions

Line functions are those activities that directly affect the principal work flow in an organization. In a manufacturing firm, for instance, all production activities—such as engineering, stamping, plating, assembly, painting, inspection, and shipping—would be considered line functions. **Staff functions** are support activities that provide service and advice to line departments. These usually include the personnel, legal, and finance departments. Figure 14–10 illustrates the distinction between line and staff functions in an organization.

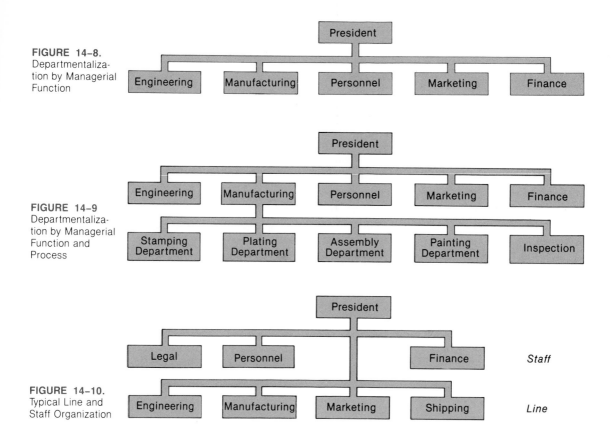

FIGURE 14–8.
Departmentalization by Managerial
Function

FIGURE 14–9
Departmentalization by Managerial
Function and
Process

FIGURE 14–10.
Typical Line and
Staff Organization

Nowhere are the problems of integrating line and staff functions more severe than in firms with manufacturing and marketing operations in a number of countries, that is, multinational corporations.

ACROSS CULTURES

Line–Staff Integration in Multinational Corporations

Physical Proximity

As the following remark by an executive in one of the companies Pitts and Daniels studied testifies, co-location of line and staff can facilitate integration between the two:

> Until recently our area managers [line] were scattered all around the globe. This kept them in close touch with local area developments. However, it isolated them from our headquarters staff (representing major functions and lines of business). To remedy this situation we brought our area heads home a few years ago. While this move created some initial difficulties for them by separating them from their areas, it has greatly improved coordination [integration] between them and our staff groups. Now, line and staff people only have to cross the hall to confer with each other. They often have lunch together in our headquarters cafeteria and socialize off-premises. The

close, personal relationships which have developed have smoothed the way for much more sensitive interaction between the two.

In another case the area manager for Europe was staff. He had been transferred to Europe to save time and transportation costs, to give on-the-spot advice to European production subsidiaries, and to analyze the overall European situation for corporate headquarters. Because he seldom went back to headquarters, he had little influence on corporate policies affecting Europe. At the advice of heads of some large European subsidiaries, he and other staff members moved back to headquarters, where they serve on corporate committees and function more effectively as spokesmen for area interests.

World Boards

The formation of *ad hoc* groups to develop worldwide strategy for individual businesses is yet another device which some companies we examined use to bring line and staff together. Called "World Boards" by one firm, each group typically includes country, area, and functional representatives along with representatives of the particular business involved.

World Boards generally have no direct authority over a company's activities, of course. This still resides with the line organization. However, as the following comment by an executive of one firm using this approach suggests, such groups can exert considerable indirect influence upon integrated strategic action:

> A World Board typically includes representatives from our international division, from corporate R&D and engineering, and from the domestic division involved with a particular line of business. Since each board must issue a written strategy statement for its business, its members are encouraged to work toward compromise. While the strategy eventually developed is not binding on either our domestic or international organization, people have a lot of explaining to do if they deviate in any major way from the plan. As a consequence, line units tend to act pretty much in accordance with the strategies determined by these Boards.

Multiple Role Assignment

Yet another device being used to improve integration is multiple role assignments of top-level executives. Typically, senior executives are assigned both a staff unit and line activity. Such an arrangement obliges them to contend with trade-offs between line and staff on an ongoing basis. As they deal with such issues over time, they gain a broader perspective of the company's world-wide needs and, in turn, communicate these to subordinates. Under such an arrangement, the latter find it difficult to espouse a narrow parochial view. To satisfy multiple-role superiors, they must also adopt a broader company viewpoint.

One of the companies that we interviewed has carried this concept throughout most of the organization so that it is not just the top-level executives who have dual responsibilities. Within Europe, for example, the British and German subsidiaries produce and sell similar products for their domestic markets. The head of the British group is also in charge of marketing staff support for Germany, while the German group head is in charge of production support in the UK. The staff duties are structured and delegated so that a large number of line managers within each of the two countries is also engaged in staff assistance in another country.[30]

Chain of Command

In addition to distinguishing line from staff functions, early writers on organization design stressed two basic ideas about the chain of command. First, in a **scalar chain of command** authority and responsibility are arranged hierarchically. They flow in a clear, unbroken vertical line from the highest executive (who holds the maximum authority and responsibility) to the lowest worker. Clarity is at the heart of the scalar chain. Second, these early writers emphasized **unity of command**, or the principle that no subordinate should receive orders from more than one superior. These ideas are similar to the points made earlier about the hierarchy of authority in a mechanistic system. Modern organizations do not always follow the unity-of-command principle throughout their structures. Yet, in general, overlapping lines of authority and responsibility can make both managing and working difficult. Without unity of command, it is not clear who may direct whom to do what, and people must do much more persuading or bargaining to accomplish their tasks.

Span of Control

Span of control is the number of people supervised by a manager. The span of control an organization uses is a major influence on its shape and structure.[31] When the span of control is broad, relatively few levels exist in the hierarchy between the top and bottom of the organization. Conversely, when the span of control is narrow, more levels are required in the hierarchy for the same number of workers. As Figure 14–11 illustrates, an organization with 19 employees requires four levels with a narrow span and three levels with a broader span.

The span of control should vary with the nature of the tasks being performed. Thus there is no one proper span of control. A supervisor of a relatively simple and repetitive operation might effectively manage 20–30 workers, as in an automobile assembly plant. At higher organizational levels, however, only four or five subordinates would report to the plant manager or department head.

Managerial Implications

No structure is without problems, but some structures are relatively better than others under certain conditions. As Table 14–1 suggests, the functional

FIGURE 14–11.
Span of Control and
Organization Shape

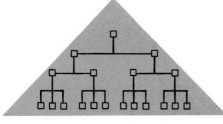

N = *19*
Narrow Span of Control
Tall Shape

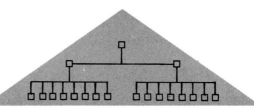

N = *19*
Broad Span of Control
Flat Shape

TABLE 14-1   Assessment of the Functional Structure

Advantages
- Promotes skill specialization.
- Reduces duplication of scarce resources and uses resources full-time.
- Enhances career advancement for specialists within large departments.
- Facilitates communication and performance, because superiors share expertise with their subordinates.
- Exposes specialists to others within the same specialty.

Disadvantages
- Emphasizes routine tasks, which encourages short time horizons.
- Fosters parochial perspectives by managers, which limit their capacities for top-management positions.
- Reduces communication and cooperation between departments.
- Multiplies interdepartmental dependencies, which can make coordination and scheduling difficult.
- Obscures accountability for overall outcomes.

Source: Adapted from McCann, J. E. and Galbraith, J. R. Interdepartmental Relations. In *Handbook of Organizational Design*, vol. 2, *Remodeling Organizations and Their Environments.* P. C. Nystrom and W. H. Starbuck (Eds.) New York: Oxford University Press, 1981, 61.

structure has both advantages and disadvantages. For example, on the positive side, the functional structure permits the clear assignment and identification of responsibilities. Employees easily understand this structure. People doing similar work and facing similar problems work together, increasing the opportunities for interaction and mutual support.

On the negative side, the functional structure encourages a limited point of view that focuses on a narrow set of tasks and that may lose sight of the organization as a whole. Integration involving functional departments often becomes difficult as the organization increases the number of geographic areas served and range of products or services provided.

The functional structure is likely to be effective in any type of external environment so long as the firm only has a narrow product or service line and does not have to respond to extreme pressures as a result of serving different geographic areas or types of customers. The addition of specialized staff units to the functional structure may enable a firm to deal with somewhat more complex/changing environments. Staff departments can provide the line departments with the expert advice they need to make decisions about more complex problems. The addition of integrating mechanisms, such as linking roles and task forces, may also enable the continued use of the basic functional structure in dynamic/complex environments.

PRODUCT STRUCTURE

As the differentiation of an organization increases—especially in terms of its range of products or services—the product structure is often more effective than a "pure" functional structure.

Basic Characteristics

The **product structure** has relatively self-contained groups, departments, or divisions that are organized according to specific products, product groups, services, markets, customers, or major programs. This structure increases the use of and emphasis on pooled interdependence within the organization.

Organizations with multiple products or services, such as Procter & Gamble and General Foods, usually benefit from using the product structure. It reduces the complexity that would otherwise confront managers in the more typical functional structure. In the functional structure, the marketing vice-president may have to be concerned with all the products sold by the organization. When sales of different products become substantial, the resulting complexity can be effectively reduced by creating the position of marketing manager to oversee each product line. Moreover, the product structure becomes an attractive alternative when the competitive environment for each product line is dynamic/complex.[32]

Typical Evolution

Organizations that adopt the product structure usually began with the functional structure. They found that growth, complexity, and increasing rate of environmental change create management problems that the functional structure alone cannot efficiently or effectively deal with. When changing to a product structure, however, these companies usually do not discard altogether the functional structure. Instead, the product structure may incorporate functional departments within each product division or group.

Managerial Implications

Structuring by product or service line eases problems of integration by focusing on individual expertise and knowledge in specific areas. For example, the sales efforts of a marketing department may not be particularly effective if that department has to deal with nuclear power, solar energy, and laser beam products, each of which is best handled by a department thoroughly familiar with each product line and set of customers.

One potential disadvantage of the product structure is that a firm must have a large number of personnel with the needed managerial talent available to serve each product line. Another is the higher costs that result from the necessary duplication of certain activities. Table 14–2 provides an overview of the advantages and disadvantages of the product structure.

TABLE 14–2   Assessment of the Product Structure

Advantages

- Recognizes sources of interdepartmental interdependence.
- Fosters an orientation toward overall outcomes and toward clients.
- Allows diversification and expansion of skills and training.
- Ensures accountability by departmental managers and so promotes delegation of authority and responsibility.
- Heightens departmental cohesion and involvement in work.

Disadvantages

- May use skills and resources inefficiently.
- Limits career advancement by specialists to movements out of their departments.
- Impedes specialists' exposure to others within the same specialties.
- Puts multiple role demands on people and so creates stress.
- May promote departmental objectives as opposed to overall organizational objectives.

Source: Adapted from McCann, J. E. and Galbraith, J. R. Interdepartmental Relations. In *Handbook of Organizational Design*, vol. 2, *Remodeling Organizations and Their Environments*. P. C. Nystrom and W. H. Starbuck (Eds.) New York: Oxford University Press, 1981, 61.

Adoption of the product structure often reduces the complexity of the environment facing any one department, division, or manager. The manager of a product group needs to focus only on the environment for one product or service line rather than on those for multiple products or services. As with the functional structure, an organization with a product structure can further deal with complex/dynamic environments through the addition of integrating mechanisms, such as linking roles, task forces, and integrating roles and groups.

Eastman Kodak Company provides an example of how organizational structure can and should change over time as a company faces new problems. Kodak adopted a product structure while retaining some elements of its functional structure.

In Practice: Eastman Kodak Company

When Eastman Kodak Company Chairman Colby H. Chandler commissioned a sweeping review of the company's management structure, he flippantly told his two top executives that he already knew the outcome. After all, Chandler had been operating in Kodak's ponderous bureaucracy since 1950, when he started as a product engineer. And for a decade he'd been hearing arguments for breaking up Kodak's monolithic management into small, nimble groups that could charge into such fast-paced markets as electronics and biotechnology.

Ever a Kodak man, Chandler couldn't bring himself to decide hastily. Worried about traumatizing the company, he kept the plan under wraps. It was known only to seven hand-picked executives at the Rochester (N.Y.) headquarters. Over the next nine months, Kodak polled a widening corps of its managers and called in outside consultants . . ., McKinney & Company, [who] even conducted "trap teams," where managers were invited to test out scenarios that might cause problems.

Change came swiftly in January, 1985. The company reorganized its $8.3 billion Photographic Division into 17 operating units. Each is a separate profit center, managed by a young executive with authority over everything from design to production. Most of Kodak's technology-based acquisitions and other new corporate ties are part of this new Photographic & Information Management Division. "We wanted to keep the train moving at a high speed," says J. Phillip Samper (Executive Vice-president), "but we wanted to change some of the cars and perhaps lay new rails while the train was under way." At 50, Samper is the youngest of Kodak's top three executives and, as general manager of the new division, the driving force behind the shakeup.

By opting for decentralization, Kodak abandoned a decades-old management structure in which marketing and manufacturing executives reported through separate chains of command. At the old Kodak, a suggestion from a marketing manager for altering a manufacturing process would have to filter all the way up the management ladder and back down the manufacturing ranks. "By the time [a decision] got back down, it was distorted, there were hard feelings, and you didn't solve the problem," says Charles L. Trowbridge, vice-president for copy products and one of the 17 new "entrepreneurs."

Trowbridge, a 44-year-old chemical engineer and MBA, says similar decisions can now be made in a matter of days. In one case, an idea for a new district office bounced around for weeks. After the reorganization, Trowbridge and another manager decided in a half-hour to go ahead. "They [the 17] have a willingness to step out and do things differently," says Lawrence J. Matteson, Trowbridge's boss and group vice-president for Commercial and Information Systems.

There are even physical signs that mark the merger of marketing and manufacturing, says John A. Lacy, a vice-president and 28-year Kodak veteran. One is the computer showroom in the middle of a manufacturing complex. Kodak invites customers to view several of its new products on site.[33]

MATRIX STRUCTURE

The matrix structure is the most difficult form of organization to manage because of its unique characteristics. However, under special conditions, it can be an effective structure.

Basic Characteristics

In the **matrix structure,** some employees, usually managers or skilled specialists, report to two higher-level managers rather than to a single manager.[34] Figure 14–12 illustrates this key feature. The matrix structure usually involves a combination of both functional and product forms of departmentalization through the use of dual authority, information, and reporting relationships and systems. Every matrix contains three unique sets of role relationships: (1) the top manager, who heads up and balances the dual chains of command; (2) the managers of functional and product departments, who share subordinates; and (3) the managers (or skilled specialists) who report to both a functional manager and a product manager.[35] In an organization that has major operations throughout the world, matrix managers could be

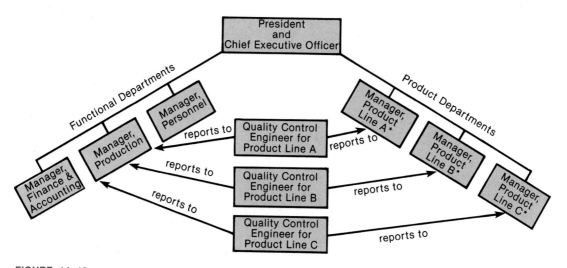

FIGURE 14–12.
Partial Illustration of Basic Matrix Structure

*These product managers also have full responsibility for the marketing activities associated with their own product lines.

designated for each of the firm's major geographic areas: Europe, South America, North America, Pacific Rim, the Middle East.

Aerospace companies were the first to use the matrix structure. Today, organizations in many industries (chemical, banking, insurance, packaged goods, electronics, and computer) and fields (hospitals, government agencies, and professional organizations) have adopted various forms of the matrix structure.

Typical Evolution

Matrix structures typically evolve in stages. The first stage may be the use of a temporary task force. Composed of representatives from the different departments or divisions of the organization, the task force is created to study a problem and make recommendations. Team members retain their usual departmental affiliations (an engineer continues to report to the head of engineering and a marketing representative to the head of marketing), but these temporary team members are also accountable to the leader of the task force.

The second stage usually involves the creation of permanent teams or committees organized to address specific needs or problems. Again, representatives from the various functional and product departments make up the team or committee, each representing the view of the home department.

The third stage may occur when a project manager is appointed and held accountable for integrating the activities and inputs of the team or committee. Project managers also are accountable for the final project output. They often must negotiate or "buy" the human resources necessary to carry out the tasks from the managers of functional departments. With the appointment of project managers, an organization is well on the way to a matrix structure and faces all the difficulties and benefits of multiple-authority relationships.

The simple, straightforward, single chain of command is replaced by new multiple-authority relationships, which are a distinguishing characteristic of the matrix structure. While the traditional hierarchical structure rests on formal reward or position power, the matrix structure demands negotiation by peers with high tolerances for ambiguous power relationships.[36] The problem of managing the power relationships is one of the most troublesome aspects of the matrix structure. Consider the case of the Xerox Corporation.

In Practice: Xerox Corporation

Xerox executives now freely admit that the company had strangled itself with a matrix organization. The heads of groups such as product planning, design, service, and manufacturing were based in Rochester, N.Y., but reported to separate executives at corporate headquarters in Stamford, Connecticut. Each group worked products through its own hierarchy, then handed them off to the next one. The groups had endless debates over feature and design trade-offs, and "no one had the priority for getting products out," Hicks recalls. Disagreements often reached all the way to the president's office in Stamford.

Now four strategic business units (SBUs) run the copier business. General managers, who each set long-range strategy and oversee product development, report to Hicks. He in turn answers to one executive at headquarters. This has resulted in an immediate 10 percent productivity gain, Hicks says. Engineering cycles for some products have been shortened by 50 percent.

These days, the development process at Xerox usually begins with ideas generated by an SBU. These are immediately tested for feasibility by small "product-synthesis" teams that quickly weed out the losers. Several competing teams of designers produce a prototype, sometimes taking up to six months. If the model cannot meet pre-set goals, the project is killed. "We've learned not to fear failure," says Hicks. The old system tended to prevent early mercy killing. "We used to have 200 or 300 people working on a project and sometimes ended up killing it," recalls Hicks.

If a "go" decision is reached, a product "delivery" team headed by a chief engineer takes the prototype through to manufacturing. Meanwhile, market research and benchmarking will have sketched out performance requirements as well as boundaries for development and manufacturing costs. The chief engineer also takes charge of developing a manufacturing process in a pilot plant housed near the design team—a practice borrowed from Japanese rivals.[37]

Managerial Implications

The matrix structure is most likely to be effective under the following conditions: (1) when it is absolutely essential that managers and others be highly responsive to both functional or product line (or geographic area) concerns; (2) when managers face complex/dynamic task environments that generate very high information processing requirements; and (3) when managers must deal with strong constraints on financial resources, human resources, or both. The potential advantages and disadvantages of the matrix structure are highlighted in Table 14–3.

The matrix structure demands substantial managerial overhead, particularly in the installation stages (which may take two to three years) while

---

TABLE 14–3   Assessment of the Matrix Structure

Advantages

- Makes specialized, functional knowledge available to all projects.
- Uses people flexibly, since departments maintain reservoirs of specialists.
- Maintains consistency between different departments and projects by forcing communication between managers.
- Recognizes and provides mechanisms for dealing with legitimate, multiple sources of power in the organization.
- Can adapt to environmental changes by shifting emphasis between project and functional aspects.

Disadvantages

- Can be very difficult to introduce without a preexisting supportive management climate.
- Increases role ambiguity, stress, and anxiety by assigning people to more than one department.
- Without power balancing between product and functional forms, lowers overall performance.
- Makes inconsistent demands, which may result in unproductive conflicts and short-term, crisis management.
- May reward political skills as opposed to technical skills.

Source: Adapted from McCann, J. E. and Galbraith, J. R. Interdepartmental Relations. In *Handbook of Organizational Design*, vol. 2, *Remodeling Organizations and Their Environments*. P. C. Nystrom and W. H. Starbuck (Eds.) New York: Oxford University Press, 1981, 61.

participants learn how to operate in the new organization. Learning may be slow, because fundamental changes in attitude are required of participants. The employees may be used to unity of command, and unambiguous authority structure, and top-down orders. The matrix structure changes all this, and special training programs are often needed to implement the new structure. In order to work properly, a matrix structure must maintain a continuing tension between multiple orientations (such as functional specialty and product line). This, in turn, requires effective interpersonal skills in confrontation, conflict resolution, bargaining, and trade-offs.

SUMMARY

The design of organizations is a complex process that is heavily influenced by the interplay of three key contingencies: environmental forces, technological factors, and strategic choices. The task environment(s) confronting an organization as a whole and its various departments can be highly variable. This variability can be assessed in terms of complexity (simple to complex) and dynamism (stable to dynamic). An organization, or its departments, with a simple/stable environment generally can effectively use the basic functional structure, where the top executive serves to integrate the various functional departments. If a firm has a single product line and the environment is complex/dynamic, the functional structure may continue to be effective if it is supplemented with the use of staff services and integrating mechanisms such as task forces, formal planning activities, linking roles, integrating groups, and the like.

Strategic choices—such as top-management's philosophy and decisions about the range of markets and types of customers to be served—have a direct impact on organization design. If top management believes in tight, centralized control of day-to-day decisions and has a general attitude of distrust of employees and lower level managers, it is more likely to use a mechanistic system rather than an organic system.

As with job design, technological considerations play a role in organization design. The potential impact of three technological variables—workflow uncertainty, task uncertainty, and task interdependence (pooled, sequential, and reciprocal)—on organization design were considered.

The characteristics of and conditions favoring the use of mechanistic and organic systems were reviewed. For our purposes here, bureaucracy is considered to be essentially synonymous with the mechanistic system. Different departments or divisions of the same organization may be mechanistic or organic. In an organization with a functional structure, it is quite possible that a production department could operate with a mechanistic system, while the research and development department operates with a relatively organic system.

Organization design is also affected by interdepartmental relationships that, in turn, are strongly influenced by three variables: differentiation, integration, and uncertainty. Diagnosis of these variables is an important aspect of organization design.

Three basic organizational structures—functional, product, and matrix—were presented and discussed. Each deals somewhat differently with the variables of interdepartmental relations. The functional and product structures can operate well under both mechanistic and organic systems, whereas the matrix structure can operate effectively only under an organic system. A number of managerial implications of each structure were presented.

KEY WORDS AND CONCEPTS

Bureaucracy
Centralization
Complexity dimension
Departmentalization
Differentiation
Division of labor
Dynamism dimension
Functional structure
Hierarchy of authority
Impersonality
Integration
Line functions

Matrix structure
Mechanistic system
Organic system
Organization design
Procedural specifications
Product structure
Rules
Scalar chain of command
Span of control
Staff functions
Task environment
Unity of command

DISCUSSION QUESTIONS

1. What problems is the functional division of labor intended to solve?
2. Describe an organization of which you are a member in terms of its mechanistic or organic characteristics.
3. Give some examples of organizational rules that you have encountered which seemed to be helpful or counterproductive from the standpoint of organizational effectiveness.
4. How might perceptions and attributions influence the diagnosis of the task environment and organization design decisions?
5. What difficulties are associated with the matrix structure? Would you like to work in a matrix structure? Why?
6. In addition to those discussed in this chapter, what other strategic choices of top management might influence the design of an organization?

MANAGEMENT INCIDENTS AND CASES

State Drug Council

Part I

The State Drug Council had, as one of its charges, to review a variety of proposals dealing with drug abuse in the state. Proposals and programs which the Council might be asked to review include requests for funding on such topics as drug treatment effectiveness, state-wide educational programs, level and extent of drug abuse within the state, factors which lead to drug abuse, evaluation of various educational efforts, evaluation and study of law enforcement efforts, support for new treatment facilities, etc. The head of the Drug Council, who readily admitted limited knowledge on the subject, decided to recruit a variety of professionals from the state to provide more valid assessments of the proposals submitted.

Several professionals concerned with drug abuse were contacted by the head of the Drug Council and asked to come to a meeting at the capital city headquarters. At the first meeting people involved in drug treatment, law enforcement, drug-related research and educators from all parts of the state were present. The head of the Drug Council chaired this meeting, which included 22 professionals, and after calling the meeting to order told the group he did not want to impose any of his ideas on the group about how it might organize. He was sensitive to the fact that the people involved were donating their time and felt he would let the group decide.

After a few minutes, the meeting quickly degenerated into several people talking at once, each proposing a different approach. The law enforcement people knew each other even though they were from different parts of the state and felt they should form a separate committee. The research methodology people felt it would be difficult to meet regularly as a separate committee because they came from different parts of the state and driving to the capital city took at least one hour each way. The educators, coming from different universities, expressed concern over driving time, while the psychologists and psychiatrists involved in treatment just wanted to be sure that adequate funds went into effective treatment programs. The first meeting was terminated with little resolved except to set up a second meeting time.

At the second meeting, the group continued to flounder as more and more individuals became frustrated and threatened to be absent from such future meetings. At the third meeting, the group demanded that the head of the Drug Council provide some direction. He told the group that he had some proposals for them to consider and suggested that they begin by looking at the proposal he had sent to them, previous to the meeting, concerning a new free treatment clinic. The people involved in treatment suggested they go off by themselves and review the proposal since this was their bailiwick. As the discussion continued, a police chief stated that he perceived real problems with law enforcement officials accepting free and private clinics. He felt that police would see them merely as "crash pads." The educators expressed concern over having the funding sufficient enough to provide adequate publicity in local schools. The research methodology people attacked the lack of effective assessment measures in the proposal and proposed it be sent back for revision. The meeting continued with accusations of "grand-standing" and several people departed early. Most people left this meeting angry and frustrated and several members told the head of the Drug Council that something had to be done or they would not be returning. Prior to the next meeting, the head of the Drug Council sent out a state memo detailing what he believed to be the objectives of the group and how he hoped to deal with the problems they had proposed.

STATE MEMO

TO: Members of Drug Council
      Advisory Board
      (22 members)
FROM: Head of Drug Council
SUBJECT: Council Objectives

The objective of the Advisory Board as I see it is to provide recommendations to the State Drug Council concerning various proposals involved with drug abuse. As I see it, some proposals may require specific expertise for evaluation such as those that deal with education. On the other hand, as we discussed last week, most proposals seem to overlap all of our areas of expertise to some extent and effective recommendations require several inputs. Therefore, it is imperative for all of you to contribute your ideas.

I have asked a management consultant to attend our next meeting and to propose to us how we might organize ourselves. I would appreciate it if everyone would come and cooperate with him.

Part II

After the consultant attended the next meeting of the board, he requested a list of the Board members, their areas of expertise and their geographic locations. In addition, after discussing the Board's objectives and past performance with the head of the Drug Council, he met privately with several members and listened to their complaints. The following represents the data he gathered:

Member	Area of Expertise	Geographic Location*
1. A. Alfred	Research Methodology	Central
2. T. Brougham	Law Enforcement	Northeast
3. Ms. N. Brown	Treatment	Central
4. R. J. Crousee	Research Methodology	Northeast
5. J. F. Donley	Treatment	Southern
6. P. W. Everett	Education	Central
7. J. Francis	Treatment	Northeast
8. T. French	Research Methodology	Southern
9. S. Gant	Education	Southern
10. N. Hughes	Research Methodology	Southern
11. J. L. Hughes	Research Methodology	Central
12. S. Islay	Treatment	Central
13. G. Jones	Treatment	Northeast
14. H. Kronsel	Research Methodology	Northeast
15. M. Listro	Law Enforcement	Central
16. R. Nunes	Research Methodology	Southern
17. L. M. Lacey	Treatment	Southern
18. G. Turner	Research Methodology	Northeast
19. P. Vail	Treatment	Northeast
20. W. Walters	Education	Northeast
21. J. Verna	Law Enforcement	Southern
22. S. Yates	Research Methodology	Central

*Grouped by general location within the state.

Complaint List

1. "A one hour drive each way to a meeting is too much given the amount of time we waste at the meeting."
2. "You can't do a thing with 22 people all talking at once."
3. "Some of the proposals could really benefit from the people in my area (Treatment) getting together separately."
4. "Some of these people don't realize the value of sharing ideas with professionals outside of their own area. They act as if they have the only answer."

With these data the consultant pondered what to recommend to the board and the head of the Drug Council.[38]

Questions

1. What factors should be diagnosed by the consultant in thinking about an organization design for the Council? Why?
2. What structure do you think the consultant should recommend? Why? (You should develop an organization chart.)
3. What is your assessment of the head of the State Drug Council? Explain.

References

1. Developed from Uttal, B. Mettle Test Time for John Young. *Fortune*, June 29, 1985, 242–244, 248. Used with permission. Why Hewlett-Packard Overhauled Its Management. *Business Week*, July 30, 1984, 111–112; Saporito, B. Hewlett-Packard Discovers Marketing. *Fortune*, October 1, 1984, 50–54; Uttal, B. Delays and Defections at Hewlett-Packard. *Fortune*, October 29, 1984, 62.

2. Mintzberg, H. Power and Organization Life Cycles. *Academy of Management Review*, 1984, 9:207–224.

3. Szilagyi Jr., A. D., and Schweiger, D. M. Matching Managers to Strategies: A Review and Suggested Framework. *Academy of Management Review*, 1984, 9:626–637; Bobbitt Jr., H. R., and Ford, J. D. Decision-Maker Choice as a Determinant of Organizational Structure. *Academy of Management Review*, 1980, 5:13–23.

4. Daft, R. L. *Organization Theory and Design*, 2d ed. St. Paul, Minn.: West, 1986; Galbraith, J. R. *Strategy Implementation: The Role of Structure and Process*, 2d ed. St. Paul, Minn.: West, 1986; Astley, W. G., and Van de Ven, A. H. Central Perspectives and Debates in Organization Theory. *Administrative Science Quarterly*, 1983, 18:248–273.

5. For example, see Gerloff, E. *Organization Theory and Design: A Strategic Approach*. New York: McGraw-Hill, 1985; Dessler, G. *Organization Theory: Integrating Structure and Behavior*. Englewood Cliffs, N.J.: Prentice-Hall, 1985; Jackson, J., Morgan, C., and Paolillo, J. G. *Organization Theory: A Macro Perspective for Management*, 3d ed. Englewood Cliffs, N.J.: Prentice-Hall, 1986; Robey, D. *Designing Organizations*. Homewood, Ill.: Irwin, 1986.

6. Kimberly, J. R. The Anatomy of Organizational Design. *Journal of Management*, 1984, 10:109–126; Aldrich, H., McKelvey, B., and Ulrich, D. Design Strategy from the Population Perspective. *Journal of Management*, 1984, 10:67–86; Ulrich, D., and Barney, J. B. Perspectives in Organizations: Resource Dependence, Efficiency, and Population. *Academy of Management Review*, 1984, 9:471–481.

7. Duncan, R. Characteristics of Organizational Environments and Perceived Environmental Uncertainty. *Administrative Science Quarterly*, 1972, 17:314. Also see Lawrence, P. R., and Dyer, D. *Renewing American Industry*. New York: Free Press, 1983; Baird, I. S., and Thomas, H. Toward a Contingency Model of Strategic Risk Taking. *Academy of Management Review*, 1985, 10:230–243.

8. Dess, G. G., and Beard, D. W. Dimensions of Organizational Task Environments. *Administrative Science Quarterly*, 1984, 29:52–53; Downey, H. K., and Ireland, R. D. Quantitative versus Qualitative: Environmental Assessment in Organizational Studies. *Administrative Science Quarterly*, 1979, 24:630–637; Ungson, G. R., James, C., and Spicer, B. H. The Effects of Regulatory Agencies on Organizations in Wood Products and High Technology/Electronics Industries. *Academy of Management Journal*, 1985, 28:426–445.

9. Wilson, I. Evaluating the Environment: Social and Political Factors. In W. D. Guth (Ed.) *Handbook of Business Strategy*. Boston: Warren, Gorham and Lamont, 1985, 3-2. Also see Porter, M. E., and Millar, V. E. How Information Gives You the Competitive Advantage. *Harvard Business Review*, July–August 1985, 149–160.

10. Hambrick, D. C., and Mason, P. A. Upper Echelons: The Organization as a Reflection of Its Top Managers. *Academy of Management Review*, 1984, 9:193–206; Bourgeois III, L. J. Strategic Management and Determinism. *Academy of Management Review*, 1984, 9:586–596.

11. Child, J. *Organizations: A Guide to Problems and Practice*, 2d ed. London: Harper & Row, 1984; Lorange, P. Organizational Structure and Management Process. In W. D. Guth (Ed.) *Handbook of Business Strategy*. Boston: Warren, Gorham, and Lamont, 1985, 23-1–23-31; Harrigan, K. R. Vertical Integration and Corporate Strategy. *Academy of Management Journal*, 1985, 28:397–425; Daniels, J. D., Pitts, R. A., and Tretter, M. J. Strategy and Structure of U. S. Multinationals: An Exploratory Study. *Academy of Management Journal*, 1984, 27:292–307; Kanter, R. M., and Buck, J. D. Reorganizing Part of Honeywell: From Strategy to Structure. *Organizational Dynamics*, Winter 1985, 4–25.

12. Developed from Lawrence, P. R., and Dyer, D. *Renewing American Industry*. New York: Free Press, 1983, 146–165; Eccles, R. G. Bureaucratic versus Craft Administration: The Relationships of Market Structure to the Construction Firm. *Administrative Science Quarterly*, 1981, 26, 449–469; Mayer, M. *The Builders: Houses, People, Neighborhoods, Governments, Money*. New York: Norton, 1978.

13. Fry, L. W. Technology-Structure Research: Three Critical Issues. *Academy of Management Journal*, 1982, 25, 532–552; Fry, L. W., and Slocum Jr., J. W. Technology, Structure, and Workgroup Effective-

ness: A Test of a Contingency Model. *Academy of Management Journal,* 1984, *17,* 221–246.

14. Carter, N. M. Computerization as a Predominant Technology: Its Influence on the Structure of Newspaper Organizations. *Academy of Management Journal,* 1984, *27,* 247–270; Ovalle II, N. K. Organizational/Managerial Control Processes: A Reconceptualization of the Linkage Between Technology and Peformance. *Human Relations,,* 1984, *37,* 1047–1062; Rousseau, D. M., and Cooke, R. A. Technology and Structure: The Concrete, Abstract, and Activity Systems of Organizations. *Journal of Management,* 1984, *10,* 345–362: Woodward, J. *Industrial Organization: Theory and Practice,* 2d ed. New York: Oxford University Press, 1980.

15. Kmetz. J. L. An Information-Processing Study of a Complex Workflow in Aircraft Electronics Repair. *Administrative Science Quarterly,* 1984, *29,* 255–280; Lengnick-Hall, C. A., and Futterman, D. H. Getting a Handle on Complex Units. *Personnel,* March 1985, 57–63; Randolph, W. A. Matching Technology and the Design of Organizational Units. *California Management Review,* Summer 1981, 39–48.

16. Dun's Marketing Series. *Million Dollar Directory.* Parsippany, N.J.: Dun & Bradstreet, 1985, 2183–2184.

17. Burns, T., and Stalker, G. M. *The Management of Innovation.* London: Social Science Paperbacks, 1961, 96–125; Daft, R. L. Bureaucratic versus Nonbureaucratic Structure and the Process of Innovation and Change. In S. B. Bacharach (Ed.) *Research in the Sociology of Organizations.* Greenwich, Conn.: JAI Press, 1982, 129–166.

18. Adapted from Weber, M. *The Theory of Social and Economic Organization* (trans., T. Parsons). New York: Oxford University Press, 1947, 329–334.

19. Rogers, R. E. *Max Weber's Ideal Type Theory.* New York: Philosophical Library, 1969; Weiss, R. M. Weber on Bureaucracy: Management Consultant or Political Theorist? *Academy of Management Review,* 1983, *8,* 242–248.

20. Rubenstein, D., and Woodman, R. W. Spiderman and the Burma Raiders: Collateral Organization in Action. *Journal of Applied Behavioral Science,* 1984, *20,* 1–21; Vaughan, T. R., and Sjoberg, G. The Individual and Bureaucracy: An Alternative Meadian Perspective. *Journal of Applied Behavioral Science,* 1984, *20,* 57–69; Sjoberg, G., Vaughan, T. R., and Williams, N. Bureaucracy as a Moral Maze. *Journal of Applied Behavioral Science,* 1984, *20,* 441–453.

21. Carter, N. M., and Cullen, J. B. A Comparison of Centralization/Decentralization of Decision Making Concepts and Measures. *Journal of Management,* 1984, *10,* 259–268; Sherman, J. D., and Smith, H. L. The Influence of Organizational Structure on Intrinsic versus Extrinsic Motivation. *Academy of Management Journal,* 1984, *27,* 877–885.

22. Blackburn, R. S. Dimensions of Structure: A Review and Reappraisal. *Academy of Management Review,* 1982, *7,* 59–66.

23. Connor, P. E. *Organizations: Theory and Design.* Palo Alto, Calif.: SRA, 1980, 347–353.

24. Smith, A. *An Inquiry into the Nature and Causes of the Wealth of Nations.* (1776) Reprinted ed., New York: Modern Library, 1937, 48.

25 Ford, J. D. Departmental Context and Formal Structure as Constraints on Leader Behavior. *Academy of Management Journal,* 1981, *24,* 274–288.

26. Lorsch, J. W., and Allen III, S. A. *Managing Diversity and Interdependence: An Organizational Study of Multidivisional Firms.* Cambridge, Mass.: Harvard University Graduate School of Business Administration, 1973. Also see Lawrence, P., and Lorsch, J. W. *Organization and Environment: Managing Differentiation and Integration.* Homewood, Ill.: Irwin, 1969.

27. Lorsch and Allen.

28. Dollinger, M. C. Environmental Boundary Spanning and Information Processing Effects on Organizational Performance. *Academy of Management Journal,* 1984, *27,* 351–368; Pearce II, J. A., and David, F. R. A Social Network Approach to Organization Design Performance. *Academy of Management Review,* 1983, *8,* 436–444; Randolph, W. A., and Dess, G. G. The Congruence Perspective of Organization Design: A Conceptual Model and Multivariate Research Approach. *Academy of Management Review,* 1984, *9,* 114–127; McDonough III, E. F., and Leifer, R. Using Simultaneous Structures to Cope with Uncertainty. *Academy of Management Journal,* 1983, *26,* 727–735.

29. Lawrence, P. Organization and Environment Perspective: The Harvard Research Program. In A. Van de Ven and W. Joyce (Eds.) *Perspectives on Organization Design and Behavior.* New York: Wiley, 1981, 311–337.

30. Excerpted from Pitts, R. A., and Daniels, J. D. Aftermath of the Matrix Mania. *Columbia Journal of World Business,* Summer 1984, 48–54. Reprinted with permission of *Columbia Journal of World Business.* Also see Berenbeim, R. E. *Man-*

aging the International Company: Building a Global Perspective. New York: The Conference Board, 1982; Mansfield, R., and Zeffane, R. A. Organizational Structure and National Contingencies. Hampshire, England: Gower, 1983; Garnier, G. H. Context and Decision Making Autonomy in the Foreign Affiliates of U. S. Multinational Corporations. Academy of Management Journal, 1982, 25, 893–908.

31. Van Fleet, D. D. Span of Management Research and Issues. Academy of Management Journal, 1983, 26, 546–552; Dewar, R. D., and Simet, D. P. A Level Specific Prediction of Spans of Control Examining the Effects of Size, Technology, and Specialization. Academy of Management Journal, 1981, 24, 5–24.

32. Jelinek, M., Litterer, J. A., and Miles, R. E. (Eds.) Organizations by Design: Theory and Practice. Plano, Texas: Business Publications, 1981; Gordon, J. R., Corsini, L. S., and Fetters, M. L. Restructuring Accounting Firms for Better Client Service. Sloan Management Review, Spring 1985, 43–55.

33. Developed from: Kodak is Trying to Break Out of Its Shell. Business Week, June 10, 1985, 92–95; Eastman Kodak Announces Reorganization of Photographic Division. Wall Street Journal, November 19, 1984, 26.

34. Davis, S. M., and Lawrence, P. R. Matrix. Reading, Mass.: Addison-Wesley, 1977.

35. Davis, S. M., and Lawrence, P. R. Problems of Matrix Organizations. Harvard Business Review, May–June 1978, 131–142.

36. Kolodny, H. F. Managing in a Matrix. Business Horizons, March–April 1981, 17–35.

37. Developed from How Xerox Speeds up the Birth of New Products. Business Week, March 14, 1984, 58–59; Xerox Plans New Series of Products, Systems, and Strategies to Transform Business. Forbes, April 22, 1985, 41.

38. Case prepared by Jack Veiga, School of Business, The University of Connecticut, Storrs, Conn., and used with his permission.

PART V

Dynamics of the Work Environment: The Interaction of Individual, Group and Organizational Processes

15 Decision Making and Goal Setting

LEARNING OBJECTIVES

After you have finished studying this chapter, you should be able to:

■ Describe the five phases of managerial decision making as streams of decisions.

■ Explain the scope and functions of goal setting and how it can be used to influence individual effort and performance.

■ State how management by objectives (MBO) can be applied as a management philosophy and system.

■ Describe the purposes and importance of performance appraisal in MBO and two of the frequently used methods for rating performance.

OUTLINE

Preview Case

Rolm Corporation

Co-founder Kenneth Oshman, 44, of Rolm Corporation—a classic Silicon Valley success, acquired last year by IBM for $1.9 billion—believes a chief executive's job is to peer intently three to five years into the future, looking for problems. In 1971 the first flicker of an adverse change in Rolm's environment galvanized him into furious activity. Rolm was then a fast-growing $1.5 million-a-year maker of heavy-duty computers, 60% of which were sold to the military—"not a totally rational customer," Oshman recalls. That year, as he began to worry that the market for his specialized product would soon be saturated at around $15 million in annual sales, the Navy announced plans to use only one standard computer design, with specifications identical to a machine made by Sperry Univac. Oshman scrambled to find a second, related product line.

Well, remarked two employees, there's always the computerized telephone business, though that's now grinding up our former employer, Arcata Communications Inc., which distributes such gear. Oshman decided to investigate. Surely, he thought, the Federal Communication Commission's 1968 decision to let non-Bell equipment be hooked up to the phone company's network must create a major opportunity. Six months of research produced a disappointing conclusion: to gain a worthwhile share of the potentially giant market, you'd have to stride in as a full-blown manufacturing, sales, and service behemoth, a task far beyond Rolm's capacity.

"But we didn't have a strong enough gut feeling that anything else was right for us," says Oshman. "So we decided to see how we could turn this into a business." After more months of sounding out skeptical telephone experts, he called in reinforcements by hiring a technical expert and a marketing veteran, making Rolm's top management feel even more committed to the decision.

Oshman believed Rolm could develop digital switching equipment much more sophisticated than the equipment AT&T and a handful of competitors were supplying to businesses. What big companies really wanted, Rolm's talks with potential customers found, was a phone system that would route calls over the cheapest available lines, monitor phone use to control costs, and make it easy to let employees keep the same phone number when they changed offices—tasks made to order for a computer-controlled system. The same system could solve Rolm's service problems by having a built-in diagnostic capability that would pinpoint malfunctions on its own.

"As the Boston Consulting Group would tell you," says marketing vice president Richard Moley, 45, "the last thing you ever do is go into a new market with a completely new product." That's true—if you don't want to take the risk of building a giant new business. In this case the product worked, customers bought it, and in nine years Rolm grew at an annual compound rate of 57% to the $660 million in annual sales it reached just before IBM acquired it.

And the premises that set this whole beautifully logical process in motion turned out to be completely wrong. The military-specification computer market did not stop at $15 million a year but grew to an esti-

> mated $200 million, of which Rolm today has around half. And the Navy began to loosen its single computer standard in 1976. Says Oshman: "I'd rather be lucky than right."[1]

The real world of managerial decision making is anything but orderly, undertaken with a sense of certainty, and totally within the control of managers. The chancy and somewhat turbulent world of managerial decision making is nicely illustrated in the Preview Case. Of course, managers do *try* to bring a greater sense of order to, reduce risks and uncertainties of, and increase control over the forces that affect the processes and results of decision making. In other chapters we have already presented a number of recommendations for improving the success rate in making decisions about particular issues and problem areas. For example, Chapter 7 provided guidance about the process that should be followed for diagnosing problems of work motivation and the types of decisions that are likely to improve work motivation and productivity. Chapter 9 identified and discussed the six phases of group decision making that should be followed for greater effectiveness. Chapter 11 presented the Vroom and Yetton normative model, which provides an insight into the leadership styles that should result in acceptable and high quality decisions.

In the first section of this chapter, we attempt to capture the real-world flows and crosscurrents of managerial decision making. In the second section, we address goal setting, a process by which managers attempt to bring a greater degree of order, controllability, and direction to decision making. And in the third section, we discuss management by objectives as a management philosophy and system that attempt to integrate goal setting into the life of organizations. We also present the use of performance appraisal within the framework of management by objectives in this section.

STREAMS OF MANAGERIAL DECISION MAKING

For our purposes, **managerial decision making** is a complex process and set of activities that begins with a recognition or awareness of problems and concludes with an assessment of the results and consequences of the actions taken to solve them. Figure 15–1 provides a model of managerial decision making that involves streams of decisions.[2] Although this flow is shown as proceeding step-by-step, managerial decision making is often quite disorderly and complex as it unfolds.[3] Managerial decision making has been generally described as follows:

> Decisions are made and problems solved in fits and starts. The process is like a flowing stream, filled with debris, meandering through the terrain of managers and their organizations. There is no beginning or end.[4] Also, . . . management, in large measure, is dealing with the unexpected crises and petty little problems that require much more time than they're worth. . . . The manager may well go from a budget meeting involving millions to a discussion of what to do about a broken decorative water fountain.[5] . . . Thus, managerial work is hectic and fragmented and requires the ability to shift continually from person to person, from one subject or problem to another.[6]

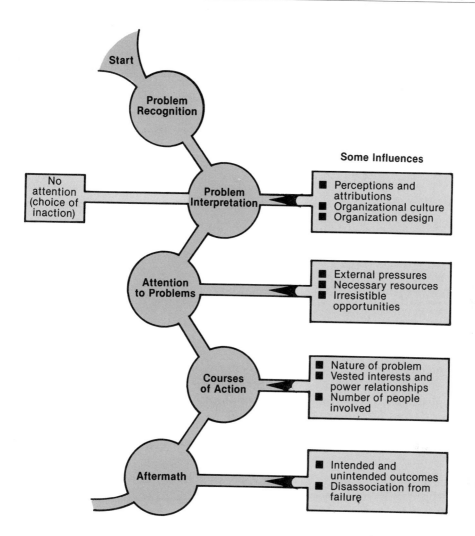

FIGURE 15-1.
Managerial Decision Making as Streams of Decisions

Source: Adapted from McCall Jr., M. W. and Kaplan, R. E. *Whatever It Takes: Decision Makers at Work.* Englewood Cliffs, N.J.: Prentice-Hall, 1985, xvii.

Given this description, it is apparent that Figure 15-1 illustrates only part of the puzzle-like qualities of managerial decision making. Similarly, the following presentation of each of the major elements in managerial decision making serves to sketch only the broad outlines of the managerial decision-making process.

Problem Recognition

Managerial decision making rarely begins with a clean slate. Previous decisions and experiences of managers and new information have a significant impact on whether there is any awareness or recognition that a problem exists. Moreover, the characteristics of individual managers also play an important role in problem recognition.[7] (See Chapter 5.)

With **structured problems,** the recognition stage is straightforward. For example, a marketing manager promises the delivery of an order within 30 days. After 45 days, the customer calls and, in a state of irritation states: "The order hasn't arrived. I need it pronto. What are you going to do?" The marketing manager is suddenly and forcefully made aware that a problem exists and that it must be resolved.

With **unstructured problems**, the recognition of problems is often, itself, a problem. The "problem" of problem recognition can result from unclear or inadequate information about developments and trends in the environment and organization. For example, many organizations create marketing research departments to collect information about their customers or potential customers to determine whether changing customer tastes and preferences are likely to create new problems.

Let us return to the marketing manager who was called by an irate customer. Suppose that this manager has been experiencing a 200 percent turnover in sales representatives. When asked about this level of turnover, the marketing manager replies: "That's the way it's always been, even before I became the marketing manager. I guess it's just part of the cost of doing business and the nomadic nature of sales reps. . . ." This response shows no awareness that a problem with turnover might exist. Six months later a new marketing manager is appointed. When reviewing the personnel files, she is astounded by the "major turnover problem, which must be corrected if we are ever to establish long-term and trusting relationships with our customers and eventually increase our sales to them."

The recognition of a problem usually triggers activities that may lead to a quick solution or may be part of a long, drawn out process, depending on the nature and complexity of the problem. For example, the new marketing manager may be confronted with a problem like this by a subordinate: "We are 15 days late in the delivery of the West Publishing Company order. Should we ship it by our regular freight line, air express it, or what?" The marketing manager may immediately respond: "Air express it." On the other hand, her recognition that the 200 percent annual turnover in sales personnel represents a major problem may require a year to: (1) determine the reasons for the turnover; (2) implement a program to reduce turnover; and (3) assess the results of the program.

Problem Interpretation

The second phase in the decision-making process requires an *interpretation* of the problem. For example, the high turnover rate for sales representatives might be the result of looking for applicants in the wrong places, inadequate selection procedures, poor training, lack of supervision, a poor compensation system, or some combination of these factors. **Problem interpretation** refers to the process of giving meaning and definition to those problems that are recognized.[8] However, recognition of a problem does not ensure that it will be given sufficient, if any, attention. Thus Figure 15–1 indicates that one option for managers is to simply not give a recognized problem any attention. This is the choice of inaction. This choice may be a consequence of demands on the manager to deal with too many other high priority problems, a belief that the problem will go away with time, the judgment that an attempt to do something about the problem will only worsen the situation, and the like.

Preconceptions, the filtering out of new information, and defensiveness are key ingredients in ineffective problem interpretation.[9] As suggested in Figure 15–1, some of the key influences on the process of problem interpretation include perceptions and attributions (Chapters 4 and 5), organizational culture (Chapter 12), and organization design (Chapter 14). A common thread in these influences is the way information is processed and how it is used to interpret problems.[10] There is no simple one-to-one relationship between the availability of "objective" information and how it is processed in the problem interpretation phase. Table 15–1 serves as a reminder of some of the information processing biases that enter into the decision-making process, particularly in this phase.

Effective organizations with strong organizational cultures are characterized as having managers and nonmanagers who are *active listeners*. It has been suggested that managers of organizations that exhibit superior performance tend:

> To "wander," with customers and vendors and our own people, . . . to be in touch with the first vibrations of the new. Hard data-driven information is usually a day late and always sterile. The adaptive organization is one that is in touch with the outside world via living data. The No. 1 managerial productivity problem in America is, quite simply, managers who are out of touch with their people and out of touch with their customers.[11]

Through active listening and the seeking of information from customers, suppliers, employees, and others, managers have a much better chance of effective problem interpretation. A strong organizational culture that supports and reinforces such listening presumably reduces the risk of poor problem interpretation.

Specialization results in the channeling of information and problems to particular positions and departments. It can both aid and hinder problem recognition and interpretation. For example, when the marketing manager

---

TABLE 15–1 Examples of Potential Biases in Information Processing

Potential Biases	Description/Example
■ Availability	If a person can easily recall specific instances of an event, he or she may overestimate how frequently the event occurs (and vice versa).
■ Selective perception	What people expect to see biases what they do see. People seek information consistent with their own views. People downplay information that conflicts with their preconceptions.
■ Concrete information	Vivid, direct experience dominates abstract information; a single personal experience can outweigh more valid statistical information.
■ Law of small numbers	Small samples are deemed representative of the larger population (a few cases "prove the rule"), even when they are not.
■ Complexity	Under time pressure, processing of complex information may be quite superficial.
■ Gambler's fallacy	Seeing an unexpected number of similar chance events leads to the belief that an event not seen will occur (such as, after observing 9 successive reds in roulette, believing that chances for a black on the next spin are greater than 50/50).

Source: Excerpted and adapted from Hogarth, R. M., and Makridakis, S. Forecasting and Planning: An Evaluation. *Management Science*, 1981, 27:117–120.

and her staff have been assigned goals to ensure customer satisfaction—such as "98 percent of all orders are to reach customers on the promised date of delivery"—and to initiate corrective action when the goals are not achieved, specialization probably aids problem recognition and interpretation. However, unless accompanied by effective integrating mechanisms, specialization may well lead to counterproductive efforts and conflicts between specialties and departments, perhaps even concealing and distorting information to advance individual and departmental goals. There may also be a failure to recognize the importance of new information that does not clearly fall within an existing specialty or the area of responsibility of one of the departments. Unfortunately, this tendency is most likely to occur in complex and dynamic environments, or the very conditions for which effective problem recognition and problem interpretation become most critical.[12]

The likelihood that managers will learn to recognize and interpret problems more effectively is strongly influenced by the characteristics of and processes within the culture of the organization. **Organizational learning** can be defined as the process within an organization by which knowledge about action–outcome relationships and the effect of the environment on these relationships is developed. This requires a process through which an individual's knowledge can be shared, evaluated, and integrated with that of others in the organization.[13] Let us consider briefly how Japanese firms support organizational learning to enhance problem interpretation and other managerial decision-making skills.

ACROSS CULTURES

Organizational Learning in Japanese Firms

The importance of management skills in the success of Japanese organizations has been underlined in a number of recent publications. Japanese management in these writings serves mainly as a foil for the development of a general argument for the superiority of a management style synthesizing the best of both Japanese and American management. Briefly, this synthesis consists of a combination of structural factors (the American type of "hard" S's: Strategy, Structure, and Systems) with the human resources of the organization (the Japanese type of "soft" S's: Skills, Staff, Style, and Superordinate goals). The degree of consistency achieved in the relationships between these two areas is supposedly an indicator of the strength of managerial performance in the organization. One lesson from the Japanese managers is that both "soft" and "hard" factors are important for success. The focus here is on the "hard" factors.

Basically it is thought that Japanese companies are usually adept at organizational learning and that this learning makes Japanese managers very good at "hard" decision making. Faced with a complex and uncertain environment, the Japanese organization's first step in the learning process is to develop various means for scanning the task environment. The incoming stimuli are filtered through an organizational culture that is characterized by high levels of information sharing, consensus building, and wide participation in decision making. The soft management skills provide the "oil" for the internal mechanisms that serve to disperse the information throughout the firm. The organization "learns." Over time, continuous interaction with the environment generates more information feedback and new stimuli, and the organizational members gradually learn the requisite hard skills for coping successfully with forces in the environment. The process is in the spirit of, but not limited to, on-the-job training. The incentive to stay with the same Japanese company generally is very strong, and the organization can count on the individual for long-term future contributions. The hard management skills in the Japanese company thus might be relatively slow to emerge, but in firms with extensive experience in an industry these skills will be very competitive indeed.

Several factors specific to Japanese organizations are at work. The group sharing process leads naturally to an exposure of junior members to higher echelon executives, and learning by example is a standard experience of new arrivals. With slow promotion policies, the younger members are given plenty of time to absorb new information. Specific assignments of teacher–pupil (sempai–kohai) pairs also account for attention to an individual's learning and skills development. The common practice of job rotation also enables the individual to develop skills in a wide variety of areas, making a professional type of skill development less common but also enabling the individual to share in-depth in company operations as a whole. The standard practice of promotions based on seniority in the company, although sometimes challenged, still is common and contributes to an openness on the part of senior managers to their juniors' suggestions and allows the latter to participate in many of the crucial decisions made by the company.

Other more mundane differences also contribute to this on-the-job education. It is well known that briefings by foreign suppliers and buyers often require the attendance of many employees from the Japanese company. At such meetings the Japanese often overwhelm the presenters with requests for all possibly relevant information. After the meetings the Japanese attempt an immediate digestion of the information, allowing divergent interpretations to emerge and be discussed intensively. There is no doubt that this "technique" serves primarily as an insurance policy against possible mistakes (similar to the consensus decision-making process), but it also provides education, information, and knowledge for the managers. As a result, one can argue, the typical "low profile" of the Japanese managers should be seen more as a reflection of the need to consult other people before making a final decision and much less as a consequence of the traditional view of Japanese managers as "only figureheads." This is especially important to keep in mind because the lack of ability to communicate in a foreign language often makes the Japanese representative in an international meeting seem a less formidable friend or foe than frequently is the case.

The managed interactions between a complex and uncertain environment and the internal workings of the Japanese organization represent a very effective organizational learning mechanism. Generally speaking, the accumulated information and experiences of the large Japanese company (from domestic as well as overseas operations) are continually processed, integrated, shared, and revised.[14]

Attention to Problems

After problems have been recognized and interpreted, judgments need to be made as to which problems receive attention, how much, and in what order. Unlike most of the other employees in organizations, managers must be cognizant of the *relative priorities* they place on the problems they attend to. As suggested in Figure 15-1, the problems receiving the highest priority are likely to meet the following criteria:

■ Attention to the problem is supported by strong external pressure (the executive vice-president insists that the report be completed within two weeks).

■ Attention to the problem is supported by the resources necessary to take action (you are authorized to approve overtime pay and hire temporary workers to complete the report within two weeks).

■ Attention to the problem represents an irresistible opportunity (the report deals with assessing an expansion in production capacity that could lead to a larger and more profitable firm, a promotion from production manager to vice president of production, or the potential for bigger bonuses).

A key to understanding the demands of managerial decision making is that the volume and variety of recognized problems needing attention almost always exceed the manager's capacity for addressing and resolving all of them within the desired time frame. Crises from the external environment can shift the most carefully planned sequence of priorities for attending to already recognized problems.[15] Consider the managerial impact of Union Carbide's Bhopal catastrophe. Thousands of managerial hours were abruptly shifted from other issues to the problems triggered by this catastrophe.

In Practice: **Union Carbide and the Bhopal Catastrophe**

Well before the death toll crept past 1,200, the disaster at Union Carbide Corporation's pesticide plant in Bhopal, India, was already seen as history's worst industrial accident. On December 3, 1984, a valve on an underground storage tank gave way under pressure, spewing a cloud of deadly gas over the sleeping city of more than half a million. Several days later, hospitals were still jammed with the dying and injured.

Half a world away, in Danbury, Connecticut, shocked officials at Union Carbide's headquarters struggled to cope with a tragedy that they would certainly be held responsible for but one that they knew little about. The company's executives faced a string of management problems: how best to aid the victims; how to be sure that whatever happened at Bhopal doesn't happen again somewhere else; how to help employees keep up morale; how to reassure investors about the corporation's financial stability; and how to begin protecting the company from excessive legal liabilities. They had to face these questions all at once, and in circumstances that made calm deliberation virtually impossible. Every issue had a public relations side to it.

The company was hampered initially by two things: facts were hard to come by, and even when they did filter into Danbury, they were hard to believe. With only two phone lines into Bhopal and the plant supervisors there under arrest, Union Carbide was reduced to relying on Indian news reports relayed by phone from employees at its subsidiary in Bombay.

Chairman Anderson professed to be personally "shattered" by the events in Bhopal. Asked on his return from India about his plans for getting his company "back on the track," Anderson answered wistfully: "I *do* worry about that once in a while." The 63-year-old executive went on to predict that "the balance of my professional career will be spent having to sort out this incident."[16]

Courses of Action

The development and evaluation of courses of action (alternatives) and the implementation of the selected alternative can range from a *quick action* process to a *convoluted action* process.

A *quick action* process is appropriate when (1) the nature of the problem is well structured (two subordinates fail to show up for work, creating a problem in meeting a deadline for the next day); (2) a single manager (or at most, two managers) is clearly recognized as having the authority and responsibility to resolve the problem (the manager authorizes overtime for some of the other employees to meet the deadline); and (3) the search for information about the problem and alternatives is quite limited (the manager might call the customer to determine whether the deadline can be pushed back by another day or two and, if not, considers whether to schedule overtime, bring in help from a temporary employment service, or check with other managers to see if any of them are less busy and could loan some workers). This quick action process may well take place within ten minutes or less.

At the other extreme, is the *convoluted action* process.[17] The Bhopal catastrophe, for example, undoubtedly triggered a convoluted action process within Union Carbide. A convoluted action process is usually necessary when:

- The nature of the problem is unstructured. (Union Carbide managers had never faced a catastrophe like the one at Bhopal.)
- A long period of time is required for problem solution. (Some authorities estimate that the Bhopal incident will require years before all of the law suits and other issues are finally resolved.)
- Many vested interests and power relationships are involved. (Among those included in the Bhopal incident are the governments of India and the United States, the heirs of the 1,200 people who died, the thousands who were injured, and company management and shareholders.)
- Many people are involved in an extensive search for solutions. (In the Bhopal incident, managers, lawyers, accountants, Indian and U.S. government officials, public relations representatives, engineers, and others are involved to fix responsibility, to avoid repetition of this type of accident, to compensate victims and heirs, and so on.)

In the convoluted action process, tradeoffs, negotiations, conflicts, and political processes are usually evident. (See, especially, Chapters 16 and 17.) Although managers are continuously involved with a variety of problems, many can be addressed by the quick action process, far fewer require involvement in the convoluted action process.

Aftermath

During the **aftermath** phase, outcomes and consequences of the actions taken are evaluated. With structured problems, this is usually a simple matter. Recall the example of the manager who scheduled overtime to meet a deadline when two workers failed to show up. If the overtime hours resulted in meeting the deadline, there is clear feedback that the decision led to the intended outcome.

However, selection of a course of action and its implementation to deal with an unstructured problem may involve many individuals and departments and qualitative judgments. Moreover, the assessment of the course of action taken may require further use of qualitative judgments and a long wait before the outcomes are known and their consequences can be determined.[18] Unstructured problems usually require the implementation of a course of action in the face of risk and uncertainty. Thus it is not surprising when both intended and unintended outcomes occur. One notable unintended outcome of a corporate decision caused the Coca-Cola Company to announce reintroduction of its original-formula soft drink only a few months after replacing it (with much attendant publicity) with "New Coke."

In Practice: Reintroduction of Coca-Cola "Classic"

The management of the Coca-Cola Company had no intention of introducing a new taste for Coke that would meet with widespread public hostility. Because of the unintended outcome and the belief that a "no action" response would not help, top management soon announced a reintroduction of the original Coke flavor (renamed "Coca-Cola Classic"). While resting at home on July 4, 1985, Gerald Keough, the company president, decided that regardless of the embarrassment it might cause, the company had to quickly bring back its old formula. Why? It was more than just public hostility by a few noisy Coke diehards. In some key markets, shipments had fallen by as much as 15 percent in June. In addition, the worst was confirmed by two different marketing research studies conducted that same month, involving samples of 900 and 5,000 Coke drinkers. When these consumers were asked which Coke they liked better, 60 percent said "old" and only 30 percent "new." Keough concluded: "Some critic will say Coca-Cola made a marketing mistake. Some cynic will say that we planned the whole thing [for the publicity value]. The truth is we are not that dumb and we are not that smart."

When Coca-Cola Company executives first announced the return of old Coke, competitors were overjoyed. After all, the mighty Atlanta marketing machine had bogged down. They reasoned that the company would suffer from consumer confusion, diluted promotional efforts, and a lack of space on retailers' shelves. Coca-Cola, of course, may still end up taking a beating because of its hastily concocted change in strategy. But the longer its soft-drink competitors think about the company's desperation move, the more worried they become. That's because Coca-Cola has suddenly shifted the battleground on its rivals. By bringing back old Coke—and naming it Coca-Cola Classic—the soft-drink giant has bullied the competition into a much more difficult fight. Instead of selling against "new" Coke, which was intended to hurt Pepsi but has met with seemingly universal indifference, competitors must now battle a chastened Coca-Cola that will concentrate on its traditional strengths: selling sodas and winning shelf space.

Meeting Coca-Cola on that battleground will not be easy. It commands a $100 million budget to promote the two Cokes, enough to drown out messages from all competitors except free-spending PepsiCo, Inc.[19]

In retrospect, Coca Cola management probably made a mistake in attempting to completely drop the original Coke from the market. But even the best managers make mistakes, and the challenge is to learn from these mistakes—not to deny them or engage in self-delusions that they were not a part of the mistake. Most employees and managers guard their reputations as capable people and may go to extremes not to acknowledge their mistakes. In addition, research generally supports the view that individuals and groups tend to overestimate the effectiveness of their judgment decisions.[20]

The following comments by two managers are instructive of the need to learn from the aftermath of a course of action, including those that turned out to be mistakes:

> Everybody knows you make mistakes, so why not admit it. I make it a point to admit the blunders. Once I admit it, I feel better about it. It doesn't bother me. It's really a painful thing to keep trying to not admit some things. You have to carry that around as a burden until you get it off your chest.[21]

> When one's decisions turn out alright, one should resist the temptation to spend very much time basking in the glory of those right decisions. They need to be reexamined on a continuous basis to be sure that the decision that was right yesterday continues to be right today.[22]

Intuition and Creativity

The most difficult problem situation faced by managers is likely to be one of disagreement over the best course of action to take, as well as the goals that should be achieved.[23] A variety of decision-making techniques and processes may be used in such a situation. We briefly discuss two of them: intuition and creativity.

Intuition consists of hunches, images, insights, or thoughts that often spontaneously surface to conscious awareness.[24] (Recall the discussion of intuitive thinkers and intuitive feelers in Chapter 5.) Two managers commented on intuition as follows:

> "In a business that depends entirely on people and not machinery," says Robert Bernstein, chairman of Random House, "only intuition can protect you against the most dangerous individual of all—the articulate incompetent. That's what frightens me about business schools. They train their students to sound wonderful. But it's necessary to find out if there's 'judgment' behind the language."

> Confronted in 1960 with what his lawyer called a bad deal—$2.7 million for the McDonald name—Ray Kroc says: "I closed my office door, cussed up and down, threw things out of the window, called my lawyer back, and said, 'Take it!' I felt in my funny bone it was a sure thing".[25]

Intuition may or may not be a result of creativity, which is the more involved process of the two. In brief, **creativity** is defined as applied imagination. The four basic phases in the creative process include:

- *Preparation*—saturating yourself in the problem.
- *Incubation*—interruption of conscious effort to solve the problem.
- *Illumination*—the floating up to consciousness of an essential element of the solution.
- *Elaboration*—the process of confirming, expanding, tightening, reformulating, and revising the new idea so that it meshes with what is known and what is needed.[26]

Creativity helps managers and others to uncover problems, identify opportunities, and undertake novel courses of action to solve problems. Several approaches for stimulating creativity within organizations were presented in Chapter 9.

GOAL SETTING

Goal setting is a process intended to increase efficiency and effectiveness by specifying the desired outcomes toward which individuals, departments, and organizations should work. Goals are the main ingredients in goal setting. **Goals** are the future outcomes (results) that individuals, departments, and organizations desire and strive to achieve.[27] The following is an example of an individual's goal: "I am shooting to graduate with a 2.8 grade-point average by the end of the spring semester, 1989."

Stakeholders and Goal Setting

Goals and goal setting are often the object of disagreement and conflict. Because diverse groups have a stake in organizational decisions, managers are faced with the continuing need to develop, modify, and discard goals. The intensity of goal setting activities is strongly influenced by the dynamism and complexity of the environment. In a simple/stable environment (such as that of the baking industry), goal setting tends to focus on revising existing goals, such as "increase sales of product X by 4 percent over the next 12 months." In a complex/dynamic environment (such as that of the computer industry), managers will more frequently devise entirely new goals, significantly revise existing goals, and discard outdated goals. Such changes—often in rapid sequence—are likely to reflect (1) new *opportunities,* such as IBM's program of linking computer technology with telecommunication technology; (2) new *threats,* such as the strong entry of retailers (Sears and Kmart) into financial services, which poses a threat to banks; and (3) new *weaknesses,* such as the relatively high labor costs of established airlines (American, Eastern, United) after deregulation as a result of the entry of new, low-labor-cost airlines into the industry (People Express).

Table 15–2 contains several categories of goals of particular interest to various stakeholders of organizations, some of which are obviously incompatible. The creation of a unified and logical system of goal setting for an organization is very difficult in the following situations:

TABLE 15-2   Examples of Categories of Goals of Interest to Stakeholders

Shareholders	Employees
■ Growth in dividend payments ■ Growth in share price ■ Growth in net asset value	■ Good compensation and job security ■ Sense of meaning or purpose in the job ■ Opportunities for personal development

Customers	Government
■ Price always competitive ■ Emphasis on quality ■ Return and replacement policies	■ Being an efficient user of energy and natural resources ■ Adhering to the country's laws ■ Provision of employment

Lenders	Suppliers
■ Liquidity of the company ■ Character and standing of the borrowing firm's managment ■ Quality of the borrowing company's assets available for security	■ Degree to which the company is seen to be professionally managed ■ Timely payment of debts ■ Adequate liquidity

Source: Adapted from Mendelow, A. L. Setting Corporate Goals and Measuring Organizational Effectivenewss: A Practical Approach. *Long Range Planning*, February 1983, 75–76.

- Each stakeholder group has substantial power in relation to the organization.
- Each stakeholder group pushes to maximize its own interests and perceives the interests of some or all other groups as incompatible with its own.
- The stakeholders keep changing what they expect (want) from the organization.
- The management team itself is divided into competing groups (coalitions).[28]

Taken together, these situations present a profile of the "worst case scenario." Fortunately, managers are not usually confronted with such a diversity and incompatibility of demands in setting goals. Nonetheless, Table 15–2 and this worst case scenario serve to illustrate that goal setting is in and of itself a major problem area in the decision-making process and often requires the use of keen judgment and negotiation skills.

Functions of Goal Setting

Even though goal setting is no easy task, the purposes served by the establishment of goals generally make the effort worthwhile. The establishment of goals has often been found to increase the efficiency and effectiveness of individuals, departments, and organizations. The following are among the more important functions of goals:

- Goals guide and direct behavior. They increase role clarity by focusing effort and attention in specific directions, thereby serving to reduce uncertainty in day-to-day decision making.
- Goals provide challenges and standards against which assessments of individual, departmental, or organizational performance can be made.

- Goals serve as a source of legitimacy. They justify various activities and the use of resources to pursue them.
- Goals define the rationale for the structure of an organization. They determine, in part, communication patterns, authority relationships, power relationships, and division of labor. Goals thus serve an organizing function.
- Goals reflect what the goal setters consider important, thereby providing a framework for planning and control activities.
- The study of goals and goal setting can provide insights into the behavior of groups and individuals.[29]

Individual Goal Setting

For the remainder of this section, we narrow our discussion to focus on key elements of goal setting for the individual employee or manager. We will hold in the background the types of issues and factors mentioned earlier that can complicate goal setting from an organization perspective. In addition, our discussion of management by objectives in the following section will address in more detail the setting of individual goals when employees work relatively independently of others (pooled interdependence) or are highly interdependent with others in performing their tasks (sequential and reciprocal interdependence).

Figure 15–2 presents a goal-setting model for individuals. It shows the key variables and sequence of relationships between them that should result in focused efforts and improved performance.

GOAL ATTRIBUTES   For the individual, *goal setting* is the process of developing, negotiating, and formalizing targets that he or she is responsible for accomplishing. Employees with unclear goals or no goals are more prone to work slowly, perform poorly, lack interest, and accomplish little. On the other hand, employees with clearly defined goals appear to be more energetic, challenged, and productive. They get things done on time and then move on to other activities (and goals).

FIGURE 15–2.
Goal-Setting Model for Individuals

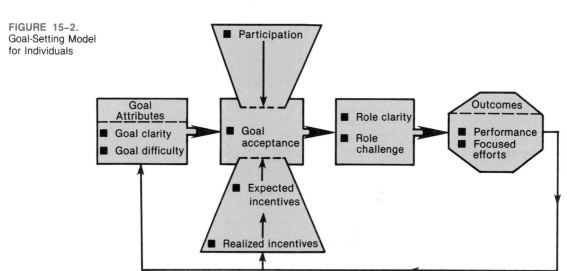

Goals can be implicit or explicit, vague or clearly defined, and self-imposed or externally imposed. Whatever their form, they serve to structure time and efforts for employees. Two key attributes of goals should be considered from the very beginning of individual goal setting:

- **Goal clarity.** Goals must be clear and specific if they are to be useful for directing effort. The employee thus will have clear knowledge of expectations which lead to role clarity.
- **Goal difficulty.** Goals should be moderately challenging. If they are too easy to attain, the employee may procrastinate or approach the goal lackadaisically. The employee may not accept too difficult a goal and, thus, not try to meet it.[30]

In general, clear and specific goals lead to higher performance than do vague or general goals. For example, it would be better to set a salesperson's goal at a specific amount to be sold than to set a goal of "trying to increase sales" or "doing your best." Also, goals that are difficult to attain will lead to higher performance than will easy goals. However, unrealistically high goals that can't be reached may not be accepted or may lead to high performance only in the short run, as employees eventually get discouraged and stop trying.

GOAL ACCEPTANCE, PARTICIPATION, AND INCENTIVES   Setting clear and challenging, but not impossible, goals may be thought of as necessary but *not* sufficient conditions for outcomes of high performance and focused efforts by individuals. **Goal acceptance** refers to the extent to which a goal is approved, favored, and recognized by the employee. The degree of acceptance could range from a deep personal commitment to the goal to rejection of and hostility towards it. In general, positive goal acceptance is more likely if the employee participates in setting the goal. If the employee does not expect or want to be involved in goal setting, the importance of participation on goal acceptance obviously would be substantially diminished.[31] However, even when it is necessary to assign the goal and thus not develop it with the participation of the employee, research suggests that more focused efforts and better performance will result than if no goal were set.[32]

The *expected incentives* for achieving the goal—whether it was one the employee participated in setting or was assigned to the employee—will play an important part in the degree of goal acceptance. The greater the extent to which the employee believes that positive incentives (merit pay raises, bonuses, promotions, opportunities to perform interesting tasks, and the like) are contingent on achieving the goal(s), the greater is the likelihood of goal acceptance.[33] Similarly, if the employee expects punishment as a result of not achieving the goal, there is a higher probability—everything else being equal—of goal acceptance.[34] However, recall that in Chapters 6 and 7, we discussed why punishment and the fear of punishment as a primary means of guiding behavior has a number of problems associated with it.

As suggested in Figure 15-2, the employee will compare expected incentives against the actual incentives realized (rewards). This comparison is based on the perceptions of the employee. If the perceived realized and expected incentives are in substantial agreement and positive, the incentive system is likely to continue to support goal acceptance. However, if the em-

TABLE 15-3   Some Relationships between Goal Setting and Performance

When Goals are	Performance will tend to be
■ Specific and clear	Higher
■ Vague	Lower
■ Difficult and challenging	Higher
■ Easy	Lower
■ Set participatively	Higher
■ Assigned	Lower
■ Accepted by employees	Higher
■ Rejected by employees	Lower
■ Accompanied by positive incentives	Higher
■ Accompanied by no incentives	Lower

ployee perceives that the realized incentives are much less than the expected incentives, he or she may experience a sense of inequity (Chapter 7) and eventually develop a lower level of goal acceptance.

ROLE CLARITY, CHALLENGE, AND OUTCOMES With specific, clear, and acceptable goals, the employee is more likely to comprehend the tasks that need to be performed and their relative priorities. In addition, these goals should provide a sense of motivation or role challenge. Thus, with a sense of role clarity and role challenge, the employee's efforts are more likely to be focused on job-related tasks, high levels of performance, and goal achievement. Table 15-3 provides a summary of a number of these ideas about the most likely links between goal setting and individual performance.

FEEDBACK Feedback serves as the mechanism for making goal setting and employee responses to their perceived levels of goal achievement a dynamic process that can change over time.[35] *Feedback* provides information to an employee and others about the outcomes and degree of goal achievement by the employee. With feedback, the individual is able to compare perceptions of expected incentives against realized incentives, which, in turn, can influence changes in the degree of goal acceptance.[36]

MANAGEMENT BY OBJECTIVES (MBO)

Management by objectives (MBO) is a philosophy and system of management that serves as both a planning aid and a way of organizational life, reflecting a positive philosophy about people and a participative management style. It is a widely used management approach; Hewlett-Packard and IBM are among the successful organizations with strong corporate cultures that use MBO.

Management by objectives involves managers and their subordinates in jointly setting goals for work performance and personal development;

evaluating progress toward these goals; and integrating individual, departmental, and organizational goals. At specified times in the future, the success of the employees in attaining the goals is evaluated.

While many people have contributed to the development of MBO, Peter Drucker coined the term *management by objectives* sometime between 1948 and 1951.[37] A variety of forms of MBO are used in practice. In this section we discuss two models of MBO: one that emphasizes the individual, and a second that focuses on the work team and interdependent groups. Goals and goal setting are important in both of these two models.[38]

Individual-Focused MBO

The **individual-focused MBO model** contains four basic components, each of which consists of a number of dimensions. As Figure 15–3 shows, these variables are goal setting, subordinate participation, implementation, and performance appraisal and feedback. The arrows indicate that a strong interrelationship exists among the components and that all should operate simultaneously to make the MBO process effective.

GOAL SETTING   Subordinates and superiors define and focus on goals of jobs rather than just on rules, activities, and procedures. *Goals* is used synonymously with *objectives, outputs, results, ends,* or *performance standards.* The objective-setting (goal-setting) process includes identifying specific areas of responsibility for jobs, developing standards of performance in each area, and, possibly, formulating a work plan for achieving the desired results. Table 15–4 provides a hypothetical example of selected task-related responsibility areas for a salesperson and possible specific goals in each area.

The responsibility areas in a particular job usually change less dramatically and less frequently over time than do the specific goals associated with each responsibility area. In Table 15–4, the salesperson will continually have sales volume as a responsibility area, but the specific levels and changes in

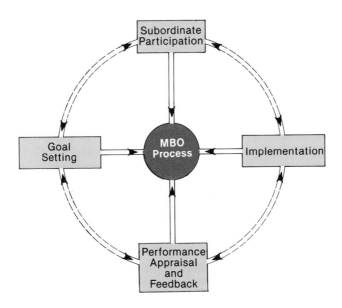

FIGURE 15–3.
Individual-Focused
MBO Model

TABLE 15-4   Hypothetical Responsibility Areas and Goals for a Salesperson

Selected Responsibility Area	Specific Goals
Sales volume	Increase sales volume by 8 percent.
Gross margin of goods sold	Keep average gross margin on goods sold at 40 percent.
Number of calls per day	Increase to 7 the average number of calls per day.
Order/call ratio	Increase order/call ratio to 20 percent.
Average order size	Increase average order size to $300.
New accounts	Generate 24 new accounts.

---

sales volume can vary dramatically because of general economic conditions, changed market acceptance, more or fewer opportunities in a sales territory, and so on.

A variety of prescriptions have been offered as to *how* managers should set goals with subordinates, of which the following is one set:

- *State what must be done.* If you are setting goals with a subordinate, you may find a job description helpful. It should list the tasks to be performed, the outcomes expected, the other jobs with which this one coordinates, necessary equipment, supervisory duties, and so on. Critical job requirements, upon which job success depends, can further clarify the job description.

- *Specify how performance will be measured.* Often you can use time, money, or physical units. Sometimes, though, success is more qualitative and cannot be measured in numbers. Yet you can still define it by specifying behaviors or actions that you know will lead to success.

- *Specify the standard of performance.* A readily accepted, but not the most precise approach, is to start goal setting by letting previous performance set the standard. Most employees consider their average previous performance, or that of their group, to be a fair goal. Performance in some jobs, though, cannot be measured so precisely. Or, the job may be unique or so new that no previous performance measures are available. If so, goal setting becomes a matter of judgment, in which you should involve the workers.

- *Set a deadline to reach the goal.* Some goals lend themselves to daily or weekly accomplishment. Others call for monthly, quarterly, or annual time spans for accomplishment.

- *Rank goals in order of their importance.* Manager and subordinate must agree on goal priority to avoid misunderstandings.

- *Optional step: Rate goals as to difficulty and importance.* You may need to be more precise when you deal with multiple goals, as in the case of an employee's job description or a departmental goal. If so, follow this procedure:
  1. Rate each goal's importance. Give the most important goal a 10 and the least important goal a 1. Continue by assigning numbers between 1 and 10 to intermediate goals to show their relative importance compared to 1 and 10.
  2. Rate each goal's difficulty in the same manner.

3. Calculate the employee's fulfillment of each goal as a percentage.
4. Multiply difficulty of achievement by percent fulfillment to get a score. Add the scores for the multiple goals to get a total performance score.
5. Compute an absolute score by dividing the total performance score by the highest possible score (the score that the worker would get if attainment of each goal was 100%).[39]

PARTICIPATION   A moderate-to-high level of participation by subordinates in the goal setting process may be most effective. Before subordinates can participate significantly, sufficient discretionary content in the job must already exist or an increase be planned. Discretionary content enables employees to plan and control in addition to merely doing what they are told. Management by objectives requires increasing or stimulating subordinates' planning and control tasks. Thus highly routine and programmed jobs usually require redesign before applying the MBO approach to them.

IMPLEMENTATION   Implementation of the individual-focused MBO model requires translating the outcomes from the goal setting process into new day-to-day behaviors that ultimately will lead to the attainment of the desired goals. The implementation phase is often accompanied by action planning that focuses on how goals are to be achieved. In the implementation step, superiors must give greater latitude and choice to subordinates, perhaps by discontinuing the hour-by-hour and day-to-day management of their activities. Superiors must be available to coach and counsel subordinates, as needed. They must play a more helping or facilitating role and less of a judgmental role. Superiors should hold periodic meetings during the year with subordinates to review progress, discuss any assistance needed, and make any necessary changes in goals. Goals should be changed or modified as needed. This prevents employees from perceiving MBO as a rigid system and encourages them to address major new problems or changes as they occur.

PERFORMANCE APPRAISAL AND FEEDBACK   In the individual-focused MBO model, subordinates develop a clear understanding of their progress through performance appraisal and feedback. Feedback is a key element of MBO because it provides knowledge of the correspondence between the employees' goals and the extent to which they attained them. The knowledge of behavioral results is often essential to changes in job performance and personal development in the form of new skills, attitudes, and motivation. **Performance appraisal** refers to: (1) the *identification* of measurement factors or criteria (such as goals) against which to evaluate performance; (2) the *measurement* of performance against such criteria; (3) the *review* of performance levels attained by individuals; and (4) the *development* of future performance.[40]

Unlike some other approaches, MBO places heavy emphasis on subordinates' evaluating their own performance. Subordinates who know their own goals and the measures of achievement indicators for these goals should gain substantial insight into their performance and the possible need for modified behaviors. For example, two goals for the salesperson in Table 15–4 were an increase of 8 percent in sales volume and maintenance of the average gross margin on goods sold at 40 percent. So long as the salesperson receives feedback about performance in these areas, a concrete self-understanding of outcomes in relation to these goals is possible.

Unfortunately, the review process is often not this simple. Factors other than the salesperson's own behavior, such as product quality, may create gaps between the stated goals and the outcomes. Also, significant parts of many jobs may not lend themselves to the development of goals that can serve as indicators of performance. As we noted earlier, evaluations of goals based on judgement can vary from person to person. Thus the problem of determining whether a goal was achieved may exist even before questions of why it was or was not attained can be answered.

Although MBO does not prescribe a passive role for superiors in the performance review and feedback process, it does require superiors to play more of a helping and mutual problem-solving role than a judgmental role. Some managers have interpreted this element, and thus the whole MBO process, as managerially weak. This criticism is not valid; managers can discipline, demote, and dismiss individuals under the MBO system. In fact, the rationale for any such action should be readily apparent under the system; therefore it should be easier for superiors to confront the necessity of making such decisions. On the other hand, the MBO process should minimize the need for such decisions.

Five of the major characteristics of effective performance appraisals under MBO (or any management approach) are as follows:

- High levels of subordinate participation in the performance-appraisal process result in employees being satisfied with both the appraisal process and the manager who conducted it.

- Employee acceptance of the appraisal and satisfaction with the manager increases to the extent that the manager is supportive of the employee.

- Discussing problems that may be hampering the subordinate's current job performance and working toward solutions has a positive effect on productivity.

- The number of criticisms in an appraisal interview correlates positively with the number of defensive reactions shown by the employee. Those areas of job performance that are most criticized are least likely to show an improvement. There appears to be a chain reaction between criticisms made by the manager and defensive reactions shown by the subordinate, with little or no change in the subordinate's behavior.

- The more that subordinates are allowed to voice opinions during the appraisal, the more satisfied they will feel with the appraisal.[41]

Effective and accurate performance appraisal is very difficult to achieve.[42] Virtually all the problems, individual differences, and biases associated with human judgments and interactions that have been discussed in previous chapters (see, especially, Chapter 4) and earlier in this chapter seem to find their way into the performance appraisal process. Although these problems and biases probably cannot be eliminated, they can be substantially reduced by following the guidelines we have presented.

ASSESSMENT Critics have attacked the individual-focused MBO model, particularly with respect to ways that organizations actually apply it. These criticisms relate mainly to how individuals actually use the process rather than to how it is supposed to be used. Some of these criticisms are:

- Too much emphasis is placed on a reward–punishment psychology (that is, people are rewarded for accomplishing goals and punished for not doing so).

- An excessive amount of paperwork and red tape develops—the very things that MBO is supposed to reduce.

- The process is really controlled and imposed from the top, allowing little opportunity for real employee participation.

- The process turns into a zero-sum (win–lose) game between superiors and subordinates.

- Aspects of jobs that can be assessed quantitatively rather than qualitatively receive undue emphasis.

- Too much emphasis on individual goals and performance drives out recognition of the need for collaborative teamwork and group goals. Individuals may optimize their own goals to the detriment of overall goals.[43]

The experience of a certain engineering department provides one example of a successful application of goal setting within the basic framework of the individual-focused MBO model.

In Practice: The Engineering Department

The study was conducted in a company engaged in the design and manufacture of various types of walk-in vans, parcel delivery vans, truck bodies, cargo haulers, flat-bed carries and mobile classrooms. Many of the products were custom designed in the company's engineering department to meet customer specifications. The changes involved the entire engineering department, which consisted of twelve people including the department manager. Three of the staff members were engineers who had responsibility for the customer engineering designs for the company's products. Of the remaining eight staff members, four were in drafting, one was the drafting supervisor, one was responsible for cost estimates on the engineering projects, another was the bill-of-materials writer, and one was the departmental secretary.

Prior to the changes, all projects within the department were assigned to subordinates by the manager. Project due dates were established unilaterally by the manager, taking into consideration each subordinate's existing workload. There was little, if any, input from subordinates concerning project assignments and no input regarding project due dates.

Problem definition

The engineers' missed completion dates and project design errors were the key problem areas facing the department manager. Because of the sequencing of work activities, the effectiveness and efficiency of the entire engineering department and of the purchasing and production departments depended on the engineers completing their designs accurately and on time.

Outcome measures

The effectiveness of the changes were evaluated with two measures which reflected the three engineers' work output. The first measure was the number of missed completion dates per week. The second measure was the number of engineering design errors discovered during the work week.

Feedback apparatus

The feedback apparatus used in the study was an Engineer Project Scheduling Board (EPSB). It measured four feet by six feet and was faced with over fifty movable magnetic strips. Each strip measured one and one-half inches wide by thirty-three inches long. Information about special projects within the engineering department was written on these strips with erasable ink. The information pertained to the project due date, the person who was responsible for the project, and a brief project description. Each strip was then physically moved into one of three distinct areas of the EPSB to indicate the project's current status. Via the movable magnetic strips, the EPSB provided public feedback about the current status of all special projects.

Procedures

The changes occurred over a 20 week period. The engineering manager met with departmental personnel to explain the project. First, the purpose of the project was described. Second, the participative goal setting procedure was explained to the employees. To initiate participative goal setting, the manager asked each departmental member whose projects would be listed on the EPSB to continue keeping his or her project list from the previous attempt at dealing with the problems. However, contrary to previous use of these lists, a person's project list now would consist of all assigned projects and any projects voluntarily initiated by the staff member. The project lists would provide the basic information for the participative goal setting part of the change. The participative goal setting would occur during a weekly meeting between the department manager and each individual whose projects would be placed on the EPSB. During this meeting they would review the individual's project list and jointly decide which projects fulfilled the criteria for being placed on the EPSB. Once the manager and the employee mutually agreed that a given project was to be placed on the EPSB, they would then negotiate a realistic project due date for which the subordinate would be held accountable. Provision was made for renegotiating due dates in the event unanticipated problems arose. Third, the physical layout of the EPSB, the procedure for using the EPSB, and its relationship to the participative goal setting procedures were explained to the employees. Next, the department manager answered any questions the staff members had concerning the goal setting procedures, the EPSB, or the procedure for using the EPSB. Finally, the manager solicited suggestions for improving any of the changes. After the meeting, the manager distributed to the staff members a memo summarizing the information presented during the meeting.

The departmental secretary updated the EPSB on a daily basis and compiled records of missed completion dates and project design errors for the three engineers. These records were submitted to the department manager for his review and for the researcher's use in evaluating the effectiveness of the changes. The department manager reviewed each week's figures with the appropriate person during the individual goal setting meeting at the beginning of the following week. He also conducted informal daily reviews.

Outcomes and follow-up

The engineering department has used, with some modification, the new goal setting and feedback procedures for more than a year. The department manager reported continued success in keeping project errors and missed completion dates at a level which was consistent with the pattern of results found during the last six weeks of the change period. The changes were considered a success and departmental personnel continued to exercise much greater self-management.[44]

Team-Focused MBO

The **team- focused MBO model** is fundamentally consistent with the key elements of the individual-focused MBO model. However, the goal-setting process includes entire work groups, as well as individuals. The team-focused model attempts to overcome two major deficiencies in the individual-focused MBO model. First, the team model explicitly recognizes the sequential and reciprocal interdependencies between jobs, especially at the supervisory and managerial levels. Second, it encourages integration of goals among the individuals occupying the interdependent jobs instead of placing the entire responsibility for integration upon the common superior.

IMPLEMENTATION As with the individual-focused MBO model, the degree of participation and influence of work groups in setting goals can vary widely in the team-focused MBO model. One process for implementing the team-focused MBO model can be summarized as follows:

- In team meetings, top executives develop overall organization goals to be achieved within a certain time period, primarily on the basis of consensus. (Prior inputs and interaction from lower levels is assumed.)
- Departmental or unit goals to facilitate the attainment of overall organizational goals are again developed in team or group sessions, primarily through consensus.
- Individuals develop their own goals within this framework. However, a major difference from the individual-focused MBO model in this phase is that in the team-focused model, team members may discuss one another's goals, suggest changes, and openly discuss the interdependent nature of their responsibilities.
- While performance reviews take place between superiors and subordinates, matters of concern to the team are discussed in regularly scheduled team meetings.[45]

ASSESSMENT The team-focused MBO model probably has the greatest potential for success only if certain conditions exist. First, a real need for integration among individuals must exist. Second, the top-management group must cooperate and offer mutual assistance instead of engaging in political power struggles. Third, the participants must have some degree of skill in group processes and interpersonal relations.

SUMMARY

This chapter focused on decision making and goal setting within organizations, primarily from a managerial perspective. Managerial decision making was characterized as involving unending flows and crosscurrents of decisions. Five phases of managerial decision making were presented: problem recognition, problem interpretation, attention to problems, courses of action, and aftermath. We emphasized that these phases do not unfold for real-world managers in the neat and orderly sequence presented in this chapter. We also noted that intuition and creativity are likely to be very important in addressing the most difficult type of decision problem: when there is disagreement over the best course of action to pursue, as well as the goals to be sought.

The functions of goal setting and the potential impact of stakeholders on this process were examined. An individual-focused model of goal setting was presented. The variables included in this model are goal clarity, goal difficulty, goal acceptance, participation, expected and realized incentives, role clarity and challenge, outcomes that include focused efforts and improved performance, and feedback. The key sequential relationships between these variables were discussed.

Management by objectives (MBO) was described as both a philosophy and system of management. Two models of MBO were discussed: the individual-focused MBO model, and the team-focused MBO model. A set of specific prescriptions that can be used by a manager in setting goals with a subordinate were presented. Performance appraisal and feedback under MBO was discussed, including the five major characteristics of effective performance appraisals. Some of the criticisms of MBO applications were also noted.

KEY WORDS AND CONCEPTS

Aftermath
Creativity
Goal acceptance
Goal clarity
Goal difficulty
Goal setting
Goals
Individual-focused MBO model
Intuition

Management by objectives (MBO)
Managerial decision making
Organizational learning
Performance appraisal
Problem interpretation
Structured problems
Team-focused MBO model
Unstructured problems

DISCUSSION QUESTIONS

1. How is the decision-making process for managers likely to differ from that of non-managerial employees within organizations?

2. How might intuition and creativity help managers who experience difficulties in problem identification and problem interpretation?

3. Do you think that U.S. firms could adopt the practices used in Japanese firms to maintain and increase "organizational learning"? Explain.

4. How might technology and the design of jobs influence a manager's ability to engage in setting goals with an individual employee?

5. What relationships exist between the expectancy theory of motivation (see Chapter 7) and the individual-focused goal-setting model?

6. Can Management by objectives operate in both mechanistic and organic systems? (See chapter 14.) Explain.

7. Why is performance appraisal one of the most difficult, controversial, and emotionally laden areas of managerial decision making?

MANAGEMENT INCIDENTS AND CASES

Custom Scales, Inc.

Company History

Custom Scales, Inc. (CSI) was formally established in St. Louis in 1964 as a manufacturer of industrial scales. During that year, George Babb's small operation (Babb's Scales) was taken over by a local group of bankers that offered him 12.5% of the stock of CSI, the position of the Chief Executive Officer, and a sizable salary in return for his business. His business was more or less a family concern. He owned 100% of it, had no loans whatsoever, and additionally had a significant number of patented designs that were making unique inroads in the Benelux (Belgium, Netherlands, Luxemberg) markets. In fact, in 1963 his brother Steve, who was living in Brussels, had sold the Babb's Scales' entire production, almost $250,000 worth of industrial scales. At that point George Babb's operation employed a total of 16 workers, plus his wife and his sister-in-law, for general administration and accounting purposes.

CSI proved to be an engineering and marketing success. Over the years, CSI increased by almost 20% annually and expanded both in the domestic and in the foreign markets (see Exhibit 1). However, it must be stated that CSI never developed a management system for a corporation of its new size. Most practices and policies continued to be loosely administered with most departments growing independently and often instituting conflicting objectives. CSI's key personnel, their respective position, and some information with respect to them are presented in Exhibit 2.

In January 1985, almost 60% of CSI's 424 employees were unionized by the International Brotherhood of Engineering Workers (Local 76), the rest being made up of salaried administrative and engineering employees along with non-union foremen and technicians. Basically, however, all of them were enjoying the same fringe benefits package (insurance, vacation, sick leave, and so on) although the company had a less

---

EXHIBIT 1   Sales Volume ($000)

	1975	1977	1979	1981	1983	1985
Domestic	3,976	5,078	6,204	7,229	8,677	9,371
Foreign	790	816	1,220	2,421	4,421	6,974
Total	4,766	5,894	7,424	9,650	12,891	16,345

EXHIBIT 2   Key Personnel

Name	Position	Age	Years with CSI	Education
George Babb	CEO	61	27	B.S.M.E.
Dennis Hrebec	Production Manager	51	16	B.S.I.E.
Don Black	Engineering Manager	44	2	B.S.M.E.
Steve Babb	Sales Manager	58	24	B.S.B.A.
Andy Parker	Treasurer	36	3	M.B.A., CPA
Ralph Towne	Personnel Director	49	14	M.S. (School Admin.)

closely supervised attitude towards the non-union employees (coffee breaks, time off, no time-clock punching, etc.)

The Situation

On August 9, 1981, Jim Wymann (then age 28) was hired as an engineering technician at (pay) Grade 4. Exactly two weeks later, Martin Turner, 26, was hired also as a Grade 4 engineering technician. Both men were employed in parallel positions within CSI's Engineering Department.

In January 1983, Jim's wife and daughter were involved in a serious automobile accident. As a result of his family's mishap and in order to be of assistance during that period of suffering, Jim first took all his sick leave. Then, he exhausted his 2-week vacation and finally asked for a 30-day leave of absence without pay. Under the circumstances this leave of absence was granted, and Jim returned promptly to his post in the first week of March.

In July 1983, Donald Black was hired by CSI as Engineering Manager. During the following two years, Mr. Black had ample opportunities to evaluate Jim and Martin, and he was convinced that both men were of equal talent and work ability. Further, he was aware of the unfortunate accident that Jim's family had experienced, but he was not aware of the leave of absence that Jim had taken in February, 1983.

Within the Engineering Department two positions were to open for Grade 5. The first, on June 1, 1985, was due to the resignation of Todd Johnson; and the second, on September 1, 1985, was due to the retirement of Ed Hayes. Mr. Black had concluded that Martin and Jim were excellent choices for these positions. Since no promotion policies were established in CSI, the Engineering Manager decided to use seniority as the only determining factor of promotion (Grade 5 salary was about 15% above Grade 4).

Don Black decided to handle the promotion issue by himself. On June 9, 1985, he called the Personnel Department. Since Ralph Towne, the Personnel Director, was (often) extending his weekend by one day, Black asked Towne's secretary Sally Gossupton for some specific information. He wanted to know the exact dates and at which pay grades his nine technicians had entered the company.

Half an hour later, Sally called Black and gave him a complete list with names, ages, dates of entrance at CSI, and respective grades. The next morning, the Engineering Manager, confident that he knew exactly what he was doing, called both Jim and Martin into his office and said, "As you probably can guess, I need a new Grade 5 technician on July 1 to take Todd's place. He is leaving us at the end of this month. Since you have both been good employees of equal ability, I will follow strict seniority and promote you, Jim, on July 1 and you, Martin, on September 1 to replace Ed Hayes who is retiring." Neither Martin nor Jim expressed any feelings about the promotions, and the discussion was quickly diverted to a drafting issue.

After discussing the matter that evening with his personal friend and lawyer, Roger Carter, Jim decided that he was (as Roger said) "getting the wrong end of the stick!" The next morning, Martin entered Mr. Black's office and adamantly complained that he had seniority, ". . . I like Jim, he's a nice guy, but I have seniority over him; he took 30 days off when Sarah and his daughter damn near died when some drunk (expletive deleted) ran 'em off the road in a snowstorm." Before Martin could explain his case in detail, Black interrupted him by saying, "Settle down, Martin, I admit I didn't know about the 30 days . . . let me check it out with Ralph Towne;

I'll let you know by noon tomorrow at the latest." Seeing that it was not wise to prolong the conversation at that time, Martin left the Engineering Manager's office.

The Engineering Manager immediately went to Ralph Towne's office and closed the door behind him (so that Sally could not hear). Black explained the problem, and the two managers openly discussed the situation, quickly agreeing to the facts. Towne then replied, "Don, it's your problem, not mine! You'll have to make the ultimate decision." Black countered, "I can't! This is a personnel matter. What do you think Custom Scales pays you for, keeping a muzzle on Sally and playing golf two or three times a week on company time?" Towne snapped back, "I'm not going to sit here and listen to that line. Just leave my office and make your decision. Leave me out of this. I'll support you either way." The Engineering Manager stormed out muttering to himself as he drew a peculiar stare from Sally Gossupton.

Immediately, Don Black called Martin into his office and told him that Jim and he were both being promoted to Grade 5 on July 1. Martin said, "fine" and considered the matter as closed. The next morning the Engineering Manager issued a memo to both Jim and Martin confirming the July 1 date and sent two copies to accounting and a copy to personnel.

About one week later, Andy Parker, Treasurer, called Don Black stating, "You can't promote both men in July, you'll be overexpended on your payroll; we can't tolerate that!" Don Black replied, "I'm in charge of engineering. I have to run my department and have to get the most work out of my employees; I'm sure you can figure out a way to please those beancounters from Ross and Pickering (CSI's audit firm). Besides, that's your problem, not mine." Black hung up before Parker had time to reply.

George Babb was out of town on a personal vacation in South Africa when all of this took place. As was customary, Dennis Hrebec, Production Manager, was left in charge of CSI during his absence. Hrebec became aware of the situation through a conversation with Parker over lunch the next day (Friday). The following Monday morning, he summoned Black, Parker, and Towne for a meeting. Black half-heartedly apologized to both Parker and Towne but insisted that there must be an easy way out of the situation and pleaded that July 1 stand as promotion date for both technicians. All four men expressed a desire to keep the word of the incident from spreading and not to let George Babb find out. They agreed to meet and work out a solution over drinks around 5:30 at the nearby "Aqua-Gate Lounge."[46]

Questions

1. Study the origin of the promotion problem. How could it have been avoided? Who was at fault?

2. List the possible options that the Engineering Manager has: (a) before making any announcements on promotions; and (b) after the incident with the Personnel Director and his refusal to intervene.

3. Consider yourself in the position of the Engineering Manager (new in the corporation, basically design oriented, etc.). What would you have done differently? What kinds of information and from what sources would you have sought?

4. Do you think Martin has any grounds (legal or otherwise) to stand on if Jim is promoted before him?

5. Explore the issue of Black's responsibility in decision making outside of his professional exper-

tise. What are his added obligations because of his present management post?

6. Study the origin of the promotion problem in the corporate framework. Pinpoint the areas that lack coordinated policies and complete communication lines.

Make a list of guidelines that should prevent similar incidents.

7. Comment on Black's remarks to both Towne and Parker. What effects (both direct and indirect) might these remarks have on the case?

REFERENCES

1. Excerpted from Magnet, M. How Top Managers Make a Company's Toughest Decision. *Fortune*, March 18, 1985, 52–59. Used with permission. © 1985 Time Inc. All rights reserved.

2. The perspective of this discussion was developed from McCall Jr., M. W., and Kaplan, R. E. *Whatever It Takes: Decision Makers at Work*. Englewood Cliffs, N.J.: Prentice-Hall, 1985.

3. Huber, G. *Managerial Decision Making*. Glenview, Ill.: Scott, Foresman, 1980; McCann, J. E. Design Guidelines for Social Problem-Solving Interventions. *Journal of Applied Behavioral Science*, 1983, *19*, 177–192; Meyer, A. D. Mingling Decision-Making Metaphors. *Academy of Management Review*, 1984, *9*, 6–17; Nutt, P. C. Types of Organizational Decision Processes. *Administrative Science Quarterly*, 1984, *29*, 414–450.

4. McCall Jr., M. W., and Kaplan, R. *Whatever It Takes: Decision Makers at Work*. Englewood Cliffs, N.J.: Prentice-Hall, 1985, xv.

5. Sayles, L. *Leadership: What Effective Managers Really Do . . . and How They Do It*. New York: McGraw-Hill, 1979, 15.

6. Sayles, 17.

7. Hambrick, D. C., and Mason, P. A. Upper Echelons: The Organizations as a Reflection of Its Top Managers. *Academy of Management Review*, 1984, *9*, 193–206; Ramaprasad, A., and Mitroff, I. I. On Formulating Strategic Problems. *Academy of Management Review*, 1984, 9, 597–605.

8. Janis, I. L., and Mann, L. *Decision Making: A Psychological Analysis of Conflict, Choice, and Commitment*. New York: Free Press, 1977, 81–106.

9. Daft, R. L., and Weick, K. E. Toward a Model of Organizations as Interpretation Systems. *Academy of Management Review*, 1984, *9*, 284–295; Gioia, D. A., and Poole, P. P. Scripts in Organizational Behavior. *Academy of Management Review*, 1984, *9*, 449–459; Shrivastava, P. Knowledge Systems for Strategic Decision Making. *Journal of Applied Behavioral Science*, 1985, *21*, 95–107; Weiner, B.

"Spontaneous" Causal Thinking. *Psychological Bulletin*, 1985, *97*, 74–84.

10. Basadur, M., and Finkbeiner, C. T. Measuring Preference for Ideation in Creative Problem-Solving Training. *Journal of Applied Behavioral Science*, 1985, *21*, 37–49; Eden, C., Jones, S., and Sims, D. *Messing About in Problems: An Informal Structured Approach to Their Identification and Management*. New York: Pergamon, 1983; O'Reilly III, C. A. The Use of Information in Organizational Decision Making: A Model and Some Propositions. In L. L. Cummings and B. M. Staw (Eds.) *Research in Organizational Behavior*. Greenwich, Conn.: JAI Press, 1983, 103–139.

11. Peters, T., and Austin, N. A Passion for Excellence. *Fortune*, May 13, 1985, 20.

12. Anderson, P. A. Decision Making by Objection and the Cuban Missile Crisis. *Administrative Science Quarterly*, 1983, *28*, 201–222; Osigweh, C. A. Puzzles or Problems? Cutting Through the Manager's Dilemma. *Business Horizons*, May–June 1985, 69–73.

13. Nonaka, I., and Johansson, J. K. Japanese Management: What About the "Hard" Skills? *Academy of Management Review*, 1985, *10*, 183. Also see Smith, L. Creativity Starts to Blossom in Japan. *Fortune*, October 29, 1984, 144–153.

14. Adapted from Nonaka and Johansson, 181–191. Used with permission.

15. Tjosvold, D. Effects of Crisis Orientation on Managers' Approach to Controversy in Decision Making. *Academy of Management Journal*, 1984, *27*, 130–138.

16. Developed from The Bhopal Tragedy Has Union Carbide Reeling. *Business Week*, December 14, 1984, 32; Kirkland Jr., R. I. Union Carbide: Coping with Catastrophe. *Fortune*, January 7, 1985, 50–53; Union Carbide Fights for its Life. *Business Week*, December 24, 1984, 52–56.

17. Taylor, R. N. *Behavioral Decision Making*. Glenview, Ill.: Scott, Foresman, 1984; Grandori, A. A Prescriptive Contingency View of Organizational Decision Making. *Administrative Science Quarterly*, 1984, *29*, 192–209; Mintzberg, H. Raisinghani,

D., and Theoret, A. The Structure of "Unstructured" Decision Processes. *Administrative Science Quarterly,* 1976, *21,* 246–275.

18. Stahl, M. J., and Zimmerer, T. W. Modeling Strategic Acquisition Policies: A Simulation of Executives' Acquisition Decisions. *Academy of Management Journal,* 1984, *27,* 369–383; Harrison, J. R., and March, J. G. Decision Making and Postdecision Surprises. *Administrative Science Quarterly,* 1984, *29,* 26–42.

19. Developed from Koten, J., and Kelman, S. How Coke's Decision to offer 2 Colas Undid 4½ Years of Planning. *Wall Street Journal,* July 15, 1985, 1, 10; Coke's Man on the Spot. *Business Week,* July 29, 1985, 56–61; Fisher, A. B. Coke's Brand-Loyalty Lesson. *Fortune,* August 5, 1985, 44–46.

20. Nystrom, P. C., and Starbuck, W. H. To Avoid Organizational Crises, Unlearn. *Organizational Dynamics,* Spring 1984, 53–65; Sims Jr., H. P. and Gioia, D. A. Performance Failure: Executive Response to Self-Serving Bias. *Business Horizons,* January–February 1984, 64–71.

21. McCall, M. W., and Kaplan, R. E. Consequences. *Issues and Observations.* Greensboro, NC: Center for Creative Leadership, February 1985, 7.

22. McCall and Kaplan, 8.

23. Thompson, J., and Tuden, A. Strategies, Structures and Processes of Organizational Decision. In J. Thompson et al, 3d ed., *Comparative Studies in Administration.* Pittsburgh: University of Pittsburgh Press, 1959.

24. Agor, W. H. *Intuitive Management: Integrating Left and Right Brain Management Skills.* Englewood Cliffs, N.J.: Prentice-Hall, 1984; Isenberg, D. J. How Senior Managers Think. *Harvard Business Review,* November–December 1984, 81–90; Keegan, W. J. *Judgments, Choices, and Decisions: Effective Management through Self-Knowledge.* New York: John Wiley, 1984.

25. Rowan, R. Those Business Hunches are More than Blind Faith. *Fortune,* May 23, 1979, 111–114.

26. Oxenfeldt, A., Miller, A., and Dickinson, R. *A Basic Approach to Executive Decision Making.* New York: AMACOM, 1978, 157. Also see Bessinger, R. C., and Svojanen, W. W. (Eds.) *Management and the Brain: An Integrative Approach to Organizational Behavior.* Atlanta: Business Publishing Division, Georgia State University, 1983; Rice, B. Imagination to Go. *Psychology Today,* May 1984, 48–56; Sinetar, M. Entrepreneurs, Chaos, and Creativity—Can Creative People Really Survive Large Company Structure? *Sloan Management Review,* Winter 1985,

57–62; Ward, B. Centers of Imagination. *Sky,* June 1985, 72–80.

27. French, W. L., Kast, F. E., Rosenzweig, J. E. *Understanding Human Behavior in Organizations.* New York: Harper & Row, 1985, 68–71; Donaldson, G., and Lorsch, J. W. *Decision Making at the Top: The Shaping of Strategic Direction.* New York: Basic Books, 1983; Donaldson, G. Financial Goals and Strategic Consequences. *Harvard Business Review,* May–June 1985, 57–66.

28. Bazerman, M. H., and Lewicki, R. J. Contemporary Research Directions in the Study of Negotiating in Organizations: A Selective Review. *Journal of Occupational Behavior,* 1985, *6,* 1–17; Gaertner, G. H., and Ramnarayan, S. Organizational Effectiveness: An Alternative Perspective. *Academy of Management Review,* 1983, *8,* 97–107; Murnighan, J. K. Coalitions in Decision-Making Groups: Organizational Analogs. *Organizational Behavior and Human Performance,* 1985, *35,* 1–26; Zammuto, R. F. A Comparison of Multiple Constituency Models of Organizational Effectiveness. *Academy of Management Review,* 1984, *9,* 606–616.

29. Hrebniak, L. G. *Complex Organizations.* St. Paul, Minn.: West, 1978; Richards, M. D. *Setting Strategic Goals and Objectives,* 2d ed. St. Paul, Minn.: West, 1986.

30. Fellner, D. J., and Sulzer-Azaroff, B. A Behavioral Analysis of Goal Setting. *Journal of Organizational Behavior Management,* 1984, *6,* 33–51; Naylor, J. D., and Ilgen, D. R. Goal Setting: A Theoretical Analysis of Motivational Technology. In B. M. Staw and L. L. Cummings (Eds.) *Research in Organizational Behavior.* Greenwich, Conn.: JAI Press, 1984, 95–140.

31. Erez, M., Early, P. C., and Hulin, C. L. The Impact of Participation on Goal Acceptance and Performance: A Two-Step Model. *Academy of Management Journal,* 1985, *28,* 50–66; Erez, M., and Kanfer, F. H. The Role of Goal Acceptance in Goal Setting and Task Performance. *Academy of Management Review,* 1983, *8,* 454–463.

32. Locke, E. A., Frederick, E., Buckner, E., and Bobko, P. Effect of Previously Assigned Goals on Self-Set Goals and Performance. *Journal of Applied Psychology,* 1984, *69,* 694–699; Latham, G. P., and Steels, T. P. The Motivational Effects of Participation versus Goal Setting on Performance. *Academy of Management Journal,* 1983, *26,* 406–417; Shing-Yung Chang, G., and Lorenzi, P. The Effects of Participation versus Assigned Goal Setting on Intrinsic Motivation. *Journal of Management,* 1983, *9,* 55–64; Erez, M., and Zidon, I. Effect of Goal Acceptance on the Relationship of Goal Difficulty to Perfor-

mance. *Journal of Applied Psychology,* 1984, *69,* 69–78.

33. McElroy, J. C. Inside the Teaching Machine: Integrating Attribution and Reinforcement Theories. *Journal of Management,* 1985, *11,* 123–141; Tolchinsky, P. D., and King, D. C. Do Goals Mediate the Effects of Incentives on Performance? *Academy of Management Review,* 1980, *5,* 455–467; Overstreet, J. S. The Case for Merit Bonuses. *Business Horizons,* May–June 1985, 53–58.

34. Arvey, R. D., and Ivancevich, J. M. Punishment in Organizations: A Review, Propositions, and Research Suggestions. *Academy of Management Review,* 1980, *5,* 123–132.

35. Crino, M. D., and White, M. C. Feedback Effects in Intrinsic/Extrinsic Reward Paradigms. *Journal of Management,* 1982, *8,* 95–108; Kim, J. S. Effect of Behavior Plus Outcome Goal Setting and Feedback on Employee Satisfaction and Performance. *Academy of Management Journal,* 1984, *27,* 139–149; Refer, R. A., and Wallin, J. A. The Effects of Training, Goal Setting, and Knowledge of Results on Safe Behavior: A Component Analysis. *Academy of Management Journal,* 1984, *27,* 544–560.

36. Abelson, M. A. The Impact of Goal Change on Prominent Perceptions and Behaviors of Employees. *Journal of Management,* 1983, *9,* 65–79; Liden, R. C., and Mitchell, T. R. Reactions to Feedback: The Role of Attributions. *Academy of Management Journal,* 1985, *28,* 291–308; Garland, H. Relation of Effort-Performance Expectancy to Performance in Goal-Setting Experiments. *Journal of Applied Psychology,* 1984, *69,* 79–84.

37. Greenwood, R. G. Management by Objectives: As Developed by Peter Drucker, Assisted by Harold Smiddy. *Academy of Management Review,* 1981, *6,* 225–230. Also see Wechrich, H. *Management Excellence: Productivity through MBO.* New York: McGraw-Hill, 1985.

38. Locke, E. A., Shaw, K. N., Saari, L. M., and Latham, G. P. Goal Setting and Task Performance: 1969–1980. *Psychological Bulletin,* 1981, *90,* 125–152.

39. Locke, E. A., and Latham, G. P. *Goal Setting: A Motivational Technique that Works!* Englewood Cliffs, N.J.: Prentice-Hall, 1984, 27–40.

40. Carroll, S. J., and Schneier, C. E. *Performance Appraisal and Review Systems.* Glenview, Ill.: Scott, Foresman, 1982, 3. Also see Ilgen, D. R., and Feldman, J. M. Performance Appraisal: A Process Focus. In L. L. Cummings and B. M. Staw (Eds.) *Research in Organizational Behavior.* Greenwich, Conn.: JAI Press, 1983, 141–197; Lee, C. Increasing Performance Appraisal Effectiveness: Matching Task Types of Appraisal Process and Rater Training. *Academy of Management Review,* 1985, *10,* 322–331.

41. Burke, R. J., Weitzel, W., and Weir, T. Characteristics of Effective Employee Performance Review and Development Interviews: Replication and Extension. *Personnel Psychology,* 1978, *31,* 903–919; Edwards, M. R., Borman, W. C., and Sproull, J. R. Solving the Double Bind in Performance Appraisal: A Saga of Wolves, Sloths, and Eagles. *Business Horizons,* May–June 1985, 59–68; Sashkin, M. *Assessing Performance Appraisal* San Diego, Calif.: University Associates, 1981.

42. Cardy, A. L., and Kehoe, J. F. Rater Selective Attention Ability and Appraisal Effectiveness: The Effect of a Cognitive Style on the Accuracy of Differentiation among Ratees. *Journal of Applied Psychology,* 1984, *69,* 589–594; Peters, L. H., O'Connor, E. J., Weekley, J., Pooyan, A., Frank, B., and Erenkrantz, B. Sex Bias and Managerial Evaluations: A Replication and Extension. *Journal of Applied Psychology,* 1984, *69,* 349–352; Banks, C. G. and Roberson, L. Performance Appraisers as Test Developers. *Academy of Management Review,* 1985, *10,* 128–142.

43. Kondrasuk, J. N., Flager, K., Morrow, D., and Thompson, R. The Effect of Management by Objectives on Organization Results. *Group and Organization Studies,* 1984, *9,* 531–539; Pringle, C. D., and Longenecker, J. G. The Ethics of MBO. *Academy of Management Review,* 1982, *7,* 305–312; Kelly, C. M. Remedial MBO. *Business Horizons,* September–October 1983, 62–67; Kondrasuk, J. N. Studies in MBO Effectiveness. *Academy of Management Review,* 1981, *6,* 419–430.

44. Excerpted from McCuddy, M. K., and Griggs, M. H. Goal Setting and Feedback in the Management of a Professional Department: A Case Study. *Journal of Organizational Behavior Management,* 1984, *6,* 53–64. Used with permission of the Haworth Press, Inc., 28 East 22 Street, New York, N.Y. 10010. Copyright 1984.

45. French, W. L., and Hollmann, R. Management by Objectives: The Team Approach. *California Management Review,* 1975, 16, 13–22.

46. Case prepared by J. W. Leonard of Miami University and John Thanopoulos of the University of Akron as a basis for class discussion and analysis. Dates have been modified from the original case. This case was based on personally conducted field research. Names have been disguised at the request of the company. Copyright 1981 by the authors. Used with permission.

16 Power and Political Behavior

LEARNING OBJECTIVES

When you have finished studying this chapter, you should be able to:

- Describe the concepts of organizational power and organizational politics.
- Diagnose the structural, situational, and interpersonal sources of power in organizations.
- State the effective and ineffective uses of power.
- Explain why political behavior is not necessarily undesirable.
- Diagnose the personal and situational factors that contribute to the occurrence of political behavior.

OUTLINE

Preview Case

The Staff Assistant

Linda was staff assistant to the president of a fairly large financial organization. She worked in an office with 14 other staff and research assistants. Superficially, this research staff seemed to be a powerless lot; their work consisted chiefly of preparing background reports, preparing summary analyses of progress reports, and generally providing routine staff assistance to members of the organization's executive committee, made up of the heads of the major operating and support units of the firm.

One of Linda's major duties was assisting the president in preparing the agenda for the meetings of the executive committee. This control over the agenda ensured that issues would be discussed only when the president and her staff were ready with prepared reports and that strategy and planning would be done only when similar staff work had been performed. This meant that the president carried even more power than might be suggested by her formal position, because she controlled the content and timing of items for discussion. She brought up topics when and only when she was prepared with a position and supporting documentation. At the same time, other executives found raising items for discussion difficult. The ordered agenda, like many procedures, had been instituted as a device to rationalize the decision-making process. It was considered bad taste and not proper for another executive to insist on attention to some special issue. Under such circumstances, Linda had more power over the organization's decisions than most of the operating executives with their formally higher ranks. The president and Linda thus exerted substantial power over decision outcomes.[1]

This chapter defines and describes power and political behavior in organizations. As described in the Preview Case, one part of Linda's duties gave her power much greater than would be expected from either her position in the organization or her job description. Managers and employees must understand the characteristics and sources of power in their organizations and the effective and ineffective uses of that power.

People often are uncomfortable discussing the concept of power, and the same feeling exists when managers talk about "office politics." Both power and politics carry an emotional, perhaps negative, implication. This need not be the case; these labels are simply descriptive terms that apply to certain aspects of the behavior of people in organizations.[2] Certainly political behavior can be unproductive for the organization, and people can use power in unfair or harmful ways. Managers must try to avoid these outcomes, but they cannot change reality by refusing to accept the existence of power differences or political behavior.

POWER: AN INTRODUCTION

Power is the ability of one individual to influence others and affect their behavior.[3] The term *power* can also be used in reference to groups, organizations, and countries. For example, a certain group or department within an organization might be labeled as powerful, which suggests that the group or department has the ability to influence the behavior of individuals in other departments. This influence may affect budgetary decisions, the setting of goals, hiring decisions, or many other behaviors and outcomes in the organization.

People naturally attempt to influence the behavior of others. For example, using the terminology and concepts of learning and reinforcement introduced in Chapter 6, people quite naturally attempt to *reinforce* the behaviors of family members and friends that please or satisfy them. Likewise, often without conscious awareness, people will fail to reinforce or even attempt to *punish* undesirable behavior. Certainly the behavior of people at work is no different.

Figure 16-1 illustrates an attempt by Anna to influence the actions of David. If this attempt is successful, Anna has *power* with respect to David; that is, Anna has the ability or capacity to *influence* David's behavior in at least this specific instance. This seemingly simple diagram implies several critical characteristics of the concept of power:

- Power is a *social* term; that is, an individual has power in relation to other people, a group has power in relation to other groups, and so on. The concept of power characterizes interactions among people—more than one person must be involved for the concept to apply.

- Power is never absolute or unchanging. It is a dynamic relationship that changes as situations and individuals change. For example, even though Anna is David's supervisor, she generally will be able to influence only some of David's behavior some of the time. Also, Anna may be very powerful with respect to David but have no ability to influence the behavior of some other employee. In addition, relationships change with time. Last month's successful influence attempt may fail tomorrow, even though the same people are the key actors. Thus understanding power relationships requires specifying the situation and individuals involved.

- The terms *power* and *authority*, while closely related, do not mean exactly the same thing. **Authority** is *power legitimated* through its acceptance by employees as being right and proper.[4] The most obvious organizational example is the superior–subordinate relationship. When individuals join an organization, they generally recognize the authority structure as legitimate; that is, employees accept the manager's right to give orders, directives, and so on. As long as these orders are reasonable and related to the job, employees generally obey them. Authority is narrower in scope than power and applies to a smaller percentage of behaviors in an organization.

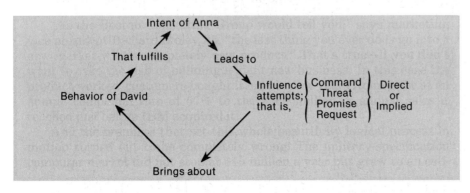

FIGURE 16-1.
The Power of One Person over Another

Source: Lawless, David J. *Organizational Behavior: The Psychology of Effective Management,* 2d ed., copyright © 1979, p. 362. Reprinted by permission of Prentice-Hall, Inc., Englewood Cliffs, N.J.

Suppose that the influence attempt diagramed in Figure 16-1 is successful, and David behaves the way that Anna intends. David may do this because of Anna's authority; that is, the source of her power may lie in David's recognition and acceptance of an authority relationship. However, there are many other possible reasons for an individual's ability to influence the behavior of other people in an organization.

In general, power sources in an organization can be grouped as (1) interpersonal sources of power and (2) structural and situational sources of power. The various sources of power that we will discuss in the following two sections are illustrated in Figure 16-2.

INTERPERSONAL SOURCES OF POWER

Many studies of power in organizations have focused on interpersonal relationships between manager and subordinate or leader and follower. French and Raven identified five **interpersonal sources of power**: reward power, coercive power, legitimate power, expert power, and referent power.[5]

Reward Power

Reward power is a manager's ability to influence subordinates' behavior by rewarding subordinates for desirable behavior. To the extent that subordinates value rewards that the manager can give—praise, promotions, money, time off, and so on—they may comply with requests and orders. For example, a manager who controls the allocation of merit pay raises in a department has reward power over the employees in that department. Employees may comply with some influence attempts by the manager because they expect to be rewarded for compliance.

Coercive Power

Coercive power is a manager's ability to influence subordinates' behavior by means of punishment for undesirable behavior. Subordinates may comply because they expect to be punished for failure to respond favorably to a manager's influence attempts. Punishment may take the form of reprimands, undesirable work assignments, stricter supervision or enforcement of work

FIGURE 16-2.
Sources of Power in
Organizations

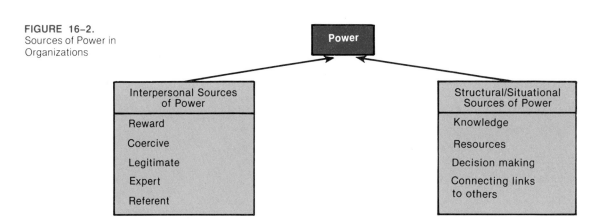

rules, suspension without pay, and the like. The ultimate punishment, from the organization's perspective, is firing the employee.

Recall from Chapter 6, however, that punishment can have undesirable side effects. The worker who receives an official reprimand for shoddy work, for example, may find other ways to avoid the punishment, such as not performing the task at all, falsifying performance reports, or being absent frequently.

Legitimate Power

Legitimate power is a manager's ability to influence subordinates' behavior because of the manager's position in the organizational hierarchy. Subordinates may respond to a manager's influence attempts because they acknowledge the manager's legitimate right to prescribe certain behaviors.

Legitimate power is an important managerial concept. Each manager is empowered to make decisions within a specific area of responsibility. This area of responsibility, in effect, defines the activities for which the manager can expect to have legitimate power to influence behavior. The farther a manager gets from this specific area of responsibility, the weaker his or her legitimate power becomes. Employees have a **zone of indifference** with respect to the exercise of managerial power. Employees will accept certain directives without consciously questioning the manager's power.[6] Within the zone of indifference, a manager may have considerable legitimate power to influence subordinates' behavior. Outside this zone, however, legitimate power disappears rapidly. For example, a secretary will type letters, answer the phone, open the mail, and the like without question. If the manager asks the secretary to go out for a drink after work, however, the secretary may refuse. The manager's request clearly falls outside the secretary's zone of indifference. The manager has no legitimate right to expect the secretary to comply.

Expert Power

Expert power refers to the ability of managers to influence their subordinates' behavior because of the managers' perceived skills, talents, or knowledge. To the extent that managers can demonstrate competence in implementing, analyzing, evaluating, and controlling the tasks of subordinates, they will acquire expert power. Expert power usually has a very narrow scope. For example, dentists have recognized expertise with regard to teeth and thus the ability to influence their patients' dental care behavior. They have much less influence in giving tax advice, where their knowledge is less complete. A lack of expert power often plagues the first-time supervisor or new manager. Even a young manager with a great deal of knowledge concerning subordinates' jobs needs time for that expertise to become known and accepted.

Referent Power

Referent power is a manager's ability to influence subordinates' behavior as a result of the employees' personal liking or admiration for the manager or the manager's charisma. Subordinates' identification with a manager often forms the basis for referent power. This identification may include the subordinates' desire to emulate the manager. For example, a young manager may copy the leadership style of an older, admired, more experienced manager. The older manager thus has some ability to influence the behavior of the younger manager—some referent power. Referent power usually is associated with individuals who possess admired personality characteristics, charisma, or a good reputation. Referent power is often associated with political leaders, movie stars, or other well-known individuals, but managers can also have considerable referent power with subordinates because of the strength of their personalities.

Interactions among Sources of Power

Managers possess varying amounts of these interpersonal sources of power, and power from different sources is not necessarily independent. The way in which managers use one type of power can either enhance or limit the effectiveness of power from another source. For example, managers who administer rewards to subordinates also tend to be well-liked and seem to have greater referent power. However, the use of coercive power can reduce referent power.[7] Employees may view managers who possess knowledge valuable to them as having greater legitimate power in addition to expert power.

A study conducted in two paper mills provides another example of power source interdependence.[8] One of the mills dropped an incentive pay plan based on performance in favor of a pay plan based strictly on seniority. Compared with the second plant, which retained the incentive system, noticeable changes in subordinates' perceptions of the use of various sources of power by supervisors occurred in the first plant. Discontinuing the incentive plan resulted in a decrease in the perceived reward power of supervisors, as might be expected, but other results were more complex. Perceptions of supervisors' use of punishment increased (attributable perhaps to less control over rewards), and the perceived use of referent and legitimate power decreased. Expert power appeared to be unaffected. These interdependencies imply that managers' power to influence behavior is complex and depends on a variety of sources. Changes in one source can cause changes in the effective use of others.

These five sources of interpersonal power divide into two broad categories: organizational and personal. Reward power, coercive power, and legitimate power have organizational bases; that is, higher-level managers or the board of directors of the organization can give to or take away from managers the right to administer rewards and punishments. The organization can change managers' legitimate power by changing managers' locations in the formal hierarchy or by changing job descriptions, rules, and procedures. However, referent power and expert power depend much more on the personal characteristics of managers—personalities, leadership styles, and knowledge brought to the job. In the long run, the organization may influence managers' expert power by, for example, making additional training available; however, the individuals determine how they use that training. In summary, some sources of interpersonal power to influence employee behavior are under the direct control of the organization, and other sources depend more on the personal characteristics of individual managers.

STRUCTURAL AND SITUATIONAL SOURCES OF POWER

Much of the attention directed toward power in organizations has tended to focus on hierarchical relationships, that is, the power of managers over subordinates. This power is important, but it is not the only dimension of power. Another perspective is that power is determined, in part, by many aspects of the situation, including the design of the organization's or department's structure, the opportunity to influence, access to powerful individuals and critical resources, and so on.[9] For example, **structural and situational sources of power** are created by division of labor and departmentalization in an organization, which naturally results in unequal access to information, resources, and decision making. These sources of power include **knowledge as power, resources as power,** and **decision making as power.**

Knowledge as Power

Knowledge is extremely important in most organizations. In fact, Zand suggests that managers' effective power is the product of their legitimate power multiplied by their ability to use knowledge competently. If managers are seriously lacking in either capacity, they have little effective power. In other words, Zand contends that organizational power can be destroyed or wasted if managers do not understand the importance and correct utilization of information and vice versa.[10]

Organizations are information processors that must use knowledge to produce goods and services. Thus individuals, groups, departments, or divisions of a firm that possess knowledge critical to the attainment of the organization's goals have power. People and groups in a position to control information about current operations, develop information about alternatives, or acquire knowledge about future events and plans have enormous power to influence the behavior of others. This explains why certain staff and support activities—a data processing center, for example—sometimes seem to have influence in the organization disproportionate to their relationship to its major goals and activities.

The increasing use of the personal computer is having an impact on access to and use of information, and thus on power relationships, in many firms. For example, a recent report stated:

> The most far-reaching effect of computers may be on the power structure of the office—flattening the hierarchy, making it more difficult to hoard authority. Managers with computers quickly notice that they delegate fewer typing chores and less statistical analysis.[11]

Resources as Power

Organizations need a variety of resources to survive, including employees, money, equipment, materials, supplies, customers, and so on. The importance of resources to a firm's success and the difficulty of obtaining them vary. Departments, groups, or individuals in the organization who can provide the resources that are the most critical or are the most difficult to obtain acquire power. Many resources can potentially affect the distribution of power in an organization; which resources are the most important depends on the situation, the goals of the firm, the state of the economy, and the product or service being offered. The old saying that "he who has the gold makes the rules" sums up the idea that resources are power.

Decision Making as Power

Decisions in organizations often are made sequentially, with many individuals or groups participating (Chapter 15). The decision-making process creates additional power differences among groups or individuals. To the extent that individuals or groups can affect some part of the process, they acquire power. They might influence the objectives being developed, the premises being used in making the decision (for example, estimates of resource availability), the alternatives being considered, the outcomes being projected, and so on. For example, a task force charged with studying a problem and making recommendations for action may have a great deal of power. Even if the task force is not going to make the final decision, it may control the consideration of possible solutions. A powerful machine politician in New York City is reputed to have said, "I don't care who does the electing, as long as I have the power to do the nominating."

The ability to influence the decision-making process is a subtle and often overlooked source of power. Decision-making power does not necessarily reside with the final decision maker in an organization or society. A clear example of the application of power in the decision-making process is provided by elections in the Soviet Union, where citizens dutifully line up to vote for political candidates—all of whom have been carefully selected by one party. Where does the power lie in this process? With those making the final decision or with those who construct the lists of candidates?

Note the relationship of knowledge, resources, and decision making to power in the description of nonprofit organizations.

In Practice: The New Power Game

The nonprofit sector has become big business—one of the biggest, in fact. Twenty-three percent of all workers are employed in government or other nonprofit agencies. As a result, a career in nonprofits is not the noble mix of idealism and self-sacrifice popularized in the 1960s. You don't have to leave your ambition at the door when you enter nonprofit work. If you do, there's a strong chance you'll stay by the door for the rest of your career.

Power in nonprofits comes from access to those who have power. As public resources dwindle, nonprofit organizations are increasingly dominated by corporate types and lawyers who serve as board members, by politicians dispensing funds and influence, and by the media. All three groups control the flow of money to a nonprofit agency or government department; this ability to raise or decrease the annual budget is power. And the closer you can get to that power, the more it will benefit your own career.

With all these forces affecting nonprofit institutions, change is an integral part of one's career. Turnover in political administrations can radically alter the nature of a government department and, by ripple effect, the nonprofit agencies within its sphere of influence. Media coverage, or the lack of it, can determine the outcome of fund-raising efforts or alter a city-council vote on appropriations. And most unpredictable of all, the board of a nonprofit agency is empowered to determine priorities, allocate resources, and hire and fire leadership. Anticipating changes, preparing for them, and above all being focused in the midst of change are the operative criteria for success.

Handling change is one aspect of the principle that dominates a nonprofit career, particularly in government. That principle, known colloquially as "cover your ass," means maintaining friends in high places, disassociating yourself from those on the way out, and documenting what you do. Putting it in writing has become the government equivalent of no-fault insurance.

Since few nonprofit organizations have built-in mechanisms for regular salary increases and promotions, the quickest way to build a strong base is to determine where the power and perks lie. Central management is usually not the best place to be. Some of the most powerful and upwardly mobile people in the nonprofit sector stay on the edges of organizations by managing special projects or performing specific functions, such as planning or fund raising. Both allow for visibility and independence and easy access to those with power. Most important, those two areas remain aloof from the mistakes that the leadership of an organization makes.

Organizational skills are at a premium in nonprofit life. Similarly blessed are successful fund raisers, since they directly affect an organization's annual budget and there is intense competition for the best people. Public-relations abilities are also valuable—both to control the effect of media on an agency and to promote your own image. The preferred management style is consensus management because it avoids controversy.[12]

Connecting Links as Power

The existence of structural and situational power depends not only on access to information, resources, and decision making, but also on the ability to get cooperation in carrying out tasks. Managers and departments need connecting links with other individuals and departments in the organization. Structural and situational sources of power can be regarded as consisting of three connecting links.[13] Each of these links relates to factors already discussed:

- *Information links.* To be effective, managers must be "in the know" in both the formal and informal sense (knowledge is power).

- *Supply links.* Influence outward, over others and the environment, means that managers can bring in what their own organizational domain needs, such as materials, money, resources to distribute as rewards, and perhaps even prestige (resources are power).

- *Support links.* In a formal sense, a manager's job must allow for decision-making discretion—the exercise of judgment. Managers must know that they can make decisions and assume innovative, risk-taking activities without each decision or action having to go through a stifling, multilayered approval process. In an informal sense, managers need the backing of other important figures in the organization, whose tacit approval becomes another resource they bring to their own work unit (participation in decision making is power and an important indicator of support links).

Note how the concepts of information, supply, and support links also appear in the description of nonprofit organizations. Although we have discussed several major categories of factors, an almost infinite variety of specific situational factors could become a source of power in an organization. Table 16-1 lists some of these factors.

TABLE 16-1 Some Ways Organizational Factors Contribute to Power or Powerlessness

Factors	Generates Power When Factor Is	Generates Powerlessness When Factor Is
Rules inherent in the job	Few	Many
Predecessors in the job	Few	Many
Established routines	Few	Many
Task variety	High	Low
Rewards for reliability/predictability	Few	Many
Rewards for unusual performance/innovation	Many	Few
Flexibility around use of people	High	Low
Approvals needed for nonroutine decisions	Few	Many
Physical location	Central	Distant
Publicity about job activities	High	Low
Relations of tasks to current problem areas	Central	Peripheral
Focus of tasks	Outside work unit	Inside work unit
Interpersonal contact in the job	High	Low
Contact with senior officials	High	Low
Participation in programs, conferences, meetings	High	Low
Participation on problem-solving task forces	High	Low
Advancement prospects of subordinates	High	Low

Source: Reprinted by permission of the *Harvard Business Review*. Kanter, R. M. Power Failure in Management Circuits. *Harvard Business Review*, 1979, 57(7), 67. Copyright © 1979 by the President and Fellows of Harvard College. All rights reserved.

The Power of Lower-Level Employees

As the Preview Case showed, *lower-level participants*—employees located lower in an organization's hierarchy—commonly wield considerable power.[14] Some sources of interpersonal power, expert power in particular, may allow subordinates to influence their managers. While lower-level employees may have interpersonal power, their ability to influence behavior more likely stems from structural or situational sources.

Figure 16-3 suggests that the power of lower-level employees is a result of their locations in the organization. When in certain locations, they may be able to control access to information or resources, as well as important aspects of the decision-making process. In addition, the expertise of employees and the amount of effort they expend also influences the extent of their power. As Figure 16-3 illustrates, whether the expertise and effort of employees increases their power depends, in part, on the expertise and effort of their managers. For example, if an employee's supervisor has little knowledge about a certain task and the employee has considerable knowledge, the power of the employee increases. Employees also can acquire power by expending effort in areas in which management puts little effort.

THE EFFECTIVE USE OF POWER

Managers who believe that they can effectively influence the behavior of others by acquiring enough power to order other people around are generally unsuccessful. In addition, there is considerable evidence that the misuse of power in an organization changes people's views of themselves and others.[15] If the use of power is not carefully managed, powerful individuals may exploit those in the organization with less power, overvalue their own importance to the organization, and confuse their self-interests with the legitimate

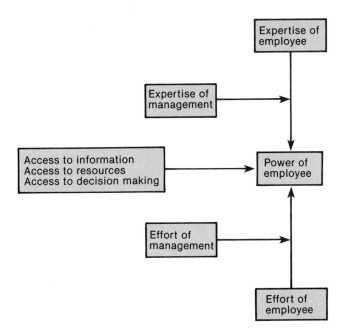

FIGURE 16-3.
Model of Lower-Level Employee Power

interests of the firm. To the contrary, managers who are successful and effectively influence others in ways consistent with the needs of the organization often have some or all of the following characteristics:

- They understand what is and what is not legitimate behavior in acquiring and using power. Different sources of power demand certain obligations in terms of how they may be used, and the misuse or lack of understanding of a source of power can destroy its effectiveness. For example, individuals erode expert power if they attempt to draw on expertise in an area in which they do not have the required knowledge. Individuals may lose referent power by behaving in ways that are inconsistent with characteristics or traits that are attractive to others. Others may perceive a person with referent power as ideal; if this ideal person misbehaves, subordinates or peers feel betrayed, and the person loses referent power.

- They understand the interpersonal as well as the situational and structural sources of power and the most effective methods of influencing people using these different sources. For example, professionals such as research and development scientists, engineers, lawyers, or professors tend to be more readily influenced by expertise than by other sources of power. Effective managers often recognize the structural and situational problems that exist in a power relationship and modify their own behavior to fit the actual situation. As a result, they tend to develop and use a wide variety of power sources and influence methods. Some unsuccessful managers rely too much on one or a few power bases.

- They tend to seek managerial positions that allow the development and use of power. In other words, they choose jobs in the mainstream of critical issues and concerns of an organization. These jobs provide opportunities for and, indeed, demand influencing the behavior of others. Successful performance in these positions, in turn, allows the managers to acquire power.

- They temper their power-oriented behavior with maturity and self-control. They recognize that their actions influence the behaviors and lives of others. While they are not necessarily reluctant or afraid to use their power—recognizing that influencing the behavior of employees is a legitimate and necessary part of the manager's role—they nevertheless apply power carefully, in principled and fair ways that are consistent with organizational needs and goals.[16]

When managers face a situation in which they wish to influence the behavior of others, they must decide among a variety of strategies that may or may not be effective in any given instance. In a recent study, Kipnis, Schmidt, Swaffin-Smith, and Wilkinson examined seven dimensions, or strategies of influence, used by managers in England, Australia, and the United States. They found no basic differences in the ways that managers exercise influence in these three countries.

ACROSS CULTURES

Patterns of Managerial Influence

Managers from firms in England, Australia, and the United States were surveyed to measure the ways in which they try to influence their superiors and their subordinates. In total, 360 first- and second-line managers participated in the international comparison: 113 from the United States, 126 from Australia, and 121 from England.

The study examined seven dimensions or strategies of managerial influence:

- *Reason.* This strategy involves the use of facts and data to support the development of a logical argument.
- *Friendliness.* This strategy involves the use of impression management, flattery, and the creation of goodwill.
- *Coalition.* This strategy involves the mobilization of other people in the organization.
- *Bargaining.* This strategy involves the use of negotiation through the exchange of benefits or favors.
- *Assertiveness.* This strategy involves the use of a direct and forceful approach.
- *Higher authority.* This strategy involves gaining the support of higher levels in the organization to back up requests.
- *Sanctions.* This strategy involves the use of organizationally derived rewards and punishments.

The study essentially found no difference among these countries in how managers exercised influence. In all three countries, the frequency with which managers used the various influence strategies was virtually identical. These results are presented in Table 16-2. When seeking to influence their superiors, managers reported that they relied most often on reason, followed by coalitions, and then by friendliness. Going over the "boss's head" or resorting to higher authority was used least often to influence superiors.

TABLE 16-2   Most-to-Least Popular Strategies

	When Managers Influenced Superiors*	When Managers Influenced Subordinates
Most	Reason	Reason
Popular	Coalition	Assertiveness
	Friendliness	Friendliness
to	Bargaining	Coalition
	Assertiveness	Bargaining
Least	Higher Authority	Higher Authority
Popular		Sanctions

*The strategy of sanctions is omitted in the scale that measures upward influence.

The rank order of preferred strategies was somewhat different when influencing subordinates. Once again managers reported that the most frequently used strategy was reason. Interestingly, however, the second most popular strategy was assertiveness. While perhaps not surprising, this finding confirms the common belief that managers can assert themselves aggressively when they demand compliance from their subordinates, but not when they are seeking compliance with their requests from their superiors.

While there were no differences in influence styles among managers in these English-speaking countries, the study did uncover some variables that affected the selection of influence strategies in all three countries: the manager's relative power, the manager's objectives for wanting to use influence, and the manager's expectation of the target person's willingness to comply. A summary of the findings with regard to three of the influence strategies is shown in Table 16-3.

The Manager's Power   Power enters into the selection of strategies in two ways. First, managers who control resources that are valued by others, or who are perceived to be in positions of dominance, use a greater variety of influence strategies than those with less power. Second, managers with power use assertiveness with greater frequency than those with less power.

TABLE 16-3   Use of Influence Strategies

Assertiveness is frequently used when:
- Objectives are to benefit the organization.
- Expectations for success are *low*.
- Organizational power is *high*.

Reason is frequently used when:
- Objectives are to benefit the organization.
- Expectations for success are *high*.
- Organizational power is *high*.

Friendliness is frequently used when:
- Objectives are to benefit the person.
- Expectations for success are *low*.
- Organizational power is *low*.

The Manager's Objectives   Managers vary their strategies in relation to their objectives. When managers seek benefits from a superior, they often rely on the use of soft words, impression management, and the promotion of pleasant relationships—that is, tactics encompassed by the strategy of friendliness. In comparison, managers attempting to persuade their superiors to accept new ideas usually rely on the use of data, explanations, and logical arguments—that is, tactics encompassed by the strategy of reason. In addition, such managers are likely to use assertiveness to gain organizational objectives, but not personal objectives.

The Manager's Expectations of Success   Managers also vary strategies according to how successful they expect to be in influencing the target. When past experience indicates a high probability of success, managers use simple requests to gain compliance. In contrast, where success is less predictable, managers are more tempted to use assertiveness and sanctions to achieve objectives.[17]

POLITICAL BEHAVIOR

Political behavior of individuals and groups consists of their attempts to influence the behavior of others and the course of events in the organization in order to protect their self-interests, meet their own needs, and advance their own goals. Described in this way, almost all behavior may be regarded as political. Labeling behavior as political, however, usually implies a judgment that individuals or groups are gaining something at the expense of other employees, groups, or the organization. People often are self-centered when labeling actions as political behavior. For example, employees may perceive their own behavior as defending legitimate rights or interests; yet they call a similar behavior by others as "playing politics."

Organizational Politics

Organizational politics involves actions of individuals or groups to acquire, develop, and use power and other resources in order to obtain preferred outcomes when there is uncertainty or disagreement about choices.[18] Managers must recognize the inevitability of much political behavior in organizations. "In circumstances in which people share power, differ about what must be done and where these differences are of some consequence, decisions and actions will be the result of a political process."[19] Factors that increase the probability of political behavior include disagreements over goals, unclear goals, different ideas about the organization and its problems, different information about the situation, the need to allocate scarce resources, and so on. After all, if everyone knew what was best for the organization and its employees, if resources were infinite, and if people agreed completely on objectives and how to achieve them, perhaps there would be no political behavior in organizations. However, it is often not possible to know the best course of action in advance; resources are never infinite; and people must make difficult allocation decisions among competing needs, departments, and divisions of a company. Thus political behavior will occur as employees and groups attempt to obtain their preferred outcomes. Managers should not try to prevent the inevitable—organizational politics—but rather try to ensure that these activities do not have negative consequences for the organization.

People tend to assume that political behavior does not result in the best decisions or outcomes from the organization's viewpoint and that somehow, by advocating their own position, individuals or groups produce inferior actions or decisions. This is not necessarily true as the situation at General Rubber indicates.

In Practice: **Merit or Politics?**

Lori and Bob are highly motivated research scientists who work in the new-product development lab at General Rubber. Lori is by far the most technically competent scientist in the lab, and she has been responsible for several patents that have netted the company nearly $6 million in the past decade. She is quiet, serious, and socially reserved. In contrast, Bob is outgoing and demonstrative. He lacks Lori's technical track record, but his work has been solid, though unimaginative. Rumor has it that Bob will be moved into an administrative position in the lab in the next few years.

According to lab policy, a $300,000 fund is available every year for the best new-product development idea proposed by a lab scientist in the form of a competitive bid. Accordingly, this year Lori and Bob both prepare proposals. Each proposal is carefully constructed to detail the benefits to the company and to society if the proposal is accepted, and it is the consensus of other scientists from blind reviews that both proposals are equally meritorious. Both proposals require the entire $300,000 to realize any significant results. Moreover, the proposed line of research in each requires significant mastery of the technical issues involved and minimal need to supervise the work of others.

After submitting her proposal, Lori takes no further action aside from periodically inquiring about the outcome of the bidding process. In contrast, Bob begins to wage what might be called an open campaign in support of his proposal. After freely admitting his intentions to Lori and others, Bob seizes every opportunity he can to point out the relative advantages of his proposal to individuals who might have some influence over the decision. So effective is this open campaign that considerable informal pressure is placed on those authorized to make the decision on behalf of Bob's proposal. Bob's proposal is funded, and Lori's is not.[20]

In this situation, whether the decision to fund Bob's proposal (and, hence, to not fund Lori's) is in the best interests of the company is not at all clear: it depends on how the project turns out, what Lori does with the time she would have spent working on her project had it been funded, the future career paths of both Bob and Lori in the company, and many other unknowns. What is clear, however, is that political behavior is not necessarily detrimental to an organization. It can and does meet appropriate and legitimate individual and organizational needs. In any event, managers and employees must understand political behavior because it commonly occurs in organizations.

Occurrence of Political Behavior

Employees are often concerned about office politics. Like power, politics is a subject more often discussed than understood. People commonly agree on the existence of organizational politics and, perhaps just as often, believe that an ideal worksetting would be free of political behavior.

In one research study, 428 managers were asked to rank organizational decisions from the most to the least political.[21] They ranked decisions related to interdepartmental coordination, promotions and transfers, and delegation of authority first, second, and third, respectively. Decisions in these areas are characterized by a lack of established rules and procedures and reliance on subjective, ambiguous criteria. Areas the managers ranked as least political are characterized by established policies, precedents, and more objective criteria. Examples of less politically sensitive areas were personnel policies, hiring, and disciplinary penalties.

Decisions in some areas can be made less political by strategies such as increasing the resources available (thus reducing conflict over scarce resources) or by making the decisions seem less important than they really are.[22] However, strategies to reduce the political behavior associated with organizational decisions may have some unintended consequences, which translate into real costs for the firm. Table 16-4 shows examples of strategies used to avoid organizational politics and the potential costs associated with each strategy.

The same 428 managers were also asked about the location of political behavior in their organization. In general, they believed more politics occurred at higher managerial levels than at lower managerial levels and among nonmanagerial employees. A slight majority (55 percent) considered political behavior detrimental in terms of organizational effectiveness. Another study involving 90 managers in 30 organizations reported similar results.[23] More than 90 percent of these managers reported that organizational politics is more frequent at middle and upper levels of management than at lower levels of management. In addition, this group of 90 managers identified both harmful and beneficial effects of political behavior. Table 16-5 lists these effects.

These and other studies often agree on two points: (1) in spite of the negative connotation of political behavior, many managers and employees rec-

---

TABLE 16-4 Strategies for Avoiding the Use of Power and Politics in Decision Making and Their Costs

Strategy	Costs
■ Slack or excess resources, including additional administrative positions or titles	■ Inventory costs, costs of excess capacity, costs of extra personnel and extra salary
■ Similarity in goals and beliefs about technology produced through recruitment practices, socialization, and use of rewards and sanctions	■ Fewer points of view, less diverse information represented in decision making; potentially lower quality decisions
■ Make decisions appear less important	■ Decision may be avoided; subterfuge may be discovered; analysis and information may not be uncovered

Source: Pfeffer, J. *Power in Organizations.* Marshfield, Mass.: Pitman, 1981, 93. Reprinted with permission.

TABLE 16-5   Perceived Ways Organizational Politics Can Be Helpful or Harmful to the Individual or the Organization

Factors Affecting Individual	Percentage Response by Managers in Study
Helpful	
Career advancement	60.9
Recognition, status	21.8
Power, position enhancement	19.5
Personal goal accomplishment	14.9
Getting the job done	11.5
Ideas, projects, programs sold	10.3
Feelings (achievement, ego, control, success, and so on)	8.1
Survival	4.7
Harmful	
Loss of power, strategic position, credibility	39.1
Loss of job, demotion, and so on	31.0
Negative feelings of others	21.8
Passive loss of promotion, transfers, and so on	19.5
Internal feelings, guilt	12.6
Promotion to level of incompetence	9.2
Job performance hampered	3.5

Factors Affecting Organization	Percentage Response by Managers in Study
Helpful	
Organization goals achieved, getting the job done	26.4
Organization survival, health, processes	26.4
Visibility of ideas, people, and so on	19.5
Coordination, communication	18.4
Team development, group functioning	11.5
Esprit de corps, energy channeling	10.3
Decision making, analysis	6.9
No response (unable to mention helpful result)	14.9
Harmful	
Distraction from organization goals	44.8
Misuse of resources	32.3
Divisiveness, splits, fights	21.8
Climate: tension, frustration	19.5
Incompetents advanced	14.9
Lower coordination, communication	10.3
Organization's image and reputation damaged	10.3
No response (no harm mentioned)	3.5

Source: Adapted with permission from Madison, D. L., Allen, R. W., Porter, L. W., Renwick, P. A. and Mayes, B.T. Organizational Politics: An Exploration of Managers' Perceptions. *Human Relations*, 1980, *33*, 92, Plenum Publishing Corporation.

ognize its prevalence and realize that it can have either positive or negative effects on both individuals and organizations; and (2) people expect the occurrence of political behavior to be greater at top-management levels than at middle- or lower-levels of the organization.

Another interesting issue concerns the specific kinds of behaviors that organizational members consider political. A sample of chief executive officers, high-level staff managers, and supervisors were asked to describe the most commonly used organizational political tactics. Their responses indicated that attacking or blaming others when things go wrong, withholding or restricting access to information, and engaging in image building or "impression management" were behaviors that they most readily perceived as political.[24]

POLITICAL BEHAVIOR AND PERSONALITY

In the chapter so far, we have stressed the situational and structural determinants of political behavior. However, just as power has personal as well as situational sources, evidence indicates that some individuals are more likely to engage in political behavior than others. Before reading further, respond to the questionnaire in Table 16-6.

Several personal traits are related to a willingness to engage in political behavior (and in some cases, a willingness to use power). We will discuss four of these: the need for power, Machiavellianism, locus of control, and risk-seeking propensity.[25]

Need for Power

The **need for power** is a motive, or basic desire, to influence and lead others and to be in control of one's environment. As a result, individuals with a high need for power are more likely to engage in political behavior in organizations. In addition, successful managers often have high needs for power.[26] The desire to have an impact, to control events, and to have an influence over others is frequently associated with effective managerial behaviors, equitable treatment of subordinates, and, hence, higher morale.

However, some aspects of strong power needs may not be particularly useful for effective management. The need for power may take two different forms: personal power and institutional power.[27] Managers who emphasize personal power strive for dominance over others; they create loyalty to themselves rather than the organization. When this type of manager leaves the organization, the work group may fall apart. On the other hand, managers who emphasize institutional power demonstrate a more socially acceptable need for power. They create a good climate for effective work, and their subordinates develop an understanding of and loyalty to the organization. Thus not all characteristics of a need for power contribute to effective management, but better managers frequently have strong desires to influence behavior and to play leadership roles.

Machiavellianism

Niccolò Machiavelli was a sixteenth-century Italian philosopher and statesman whose best-known writings include a set of suggestions for obtaining

---

TABLE 16-6   Political Orientation Questionnaire

Answer each question according to whether you mostly agree or mostly disagree, even if it is difficult for you to decide which alternative best describes your opinion.

	Mostly Agree	Mostly Disagree
1. Only a fool would correct a boss's mistakes.	_____	_____
2. If I have certain confidential information, I release it to my advantage.	_____	_____
3. I would be careful not to hire a subordinate who had more formal education than I.	_____	_____

	Mostly Agree	Mostly Disagree
4. If I do somebody a favor, I remember to cash in on it.	_____	_____
5. Given the opportunity, I would cultivate friendships with powerful people.	_____	_____
6. I like the idea of saying nice things about a rival in order to get that person transferred from my department.	_____	_____
7. Why not take credit for other people's work? They would do the same to me.	_____	_____
8. Given the chance, I would offer to help my boss build some shelves at home.	_____	_____
9. I laugh heartily at my boss's jokes, even when they are not funny.	_____	_____
10. I would be sure to attend a company picnic even if I had the chance to do something I enjoyed more that day.	_____	_____
11. If I knew an executive in my company was stealing money, I would use it against him or her in asking for favors.	_____	_____
12. I would first find out my boss's political preferences before discussing politics with him or her.	_____	_____
13. I think using memos to zap people for their mistakes is a good idea (especially when I want to show that person up).	_____	_____
14. If I wanted something done by a co-worker, I would be willing to say "If you don't get this done, our boss might be very unhappy."	_____	_____
15. I would invite my boss to a party at my house, even if I did not like him or her.	_____	_____
16. If I were in a position to, I would have lunch with the "right people" at least twice a week.	_____	_____
17. Richard M. Nixon's bugging the democratic headquarters would have been a clever idea if he had not been caught.	_____	_____
18. Power for its own sake is one of life's most precious commodities.	_____	_____
19. Having a high school named after me would be an incredible thrill.	_____	_____
20. Reading about job politics is as much fun as reading an adventure story.	_____	_____

Interpretation of Scores

Each statement you checked "Mostly Agree" is worth 1 point toward your political orientation score. A score of 16 or over suggests that you have a strong inclination toward playing politics. A high score of this nature also suggests that you have strong needs for power. Scores of 5 or less suggest that you are not inclined toward political maneuvering and that you are not strongly power driven.

This questionnaire is designed primarily for discussion purposes and to encourage you to think about the topic under study. The Political Orientation Questionnaire lacks the scientific properties of a validated personality or interest test.

Source: From DuBrin, A. J. *Human Relations: A Job Oriented Approach*, 1978, Fig. 14–3. Reprinted with permission of Reston Publishing Company, a Prentice-Hall Co., 11480 Sunset Hills Road, Reston, VA 22090.

and holding governmental power. Over the centuries Machiavelli has come to be associated with the use of deceit and opportunism in interpersonal relations. Thus *Machiavellians* are people who view and manipulate others for their own purposes.

It is possible to measure **Machiavellianism** as a personal trait or style of behavior toward others characterized by (1) the use of guile and deceit in interpersonal relationships; (2) a cynical view of the nature of other people; and (3) a lack of concern with conventional morality.[28] For example, a person who scores high on a test to measure Machiavellianism would probably agree with the following statements:

- The best way to handle people is to tell them what they want to hear.
- Anyone who completely trusts anyone else is asking for trouble.
- Never tell anyone the real reason you did something unless it is useful to do so.
- It is wise to flatter important people.

Machiavellians are likely to be effective manipulators of other people. They often effectively influence others, particularly in face-to-face contacts, and tend to initiate and control social interactions. As a result, Machiavellianism can be associated with a tendency to engage in political behavior. For example, a study that examined the relationship between a propensity to engage in political behavior in organizations and a variety of individual differences, reported that Machiavellianism was the strongest correlate of political behavior among the variables investigated.[29] The study concluded that Machiavellianism may be a good predictor of political behavior in many organizational situations.

Locus of Control

As described in Chapter 3, **locus of control** refers to the extent to which individuals believe that they can control events that affect them. Individuals with a high internal locus of control believe that events result primarily from their own behavior. Those with a high external locus of control believe that powerful others, fate, or chance primarily determine events. Those with a high internal locus of control tend to exhibit more political behaviors than externals and are more likely to attempt to influence other people; they are more likely to assume that their efforts will be successful. The study of relationships among political behavior and individual differences referred to in the preceding section also supported the notion that the propensity to engage in political behavior is stronger for individuals who have a high internal locus of control than for those who have a high external locus of control.

Risk-Seeking Propensity

Individuals differ (sometimes markedly) in their willingness to take risks, or their **risk-seeking propensity**. Some people are risk avoiders, and others can be described as risk seekers. Some studies have identified negative outcomes for individuals and groups that engage or appear to engage in political behavior in organizations.[30] Thus engaging in political activity would not seem to be risk free; to advocate a position and to seek support for it is to risk being perceived as opposing some other position. In many situations, risk seekers more willingly engage in political behavior while risk avoiders tend to avoid such behavior because of its risky nature.

SUMMARY

Power is the ability of individuals or groups in an organization to influence the behavior of other individuals or groups. Sources of power stem from interpersonal as well as structural and situational factors in an organization. Interpersonal power bases can be categorized as reward power, coercive power, legitimate power, expert power, and referent power. Situational or structural power differences stem from unequal access to information, resources, and decision making. Lower-level employees, in spite of their location in the organizational hierarchy, can have considerable power to influence events and behavior. Managers who are effective in influencing the behavior of employees usually understand clearly the sources of power in the organization, as well as their appropriate and fair uses.

Organizational politics involves the use of power and other resources by individuals or groups to obtain their own preferred outcomes. Political behavior is inevitable, owing to naturally occurring disagreements and uncertainty about choices and actions. Political behavior has both positive and negative consequences; it may or may not result in optimal decisions, and there are some real costs associated with avoiding political behavior.

There is evidence from various studies that some personality traits predispose people toward political behavior. Specifically, the probability that individuals will engage in political influence attempts increases if they have (1) a high need for power; (2) a Machiavellian interpersonal style; (3) a high internal locus of control; or (4) a preference for risk taking. These are not the only personal factors that can influence political behavior, but current evidence indicates they may be among the most important.

KEY WORDS AND CONCEPTS

Authority
Coercive power
Decision making as power
Expert power
Interpersonal sources of power
Knowledge as power
Legitimate power
Locus of control
Machiavellianism
Need for power
Organizational politics

Political behavior
Power
Referent power
Resources as power
Reward power
Risk-seeking propensity
Structural and situational sources of
  power
Zone of indifference

DISCUSSION QUESTIONS

1. Why is it important for a manager to understand the characteristics and sources of power in organizations?

2. In a work situation in which you had the power to influence the behavior of others, what was the source or sources of your power?

3. In a work situation in which someone else had the power to influence your behavior, what was the source or sources of that power?

4. Why do individuals or groups sometimes have power out of proportion to their location in the organizational hierarchy? Give some examples.

5. Why are the various sources of power not independent of each other? Give an example of how power from one source can enhance or reduce power from another source.

6. Based on your own experiences, describe a situation in which an individual had the power to influence others but used it ineffectively.

7. Give an example of the effective use of power.

8. Describe some factors that can contribute to the occurrence of political behavior in an organization.

9. Describe some of the likely consequences of political behavior in organizations. Give examples of some potential consequences of avoiding political behavior.

10. Are power differences and political behavior related in any way? If so, how?

MANAGEMENT INCIDENTS AND CASES

Barbara DiBella

Part I

Barbara DiBella began work in Spartan Corporation's management trainee program immediately after graduating from college with a major in marketing. Spartan had recruited her very vigorously as part of its affirmative action efforts to increase the number of women in management positions. While Barbara had had work experience in summer jobs, this was her first full-time position. In the trainee program Barbara would be assigned to the various departments of the corporation for periods of six weeks to six months, so that she could receive an introduction to the complete scope of the organization's activities and also meet the key people. While assigned to each department she would be under the direct supervision of the Department Manager.

Paul Platowski was the corporation's Marketing Manager. He had joined the firm just seven years ago, following completion of an MBA program, and had progressed very rapidly to his current position of power and prominence. He, too, had gone through the management trainee program, following which he had selected marketing for his initial permanent assignment.

As Barbara's training assignment to the Marketing Department approached she became increasingly apprehensive. Her fellow trainees and graduates of previous years' trainee programs told her many stories of Paul's interest in and involvement with young women in the trainee program. Barbara heard of no fewer than three former trainees with whom the grapevine said Paul had been or was intimately involved. Two of the three had excellent positions in the Marketing Department and the third was progressing quickly in one of the Product Groups. The grapevine also indicated that Paul had sought relationships with two other women trainees but had been rejected. One of these women was mired in an undesirable field sales job and the other had left Spartan.

The Manager of the Accounting Department, whom Barbara did not know particularly well but to whom she was assigned just prior to her rotation through Marketing, warned her to be careful of Paul. He said he wouldn't be surprised if top management had stalled the Marketing Manager's rise at its current level until he "cleans up his act."

Barbara was also concerned about her upcoming contact with Paul because he seemed to always have his arm around women when he was with them in the halls, at lunch, and at social gatherings.

Questions for Part I

1. What risks are there to Barbara in getting "involved" with Paul?
2. Are there any risks for Paul in getting "involved" with Barbara?
3. What would you do if you were Barbara?

Part II

On the first day of her assignment in Marketing, Barbara had an early morning meeting with the Department Manager, as was typical when a trainee entered a new department. Paul welcomed her to his office by putting his arm around her and ushering her to a seat on the couch, where he joined her. Paul was extremely warm and animated in their conversation, telling Barbara he was extremely impressed by her credentials. He promised that her stay in Marketing could be an exciting, challenging experience and that a permanent position and unequalled career progress were possible if things worked out. Paul explained her first assignment, which Barbara recognized to be the most exciting she had had by far. After inviting and responding to Barbara's questions and explaining some of the mechanics of the department, Paul wrapped up the meeting by urging her to come to him at any time with questions, problems, or concerns. With that he helped her up from the couch and again put his arm around her as they walked toward the door of his office.

Barbara emerged from the meeting with very mixed emotions. On the one hand she was elated about the assignment she had and the description of how the department operated. On the other hand, she was frightened by the possibility that Paul wanted an intimate relationship with her. She was clear that both personally and professionally she did not want a romantic relationship with her boss. It seemed to her that any short-term benefits would be more than outweighed by long-term consequences.

Barbara decided she would keep her relationship with Paul strictly business. She would work very hard at her marketing assignments, but would keep the relationship cool and impersonal. She planned to take full advantage of the opportunity that Paul and his department offered for professional development, but be very sure that she was not drawn into the complexities of a personal relationship.

As Barbara considered her future with Paul, she rehearsed in her head a conversation in which she would tell him that she was very interested in an intense professional relationship, but totally uninterested in any kind of intimate relationship. Ultimately, though, she decided against actually having that talk with Paul. She would avoid the chance for things to get personal, but she would not confront the issue directly with Paul.

Questions for Part II

1. What are the costs and benefits of the strategy Barbara has chosen for managing her relationship with Paul?
2. What other strategies were available to her? What would their costs and benefits have been?

Part III

Over the next couple of months Barbara became more and more comfortable in her relationship with Paul. In fact, as she thought back to her first days in the Marketing Department she almost couldn't remember what she had been so upset about. She was working very hard at her assignments and producing work that Paul acknowledged to be top quality.

There had been a few occasions when her plan for keeping the relationship with her boss businesslike had been tested. For example, he had invited her to accompany him on a two-day trip for the presentation of a marketing plan at one of the key subsidiaries, but the deadline on another project was close enough that she was able to beg off. A couple of times at the beginning Paul had asked her to go to lunch, but again she had been able to use the press of work as an excuse for declining. She had dealt with Paul's touching by simply keeping her physical distance from him, joking about him "keeping his hands off the merchandise," and choosing a chair rather than the couch when meeting with him in his office.

Overall, Barbara was feeling very good about her situation in Marketing and the early threat of a personal relationship with Paul had become a non-issue.

Questions for Part III

1. How has Barbara's plan worked?
2. Should she have any further concerns?

Part IV

As time passed Barbara noticed that her assignments began to take on a certain sameness. Paul did not seem to be giving her anything new to do. There was nothing wrong with the work she was given—it was interesting and important—but it was not particularly challenging anymore because she had done it several times before. She decided to set up a meeting with Paul to discuss her concerns. Paul had some difficulty finding a time for them to meet but ultimately found fifteen minutes to "squeeze her in." During the meeting he was continually interrupted by phone calls and questions from his secretary. In response to Barbara's concerns Paul said he was sorry to hear she was dissatisfied, but he also indicated that it was really too late to get into anything very new because she had only one month left in the Marketing Department. Barbara decided to raise the issue of a permanent position in Marketing. Paul responded by suggesting that they hold off on any decision about that until she had completed her other assignments and knew what else was available. Rather abruptly Paul stood and thanked Barbara for coming in and walked to the door to discuss something with his secretary.

Questions for Part IV

1. What is happening? How does Paul view the situation?
2. What should Barbara do about it?

Part V

Barbara was quite disappointed with her meeting with Paul, but resigned herself to a final month of the same type of assignments and a delay in discussion of a career in marketing.

During her final month Barbara was involved with a project that was supervised by one of "Paul's women" in the Marketing Department. Judy had been through the trainee program two years earlier and was now doing extremely well. One evening after Barbara and Judy had been finishing up some work on the project, Judy took a bottle of wine from her desk, poured a glass for Barbara and one for herself, and they began to talk. Three hours and a bottle of wine later Barbara had learned that Judy was not romantically involved with Paul and never had been. In addition, Judy assured her that the other two trainees about whom Barbara had heard rumors of a relationship with Paul were not romantically involved either. Judy acknowledged that Paul was "too touchy" and that she had talked with him about it to no avail, but added that she had learned to live with it. She described Paul as her mentor and close friend and made an impassioned statement about the centrality of Paul to her career success.[31]

Questions for Part V

1. How do you explain what happened to Barbara? What mistakes did she make?
2. What should she do now?

REFERENCES

1. Adapted with permission from Pfeffer, J. *Power in Organizations.* Marshfield, Mass.: Pitman, 1981, 150.

2. See, for example, Bacharach, S. B., and Lawler, E. J. *Power and Politics in Organizations.* San Francisco: Jossey-Bass, 1980; Cobb, A. T. An Episodic Model of Power: Toward an Integration of Theory and Research. *Academy of Management Review,* 1984, *9,* 482–493; Hamilton, G. G., and Biggart, N. W. Why People Obey: Theoretical Observations on Power and Obedience in Complex Organizations. *Sociological Perspectives,* 1985, *28,* 3–28; Rubin, I. M., and Berlew, D. E. The Power Failure in Organizations. *Training and Development Journal,* January 1984, 34–38.

3. Huber, V. L. The Sources, Uses, and Conservation of Managerial Power. *Personnel,* 1981, *51*(4), 62.

4. Pfeffer, *Power in Organizations,* 4–6. Also see Biggart, N. W., and Hamilton, G. G. The Power of Obedience. *Administrative Science Quarterly,* 1984, *29,* 540–549.

5. French, J. R. P., and Raven, B. The Bases of Social Power. In D. Cartwright (Ed.) *Studies in Social Power.* Ann Arbor, Mich.: University of Michigan Institute for Social Research, 1959, 150–167.

6. Barnard, C. I., *The Functions of the Executive.* Cambridge, Mass.: Harvard University Press, 1938. For additional perspectives on this issue, see Zelditch, M., and Walker, H. A. Legitimacy and the Stability of Authority. In Bacharach, S. B. and Lawler, E. J. (Eds.) *Advances in Group Processes,* vol. 1. JAI Press, 1984, 1–25.

7. Huber, The Sources, Uses, and Conservation of Managerial Power, 66–67.

8. Greene, C. N., and Podsakoff, P. M. Effects of Withdrawal of a Performance-Contingent Reward on Supervisory Influence and Power. *Academy of Management Journal,* 1981, *24,* 527–542.

9. Bacharach and Lawler, *Power and Politics in Organizations,* 33–38; Pfeffer, *Power in Organizations,* 101–122; Tushman, M. L., and Nadler, D. A. Implications of Political Models of Organization. In R. H. Miles (Ed.) *Resourcebook in Macro Organizational Behavior.* Santa Monica, Calif.: Goodyear, 1980, 177–190.

10. Zand, D. E. *Information, Organization, and Power: Effective Management in the Knowledge Society.* New York: McGraw-Hill, 1981, x.

11. Nulty, P. How Personal Computers Change Managers' Lives. *Fortune.* September 3, 1984, 44.

12. Reprinted with permission of Macmillan Publishing Company from *Powerbase: How to Get It/How to Keep It* by M. M. Kennedy. Copyright © 1984 by Macmillan Publishing Company.

13. Kanter, R. M. Power Failure in Management Circuits. *Harvard Business Review,* 1979, *57*(7), 66.

14. See, for example, Blackburn, R. S. Lower Participant Power: Toward a Conceptual Integration. *Academy of Management Review,* 1981, *6,* 127–131; Mechanic, D. Sources of Power of Lower Participants in Complex Organizations. *Administrative Science Quarterly,* 1962, *7,* 349–364; Porter, L. W., Allen, R. W., and Angle, L. L. The Politics of Upward Influence in Organizations. *Research in Organizational Behavior,* 1981, *3,* 109–49.

15. Clarke, N. K. The Sadistic Manager. *Personnel,* February 1985, 34–38; Kipnis, D. The View From the Top. *Psychology Today,* December 1984, 30–36.

16. These characteristics of managerial effectiveness are based on Kotter, J. P. Power, Dependence, and Effective Management. *Harvard Business Review,* April 1977, 125–136. Also see Gioia, D. A., and Sims, H. P. Perceptions of Managerial Power as a Consequence of Managerial Behavior and Reputation. *Journal of Management,* 1983, *9,* 7–26.

17. Excerpted with permission of the publisher from Kipnis, D., Schmidt, S. M., Swaffin-Smith, C., and Wilkinson, I. Pat-

terns of Managerial Influence: Shotgun Managers, Tacticians, and Bystanders. *Organizational Dynamics*, Winter 1984, 58–67. Copyright © 1984 Periodicals Division, American Management Associations, New York. All rights reserved.

18. Pfeffer, *Power in Organizations*, 7.

19. Mangham, I. *The Politics of Organizational Change*. Westport, Conn.: Greenwood, 1979, 17.

20. Adapted with permission from Cavanagh, G. F., Moberg, D. J., and Velasquez, M. The Ethics of Organizational Politics. *Academy of Management Review*, 1981, 6, 369.

21. Gandz, J., and Murray, V. V. The Experience of Workplace Politics. *Academy of Management Journal*, 1980, 23, 237–251.

22. Pfeffer, *Power in Organizations*, 88–94.

23. Madison, D. L., Allen, R. W., Porter, L. W., Renwick, P. A., and Mayes, B. T. Organizational Politics: An Exploration of Managers' Perceptions. *Human Relations*, 1980, 33, 79–100.

24. Allen, R. W., Madison, D. L., Porter, L. W., Renwick, P. A. and Mayes, B. T. Organizational Politics: Tactics and Characteristics of Its Actors. *California Management Review*, 1979, 22(1), 77–83. For a description of impression management, see Tedeschi, J. T., and Melburg, V. Impression Management and Influence in the Organization. In Lawler, E. J. (Ed.) *Research in the Sociology of Organizations*, vol. 3. JAI Press, 1984, 31–58.

25. The sections on these personal traits are based, in part, on Porter, Allen, and An-

gle, The Politics of Upward Influence in Organizations, 120–122.

26. See, for example, McClelland, D. C., and Burnham, D. H. Power is the Great Motivator. *Harvard Business Review*, February 1976, 100–110; Miner, J. B. *Theories of Organizational Behavior*. Hinsdale, Ill.: Dryden, 1980, 50–53.

27. For the conceptual background of these ideas, see, McClelland, D. C. The Two Faces of Power. *Journal of International Affairs*, 1970, 24(1), 29–47; McClelland, D. C., and Burnham, D. H. Good Guys Make Bum Bosses. *Psychology Today*, July 1975, 69–70.

28. Christie, R., and Geis, F. L. *Studies in Machiavellianism*. New York: Academic Press, 1970.

29. Woodman, R. W., Wayne, S. J., and Rubinstein, D. Personality Correlates of a Propensity to Engage in Political Behavior in Organizations. *Proceedings of the Southwest Academy of Management*, 1985, 131–135.

30. See, for example, Madison, *et al.*, Organizational Politics: An Exploration of Manager's Perceptions; Schilit, W. K., and Locke, E. A. A Study of Upward Influence in Organizations. *Administrative Science Quarterly*, 1982, 27, 304–316.

31. Spelman, D. and Crary, M. Intimacy or Distance? A Case of Male-Female Attraction at Work. *Organizational Behavior Teaching Review*, 1984, 9 (2), 72–85. Reprinted with the permission of the Organizational Behavior Teaching Society.

17 Conflict within Organizations

LEARNING OBJECTIVES

When you have finished studying this chapter, you should be able to:

- Define *conflict* and distinguish when it is a negative or a positive force.
- Identify five major levels and sources of conflict within organizations.
- Use different interpersonal conflict-handling styles and identify their probable effects.
- Explain the difference between vertical and horizontal conflict within organizations.
- Describe the causes and effects of role conflict and role ambiguity.
- State how structural, interpersonal, and promotional approaches can be used for managing conflicts within organizations.

OUTLINE

Preview Case

The German Manager

A plant in southern Germany produced a simple time-keeping device on an assembly line. The new plant manager, Mr. G., was faced with a problem. The assembly line production workers, all women from the local community, had a high turnover rate. He inquired about this, and gradually, as he lived in the community, he got to know all their families. What he found out was that the women felt it was hard to work a standard eight-hour day (8 A.M. to 5 P.M.), Monday through Friday, and keep up with household chores, shopping, and family emergencies. After a few months of work, a woman would give up trying to juggle the two spheres and quit.

Mr. G. realized that the plant was a revolving door. Women worked until the conflicts and resulting stresses of juggling family and job became too much, and then quit. After a year or so, a woman might return to work but eventually would quit once more.

Mr. G. thought the situation over and came up with an unusual motivational plan. He had each worker learn all of the assembly line jobs. This was not a difficult achievement for any of the women, and was soon accomplished. Next, each woman was taught how to slow down or speed up the assembly line. Finally, he gave each worker a key to the plant door. The women were free to come and go on their own, that is, to decide on their own work hours.

What happened? The women trickled in and out all hours of the day, from early morning until midnight. The workers who were there could easily organize themselves into an assembly group. If a worker came alone (perhaps on a late Sunday evening), she slowed down the assembly line (as she had been trained) and did each of the jobs in sequence.

The turnover problem was solved. Soon women who had "quit for good" were back at the plant. Eventually, most of the women in the community worked at the plant. There was a family sense that it was their plant. They liked organizing themselves. Most of the families in the community had gotten to know the plant manager. He was well liked and a sense of loyalty developed toward him. As the number of workers increased and turnover went down, production per worker went up.

A top manager from headquarters—Mr. T.—eventually made a visit to the plant. Mr. T. was terribly offended by what he saw. He was shocked by the "informality," "the lack of rules and discipline," and "the lack of structure and order." Statistics which proved the rise in production and statistics that showed this plant to have better profit figures than other comparable plants in Germany were shown to Mr. T. They did not alter his negative judgment. To Mr. T., the plant appeared to be run "sloppily" and sadly needed many improvements to put it "in order."

The conflict between Mr. T. from headquarters and Mr. G. grew to the point where it was quite clear to Mr. G. that he had no future in the corporation. Curiously enough, the very success of Mr. G's plant seemed to rankle Mr. T. the most. By mutual agreement, Mr. G. left the corporation.[1]

The Preview Case reports an actual situation encountered by a German manager of a production plant located in southern Germany. We will occasionally refer back to this situation to analyze the types of conflicts encountered by Mr. G. In this chapter we examine conflict from a variety of viewpoints. First we consider the positive and negative aspects of conflict.[2] Next, we discuss the levels and sources of conflict that can occur within organizations.[3] Finally, we identify some of the basic methods for managing conflict.[4]

The effective management of conflict involves more than specific techniques. The ability to understand and correctly diagnose conflict is a prerequisite to its management.[5] Thus most of this chapter is directed toward developing a better understanding of how to manage conflict processes within organizations.

INTRODUCTION TO CONFLICT

Conflict Defined

Conflict is difficult to define. This is because it occurs in many different forms and settings. The essence of conflict seems to be disagreement, contradiction, or incompatibility. For our purposes, **conflict** refers to any situation in which there are incompatible goals, cognitions, or emotions within or between individuals or groups that lead to opposition or antagonistic interaction. This general definition recognizes three basic types of conflict:

- **Goal conflict** is a situation in which desired end states or preferred outcomes appear to be incompatible.
- **Cognitive conflict** is a situation in which ideas or thoughts are perceived as incompatible.
- **Affective conflict** is a situation in which feelings or emotions are incompatible; that is, people literally become angry with one another.

All three types of conflict are present in the Preview Case. The women production workers initially experienced severe conflicts between the goals of being a good employee and a good homemaker. When the conflicts and resulting stresses became too great, the women workers simply quit their jobs. The plant manager came up with a novel idea for substantially reducing this goal conflict. The flexible work schedule seemed to reduce the goal conflicts of the women, reduce turnover, and create the unexpected benefit of increased work motivation and commitment. The plant manager, Mr. G., soon experienced a new type of conflict—cognitive conflict. The ideas and thoughts he held about good human resource management practices were in sharp contrast to the thoughts and ideas of Mr. T., from headquarters. These cognitive conflicts were not resolved. They were soon accompanied by negative feelings of Mr. G. and Mr. T. toward each other. This affective conflict became so severe that Mr. G. came to feel that his future with the corporation was questionable. Given the high power of Mr. T. relative to Mr. G. and the depth of their cognitive and affective conflicts, it was "agreed" that the best course of action was for Mr. G. to resign.

Conflict as a Positive Force

Conflict is common in organizations and can be a positive force. The creation and/or resolution of conflict often leads to constructive problem solving. The need to resolve conflict can cause people to search for means of changing the way they do things. Thus the conflict-resolution process can stimulate positive change within an organization. The search for ways to resolve conflict may not only lead to innovation and change, but it may make change more acceptable.[6]

Sears, Roebuck and Co. provides an example of an organization that benefited from effective conflict resolution. In 1925, Sears established retail stores to sell directly to the public, a marked change from its previously exclusive focus on catalog sales. The new sales strategy was accompanied by substantial conflict. Sears had a highly centralized structure with an implicit goal of limiting decision-making discretion at the retail store level. This was in direct conflict with the goal for each retail store to serve its customers' needs because to do so successfully retail store management needed more autonomy. The resolution of this conflict led to a new, decentralized structure at Sears in the early 1940s, which apparently contributed to Sears' retailing success.[7] However, Sears has now recentralized some of its activities in order to achieve better integration.

The intentional introduction of conflict into the decision-making process can be beneficial. For example, in group decision making, a problem may arise when a cohesive group's desire for agreement interferes with its consideration of alternative solutions. As discussed in Chapter 9, a group may encounter the problem of *groupthink*, which it can reduce if the introduction of conflict takes the form of one or more dissenting opinions.

Competition that leads to conflict over one or more goals sometimes can have beneficial effects. Employees who perceive a competitive atmosphere among fellow workers with respect to performance may sometimes be motivated to put forth greater effort to come out ahead in the competition.[8] Empirical evidence suggests that competition enhances the quantity of products produced during a given time period.[9] Thus an organization whose primary goal is to produce a large number of units in a given time period—and where the employees do not have to cooperate with each other—may benefit from a mildly competitive atmosphere. For example, it could give bonuses to employees who produce the most units.

Conflict as a Negative Force

Conflict also can have serious negative effects and may divert efforts from goal attainment. Instead of directing organizational resources primarily toward reaching prescribed goals, the conflict may deplete resources, especially time and money.

Conflict can also negatively affect the psychological well-being of employees. If they are severe, conflicting thoughts, ideas, and beliefs can result in resentment, tension, and anxiety. These feelings appear to result from the threat that conflict poses to important personal goals and beliefs. Over an extended period of time, conditions of conflict may make the establishment of supportive and trusting relationships difficult.[10]

Finally, deep conflicts where interaction between the parties is required appears to negatively affect results.[11] For example, pressure for results tends to emphasize immediate and measurable goals (such as product quantity) at the expense of longer range and more important goals (such as product quality). When high product quality is a primary organizational goal, competition may be ill-advised.

LEVELS AND SOURCES OF CONFLICT

There are five major levels and sources of conflicts within organizations, as illustrated in Figure 17-1. They are *intrapersonal* (within an individual), *interpersonal* (between individuals), *intragroup* (within a group), *intergroup* (between groups), and *intraorganizational* (within an organization). All can occur at a sixth level, *interorganizational* (between organizations), which is beyond the scope of this chapter. These levels and sources of conflicts are of-

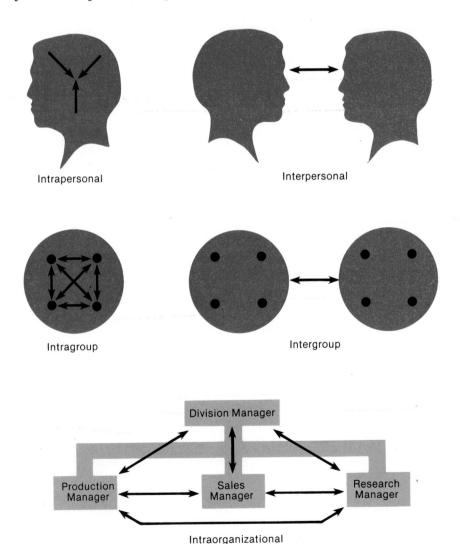

Intrapersonal

Interpersonal

Intragroup

Intergroup

Intraorganizational

FIGURE 17-1.
Levels and Sources
of Conflict

ten interrelated. For example, conflicts within individuals (intrapersonal) may cause them to act in an aggressive or hostile manner toward others, thus triggering interpersonal conflicts.

Intrapersonal Conflict

Intrapersonal conflict occurs within an individual and often involves some form of goal conflict or cognitive conflict. Goal conflict exists for individuals when their behavior will result in outcomes that are mutually exclusive or have incompatible elements (both positive and negative outcomes). College graduates may have to decide whether to take jobs in business or in government (mutually exclusive outcomes). Further, if they take certain jobs in business they may make more money but have less security (incompatible elements) than with certain jobs in government. Intrapersonal goal conflict involves an interplay of positive outcomes, negative outcomes, or both. Three basic types of intrapersonal goal conflict can be identified:

- **Approach–approach conflict** is a situation in which individuals have a choice among two or more alternatives that have positive outcomes (such as a choice between two jobs that appear to be equally attractive).
- **Avoidance–avoidance conflict** is a situation in which individuals must choose among two or more alternatives that have negative outcomes (such as a threatened demotion or increased out-of-town traveling).
- **Approach–avoidance conflict** is a situation in which individuals must decide whether to do something that has both positive and negative outcomes (such as an offer of a good job in a bad location).

Day-to-day decisions frequently involve the resolution of intrapersonal goal conflict and particularly approach–avoidance conflict. The intensity of intrapersonal conflict generally increases under the following conditions:

- There are several-to-many realistic alternative courses of action for coping with the conflict.
- The alternative courses of action are perceived as roughly equal in their positive and negative consequences.
- The source of the conflict is perceived as important to the decision maker.

COGNITIVE DISSONANCE   Intrapersonal conflict is often associated with cognitive dissonance. In general, **cognitive dissonance** exists when individuals recognize inconsistencies in their thoughts, attitudes, values, and/or behaviors.[12] The existence of substantial and recognized inconsistencies is usually stressful or uncomfortable. Sufficient discomfort usually motivates a person to reduce the inconsistency (dissonance) and achieve a state of equilibrium (consonance). In brief, consonance can be achieved (1) by changing thoughts, attitudes, values, and/or behaviors; or (2) by obtaining more information about the issue that is causing the dissonance.

Suppose, for example, that a group of salespeople consider themselves very effective at selling. If they fail to achieve their sales quotas, they may experience cognitive dissonance. They can reduce this dissonance in a number of ways. Some individuals may change their attitudes about their sales abilities, acknowledging the fact that they might not be so great, after all. Others may change their attitudes toward their customers, thinking that the customers did not recognize a good deal. Still others may change their attitudes about what they have to do, resolving to work harder next time to make the sale. Finally, some individuals may realize that their product does not match the competition's, concluding that some improvements are needed in the product rather than in their sales efforts.

Both goal conflict and cognitive conflict exist for many important personal decisions. Some authorities suggest that the greater the goal conflict is before the decision, the greater will be the cognitive dissonance following the decision. We experience post-decision dissonance because we know that the alternative accepted has negative (avoidance) elements, and the alternative rejected has positive (approach) elements. Thus the more difficulty we have in arriving at the original decision, the greater is our need to justify the decision afterward. Some cognitive dissonance is inevitable in life. Otherwise, with total consistency, our own inner world and the external world as we interpret it would be in perfect harmony.

NEUROTIC TENDENCIES **Neurotic tendencies** refer to personality-based mechanisms used by the individual—often unconsciously—that are irrational and create inner conflicts. In turn, these inner conflicts frequently result in behaviors that lead to conflicts with others. The psychological sources of neurotic tendencies is beyond the scope of this discussion.[13]

Let us briefly consider some ways that managers with strong neurotic tendencies might think and act within the organization.[14] Neurotic managers might make excessive use of tight organizational controls (budgets, rules and regulations, monitoring systems) because they distrust people in and outside of the organization. Some neurotic managers may be fearful of uncertainty and risk, not necessarily distrustful of others. Thus they are driven to plan and standardize every detail of their operation. Again, they emphasize formal controls. Still other neurotic managers may be excessively bold and impulsive in their actions. They may be predisposed to rely on hunches and impressions rather than to seek out available facts. These managers may not use participation and consultation in their decision making unless required to do so.

Managers—and people in general—with strong neurotic tendencies usually struggle unsuccessfully with their inner conflicts. Through their dysfunctional behaviors, they often trigger interpersonal conflict with others. For example, the excessive distrust and need to control exhibited by neurotic managers is likely to trigger conflicts with others, especially their subordinates who come to feel overcontrolled and distrusted. Fortunately, there is no evidence to suggest that most managers—or employees in general— show excessive neurotic tendencies.

Interpersonal Conflict

Interpersonal conflict involves two or more individuals who perceive themselves as being in opposition to each other regarding preferred outcomes (goals) and/or attitudes, values, or behaviors. This can be illustrated by what is known as the *prisoner's dilemma.*

In Practice: Prisoner's Dilemma

Two suspects are taken into custody and separated. The district attorney is certain that they are guilty of a specific crime, but she does not have adequate evidence to convict them at a trial. She points out the alternatives to each prisoner: to confess to the crime that the police are sure they have committed or not to confess. If they both do not confess, the district attorney states she will book them on some minor charge, such as petty larceny or illegal possession of a weapon, for which they both will receive minor punishments. If they both confess they will be prosecuted, but she will recommend less than the most severe sentence. If one confesses and the other does not, the confessor will receive lenient treatment for turning state's evidence, whereas the other will get a stiff sentence.[15]

In this situation, each prisoner must decide what to do without knowing the other's decision. Figure 17–2 shows the possible outcomes. If both prisoners confess, they will each be sentenced to six years in jail. If they both remain silent, they will each receive sentences of three years. If one confesses while the other remains silent, the confessor will get off with only a year, whereas the nonconfessor will receive ten years in jail.

This type of situation includes many of the features of interpersonal conflict. First, the dilemma is based on the interdependencies and contingencies present in the payoff matrix shown in Figure 17–2. The outcomes for each person depends on what the other does. Second, the dilemma emphasizes the distinction between individual outcomes and joint outcomes. For each person, the best individual outcome results from confessing. However, the best joint outcome results from both remaining silent. Third, the dilemma involves the role of trust. Assume that the district attorney allows the two prisoners to meet before they reach their separate decisions, and the prisoners agree to remain silent. When they return to their separate cells and reconsider the payoff matrix, it is still in their best individual interest to confess, because neither one knows whether to trust the other.

COMPETITIVE VERSUS COOPERATIVE RESPONSES The prisoner's dilemma shows several interesting aspects of interpersonal conflict in a relatively

A's Choices

		Confess	Remain silent
B's Choices	Confess	− 6 for A − 6 for B	− 10 for A − 1 for B
	Remain silent	− 1 for A − 10 for B	− 3 for A − 3 for B

FIGURE 17–2.
Prisoner's Dilemma
Payoff Matrix

simple format. The two alternatives—confess or remain silent—represent *competitive* versus *cooperative* responses to conflict. Confession is a competitive response. One party attempts to achieve the best outcome at the expense of the other. A number of factors affect the level of cooperation between two people in the prisoner's dilemma, including the following:

- When the situation involves a series of decisions (a number of trials), cooperation tends to be low or to decline at first and then to rise.

- A person responds more to changes in the other's strategy than to fixed strategies. For example, a person is more likely to cooperate if the other person shifts from competition to cooperation than if the other has been consistently cooperative from the start.

- Opportunities for feedback and communication usually increase the probability of cooperation. Of course, since communication can be used to deceive, the effects of communication must be considered in the broader context of the person's intent.[16]

The prisoner's dilemma format is useful for studying some aspects of interpersonal conflict. However, it tends to oversimplify the possible responses available in an interpersonal conflict, allowing only two possible responses: competitive or cooperative behaviors. In actual interpersonal conflict, other responses are possible.

INTERPERSONAL CONFLICT-HANDLING STYLES We respond to interpersonal conflict in at least five different ways.[17] Figure 17–3 provides a useful model for understanding and comparing these five interpersonal conflict-handling styles. They are identified according to their locations in two dimensions, which are based on the distinction between the desire to satisfy our own concerns and the desire to satisfy the concerns of others. The desire to satisfy our own concerns depends on the extent to which we are *assertive* in pursuing personal goals. Our desire to satisfy the concerns of others depends on the extent to which we exhibit a *cooperative* stance. Thus the five interpersonal conflict-handling styles represent different combinations of assertiveness and cooperativeness.

The **avoidance style** involves behavior that is unassertive and uncooperative. People use this style to stay out of conflicts, ignore disagreements, or remain neutral. This approach might reflect a decision to let the conflict work itself out, or it might reflect an aversion to tension and frustration.

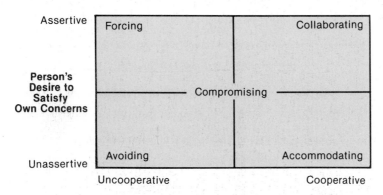

FIGURE 17–3.
Model of Interpersonal Conflict-Handling Styles

Source: Adapted with permission from Thomas, K. W., Conflict and Conflict Management. In *Handbook of Industrial and Organizational Psychology*, M. D. Dunnette (Ed.) Chicago: Rand McNally, 1976, 900.

Sometimes avoidance can be useful in minimizing the possibility of conflict escalation. However, ignoring important issues often frustrates others. Consistent use of this interpersonal conflict-handling style usually results in unfavorable evaluations by others.

The **forcing style** is behavior that is assertive and uncooperative, and it reflects a win–lose approach to interpersonal conflict. Those who use this style try to achieve their own goals without concern for others. Thus the forcing style often involves elements of power and dominance. The forcing person feels that one side must win and, by necessity, one side must lose. This style can sometimes help a person to achieve individual goals. However, like avoidance, forcing tends to result in unfavorable evaluations by others.

In the Preview Case, Mr. T., the manager from headquarters, used a forcing style on Mr. G., the plant manager. Mr. T. insisted on changes in the flexible work schedule because of what he defined as a "lack of rules and discipline" and a "lack of structure and order." He held this view despite the dramatic increases in production, efficiency, and profitability at the plant. Mr. T. may have had a compulsive neurotic tendency.

The **accommodating style** represents behavior that is cooperative but not assertive. Accommodation may represent an altruistic act, a long-term strategy to encourage cooperation by others, or a submission to the wishes of others. Accommodators are usually favorably evaluated by others but also are perceived as weak.

The **collaborative style** is behavior that is strongly cooperative and assertive. It reflects a win–win approach to interpersonal conflict. Thus the collaborative style represents a desire to maximize joint outcomes. People who use the collaborative style tend to have the following characteristics:

- They see conflict as natural, helpful, and even leading to a more creative solution if handled properly.
- They show trust and candor with others.
- They recognize that, when conflict is resolved to the satisfaction of all, commitment to the solution is likely.
- They believe that everyone has an equal role in resolving the conflict and view the opinions of everyone as equally legitimate.
- They do not sacrifice anyone simply for the good of the group.[18]

Others perceive people using the collaborative style as dynamic individuals and evaluate them favorably.

In the Preview Case, Mr. G. recognized the work versus family conflicts being experienced by the women workers. He developed a course of action to meet their concerns and those of the company. The solution of flexible work hours and increased training so that the workers could perform all the jobs on the assembly line was effective. A win–win (collaborative) solution had been reached until Mr. T. visited the plant.

The **compromise style** represents behavior that is intermediately cooperative and assertive. This style is based on a give-and-take process and typically involves negotiation and a series of concessions. Compromise is commonly used and widely accepted as a means of resolving conflict. Those who compromise with others tend to be evaluated favorably. Compared with the collaborative style, compromise does not tend to maximize joint satisfaction. Rather, compromise achieves moderate, but only partial, satisfaction for each party. In the Preview Case, Mr. T. was not receptive to Mr. G.'s efforts to work out a compromise between his demands for order and control and the women production workers' needs for some flexibility in their work schedules.

FINDINGS ON INTERPERSONAL CONFLICT-HANDLING STYLES A number of studies have been conducted on the use of different interpersonal conflict-handling styles. They found that people tend to claim using collaboration more often than the other styles. Collaboration tends to be characteristic of (1) more successful managers compared with less successful managers; and (2) higher-performing organizations compared with medium- and lower-performing organizations. In addition, they found that people tend to perceive collaboration in terms of the constructive use of conflict. Finally, the use of collaboration seems to result in positive feelings in others as well as favorable self-evaluations of performance and abilities.

In contrast to collaboration, forcing and avoidance apparently have negative effects. Forcing and avoidance tend to be associated with decreases in the constructive use of conflict, negative feelings from others, and unfavorable self-evaluations of performance and abilities. The effects of accommodation and compromise appear to be mixed. For example, in one study, the use of accommodation seemed to elicit positive feelings from others but did not lead to favorable evaluations of performance and abilities by others. Another study found no significant effects of compromise, but a third study found that compromise was followed by positive feelings from others.[19]

Intragroup Conflict

A group is greater than and different from the sum of its individual parts. Likewise, intragroup conflict involves more than a sum of intrapersonal and interpersonal conflicts. **Intragroup conflict** refers to clashes among some or all of the individual group members. Thus intragroup conflict often affects the group's processes and outputs. In addition, the task and social–emotional processes within the group influence the causes or resolution of intragroup conflict.

In a classic study, Deutsch investigated the effects of cooperation and competition on group process and productivity.[20] As part of a college course, 50 students were divided into 10 teams. The teams were assigned problems each week and graded on their performance. The method of grading allowed the researcher to create two very different social situations. Five of the groups were assigned to a cooperative situation and were graded as units. That is, each group as a whole received a grade depending on how well it did in comparison with the other groups. The remaining five groups were assigned to a competitive situation, and each person was graded. Within each of these groups, the person who contributed the most received the highest grade. Moreover, the grade was based on a ranking system so the individual contributing most received a 1, the next highest contributor received a 2, and so on down to a 5 for the person contributing the least. In the cooperative situation, the group members shared a common goal: to maximize the group's grade. In the competitive situation, the members did not share any goals; each member tried to maximize his or her own grade.

By the end of the five-week study, the two grading systems resulted in different effects on the group's processes and output. Compared with groups in the competitive situation, groups in the cooperative situation showed the following characteristics: (1) greater coordination of effort; (2) better understanding of communication; (3) greater friendliness; (4) more favorable evaluations of the group; (5) greater productivity per unit of time; and (6) higher-quality solutions.

From the results of this study, Deutsch concluded that intragroup cooperation facilitates positive group processes such as coordination and communication, while also improving the quantity and quality of group output. Criticism of Deutsch's conclusions, however, included the point that his situation of intragroup cooperation also involved intergroup competition. Thus the element of competition between groups may have stimulated each group to try harder. Intragroup cooperation seems to positively affect group process, with or without intergroup competition. However, intergroup competition seems to stimulate productivity. Competition apparently facilitates performance on some tasks.[21]

Intergroup Conflict

Intergroup conflict refers to opposition and clashes between two or more groups. Intergroup competition can stimulate groups to perform better. Thus intergroup conflict can involve benefits as well as costs. The following study, conducted as part of a management training program, illustrates the potential effects of intergroup competition.

In Practice: The Competing Managers

In a management training program, the participating managers were assigned to one of two groups to work on a number of managerial dilemmas. After the groups had been working together for twelve to fourteen hours, they were given a problem that supposedly measured their effectiveness in group problem solving. The problem was presented so that each group was competing with the other group to find the best solution. Thus, one group would be a winner and the other group would be a loser. Once the problem was assigned, the element of competition began to affect behavior within each group as well as relations between the groups.

Behavior within groups   As work on the problem got underway, each group became closer and a sense of group loyalty developed. Each group experienced a rapid increase in cohesion. Associated with the increased cohesiveness was pressure toward conformity (the groupthink phenomenon) and a suppression of interpersonal conflict. Each group was primarily concerned with task goals. Members became more willing to follow autocratic leaders. The net result of all these trends was that group members felt satisfied with their group and rated the group in very positive terms. The researchers referred to the members' high rating of their group as a natural "superiority complex". That is, group members tended to regard their group as superior to the other group.

Relations between groups   Hostility developed between the groups. Each viewed the other as an "enemy." Perceptions of the other group tended to be distorted, and inaccurate stereotypes developed. These distorted and inaccurate perceptions were maintained as interaction and communication between the groups decreased. The hostility, misperceptions, and reduced communication seemed to reinforce one another. The intensity of the conflict escalated.

Reactions to the choice of a winner   When a neutral judge chose the "best" solution, the two groups' reactions, predictably, were different. The winning group considered the decision to be fair and impartial. After the decision, the winning group became even more cohesive. Winning had validated the members' positive views of the group. The leaders became even more established in their positions. Group members became self-satisfied and engaged in playful tension; they became "fat and happy." This self-satisfaction led to a complacent attitude in future competition. As a result of such complacency, a winning group may not improve much over its past performance.

In contrast, the losing group considered the judge's decision unfair and biased. After hearing they had lost, the losing group often became disorganized. Unresolved intragroup conflict began to surface. The group looked for something or someone to blame for their defeat. Often the members considered the leaders responsible for the loss, and a new leadership structure emerged.[22]

If further competition were scheduled, the losing group probably would reorganize and become more cohesive. If it found valid reasons for its previous failure, it might learn valuable lessons from the loss. Thus it might improve its performance in later problem-solving situations. On the other hand, intragroup dissension following a loss may cause the losing group to become demoralized and adopt a defeatist attitude. The group may miss valuable learning opportunities if it simply tries to shift the blame for its loss.[23] Of course, winning groups may also ignore the opportunity to learn as a result of the "fat and happy" state that sometimes follows success.

Intraorganizational Conflict

Intraorganizational conflict arises from opposition and clashes that are based primarily on the way jobs are designed, the organization is structured, and formal authority is allocated. There are four major types of intraorganizational conflict: (1) vertical conflict; (2) horizontal conflict; (3) line–staff conflict; and (4) role conflict. These types of conflict—especially role conflict—can overlap, but each type has some distinctive characteristics. In addition, they often are nestled within one or more of the levels of conflict previously discussed (intrapersonal, interpersonal, intragroup, and intergroup).

VERTICAL CONFLICT   Vertical conflict refers to clashes between levels in an organization. The conflict experienced between Mr. G., the plant manager, and Mr. T., the manager from headquarters, in the Preview Case is one example. Vertical conflicts often arise because superiors attempt to control subordinates too tightly and subordinates tend to resist.[24] Subordinates may resist because they believe that control infringes on their personal freedom. Vertical conflict can also arise because of inadequate communication, conflicts of goals, or a lack of consensus concerning perceptions of information and values (cognitive conflict).[25]

HORIZONTAL CONFLICT   Horizontal conflict refers to clashes among employees or departments at the same hierarchical level in an organization. A fundamental cause of horizontal conflict is the presence of suboptimization in many organizations. Each department may suboptimize by independently striving for its own departmental goals. These goals may be incompatible across departments, causing goal conflict. Contrasting attitudes of employees in different departments also may lead to conflict.

LINE–STAFF CONFLICT   Most organizations have staff departments to assist the line departments. Line managers normally are responsible for some process that creates a part or all of the firm's product. Staff managers often serve an advisory or control function that requires specialized technical knowledge.

The line–staff relationship frequently involves conflict. Staff managers and line managers typically have different personal characteristics. Staff managers tend to have a higher level of education, come from different backgrounds, and are younger than line managers.[26] These differences in personal characteristics are frequently associated with different values and attitudes. The surfacing of these different values and attitudes tends to create conflict.

Line managers often feel that staff managers are infringing on their areas of legitimate authority.[27] Staff people may specify the methods and partially control the resources used by line managers. For example, in many manufacturing organizations, staff engineers specify how each product should be made and what materials should be used. At the same time, line managers are held responsible for the output. Thus line managers may experience conflict when they perceive that the engineers are directing production activities. Line managers often reason that staff managers reduce their authority over workers but that their responsibility for the output remains unchanged; that is, their perceived authority is less than their perceived responsibility because of staff involvement.

ROLE CONFLICT   A **role** is the cluster of activities that others expect a person to perform in his or her position and frequently involves conflict. Figure 17–4 presents a model of a role episode. Prior to a message being sent, role senders have expectations, perceptions, and evaluations of the focal person's activities. These, in turn, influence the actual role messages that senders

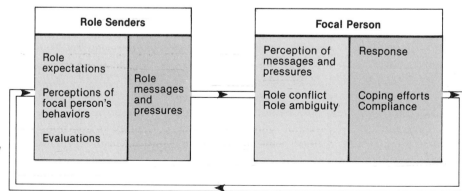

FIGURE 17–4.
Role Espisode
Model

Source: Based on Kahn, R. L., *et al. Organizational Stress: Studies in Role Conflict and Ambiguity.* New York: John Wiley, 1964, 26.

transmit. The focal person's perceptions of these messages and pressures may then lead to role conflict. Accordingly, **role conflict** occurs when a focal person perceives incompatible messages and pressures from the role senders. Finally, the focal person responds with coping behaviors that serve as inputs to the role senders' experiences.

A **role set** is the group of role senders for the focal person. As an example, a role set usually includes your manager, perhaps your manager's immediate supervisor, and other employees with whom you work closely. Four types of role conflict often result from incompatible messages and pressures from the role set:

- **Intrasender role conflict** means that different messages and pressures from a single member of the role set are incompatible.

- **Intersender role conflict** means that messages and pressures from one role sender oppose messages and pressures from one or more other senders.

- **Interrole conflict** means that role pressures associated with membership in one group are incompatible with pressures stemming from membership in other groups.

- **Person–role conflict** means that role requirements are incompatible with the focal person's own attitudes, values, or notions of acceptable behavior.[28]

In addition to experiencing one or more of the four types of role conflict, an individual may experience conflict due to role ambiguity. **Role ambiguity** is the focal person's perception of a lack of clear, consistent information about the required activities and tasks of the job. Like role conflict, severe role ambiguity often causes stress and subsequent coping behaviors. These behaviors may include (1) aggressive action and hostile communication; (2) withdrawal; and (3) approaching the role sender or senders to attempt joint problem solving. However, research on the relationships among role conflict, role ambiguity, and outcomes such as stress reactions, aggression, hostility, withdrawal behavior (turnover and absenteeism), and the like is far from clear-cut.[29] Stress is a common reaction to severe role conflict and role ambiguity. Chapter 18 focuses on the sources of and ways for dealing with work stress.

STRUCTURAL METHODS OF CONFLICT MANAGEMENT

The preceding discussion on the levels and sources of conflict within organizations provided some hints about ways to avoid unnecessary conflict and to deal with those conflicts that are an inevitable part of life. In this section and the next two, we develop and build on those hints by proposing specific approaches to managing conflict within organizations. Because the levels and sources of conflict within organizations are wide-ranging, there is no single approach or set of methods for managing conflict.

The three major approaches to managing conflict within organizations are: structural, interpersonal, and promotional. A variety of methods has been used successfully with each approach. A representative sampling of these methods, rather than a complete inventory, is presented.

The structural approach is used when conflict is already present and requires management. The methods used in this approach tend to minimize the direct expression of conflict by separating the parties. Organizations commonly use five structural methods in managing conflicts: dominance through position, decoupling, buffering with inventory, buffering with a linking pin, and buffering with an integrating department. As Figure 17–5 suggests, an organization may use all of these methods.

Dominance through Position

Managers may attempt to resolve conflict within their respective areas of authority by simply issuing a directive that specifies the course of action subordinates are expected to follow. For example, two vice-presidents in the same firm are working on the organization's strategy. One vice-president advocates a strategy of growth based on decentralized decision making. The other vice-president desires a strategy that requires authority to be concentrated at the top levels of the organization. The growth objective conflicts directly with the centralized authority objective and the president exercises positional authority to select the strategy to be followed.

Managers can use positional authority to settle conflicts within or between departments. Within a department, the supervisor can issue a directive to resolve the conflict. Between departments, a higher-level manager with responsibility for the departments can issue a directive to resolve the conflict. Of course, dominance through position can also increase conflict, as we saw in the Preview Case.

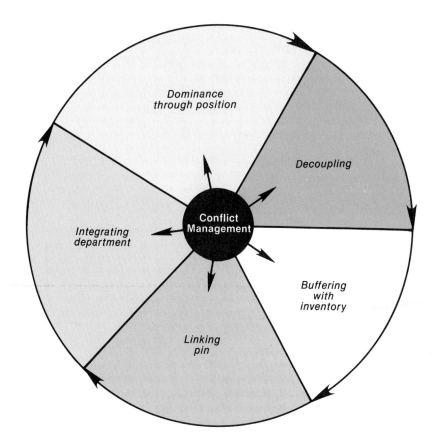

FIGURE 17–5.
Common Structural Methods of Conflict Management

Positional authority does not always effectively resolve interdepartmental conflict. It is unrealistic to expect a vice-president to resolve all the conflict issues that arise among lower-level departments. Furthermore, the dominance method does little to prevent conflict from occurring again. This method serves primarily to resolve a specific conflict after it has already occurred.

Decoupling

Organization design can directly reduce interdependence among departments. Providing departments with resources and inventories that are independent of those of other departments can *decouple* them and thus reduce the propensity for interdepartmental conflict. However, independence may increase costs because of duplication of efforts and equipment. The product form of organization (Chapter 14) is a structural way of decoupling.

Buffering with Inventory

Completely decoupling departments, or making them totally independent, may be too costly. Thus an organization may want to buffer the work flow between departments with inventory. If Department A produces a product that serves as an input to Department B, an inventory buffer can prevent Department B from being severely affected by a temporary shutdown or slowdown in Department A. Thus the likelihood that employees in Department B will become upset with Department A declines.

Linking Pin

An organization can incorporate linking pins into its structure when poor departmental integration and unnecessary conflict exist.[30] A **linking pin** is an individual assigned to help integrate two departments that have overlapping activities. This person is expected to understand the operations of both departments and coordinate the departmental activities that interface. The linking pin must keep information flowing between the departments. In order to do this, the person must be perceived as someone who can be trusted by both departments and not as someone who is a member of either department. The linking pin must often remind both departments of their commitments and loyalties to the overall organization and its goals. This reduces the tendency of the departments to focus on their own subgoals and lose sight of the bigger picture in conflict situations. The linking pin must also discourage each department from taking unilateral action on those issues that may affect—directly or indirectly—the other department. An effective linking pin must be a strong advocate and user of the collaboration and compromise conflict management styles. Moreover, this person is doomed to failure if any of the neurotic tendencies mentioned earlier are part of his or her personality.

Integrating Department

An integrating department typically has formal authority to issue orders to two or more interdependent departments with respect to those activities that affect their ability to act in an integrated manner. Thus an integrating department generally has much more formal authority than a linking pin to direct the activities of other departments and to resolve conflicts that might arise among them. Consider the tasks of the distribution and product planning department of an integrated paper company, as described by its vice-president.

In Practice: Distribution and Product Planning Department

My department schedules all paper machines in the mill side of the business. For instance, with respect to the container division's business, we schedule the mill's machines which make paperboard and corrugating medium and we are responsible for controlling inventory at this stage of production. Of course, we do not schedule the actual converting operations for containers or packaging; that is their responsibility.

We must know both on a daily and future basis what the container and packaging people are converting so that we can insure that they don't run out of paper and board. This requires a tremendous amount of close work because we have a wide variety of products and the converting divisions' business can shift drastically over time. There is always a danger that inventory at the mill level will become very high by grade; and our job is to balance the need for a reasonable level of this inventory with the danger of running out of paper.

The basic issue is to keep everything going. The paper machines must run 100% of the time if the mills are to make a reasonable cost showing. If we come in with a lot of shifts in scheduling, the mill costs suffer. We try to be responsive to those cost requirements, but at the same time we have to take care of our market demand. Unanticipated market shifts in one area can also raise hell above and beyond their impact on the mills. Over the last few years we've been fairly tight on mill capacity; we have virtually no unused capacity. Thus, an emergency change in schedules for one converting unit can put another converting unit on the spot.

Because of our intimate involvement in day-to-day planning of product flow we are in a position to play a central role in planning long-range facilities expansions along with the mills. We secure forecasts of future needs on a two-, five-, and ten-year basis and then pull together the capital projects which will be presented to the corporate officers. In this side of the business long-range planning cannot be an "ivory tower" sort of thing; it is closely tied to our day-to-day planning and scheduling.[31]

The distribution and product planning department provided the major means of integration between the container division and the converting divisions. This department almost eliminated the need for the container division to interact with the converting divisions. Thus the conflict between these manufacturing divisions was also minimal.

INTERPERSONAL METHODS OF CONFLICT MANAGEMENT

The interpersonal approach to conflict management also is used when conflict is evident and requires management. In contrast to the methods used in the structural approach, interpersonal methods are aimed at causing conflict to surface by bringing the parties together. The primary interpersonal methods of conflict management include collaboration, negotiation, and third-party consultation.

Collaboration

As implied in the earlier discussion of the collaborative conflict-handling style, **collaboration** is a process by which individuals directly engage one another, openly exchange information on the issues, and try to identify a course of action that will result in a mutually desirable (win–win) outcome. Collaboration is a *process* and set of interactions engaged in by all of the parties. Thus it is more than the characteristics and personal inclinations of the individuals involved. Collaboration should have been used in the situation related in the Preview Case to attempt to resolve the conflict between Mr. G. and Mr. T. Of course, Mr. T., who had much more power than Mr. G., appeared to be satisfied with his forcing strategy, even though it was likely to revive the turnover and productivity problems at the plant.

Collaboration is most practical when there is

- sufficient *required interdependence* so that it makes sense to expend the extra time and energy needed with collaboration to work through individual differences;

- sufficient *parity in power* among individuals so that they feel free to interact candidly, regardless of their formal superior/subordinate status;

- the potential for *mutual benefits,* especially over the long run, for resolving the dispute through a win–win process; and

- sufficient *organizational support* for taking the time and energy to resolve disputes through collaboration. Thus the norms, rewards, and punishments of the organization—especially as set by top management—provide the framework for encouraging or discouraging the use of collaboration.[32]

Collaboration does not automatically occur when people directly engage each other. Adoption of a win–lose strategy leads to forcing rather than collaborative interaction. The use of collaboration depends heavily on the parties' attitudes and goals. The assumption that both sides can win distinguishes collaboration from other responses to conflict. This is not to suggest that collaboration is an easy process, which depends only on the participants having the *right* attitudes. Collaboration can be a tense and emotionally draining process.

Negotiation

Negotiation is a process in which two or more parties, having both common and conflicting interests, state and discuss proposals concerning specific terms of a possible agreement. Negotiation normally includes a combination of compromise, collaboration, and possibly some forcing on particular issues that are vital to one or more of the parties.

It is impossible to consider here all of the strategies, tactics, and other aspects of negotiations.[33] However, it is useful to understand that most successful negotiations proceed through three stages:

- *Establishing the negotiation range.* The negotiators spend time on clearly identifying the relevant issues and the range (upper and lower limits) within which they will negotiate. This stage is often characterized by tough talk and the stressing of differences in the positions of the parties.

- *Probing the negotiation range.* The negotiators ask questions about their "opponent's" positions and the outcomes that various positions might create for them. There is more listening and sharing of information during this stage but not total openness. Retreats are made from the initially stated firm positions and trial concessions are floated that can be withdrawn quickly if need be. Win–win possibilities are explored on those issues involving conflict over common interests, and potential compromises are considered for distributive issues. The process figuratively "goes in circles," working ever closer to more concrete potential agreements, but not reaching agreement on any one issue.

- *Precipitating the agreement or crisis.* This stage might actually result in an increase in sporadic heated exchanges as the negotiators try to bring together all of the issues in an attempt to reach agreement. Tensions and anxiety are usually heightened during this stage as the negotiators realize that they will have to live with the agreement. Second thoughts (especially cognitive dissonance) about the commitments they are about to make surface. This is also a delicate stage in which the negotiations can quickly swing in one of two directions: toward either agreement or crisis and stalemate.[34]

Broader cultural norms and expected patterns of behavior can influence the process of negotiations. This is illustrated in the description of negotiating with the Japanese.

ACROSS CULTURES

Negotiating with the Japanese

To the Japanese businessperson, negotiation is the beginning of business, the start of a relationship and not the end of a transaction, as it usually is in the West. Japanese very rarely present their best and/or final plan until the end when they feel they absolutely must. Negotiations are usually conducted in stages in Japan so that clarifying questions can be posed along the way or so that counterparts can make counterclaims or demands regarding the issue at hand. This can make negotiation a somewhat drawn-out affair in Japan, where patience is a virtue.

The Japanese negotiator more often than not is concerned primarily with data, price, and quality of the product but tends to develop a relationship first, providing the relationship has the potential for mutual benefit. To the Japanese these are the essential factors involved in deciding which way the negotiation will go. If you don't take time to develop some sort of interpersonal relationship with the Japanese you are dealing with, you may very well end up with some very negative results. Japanese have been known to throw away millions in profits by rejecting possible joint ventures and other business transactions because they felt the *Gaijin* (foreigners) didn't like them.

Japanese businesspeople are usually very calm but formal in negotiation. Expressions of emotion are considered a weakness in Japan and unforgivable in business transactions. They rarely get angry or resort to heated argument, trying always to respect or maintain the face and dignity of their counterparts as well as themselves. Aggressive behavior in negotiation is rare and the presentation of arguments is usually confined to group causes and interests in an effort always to maintain group identity. Presentations are often primarily concerned with factual analysis and data interpretation. Policy and/or plan implementation are rarely presented or discussed until negotiations have been finalized. There is usually a lack of persuasion in Japanese negotiations as we know it. Transactional matters are discussed in very general and sometimes vague, even ambiguous, terms. The details in many instances are adjusted in the process of implementation. To the Japanese, the policies and plans in any particular transaction are subject to current conditions. As current conditions have a tendency to change, so do the policies and plans. This makes contracting a very difficult, if not sometimes impossible, process. To the Japanese, the contract is often oral and almost always is limited in written form.

Business logic for the Japanese often has a dual aspect. One is the logic of ritual used to maintain *wa* (harmony, the absence of conflict) and the other is the logic of problem solving, which lacks the element of negative reasoning resulting from the first type of logic. The lack and avoidance of negative reasoning makes negotiations for Japanese on an international level extremely difficult.[35]

Third-Party Consultation

Most negotiation occurs directly between the involved parties. When the parties are likely to get locked into win–lose conflict, a third-party consultant, acting as a *neutral* party, can help the parties resolve their differences.

SKILLS AND FUNCTIONS It is quite easy to take on the role of a third-party consultant. However, it is not at all easy to act effectively in that role. Effective third-party consultants need particular conceptual and behavioral skills. First, they must be able to diagnose the conflict. Second, they must be skilled in breaking deadlocks and interrupting interaction at the right time. Finally, they must show mutual acceptance and have the personal capacity to provide emotional support and reassurance. Thus the style of a third-party consultant must instill confidence and acceptance by parties in conflict. Key functions of this role are to

- *ensure mutual motivation.* Each party should have incentives for resolving the conflict.
- *achieve a balance in situational power.* If the situational power of the parties is not approximately equal, it may be difficult to establish trust and maintain open lines of communication.
- *coordinate confrontation efforts.* One party's positive overtures must be coordinated with the other party's readiness to reciprocate. A fail-

ure to coordinate positive initiatives and readiness to respond can undermine future efforts to work out differences.

- *promote openness in dialogue.* The third party can help to establish norms of openness, provide reassurance and support, and decrease the risks associated with openness.

- *maintain an optimum level of tension.* If threat and tension are too low, the incentive for change or finding a solution is minimal. However, if threat and tension are too high, the parties may be unable to process information and see creative alternatives. They may begin to polarize and take rigid positions.[36]

INTERGROUP CONFRONTATION TECHNIQUE A third-party consultant usually tries to facilitate conflict resolution without setting down a specific set of procedures for the parties to follow. Occasionally, however, this is useful to ensure that the parties concentrate on the appropriate issues and direct their efforts toward resolving them. One example of such a structured approach is the *intergroup confrontation technique.*[37] One procedure for such a confrontation includes the following steps:

- Each group meets in a separate room and develops two lists. On one list they indicate how they perceive themselves as a group, particularly in their relationship with the other group. On the second list they indicate how they view the other group.

- The two groups come together and share perceptions. The third-party consultant helps them to clarify their views and, it is hoped, better understand themselves and the other group.

- The groups return to their separate rooms to look deeper into the issues, diagnose the current problem, and determine what each group contributes to the conflict.

- The groups meet together again to share their new insights. The third-party consultant urges them to identify common issues and plan the next stages for seeking solutions.

Like most methods of conflict management, the intergroup confrontation technique does not guarantee a successful resolution of conflict. Instead, it provides a process for parties in conflict to explore and work through their differences. A skillfull third-party consultant uses the technique to move the parties toward a resolution of their conflicts.

PROMOTIONAL METHODS OF CONFLICT MANAGEMENT

The promotional approach to conflict management is based on the assumption that "adequate" conflict is lacking. As noted earlier, cognitive conflict can help avoid groupthink and sloppiness in considering problems and alternative courses of action. Hence, promoting functional cognitive conflict may actually be a useful approach to managing conflict. A variety of methods can be used to promote constructive conflict.[38] The two highlighted here are the dialectical inquiry method and the devil's advocate method.

Dialectical Inquiry Method

The **dialectical inquiry method** involves the development and recommendation of a course of action by one advocate or subgroup of advocates and the development and recommendation of a contradictory course of action by another advocate or subgroup of advocates.[39] The decision maker or group as a whole considers the recommendations of both advocates or subgroups before choosing one alternative or a composite alternative. The two recommended courses of action stem from opposing viewpoints of the same situation. Thus cognitive conflict occurs when both sets of recommendations are considered. Through this process, the decision makers are more likely to reach decisions that have considered all of the facts, possibilities, and viewpoints.

Devil's Advocate Method

The **devil's advocate method** calls for a person or a small group to develop a systematic critique of a recommended course of action.[40] The *devil's advocate* attempts to point out weaknesses in the assumptions underlying the proposal, internal inconsistencies in it, and problems that could lead to failure if it were followed. Unlike the dialectical inquiry method, this method does not promote an alternative course of action; the criticism alone promotes cognitive conflict for the decision maker. The need to resolve the cognitive conflict leads to a better understanding of the problem and, it is hoped, a better decision. In some situations the devil's advocate method appears to lead to better decisions than does the dialectical inquiry method. It may cause the decision maker not to take the recommendations from any one person or group as a given and to be especially sensitive to data that either confirm or dispute the recommended course of action.

SUMMARY

Conflict is inevitable in organizational life, but it need not have destructive consequences for the organization. Depending on how the conflict is managed, the negative effects may be minimized, and positive effects may result from the conflict. The effective management of conflict is based, in part, on a solid understanding of the different ways conflict emerges and is resolved.

Conflict occurs at five different levels within organizations: intrapersonal, interpersonal, intragroup, intergroup, and intraorganizational. Intrapersonal conflict occurs when we experience goal conflict or cognitive conflict within ourselves. Conflict at this level can lead to personal stress, anxiety, and tension. Interpersonal conflict occurs between two or more people. Depending on the interpersonal conflict-handling styles used, the outcomes of interpersonal conflict may represent integrative solutions (win–win outcomes) or distributive solutions (win–lose outcomes). A collaborative style, which is both assertive and cooperative, is generally considered the best way to achieve integrative solutions.

Minimizing intragroup conflict seems to promote more favorable interpersonal relations within groups. However, such conditions may not be sufficient to produce an increased quantity and/or quality of output. In some cases intergroup conflict leads to greater productivity through competition. However, intergroup conflict also can have negative side effects: hostility, misperception, and reduced communication between groups.

The four types of intraorganizational conflict—vertical, horizontal, line–staff, and role—are based, in part, on the interdependencies inherent in organizations. While an organization cannot totally eliminate interdependencies, it can manage intraorganizational and other levels of conflict by structural, interpersonal, or promotional approaches. Five structural methods for managing conflict—dominance through position, decoupling, buffering with inventory, linking pin, and the use of integrating departments—were presented. The interpersonal methods of conflict management highlighted include collaboration, negotiation, and third-party consultation. Finally, promoting conflict may be useful at times. The dialectical inquiry and devil's advocate methods can enhance decision making through the intentional introduction of conflicting points of view.

KEY WORDS AND CONCEPTS

Accommodating style
Affective conflict
Approach–approach conflict
Approach–avoidance conflict
Avoidance–avoidance conflict
Avoidance style
Cognitive conflict
Cognitive dissonance
Collaborative style
Compromise style
Conflict
Devil's advocate method
Dialectical inquiry method
Forcing style
Goal conflict

Intergroup conflict
Interpersonal conflict
Interrole conflict
Intersender role conflict
Intragroup conflict
Intraorganizational conflict
Intrapersonal conflict
Intrasender role conflict
Negotiation
Neurotic tendencies
Person–role conflict
Role
Role ambiguity
Role conflict
Role set

DISCUSSION QUESTIONS

1. Cite some differences between conflict, competition, and cooperation.

2. Conflict is often considered a negative feature in organizations. What are some of the positive features of conflict? Provide an example of beneficial conflict from your personal experience.

3. If you were involved in a prisoner's dilemma situation, what would you do to encourage a cooperative response from the other party? If you had a guarantee of cooperation from the other party, what would you do? Why?

4. Identify the five interpersonal conflict-handling styles, and give examples of situations in which each style would be appropriate. What criteria did you use to decide what is appropriate behavior?

5. What advantages and problems could be associated with intergroup conflict? As a manager, would you promote this type of conflict? Why or why not?

6. What were the major findings of the Lawrence and Lorsch study of horizontal organizational conflict? When would a formal integrative department be desirable or undesirable?

7. What are the different types of role conflict? Name the options for coping with role conflict.

8. What is decoupling in conflict management? What is an inventory buffer in an organization? How do these features in organization design lower the likelihood of conflict?

MANAGEMENT INCIDENTS AND CASES

The Reluctant Loan Officer

Betty Hampton graduated from State College with a bachelor's degree in English. For three years she had worked for a local bank during the day and attended classes at night. At this bank Betty had held various jobs, such as teller, loan clerk, secretary, new accounts clerk, and loan processor. Although her major area was English, she had taken enough courses to have a second, unofficial major in business administration. Upon graduation, Betty had difficulty finding a challenging job. Finally, in desperation, she accepted a secretarial position with Third National Bank of Brookfield, Betty's hometown. She was easily able to master the routine secretarial work as well as handle some other areas of responsibility, such as new accounts, loan documentation, statement analysis, and computer output.

Betty's work was soon noticed by Ralph Wheelen, the senior commercial loan officer, who remarked to others that since Betty seemed to be doing such a good job processing loan applications, she might make a good loan officer. Top management was somewhat reluctant to have a female loan officer, since they felt it was "well known" that women are easily swayed by their emotions. Some feared that customers might take advantage of Betty. Carlos Louis, the bank president, feared that a young, attractive woman might not project the stable and conservative image he felt was necessary in a good loan officer. At that time, only three women in the bank had supervisory responsibilities. Two women were in operations—one supervising the bookkeeping department and the other overseeing tellers. There was also one female branch manager, Susan Spriggs (with whom Carlos quite openly had more than a simple business rela-tionship). Carlos believed these women to be appropriately placed, since they primarily supervised other women and had nothing to do with what he considered to be the key profit area in the bank—commercial loans. Nevertheless, on the basis of Ralph's recommendation and Equal Employment Opportunity consider-ations, Carlos gave Betty the chance to move up to the position of loan officer.

Betty realized that the bank was using her as a test case and that the president was concerned she project the proper image. Consequently, she dressed in long-sleeved blouses with high-neck collars. She wore mainly dark colors and attempted to main-tain a serious appearance and demeanor at all times, both on the job and in the community. Of eight banks in the city, only Third National had a female lender.

The first few months on the job were challenging ones for Betty. She enjoyed her job and seemed to be progressing well. She was having no real problems getting commercial customers to accept her as a lender or in conducting her officer calls, during which she visited local business people to encourage them to do business with Third National.

One morning Betty joined eleven other loan officers and branch managers in the conference room for the weekly business development meeting. The meeting was conducted, as usual, by the senior vice-president, Bill Weber. After discussing the week's officer call reports, Bill asked the group how the bank could increase its holdings of mortgage loans. John Sullivan, a loan officer of many years, suggested that someone talk with Amos McLaren, a successful realtor in the community. "If someone could just talk Amos into mentioning Third National to his customers," suggested John, "we could really pick up business!"

"That's an excellent idea," responded Bill, "but we have to be careful how we approach him." Turning to Betty, Bill said, "Betty, I think you ought to take Amos out tommorrow night and do whatever is necessary to get his business."

Betty was astounded at the implications of Weber's statement. "Who does he think I am?" she wondered to herself as she looked at the eleven other people in the conference room. Susan, the branch manager and the only other female in the room, was looking at the floor and nervously adjusting her watch. No one else seemed to be reacting except for Joe Bibbins, a young but experienced loan officer, who seemed to have a slight smirk on his face. Betty had heard the rumors circulating around the bank of various people sleeping together, but she never realized how far things seemed to have gone!

After a moment's hesitation, Betty looked the senior vice-president in the eye and said, "You have other women on the staff you've hired for that purpose. Let them do it."[41]

Questions

1. What types of conflicts exist in this case study?
2. What are the basic causes of these conflicts?
3. Did Betty say the right thing? What is the basis for your response?

GTE of the Central States

GTE of the Central States serves the outskirts of a large metropolitan area. The company's recent request for a rate increase was rejected by the state's Public Service Commission primarily because of customer complaints regarding poor service. Many of the complaints were aimed at repeated trouble reports.

Each reporting center is made up of two employee groups: craft and management. Supervisory personnel are assigned to each reporting center and are managed by one second-line supervisor, who is in most cases identified as "hipo"—a high-potential graduate of the company's highly touted management training program.

According to company practice, second-line supervisors oversee those who supervise each craft group and whose primary functions include assigning work, establishing priorities, and completing quality inspections. Since some of the stations are understaffed in terms of supervisory personnel, selected craft personnel also perform some of the supervisory functions, including scheduling and quality inspections.

This type of cooperation had been going on smoothly for many years until recently, when some of the craft personnel refused to do any supervisory work. The acting supervisors indicated that company policy on such factors as work schedules, parking privileges, and work breaks favors the second-line supervisors, whose work schedules fit their personal needs rather than service needs. The first-line supervisory personnel claim that second-line supervisors are given preferred parking locations, while they and craft employees are required to park in an area further from the reporting location in unpaved and poorly lighted lots. The first-line supervisors and craft employees have complained to the area service manager, but she explained that these privileges had existed for several years and were designed to recognize the more professional, demanding nature of the second-line supervisor's job.

The pressures from the area service manager regarding repeated trouble reports have caused regular supervisory personnel to complain about a lack of understanding. The area service manager claims that since the Public Service Commission refused the requested rate increase, there is no money available to hire more supervisory personnel.

The ill feelings among craft employees, first-line supervisors, and the second-line supervisors are resulting in a continuing reduction of the quality of service, as well as a loss of morale.[42]

Questions

1. What types of conflict exist at GTE?
2. What are the underlying causes of these conflicts?
3. What actions would you take if you were the area service manager? Why?

REFERENCES

1. Excerpted from Elbing, C. J. 'Yes, but...': Hidden Criteria for Judging Managerial Innovations. *Business Horizons,* November/December, 1984, 10–14. Copyright, 1984, by the Foundation for the School of Business at Indiana University. Reprinted by permission.

2. Fraser, N. M., and Hipel, K. W. *Conflict Analysis: Models and Resolutions.* New York: North-Holland, 1984.

3. Deutsch, M. Conflicts: Productive and Destructive. *Journal of Social Issues,* 1969, *25,* 4–41.

4. Imberman, W. Who Strikes—and Why? *Harvard Business Review,* November–December 1983, 18–20ff; Turney, J. R. *Identifying Sources of Organizational Conflict.* Washington, D.C.: U.S. Government Printing Office, 1981.

5. Cole, D. W. (Ed.) *Conflict Resolution Technology.* Cleveland: Organization Development Institute, 1983; Schultz, B., and Anderson, J. Training in the Management of Conflict: A Communication Theory Perspective. *Small Group Behavior,* 1984, 333–348.

6. van de Vliert, E. Escalative Intervention in Small-Group Conflicts. *Journal of Applied Behavioral Science,* 1985, *21,* 19–36; Litterer, J. A. Conflict in Organizations: A Reexamination. *Academy of Management Journal,* 1966, *9,* 178–186.

7. Brown, K. H., and Slocum, Jr., J. W. An Application of Systems Concepts in Diagnosing Organizational Strategies. In D. Hellriegel and J. W. Slocum Jr. (Eds.) *Management in the World Today: A Book of Readings.* Reading, Mass.: Addison-Wesley, 1975, 54–70.

8. Locke, E. A., and Latham, G. P. *Goal Setting: A Motivational Technique that Works.* Englewood Cliffs, N.J.: Prentice-Hall, 1984, 18–19, 53–54, 112, 126; Steers, R. M., and Porter, L. W. Task-Goal Attributes in Performance. *Psychological Bulletin,* 1974, *81,* 434–452.

9. Cosier, R. A., and Rose, G. L. Cognitive Conflict and Goal Conflict Effects on Task Performance. *Organizational Behavior and Human Performance,* 1977, *19,* 378–391.

10. Huse, E. F., and Cummings, T. G. *Organizational Development and Change,* 3d ed. St. Paul, Minn.: West, 1985.

11. Richardson, B. The Zero-Sum Management Disease and the von Thünen Prescription. *Business Horizons,* November–December, 1984, 15–20; Maier, N. R. F. Assets and Liabilities in Group Problem Solving: The Need for an Integrative Function. *Psychological Review,* 1967, *74,* 239–249.

12. Festinger, L. *A Theory of Cognitive Dissonance.* Evanston, Ill.: Row, Peterson, 1957.

13. For further information about psychological sources, see Lewis, H. B. *Shame and Guilt in Neurosis.* New York: International Universities Press, 1971; Shapiro, D. *Neurotic Styles.* New York: Basic Books, 1965; Kets de Vries, M. F. R. *Organizational Paradoxes: Clinical Approaches to Management.* London: Tavestock, 1980.

14. Kets de Vries, M. F. R., and Miller, D. *The Neurotic Organization.* San Francisco: Jossey-Bass, 1984.

15. Adapted from Luce, R. D., and Raiffa, H. *Games and Decisions.* New York: McGraw-Hill, 1957, 95.

16. Vinacke, W. E. Variables in Experimental Games: Toward a Field Theory. *Psychological Bulletin,* 1969, *71,* 293–318; Friedman, S. R. Game Theory and Labor Con-

flict: Limits of Rational Choice Models. *Sociological Perspectives,* 1983, *26,* 375–397; Lindskold, S., Walters, P. S., and Koutsourais, H. Cooperators, Competitors, and Responses to GRIT. *Journal of Conflict Resolution,* 1983, *27,* 521–532.

17. Cosier, R. A., and Ruble, T. L. Research on Conflict-handling Behavior: An Experimental Approach. *Academy of Management Journal,* 1981, *24,* 816–831; Rahim, M. A. A Measure of Styles of Handling Interpersonal Conflict. *Academy of Management Journal,* 1983, *26,* 368–376.

18. Filley, A. C. *Interpersonal Conflict Resolution.* Glenview, Ill.: Scott, Foresman, 1975, 52.

19. Blake, R. R., and Mouton, J. S. *Solving Costly Organizational Conflicts.* San Francisco: Jossey-Bass, 1984; Thomas, K. W. Conflict and Conflict Management. In M. D. Dunnette (Ed.) *Handbook of Industrial and Organizational Psychology.* Chicago: Rand McNally, 1976, 889–935; Tjosvold, D. Effects of Crisis Orientation on Managers' Approach to Controversy in Decision Making. *Academy of Management Journal,* 1984, *27,* 130–138.

20. Deutsch, M. A Theory of Cooperation and Competition. *Human Relations,* 1949, *2,* 129–152; Deutsch, M. An Experimental Study of the Effects of Cooperation and Competition on Group Process. *Human Relations,* 1949, *2,* 199–232.

21. Julian, H. W., and Perry, F. A. Cooperation Contrasted with Intragroup and Intergroup Competition. *Sociometry,* 1967, *30,* 79–90.

22. Blake, R. R., and Mouton, J. S. Reactions to Intergroup Competition under Win–Lose Conditions. *Management Science,* 1961, *4,* 420–425.

23. Blake, R. R., and Mouton, J. S. How to Achieve Integration on the Human Side of the Merger. *Organizational Dynamics,* Winter 1985, 41–56; Brown, L. D. *Managing Conflict at Organizational Interfaces.* Reading, Mass.: Addison-Wesley, 1983; Nystrom, P.C., and Starbuck, W. H. To Avoid Organizational Crises, Unlearn. *Organizational Dynamics,* Spring 1984, 53–65.

24. Pondy. L. R. Organizational Conflict: Concept and Models. *Administrative Science Quarterly,* 1967, *12,* 296–320.

25. Aram, J. D., and Jalispante Jr., P. F. An Evaluation of Organizational Due Process in the Resolution of Employee/Employer Conflict. *Academy of Management Review,* 1981, *6,* 197–204; Walters, R. S. Union–Management Ideological Frames of Reference. *Journal of Management,* 1982, *8,* 21–33.

26. Dalton, M. Conflict between Staff and Line Managerial Officers. *American Sociological Review,* 1966, *15,* 3–15.

27. Simon, J. R., Norton, C., and Lonergan, N. J. Accounting for the Conflict between Line Management and the Controller's Office. *S.A.M. Advanced Management Journal,* Winter 1979, 4–14.

28. Kahn, R. L., et al. *Organizational Stress: Studies in Role Conflict and Role Ambiguity.* New York: John Wiley, 1964.

29. Berger-Gross, V., and Kraut, A. I. 'Great Expectations': A No-Conflict Explanation of Role Conflict. *Journal of Applied Psychology,* 1984, *69,* 261–271; Fisher, C. D., and Gitelson, R. A Meta-Analysis of the Correlates of Role Conflict and Ambiguity. *Journal of Applied Psychology,* 1983, *68,* 320–333; Jackson, S. E., and Schuler, R. S. A Meta-Analysis and Conceptual Critique of Research on Role Ambiguity and Role Conflict in Work Settings. *Organizational Behavior and Human Decision Processes,* 1985, 36, 16–78; Greenhaus, J. H., and Beutell, N. J. Sources of Conflict Between Work and Family Roles. *Academy of Management Review,* 1985, *10,* 76–88.

30. Likert, R., and Likert, J. G. *New Ways of Managing Conflict.* New York: McGraw-Hill, 1976.

31. Excerpted by permission of the Harvard Business School from Lorsch, J. W., and Allen III, S. A. *Managing Diversity and Interdependence: An Organizational Study of Multidivisional Firms.* Boston: Division of Research; Harvard Business School, Harvard University, 1973, 125–126. Copyright © 1973 by the President and Fellows of Harvard College. All rights reserved.

32. Derr, C. B. Managing Organizational Conflict. *California Management Review,* Winter 1978, 78–63; Shea, G. F. *Creative Negotiating.* Boston: CBI, 1983.

33. For further information on negotiation, see Bazerman, M. H., and Lewicki, R. J. (Eds.) *Negotiating in Organizations.* Beverly Hills, Cal.: Sage, 1983; Brooks, E., and Odiorne, G. S. *Managing by Negotiations.* New York: Van Nostrand Reinhold, 1984; Fisher, R., and Ury, W. *Getting to Yes: Negotiating Agreement without Giving In.* Boston: Houghton Mifflin, 1981; Greenhalgh, L., Neslin, S. A., and Gilkey, R. W. The Effects of Negotiator Preferences, Situational Power, and Negotiator Personality on Outcomes of Business Negotiations. *Academy of Management Journal,* 1985, *28,* 9–33; Raiffa, H. *The Art and Science of Negotiation.* Cambridge, Mass.: Harvard University Press, 1982; Winkler, J. *Bargaining for Results.* New York: John Wiley, 1984.

34. Wall, Jr., J. A. *Negotiation: Theory and Practice.* Glenview, Ill.: Scott, Foresman, 1985; Douglas, A. *Industrial Peacemaking.* New York: Columbia University Press, 1962.

35. Smith, J. M. The Japan Syndrome: Demystifying Japanese Management. *Management Decision,* 1983, *21*(3), 25–33. Copyright, 1983, by MCB University Press. Used with permission. Also see Deutsch, M. F. *Doing Business with the Japanese.* New York: New American Library, 1983, 99–124; Tung, R. L. How to Negotiate with the Japanese. *California Management Review,* Summer 1984, 62–77.

36. Walton, R. E. *Interpersonal Peacemaking: Confrontation and Third-Party Consultation.* Reading, Mass.: Addison-Wesley, 1969; Fisher R. J. Third Party Consultation as a Method of Intergroup Conflict Resolution. *Journal of Conflict Resolution,* 1983, *27*, 301–334; Sheppard, B. H. Third Party Conflict Intervention: A Procedural Framework. In B. M. Staw and L. L. Cummings (eds.) *Research in Organizational Behavior,* vol. 6. Greenwich, Conn.: JAI Press, 1984, 141–190; Wall Jr., J. A. Mediation: The Effects of Mediator Proposals, Number of Issues, and Altered Aspirations. *Journal of Management,* 1984, *10,* 293–304.

37. Blake, R. R., Shepard, H. A., and Mouton, J.S. *Managing Intergroup Conflict in Industry.* Houston: Gulf, 1964; Blake, R. R., and Mouton, J. S. *Solving Costly Organizational Conflicts.* San Francisco: Jossey-Bass, 1984.

38. Bazerman, M. H. The Relevance of Kahneman and Tversky's Concept of Framing to Organizational Behavior. *Journal of Management,* 1984, *10,* 333–344; Neale, M. A., and Bazerman, M. H. The Effects of Framing and Negotiator Overconfidence on Bargaining Behaviors and Outcomes. *Academy of Management Journal,* 1985, 28, 34–49; van de Vliert, E. Escalative Intervention in Small-Group Conflict. *Journal of Applied Behavioral Science,* 1985, *21,* 19–36.

39. Mason, R. O. A Dialectical Approach to Strategic Planning. *Management Science,* 1969, *15,* B403–B414; Mason, R. D., and Mitroff, I I. *Challenging Strategic Planning Assumptions.* New York: John Wiley, 1981.

40. Cosier, R. A., and Aplin, J. C. A Critical View of Dialectical Inquiry as a Tool in Strategic Planning. *Strategic Management Journal,* 1980, *1,* 343–356; Schwenk, C. R. Giving the Devil Its Due. *The Warton Annual,* 1985, 104–108.

41. Adapted with permission from J. D. Hunger, McIntire School of Commerce, University of Virginia. Copyright © 1979 by J. D. Hunger. Distributed by the Intercollegiate Case Clearing House, Soldiers Field, Boston, MA 02163. All rights reserved to the contributors. Printed in the U.S.A.

42. Prepared by R. Price, manager of curriculum development, GTE Service Corporation, Dallas, Texas, 1982. Used with permission.

18 Work Stress

LEARNING OBJECTIVES

When you have finished studying this chapter, you should be able to:

- Explain the concept of stress.
- Describe the general nature of the body's response to stressors.
- Diagnose the sources of stress in organizations.
- Describe the positive and negative effects of stress.
- Understand the nature and causes of job burnout.
- Explain the general relationship between stress and job performance.

OUTLINE

Preview Case

Chester Martin

Chester Martin awakens at 7:00 A.M. having overslept by forty-five minutes. Panic-stricken, he realizes he will be late for the second time in as many weeks. In his effort to hurry he cuts himself while shaving, scalds his tongue on too hot coffee, and worries what the boss will say. On the freeway, unable to change lanes, he is caught behind a slow-moving vehicle. He honks, stays within inches of the other vehicle, and mutters uncomplimentary remarks about the other driver, unconsciously tensing his entire body and tightening his grip on the steering wheel.

Once at the office he finds dictation from yesterday still not transcribed and chews out his secretary without waiting for her explanation of the delay. Overhearing the exchange, Chester's boss explains that the secretary had been handling a special assignment for him and reprimands Chester for his discourtesy. Upset over the reprimand, Chester slams down his coffee cup, spilling coffee over important papers on his desk. Later that day, preoccupied with his thoughts in a staff meeting, he fails to recognize that a question is being directed at him and suffers the embarrassment of having everyone's attention focused on him as the boss suggests that if Chester would pay attention, he might have a better idea of what was going on in the company.

That evening, after several more incidents, Chester drives home an hour late. Tired, tense, and irritable, he is short-tempered with his children, upsetting his wife, which in turn provokes an argument. Chester ends up spending the night on the couch, staring at the ceiling until the early hours of the morning. Consequently, he oversleeps again, awaking tired and irritable.[1]

It is very easy for most people to empathize with Chester in the Preview Case—most of us have a "bad day" from time to time and experience stress. Sometimes stress can have positive effects, and sometimes it can be harmful. Work stress, in particular, can be both positive and negative. Having enough stress to work at peak efficiency can create satisfaction and a sense of well-being and accomplishment, and bring the rewards associated with career success. On the other hand, excessive stress at work can result in a loss of efficiency, a failure to perform well, and adverse effects on mental and physical health. People need a balance in the amount of stress experienced in their personal and work lives. Unfortunately, recognizing the appropriate balance and achieving it are not easy to do.

Managers and employees need to understand the nature of work stress, the relationship between stress and performance, and the sources of stress within an organization. Everyone should have an appreciation for the relationships between stress and health. In this chapter, we will examine the general nature of stress, the sources of stress at work, the effects of stress, and ways that employees and organizations can cope with stress. People react differently to and can handle effectively varying amounts of stress; we will also explore some of these individual differences in this chapter.

NATURE OF STRESS

Stress is a consequence of or a general response to an action or situation that places special physical or psychological demands, or both, on a person. Stress involves the interaction of a person and that person's environment. The physical or psychological demands from the environment that cause stress are called **stressors**.[2] Stressors can take a variety of forms and can stem from a job, family, friends, co-workers, or internal demands. However, stressors have one thing in common: they create stress or the potential for stress when an individual perceives them as representing a demand that may exceed his or her ability or capacity to respond.

Fight-or-Flight Response

Suppose you come home late one night after an extremely exhausting day at work or school. You are so tired that you have been hardly able to stay awake during the drive home. As you open your front door, you suddenly see flashlights inside and you hear hushed voices. Immediately and spontaneously, you become wide awake. A complex biochemical process has been set off in your body, and the following kinds of reactions occur: Photochemical changes take place in your retinas so that your eyes adjust to the darkness more quickly than they would have under normal circumstances; your hearing becomes momentarily more acute; your breathing and heart rates alter; blood rushes from the extremities to your chest cavity so that your vital organs will have all the blood necessary to operate at peak capacity; your brain wave activity goes up as extra supplies of blood rush to your head to allow your brain to function maximally; your muscles ready themselves for action.[3]

These biochemical and bodily changes represent a natural response to an environmental stressor: the **fight-or-flight response**.[4] An animal attacked by a predator in the wild has basically two choices: to fight or to flee. The animal's bodily responses to the stressor (the predator) increase its chances of survival. Similarly, our cave-dwelling ancestors benefitted from this biological response mechanism. People away from their cave gathering food would have experienced a great deal of stress upon meeting a saber-toothed tiger. In dealing with the tiger they could have run away or stayed and fought. The biochemical changes in their body prepared them for either alternative and contributed to the probability of their survival.

Even today, the human nervous system still responds the same way to environmental stressors. While this may sometimes have survival value in a true emergency, for most people the "tigers" are imaginary rather than real, and a fight-or-flight response is no longer appropriate. For example, if an employee receives an unpleasant work assignment from a supervisor, it is not appropriate for the employee to assault the supervisor physically or to storm angrily out of the office. Instead, the employee is expected to calmly accept the assignment and do the best job possible. This may be especially difficult when a negative perception of the assignment as a threat, or stressor, has prepared the body to act accordingly.

What is the nature of this biochemical response to environmental demands? Do different environmental stressors evoke different kinds of physiological responses? Medical science has discovered that the human body has a standard response to demands placed on it—whether psychological or physical. In other words, the gross biological response to different stressors is the same. Medical researcher Hans Selye first used the term *stress* to describe the body's biological response mechanisms. Selye considers stress as the nonspecific response of the human body to any demand made on it.[5] The body has only a limited capacity to respond to stress, which is extremely important from a medical perspective. The workplace makes a variety of demands on people, and too much stress over too long a period of time will exhaust their ability to cope with environmental stressors.

Experience of Work Stress

Whether an individual experiences work stress is determined by the following factors: (1) the person's perception of the situation; (2) his or her past experiences; (3) the relationship between stress and task performance; (4) interpersonal relationships among the people involved; and (5) individual differences with regard to stress reactions.[6]

PERCEPTION   In Chapter 4, perception was defined as a key psychological process whereby a person selects and organizes environmental information into a concept of reality. Employees' perceptions of a situation influence how they experience stress. For example, two supervisors had their job duties substantially changed—a situation likely to be stressful for many people. The first supervisor saw the new duties as an opportunity to learn new skills and perceived the change as a vote of confidence from higher management on her ability to be flexible. However, the second supervisor perceived the same situation as extremely threatening and concluded that higher management was unhappy with his performance in the original job.

PAST EXPERIENCE   A person may experience a situation as more or less stressful, depending on how familiar the person is with the situation and what prior experience he or she has had with the particular stressors involved. Past practice or training may allow some employees in an organization to deal calmly and competently with stressors that would greatly intimidate less experienced employees. The relationship between experience and stress is based on reinforcement (Chapter 6). Positive reinforcement or success in a similar situation can reduce the level of stress that a person experiences in the present situation; past failure under similar conditions can increase stress in the present situation.

STRESS AND PERFORMANCE   A relationship exists between the degree of stress involved in some jobs or tasks and the quality and level of performance. An optimum level of stress probably exists for maximum performance of any task. Too little or too much stress may result in lowered performance. A good example is the performance of the members of a football team. Not taking an opponent seriously enough (experiencing too little stress) may cause the team to perform poorly. On the other hand, becoming too excited or angry (experiencing too much stress) may cause the players to lose their poise and not perform at their best. The important relationship between stress and performance will be examined in more detail later in the chapter.

INTERPERSONAL RELATIONSHIPS The presence or absence of other people influences how individuals in work settings experience stress, as well as their behavior in response to stressors. The presence of co-workers may increase an individual's confidence, allowing that person to cope more effectively with stress. For example, working alongside a person who performs confidently and competently in a stressful situation may help an employee behave in a similar manner. Alternatively, the presence of fellow workers may irritate people, reducing their capability to cope with stress.

INDIVIDUAL DIFFERENCES Personality characteristics may explain some of the differences in the ways that employees experience and respond to stress. Individual differences in needs, values, and abilities also influence how employees experience work stress. Simply stated, people are different. What one person considers a major source of stress, another may hardly notice. Relationships between personality and stress will also be discussed later in the chapter.

SOURCES OF STRESS

Individuals commonly experience stress both from their personal and work lives. It is important to understand both of these sources of stress and their possible interaction. For example, it has been demonstrated that a greater understanding of the effects of stress on employee well-being is achieved by taking into account the combined effects of job stress and personal life stress.[7]

Stressors at Work

Work stressors can take a variety of forms. Almost anything in the work environment can be a source of stress for someone. A number of studies have been performed in organizations to identify specific stressors and their effects.[8]

Figure 18-1 identifies a variety of sources of work stress. As previously discussed, factors internal to the person—such as personality, perceptions, and past experience—influence the ways in which individuals experience these stressors in a given situation. Figure 18-1 divides the sources of work stress into six general categories, which can overlap. The stressors in each category are examples and are not intended to be a complete listing of the stressors that could exist in an organization.[9]

STRESSORS INTRINSIC TO THE JOB For many people, having too much work to do can obviously be stressful. Interestingly, having too little work can also create stress. In addition to overload or underload situations, the nature of the work itself has a great deal to do with the experience of stress. Some jobs inherently contain more stress than others. For example, the jobs of police officer, fire fighter, and air traffic controller are often considered to be particularly stressful.

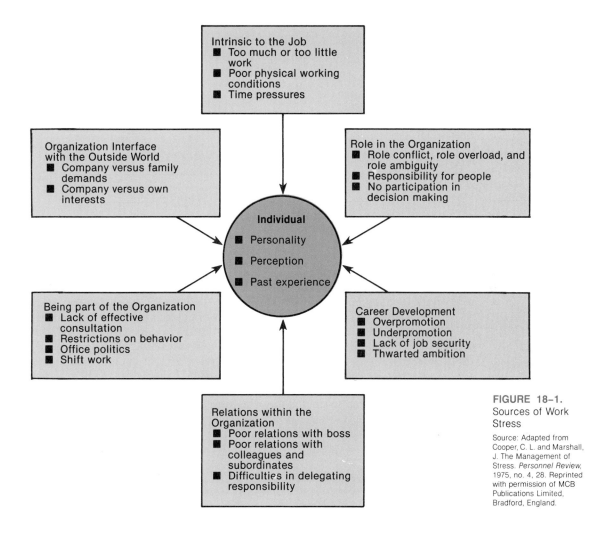

FIGURE 18–1.
Sources of Work Stress

Source: Adapted from Cooper, C. L. and Marshall, J. The Management of Stress. *Personnel Review,* 1975, no. 4, 28. Reprinted with permission of MCB Publications Limited, Bradford, England.

Another important set of job stressors is related to poor working conditions. Temperature extremes, loud noise, too much or too little lighting, radiation, and air pollution are just a few examples of the working conditions that can cause stress for employees.[10]

Let us consider the types and amounts of work stress that executives in one industry face.

In Practice: Stress on Independent Oil and Gas Company Executives

Recently researchers conducted a large-scale survey of attitudes, opinions, lifestyles, and backgrounds of executives of independent oil and gas producing firms. An independent oil and gas producing firm engages primarily in the exploration for and production of oil and gas, as opposed to refining and marketing petroleum products. While some of these firms are fairly large, they are generally much smaller than the giant oil corporations, such as Exxon or Texaco, that engage in all phases of the oil business, from finding oil to selling gasoline to the public. The independent oil and gas business is quite risky; new firms form and

TABLE 18-1   Responses of executives to the question: Is your job stressful?

	Number of Executives Answering	Frequency of Response
Never	10	1.3%
Seldom	68	8.6
Moderately	323	40.7
Often	267	33.6
Very often	111	14.0
No response	15	1.9

others go bankrupt on a regular basis. Fortunes can be made quickly and lost just as suddenly. The survey aimed to profile the key executives of these firms.

The researchers gathered questionnaire data from 794 executives of independent oil and gas producers. Part of the survey asked these executives several questions about their work stress. Executives responded as shown in Table 18-1 to the question: Is your job stressful?

Few of these executives never found their work stressful. Over 88 percent of them reported that their work was moderately, often, or very often stressful. A significant number (111 people) selected the most stressful response category, "very often."

The survey also asked executives what kinds of things caused them to feel stressed. The most frequently mentioned stressors were deadlines and work load ("I have too little time to do the job," "multiple decisions that must be made quickly," and "too many deadlines and insufficient data"); people problems ("the failure of people to perform" and "dumb employees"); dry wells ("having to report dry holes to investors"); and self-induced stress ("I do it to myself" and "me").

Finally, the researchers asked executives what they did when they felt stressed. The most frequently mentioned coping mechanisms were exercise ("walk and exercise," "jog," and "play golf"); "personal" coping strategies ("reflect, meditate, work on something else," "I use biofeedback to relax," "drink," "swear," and "pray and read the Bible"); hard work ("work faster, concentrate harder" and "work like hell to catch up"); and social activity ("relax with coffee and light conversation" and "go to church").[11]

ROLE IN THE ORGANIZATION   The specific roles played by employees are a prime source of stress in an organization. **Role conflict** (Chapter 17) exists whenever differing expectations or demands are placed on a person's role. A particular form of role conflict, called **role overload**, exists when demands exceed the capacity of a manager or employee to perform or meet all of them adequately. Role overload can also be considered as simply having too much work to do and thus overlaps with the category of stressors intrinsic to the job. **Role ambiguity** describes the situation in which there is uncertainty about job duties and responsibilities. Role conflict and role ambiguity are particularly important sources of much organizational stress.[12] Having responsibility for the behavior of others, as well as a lack of opportunity to participate in important decisions affecting the job, are other aspects of employees' roles that may serve as stressors.

CAREER DEVELOPMENT Major stressors related to career planning and development involve job security, promotions, transfers, and developmental opportunities (Chapter 19). As with too much or too little work, an employee can feel stressed by **underpromotion** (failure to advance as rapidly as desired) or **overpromotion** (promotion to a job that exceeds the individual's capabilities).

RELATIONS WITHIN THE ORGANIZATION Groups have a tremendous impact on the behavior of people in organizations (Chapter 9 and 10). Relationships with others are a critical part of organizational life and a potential source of stress. Good interpersonal relationships facilitate the achievement of many personal and organizational goals; poor interpersonal relationships cause considerable stress and other unpleasant outcomes.

BEING PART OF THE ORGANIZATION Simply being a part of an organization can create stress for some employees. In particular, being in a work environment where behavior is restricted or the individual's opinions do not seem to matter can be stressful for many people. Office politics is another potential source of stress for some (Chapter 16).

An aspect of many employees' work experience that has only recently received much attention is shift work. **Shift work** is defined as a work period that extends the organization's hours of operation beyond the normal workday.[13] A typical shift-work schedule is from four P.M. to midnight and/or from midnight to eight A.M. Shift work is common in organizations that require continuous operations or that utilize particularly expensive equipment so that continuous production is necessary in order to be profitable. Examples include food processing, steelmaking, oil refining, and health care. Some aspects of shift work have advantages for employees. Employees may be paid more to work evening or night shifts, may have more daylight hours to handle personal business, may enjoy the greater autonomy of shift work, and so on. Among the negative consequences of shift work are a possible disruption of family and social relations, fatigue caused by the disruption of normal sleep patterns, organizational problems such as poor performance and communication difficulties, and poorer overall employee health. These and other potentially negative consequences of shift work may be quite stressful for some individuals. For example, a recent study reported that nurses on a night shift reported considerably more stress symptoms and conflict between work and family roles than did day-shift nurses.[14] Shift work is also related to the following category of work stressors.

ORGANIZATION'S INTERFACE WITH THE OUTSIDE WORLD A person plays many roles in life, only one of which is typically associated with work (although some individuals may hold more than one job at a time). These roles may present conflicting demands that serve as a source of stress. Furthermore, work typically meets only some of an employee's goals and needs. Other personal goals and needs may conflict with career goals, which presents an additional source of stress. For example, a manager's personal needs to spend time with the family may conflict with the extra hours the person must work to advance his or her career.

The questionnaire in Table 18-2 contains sets of items that measure several of the stressors identified in Figure 18-1: role ambiguity, role con-

---

TABLE 18-2   Stress Diagnostic Survey ©

The following questionnaire is designed to provide you with an indication of the extent to which various individual level stressors are sources of stress to you. For each item you should indicate the frequency with which the condition described is a source of stress. Next to each item write the appropriate number (1–7) which best describes how frequently the condition is a source of stress.

Write *1* if the condition described is *never* a source of stress
Write *2* if it is *rarely* a source of stress
Write *3* if it is *occasionally* a source of stress
Write *4* if it is *sometimes* a source of stress
Write *5* if it is *often* a source of stress
Write *6* if it is *usually* a source of stress
Write *7* if it is *always* a source of stress

	Answer
1. My job duties and work objectives are unclear to me.	_____
2. I work on unnecessary tasks or projects.	_____
3. I have to take work home in the evenings or on weekends to stay caught up.	_____
4. The demands for work quality made upon me are unreasonable.	_____
5. I lack the proper opportunities to advance in this organization.	_____
6. I am held accountable for the development of other employees.	_____
7. I am unclear about whom I report to and/or who reports to me.	_____
8. I get caught in the middle between my supervisors and my subordinates.	_____
9. I spend too much time in unimportant meetings that take me away from my work.	_____
10. My assigned tasks are sometimes too difficult and/or complex.	_____
11. If I want to get promoted I have to look for a job with another organization.	_____
12. I am responsible for counseling with my subordinates and/or helping them solve their problems.	_____
13. I lack the authority to carry out my job responsibilities.	_____
14. The formal chain of command is not adhered to.	_____
15. I am responsible for an almost unmanageable number of projects or assignments at the same time.	_____
16. Tasks seem to be getting more and more complex.	_____
17. I am hurting my career progress by staying with this organization.	_____
18. I take action or make decisions that affect the safety or well-being of others.	_____
19. I do not fully understand what is expected of me.	_____
20. I do things on the job that are accepted by one person and not by others.	_____
21. I simply have more work to do than can be done in an ordinary day.	_____
22. The organization expects more of me than my skills and/or abilities provide.	_____
23. I have few opportunities to grow and learn new knowledge and skills in my job.	_____
24. My responsibilities in this organization are more for *people* than for *things*.	_____
25. I do not understand the part my job plays in meeting overall organizational objectives.	_____
26. I receive conflicting requests from two or more people.	_____
27. I feel that I just don't have time to take an occasional break.	_____
28. I have insufficient training and/or experience to discharge my duties properly.	_____
29. I feel that I am at a standstill in my career.	_____
30. I have responsibility for the future (careers) of others.	_____

TABLE 18-2   Continued

Scoring

Each item is associated with a specific individual level stressor. The item numbers and the appropriate categories are listed below. Add your responses for each item within each category to arrive at a total category score.

Your Score

Role Ambiguity: 1, 7, 13, 19, 25   ____ + ___ + ___ + ___ + ___ = _____
Role Conflict: 2, 8, 14, 20, 26   ____ + ___ + ___ + ___ + ___ = _____
Role Overload—Quantitative: 3, 9, 15, 21, 27   ____ + ___ + ___ + ___ + ___ = _____
Role Overload—Qualitative: 4, 10, 16, 22, 28   ____ + ___ + ___ + ___ + ___ = _____
Career Development: 5, 11, 17, 23, 29   ____ + ___ + ___ + ___ + ___ = _____
Responsibility for People: 6, 12, 18, 24, 30   ____ + ___ + ___ + ___ + ___ = _____

The significance of the total score in each of the stressor categories will, of course, vary from individual to individual. In general, however, the following guidelines may be used to provide a perspective for each score:

Total scores of less than 10 are indicators of low stress levels.

Total scores between 10 and 24 are indicative of moderate stress levels.

Total scores of 25 and greater are indicative of high stress levels.

Source: Ivancevich, J. M. and Matteson, M. T. *Stress and Work: A Managerial Perspective*, 1980, 118–120. Reprinted by permission.

flict, role overload, career development, and responsibility for people. Thinking of the job you currently hold or one that you held in the past, respond to the statements and calculate your score.

Our discussion of sources of work stress has been oriented to experiences in U.S. organizations, but there is evidence that managers in many countries around the world perceive similar stressors in their work. Some interesting differences also exist, as the results of a recent survey of executive stress indicates.

ACROSS CULTURES

A Ten Nation Survey of Executive Stress

In 1984 the journal *International Management* sponsored what was probably the first worldwide comparative study of executive stress. Researchers gathered information from 1,065 executives in ten countries on five continents: Brazil, Great Britain, Egypt, Germany, Japan, Nigeria, Singapore, South Africa, Sweden, and the United States. A portion of the survey asked these managers about their perceptions of the major causes or sources of job stress. Table 18-3 shows the 15 sources of stress most frequently mentioned by the managers and, by way of comparison, the country from which each source was most frequently and least frequently mentioned.

Time pressures and deadlines were the most frequently cited source of work stress, being mentioned as a stressor by 55 percent of all respondents. This was closely followed by work overload (which we call role overload), mentioned by almost 52 percent of the managers in the study. Many of the stressors listed in Table 18-3 can be found in Figure 18-1 and have already been discussed.

TABLE 18-3   A Ten-Country Comparison of Work Stressors

Source of Stress	Percentage of Respondents Mentioning Source	Most Often Mentioned by Managers in	Least Often Mentioned by Managers in
1. Time pressures and deadlines	55.3%	Germany (65.4%)	Japan (41.8%)
2. Work overload	51.6	Egypt (76.7%)	Brazil (38.1%)
3. Inadequately trained subordinates	36.4	Egypt (65.0%)	Britain (13.1%)
4. Long working hours	29.0	Nigeria (40.5%)	Brazil (19.6%)
5. Attending meetings	23.6	South Africa (28.5%)	United States (16.3%)
6. Demands of work on my private and social life	22.1	Sweden (31.7%)	Singapore (12.9%)
7. Demands of work on my relationship with my family	21.4	Nigeria (29.7%)	Brazil (8.2%)
8. Keeping up with new technology	21.4	Japan (32.8%)	Egypt (10.0%)
9. My beliefs conflicting with those of the organization	20.6	United States (30.2%)	Egypt (13.3%)
10. Taking my work home	19.7	Egypt (30.0%)	Japan (13.4%)
11. Lack of power and influence	19.5	United States (46.5%)	Sweden (11.0%)
12. Interpersonal relations	19.4	Japan (29.8%)	Singapore (12.9%)
13. The amount of travel required by my work	18.4	Nigeria (29.7%)	Brazil (9.3%)
14. Doing a job below the level of my competence	17.7	Brazil (23.7%)	Sweden (10.3%)
15. Incompetent boss	15.6	United States (30.2%)	Britain (9.1%)

Source: Adapted from Cooper, C., and Arbose, J. Executive Stress Goes Global. *International Management,* May 1984, 48.

The comparisons among countries shown in Table 18–3, while interesting, must be interpreted carefully. For example, even though U.S. managers seemed to perceive attending meetings as less stressful than their counterparts in the other nine countries (see line 5), this should not be interpreted to mean that they attend less meetings. We do not know, from this data, whether managers in the United States attend more, less, or roughly the same amount of meetings as executives in these other nations. As another example, we would not want to conclude that Nigerian executives travel more than others (line 13), only that they find it somewhat more stressful (perhaps due to the level of development of their transportation system). With this note of caution, it is nevertheless interesting to observe that U.S. managers mentioned three of these sources of stress more frequently than did their counterparts in other countries: conflict between personal and organizational beliefs (line 9), lack of power and influence (line 11), and an incompetent boss (line 15). Again, a conclusion that U.S executives have, for example, less power in their organizations than others would not necessarily follow from this. Perhaps managers in the U.S. have somewhat higher expectations of being able to influence people and events, and thus find it more stressful when these expectations are not always met.

An examination of the last column in Table 18-3, might lead to the conclusion that Brazilian executives experienced less stress than others, since four of the sources of stress were mentioned less often by them. However, this interpretation would be wrong. In addition to the kinds of data shown in Table 18-3, researchers also gathered information concerning stress symptoms—examples would be depression and anxiety—exhibited by the executives. Brazilian executives scored second highest in the survey in terms of stress symptoms. Indeed, an interesting, and somewhat surprising, result from this portion of the study was that executives in emerging countries—Brazil, Egypt, Nigeria, and Singapore—showed more symptoms of stress than did executives in industrialized countries. The researchers speculated that managers in these nations are having to perform in an environment undergoing rapid economic, sociological, and technological change, and this may account for their higher levels of perceived stress. Among industrialized countries, Japanese executives had the highest levels of stress. Overall, executives in Egypt had the highest levels of stress symptoms, followed, in order, by Brazil, Nigeria, Singapore, Japan, Great Britain, South Africa, the United States, Germany, and Sweden. The level of stress symptoms was almost twice as high in Egypt—in first place—as in Sweden, which had the lowest level of stress symptoms.[15]

Life Stressors

The distinction between work and nonwork stressors is not always clear. For example, as Figure 18-1 shows, one source of stress lies in possible conflicts between work and family demands. Managers must understand that much of the stress felt by employees may stem from stressors in their personal lives, or **life stressors**. In addition, studies indicate that job stress and life stress are often related in that high stress in one area can reduce a person's ability to cope with stress in the other.[16]

Much of the stress in an individual's personal life seems to be caused by major changes, such as divorce, marriage, the death of a family member, and so on.[17] A study of more than 5,000 patients suffering from stress-related illnesses attempted to isolate the major changes in their lives.[18] The study generated the social readjustment rating scale shown in Table 18-4. These life events have been assigned a numerical rating according to their expected relative impact on an individual or the degree of readjustment required following the event. For example, the death of a spouse (first in the list in Table 18-4) with a score of 100 requires twice as much readjustment as a marriage (seventh in the list) with a score of 50. A retirement (tenth in the list) is approximately twice as stressful as having trouble with a boss (thirtieth in the list).

Recall that Selye's medical science definition emphasized that stress is the body's general response to any demand made on it. Note that the list of stressful life events in Table 18-4 contains both unpleasant events, such as a divorce, and events normally considered pleasant, such as vacations and Christmas.

TABLE 18-4   The Social Readjustment Rating Scale

Life Event	Mean Value
1. Death of spouse	100
2. Divorce	73
3. Marital separation	65
4. Jail term	63
5. Death of close family member	63
6. Personal injury or illness	53
7. Marriage	50
8. Fired at work	47
9. Marital reconciliation	45
10. Retirement	45
11. Change in health of family member	44
12. Pregnancy	40
13. Sex difficulties	39
14. Gain of new family member	39
15. Business readjustment	39
16. Change in financial state	38
17. Death of close friend	37
18. Change to different line of work	36
19. Change in number of arguments with spouse	35
20. Mortgage over $10,000	31
21. Foreclosure of mortgage or loan	30
22. Change in responsibilities at work	29
23. Son or daughter leaving home	29
24. Trouble with in-laws	29
25. Outstanding personal achievement	28
26. Wife begins or stops work	26
27. Begin or end school	26
28. Change in living conditions	25
29. Revision of personal habits	24
30. Trouble with boss	23
31. Change in work hours or conditions	20
32. Change in residence	20
33. Change in schools	20
34. Change in recreation	19
35. Change in church activities	19
36. Change in social activities	18
37. Mortgage or loan less than $10,000	17
38. Change in sleeping habits	16
39. Change in number of family get-togethers	15
40. Change in eating habits	15
41. Vacation	13
42. Christmas	12
43. Minor violations of the law	11

Source: Reprinted by permission of the publisher from Holmes, T. H. and Rahe, R. H. The Social Readjustment Rating Scale. *Journal of Psychosomatic Medicine, 11*, 213–218. Copyright © 1967 by The American Psychosomatic Society, Inc.

You may be surprised to find out that vacations and Christmas exact a toll, in stress, but consider what they are often like. You may save up many household chores as well as fun activities until your vacation time so that you end up cramming so much into your vacation period that you literally wear yourself out. A vacation is supposed to be refreshing and relaxing, yet you can turn it into two of the most hectic, fast-paced weeks of the year. Christmas is an exciting time of the year for almost everyone—there are parties, family gatherings with loved ones, shopping sprees, and a general excitement in the air—but in our efforts to get into the spirit of the season and enjoy ourselves, we sometimes push ourselves too far. As with our vacations, we can damage our health by squeezing too much activity into too short a time period.[19]

Patients in stress-related counseling are often asked to calculate their susceptibility to health changes by examining the events in their lives over the past year. People with high scores on the life-change index are more likely to contract illness following a major life event. A score of 150 or less from the list in Table 18–4 indicates a relatively manageable degree of readjustment and low susceptibility to a stress-related illness. However, a score in the range of 150–300 indicates a 50-percent probability of a stress-induced major health breakdown during the next two years. The chances of health problems rise to about 80 percent for scores greater than 300. However, viewing life events as having only negative effects is incorrect. People often can cope with unpleasant events and, to a certain extent, need the stimulation of pleasurable events.

EFFECTS OF STRESS

As stated previously, work stress has both positive and negative effects. However, research on work stress has focused on its negative effects. This focus seems well-directed because the cost of stress-related illnesses in the United States is currently estimated to be about 3 percent of the gross national product. In Western industrialized countries, some five to ten times as many work days are lost from stress-related illnesses as are lost from strikes and other industrial strife.[20]

The effects of work stress occur in three major areas: physiological, emotional, and behavioral.[21] Examples of the effects of excessive stress in these three areas are as follows:

- **Physiological effects of stress** include increased blood pressure, increased heart rate, sweating, hot and cold spells, breathing difficulties, muscular tension, and increased gastrointestinal disorders.
- **Emotional effects of stress** include anger, anxiety, depression, lowered self-esteem, poorer intellectual functioning, including an inability to concentrate and make decisions, nervousness, irritability, resentment of supervision, and job dissatisfaction.
- **Behavioral effects of stress** include decreased performance, absenteeism, higher accident rates, higher turnover rates, higher alcohol and other drug abuse, impulsive behavior, and difficulties in communication.

Health and Stress

Considerable research links stress to coronary heart disease. Other major health problems commonly associated with stress include alcohol and other drug abuse, physical ailments like back pain, and a variety of mental problems. Medical researchers have recently discovered possible links between stress and cancer. Although it is difficult to determine the precise role stress plays in health, it is becoming increasingly clear that a great many illnesses are stress-related.[22]

Stress-related illnesses place a considerable burden on people and organizations. The costs to individuals are sometimes more obvious than the costs to organizations, but it is possible to measure at least some of the organizational costs associated with stress-related disease. For example, recent research studies on stress from the National Safety Council, and the National Institute for Occupational Safety and Health revealed the following:

- The total cost of work-related accidents in the United States is currently about $32 billion per year. It is estimated that 75–85 percent of all industrial accidents are caused by an inability to cope with emotional distress.

- Heart disease, which is related to stress, causes an annual loss of more than 135 million workdays.

- Stress-related headaches are the leading cause of lost work time in U.S. industry.

- More than 60 percent of long-term employee disability is related to psychological or psychosomatic problems often brought on or made worse by stress. Currently $26 billion is spent each year on disability payments and medical bills.[23]

Performance and Stress

Nowhere are both the positive and negative aspects of stress more apparent than in the relationship between stress and performance.[24] Figure 18–2 provides a graph of the performance–stress relationship. The vertical axis shows the level of performance from low (poor) to high (excellent). The horizontal axis shows the amount of stress experienced from low to high. At low levels of stress, a person may not be sufficiently alert, challenged, or involved to perform at his or her best. As the curve in Figure 18–2 indicates, increasing a low amount of stress can improve performance—up to a point. An optimum level of stress exists for any task. Past this point, performance begins to deteriorate. At excessive levels of stress, a person is too agitated, aroused, or threatened to perform at his or her best.

In Practice: Optimum Stress

The Olympic Diver

All cameras focus on the Olympic diver as she warms up. Her muscles taut, she paces up and down while gulping air and shaking her arms. Keyed up by the stress of competition, her entire body is in a state of tense readiness for the immediate task ahead.

She concentrates intensely on the dive, completely oblivious to all the excitement around her. Spectators follow her every move as she steps on the diving board almost 36 feet above the water. Diving from that height, she will hit the water at thirty-five miles an hour.

Tension is near the breaking point for the diver and spectators alike. A silent hush fills the stadium as she prepares to dive.

The athlete dashes forward, jumps off the high board to do three and a half flips, and hits the water like an arrow. It is a perfect dive, a fitting outcome and reward for the months and years when she prepared four to six hours every day so she would be ready for this very event.

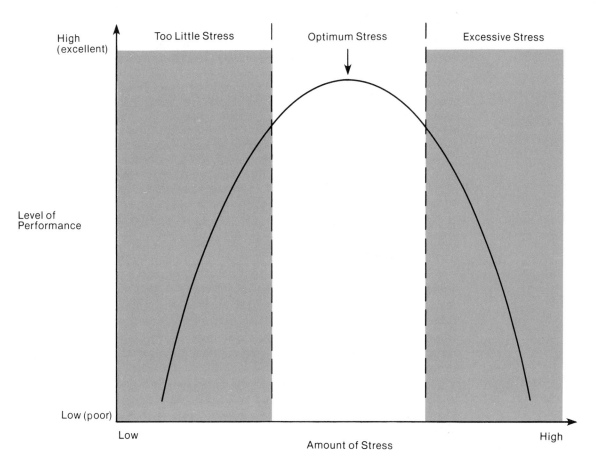

FIGURE 18-2.
Typical Relationship between Performance and Stress

The diver has learned through trial and error to find her optimum level of stress. By channeling this delicate balance of tension, she is able to utilize it for top performance.

A Sales Manager

A sales manager prepares to lead his company's national sales meeting. His pulse quickens and there is a fluttering feeling in his stomach as he readies himself for the talk. In the past he would have tried to bolster his confidence with one or two martinis or even with a tranquilizer, but although they reduced tension, they also reduced his mental alertness.

Although he can feel the tension mounting, he is still confident and in control of the situation. Experience has taught him that the right amount of stress can actually give him that extra push that makes the difference between superior and mediocre performance. He is not afraid of the tension. In fact, he welcomes it.

In the few minutes before his presentation, he glances at his audience. Most of the top brass in the company are there. Everything he says will be weighed carefully. There is a great deal at stake, and he realizes it.

The sales manager prepares himself by reviewing the presentation in his mind. This gives him a psychological set, which results in maximum concentration.

As he gets up to speak, his entire body becomes tense. His blood pressure rises slightly, his palms are sweaty, and adrenalin pours into his bloodstream to give him extra energy. He feels somewhat anxious, but the stress of the situation energizes him into a state of tense readiness.

As he begins to speak, he notices that his words are flowing smoothly. Memory, recall, and concentration are razor-sharp. He swiftly gains the interest and attention of his audience. People are nodding and smiling by the time he makes his closing remarks, and a round of applause follows as he sits down.

The talk is over. He lets out a sigh and begins to come down, feeling good about his performance. Within an hour he is relaxed and calm again.[25]

Both the Olympic diver and the sales manager understand the amount of stress they need for optimum performance. Managers also often want to know the optimum stress points for both themselves and their subordinates. However, this information is difficult to obtain. For example, an employee may be absent from work frequently because of boredom (too little stress) or because of overwork (excessive stress). Also, the curve shown in Figure 18–2 changes with the situation; that is, the curve varies for different people and different tasks. Too little stress for one employee may be just right for another on a particular task. The optimum amount of stress for a specific individual for one task may be too much or too little for that person's effective performance on other tasks.

Job Burnout

Job burnout refers to the adverse effects of working conditions where stressors seem unavoidable and sources of satisfaction or relief seem unavailable.[26] Job burnout commonly results in a state of physical, emotional, and mental exhaustion.[27]

Only recently has job burnout come to be recognized as a major work stress problem. Burnout seems to be most common among professionals who must deal extensively with other people—clients, subordinates, peers—on the job. The professionals who may be most vulnerable to job burnout include accountants, lawyers, managers, nurses, police officers, social workers, and teachers. While reliable statistics are not available, it has been estimated that about 20% of owners, managers, professionals, and technical people in the U.S. suffer from job burnout.[28]

In Practice: The Road to Job Burnout

"I told you not to do it that way," shouted Frank Halpern, a product manager at a major electronics firm. He was directing his annoyance at his design engineer, Jerry.

At thirty-three, Jerry Rasmussen seemed well on the road to success and personal happiness. A graduate of M.I.T., he began his career with a small New England company so that, as he said, "I wouldn't be hassled by big business bureaucracies." He got married about a year later and was able to put a down payment on a house just one hour's drive from the White Mountains of New Hampshire, where he and his wife enjoyed camping and fishing on weekends. He designed various electronic components at work and was instrumental in the design of a breakthrough product, which brought him to the attention of a major firm in Dallas.

The Dallas firm made Jerry a generous offer, which he agonized over but ultimately accepted. Jerry consequently sold his house and moved his family, which then included a son, to Texas.

Initially, Frank Halpern, Jerry's boss, was all smiles and enthusiasm at having a talented engineer "join my team." That quickly faded as Jerry learned the meaning of Frank's reference to "my team." Within fifteen months, Frank was constantly shouting at Jerry.

"Yes, but just look at the results," retorted Jerry. "No buts! Just do it the way I said."

Over time, similar scenes led Jerry to give up trying. Frustrated, Jerry did consider taking his talents elsewhere, preferably to a small company once again. However, he saw that as a career move backwards since smaller firms could not match his present salary, and not that many firms were hiring during the current recession. Further complicating the matter was the newest addition to his family, a daughter, and the fact that the family were really happy with their new home and Texas lifestyle. He, alone, longed for the White Mountains.

Time passed slowly. Frustration became cynicism at work and outbursts of irritability at home. He began to wake up tired and to dread the drive to work. Jerry was on the road to job burnout.[29]

Individuals who experience job burnout seem to have some common characteristics. Three characteristics in particular seem to be associated with a high probability of burnout:

- Burnout candidates experience a great deal of stress as a result of job-related stressors.
- Burnout candidates tend to be idealistic and/or self-motivating achievers.
- Burnout candidates tend to seek unattainable goals.[30]

The burnout syndrome thus represents an interaction of certain individual characteristics and the job situation. Individuals who suffer from burnout tend to have unrealistic expectations concerning their work and their ability to accomplish desired goals, given the nature of the situation in which they find themselves. Job burnout is not something that happens overnight: the entire process typically takes a great deal of time. The path to job burnout is illustrated by Figure 18–3. One or more of the working conditions listed, coupled with the unrealistic expectations or ambitions of the individual, can lead eventually to a state of complete physical, mental, and emotional exhaustion. Under conditions of burnout, the individual can no longer cope with the demands of the job and a willingness to try to do so drops dramatically.

The costs of job burnout, both to the employees suffering from this syndrome and to their organizations, can be high. Strategies for coping with stress, which we will examine in the last section of this chapter, are often useful in reducing causes and symptoms of job burnout.

PERSONALITY AND STRESS

Personality is the stable set of characteristics and traits that account for consistent patterns of behavior by a person in various situations (Chapter 3).

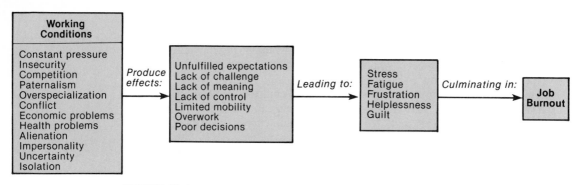

FIGURE 18–3.
The Path to Job Burnout

Source: Reprinted by permission from *Business* Magazine. "Helping Employees Cope with Job Burnout," by D. P. Rogers, October–December, 1984.

At work, personality influences (1) how individuals are likely to perceive situations and stressors, and (2) how they will react to these environmental stressors.

One study illustrates the way in which personality influences perceptions of and reactions to stressors. Information gathered from 90 owner–managers of small businesses in a Pennsylvania community indicated that locus of control (a personality dimension described in Chapter 3) was highly related to the perception of stress and the choice of coping behaviors.[31] The owner–managers with a high external locus of control perceived greater stress stemming from a flood that struck their community and displayed more emotional coping behaviors (for example, hostility and withdrawal). Those with a high internal locus of control perceived less stress in the same situation and used more task-oriented coping behaviors (like problem solving and acquiring the resources to maintain operations).

Many personality dimensions or traits can be related to stress including self-esteem, tolerance for ambiguity, introversion/extraversion, and dogmatism.[32] Often the presence or absence of a trait may increase or decrease the probability that a situation or event will act as a stressor. For example, an individual with low self-esteem may be more likely to experience stress in demanding work situations. Combinations of certain behaviors and tendencies characterize two distinctive personality types: Type A and Type B. They also have a bearing on the ways in which a person experiences stress.

Before reading further, however, take a few minutes and respond to the questions in Table 18–5.

Type A Personality

People with a **Type A personality** are involved in a never-ending struggle to achieve more and more in less and less time. Characteristics of this personality type include (1) a chronic sense of urgency about time; (2) an extremely competitive, almost hostile orientation; (3) an aversion to idleness; and (4) an impatience with barriers to task accomplishment. Two medical researchers,

TABLE 18-5   A Self-Assessment Exercise

Choose from the following responses to answer the questions below:

a. Almost always true   c. Seldom true
b. Usually true   d. Never true

Answer each question according to what is generally true for you:

_____ 1. I do not like to wait for other people to complete their work before I can proceed with my own.

_____ 2. I hate to wait in most lines.

_____ 3. People tell me that I tend to get irritated too easily.

_____ 4. Whenever possible I try to make activities competitive.

_____ 5. I have a tendency to rush into work that needs to be done before knowing the procedure I will use to complete the job.

_____ 6. Even when I go on vacation, I usually take some work along.

_____ 7. When I make a mistake, it is usually due to the fact that I have rushed into the job before completely planning it through.

_____ 8. I feel guilty for taking time off from work.

_____ 9. People tell me I have a bad temper when it comes to competitive situations.

_____ 10. I tend to lose my temper when I am under a lot of pressure at work.

_____ 11. Whenever possible, I will attempt to complete two or more tasks at once.

_____ 12. I tend to race against the clock.

_____ 13. I have no patience for lateness.

_____ 14. I catch myself rushing when there is no need.

Score your responses according to the following key:

■ *An intense sense of time urgency* is a tendency to race against the clock, even when there is little reason to. The person feels a need to hurry for hurry's sake alone, and this tendency has appropriately been called "hurry sickness." Time urgency is measured by Items 1, 2, 8, 12, 13, and 14. Every A or B answer to these six questions scores one point.
Your Score = _____

■ *Inappropriate aggression and hostility* reveals itself in a person who is excessively competitive and who cannot do anything for fun. This inappropriately aggressive behavior easily evolves into frequent displays of hostility, usually at the slightest provocation or frustration. Competitiveness and hostility is measured by Items 3, 4, 9, and 10. Every A or B answer scores one point.
Your Score = _____

■ *Polyphasic behavior* refers to the tendency to undertake two or more tasks simultaneously at inappropriate times. It usually results in wasted time due to an inability to complete the tasks. This behavior is measured by Items 6 and 11. Every A or B answer scores one point.
Your Score = _____

■ *Goal directedness without proper planning* refers to the tendency of an individual to rush into work without really knowing how to accomplish the desired result. This usually results in incomplete work or work with many errors, which in turn leads to wasted time, energy, and money. Lack of planning is measured by Items 5 and 7. Every A or B response scores one point.
Your Score = _____
TOTAL SCORE = _____

If your total score is 5 or greater, you may possess some basic components of the Type A personality.

Source: Reproduced with permission of the Robert J. Brady Co., Bowie, Maryland, 20715, from their copyrighted work *The Stress Mess Solution: The Causes and Cures of Stress on the Job,* by Everly, G. S., and Girdano, D. A. 1980, 55.

Friedman and Rosenman, first identified the Type A personality when they noticed a recurrent personality pattern in their patients who suffered from premature heart disease.[33] Specific behaviors typically exhibited by a Type A individual include:

- explosive, accelerated speech;
- a heightened pace of living;
- impatience with slowness;
- concentration on more than one activity at a time;
- self-preoccupation;
- dissatisfaction with life;
- evaluation of the worthiness of one's activities in terms of numbers;
- a tendency to challenge and compete with others, even in noncompetitive situations; and
- a free-floating hostility.[34]

The questionnaire in Table 18-5 measures four sets of behaviors and tendencies associated with the Type A personality: (1) time urgency; (2) competitiveness and hostility; (3) polyphasic behavior (trying to do too many things at once); and (4) a lack of planning. Medical researchers have discovered that these behaviors or tendencies often relate to work stress. They tend to cause stress or to make stressful situations worse than they otherwise might be.

Type B Personality

People with a **Type B personality** seldom desire to accomplish increasingly large numbers of objectives or to participate in more and more activities. This personality type has characteristics opposite from those of the Type A personality.[35] Type B individuals are less likely to overreact to situations and less likely to behave competitively or aggressively in situations where competitive behavior is inappropriate or unimportant. Type B individuals are less status conscious and insist less on recognition for achievement than Type A individuals.

Work events bothersome to Type A individuals may be considered unimportant by Type B individuals. People with a Type B personality contemplate more when setting goals and tend to examine more alternatives. They often feel that there is sufficient time to get things done, but this does not imply that Type B individuals lack desire for career success or goal accomplishment based on specific tasks.

As with other personality dimensions (such as introversion/extraversion), Type A and Type B personalities represent extremes on a continuum, and most people have some characteristics of both types. Considerable evidence links Type A behavior with vulnerability to heart attacks. Comparing extremes, Type A individuals are three times more likely to develop heart disease than Type B individuals. Of course, the traits Type A individuals possess also may represent behaviors related to success. Being conscious of time, highly motivated, and goal directed are all reasonable businesslike behaviors. It is when these behaviors are carried to extremes that they create or contribute to stress and its harmful effects on health.

Recently, some medical researchers have criticized the Type A label and suggested that the Type A characterization may be too broad. They argue that only some specific dimensions of the Type A personality, particularly hostility, have a strong relationship to heart disease.[36]

COPING WITH STRESS

Articles in newspapers and popular magazines often suggest various ways of coping with stress. The pervasiveness of these articles illustrates the prevalence of stress in U.S. society. The obvious shallowness of some of the techniques proposed in these articles should not blind readers to the benefits of understanding stress better and the use of reasonable, thoughtful methods to reduce stress.

Stress management by individuals and organizations usually is designed to (1) eliminate or control the sources of stress; or (2) make the individual more resistant to stress or better able to cope with stress. Methods used by individuals to cope with stress include therapy, exercise, planning ahead, a proper diet, adequate sleep, meditation and relaxation, and recreational activity.

Managers in an organization will find that being able to identify stressors at work and pinpoint their effects on themselves and their subordinates is a useful skill. Effective managers recognize the symptoms of too much stress on an employee: changes in personality, work habits, or behavior patterns. Changes in behavior patterns that may indicate too much stress include:

- working late much more or much less than usual;
- increased tardiness;
- increased absenteeism;
- difficulty in making decisions;
- increased number of careless mistakes;
- missed deadlines;
- forgetting appointments;
- difficulties in getting along with others; and
- preoccupation with mistakes and personal failures.[37]

The effective manager does not focus on isolated events—everyone makes mistakes—but, instead, looks for *patterns* of employee behaviors that may indicate too much stress.

Organizational programs to help employees cope with stress have become increasingly popular as the tremendous toll taken by stress has become more widely known.[38] Programs of stress management often include one or more of the following:

- Behavior modification (Chapter 6).
- Career counseling (Chapter 19).
- Greater levels of employee participation, particularly in planning changes that affect them (Chapter 21).
- Improvements in the physical environment at work.
- Job redesign (Chapter 13).

- Management by objectives (Chapter 15).
- Physical fitness or "wellness" programs.
- Redesign of organizational structure (Chapter 14).
- Seminars on job burnout to help employees understand its nature and symptoms.
- Workshops dealing with role clarity and role analysis (Chapter 17).

Programs that promote role clarity and role analysis can be particularly useful in removing role ambiguity and role conflict, which are major sources of stress. The New York Telephone Company has had success with a companywide stress management program designed to teach meditation and relaxation techniques to employees.[39] Many employees of the company believe that regular meditation helps them to cope with work stress and increases their efficiency on the job. Wellness programs, which often have a stress management component, are extremely popular currently. A number of large corporations—including New York Telephone, Mesa Petroleum Company, Kimberly-Clark Corporation, General Motors, Kennecott Copper Company, The Times Publishing Company, Burlington Industries, Campbell Soup Company, Xerox, IBM, Control Data, and Johnson & Johnson—have recently reported substantial reductions in stress-related illnesses and associated costs as a result of their corporate wellness programs.[40]

SUMMARY

Stress is a consequence of or a response to a situation that places either physical or psychological demands, or stressors, on a person. The body's general biological response to stressors prepares people to fight or flee, behavior generally inappropriate in work settings. Many factors determine how employees experience work stress, including their perception of the situation, past experiences, the presence or absence of other employees, and a variety of individual differences.

Stressors at work take many forms. The general categories discussed included stressors intrinsic to the job, stressors stemming from roles in the organization, stressors associated with career development, stressors dealing with interpersonal relations in the organization, stressors associated with just being at work, including shift work, and stressors related to necessary interfaces outside the organization. In addition, stress may arise from major changes in an individual's personal life, or life events.

Stress affects people physiologically, emotionally, and behaviorally. Researchers have linked stress to several major health problems, particularly coronary heart disease. An inverted U-shaped relationship exists between stress and performance. An optimum level of stress probably exists for any given task, and less or more stress than the optimum level leads to reduced performance. Job burnout has been identified as a major result of stress in organizations.

Several personality traits can be related to stress. Individuals having a Type A personality are particularly prone to stress and have an increased chance of heart disease.

For all these reasons, stress is an important factor in people's behavior in organizations. Fortunately, various techniques and programs can help manage stress in the work environment.

KEY WORDS AND CONCEPTS

Behavioral effects of stress
Emotional effects of stress
Fight-or-flight response
Job burnout
Life stressors
Overpromotion
Physiological effects of stress
Role ambiguity

Role conflict
Role overload
Shift work
Stress
Stressor
Type A personality
Type B personality
Underpromotion

DISCUSSION QUESTIONS

1. Why should managers and employees be concerned about work stress?

2. Explain how individual differences affect the ways in which people experience work stress.

3. Look again at your responses to the questionnaire contained in Table 18–2. Describe the sources of stress in the job you used as a reference point. Which stressors were most difficult to deal with?

4. Give an example of a time when the fight-or-flight response seemed particularly inappropriate for your own behavior.

5. Suggest some actions that an organization might take to identify stressors. What things might be done to help employees cope with stress?

6. Describe the conditions and circumstances leading to job burnout. How can individuals and organizations cope with this consequence of stress?

7. What strategies or techniques do you use to cope with stress in your personal life? In your work?

MANAGEMENT INCIDENTS AND CASES

Stress and the Woman Manager

I am the Officer in Charge of a small, but busy Job Center. I have been in the British Civil Service since 1978, since 1981 as an Executive Officer. I was deputy Officer in Charge at my present office since 1982. Taking up full command in July 1985, I have charge of seven staff, of which only two are men. (This reflects the usual female:male ratio in the British Civil Service, where the lower clerical grades are predominantly female.) At present I am blessed with a group of staff who are uniformly bright and cooperative. This enables me to get by with a "low-profile" as a manager, so that I only need to emerge as a "leader" when the situation requires me to make decisions. I believe that a man in this position would perhaps feel he had to exert his authority more and be "seen" to manage. I believe that being in the management role panders to the male ego. The female doesn't believe in wasting energy in striking attitudes about her job as a manager. Women regard management as a job to be done while men see it as something that enhances their status. I find that my female colleagues are less concerned with status than with doing an efficient job. They feel that as women they have to be so much better than men in a similar role in order to prove their capabilities to higher management which, in the Civil Service, is predominantly male.

In the past five years all my immediate managers have been male.

Their styles have demonstrated a wide variety of attitudes. There was an elderly gentleman, near retirement, who was one of the "old school." I was treated with a paternal kindness by him which was rather more bearable than being made to feel like a silly female irritant by the next, aggressive, go-getting manager I had. One manager known for his chauvinism, who frequently pestered female staff, treated me reasonably, mainly because I did a good job for him and had an intellectual approach to the job which probably alarmed him so that he kept his distance. My present manager is a model to all those who seek to deal with female staff. He never makes the sexist jokes that one has heard so often before; he treats me as his equal in every respect and consults me as one of his management team rather than as a mere woman. My views are listened to and valued, and this is a rare treat. Unfortunately this situation does not extend to my senior manager who seems ill at ease when he is with his women managers. My constant problem is lack of staff resources, yet if I mention this to him he responds as though I were a nagging wife. It's the "Oh, Hilary, not that again" approach, as though he were chiding his wife for bringing up the price of the children's shoes again. I rather doubt if his male managers get this approach. I have to attend management meetings at which I am frequently the only female. At first it was rather like entering an exclusive Men's Club. I was tolerated but not taken seriously. When the tea arrived I was obviously expected to get up and hand the cups round, this I have steadfastly refused to do! During the course of these meetings I am able to observe how many vacillating, boorish and silly men have wormed their way to the top. Unfortunately this observation has not yet given me sufficient confidence to present myself at their meetings in a really forceful way, even though I

know that I am the intellectual superior of most of those present.

Of course the main difference between male and female managers is that for most women their working day does not end at 5:00 P.M. Even in these supposedly enlightened times, it is the rare man who contributes significantly to the running of the home. How many men spend their lunch times queueing in the supermarket or dashing round to collect the dry-cleaning? Running even a two-person household takes more time and energy than is generally realized and it is not uncommon for me to spend four or five hours a day on matters connected with a home. The only fringe benefit of this kind of life is that you do get used to organizing your time and energy with a military precision that makes the average male manager seem, by comparison, a ditherer. For women with young families the demands on their energy and patience must be enormous and we should hardly be surprised if they do complain of fatigue and feel torn between the demands of home and work. Personally, I always try to encourage the suitably able female members of my staff to look at their job in terms of a career. I encourage and advise them to find that quite often they have a poor image of themselves in relation to their work and lack the confidence to put themselves forward as candidates for promotion. Where their husbands are engaged in manual work, it is common to find that they regard their wives as sort of "non-workers" simply because they sit at a desk all day rather than being engaged in some sort of "productive" work.

The general feeling is then that to succeed in management one has to be positively better than one's male counterpart. The road to success is not easy. Some women adopt a simpering and fawning attitude to their superiors in an effort to please. The woman who is independent and wants to be treated on equal terms is still regarded as something of an oddity.

Having read through what I've just written, I wonder if I'm perhaps taking an over-sensitive line, but I have to attend a managers' meeting tomorrow and I know I shall encounter there all the attitudes I have described that make it so difficult to be a woman manager.[41]

How to Increase Employee Stress

There is a theory making the rounds that stress is an effective incentive and can be a challenging influence in one's life. Therefore, stress can motivate your subordinates to consider creative ways to work productively and effectively in order to please you—the manager.

The following techniques are guaranteed to increase your employee's stress:

1. Delegate work at the last minute and say it must be done by tomorrow. Then don't look at it for several days.
2. Transfer decision-making powers to your assistant and then state you should have been contacted on three of the five decisions that have been rendered.
3. Give only negative feedback and don't tell how you would like something to be improved. Just say, "I don't like the way you have written this report. Change it."
4. Hand five reports over to be typed immediately. When you are asked the order in which they should be typed, say, "I don't care." Then keep asking "Have you finished the report on the Solway Account? Have you completed the figures for the budget?"
5. Play favorites. Instead of building a team, assign projects according to how you feel personally about each employee.

Questions

1. List the stressors that are perceived by this woman manager.
2. To be successful, must women really outperform men? Justify your answer.
3. What coping strategies might be useful for the manager who wrote the above description?

6. Play one person against the other. Ten days before a deadline, tell Sally that John has almost finished his part of the project and ask her, "When will you be finished?" Then say the opposite to John: "Sally is almost finished. When will you complete your part of the project?" Be manipulative, even though you know the information that you have given is not true.
7. Give a poor performance appraisal with the idea that an individual needs to improve in all areas of work because no one is perfect. Do not set any goals with the employee.
8. Block transfers to other departments where employees would learn more skills, have greater responsibility and earn a better salary, under the guise that they are needed in your department and you can't do without them.
9. Send out memos every three days that contradict previous memos.
10. Give employees who have transferred into your department more responsibility than they can handle and do not train them in their new positions.
11. Create rumors by telling the staff that the department will be moving. But don't say when. Make different statements to different individuals so that no one has a clear understanding of what will occur. Spring changes

without giving anyone a chance to assimilate the new information. State the changes will start within three days. Do not provide explanations and do not allow input from anyone.

Get the idea? If you faithfully follow these suggestions, I promise that you will have very stressed employees who will appreciate the many opportunities you have given them for creative growth under duress.[42]

Questions

1. For each of the 11 suggestions for creating stress made above, restate the issue in a way that would tend to reduce or minimize employee stress and foster managerial effectiveness. In each case explain and justify your statement.

REFERENCES

1. Ivancevich, J. M., and Matteson, M. T. *Stress and Work: A Managerial Perspective.* Glenview, Ill.: Scott, Foresman, 1980, 76. Copyright © 1980 Scott, Foresman and Company. Reprinted with permission.

2. Quick, J. C., and Quick, J. D. *Organizational Stress and Preventive Management.* New York: McGraw-Hill, 1984, 2–6.

3. Yates, J. E. *Managing Stress: A Businessperson's Guide.* New York: AMACOM, a division of American Management Associations, 1979, 20.

4. This section is based on the description of the fight-or-flight syndrome found in Ivancevich and Matteson, *Stress and Work,* 10–11.

5. Selye, H. The Stress Concept and Some of Its Implications. In Hamilton, V., and Warburton, D. M. (Eds.) *Human Stress and Cognition.* New York: Wiley, 1979, 12; Selye, H. *The Stress of Life,* rev. ed. New York: McGraw-Hill, 1976, 1.

6. The discussion of these factors in work stress is based, in part, on McGrath, J. E. Stress and Behavior in Organizations. In Dunnette, M. D. (Ed.) *Handbook of Industrial and Organizational Psychology.* Chicago: Rand McNally, 1976, 1351–1395; Quick and Quick, *Organizational Stress and Preventive Management.*

7. Bhagat, R. S., McQuaid, S. J., Lindholm, H., and Segovis, J. Total Life Stress: A Multimethod Validation of the Construct and its Effects on Organizationally Valued Outcomes and Withdrawal Behaviors. *Journal of Applied Psychology,* 1985, *70,* 202–214.

8. See, for example, Frese, M. Stress At Work and Psychosomatic Complaints: A Causal Interpretation. *Journal of Applied Psychology,* 1985, *70,* 314–328; Hendrix, W. H., Ovalle, N. K., and Troxler, R. G. Behavioral and Physiological Consequences of Stress and its Antecedent Factors. *Journal of Applied Psychology,* 1985, *70,* 188–201; Parasuraman, S., and Alutto, J. A. An Examination of the Organizational Antecedents of Stressors at Work. *Academy of Management Journal,* 1981, *24,* 48–67; Parasuraman, S., and Alutto, J. A. Sources and Outcomes of Stress in Organizational Settings: Toward the Development of a Structural Model. *Academy of Management Journal,* 1984, *27,* 330–350.

9. The categorization of work stressors presented here is adapted from Cooper, C. L., and Marshall, J. The Management of Stress. *Personnel Review,* 1975, *4*(4), 26–31.

10. Shostak, A. B. *Blue-Collar Stress.* Reading, Mass.: Addison-Wesley, 1980, 19–28.

11. Youngblood, S., Lyon, L., Allen, J., Boyd, J., Molleston, J., Senia, S., and Woodman, R. *A Survey of Senior Executives of United States Independent Oil and Gas Producing Firms.* Technical report prepared for Korn/Ferry International, April 1982.

12. Kahn, R. L., Wolfe, D. M., Quinn, R. P., Snoek, J. D., and Rosenthal, R. A. *Organizational Stress: Studies in Role Conflict and Ambiguity.* New York: Wiley, 1964.

13. Benjamin, G. A. Shift Workers. *Personnel Journal,* June 1984, 74.

14. Hood, J. C., and Milazzo, N. Shiftwork, Stress, and Wellbeing. *Personnel Administrator,* December 1984, 95–105.

15. Based on data reported in Cooper, C., and Arbose, J. Executive Stress Goes Global. *International Management,* May 1984, 42–48.

16. See, for example, Cooke, R. A., and Rousseau, D. M. Stress and Strain from Family Roles and Work-Role Expectations. *Journal of Applied Psychology,* 1984, *69,* 252–260; Hendrix, Ovalle, and Troxler. Behavioral and Physiological Consequences of Stress and its Antecedent Factors.

17. Johnson, J. H., and Sarason, I. G. Recent Developments in Research on Life Stress. In *Human Stress and Cognition*, 205–233; Kessler, R. C., Price, R. H., and Wortman, C. B. Social Factors in Psychopathology: Stress, Social Support, and Coping Processes. *Annual Review of Psychology*, 1985, *36*, 531–572.

18. Holmes, T. H., and Rahe, R. H. The Social Readjustment Rating Scale. *Journal of Psychosomatic Medicine*, 1967, *11*, 213–218.

19. Yates, *Managing Stress*, 80.

20. Cooper and Arbose, Executive Stress Goes Global, 42.

21. Many of the effects of work stress are discussed in Beehr, T. A., and Newman, J. E. Job Stress, Employee Health, and Organizational Effectiveness: A Facet Analysis, Model, and Literature Review. *Personnel Psychology*, 1979, *31*, 665–699; Levi, L. *Preventing Work Stress*. Reading, Mass.: Addison-Wesley, 1981, 71–80; Quick and Quick, *Organizational Stress and Preventive Management*, 43–74.

22. Bammer, K., and Newberry, B. H. (Ed.) *Stress and Cancer*. Toronto: C. J. Hogrefe, 1982; Matteson, M. T., and Ivancevich, J. M. Organizational Stressors and Heart Disease: A Research Model. *Academy of Management Review*, 1979, *4*, 347–357; Selye, *The Stress of Life*; Shostak, *Blue-Collar Stress*, 113–133; Warshaw, L. J. *Managing Stress*. Reading, Mass.: Addison-Wesley, 1979, 95–121.

23. Jones, J. W. A Cost Evaluation for Stress Management. *EAP Digest*, November–December 1984, 34.

24. For reviews of the relationships between performance and stress, see Cohen, S. Aftereffects of Stress on Human Performance and Social Behavior: A Review of Research and Theory. *Psychological Bulletin*, 1980, *88*, 82–108; Hockey, R. Stress and the Cognitive Components of Skilled Performance. In *Human Stress and Cognition*, 141–177; Ivancevich and Matteson, *Stress and Work*, 191–204.

25. Excerpted from *Corporate Stress* by Rosalind Forbes, pp. 9–10. Copyright © 1979 by Rosalind Forbes. Reprinted by permission of Doubleday & Company, Inc.

26. Moss, L. *Management Stress*. Reading, Mass.: Addison-Wesley, 1981, 66.

27. Etzion, D. Moderating Effect of Social Support on the Stress–Burnout Relationship. *Journal of Applied Psychology*, 1984, *69*, 615–622.

28. Rogers, D. P. Helping Employees Cope With Burnout. *Business*, October–December 1984, 3–7.

29. Niehouse, O. I. Controlling Burnout: A Leadership Guide for Managers. *Business Horizons*, July–August 1984, 80–81. Copyright, 1984, by the Foundation for the School of Business at Indiana University. Used with permission.

30. Niehouse, Controlling Burnout: A Leadership Guide for Managers, 81–82.

31. Anderson, C. R., Hellriegel, D., and Slocum, J. W. Jr. Managerial Response to Environmentally Induced Stress. *Academy of Management Journal*, 1977, *20*, 260–272.

32. Descriptions of individual differences can be found in Quick and Quick, *Organizational Stress and Preventive Management*, 63–74; Schuler, R. S. Definition and Conceptualization of Stress in Organizations. *Organizational Behavior and Human Performance*, 1980, *25*, 184–215.

33. Friedman, M., and Rosenman, R. *Type A Behavior and Your Heart*. New York: Knopf, 1974.

34. Matthews, K. A. Psychological Perspectives on the Type A Behavior Pattern. *Psychological Bulletin*, 1982, *91*, 293–323.

35. The comparisons between Type A and Type B individuals are based on McLean, A. A. *Work Stress*. Reading, Mass.: Addison-Wesley, 1979, 68–71.

36. Tierney, J. Type A's Maybe Now You Can Relax. *Science 85*, June 1985, 12.

37. Ivancevich and Matteson, *Stress and Work*, 208.

38. For descriptions of organizational stress management programs and their effects, see Newman, J. E., and Beehr, T. A. Personal and Organizational Strategies for Handling Job Stress: A Review of Research and Opinion. *Personnel Psychology*, 1979, *32*, 1–43; Rose, R. L., and Veiga, J. F. Assessing the Sustained Effects of a Stress Management Intervention on Anxiety and Locus of Control. *Academy of Management Journal*, 1984, *27*, 190–198; Stoner, C. R., and Fry, F. L. Developing a Corporate Policy for Managing Stress. *Personnel*, May–June 1983, 66–76; Warshaw, *Managing Stress*, 159–189.

39. McGeveran, W. A. Meditation at the Telephone Company. *Wharton Magazine*, 1981, *6*(1), 29–32.

40. Hartman, S. W., and Cozzetto, J. Wellness in the Workplace. *Personnel Administrator*, August 1984, 108–117.

41. From *Stress and the Woman Manager* by Marilyn Davidson and Cary Cooper. Copyright © Marilyn Davidson and Cary Cooper, 1983, and reprinted by permission of St. Martin's Press, Inc.

42. Schulman, D. How to Stress Your Employees. *Supervisory Management*, January 1984, 20–21. Reprinted with permission.

PART VI

INDIVIDUAL AND ORGANIZATIONAL CHANGE

19 Career Planning and Development

LEARNING OBJECTIVES

When you have finished studying this chapter, you should be able to:

■ Define career and describe its components.

■ State the factors that influence a person's choices of career and occupation.

■ State the four career stages that most people go through.

■ Identify the central activities and career concerns associated with each career stage.

■ State the factors that affect career planning.

OUTLINE

Preview Case

John Akers, IBM's Chief Executive Officer

When John Akers joined IBM as a sales trainee in 1960, he did not seriously entertain the idea that on February 1, 1985, he would be named chief executive officer of IBM. Out of the Navy with a B.S. degree in engineering, he was one of several hundred new hires for IBM in 1960. At that time, IBM was small, with sales of around $1.8 billion (sales in 1984 were $44.3 billion). As a sales trainee for IBM, he was assigned to San Francisco and made $6,500 a year, an adequate salary for him and his wife to live on in the bay area at that time.

After spending 18 months as a trainee in San Francisco, he got his first assignment as a marketing representative in western Massachusetts and Vermont. For the next five years, he worked that territory, handing out IBM cards to anyone who would take one. In a good year, he made $30,000. While on this assignment, he made IBM's "Hundred Percent Club" each year. This club is composed of sales reps who meet or exceed sales goals. The Hundred Percent pin in IBM is essential for advancement. Most people, if they stay with IBM for a few years, will make the club at least once. Each year, Akers would be honored at sales meetings and conventions for his outstanding sales. Akers went even further, gaining entry into the elite Golden Circle, a most prestigious sales honor at IBM.

In 1967, he started to make a series of rapid advancements. He was promoted to marketing manager in the Boston office in 1967, and then on to branch manager in New York City in 1969. It was during this assignment that he caught the attention of then president Frank Carey. Carey reassigned Akers to corporate headquarters in Armonk, New York and named him his administrative assistant in 1971.

According to insiders at IBM, the administrative assistant job is the beginning or end of your career. If you survive, it means you've got executive material and people at headquarters are going to look you over very carefully. It also requires the person to work 16-hour days, seven days a week. The administrative assistant job for Akers involved everything from arranging dinners to writing speeches for Carey. Akers passed this survival test and at 36 was assigned the job as industry director of IBM's data processing division. At this level, he became acquainted with other IBMers who had also arrived at their managerial position by following the classic path from salesman up without significant business experience outside of IBM.

In less than a year, he was promoted to vice-president and regional manager of IBM's western region data processing territory in Los Angeles. Little more than a year later, he was reassigned to White Plains, New York and became president of that division, a post that Carey had held ten years earlier. As president of the data processing division, he had become part of IBM's inner circle: those selected few people who benefitted from IBM's executive bonus plan and other perks, as well as making strategic decisions for the company.

Because IBM has a culture that says that up-and-coming executives are seldom, if ever, quoted in the press, few people outside of IBM were aware of his career. However, within the organization, he was becoming something of a legend. One story is that Akers made a presentation before the president and executive vice-presidents of New England Mutual Life Insurance in an attempt to take that company's business from Univac, who had it for over ten years. His presentation was so powerful that, soon afterwards, IBM won that account.

Akers' name appeared for the first time in IBM's 1974 annual report when he became president of the data processing division. Little more than two years later, he was named one of 25 IBM vice-presidents. In 1978, he became one of only three group executives, vice-president and group executive for Data Processing.

To those outside of IBM, it might appear that Akers' career strategy was to get to the top as fast as possible. But to those inside IBM, this is not the way to the top. To succeed at IBM, you have to do it in a group, as part of a team. IBM recognizes the team through its reward system. Akers is careful to give the credit to his team, and is careful not to allow individuals to take all the credit for the success of a project.[1]

Most people would regard John Akers as successful. Within a period of 25 years, he moved through the ranks from management trainee to chief executive officer of one of the world's most successful companies. Akers got to the top because the people for whom he worked and who worked for him during his career rise thought very highly of him, and people had opened doors for him. However, he was successful also because he planned his career. He looked to IBM for challenging opportunities, satisfying work experiences, and the chance for personal and professional growth.

The purpose of this chapter is to make you aware of some of the important concepts involved in managing your own career. We cannot promise you that, after studying this chapter, you will be another John Akers, but we do hope that you will learn from his experiences at IBM and the ideas that we present in this chapter.

THE CONCEPT OF CAREER

Many people may not think of their life and work experiences as comprising a career, but they do. A **career** basically is a sequence of work-related positions occupied by a person during the course of a lifetime.[2] The popular view of a career is usually restricted to the idea of moving up the organization ladder, as John Akers did. However, a career also consists of attitudes and behaviors that are a part of an on-going sequence of work-related activities and experiences. People can remain in the same job, acquiring and developing skills, and have a successful career without ever getting promoted. Or people can build a career by moving among various jobs in different fields and organizations. Thus our concept of career encompasses not only traditional work experiences, but also the diversity of career alternatives, individual choices, and individual experiences.

Four assumptions about career can help to clarify the concept of career:

- The *nature* of career does not in itself imply success or failure or fast or slow advancement. Career success or failure is best determined by the individual, rather than by other interested parties such as researchers, employers, parents, spouse, or friends.

■ No absolute standards exist for evaluating a career.[3] Career success or failure is related to the concept of self-actualization in the needs hierarchy (Chapter 7). Individuals should evaluate their own career goals and progress in terms of what is personally meaningful and satisfying. The measurement of an individual's career success or failure is as unique as the person.

■ A career consists of both behaviors and attitudes, that is, things a person does and feels. A career has subjective aspects: values, attitudes, personality, and motivations, which change as people pass through their careers. A career also has more objective characteristics: activities and behaviors, job choices, specific positions held, and so on. A complete understanding of an individual's career requires examination of both its subjective and objective aspects.

■ A career is made up of work-related experiences, which includes more than the work that is performed for pay. Volunteer work, work around the house, school work, or political activities are also an important part of many careers.[4]

Career development requires an individual to make decisions and engage in activities to attain career goals. The central idea in the career development process is time.[5] The shape of a person's career over time is influenced by several factors. Let us consider one pair of these factors—costs and benefits—within the context of job opportunities in an organization. When someone accepts a position, there are costs and benefits both to the individual and the organization. The individual gives time, talent, and effort in return for a salary. The organization gives up financial resources and gains human resources. In this arrangement, both parties either implicitly or explicitly attempt to match costs and benefits. In reality, these costs and benefits change in various ways over time, and both parties attempt to manage the fit continuously. When changes occur, individual and/or organizational decisions are made. These decisions by either or both parties have a direct impact on the career-development process of the individual. Finally, career development processes also vary by culture. That is, various cultural norms from countries, such as Spain, France, Japan, United States, and Israel, also impact the direction of a person's career. Let's look at how women's careers in Israel develop.

ACROSS CULTURES

Careers for Israeli Women

Israeli society is multicultural and the attitudes and norms relevant to careers are influenced by many things. Besides the formal value system, there are three variables that influence a woman's career path in Israel. First, the general cultural background of values, norms, and social customs form a continuum from the traditional rural Jewish and Arab society to the extremely modern urban society of native-born Israelis and immigrants from Western Europe and the United States. Women raised in the more traditional culture have fewer years of schooling, a lower average age at marriage, higher rates of fertility, and lower participation rates in the labor force than more modern Israeli women. Sixty percent of the urban women work outside their homes, compared to 27 percent of the traditional women. As the country has moved toward a standard that resembles the modern "Western" mode in education and occupations, education has become the great modernizing factor for many Israeli women. Second, the rural population is highly differentiated. Many Jewish women live in villages similar to traditional peasant societies; yet right next to them resides a large farm population organized as socialist cooperatives that are based on egalitarian ideas. Third, religion and ideology have considerable impact. Those women living in rural areas tend to be very religious and assume the dominant role in the home and family. In urban areas, many women have greater autonomy and responsibility. Many of these women want to work in order to raise their standard of living and to have a career outside of the home.

Women do not try to enter every type of occupation and often prefer typical women's jobs. Women are found in clerical and administrative jobs (31 percent), professional and technical jobs (24 percent), and service jobs (16 percent). Approximately equal ratios of men and women are found in scientific and academic jobs (about 8.5 percent each). Many Israeli women prefer part-time to full-time work. Part-time work undoubtedly deters companies from promoting them into higher-level managerial jobs. Choosing between a career and the relative comfort of part-time work is a major dilemma for many. Most part-time workers do not see themselves as career women responsible for family support, but as helpers working to supplement the family's income.

Israeli women tend to earn less than men. A woman's pay is about 80 percent of the average for men. However, in the civil service, women are better educated than men, have only slightly less seniority, and generally are continuously employed. Women rank family interests higher than do men. The majority of women, even those raising modern as opposed to traditional families, feel a stronger commitment to their families than do the husbands. Even in the Kibbutz, which is a strongly work-oriented community, work is less central in the lives of women than in the lives of men. Many employers recognize this feeling and have established day care centers and holiday camps and are seeking other means of integrating family and work commitments.

Source: Adapted from Bar-Yosef, R. Israel. In *Woman Workers in Fifteen Countries*. J. Farley (Ed.) Ithaca, N.Y.: ILR Press, New York State School of Industrial Relations, 1985, 68–81.

Matching Organizational and Individual Needs

Effective career development requires a fit between the individual and the organization over time. Recall that the individual's career is a process, or sequence, of work-related experiences. The organization has an important stake in this process, and organizational needs must be matched with the employee's needs and career goals. To the extent that the matching process is done well, both organization and employee benefit. The organization is more effective and productive, and the individual is more satisfied, happy, and successful.

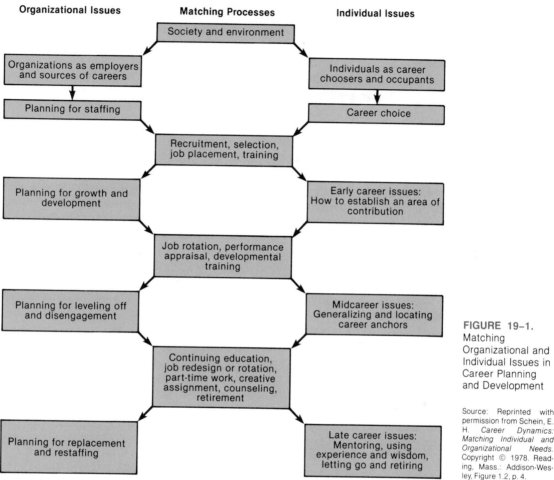

Organizational Issues   **Matching Processes**   **Individual Issues**

Society and environment

Organizations as employers and sources of careers

Individuals as career choosers and occupants

Planning for staffing

Career choice

Recruitment, selection, job placement, training

Planning for growth and development

Early career issues: How to establish an area of contribution

Job rotation, performance appraisal, developmental training

Planning for leveling off and disengagement

Midcareer issues: Generalizing and locating career anchors

Continuing education, job redesign or rotation, part-time work, creative assignment, counseling, retirement

Planning for replacement and restaffing

Late career issues: Mentoring, using experience and wisdom, letting go and retiring

FIGURE 19–1.
Matching Organizational and Individual Issues in Career Planning and Development

Source: Reprinted with permission from Schein, E. H. *Career Dynamics: Matching Individual and Organizational Needs.* Copyright © 1978. Reading, Mass.: Addison-Wesley, Figure 1.2, p. 4.

Figure 19–1 highlights the organizational and individual issues inherent in career planning and development. It also shows some of the ongoing matching processes needed to integrate organizational needs and individual needs and career goals.

ORGANIZATIONAL NEEDS   A society's technology and cultural values—and its laws and institutions—determine the labor market and strongly influence the structure of occupations. The environment within which a company must operate broadens or constrains the career opportunities that the company can make available to its employees. Thus an important organizational activity is identifying human resource needs and making plans for meeting them. How many people will be needed? When will they be needed? Where will they come from? What skills will they need to have? Organizations must continuously recruit, develop, transfer, and promote people to perform its functions. These planning and managing activities never stop unless the firm goes out of business.

INDIVIDUAL NEEDS AND GOALS   Whereas an organization must meet its human resource and staffing needs if it is to be successful, the individual must develop a career plan in order to be successful. A **career plan** is the individual's choice of occupation, organization, and career path. (Career planning is discussed in detail at the end of this chapter.) If opportunities provided by the organization are not attractive career alternatives for individuals, the organization will be plagued by personnel problems, including those of recruiting and retaining qualified employees.

THE MATCHING PROCESS   The central portion of Figure 19–1 shows ways in which an organization can attempt to match its human resource needs with the career stages of employees. The careers of most people seem to go through similar stages, with a beginning, a middle, and an end. (Career stages are discussed in more detail later in this chapter.) People's needs, values, and goals change as they progress through these stages. The staffing needs of the organization also change over time. All of these changes—both individual and organizational—make matching organizational and individual needs and goals complex.

Thus organizations strive to translate needs for personnel into opportunities that employees will view as attractive in terms of their own needs and career goals. The extent of this matching, in part, determines organizational effectiveness.

CAREER CHOICES

Why do people make the career decisions they do? Consider the dilemma faced by Steve and Mary and try to decide what you would do in a similar situation.

In Practice: What Would You Do?

Steve and Mary were seniors at a large midwestern university majoring in business administration. On April 10th, they were sitting in Mary's apartment discussing the decisions that were facing them. They had met during their junior year and had become engaged to be married. They faced different career and life style options and were wrestling with the choices they had to make.

Steve's Background and Options

Steve had been raised on Chicago's north side. His father had a law degree from Northwestern University and was a lawyer with a prestigious Chicago firm. His mother had earned a degree in criminal justice and now did some part-time work in Chicago. Steve was the middle of three boys. Between Steve's high school graduation and first year of college, he took some time off to "find himself." During this time, he worked at a variety of manual labor jobs. Now he had the following job options:

- Levi Strauss had offered Steve a job as a management trainee. He would be responsible for working with a senior salesperson in the Seattle area and within a year or so, would be responsible for developing a computer-assisted software program for estimating sales revenue from a sales territory.
- KVIL was a major radio broadcasting station in the Dallas-Forth Worth area. KVIL had offered Steve his choice of two positions, one in sales and the other in promotion and advertising.

- Sunset Energy was a newly formed firm located in Houston. It had been founded two years earlier by several engineers who worked on problems of solar-produced electrical energy. This firm wanted Steve to work in its accounting department.

- Steve had received a scholarship to attend Northwestern University's MBA program. Steve's parents indicated that they would help him financially if he chose to continue his education.

Mary's Background and Options

Mary was born on a farm on the outskirts of Lincoln, Nebraska and was raised as an only child. Mary's mother worked as a school teacher in the Lincoln school system, and her father managed the local State Farm Insurance Agency. During the summers, Mary had worked in a local bank as a teller and had impressed the bank president with her interpersonal and administrative skills. Now she had the following options:

- Mary could accept a position in the local bank where she had worked during the summers. Her salary would be greatly increased, and she knew everyone at the bank. Her initial position would be as a trainee in the loan department, with a promised move into a management position quickly.

- Mary had received an offer from the University of Nebraska to work as an assistant director of admissions. This position would require her to travel around the state talking with high school seniors about educational opportunities at the University of Nebraska. She would also be in charge of two individuals who processed applications for admissions. One fringe benefit of this job was that the University would let her pursue her MBA for free.

- Mary had also received an offer from a Wall Street firm to work as a Research Analyst. This would require her to research industries and firms that brokers thought might be good prospects for their clients. This job offered the possibility of moving into a broker's job in the near future. She had visited New York City several times and thought it might be exciting to live there.

- Mary could also decide to stay at home and manage the household while Steve worked. If they decided to have children, she would be there to raise them in a "traditional" household.[6]

Steve and Mary, like all of us, have to make two initial career choices: (1) an occupation; and (2) an organization. These choices will have to be made in the midst of other decisions, such as the kind of life style they want to create in their marriage, where they want to live, whether they should rent an apartment or buy a house, and the like.

During the course of your career, you will have to make many such choices. These decisions are seldom irreversible. People like Mary and Steve need not feel locked into these choices for life; instead, they can create or find other career opportunities. People's careers frequently involve working in many organizations, commuting long distances, and sometimes pursuing multiple occupations during their lifetime. Studies of college graduates indicate that, five years after graduation, at least 50 percent have changed organizations at least once, and 20 percent had changed occupations.[7]

Occupational Choice

Researchers and managers have long been fascinated by the possibility that individuals attracted to a specific occupation might have certain common characteristics or attributes. They also have studied whether certain sets of characteristics might be used to predict specific career choices and effective performance in those careers. While finer distinctions might be made, at least two general categories of personal characteristics seem to be related to career choices: personality and social background.

PERSONALITY: VOCATIONAL BEHAVIOR   John Holland advanced the most detailed theory relating personality to vocational behavior.[8] He proposed the existence of six basic personality types—**Holland's personality types**—each of which has a particular type of work environment with which it will be most congruent. In a congruent situation, the basic orientation of the personality matches the demands and expectations needed for success in a particular work environment. Holland claims that these six classifications of personality types are good predictors of career aspiration and choice. For example, the enterprising personality type is likely to be attracted to an enterprising type of work environment, such as management. Empirical research supports the existence of a relationship between personality orientation and career choice. Some evidence also shows that a person is more likely to remain in a chosen occupation if it is congruent with his or her personality orientation. When placed in incongruent environments, people will be less satisfied with the job, their job performance will be lower, and they will be more likely to quit.[9]

Table 19-1 lists the six basic personality types in Holland's theory, along with some of their corresponding personality traits, interests, and representative occupations. Column 2 contains the problem-solving style (Chapter 5) that seems to best fit each personality type. Note that no single problem-solving style appears to be typical of the enterprising personality type.

PERSONALITY INTERESTS   Column 4 of Table 19-1 lists some of the occupational interests that are often displayed by each of the six personality types. Since an occupation involves specific activities, people having the same occupation may share certain interests to a greater extent than do people in general. Thus an individual's interests can be identified and compared to the profile of interests held by samples of individuals in various occupations. This information can help an individual choose a vocation. There is considerable evidence that people tend to pursue careers that match their interests; there is some evidence that such interests play a part in career success or, at the least, in a person's remaining in a chosen occupation.

PERSONALITY: SELF-ESTEEM   Another personality dimension related to occupational choice is a person's self-esteem (Chapter 3). **Self-esteem** is a person's general self-image, including opinions of his or her behavior, ability, appearance, and overall worth as a person. A person's self-esteem may strongly influence the initial vocational choice. A person's self-concept may change over time as a result of the value placed on a chosen occupation and career by others and the person's performance in them.

TABLE 19–1   **Holland's Personality Type Descriptions**

Personality Type	Corresponding Problem-Solving Style	Personality Traits	Interests	Representative Occupations
Realistic	Sensation-thinker (ST)	Stable, materialistic, persistent, practical	Manual skills, mechanics, agriculture, electronics, technology	Architecture, trades (plumber, electrician), machinist, forest ranger
Investigative	Intuitive thinker (NT)	Analytical, critical, curious, intellectual, rational	Science, math	Physicist, anthropologist, chemist, mathematician, biologist
Artistic	Intuitive feeler (NF)	Emotional, idealistic, imaginative, impulsive	Language, art, music, drama, writing	Poet, novelist, musician, sculptor, playwright, composer, stage director
Social	Sensation-feeler (SF)	Cooperative, friendly, sociable, understanding	Human relations, interpersonal skills, education	Professor, psychologist, counselor, missionary, teacher
Enterprising	?	Adventurous, ambitious, energetic, optimistic, self-confident, talkative	Leadership, interpersonal skills, influence	Manager, salesperson, politician, lawyer, buyer
Conventional	Sensation-thinker (ST)	Conscientious, obedient, orderly, self-controlled	Clerical and computational skills, business systems	Certified public accountant, statistician, bookkeeper, administrative assistant, post office clerk

Source: Adapted from Holland, J. *Making Vocational Choices: A Theory of Careers.* Englewood Cliffs, N.J.: Prentice-Hall, 1973, 111–117; Spokane, A. A Review of Research on Person–Environment Congruence in Holland's Theory of Careers. *Journal of Vocational Behavior*, 1985, 26:306–343.

SOCIAL BACKGROUND   The social background of the individual also influences career choice. **Social background** refers to early childhood experiences, the socioeconomic status of the family, the educational level and occupations of parents, and so on. All these factors affect the occupational goals set and career choices made by an individual by providing socialization experiences and setting practical constraints. For example, people may be more likely to consider a white-collar or professional career if one or both of parents have such a career. The practical constraint of parents being unable to afford a college education for their children may, in turn, limit the occupational choices available later to those children. Other, more subtle constraints include the socialization of girls to expect adult roles different from those of men (for example, the roles of wife and mother). This early socialization later may influence the vocational choices made by many women.[10]

Organizational Choice

Choosing an organization is the second major career decision that most people must make.[11] A major factor in choosing a specific organization is the availability of opportunities for individuals at any given time. (What if Mary and Steve had had no offers?)

The amount of information available concerning job opportunities is also a constraint. In an attempt to overcome it, college placement services, state employment offices, private placement firms, and other agencies provide aid in matching individuals and organizations. People also obtain information about organizations from a variety of other sources, including the organizations themselves, friends, acquaintances, family, the organizations' current and former employees, and newspapers. For example, one research study determined that job applicants at an aerospace firm were receiving a considerable amount of their information about the firm from former employees.

Individuals use information about an organization to form opinions about working there. Some typical questions that people have regarding an organization are shown in Table 19-2. People tend to judge an organization by how well it fits their career goals and plans and base their choice of an organization on their perceptions of a fit between known organizational characteristics and their personal characteristics, values, and goals.

CAREER STAGES

A **career stage** in a person's life is a period of time characterized by distinctive and fairly predictable developmental tasks, concerns, needs, values, and activities.[12] The following sections examine career stages from two perspectives: (1) career movement of an individual within a specific organization; and (2) an individual's passage through career stages spanning his or her entire working life.

Career Movement within an Organization

People most often think of career movement as advancement up some management or technical hierarchy with ever-increasing salary, status, and responsibilities. For example, at one petroleum company, new college graduates with an engineering degree begin their employment as associate

---

TABLE 19-2   Questions Often Asked by Individuals When Assessing an Organization

1. How large is the organization's industry and what are its prospects for growth?

2. What goods and services does it produce?

3. How large is the organization (people, assets, sales volume)?

4. Where does it have other plants or divisions?

5. What are the organization's compensation policies? Performance Appraisal practices? Training and development practices?

6. What do people generally like or dislike about the organization?

7. What are the organization's plans for the future?

8. What jobs have top executives held during their careers with the organization?

Source: Adapted from Clawson, J., Kotter, J., Faux, V., and McArthur, C. *Self Assessment and Career Development,* 2d ed. Englewood Cliffs, N.J.: Prentice-Hall, 1985, 295.

engineers. They advance to positions such as production engineer, senior production engineer, and district production engineer. However, career moves in an organization actually are considerably more complex than this.[13] Individuals really move in three directions in an organization: vertical, horizontal, and (more subtly) inclusion.[14] An understanding of the complexity of career moves in an organization can be extremely valuable in aiding an individual's career planning and development.

VERTICAL MOVEMENT   **Vertical career movement** refers to increases or decreases in the formal rank or level of individuals in organizations. During the course of a career in a particular organization, most people move vertically, typically receiving a series of raises and promotions. Of course, in this highly variable process, only a few individuals rise to the very top ranks of the organization, and some individuals reach their final hierarchical level early in their careers. Organizations differ dramatically in the number of hierarchical opportunities available: some may be quite "flat" in terms of hierarchical steps to the top, and others may have many levels or ranks.

HORIZONTAL MOVEMENT   **Horizontal career movement** refers to the movement of individuals laterally in an organization in functional or technical areas. The horizontal movement relates to individuals' areas of knowledge, skills, and expertise. Common functional areas in business firms include production, marketing, finance, engineering, accounting, and personnel. Here, too, individual careers vary considerably; some employees stay in the same functional or technical area for their entire careers, whereas others make frequent changes. The middle manager who is rotated among positions in production, marketing, and personnel provides an example of horizontal movement. Organizations sometimes design this rotation to groom people for eventual promotion to the general management ranks, where managers need the ability to see and understand overall operations.

INCLUSION: MOVEMENT TOWARD THE CENTER   The **inclusion career movement** refers to movement toward the inner circle, or core, of an organization. This occurs when a manager becomes more trusted, comprehends the organization, gains greater responsibility, and is more frequently consulted on important matters. A relationship often exists between vertical and inclusion movement; yet a person often can make one move without the other. A person can become more "central" to the organization without being promoted to a higher rank by acquiring experience and the trust and confidence of a top manager and co-workers. Similarly, a person can move up in the hierarchy and yet still not be included in important core activities and decisions, as illustrated by the phrase "being kicked upstairs."

Inclusion is the most subtle and confusing aspect of career moves within an organization. People may go through their entire careers completely unaware of their position in terms of inclusion or, perhaps, even be oblivious to the existence of inclusion.

The model illustrated in Figure 19–2 combines the three directions in which career moves can be made. Vertical movement is represented by a move up or down the cone. Horizontal movement is represented by a move around the circumference of the cone from one functional or technical area to another. Inclusion movement is a move from the outer surface of the cone toward the center.

We can use this model of career movement to trace John Akers' movement through IBM. His career was marked by significant *vertical* movement. His promotion from marketing representative to marketing manager in 1967 was the first vertical movement. From there he was promoted to district manager, administrative assistant to Frank Carey, and so on up the line. At each move, his salary and responsibilities increased. Akers moved

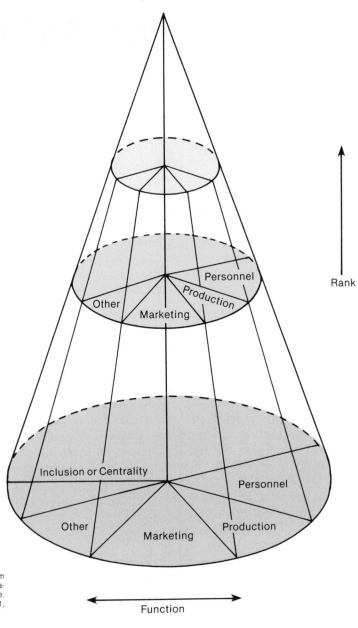

FIGURE 19–2.
A Model of Career
Movement in
Organizations

Source: Reprinted with permission from
Schein, E. H. The Individual, the Organization, and the Career: A Conceptual Scheme.
Journal of Applied Behavioral Science, 1971,
7:404. Copyright © 1971 by NTL Institute.

horizontally from engineering to sales to marketing to general management—all phases of IBM's operations. The *inclusion* movement began when Akers performed well as Carey's administrative assistant and was completed with his selection as president of the data processing division. At that time, he became part of the inner circle at IBM.

Working-Life Career Stages

Individuals typically move through four distinct career stages during their working lives: establishment, advancement, maintenance, and withdrawal.[15] Figure 19-3 summarizes these stages and indicates the expected relative levels of performance as employees move through their careers. Not all careers will be like those shown in Figure 19-3 because there will always be individual differences. For example, some people may take longer to decide about what to do than others; similarly, others may start another career when they are 40 and thus have to learn new skills that others learned earlier in their careers.

ESTABLISHMENT CAREER STAGE   When first joining an organization, a person is immediately faced with several challenges. First, the new employee must learn to perform at least some work tasks competently and which tasks are essential and which require less attention.[16] At the same time the newcomer must also learn how to get things done, using both the formal and informal channels of communication. Finally, the new employee must do these things while being closely watched by a manager for competency and indications of future potential.

   Much of a new employee's work in this career stage involves fairly routine duties. It is important for a person not to become completely bogged down in this detail work, but to show some initiative and be innovative in

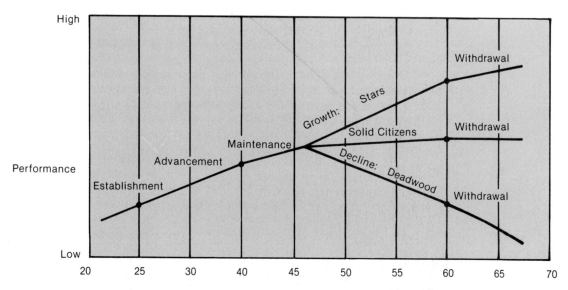

FIGURE 19-3.
Working-Life Career Stages

Source: Adapted from Hall, T. *Careers in Organizations*. Santa Monica, Calif.:Goodyear, 1976, 57.

finding solutions to problems. New employees are typically assigned parts of larger projects that are being directed by managers which many people find frustrating. Such a reaction is understandable, but those who try to escape subordinate positions too quickly will miss an important aspect of career development: they will fail to learn what others have gained by experience. More importantly, if they were to undertake tasks for which they are not prepared, the newcomers may acquire the reputation of being mediocre performers, a reputation that is hard to overcome. Effectively handling the subordinate-superior relationship and the types of tasks assigned may be critical to building an effective career.

Ideally, newcomers will be assigned to a mentor who knows the organization, is successful, and has been trained to work with newly hired employees. A **mentor** is a person who will sponsor and speak to others about employees' accomplishments.[17] The mentor suggests what to do and what not to do and offers advice about organizational life that is not found in organizational charts and orientation brochures. At IBM, Frank Carey served as John Akers' mentor. Carey helped Akers gain the skills, experience, and visibility necessary for advancement in IBM.

The concerns of managers at this career stage are summarized in Table 19-3. This stage requires time for adjustment to the reality of the job, orientation to the organization, and establishment of a mentoring relationship with a supervisor. Completing routine jobs successfully can quickly lead to more challenging assignments. If new employees can pass through this stage successfully, their career goals can usually be reached more easily.

ADVANCEMENT CAREER STAGE   The second career stage often involves new experiences: special assignments, transfers, promotions, offers from other organizations, and chances for visibility to higher management. Performance feedback becomes critical to development of feelings of success or failure. With greater self-confidence and knowledge of the organization, people are more likely to be concerned about promotion and advancement than about their ability to get the work done. With a track record developing, they will be looking ahead to having their own projects. Although they will not be allowed to work alone, they are no longer closely supervised or given specific methods to use in doing tasks.

An important individual decision to be made is how much to specialize. Specializing in one area (quality control, tax accounting, purchasing) allows a person to become an expert in it; the potential danger, though, is that of being pigeonholed. The other option is to develop a set of specialized skills and apply them in a variety of areas. For example, a computer specialist (programmer or systems analyst) can apply his or her skills in marketing, accounting, personnel, manufacturing, and finance. The risk here is that of becoming a jack of all trades and a master of none.

TABLE 19-3   Concerns of Managers at the Establishment Stage—Ages 20-25

■ Central activity: Helping, learning, and following directions

■ Primary relationship: Being a subordinate and finding a mentor

■ Needed from superior: Coaching, feedback, visibility

As people approach the age of 35, most feel a greater commitment to the organization than they did when they were 21. Top managers recognize this and use golden handcuffs to retain valued employees. **Golden handcuffs** are the salary, perks (country club memberships, company car) and fringe benefits (deferred compensation plans, stock options) that companies use to tie employees to the company. The independence once sought by the recent college graduate has now been replaced by a growing commitment to and dependence on the organization.

Peer relationships take on great importance. A person relies less and less on a mentor for direction and advice and, instead, turns to the peer group. It provides an outlet for discussion of inequalities, such as who did and didn't get promoted and why, the size of pay increases and bonuses, and the like. The transition from relating to a mentor to relating to a peer group is not easy. Peer group members may exploit flaws in other group members to their advantage when the opportunity arises. For example, if a person fails to receive an expected promotion, the individual will likely turn to the peer group for emotional support. The individual hopes that they agree that the wrong person was promoted and offer advice that will boost his or her self-esteem. However, some of them may secretly be glad that the person was not promoted because this opens opportunities for them to get promoted faster. Once someone has been passed over, the chances for being considered again decrease.[18]

During the advancement stage, a person's struggles to make decisions at work are often compounded by struggles to make important personal decisions. Work and personal decisions are often interrelated, such as whether to take a promotion with its possible effects (relocation, longer hours, a lot more travel, increased stress) on an individual's personal and family life.[19] Whether to stay with an organization and become increasingly tied to it by golden handcuffs is yet another consideration. College graduates will change jobs an average of four times during their careers; many of those job changes occur during the advancement stage.

The concerns of managers at this career stage are summarized in Table 19–4. As the potential for advancement is either realized or not, self-esteem and the probability for future advancement are determined.

MAINTENANCE CAREER STAGE Moving into the maintenance stage is often associated with a number of personal changes. Changes in physical appearance and stamina occur more rapidly after age 40: hair begins to turn gray, skin begins to wrinkle, muscles begin to complain during tennis and racketball games. In addition to these types of changes, 35 percent of today's managers will probably experience a mid-life crisis. A **mid-life crisis** results in radical changes in a person's behavior and usually occurs between the ages of 39–44.[20] A career that has not lived up to a person's dreams and expecta-

---

TABLE 19-4 Concerns of Managers at the Advancement Stage—Ages 25-40

■ Central activity: Specialization, independent contributor, professional standing

■ Primary relationship: Peers

■ Needed from superior: Exposure, challenging work, sponsorship

---

tions can lead to feelings of resentment, sadness, frustration and severe personal problems. Someone experiencing such a crisis may quit a stable job and take a less secure one, becoming a middle-aged drop-out, be unable to cope with family problems, or get divorced.

During the maintenance stage, a person may take one of three typical career paths: star, solid citizen, or deadwood. The path taken will depend largely on the direction a career has taken during the first two stages. Those who have been picked by top managers as **stars** will continue to receive promotions, new job assignments, greater responsibility, and higher status.[21] These people feel that they have almost made it. Special assignments and expanded mentoring roles are important to stars. Assignments may entail dealing with others outside the organization, such as governmental agencies and large customer accounts.

Many employees are **solid citizens**. They are reliable and do good work but, for one reason or another, have little chance for promotion within the organization. They may lack the technical skills needed to move to a higher position, the desire for further promotion, or the interpersonal skills needed to play the political game in the company; or they may be too valuable to the company in their present positions for the organization to move them to other jobs. Managers who have these characteristics constitute the largest group of managers in most organizations and accomplish most of its work.

Regardless of the reason, they have reached a **career plateau**. This is a level at which the likelihood of future promotions is very low.[22] Plateauing does not ordinarily lead to poor performance. A plateau is reached in most cases simply because there are far more qualified people for higher-level positions than there are positions available.

Solid citizens are faced with doing the same job for many years. This involves being patient, trying not to overreact to mistakes, and helping newcomers learn from their mistakes. Many develop outside interests; community and family activities become important to these people.

Deadwood have little chance for promotion. They are often given staff jobs that top managers have labeled dead-end positions. The performance of these managers is likely to decline to a point where it becomes marginal. They simply try not to make mistakes that will result in their getting fired. Deadwood have few relationships at work. Because they lack influence in the organization, their attempts at mentoring fail. They do not receive challenging assignments, and salary increases are minimal. By accepting positions out of the mainstream of decision making, they hope to hang on until retirement.

In summary, the maintenance stage is the time when most people review their career progress. The concerns of managers at this career stage are shown in Table 19-5. Stars continue to receive promotions within the company and are assigned to increasingly challenging and important tasks. Sol-

---

TABLE 19-5   Concerns of Managers at the Maintenance Stage—Ages 40-60

■ Central activity: Training and directing others

■ Primary relationship: Mentoring

■ Needed from superior: Autonomy, opportunity to develop others

id citizens are satisfied with their careers, demonstrate loyalty to the company, and can serve as mentors to others. Deadwood are assigned duties that are out of the mainstream of the organization.

WITHDRAWAL CAREER STAGE   This stage occurs for most people when they reach about 60 years of age. Many managers who have been around an organization for a long time can bring together the resources and people to push new ideas to a successful conclusion, playing the role of maverick or internal entrepreneur. These roles are legitimate so long as they can be played successfully. A person's identity as a maverick or entrepreneur can often be established on the basis of a solid reputation in the company.

It is important for older managers to establish mentor relationships with younger managers in a firm. Many will spend considerable time and energy in the development of key people to replace themselves upon their retirement. They learn to think about the needs of the organization beyond the time of their involvement in it. Others will dedicate time to establishing relationships outside their organization and representing the company in business, professional, and community organizations.

CAREER PLANNING ISSUES

Many of today's employees want more than money from their jobs. This new breed of employee includes women and minorities who are in the work force looking for the challenging careers they never had access to before. In a recent survey of some 100 Fortune 500 companies, 86 percent of the companies indicated that they have started career planning programs for employees to follow.[23] **Career planning** is the process of choosing occupations, organizations, and career paths.[24] It entails evaluating abilities and interests, considering alternative career opportunities, establishing career goals, and planning practical career development activities. The process results in decisions to enter a certain occupation, join a particular company, accept or decline new job opportunities (relocations, promotions, or transfers), and ultimately leave a company for another job or retirement.

Effects of Career Planning

A career planning program is an important means of helping a company meet its continuing staff requirements. In large companies, a typical career planning program might include some or all of the following activities:

- Career counseling by members of the human resources department.
- Career workshops to help employees evaluate their skills, abilities, and interests and to formulate development plans.
- Self-directed programs aimed at helping employees to guide their own careers through self-assessment.
- Communication of job opportunities through job postings, videotapes, reading materials, and publications.

Career planning has both positive and negative effects, as shown in Figure 19–4. In some companies, managers are concerned that career planning will increase their work loads by requiring them to provide counseling and

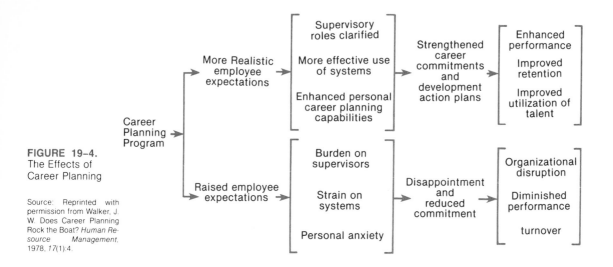

FIGURE 19-4.
The Effects of
Career Planning

Source: Reprinted with permission from Walker, J. W. Does Career Planning Rock the Boat? *Human Resource Management*, 1978, *17*(1):4.

on-the-job development. Career planning may also lead to greater employee demand for career development resources. Participants in career planning programs rely on the company for training, education assistance (tuition reimbursement), and staff counseling. In addition, employees may request more information on job vacancies, pay practices, and career opportunities. Finally, raised expectations may increase employee anxiety: fundamental questions regarding individual strengths, weaknesses, and goals sometimes are raised for the first time; group training sessions are rarely equipped to handle these issues. Unfulfilled expectations sometimes can lead to employee disappointment and reduced commitment to the firm. As a result, some employees may become less motivated to perform well, and others may seek work elsewhere.

Despite these negative aspects, Gulf Oil, IBM, GE, Xerox, TRW, and GM have developed career planning programs to reduce turnover, improve the quality of working life, and improve on-the-job performance. These companies have found that it is in their best interests—and those of their employees—to stimulate realistic career aspirations. Moreover, these companies have tried to dispel the "up-or-out" notion of career because many employees ultimately will be plateaued. Therefore lateral career moves within specialized job areas can be attractive to many employees if career information focuses on personal development, work content, and job importance rather than solely on promotability.

As shown in Figure 19-4, rather than burdening managers, career planning can clarify and support supervisory responsibilities. After all, the bases for realistic career planning are current job responsibilities and mastery of job requirements. The manager therefore should focus on the employees' current job performance.

Career planning can also provide employees with information to enable them to make better career decisions. Rather than raising expectations with promises that probably will not be fulfilled, many companies candidly describe what their programs can and cannot do and anticipated job opportunities. Consider one individual's assessment of the career planning program of his company, Pacific Telephone Company.

In Practice: J. M. Suozzo, Pacific Telephone Company

When I started with the telephone company in San Diego, I strongly believed that a career with the company would provide opportunity and security, and that it would be interesting working with an organization that had an excellent public image. As a result of my previous job experience (I had had four jobs during the preceding five years), I had the background needed to make an objective evaluation of what my requirements would be for a permanent lifetime job.

When I was interviewed, the various career options were described to me in detail. So when I was hired and on the new job, I set some preliminary career goals that I hoped to meet. My short-term goal was to be promoted to management in the company's sales organization, although a promotion would have required moving to Los Angeles, a move my family was not in favor of.

Although the company provided opportunities for career development, I realized that I had to make some effort on my own in this area as well. So I took correspondence courses, got involved in forming an alumni association for my college, and participated in community activities.

The company's offer to assign me to another department caused the first adjustment to my career plan. Shortly after the move, I was promoted to management, but I only held the position for a short time. The United States Navy recalled me to active duty for two years.

Two career options became available simultaneously, necessitating far more realistic career planning. I could remain in the navy or return to civilian life. After comparing the growth potential, job satisfaction, earnings potential, and sacrifices required in both careers, I decided to return to civilian life and to resume my career with the telephone company.

In the next eight years, I was promoted three times and had to move to six different cities in southern California. This mobility requirement for promotion, though considered in my planning, meant uprooting my children from schools and making new friends and was more of a problem than I had anticipated.

During this time, I became a member of the Society for the Advancement of Management, the Personnel Managers' Association, and a number of civic groups. As part of my self-development program, I took several courses at local colleges and read books and articles on management. My company also sent me to two executive training programs.

My own career grew from a combination of flexibility and self-development efforts on my part and quite a bit of career planning on my company's. As for the latter, I think that more might have been done in broader cross-discipline training sooner, but I would grade the company's overall career planning effort as superior to my personal effort.[25]

Dual-Career Couples

Approximately 60 percent of all American couples have dual careers outside the family. A **dual career** is one where both people have careers, as opposed to jobs.[26] When both people have outside careers, both may travel, both may relocate, both are on tight schedules, and both earn better-than-average incomes.

Table 19–6 shows a continuum of couple career relationships. At the extreme left is the traditional relationship: the husband has an outside career and the wife's career is homemaker and child-raiser. Moving from left to right across the continuum, we note that male and female roles change to-

TABLE 19-6   Continuum of Dual-Career Couple Relationships

The Traditional Couple	The Semi-Traditional Couple	The Typical Couple Dual Outside Careers	The Egalitarian Couple
HE is the breadwinner. SHE is the homemaker and child-raiser. HE competes and succeeds for both. SHE provides child care, social, and maintenance for both.	HE is the breadwinner (with some involvement in family and home). SHE is the homemaker and child-raiser but she also works, usually for a specific purpose (such as better vacations for the family, college tuition, braces for someone's teeth, her own personal satisfaction.) HE has the dominant career but acknowledges her contribution to their quality of life, and her need for some kind of outside activity. SHE works, but neither of them thinks of her as having an outside career.	HE is committed to a professional career. SHE is committed to a professional career. The couple think of themselves as having dual outside careers. BUT, one of them (almost always the woman) takes on more than 50 percent of the responsibility for housekeeping and child-raising, and provides less than 50 percent of the income.	HIS and HER roles vis-à-vis outside career and home are essentially the same. BOTH have equal commitments to their outside careers and the home. BOTH do 50 percent of the housework. BOTH do 50 percent of the child-raising.

Source: Adapted from Clawson, J., Kotter, J., Faux, V. and McArthur, C. *Self-Assessment and Career Development.* Englewood Cliffs, N.J.: Prentice-Hall, 1985, 311.

ward more equal participation in family and outside careers. The job selection process tends to become increasingly complex and the individuals' careers must become more integrated and be better managed. Two of the major sources of concern for couples with dual careers outside the home are relocation and child care.

RELOCATION   The increase in the number of couples that have dual careers outside the home has posed problems for companies when trying to relocate employees. In 1977, Merrill Lynch conducted a relocation survey and asked companies whether employees were resisting transfers because of working spouses. At that time, less than 20 percent indicated that this was a concern. In 1981, that figure increased to 26 percent and Merrill Lynch estimates that, by 1986, it will rise to more than 30 percent.[27] Seventy percent of companies surveyed believed that the spouse's job will play a larger role in relocation decisions in the future. To ease the relocation decision, job-finding assistance for the spouse is typically provided. This involves services ranging from informational contacts with other employers in the area, to more elaborate outside agency programs that offer much more formal assistance. These agencies generally guide spouses in the art of finding positions, including résumé preparation and review, specific job guidance and counseling, and actual employment search assistance. The cost of these assistance programs ranges from $500–$2,000 per spouse. Let us look at how GE tries to help such couples make a relocation decision.

In Practice: **General Electric's Dual-Career Philosophy**

The relocation of dual-career couples is "not just a women's issue," says Ross Bailey, manager of employee relations at General Electric. In 1983, GE issued a set of guidelines for managing this process. The underlying philosophy is that neither spouse should have to give up a position: GE must be aware of, and willing to understand, the realities of dual-career couples.

Michael Schiavoni, manager of organization and staffing at GE's Plastic Business Group, described how his division implemented this philosophy. "First we conducted a survey of dual-career couples among our labor force to determine what we should do, if anything. We found that the average age of our labor force was 33, and that there were more people involved in dual-career marriages than we had thought. Employees wanted help in premove counseling, and job seeking assistance for spouses. The program was aimed at helping the spouse adjust to the new community. As a result, people feel they are not unique, and a support system is created to alleviate the trauma of relocating. An outside facilitator conducts a series of eight different evening meetings. We try to make it an open issue; to make people comfortable talking about it. The workshop for couples provides information about the new community. We invite the spouse on the employment interview so they can see the area as well."[28]

CHILD CARE   Alisa Rogers, an engineer at Lockheed Corporation in Burbank, California, was near her wit's end last summer after her babysitter retired. She had searched for a day-care center for her two-year-old son, but had had no luck. She thought about quitting her job, but quickly realized that this was not a realistic solution. She received help from a newly formed association of companies. Lockheed, along with Disney Studios, NBC, Warner Brothers, and others, had established an association and built a day-care center for its employees. Each sponsoring company is allowed to place 20 children in the day-care center. The sponsoring companies provide financial assistance to help keep tuition within reasonable limits for each employee. Now dozens of other companies are forming similar associations to help couples with dual outside careers.[29]

Why are companies getting into the child-care business? First, it has been estimated that 80 percent of employed women will become pregnant during their working careers. Employers are also aware that worries about who is minding the children can weigh heavily on the minds of mothers and fathers alike and can affect worker productivity. Second, 85 percent of the companies that have established day-care centers believe that they have had a positive impact on recruitment; 65 percent said that it has decreased turnover; 53 percent report it reduced absenteeism and tardiness. Third, many companies permit employees to have prespecified amounts withheld from their paychecks and deposited into accounts for child-care expense. These are generally called salary-reduction programs since the amounts targeted for day care are taken from pretax dollars.

Women and Minorities

Having equal access to career opportunities is a major issue in career planning for many individuals. While organizations are employing increasing numbers of women and minority managers, not many of these people are in top-management positions. For example, only 367 women (but some 15,000 men) sit on the boards of the country's largest 1,300 companies whose stock is publicly held and traded on one of the exchanges. Of the top 50,000 management jobs in the United States, perhaps only 1,000 are held by women and minority group members.[30]

During the 1970s and so far in the 1980s, three important trends have emerged. First, the educational level for women has risen and will continue to rise. In 1984, 86 percent of the women between the ages of 20–24 who were college graduates were employed, while only 55 percent of the women between the ages of 55–64, who had the same amount of education, were employed. Thus, as younger workers age and older workers drop out of the work force, the overall educational level for working women will rise. Second, women are getting more experience on the job. The Rand Corporation predicts by the year 2000, a 40-year-old woman will have 5.2 more years of experience than her counterpart had in 1980. Since U.S. women are having fewer children, they tend to spend less time at home and more time on the job. Third, women are slowly moving into higher-paying professions still dominated by men. In 1983, there were 12 times as many women accountants and 6 times as many women computer-systems analysts than in 1972.

Despite these impressive trends, the problem for women and minorities is that decisions about who goes on to the top-management jobs tends to be more subjective than promotion decisions involving lower- and middle-management positions. According to one large recruiting firm, women and minorities tend to make up about 50 percent of entry-level management and about 25 percent of middle management. For example, the promotion from product brand manager depends primarily on the manager's sales record. But the promotion from marketing manager to vice-president depends on both performance and compatability with the chief executive officer.

If promotions do not come, frustration can result. Some of the reasons for lack of upward mobility include education, language, dress, informal exclusion from social events, including fishing and hunting trips and golf games, lack of a sponsor, and stereotypes.[31] Many executive recruiting firms, or so-called headhunters, report that an increasing number of women are using their services to job-hop, rather than remain with their present company. However, many women have cracked barriers to jobs traditionally held by men, as in the case of Wall Street.

In Practice: Women on Wall Street

Forbes magazine invited women to discuss their thoughts on what it takes to make it on Wall Street. Following are questions they asked Cheryl Grandfield, a partner with the investment counsel of Brundage, Story and Rose, and her answers.

F: Do you feel you have to be "one of the boys" to succeed on Wall Street?

CG: A lot of young women believe it, but I never found that to be the case. You have to work real hard. And to the extent that you're traveling with men, you have to be able to get along with them. But you also have to be a reasonable professional, which generally means not letting down your hair all the way. It means you don't slide into too casual a conversation after having three drinks at the bar.

F: Some women believe they have to be better than men to be considered equals. Do they?

CG: Probably between 25–28 percent of the women believe that it's true. But seriously, Wall Street is wonderfully bottom-line oriented, and it will not pass up people with talent and brains if they can make money.

F: Have you had to deal with discrimination on Wall Street?

CG: You ignore it until it gets overt enough that it really becomes an obstacle. Then you deal with it up front. Not in a nasty, obnoxious or tearful way, and you don't take it personally. You just say, "Hey, let's get past this. It's not doing anyone any good, and it's a diversion." But it hardly ever happens.

F: Do women, as has been suggested, need the "killer instinct" to succeed?

CG: The same could be said for a lot of men. How many men who are chairmen of companies don't have the killer instinct?

F: Success requires long hours, travel, dedication and skill. Hasn't that meant disruption of family life?

CG: Most of the qualities, except for disruption of family life, are exactly the same old ones that have been given as a standard recipe for male success for umpteen years. So what's the difference? How can a woman expect to walk into a profession and be successful by completely different rules? That is not realistic. The ridiculous disruption of the personal life is something that is exclusive to a few types of professions and investment banking is one of them. But that's what it takes for men. If part of the recipe for success means that you have to be there 180 percent of the time, then obviously you are sacrificing something else. My guess is that nine out of ten investment bankers on Wall Street are on their second or third marriages.[32]

SUMMARY

Gaining an understanding of why certain events occur somewhat predictably over the course of a career was the focus of this chapter. Individual and organizational factors affect the choice of a career, including the probability that a person will choose one in which he or she is likely to be successful. Individual factors that affect occupational choice include personality, vocational interests, self-esteem, and social background. Organizational factors include the type of industry, nature of the business, organizational culture, characteristics of the job, and the like. When there is a good match between the person and the organization, the employee is more likely to be satisfied with the job, be a high performer, and develop a solid commitment to the firm.

There are three distinct career movements within an organization: vertical, horizontal, and inclusion. Each type of career movement presents an individual with a new series of challenges and career issues.

A person's working life can be broken down into four career stages. Each of these stages presents certain problems that have to be resolved. In the establishment stage, the newcomer is a subordinate and will be expected to follow orders and perform routine tasks well. During this stage, the newcomer should find a mentor who will sponsor him or her in the organization.

After passing through the establishment stage, the individual moves into the advancement stage. The central activity at this stage involves specialization and making an independent contribution to the firm. Instead of relying solely on a mentor for sponsorship, the individual will likely turn to a peer group for encouragement and support.

As a person approaches 40, he or she will probably enter the maintenance career stage. One of three paths can be followed during this stage: (1) those who are selected as stars will continue to receive assignments that involve greater levels of challenge, authority, and responsibility; (2) others become known as solid citizens, with little chance for further promotion because they have reached a career plateau, but who will continue to perform well; and (3) others who become deadwood when they plateau because they let their performance slip, become indifferent and who will be bypassed and cut off from the mainstream of decision making.

In the withdrawal stage, the individual begins to think about retiring. Some play the maverick role; others, the internal entrepreneurial role; still others spend time establishing relationships outside the organization. As managers proceed through the withdrawal stage, they begin to feel the loss of power and have to learn not to second-guess the decisions of subordinates.

In the final section of the chapter, we addressed three issues in career planning: (1) the effects of career planning on the organization and the individual; (2) couples that have dual careers outside the home; and (3) problems facing women and minorities in their efforts to move up in organizations.

KEY WORDS AND CONCEPTS

Advancement career stage	Horizontal career movement
Career	Inclusion career movement
Career development	Maintenance career stage
Career planning	Mentor
Career plateau	Mid-life crisis
Career stage	Self-esteem
Deadwood	Social background
Dual career	Solid citizens
Establishment career stage	Stars
Golden handcuffs	Vertical career movement
Holland's personality types	Withdrawal career stage

DISCUSSION QUESTIONS

1. Describe the phases of your career to date. What have been some important milestones for you?

2. What advice would you give to Steve and Mary? Their dilemma was described in the In Practice, "What Would You Do?" How does your answer reflect your own career concerns?

3. What are the three types of career movements within the typical organization and how do they influence a person's career?

4. How can career planning help people?

5. What are some potential problems for a manager who is managing people at different career stages?

6. Why can a career plateau be so traumatic for a person?

7. How would you motivate the solid citizen; the star; deadwood?

8. What are some major problems facing couples who have dual outside careers?

9. Why are managers and peers so important in the mentoring process?

MANAGEMENT INCIDENTS AND CASES

Margaret Jardine

Margaret Jardine was sure when she completed her bachelor's degree in business at Oregon State over thirteen years ago that she would go places at Pacific Security Bank. She had graduated with honors from OSU with an emphasis in finance and had joined PSB because she had felt it was a very progressive bank and sufficiently large to allow for movement into a variety of areas. She had done very well in the bank's credit training program and had gone, after one year with the bank, directly to the position of loan officer at the Albany branch of PSB. Albany was located in central Oregon about 100 miles south of Portland, where PSB had its headquarters.

She had been successful in her first assignment, she felt, because she had been able to work closely with Ben Compton, the branch manager, who had given her a good deal of direction and guidance on handling accounts during her first year or two. She had also put in a great deal of extra time in that assignment keeping up with pending loan requests and making sure of each analysis. The only disconcerting thing to Margaret was that she had spent a full seven years in the assignment. This, she felt, had been too long.

When Ben Compton left the bank, Margaret felt there were a lot of reasons why she should be his replacement. When she did get the position as Albany branch manager, this confirmed her faith that she was on her way up in the bank. She was only the second woman in PSB to attain the position of branch manager. Recently, though, she had begun again to wonder about her future with the bank.

She had now been branch manager for over five years, and from her current perspective she could see what kind of opportunities were open to her in the bank. The fact was that there was very little movement among officers in the bank. There was only one other branch manager in the division who had been in his position less time than she had, and there were several who had been branch manager for ten years or more. The division manager, Dan Martin, was new but had himself been a branch manager for twelve years at Corvallis before becoming division manager. Recently at a bank dinner, Dan had introduced her to someone from another division and had referred to her as "one of our new branch managers."

In her four years at Albany, the branch had done well, with substantial increases in loans outstanding and earnings. Recently, though, she felt that she had lost some of her motivation. Now if she put in extra time, it was only out of necessity of getting something done that had to be done. It certainly was not voluntary.

Margaret felt trapped, pigeonholed in some way. She felt like she had no idea where she was going in the bank. Others who had joined the bank and gone through the training program with her had stayed near PSB headquarters in Portland and had gotten a somewhat broader experience than she had. They were probably more promotable now than she was. She as at the stage with the bank where, although her market value was still high, her salary increases were getting smaller and smaller and her options were becoming more limited. Recently, Margaret had turned down a very attractive offer from Northwestern Security and Exchange, a small finance company in Salem near Albany, because there, too, she thought there would be little opportunity for advancement. Now she wondered if it would have been better to take the opportunity.

Still, there was an ambiguity in Margaret's feelings about the bank. She felt that a move to corporate headquarters would be advantageous for her at this point in her career. At least that seemed like the next logical move; and if she could do that, there was a great likelihood she would be made an Assistant Vice-President. Yet she had really come to enjoy living in Albany. She was not sure that she wanted to leave Albany for the big-city atmosphere of Portland even if a better opportunity presented itself there. Her dilemma was that as long as she stayed in Albany, there was no place for her to go in the bank, and realistically speaking, an offer to go to Portland was not exactly imminent.

After dialing Northwestern's number, only to hang up before it rang, Margaret decided she would put off any decision for at least a month so she could have plenty of time to think over her situation. Besides, Dan Martin had called from division headquarters and asked to see her on Monday morning. This would be a good time, she felt, to raise her concerns with Dan and to get his ideas.

Dan Martin had felt like he had it coming. After twelve years as man-

ager of the Corvallis, Oregon, branch office of Pacific Security Bank, Dan had been made division manager of PSB's southern division. PSB was a large northwestern bank centered at Portland and the southern division covered most of the southern half of Oregon. Since division headquarters were in Corvallis, Dan had not had to move with the promotion.

Along with the benefits, the new position had brought its share of headaches. Dan's biggest challenge, he felt, was keeping the branch managers in his division motivated. Margaret was a very promising young employee who, at 36, still had a bright future with the bank. Margaret's problem was not exactly motivation, since she was one of the outstanding performers in the division and her branch had significantly bettered its financial position during her term as branch manager. Nor was her problem one of complacency or stagnation. While several of the other branch managers had been in their positions for ten years or more, Margaret had only been a branch manager for five years or so.

From Dan's point of view, Margaret's problem was simply that she had become dissatisfied with the bank. She apparently felt, from comments she had made to Dan and Ed Finnerty, the former division manager, that she had not had sufficient opportunity to move around within the bank and to gain a broad exposure of PSB's operation. She also felt, according to Ed, that her advancement opportunities had not come quickly enough. Ed had said that he expected her to leave PSB sometime in the near future if she could not get the kind of opportunity she wanted within the bank. Of late, Dan had noticed a subtle change in her attitude. Margaret seemed to be less enthusiastic than Dan had come to expect of her and had been, on occasion, very critical of PSB's operations. One or two of the other branch managers in the division had described her as being "cynical" and even "apathetic."

Dan decided he had better bring her in to talk over her situation.

Dan turned to her file to learn more about her background and her history with PSB. Margaret had been at the Albany branch for twelve of her thirteen years with the bank. She had spent only seven years as a loan officer before becoming the branch manager. That she had been very highly rated in her appraisals throughout her career also corroborated Dan's impression of her. Her salary increases had been generally quite high. Considering the age at which she had become a branch manager and the kind of increases she had received, it was difficult to understand her dissatisfaction.

Dan read through the appraisals Ed Finnerty had written on her in the last five years. The following comment from her most recent appraisal was typical:

> Margaret is a highly competent professional with sound quantitative skills and credit judgment as well as the skills necessary for bank leadership. She gets along well with the people who work with and for her and the Albany branch has shown consistent improvement under her direction.

Dan found some of Ed's concluding remarks interesting:

> Margaret is anxious to continue her career at Pacific Security and looks forward in the future

to taking on new and diverse assignments within the bank. She would like, however, to remain in the southern division and her preference would be to remain in or around Albany, where she has lived for some time.

It occurred to Dan that Margaret wanted to have her cake and eat it, too. She could never really advance in the bank without moving close to Portland. To remain in Albany was impossible if she really wanted to develop her career at the bank. Dan might be able to offer her a divisional assignment in Corvallis sometime down the line, but this would not really be a step up for her, and Dan was not sure she would want to move to Corvallis. Dan did not want to see her leave the bank, and he also felt that her present frame of mind needed to be changed if she ever wanted to advance beyond her present position at the bank. Not knowing exactly what he planned to say to Margaret or what he could do for her, Dan phoned her and arranged an appointment for the following Monday morning.[33]

Questions

1. What are some of the career concerns facing Margaret?
2. How does her career stage influence her actions?
3. What advice should Dan Martin give to Margaret?

REFERENCES

1. Byrne, J. Be Nice to Everybody. Forbes, November 5, 1984, 244–246.

2. Super, D., and Hall, T. Career Development: Exploration and Planning. *Annual Review of Psychology*, 1978, *29,* 334.

3. Jaskolka, G., and Beyer, J. Measuring and Predicting Managerial Success. *Journal of Vocational Behavior*, 1985, *26,* 189–205.

4. Hall, D. *Careers in Organizations*. Santa Monica, Calif.: Goodyear, 1976, 3–4.

5. Super, D. A Life-span, Life-space Approach to Career Development. *Journal of Vocational Behavior*, 1980, *16,* 282–298.

6. Adapted from Clawson, J., Kotter, J., Faux, V., and McArthur, C. *Self-Assessment and Career Development*. Englewood Cliffs, N.J.: Prentice-Hall, 1985, 9–11.

7. Porter, L., Lawler, E., and Hackman, R. *Behavior in Organizations*. New York: McGraw-Hill, 1975, 200.

8. Holland, J. *Making Vocational Choices: A Theory of Careers.* Englewood Cliffs, N.J.: Prentice-Hall, 1973.

9. For an excellent review of the research on Holland's theory, see Spokane, A. A Review of Research on Person-Environment Congruence in Holland's Theory of Careers. *Journal of Vocational Behavior,* 1985, *26,* 306–343.

10. Brief, A., Sell, M., and Aldag, R. Vocational Decision Making among Women: Implications for Organizational Behavior. *Academy of Management Review,* 1979, *4,* 521–530; Feldman, D., and Arnold, H. Personality Types and Career Patterns: Some Empirical Evidence on Holland's Model. *Canadian Journal of Administrative Sciences,* 1985, 2, 192–210.

11. Wanous, J. *Organizational Entry: Recruitment, Selection, and Socialization of Newcomers.* Reading, Mass.: Addison-Wesley, 1980.

12. Super, D. *The Psychology of Careers,* New York: Harper & Row, 1957; Slocum, J., and Cron, Wm. Job Attitudes and Performance During Three Career Stages. *Journal of Vocational Behavior,* 1985, *26,* 126–145; Mount, M. Managerial Career Stage and Facets of Job Satisfaction. *Journal of Vocational Behavior,* 1984, *24,* 340–354.

13. London, M., and Stumpf, S. *Managing Careers.* Reading, Mass.: Addison-Wesley, 1982; Sonnenfeld, J., and Kotter, J. The Maturation of Career Theory. *Human Relations,* 1982, *35,* 19–46.

14. Schein, E. *Career Dynamics: Matching Individual and Organizational Needs.* Reading, Mass.: Addison-Wesley, 1978, 37–39; Von Glinow, M., Driver, M., Brousseau, K., and Prince, J. The Design of a Career Oriented Human Resource System. *Academy of Management Review,* 1983, *8,* 23–32.

15. Super, D. *The Psychology of Careers.* New York: Harper & Row, 1957.

16. Baird, L., and Kram, K. Career Dynamics: Matching the Superior/Subordinate Relationship. *Organizational Dynamics,* Spring 1983, 46–64.

17. Kram, K., and Isabella, L. Mentoring Alternatives: The Role of Peer Relationships in Career Development. *Academy of Management Journal,* 1985, *28,* 110–132; Kram, K. *Mentoring at Work: Developmental Relationships in Organizational Life.* Glenview, Ill.: Scott, Foresman, 1985; Hunt, M., and Michael, C. Mentorship: A Career Training Tool. *Academy of Management Review,* 1983, *8,* 475–485.

18. Rosenbaum, J. Tournament Mobility: Career Patterns in a Corporation. *Administrative Science Quarterly,* 1979, *24,* 220–241; Cochran, P., and Wartick, S. Golden Parachutes: A Closer Look. *California Management Review,* 1984, *26*(4), 111–120.

19. Greiff, B., and Munter, P. *Tradeoffs: Executive, Family and Organizational Life.* New York: Mentor, 1980; Korman, A., and Korman, R. *Career Success/Personal Failure.* Englewood Cliffs, N.J.: Prentice-Hall, 1980.

20. McGill, M. *The 40- to 60-Year-Old Male.* New York: Simon and Schuster, 1980.

21. Slocum, J., Cron, Wm., Hansen, R., and Rawlings, S. Business Strategy and the Management of the Plateaued Performer. *Academy of Management Journal.* 1985, *28,* 133–154.

22. Near, J. A Discriminant Analysis of Plateaued versus Nonplateaued Managers. *Journal of Vocational Behavior,* 1985, *26,* 177–188; Veiga, J. Plateaued versus Nonplateaued Managers: Career Patterns, Attitudes, and Path Potential. *Academy of Management Journal.* 1981, *24,* 566–578.

23. Moravec, M. A Cost-effective Career Planning Program Requires a Strategy. *Personnel Administrator,* January 1982, 28–32; Levine, H. Consensus on Career Planning. *Personnel,* March 1985, 67–72.

24. Walker, J. Does Career Planning Rock the Boat? *Human Resource Management,* Spring 1978, *17,* 2–7.

25. Abstracted from Is Career Planning a Useless Exercise? *S.A.M. Advanced Management Journal,* Summer 1975, 52–62.

26. Sekas, M. Dual-Career Couples—A Corporate Challenge. *Personnel Administrator,* March/April 1984, 37–45.

27. Merrill Lynch Relocation Management, Inc., Life-Style Related Trends: Dual-Career Couples. *Merrill Lynch Relocation Management Quarterly,* 1982, *30,* 13.

28. Sekas, M. Dual-Career Couples, . . . 40.

29. Peterson, N. Here's Looking After You, Kid. *American Way,* July 9, 1985, 42–47.

30. You've Come a Long Way, Baby—But Not As Far As You Thought. *Business Week,* October 1, 1984, 126–131; Arnold, B. Women at Work. *Business Week,* January 28, 1985, 80–85.

31. Larwood, L., Wood, M., and Inderlied, S. Training Women for Management: New Problems, New Solutions. *Academy of Management Review,* 1978, *3,* 584–594.

32. Adapted from Byrne, J. No Time to Waste on Nonsense. *Forbes,* May 6, 1985, 110–114.

33. Ritchie, J., and Thompson, P. *Organization and People.* 3d ed. St. Paul, Minn.: West, 1984, 152–155. Reprinted by permission.

20 Nature of Planned Organizational Change

LEARNING OBJECTIVES

When you have finished studying this chapter, you should be able to:

- Describe the objectives of planned organizational change.
- Discuss the sources of pressures on organizations to change.
- Explain reasons for individual and organizational resistance to change.
- Diagnose the pressure for and resistance to change in a work setting.
- Describe some general models or approaches for organizational change.

OUTLINE

Preview Case

The Limits of Tradition

In June 1985, after 153 years of production, the last fire truck rolled off the quarter-mile-long assembly line at American LaFrance in Elmira, N.Y. American LaFrance once ruled its marketplace as well as any American company ever dominated a business. But the parking lot is mostly empty now, and it's hard to find a person in Elmira who clearly understands why the company is closing up shop. Executives directly in charge at LaFrance offer no explanations. Figgie International, the conglomerate that has owned it since 1966, cites LaFrance's dated truck designs, high overhead and a string of losses, culminating last year with a pretax loss of $7.6 million on flagging sales of $21.5 million.

Why does a company like American LaFrance fail? How could the company allow its products, identified by the familiar American LaFrance chrome eagle, to fall woefully behind the competition? How, in the last few years, could it blow a preeminent franchise built on the sweaty brows of eight generations of craftsmen?

The answer will be found 1,000 miles south, in Ocala Florida, home of Emergency One, an upstart in the fire truck business. In only 11 years Emergency One has grown from a tiny operation in an entrepreneur's barn to a $51 million enterprise. The company has become the leading maker of American fire trucks and last year earned $3.4 million pretax doing it.

More than 50 fire trucks a month roll out of Emergency One's bustling factory, bordering busy I-75 in central Florida. The reason for the bustle is disarmingly simple—a new idea. The bodies of Emergency One's trucks are aluminum, mounted on steel chassis. That doesn't sound like a big deal, unless you're running a fire department on a tight budget. Unlike steel trucks, made for years by American LaFrance and others, aluminum doesn't corrode when exposed to salt and water. Though aluminum is more expensive than steel initially, fire departments in brutal proving grounds such as Chicago and Boston have reason to believe aluminum will be cheaper in the long run.

So here is point one. Undeterred by the no-growth nature of the fire truck market and seeing a chance to catch hidebound competition asleep at the wheel, Emergency One levered itself into the market with an innovation. It has already captured about 15% of a fragmented market and aims to raise that to 25% in a few years. As Robert Wormser, a gruff, self-taught metal designer and founder of Emergency One, succinctly puts it, "We weren't confused by tradition."

Point two: While American LaFrance required six months to turn out a basic fire truck, Emergency One assembles one in 45 days. Why the difference? Revolutionary design and assembly by Emergency One. For example, American LaFrance hand-drafted blueprints of each order. The process can take a week. Emergency One does the same thing in a few hours on IBM computer-aided design (CAD) machines.

Point three: Even Emergency One's selling efforts smack of creativity absent from American LaFrance. Last year Emergency One gained a toehold in Boston by lending the fire department there several new-model trucks. Sales executives lived at the firehouse and went out on 60 fire

> calls. Boston bought. Another example: The company flew 20 West Coast fire chiefs to Florida to drive trucks purchased by other departments back out to the coast. Five of those fire chiefs have already bought and another five are nibbling. Emergency One even gives away a small fire truck each year in a drawing from sales card leads returned by mail, a relatively inexpensive way to build a prospect list.[1]

A major challenge facing organizations is to manage change effectively.[2] When organizations fail to change in necessary ways, the costs of that failure may be quite high, as they were for American LaFrance. In many sectors of the economy, organizations must have the capacity to adapt quickly in order to survive. Often the speed and complexity of change severely test the capabilities of managers and employees. Unless people are emotionally and intellectually prepared for change, the sheer speed with which it rushes at them can be overwhelming.

To a certain extent, all organizations exist in a changing environment and are themselves constantly changing. In an increasing number of situations, the mechanistic system—with its emphasis on rigid structure; functional specialization; hierarchy of authority; fixed systems of rights, duties, and procedures; and impersonal human relationships—is responding inadequately to the demands placed upon it from within and outside the organization. There is an increasing need for experimentation with new organizational forms, learning from experience, flexibility and adaptability, and personal growth for employees.

While we may tend to think that business organizations confront the most turbulent environments, the forces of change are not limited to the business sector of the economy. Nonbusiness organizations, such as educational institutions, hospitals, governments, and religious institutions, also face rapid change. The proliferation of social demands, together with costs that threaten to exceed available resources, requires that organizations operate more effectively today than ever before.

Furthermore, not just organizations are changing. People are ceasing to be objects used by organizations and increasingly assert themselves for numerous and complex reasons. Levels of educational attainment are rising. An increased availability of technology is both freeing people from the burdens of physical and routine labor and making them more dependent on society. An increasing rate of change is affecting their environments, which both threatens and challenges them. Finally, greater affluence is opening up opportunities for many experiences never before so generally available.

In this chapter, we will examine the objectives of planned change, the pressures for and resistances to change that exist in organizations, and some models and processes for making changes in organizations. The final chapter—Chapter 21—will explore a number of specific approaches to and techniques for making organizational changes.

OBJECTIVES OF PLANNED ORGANIZATIONAL CHANGE

It is important to distinguish between change that inevitably happens to all organizations and change that is *planned* by members of an organization.[3]

Our focus is primarily on intentional, purposeful organizational change, although it is valuable as well to understand the nature of all organizational change. "**Planned organizational change** refers to a set of activities and processes designed to change individuals, groups, and organization structure and processes."⁴ Because the management of an organization cannot control its environment, it must continually introduce internal organizational changes that allow it to cope more effectively with new challenges; challenges presented by employees and from sources outside the firm, such as increased competition, advances in technology, new governmental legislation, and pressing social demands. Most frequently, organizations introduce change in reaction to these pressures. In some cases, however, they make changes in anticipation of future problems (for example, impending governmental regulations or a competitor introducing new products).

Planned organizational change represents the intentional attempt by managers and employees to improve the functioning of groups, departments, or an entire organization in some important way. Thus there will always be specific goals for planned change efforts, such as higher productivity, employee acceptance of new technology, greater employee motivation, more innovative employee behaviors, increased market share, and so on. However, in a very real sense, these and other improvement goals rest on two basic underlying objectives: (1) to improve the capacity or ability of the organization to adapt to changes in its environment; and (2) to change patterns of employee behaviors.

Improving Organizational Adaptability

The United States is changing in a number of important ways that have significant impacts on organizations. For example, John Naisbitt spent 12 years carefully identifying and studying indicators of broad trends that affect individuals, organizations and the society. His work indicated that the most significant trends included the following changes:

- from an industrial society to an information society (an economy based on the creation and distribution of information);
- from high technology that was imposing in its complexity to using high technology with a more personal touch;
- from a predominantly national economy to a more interdependent world economy;
- from a short-term managerial orientation to a focus on long-range planning;
- from centralized institutional and corporate structures to greater decentralization;
- from an emphasis on organizational hierarchy to an emphasis on networking (greater sharing of ideas, information, and resources);
- from limited personal choices to a greater variety of options in life styles, careers and so on.⁵

Similar trends are apparent in countries other than the United States as well. Organizations that cannot or will not adapt to these and other changes in their environments will eventually die. For example, Table 20-1 contains current survival rates for U.S. corporations: 62 percent have failed within

TABLE 20-1   **Survival Rates for U.S. Corporations**

Age in Years	Percentage Surviving to This Age
5	38
10	21
15	14
20	10
25	7
50	2
75	1
100	0.5

Source: Adapted from Nystrom, P. C., and Starbuck, W. H. To Avoid Organizational Crises, Unlearn. *Organizational Dynamics,* Spring 1984, 54.

the first 5 years of their existence; only 10 percent have survived even 20 years. Organizations must have effective mechanisms or ways to adapt to changing markets, labor supplies, expectations of society, legal requirements, ideas, and so on. Adaptive mechanisms that are components of an organization have names such as product research, market research, long-range planning staffs, research and development departments, public affairs departments, organization development staffs, and the like.[6] These staffs and departments maintain contact with a wide variety of organizations, including governmental agencies, centers of research on the future, planning staffs of other companies, professional societies, and universities. In addition, organizational culture (Chapter 12) has an important influence on the organization's adaptability. The necessity for organizational adaptation is a major theme of this and the next chapter.

Changing Individual Behaviors

The second major objective of planned organizational change is achieving changes in the behavioral patterns of individuals within the organization. An organization may not be able to change its adaptation strategy for reacting to its relevant environment unless its members behave differently in their relationships with one another and to their jobs. In the final analysis, organizations survive, grow, prosper, decline, or fail because of employee behaviors—the things they do or fail to do.

Any organizational change, whether introduced through a new structural design or a company training program, basically tries to make employees change their behaviors. In a frequently changing environment, such as the aerospace, electronics, and pharmaceutical industries, a rigid-authority hierarchy may restrict the channels of communication and thus reduce the amount of information reaching the organization's top managers. Even if the structure of an organization shifts to a more decentralized one, unless the employees' behavioral patterns change, the new structure may have little impact on organizational effectiveness. For effects of change efforts to be apparent throughout the organization, new employee behavior patterns consistent with the demands of the organization's environment must emerge. (Chapter 21 will examine strategies for changing the behaviors of employees.)

PRESSURES FOR CHANGE

A striking feature of the U.S. economy is its constant change. One hundred years ago the country's biggest industry was agriculture; a few decades later, manufacturing engaged the largest number of people. However, by 1984, about 70 percent of all workers were involved not in producing goods, but in delivering services.[7] Automation and the increasing use of computers certainly will accelerate this trend. Some experts predict that by the year 2000, more than 80 percent of the U.S. labor force may be employed in the service sector of the economy.

Managers and employees operating in this constantly changing environment need to understand the factors that contribute to pressures on organizations to change. Figure 20-1 shows the major categories of **pressures for change** facing organizations in the United States.

Changing Technology

The rate of technological change is greater today than at any time in the past. Technology changes the nature of work performed at all levels of the organization.[8] In the near future, firms will need fewer employees for purely repetitive work in conventional factories. For example, there is a clear trend toward greater use of robots in many U.S. manufacturing and assembly facilities and increasing concern about the impact this trend may have on employees.[9] **Robots** are defined as "combinations of sophisticated microelectronic technology, usually involving a computer, and various mechanical devices that perform functions ordinarily ascribed to human beings and that operate with what appears to be almost human intelligence."[10] It has been projected that there may be as many as 150,000 robots at work in the United States by 1990.

In addition to manufacturing, many other industries will also require less direct labor. A single worker may be able to operate a large hydroelectric plant, oil refinery, or cement plant with the assistance of automated machinery directed by computer. Organizations will still need people to operate and service highly complex automatic equipment, but they will employ far fewer people.

The role of middle management may change dramatically in organizations of the future as machines take over more and more routine tasks. The middle managers' jobs will become more unstructured and focus on the important role of providing communication links between task groups. Middle managers will strive to promote high levels of cooperation among technically trained personnel and provide them with a work environment conducive

FIGURE 20–1.
Pressures on
Organizations to
Change

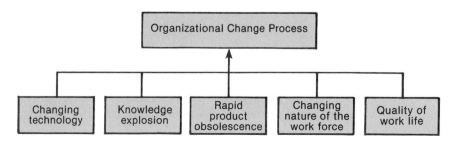

to group collaboration. To search for better decision rules, managers will study the relationship between their areas of responsibility and the rest of the organization. Future middle managers will spend most of their time **managing by exception**: when unexpected problems arise, when a change in rules is needed, or when a computer breaks down, the middle manager will take over. As middle management positions become less structured, innovation and creativity are likely to become more important managerial skills.

Among the most dramatic technological changes in organizations is the rapid expansion of **information systems technology** (that is, complex networks of computers, telecommunications systems, and remote-controlled devices).[11] As information-systems technology develops, top management will probably rely less on middle managers and will be able to focus more attention on organizational goals, long range planning, and organizational relations with the external environment. The traditional use of a single chief executive officer may become impractical. To make complex decisions, chief executives will either have to expand their staffs greatly to include a variety of diverse specialists or allow the decision-making process to flow through an executive team. The increase in the use of sophisticated information-systems technology in organizations is, in part, a response to the knowledge explosion.

Knowledge Explosion

The rate at which society stores useful information about itself has been spiraling upward exponentially. Today, for example, the number of scientific journals and articles doubles about every 15 years, and about 1,000 book titles are produced each *day*. As a result, knowledge in a particular field quickly becomes obsolete.

The availability of knowledge profoundly affects everyone's life, from how to earn a living to ways to spend leisure time. In the agricultural society of the early United States, the major work activity was the production or distribution of agricultural products. In the nineteenth century the transition to an industrial capitalist society began. Great numbers of people became involved in the production of goods, which created the current U.S. wealth. In the 1980s the United States is in transition to a knowledge-based society. Less than 3 percent of the U.S. population works on farms or ranches, and less than 12 percent produces the entire U.S. industrial output. However, more than 30 percent of the population of the United States attend schools.[12]

Business organizations both stimulate the knowledge explosion and are, in turn, affected by it. Organizations demand well-educated employees to perform their increasingly complex work. Within an organization, the knowledge explosion presents new challenges for managers to:

- Find and disseminate knowledge that already exists in the organization.
- Acquire and create new knowledge.
- Convert knowledge into profitable products and services.
- Manage people who work with knowledge.[13]

Knowledge is converted into products and services through the process of organizational innovation.[14] **Innovation** is the creation or adoption of new products, services, processes, or procedures by an organization. The capacity to innovate is central to the ability of an organization to adapt to changes in its environment.

Rapid Product Obsolescence

Fast-shifting consumer preferences, combined with frequent technological changes and innovations, have shortened the life cycle of many products and services. You may have tried to buy a certain item only to find that the product or brand no longer exists. Approximately 55 percent of the items sold today did not exist ten years ago; of the products sold then, about 40 percent have been taken off the shelf. In the volatile pharmaceutical and electronics fields, a product often becomes obsolete in as little as six months. As the pace of product obsolescence accelerates, managers may well participate in the creation of products with the knowledge that these products will remain on the market for only a few months. When Bowmar introduced the pocket calculator in 1971, it sold for $247. Today a small pocket calculator, having all the functions of the first models, can be purchased for less than $10. Almost every month, less expensive but more complex electronic equipment—stereos, VCRs, home computers—are introduced into the market, rendering older versions obsolete to some extent.

When product life cycles become shorter, organizations must be able to shorten their production lead times. Thus organizations, or at least subsystems, will need flexibility to remain viable in the future. The capacity to adapt rapidly to change will be increased by using temporary or flexible structures to permit managers to assemble small groups of personnel to develop ideas, determine strategies, and analyze decisions. In addition to the value of temporary structures in permitting flexibility and adaptation for the corporation, they also enable the corporation to react quickly to information gathered by an early warning system, facilitate transitions to new forms of operations, encourage broad-based and participative decision making, and provide a multitude of situations in which organizations can observe and develop potential future leaders.

Changing Nature of the Work Force

In addition to coping with technology, knowledge, product, and other changes, organizations must attract employees from a rapidly changing work force. Between now and the year 2000, the nature of the work force in the United States is projected to show the changes described in the following In Practice.

In Practice: **The Work Force of Tomorrow**

Tomorrow's work force will probably be older, more diverse in terms of gender and race, marked by intense competition for jobs and promotions, less unionized, and better educated. The realignment of values and aspirations resulting from these changes is likely to exert considerable influence on the nature of work in coming years.

As the large post-World War II "baby boom" generation matures, the average age of American workers will increase steadily through the end of this century. Just as this generation's entrance into the labor force lowered the average age of workers, the aging of the same generation will raise the average age from 34.8 years in 1982 to 37.3 years by 1995.

As this generation reaches and passes middle age, the shortage of advancement opportunities may result in significant job discontent and eventually a demand for young workers to fill vacancies at entry level positions. Even without promotion, the demand for increased earnings resulting from seniority, experience and the economic needs of mid-life will push wage levels up despite competition for employment opportunities.

The growing participation of women in the labor force will also have significant effect. As the percentage of women in the labor force climbed from 31.8% in 1947 to 52.6% in 1982, the female proportion of the total labor force has increased from 27.4% to 43.3% during the same period. By 1995, the labor force participation of women is projected to reach 60.3%, as compared to 76.1% for men. The average woman of the future is likely to work during all stages of the life and family cycle. The dual-income household is well on its way to becoming the norm of the future, creating a need for new relations between home and work and demanding changes in both areas.

Minorities as a proportion of the American labor force increased from 10.7% to 12.8% between 1954 and 1982, and a combination of demographic and immigration trends are expected to increase this proportion to 14.5% by 1995. Unemployment for minorities has been almost twice that of non-minorities. Therefore, pressures for equal opportunity from groups that have historically been disenfranchised will persist.

Other longstanding characteristics of the work force are also likely to change. Current trends suggest that the extent of union affiliation may decline. The proportion of American workers affiliated with a union declined from a peak of 35% in 1955 to around 20% in 1982. Although union policies, coupled with social and political conditions, could reverse this process, current trends suggest a largely unorganized work force in the future.

Finally, the educational background of the American labor force has been rising steadily. High school graduation has now become the norm for most entry level jobs, and the proportion of the U.S. labor force that has completed four years of college or more grew from 14.7% to 24.2% between 1970 and 1983.

During the past two decades, assumed conditions of economic affluence and security, coupled with political pressures for social equality, fostered values that were commonly perceived to change the traditional American "work ethic." Key trends in this shift seemed to include the de-emphasized importance of material wealth as a motivator of work activity, pressures for equality and resistance to authority, desire to realign the balance between work and other aspects of life, and increased concern with finding intrinsically interesting and personally rewarding work.

Most studies indicate that these trends have not reduced the motivation to work, but instead increased expectations concerning the conditions and rewards of work. Although many of these "new" values are not likely to disappear, turbulent economic conditions, changes in the work force, and progression of the baby boom generation through the life cycle are likely to force a compromise between aspirations and reality during the next few decades.

Unstable economic conditions and the demands of mid-life expenditures will reassert the importance of income as a motivator for work. At the same time, social values developed during the 1960s and 1970s will create a high priority for work environment reforms, such as participative decision making, pleasant work conditions, considerate management, and such supportive facilities as day care centers.[15]

Not only will the composition and values of the work force continue to change, but interorganizational mobility will increase. Plans that enable workers to move their pension contributions with them from company to company without losing future benefits will aid occupational mobility. If an organization cannot meet an employee's need for vocational or personal development, the person may simply leave. Employees are likely to become more cosmopolitan and less loyal to an individual employer or company. Their strongest ties will be to their profession or skill rather than to an organization. However, people may be forced to change occupations several times during their working lives to adjust to changing occupational demands. As a result it will become more common for individuals to have several different careers during their lives. (See Chapter 19.)

Managers will need a broader and more intensive education as work becomes increasingly intellectual and the level of education in the general population increases. Their education will have to provide them with skills and tools for a lifetime of career moves. Businesses and government will need to make large-scale provision for the continual reeducation of the work force. Many organizations, such as IBM, Xerox, GE, Westinghouse, B.F. Goodrich, and Exxon already have established their own educational centers. Using advanced educational and technological systems, these companies offer programs ranging from basic educational and vocational training to executive development.

Quality of Work Life

Quality of work life is the degree to which members of an organization are able to satisfy important personal needs through their work experiences in the organization.[16] This has become a major issue in the labor force, not only in the United States but throughout Western industrial society. Management, organized labor, and even government are interested in participating in the design of organizational change activities aimed at improving the quality of work life.

Little direct data are available on the seriousness or the scope of the problem of quality of work life. Those who argue that it is important generally contend that:

- Worker alienation and job dissatisfaction are increasing, primarily as a result of meaningless jobs and autocratic managers.
- The productivity of U.S. workers is declining, while counterproductive behaviors (such as turnover, sabotage, union militancy, theft, drug abuse, and alcoholism) at work are increasing.
- Confidence in big organizations is eroding.

The quality of an individual's work life has been linked to many behaviors both on and off the job. In addition, it is an important component of the quality of life in general for most people.[17] For example, improvements in the quality of a person's work life may lead to more positive feelings about himself or herself (greater self-esteem), the job (improved job satisfaction and involvement), and the organization (stronger commitment to organizational goals). Better physical health, fewer mental health problems and less drug abuse, and greater growth and development of the individual, both as a person and a productive member of the organization, may result from improvements in the quality of work life. Finally, a higher quality of work life may lead to decreased absenteeism and turnover, fewer industrial accidents, and a high level of job performance.[18]

RESISTANCE TO CHANGE

Pressures on organizations to change are never-ending. However, it is also inevitable that change will be resisted, at least to some extent, by both individuals and organizations. **Resistance to change** is one of the most baffling problems managers face because it can take so many forms. Overt or explicit resistance may take the form of strikes, reduction in productivity, shoddy work, and even sabotage. Covert or implicit resistance may be manifested in increased tardiness and absenteeism, requests for transfers, resignations, loss of motivation, lower morale, and higher accident or error rates. The effects of resistance, whether explicit or implicit, may be subtle and cumulative. That is, minimal reactions to a small change (for example, a change in the location of an office machine or a change in office routine) may occur without a manager being aware of employee resistance. In contrast, a wildcat strike or a work slowdown may occur as a major overt indicator of resistance. It is important for managers and employees alike to understand the reasons for and sources of resistance to change.[19]

Individual Resistance to Change

Figure 20-2 shows several sources of resistance to change that may operate within the individual. Figure 20-2 provides examples of some of the more important sources but is not intended to suggest that these are the only reasons why individuals may resist change at work.

SELECTIVE ATTENTION AND RETENTION As Chapter 4 indicated, people tend to perceive selectively those things that fit most comfortably into their cognitive maps, or their current understanding of the world. Once an individual establishes his or her understanding of reality, that understanding re-

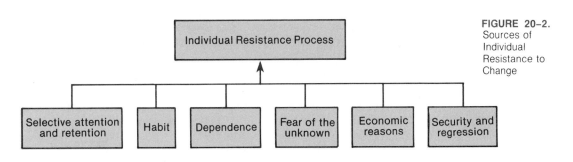

FIGURE 20–2. Sources of Individual Resistance to Change

sists change. Among other things, this means that people tend to resist the possible impact of change on their lives by reading or listening only to what they agree with, by conveniently forgetting any knowledge that could lead to other viewpoints, and by misunderstanding communication that, if correctly perceived, would be incongruent with preestablished attitudes and values. For example, managers enrolled in management training programs are exposed to different managerial philosophies and techniques. They may ably discuss and answer questions about these philosophies, but they may carefully segregate in their minds the new approaches that they feel would not work in their job and those that they already practice.

HABIT Unless a situation changes noticeably, individuals may continue to respond to stimuli in their accustomed way. An established habit may be a source of satisfaction for an individual. Habits allow people to adjust to and cope with their world and provide a certain comfort and security. Whether a habit becomes a major source of resistance to change depends, to a certain extent, on whether individuals immediately perceive advantages from changing some habitual behavior. For example, if an organization suddenly announced that all employees would immediately receive a 20-percent pay raise, few would object, although this might mean that changes in life styles would become possible. However, if the company suddenly announced that all employees would immediately receive a 20-percent pay raise only if they switched from flexible hours to set hours of work, many would object. Employees would have to change many habits: sleeping late when they were tired, driving on expressways free of rush hour traffic, working late at night if they needed a quiet office, and so on.

DEPENDENCE All human beings begin life dependent on adults. Parents sustain life in the helpless infant and provide major satisfactions to their children. Thus dependence is instilled in all people to a certain extent. Dependency is not a bad thing, indeed to care deeply about another person is to allow yourself to be, in a sense, dependent on them. However, dependency on others can lead to resistance to change if carried to extremes. People who are highly dependent on others often lack self-esteem (Chapter 3), and they may resist changes until those they depend on endorse the changes and incorporate them into their behavior. For example, workers who are highly dependent on their superior for feedback on performance will probably not adopt any new techniques or methods unless the superior personally endorses them and indicates to the employees how these changes will improve performance.

FEAR OF THE UNKNOWN Confronting the unknown makes most people anxious. Each major change in a work situation carries with it an element of uncertainty. Women starting a second career after raising a family may be anxious about how they will fit in with other workers after a long absence from the work environment. An employee may wonder what might happen if he or she relocated to company headquarters in another state. Would my family like it? Will I be able to find friends? What will the company think of me if I refuse to relocate? Uncertainty in this situation arises not from the change itself, but from the consequences surrounding the change. In order to avoid making more demanding types of decisions and the fear of the unknown, some managers may refuse promotions that require relocating or that require major changes in job duties and responsibilities.

ECONOMIC REASONS Money weighs heavily in people's considerations. They usually resist changes that could lower their income directly or indirectly. Employees have invested in the status quo in their jobs. That is, they have learned how to perform the work successfully, perhaps how to get good performance evaluations, how to interact with peers, and so on. Changes in established work routines or job duties may threaten their economic security. Employees may fear that, after changes are made, they will not be able to perform up to their previous standards, and subsequently will not be as valuable to the organization, their superiors, or co-workers.

SECURITY AND REGRESSION Another obstacle to change is the tendency of some people to seek security by regressing to the past. When life becomes frustrating, people think about a happier past and may want to cling to old, comfortable behaviors. Ironically, this frustration–regression sequence usually occurs just when old ways no longer produce the desired outcome and experimentation with new approaches is most needed. Even so, highly insecure people are apt to cling even more desperately to old, unproductive behavior patterns. For example, a manager who does not recognize or value the effects of equal opportunity legislation on his policy of hiring only white males may seek to return to the "old days," when he ran the shop according to his personal inclinations.

Organizational Resistance to Change

To a certain extent it is the nature of organizations to resist change and innovation as shown by the American LaFrance experience in the Preview Case. Organizations are often most efficient when doing routine things and tend to perform more poorly, at least initially, when doing anything for the first time. Like fully automated factories, they are designed to perform reliably a narrowly prescribed set of functions. To ensure operational efficiency and effectiveness, organizations may create strong defenses against change. Moreover, change often opposes vested interests and violates certain territorial rights or decision-making prerogatives that have been established and accepted over time. Figure 20-3 shows several of the more significant organizational resistances to change.

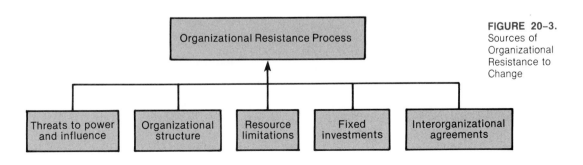

FIGURE 20–3. Sources of Organizational Resistance to Change

THREATS TO POWER AND INFLUENCE   Some people in organizations may view change as a threat to their power or influence. One source of power in organizations is the control of something other people need, such as information or resources. (See Chapter 16.) Once a power position has been established in an organization, the individual will resist change that is perceived as reducing his or her power and influence. For example, programs to improve the quality of work life (QWL programs) in organizations tend to focus on nonmanagerial employees and are often perceived as increasing the power of such people. As a result, they may be resisted by managers and supervisors as the following quotation indicates.

> I've killed myself for the last two years trying to get this QWL project going. I've attended meetings, had lots of one-to-ones, put in lots of extra time, and so forth. And the more I put in, the more the organization seemed to demand of me. I just couldn't take it any more. I am beginning to believe that all of this participation stuff is just a bunch of garbage that will never work in the long haul. I am not interested in improving someone else's QWL at my expense. There is just no way it will work![20]

This statement was made by a disgruntled middle manager who later resigned. He perceived (perhaps correctly) the QWL change program as a threat to his own position and power.

In addition, novel ideas or a new use for resources can disrupt the power relationships among individuals and departments in an organization and therefore are often resisted.

ORGANIZATION STRUCTURE   Organizations need stability and continuity in order to function effectively. Indeed, the very meaning of organization implies that a certain structure must be given to group activities. Individuals must have assigned roles, established procedures for getting the job done, consistent ways of getting needed information, and so forth. However, this legitimate need for structure also can serve as a major resistance to change. Organizations may have narrowly defined jobs; clearly spelled out lines of authority, responsibility, and accountability; and strictly limited flows of information from the top to the bottom. An emphasis on the hierarchy of authority usually causes employees to adhere only to specific channels of communication and to feed back only positive information regarding their jobs. They may neglect to give any negative feedback that might actually help management to better identify both the need and means for change. The more mechanistic the organization is, the more numerous are the channels of communication through which an idea must travel. This, then, increases the probability that any new idea will be screened out because it violates the status quo in the organization.

RESOURCE LIMITATIONS   Whereas some companies want to maintain the status quo, others would change if they had the available resources to do so. The U.S. steel industry provides a good example. Its problems include formidable competition from abroad, slack demand, high labor costs, aging mills, and rigorous antipollution laws that require huge investments in nonproductive equipment. The continuing inability of U.S. steel firms to generate adequate profits for reinvestment has sharply limited their capacity for organizational change.

In general, change requires resources: capital, time, people with the necessary skills, and so on. At any point in time, an organization's managers may have identified a number of changes that could (and, perhaps, should) be made, but they may have to make difficult decisions concerning the relative importance of desired changes because of resource limitations.

FIXED INVESTMENTS Resource limitations are not confined to organizations that lack assets. Wealthy organizations may experience difficulty and be unable to change because of fixed capital investments in assets that are not easily altered (such as equipment, buildings, and land). The plight of the central business districts in many U.S. cities illustrates this resistance to change. Most larger U.S. cities evolved before automobiles, so they cannot begin to accommodate today's traffic volumes and parking demands. The fixed investments in buildings, streets, and utilities is enormous and usually prevents rapid and substantial change. Therefore the older central areas have experienced increasing difficulty in meeting the competition of suburban shopping centers.

Fixed investments are not always limited to physical things; they also can be expressed in terms of people. For example, consider employees who no longer are making a significant contribution to an organization but have enough seniority to maintain their jobs. Unless they can be motivated to higher task performance, or retrained for other positions, their salaries and fringe benefits represent, from the company's perspective, fixed investments that cannot easily be changed.

INTERORGANIZATIONAL AGREEMENTS Agreements between organizations usually impose obligations on people that can restrain their behaviors. Labor negotiations and contracts are the most pertinent example: some ways of doing things that were once considered major prerogatives of management (the right to hire and fire, assignment of personnel to tasks, promotions, and so on) become subject to negotiation and become fixed in the negotiated contract. Other kinds of contracts also restrain management. Proponents of change in an organization may face delay because of arrangements with competitors, commitments to suppliers and other contractors, and pledges to public officials in return for licenses or permits. While agreements can be ignored or violated, potential legal costs may be very expensive, lost customers may hesitate to buy the product again, and a lowered credit rating can be disastrous.

SUMMARY Resistance to change stems from a variety of sources, some involves the resistance of individuals and some involves the nature and structure of organizations. Realistically, we should not expect resistance to change ever to cease completely. However, managers can learn to identify and overcome many resistances and thus become more effective agents for change in an organization.

An interesting example of resistance to change is provided by the current experience of Soviet managers. These managers, their organizations, and the Soviet regime are reported to be highly resistant to the use of computers.

ACROSS CULTURES

The Great Soviet Computer Screw-Up

Soviet industry is in big trouble with computers. Its hardware isn't modern. Breakdowns occur endlessly. The telecommunications are terrible. And Soviet managers have lots of sneaky reasons for not wanting effective information systems.

With some kicking and screaming along the way, the business managers of the Western world have long since adapted to computers. No sizable capitalist enterprise could be competitive nowadays without computer-driven management information systems—what the data-processing department calls MIS. A problem that Mikhail Gorbachev must find maddening these days, as he looks around for ways to cure the sick Soviet economy, is his country's broad failure in MIS. With every year that goes by, it is increasingly apparent that Soviet industry has fundamental problems with computers. Russian managers aren't exactly kicking and screaming, but they also aren't adapting very well.

Computers present several challenges to the Soviet leadership. Presumably it worries about the military implications of the U.S.S.R.'s inferiority in computer hardware. Gorbachev must also be concerned about the computer's implicit threat to the official Communist monopoly on ideas: a few Apple II computers hooked up to printers could make instant best-sellers out of dissident literature. So just about all computers in the Soviet Union are closely guarded in state-run institutions. Americans worry about hackers electronically breaking into institutions and gaining access to various business and military secrets. In the Soviet Union, things are reversed: the state's problem is to prevent any computer users from *breaking out* of the institutions.

Thus far, at least, the regime seems to have dealt effectively with these widely publicized problems. It has been reasonably successful in stealing and otherwise acquiring Western technologies with military applications. And the KGB seems to have had little difficulty in preventing dissidents from getting their hands on printers and other duplicating devices. But the problem posed by computers for Soviet enterprises—the state-owned counterparts of Western corporations—is another matter. At the enterprise level, the Russians have generally failed to exploit the fantastic efficiencies made possible by the new electronic technology, and this failure is a major reason for expecting the gap between the Soviet and Western economies to keep widening.

Among those who have been most closely tracking the record at the enterprise level is a team at the University of Arizona's College of Business and Public Administration, under the direction of Seymour E. Goodman. The team's members have worked hard at interviewing the occasional Soviet emigré who is knowledgeable about information systems; most of their data, however, are based on exhaustive analysis of Soviet technical journals. Professor Goodman, who was recently in Brussels briefing NATO officials on Soviet computers, believes the Russians are deeply distressed by their shortcomings. "They sit there and watch this competition between Japan and the West over development of a fifth generation of computers," he observed recently. "They know they can't just sit out the contest. They know they have to at least look as though they're doing the same kinds of things, but that's not easy."

Most Soviet enterprises still lack mainframes of any kind. William K. McHenry, a colleague of Goodman's and author of a recent prodigious Ph.D. dissertation on management information systems in the Soviet Union, estimates that only 7.5% of the country's industrial enterprises— 3,300 out of 44,000—had mainframes in 1984. To be sure, this minority includes a disproportionate number of large, high-priority enterprises. Even so, the evidence suggests that most sizable plants in the Soviet Union are still getting by without mainframes. McHenry, who will be an assistant professor at Georgetown's School of Business Administration beginning this fall, has assembled data showing that only one-third of large plants ("large" meaning at least 500 employees) had mainframes in 1984. With or maybe even without rounding, the comparable figure for the U.S. would be 100%.

The systems in use in the U.S. typically enable managers to instantly call up an infinity of data about payrolls, inventories, production, sales, and anything else useful. American managers take it for granted that they can function more effectively if these data are accurate and timely. But Soviet managers are frequently under pressures to falsify data, and so they are understandably nervous about computerized systems for keeping track of what's happening.

Soviet managers have many perverse incentives to misuse computers. One that nullifies productivity gains in many sectors of the economy is the regime's guarantee of employment to all workers. This means that the manager who acquires a mainframe can't easily use it to replace all the workers with abacuses who are now on his payroll—and his plant might literally have hundreds of them. Soviet enterprises typically consist of numerous small fiefdoms, each with its own statistical department, and the evidence thus far suggests that management information systems have not really dented these fiefdoms. Their survival is additionally ensured by the organizational rigidity of Soviet enterprises: an enterprise of a given size in a given industry is ordinarily required to have certain well-defined line and staff relationships. These requirements are intended to make it easier for the ministries to supervise the many enterprises under their jurisdiction, but, of course, the effect is to prevent managers from devising new organizational arrangements suitable to the computer age.

As you might assume, the overriding obstacle to rational use of computers in the enterprises is the managers' recurring need to falsify much of their data. The garbage-in, garbage-out phenomenon is pervasive, and there is little the ministries can do about it. Soviet managers frequently have to make purchases in various black markets to get needed supplies. Knowing that such illegal purchases are often necessary, they may set up a slush fund by diverting money from, say, the payroll account; to make this possible they might overstate the number of workers at the enterprise, which would enable them to get extra wages from the ministry in charge. Meanwhile, their computers would inevitably be spitting out garbage.

The pressures that drive managers to cook the books are clear enough. The economic system in which they operate features unrealistic planning targets, causing chronic shortages of resources—so they hoard resources, doing their best to conceal from the ministries the true state of inventories and the true number of production workers. The system provides bonuses for fulfillment of the plan but also tends to raise required norms for anyone who overfulfills it—so the managers suppress any data that might suggest they were capable of increased output. On the other hand, they tend to overstate performance when norms are not being met.

The Soviet economy's failure to assimilate computers is not only an economic disaster. The failure also has a symbolic dimension. Communism is, after all, an idea claiming to stand for progress, and computers are the quintessential symbol of progress. The performance of Soviet managers in the face of the new technology can be taken as another threat to the legitimacy of the regime.[21]

Overcoming Resistance to Change

Managers often encounter difficulty in clearly understanding situations that involve change. Analyzing a change problem can become quite complex because of the large number of variables that must be considered. Kurt Lewin, a pioneering social psychologist, developed a way of looking at change, called **force field analysis**, that has proved to be highly useful to action-oriented managers.[22] Lewin saw change not as an event, but as a dynamic balance of forces working in opposite directions. Any situation can be considered to be a state of equilibrium resulting from a balance of forces constantly pushing against each other. Certain forces in the situation—the resistances to change—tend to maintain the status quo. At the same time, the pressures for change are acting opposite to these forces and are pushing for

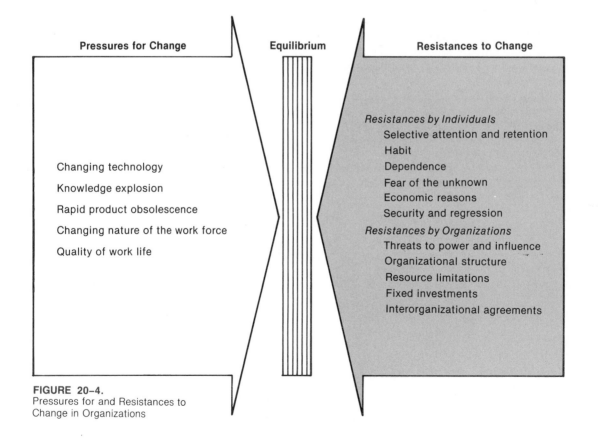

FIGURE 20–4.
Pressures for and Resistances to
Change in Organizations

change. The combined effect of these two sets of forces results in the situation depicted in Figure 20-4. By way of illustration, Figure 20-4 shows the various pressures and resistances that have been discussed in this chapter.

In order to initiate change, a manager must act to modify the current equilibrium of forces. The manager might attempt to change the situation by:

- Increasing the strength of the pressures for change.
- Reducing the strength of the resisting forces or removing them completely.
- Changing the direction of a force—that is, change a resistance into a pressure for change.

Using this model to understand the processes of change has two primary benefits. First, it requires that managers analyze the current situation. By becoming skillful at diagnosing the forces pressing for change and the resistances to change, managers should be better able to understand the relevant forces in any situation. Second, the model highlights the factors that can be changed and those that cannot. Managers often waste a great deal of time considering actions related to forces over which they have little, if any, control. When managers direct their attention to those forces over which they do have some control, they increase the likelihood that the options they choose will be the most effective.

To demonstrate the application of force field analysis, consider the situation where a manager wants to delegate more authority to subordinates. The manager starts by identifying the pressures for and resistances to change that exist, as shown in Figure 20-5. With this analysis as a starting point, the manager might go on to analyze which of the resistances are most easily reduced or removed and begin to take action accordingly.

Careful analysis of a situation, however, does not guarantee successful change. For example, there is a natural tendency to increase the pressures for change in any situation in order to produce the desired change. While increasing such pressure may result in changes in the short run, these changes may have a high cost: strong pressures on individuals and groups may disrupt and unbalance the organization. Often, the most effective way to make needed changes is to identify existing resistances to change and to focus efforts on removing or reducing as many of them as possible.

In addition, an important part of Lewin's approach to changing behaviors consists of carefully managing and guiding change through a three-step process:

- **Unfreezing.** This step usually involves reducing those forces maintaining the organization's behavior at its present level. Unfreezing is sometimes accomplished by introducing information that shows discrepancies between behaviors desired by organizational members and those behaviors they currently exhibit.
- **Moving.** This step shifts the behavior of the organization or department to a new level. It involves developing new behaviors, values, and attitudes through changes in organizational structures and processes.
- **Refreezing.** This step stabilizes the organization at a new state of equilibrium. It is frequently accomplished through the use of supporting mechanisms that reinforce the new organizational state, such as organizational culture, norms, policies, and structures.[23]

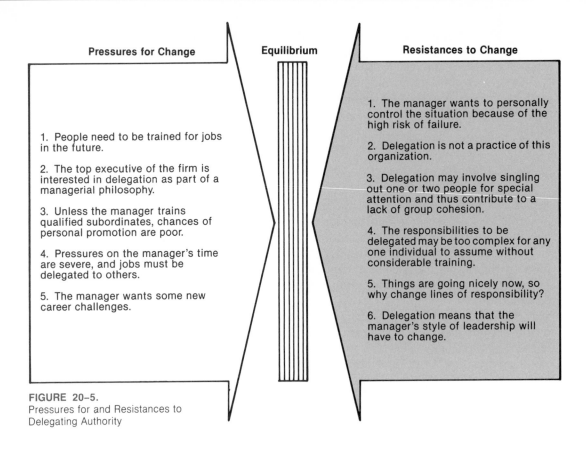

Pressures for Change	Equilibrium	Resistances to Change

Pressures for Change

1. People need to be trained for jobs in the future.

2. The top executive of the firm is interested in delegation as part of a managerial philosophy.

3. Unless the manager trains qualified subordinates, chances of personal promotion are poor.

4. Pressures on the manager's time are severe, and jobs must be delegated to others.

5. The manager wants some new career challenges.

Resistances to Change

1. The manager wants to personally control the situation because of the high risk of failure.

2. Delegation is not a practice of this organization.

3. Delegation may involve singling out one or two people for special attention and thus contribute to a lack of group cohesion.

4. The responsibilities to be delegated may be too complex for any one individual to assume without considerable training.

5. Things are going nicely now, so why change lines of responsibility?

6. Delegation means that the manager's style of leadership will have to change.

FIGURE 20-5.
Pressures for and Resistances to
Delegating Authority

MODELS AND PROCESSES FOR ORGANIZATIONAL CHANGE

Although there are many models and processes that can be used to foster organizational change, we will consider only one model (systems) and two processes (action research and organization development); these are among the most important and widely used approaches for initiating change in organizations.

A Systems Model of Change

A widely-used systems model of change is comprised of four interacting variables that could serve as the focus of planned change in an organization: task, structure, people, and technology.[24] The **task variable** refers to whether the job is simple or complex, novel or repetitive, or standardized or unique. Some tasks, such as the placement of a bumper on an automobile, are highly standardized, repetitive, and simple, whereas the design of a new safety bumper is unique, novel, and complex. A task's nature can affect the relationships among individuals and departments in an organization. The **structure variable** is the system of communication, authority, and responsibility in the organization. Each organization has its own structure, which specifies power and working relationships among the individuals in it. The **people**

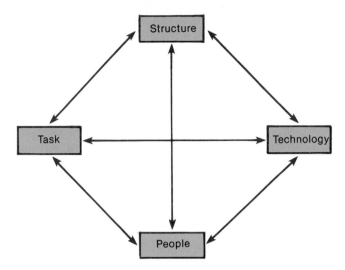

FIGURE 20–6.
Variables in Organizational Change

variable applies to the individuals working within the organization, including their attitudes, personalities, and motivations. Finally, the **technology variable** encompasses the problem-solving methods or techniques used in the organization, such as computers, typewriters, and drill presses. As Figure 20-6 indicates, these four variables are highly interdependent. A change in any one variable usually results in a change in one or more of the others. For example, a structural change toward decentralization of decision making could result in the assignment of different people to certain organizational tasks. However, decentralization of decision making may also change the technology for performing the tasks, and affect the attitudes and values of the employees involved.

Organizational change can be introduced by altering these variables singly or in combination. However, all four variables of organizational change are usually present in a change process. A systems approach to change requires that managers understand all four variables before disturbing any one of them. The systems model shown in Figure 20-6 provides the framework for examining some specific approaches and techniques of organizational change in Chapter 21.

Action Research

Action research is a data-based, problem-solving process of organizational change that replicates the steps involved in the scientific method described in Chapter 2.[25] It represents a powerful approach to organizational change, and it underlies many successful change programs. The process of action research consists of three essential steps:

- Gathering information about problems, concerns, and needed changes from the members of an organization.
- Organizing this information in some meaningful way and sharing it with the employees involved in the change effort.
- Planning and carrying out specific actions to correct identified problems.

The action-research sequence often includes an evaluation of the agreed-on actions that have been carried out. An organizational change program may go through repeated cycles of data gathering, information sharing, and action planning before its conclusion.[26]

The strength of the action-research approach to change lies in (1) its involvement of employees in the change process; and (2) the fact that it bases change on a careful diagnosis of the current situation in the organization. Managers can effectively change an organization or task group only if they understand the current situation, determining in the process what things are done well and what things need to be improved. In addition, employee involvement can present a powerful force for change for at least two reasons. First, people are more likely to implement and support a change that they have helped create. Second, once managers have identified the need for change and have widely shared this information, the need becomes difficult for employees to ignore. The pressure for change thus comes from within the group or department rather than from outside. This internal pressure is a particularly powerful force for change.[27] Note the application of the action-research process in a mental health hospital.

In Practice: Action Research in a Mental Health Hospital

A large mental health hospital in Florida was forced into a major reorganization mandated by the state agency that controlled its budget and directed the operation of all similar state facilities. The reorganization resulted in the decentralization of the hospital into a number of smaller, semiautonomous units, each with its own patients and staff. Following the reorganization, both morale and performance declined markedly in some units of the hospital. The hospital administrator decided to implement an organizational change program designed to increase performance and managerial effectiveness in the units having difficulties. He hired two outside consultants who specialized in organizational change problems to help.

The consultants and the management of the affected units decided to follow an action-research approach to change. First, using questionnaires and personal interviews, they gathered information from the staffs of two units, who were to serve as models for the rest of the hospital. This information focused on a variety of issues facing the units, including communication problems between shifts, disagreements over new roles, and difficulties in managing and working within the new organizational structure (which was essentially a matrix). Summaries were made of people's concerns and work problems, and this information was shared with all participating employees at a series of workshops and meetings. Following this, detailed action plans were drawn up to solve the problems facing the units. Employees were organized into teams, which took responsibility to accomplish specific actions. A significant number of changes were made in communication patterns and procedures, role assignments, and the administrative structure of the units.

The action research process worked because (1) all the employees of the units were involved; (2) once problems surfaced it was no longer possible to pretend they did not exist; and (3) the organizational change program "belonged" to the employees and not to the consultants or some staff experts.[28]

Organization Development

Organization development (OD) is a planned, systematic process of organizational change based on behavioral science technology, research, and theory.[29] OD is a relatively new field of behavioral science that focuses on the management of change in organizations. As a field of behavioral science, it draws heavily on psychology, sociology, and anthropology. In its concern with organizations, OD relies on information from motivation theory (Chapter 7), personality theory (Chapter 3), and learning theory (Chapter 6), as well as on research on group dynamics (Chapters 9 and 10), leadership (Chapter 11), power (Chapter 16), and organization design (Chapter 14). It is based on many well-established principles regarding the behaviors of individuals and groups in organizations; in short, the field of organization development rests on many of the facets of organizational behavior covered in this book.

Organization development is not a single technique, but a collection of techniques that have a certain philosophy and body of knowledge in common. In addition, some basic tenets of OD set it apart from other organizational change approaches. Among these are the following:

- OD seeks to create self-directed change to which people are committed. The problems and issues to be solved are those identified by the organization members directly concerned.

- OD is a systemwide change effort. To make lasting changes that create a more effective organization requires an understanding of the entire organization. It is not possible to change part of the organization without changing the whole organization in some sense.

- OD typically places equal emphasis on solving immediate problems and the long-term development of an adaptive organization. The most effective change program is not just one that solves present problems, but one that also prepares employees to solve future problems.

- OD places more emphasis than do other approaches on a collaborative process of data collection, diagnosis, and action for arriving at solutions to problems. Action research, discussed in the previous section, is a primary change process used in most OD programs.

- OD often leads to new organizational arrangements and relationships that break with traditional bureaucratic patterns.[30]

Many of the techniques and methods for organizational change described in Chapter 21 often make up part of an OD program.

SUMMARY

A rapidly changing world places many demands on managers, including the need to manage organizational change effectively. Planned organizational change is the intentional attempt to alter the structure and processes of an organization in order to make it more effective. Organizational change requires adaptation by the organization as a whole and by individuals in the organization, who must alter their patterns of behavior.

Pressures for change stem from changing technology, the knowledge explosion, rapid product obsolescence, the changing nature of the work force, and demands for higher quality of work life. Individuals resist change through selective attention and retention or through the effects of habit, dependence, and fear of the unknown. Economic reasons—the fear of loss of income—and the need for security, which can result in regression, also act as individual resistances to change. Organizational resistances to change can be caused by a threat to power and influence, the organizational structure itself, resource limitations, fixed investments not easily altered, and interorganizational agreements.

Force field analysis can help managers overcome resistance to change. Managers must encourage pressures for change and discourage resistances to change or convert them into pressures for change. The change process passes through three stages: unfreezing, moving, and refreezing.

The major systems variables in the change process are task, structure, people, and technology. A systems approach to change recognizes the interdependent nature of these variables. Successful change programs often utilize an action-research sequence of information gathering, feedback, and action planning. Organization development (OD) is a field of applied behavioral science that involves a planned, systematic approach to change and often includes the action-research process.

KEY WORDS AND CONCEPTS

Action research
Force field analysis
Information systems technology
Innovation
Managing by exception
Moving
Organization development (OD)
People variable
Planned organizational change

Pressures for change
Quality of work life
Refreezing
Resistance to change
Robots
Structure variable
Task variable
Technology variable
Unfreezing

DISCUSSION QUESTIONS

1. Describe the two basic underlying objectives of every organizational planned change program. Which is the more fundamental? Explain your answer.

2. Identify some internal and external sources of pressure for change within the college or university you are attending.

3. How do individuals resist change? Why do they do so?

4. Why do many people involved in change efforts refer to organizations as "innovation resisting"?

5. Use force field analysis to analyze some situation that needed changing from your own work experience. Start by describing the setting and situation. Then identify the major pressures and resistances to change operating in the situation.

6. Using the three step process model of unfreezing, moving, and refreezing, describe some major behavioral change from your own experience.

7. Describe the four major systems variables that affect an organization's ability to achieve change. Give an example that shows how they are interrelated.

MANAGEMENT INCIDENTS AND CASES

Le Master Utility, Incorporated

Le Master is a large national utility company with a 5500 person divisional office located in the New England area. The New England Division Accounting Department consists of the functions illustrated in Figure 20-7. The company is strongly unionized at all non-managerial levels. The Accounting Department is the third largest of the ten departments assigned to the New England Division.

In 1985, a reorganization plan was presented by the Accounting Department Manager, Mr. Bill Wilcox. The plan called for the centralization of all data processing work in the New England Division. All manual accounting work units were to be transferred to the Mid-Atlantic Division. The centralization was to take place in three steps. Each manual accounting work unit was to move according to a fixed schedule. The first step called for the move of the Reports and Vouchers Unit at the close of September's business, the end of the third quarter. The second step included the move of the Payroll Unit after the fourth quarter close in December. This timing was necessary so that all wage reports and W-2's would be issued before the records were packed for shipment. Finally, all revenue units—the Traffic Unit, Service Order Unit, and Cash Unit—would be transferred together in time to start July's business.

On August 23, the managers of the Accounting Department were called together for a meeting with Y. A.

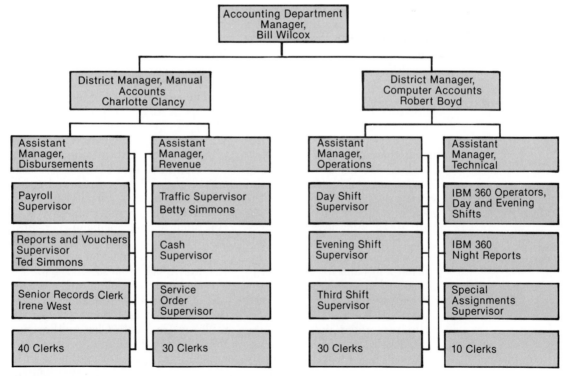

FIGURE 20-7.
Le Master Utility, Incorporated: Accounting Department, New England Division

Bernard, Vice President of the Eastern Operations Region. This was a special visit by Mr. Bernard who rarely left the corporate headquarters, except to handle difficult reorganization or labor problems. Many rumors had circulated throughout the department since the announcement of his scheduled stop at the division offices. Rumors linked his scheduled appearance with recent efficiency problems revealed by the company's inter-departmental efficiency and cost indices. These indices showed that the Accounting Department's manual section had the highest company costs in the eastern region for the past two years.

Mr. Bernard started the meeting:

The company headquarters staff has been studying the operations of the Accounting Department here for the past year. We have had systems management consultants assist us in this study designed to improve the operational efficiency in this area. At this very moment, my assistant is explaining exactly what I say here to the Mid-Atlantic Division.

Systems management has presented a plan that the Board of Directors has accepted to take place at the close of September's business. It calls for the simultaneous reorganization of the New England Division's Accounting Department and the type of work performed relative to the new structure here. I'm sure you will see a significant improvement that will result after this plan's completion.

The plan calls for the centralization of most of the data processing functions now performed by both divisions. Also, the manually performed duties will be centralized as a result. The company will benefit by this plan by eliminating the computer hardware duplication in both divisions, more fully utilizing such equipment, and reducing the personnel needs necessary to perform the accounting functions.

However, let it be known to your clerks, that no one will be laid-off. Each person will receive a comparable job upon the completion of their present duties. By comparable, we mean comparable in terms of wages, hours, and type of work. A refusal to accept a comparable job will result in the termination of the refusing employee.

It is a very fair plan. Please assure your people that we are doing everything we possibly can to make this reorganization pleasant for employees and profitable to the company. You will all receive a copy of this plan as you leave the room. Mr. Wilcox, your Division Manager will have the authority to revise this plan as he feels necessary. Thank you.

For the most part, the seventy manual operations clerks were upset at the idea of losing their jobs. Twenty-two had held their accounting jobs for at least fifteen years. Some of the younger clerks doubted the "comparable job" promise of management. The poor morale of the unit affected the operations efficiency even more in September. Since the September business officially closed on the 8th of October, the four senior clerks, averaging 28 years of service, decided to resign. The plan offered them twice the regular termination pay (years of service times weekly salary) plus normal pension benefits. The fifth most senior clerk, Irene West, who was classified as a Senior Records Clerk, was offered a job in the Commercial Department at the Mid-Atlantic Division as a "Verifier." This job was considered comparable by Charlotte Clancy, the District Manager—Manual. Charlotte was 28 years old and had been with the company for five years. She had been promoted to the district manager position two weeks earlier. She had a college degree in business from a Texas school. It was unusual to be promoted to a district manager's position before one had been with the company for 8 to 10 years. Her judgment concerning the recommended job was endorsed by Mr. Wilcox.

Irene was 51 years old and had been with the company for 30 years. She was a high school graduate, pleasant, somewhat pessimistic, but self-confident about her work. Irene's salary as Senior Records Clerk was $303 per week. Her current job consisted of maintaining seven expense accounts. It involved the receipt of voucher forms, checking signatures for verification, adding amounts to master account files, and drawing up checks manually for the amount vouchered. She then passed the checks to her supervisor for signature and delivery to the respective department.

The new Verifier duties involved checking for completeness of reports filed daily by the service coordinators, compiling daily reports for a weekly report, investigating and reporting any unusual fluctuations in figures submitted. The pay for this job was $295 per week and the hours were the same as Senior Records Clerk.

Charlotte Clancy attached a note to the job offer sent to Irene that said: "Looks like we found your job. Hurry the affirmation response by signing the appropriate places. Any questions? Just call me!"

Irene felt uneasy about the new job and informed Ted Simmons, her supervisor, that she would not take it. She contended that the job was not "comparable" for the following reasons: (1) verifying reports requires little thought; (2) the pay is $8 less a week amounting to $416 less a year; (3) she has been with the Accounting Department for 22 years; and (4) she believed she could be trained for a data processing job so that she could stay at the New England Division.

Irene's supervisor, 24-year-old Ted Simmons, had joined the depart-

ment on June 1. This rather sensitive, independent thinking, new supervisor had a B.S. degree in management having graduated with a B plus average. He liked people and would go out of his way to help his employees. He often allowed rescheduled work hours so that employees could attend to personal business. He was not above coming to work at 6:30 A.M. to supervise workers who came in early because they wished to leave early to attend to personal business. In a short time Ted had won the respect and cooperation of his workers. They trusted him so much that some would even seek confidential help from him concerning family or personal problems. He would listen to the employee's predicament and try to help solve the problem as best he could. Ted's wife, Betty, was a Traffic Supervisor in the Manual section. Betty was known to be an intelligent high achiever, who looked forward to moving ahead at Le Master.

After Ted announced the reorganization plan he told his workers that he would not give any counsel for or against the job transfers. In his view this was a "too important" issue to have supervisory involvement. Ted was a management employee and each manager was graded on the "image" displayed in the department. At Ted's first appraisal he was warned about his closeness to the non-management employees. He tried to argue that improved efficiency resulted from his personal touch. He now realized that helping his workers could seriously hurt him in the reorganization if he expressed views not consistent with the management's goals and objectives. To avoid possible conflict, Ted chose to remain silent about the individual's possible choices on specific jobs. He did say he would help clarify the worker's questions concerning the new position and would provide direction according to the worker's expressed desires.

Ted took the job offer sheet into Charlotte's office and explained

Irene's reasons for rejecting it. Charlotte dismissed Ted saying, "I'll handle this one." That afternoon, Irene received a note from Charlotte that said: "Just read the report again, Irene, and your refusal has put me in an ugly position. I will have to ask for your resignation and give you your termination pay if you don't reconsider."

Irene approached Ted with the note and said, "I will have to notify an attorney and the union steward if that's the way she wants to play. You tell Charlotte that she better reconsider or we'll be off to court." This was an alarming statement to company management since court action was considered damaging to the public image of the company. Although Ted was new to this company, he already understood that the company's public image was a very important consideration at Le Master. Utilities have a monopoly position and procedures for developing acceptable level profits are provided through the regulatory commission rate adjustments. If utility costs rise, a petition is filed with the regulatory agency requesting a rate increase. A poor public image decreased the likelihood of rate increases.

At a hastily called meeting Charlotte, Mr. Wilcox, and Ted discussed Irene's threat. Mr. Wilcox decided to revise the plan to allow transfers within the Manual District and providing more time for the employees to decide on interdepartmental transfer. This action would initially result in the overstaffing of the other units. Mr. Wilcox reasoned the added time would make the transfer to another department easier for employees. If Irene and possibly others refused to cooperate, training for less important data processing functions would be initiated. Mr. Wilcox's strategy was based on the fear of public charges of unfair dismissal procedures in the courts. The revised plan was presented to the Accounting Depart-

ment and Irene's casual response was, "Guess we can take any job we want."

Six months later Ted Simmons resigned to return to graduate school to work on his MBA degree in a different city. Betty Simmons requested and received a transfer in order to be with Ted.[31]

Questions

1. Was the reorganization plan thought out adequately enough by management to promote an efficient as well as equitable move to the Mid-Atlantic Division? Justify your answer.

2. What type of influence method did management attempt to use to gain employee cooperation and compliance with the plan?

3. Consider Irene's behavior and her possible motivations for wanting a comparable job in a data processing unit in the New England Division. Explain why management's influence attempts failed to sway her. How should the Division Manager, Mr. Wilcox, have handled the implementation of the plan so as to minimize resistance to it?

4. Consider Ted's behavior and his apparent reasons for not aiding his employees in making their choices. Does his behavior demonstrate that he has acted as an effective manager in the past and in this situation? Justify your answer.

5. Discuss the short-run benefits and possible ramifications of Mr. Wilcox's decision to modify the implementing procedures on the basis of Irene's refusal to accept the job offer. Do you justify his revised strategy for implementing the plan on the basis of specific criteria to benefit the company, the employees, or both? Explain.

REFERENCES

1. Merwin, J. The Limits of Tradition. *Forbes,* May 20, 1985, 112–115. Reprinted with permission of *Forbes* Magazine. Copyright © Forbes, Inc., 1985.

2. Lippit, G. L., Langseth, P., and Mossop, J. *Implementing Organizational Change.* San Francisco: Jossey-Bass, 1985; McCaskey, M. B. *The Executive Challenge: Managing Change and Ambiguity.* Boston: Pitman, 1982.

3. See, for example, Huse, E. F., and Cummings, T. G. *Organization Development and Change,* 3d ed. St. Paul, Minn: West, 1985, 19–32.

4. Goodman, P. S., and Kurke, L. B. Studies of Change in Organizations: A Status Report. In P. S. Goodman and Associates (Eds.) *Change in Organizations: New Perspectives on Theory, Research, and Practice.* San Francisco: Jossey-Bass, 1982, 4.

5. Naisbitt, J. *Megatrends.* New York: Warner, 1982.

6. Katz, D., and Kahn, R. L. *The Social Psychology of Organizations,* 2d ed. New York: Wiley, 1978, 54–55.

7. Kirkland, R. I. Are Service Jobs Good Jobs? *Fortune,* June 10, 1985, 38–43.

8. Finklestein, J., and Newman, D. The Third Industrial Revolution: A Special Challenge to Managers. *Organizational Dynamics,* Summer 1984, 53–65; Handy, C. The Changing Shape of Work. *Organizational Dynamics,* Autumn 1980, 26–34.

9. Foulkes, F. K., and Hirsch, J. L. People Make Robots Work. *Harvard Business Review*, January–February 1984, 94–102; Hollon, C. J., and Rogol, G. N. How Robotization Affects People. *Business Horizons,* May–June 1985, 74–80.

10. Foulkes and Hirsch, People Make Robots Work, 96.

11. McFarlan, F. W. Information Technology Changes the Way You Compete. *Harvard Business Review,* May–June 1984, 98–103.

12. Zand, D. E. *Information, Organization, and Power.* New York: McGraw-Hill, 1981, 3–5.

13. Zand, 6–7.

14. Drucker, P. F. The Discipline of Innovation. *Harvard Business Review,* May–June 1985, 67–72.

15. Best, F. The Nature of Work in a Changing Society. *Personnel Journal,* January 1985, 37–42. Copyright © January 1985. Reprinted with permission of *Personnel Journal,* Costa Mesa, Calif. All rights reserved.

16. Hackman, J., and Suttle, J. *Improving Life at Work: Behavioral Science Approaches to Organizational Change.* Santa Monica, Calif.: Goodyear, 1977, 4.

17. Rice, R. W., McFarlin, D. B., Hunt, R. G., and Near, J. P. Organizational Work and the Perceived Quality of Life: Toward a Conceptual Model. *Academy of Management Review,* 1985, *10,* 296–310.

18. Lawler, E. E. Strategies for Improving the Quality of Work Life. *American Psychologist,* 1982, *37,* 486–493; Lawler, E. E., and Ledford, G. E. Productivity and the Quality of Work Life. *National Productivity Review,* Winter 1981–1982, 23–36.

19. For additional perspectives on resistance to change, see Argyris, C. *Strategy, Change and Defensive Routines.* Boston: Pitman, 1985; Elbing, C. J. Yes, but . . . Hidden Criteria for Judging Managerial Innovations. *Business Horizons,* November–December 1984, 10–14; Staw, B. M. Counterforces to Change. In *Change in Organizations,* 87–121; Zaltman, G., and Duncan, R. *Strategies for Planned Change.* New York: Wiley Interscience, 1977.

20. Schlesinger, L. A., and Oshry, B. Quality of Work Life and the Manager: Muddle in the Middle. *Organizational Dynamics,* Summer 1984, 6.

21. Seligman, D. The Great Soviet Computer Screw-Up. *Fortune,* July 8, 1985, 32–36. Reprinted with permission from *Fortune* Magazine. Copyright © 1985 Time, Inc. All rights reserved.

22. Lewin, K. *Field Theory in Social Science.* New York: Harper & Row, 1951; Lewin, K. Frontiers in Group Dynamics. *Human Relations,* 1947, *1,* 5–41.

23. Huse and Cummings, *Organization Development and Change,* 20.

24. Leavitt, H. Applied Organizational Change in Industry: Structural, Technological, and Humanistic Approaches. In J. March (Ed.) *Handbook of Organizations.* Chicago: Rand McNally, 1965, 1144–1170.

25. French, W. L., and Bell, C. H. *Organization Development: Behavioral Science Interventions for Organization Improvement,* 3d ed. Englewood Cliffs, N.J.: Prentice-Hall, 1984, 107.

26. For descriptions of action research, see French and Bell, *Organization Development,* 107–119; Huse and Cummings, *Organization Development and Change,* 21–28; Margulies, N., and Raia, A. P. *Conceptual Foundations of Organizational Development.* New York: McGraw-Hill,

1978, 55–81; Peters, M., and Robinson, V. The Origins and Status of Action Research. *Journal of Applied Behavioral Science,* 1984, *20,* 113–124.

27. See, for example, the classic statement by Cartwright, D. Achieving Change in People: Some Applications of Group Dynamics Theory. *Human Relations,* 1951, *4,* 381–392.

28. Tolchinsky, P. D., and Woodman, R. W. *Facilitating Matrix Structures in Mental Health Using OD Techniques.* Technical report for the Florida Department of Health and Rehabilitative Services, 1981.

29. Burke, W. W. *Organization Development: Principles and Practices.* Boston: Little, Brown, 1982, 10.

30. Beer, M. *Organization Change and Development: A Systems View.* Santa Monica, Calif.: Goodyear, 1980, 10.

31. Case prepared by Craig Zerresch, an MBA student, under the direction of James E. Weir, Associate Professor, Southern Illinois University-Edwardsville, and reprinted with permission.

21 Approaches to Planned Organizational Change

LEARNING OBJECTIVES

When you have finished studying this chapter, you should be able to:

- Explain and provide examples of several people-focused, task- and technology-focused, and structure-focused approaches to organizational change.
- Discuss the importance to planned organizational change of an accurate diagnosis of organizational problems.
- Identify the key contingencies that influence the choice of a change approach.
- Explain the likely effects of each of the organizational change approaches presented.
- Respond effectively to various types of change efforts.

OUTLINE

Preview Case

Organizational Change at Mot Surgical Corporation

Mot Surgical Corporation is a subsidiary of a large pharmaceutical company that produces drugs and related medical products. Mot specializes in surgical equipment and had three manufacturing plants with plans to open a new plant in the southwestern United States. Mot's parent corporation had supported employee quality of work life for several years. It had encouraged its subsidiaries to increase employee involvement and to design meaningful jobs. The new plant in the southwest was seen by Mot as a potential site to enrich jobs and increase employee participation. At Mot's older plants jobs were very routinized and employee involvement in decision making was minimal.

For the new plant Mot made great efforts to recruit people who were likely to respond favorably to enriched jobs. Newspaper advertisements and job interviews explicitly mentioned the enriched nature of the new jobs and the promise that employees would be involved in decision making. Potential recruits were shown the new plant setup, and asked about their desire to learn new things and to be involved in decision making. About 30 people were hired and trained in the new jobs initially; additional employees were assimilated into the new plant over the next few months. The training program was oriented to learning several new jobs (job rotation was to be used extensively), and to gaining problem-solving skills.

As training progressed and the plant gradually started production, several unexpected problems emerged. First, employees found it difficult to rotate among the different jobs without a considerable loss of production. The jobs involved entirely different kinds of manual dexterity and mental concentration. Each time people switched from one job to another, much relearning and practice was necessary for them to achieve a normal level of production. The net result of this rotation was lower-than-expected productivity. When this problem persisted, workers were urged to stay on one particular job.

A second problem concerned employee involvement in decision making. During the early stages of the plant start-up, workers had ample opportunities for decision making. They were involved in solving certain break-in problems and deciding housekeeping, personnel, and operating issues. They were undergoing training and had time to devote to problem solving without heavy pressures for production. Over time, however, plant operations became more routine and predictable, and there was less need for employee decision making. Moreover, increased pressures for production cut into the limited time devoted to decision making.

A third problem involved employee behaviors and attitudes. After six months of operation, employee absenteeism and turnover were higher than the local industry average. People complained that the job was more routine and boring than they had expected. They felt that management had sold them a bill of goods about opportunities for decision making. These behaviors and attitudes were especially prevalent among those who were hired first and had participated in the initial recruiting and start-up.[1]

Managing organizational change is a complex undertaking. Planned changes that are expected to work may not, or they may have consequences different from those intended. When trying to improve organizational adaptability and employee behaviors, managers must understand the nature of the changes needed and the likely effects of alternative approaches to bringing about that change.

In Chapter 20, we discussed individual and organizational resistances to change, as well as the pressures and needs for change in organizations. In this chapter, we discuss specific approaches and techniques available to managers for effecting changes in organizations and their employees. Each of these approaches may be valuable under certain conditions. However, organizational change is never easy, risk-free, or obtained at no cost. But the choice for management over the long run is obvious: innovate and adapt, or stagnate and die.

Controversy exists over the best approach for changing an organization and/or employee behaviors. Many different approaches have been used successfully in organizational change efforts, but a successful approach to change in one organization may not necessarily work in another. Thus we will emphasize a contingency perspective on organizational change, which suggests that there is no single best approach to change; no one approach is likely to be effective under all circumstances.

OVERVIEW OF CHANGE APPROACHES

Chapter 20 introduced a systems model of change consisting of four variables: people, task, technology, and structure. Here, we will use this sytems model to organize approaches to change into three major categories: people-focused approaches, task- and technology-focused approaches, and structure-focused approaches. Task and technology are presented together because the change programs which focus on these variables tend to impact both areas. A number of specific change strategies and techniques will be explored within each of the general categories. While the chapter is organized as if each approach to organizational change discussed were independent and mutually exclusive of the others, nothing could be further from the truth. Successful organizational change programs frequently require the use of a variety of approaches and many of these techniques are commonly used together to effect needed changes.

Relative Impact on Major System Variables

Table 21-1 provides a summary of the change approaches discussed in this chapter, the primary focus of each approach, and the relative direct impact of each on the four major system variables: people, task, technology, and structure. Each approach is characterized as usually having a high, moderate, or low *direct* impact on each of the four system variables. For those approaches that frequently have different degrees of direct impact on a system variable, the table indicates a range. For example, team building can vary from having a low to a high direct impact on the task variable, depending on the focus and goals of the team-building activities.

TABLE 21-1   Comparison of Relative Direct Impact of Selected Change Approaches on Major System Variables

| Change Approach | Relative Direct Impact on Major System Variables | | | |
	People	Task	Technology	Structure
People Focus				
Survey feedback	High	Low to moderate	Low	Low to moderate
Team building	High	Low to high	Low	Low to moderate
Process consultation	High	Low to moderate	Low	Low
Quality of work life	High	Low to moderate	Low to moderate	Low to moderate
Task and Technology Focus				
Job design	Low to high	High	Low to high	Low
Sociotechnical systems	High	Moderate to high	High	Low to moderate
Quality circles	Low to moderate	Moderate to high	Low to high	Low
Structure Focus				
Matrix organization	Low to high	Low to moderate	Low	High
Collateral organization	Low to high	Low to moderate	Low	High

The direct impact shown in Table 21-1 represents the initial focus or target of the change effort.[2] Remember, however, that the systems perspective means that to change part of an organization, in the long run, is to change the whole. Thus each change approach, if successful, will ultimately impact all four major system variables.

Organizational Diagnosis

The key contingency that influences the choice of approach or combination of approaches is the nature of the problem the organization is trying to solve. Thus a careful analysis must be made of the current situation. The intent of planned change is to solve problems rather than to make them worse. For example, an approach that emphasized the development of group problem-solving skills for production workers who are dissatisfied and frustrated with highly controlled, boring, and routine jobs could easily increase the problem. The opportunity for the production workers to openly and explicitly discuss the nature of their work without the chance to change the way they perform tasks could easily increase their dissatisfaction and frustration. The approach to change in this situation probably should focus on the nature of the production workers' jobs and opportunities to enrich the tasks they perform. Group problem-solving sessions involving managers and the production workers might be an effective supplemental approach to gain the workers' assistance and embrace their ideas in redesigning tasks to be included in their jobs.

There is no one best way to identify the problems facing work groups, departments, or organizations. Nor is there any magic formula for matching specific change programs or approaches to specific problems or issues after they have been identified. However, it is clear that an accurate diagnosis of organizational problems is absolutely essential in an effective organizational change program.[3] Four basic issues that must be addressed in **organizational diagnosis** are:

- Recognition and interpretation of the problem and assessment of the need for change.
- Determination of the organization's readiness and capability for change.
- Identification of managers' and employees' resources and motivations for change.
- Determination of the change strategy and goals.[4]

Information needed to diagnose organizational problems may be gathered by questionnaires, interviews, observation, or from the firm's records. (See Chapter 2.) Most frequently some combination of these data-gathering methods is employed. A major advantage of the information-collecting process is to increase awareness of the need for change on the part of both managers and employees. However, even when widespread agreement exists among an organization's members concerning the need for change, people may have different ideas about the change approaches that should be used and when and where they should be implemented. It is important that some systematic attempt be made to determine the initial focus of the change effort. For example, using the systems model, managers might begin by placing problems in people, task, technology, or structure categories. Of course, regardless of the analysis scheme used, real problems may not fit neatly into a single category.

Any change program requires a careful assessment of individual and organizational *capacity* for change. With regard to individual readiness for change, a critical variable is employee expectations regarding the change effort.[5] Expectations play a key role in behavior (Chapters 4 and 7). If people expect that nothing of significance will change regardless of the amount of time and effort they devote, this belief can act as a self-fulfilling prophecy. On the other hand, employee expectations for improvement might sometimes be unrealistically high, thus creating a situation where unfulfilled expectations make matters worse. Ideally, expectations regarding change should be positive yet realistic. In addition, there must be an accurate assessment of the organization's physical and financial capacity to make the change. Approaches that require a massive commitment of personal energy and organizational resources will probably fail if the company has few resources and its people do not have time to think through the issues. Under such circumstances, the organization may benefit most from starting with a more moderate, less demanding approach. Then, as the organization develops the necessary resources and commitment, it can increase the depth and breadth of the change.

When managers and employees conduct an organizational diagnosis, they should recognize two important factors. First, organizational behavior is the product of many interacting forces. Therefore what is observed or diagnosed—employee behaviors, problems, and the current state of the organization—has multiple causes. Trying to isolate single causes for complex problems can lead to simplistic change strategies that are not effective. Second, much of the information gathered about an organization during a diagnosis will represent symptoms of problems rather than causes of problems. Needless to say, focusing change strategies on symptoms will not solve underlying problems. For example, in an organization an awards program recognizing perfect attendance failed to reduce absenteeism because it failed to deal with the cause of the problem. Employees were absent from work in a particular department because of pressures created by excessive work loads and an inefficient, frustrating set of procedures for doing their jobs. Absenteeism thus was a symptom of this overload problem, and the awards offered were not sufficient to change employee behaviors and did not address the real problem.

PEOPLE-FOCUSED APPROACHES TO CHANGE

People-focused approaches to change tend to rely a great deal on active involvement and participation by many members of the organization. People-focused approaches, if successful, may bring improvements in individual and group processes such as decision-making skills, abilities to identify and solve problems, communication skills, working relationships, and the like. We will examine four people-focused approaches to organizational change: survey feedback, team building, process consultation, and quality of work life (QWL) programs.

Survey Feedback

Survey feedback is an organizational change process that consists of (1) collecting information (usually by questionnaire) from members of an organization or work group; (2) organizing the data into an understandable and useful form; and (3) feeding it back to the employees who generated the data.[6] Some or all of the participants then use this information as a basis for planning actions to deal with specific issues and problems. Survey feedback follows the action-research change process described in Chapter 20. The primary objective of the survey–feedback approach is not to introduce a specific change (such as a new computer system), but to improve the relationships among the members of groups and between departments through the discussion of common problems. Survey feedback is also frequently used as a diagnostic tool to identify group and organizational problems. Because of its value in organizational diagnosis, survey feedback is often employed as part of large-scale, long-term change programs in conjunction with other techniques. Since survey feedback is used so often to diagnose organizational problems, and appears so frequently in conjunction with other approaches, it may well be the single most frequently used organizational change approach.

The survey–feedback approach typically begins with the commitment and endorsement of top management. Participants then complete a standardized questionnaire. Generally, surveying members of the entire organization, or at least everyone in a department or work group, yields the best results. The questionnaire, which people answer anonymously, may ask for employees' perceptions and attitudes about a wide range of conditions, including communication processes, motivational incentives, decision-making practices, coordination between departments and individuals, job satisfaction, and so on. Table 21-2 presents a sample of items included on a questionnaire that has been used in a wide variety of survey–feedback programs.

A survey–feedback questionnaire may include standardized items that all employees in many organizations can complete; it also may include items

---

TABLE 21-2   Sample Questions in a Survey-Feedback Program

Instructions: To indicate how descriptive each statement is (or should be) of your situation, write a number in the blank beside each statement, based on the following scale:

1 To a very little extent	2 To a little extent	3 To some extent	4 To a great extent	5 To a very great extent

_____ 1. To what extent is this organization generally quick to use improved work methods?

_____ 2. To what extent does this organization have a real interest in the welfare and happiness of those who work here?

_____ 3. How much does this organization try to improve working conditions?

_____ 4. To what extent does this organization have clear-cut, reasonable goals and objectives?

_____ 5. To what extent are work activities sensibly organized in this organization?

_____ 6. In this organization to what extent are decisions made at levels where the most adequate and accurate information is available?

_____ 7. When decisions are being made, to what extent are the people affected asked for their ideas?

_____ 8. People at all levels of an organization usually have know-how that could be of use to decision makers. To what extent is information widely shared in this organization so that those who make decisions have access to all available know-how?

_____ 9. To what extent do different units or departments plan together and coordinate their efforts?

How friendly and easy to approach are the people in your work group?

_____ 10. This is how it is _now._

_____ 11. This is how I would _like_ it to be.

When you talk with people in your work group, to what extent do they pay attention to what you are saying?

_____ 12. This is how it is _now._

_____ 13. This is how I would _like_ it to be.

To what extent are people in your work group willing to listen to your problems?

_____ 14. This is how it is _now._

_____ 15. This is how I would _like_ it to be.

To what extent does your supervisor offer new ideas for solving job-related problems?

_____ 16. This is how it is _now._

_____ 17. This is how I would _like_ it to be.

To what extent does your supervisor encourage the people who work for him or her to work as a team?

_____ 18. This is how it is _now._

_____ 19. This is how I would _like_ it to be.

Source: Adapted with permission from Taylor, J. C. and Bowers, D. G. _Survey of Organizations: A Machine-scored Standardized Questionnaire Instrument._ Ann Arbor, Mich.: Institute for Social Research, The University of Michigan, 1972. No further reproduction in any form authorized without written permission of the copyright holders.

developed for a particular organization or department. The questionnaire normally contains items that focus on the respondents' work group, as well as on processes that may characterize the organization as a whole. Top management may want to use only questionnaire items that relate to practices and processes that they are willing and able to change. Since the survey feedback typically requires the feedback of data from the completed questionnaires to all respondents, top management should not raise the expectations of employees in areas that it has no intention of modifying.

All respondents receive a report of data from the questionnaire, which usually summarizes the responses for the entire organization, department, or work group, as well as their own individual responses. Group discussion and problem-solving meetings are then held to discuss the data being fed back. Under ideal conditions, these group sessions move from discussing the tabulated perceptions and attitudes to identifying various action steps. A single group session may deal only with particular parts of the data fed back, and groups may hold several meetings over a period of time to consider the data fully. The task-oriented and problem-solving emphasis of these meetings usually avoids focusing on personalities.

Prior to these meetings, a consultant often counsels the immediate superior in each organizational group on the nature of the responses, the basis and meaning of the questionnaire measures, interpretation and use of the data, and conducting the group problem-solving sessions. Three basic timing methods for feedback of the data exist, in which everyone can obtain the data (1) almost simultaneously; (2) in a "waterfall" pattern, when group meetings are held at the highest organizational levels first, followed by group meetings at each succeeding lower level; or (3) in a "bottom-up" fashion, when group meetings are held first at the lowest participating levels of the organization.

CONDITIONS FOR SUCCESS WITH SURVEY FEEDBACK Several conditions should exist for maximum impact of the survey–feedback approach. First, the sessions should be conducted in a factual, task-oriented manner. Second, each group must have sufficient discretion to consider and take actions based on its findings and analysis. The approach may be counterproductive if the group can only discuss problems and perceptions without actually determining or strongly influencing corrective actions. Under such conditions, participants will probably feel that they were deceived and manipulated and that the process was misrepresented. A third condition for successful survey feedback is reporting up the line the results of the problem-solving meetings from the lower organizational groups. This serves several purposes. Higher management is more likely to become rapidly involved in recommendations requiring some action on its part. Recognition at all levels that the process is important and is to be taken seriously is more likely. Thus the commitment by all parties may be greater if they believe their efforts can make a difference.

ASSESSMENT OF SURVEY FEEDBACK The survey–feedback approach, in contrast to traditional training courses, considers the system of human relationships as a whole; that is, it assumes superior and subordinate can change together. It deals with managers and employees in the context of their own jobs, problems, and work relationships.

A strength, but also a limitation, of this approach is its reliance on the existing organizational structure. It emphasizes improving working relationships and two-way communication between the various levels within the present structure. The survey–feedback approach can increase the influence of lower-level employees. At the same time, management also can develop greater influence since employees may better understand the reasons for management policies. Decision making and problem solving can improve, because this approach applies competency and knowledge from throughout the organization to important issues identified by the employees themselves. The effectiveness of survey feedback has been attributed to (1) the broad coverage of the process, which includes virtually all members of an organization or department; (2) the amount of unfreezing that the approach stimulates; and (3) the tendency of employees to perceive the data generated and the process as relating directly to their problems and goals and those of the organization and its work groups.[7]

Thus survey feedback can effectively meet both organizational goals and individual needs. It does not usually bring about fundamental changes in the structure, task design, or technology of the organization. However, survey feedback may bring problems to the surface and clarify issues, which, in turn, indicate the need for major changes in structure, tasks, or technology.

Team Building

Team building is an organizational change process by which members of a work group diagnose how they work together and plan changes that will improve their effectiveness.[8] Organizations produce little solely from individual effort. Many different work groups make up an organization, and the success of most organizations ultimately depends on how effectively people can work together in groups (Chapters 9 and 10).

Team building attempts to improve the effectiveness of work groups by having group members focus on one or more of the following four purposes:

- Setting goals or priorities for the group.
- Analyzing or allocating the way work is performed.
- Examining the way the group is working.
- Examining relationships among the people doing the work.[9]

Team building usually follows a cycle similar to that shown in Figure 21-1. A team-building sequence begins when group members recognize a problem in group functioning for which team building seems appropriate. During a team-building program, members of the work group contribute information concerning their perceptions of issues, problems, and working relationships. Data may be gathered informally during group meetings or prior to meetings using interviews or questionnaires. These data are analyzed, and work-group problems are diagnosed. Using problem diagnosis as the starting point, members of the group plan specific actions and assign individuals to implement them. At some later stage, members of the team must evaluate their progress and determine whether their action plans solved the problems. Notice that the team-building sequence depicted in Figure 21-1 also includes the action-research process described in Chapter 20.

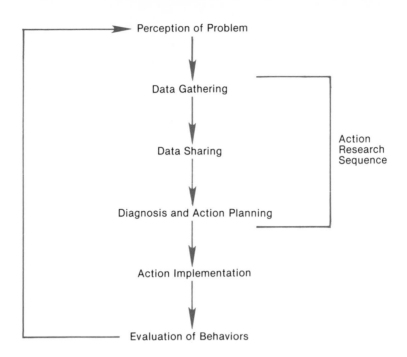

FIGURE 21–1.
The Team-Building
Cycle

A team-building program deals with immediate group problems and helps the members learn how to deal with new problems on an ongoing basis. An effective work group recognizes barriers to effectiveness and designs and carries out actions to remove those barriers.

CONDITIONS FOR SUCCESS WITH TEAM BUILDING   Before a group attempts team building, a basic interdependence among the group members must exist. That is, the work activities of team members must require group effort, and effective performance by one group member must depend on that of the others. When such task interdependencies do not exist, team building is inappropriate, and the group should use other change programs.

Team building is more successful when goals have been clearly stated. The team members must understand the reasons for engaging in team building and basically agree with the goals of the effort. In other words, the goals of team building need to be the goals of the members and not the goals imposed by higher management, staff experts, or outside consultants. In addition, there is evidence that team building frequently is most successful when it focuses on goal-setting and problem-solving activities that are closely related to the group's primary tasks, rather than on interpersonal issues.[10]

However, interpersonal problems can and do reduce group effectiveness, and they must be dealt with. Team building provides a useful way for the group to examine interpersonal issues. Managers must be aware that people problems are sometimes more threatening than task-related problems, and the probability of successful change is somewhat reduced unless employee concerns are handled well. Sometimes a skilled third party, such as an outside consultant or a human resource professional from the firm's personnel staff, can help a work group deal with interpersonal issues that surface during a team-building program.

Another important condition for success in team building is the ability of the work group to take action to correct the problems identified or, at the very least, to tackle some reasonable percentage of them. Making everyone aware of issues facing the group and raising expectations of change is pointless if the team lacks sufficient power to institute needed improvements.

ASSESSMENT OF TEAM BUILDING   Team building has resulted in many positive outcomes for work groups and organizations. As a result of team-building programs, organizations have reported positive changes in employee participation, involvement, and attitudes, job satisfaction, organizational climate, group decision-making and problem-solving skills, and other aspects of group behavior.[11] While some disagreement exists, there is much less evidence that team building can be linked directly to productivity or performance gains.[12]

Team building frequently is an important part of an organization development (OD) program, as described in Chapter 20. Organization development practitioners place great value on collaborative behaviors in the process of organizational change. In addition, many OD programs are based on the assumption that widespread participation by employees is necessary to effect and sustain meaningful change in an organization. Increased involvement and participation is among the strongest expected outcomes of team building.[13] As such, team building often can provide a useful way to involve employees in an organizational change program and to increase the occurrence of collaborative behavior.

Many managers and consultants consider team building to be one of the most powerful and well-developed organizational change approaches: "The basic building blocks of organizations are groups of people; therefore, the basic units of change are also groups, not simply individuals."[14] Let us turn to an example of a successful team building program.

In Practice: **Team Building with the PAL Management Team**

The PAL management team was responsible for running a new plant producing military equipment. The plant, located in the Midwest, was part of a diversified corporation specializing in electronics. The management team consisted of the plant manager and the heads of the functional departments at the plant. At the time of this example, the team had been together only the few weeks since the plant had begun start-up operations. Already, however, the team was experiencing problems defining its task and making timely decisions. Members complained that they were unsure what decisions and problems the team should handle as distinguished from those resolved by the functional departments. Also, members felt that team meetings were ineffective—for example, complex problems were either resolved too quickly without full discussion or they were put off indefinitely when members became bogged down in too many details.

External OD consultants had been working with management to design the new plant and to help start it. The growing complaints about team effectiveness led the consultants to suggest a two-day team building session as a start towards developing a more effective management team. Although team members were overloaded with start-up problems, they agreed to take the necessary time to build their team. The plant manager and the consultants jointly designed the session, which took place at a local hotel.

Prior to the team building session, the consultants interviewed each member of the team, including the plant manager. They asked questions about how members saw the task of the team—for example, what decisions and problems should be resolved by the team and what issues should be left to the departments. They also asked questions about team functioning, including its good and bad performance and what problems plagued it and their likely causes. The consultants summarized this information and placed it on large sheets of newsprint for viewing by team members.

At the start of the session, the plant manager reviewed the reasons for the team building and shared his expectations for the session. Members were encouraged to ask questions and to share their own expectations. Next, the consultants helped members set specific norms which would guide their behaviors during the two-day meeting. These included norms of being open with opinions and feelings, of listening to others, and of participating actively in the session. The norms were placed on newsprint, which was then affixed to the wall of the meeting room. All members agreed to try to behave according to the norms and to periodically assess how well the norms were being followed. The consultants agreed to provide feedback on norm compliance during the session.

The next part of the meeting was devoted to examining the interview data. Members started with the information about the group's tasks. They examined the responses to the task question, and both sought and offered fuller explanations of the interview data. Over a three- to four-hour period, members gained a clearer understanding of each person's perceptions of the decisions and problems that the team should deal with versus those issues that departments should handle. As might be expected, there was some disagreement on which issues should belong to the team and which should be delegated to the departments. The team also did an initial assessment of how well members were following the norms. They agreed that member participation and openness were sufficient but that listening to one another could improve.

Before examining the rest of the interview data, the consultants suggested that members might want to try to resolve their task disagreements. Members agreed and began to talk through their differences and to negotiate an acceptable team task definition. The consultants served both as process consultants and third-party facilitators during this period. They helped to clarify members' views and to see that personal issues were identified and listened to. By the end of the first day of the session, the team had arrived at a clear set of statements defining its task. Moreover, members had begun to examine group process and to improve their listening and problem-solving abilities.

The second day of the session was devoted to examining the rest of the interview data about team functioning. Like the previous day, members asked questions and shared opinions about the interview responses. This resulted in a clearer understanding of things the group did well, of things it did poorly, and of problems hampering group problem solving and their likely causes. Members again assessed how well they were following the norms and agreed that behaviors were becoming more acceptable. The consultants also gave feedback to members about the norms. They then suggested that based on members' diagnosis of the interview data, members might want to develop specific action plans for resolving the barriers to group problem solving. This resulted in a lively discussion of ways to improve group meetings, including setting agendas, examining group process, and following a more orderly problem-solving process. Members agreed to implement some of these suggestions over the next few weeks; they set specific dates for implementing them, as well as assignments of who was responsible for each of the changes.

The session ended with members assessing the meeting in light of their initial expectations. All agreed that most of their expectations were met. Members also did a final assessment of how well they had followed group norms. Interestingly, they all agreed that the norms governing behaviors during the team building should also apply to future team meetings back at the plant.[15]

Process Consultation

Process consultation is guidance provided by a consultant to help members of an organization perceive, understand, and act on process events that occur in their work environment.[16] *Process events* refer to the human actions within groups and organizations to perform work, or the ways in which work gets done. Process events include the behaviors of people at meetings; formal and informal encounters among employees at work; and, in general, any of the behavioral steps involved in performing a task. Process consultation is characterized by the use of a skilled third party—a consultant or facilitator—who helps individuals and groups examine the process by which they are working toward task accomplishment. This skilled third party may be an outsider to the organization, such as an external behavioral science consultant; or a member of the organization, such as a human resource professional or a manager skilled in process activities.

Process consultation programs typically address one or more of the following areas of concern:

- *Communication.* Managers must understand the nature and style of the communication process in the organization and make this process as open and valid as possible. In particular, communication patterns of meetings can contribute to or reduce group effectiveness.

- *Leadership.* Process consultation can help a work group understand leadership styles and help individual managers adjust their style to better fit different situations. In addition, by understanding influence processes, members of a group can learn to rotate leadership according to individual expertise; this is an important group skill.

- *Decision making and problem solving.* Efficient decision-making and problem-solving processes are critical for individual and group effectiveness in organizations. Managers must understand how decisions are made in their organizations and learn effective problem-solving behaviors.

- *Group norms and roles.* Managers should be aware of the processes by which employees take on certain roles in groups and organizations. In addition, process consultation can help a group examine the appropriateness of norms that influence individuals' behavior. It is possible to change norms by a conscious process.

- *Conflict resolution.* How organizations resolve conflicts between individuals and groups is another important process. Process consultation provides an often effective approach to diagnosing, understanding, and resolving organizational conflict.[17]

The specific activities of process consultation often are not as clear-cut as those in the team-building or survey–feedback approaches to change. In general, process consultation follows an action-research cycle that includes gathering data about some organizational or group process, sharing this information with the employees involved, and planning actions designed to improve the process. Some form of practice or experimenting with different process-related behaviors may be included in the change program prior to implementation of the improved processes by the group or organization.

ASSESSMENT OF PROCESS CONSULTATION   Process consultation is designed to change attitudes, values, interpersonal skills, group norms and cohesiveness, and other process variables, and it often is effective in facilitating these kinds of changes.[18] On the other hand, there is no evidence that process consultation *directly* affects outcome variables, such as task performance.[19] However, process consultation is seldom the sole component of an organizational change program; it often is used in combination with other approaches. For example, in the In Practice description of team building, at one point the consultants played the role of process consultants to help team members make a decision concerning the nature of the management team's task.

Quality-of-Work-Life Programs

Quality-of-work-life (QWL) programs have become increasingly popular during the 1980s in response to demands for improvements in the quality of work life. In addition, QWL programs have been perceived as a way to increase productivity and quality of output through greater involvement and participation by employees in decisions that affect their jobs. QWL programs are typically broad-based and, to a certain extent, lack the precise definition and focus of other change approaches (such as survey feedback and team building). However, the following description captures the general concerns of QWL change programs.

> **Quality-of-work-life programs** refer to any activity undertaken by an organization for the expressed purpose of improving one or more of the following conditions that affect an employee's experience with an organization:
>
> - security
> - equity
> - individual choice
> - participation in decisions
> - safety and health
> - opportunities to use and develop human capacities
> - meaningful work
> - control over work time or place
> - protection from arbitrary or unfair treatment
> - opportunities to satisfy social needs.[20]

Organizations that have active QWL programs include GM, Ford, Chrysler, Motorola, Honeywell, Westinghouse, Digital Equipment, Hewlett-Packard, AT&T, Bethlehem Steel, Polaroid, and GE.[21] Quality-of-work-life programs usually have two major objectives: (1) improvements in employee quality of work life; and (2) improvements in group or organizational productivity.[22] Such change programs may include a wide variety of specific techniques such as team building, job redesign, participative management and employee involvement programs, quality circles, work environment improvements, and flextime programs. **Flextime** programs give employees some control over their own work schedules. For example, employees might be allowed to begin their workdays anytime between 7 A.M. and 9 A.M. and to end their work between 4 P.M. and 6 P.M., depending on their starting times. Or employees might have the option of working four ten-hour days instead of five eight-hour days.

ASSESSMENT OF QWL PROGRAMS   QWL programs are so new and encompass such a wide variety of change activities that it is difficult to document their precise effects. However, considerable success has been reported in improving employee work attitudes, increasing levels of employee involvement, improving working conditions, and changing organizational culture. Improvements in productivity have also been reported, although the relationship between QWL programs and productivity changes is complex and not easily measured. For example, Figure 21-2 suggests that QWL programs have the potential for improving communication and coordination, motivation, and capabilities of individuals and groups to perform. These improvements, in turn, may translate into improvements in productivity.

It is important to note that QWL programs can have negative outcomes as well. For example, middle managers and supervisors sometimes resist QWL programs, perceiving them as increasing employee participation at the expense of their management prerogatives. Unless such resistance is overcome, a QWL program may fail or be achieved at a high cost in terms of managerial or supervisory turnover.[23]

TASK- AND TECHNOLOGY-FOCUSED APPROACHES TO CHANGE

This section examines three approaches to organizational change that focus on task and technology: job design, sociotechnical systems, and quality circles. The task-focused approach emphasizes making changes in the activities or tasks each person or work group does: what, when, where, with whom, for how long, and how often. The technology-focused approach concentrates

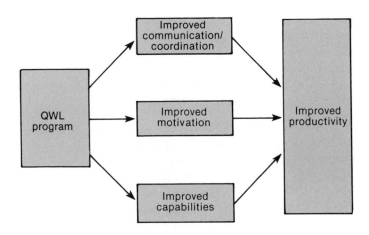

FIGURE 21–2.
Potential Effects of QWL Programs on Productivity

Source: Lawler, E. E., and Ledford, G. E. Productivity and the Quality of Work Life. *National Productivity Review,* Winter 1981–1982, 29. Reprinted with permission of the publisher. National Productivity Review, 33 West 60th St., New York, NY 10023.

on the technological tools used to perform the work: computers, other machines, processes, mathematical procedures, and the like. In practice, changing specific tasks when redesigning work or working relationships is difficult without also changing the technological tools used to perform that work. Thus we group task and technology together when discussing specific approaches to organizational change in these areas.

Job Design

Job Design represents a deliberate, planned restructuring of the way work is performed in order to increase employee motivation, involvement, and efficiency—and, hence, to improve performance. Job design represents a whole family of specific organizational change techniques, including job engineering, job rotation, job enlargement, job enrichment, and the redesign of core task characteristics, which were described fully in Chapter 13.

Each of these job-design techniques has been demonstrated to be an effective approach to organizational change under certain conditions. All can positively affect task performance, absenteeism, turnover, and job satisfaction. Managers sometimes use specific job-design techniques inappropriately, however. For example, job enrichment can fail if managers erroneously assume that all employees want enriched work and do not allow for differences in employee needs and values. Job-design techniques are perhaps most successful in the context of a comprehensive organizational change program that examines the complex fit among the tasks to be performed, the types of technology used, the structure and climate of the organization or group, and the nature and characteristics of the people doing the work.[24]

Sociotechnical Systems

Sociotechnical systems represent a planned approach to organizational change that simultaneously focuses on changing both the technical and social aspects of the organization in ways designed to optimize their relationship and thus to increase organizational effectiveness. Sociotechnical systems theory regards the organization as more than just a technical system for making products and providing services. Ultimately, the organization is a collection of human beings—a social system. Changes made in the technical system affect the social fabric of the organization. Thus, in order to manage organizational change effectively, managers must deal with both the social and technical aspects of that change.

Sociotechnical approaches to organizational change usually incorporate a major redesign of the way work is done—the task variable—in addition to emphasizing the technical and people dimensions of the organization. A sociotechnical model of job design was presented in Chapter 13.

AUTONOMOUS GROUPS   From the perspective of organizational change, the idea of autonomous or self-managing work groups is a major contribution of sociotechnical systems theory. **Autonomous groups** are work groups that are self-managing in terms of planning their work, controlling its pace and quality, and making many of the decisions traditionally reserved for management. An autonomous group may determine its own job assignments, work schedules, and even quantity and quality of output. This approach redesigns work groups to give them a greater measure of control over virtually all the resources and skills needed to produce a specific output, to serve customers in a particular geographic area, or both.

Two features distinguish autonomous groups from more traditional ways of organizing tasks and controlling employees. First, autonomous groups organize people performing interdependent tasks into relatively small groups of from 7–25 individuals. Second, employees within the autonomous group have much greater control of their tasks.

ASSESSMENT OF SOCIOTECHNICAL SYSTEMS   Individuals in autonomous groups participate extensively in task-related decision making and may, as a result, find their jobs to be more meaningful and satisfying. From the standpoint of the organization, productivity of autonomous groups is usually equal to or better than that of other types of groups. Other factors, such as labor–management relations, absenteeism, turnover, and cooperation among workers, may also improve.[25]

The greatest appeal of sociotechnical change strategies is their potential effects on group and organizational performance. For example, a study over two and one-half years in a food-processing plant compared the effects of the sociotechnical systems, job design, and survey–feedback approaches to organizational change. The three approaches had similar positive effects on worker attitudes. However, only the sociotechnical approach resulted in productivity improvements and cost savings.[26]

Sociotechnical approaches to organizational change were originally developed in England at the Tavistock Institute, and for many years most sociotechnical change programs took place in Europe. The Volvo Kalmar Plant in Sweden is a well-known European example of sociotechnical change. (See Chapter 13.) During the past two decades sociotechnical systems approaches have also been used extensively in the United States and Canada to design, build, and manage new plants. For example, General Foods, Procter & Gamble, Sherwin-Williams, the Mead Corporation, Shell Canada, and Westinghouse have recently built new facilities utilizing sociotechnical systems concepts.[27]

Sociotechnical systems approaches to organizational change promise to be one of the more popular approaches in the years ahead. Many aspects of the organization must be managed in an interrelated way if change is to be effective, and sociotechnical systems enable managers to tie them together.

Quality Circles

Quality circles are semiautonomous work groups, generally containing less than a dozen volunteers from the same work area, who meet regularly to solve and monitor job-related quality and/or production problems. Quality circles are also designed to improve working conditions and encourage self-development of employees.[28] As such, they are frequently an important component of QWL programs. Adapted initially from Japanese quality-control practices, quality circles represent a recent organizational change approach. The first quality circle was implemented in the United States in 1974, and their use has spread rapidly with an estimated 500 U.S. firms currently using quality circles.[29]

A recent critical examination of quality circles described their typical activities, focus, and limitations as follows:

> The [quality-circle] members receive training in problem solving, statistical quality control, and group process. Quality circles generally recommend solutions for quality and productivity problems which management then may implement. A facilitator, usually a specially trained member of management, helps train circle members and ensures that things run smoothly. Typical objectives of QC programs include quality improvement, productivity enhancement, and employee involvement. Circles generally meet four hours a month on company time. Members may get recognition but rarely receive financial rewards.[30]

Quality circles typically have a narrower focus than many of the other change techniques. They also differ from other approaches in that management retains more control over the activities of the participants than is possible, or desirable, in most other approaches to organizational change. There are both advantages and disadvantages to this tight control and focus.

Quality circles have attracted a great deal of attention in a short period of time. While careful evaluations of the effects of quality circles often are not done, evidence comparing expected to actual outcomes is beginning to accumulate.[31] So far, the results seem to be mixed. Productivity and quality gains—sometimes of a substantial magnitude—have been reported. Quality circles also fit well into comprehensive QWL programs and can foster greater employee involvement in decision making and other aspects of work. However, a number of failures have also been reported. Quality circles may not fit well into the culture of an organization. It appears that quality circles can cope successfully with only a limited range of problems; accurate diagnosis is essential to ensure that the problems facing the organization are best addressed by this change approach.

The popularity of quality circles is not limited to the United States. Consider the experience of a Welsh firm with a new quality-circle program.

ACROSS CULTURES

Quality Circles in a Welsh Factory

Toys and games are fast-moving consumer goods in a highly seasonal market where price level and quality standards are essential to success. A British toy and game manufacturer became concerned about the need to improve productivity and quality in their manufacturing facilities. A factory in South Wales was selected to implement the firm's new quality circle program. The site contained some 1,800 people, comprising a manufacturing complex, a distribution operation and the greater part of the company's administration activity, including mainframe computer operations.

It was believed that productivity improvement would stem from the workforce gaining a better understanding of the organization and the factors which affected it, from improved standards of supervision, improved methods of communication and improved workforce involvement. Achievement of these objectives, it was thought, would lead to improvements in quality and efficiency and to a lowering of scrap and re-work costs.

A timetable was established for the implementation of a pilot quality circles program, with the intention of establishing three circle groups only so that they could be given the specific consultant and in-house attention needed to ensure success, which should in its turn encourage an extension of circle activity. The timetable required a series of presentations to all levels of management down to and including every first-line supervisor. These presentations were supported by a continuing process of follow-ups with the skeptics who emerged during the presentation sessions.

In addition, all the union representatives in the company were given the same presentation and the same opportunity to address questions to directors of the company in order to satisfy themselves in particular that any quality circles activity would not be allowed to cut across established union negotiation and consultation procedures, and that quality circles would not be allowed to pursue subjects which unions and the company would normally consider to be within the established lines of industrial relations and communication.

After the first three circle groups were selected, training began under the control of the company facilitator. Each circle group took one hour per week to learn the basic skills to make them effective circle contributors. This training was specifically related to their work situation, as distinct from non-work related theoretical exercises, and as a result, concurrent with the training, the circles were encouraged to identify a first project and to look for proposed solutions to the chosen problem for presentation to their manager at the end of the training period. Perhaps the greatest initial difficulty here was to guide the circles into identifying problems for correction which were directly concerned with the production operation.

For the first three months of circle activity, the facilitator would attend each and every circle meeting to ensure that training was being adequately provided by the supervisor, and that the circles were applying their newly-learned skills in an objective manner. Equally the facilitator, as an experienced production manager, was able during the course of circle meetings to explain and expand on points being raised about which the circle members had insufficient knowledge, and where he did not have such knowledge he was able to act as a catalyst, encouraging the supervisor to go to industrial engineering and other technical departments to ask for support and assistance. While in some cases there was an initial resistance to providing such assistance, generally speaking technical departments were very willing to visit the circle groups to discuss with them problems arising or to clarify with them any points of misunderstanding.

The first circle groups took about twelve weeks to achieve their first successes. In one case, an annual saving of £12,500 was identified in recycling cardboard work-in-progress containers, instead of throwing them away. In another case an even more substantial saving was identified in the labelling department, where the group significantly reduced waste and increased labor efficiency. However, one of the initial circles also experienced its first failure. A project they had pursued with considerable vigor was found at the end to bring such small savings that it destroyed the enthusiasm of the group, and a great deal of concerted effort had to be put behind reforming the quality circle in this section.

> The circles quickly became close teams with an obvious interdependence, which led to another problem. When a circle member left the group, the rest of the team sometimes found it difficult to accept a new member even when there was no shortage of volunteers. Equally in production environments where flexibility and movement of labor is important, circle continuity can become difficult, and in one or two cases this was found to be disadvantageous to the confidence of the circle group. Circles need stability. They need to feel the confidence of the company in what they do, and they certainly need the confidence of a coordinator whom they can turn to at any time for advice and assistance.
>
> The organization concluded that their circles generated more effective communication and participation, and workforce attitudes improved with a clearer understanding by the workforce of the problems that the company faced. Equally management was seen as being significantly more sympathetic to the workforce since it associated with them more closely due to the existence of quality circles.[32]

STRUCTURE-FOCUSED APPROACHES TO CHANGE

Structure-focused approaches to organizational change involve the redefinition of positions or roles, relationships among positions, and the expected behaviors of people in those positions. This is accomplished through modification of the organizational structure and its design characteristics. A list of some of the elements often regarded as essential parts of structural approaches to organizational change is contained in Table 21-3. We will examine two structure-focused approaches to change: matrix organization and collateral (or parallel) organization.

Matrix Organization

As organizations grow increasingly complex, they need new ways of organizing their activities. They particularly need more flexible and adaptive structures than those of the traditional mechanistic system with its rigid hierarchy and standardized procedures. A detailed description of matrix organization was presented in Chapter 14. As described there, a **matrix organization** represents a balance between organizing resources according to products, programs, or projects and functional departments, such as marketing, production, finance, personnel, and research.

TABLE 21-3   Elements Often Included in Structural Approaches to Change

Rules	Number of organizational levels
Procedures	Committees
Formal rewards system	Staff–Line functions
Reporting requirements	Performance criteria
Plans	Formal decision-making authority
Basis of departmentalization	Promotion criteria
Span of control	Selection criteria
Schedules	Project Groups
Communication systems	Budgets
Task teams	Formal Training
	Chain of command

A mutually beneficial relationship often exists between the matrix form of organization and other approaches to organizational change. The matrix form helps to create a culture receptive to organizational improvement efforts. Many features of OD programs, such as an emphasis on collaborative behavior and the effective use of groups, are also important for implementing a matrix structure with its decentralized decision making and extensive use of temporary task forces and teams.

Changing an organization to a matrix form is never easy. Often managers need a people-focused change strategy to facilitate the transition. For example, team building has successfully helped organizations introduce matrix structures.[33]

The matrix structure is appealing, and it may be superior to other organizational forms when the organization uses complex technology, faces rapidly changing market conditions, and needs a high degree of cooperation among projects or functions. However, a matrix structure is costly to implement and maintain and can be extremely difficult to manage effectively, as pointed out in Chapter 14.

Collateral Organization

A **collateral organization** is a parallel, coexisting organization that a manager can use to supplement the existing formal organization.[34] This organizational form utilizes groups of people outside normal communication and authority channels to identify and solve difficult problems that the formal organization may be unwilling or unable to solve. A collateral organization has different norms—ways of working together, making decisions, and solving problems—than the rest of the organization. However, the collateral organization requires no new people and is carefully linked to the formal organization and coexists with it.

Collateral organizations have the following characteristics:

- All communication channels are open and connected. Managers and specialists freely communicate without being restricted to the formal channels of the organizational hierarchy.

- There is a rapid and complete exchange of relevant information on problems and issues.

- The norms in use encourage careful questioning and analysis of goals, assumptions, methods, alternatives, and criteria for evaluation.

- Managers can approach and enlist others in the organization to help solve a problem; they are not restricted to their formal subordinates.[35]

Let us look at the way in which a collateral organization functions at General Motors Corporation.

In Practice: GM's Collateral Organization

Managers of the Central Foundry Division of General Motors established a collateral organization, which they refer to as a "parallel" organization structure. The parallel organization was established when the managers became convinced that the division's more traditional structure was not allowing its members to

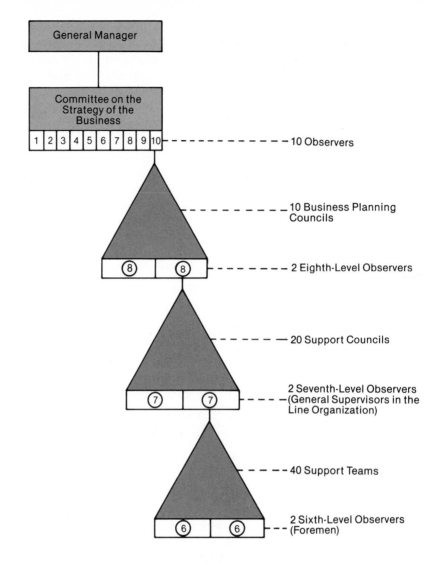

work together effectively. This collateral organization structure has been described as follows:

> The parallel organization is a structure that is flat, permanent, as inviolate and important as the line organization, and unbounded. Every unit in the organization is structured across function and across location. It is linked vertically as well as horizontally but it is different from a matrix organization, which offers only horizontal integration.[36]

The primary function of this parallel organization is strategic planning, which involves almost all salaried, management-level employees of the division. Councils at various managerial levels in the organization provide linkage, as indicated in Figure 21-3.

The Committee on the Strategy of the Business reports directly to the general manager of the division. It consists of the general manager's immediate staff and the division's five plant managers. Attached to this committee are ten observers, each of whom heads a business planning council. Each of these councils has two observers from middle management, who in turn head support councils, and so on. As Figure 21-3 shows, the observers for the support teams have reached as far down in the organizational hierarchy as first-line supervisors. The lines of communication for this parallel organization need to go through only 4 levels versus 8–12 levels for the formal line and staff organization.

Managers in the division reportedly spend 80–85 percent of their time working in the formal system and 15–20 percent on parallel organization activities. This parallel organization can only study problems and recommend changes; the line organization must approve and implement any actual change. However, perhaps because the same people who did the planning are also responsible for implementing the recommendations, GM reports that the division has achieved "phenomenal" rates of change in areas previously resistant to innovation.[37]

Postscript: This parallel structure operated successfully at GM from the mid-1970s through 1984. In 1985 the Central Foundry Division underwent a major reorganization and the collateral groups were placed on "hold." At the time of this writing it remains to be seen whether GM will continue this structural innovation.

Collateral organizations seem appealing, but improvements stemming from this approach are not yet well-documented. Perhaps a major advantage of the collateral form of organization is that it gives managers a way to match problems with the organizational structures suited to solve them. For example, the formal organization may best deal with routine production problems, whereas poorly structured or defined problems may best be handled by problem-solving groups operating outside the formal structure. However, some evidence suggests that the real advantages of collateral organizations may be other than problem solving.[38] Collateral organizations create complex role sets for employees, which may provide more opportunities for individuals to be involved, engage in meaningful work, have control over their jobs, and gain needed satisfaction from their work. In addition, collateral organizations may be particularly good at developing managerial skills, coping with crises requiring decentralized decision making, and fostering organizational innovation.

Stein and Kanter reported on the successful use of a collateral organization in a firm manufacturing high technology electrical equipment.[39] Based on their experiences, Stein and Kanter suggest that collateral or parallel organizational forms may provide an important solution to problems facing organizations in the future. Since a collateral organization can function side by side with a bureaucracy, it allows a firm to successfully use the bureaucratic structure's strengths while perhaps avoiding some of its weaknesses.

SUMMARY

An accurate diagnosis of organizational problems is the starting point for any effective organizational change effort. Based on this diagnosis, managers may choose among a variety of change strategies. Often a combination of approaches is most effective in bringing about changes in an organization. Managers and employees must understand the likely effects of various change approaches, and carefully match change programs with the problems they are intended to solve.

In this chapter, we discussed four people-focused approaches to organizational change: survey–feedback, team-building, process-consultation, and quality-of-work-life programs. In addition, three task- and technology-focused approaches were presented: job design, sociotechnical systems, and quality circles. Finally, two structure-focused approaches to change were reviewed: matrix and collateral organizations.

No single approach to organizational change can be completely successful without addressing some aspects of several, if not all, of the people, task, technology, and structure variables. Comprehensive organizational change programs, regardless of their initial focus, often make congruent changes in several aspects of the organization. The approaches presented in this chapter are often used in combination to manage organizational change.

KEY WORDS AND CONCEPTS

Autonomous groups
Collateral organization
Flextime
Job design
Matrix organization
Organizational diagnosis

Process consultation
Quality circles
Quality-of-work-life (QWL) programs
Sociotechnical systems
Survey feedback
Team building

DISCUSSION QUESTIONS

1. Explain the rationale for an accurate diagnosis of organizational problems and situations prior to implementing a change program.

2. Why do you think so many different approaches to organizational change exist?

3. Which of the four people-focused approaches to organizational change is the most comprehensive? Why?

4. Is it always possible for employees to have a high level of involvement in organizational change programs? Why or why not?

5. How would you describe the values that seem to be implicit or explicit in each of the change approaches discussed in this chapter?

6. Which of the three task- and technology-focused approaches to change is the most comprehensive? Defend your answer.

7. Based on your own experiences, describe an organizational or group problem that needed changing. Which of the change approaches presented would you use? Why?

8. Explain why people-focused approaches to organizational change can sometimes be used effectively with structure-focused approaches.

MANAGEMENT INCIDENTS AND CASES

Stop Crushing My Turbine Blades

Arnold, a graduate of Louisiana State University, with a BS in mechanical engineering, considered himself fortunate to land a job in his chosen career field directly upon graduation. Lowell Dynamics offered him a position as a Technical Advisor for turbine blade production.

A shortage of engineers at Lowell prompted Dick Reilly to assign Arnold to his first out-of-the-ordinary job duty. Arnold was to investigate several complaints from customers that turbine blades were received in damaged condition. Considering the immense unit price of a turbine blade, this was an assignment of considerable magnitude. Over the 20 years that Lowell Dynamics had been producing turbine blades, numerous similar complaints had been received. Dick Reilly was at first hesitant to assign Arnold this sensitive investigation because of his limited technical and organizational experience. However, he reasoned on second thought that perhaps a fresh approach to this perennial problem might generate a workable solution.

After a brief orientation to the problem, Arnold focused his attention on the work flow design. Turbine blades of varying sizes and dimensions were cast, milled, ground, and polished in a job shop operation by experienced machine operators of the finishing work center.

The packaging work center received work from the finishing work center. As such, the packaging area was responsible for grouping the turbine blades for a particular customer and packaging them for shipment. Few methods or material changes had been made in the 20 years of the packaging center operation. Most employees of the center had worked on the same job for a number of years.

The six members of the packaging work center had similar jobs. After grouping of an order in a storage area, turbine blades were brought by pallet to the packaging work place. The packager then loaded the turbines on his work bench and proceeded to tape the critical edges of the blades with masking tape. Next, he packed cotton padding around the blade, formed a corrugated case, packed the blade in the case, placed more cotton around the blade, labeled and sealed the case, and placed it on an outgoing pallet for delivery to the loading dock. Finally, the packaging operator completed the necessary forms to indicate that the order was ready for delivery.

All six packaging operators and their foreman had a constructive working relationship and formed a cohesive group. In spite of the limited attention by management, they felt that they were needed by the company. In their perception, it was the packaging department that had final responsibility for quality. When the packaging foreman needed extra effort for peak periods and rush customer orders, the response was usually more than adequate.

In the past, engineers had been assigned to investigate the damaged turbine problems. Some changes had been recommended but the projected costs made the changes uneconomical. Arnold decided to consult with other engineers who had worked on this problem (to ask their advice) before speaking directly to members of the packaging work center. Two engineers with whom Arnold spoke presented a grim picture of his possibilities for success on this assignment. Nelson, an experienced mechanical engineer, described it this way:

> Arnold, I don't want to discourage you, but it's very difficult to get to the heart of the problem. You just can't get those people in packaging to tell you anything. I made several trips to the packaging area. I tried to be friendly and not act as if I was a corporate spy or some kind of an expert trying to tell them how to run their job. But my strategy didn't work. When I asked the packaging operators specific questions about why they did something in a particular way, the answers were misleading and trite.
>
> In frustration, I went to the foreman. He responded in an equally noncommittal and evasive fashion. I then just flat out

made some suggestions for revamping some of their procedures. They basically ignored my suggestions.

Before pressing ahead into the packaging area, Arnold decided to discuss this problem with a friend in the personnel department, Harvey Burford. After listening to Arnold's description of the situation, Harvey and Arnold discussed a possible approach to the problem. Based upon some knowledge of organizational behavior Harvey had acquired through both reading and on-the-job experience, they laid out some general ground rules for solving the human problem. Five steps were contained in their strategy:

- Let the people know what you are doing.
- Recognize the chain of command and respect its rules.
- Assure the people that you are leveling with them and that you are not a spy.
- Assure people of their job security. For instance, tell them, "You are good workers and the company needs you."
- Enlist their aid in solving the problem.

With these ground rules in mind, Arnold approached the foreman of the packaging work center. Arnold carefully explained the nature of the problem he was investigating and enlisted the foreman's aid in solving it. Arnold requested that management grant him the time to hold a meeting with the foreman and the packaging operators. Management granted his request.

During the meeting, Arnold again explained the history and nature of the damaged turbine blade problem. He assured operators that their job was not in danger and asked them for assistance in solving the problem. Together they decided to investigate and list the number of ways

damage could occur in the packaging work center. Arnold recognized instantly that the true path to resolving the crushed turbine blade enigma had been found.

Stuart Ludlow, one of the senior operators, offered a diagnosis of the problem that was supported by others:

Under normal circumstances we (the other packaging operators) are very careful in packaging the blades. It's like we are moving men packing china and crystal. But I've noticed that for years, the most difficult part of the whole job is loading the blades into the cases. It's a bit like loading a cabin cruiser into a storage rack. The blades are so darn cumbersome and heavy.

When we are in a hurry because of a rush order or a peak period, we do sometimes drop the blades into the cases. It's not that we're being malicious. Just a simple case of your best judgment slipping a little under pressure. Maybe this is the key to the problem. We told Mel (the foreman) about this problem over one year ago. Mel suggested that we add another man during peak periods. Mel then went to the Department Head with this request to allocate another helper for our busy periods. As you might suspect, it was turned down because it cost money.

Arnold gathered this information and a few related items of information from the packaging operators. A thorough analysis of existing records indicated that in 92 percent of the damaged turbine complaints, the packaging work center was working on a rush order or was experiencing a peak work period. Arnold passed this information back to the foreman and the packaging operators. He agreed with them that the problem seemed to be confined to placing the blades in the cases.

Working together on this problem in the future meetings, they generated several alternatives. Finally, they made a joint presentation of a feasible alternative to the Department Head and upper management. The idea was basic—devise a fixture that would allow the packaging operator to form the case around the taped and padded blade, eliminating placing (and sometimes dropping) the blade in the case.

As things worked out, this simple technological innovation reduced complaints about crushed turbine blades about 98 percent. Arnold is back at the drawing board trying to figure a way to salvage that remaining two percent.[40]

Questions

1. Identify the key contingencies and concepts from both chapters 20 and 21 that appear in this case.

2. What were the reasons that Arnold succeeded while his predecessors failed?

3. Why are not more change problems solved in this manner?

4. Does this case suggest any other reasons why the turbine blades might have been damaged? Explain.

REFERENCES

1. Adapted with permission from Huse, E. F., and Cummings, T. G. *Organization Development and Change*, 3d ed. St. Paul, Minn.: West, 1985, 55–56. Copyright © 1985 by West Publishing Company. All rights reserved.

2. Woodman, R. W., and Muse, W. V. Organization Development in the Profit Sector: Lessons Learned. In J. Hammons (Ed.) *Organization Development: Change Strategies*. San Francisco: Jossey-Bass, 1982, 23–44.

3. For descriptions of organizational diagnosis, see Burke, W. W. *Organization Development: Principles and Practices*. Boston: Little, Brown, 1982, 168–212; Huse and Cummings, *Organization Development and Change*, 33–61; Levinson, H. *Organizational Diagnosis*. Cambridge, Mass.: Harvard University Press, 1972; Weisbord, M. R. Organizational Diagnosis: Six Places to Look for Trouble with or without a Theory. *Group & Organization Studies*, 1976, *1*, 430–447.

4. Beckhard, R. Strategies for Large System Change. *Sloan Management Review*, 1975, *16*, 43–55.

5. Pond, S. B., Armenakis, A. A., and Green, S. B. The Importance of Employee Expectations in Organizational Diagnosis. *Journal of Applied Behavioral Science*, 1984, *20*, 167–180; Woodman, R. W., and Tolchinsky, P. D. Expectation Effects: Implications for Organization Development Interventions. In D. D. Warrick (Ed.) *Contemporary Organization Development: Current Thinking and Applications*. Glenview, Ill.: Scott, Foresman, 1985, 477–487.

6. For descriptions of survey feedback and its effects, see Bullock, R. J., and Bullock, P. F. Pure Science versus Science-Action Models of Data Feedback: A Field Experiment. *Group & Organization Studies*, 1984, *9*, 7–27; Conlon, E. J., and Short, L. O. Survey Feedback as a Large-Scale Change Device: An Empirical Examination. *Group & Organization Studies*, 1984, *9*, 399–416; French, W. L., and Bell, C. H. *Organization Development: Behavioral Science Interventions for Organization Improvement*, 3d ed. Englewood Cliffs, N.J.: Prentice-Hall, 1984, 181–185; Gavin, J. F. Observations from a Long-Term, Survey-Guided Consultation with a Mining Company. *Journal of Applied Behavioral Science*, 1985, *21*, 201–220; Nadler, D. A. *Feedback and Organization Development: Using Data-Based Methods*. Reading, Mass.: Addison-Wesley, 1977.

7. Bowers, D. G., and Hausser, D. Work Group Types and Intervention Effects in Organizational Development. *Administrative Science Quarterly*, 1977, *22*, 76–96.

8. Beer, M. *Organization Development: A Systems View*. Santa Monica, Calif.: Goodyear, 1980, 140.

9. Beckhard, R. Optimizing Team Building Efforts. *Journal of Contemporary Business*, 1972, *1*(3), 23–32.

10. Woodman, R. W., and Sherwood, J. J. The Role of Team Development in Organizational Effectiveness: A Critical Review. *Psychological Bulletin*, 1980, *88*, 166–186.

11. Beer, M. Technology of Organization Development. In M. D. Dunnette (Ed.) *Handbook of Industrial and Organiza-*

tional Psychology. Chicago: Rand McNally, 1976, 955–961; Friedlander, F., and Brown, L. D. Organization Development. *Annual Review of Psychology*, 1974, *25*, 313–341; Lundberg, C. C. Microinterventions for Team Development: Toward Their Appreciation and Use. In Warrick (Ed.) *Contemporary Organization Development*, 114–122; Woodman and Muse, Organization Development in the Profit Sector: Lessons Learned.

12. For contrasting viewpoints on the outcomes of team building, see Allender, M. C. Productivity Enhancement: A New Teamwork Approach. *National Productivity Review*, Spring 1984, 181–189; Eden, D. Team Development: A True Field Experiment at Three Levels of Rigor. *Journal of Applied Psychology*, 1985, *70*, 94–100.

13. Woodman, R. W., and Sherwood, J. J. Effects of Team Development Intervention: A Field Experiment. *Journal of Applied Behavioral Science*, 1980, *16*, 211–227.

14. Sherwood, J. J. An Introduction to Organization Development. In J. W. Pfeiffer and J. E. Jones (Eds.) *The 1972 Handbook for Group Facilitators*. La Jolla, Calif.: University Associates, 1972, 155.

15. Huse and Cummings, *Organization Development and Change*, 121–122. Reprinted with permission. Copyright © 1985 by West Publishing Company. All rights reserved.

16. Schein, E. H. *Process Consultation: Its Role in Organization Development*. Reading, Mass.: Addison-Wesley, 1969, 9.

17. Descriptions of these areas may be found in Burke, *Organization Development*, 282–286; Huse and Cummings, *Organization Development and Change*, 98–105.

18. Kaplan, R. E. The Utility of Maintaining Relationships Openly: An Experimental Study. *Journal of Applied Behavioral Science*, 1979, *15*, 41–59; Lipshitz, R., and Sherwood, J. J. The Effectiveness of Third-Party Consultation as a Function of the Consultant's Prestige and Style of Intervention. *Journal of Applied Behavioral Science*, 1978, *14*, 493–509.

19. Kaplan, R. E. The Conspicuous Absence of Evidence that Process Consultation Enhances Task Performance. *Journal of Applied Behavioral Science*, 1979 *15*, 346–360.

20. Pasmore, W. A. A Comprehensive Approach to Planning an OD/QWL Strategy. In Warrick (Ed.) *Contemporary Organization Development*, 205.

21. Cummings, T. G., and Molloy, E. S. *Improving Productivity and the Quality of Work Life*. New York: Praeger, 1977; Jick, T. D., and Ashkenas, R. N. Involving Employees in Productivity and QWL Improvements: What OD Can Learn from the Manager's Perspective. In Warrick (Ed.) *Contemporary Organization Development*, 218–230; Lawler, E. E. Increasing Worker Involvement to Enhance Organizational Effectiveness. In P. S. Goodman and Associates (Eds.) *Change in Organizations: New Perspectives on Theory, Research, and Practice*. San Francisco: Jossey-Bass, 1982, 280–315; Lawler, E. E., and Ledford, G. E. Productivity and the Quality of Work Life. *National Productivity Review*, Winter 1981–1982, 23–36.

22. Gadon, H. Making Sense of Quality of Work Life Programs. *Business Horizons*, January–February 1984, 42–46.

23. Klein, J. A. Why Supervisors Resist Employee Involvement. *Harvard Business Review*, September–October 1984, 87–95; Schlesinger, L. A., and Oshry, B. Quality of Work Life and the Manager: Muddle in the Middle. *Organizational Dynamics*, Summer 1984, 5–19.

24. Griffin, R. W., and Woodman, R. W. Utilizing Task Redesign Strategies within Organization Development Programs. In Warrick (Ed.) *Contemporary Organization Development*, 308–319.

25. Pasmore, W. A., and J. J. Sherwood (Eds.) *Sociotechnical Systems: A Sourcebook*. La Jolla, Calif.: University Associates, 1978.

26. Pasmore, W. A., and King, D. C. Understanding Organizational Change: A Comparative Study of Multifaceted Interventions. *Journal of Applied Behavioral Science*, 1978, *14*, 455–468.

27. Huse and Cummings, *Organization Development and Change*, 206.

28. Cole, R. E., and Tachiki, D. S. Forging Institutional Links: Making Quality Circles Work in the U.S. *National Productivity Review*, Autumn 1984, 417–429.

29. Meyer, G. W., and Stott, R. G. Quality Circles: Panacea or Pandora's Box? *Organizational Dynamics*, Spring, 1985, 34–50.

30. Lawler, E. E., and Mohrman, S. A. Quality Circles after the Fad. *Harvard Business Review*, January–February 1985, 66.

31. Blair, J. D., and Whitehead, C. J. Can Quality Circles Survive in the United States? *Business Horizons*, September–October 1984, 17–23; Mohrman, S. A., and Novelli, L. Beyond Testimonials: Learning from a Quality Circles Programme. *Journal of Occupational Behavior*, 1985, *6*, 93–110; Steel, R. P., Mento, A. J., Dilla, B. L., Ovalle, N. K., and Lloyd, R. F. Factors Influencing the Success and Failure of Two Quality Circle Programs. *Journal of Management*, 1985,

11, 99–119; White, D. D., and Bednar, D. A. Locating Problems with Quality Circles. *National Productivity Review*, Winter 1984–1985, 45–52.

32. Mowat, J. The Problem Solvers: Quality Circles. In M. Robson (Ed.), *Quality Circles In Action.* Aldershot, England: Gower Publishing, 1984 Reprinted with permission.

33. Tolchinsky, P. D., and Woodman, R. W. *Facilitating Matrix Structures in Mental Health Using OD Techniques.* Technical report for the Florida Department of Health and Rehabilitative Services, 1981.

34. Zand, D. E. *Information, Organization, and Power.* New York: McGraw-Hill, 1981, 58.

35. Zand, D. E. Collateral Organization: A New Change Strategy. *Journal of Applied Behavioral Science*, 1974, *10,* 63–89.

36. Miller, E. C. The Parallel Organization Structure at General Motors: An Interview with Howard C. Carlson. *Personnel*, September–October 1978, 65.

37. Based on Miller, The Parallel Organization Structure at General Motors, 64–69; and personal conversation with Howard Carlson, September 1985.

38. Rubinstein, D., and Woodman, R. W. Spiderman and the Burma Raiders: Collateral Organization Theory in Action. *Journal of Applied Behavioral Science*, 1984, *20,* 1–21.

39. Stein. B. A., and Kanter, R. M. Building the Parallel Organization: Creating Mechanisms for Permanent Quality of Work Life. *Journal of Applied Behavioral Science*, 1980, *16,* 371–388.

40. DuBrin, A. J. *Fundamentals of Organizational Behavior: An Applied Perspective,* 2d ed. New York: Pergamon, 1978, 439–442. Reprinted with permission. Copyright © 1978, Pergamon Press.

Author Index

Subject Index